D1195875

The Principles of Monasticism

The Principles of MONASTICISM

by Maurus Wolter, O.S.B.

translated, edited, and annotated by
BERNARD A. SAUSE, O.S.B.

B. HERDER BOOK CO.
15 & 17 South Broadway, St. Louis 2, Mo.
AND 2/3 Doughty Mews, London, W.C. 1

American Benedictine Academy,
Studies in Ascetical Theology, N. 1

Nihil Obstat Sebastian Weissenberger, O.S.B.
Imprimi Potest ✠ Cuthbert McDonald, O.S.B., *Abbot*
Imprimatur ✠ Joseph Cardinal Ritter
Archbishop of St. Louis
February 21, 1962

Library of Congress Catalog Card No. 62-10507
Printed in the U.S.A.

Translator's Foreword

Ancient monasteries somehow resemble fortresses. From the Liri Valley Montecassino looks impregnable. All factors would seem to work together to give validity to this impression: the enduring character of an abbey's purposes; the vow of stability by which a monastery becomes the home of its monks for all the days of their life; the imperceptible linking of generations that stretch into centuries when permitted to do so; the unhurried pace and unworried approach to all questions; the very solidity of the buildings.

Regrettably the impression has not been borne out in fact. History has demonstrated repeatedly and tragically that monasteries, stable by vow, and identified with their respective regions' permanent well-being, are of all public institutions sometimes the most peculiarly vulnerable. England, Germany, France, and Italy are dotted with stately ruins which were once thriving centers of the religious life. In the past hundred years many monasteries which flourished long ago have been re-peopled, to begin anew and very humbly the more pretentious efforts of times past. Larger religious houses have often been the first and most dramatic victims of all political upheavals; often too they are almost the last to recover, if they are ever refounded.

Before 1789 Central and Western Europe had an estimated one thousand monasteries of Benedictine men, and half again as many monasteries of nuns. Fifty years later only five per cent of that number remained, and these houses were woefully reduced in size, despoiled of their libraries and other possessions. In almost all instances the contact with the traditions which had hallowed their homes for centuries had been only imperfectly re-established; even the most dedicated and generous monks and nuns were harassed by the sense of insecurity and of being tolerated rather than welcomed or made to feel needed, hampered in their works of zeal through which monasticism had made some of its most valuable contributions to the spiritual life of the Church. Gone forever were such famous names in monasticism as the Bursfeld

Congregation, the Maurists, the Congregation of St. Vanne, that of Valladolid.

In the design of Providence, two men seem to have been chosen for the task of re-establishing contact with the intellectual appreciation of monasticism and its workings. They were to translate their knowledge into a way of life that became a most influential force in the new bid for monasticism's honored place in the Church. These two men were: Dom Prosper Guéranger who bought back Solesmes and restored it, and was later to become the first abbot president of the Congregation of France; and Maurus Wolter, whose pioneering experiences in Germany parallelled those of his friend in France. From their first encounter until Guéranger's death in 1875 the two abbots were close friends and corresponded frequently. Both were men of ability far above the average; both were former diocesan priests; each was blessed in his own way with a realization of the importance of strict adherence to the traditional principles of the monastic life. Circumstances in his own country led Guéranger to concentrate in large measure on the restoration of the sacred liturgy, whereas Wolter focused his attention more specifically on monasticism's ascetical program.

Maurus Wolter was born at Bonn on the Rhine, July 4, 1825, and at baptism was given the name Rudolph. Upon completion of his Gymnasium studies he entered the University of Bonn and devoted himself to philosophy and theology. He was awarded the doctorate in philosophy in 1849. Oxford and Breslau Universities made him flattering offers, but the young scholar declined both, entered the seminary in Cologne, and was ordained priest September 3, 1850. After six years of activity in the Archdiocese of Cologne he left his native land to enter the novitiate in the ancient abbey of St. Paul-outside-the-Walls in Rome, where he pronounced his vows November 15, 1857, receiving at that time St. Maurus as his monastic patron. He was thus following in the steps of his younger brother Ernest who had made profession in the same monastery a year earlier: Ernest received the name Placidus in religion. He was subsequently to become the founding abbot of Maredsous Abbey in Belgium.

Pope Pius IX appointed Maurus spiritual director of Countess Katharina von Hohenzollern, who was devoted to St. Benedict and his order, and longed for the refounding of monasteries in her native land. With the Holy Father's special blessing the Wolter brothers set out upon this task September 29, 1860, with the substantial material aid of the Countess and the help of her influence in high places.

Few foundations in the history of monasticism have experienced more scabrous and disheartening beginnings. In 1861 the brothers sought to locate in their native Rheinland at Materborn near Cleve in the Münster diocese. Some few of the ancient houses in Bavaria had already reopened in a humble way, but this Materborn experiment was the first really new venture after the Period of Secularization, and it proved unsuccessful.

After overcoming numerous obstacles, St. Martin's, Beuron, a former Augustinian monastery whose history mounts back to the year 777, and which had been in the possession of the Canons from 1077 until the suppression of 1802, was opened as a priory on Pentecost, May 24, 1863. It is located in southwest Germany, not far from Freiburg. Only five years later the house was elevated to the rank of an abbey, prior Maurus Wolter appointed its abbot, and the monastic congregation of Beuron simultaneously established. For the moment everything looked promising. But development continued with relative placidity for less than a decade. In 1875 disaster struck in the *Kulturkampf,* the monks were driven out of Beuron and Germany, to remain exiled for twelve years.

In one way the tragedy of the motherhouse proved a blessing: during the twelve-year absence from Beuron new foundations were made in Prague (Abbey of Emmaus), Belgium (Abbey of Maredsous), Steirmarck, Austria (Abbey of the Blessed Virgin Mary of Seckau), and elsewhere. All these are flourishing communities today. Thus when the monks were allowed to return to Beuron in 1887, they came back considerably stronger than they had left.

Beuron's experience in the 1860's parallelled all too faithfully monasticism's generally unhappy and disorganized condition. The autonomy of the individual monastery, patterned from earliest organized monastic life upon the supernatural as well as the natural ideal of the family, with the father and his spiritual sons, is the distinctive strength of Benedictinism, as well as its most vulnerable weakness. Fewer than fifty undermanned monasteries were struggling to recapture and carry on monastic tradition, each according to its own interpretation and adaptation to local needs. Monasticism is eminently identified with the life of the Church in the local scene and always wields its influence locally. Hence each abbey was handicapped by its own distinctive limitations.

In view of these difficulties the abbots and priors of some of the European houses met in 1868 at St. Peter's Abbey, Salzburg, Austria, the oldest Benedictine monastery with an uninterrupted history since its foundation. It was established by St. Rupert in the seventh century. For 200 years the episcopal and abbatial dignities were united. The immediate occasion of the congress was the discussion of common Benedictine interests in view of the forthcoming Vatican Council (1869–70). The long-range purpose was to base the already encouraging growth of the order on the most solid foundations possible (cf. Author's Preface).

After his subsequent meeting with Abbot Prosper Guéranger of

Solesmes in May, 1869, the broad lines of the fundamental principles for the monastic revival were agreed upon, and Maurus Wolter set to serious work. Actually, much of his effort was to be devoted to the project during his exile from Beuron. There were, no doubt, innumerable disadvantages in the conditions under which he conducted his research and strove to master so vast a field. Nevertheless these must have been offset, at least in part, by benefits of considerable significance to the monk-scholar—the absence of secondary work and time-consuming activities, and the possibility of complete dedication to the monastic ideal. Under these conditions the entire community collaborated in the reading, note-taking, discussing, editing. Even the novices contributed to the journeyman work. What had begun as a self-study and a statement of policy developed into a pretentious and scholarly undertaking. Two separate works were published as a result.

The smaller consisted of Archabbot Maurus Wolter's personal composition, with a brief introduction on devotion to St. Benedict, and short expositions of the seven basic and constituent elements or principles—the *elementa vitae monasticae*—of the monastic life. A gift copy of this smaller work was presented to the Pope, to the cardinals, and to each abbey on the occasion of the celebration of the fourteenth centenary of St. Benedict's birth, in 1880.

Simultaneously the extensive work was published: *Praecipua ordinis monastici elementa* (Bruges: Desclée, de Brouwer & Cie, 1880, viii, 840 pp.). This large volume, one of the most beautifully printed books ever to appear on monasticism, incorporates Wolter's statements of principle (practically identical with the smaller book just referred to). It added: (1) all pertinent passages from St. Benedict's Rule, systematically presented; (2) copious material from the Church's official pronouncements—excerpts from official letters of individual popes, canons and decrees of general councils and provincial synods, rules of religious orders which are monastic in character, statutes of individual monastic congregations (which must always have papal approval), excerpts from the Missal, the Breviary, the Pontifical, and so on; and (3) the longest part, excerpts from the writings of saints and scholars.

The finished work is as extensive and scholarly a presentation of the principles of the monastic life as has ever been assembled. Since its composition it has served as a guide for the young monks of the Beuron congregation. During two summer vacations as a young student I had the privilege of participating in the daily class for the Junior professed members of St. Joseph's Abbey, Gerleve (close to Coesfeld, in Westfalen, Germany). These classes were conducted by Prior Bonaventure Rebstock, O.S.B., a recognized authority in the ascetical field in his own right. As German was the medium of instruction, and as I was then only just establishing an acquaintance with the language, I fear that I acquired but little of factual content that I can now recall. This inability to keep pace with my companions was offset by acquiring some fundamental concepts germane to present considerations. I consider these the most valuable: (1) the adaptability of St. Benedict's Rule to almost any circumstances, presupposing good will, dedication to prayer life, and work that is not opposed to the regularity of monastic ideals, but is at the same time a contribution to the Church in its local needs; (2) the conviction of the importance of stability as the great strength of the order, and the consequent complete identification of the individual monastery with the Church and the people of any given region; (3) the necessity of reading Wolter's excerpts in context: that is, going back to the sources and studying the matter as originally proposed. This last thought explains why I have offered the most detailed references for all citations throughout the translation; and (4) the necessity of an integrated program in the study of monasticism. The seven principles elaborated by Wolter were carefully chosen after much discussion by men of outstanding ability, men whose scholarly attainments were coupled with the actual experience of directing the spiritual efforts of their abbeys under distressing conditions. I suppose other principles could be added, but this could scarcely be done without needless repetition. I am quite certain that none of the seven could be omitted.

Many religious readers are certain to disagree, both with some of the practical deductions made by Wolter and actually introduced into his congregation, and with some of the observances of ages past, which he quotes. That is understandable enough: in fact, it could not be otherwise. Each person is bound by the Rule and constitutions of his own particular institute (*Code of Canon Law,* canon 488, n. 1). For such a commitment, on which he has offered his life's work to God in profession, he is almost certain to have a love, and also a profound sentimental attachment. Of this no one would deprive him. But everyone learns to love the ideal of monasticism through the eager striving of saints and scholars in the past, working under the wise guidance of Mother Church.

Many, no doubt, will find fault with the lack of attention regarding specific secondary works (considering God's glorification in formal, common prayer as the community's prime purpose). There is very little about foreign missionary activity, the glory of the order's history; next to nothing about parochial work, which engages so many today; disappointingly meager attention to the apostolate of education, or conducting retreats, hearing confessions, or activity in general. Neither, for that matter, are any of these to be found in the *Rule of St. Benedict*—and for the same reason. Wolter, I think, much after the manner of St. Benedict himself, purposely omits specific application of his principles to concrete endeavors. He in intent on presenting the ideal of the monastic life, in terms of the principles involved. The eventual implementation is always the concern of the local abbot, who in weightier matters seeks the counsel of his spiritual sons (*RSB*, c. 3).

On the plane of ideals, in the treatment of principles, Wolter shows himself to be exceptionally gifted. He uses his extensive sources judicially. There is often a touch of genius in his method. Where he gives a short excerpt from a sermon of St. Bernard, for example, the reader may rest assured that the brief passage contains the heart of St. Bernard's teaching. It is interesting to take such a short passage, read it in the original context, study the sermon or letter, and observe the delicacy of perception that motivated the choice of the passage in the *Elementa*.

In many respects the motivation of Wolter has become ours today in the United States, and in monastic congregations that do not possess a long observed tradition. God's goodness to us has permitted a century of intense building, zealous activity, often at the conscious sacrifice of monastic tradition, and hard work. We have everything to work for, and a great deal to work with. Everywhere one sees evidence among these young peoples of a process of calming down, of more intense study of spiritual values, of eagerness to consult sources. It is because of this trend that Wolter's work promises to be of service. His problems of eighty years ago have more than a little in common with our own today.

The translator's scope has been: (1) to make available in English passages which have been the foundation on which monastic ascetical endeavor has built throughout the ages, systematically compiled by Archabbot Wolter into a carefully integrated anthology; (2) to furnish accurate references for all quotations, with the thought of encouraging today's religious to use their libraries extensively and to read in context the works from which Wolter's excerpts are taken, especially now that so many of these writings can be had in translation; (3) to give an accurate translation of the ideas into the present-day idiom; and (4) to furnish explanatory notes wherever they are considered helpful.

Even this simplicity of objective has not been wanting in difficulties. Despite their excellence, some of Wolter's sources were never printed, and copies had to be procured. Certain works are not listed in the Union Catalogue and had to be procured in Europe, or, at least, the passages controlled. In numerous instances Wolter availed himself of the ancient tomes he had at hand, from which modern critical and definitive editions have expunged the passages he quotes,—or attributed them to others. Subsequent legislation of the Church has in some areas mitigated the severity of former observance (the Eucharistic fast, Lenten observances).

Wolter purposely avoided all direct quotations of isolated excerpts from the Bible. He did this because the principal passages that have a direct bearing on the monastic life have been employed for centuries and are encountered in almost every book on the religious life. He adopted the policy also because these very passages are used so extensively by the Fathers whom he quotes.

For all biblical quotations that occur throughout the text, I have tried to use the *New Catholic Edition of the Bible:* that is, the translation of the first eight books of the Bible, the seven Sapiential books (Job to Sirach), and the entire New Testament, which is that of the Confraternity of Christian Doctrine made under the guidance of the bishops of the United States. Permission has been granted for this use. The use of the Confraternity edition of the Bible presents a problem too. Councils of the Church in former centuries, individual popes, the rules of the religious orders, and ascetical writings of the saints and scholars employed the Latin text of which the Douay version is the accepted translation. In most instances the Confraternity edition offers a far more facile reading of the thought than does the Douay version. In some instances, however, particularly in the Psalms and in the Book of Sirach the changes are so extensive as to make the present-day reading of the sources meaningless. An instance: Formerly we prayed: *Out of the depths I have cried to thee, O Lord!* (Ps. 129:1.) A Father of the Church emphasizes the idea, *I have prayed* to thee—therefore, perseverance. He enlarges on the thought. But the Confraternity has, *I cry to you!* In such cases it has been decided to indicate the Douay reading in parentheses. Otherwise the Confraternity edition is used throughout.

Wolter, and all the order's spiritual leaders of the past century have appealed with great insistence to close attention to the text of St. Benedict's Rule. Today's monks should be deeply grateful for the critical work of scholars like Morin, Butler, McCann, and Wolter himself, who have furnished excellent texts and commentaries. Abbot Justin McCann's translation of the Rule has been used throughout the present work.

During the early part of preparing this translation, my purpose had been to bring the work up to date. With a few exceptions this part of the project has been abandoned. The principal reasons for the decision are: (1) in most instances the significant contributions since Wolter's day are readily available in English; (2) the additions would have increased the size of the work to the point that it no longer would have retained the character Wolter chose to give it; (3) relatively few ideals of modern works are distinctively monastic.

Although it would be impossible to include by name all who have helped me in this work, I must thank Dom Suso Mayer, O.S.B., of Beuron, whose assistance during my visit to his abbey and in subsequent correspondence has been as gracious as it has been extensive; Father Colman Farrell, O.S.B., librarian of my own abbey, and his assistants for generous professional help; the Dominicans of the House of Studies at River Forest, Illinois, and St. Rose's Priory, Dubuque, Iowa, who placed their resources at my command; and individual staff members at the Newberry Library, the Chicago University Library, and the libraries of Loyola, Kansas, and Wisconsin Universities, who have been unfailingly cooperative.

How good God has been to the Order of St. Benedict, and to other monastic institutes in the past one hundred years! To look back to the humble and self-sacrificing efforts of the men who founded monasteries four generations ago, forces one to be optimistic and hopeful that today's revival of monasticism is only a foreshadowing of wonderful contributions to the spiritual life of the Church. May greater acquaintance with Wolter's work give some small increase to the effort!

Author's Preface

Peace! To all serving Christ under the standard of the beloved Father, Benedict, we address fraternal greetings!

The sacred festivals of the blessed Patriarch whom monks of the West have for fourteen centuries held in highest esteem as their leader, their master, and lawgiver are rapidly approaching [fourteenth centennial of St. Benedict's birth, 1880]. How brightly the blessings and the honor of the beloved Father of all who live the cenobitic life, the doctor of a school of exalted holiness, continue to shine, is evident in that everyone joins with the rejoicing families of monks, expressing the hope that the children of this blessed Father will grow in merit and numbers.

Despite our poverty we could not refrain from bestowing our little gift to honor, in grateful and loving attachment, our beloved master. We should like for this offering to be received as was the gift of that poor widow (cf. Luke 21:2 f) whose two mites cast into the treasury of the temple merited the praise of the Lord himself: *All these out of their abundance have put in as gifts to God: but she out of her want, has put in all that she had to live on* (*ibid.*, v. 4). Prostrate in the deepest sense of humility at the feet of the gloriously reigning Vicar of Christ, Pope Leo XIII, we desire to present this small gift as a token in honor of St. Peter out of sentiments of profound obedience and fidelity.

Time was in ages past when the monastic order was a particularly fruitful vine in God's house, which sent forth its branches as far as the sea, and from its stem furnished the slips by which it was transplanted to the farthest ends of the earth. But how grave the misfortunes that have befallen us! In these latter days we deplore the condition to which this same order has now been so greatly reduced and impaired. All know well the causes of this tragedy. Through the evil of the times and the iniquity of men many abbeys which formerly flourished in holy zeal are now abandoned, or even lie in ruins. The monastic family hearths of prayer and charity have been extinguished; those fountains of water springing unto eternal life have been covered over. In fact, there have been some men who, although listed among the number of monks, have dug other wells in place of those monastic springs, and have drawn other waters, for which reason the foundation of St. Benedict has ceased, in part, to be that chosen vessel of holiness set up by the Holy Spirit in the Church of God.

Precisely because the order has been reduced to such a condition, we think that nothing is more needed than to reopen those fountains and light again those sacred fires, that is, rediscover and state anew the true and solid principles and the genius of monasticism which, built on the precepts of the holy Rule, had flourished with undiminished and unshaken vigor for more than a thousand years.

A meeting of the abbots of the Order of St. Benedict in Salzburg in 1868 provided us the occasion for undertaking this restatement of principles. We had just received the paternal counsel * to unite into a federation of holy charity the monasteries which had remained until that time disunited [that is, the ancient monasteries like St. Peter's abbey, Salzburg, where the meeting was held, which had managed to struggle along through the political upheavals; the abbeys which had been restored after the French Revolution and the period of Secularization, circa 1835–68, as was the case with Solesmes in France and Metten in Germany; and the houses which had been newly founded in the same period, like the monasteries of the Beuron Congregation]. For this purpose it was necessary both to determine the projected federation's general character and the solidly founded norms on which the re-established monastic life should be made to rest.

As a result of the deliberations in this congress of abbots, seven fundamental principles were agreed upon as basic to monasticism. It is these which we present in this volume. A number of Right Reverend Abbots in attendance assented to these principles. Among them we wish to name specially Charles de Vera of Montecassino; Francis Zelli of the Abbey of St. Paul-outside-the-Walls, Rome; Albert Eder of St. Peter's Abbey, Salzburg; and Theoderic Hagn, then of the Abbey of the Blessed Virgin Mary, Lambach, now Archbishop. More particularly we wish to mention that venerable restorer of the monastic life, Dom Prosper Guéranger, Abbot of Solesmes [d. 1875], who originally proposed, in large measure, this division into seven fundamental principles. It is his undying memory that we purpose to honor by this study,

* The reference is to Pope Leo XIII's initial suggestion, communicated through Benedict Cardinal Dusmet, O.S.B., that the Black Benedictines form a federation, which counsel ultimately produced today's Confederation of Monastic Congregations of the Order of St. Benedict. Cf. *The Law proper to the Confederation of Monastic Congregations of the Order of St. Benedict,* translated by Bernard A. Sause, O.S.B. (Atchison, Kansas: Abbey Student Press, 1953), 85 pp., in which all pertinent documents are given in their entirety.

in the spirit of heartfelt gratitude. As for our own modest and insignificant contribution, we have made bold to explain and support the principles with what we have been able to gather in this brief time from a study of the holy Rule, the liturgical books and decrees of Holy Church, and from the writings of saints and Doctors, a compilation which we hope will prove useful for reading and meditation.

We beg you urgently, beloved brethren, to receive this commentary in a spirit of benevolent appreciation and indulgence. Although we know that we are the least of men and unequal to the task, we fondly hope, placing our trust in God alone, that it will produce some fruit, and better still, that it will stir someone endowed with richer gifts to take up successfully the work we have begun.

One thing I ask of the Lord; this I seek (Ps. 26:4), that I shall some day see the beloved monastic order thriving again with its former holiness, and that from it Holy Church will receive a marvelous increase of comfort and help, and heaven an intensification of joy, "that in all things God may be glorified" (*RSB,* c. 57). Then that order will again be the glorious "city of God," with its "foundations upon the holy mountains," whose gates the Lord loves more than any dwelling of Jacob. . . . *And of Sion they shall say: "One and all were born in her; and he who has established her is the Most High Lord." They shall note, when the peoples are enrolled: "This man was born there." And all shall sing, in their festive dance: "My home is within you"* (Ps. 86: 5–7).

May you, beloved Lawgiver and Patriarch, invincible bearer of the holy cross, show yourself to be our Father, blessed in name [Benedict] and in grace! At your intercession may God raise up in the monastic order the Spirit whom you served, so that filled with the same, we may strive to love what you loved, and fulfil by our deeds what you taught. May we do so to the glory of the Most Holy Trinity and to the honor and veneration of the Blessed and ever Immaculate Virgin Mary!

This I have written at Prague, in the Abbey of Montserrat-Emmaus, on the feast of the Patriarch St. Joseph, 1880.

Abbreviations

abp. — Archbishop

In Append. — *In Appendice,* included among collected works, in an appendix, doubtful work, usually attributed to the author indicated

art. — *Articulus,* article, often the lowest division of a composition or work

bp. — Bishop

BR — *Bullarium Romanum,* 25 vols. Bibliography: *Bullarium Diplomatum . . .*

BRC — *Bullarii Romani Continuatio,* 14 vols.

c. — *capitulum,* chapter. Also: *caput,* canon

Can. et decr., Richter — *Canones et decreta Concilii Tridentini,* Richter

Canivez. O.Cist. — Canivez, *Statuta Capitulorum Generalium Ordinis Cisterciensis*

CJC Fontes — *Codicis Juris Canonici Fontes,* 9 vols.

CJC Richter — *Corpus Juris Canonici,* ed. A. L. Richter, 2 vols.

CL — *Acta et Decreta Sacrorum Conciliorum Recentiorum, Collectio Lacensis,* 7 vols.

col. — *columna,* column, reference where page is divided into two columns

Comment. — *Commentarium,* a commentary on

Concil. Coll. Labbei — *Conciliorum Collectio Labbei . . .* 12 vols.

Congr. — *Congregatio monastica,* monastic congregation

Const. — *Constitutiones,* the constitutions of a given order or monastic congregation

Const. Apost. — (following the name of a pope) *constitutio apostolica,* an Apostolic Constitution

CR — *Codex Regularum,* Holstenius-Brockie, 6 vols.

Declar. — *Declarationes in RSB,* adaptations by monastic congregations, usually geographically united, e.g., Bursfeld Congregation,

Swabian Congregation of St. Joseph, American-Cassinese Congregation. These modifications, which are designed to apply the principles of *RSB* to local conditions, and as a consequence form an important part of each monastic congregation's law, have the approval of the Apostolic See

Decr. — *Decretum,* decree

Dist. — *Distinctio,* section, division of a work

Div. — *Divisio,* section of a work

Dom. — *Dominica,* Sunday, e.g., *Dom. XI p. Pent.,* Eleventh Sunday after Pentecost

Enarr. — *Enarratio,* commentary on

Ep. — *Epistola,* letter

Episc. — *Episcopus,* bishop

Expos. — *Expositio,* treatise on

fol. — *folium,* leaf, page of an unpublished manuscript

Hom. — *Homilia,* homily, sermon

Lib. — *Liber,* book

Mansi — *Sacrorum Conciliorum nova et amplissima collectio*

Miss. Rom. — *Missale Romanum,* Roman Missal

n. — *numerus,* number, or paragraph

Op. Om. — *Opera Omnia,* the collected works of an author

Opusc. — *Opusculum,* minor work

PG — *Patrologia Graeca,* Migne

PL — *Patrologia Latina,* Migne

Praef. — *Praefatio,* preface

Prov. — *Provincialis,* used especially in connection with Provincial Councils

Reg. — *Regula,* the rule of a religious order

RSB — *Regula Sancti Benedicti,* Rule of St. Benedict

Schroeder, Councils — *Disciplinary Decrees of the General Councils,* Schroeder

Schroeder, Trent — *Canons and Decrees of the Council of Trent,* Schroeder

semicolon [;] — followed by an author's name and number of page, after the citation of an excerpt: added available texts or translations, without being, necessarily, a direct quotation

Serm. — *Sermo,* sermon, treatise

Stat. — *Statuta,* Statutes, in monastic law, usually the combination of Declar. to *RSB,* and the Constitutions of a monastic congregation

tit. — *Titulus,* title, subdivision of a work

Tr. — Translator

Tract. — *Tractatus,* a treatise

Contents

Introduction

I. STATEMENT BY WOLTER

The holy Father, Benedict

1. *Honor your father and your mother, that you may have a long life in the land which the Lord, your God, is giving you* (Exod. 20:12). You, soldier of Christ under the *Rule of St. Benedict,* have for a Father the loving and glorious Patriarch of Monks, and the holy Rule and the community of the order which he established for a mother. Thousands of saintly and trustworthy witnesses have proclaimed for fourteen centuries the admiration and esteem the holy Patriarch has merited. He was a man of saintly life, blessed both in his name and in grace, the wonderfully blessed Benedict * who shone in his days *like a star shining among the clouds, like the full moon at the holyday season; like the sun shining upon the temple* (Sir. 50:6–7, used in the Epistle of the Mass in honor of St. Benedict).

2. He was filled with the spirit of all the just and endowed with the power of the saints *(Antiph. 4 ad Vesp., In Transitu S. Benedicti,* 21 Mar. *Breviar. monastic.* 1:851, *alibi*). He shone with the splendor of virtue and was adorned with the power of almost unheard-of miracles. He became a Father blessed with countless posterity; in fact, he is justly called the Father of fathers, a second Abraham. He gave to the religious state and to his order many thousands of children. He was the founder of all monasticism in the West. His children became the apostles of many nations, and through them he brought almost all of Europe under Christ the King. In filial pride and gratitude we may justly name him, who is the prince, the leader, and master of monks, the Father as well, and the patron of the whole Christian family of nations.†

* Many writers have adverted to the significance of St. Benedict's name, which means blessed. The phrase, "blessed by God both in grace and in name," coined by Pope St. Gregory the Great, St. Benedict's biographer, occurs repeatedly.

† Pope Pius XII stated: "St. Benedict is the Father of Europe" (Homily preached on September 18, 1947, in the Basilica of St. Paul-outside-the-Walls, which from

Filial devotion to St. Benedict

3. From these considerations it is easy to understand what sentiments you as a member of the monastic order should cherish for this holy and benevolent Father. You must neglect no opportunity to give expression to a filial debt of gratitude, to celebrate the praises of your exalted and loving Father in Christ; to venerate him with due esteem; have recourse to him in holy reverence and deep confidence, both in life and at the hour of death; love him in the depth of your heart, and with joy hold his memory, his image, and his glory dear to you. "Honor your Father; for the Father's blessing confirms the houses of the children."

The Holy Rule

4. Our beloved Father merited the praises to which we have referred, particularly in his role of lawgiver of the monastic life, and in his capacity of teacher in the school of holiness. Under the guidance of the Holy Spirit, he wrote a Rule for monks, a truly blessed book which, according to the generally accepted conviction, has come down to us from the Father of Lights. This is the holy Rule, a work marvelous for its discretion. Supreme Pontiffs, sacred councils, and Doctors of the Church have honored it with words of unstinted praise. It is the cherished legacy of our benevolent Father; the noble monument of our leader; our teacher's voice resounding through the centuries. It is in a certain sense the Magna Charta, the constitution and declaration of liberty for monks; their code of law, their road marker, their battle standard. Like Moses from Mount Sinai, Benedict from Montecassino has made known the will of God to a new Israel. Hence we exclaim: *We are happy, O Israel; because the things that are pleasing to God, are made known to us* (Bar. 4:4).

Binding force of rule and constitutions

5. This, then, brother, is the law to which you have bound yourself, according to which you have solemnly engaged yourself, under which you have promised to serve. This law of the Rule—and what is said of the Rule holds true as well of the constitutions approved by the

---

early Cluniac days has been entrusted to the sons of St. Benedict. This sermon was delivered before the assembled abbots of the Benedictine Confederation, on the occasion of the fourteenth centennial of the death of the Patriarch. *Acta Apostolicae Sedis,* 39:453). See also Pope Pius XII, Encyclical Letter *Fulgens radiatur,* March 21, 1947, in praise of St. Benedict, *ibid.,* 39:137–155.—This statement was repeated by His Holiness in his message, July 4, 1958, to the people of Norcia, Italy, on the completion of the restoration of St. Benedict's church, built on the site of his birthplace. *L'Osservatore Romano,* August 29, 1958, p. 4. [*Tr.*]

Apostolic See—does not bind you under sin except in those portions which pertain to the vows. Be on your guard, nevertheless, against rashly violating even its least precepts. *He who breaks through a wall may be bitten by a serpent* (Eccles. 10:8), and *He who wastes the little he has will be stripped bare* (Sir. 19:1; the Douay reading is: *He that contemneth small things, shall fall by little and little*). If the vows are thought of as a fortress guarding Christian perfection, the other prescriptions of the Rule are its outer wall and bulwark (cf. Isa. 26:1). They are the unshorn hair of the Nazarites (cf. Num. 6:1 f), the locks of Samson, wings for flight, the warrior's breastplate. In a certain sense, it can be stated of the whole monastic law: *Not one jot or tittle shall be lost from the Law till all things have been accomplished* (Matt. 5:18). And: *Whoever follow this rule, peace and mercy upon them* (Gal. 6:16), and the joy of the Holy Spirit. On regular observance depends the salvation of the individual religious, the strength of the monastery, the stability and honor of the monastic congregation.

6. Consider the holy Rule as entrusted to you from the hand of God and from your Father, Benedict. Devote your whole effort to its study, in order that you may know this Rule, so rich in blessings, and day by day grow in reverence, appreciation, and esteem for it. By reading it and meditating on it, seek to penetrate deeply into its meaning and spirit. Listen with close attention, devotion, and gratitude when it is read in the chapter each day * and in the refectory, and say to yourself: *In the written scroll it is prescribed for me. To do your will, O my God, is my delight, and your law is within my heart!* (Ps. 39:8–9.)

Devotional renewal of vows

7. The vows, or the evangelical counsels, by which you have bound yourself to God, have their origin and sanction from the teaching and the example of the Savior himself. Consider carefully that the words: *And Jesus, looking on him, loved him, and said to him: . . . "Come, follow me . . ."* (Mark 10:21) are applicable to you too. With ardent love and generosity of spirit frequently renew your vows.† Consider

* According to the universal monastic practice of many centuries, an excerpt from the *Rule of St. Benedict* was daily read in Latin during the second half of Prime. The discontinuance of the custom was included as part of the petition addressed to the Sacred Congregation of Rites by the newly-elected Abbot Primate, Benno Gut, O.S.B., acting in the name of the congress of abbots, that Prime be made uniform with the other Day-Hours, by dropping everything after the first oration. The petition was granted November 12, 1959. Excerpts of the Rule, with the corresponding "Declarations" are still read in the vernacular at the evening meal. The readings are so arranged that the Rule is heard in its entirety three times a year. [*Tr.*]

† Many religious cultivate the practice of kneeling in God's presence to renew their profession before retiring at night. Others do so mentally at the time of the Offertory, in the environment and at the time of their original offering on the

yourself fortunate and truly blessed, for God has chosen you from among thousands, *and you will be a people sacred to the Lord your God* (Deut. 26:19). Unceasingly give thanks to your heavenly Bridegroom from the depths of your heart, until the angels summon you: "Come, receive the crown which the Lord has prepared for you."

II. EVIDENCE FROM THE RULE OF ST. BENEDICT

8. Hearken, my son, to the precepts of the master and incline the ear of your heart; freely accept and faithfully fulfil the instructions of a loving Father (*RSB, Prolog.,* opening sentence). Therefore we must establish a school of the Lord's service; in making this foundation we hope to ordain nothing that is harsh or burdensome (*ibid.,* last paragraph). This Rule has been written in order that, by practicing it in monasteries, we may show that we have attained to some degree of virtue and the rudiments of monastic observance. . . . Whoever, therefore, you are, hastening to your heavenly country, fulfil first of all by the help of Christ this little Rule for beginners (*ibid.,* c. 73). In all things therefore, let all follow the Rule as master, nor let anyone rashly depart from it (*ibid.,* c. 3). Let a monk do nothing except what is commended by the common rule of the monastery and the example of his superiors (*ibid.,* c. 7, eighth degree of humility).

9. Should a brother be found contumacious, or disobedient, or proud, or a murmurer, or in any way despising and setting himself in opposition to the holy Rule and the orders of his superiors; let such a one, according to our Lord's commandment, be admonished secretly by his superiors for a first and second time (*ibid.,* c. 23). To one who has recently arrived in order to become a monk, let this Rule be read through to him [three times], and let him be addressed thus: "Behold the law under which you wish to serve; if you can observe it, enter; if you cannot, freely depart." And if, after mature deliberation, he promises to observe all things and to obey all the commands that are given to him, let him be received into the community. But let him understand that according to the law of the Rule he is no longer free to leave the monastery, or to withdraw his neck from under the yoke of the Rule (*ibid.,* c. 58).

10. Let [a priest] know that he will have to observe the full discipline of the Rule, and that nothing will be abated for him. As the Scripture says: *Friend, for what purpose hast thou come?* (Matt. 26:50.) Let him know that he is subject to the discipline of the Rule, and must

---

morning they took vows. Others recite the formula given in the Appendix of most editions of the Breviary and Missal as part of their thanksgiving after receiving Holy Communion (*Oratio ad renovandam professionem, Breviar. monastic.* 1:284*). [*Tr.*]

rather give to all an example of humility (*ibid.*, c. 60). Let him not because of his priesthood forget the obedience and discipline of the Rule, but make ever more and more progress toward God. . . . Should he presume to act otherwise, let him be judged not as a priest, but as a rebel. . . . Let him be dismissed from the monastery, provided that his contumacy be such that he refuse to submit and to obey the Rule (*ibid.*, c. 62). For the more the prior is set above the rest, the more scrupulously should he observe the precepts of the Rule (*ibid.*, c. 65). And especially let [the abbot] keep this present Rule in all things (*ibid.*, c. 64). We desire that this Rule be read aloud often in the community, so that no brother may excuse himself on the ground of ignorance (*ibid.*, c. 66).

11. *Life of St. Benedict:* Yet I would not have you ignorant of this fact, that besides the many miracles that made the man of God famous in the world he was quite renowned also for his teaching. For he wrote a Rule for monks which is remarkable both for its discretion and for the lucidity of its style. If anyone wishes to know his character and life more precisely, he may find in the ordinances of that Rule a complete account of the abbot's observance; for the holy man was incapable of teaching a doctrine at variance with his life (*S. Greg. Magni Dialogorum Lib. II,* c. 36, *PL* 66:200). While they were still sitting at table and the hour grew late as they continued to converse on spiritual matters, the holy woman petitioned him: "Do not leave me this night, my brother, so that we may talk till morning of the joys of heavenly life." "What is it that you are asking, sister?" Benedict replied. "I cannot remain out of the monastery" (*ibid.*, c. 33, col. 194. Nothing short of a miracle could cause Benedict not to observe his Rule, and force him to remain with his sister, who died three days later). They saw a path, strewn with rich coverings and brilliantly lighted with innumerable lamps, stretching eastward from his monastery to the sky. And beside it above stood a man in venerable garments, who asked them whose path it was they saw. When they said that they did not know, he told them: "This is the path by which Benedict, the beloved of the Lord, ascended to heaven" (*ibid.*, c. 37, col. 202).

III. DECREES AND DOCUMENTS OF THE CHURCH

St. Benedict

12. MONASTIC OFFICE. O heaven-given pattern of life, teacher and guide, Benedict, whose spirit rejoices with Christ in heaven! Preserve your flock, loving shepherd; strengthen it with your holy prayers; help it, under your leadership, to enter heaven by the shining path (*Antiph.*

ad Magnificat, II Vesp. In Solemnitate S.P. Benedicti Abb., 11 Jul., *Breviar. Monastic.* 2:502).

13. MONASTIC MISSAL. . . . who [God] appointed the most blessed confessor Benedict to be the leader and spiritual master of an innumerable multitude of sons. When he was filled with the spirit of all the just and rapt out of himself, you [God] illumined him with the splendor of your light, so that, in the brilliance of a vision from heaven his soul, freed from all hindrance, might learn how mean are all things here below, through Christ our Lord. Therefore with shouting gladness the whole throng of monks all over the world rejoices; and the heavenly hosts and angelic powers join in singing the hymn of your glory, saying again and again, "Holy, Holy, Holy . . ." (*Praef. de S. Benedicto,* 21 Mar., *Missae propriae et Kalendarium,* p. 22).

Rule of St. Benedict

14. II COUNCIL OF DOUZY (874). In harmony with the Sacred Scriptures, and the teaching of the holy Fathers, Benedict, blessed both in grace and in name, inspired by the Holy Ghost, states in his Rule that . . . (c. 8, *Mansi* 17A:295). Through Benedict the Holy Ghost published the Rule for monks by the same inspiration in which the sacred canons were previously composed. . . . For the rest, it is decreed that this same Rule, promulgated by the Holy Spirit and by the authority and praise of the Blessed Pope Gregory [the Great] is to be reputed as among the Canonical Scriptures and the writings of the Catholic Doctors . . . (*ibid.,* c. 7, col. 293).

15. POPE URBAN VIII (d. 1644). All that is admirable in the lives of the saints, all that is profound under the light of faith, belongs to your calling. The spiritual graces that render other orders holy in an innumerable variety of differences, constitute a part of that whole which is communicated to your order, for its founder [Benedict] was filled with the spirit of all the just (In *Bulla ad Sanctimoniales Xanctonenses.* This excerpt is included among the encomiums of the Rule in the preface to the *Declarations of the Congr. of the Maurists,* and has been subsequently copied in the commentaries on the Rule by Martène, Calmet, etc. The Bull is not found in the standard Bullaria or other sources (*Regula S.B. cum declarationibus Congr. S. Mauri,* p. [IV])).

Regular observance

16. COUNCIL OF AUTUN (670, conducted under St. Leodegar). With reference to abbots and monks, it is proper to observe that they must fulfil and preserve intact whatever the canonical regulations or the *Rule of St. Benedict* teaches. If all these regulations are legitimately kept by abbots and monasteries, the number of monks will increase

under God's favor, and the whole world will be spared evil influences by virtue of their assiduous prayers (c. 15, *Mansi* 11:124).

17. COUNCIL OF LONDON (1268). In the kingdom of heaven there are many mansions, as he who is Truth itself has testified (cf. John 14:2). It gathers its citizens from the whole world, as though it had pressed them in the wine press—people who follow different paths of virtue, who are intent on avoiding the evils of the world, who ascend the different levels of penitence, all to enter the tabernacles of the heavenly mansion, there to receive their respective rewards. Among them all, the more we consider the holy order of monks, made dear to God through Benedict, that man of venerable life, blessed both in grace and in name, instructed as he was and elevated to worthier charismata under the inspiration of the Holy Spirit, triumphing by his dedication to the higher life over the things of earth even from his earliest youth, and bearing away the kingdom of God with a holy violence, the greater the charge weighs upon us to keep this beauty from perishing, to defend its holiness of life, to shield it from the influences of the wicked angels, and to heal the wounds inflicted with sword and temptation by enemies (c. 38, *De monachis, et canonicis regularibus, et monialibus. Mansi* 23: 1250).

18. COUNCIL OF TRENT. Since the holy council is not ignorant of how great a splendor and usefulness accrues to the Church of God from monasteries piously regulated and properly administered, it has, to the end that the old and regular discipline may be the more easily and promptly restored where it has collapsed, and may be the more firmly maintained where it has been preserved, thought it necessary to command, as by this decree it does command, that all regulars, men as well as women, adjust and regulate their life in accordance with the requirements of the rule which they have professed, and especially that they observe faithfully whatever pertains to the perfection of their profession, as the vows of obedience, poverty, and chastity, and any other vows and precepts peculiar to any rule and order and belonging to the essence thereof, as well as the preservation of the common life, food and clothing. Superiors shall use all care and diligence, in general and provincial chapters as well as in their visitations, which they shall not neglect to make at the proper times, that these things are not departed from; for it is evident that they cannot make any relaxations in those things that pertain to the substance of the regular life. For if those things that constitute the basis and foundation of all regular discipline are not strictly observed, the whole edifice must necessarily fall (Sess. XXV, *de regularibus et monialibus,* c. 1, *Can. et decret.* Richter, p. 394; Schroeder, p. 217).

19. COUNCIL OF BEZIERS (1233). With regard to the vows and ob-

servances by which order and regular discipline are preserved, monks . . . are to follow as their guide their rule according to which they have professed to live. Without its observance they are neither in the state nor in the order of those who are to be saved (c. 14, *De observantia regularium. Mansi* 23:274).

20. POPE CLEMENT XIV (d. 1774). Acknowledge, brethren, your weakness before God. Zealously and earnestly implore the divine mercy. Observe your rule, your constitutions, and the decrees [of the Apostolic See]; love the regular discipline, and be ever subject to it, and your holiness of life and purity of religious observance will be such as to be held up to all as an example of piety and worthiness of life, not only for the faithful in general, but for religious as well (*Const. Apost. In vinea Domini,* § 11, 4 Jul. 1772; *confirmatio decretorum pro Cappuccinis prov. Subalpinae. BRC* 5:462).

Rule and constitutions

21. PROV. COUNCIL OF PRAGUE (1860). Let the rule be the distinctive treasure of regulars, for according to its precepts and the accompanying explanations of the statutes, the individual families of religious, each in its own way, imitate the holy founders of their orders, in whom different gifts of the Holy Spirit have produced most varied and beautiful fruits of charity . . . (Decr., tit. 7, c. 3, *De obligationibus regularium, CL* 5:575).

22. PROV. COUNCIL OF COLOCZA (Hungary, 1863). Individually and collectively, religious are to observe, in the manner in which they have vowed to God, the statutes of their order, their traditions, and the discipline of their ancestors, so that by following their footsteps they may merit to attain the same eternal reward they did (Decr., tit. 5, c. *unicum, De regularibus, CL* 5:688).

23. PROV. COUNCIL OF GRAN (Hungary, 1858). Obedience must be perfect in the sense that everyone from the highest superior to the most recently received novice must offer full submission to the laws, constitutions, and regulations of their order which have been confirmed by the Apostolic See; hold in veneration as their code of laws the book which contains these documents; reread it frequently; meditate on its content; and strive to enter profoundly into its meaning. Local superiors will see to it that it is publicly read at the prescribed times; and novice masters are frequently to explain it according to the understanding of each novice (Decr., tit. 7, *De regularibus,* § 2, *CL* 5:65).

24. PROV. COUNCIL OF UTRECHT (1865). A. Only then can religious institutes produce fruits of a distinguished character when regulars, men and women alike, establish and conduct their lives according to the precepts of the rule they have professed (Decr., tit. 7, c. 1, *De perfectione religiosa, CL* 5:890). B. It is the solemn duty of regular su-

periors to see to it that in monasteries the rule and the constitutions approved by the Holy See are strictly observed in all things; nor are they to change anything at all. If they discover any deviation from the primitive observance of the rule, they must make it their concern to restore discipline without delay (*ibid.,* c. 2, *De regularium regimine et disciplina,* col. 892).

25. POPE PIUS IX. A. In the numerous forms they have assumed, religious families, founded by men of outstanding holiness under the inspiration of the Holy Ghost and with the approval of this Apostolic See for achieving the greater glory of God and the welfare of souls, make up that exceedingly beautiful variety which adorns the Church so marvelously. They are the select troops of soldiers that have ever been of the greatest service, honor, and defense of both Christian and civil society (Ep. Encycl. *Ubi primum arcano,* § 1, 17 Jun., 1847, *de instauranda regulari disciplina. Pii IX Acta* 1:47; available also in Bizzarri, *Collectanea,* p. 816). B. Most earnestly do we exhort the superiors of orders and all regulars . . . faithfully to fulfil the vows they have offered to God in profession; to preserve regular observance and discipline; and to show that they are religious not only by the wearing of their habit but by their virtue and in the spirit with which their saintly founders were animated, in order that they may achieve personal sanctification and also for the service of the Church and the edification of the faithful (*Acta et decr. Concil. Vaticani,* XV, *Schema Constitutionis pro regularibus, CL* 7:672).

IV. WRITINGS OF SAINTS AND DOCTORS

St. Benedict

26. ST. ODO, abbot of Cluny (d. 942). Benedict's praise is sung wherever Holy Church has spread, among all tribes, nations, and tongues. For if *in many subjects lies the glory of the king* (Prov. 14:28), how exalted must we consider the glory of a leader whom so huge an army of monks has followed! What king or emperor ever commanded in so many different parts of the world, or drew to himself so many legions from different peoples, as has Benedict gathered from both sexes and all ages, persons voluntarily sworn into the army of Christ? Looking up to him as though he were present, and following the standard of his teaching, they have manfully taken up arms against the devil's hordes. . . . It is an orthodox belief that at the Resurrection every saint will rise with those whom he has gained for the Lord. When all the disciples of this order foregather, what a miracle of the apostolate will that numerous army show itself in Benedict's honor! With what joy will he then dance at having been able to assemble these

cohorts! . . . May Benedict be always in our heart, may Benedict be in our words, may Benedict be in our deeds. In the words of the Apostle, may we be imitators of him (cf. Phil. 3:17), imitating what we have seen in him, and have heard through him, and have heard about him, so that through him in all virtue and all commendation of discipline, the God of peace may be with us forever and ever. Amen (Serm. 3, *De S. Benedicto abbate, PL* 133:728).

27. ST. PETER DAMIAN, monk, cardinal, Doctor of the Church (d. 1072). More abundantly than others our father and master, Benedict, will present a soldier's spoils to the exalted Prince, and will people the palaces of heaven with bands of monks who have led angelic lives. . . . What a resplendent and impressive soldier he will appear before the throne of the Emperor, filled with all virtues, surrounded by countless soldiers, counsellor to the King, friend of the Judge, adversary of the enemy of old. . . . As a boy our father and master, Benedict, abandoned the world with its promises and followed in the footsteps of the running Christ with swift pace which he did not slacken until he caught up with him. Who among those sitting in judgment will pronounce sentence more eminently? Who ever received the hundredfold of this life more abundantly? Who will possess eternal life more gloriously? May our Lord Jesus Christ, who came that we might have life (cf. John 10:10), who is blessed forever, deign to minister to us, at Benedict's intercession, the plenitude of his grace for our present consolation, and the possession of that life which is eternal. Amen (*Hom. ad honorem et laudem S. Benedicti abbatis, PL* 144:548, 553).

28. ST. BERNARD, abbot of Clairvaux, Doctor of the Church (d. 1053). A. The most sweet name of Benedict ought to awaken in our hearts sentiments of gladness and respect, because it is the name of our guide, our master, and our lawgiver (*Serm. de temp. Serm. in natali S. Benedicti abbatis,* n. 2. *PL* 183:377).

B. A noble tree was the blessed Benedict, tall and fruitbearing, like a tree which is planted near the running waters (Ps. 1:3; *ibid.,* n. 4). . . .

C. To its fruit belong the three things of which I have already made mention: his sanctity, his justice, and his piety. His sanctity is proved by his miracles, his piety by his teaching, and his justices by his life. To what purpose do I place the holy man's miracles before you? Is it that you may desire to emulate them? Certainly not, but that you may stand upon them for support, in other words, in order that you may feel confidence and joy in the thought that you are placed under the care of such a pastor and have merited to have the assistance of so powerful a patron. . . . By his teaching, on the other hand, he enlightens us, and guides *our feet into the way of peace* (Luke 1:79). Furthermore, by the justice of his life he fortifies and encourages us.

For we feel the more animated to practice what he teaches because of our assurance that he teaches only what he practiced himself (*ibid.*, n. 7).

D. In this way, then, the sanctity [of our blessed Father] consoles us, his piety enlightens us, and his justice strengthens us. How great was the piety of that holy man, who not only benefited those of his own time, but showed himself solicitous also for the generations to come! It was not alone for his contemporaries that this spiritual tree produced its fruit: even to this present hour its fruit abides and increases. Surely we may call him "dear to God and men," since not only was his presence held in benediction while he lived among men, but his memory still is (cf. Sir. 45:1). In this he is unlike so many other saints who are now beloved of God alone, because known as yet to God alone. For to this hour, as a threefold profession of his love for his Lord (cf. John 21:15 f.), Benedict continues to feed the flock of the Lord with his threefold fruit. He feeds it by his life, he feeds it by his teaching, and he feeds it too by his intercession. Assisted continually by the prayers of so powerful an advocate, do you also, dear brethren, render yourselves faithful, because for this you have been appointed to go forth and bear fruit (cf. John 15:16; *ibid.*, n. 8).

29. ST. GERTRUDE, virgin of the monastery of Helfta (d. 1302). On the feast of the glorious father St. Benedict, as [Gertrude] assisted at Matins with special devotion to honor so excellent a saint, she beheld him in spirit, radiant with glory, standing in the presence of the ever-peaceful Trinity. His countenance was full of majesty and beauty; his habit shone surpassingly. Bright living roses seemed to spring forth from his limbs, each rose producing another, and this one a third, and so on, the last surpassing the former in fragrance and beauty. Thus adorned, the holy Father, truly blessed both by grace and in name, gave the greatest pleasure to the adorable Trinity and to the whole heavenly court as all rejoiced with him because of his beatitude.

The roses which bloomed from his limbs signified the practices by which he had subdued his flesh to his spirit, and all the virtuous deeds which he had performed. They represented also the good works of all his disciples who, inspired by his example and doctrine, had renounced the world in order to live under the discipline of the Rule; those namely who, following him on this royal road, have already attained the heavenly fatherland, or who are yet to attain it in the course of the centuries. For each of these persons this great patriarch receives a distinctive honor. All the saints share in his triumph and joy, and because of them praise God forever.

The blessed Benedict also carried a scepter after the manner of a staff, beautifully embellished on either side with precious stones of great brilliancy. As he held this scepter in his hand, the jewels on the part of the scepter turned toward him gave off a glorious light, signifying the happiness of all those who had professed his Rule and amended and perfected their lives. God overwhelmed him with incomparable joy because of these saints.

The other side of the scepter, turned toward God, reflected the divine justice which has been magnified in the condemnation of those who had been admitted to this holy order through the gratuitous gift of God, but had rendered themselves unworthy of it, and therefore had been consigned to eternal flames. For the higher the Lord elevates a soul to a holy order, the more justly he condemns and the more severely he punishes when the soul conducts itself in an unworthy manner. . . .

Gertrude asked St. Benedict: "Holy Father, what special reward has been yours in heaven as a result of your glorious death?" He replied: "Because I gave up my last breath as I was in the act of praying, I now give forth a fragrance of such sweetness that the saints delight to be near me." Then Gertrude besought him, by reason of that glorious death, to deign to assist the religious of her monastery, each in her final hour. The venerable Father replied: "Whoever will call upon me in prayer, recalling the glorious death with which God honored me, shall have my assistance at his own death, with such fidelity that I will protect him from the insidious temptations of the enemies of salvation wherever I see them threatening him. Fortified and protected by my presence he will avoid the snares of the enemies, and depart happily and peacefully to the joys of eternal blessedness" (*Insinuationes divinae pietatis, Lib. IV,* c. 20, p. 469).

30. ST. BIRGITTA of Sweden (d. 1373). In a vision the Mother of God revealed to St. Birgitta: "The soul of that blessed man, the holy abbot Benedict, was like an angel who passed on to others intense heat and flame, as I shall show you by means of this illustration: It is as though there were three fires, the first was set to myrrh wood, giving off an odor of sweetness. The second was as though it had been lighted in dry wood, which produced glowing coals and shining light. The third was put to olive wood, which gave off flame, light, and heat. I understand these three fires to be the three states of monks, confessors, and martyrs. . . . Now Benedict was sent to forge these three flames into one, insofar as those who were lacking in wisdom were enlightened, the indolent inflamed, the fervent made more fervent still. And thus with these three fires began the religious order of Benedict which directed every member on the way of eternal salvation and happiness, each according to his disposition and ability" (*Revelationes, Lib. III,* c. 21).

31. ST. BRUNO, abbot of Cassino, bp. of Segni (d. 1125). *Behold, a greater than Solomon is here* (Matt. 12:42). Perhaps you will inquire: In what is Benedict greater? In wisdom, in righteousness, in fortitude,

in temperance, and beyond all these considerations, he is richer and more powerful. I am not speaking of the wisdom of this world, which is foolishness in God's sight—for to this Benedict never devoted his attention—but of that true wisdom which leads man to eternal life. Nor do I speak of temporal wealth, which was stolen from the temple by the Egyptians and Chaldeans, but of those everlasting riches which are borne by angels to heaven. In such riches Benedict truly abounded; in them he was extremely wealthy, and deposited his wealth in heaven, where thieves cannot break in and steal (cf. Matt. 6:19; *Sententiarum Lib. VI,* c. 2, *de confessoribus,* Serm. 2, *de S. Benedicto, PL* 165:1053).

32. PAUL WARNEFRIED, deacon, monk of Montecassino (d. circa 800). Who, after the apostles, my dear brethren, can more deservedly be called *the salt of the earth* (Matt. 5:13), than our most blessed Father? He had fled the city of Romulus [Rome] as though from the raging and calamitous waters of a flood. Whatever little of the world's instability remained in his character—and it was little indeed—that which, as it were, was still fluid, he changed into the solidity and nature of salt while he dwelt within his cave. Brought to intense heat by the rays of the true Sun through the fervor of charity, he attained the splendor of righteousness. By his pious words and virtuous deeds he not only preserved the life of the many who knew him personally, but he continues to instruct his followers, especially throughout the West, down to the present day. By his salutary Rule, filled with good sense and saving doctrine, the spirit of restraint summons the way of life of carnal men, decaying with the taint of dissolution, back to salvation. Although, as is true of salt, the severity of the life seems bitingly severe to festering wounds, it will certainly prove a medicine from heaven if borne patiently.

Has there ever been a light more brilliant (cf. Matt. 5:14) than that of this master, which, placed on the lampstand of the higher way of life, cast forth its rays to all the provinces of the West? . . . When, under God's providence, this light was placed on the lampstand of governing, it sent forth its brilliance to all who sought to be enlightened. Even today, through almost all the regions dedicated to Christian worship, once men have heard the wonders of his miracles and have learned to know the light of so great a holiness, these marvels contribute to God's praise by all the faithful whom they have reached. . . . Now whence did this excellent Father merit the grace to perform these wonders, so that in imitation of the holy apostles he shone with so many miracles to the admiration of the whole world, except that he followed the life of those same apostles, and received the doctrine of the heavenly Master with willingness of heart and the firm resolve to keep it? Not even to the slightest degree could the pleasures of the flesh or the joys of the world with all their attraction, nor the clever suggestions of the enemy turn him aside from his longing for eternal reward. Hence dear brethren, we who have gathered together from different walks of life in the world under his teaching, must learn to spurn what he spurned, and love what he loved. If we desire to follow him to glory, we must, by our imitation, follow now in his footsteps, lest, deviating from his pattern of righteousness now, we shall later be forcefully separated from companionship with him (*Hom. 3, de S. Benedicto, PL* 95:1574).

33. BL. GUERRICUS, abbot of Igny, diocese of Rheims (d. 1157). A. *Blessed is the man that trusteth in the Lord* (Jer. 17:7). Our holy Father, blessed by grace and in name, whose memory is held in benediction, was indeed a blessed man who placed his confidence in the Lord. . . . Where in all the world is the memory of the blessed of the Lord, Benedict, not held in benediction? Surely, *Blessings are for the head of the just* (Prov. 10:6), upon whom the grace of God has showered so many blessings of heaven and earth. This blessing is not like that of Esau, *dew from heaven, and fruitfulness of earth, abundance of grain and wine* (Gen. 27:28), but in the fulness of the spirit and in the Maker of the heavens, who spoke by the prophet, *I will be as dew* (Osee 14:6) and to whom it was said: *for thy dew is the dew of light* (Isa. 26:19). . . . Deservedly blessed in the Lord is the man who has reposed his confidence in the Lord, for he who trusts in God attaches himself to God, and is like a tree, for where the tree attaches its root, there it drinks the sap of life and the moisture of fruitfulness (*Serm. II in festo S. Benedicti; de fiducia in Deum,* n. 1, *PL* 185:103).

B. *For his trustworthiness and meekness, God selected him from all mankind* (Sir. 45:4). This was said of Moses but today is, I think, capable of accommodation to Blessed Benedict without incongruity. For since he was filled with the spirit of all the just (*Antiph. 4 ad Vesp. In Transitu S.P. Benedicti,* 21 Mar., *Breviar. monastic.* 1:851), we must believe that he enjoyed not a little of the spirit of Moses. For if the Lord took of the spirit of Moses and conferred it on all that chosen group of elders (cf. Num. 11:24–27), who thereby claimed for themselves a share in the office of Moses, how much more is that spirit conferred on him who enjoys the fulness of that office more truly because he possesses it more spiritually. Moses was the leader of those who went out from Egypt; Benedict, of those who renounce the world. Moses was a lawgiver, as was Benedict as well. Moses was merely the servant of the letter, which kills; Benedict, the minister of the spirit, which vivifies. Because of the hardness of the Jews' hearts, Moses gave them no elevated principles of justification beyond a few moral rules; Benedict bequeathed Gospel purity and a simple moral training. Moses wrote many things that are difficult to understand and impossible or unprofitable to fulfil; Benedict composed a Rule of life remarkable for its discretion and its clarity. Finally, Moses is the leader of the sons of Israel, whom he led out of Egypt but failed to lead into the Promised Land; our leader precedes us into the kingdom of heaven as the standard-bearer of the army of monks, on the straight path, the road of glory (*ibid.*, Serm. IV, *De lenitate et fide,* n. 1, col. 111).

34. POPE STEPHEN III (d. 757). Hail, Benedict, disciple of Christ! Hail, friend of the true Bridegroom! Hail, preacher of truth and leader of nations! Hail, universal lawgiver! Hail, abbot of abbots! Hail, universal archimandrite! Hail, pillar of orthodoxy, I who am numbered among your followers, and even these seven bishops, your clergy, your people of Rome and their princes, your Lateran church in which you were instructed and trained, your monastery of Montecassino, where you dwell in body as well as in spirit. Do not suffer us to be excluded from among your sheep. Protect the Apostolic See! Defend the Roman Empire and these glorious princes, prostrate in mind and body before you, from enemies visible and invisible; pour out your prayers to Christ for all, insofar as we all rejoice in your reward, now and forever. Amen (*Serm. in honorem S. Benedicti,* apud Haeften, *Disquisitiones monasticae, Prolegomenon* 17, p. 31).

35. ST. BERTHARIUS, abbot of Montecassino, martyr (d. 883).

O Benedict, Father enjoying renown in every land,
You have received the highest honors bestowed on men who bear witness to God. . . .
You are the way, the leader, the shepherd, the teacher of all
Who, having spurned the things of earth, seek the kingdom of heaven. . . .
Hail, blessed Father, you who stand forth in a light so strong,
And shine with such loving kindness from among the thrones above,
Be for ever your servants' protector and teacher,
So that the deceptive wolf, the disease-bearing enemy, may never
Seize a lamb from the flock over which you watch in your own right.*

36. ALCUIN OF YORK (d. 804).

Hail, O Benedict, great shepherd of monks!
Govern now by your prayers those whom you have given birth by your teaching. . . .
Aid your followers everywhere by your intercession.
May your flock, beloved shepherd, increase in number. . . .
For the glory of the shepherd grows with the size of the flock.
By your merits preserve your subjects.†

37. CARDINAL BARONIUS (d. 1617). A. God's infinite providence in caring for the needs of his Church was manifest in St. Benedict's voca-

* *Carmen de S. Benedicto, PL* 126:975, 976.

† *Carmen* 254, *ad S. Benedictum, PL* 101:795.

tion, a circumstance to claim the attention of all. In the midst of the deep uncertainty and dense darkness of this horrible night [when so many regions of the Western Church were infected with heresy], a brilliant light shone forth, a light by which the whole Catholic world was to be illumined . . . (*Annales Ecclesiastici,* ann. 494, § 75, tom. 8:549). B. As from a tender shoot there sprang up tracts of fertile trees which spread over the entire Church of the West. This order [of St. Benedict] became a fruitful seminary from which numerous saintly bishops went forth to different dioceses. Nor were there wanting among its members men who, having ascended the apostolic throne, governed the Universal Church with unusual constancy in times when disturbances of intense violence were raging. From the same order of monks others went forth by apostolic appointment to convert pagan peoples who were eager to bear the yoke of Christ, and finally submit of their own accord to the faith of Christ. . . . Others won the martyrs' crown of victory in waging the battle for religion. For the time being we shall pass over those who flourished among ecclesiastical writers by reason of their excellence in sacred studies. Nor shall we attempt to enumerate—for they could hardly be counted—the monasteries of holy virgins. For that matter, it is not easy even to tabulate the many great streams that trace their source to this one small spring, that is to say, the many orders of monks who, although they are now designated by different names in the Church of God, were established by St. Benedict and glory in having taken their origin from him (*ibid.,* ann. 529, § 11, tom. 9:379).

38. JOHN OF TRITHEIM, abbot of Sponheim (d. 1516). A. *Like a lamp put upon the lamp-stand* (Matt. 5:15), the holy man Benedict enlightened the world by his life and doctrine. Of such a man it is stated in Zacharias: *Behold a man, the Orient is his name; and under him shall he spring up, and shall build a temple to the Lord; and he shall bear the glory, and shall sit, and rule upon his throne* (Zach. 6:12–13). . . . He sowed peace and tranquillity. . . . The whole world has merited his blessing. . . . Who would not rejoice to have such an advocate before God? (*Comm. in RSB, Praef., Opera pia et spiritualia,* p. 154.) B. The holy Father Benedict was a man of great renown . . . spreading his order to the sea and sending his descendants to distant regions. He performed his work, not for himself alone, but for all who seek truth. As regards his personal life, he was firm in faith, strong in hope, fervent in the love of God and man, pure of mind, outstanding in devotion, ardent in prayer, his mind inflamed in meditation, zealous in reading Sacred Scripture, and elevated in contemplation. To conclude, in a word, he was distinguished with the beauty of all virtues: humble, sober, chaste, and modest (*De viris illustribus O.S.B., Lib. I,* c. 1, *ibid.,* p. 17).

39. ROLEVINCK, WERNER, Carthusian (d. 1502). Excellent lawgiver

that he was, and Father, support of the Universal Church, and model of the religious ideal, Benedict had illustrious disciples, and in great numbers; in fact, he won the admiration of the whole world. . . . The fact, too, that not just any of the Church's teachers, but the renowned and eloquent Pope Gregory [the Great] wrote his life (*Dialogorum Lib. II, PL* 66:125 ff.) contributed to the honor in which he is held, for all that he did has been made to shine like gold. For it was divinely arranged that since this same excellent legislator had been signalized by God in many ways, both he and his Rule should be strengthened with greater prestige from the fact that the Supreme Pontiff of the Apostolic See should record his life (*Fasciculus temporum,* ann. 504, fol. 39, page numbers written in ink [in: Rolevinck, Werner, *Fasciculus temporum.* Coloniae: 1470].

40. BONIFACE SIMONETTA, Cistercian abbot of St. Stephen's, diocese of Cremona (d. circa 1490). Benedict's garden has produced beautiful flowers in profusion, abundant crops, and wonderful provisions for souls on their final journey! From Benedict's spring, many streams and great rivers have taken their origin, so that the Catholic faith, watered by such irrigation, can never again experience the drought of fruitlessness (*De Christianae fidei et Romanorum pontificum persecutionibus,* ep. 20).

41. DOM PROSPER GUÉRANGER, restorer and abbot of Solesmes, whom Pope Pius IX called a brilliant ornament of the family of St. Benedict, a true disciple of the master (d. 1875). The life of our most holy Patriarch is for us a brilliantly polished and flawless mirror reflecting the image of the perfect monk. It is a golden key opening the way to his Rule. It is a theater in which the deeds of its author shine forth; . . . a living image of a most loving father who makes himself known to his sons in deed and in word. There you can find the distinguishing marks of his monastic apostolate, wonderful works which we can only call miraculous, by means of which God has never ceased to glorify him, and as it were to encompass him, so that there was bestowed on Benedict a credence almost similar to that given to the Lord of all things himself, who directed him and worked through him (*Enchiridion Benedictinum, Introd.,* p. ix).

42. GERARD THE BELGIAN, abbot (15th century). With good reason we say that our holy Patriarch and lawgiver, Benedict, is a Father worthy of all admiration. He is the Father of many thousands of heavenly citizens, his sons who are monks; he is so renowned for his miracles that he seems scarcely to have an equal among the citizens of heaven. Then, too, for many centuries he has been venerated because of the honors bestowed on his children, and because of many holy practices and foundations established in the Church through him. You, my sons, must know that it is a mark of your vocation and of your destiny to love

your Father with deep affection. . . . Now to whom, I ask, should I rather commit myself than to him who is, I realize, more loving to me than I am myself; to whom no one has ever entrusted his welfare and failed to experience confidence; in whom no son, when attacked, has ever failed to find a defender; and, more than all else, to a leader of so great a courage. Who else, in order to protect his followers, has crushed armies, destroyed fleets, conquered demons time and again, terrorized and overthrown kings and princes, turned floods aside, extinguished fires, cured illnesses, assisted the dying, and introduced them into heaven? How much I owe him! For I know that he never fails to plead my cause before God, the Supreme Judge. I realize that he never desists in watching over me even when I sleep, to help me wherever I may be. He is never wanting in interest, but averts all evils, wherever I am, and draws blessings upon me (*Dicta et facta Gerardi monachi, Opusculorum piorum* 2:214 f.).

43. HUGH CAPET, King of France, who cultivated a particular devotion to St. Benedict, is reported to have spoken to his son, when dying (996), in the presence of a number of persons: "By the holy and undivided Trinity, I entreat you never to acquiesce to the counsel of flatterers or to be moved to grant their evil desires because of their obsequious services or poisoned gifts. Never allow them to draw you away from those abbeys which, after God, I entrust to you forever. Do not thoughtlessly divide, plunder, or destroy any of them in anger. I specially want to impress this upon you: under no consideration allow yourself to be separated from the leader of them all—I mean the Father Benedict—for he is a sanctuary of the Judge of universal salvation, a haven of tranquillity, an asylum of safety after the death of the body." [To these utterances Baronius, the historian, adds]: "You see, dear reader, to use Job's terminology, the foundations upon which this kingdom has been built (cf. Job 38:6), namely upon the saints, so that one could rightly say of it: *His foundation upon the holy mountain the Lord loves*" (Ps. 86:1; Baronius, *Annales ecclesiastici,* ann. 1029, § 2, 16:536).

44. PHILIP I, also King of France, when dying (1108) made the following statement in the presence of his friends after he had confessed: "I know that it is customary to conduct the funerals of the kings of the Franks at the church of St. Denis; but because I realize I am so great a sinner, I do not dare to be buried beside the body of so great a martyr. I love St. Benedict, I humbly beg the kind Father of monks, and desire to be buried in his church on the Loire (Fleury-sur-Loire). For he is merciful and benign, and compassionately receives all sinners who seek a worthier life and who earnestly strive to be reconciled with God according to the discipline of his Rule" (*Orderici Vitalis Historia ecclesiastica, Pars III, Lib. 11,* c. 18. *PL* 188:838).

The rule of St. Benedict

45. VEN. BENEDICT, abbot of St. Michael's of Chiusa, diocese of Turin (d. 1091). In the Rule of our holy Father Benedict is found all the perfection of the Gospel and of the apostles (*Vita V. Benedicti abbatis Clusiensis, auctore Willelmo mon., ejus discipulo,* § 9, *PL* 150:1467).

46. GEOFFREY, abbot of Clairvaux (d. 1166). What the Rule of our blessed Father Benedict taught, the study of the Gospel commends to us; the herald of Truth does not present a different doctrine from that which Truth itself had already taught (*Testimonia veterum de RSB, PL* 66:215).

Holy Spirit, author of the rule

47. RUPERT, abbot of Deutz (d. 1135). The Holy Spirit, with whom Benedict was filled, produced the Rule by his mind and spoke through his mouth. The Rule is composed entirely on divine revelation, the foundation of evangelical authority, upon which this author kept the eye of his mind firmly fixed all the while he was writing (*Super quaedam capitula RSB., Lib. I, PL* 170:478).

48. PETER THE VENERABLE, abbot of Cluny (d. 1158). A. Hearken to the author of the Rule, but more importantly, hearken to the one who dictated the Rule, the Holy Spirit. . . . You have Benedict as the author of the principles of your way of life, who commanded that all his writings be directed to one end, the achieving of charity at whatever cost, by one method or another, and serving the welfare of souls. . . . The Rule of this holy Father is an expression of that sublime and universal law of charity on which, according to the statement of Truth itself, *depend the whole Law and the Prophets* (Matt. 22:40). If the whole Law, then certainly the law of his Rule. The monk, therefore, fulfils in very truth, the Rule of our holy Father Benedict which he has professed, when he fulfils the law of charity in all that he does, whether in observing the letter of the law, or in modifying some of the chapters of that Rule (*Lib. IV,* ep. 17, D. Bernardo Claraevall. *abb., PL* 189:328–330). B. And in another place [Augustine] says: "Have charity and do what you will." If [Benedict] could do what he willed, he could write the Rule, he could change that Rule. Nor is it to be considered an injustice to the saint to say that [the Rule] was changed, not by another, but by that charity which, diffused in his heart by the Holy Spirit who had been communicated to him, and that he drew upon that Holy Spirit as upon an organ in composing the Rule (*Lib. I,* ep. 28, *D. Bernardo,* col. 156).

49. ST. BIRGITTA of Sweden (d. 1373). Saint Birgitta heard from the lips of the Blessed Virgin Mary: "God summoned Benedict to the

mountain so that the good flame that was in him would ignite many. Having gathered many lesser fires about him, he made of them, through the Spirit of God, one huge conflagration. He composed for them the Rule of the Spirit of God by which many have been made perfect, as was Benedict himself" (*Revelationes, Lib. III,* c. 20).

50. TURSTIN, abp. of York. Finally, whatever Benedict taught in his Rule was so completely directed by the providence of the Holy Spirit that it is impossible to think of anything holier or more blessed (*Ep. Turstini archiepiscopi Eboracensis ad Willelmum Cantuariensem pontificem., In Append. ad S. Bernardi Epistolas,* n. 490, § 2, *PL* 182: 699).

51. ST. PETER DAMIAN, monk, cardinal (d. 1072). Sharp attention must be given to the opening part of the Rule in order to note to whom the Holy Spirit addresses his words. Observe that I say "the Holy Spirit." For the saintly man [Benedict], who cherished humility so zealously, would certainly never have broken into speech so sharply, forthwith usurping for himself the master's chair, and particularly the privilege of the loving father, by saying: "Hearken, my son, to the precepts of the master, and incline the ear of your heart; willingly accept and faithfully fulfil the instructions of a loving father" (*RSB, Prolog., initium*). But the Holy Spirit, who had done much the same thing at the beginning of the prophecy by exclaiming through Isaias, *I have brought up children, and exalted them* (Isa. 1:2), appoints Benedict, his servant, to be the instrument of his own voice. . . . The holy Rule was made into a sort of large, roomy, impressive house to accommodate all kinds of persons, children and elderly men, the strong and the weak . . . (*Opusc. 13, De perfectione monachorum,* c. 6–7, *PL* 145:300–301).

St. Benedict, excellent lawgiver; his doctrine

52. GEOFFREY, abbot of Vendôme, diocese of Chartres, cardinal (d. 1132). Moses gave a good and holy law indeed to the Jewish people, but Christ gave a far better one to his followers. In the same way, saintly men of earlier monasticism legislated for monks according to the grace that they had received from God, but because he had received greater grace our Father and lawgiver, Benedict, established a better law. . . . The laws which the saints established before his time, as had been the case with the law of Moses, were harsh and difficult. But the sacred provisions of prudent Benedict were appealing to reason, easy of fulfilment, and filled with discretion, the mother of virtues. The sanctions of the ancient monastic leaders were, in a sense, like elaborations of the Old Testament. But our loving Father, Benedict, brought us forth, sons of the new grace, by tempering the severity of those harsh statutes. All, or nearly all of the old legislation had passed out of existence when Benedict published the new law for monks. The former seem to have

been a foreshadowing or prefiguring of the future monastic life; through the renowned Benedict, writing under the guidance of the Holy Spirit, the truth has been made known to us. Out of his great humility, however, he praises and expresses admiration for the lives and works of St. Basil and other early Fathers, passing over in silence or referring only casually to anything personal, as a worthy disciple of the worthiest of all teachers, who had enjoined silence on him, since Benedict accomplished what no one is able to accomplish without the divine Master's aid. . . . Just as after the three blessed Evangelists, Matthew, Mark, and Luke, there came another, John, who wrote more worthily, so also this holy man, following upon the other Fathers of monks, wrote a Rule in which he lovingly united men to *the chief corner stone* (Eph. 2:20), Christ Jesus, with the cement of sweet charity. We may properly say, therefore, and must firmly believe, that he was destined to be God's apostle and messenger for us. For God sent him to us in order that by means of the example of his own well-ordered and beautiful life he might fashion us in a distinctive and extraordinary manner, and that he might make known to us what is virtuous through the doctrine of his wisdom. For the Lord had decreed that Benedict should be second to none but himself as Father, shepherd, physician, and teacher of monks.

Therefore, beloved friends and confreres, since this blessed man is thus worthy to be our Father, shepherd, physician, and teacher, let us beseech him in our hearts and by our words to nourish us as a loving father, feed our souls with the bread of virtue, and heal the wounds of our sins and offenses. When we have learned diligently at his feet the things that are to be sought after, let us labor and merit to come to him who is the giver of all good gifts and the rewarder of good works, our God and Lord Jesus Christ, who with the Father and the Holy Spirit lives and reigns forever (Serm. 11, *in festivitate B. Benedicti, PL* 157:279 f.).

53. AUGUSTINE, Cistercian monk (date of death undetermined). Because of the prerogative of his sanctity, the excellence of his purity of life, and the glory of his miracles, our holy Father Benedict, shines after the manner of a pure and brilliant star from west to east; so that whatever the east rejoices at possessing in any of its regions, and in its treasures of grace, the west justly glories in possessing in this holy Father, Benedict, filled with the spirit of all the just. This highly revered father who wrote a Rule for monks whose doctrine and provisions he had learned by the long practice of virtues, not from man, but by the anointing of him who teaches men knowledge. In this Rule, the wonder-builder, the Holy Spirit, united in a most marvelous manner the height of perfection and the discretion of great moderation (*Citat. a Constantino Cajetano, O.S.B.,* 1650).

54. ST. HILDEGARDE, abbess of St. Rupert's monastery (d. 1179). A. [God thus spoke to St. Hildegarde]: "The first rays of the new day's light represent the faithful words of the apostles' preaching. Dawn signifies the origins of the way of life based upon that apostolic teaching which had its beginnings in the desert and in caves [the eremitical life]. But the full sun rises on the discreetly governed and well-regulated pattern of life of my servant Benedict. I inspired him with an ardent flame of love and taught him to adore, through the garb of his order, the Incarnation of my Son and to act in imitation of my Son's passion through the abandonment of his own will. Benedict, who took up his abode in a cave and tortured his body and brought it into subjection out of love of the higher life, is like another Moses. At my command the first Moses wrote on tables of stone the harsh and severe Law of my commandments and gave it to the Jews. But as my Son perfected the Law of Moses with the sweetness of the Gospel, so my servant Benedict, under the gentle inspiration of the Holy Spirit made the basic principles of the monastic form of life a way of moderation and smoothness, which up to his time had been quite different. By so doing he assembled a huge throng of religious brethren about him, as had also my Son by the sweetness of his perfume drawn the Christian people to himself" (*Scivias, sive visiones ac revelationes, Lib. II, Visio 5, PL* 197:487).

B. I heard the voice of the true Light addressing me: "The Holy Spirit produced in Benedict a brilliant and spiritual doctrine so that what glowed in his mind he carried to perfection through the love of God, never allowing the cunning temptations of the devil to interfere with his works. So completely was he filled with grace of the Holy Spirit that in none of his work, never for even a moment, or for the twinkling of an eye, was he wanting in strength drawn from him. The source was enclosed, and he poured out his doctrine in the discretion received from God, accurately establishing the level of his doctrine, neither too high nor too low, but at the very center, so that everyone, strong and weak, could profitably draw from it, each according to his capacity. . . . With meekness Blessed Benedict drew forth his doctrine in the fear of God; he taught the divine commandments in loving-kindness; built the wall of the Rule's holiness in charity; and in his chastity he kept himself a stranger to all the enticements and pleasures of the world. And since he thus wrote his doctrine in fear and love, in charity and chastity, nothing may be added to it or taken from it. It is wanting in nothing whatever, since it was made and completed in the Holy Spirit" (*RSB explanatio, Prooem., PL* 197:1055).

C. Under the inspiration of the Holy Spirit, our holy Father Benedict composed a Rule designed for the direction of persons dedicated to the spiritual life, drawn from the lives of all the saints (*Vita S.*

Disibodi, episc. et confessoris, c. 2, n. 22. *Acta Sanctorum Bolland.* Jul. tom. 2, die 8, p. 592).

55. ST. BRUNO, bp. of Segni (d. 1123). Moses, or rather God himself, who is represented by Moses, commanded that the chiefs of the people, and those who carried staves, should dig wells (cf. Num. 21:16 f.), and explain the Scriptures. . . . What capable men there were in former times, for this task of digging! How many wells they dug, and how deep! What waters they drew forth from the depths—living waters, leaping to eternal life! . . . What shall I say of Blessed Benedict, who has dug us a famous well in his Rule, whose wholesome and pleasant-tasting water slakes the thirst and ministers to the health of all who wish to drink. After the apostles and the evangelists, no well has been dug which has satisfied more men and freed them from the danger of death and all passions. Whoever we may be, brethren, no matter with what toil we are fatigued, let us hasten to these wells: there we shall find Jesus, worn out too, sitting beside the well, and speaking with the Samaritan woman (*Sentent. Lib. VI,* p. 2. *Serm. 3, PL* 165:1057).

56. FREPPEL, Charles-Émile, bp. of Angers (d. 1891). Nothing is more simple than the *Rule of St. Benedict;* but this simplicity is that of the Gospel, which accommodates itself to the understanding of every person, just as it appeals to everyone's heart. To smoothe the way of the evangelical counsels with the forces of moderation and discretion —such was Benedict's purpose. As St. Hildegarde, one of his more inspired interpreters, stated it: "He plotted a course that is discreet in its demands and smooth" (see n. 54-A). It is not the perfect whom he addresses, but those who desire to become perfect. What he seeks to found, in all simplicity, is a school where a person will learn to serve the Lord to the best of his ability, a school of the Lord's service (*RSB, Prolog.*), in which he will introduce nothing harsh, nor anything too arduous for human weakness. Yes, it is with ease, and in complete freedom, sweetly and without fear, that his disciple will follow the very way outlined by the Gospel and arrive at perfection, aiming neither too high nor too low, but allowing himself to move along with the breath of grace which will lead him forward on his path to the goal he must reach.

There you have the Rule of Benedict, an admirable work, my brethren, in which, under light from on high there shines the genius of a man with vast and deep perception. In his legislation for souls summoned to the way of perfection, in this masterpiece of prudence and discretion, as St. Gregory expresses the thought (*Dialogorum Lib. II,* c. 36, *PL* 66:200), there is, beyond doubt, lofty clarity of view illumined by faith. But one finds there too, unless I am mistaken, characteristics of the patricians of ancient Rome, who had conquered the world with wisdom rather than by force, who knew how to govern that world after having conquered it, and who, in so doing, although they were unaware of their role, prepared for the universal kingdom of Christ. It is by his wisdom, which is distinctively Roman, that the Patriarch of Montecassino won for himself a posterity as numerous as the stars of heaven and the sands of the seashore.

The sons of St. Benedict have been able to carry this Rule, which is adaptable to the most diverse conditions, this Rule which excludes nothing and accommodates itself to all, to all countries, and into whatever social environment they willed. Everywhere it will form perfect Christians—wherever, that is, it finds souls to consecrate themselves to God and an enclosure for chanting the divine praises (*Discours sur l'ordre monastique, prononcé dans l'église abbatiale de Solesmes a l'anniversaire des obsèques de Dom Guéranger,* le 16 mars 1876. *Le Semaine du fidèle,* 1876, pp. 416–417).

57. GEOFFREY, abbot of Clairvaux (d. 1166). "This is the way by which Benedict, the beloved of the Lord, ascended into heaven" (*S. Greg. Magn., Dialogorum Lib. II,* c. 37. *PL* 66:202). What is this way leading from his cell other than the order which the holy man founded, and the way of life which took its beginning from him? The beloved of the Lord ascended this way because "he cannot have taught a doctrine at variance with his way of life" (*ibid.,* c. 36). And this is the chief confidence of those who are zealous in treading in his footsteps, following their leader and teacher. No one can doubt the holiness of this manner of living by which Benedict obtained so great a grace of sanctity during his life here, so great a glory of blessedness after death, formed as it is more on divine inspiration and counsel than on human prudence and learning (*Declamationes de colloquiis Simonis cum Jesu, ex S. Bernardi serm. collectae,* 38, n. 45. *PL* 184:461).

58. LEO, abp. of Ravenna (d. circa 1000). Observe, my dear friend, . . . the well-loved Rule drawn up by Blessed Benedict and dictated by the Holy Spirit, cherished by the illustrious doctor and Supreme Pontiff [Gregory], and imitated by men seeking perfection, for it leads its followers to the kingdom of heaven (*Mabillon, Acta Sanctorum O.S.B., de Leone Abb. Nonantulano, ep. ad Durandum monachum,* tom. 7:873).

59. TORQUEMADA, JUAN, O.P., cardinal (d. 1468). The ideal of all monastic perfection is presented in [the Rule of holy Father Benedict], for it contains all the instruments of virtues and all the precepts of religion, as is abundantly evident to those who contemplate its individual chapters, so that we may apply to it the words of the Book of Wisdom: *For she* [wisdom] *is the instructress in the understanding of God, the selector of his works* (Wisd. 8:4; *De commendatione RSB, c. unicum* [in: *Regula S. Benedicti, cum doctiss. et piiss. commentariis*

Joannis de Turre Cremata . . . et Smaragdi abbatis; Coloniae Agrippinae, 1575. p. 37]).

60. ST. ANTONINUS, O.P., abp. of Florence (d. 1459). The most blessed Benedict, Father of the monks of the West, wrote a Rule which excels, as I may say, in detailed directiveness. It is presented in the decrees of the Church as approved. All monks of the west hold it in veneration as the foundation [on which monastic legislation rests] (*Summa Theologica, Pars III, tit. 16, De regulis religiosorum,* § 7, 3:851 f., somewhat modified).

61. SMARAGDUS, abbot of St. Michel's, Verdun (d. circa 800). The Rule of the holy Father Benedict is, for tried and tested monks, a palm of victory, a pleasant and broad highway; but to young persons and novices who have long been nurtured and provided for in comfort, it seems harsh and stringent.

This is the sacred road along which God's blessed forces seek to hasten, the narrow path to heaven, surpassing all others in splendor. This lofty Rule admonishes all monks to be detached from personal possessions and to seek the kingdom of heaven. . . . In the terminology of the sacred law this is called by our Fathers the royal way for those who pursue its course worthily. To the virtuous it is life itself, nothing less than the rule of salvation; to those inspired by love, the arms of defense; to the evil a gleaming spear.

The Rule trains monks to hope for the region of light in the paradise of heaven. It maps out the journey for our brethren, and opens the heavens to those who have proved themselves friends [*You are my friends if you do the things I command you* (John 15:14)]. Hence they must not be lazy, but must "run . . . in the way of God's commandments . . . in patience" (*RSB, Prolog.*). It serves to check on the monk's life, regulates his conduct and makes it pleasing, shakes it violently [in the conversion of morals], makes it conform [to what others are doing in striving to give praise to God], and in this conformity draws it along the way of progress.

It destroys what is evil; it tests the just man as gold is tried by fire; it files off what is rough, weighs again, and in the process of polishing, gives balance and harmony to the way of life. . . .

It reproves, entreats, rebukes (cf. II Tim. 4:2 and *RSB,* c. 2), and is ever ready to correct those whom it has admitted to the brotherhood. It has the power to lead monks to the eternal kingdom and unite them happily with the angelic choir . . .

Let no monk fear to enter upon the narrow way; for it leads to the star-studded goal, to the regions of the blessed. . . .

But in all he does let discretion govern the monk's heart, and lead him in the mid-course [virtue's avoidance of extremes] along the royal road. The obligations of the sacred law spur him on, but so that he will adroitly avoid one side of the road and fearfully keep his distance from the other.

Whoever longs to gather the mature fruits of holiness must identify himself with them by his deeds. If his life is adorned by virtuous conduct, and a chaste body, he will ever be loved by the Lord. Let him be devoted to silence, humble, meek, and kind; patient, serious-minded, prudent, and devout. Let him proceed on this course docile of disposition, well-counselled, distrustful of his own judgment; a man marked by sorrow for sin, tranquillity, and caution. Let compunction of heart stir up in him the waters which wash away all uncleanness and filth from the soul (*Comm. in RSB, Praef. metrice dictata, PL* 102:689).

62. LOUIS THE PIOUS, emperor (d. 804), addressing the newly-elected abbot Eigil of Fulda. The man of God, Benedict, composed a Rule which is excellent in expression, in which he included nothing of occult doctrine, nothing of obscurity. Because of this quality his Rule needs not explanation so much as calling to mind. For it is the narrow portal and the straight way that leads its followers to God. It so teaches you to have discretion, appreciation for the capacity of your subjects, and love for them, that you yourself are exhorted in charity to exercise your superiorship in rooting out vices, in doing all in moderation because of the fainthearted, in being ever mindful of the discretion of Jacob, and constantly and in all things in reminding yourself of your own weakness (*Eigilis vita, auctore Candido monacho Fuldensi,* § 12. *Mabillon Acta Sanctorum O.S.B.* 5:224).

63. JACOBUS DE VARAGINE, O.P., abp. (d. 1298). As the sun which has already set gives forth its light for us to the moon, and the moon shines upon us, so with St. Benedict, in glory after the death of the body, gives us his moon, that is, the salutary Rule, which sheds its light upon the monastic form of religion (*Serm. 95,* n. 1 ex 3, *de S. Benedicto* [in: *Domini Jacobi de Voragine, S. Theologiae professoris, Ord. Praedicatorum, quondam episcopi Januen., Sermones de sanctis per anni totius circulum concurrentibus.* Lugduni: apud Jacobum Giuncti, 154 . . .]; no pagination. This work is not to be confused with the sermons on St. Benedict in the *Legenda aurea, The Golden Legend* which is readily found).

64. GUÉRANGER, Dom Prosper, abbot of Solesmes (d. 1875). It behooves us to receive the Holy Rule with filial reverence. . . . By its means St. Benedict became, like Abraham, the Father of many generations of great men, namely the members of the monastic order. By its means he equipped countless soldiers of the Lord with strong weapons to subdue demons, and with them, corruption and errors. By its means he filled the heavens with so many witnesses that their number and holiness proclaim how powerful in word and deed was that harvester of

souls. In it Benedict, although dead, still speaks; in it you will find his authentic testament; in it his sons possess a relic of their Father of inestimable worth (*Enchiridion Benedictinum, Praef.*, p. iv).

65. BOSSUET, bp. of Meaux (d. 1704). The Rule is an epitome of Christianity; a learned and mysterious abridgement of the whole Gospel teaching, of all the instructions of the holy Fathers, of all the counsels of perfection. In it prudence and simplicity, humility and courage, severity and gentleness, liberty and dependence, eminently appear. In it correction has all its proper firmness; condescension all its attractiveness; command all its vigor; and subjection its repose; silence its gravity, speech its grace, strength its exercise, and weakness its support. And yet St. Benedict calls this Rule only a beginning, in order that those who are bound to obey it may always live in a state of holy fear (*Panégyrique de Saint Benoit,* 3me point. *Oeuvres Complètes de Bossuet.* 10 v. Paris: Lefèvre, 1856, 5:49; *Panegyrics of the saints, from the French of Bossuet and Bourdaloue;* edited by Rev. D. O'Mahony; London: Kegan Paul, Trench, Trubner, 1924, p. 82).

Regular observance

66. ST. THOMAS AQUINAS, O.P. (d. 1274). As regards those things which are not included in the common obligation of a precept, the transgression thereof [the rule of a religious order] does not involve a mortal sin, except by reason of contempt. . . . An action or transgression proceeds from contempt when a man's will refuses to submit to the ordinance of the law or the rule, and from this he proceeds to act against the law or rule (*II-II, q. 186, art. 9, Utrum religiosus semper peccet mortaliter transgrediendo ea quae sunt in regula, et ad 3m. Op. Om.* 10:500, 501; Am. ed., 2:1980).

67. ST. JEROME. You have abandoned the world; more than that, besides your baptismal vow, you have taken a new one [virginity]; you have entered into a compact with your adversary, stating to him: "I renounce you, O devil, your world, your pomp, and your works." Observe, therefore, the treaty you have made, and keep terms with your adversary while you are in the way of this world (*Ep. 130, ad Demetriadem, de servanda virginitate,* § 7, *PL* 22:1113).

68. ST. BERNARD. A. I implore you, dearest brothers, so to act, so to stand firm in the Lord, as to be always careful for the observance of the order, that the order may always be careful for you (*Ep. 345, ad fratres de S. Anastasio,* § 1, *PL* 182:550; James (N. 388), p. 458). B. Is not a bird all the more buoyant for the very quantity of its feathers? Pluck them off, and it will be weighed down by its body. That is the way it is with the Rule too, the sweet yoke, the light burden of Christ. The more fully we submit ourselves to it, the more we are lifted up by

it; the more we try to avoid it, the heavier we find it; for it bears us rather than is borne by us (*Ep. 385, ad monachos Ecclesiae S. Bertini,* § 3, *PL* 182:589; James, p. 492).

69. ST. BIRGITTA (d. 1373). [Our Savior said]: "He is a monk of St. Benedict who obeys the Rule rather than flesh; who neither by the religious garb nor in his observance of morality strives to please anyone but God; who daily longs for death and prepares himself for leaving this world, concerned only about rendering his account of the Rule of Benedict (*Revelationes, Lib. IV,* c. 127).

70. ST. CAESARIUS OF ARLES, monk of Lerins, bp. (d. 542). Because I desire you to be like angels, I beg you again and again, and earnestly entreat you, by Almighty God, not to permit anything to be struck from the instruction of the Holy Rule, but with the Lord's help, to strive with all your power to keep it, in the knowledge that *each will receive his own reward according to his labor* (I Cor. 3:8). More than all else, I ask your holiness [the abbess] not to receive our admonition casually, for we are not speaking out of personal presumption but are exhorting you in deep affection and true charity, according to what is read in the canonical Scriptures and what is contained so extensively in the writings of the ancient Fathers. You read that *Whoever does away with one of these least commandments . . . shall be called least in the kingdom of heaven* (Matt. 5:19). Hence do not despise the words of our lowliness, as though they were of no consequence, for it is written: *He who rejects you, rejects me* (Luke 10:16), and *He that contemneth small things shall fall by little and little* (Ecclus. 19:1, Douay; *Regula pro virginibus, Recapitulatio,* c. 13, *CR* 1:361).

71. ST. AUGUSTINE, bp. of Hippo (d. 430). In our questions we should refer everything, especially what we say to the people from the pulpit, not to man's temporal welfare, but to his eternal salvation; and since we must also warn them against eternal damnation, everything we say is important. So true is this that whatever the Christian teacher says about financial matters, either in regard to gain or loss, or whether the amount be large or small, should not seem unimportant, and we should certainly protect it even in regard to small amounts of money, because the Lord says: *He who is faithful in a very little thing is faithful also in much* (Luke 16:10). Therefore what is a very little thing is a little thing, but to be faithful in a little thing is a great thing. Just as the nature of a circle, namely that all lines drawn from a point in the center to the circumference are equal, is the same in a large disk as it is in a little coin, so, where inconsequential matters are transacted in justice, the dignity of justice is not lessened (*De doctrina Christiana, Lib. VI,* c. 18, *Ecclesiasticus orator in materia grandi semper versatur,* n. 35, *PL* 34:105).

72. ST. ANSELM, abbot, abp. of Canterbury (d. 1109). A. Fish die if the pool where they are kept gradually and frequently is cracked, and not repaired, thus allowing the water to flow out; in a similar way the religious spirit of a monastic order is completely destroyed if its observance gradually loses fervor by contemptuous disregard of small faults (*Eadmeri monachi Lib. de S. Anselmi similitudinibus,* c. 123, *PL* 159:677). B. This is a certain fact that we have learned by experience in many communities: in a monastery where even the most detailed observances are faithfully kept, the strength of the monastic rule is preserved inviolable; peace reigns among the brethren; and in the chapter accusations are rare and are tranquilly made. In contrast, where minor points of discipline are neglected, the whole observance is gradually relaxed and disappears altogether (*Lib. III, ep. 49, ad monachos Cestrenses* [Chester], *PL* 159:80; Schmitt, *Op. Om.* 4:137). C. Your community ought to be the temple of God, and the temple of God is holy (cf. I Cor. 3:17). If you live in a holy manner, as I hope you do, you are the temple of God. You live in a holy manner when you guard the objectives of the order zealously and contemn not even the least regulation (*ibid., ep. 125, ad Eulaliam abbatissam.* 159:161; Schmitt 5:347). D. Since your love for me is so great, I should consider myself guilty of an injustice if I were not to love you. And because true love always desires the progress of the one loved, I exhort you and plead with you constantly to direct your mind toward greater progress. If you ask my advice as to how you are to do this, I state simply: Love your monastic vocation above all things (*ibid., Lib. IV, ep. 111, ad Hugonem monachum . . . quem hortatur ut culpas suas nec celet, nec defendat, ut cor suum abbati suo patere velit,* col. 259; Schmitt 4:138).

73. ST. GREGORY THE GREAT, monk, pope (d. 604). A. If we neglect to take heed to little things, being insensibly led away, we perpetrate even greater things with a bold face (*Moral., Lib. X,* c. 11, n. 21, *PL* 75:933).

Profession of vows a holocaust

B. When one has vowed to Almighty God all that he has, all that makes up his life, and all that is pleasing to him [that is, poverty, chastity, obedience], that is a holocaust. And there are some who reserve nothing whatever for themselves, but immolate to Almighty God their understanding, their speech, their life, and the very being they have received. What do these do but offer a holocaust to God, or, more properly speaking, they become a holocaust (*In Ezechiel. Proph. Lib. II, Hom. 8,* § 16, *PL* 76:1057).

74. ST. EPHRAEM, deacon, monk, of Edessa (d. 378). Consider to whom you have bound yourself, and do not underestimate that contract. You know that in that hour [of your profession] angels wrote

down the words you used, what you agreed to, what you gave up in sacrifice. . . . On the day of judgment angels will present your written record and the words of your lips before the dreaded tribunal (*Serm. de compunctione animi, Op. Om.* 3:592).

75. ST. BASIL THE GREAT, bp. of Caesarea (d. 379). Before making a promise to live the religious life, anyone who wishes may lawfully and licitly follow the way of the world and freely submit to the yoke of wedlock. When, however, by his own consent, a man has been made subject to a prior claim, he should reserve himself for God as a kind of sacred votive offering, in fear of being condemned for sacrilege by defiling again, by an ordinary way of life, the body consecrated to God by a vow (*Serm. Asceticus I,* n. 2, *PG* 31:871).

76. ST. AUGUSTINE. Do not regret having made the vow; rather rejoice that you are no longer free to do what you might have done to your own great harm. Go forward boldly, then, and turn your words into deeds; he who inspired your vow will help you. Happy the necessity which forces us to do better things! (*Ep. 127, ad Armentarium et uxorem Paulinam,* n. 8. *PL* 33:487. St. Augustine exhorts this husband and wife, who had made a vow of continence, and wanted to be released from the same, to remain faithful to their promise. Wolter applies the words in the present wider connotation.)

77. HUMBERT OF ROMANS, fifth master general of the Order of Preachers (d. 1277). Beloved brethren . . . with all my strength I pray you and urge you in conscience by him who redeemed us with his precious blood and who, by his loving death opened the door of life for us: being not unmindful of your profession and your purpose, recall the old paths along which our forefathers hastened (cf. Jer. 6:16) in the spirit of intense zeal; and now reign with Christ, consoled forever with the repose of the blessed (*Ep. de tribus votis substantialibus,* c. 57, *De vita regulari,* 1:41).

Renewal of vows

78. DENIS THE CARTHUSIAN, monk of Roermond (d. 1471). This is the teaching of St. Bernardine of Siena (*Serm. 24, De sacra religione, pro Sabb. post Dom. II in Quadr.,* c. 3, *Vovens ex voto stabilitur magis in via Dei, Op. Om.* 2:128), and of many other Doctors: As often as a religious, recalling his profession to memory, so rejoices in its having been made that if he had not as yet made it, he would, moved by the love of God, do so now—that is, he would renounce the world with all its vices and would be prepared to offer himself as a victim in the perpetual service of him who emptied himself for man's sake, taking upon himself the nature of a slave (cf. Phil. 2:7), who came not to be served but to serve—whoever calls his profession to mind with these dispositions obtains the full remission of all his sins (*Quam sit fructuosum*

*de professione facta gaudere. Append. Lib. de professione monastica).**

79. DOM GERMAIN MORIN, monk of Maredsous (d. 1946). We should be mistaken if we saw only an interesting archeological fact in this series of remarkable coincidences. They express a great and solid doctrine—namely, that in the mind of ecclesiastical tradition our profession is truly a second baptism which, like the first, remits all the penalty due to sin.

Lastly, a theologian of our order has been at pains to bring together the authorities on which this doctrine rests. And, indeed, there are few propositions, outside the truths of faith properly so-called, which rest on such solid foundations. These are, in the first place, the Fathers of the Church, who, from St. Jerome to St. Bernard, are unanimous in comparing the monastic profession sometimes to baptism, sometimes to martyrdom, which is itself only a baptism of blood. Commentators on the Rule, great monastic synods, the liturgy of divers religious institutes, echo the teaching of tradition. St. Thomas, who is followed by the whole medieval school, also pronounces in favor of the same doctrine. Canon Law itself officially sanctions it; whilst mystical writers make it the point of departure of their considerations on the excellence of the religious state.

All this, doubtless, is well calculated to inspire with a high idea of this venerable rite, at which we can never assist without fresh emotion. Let those, above all, who are preparing with all the fervor of their soul to pronounce their holy vows, profit by this teaching. And let us who have already accomplished this great act, and who sometimes fear that we have not profited by it as we should, take courage by the remembrance of this solidly established doctrine—that the power of remitting all the penalty due to sin is attached, not to the act of profession only, but even to its simple renewal, whether made in public or in private with the interior dispositions which are presupposed by the formula of the holy vows. This opinion, already known to us through the pages of those two great Saxon nuns of the thirteenth century, Gertrude and Mechtild, has since been supported by an imposing array of theologians, such as St. Bernardine of Siena, Denis the Carthusian, the Doctors of Salamanca, St. Alphonsus, and still more recently, the venerable founder of Beuron, Abbot Maurus Wolter. . . . We have in our Breviary, at the end of the Act of Thanksgiving after Mass, a formula—

* This two-page appendix to the work *De professione monastica* is not given in the 41 v. *Op. Om.*, 1896 ed., to which all subsequent references in this translation are made, but is found on p. 417 in *Opuscula insigniora D. Dionysii Carthusiani doctoris ecstatici. . . .* Coloniae Agrippinae, 1599, [xii] 960 pp., which is one of the works of Denis employed by Wolter. The reason for excluding the passage from the later more critical edition should certainly not be considered on doctrinal grounds, as is clearly evidenced by the following quotation from the great scholar, Dom Germain Morin, O.S.B.

richly indulgenced by the Church—composed by the learned Haeften, Prior of Afflighem. Let us use it as often as our devotion prompts us (*L'idéal monastique et la vie chrétienne des premiers jours,* 4me ed., Paris: Desclée de Brouwer, 1927, p. 60 f.; *The Ideal of the monastic life found in the apostolic age;* translated from the French by C. Gunning; London: R. & T. Washbourne, Ltd., 1914, p. 60 f.).

Profession a second baptism

80. ST. THOMAS AQUINAS. Moreover it may be reasonably stated that also by entrance into religion a man obtains remission of all his sins. For if by giving alms a man may forthwith satisfy for his sins, according to Daniel 4:24, *Redeem thou thy sins with alms;* much more does it suffice to satisfy for all his sins that a man devote himself wholly to the divine service by entering religion, for this surpasses all manner of satisfaction, even that of public penance . . . just as a holocaust exceeds a sacrifice, as Gregory declares (*Homily 20 on Ezechiel*). Hence we read in the lives of the Fathers (vi, libell., n. 9, 1) that by entering religion one receives the same grace as by being baptized (*II-II, q. 189, art. 3, Utrum ille qui obligatus est voto ad religionis ingressum, teneatur intrare, ad 3m, Op. Om.* 10:540; Am. Ed. 2:2008).

81. ST. PETER DAMIAN. Tell me, therefore, have you not read that the purpose of the monastic life is a second baptism? Since this is manifestly contained in the sayings of the Fathers, it cannot be denied: The profession of the monastic life is a second baptism (*Opusc. 16, adversus episcopum monachos ad saeculum revocantem, PL* 145:376).

81.[a] ST. JOHN OF DAMASCUS, monk (d. circa 754). We know that the divine profession of the monastic life drives out sin, and that it is the companion and helper of the righteousness granted to us through holy baptism (*In hist. Barlaam et Joasaph,* c. 12, *PG* 96:971).

82. ST. BERNARD. You ask me why the monastic profession is so privileged among all other works of penance as to deserve to be called a second baptism. I answer: because it implies a complete renunciation of the world, because the monastic life is the most excellent of all, making its professors and lovers more like angels than men, nay, it restores in man the original image and likeness of God (cf. Gen. 1:26), inasmuch as, like baptism, it conforms us anew to Christ. For we are in some sense baptized anew when, *mortifying our members which are on earth* (Col. 3:5), we again *put on the Lord Jesus Christ* (Rom. 13:14), being a second time *united with him in the likeness of his death* (Rom. 6:5). And just as in baptism we are rescued from the powers of darkness and transferred to the kingdom of eternal glory, so in the regeneration of the monastic vows, we are delivered from the denser darkness of multiplied personal sins and introduced into the light of virtue, so that we can say with the Apostle: *The night is far advanced; the day is at hand*

(Rom. 13:12; *Lib. de praecepto et dispensatione,* c. 17, § 54. *PL* 182: 889).

Order of St. Benedict

83. ST. MECHTILD, virgin of the monastery of Helfta (d. circa 1300), heard these words from the Lord: "The center of the Church is the order of St. Benedict; it is like a pillar on which the whole Church rests; for it holds some relation to all the ranks to be found in the Universal Church. It renders homage and obedience to superiors, namely the pope and prelates. It furnishes instruction and sets the rules for leading a good and virtuous life to religious, for other orders only imitate this order in certain points. The good and just find in it advice and help; sinners, compassion, correction, and the hearing of their sins in confession; the souls in purgatory, the help of holy prayers. Travelers and pilgrims find in it hospitality; poor people, sustenance; those who are hungry and those who thirst, food and drink; the sad, consolation; the souls of the faithful departed, deliverance (*Le livre de la grace spéciale, Iere partie,* ch. 28, p. 96).

84. JACQUES DE VITRY, cardinal (d. 1240). No other religious institute in the same degree as the order of St. Benedict has had so many saints; nor has any remained so long in holiness and rigor of discipline; nor begotten so many prelates throughout the whole world, who by their example of an outstanding way of life and their holy preaching have snatched so many souls from the devil and given the example that has helped to inspire so many other religious orders (*Historia occidentalis,* c. 20).

85. ST. ODO, abbot of Cluny (d. 942). Let him be called a lamp, . . . a star, . . . a sun. Let him be called an angel, for they seek the law from his lips. Finally, let them realize and rejoice in the appropriateness of his being called Benedict (that is, blessed), whom God so blessed with every spiritual blessing, and through whom so many will possess blessing as through an inheritance. I acknowledge that it is pleasing to those who love this great father to be identified with his name, which after the divine name Christians employ more than any other (*Serm. 3, de S. Benedicto abb., PL* 133:725).

86. BENEDICT HAEFTEN, provost of Affighem (d. 1648). The sons of the blessed Patriarch, Benedict, who have inherited from him the very name of blessedness, so follow in the footsteps of their Father, that they too may merit one day to hear the words, *Come, blessed of my Father, take possession of the kingdom prepared for you from the foundation of the world* (Matt. 25:34). The very name of Benedict demands this as a minimum from all Benedictines (*Disquisitiones monasticae. Prolog. in vitam S. Benedicti, XVI, pars 1,* p. 29).

Excellence of the religious profession

87. ST. BERNARD. A. What is that *pearl of great price* (Matt. 13:46), I ask you, my brethren, to possess which we are to give all we have—that is to say, our very selves, for he has given all to God who has offered himself? Is it not *religion pure and undefiled* (Jas. 1:27), in which a man lives more purely, falls more rarely, rises more quickly, walks more securely, is blessed with graces more frequently, sleeps more peaceably, dies more confidently, is purified more quickly, and rewarded more abundantly? (*Hom. in Matt. 13, 45, Simile est regnum coelorum homini quaerenti bonas margaritas,* § 1, *In Append., PL* 184:1131.) B. O unhappy monk that I am, that I should have lived to see the day when our order has come to such a pass. Our order was the first in the Church: in fact, it was that from which the Church arose. None on earth more nearly resembles the angelic orders, none is closer to the heavenly Jerusalem, our Mother; both because of the beauty of chastity and the ardor of charity. Its founders were the Apostles, its first members, those whom Paul so often calls saints (*Apologia ad Guglielmum S. Theodorici abbatem,* c. 10, n. 24, *PL* 182:912).*

88. ALCUIN OF YORK (d. 804). How blessed is the life of monks! It is pleasing to God, worthy of the love of angels, honorable in the sight of men. There is no doubt that he who lives this life happily among men is reigning happily among the angels (*Ep. 93, ad fratres Juvavensis Ecclesiae, PL* 100:298).

89. ANSELM, bp. of Havelberg, O.Prae. (d.1154). Following the many Fathers of monks dwelling in Egypt, Blessed Benedict arose in

* Shortly after he had succeeded the unfortunate Pons (in 1122) as archabbot of Cluny, Peter the Venerable (Peter Maurice de Montboisier) wrote a long letter, addressed to Bernard, the Abbot of Clairvaux, in which the Cistercians were severely taken to task for being scrupulously solicitous about lesser observances of the monastic law, to the neglect of its more important precepts. However well intentioned Peter may have been, and it is admitted that he was sincere in all he said, and that his purpose was to heal the lack of good relations between the two families of Benedictines, commonly known as the White Benedictines, the Cistercians, and the Black Benedictines, his discretion could certainly be questioned; for in making a strong case for the powerful Cluniacs, he leveled many serious charges against the Order of Citeaux. Urged by two friends, William of St. Thierry, himself a Cluniac abbot, and Ogerius, a Canon-Regular of St. Nicholas, Tournay, St. Bernard came forward as the spokesman for the Cistercians, and composed his famous *Apologia,* a short work consisting of an introduction and thirteen short chapters (*PL* 182:895–918), addressed to William of St. Thierry, but aimed in its every statement at the Cluniacs. By comparison with many of St. Bernard's innumerable and incomparably elevated passages on the monastic life in his other works, the *Apologia,* although immediately and eminently effective in its purpose, and universally recognized a masterpiece of polemic art which abounds in satire, can hardly be considered in context a fortunate expression of the ideals of monasticism (cf. Luddy, *Life and Teaching of St. Bernard,* c. 9, the *Apologia,* pp. 95 f.).

the monastic order, a man worthy in God's sight, filled with the Holy Spirit. Drawn forth from the desert [i.e., the status of the world] in Nursia, where he had led a sheltered life, he became the abbot of monks at Montecassino in the Campagna. He was most fervent in the practice of the religious life, and on the inspiration of the Holy Ghost, wrote a Rule for his monks, renewing and strengthening monastic discipline which was then in a precarious condition. Both personally and through his Rule after him, he restored many monasteries of monks in different regions (*Dialogi, Lib. I,* c. 10, *quod in quarto statu Ecclesiae . . . multae et variae religiones creverunt, PL* 188:1155).

90. HINCMARUS, abp. of Rheims (d. 882). Our venerable brothers, the monks, religious men, will do well if, according to what is written in the *Rule of St. Benedict,* which they have professed with an oath to observe, they render their obedience to the most holy Father Benedict, or rather to the Holy Spirit who addressed us through him. Inspired by the same Holy Spirit, the holy Rule, promulgated by the voice of Blessed Benedict, commands the same things [corporal punishment for monks who refused to be corrected by verbal admonition] as did the venerable Councils of the Church (*Collectio de una et non trina Deitate, Sanctae videlicet et inseparabilis Trinitatis unitate, Lib. I, PL* 125:498, 505).

FIRST PRINCIPLE

Conventual Character of Life in the Monastery

CONTENTS: Dangers of the world — Entrance into the enclosure — The cloister — Use of speech — Silence — Stability — The cenobitic family — Filial love of the abbot — Fraternal charity — Recreation — Reformation of life according to monastic principles (*conversio morum*).

I. STATEMENT OF PRINCIPLE

Dangers of the world

91. Before you entered the monastery, dear confrere, you stood before a deep, threatening abyss. Your very salvation was exposed to serious danger. The world surrounded you on all sides with its countless pleasures, attractions, and temptations, with its allurements and deception. Like a blind man you were plunged into fearful and difficult struggles; possibly even shipwreck threatened your soul. *Because all that is in the world is the lust of the flesh, and the lust of the eyes, and the pride of life* (I John 2:16). But see the wonderful goodness of God! He enlightened your soul with grace's clarity, and led you forth from the world, from this great number of serious dangers. [The Lord] *reached out from on high and grasped me; he drew me out of the deep waters* (Ps. 17:17): *You have rescued me from death, my feet, too, from stumbling* (Ps. 55:14).

Entrance into the enclosure

92. You have entered the monastery, you have escaped serious dangers to your spiritual welfare. Although you have not yet reached the shore of safety, your little vessel has reached the tranquil and peaceful calm of the sheltered waters of the cloister, and is sailing in a protected harbor. Here you are guarded against sunken rocks, storms, and seething waves.

The Lord is my shepherd; I shall not want. In verdant pastures he gives me repose (Ps. 22:1–2). He stands at the helm and steers the little ship that is your life. He has directed your steps in the way of holiness and peace. He is your beloved, and you his. The cloister is for you a fortress of strength, a citadel of holiness, the city and kingdom of God; an oasis in the desert, the ark in the deluge, a watch-tower in the field of battle, a treasure of graces, an armory for heaven. You have, in truth, left all things, but only to gain all.

93. Fortunate you are, indeed, many times over, for through no merit of your own, God has lovingly delivered you from the power of darkness and has translated you into the kingdom of his beloved Son (cf. Col. 1:13). Out of the richness of his goodness he has hidden you in his abode (cf. Ps. 26:5). What is there that he ought to have done more for you that he has not done? (cf. Isa. 5:4.) He has showered countless benefits on you: he created you, he redeemed you, and to these gifts has heaped upon you all the riches of his blessings. No day should be allowed to pass without your expressing your heartfelt thanks. Make this a favorite practice to cultivate the highest regard for the blessings you have received, never permitting them to be accepted as a matter of course. At every opportunity give expression of your gratitude, particularly by making your deeds evidence of your spirit of thanks. Do what lies in your power and with childlike devotion bring all the acts of your life as a perpetual sacrifice of praise to God who has loved you from all eternity, and has kept you in his heart.

The cloister

94. You must, then, with all zeal, endeavor to flee the world, on which you have turned your back, and shun all corrupting contact with it. Most of all, you must be intent on safeguarding the grace of your vocation. May the enclosure be for you a holy and inviolable protection—and I am speaking not only of the outward or material cloister, but more particularly of that internal or spiritual enclosure which is silence, the distinguishing characteristic mark of religious observance.

Dedicated speech

95. *He who guards his mouth protects his life* (Prov. 13:3). *If anyone thinks himself to be religious, not restraining his tongue, . . . that man's religion is vain* (Jas. 1:26). An undisciplined tongue reveals a dissolute disposition. Hold your tongue in check, subdue it, and keep it under control. It should be like a bell that is dedicated to divine worship, or like a harp which is never played except in such tones that it *may give grace to the hearers* (Eph. 4:29). Whether you have occasion to speak in the reception room of the monastery or in the circle of your brethren, make of your use of speech a grace that is *from God . . . in*

Christ in God's presence (II Cor. 2:17). Think how often your tongue has received, as on a golden paten, the Eucharistic Host, and how it has thus been consecrated by it!

Silence

96. Hence you should speak only when you receive permission from the superior, and at all other times keep silence faithfully and conscientiously. Masters of the spiritual life have called silence the support of the monastic life, the touchstone of discipline, the key to monastic reformation of life, the foundation of piety, the help and protection of the virtues, the heavenly Spouse's mark deeply impressed upon the soul. Without the observance of silence it is impossible to conquer our faults, preserve peace and charity, or make serious progress in the spiritual life.

More importantly than all else, be faithful about the nocturnal silence. Should you need to communicate to anyone, make yourself understood with a sign rather than with the spoken word. During the day, too, strive seriously to cultivate the spirit of recollectedness, particularly in the places where silence is prescribed. Let your motivation be both the continual avoiding of sin and the preserving of your union with God. The statutes approved by the Apostolic See dispense from silence for short periods to promote mutual charity, and for other benefits that derive from recreation.

Stability

97. You have professed stability, dear confrere, stability of attachment either to your monastery or to your monastic congregation * as well as stability in your vocation, that is, dedication to the monastic life. By profession you have placed yourself in the mystical tomb.† With your own hand [that is, by the vow of stability], you have rolled a large stone before its door and sealed it (cf. Matt. 27:60). The world is dead to you, and you to the world: now *your life is hidden with Christ in God* (Col. 3:3). *Should the anger of the ruler burst upon you, forsake not your place* (Eccles. 10:4). Do not look behind you (cf. Gen. 19:17). Never advance a step except under obedience. Love the seclusion of the enclosure, the holy solitude of your cell. See how unstable,

* Certain units of the Benedictine monastic family have, in times past, for the purpose of greater unity in monastic reforms and for undertaking works that exceeded the scope and limitation of the individual abbey, made profession, not for one abbey or priory, but for the monastic congregation as a whole. A few modifications of this practice are still to be found in present-day monastic congregations. This is recognized to be a deviation from St. Benedict's ideal, for he composed his Rule for one ideal house, one superior, one monastic family. [*Tr.*]

† Saints delighted in comparing the contemplative life, or the contemplative character of a more active interpretation of monasticism, to the tomb. [*Tr.*]

transitory, and perishable are the things of this world, and how unprincipled and changeable its men. Your life's ideal is to be found in him whose image you bear, who is eternally immutable. Eliminate all that is inconstant from your character. Be firm in your holy resolve. Vacillating only leads ultimately to ruin. Be a person of strong character, built as though upon rock, a man of God in very truth, firm, steadfast, and immovable (cf. I Cor. 15:58), glorying with the Apostle: *Who shall separate me from the love of Christ?* (Rom. 8:35.) Only *he who has persevered to the end will be saved* (Matt. 10:22); and what is more desirable than to be saved?

The monastic family

98. You have joined a family living in a monastery, acting as you have with the firm conviction that *It is not good that the man is alone* (Gen. 2:18). You have been admitted into the "strong race of the cenobites" (*RSB*, c. 1). You have an abbot as a father, and the monks for your brothers, according to provisions that are sacred, supernatural, and divine. A family of monks is a beautiful image of that family whose Father and Head both in heaven and on earth is the most loving God himself. It is a faithful likeness too of that venerable family which the Savior established with his disciples.

Filial love of the abbot

99. With full justification, therefore, faith recognizes in the abbot the representative of Christ. It is your duty to show him all veneration, esteem, and childlike devotion, for he is your loving father in Christ, your provider, teacher, and guide. After Christ no one should be dearer to you, nor held in higher esteem. Be attached to him in the spirit of sincere, humble, and grateful affection, as a willingly obedient son is to his father. His life is dedicated to you and your needs; and for your sake he allows himself no rest, day or night; he is ever concerned about providing for your salvation, your peace, your welfare.

Fraternal charity

100. After the abbot, your confreres have first claim on your love. You should possess and share all things in common with them: your joys and sorrows, your hopes, your happiness. One spirit should animate all of you: all should be one heart and one soul. Being on good terms with all your brethren and seeking their welfare should be your deepest concern, the object of your prayer, your very life. Bear them in your innermost heart, until you will be united with them forever in the Beatific Vision. You must not only profess this chaste love for your brethren in words, but express it and confirm it with your deeds, in order that by exercise it may grow stronger day by day.

Recreation

101. This spirit of chaste love for the brethren should manifest itself especially during recreation. This companionable diversion came into practice at the very beginnings of monasticism; it was adopted both in order to give a chance for relaxation and to unite the brethren more and more in the bonds of love. We must consider this interruption in the daily program of prayer and work as being also dedicated to God, in that the brethren vie with one another in the exercise of humility and charity. During recreation that mutual love which comes from the heart, which in all modesty is self-effacing, gracious, gentle, patient, unaffected, cheerful, obliging, and which strives to be all things to all, is the mark and ornament of a blessed family. It merits the approval and blessing of him who finds his delights in the sons of men (cf. Prov. 8:31). *Behold, how good it is, and how pleasant, where brethren dwell as one!* (Ps. 132:1.) By this will all men know that you are disciples of Christ (cf. John 13:35), disciples too of your kind and blessed Father and Patriarch, Benedict, truly a delightful spectacle to angels and men.

Reformation of life according to monastic principles

102. A word remains to be said regarding our precise purpose in the monastic life. Its real meaning and objective are the reformation of one's life by the operation of its own distinctive principles (*conversio morum*). It is the *one thing needful,* to use the description of our Lord himself (Luke 10:42). It is the fulfilment of another saying of the Lord: *Seek first the kingdom of God and his justice* (Matt. 6:33). To be a true monk means truly to seek God (*RSB,* c. 58), in order to return to him from whom one has wandered (*ibid., Prolog.*). The monk turns from evil and directs his heart in all its thought and desire to the Lord his God, in order that with all his energies he may from day to day develop his powers and make firm in himself God's supreme authority, kingdom and glory. Animated with virtuous zeal he works tirelessly at becoming holy. *They go from strength to strength, . . . Their hearts are set upon the pilgrimage* (Ps. 83:8–6), in order to possess divine life in its fulness. Who will give you the wings of a dove to fly, and lend wings to your feet to run as a giant on the way of perfection? Remain steadfast and *faithful unto death, and I will give you the crown of life* (Apoc. 2:10).

II. EVIDENCE FROM THE RULE OF ST. BENEDICT

Flight from the world

103. *Seek peace and follow after it* (Ps. 33:15; *RSB, Prolog.*). Now the workshop in which we shall diligently put into practice all these [instruments of good works] is the enclosure of the monastery and stability in the community (*ibid.*, c. 4, last §).

Life of St. Benedict: A man of venerable life . . . Benedict, . . . despised the empty delights of the world and spurned its allurements. . . . When he saw many of his fellow students pursuing the deadly paths of vice, he drew back the foot which he had placed on the threshold of the world, fearing that by acquiring any of its learning, he too might fall headlong into the dreadful abyss. . . . He abandoned his home and his father's wealth, and desiring to please God alone, sought for the habit of holy religion (*S. Greg. Magn. Dialogorum Lib. II, Prooemium, PL* 66:126).

Enclosure of the monastery

104. . . . so that the monks may not be compelled to wander outside [the enclosure], for that is not at all beneficial for their souls (*RSB*, c. 66). Let no one presume to tell another what he has seen or heard outside the monastery, because this causes very great harm (*ibid.*, c. 67). Let him be punished . . . who shall presume to leave the enclosure of the monastery . . . without the permission of the abbot (*loc. cit.*). The fourth kind of monks are those called the Gyrovagues, . . . ever roaming and never stable (*ibid.*, c. 1). The brethren should not associate with one another at unseasonable hours (*ibid.*, c. 48). Let no one, without special instructions, associate with or converse with guests (*ibid.*, c. 53). On no account shall a monk be allowed to receive letters, devout tokens, or any small gifts whatsoever, from his parents or other people or his brethren, or to give the same, without the abbot's permission (*ibid.*, c. 54). At the gate of the monastery let there be placed a wise old man . . . so that those who come may always find someone to answer them (*ibid.*, c. 66).

Life of St. Benedict: And with that [Benedict, the man of God] returned to his beloved solitude, and alone under the eye of God dwelt with himself . . . kept constant guard over himself, considered himself always as under the eye of God, examined himself constantly, and never allowed his thoughts to be scattered abroad (*S. Greg. Magn. Dialogorum Lib. II*, c. 3, *De vase vitreo crucis signo rupto, PL* 66:136 f.). It happened one day that a boy monk, who loved his parents excessively, left the monastery without permission and went home. He died that same day, as soon as he had reached home (*ibid.*, c. 24, *De puero monacho quem sepultum terra projecit,* col. 180).

Dedicated speech

105. Let us do as the Prophet says: *I will bless the Lord at all times; his praise shall be ever in my mouth* (Ps. 33:2; *RSB,* c. 6). Because of the great value of silence, let permission to speak be seldom granted to observant disciples, even though it be for good, holy, and edifying conversations; for it is written: *Where words are many, sin is not wanting* (Prov. 10:19). . . . It is proper for the master to speak and to teach; but it befits the disciple to be silent and listen. . . . But as for buffoonery and talk that is vain and stirs to laughter, we condemn . . . everywhere, with a perpetual ban (*loc. cit.*). When he speaks the monk is to do so gently and without laughter, humbly and seriously, in few and sensible words, and without loudness. It is written: "A wise man is known by the fewness of his words" (*ibid.*, c. 7, eleventh degree of humility). *Keep your tongue from evil and your lips from speaking guile* (Ps. 33:14; *Prolog.*).

Life of St. Benedict: The priest arose forthwith and set out on Easter day itself to find Benedict, taking with him the food that he had prepared. Over the rugged hills and down the valleys and in the pits of the earth he sought for him, and at last discovered him hidden in his cave. They prayed and blessed Almighty God, and then sat down, holding sweet converse of heavenly matters (*S. Greg. Magn. Dialogorum Lib. II,* c. 1, *PL* 66:130). [Benedict and his twin sister, Scholastica] spent the whole day in the praise of God and devout conversation, and toward evening took food together. . . . So also they spent the whole night in vigil and comforted each other with holy converse of spiritual things (*ibid.*, c. 33, col. 194 f.). Servandus, an abbot . . . a man of deep spiritual wisdom . . . was wont to come often to the monastery in order that they might delight each other with the words of life and taste at least in yearning desire that sweet food of their heavenly country which they could not yet perfectly enjoy (*ibid.*, c. 35, col. 196).

Silence

106. The ninth degree of humility is that the monk restrain his tongue and keep silence, not speaking until he is questioned (*RSB,* c. 7). Monks should practice silence at all times, but especially at night. . . . And when they come out of Compline, let there be no further permission for anyone to say anything . . . unless speech become necessary because of the arrival of guests, or the abbot gives someone an order. But even in such circumstances, this speaking should be done with the utmost gravity and the most becoming restraint (*ibid.*, c. 42).

Let there be the greatest silence [at meals] so that no whisper, and no voice but the reader's may be heard there . . . lest it give occasion to the evil one (*ibid.*, c. 38).

Stability

107. Now this is the manner of his reception. In the oratory, in the presence of all, he shall pronounce stability . . . and this before God and his saints, so that he may know that should he ever act in opposition he will be condemned by him whom he mocks. . . . Let him understand . . . that he is no longer free to leave the monastery or to withdraw his neck from under the yoke of the Rule . . . knowing that henceforward he will not have the disposition of even his own body (*RSB*, c. 58). The instruments of good works are to be employed by us unceasingly day and night. . . . Now the workshop in which we shall diligently put into practice all these [instruments] is the enclosure of the monastery and stability in the community (*ibid.*, c. 4). Wherefore the Lord says in the Gospel: *Everyone therefore who hears these my words and acts upon them, shall be likened to a wise man who built his house on rock* (Matt. 7:24) . . . . So that never abandoning his rule, but persevering in his teaching in the monastery until death, we may share by patience in the sufferings of Christ, that we may deserve to be partakers also of his kingdom (*ibid.*, *Prolog.*).

Life of St. Benedict: One of Benedict's monks was of unstable disposition and unwilling to abide in the monastery. The man of God constantly admonished and rebuked him, but without avail; the monk would not consent to persevere in the community and continually importuned [St. Benedict] to let him go. So one day the venerable abbot, wearied with his persistence, grew angry and ordered him to depart. No sooner had he left the monastery than he found confronting him on his road a dragon with open jaws. . . . He promised at once that he would never again leave the monastery, and from that time on remained faithful to his word. By the prayers of the holy man he saw the devil whom he previously had not seen but had actually followed (*S. Greg. Magn. Dialogorum Lib. II*, c. 25, *De monacho qui de monasterio discedens, draconem in itinere invenit, PL* 66:182). Benedict, the man of virtuous life . . . sent this message by his disciple [Maurus, to a hermit dwelling in a cave]: "If you are a slave of God, let not a chain of iron bind you, but the chain of Christ" (*ibid., Lib. III*, c. 16, *de Martino monacho de Monte Marsico, PL* 77:261).

Filial love of the abbot

108. The first kind of monks are the cenobites, that is, those who live in monasteries, serving under a rule and an abbot. . . . Leaving the others to one side, let us proceed with God's help to provide for the

strong race of cenobites (*RSB,* c. 1). The abbot . . . is believed to hold the place of Christ in the monastery, and for that reason is called by a name of his, according to the words of the Apostle: *You have received a spirit of adoption as sons, by virtue of which we cry, "Abba! Father!"* (Rom. 8:15.) . . . Let him show an equal love to all. . . . Let him realize also how difficult and arduous a task he has undertaken of ruling souls and adapting himself to many dispositions (*ibid.,* c. 2). Since the abbot is believed to hold the place of Christ, he is to be called lord and abbot, not for any pretension of his own, but for the honor and love of Christ (*ibid.,* c. 63). Monks dwell in monasteries and desire to have an abbot over them (*ibid.,* c. 5). Let the prior respectfully perform what is enjoined him by his abbot (*ibid.,* c. 65) . Let them love their abbot with a sincere and humble affection. Let them prefer nothing whatever to Christ (*ibid.,* c. 72).

Fraternal charity

109. . . . so there is a good zeal which separates from evil and leads to God and life everlasting. Let the monks, therefore, exercise this zeal with the most fervent love. Let them, that is, *anticipate one another with honor* (Rom. 12:10). Let them bear with the greatest patience one another's infirmities, whether of body or character. Let them vie in paying obedience to one another. Let no one follow what seems good for himself, but rather what is good for another. Let them practice fraternal charity with a pure love. Let them fear God (*RSB,* c. 72). Let [the abbot] not love one more than another (*ibid.,* c. 2). Let no one in the monastery follow the will of his own heart (*ibid.,* c. 3). The eighth degree of humility is that a monk do nothing except what is commended by the common rule of the monastery and the example of his superiors (*ibid.,* c. 7). Not to forsake charity . . . not to be a detractor . . . not to love contention . . . not to be jealous, not to give way to envy (*ibid.,* c. 4, nn. 26, 40, 67, 65, 66). Let the rest [who are not occupied in any urgent business] serve one another in charity (*ibid.,* c. 35).

Let them . . . as it were secretly, comfort the troubled brother . . . *lest perchance he be overwhelmed by too much sorrow* (II Cor. 2:7) . As the Apostle says: *Assure him of your love for him* (v. 8; *ibid.,* c. 27). . . . so that no one may be troubled or vexed in the house of God (*ibid.,* c. 31).

The Office of Lauds and Vespers shall never be allowed to end without the superior reciting, so that all can hear, the whole of the Lord's Prayer. The purpose of this is the removal of those thorns of scandal, or mutual offense, which are wont to arise in communities. For being warned by the covenant which they make in that prayer, when they say "Forgive . . . as we forgive" the brethren will cleanse their souls of such faults (*ibid.,* c. 13). The seventh degree of humility is that he should not only in his speech declare himself lower and of less account than all others, but should in his own inmost heart believe it, humbling himself (*ibid.*, c. 7). He who needs less is to thank God and not be discontented; he that needs more is to be humbled for his infirmity and not be made proud by the mercy shown to him: so will all the members be at peace (*ibid.*, c. 34).

Life of St. Benedict: Among the monks was a nobleman, whose name was Theoprobus. . . . He one day found Benedict weeping most bitterly . . . and asked him the cause of his great sorrow. The man of God answered at once: "All this monastery that I have built and all things that I have provided for the brethren are by the decree of Almighty God delivered to the barbarians. And I scarce was able to obtain the lives of my monks . . ." (*S. Greg. Magni Dialogorum Lib. II*, c. 17, *De destructione monasterii viri Dei ab ipso praedicta, PL* 66: 168).

Reformation of life according to monastic principles

110. In the oratory, in the presence of all, he shall promise . . . conversion of his life (*RSB*, c. 58). Up with us then at last, for the Scripture arouses us, saying: *It is now the hour for us to rise from sleep* (Rom. 13:11). . . . *Oh, that today you would hear his voice: 'Harden not your hearts'* (Ps. 94:8) . . . . *Walk while you have the light, that darkness may not overtake you* (John 12:35). . . . Let us therefore gird our loins with faith and the performance of good works, and following the guidance of the Gospel walk in his paths, so that we may merit to see him who has called us to his kingdom. . . . For the merciful Lord says: *I desire not the death of the wicked, but that the wicked turn from his way, and live* (Ezek. 33:11). . . . While there is still time, while we are in this body and can fulfil all these things by the light of this life, we must hasten to do now what may profit us for eternity. Therefore we must establish a school of the Lord's service. . . . Do not run from the way of salvation, of which the entrance must needs be narrow. But as we progress in our monastic life and faith, our hearts shall be enlarged, and we shall run with unspeakable sweetness of love in the way of God's commandments (*ibid.*, *Prolog.*).

The first instrument of good works is: In the first place to love the Lord God with all one's heart, all one's soul, all one's strength. Then one's neighbor as oneself. . . . To avoid worldly conduct . . . To keep constant guard over the actions of one's life (*ibid.*, c. 4, nn. 1, 2, 20, 48). To these may well be added all the other instruments of good works in the *Rule of St. Benedict*, chapter four, for it is by them that we attain holiness of life. And guarding himself always from sins and vices, whether of thought, words, hand, foot, or self-will, and checking also the desires of the flesh, let him consider that God is always beholding him from heaven (*ibid.,* c. 7, first degree of humility). Let [the priest-monk] make ever more and more progress toward God (*ibid.,* c. 62).

III. DECREES AND DOCUMENTS OF THE CHURCH

111. COUNCIL OF NICE (325). The proposition that the way of life for monks must differ from that of all others met with the approval of those taking part in the holy synod (c. XVI, q. 1, n. 1., *Apocryph.* This precise statement, quoted by Wolter from an unidentified but admittedly apocryphal source, has not been located. Substantially the same provision is found in the Council's *Varii canones Arabici,* n. 12, *Constitutio de monachis, Concil. Coll. Labbei* 1:514; *ibid.,* col. 499–500).

112. POPE ALEXANDER II (d. 1073). According to the mind of the excellent Council of Chalcedon (celebrated 451, canon 4), We command monks to dwell within the enclosure, according to the norm laid down by St. Benedict, and We forbid them to wander about in towns, castles, and cities (c. XVI, q. 1, c. 11, *ad clerum et plebem Florentinum, CJC* Richter 1:654).

113. CONGR. OF ST. MAUR (founded 1618, confirmed by Pope Gregory XV, 1621). Monks must hold themselves aloof from the ways of the world, not only in their actual external observance but also in their general attitude in such a way that they seek to avoid altogether worldly ways of acting and speaking which have a note of vanity about them, and stand in opposition to religious simplicity (*Declar.* 3 in c. 4, *RSB,* p. 36).

114. POPE EUGENE III, Cistercian, disciple of St. Bernard (d. 1153). Never lose sight of the ancient fathers who founded our holy order. Consider how, after having quitted the world and despised all it had to offer, they left the dead to bury their dead, and retired into the solitude to sit with Mary at the feet of Jesus Christ (cf. Luke 10:39 f.), there to receive the heavenly manna all the more abundantly as they were more distant from Egypt. . . . They went forth out of their country and from their kinsfolk; they forgot their own people and their father's house (cf. Gen. 12:1 f.), and because the King sought their countenance, he made them a great nation, and extended their offspring to the ends of the earth, so that the light and glory, which they shed on all sides, shone upon the whole body of the Church. It was their words which filled the cruse of the widow of Sarepta with the little drop of oil which remained therein. They, in fact, received the first fruits of the Spirit, and this divine oil which penetrated their souls, has run down to us. For this cause you must take care never to degenerate from

their virtues, in order that you may be in the branches what they were in the stem, and that having derived from them the seeds of life, you may bear the same fruit they bore (*Ep. ad Capitulum Cisterciense anni 1150, Ep. 273 S. Bernardi praemissa,* § 2, 3, *PL* 182:477).

115. POPE CLEMENT XIV (d. 1774). Let the brother learn to love intensely that solitude [the annual retreat], in which, as St. Jerome says, God speaks and deals familiarly with his own. Elsewhere, in writing to a friend in Bethlehem, Jerome explicitly calls solitude "paradise on earth." Unless a religious continuously embraces and loves solitude, he will be identified by his habit as a monk [solitary] or a cenobite [religious living in common with others], but he certainly will not be such in spirit (*Const. Apost. In vinea Domini,* § 11, die 4 Jul., 1772. *Confirmatio decretorum pro Cappuccinis provinciae Subalpinae, BRC* 5: 463).

116. POPE EUGENE II (d. 826). The monk should be content with his enclosure, because as a fish cannot live if it is taken out of water, so a monk cannot continue a monk without his monastery. *He shall sit solitary, and hold his peace* (Lam. 3:28), for he is dead to the world and lives for God (c. XVI, q. 1, c. 8, *CJC* Richter 1:654).

117. III LATERAN COUNCIL (1179). Monks . . . are not to live alone in towns and villages nor to be assigned singly to any parish church. They are to remain in a major monastery, or with some of their brethren. They shall not mingle alone with seculars, thus inviting conflict with spiritual enemies, for Solomon says: *Woe to the solitary man! For if he should fall, he has no one to lift him up* (Eccles. 4:10; c. 10, *Mansi* 22:224; Schroeder, *Disciplinary,* p. 223).

118. POPE HONORIUS III (d. 1227). Abbots and priors are either to recall to the enclosure the monks who reside alone on missions in opposition to the Statute of the General Council (preceding number), arranging for the diocesan clergy to serve these churches, or send other monks with whom those on mission may live the regular life (c. IV, *de capellis monachorum, X, Lib. III,* tit. 37. *CJC* Richter, 2:586).

119. PROV. COUNCIL OF VIENNA (1858). Foolish indeed was the wisdom of those who, under the guise of seeking the welfare of the Church and of civil society, desired religious to be so intensely dedicated to parochial care of souls, the instruction of youth, and spiritual ministrations to the sick that they declared deadly war against those very means by which the spirit of the religious life is fostered and strengthened. When the oil is cut off, the flame dies down and is snuffed out (*Decr.,* tit. 4, c. 13, *de vita religiosa, CL* 5:189).

120. POPE CLEMENT VIII (d. 1605). A. No one, not even the superior, is to have a cell apart from the common dormitory, either within or without the enclosure (*Const. Apost. Nullus omnino,* § 16, 22 Aug., 1604, *Decreta generalia pro reformatione regularium, BR* 10:665). B.

The monastery is always to be zealously protected with the clausura, and for that purpose a porter, commendable for diligence and blamelessness of conduct, is to be appointed by the superior. This porter will be on duty for guarding the door at all times; he is not to open it for any brother who is not accompanied by a companion, or who has not obtained permission to go out (*ibid.*, § 11). C. No one is to presume to leave the monastery except for a reason, with a companion, and having obtained the superior's permission and blessing, which is to be obtained each time (*ibid.*, § 12).

121. POPE ST. PIUS V, O.P. (d. 1572). All buildings of the convent are to be closed on all sides, and unnecessary doors locked. . . . Entrance to the enclosure . . . is absolutely forbidden to all women (*Const. Apost. Ex innumeris curis*, § 9, 10, 8 Mar., 1570—*reformatio totius Ordinis Cisterciensis, BR* 7:814).

122. CONGR. OF CANTERBURY (founded about 943 by Odo, abp. of Canterbury). We exhort monks and all who have offered their vow to God to devote their efforts to fulfilling the same day and night in all humility and obedience, persevering in the fear of God in the churches [abbeys] where they bound themselves by vow. They are not to be wanderers, who are deprived of the very name of monk by their want of stability, in that they contemn his obligations. But they are to imitate the example of the apostles wearing the habit of humility, devoting themselves to manual labor, sacred reading, and continual prayer, eagerly awaiting the Lord, with loins girt and lamps burning, so that when he comes he will make them dwell forever in eternal rest (*Const. S. Odonis archiepiscopi Cantuariensis*, c. VI, *Mansi* 18:393; *PL* 133:948).

123. CONGR. OF CAMALDULI (founded by St. Romuald, 1018; confirmed by Pope Alexander II, 1072; these Const., used throughout the present work, were definitively approved by Pope St. Pius V, 1571). Let our cenobites avoid all similarity with the Sarabaites, that abominable kind of monk that both Augustine and Jerome in many of their writings have striven admirably to condemn. . . . As nothing else preserves and increases monastic dignity more than to see monks dwelling perpetually within the enclosure, so too, nothing seems to lessen and destroy that dignity more than all unprofitable and needless wandering about outside the monastery. . . . The less monks are seen roaming about in the city, the more praiseworthy they are, the more they will be held in esteem by all men, and the more too they will be considered and will actually be lovers of true monastic observance (*Camaldulenses, . . . Declar., Lib. I,* in c. 1, pp. 30, 31, 34; *CR* 2:202).

124. CARTHUSIAN ORDER (founded by St. Bruno, 1086; approved by Pope Innocent II, 1176). The monk is to consider the cell as necessary to his welfare and life as water is for fish or the sheepfold is for sheep. The longer the monk has remained in his cell, the more willingly will

he continue to dwell there. For if he has been accustomed to leave it frequently on flimsy excuses, he will soon detest it (*Stat. Ordinis Carthusiensis, Consuetudines Guigonis prioris,* c. 31, *De cella, CR* 2:323; *PL* 153:703).*

125. POPE PIUS IX (d. 1878). Not only has the law governing the enclosure for religious houses of regulars of both sexes been promulgated in the sacred canons, sanctions, and constitutions of Supreme Pontiffs for the protection of the cloistral life, which is supremely necessary for regular observance, but other provisions which contribute much to the good and the guarding of the enclosure have been made with great wisdom. These regulations are established lest the religious be disturbed from the quiet of the solitude with great loss of time and danger of violating their rule, because of too many persons visiting the enclosure; it is likewise forbidden them to go out of their convents without the superior's permission and without a companion. . . .

Since these regulations which are established in so salutary a manner for protecting the chosen portion of the Lord's flock, they must be observed by everyone everywhere, and all abuses must be rooted out. With the approval of the sacred council We declare that:

I. the enclosure be observed in all houses, convents, and monasteries of men regulars, according to the sacred canons, the Apostolic Constitutions and sanctions [S. Pius V, Const. *Decet Romanum Pontificem;* Gregor. XIII, Const. *Ubi gratiae;* et Benedict. XIV, Const. *Regularis disciplinae*], so that any women of whatever rank or social condition, even infants, may not enter within their walls and the sacred enclosure, or be received into the same. . . . We severely command generals, provincials, abbots, and visitors, and others on whom this duty rests, that the enclosure be diligently preserved where it exists, and that it be re-established fully where it has been discontinued or neglected. . . .

II. Let no one presume to leave the enclosure except for a just cause, and upon having obtained permission and received the blessing from the superior each time, and with a companion. Exception is made with regard to the obligation of having a companion, in the case of some necessity, but this is to be approved by the judgment of the local superior.

Let superiors also see to it that their religious do not adopt the customs of worldlings, but that both within and outside the enclosure they so conduct themselves as to their manner of life, conduct, garb,

* Guiges, fifth prior of the Grande Chartreuse, was born about 1083, and died July 27, 1137. He was prior from 1110, three years after his profession, until 1137. He is the legislator of the Carthusian Order, and is considered its second founder and preserver. These Customs, written in 1127 or 1128, have always remained the basic pattern of the Carthusian ideal. Guiges' name appears in some older martyrologies under date of July 27, but no universal cult has been established. [*Tr.*]

and gait that enemies of the Church will have to think highly of them, having nothing evil to say of them, and that the faithful will everywhere be edified by them. Therefore these superiors are to prevent seculars from visiting the religious houses too often without just reason, lest the tranquillity of the religious family and silence be disturbed, and the spirit of observance, with which the members of regular orders must be animated, grow lukewarm, and gradually be snuffed out. Let the conscience of superiors themselves be burdened in these matters (*Schema Constitutionis de clausura Patrum Concil. Vaticani examini propositum, CL* 7:680, 681).

Silence

126. POPE INNOCENT III (d. 1216). Unbroken silence must be observed in the oratory, refectory, and dormitory; it will also be kept in the cloister at the hours and in the places established by ancient custom of the monastery which have been observed in a praiseworthy manner (c. VI, *de Statu monach.*, X, 3, 35—*abbati et conventui Sublacensibus, CJC,* Richter, 2:576).

127. CONGR. OF CLUNY (founded 910). The usefulness of silence is supremely necessary in every religious institute; in fact, unless it is properly observed, we cannot speak of the religious life at all, for there can be none. Silence's commendation is so great in Holy Scripture, that among the countless encomiums given to it, even the great Prophet Isaias has this to say of it: *The work of justice shall be peace, and the service of justice quietness, and security forever* (Isa. 32:17; *Petri Ven. Abbatis Cluniacens., IX, Stat. Congreg. Cluniacens.,* c. 19, *CR* 2:181; *PL* 189:1031).

128. CONGR. OF GRAMMONT (founded 1076 by St. Stephen of Tigerno, d. 1124, canonized 1189, approved by Clement III, 1188). Silence must be kept in the places and at the times prescribed. In these places, namely in the church, in the cloister, the refectory, the dormitory, and during the prescribed times, that is from Compline until after the chapter in the morning, the brethren are to observe unbroken silence, except some great necessity—for necessity knows no law—or some manifest utility shall have intervened. . . . Another kind of silence, which consists in abstaining from all useless concerns, and in speaking only about those which are necessary, is always and everywhere to be observed by all brethren with the utmost discretion (*Stat. Ordinis Grandimontensis,* nn. 23, 24, *CR* 2:306; *PL* 204:1154).

129. CONGR. OF STRASBURG (founded 1624). Because the virtue of silence is the preserver of peace and the guardian of the religious life and the Rule, we prescribe that unbroken silence is to be kept by everyone within the confines of the monastery, but more particularly in the refectory, the dormitory, the chapel, the cloister, and on the

stairs, except for some need or some good purpose, and even then with the permission of the superior (*Declar. in c. 6 RSB, de taciturnitate,* fol. 14).

Stability

130. CONGR. OF CAMALDULI. A. The monks are to remain steadfastly dedicated to prayer and reading in their monasteries and churches. In so doing the cell will become most gratifying to them (*Camaldulenses . . . Declar., Lib. I, in c. 4 RSB,* p. 54; *CR* 2:209). B. The monastery and the observance of silence offer the tranquil monk, who is zealous in his observance of stability, the safest and most comforting refuge from all the intensity of the world and the fires of temptations, and affords him a foretaste of the delights of paradise; in the same way the monastery becomes for the restless and unstable monk a kind of prison, a living tomb, a place of torment and an occasion for affliction (*ibid., in c. 48 RSB,* p. 201; *CR* 2:256). C. When necessity demands that they go out into the public, . . . let them be mindful of religious modesty and the custody of the eyes. Properly trained monks hold their gaze toward the ground when walking, keep their hands from gesticulating excessively when they talk, do not spread their feet wide when sitting, and make it a point to do nothing that is not proper, holy, and religious, whether walking, speaking, sitting, or resting (*ibid., in c. 4 RSB,* p. 54; *CR* 2:209). D. They strive to be serious in speech, place a guard at the door of their lips (cf. Ps. 140:3), and by every possible means avoid all idle words (*ibid., in c. 6 RSB,* p. 58; *CR* 2:209).

131. CONGR. OF BURSFELD (founded 1431). A. St. Benedict, our father, great lover and zealous promoter of silence, which is the surest means for restoring and preserving monastic discipline, does not close the lips of the religious with so severe an observance of silence that they are never allowed to speak, but prescribes that permission be seldom granted, even for conversations that are good, holy, and edifying (*RSB* c. 6). Unless another is authorized to do so, only the abbot, the prior, or in the prior's absence, the subprior, grants permission to speak within or without the monastery (*Stat.,* c. 3, *de silentio,* n. 1, p. 127). B. Care must be employed, however, that no excess be tolerated either with regard to the time allotted for speaking, or the manner of using the permission (*ibid.,* n. 3, p. 128).

132. POPE CLEMENT XIV (d. 1774). The superior is to admonish talkative brethren, correct them and, if necessary, punish them publicly in order that they and the others will learn to hate talkativeness and love silence, which is the vigorous guardian of solitude, peace, and charity; if silence is disregarded . . . the monastery is a house of confusion, not a place of religious solitude (*Const. Apost. In vinea*

Domini, § 9, 4 Jul., 1772, *confirmatio decretorum pro Cappuccinis prov. Subalpinae, BRC* 5:462).

133. SWABIAN CONGR. OF ST. JOSEPH (founded 1668, approved 1725). Interior recollectedness (*taciturnitas*) is the guardian of monastic discipline and the begetter of virtues. It is for that reason that our holy Father, knowing the many benefits recollectedness produces, and the many evils that result from talkativeness, has granted only rare permission to speak. In very few words the Apostle James enumerates these evils comprehensively in his Epistle: *The tongue is a restless evil, full of deadly poison . . . a fire, the very world of iniquity* (Jas. 3:8–6; *Const. et declar., de taciturnitate,* fol. 79).

Stability

134. POPE URBAN II (d. 1099). Do not neglect, beloved sons in Christ, the grace that is in you, which has been granted to you through the unity of a holy way of life in religion. Dwell on these truths in meditation, let them be your characteristic marks, so that your progress may be evident to all. You have become sharers with Christ, provided only that you keep the beginning of your fervor, firm until the end. Keep in mind what the Lord says: *Whoever perseveres to the end, he shall be saved* (Matt. 24:13; *Const. Apost. Cum universis sanctae Ecclesiae,* § 9, 6 Apr., 1090, *approbatio congr. Vallis Umbrosae O.S.B., quae sub protectione Sedis Apost. suscipitur, BR* 2:134; *CR* 4:363).

Fraternal charity

135. ROMAN MISSAL. Where charity and love are, God is there. The love of Christ has gathered us together. Let us exult and be joyful in him. Let us love and fear the living God. And let us love one another with sincere hearts. Being, therefore, assembled together, let us beware of being divided in mind. . . . And may Christ, our Lord, be in the midst of us! (*Fer. V. in Coena Domini, Antiph. ad lotionem pedum. Miss. Rom.,* p. 204.)

136. SWABIAN CONGR. OF ST. JOSEPH. A. Fraternal charity is the ornament of sacred orders, the support of regular discipline, the glory of monasteries, the bond of perfection, the fostering of good works, the holy zeal that unites the efforts of virtuous men. With great solicitude superiors must be watchful and subjects must cooperate in fostering and preserving peace and charity in their monasteries, for without them the observance of regular discipline can no more stand firmly than a house whose foundation and stone structure have been removed (*Const. et declar., Pars II, praef. de disciplina monastica,* fol. 36). B. If we wish to perpetuate the name of our Congregation we must exert ourselves to the utmost in cherishing among our members the spirit

of charity and love, which is produced by uniformity; * the greater that uniformity is in all things, the more firmly it unites the souls of men. For not only is *God in his holy dwelling* (Ps. 67:6), but he also *maketh men of one manner to dwell in a house* (*ibid.*, Douay version). Thus we will imitate not only our holy fathers (*RSB*, c. 7, eighth degree of humility), but hold before ourselves the very model of heavenly glory in which, although there are many mansions, all will the same, all stand in opposition to the same.

The royal Psalmist exulted for those who are so bound together when he exclaimed: *How good it is, and how pleasant, where brethren dwell at one!* (Ps. 132:1.) In so saying he seems to have referred not so much to a uniformity in choir as to the uniformity of life and moral conduct, especially when he adds the words: *It is as when the precious ointment on the head runs down over the beard, the beard of Aaron, till it runs down on the collar of his robe* (v. 2).

Our ointment is the uniformity of monastic discipline by which we become the *fragrance of Christ* (II Cor. 2:15). This discipline will then be most precious in God's sight if by its fragrance it descends, in a manner of speaking, to the hem of the garment of regular observance, completely imbuing Aaron with the precious perfume of different virtues, and fills the house of our congregation with the sweetness of perfume, so that our name will be poured out as oil, and however much the congregation may grow and whatever the number and merit of the sons of our holy father Benedict it may unite within its fold, they may always, following in the sweet perfume of the Lord's ointment, follow the Lamb, and his servant, Benedict, wherever he goes (*ibid.*, cc. 1, 2, 3, *De disciplina monastica,* fol. 33–35).

137. CONGR. OF CLUNY. Let uniformity be observed in chanting and reading, with no deviation permitted, especially in the worship of God, because being members of one congregation and order, we must strive for uniformity in all things (*Hugonis V abb. Cluniacensis, XVII, Stat.*, c. 20, *PL* 209:886).

Recreation

138. CONGR. OF BURSFELD (1433). Let each one speak freely, without fear, and according to his ability during recreation. Care is to be taken never to scorn or deride another's simplicity or lack of education. Let no one behave haughtily; when one person is speaking, the

* No word in current English seems to convey the idea adequately in translating *similitudo.* The word here employed, *uniformity,* is not intended to be limited to discipline regarding externals. Possibly the etymological use of *unanimity,* a certain oneness of mind and heart, would express the thought more exactly than any other expression. [*Tr.*]

rest are to listen to him respectfully and quietly. When the prior speaks, all should listen with polite attention. He is to encourage the timid, supplementing what they are unable to express, and with prudence and care hold in check the more impulsive, so that they will not be puffed up with their knowledge. No one is to be severely reproved or corrected during recreation (*Stat.*, c. 4, *De mutuis colloquiis*, n. 4, p. 132).

139. CONGR. OF CAMALDULI. When the brethren assemble for the purpose of recreation, inside or outside the monastery, they will make every effort to avoid shouting and frivolous conduct. They are not to touch one another. . . . They must not wrangle, nor engage in anything that is not in keeping with monastic seriousness. To make certain that these regulations will be observed, the superior or one of the seniors will always attend recreation (*Camaldulenses . . . Declar., Lib. I, in c. 6 RSB*, p. 60; *CR* 2:211).

IV. WRITINGS OF SAINTS AND DOCTORS

Detachment from the world

140. ST. AUGUSTINE, bp. of Hippo, Doctor of the Church (d. 430). A. This world is a sea, dangerous not only because of its storms and rocks, but filled as well with beasts of prey that lie in wait for one (*De cataclysmo, serm. ad catechumenos*, c. 1, *In Append., PL* 40:693). B. Consider the world as though it were the sea; the wind is violent, and there is a mighty tempest. Each man has his own particular lust, his own tempest. If you love God, you walk upon the sea, and the swelling of the earth is beneath your feet. If you love the world, it will swallow you up. It knows only how to devour those who love it, not to support them (*Serm. 76, De Domino ambulante super aquas maris, et de Petro titubante, Matt. 14,* 24 f., c. 6, n. 9, *PL* 38:482). C. How deceptive and untrustworthy, how insatiable and transitory is whatever love of this world bestows upon us, and all that appearances and short-lived beauty promise (*De spiritu et anima*, c. 49, *PL* 40:816). D. Know, my brethren, that all this misery of mankind in which the world groans, is medicinal pain, not a sentence of punishment. You see that everywhere there is pain, everywhere fear, everywhere need, everywhere toil (*Enarr. in Ps. 138*, n. 15, *PL* 37:1793). E. O life of the world, which is now deceiving so many, which has seduced and blinded so many in the past! When you move along swiftly, you are nothing; when you are seen, you are a shadow; when you raise yourself haughtily, you are nothing but smoke. You are sweet to the foolish, bitter to the

wise. He who loves you, knows you not; it is they who spurn you who understand you. You are to be feared and abandoned. . . . O empty world, why do you promise so much, and deceive us in so doing? He who wishes to be your friend will become the enemy of God. For love of the world is enmity of God (*Ad fratres in eremo, Serm. 49, de miseria carnis et falsitate praesentis vitae, In Append., PL* 40:1332). F. O unclean world! You never cease to ensnare human beings; you never allow them to rest; you desire to seize them all; you seek them only to kill them all. Woe to him who places his confidence in you. Blessed is he who resists you, but blessed far more is he who, while still unharmed, abandons you (*ibid., Serm. 31,* col. 1290).

141. ST. JOHN CHRYSOSTOM, abp. of Constantinople, Doctor of the Church (d. 407). For in worldly pursuits are continual perils, and losses one upon another, and only an uncertain hope; great is the servility, and the expenditure alike of wealth, of bodies, and of souls; and the return of the fruits is far below our expectation, should it be realized at all (*In Matt., Hom. 67,* § 5, *Moralis exhortatio ad labores vitae patienter tolerandos, PG* 58:638).

142. POPE ST. LEO THE GREAT, Doctor of the Church (d. 461). In the world dangers lurk on every side, everything presents temptations. Passionate desires arouse; allurements lie in wait to ensnare one; money makes its appeal; evil frightens one (*Serm. 43, De Quadr. V,* c. 1, *PL* 54:282).

143. ST. JOHN OF DAMASCUS, monk, Doctor of the Church (d. circa 749). The life of the world is the devil's fishhook, baited with beastly pleasures as an enticement, by which he draws to the depths of the whirlpool of hell those who are deceived (*Vita Barlaam et Joasaph,* c. 25, *PG* 96:1095).

144. HUGH OF ST. VICTOR, canon regular of the monastery of St. Victor, Paris (d. 1142). In the world the devil lies in wait to entice; the spirit of the times draws with its flattery; the flesh is attracted; the soul blinded; and man is thrown into complete disorder (*De anima, Lib. IV,* c. 5, *In Append., PL* 177:175).

145. ST. BERNARD, abbot of Clairvaux, Doctor of the Church (d. 1153). In the world we find an abundance of malice but little, if any, wisdom; here everything is slimy and slippery, and shrouded in darkness, and concealed with the snares of sinners; here our souls are ever in danger; our spirits are sorely tried, for there is nothing under the sun but *vanity and a chase after wind* (Eccles. 1:14; *Serm. de temp., Serm. V in Ascensione Dni.,* § 2, *PL* 183:316).

146. MICHAEL OF MEAUX, abp. of Sens (d. 1199). In two ways the world fights against the elect: by word and with the sword. We gain the victory over the word of falsehood by wisdom; we resist the sword

of adversity with patience (*Expos. in Ps. 34:2, inter Op. Om. S. Bonaventurae,* ed. Peltier 9:200).*

147. ST. THOMAS AQUINAS (d. 1274). For we must remember that if, on the one hand, a secular life spent in obedience to the commandments is a good preparation for the practice of the counsels, yet, on the other hand, life in the world presents a serious obstacle to observance of the counsels (*Opusc. theol. 3, Contra pestiferam doctrinam retrahentium homines a religionis ingressu,* c. 6, *Op Om.,* ed Parma 15:109; Verardo, *Opusc. Theol.* 2:167).

148. DENIS THE CARTHUSIAN, monk of Roermond (d. 1471). What is so despicable, so wicked, so dreadful, and so to be abandoned . . . as the world? What is so noxious, so wanting in gratitude, so lacking in all feeling, in fact, so mad and so foolish as the world? (*Exhortatorium noviciorum,* art. 1, *Op. Om.* 38:527.)

149. ST. ANTHONY OF PADUA (d. 1231). The world is a prison, a veritable furnace of Babylon (cf. Dan. 3; *Serm. Dom. XXII p. Trinitatem, S. Francisci Assisiatis necnon S. Antonii . . . Op., Pars II,* p. 310).

150. DIADOCUS, bp. of Photice in Illyria (d. 450). By every consideration possible withdrawal from the world is beneficial (*Capita de perfectione spirituali,* c. 18, *PG* 65:1173).

151. THEODERET, bp. of Cyrus in Syria (d. 457). Let him who wishes to be purified, even of secret thoughts, which God knows, cut himself off from the crowd (*In Jeremiam, Lib. III,* c. 12, *PG* 81:578).

152. ST. PETER DAMIAN, monk of Fonte-Avellana, cardinal, Doctor of the Church (d. 1072). We must take flight from the world, which only begets darkness. We must seek solitude where, as in the desert, light in all its fulness breaks forth (*Lib. VI, ep. 5, ad monachos monasterii Cluniacensis, PL* 144:381).

153. ST. JEROME, Doctor of the Church (d. 420). A. The love of God and fear of hell will easily break such bonds [attachment to family]. . . . What is keeping you in the world, my brother, you who are above the world? . . . You are too greedy of enjoyment, my brother, if you wish to rejoice with the world here, and to reign with Christ hereafter (*Ep. 14, ad Heliodorum monachum, peregrinationis suae comitem, quem frustra conatus erat apud se in eremo detinere,* §§ 3, 10, *PL* 22:349). B. On one side, like Charybdis the passion for luxury draws into its whirlpool the very salvation of the soul. On the

* The Franciscan scholar Fr. Fidelis da Fanna has shown conclusively that this *Expositio in Psalterium* is definitely not the work of St. Bonaventure, as previously believed and as indicated by Wolter, but should be restored to Michael of Meaux. Cf. *Op. Om. S. Bonaventurae,* ed. Quaracchi 10:21. This definitive edition of St. Bonaventure's works rules out almost 100 works formerly attributed to the saint. They are referred to in the Peltier ed. of St. Bonaventure's works as the most available source of the Latin text. [*Tr.*]

other, like Scylla, lust, with a smile on its girl's face, lures it on to destroy its chastity. The coast is savage, and the devil with a crew of pirates carries chains with which to fetter those whom he captures (*ibid.*, § 6, col. 350).

154. ST. GREGORY OF NAZIANZUS, Doctor of the Church (d. 389). Snatch your soul away from the world; flee from Sodom; take flight from the conflagration; travel on without turning back, lest you should be fixed as a pillar of salt (cf. Gen. 19:26). Escape to the mountain lest you be destroyed in the plain (*Oratio 40, in sanctum baptisma,* n. 19, *PG* 36:383).

155. JOHN OF TRITHEIM, abbot of Sponheim (d. 1516). Shun the world, for it repays those who love it in an evil way—by condemning them forever (*De vanitate et miseria humanae vitae,* c. 2, *Op. pia et spiritualia,* p. 788).

156. PETER OF BLOIS, chancellor and archdeacon, Bath, England (d. 1200). A. No one pronounces a curse on the world except in the spirit of God. (*Ep. 137, ad novitium Alexandrum de S. Albano, PL* 207:407; *Op. Om.*, p. 212).

B. The world is placed in evil, full of dangers, full of insidious temptations, full of scandals, full of depraved speech, corrupt example, treacherous words, and iniquitous counsel (*Ep. 102, ad Redingensem abbatem, qui voluit renuntiare assumptae dignitati, PL* 207:321; *Op. Om.*, p. 162).

157. HUGH OF ST. CHER, O.P., cardinal (d. 1263). A. No man, were he to understand the world perfectly, would fail to flee from it. . . . The sea casts up the dead; so does the world. And as the dead body that is cast up by the sea feels nothing, so he who is truly dead to the world has no feeling for its insults (*Sup. Gen. 31:7, 18. Commentarium* 1:44). B. The world is nothing other than confusion, a vault filled with the corpses of the dead (*Sup. Is. 25:2; ibid.*, 4:55).

158. ST. LAURENCE JUSTINIAN, can. regular, first patriarch of Venice (d. 1455). Since the world is full of confusion, he is to be considered truly blessed who, under God's preventing grace, has spurned it with the little that it has to offer, has avoided its friendships, and dwells in the holy monasteries of remote solitude (*De vita solitaria,* c. 6, *Op. Om.*, 2:135).

159. ST. BERNARD. As for us whom he has called out of the world and chosen to serve him exclusively, if, according to the Apostle *we have received not the spirit of the world, but the spirit that is from God, that we may know the things that have been given us by God* (I Cor. 2:12), we, my brethren, most particularly, shall find innumerable motives for offering unceasing thanks to the Lord (*Serm. de temp., Serm. II pro Dom. VI p. Pent.*, § 2, *PL* 183:340).

160. ST. ANSELM, abp. of Canterbury, Doctor of the Church (d.

1109). When you leave your city, imitate Lot! *Do not look behind you* (Gen. 19:17), but keep your eyes before you, in order to know the road ahead. Do not glance backward, for you must put out of your mind the thought of return, so that, in the words of the Apostle: *Forgetting what is behind, I strain forward to what is before* (Phil. 3:13; *Lib. II, ep. 25, ad Guilencum, quem obsecrat ut fugiat saeculum et Beccum veniat, PL* 158:1175; Schmitt, *Op. Om.,* 3:250).

161. ST. BONAVENTURE. A. Take flight from men and the world's distractions: for you cannot measure up to the demands of both God and men, to the things of eternity and those that are transitory (*Alphabetum religiosorum, lect. 6, Op. Om.,* ed. Peltier 12:502).* B. Since the spirit of contrition and personal acknowledgment of sin are acquired through cleanness of mind in solitude and mental prayer, it is necessary that anyone who is striving to attain this purity embrace solitude as the mother of prayer and cleanness (*De modo confitendi,* c. 16, *ibid.,* 7:578).†

162. ST. JOHN CHRYSOSTOM. A. For solitude is the mother of quiet; it is a calm and a harbor, freeing us from all turmoils (*Hom. 50 in Matt.,* § 1. *PG* 58:503). B. You will find nothing of this kind [of shipwreck] in monasteries, for although a great storm is raging, after others have been lost in the storm and the waves, religious alone, dwelling in the calm port and perfect security in monasteries, behold the shipwreck of others as though they were looking upon it from heaven itself (*Adversus oppugnatores vitae monast., Lib. III,* n. 11, *PG* 47:366). C. To be in this world as though one were a pilgrim and a stranger is the first virtue, and consequently the universal virtue to cultivate (*Hom. 24 in Ep. ad Hebr.* [11:13], n. 1, *PG* 63:165).

Holy solitude

163. ST. LAURENCE JUSTINIAN. A. Solitude [in monasticism] is a haven of tranquillity set apart from the noisy distractions of the world, an escape from evils, a nurturing of graces, the gateway to heaven, the environment of prayer, the begetter of compunction . . . the unique aid of contemplation (*De vita solitaria,* c. 1, *Op. Om.* 2:128). B. Solitude is the Bridegroom's resting place, the guardian of virtue, the intensification of peace (*ibid.,* c. 12, p. 147). C. Solitude is a school of wisdom . . . the witness of conscience, a foretaste of future blessedness, a reproacher of evils committed, a revealer of vices, the dignity of innocence, the familiar friend of heavenly secrets, ascent to heaven,

* This minor work is not contained in the critical Quaracchi ed., nor attributed to any other writer.

† The same definitive Quaracchi edition, 10:24, assigns this work to Matthew of Cracow (d. 1410).

the destroyer of spiritual passions, the ever-watchful guardian of the mind (*ibid.*, c. 18, p. 159).

164. HUGH OF ST. VICTOR. *The song of the dove is heard in our land* (Cant. 2:12). . . . Who will be found worthy to hear the dove's song? It sings only in solitude, because it always desires to be alone, and seeks the love of one only. Its song is never heard on the streets, for it does not sing out its notes. It sings to itself; none can hear it except those who are close by. They who betake themselves to the desert, who dwell in hidden recesses, and rest in silence, are the ones who hear the song of the dove (*Serm. de Assumptione B.V.M., In Append., PL* 177:1222).

165. ST. AMBROSE. The Lord said to the just man: *Enter into the ark.* That is, enter into yourself; enter into your own mind; into the purity of your soul's origin; there you will find salvation, there is guidance. Outside is the deluge, outside there is danger! (*De Noe et arca,* c. 11, n. 38, *PL* 14:397).

166. THOMAS À KEMPIS (d. 1471). Solitude is the mother of devotion; a crowd disquiets the mind (*Libell. spiritualis exercitii,* c. 4, *Op. Om.,* 2:336).

167. LIVES OF THE FATHERS. Abba Alonis stated: "Unless a man says in his heart, 'Only God and myself exist in this world,' he will not find rest" (*Aegyptiorum Patrum Sententiae, Append. ad Vitas Patrum,* n. 71, *PL* 74:391).

168. ST. PETER DAMIAN. A. When Almighty God withdrew you from the world and appointed you to serve him under monastic discipline, what else is he understood to have done than—as long ago when so many perished in the deluge—he chose you few and introduced you into the hideaway of the pitched ark (cf. Gen. 7:1 f.) in order that you might live? (*Opusc. 52, Quod monasteria vivaria sunt animarum,* c. 2, *PL* 145:766.) B. O monastery, storehouse of men who trade in heavenly values, where the treasure of those goods is laid away with which the land of the living is bought. . . . O monastery, admirable workshop of spiritual practices in which the human soul restores itself to the image of its Creator and returns to the purity of its origin; where the dulled senses return to the subtleness of their sharpness and the leaven of vitiated nature [that is, of malice and wickedness] is restored with [the unleavened bread of] sincerity and truth (cf. I Cor. 5:8). . . . You, O cell, make it possible for man, wrapped up in his own darkness, who formerly did not even know himself, now to behold God with a pure heart. You make man return to his origin, and recall him from the banishment of exile to the height of his pristine dignity. You, O monastery, enable man, dwelling in the castle of his soul, to see all things passing beneath him, and behold himself

passing along with all that is transitory. . . . O monastery, tabernacle of holy warfare, advance troops of the Conqueror's army, castle of the Lord, *David's tower girt with embattlements; a thousand bucklers hang upon it, all the shields of valiant men* (Cant. 4:4). You are the field of heavenly warfare, the arena of spiritual battle, the spectacle of angels. . . . O monastery, a kind of rival to the Lord's tomb, which receives those who have died to sin and makes them live again for God by the breath of the Holy Spirit! . . . O desert, wherein the cells of monks, like an orderly array of tents in a camp, like the towers of Sion, and like the bulwarks of Jerusalem are built up against the Assyrians and against Damascus (cf. IV Kings 16:9). In those cells various duties are performed in one spirit, for at one time they chant the Office, at another they pray [privately], at another they engage in writing, again they sweat in the performance of manual labors. Who can fail to see how appropriately the divine words are applicable to the desert [solitude, monastery]: *How goodly are your tents, O Jacob; your encampments, O Israel! They are like gardens beside a stream, like the cedars planted by the Lord* (Num. 24:5; *Opusc. 11,* c. 19, *Laus eremiticae vitae, PL* 145:247–250).

169. PETER THE VENERABLE. I propose the cell for your consideration. Such is its nature that you who are dwelling in the midst of the world are actually separated from that world. It is as though through its aid you had penetrated into the deepest recesses of a vast wilderness. I offer this cell, which, according to the saying of an early Father, can alone and in its silence teach you more eloquently than all masters. Certainly you are unable not to hear it when you will have it as the daily reminder of your salvation. "Take flight from men," says one of the Fathers [St. Jerome], "Keep silence and you will be saved." Death is to be avoided either with a shield [active combat] or with your feet [by taking flight]. *He shall sit solitary, and hold his peace: because he hath taken it up upon himself* (Lam. 3:28). And David: *You have raised for those who fear you a banner to which they may flee out of bowshot* (Ps. 59:6). It is as though they were *to go into the holes of rocks, and into the caves of the earth from the face of the fear of the Lord, and from the glory of his majesty, when he shall rise up to strike the earth* (Isa. 2:19). . . . By its enclosure the cell represents you not only dead to this life, but buried, and in a sense cries out with the words of the Apostle to you as to the Colossians: *For you have died, and your life is hidden with Christ in God* (Col. 3:3; *Lib. I, ep. 20, PL* 189:90).

170. ST. JEROME. O desert, bright with the flowers of Christ! O solitude, whence come the stones with which, according to the Apocalypse, the city of the great King is built (cf. Apoc. 21:19). O wilderness,

gladdened with God's special presence! What is keeping you in the world, my brother, you who are above the world? How long will gloomy roofs press you? How long shall the smoky cities immure you? Believe me, I have more light than you. . . . Sweet it is to lay aside the weight of the body and to soar into the pure bright ether (*Ep. 14, ad Heliodorum monachum, peregrinationis suae comitem, quem frustra conatus erat apud se in eremo detinere,* § 10, *PL* 22:353).

171. PETER DE BLOIS. In the cloister you possessed a retreat of solitude, an environment of penance, tranquillity of mind, the privacy needed for contemplation, joy in the Holy Spirit, guidance when you are in doubt, help in the time of temptation, and the efficacious medicine of kindness in everything. There you have the school of virtue, an exalted practice of modesty, the example of behavior according to the Rule, freedom for reading, love of the brotherhood . . . the force of discipline, the law of obedience, the bond of charity, and mutual regard for one another (*Invectiva in depravatorem operum Blesensis, PL* 207:1118; *Op. Om.*, p. 458).

172. ST. ANTONY, abbot (d. 357). He who lives in the desert is free from three kinds of spiritual attacks: that is to say, those which arise through hearing, speech, and sight; he has only one kind to fight, namely, that of the heart (*De vitis Patrum, Lib. V, Verba seniorum, libell. II,* n. 2, *PL* 73:858).

173. WILLIAM OF ST. THIERRY. For *coelum,* which is the Latin for heaven, and *cella,* which means cell, seem both to have their origin from *celare,* which signifies to hide. . . . That which is done in heaven is done in your cells. And what is that? To give yourself to God, to enjoy God. When you do this according to your Rule piously and faithfully in your cells, I dare say that the holy angels of God then take *cella* for *coelum* and find their delight in your cells as in heaven (*Ep. ad fratres de Monte Dei, Lib. I,* c. 4, *Quae sit vera pietas, quae solitudo,* § 10, *PL* 184:314).

174. ST. BASIL THE GREAT. If then, it should happen that circumstances force you to leave your cell and go abroad, arm yourself with the breastplate of the fear of God, clasp in your hand the love of Christ, and repulse with all continency the attacks of sensual pleasure. As soon as your business is completed, take your departure without delay and return on swift wing like a guileless dove going back to the ark which sent you forth (cf. Gen. 8:9), bearing the mercies of Christ on your lips, thus silencing interior protests and persuading yourself that saving tranquillity cannot be secured in any other place (*Serm. I, de renuntiatione saeculi,* n. 5, *PG* 31:638; Wagner, *Ascetical Works,* p. 23).

175. TURSTIN, abp. of York. The blessed Benedict does not recognize as his subject anyone who does not dwell in the monastery under

the Rule and an abbot [*RSB*, c. 5] (*Turstini Archiepisc. Eboracensis ad Willelmum, ep. 439, In Append. ad Epistolas S. Bernardi*, § 3, *PL* 182:699).

Dedicated speech

176. ST. GREGORY THE GREAT. In order for us to express outwardly the things of which we are inwardly aware, we pronounce them through the organ of the throat, by the sounds of the voice. To the eyes of other persons we stand, as it were, behind the partition of the body, within the secret dwelling place of our mind; but when we desire to make ourselves manifest, we go forth as though through the door of the tongue, that we may show what kind of persons we are within (*Moralium Lib. II*, c. VII, n. 8, *Variae Dei spirituumque locutiones, PL* 75:559).

177. JOHN OF TRITHEIM. As soon as one begins to speak, his tongue reveals what kind of person he is (*Comm. in Prolog. RSB*, c. 2, *Op. pia et spiritualia*, p. 173).

178. ST. BONAVENTURE. Man is never better known than by his speech (*De SS. Apostolis Serm. IV, Op. Om.*, ed. Peltier 14:10).*

178[a]. ST. JOHN CHRYSOSTOM. A. God gave you a tongue for the purpose of enabling you to give thanks to him, and to build up your neighbor. If you destroy that building, it were better to be silent and never speak at all (*Hom. 14 in Ep. ad Eph.* [4, 25], n. 3, *PG* 62:103). B. No organ is so serviceable for the devil's purposes of deceiving us and effecting our destruction as is an intemperate tongue or a mouth that is not guarded. From this source arise numerous sins and grave offenses (*Catechesis ad illuminandos*, n. 4, *Linguae quot et quanti lapsus, PG* 49:228). C. God willed the tongue to be hedged about, as it were, with a double wall. For the tongue is enclosed both by the barrier of the teeth and the protection of the lips, lest it easily and without reflection speak unbecoming words (*ibid.*, col. 229). D. Let not that tongue on which the divine body has been placed pronounce anything bitter, anything harsh (*Hom. VI in I Tim.* [2:1], n. 2, *PG* 62:531). E. We must put a guard over our mouth at all times and employ our reason as though it were a key, not for the purpose of keeping the mouth locked at all times, but that it be unlocked at the proper times (*Expos. in Ps. 140:3*, n. 4, *PG* 55:432).

* It would be an impossible task to trace the individual sermons attributed to St. Bonaventure. The definitive Quaracchi edition of his works retains a relatively small number of the sermons given in the Peltier edition. The latter is here cited for the sermons from which Wolter has taken excerpts because (1) they are inherently good material; (2) they are from reputable if unidentified sources; (3) Wolter desired to incorporate them into his work as integral components of his concept of monasticism; and (4) because this is the available source for the texts he employed. [*Tr.*]

179. ST. VALERIAN, bp. of Cimiez in France (5th century). A. It is impossible to judge how greatly the vices of an undisciplined tongue interfere with the way of life (*Hom. 2, De arcta et angusta via*, n. 4, *PL* 52:698).

B. The tongue is worse than any kind of poison, and can be curbed finally only in death. . . . Once a person breaks faith with his tongue in constant motion, it is useless for him to seek a doctor, for the sins of speech are without remedy. Even though a person fortify his life with faith, govern it with knowledge, set it in order as regards charity and moderation, there is nothing pleasing in a man if in his whole being the tongue alone is displeasing (*Hom. 5, De oris insolentia*, n. 4, *PL* 52:707).

180. ST. AUGUSTINE. A. *But the tongue no man can tame* (Jas. 3:8). Man tames the wild beast, yet he does not tame his tongue; he tames the lion, yet bridles not his own speech; he tames all else, yet he does not master himself (*Serm. 5. sup. Matt.* [5:22], n. 1, *PL* 38:375). B. We are daily tried in the furnace of the human tongue. And in this manner also you command us to continence: grant what you command, and command what you will (*Confessionum Lib. X*, c. 37, n. 60. *PL* 32:804; Sheed, p. 250). C. It is not without reason that the tongue is set in a moist place, but because it is so prone to slip. Perceiving therefore how hard it was for a man to be under the necessity of speaking, and still not to say something that he will wish unsaid, and filled with disgust at these sins, he seeks to avoid the like . . . Guard your ways, Idithun, and do not sin with your tongue; examine thoroughly and weigh well whatever you are about to say; refer to your inward apprehension of the truth, and only then present it to your hearer (*Enarr. in Ps. 38* [2], n. 3, *PL* 36:414).

181. ST. ALBERT THE GREAT, O.P., bp. of Regensburg, Doctor of the Church (d. 1280). Where there is no recollectedness of spirit, a person will be easily overcome by the enemy. . . . Where there is no control of the tongue there can be no perfection of life . . . (*Paradisus animae*, c. 37, *De taciturnitate*, *Op. Om.* 37:494).

182. ST. AMBROSE. Let us not utter a single evil word lest we fall into sin. But let there be a yoke and a balance to your words, that is, humility and moderation, in order to keep your tongue under the control of your mind. Let it be held in check with a tight rein; let it have its own means of restraint, whereby it can be recalled to moderation; let it utter words tried by the scales of justice, so that there may be seriousness to the meaning, weight in the speech, and due measure in the words (*De officiis ministrorum, Lib. I*, c. 3, *Non perpetuum esse debere silentium*, n. 13, *PL* 16:30).

183. ST. GREGORY OF NAZIANZUS. Speak, if you have something to say that is better and more excellent than silence. But when it is more

advisable to be still rather than to speak, embrace silence (*Oratio 32, De moderatione in disputando,* n. 13, *PG* 36:190).

184. ST. ISIDORE PELUSIOTA, abbot (d. circa 431). If you are striving to follow [the hermit] Paul's counsels, if you desire to cherish the monastic life, put a bridle on the rapidity of your tongue (*Lib. I, ep. 325, Cyro monacho, PG* 78:370).

185. ST. BERNARD. A. Guard your heart, and hold your tongue in check (*Tract. de ordine vitae,* c. 4. *Taciturnitatem et silentium praecipue convenire adolescentibus,* n. 13, *In Append., PL* 184:569). B. The tongue is a delicate member of the body, but one that is difficult to hold in control. Small it is, and weak, but to it belong duties that are important and serious. It is a little member, true, but unless you are careful, it can be a great evil. It is small and of little strength, but a most efficient tool for emptying hearts, as I believe many of your consciences will bear witness, unless we are all so perfect that, after protracted conversations, we have never found our minds somewhat blank, meditation less devout, the affections dried up, and the holocaust of prayer not so fat because of the words that we have either spoken or listened to . . . (*Serm. de div., Serm. 13, de triplici custodia manus, linguae, et cordis,* n. 5, *PL* 183:585).

186. ARNOLD OF BOHÉRIES, Cistercian monk of the abbey of Notre Dame, diocese of Laon, now Soissons (12th century). If he is called upon to speak, let the monk speak in conformity with the *Rule of St. Benedict,* gently and without laughter, humbly and seriously, in few and sensible words (*RSB,* c. 7, eleventh degree of humility). And before he utters what he has to say, let it be subjected twice to revision before being admitted once to expression. If he is called upon to speak with a person from outside the enclosure, he must exercise even greater caution lest he say anything that would fail to edify the one who hears him (*Speculum monachorum,* n. 1, *PL* 184:1175).

187. LIVES OF THE FATHERS. A. "We do not learn to shut a door made of wood, but to close the door of the tongue" [Abbot Paemen, to a brother who had feared that during the Lenten fast the abbot's door would be closed to him] (*Aegyptiorum Patrum sententiae,* n. 43, *PL* 74:388). B. It is impossible for a man to make progress in even only one virtue without placing a guard over his mouth; for the first virtue is in guarding one's mouth (*ibid.,* n. 96, col. 392). C. A certain brother questioned the old man: "Up to what point is silence to be observed, Father?" The old man replied: "Until you are questioned. For in all places, if you have kept the spirit of silence, you will enjoy *peace*" (*De vitis Patrum, Lib. VII,* c. 32, n. 3, *PL* 73:1051).

188. ST. AUGUSTINE. A man's talkativeness reveals what he is in the depth of his heart. . . . Blush for shame, talkative man! Know

yourself for what you are, you who are full of words (*Serm. 3 ad fratres in eremo, In Append., PL* 40:1239).

189. ST. GREGORY THE GREAT. A. Hence the mind is unable to turn back within to the knowledge of itself, in that being dissipated without through much talking, it loses the strength of interior recollection. . . . Because it is without the wall of silence, the city of the mind lies open to the attacks of the enemy (*Moral., Lib. VII,* c. 17, n. 59, *Sine silentii censura mens tota patet hosti, PL* 75:800). B. The righteousness of the interior is desolated when we do not withhold ourselves from immoderate talking. . . . The adversary gets the mastery of the city of the mind without effort, in proportion as the soul that he has to overcome wages war against itself by excessive talking (*ibid.,* n. 58, 59). C. It is a certain truth that a man full of words cannot be justified (*ibid., Lib. X,* c. 2, n. 2, col. 919). D. Deceptions result from too much talking, for it is very difficult for a person who talks too much not to be guilty of lying (*Lib. I, Hom. 12 sup. Ezech.* [4:2], n. 27, *PL* 76:931). E. For we are drawn too much down toward earth by continual talking of secular business (*Dialogorum Lib. III,* c. 15, *de Eutychio et Florentio servis Dei, PL* 77:256). F. But those who are addicted to much talking, are to be admonished to observe vigilantly from how great a degree of rectitude they lapse, when they fall to using a multitude of words. For the human mind behaves after the manner of water: when enclosed, it collects itself to higher levels, because it seeks again the height from which it came down. But, when released, it loses itself, in that it scatters itself to no purpose through the lowest levels; indeed, all the superfluous words wasted when it relaxes its censorship of silence, are so many streams carrying the mind away from itself. Consequently, it does not have the power to turn inwardly to self-knowledge, because, dissipated as it is by much talking, it is diverted from the secret places of inward considerations. It lays itself completely exposed to wounds from the enemy lying in wait for it, in that it does not encompass itself with a barrier of watchfulness (*Reg. pastoralis lib., Pars III,* c. 14, *Quomodo admonendi taciturni et verbosi, PL* 77:73; Davis, p. 132). G. He is skilled in speaking truthfully who has first learned well to observe silence (*Lib. I, Hom. 11 sup. Ezech.* [3:16], n. 3, *PL* 76:907).

190. ST. EPHRAEM. Excessive talking darkens the mind and dulls the senses (*Paraenesis seu adhortationes ad monachos, Paraen. 7, Op. Om.* 2:348).

191. ST. JOHN CLIMACUS. A. Talkativeness is the throne of vainglory on which it loves to show itself and make a display. Talkativeness is a sign of ignorance, a door to slander, a guide to jesting, a servant of falsehood, the ruin of compunction, a creator of despond-

ency, a precursor of sleep, the dissipation of recollection, the abolition of watchfulness, the cooling of ardor, the darkening of prayer (*Scala paradisi, Grad. 11, De loquacitate et silentio, PG* 88:851; Moore, p. 134; Robert, p. 190). B. Control your wondering mind in your distracted body. Amidst the actions and movements of your limbs, practice mental quiet. And, most paradoxical of all, in the midst of commotion be unmoved in soul. Curb your tongue which rages to leap into arguments. Seventy times seven in the day wrestle with this tyrant (*ibid., Grad. 4, De beata . . . obedientia,* col. 699; Moore, p. 80; Robert, p. 67).

192. ST. ISIDORE OF SEVILLE, bp., Doctor of the Church (d. 636). Excessive talking does not escape fault, nor avoid sin; a river in flood stage quickly carries much mud with it (*Synonymorum Lib. II,* c. 49, *PL* 83:856).

193. ST. DOROTHEUS, monk of Palestine (7th century). Avoid excessive speaking for it extinguishes all reasonable thoughts and those which come to the heart from heaven (*Doctrina 24, De compositione monachi, PG* 88:1838).

194. ST. BONAVENTURE. I would not hesitate to state that it is all to no purpose for a religious to take any pride in the virtue which he has acquired [by regular observance] if by the disturbance of excessive talking he disrupts the rule of silence (*De perfectione vitae, ad sorores,* c. 4, *Op. Om.,* ed. Quaracchi 8:116).*

195. ST. ISIDORE OF SEVILLE. A. Let your speech be marked by seriousness and sound doctrine; keep it above reproach; let it be profitable according to the expectations of those who hear it; strive to say, not what is pleasing, but what needs to be said. Determine well what you are going to say, and what you are to leave unsaid: be skilled both in speaking and in keeping silence. Deliberate beforehand on what you are to say, lest afterward you will be unable to retract it. Avoid slips of the tongue; do not let your tongue betray you (*Synonymorum Lib. II,* § 47, *PL* 83:856). B. A man full of words is unskilled; the wise man uses few words; wisdom makes for brevity (*ibid.,* § 49).

196. ST. BERNARD. A. It is a monstrous inconsistency to be the highest in rank and the lowest in character; to be first in dignity and last in virtue; to have a boastful tongue and idle hands; to abound in words and to be wanting in action; to be grave in looks and frivolous in conduct; to be supreme in power and lacking in constancy (*De Consideratione, Lib. II,* c. 7, n. 15, *PL* 182:750). B. How utterly constant unbridling of the tongue deprives religious persons of interior devotion! How extensive the destruction it causes! As a furnace whose door stands always open cannot retain its heat, so also a heart whose

* This work was written to a certain abbess of St. Claire's monastery, probably to Bl. Isabella, sister of St. Louis, King of France. Ed. Quaracchi 10:15.

mouth is not closed with the door of silence cannot preserve the grace of devotion (*Vitis mystica, seu. tract. de Passione Domini,* c. 27, n. 89, *In Append., PL* 184:688).

197. DENIS THE CARTHUSIAN. Excessive talking is the pulpit of vainglory, the gateway to detraction, the beginning of telling lies, the abandonment of compunction, an obstacle to divine enlightenment, the begetter of sloth, the rejection of interior recollection, that which renders fervor lifeless, the disposition that makes prayer unintelligible, the cause of distraction, the want of devotion (*De professione monastica,* art. 19, *Op. Om.* 38:579).

The excellence of silence

198. THOMAS À KEMPIS. A. It is no slight loss to forfeit the grace of devotion through overmuch talking (*Serm. ad novitios, Serm. 19, Op. Om.* 6:172; Scully, p. 139). B. The mouth's silence is the dwelling place of peace (*Hortulus rosarum,* c. 8, *Op. Om.* 4:15).

199. ST. AMBROSE. A. What need is there, then, for you to rush in undergoing the danger of condemnation by speaking when you can be more safe by keeping silent? I have seen many fall into sin by speaking, but scarcely ever have I seen anyone sin by keeping silent: and so it is more difficult to know how to keep silent than how to speak. . . . Therefore the saints of the Lord loved to observe silence, because they knew that man's voice is often the utterance of sin, and man's speech is the beginning of human error (*De officiis ministrorum, Lib. I,* c. 2, *Multiplex loquendo incurri periculum,* nn. 5–6, *PL* 16:28). B. O silence, reliable shield of the protection of prudence! Most trustworthy foundation of stability on which, if a person can stand, he need not fear the incautious word. For many who are even stable of heart have frequently fallen into error through the incautiously spoken word (*Enarr. in Ps. 38,* n. 2, *PL* 14:1089).

200. ST. DIADOCHUS. Silence is an excellent thing—in fact, it is nothing other than the mother of the wisest thoughts (*Capita de perfectione spirituali,* c. 70, *PG* 65:1192).

201. JOHN CASSIAN, abbot of Marseilles (d. 430). Be solicitous, therefore, in the first place, and especially you, John, as your more youthful age demands that you be quite careful about what I am going to say: that you may impose absolute silence on your lips, in order that your zeal for reading and the efforts expended in your purpose may not be destroyed by vainglory. For this is the first practical step toward learning: to receive the regulations and sentences of all the elders in earnestness of heart, and with closed lips; and diligently to store them up in your heart, and endeavor rather to perform them than to teach them (*Collatio 14, Coll. I Abbatis Nesterotis, de spirituali scientia,* c. 9, *PL* 49:966).

202. ST. ARSENIUS. While Arsenius was still a secular, dwelling in the palace, he prayed to God with these words: "O Lord, direct me along the way by which I may be saved." And he heard a voice saying: "Arsenius, flee from men, and you will live." When he had withdrawn to the desert and was living the ascetic life in the monastery, he prayed the same prayer to God, and again heard a voice saying to him: "Arsenius, flee, keep silence, and lead a life of silent contemplation, for these are the principles of salvation which prevent a man from committing sin" (*De vitis Patrum, Lib. III,* n. 190, *PL* 73:801; Budge, *Wit and wisdom,* p. 3).

203. ST. MACARIUS, monk of Alexandria (d. 390). "Take flight, brethren, take flight!" One of the brethren asked him: "What flight, whither? Where can we take flight from this desert?" And placing his finger on his lips, he answered: "Take flight from this!" And he closed the door of his cell (*ibid., Lib. V,* n. 27, col. 868).

204. ST. JOHN CLIMACUS. A. Deliberate silence is the mother of prayer, a recall from captivity, preservation of fire, a supervisor of thoughts, a watch against enemies, a prison of mourning, a friend of tears, effective remembrance of death, a depicter of punishment, a meddler with judgment, an aid to anguish, an enemy of freedom of speech, a companion of quiet, an opponent of desire to teach, increase of knowledge, a creator of contemplation, unseen progress, secret ascent (*Scala paradisi, Grad. 11, De loquacitate et silentio,* § 3, *PG* 88:851; Moore, p. 135; Robert, p. 191). B. The friend of silence draws near to God, and by secretly conversing with him, is enlightened by God (*ibid.,* § 5).

205. ST. EPHRAEM. Possess silence, brother, like a strong wall. Silence will enable you to gain the victory over your passions, for you will be fighting from above, and they will be subjected under foot.

Cultivate silence in the fear of the Lord, and no weapons of the enemy will harm you. Silence joined to fear of the Lord is a fiery chariot transporting its occupant to heaven. Let Elias the Prophet teach you this, for in his love of silence, joined with the fear of the Lord, he was taken up to heaven (cf. IV Kgs. 2:1–11).

O silence, progress of monks; ladder of heaven, the way to the heavenly kingdom! Silence, mother of compunction, mirror revealing his faults to the sinner. Silence, which stops not the flow of tears, begets meekness, makes itself the companion of the lowly-minded. Silence, spouse of humility and enlightenment of the soul! Silence, which puts a check on thoughts, and cooperates in forming judgments! Silence, mother of all that is good, support of fasting, and preventer of gluttony! Silence, school of reading and of prayer! Silence, tranquillity in thought and safe harbor! Silence, which casts aside all cares of the soul!

Silence, sweet yoke and light burden, refreshing and carrying him that carries it, joy of mind and heart, restraint of ears, and eyes, and tongue. Silence, destruction of artificiality and adversary of all shameless conduct! Mother of reverence! Silence, which imprisons the passions, cooperates with every virtue, fosters poverty, the garden of Christ bringing forth good fruit! Silence, joined to the fear of the Lord, the wall and defense of those who seek to do battle for the kingdom of heaven!

Most of all, brother, cultivate this *best part which Mary chose* (Luke 10:42). Mary, the model of silence, sits at the feet of the Lord and clings to him alone. For that reason he praises her saying: *Mary has chosen the best part, and it will not be taken away from her* (*Serm. de patientia et consummatione saeculi, Op. Om.* 1:166).

206. DENIS THE CARTHUSIAN. *The service of justice* [shall be] *quietness* (Isa. 32:17). Quietness, silence, that is, the freeing of self for God, the withdrawal of the heart from the multitude, the bridling of the tongue from all idle words. We see this realized especially among the cloistered who build up their cultivation of righteousness on the observance of silence (*Enarr. in c. 32 Isaiae,* art. 58, *Op. Om.* 8:560).

207. ST. PETER DAMIAN. A. As long as he keeps his mouth closed under the austere observance of silence, the monk is living [as he should], but he ceases to be the monk the moment he opens his lips for immoderate speech (*Opusc. 52, De bono religiosi status,* c. 23, *PL* 145:788). B. Once the noise of human discourse ceases, the temple of the Holy Spirit is built up within you by silence. Sacred history bears witness to something similar in recording the erection of the temple of the Israelites, for neither hammer, nor axe, nor any tool of iron was heard when the house of God was building (III Kgs. 6:7). The temple of God grows in silence, for if the human mind does not empty itself through the use of external words, the structure of the temple rises to its very pinnacle; and the more deeply its foundations are laid the higher it rises in that it is prevented from destroying itself by being guarded on every side through the preservation of silence. *The work of justice shall be peace, and the service of justice quietness* (Isa. 32:17). *It is good for a man, when he hath borne the yoke from his youth. He shall sit solitary, and hold his peace, because he hath taken it up upon himself* (Lam. 3:27–28).

While he observes silence, the solitary is indeed lifted up above himself; because the human mind, when it is enclosed on all sides within the clausura of silence, is elevated on high, is caught up to God in its longing for heaven, and is inflamed with the love of God by the ardor of the Holy Spirit. What takes place is something like a spring which is kept from flowing in this direction and that in rivulets of words, and forms into a deep lake with the mounting volumes of water. May the temple of your heart grow through silence! May the building of spiritual virtues grow tall in you, as with the structure of many spiritual stones, wherein the heavenly Bridegroom, whom you love with your whole being, may joyfully repose as in his bridal chamber (*Lib. VII, ep. 6, ad Agnetem Imperatricem, Henrici II uxorem, PL* 144:444).

208. JOHN BONA, Cistercian, cardinal (d. 1674). The spirit of recollectedness is a great thing, because by withdrawing from the companionship of men we learn to converse with God. For it is in vain that the tongue remains silent unless the spirit addresses itself to God. Silence sanctifies all that we suffer: calumny, persecution, sickness, and affliction of spirit, for he who bears these things and remains silent, consecrates to God his body, his soul, his judgment, his powers, and all his goods. It is then that he imitates Christ, who was *dumb as a lamb before his shearer* (Isa. 53:7), not opening his mouth. Freed of all disturbance, it calmly rejoices in self-possession. . . . *I kept silence from good things* (Ps. 38:3, Douay version). If at times we must abstain even from speech about that which is virtuous, how much more so from that which is harmful and useless? He is wise who knows how to observe silence, for it is far more difficult to know how to keep silence than to speak (*Principia et documenta vitae christianae, Pars II,* c. 8, *Op. Om.,* p. 46).

209. ST. BERNARD. A. There are three foreskins that are cut away: that of the flesh in the Jew; of the heart in the Christian; and of the tongue in the perfect man (*Lib. Sententiarum,* n. 91, *In Append., PL* 184:146). B. Isaias calls silence [quietness] *the service of justice* (Isa. 32:17), and Jeremias says that *it is good to wait with silence for the salvation of God* (Lam. 3:26). Therefore, so that I shall not seem entirely to ignore your request, I invite and incite you, who by speaking press me to teach what I do not know, and, if not by my teaching, at any rate by the example of my silence, all those who like you wish to grow in virtue, to foster this *service of justice,* the mother, the support, the guardian of all other virtues (*Ep. 89, ad Ogerium Canonicum Regularem,* n. 2, *PL* 182:221; James, p. 138; Gasquet, p. 114). C. If you desire to be a religious, put a check on your tongue, for without restraining the tongue, religion is in vain (*Vitis mystica, seu tract. de Passione Dni,* c. 27, n. 89, *In Append., PL* 184:688). D. But if detraction and quarrels find their way into the enclosure, where is the spirit of recollectedness and the rule? where the holiness of religious life? where the godliness of the order? where the religious spirit of the monastery? where the bond of charity? where the peace of unity? where the oneness of heart of the brotherhood? where the bond of love? Alas! the rule's spirit of recollectedness has ceased; the holiness of the religious life has been taken away; . . . the religious spirit of the monastery has been reduced to nothingness; the charity of the brotherhood has been lost (*Lib. de modo bene vivendi, ad sororem,* c. 17, *de contentione,* n. 46, *In Append., PL* 184:1229). E. Silence is the guardian of the religious life and the source

of our spiritual strength (*Serm. de temp., Serm. 2 de Dom. I post Oct. Epiphaniae,* § 7, *PL* 183:161). F. . . . for the observance of silence, in which there is the freedom of other virtues, is the supreme act of modesty (*Tract. de ordine vitae,* c. 4, *Taciturnitatem et silentium praecipue convenire adolescentibus,* n. 12, *In Append., PL* 184:568). G. A thoughtless word which escapes one, or laughter into which one breaks spontaneously, without really adverting to what he is doing, even during a time of silence, or in a place where silence is to be kept, is one thing—whereas the same actions done with the intention of violating the precept is in truth an indication of carelessness, of a spirit little given to recollection (*De praecepto et dispensatione,* c. 8, *gravius peccari legum contemptu quam neglectu,* n. 18, *PL* 182:871).

210. ST. LAURENCE JUSTINIAN. The peaceful mind, dedicated to the worship of God and love of virtue, desiring to stand in purity and devotion before the Lord, prudently confines the tongue within the enclosure of silence (*De disciplina monasticae conversations,* c. 15, *Op. Om.* 1:133).

211. HUMBERT OF ROMANS. By observance of silence, the conscience is made clear and bright, punishment is avoided, peace preserved, and the mind elevated to contemplation with less difficulty (*Ep. de tribus votis substantialibus,* c. 52, *De Vita regulari,* p. 36).

212. GILBERT OF HOILAND, English Cistercian who had received the habit from St. Bernard, his master, diocese of Lincoln (d. 1172). Do not the constant observance of silence and seriousness of disposition make for graciousness, add charm to one's whole character, and clothe it with a beautiful appearance of holiness? (*Serm. 23 in Cant. Salomonis* [4:1], n. 3, *PL* 184:121.)

213. JOHN GERSON, chancellor of Paris (d. 1429). Where the severity of silence is strictly observed, religion thrives most commendably and fully (*Tract. ad mysticam vitam, Pars II, Quattuor quaest.,* n. 33, *sub littera* "G," q. 1, conclusio 3).

214. THOMAS À KEMPIS. By the conscientious observance of silence you preserve obedience as well, guard humility, adorn modesty, show reverence for elders, give good example to the young, strike fear into the frivolous and negligent, and create a high regard for the religious state among outsiders and peace and concord among the members of the community (*Ed. ad quemdam a ministerio suo absolutum de recommendatione solitudinis et custodia silentii, Op. Om.* 4:419).

215. VEN. LOUIS DE BLOIS, abbot of Liessies (d. 1516). If you cannot endure solitude and silence, but are delighted with idle speech and inordinate laughter, you are no monk (*Speculum monachorum,* div. 1, *Op. Om.* 3:652).

216. JOHN, monk of Cluny (10th century). Without the observance of silence, the life of the monk is to be considered valueless. For his life

amounts to something only as long as he strives to be under the discipline of silence. Once that effort is abandoned, whatever else he may have judged himself to have done well or virtuously, is nothing, according to the teaching of the Fathers (*Vita S. Odonis, Abb. Cluniacensis, Lib. II,* c. 11, *PL* 133:67).

217. ST. GREGORY THE GREAT. The tongue, then, must be prudently curbed, but not completely tied up. For it is written; *A wise man is silent till the right time comes* (Sir. 20:6), that is to say, when he sees it opportune to speak what is fitting, he sets aside the rigorous observance of silence and directs his effort to be of assistance. . . . In other words, the various occasions are prudently to be judged; when the tongue ought to be restrained, it should not be unprofitably loosened in speech, or when it could speak with profit, it should not indolently withhold speech. The prophet considers this matter well when he says: *O Lord, set a watch before my mouth, a guard* [*a door,* Douay] *at the door of my lips* (Ps. 140:3). He does not ask that a wall be set before his mouth, but a door, which, you see, can be opened and closed. Wherefore we must take care to learn when speech should open the mouth discreetly and at the proper time, and when, on the contrary, silence should becomingly keep it closed (*Regulae pastoralis Lib., Pars II,* c. 14, *Quomodo admonendi sunt taciturni et verbosi, PL* 77:72; Davis, p. 131).

218. ST. BASIL THE GREAT. There is, indeed, a tone of voice, a moderateness in length, a propriety of time, and a specific appropriateness in the use of words which are especially characteristic of those leading the devout life, and these qualities cannot be taught to one who has not acquired them by constant practice (*Reg. fusius tractatae, Interrogatio 13, PG* 31:950; Wagner, p. 263).

The vow of stability

219. BENEDICT HAEFTEN, provost of Afflighem (d. 1648). Two things are included under the vow of stability: the first is that it is not permitted to leave the monastery; the other, not to withdraw one's neck from under the yoke of the Rule [cf. *RSB,* c. 58] (*Disquisitiones monasticae, Lib. IV, tract. 6, De votorum explicatione, disq. 3,* p. 147).

220. ST. PALDO, first abbot of the monastery of St. Vincent on the Voltorno, near Beneventum (d. circa 720), regularly exhorted his monks: "Believe me, brethren, the monk who will have persevered steadfastly to the end of his days in this monastery will never suffer eternal punishment, but will possess eternal life" (*Vita S. Paldonis,* § 13, *Mabillon, Acta SS. O.S.B., saec. III,* 3:406).

221. ST. BASIL THE GREAT. First of all, it behooves him who presents himself for this [monastic] life to be of stable, firm, unshakable constancy of will, and of such a purpose that the malevolent spirits can neither invade nor corrupt it. He must show such firmness of mind that

he possess a constancy even to the death of the martyrs, both in keeping the divine commandments and in preserving obedience toward his masters. For this is the very substance of the whole life of the institute (*Const. monasticae*, c. 19, *Quod oportet ascetam cum firmo proposito accedere ad asceticam vitam*, *PG* 31:1387).

222. ST. BERNARD. A. There are two things handed down to us who dwell in monasteries for special observance: one is submission to the abbot; the other is stability in our monastery. And these two are so to be observed that there is no conflict between them. That is to say, we should not be led by our stability to disdain subjection to the abbot, nor by our subjection to the abbot, to lose stability (*Ep. 7, ad Adam monachum, quem hortatur ut redeat, mortuo abbate*, n. 15, *PL* 182:102; James, p. 35).

B. Without perseverance there can be no victory for the soldier nor honor for the victor. This perseverance is the backbone of character, and the crown of virtue; it is the mother of merits and the mediator of rewards. It is the sister of patience, the daughter of endurance, the friend of peace, the link of friendship, the bond of concord, and the bulwark of holiness. Take away perseverance and service will be without reward, kindness without favor, and valor without renown. It is not the man who begins, but the man who perseveres unto the end that shall be saved. . . . I exhort you and pray you to hold firmly on to this mark of the highest honor, this sole reliable protection of integrity (*Ep. 129, ad Januenses*, n. 2, col. 283; James, p. 200).

C. It may be that a monk of one of the Cluniac monasteries desires to bind himself to the poverty of the Cistercians, seeking to follow the purity of the Rule more accurately than he can according to the custom as observed among them. Should he consult me, I would advise against it, particularly if he has not obtained the consent of his abbot in the matter. Why do I answer thus? First, because of the scandal to those whom he is leaving. Second, because there is no security in giving up what is certain for what is doubtful—for it may well be that he can keep the one [the Cluniac observance] and not be able to keep the other [the Cistercian]. Then, in the third place, I fear his motive shows want of constancy; for that which we ardently desire before we have given it a trial we often dislike once we have learned to know it through experience, thus showing a lack of constancy and reasonableness as well by simultaneously desiring and rejecting the same thing (*De praecepto et dispensatione*, c. 16, *Transitus et mutatio monasterii quatenus probanda*, n. 46, col. 886).

223. ST. PETER CHRYSOLOGUS, abp. of Ravenna, Doctor of the Church (d. 450). It is not change of place, but reformation of the moral sense which removes misfortunes, puts sadness to flight, casts off inclination to despair, prevents worries, takes possession of the sincere heart,

and prepares the mansion of joy in God (*Serm. 46, De exultatione spirituali et confessione peccatorum, PL* 52:328).

224. ST. AUGUSTINE. Therefore the less the soul clings to God, the Supreme Being, the less steadfast it feels itself to be (*Ep. 118, Dioscoro,* c. III, § 15, *PL* 33:439; Parsons, p. 276).

225. ST. ANSELM, abp. of Canterbury (d. 1109). You have entered the monastery, my dear friend, and have professed as a soldier in Christ's service: in this military duty you are under obligation not only to repel all open attack of the declared enemy, but also to be on your guard against the wiles of his temptations. Often enough when the enemy cannot mortally wound the novice of Christ by perverting his will, his malevolent cunning seeks to destroy him by offering him the cup of poisoned reason when he thirsts. For when he cannot ruin the monk with a hatred for the life that he has professed, he sets out to overwhelm him with an aversion for his surroundings. . . .

Regardless of the monastery where he has professed, a person who undertakes the cenobitic way of life must devote all effort and the whole concentration of his mind toward taking root in that place, the roots of love—unless, of course, he would be forced to commit evil there against his will. He is to refrain from passing judgment on the actions of others, or on the customs of the place, no matter how useless and unprofitable they may seem to him, provided that they are not contrary to the divine law. . . .

But if his spiritual fervor causes him to long for more advanced and salutary exercises than those permitted by the rule of the monastery where he dwells, he must be convinced that he is making a mistake—of preferring equal things to those which are only equal, or lesser ones to those that are greater—or that he is presumptuous in assuming that he can perform what in reality he is incapable of undertaking properly. Or let him be convinced simply that he has not deserved that which he would like to do. If he is wrong in so judging, let him thank the Divine Mercy, for by it he is preserved from his own error. He must not change his stability and his present ordered rule of life without advantage to himself, or even with the risk of spiritual harm—for he would then be guilty of instability and levity of character to no purpose. It is quite possible that, wearied by his attempt at a more difficult form of life, he would be forced to return to his former status, or even that he would have fallen to worse than his former condition (*Lib. I, ep. 29, ad Lanzonem novitium, PL* 158:1095; Schmitt, *Op. Om.* 3:145).

226. WILLIAM OF ST. THIERRY. For it is impossible that a man should faithfully fix in his mind on one thing without first having steadfastly fixed his body in one place. For he who seeks to flee from disease of mind by changing from place to place, is like a man that flees from his own body's shadow; he flees from himself but bears himself wherever

he goes; he changes his place, but not his mind. In all places he finds himself the same, save that the very changing makes him worse; even as it is harmful to move a sick person about and disturb him (*Ep. ad fratres de Monte Dei, Lib. I,* c. 9, *Stabilitas in cella commendatur,* n. 25, *PL* 184:324).

227. ST. BERNARD. Let no gust of wind, however strong, have power to remove us from our place, as it is written, *Should the anger of the ruler burst upon you, forsake not your place* (Eccles. 10:4). For no temptation can prevail against us so long as we do not *busy ourselves with great things* (Ps. 130:1), but remain firmly and irremovably *rooted and founded* (Eph. 3:17) in humility. Thus was this holy confessor of the Lord [Benedict], whose feast we are celebrating, *planted near running waters,* and so he *yielded fruit in due season* (Ps. 1:3; *Serm. de temp., Serm. in natali S. Benedicti abb.,* § 4, *PL* 183:378).

228. VEN. LOUIS DE BLOIS. A. Being founded therefore on rock (cf. Matt. 7:25), [monks] persist steadfast in the love of God, as persons whose chief comfort is in his good pleasure (*Speculum monachorum,* div. 2, *Op. Om.* 3:655). B. They build not on solid rock, but on unstable sand, and therefore their buildings easily fall down at every puff of wind and push of the floods (*ibid.,* div. 8, p. 673). C. Being comforted by the example of this strong and invincible champion [St. Paul], do not give way to faintheartedness in temptation, but endure manfully, fixed and immovable in this holy purpose; for without doubt this labor of yours is pleasing to God, even though it seem hard and insufferable to you (*ibid.,* div. 1, p. 652).

229. A CERTAIN MONK. I once went to him when weariness of the ascetic life had laid hold upon me, and I said to him: "Father, what shall I do? For my thoughts vex me and say to me, 'You are accomplishing nothing here, be gone from here.' " And he said to me: "Say to your thoughts: 'For the sake of Christ I will guard these walls' " (*De vitis Patrum, Lib. VIII, Historia Lausiaca, auctore Palladio,* c. 20, *PL* 73: 1119; Budge, *Stories of the Holy Fathers,* p. 165).

230. ST. JOHN CLIMACUS. Let the monastery be your tomb before the tomb. For no one will come out of the grave until the general resurrection. And if some religious have left their tomb, see! they are dead. Let us implore the Lord that this may not happen to us (*Scala paradisi, Grad. IV, de beata . . . obedientia, PG* 88:715; Moore, § 94, p. 90; Robert, p. 89).

231. HUGH OF ST. VICTOR. Stand firmly, not in the sense that you are not to progress, but so that you will not fail. Be firm, persevering in that which you have begun, not returning to that which you were. Stand firm, then, but stand in fear. . . . Prepare your soul against temptations; strengthen it with your resolve, exercise it in the practice of virtue, protect it with foresight. Give it strength so that it will not give

way to enticement; exercise it in order that it will be able to resist temptation; protect it, in order that if it cannot obtain the victory, it will at least be able to avoid defeat (*Miscellanea, Lib. I,* tit. 69, *De servitute et timore Dei, PL* 177:506).

The cenobitic family

232. ST. BASIL THE GREAT. A. I consider that life passed in company with a number of persons in the same habitation [striving for the same objective, namely, that of pleasing God], is more advantageous than the life of the solitary in many respects. My reasons are [1] that no one of us is self-sufficient as regards corporeal necessities, but we require one another's aid in supplying our needs. . . . Similarly [2], in the solitary life, what is at hand becomes useless to us and what is wanting cannot be provided, since God, the Creator, decreed that we should require the help of one another, as it is written, so that we might associate with one another (cf. Eccles. 13:20, Douay version; cf. Sir. 13:15). . . . And again [3], the doctrine of charity of Christ does not permit the individual to be concerned solely with his own private interests. . . . Furthermore [4], a person living in solitary retirement will not readily discern his own defects, since he has no one to admonish and correct him with mildness and compassion. . . . Moreover [5], the majority of the commandments are easily observed by several persons living together, but not so in the case of one living alone. . . . Besides [6], if all we who are united in the hope of our calling (cf. Eph. 4:4) are one body with Christ as our Head, we are also members, one of another (cf. I Cor. 12:12). If we are not joined together by union in the Holy Spirit in the harmony of one body . . . we would not serve the common good in the ministry according to God's good pleasure, but would be satisfying our own passion for self-gratification. . . . In addition [7], since no one has the capacity to receive all spiritual gifts, but the grace of the Spirit is given proportionately to the faith of each (cf. Rom. 12:6), when one is living in association with others, the grace privately bestowed on each individual becomes the common possession of his fellows . . . each employs his own gift and enhances it by giving others a share, besides reaping benefit from the gifts of others as if they were his own. Community life offers more blessings than can fully and easily be enumerated. . . . It is more advantageous than the solitary life [8] both for preserving the gifts bestowed on us by God, and for warding off the external attacks of the enemy (*Reg. fusius tractatae, Interrogatio 7, Quod vita agenda sit cum eis qui eodem animo impulsi, Deo placere sibi proponunt, PG* 31:927; Wagner, p. 248). B. Just as the spiritual law would have no fewer than ten partake of the mystic pasch, so they who practice the spiritual life in common should properly exceed rather than fall short of this number (*Serm. Asceticus I,* n. 3, col. 874; Wagner,

p. 210). C. Whenever, therefore, a group of persons aiming at the same goal of salvation adopt the life in common, this principle above all others must prevail among them—that they be in all one heart, one will, one desire, and that the entire community be, as the Apostle enjoins, one body that has many members (I Cor. 12:12; *ibid., Serm. II,* n. 1, col. 882; Wagner, p. 217). D. [Monks] are true imitators of the Savior and of the way of life he led while he dwelt among us. Patterning their observance on the manner in which, after he had constituted the body of his disciples, Christ gave all things and himself common to the apostles, so monks also, when they live in obedience to their superior, imitate the manner of life of the Apostles and the Lord himself (*Const. monastic.,* c. 18, *ad canonicos in coenobio versantes,* n. 2, col. 1383).

233. ST. VICTORIAN, abbot of Asán (in today's diocese of Barbastro, Spain, d. 558). When he had assumed the office of abbot, he was most vigilant over the flock committed to him. Some of the monks were living an eremitical form of life outside the monastery in individual oratories and cells. He summoned them back to the monastery and wrote a rule and norm of life for them, saying *how good it is, and how pleasant, where brethren dwell at one!* (Ps. 132:1), *where the brethren are of one heart and one soul* (Acts 4:32), and that it is necessary to fight with united forces against the ancient and cunning enemy and that such combined effort was of supreme importance . . . (*Acta Sanctorum Bolland., Jan., tom. 2, die 12,* p. 23).

234. ALCUIN OF YORK (d. 804). The devil can more easily overcome one who stands alone than another who is supported on all sides by the aid of his brethren, as the Scripture states: *A brother is a better defense than a strong city* (Prov. 18:19; *Ep. ad fratres ecclesiae S. Petri, PL* 100:168).

235. ST. DOROTHEUS. What, I ask you, do monasteries impress you as being? Do they not seem like a single body, with its respective members? They who administer and govern it represent the head; they who keep watch over the discipline and give corrections, are like its eyes; they who aid by their words take over the functions of the mouth; the monks who receive commands of obedience are its ears; the ones who perform the works assigned are like hands; they who answer the door and are sent hither and thither on errands are like feet (*Doctrina VI, Ne proximum judicemus,* c. 8, *PG* 88:1695).

236. ST. AUGUSTINE. A. David has made known to us what is God's holy place when he said: *God who maketh men of one manner to dwell in a house* (Ps. 67:7, Douay); men of one mind, of one sentiment; this is the holy place of the Lord (*Enarr. in Ps. 67:7, PL* 36:815). B. Consider, brethren, this one thing, and see if even in multitude itself anything is pleasing but this "oneness." See how great a number, through

God's mercy, you are; who could bear you, if you were not intent upon the one thing? Whence in this many, is this quiet? Give oneness, and it is a people; take away oneness, and it is a crowd. . . . See how the praise of unity is commended to us. Undoubtedly our God is Trinity. The Father is not the Son, nor is the Son the Father, the Holy Spirit is neither the Father nor the Son, but the Spirit of both; and yet these Three are not three gods, nor three almighties, but One God, Almighty, the whole Trinity is One God; because One is necessary. Nothing brings us to this one thing except being so many we have one heart (*Serm. 103, De verbis Luc. 10:38 sq., Et mulier quaedam Martha nomine excepit Illum,* c. 3, *PL* 38:614). C. God dwells in individuals as in his temples; but he dwells in all who are united together as into one body, as in his temple (*Ep. 187, De Dei praesentia,* c. 13, § 38, *PL* 33:847).

237. ST. JEROME. Certainly there is no life worse than to dwell together bodily without being united in mind. . . . In order for you to live together in one spirit, let there be affection in common, one brotherhood in common, observance of monastic discipline in common, joyfulness in common, sorrow in common (*Reg. monachorum,* c. 1, *De charitate et unitate servanda, PL* 30:394).

238. CASSIODORUS, former senator of Rome, monk, abbot of Vivarium in Calabria (d. 560). The oneness of the saints is the chariot of the Lord, in which he sits as charioteer and guides by his salutary law the observance of the saints (*Sup. Ps. 67:20, PL* 70:468).

239. JEAN RIGAUD, Franciscan theologian (d. 1323). The religious must love the community, because the larger the number banded together, the more securely they walk, the more bravely they resist [temptations], the more pleasantly they lessen the burden for one another. . . . Several united in the bond of charity shine forth more effectively by their example, and are kindled to a higher degree in their love of God than would be so many individuals. There is no doubt that there is a greater abundance of merit where many are united in the bond of love (*Diaeta salutis,* tit. 4, c. 1, *Op. Om. S. Bonaventurae,* ed. Peltier 8:283).*

240. THOMAS À KEMPIS. A. Where there is peace and harmony, there is God, and all good things. . . . Where there is harmony, there is a pleasing melody; where discord, there is the devil, and all evils (*Hortulus rosarum,* c. 16, *De amore Christi et odio mundi, Op. Om.* 4:37). B. He who comes to the aid of a brother in need, clings to the hand of Jesus (*ibid.,* c. 17). C. For [in a religious community] a man lives

* This work, often attributed to St. Bonaventure, has been published under ten different titles. It is taken almost entirely from the *Compendium theologiae pauperis* of Fr. Joannis Rigaldi (Jean Rigaud), O. Min. Cf. ed. Quaracchi 10:24, *De scriptis Seraphici Doctoris.* The Peltier text is retained as the best available for the Latin. [*Tr.*]

with greater safety, there he is aided by many. And if at times he is troubled by one of the brethren, again he is comforted by another. He who is of good will and intent on seeking God will make greater progress and stand more firmly among them that seek God. In a community a man is more tried, and exercised in virtue; he is more frequently reproved for negligence. There he is drawn to higher perfection by word and example, and forced to consider and lament his own imperfection. There he is roused by the fervor of one; taught by the humility of another; moved by the obedience of this one; edified by the patience of that. There he blushes to be less generous; there he has shame to be found less eager. In the community he finds some to fear; some to love; and thus he profits by all. There the correction of another is his own warning; another's danger is his mirror. There one is the warden of another; and one tests another in patience. In the community a man bears and is borne; he hears and sees much from which he may learn. There the rule and holy customs foster the practice of virtue; there confession and discipline correct excesses. There the good are commended that they may become better; the careless are rebuked that they may grow fervent again (*Serm. ad novitios, Serm.* 2, *Op. Om.* 6:14; Scully 5:13).

241. ST. JOHN CHRYSOSTOM. Monks have chosen a manner of existence worthy of heaven itself and have placed themselves on a level equal to that of the angels. For as there is no inequality among angels, but all alike exult in the same peace, joy, and glory, so also you find the same in monasteries. There no one complains of the lot of his poverty, none boasts of wealth. Hence that which disturbs and corrupts all things, namely "mine" and "thine," is entirely eliminated among them. All things are common to them—table, dwelling, clothing, and, what is more wonderful, one and the same spirit is common to all. All are noble with the same nobility; all servants with a common servitude; all free with the same freedom. Only one wealth is found among them, the true wealth; one glory, which is really glory—for they are all concerned with reality, not terminology. A common cheerfulness, a common delight, a common longing, a common hope is in them all. . . . There is among them no inequality. For the rest, perfect order and moderation and agreement and an indescribable love of preserving harmony are the material of perennial and everlasting joy. All undergo the same difficulties, all perform the same tasks, in order that in oneness they may rejoice and be glad (*Adversus oppugnatores vitae monast., Lib. III,* § 11, *PG* 47:366).

242. HUGH OF ST. VICTOR. Brethren dwell in unity in a threefold manner: in oneness of place only, in oneness of place and spirit, and in spirit only. To be in one place, but not one in spirit is punishment; to be one in spirit, but not together in one place, is goodness; to be both

in one place and one in spirit, is happiness (*Miscellanea, Lib. V,* c. 20, *PL* 177:758).

243. ST. PETER DAMIAN. The voice of the Lord commanded that the ark which housed eight souls through the Deluge be covered with pitch inside and out (cf. Gen. 6:14). . . . Be covered by the discipline of spiritual exercises; be lined with pitch by the harmony of fraternal charity. But this bond of fraternal charity cannot harmonize perfectly until the roof of the ark is completed, that is, when one is placed over many as the representative of Christ (*RSB,* c. 2). Oneness effects that many things harmonize, that men's different wills meet in joining together in charity and the unanimity of a common spirit. . . . Bees make honey together as long as they remain under their king bee. . . . So after the manner of shepherd and flock, commander and groups of soldiers, the monks are to be united in one spirit, in order that charity, which is God (cf. I John 4:16), hold the first place of undivided unity among them (*Opusc. 13,* c. 24, *ubi omnes in communi ad charitatis studium provocat, PL* 145:326 f.).

Filial love of the abbot

244. VEN. LOUIS DE BLOIS. If you neglect to obey your spiritual father readily and faithfully in all that is not evil, if you refuse to reverence him and to love him sincerely as God's representative, you are no monk (*Speculum monachorum,* div. 1, *Op. Om.* 3:652).

245. ST. FRANCES OF ROME, foundress of the community of Oblates O.S.B., at Tor de' Specchi, Rome (d. 1440); while rapt in ecstasy, heard from St. Benedict's lips: "A good son is ever reverent and on his guard against whatever might be displeasing to his father. He keeps himself ever in readiness to obey his father's orders; he is at great pains and does all in his power to make himself pleasing to his father; he is even willing to face death in order to serve him. In its secret counsels the divine wisdom always keeps him" (*Visio 62, in Guéranger, Enchiridion Benedictinum,* p. 292).

246. ALCUIN OF YORK (d. 804). [The abbot] must render an account of his solicitude for you, and in the same way, you must render an account of your obedience to him. For your sake he is placed in grave danger. With great charity be intent on interceding in his behalf, that he may receive a blessed reward before God because of his solicitude for you, and that you will attain rest with him in God's kingdom. The children's discipline is the praise of teachers; the increase of the flock is the shepherd's reward (*Ep. 93, ad fratres Juvavensis eccl., PL* 100:299).

The monastery a family of God

247. DAVID OF AUGSBURG, Franciscan mystic, preacher and writer (d. 1272). Whenever you are among laymen, as far as lies in your power, guard against everything that may not be a good example to them, as it is becoming to the faithful servant of God who must, whenever he can do so, promote the honor of his Lord and prevent everything that is to his dishonor. We are his family. Hence as the father of a family is held in honor because of the good discipline of his household, or is dishonored because of its lack, you must realize that whatever we do among laymen redounds in some degree to the praise of the Lord, or to his contempt (*De institutione novitiorum, Pars I,* c. 38, *Op. Om. S. Bonaventurae,* ed. Peltier 12:303).*

Charity in the community

248. ST. JOHN CHRYSOSTOM. A. For if *where two or three,* he says, *are gathered together for my sake* (Matt. 18:20), they prevail much, how much more will they prevail who are many! And yet even one may prevail, though he be but one; but not in the same proportion as many. . . . For he is wanting in the principal excellence of virtue, charity within the community (*In Act. Apost. Hom. 37,* n. 3, *PG* 60:266). B. What then, I pray you, can be equal to this man who possesses the spirit of charity? Such a man is like a walled city, walled on every side (*ibid., Hom. 40,* n. 4, col. 287). C. For the assembling is a great good, since it makes love more ardent, and out of love all good things arise (*Hom. 19 in Ep. ad Hebraeos,* n. 2, *PG* 63:141). D. Where there are holy doctrine and prayers, where there are the blessings of the Fathers and the hearing of the word of God, where there is an assembly of the brethren and the bond of the twofold charity [that is, love of God and of neighbor], where there is the speaking with God and God's speaking to men, what can prevent there being a solemn, sacred festival? (*De fide Annae, Hom. 5,* § 1, *Festorum ornatus veri, PG* 54:669.) E. *A brother is a better defense than a strong city* (Prov. 18:19). The more strongly the members of a community are joined by the powerful bond of charity, the more powerfully they withstand all the insidious temptations of demons (*De profectu Evangelii,* n. 5, *PG* 51:315). F. This spirit of concord in a family is then of the highest importance, and of greater consequence than wealth, or rank, or power, or anything else (*In Ep. ad Tit.* [2:2], *Hom. IV,* n. 2, *PG* 62:683). G. There is nothing to equal unanimity and concord, for when they are present, one person is manifold. If two or ten are of one mind, then each one is one no longer, but each one is multiplied tenfold, and you will find the one in the ten, and the

* The editors of the scholarly Quaracchi edition of St. Bonaventure's works, *Op. Om.* 10:17, definitely assign David of Augsburg as the author of this work. [*Tr.*]

ten in the one. And if they have an enemy, he who attacks the one, as having attacked the ten, is vanquished; for he is the mark not for one, but for ten opponents (*Hom. 78 in Joan.* [16:5], n. 4, *PG* 59:425). H. For as it is the nature of strife to separate, so it is that of agreement to weld together (*Hom. 82* [on John 17:14], n. 2, col. 444). I. Where there is no peace, neither will prayer be heard, nor any offering accepted, for God is not present where discord reigns (*Opus imperf. in Matt., Hom. 10, In Append., PG* 56:685). J. Hence we pray, and express the desire for the angel of peace—everywhere petitioning for peace. Nothing whatever can equal this gift of peace. We utter it in the churches, we ask for it in our prayers, we use it in our greetings. Once, and again, and a third time, and repeatedly he who presides over the assembly in the church addresses us: "Peace be to you." Why is this? It is the mother of all good, the foundation of all joy. Hence Christ commanded the Apostles to say this immediately on entering a home, as a symbol of all good things (cf. Matt. 10:12; *In Ep. ad Coloss. Hom. 3,* n. 4, *PG* 62:322).

249. ST. PETER CHRYSOLOGUS. A. Peace among the brethren is the will of God, the pleasure of Christ, the perfection of holiness, the rule of justice. This peace is the mistress of doctrine, protection of moral life, praiseworthy discipline in all things. It is that which imprints the stamp of approval on prayer; it is the easy and successful manner of obtaining the object of supplications, the perfect realization of all hopes. Peace is the mother of love, the bond of harmony, the obvious proof of a pure mind. . . . To plant peace is the work of God, to overthrow it, the work of the enemy (*Serm. 53, de pace, PL* 52:347). B. Peace is nourished by the rich fruitfulness of charity. It is the daughter of faith, the supporting column of justice. Peace is a suitable pledge of future hope. It is peace which unites those present, invites the absent. This peace reconciles earthly things with the heavenly, and human matters with the divine (*Serm. 138, de pace,* col. 572).

250. ST. GREGORY THE GREAT. A. How great is the virtue of oneness of heart is evidenced in that without it, other virtues are discovered really not to be virtues at all (*Lib. I, Hom. 8 sup. Ezech.,* n. 8, *PL* 76:857). B. He who neglects to refrain his tongue, dissipates concord (*Moral., Lib. VII,* c. 17, n. 57, *PL* 75:800). C. For never can concord be preserved, excepting through patience only (*ibid., Lib. XXI,* c. 21, n. 33, *PL* 76:209). D. It is better to cast forth a sickly sheep from the Lord's flock than to lose those which are healthy through the evil conduct of the one (*Lib. XI, ep. 74, ad Eusebium Thessalonicensem episc., PL* 77:1214).

The disease of disharmony

251. ST. BEDE, monk of Jarrow, Doctor of the Church (d. 735). When they defile the society of the brotherhood with some form of the

disease of discord, they betray the Lord, for *God is love* (I John 4:8). They, therefore, who despise the commands of love and truth, abandon God, who is love and truth. This is particularly the case when they sin not out of weakness or ignorance, but in imitation of Judas, seeking the opportunity in whatever manner, in the absence of judges to substitute truth with a lie, and virtue with sin (*In Marci evang. expos., Lib. IV,* c. 14, *PL* 92:270).

Nothing to be preferred to oneness of heart

252. WALAFRID STRABO, monk of Fulda (d. 849). We are also to give preference to nothing over the spirit of harmony and charity, but are to persevere in peace and love, whether we are proceeding to the right in prosperity or to the left in adversity (*Glossa ordinaria in Gen. 13:6–9, PL* 113:117).

253. HAYMO, bp. of Halberstadt (O.S.B., d. 853). The oneness of mind of the brotherhood is like an unassailable city: it is not subject to the attack of enemies (*Hom. 16, Dom. VI p. Pent, PL* 118:622).

254. ST. BERNARD. A. From such time as the monk spurns the spirit of peace among the brethren and questions the judgment of his superior, he can do nothing else in the monastery but give scandal (*Tract. de gradibus humilitatis et superbiae,* c. 19, *de decimo grad. superbiae, qui est rebellio,* n. 49, *PL* 182:968). B. Have no fear that by thus preserving the peace of all at the cost of one, you will be acting contrary to charity. . . . It is better that one should perish than the charity of all (*Ep. 102, ad quemdam abbatem,* n. 2, col. 237). C. What is there coming from without [the monastic enclosure] which should be able to trouble or distress you if all is well with you within, if you rejoice in brotherly love? (*Serm. 29 in Cant.,* n. 3, *PL* 183:930; Eales, p. 188.)

255. HUGH OF ST. VICTOR. The spirit of charity renders powerless all the weapons of the devil (*Expos. Reg. S. Augustini,* c. 1, *de charitate Dei et proximi, PL* 176:883).

256. RUDOLPH OF BIBERACH, Franciscan mystic (d. 1360). The peace which exists forever among the elect of the heavenly kingdom in the future glory, begins here below. This peace greatly strengthens the good, gains victory in battle, fills with comfort, unites with God, intensifies with love (*De septem itineribus aeternitatis, Iter 7, dist. 6, Inter Op. Om. S. Bonaventurae,* ed. Peltier 8:479).*

257. ST. ANTHONY OF PADUA (d. 1231). Harmony (*con-cordia*) is derived from "one" and "heart"; to be in harmony is to be one in heart (*Serm. Dom. XI p. Trinit. Sancti Francisci Assisiatis necnon S. Antonii . . . Op., Pars II,* p. 262).

* This work is definitely assigned to Fr. Rudolph of Biberach, Franciscan mystic, by the editors of the definitive Quaracchi edition of the works of St. Bonaventure, 10:23, *De scriptis Seraphici Doctoris.* [*Tr.*]

258. ST. PACHOMIUS, abbot (4th century). Let there be peace and harmony among the brethren. They are willingly to obey their superior. They must sit, walk, and stand according to rank. They are to vie with one another in practicing humility (*Praecepta et leges Patris N. Pachomii,* n. 179, *CR* 1:36; *PL* 23:87).

259. ST. ORSIESIUS, abbot of Tabenna (d. 365). The Apostle taught us that our fellowship and the common bond by which we are united is from God, stating: *Do not forget kindness and charity, for by such sacrifices God's favor is obtained* (Heb. 13:16). . . . Dwelling in monasteries and joined in mutual love, let us devote our efforts that as we have merited to be associated with the holy Fathers in this life, we may also be sharers with them in the life to come . . . (*Doctrina de institutione monachorum,* c. 50, *CR* 1:58; *PL* 103:473).

260. ST. AUGUSTINE. A. Now we dwell in him when we are his members, and he dwells in us when we are his temple. But it is unity that knits and compacts us together in order that we should be his members. But what besides charity will produce the effect of knitting us into this oneness? And whence comes the love of God? Ask the Apostle: *The charity of God,* he says, is poured *forth in our hearts by the Holy Spirit who has been given to us* (Rom. 5:5; *Tract. 27 in Joan,* c. 6, *PL* 35:1618). B. *Behold, how good it is, and how pleasant, where brethren dwell at one!* (Ps. 132:1.) . . . From these same words of the Psalter, this sweet sound, this honeyed melody of the mind as well as of the hymn, has brought monasteries into being. This is the passage which stirred up brethren who longed to dwell together in oneness. This verse was their trumpet. It sounded through the whole world, and they who had been divided were gathered together. The summons of God, the summons of the Holy Spirit, the summons of the prophets, were not heard in Juda, yet were heard throughout the whole world (*Enarr. in Ps. 132:1,* § 2, *PL* 37:1729). C. And what is meant by "dwelling at one"? (*Ibid.,* § 3.) D. They who thus live together as though to make one man, so that they really possess what is written; *One heart and one soul* (Acts 4:32) . . . many bodies, but not many minds; many bodies, but not many hearts (*ibid.,* § 6, col. 1733). E. How good and how pleasant! Nothing sweeter has been heard, nothing more gratifying has been hoped for, nothing more beneficial has been possessed. . . .

261. ST. PETER CHRYSOLOGUS. Let the brotherhood maintain itself by the bonds of deeply rooted peace and in mutual love hold itself in check with the salutary oneness of charity (*Serm. 53, De pace, PL* 52:348).

262. ST. BERNARD. A. I think that you are living in a community as you should if you are leading an orderly, sociable, and humble life; an orderly life with regard to yourself, a sociable life with regard to your

brethren, a humble life before God (*Serm. de temp., Serm. I de festo SS. Petri et Pauli,* n. 4, *PL* 183:407). B. The third night-watch [at which, if the Lord comes, he will find us ready], is zeal for the preservation of concord and unity. And you keep this when, living in the community, you give your confreres' wishes preference over your own: in so doing you not only live among them without blame, but with the kindness of charity, supporting all, and praying for all (*ibid., Serm. 3 in vigilia Nativitatis Dni,* § 6, col. 97). C. May I die before I should ever hear one of you cry out with justification: *My brothers have been angry with me* (Cant. 1:6). Are not all of you sons of one community and, as it were, of the same mother, and therefore brethren one of the other? What is there that coming from without [the monastic enclosure] should be able to trouble or distress you if all is well with you within, if you rejoice in brotherly love? *Who is there to harm you,* it is said, *if you are zealous for* what is good? (I Pet. 3:13.) *Strive after the greater gifts* (I Cor. 12:31), and you shall prove yourselves to be the followers of what is good. Now, the greatest gift of all is charity; assuredly no other gift can be compared with that which the heavenly Bridegroom of a new Bride took occasion so often to inculcate, once saying, indeed: *By this shall all men know that you are my disciples, if you have love one for another* (John 13:35); and again, *A new commandment I give you, that you love one another* (*ibid.,* v. 34); and, *This is my commandment, that you love one another* (*ibid.,* 15:12), also praying that they might be one, as he and the Father are One (*ibid.,* 17:11). See also if St. Paul himself, who invites you to seek the greatest gifts, does not place charity above all others, as when he says that it is greater than faith and hope, and far above knowledge; and also when, after having enumerated many and wonderful gifts of grace, he leads us at length to *a more excellent way,* and explains that this is no other than the gift of charity. Lastly, what can we regard as comparable to a virtue which is preferred to martyrdom itself, and to faith which removes mountains? (I Cor. 12:31; 13:2–3.)

Therefore, dear brethren, let there be peace among you; do not harm or give pain to one another by word, by action, or even by any sign, for fear lest anyone among you, being embittered and preoccupied by his own weakness of spirit, and by the persecution he endures, should be driven to appeal to God to come to his aid against those who injure or distress him, and it should come to pass that he break forth into that grave complaint: *My brothers have been angry with me* (Cant. 1:6). For in thus sinning against your brother, you sin against Christ, who has said: *Amen I say to you, as long as you did it for one of these, the least of my brethren, you did it for me* (Matt. 25:40; *Serm. 29 in Cant.,* nn. 3–4, col. 930). D. But in order for our sanctification to be made perfect, it is also clearly incumbent on us to learn from the Saint of saints the considerateness and kindliness which are necessary in human society. He himself has said: *Learn from me, for I am meek and humble of heart* (Matt. 11:29). But of him who has thus made perfect his sanctification; who is *good and forgiving, abounding in kindness* (Ps. 85:5), like God himself; who is *all things to all men* (I Cor. 9:22) like the Apostle; who, in like manner, anoints all his brethren with that ointment of gentleness and meekness with which he himself is saturated, so full, so brimming over that he seems to diffuse it on every side—why should I not say of such a one that he is *flowing with delights?* (Cant. 8:5, Douay version; *Serm. V in vigilia Nativitatis Dni,* n. 6, col. 108.)

263. WILLIAM OF ST. THIERRY. *I pray . . . that all may be one, even as thou, Father, in me, and I in thee* (John 17:21). This is the end, this the consummation, this the perfection, this peace, this is the joy in the Lord, joy in the Holy Spirit, silence in heaven (*Lib. de contemplando Deo,* c. 4, *Deum propter se, caetera omnia nonnisi propter Deum diligi debere,* n. 10, *PL* 184:372).

264. GILBERT, abbot of St. Mary in Hoiland. Love constitutes a good wall, but it also has a bulwark. Love is the wall, and its bulwark (cf. Isa. 26:1) is the severity of the Rule. The former encloses holy thoughts and sweet affections; the latter holds off and excludes the occasions of sinning (*Serm. 35 in Cant. Salomonis,* n. 2, *PL* 184:184).

Unanimity, oneness of mind

265. RULE OF THE MONASTERY OF TARNADAE (circa 750). Because you are gathered together out of fear of the Lord, you should dwell in one spirit in the house of the Lord, and have one soul and one heart, ever vigilant in the fear of God. . . . All remaining steadfast in oneness of mind, adore in your very midst the God whose temple you have merited to become. First of all, let us love God with all the strength of our spirit, and then our neighbor. These are commandments that were specially given for us (*Reg. monasterii Tarnatensis,* c. 14, *CR* 1:183; *PL* 66:983).

266. ST. SERAPION, monk of Egypt (4th century). We desire that the brethren dwell in the house in oneness of spirit, and joyously, but, under God's assistance, we command that the very oneness of spirit and the joy be kept within the proper bounds (*Reg. S.S. Serapionis, Macarii, Paphnutii, et alterius Macarii,* c. 3, *CR* 1:11; *PL* 103:436).

267. ST. CAESARIUS OF ARLES, monk of Lerins, bp. of Arles (d. 542). Let this rivalry exist among you, that each strive to gain the victory over his neighbor in being humble and practicing charity; let him seek to be more humble, more devoted to the work of God, possessed of greater patience, more recollected in spirit, more meek, affable, and devoted to contrition, in order that thus God and his angels will take pleasure in your holy way of life, and the devil, the ancient enemy, will be confounded (*Reg. ad monachos,* c. 19, *CR* 1:146; *PL* 67:1101).

268. ALCUIN OF YORK (d. 804). Keep yourselves, with the aid of divine grace, in all purity, humility, and oneness of heart, bearing one another's burdens in the spirit of charity (cf. Gal. 6:2). Let no ill or immodest speech, or that which is impatient or useless pass your lips, but only that which is good, charitable, just, and worthy of your sacred state. Speak unto the exhortation of those who hear you; and may God always be glorified in your speech (cf. Rom. 15:6). Pursue with the whole intent of your mind the things that pertain to true peace, and the peace of God will be with you (cf. Phil. 4:7–9; *Ep. 93, ad fratres Juvavensis eccl., PL* 100:299).

269. ANTIOCHUS, monk of St. Saba in Palestine (d. 614). A. Blessed is the monk who holds all others in admiration in all that is according to God. Blessed indeed is the monk who, with all joy and willingness of mind, seeks the welfare and progress of all others, as well as his own. He is a monk who considers himself one with all others in this, that he believes beyond all doubt that he sees himself in each of his brethren (*Hom. 80, De concordia, PG* 89:1675). B. We are urged by the commandment of God to forgive one another our offenses, and to pray for one another. In the same manner we are also to avoid greedily seeking what is to our advantage, but must rather be intent on that which is to the advantage of the brethren who are members of the same body, lest our vice [of selfishness] become the occasion of fault or harm for anyone. . . . Thus brethren, let us put a check on our will, in all things, denying it for the sake of our neighbor, in order that we may never cause the scandal or subversion of those who hear us. . . . St. Paul stated: *Let no one seek his own interests, but those of his neighbor* (I Cor. 10:24). *Do not be a stumbling-block to Jews and Greeks and to the church of God; even as I myself in all things please all men, not seeking what is profitable to myself, but to the many, that they may be saved* (*ibid.*, vv. 32–33). He added the verses: *Charity . . . is not self-seeking, is not provoked . . . bears with all things . . . endures all things* (*ibid.*, 13:5–7; *Hom. 73, De non quaerenda quae sua sunt,* col. 1646).

270. JOHN CASSIAN. A. St. Paul speaks of *the breastplate of charity* (I Thess. 5:8). This it is which, enveloping the vital parts of the breast and protecting what is exposed to the death-dealing wounds of swelling pride, wards off the blows that are hurled against it, and does not allow the darts of the devil to penetrate to our inner man. For it *bears with all things . . . endures all things* (I Cor. 13:7); *Collatio VII* [*I coll. abbatis Sereni*], *De animae nobilitate et spiritualibus nequitiis,* c. 5, *PL* 49:674.) B. This is true and unbroken love which grows strong by means of the mutual perfection and goodness of friends and which, when once its bonds have been entered, no difference of liking and no disturbing opposition of wishes can sever. . . . This is the sure and

indissoluble union of friendship, whose bond can only consist of likeness in goodness. . . . Therefore love can only continue undisturbed in those in whom there is a single purpose, and the mind to will and to refuse the same things (*Collatio XVI* [*coll. I abbatis Joseph*], *De amicitia,* c. 3, col. 1015).

Preservation of peace

271. POPE ST. LEO THE GREAT (d. 461). The true peace, which was first proclaimed by the angels at the Lord's Nativity . . . is that which brings forth the sons of God; it is the nurse of love, the mother of unity, the rest of the blessed, and our eternal home; its proper work and special office is to join to God those whom it separates from the world. Whence the Apostle incites us to this good end, saying: *Having been justified therefore by faith, let us have peace with God* (Rom. 5:1). In this brief sentence are summed up neatly all the commandments; for where there is true peace, there can be no lack of virtue. For what, dearly beloved, does "have peace with God" mean except to wish what he commands and not to will what he forbids? (*Serm. 26, in Nativitate Dni, VI,* § 3, *PL* 54:214.)

272. JEAN RIGAUD. Peace is the language of heaven, Christ's legacy, the token of God's presence (*Diaeta salutis, tit.* 7, c. 6, *inter Op. Om. S. Bonaventurae,* ed. Peltier 8:323).

273. DENIS THE CARTHUSIAN. The preservation of peace is in truth a most precious treasure (*De profectu spirituali et custodia cordis,* art. 21, *Op. Om.* 40:497).

274. JOHN OF TRITHEIM. No good will continue where peace is wanting. . . . As soon as peace has been destroyed in a community of monks, the whole strength of the monastic discipline wastes away (*Comm. in Prolog. RSB,* c. 2, *Op. pia et spiritualia,* p. 174).

Recreation

275. ST. HILDEGARDE, abbess of Mount St. Rupert (d. 1179). Because it is inhuman for man to guard silence continually and never speak, the same father [Benedict] left it in the power and discretion of the abbot (as he granted him the making of many similar decisions) to appoint an appropriate hour for his disciples at which they could speak together of proper and necessary matters, and also so that they would not be wearied by silence observed beyond the bonds of discretion; for after such permission to speak, they can more reasonably and more strictly be admonished and constrained to observe the recollectedness of silence (*Reg. S. Benedicti explanatio, PL* 197:1056).

276. ST. BIRGITTA (d. 1373). The Virgin Mother spoke thus to St. Birgitta: "The friends of God can at times enjoy relaxation by means of edifying words, innocent amusements, and other works in which

there is no element of detraction or deceit. You will understand this by way of an illustration: If the hand were always held tightly closed in a fist, the nerves would be contracted and the hand weakened. It is the same in spiritual matters" (*Revelationes, Lib. IV,* c. 126).

277. ST. THOMAS AQUINAS. Man's mind would break if its tension were never relaxed (*II-II,* q. 168, art. 2, *Utrum in ludis possit esse aliqua virtus, Op. Om.* 10:351; Am. ed. 2:1878).

278. JOHN CASSIAN. A. That most refreshing interlude of relaxation and courtesy which sometimes is wont to intervene because of the arrival of brethren, although it may seem tiresome to you and something which you should avoid [is, nevertheless] useful and good for your bodies as well as for your souls . . . (*Collatio XXIV* [*coll. III abbatis Abrahae*], *De mortificatione,* c. 20, *PL* 49:1311). B. It would not do always to carry the bow bent, for the force of its stiffness would be relaxed by its being continually tightened, and it would be lessened and destroyed, and when the time came for it to shoot heavier arrows after some beast, its stiffness would be lost by excessive and continuous strain, and it would be impossible for the more powerful bolts to be shot. "And, my lad," said the Blessed John, "do not let this slight and short recreation of mind disturb you, because unless the rigor of its purpose is sometimes relieved by some form of relaxation, the spirit would lose its spring owing to the unbroken strain, and would be unable, when need required, implicitly to follow what is right" (*ibid.,* c. 21, col. 1314).

279. JEAN RIGAUD. As the eagle rests its wings so that it can spread them better . . . discipline is to be relaxed from time to time so that afterward it can be intensified (*Diaeta salutis,* tit. 4, c. 1, *Op. Om. S. Bonaventurae,* ed. Peltier 8:284).

280. VEN. LOUIS DE BLOIS (Blosius). Take care not to abuse the liberty of recreation and the walks which you are permitted to take outside the enclosure. Use these opportunities with such caution that they not only do not hinder your spiritual advancement, but rather foster it. You are indeed allowed to refresh your mind unto God's honor, but you may not abandon control over it, lest, as you wander outside the enclosure, being drawn out of yourself, some delight in opposition to the spirit, or some passion lay hold of you, disturb your interior senses, and fill them with bitterness. Carefully learn, by a studied simplicity of mind, to dwell within yourself, in order to preserve recollectedness and freedom in your heart by repressing all the clamorous insistence of distracting thoughts and the disturbance of inordinate affections. Let God be your dominant thought, nay, your whole thought, for it is not always enough for you that he be your whole intention (*Speculum monachorum,* div. 8, *Op. Om.* 3:668).

281. ST. ANSELM. There is something else that greatly contributes toward peace and charity among the brethren: that is, if no one ever

says anything to one brother regarding another which would cause his hearer to take offense; but always, if he can do so, speaks of his confrere in such a way that the heart of the one to whom he is speaking is warmed to love (*Lib. III, ep. 151, ad Joannem priorem et monachos Batenses* [Bath, England], *PL* 159:184; Schmitt, *Op. Om.* [n. 450] 5:397).

282. ST. JEROME. A. Let your tongue know no theme but Christ, let it pronounce no sound but what is holy (*Ep. 130, ad Demetriadem, de servanda virginitate,* n. 20, *PL* 22:1124). B. That tongue which knows only how to pronounce words regarding things of God is precious in the Lord's sight, and holy is the mouth from which heavenly praises always issue forth . . . Accustom your tongue to speak of the good; adapt your hearing more to the praise of good men than the condemnation of the evil (*Ep. 13, Virginitatis laus,* § 14, *In Append., PL* 30:174).

283. SULPICIUS SEVERUS, priest and solitary of Aquitaine (d. circa 420). No one ever saw Martin angered or excited, sorrowful or laughing. Ever the same, his countenance shining with a sort of heavenly radiance, he seemed raised above the things of this world. In his mouth was the name of Christ alone; in his heart, nought but kindness, peace, and mercy (*De vita B. Martini, Lib. unus,* c. 27, *PL* 20:176).

284. ST. AMBROSE. Let us speak of the Lord Jesus who is himself Wisdom, who is himself the Word, the Word of God (*Enarr. in Ps. 36,* n. 65, *PL* 14:1048).

285. HUGH OF ST. CHER, O.P. A. Nothing makes a man gracious as does modesty of speech (*Sup. Ecclesiasticum* [Sir. 42:1], *Comm. 3:252*). B. If it is governed properly, the tongue will merit the rewards of eternal bliss (*Sup. Jac. 3:6, Comm.* 7:317).

286. SECOND RULE OF THE FATHERS. Let the brethren not disturb one another with idle talking, but let each one be concerned about and keep to his own work, and direct his thoughts to God. When all are gathered together in an assembly [for recreation], no one of the younger monks is to speak unless he has been addressed. . . . When a pilgrim arrives, a brother is to concern himself only with greeting him and giving him the sign of peace, and not about whence he came, or why he has come, or when he is going for a walk; nor is he to spend his time gossipping with him (*Alia Reg. Patrum ad monachos,* cc. 2–3. *CR* 1:15; *PL* 103:441).

287. CLEMENT OF ALEXANDRIA, priest (d. circa 200). . . . for the tongue is the psaltery of the Lord (*Pedagogus, Lib. II,* c. 4, *quomodo in conviviis se recreare oporteat, PG* 8:442).

288. ST. BERNARD. A. Everyone among you who not only patiently bears with the infirmities of his brethren, whether these unpleasantnesses be of body or of mind, but who also, if it is permitted him, and if he has the ability to do it, assists them by his services, strengthens them

by his exhortations, trains them by his wise counsels; and if discipline does not permit him to do this, at least does not cease to assist them in their weakness by his earnest prayers; everyone, I say, who among you acts in this manner, exercises a precious influence among the brethren, sprinkles over them, so to speak, the costliest perfumes (*Serm. 12 in Cant., De pretioso unguento pietatis,* n. 5, *PL* 183:830; Eales, p. 63). B. For of what commendation is he not worthy, and with what affection does that monk not deserve to be regarded who, *leading a blameless life* (Phil. 3:6) among his brethren, guards himself with all solicitude so that he will not in any manner cause annoyance to others, and endures with utmost patience whatever he finds troublesome in them (*Serm. de temp., Serm. I in festo Omnium Sanctorum,* n. 14, col. 461).

289. RULE OF THE MONASTERY OF TARNADAE. When you walk, go together. When, under the Lord's protection, you arrive at your destination, let the whole brotherhood remain together. Nothing unbecoming or offensive is to be seen in your manner of walking or standing, or in any movement of the body. Be intent on those things which harmonize with the holiness of your way of life (*Reg. monasterii Tarnatensis,* c. 17, *CR* 1:184; *PL* 66:984).

Particular friendships and singularity to be avoided

290. ST. BASIL THE GREAT. A. The law of charity does not allow particular friendships or exclusive groups in community life, for particular affection inevitably works great harm to communal union. Consequently, all should regard one another with equal affection and one and the same degree of charity should prevail in the entire group (*Serm. Asceticus I,* n. 5, *PG* 31:879; Wagner, p. 213). B. In every instance the loss of equality is the origin and foundation of envy and hatred on the part of those who are slighted thereby. On this account we have received a command from the Lord to imitate the goodness of him who *makes his sun to rise on the good and the evil* (Matt. 5:45). As, therefore, God grants a share of light impartially to all, so his followers should send forth a ray of charity equally brilliant for all alike (*ibid., Serm. II,* n. 2, col. 886; Wagner, p. 219). C. It is proper indeed for the brethren to practice mutual charity, but not in such a manner that two or three, conspiring together, form a clique. For this is not charity, but dissension, separation, and the proof of the wickedness of those who thus assemble (*Const. monastic.,* c. 29, col. 1418).

291. ST. PACHOMIUS. Monks who desire to be of one spirit, and have proposed to live according to oneness of purpose, must obey the counsels of their superiors. They are to do what has been handed down from the counsels of the Fathers (*Praecepta et leges Patris N. Pachomii,* n. 191, *CR* 1:36; *PL* 23:90).

292. VEN. LOUIS DE BLOIS. Conform yourself to the observance of

the community in all things that are not at variance with the ideal of the monastic life, being careful to avoid all vicious irregularity. And because you dwell among monks whose lives are commendably governed according to the sweet austerity of the holy Rule, avoid singularity in abstaining or watching. Nor must you attempt to exceed the other monks in these observances, unless by the revelation of the Holy Spirit you know that it is the will and pleasure of God. But even then you must not undertake anything without the counsel and consent of your superior, lest while you presume on your own initiative to afflict your body beyond measure, you render yourself incapable for good works, and wholly deprive yourself of the fruit of your own labor. God demands purity of heart of you, not the overthrow of your body. He would that you should subject it to the spirit, not oppress it. Therefore, as well in external exercises as internal, temper the fervor of your mind with a holy discretion (*Speculum monachorum,* div. 7, *Op. Om.* 3:669).

Reformation of life according to monastic principles (conversio morum)

293. BENEDICT HAEFTEN. A. Conversion is to be made from the world to religion; . . . from sins to repentance; . . . from vices to virtues; . . . from pleasures to continence; . . . from pride to humility; . . . from vanity to truth; . . . from cupidity to charity; . . . from self-will to the will of God; . . . from the flesh to the spirit; . . . from externals to interior things; . . . from the many to the one; . . . from the creature to the Creator (*Catechismus monastic., Pars II, monachi officia,* disq. 9, *Disquisitiones monasticae,* p. 252).* B. It is to be noted that by the vow of conversion of morals [that is, the reformation of one's life according to monastic principles], perfect conversion is not vowed as an accomplished fact, but only the serious striving for reformation. He therefore who has departed from the Rule in some point is not forthwith to be judged a violator of this vow, but only when he breaks it with a certain loathing and manifests by his actions, intentions or deeds that he knowingly and willingly abandons the effort and zealous striving to correct his moral life and live according to the Rule (*Disquisitiones monastic., Lib. IV, tract. 6, De votorum explicatione,* disq. 5, p. 422).

294. ST. THOMAS AQUINAS. A. The religious state is a school or exercise for the attainment of perfection, which men strive to reach by various practices, just as a physician may use various remedies in order to heal. But it is evident that for him who works for an end it is not necessary that he should already have attained the end, but it is requisite that he should by some means tend thereto. Hence he who enters

* Wolter gives only the paragraph headings here: they contain adequate indication of the complete thought for present purposes. [*Tr.*]

the religious state is not bound to have perfect charity, but he is bound to this, to use his endeavors to have perfect charity (*II-II, q. 186, art. 2, Utrum quilibet religiosus teneatur ad omnia consilia, Op. Om.* 10:488; Am. ed. 2:1972). B. While he is in the state of a wayfarer, man's charity can always increase (*ibid., q. 24, art. 7, Utrum caritas augeatur in infinitum, Op. Om.* 8:182; Am. ed. 2:1280). C. It is, therefore, evident that it is not possible to fix any limits to the increase of charity in this life (*ibid*).

295. JOHN CASSIAN. Hear then, in few words, how you can mount up to the heights of perfection, without effort or difficulty. *The fear of the Lord is the beginning of wisdom* (Ps. 110:10), and of our salvation, according to the Scriptures (cf. Prov. 1:7). From the fear of the Lord arises salutary compunction. From compunction of heart springs renunciation, that is, the total absence and contempt of all possessions. From want of provisions is begotten humility; from humility, the mortification of desires. Through the mortification of desires all faults are extirpated and wither away. By driving out faults, virtues shoot up and increase. By the budding of virtues purity of heart is gained. By purity of heart the perfection of apostolic love is acquired (*De coenobitorum institutis, Lib. IV*, c. 43, *PL* 49:202).

Monasticism as a seeking of God

296. VEN. LOUIS DE BLOIS. A. First and foremost, therefore, I admonish you often and seriously to consider your purpose in entering the monastery, that being dead to the world and to yourself, you may live to God alone. . . . If you seek any other thing in the monastery but God, and with might and main aspire not to perfection, you are no monk (*Speculum monachorum*, div. 1, *Op. Om.* 3:651). B. Blessed indeed are those monks who, although they are not held in high regard, and are as yet quite imperfect, nevertheless hope for perfection and strive for it with might and main; for they are certainly the adopted sons of God, whom our loving Savior Jesus comforts with the words: *Do not be afraid, little flock, for it has pleased your Father to give you the kingdom* (Luke 12:32). They may await death with security, even though they are as yet only in the beginning of their holy resolve. *Precious in the eyes of the Lord is the death of his faithful ones* (Ps. 115:6); hence they may surely look forward with confidence to death; and yet not death, but the sleep of peace, the end of death, and a passage from death to life (*ibid.*, div. 8, p. 673).

297. ST. BERNARD. A. It is a great good to seek God. I think that among all the blessings of the soul, there is none greater than this. It is the first of the gifts of God; the last degree of the soul's progress. By no virtue is it preceded; to none does it give place. To what virtue is that added which is not preceded by any? And to which should that give

way which is the consummation of all virtues? For what virtue can be ascribed to him who is not seeking God, or what limit prescribed to one who is seeking him? *Look to the Lord in his strength; seek to serve him constantly* (Ps. 104:4), says the Psalmist; nor do I think that when a soul has found him, it will cease from seeking. God is sought, not by movement of the feet, but by desire of the heart; and when a soul has been so happy as to find him, that sacred desire is not extinguished, but, on the contrary, is increased. Is the consummation of the joy the extinction of the desire? It is rather like oil poured upon a flame; for desire is, as it were, a flame. This is, indeed, the case. The joy will be fulfilled; but the fulfilment will not be the ending of the desire, nor therefore of the seeking. But think, if you can, of this earnest love of seeking God as being without any deprivation of him, and of the desire for him as without any anxiety or trouble of mind. His presence excludes the one, and the abundance of his grace prevents the other (*Serm. 84 in Cant., Quod anima quaerens Deum, preventa est ab eo,* n. 1, *PL* 183:1184).

B. The soul seeks the Word, but it has been previously sought by the Word (*ibid.,* n. 3).

C. The soul seeks the Word, and accepts his corrections with willingness and joy, so that she may obtain enlightenment and the knowledge of him, that by his support she may attain to virtue, and be reformed according to wisdom, that she may be conformed unto his likeness and rendered by him fruitful in good works, and, finally, may be happy in the enjoyment of his Presence. For all these causes the soul seeks the Word (*ibid., Serm. 85, De septem necessitatibus propter quas anima quaerit Verbum,* n. 1, col. 1187).

D. Therefore, my brothers, since this is in truth and most certainly *the race that seeks for him, that seeks the face of the God of Jacob* (Ps. 23:6), what else can I say than what was said by the same Prophet: *Rejoice, O hearts that seek the Lord! Look to the Lord in his strength; seek to serve him constantly* (Ps. 104:3, 4). And what another says: *If you seek, seek* (Isa. 21:12). Now, what does that mean: *If you seek him, seek? Seek him in integrity of heart* (Wisd. 1:1). Seek nothing else as you seek him, nothing besides him, nothing after him. *Seek him in integrity of heart.* Integrity of heart demands a simple nature. Finally, its behavior is with the unaffected. *A double-minded man is unstable in all his ways* (Jas. 1:8). God is not to be found by them *who believe for a while and in the time of temptation fall away* (Luke 8:13). He is eternity, which will not be found except by him who seeks with perseverance. . . . *Woe to the sinner who treads a double path* (Sir. 2:12). *No servant can serve two masters* (Luke 16:13). Nor does integrity, perfection, fulness have any liking for such duplicity. It considers as something unworthy to pretend to be a seeker without seeking with perfection of heart (*Serm. de div., Serm. 37,* n. 9, col. 643).

E. If God is about to vomit out of his mouth him whom he finds lukewarm (cf. Apoc. 3:16), what will happen to the hypocrite and the traitor? If he is cursed who does the work of the Lord deceitfully (cf. Jer. 48:10), what will be the merit of him who does it fraudulently? . . . God is truth, and he looks for those who seek him in spirit and truth. If we wish to seek God not in vain, we must seek him in truth, we must seek him frequently, we must seek him perseveringly, so that we seek nothing in place of him, nothing with him, and especially that we do not turn from him to seek anything else. It is easier for heaven and earth to pass away than for one who has thus sought him not to find him, for one who petitions thus not to have the favor granted, for one who knocks in this manner not to have the door opened to him (*ibid.*).

F. Consider carefully what is the object of your love and of your fear, what is the source of your joy and of your sadness, and you will find a worldly spirit under the habit of religion, and under the tattered covering of an exterior conversion and penitence, a perverted heart. For the whole heart is made up of these four affections: and so it seems to me, it is with reference to them that we must understand the precept to turn to the Lord with all our heart. Therefore let your love be converted to God, so that henceforth you will love nothing besides him, or at least nothing except for his sake. Let your fear, too, be converted to the Lord, because every fear is perverted wherein you fear anything besides him, or anything but on account of him. To him let your joy also and your sadness as well be converted. This will have been done when you will not longer either grieve or rejoice except according to God (*Serm. de temp., Serm. II in capite jejunii,* n. 3, col. 172).

298. DENIS THE CARTHUSIAN. It is the purpose of the conversion of morals to reform the individual powers of the soul and to regulate them in an orderly manner with regard to words and deeds; and to repress the inclinations of both interior and external senses, in order that the religious, who has received from God all that he is and all that he has in body and soul, may dedicate it all to the worship, love, and honor of God, reserving nothing of himself for himself (*De professione monastic.,* art. 6. *Op. Om.* 38:558).

299. ORIGEN, priest of Alexandria (d. 253). Do not think that renewal of life, as it is called, having once been made, suffices; always and daily, if I may so state it, the newness must be renewed (*In Ep. ad Rom., Lib. V,* n. 8, *PG* 14:1042).

300. ST. BERNARD. Believe me, those [evil tendencies] which are cut down shoot up again, and those which have been driven away return; the fires which have been extinguished are, in a while, rekindled; and those desires which seemed fast asleep wake once more. It is of little avail, therefore, to have pruned once; we must prune frequently, nay, if it were possible, always; because if you are honest with yourself, you

will always find something within requiring to be sternly repressed. Whatever spiritual progress you may make while you remain in this body, you err if you suppose that sins and vices are dead in you because they have been suppressed (*Serm. 58 in Cant., De putatione vitiorum,* n. 10, *PL* 183:1060; Eales, p. 352).

301. ST. JEROME. Not to aim at perfection is itself a sin (*Ep. 14, ad Heliodorum monachum, quem frustra conatus erat apud se in eremo detinere,* § 7, *PL* 22:352).

302. ST. AMBROSE. The grace of the Holy Spirit does not recognize sluggish efforts (*Expos. in Luc., Lib. II,* n. 19, *PL* 15:1640).

303. ST. BERNARD. The proper motive for loving God is that he is God; the measure in which we are to love him is to love him without measure (*De diligendo Deo,* c. 1, n. 1, *PL* 182:974).

304. IMITATION OF CHRIST (Thomas à Kempis). The noble love of Jesus perfectly imprinted in man's soul makes a man do great things, and stirs him always to desire perfection and to grow more and more in grace and goodness. Love will always have a man's mind raised to God and not occupied with the things of the world. . . . It feels no burden; it regards no labor; it desires more than it can obtain. . . . Love is swift, pure, humble, joyful, and glad; strong, patient, faithful, wise, forbearing, manly . . . devout and thankful to God (*De imitatione Christi, Lib. III,* c. 5, *Op. Om.* 2:152; Gardiner, p. 110 f.).

305. JOHN CASSIAN. A. Wherefore it is good and profitable for each person to strive with might and main to attain perfection in the work undertaken, according to the goal which he has set for himself and the grace he has received; and while he praises and admires the virtues of others, not to swerve from the goal which he has chosen once for all (*Collatio 14* [*coll. I Abbatis Nesterotis*], *De spiritali scientia,* c. 5, *PL* 49:959). B. We ought always with incessant care and anxiety give ourselves up to the acquisition of virtue, and constantly occupy ourselves with its practice, lest, if we cease to go forward, the result should immediately be a going back. For, as we said, the mind cannot continue in one and the same condition, that is to say, without receiving addition to or diminution of its good qualities. For to fail to gain new ones is to lose them; when the desire of making progress ceases, there the danger of going back is always present (*Coll. VI. Abbatis Theodori, De nece sanctorum,* c. 14, col. 665). C. Rightly then is he said to be worse, because the carnal man, that is, the worldly man and the heathen is more readily brought to salutary conversion and to the heights of perfection than one who has professed as a monk, but has not, as his rule directs that he should, laid hold of the way of perfection, and so has once for all drawn back from that fire of spiritual fervor. . . . And he is so far in a worse condition than a worldly man, precisely because he has no idea that he is wretched or blind or naked or needs to be directed or

taught by anyone (*Coll. IV., Abbatis Daniel, De concupiscentia carnis et spiritus,* c. 19, col. 606).

Fervor to be intensified

306. ST. ATHANASIUS. A. St. Antony . . . [thus exhorted his disciples]: "Let this be the common striving of all, that none of us ever abandon what we have undertaken, or become disheartened because of its difficulty. Nor should we ever say: 'We have already led the ascetical life for a long time,' but we should rather intensify our zeal as though we were beginning anew each day" (*Vita S. Antonii,* c. 16, *PG* 26:867). B. [When he was dying, Antony] . . . cried out to the brethren—there were two of them, who had been with him from the time when his old age had set in, which had been nearly fifteen years before, who ministered to him with utmost care—and said to them, even as it is written: *"Today, I am going the way of all men* (Josh. 23:14), for I have felt within myself for some days past, that I have been called by my Lord. Observe now how carefully you can maintain this contest, and take good heed that you do not lose the fruit of your long and patiently borne trial, but rather, like men who are only just beginning the strife, increase that fruit more and more, and add to it day by day" (*ibid.,* c. 91, col. 970).

307. ST. JOHN CLIMACUS. A. It is impossible to look at the sky with one eye and at the earth with the other, and it is equally impossible for anyone not to expose his soul to danger who has not separated himself completely, both in thought and body, from his own relatives and from others (*Scala paradisi, Grad. III, De peregrinatione, PG* 88:670; Moore, p. 64, n. 23; Robert, p. 34). B. So who is a faithful and wise monk? He who has kept his fervor unabated, and to the end of his life has not ceased daily to add fire to fire, fervor to fervor, zeal to zeal, love to love (*ibid., Grad. I,* col. 643; Moore, p. 56; Robert, p. 18).

308. ST. JOHN CHRYSOSTOM thus interprets the passage of St. Paul in Phil. 3:13 f.: "If Paul, after innumerable deaths, after so many dangers, considered that he was still far from the goal, how much more should we! . . . We should forget our successes and cast them behind us. For the runner does not dwell on how many laps he has completed, but how much farther he must run. We too should take account not how far we have advanced in virtue, but how much remains for us. For what will that which we have finished profit us, unless we also complete that which lies before us? St. Paul did not say: 'I do not think of what has been accomplished,' or 'I do not recall,' but *Forgetting . . . !* He said this in order to make us more zealous, for we then become eager when we apply all diligence to what lies before us, when we have committed everything else to oblivion. *Forgetting what is behind,* he says, *I strain forward to what is before.* We too must strive to attain the goal

in this manner. For he 'strains forward' who endeavors to go faster than his feet, as though running with the rest of his body, stretching himself forward, and reaching out his hands, that he may cover that much more of the course. But this comes from intense eagerness, from much warmth. In this way the athlete should run with great eagerness, intensely, without relaxation" (*In Ep. ad Phil. 3:13 f., Hom. 12,* § 1, *PG* 62:271).

309. ST. AUGUSTINE. A. If anyone has charity so intense that he is prepared even to die for his brethren, in that man there is perfect charity. But is it already quite perfect as soon as it is born? It is born in order that it may become perfect: when born it is nourished; when nourished, it is strengthened; when strengthened, it is perfected; when it has come to perfection, what does it say? *For to me to live is Christ, and to die is gain* (Phil. 1:21; *Tract. V in Ep. Joan. ad Parthos,* § 4, *PL* 35:2014). B. The whole life of a good Christian is one of holy desire. Now anything that you are longing for, you do not see; but by your very longing, you become capable of being filled by it when it comes, so that in a sense you can see it. Now if you desire to fill a bag, and know the quantity that is to be poured into it, you hold wide open the mouth of the sack, or the skin, or whatever container you are using; you know how much you want to put into it, and you see that the sack is narrow. You make it capable of holding more by stretching it. So also God, deferring our hope, stretches our desire; by our desiring he stretches our mind; by stretching it, makes it more capacious. Let us therefore desire, my brethren, for we shall be filled. See Paul widening, as it were, his bosom, that it may receive that which is to come. He says: *Brethren, I do not consider that I have laid hold of it already. But one thing I do: forgetting what is behind, I strain forward to what is before. I press on towards the goal, to the prize of God's heavenly call in Christ Jesus* (Phil. 3:13–14; *ibid., tract. IV,* § 6, col. 2008). C. Make progress, my brethren, examine yourselves well, always without deceit, without flattery, without complacency. For there is no one within you, before whom you have any need to blush, or to vaunt yourselves. There is One there, but One whom humility pleases. Let him be your examiner. And test yourselves as well. Let what you see ever be displeasing to you, if you seek to attain what you have not yet become. For once you are pleased with yourselves, there you have halted. If you have said: "It is enough," then you are lost. Be ever adding, be ever going forward, ever making progress; do not stand still on the way, do not turn back, do not go apart from the way! (*Serm. 169,* c. 15, n. 18, *Proficiendum semper in via ad Deum, PL* 38:926.) D. As far as a shipwreck is concerned, what difference does it make whether the boat capsizes with one mighty wave, or the water, to which no attention has been paid, gradually fills up the boat and sinks it? (*Ep. 266,* § 8, *PL* 33:1089.)

310. ST. GREGORY THE GREAT. For if that which evidently must be done is not advanced with assiduous application, even what has been done well deteriorates. For in this world the human soul is like a ship going upstream: it is not allowed to stay still in one place, because it will drop away to the lower reaches unless it strives to gain the upper (*Reg. pastoralis lib., Pars III,* c. 34, *PL* 77:118; Davis, p. 220).

311. ST. ANSELM. A. The present life is like a highway. For as long as man lives, he is constantly on the move. Always he is going forward or backward. He is always either ascending toward heaven, or descending toward hell. Every time he performs a good work, he takes one step upward, but when he sins in any way, he descends a step. The final result of this ascending and descending will be known by each soul when it departs from the body. He who strives zealously during the time of his life on earth to ascend by his virtuous conduct and good deeds will be placed among the holy angels in heaven and he who descends by his evil actions will be buried in hell with the fallen angels. This should be noted: one goes downward much more rapidly and easily than one ascends (*Lib. III, ep. 138, Ad Basiliam, PL* 159:171; Schmitt, *Op. Om.* 5:365).

B. You vowed to the Lord to amend your life:
Let there now be an end to sins and vices.
Let him now live humbly who used to be proud.
Let whoever was in times past given to luxury, now be dedicated to chastity.
Another sought material goods, strove for recognition:
Let neither wealth nor honor now have value in his sight.
This man delighted in banquets and found his pleasure in the richly laden table;
Now he will nourish himself with the scanty fare at temperate repasts.
Such is true conversion, brethren, such merits pardon.
Such a life has in it the power to please the offended God.*

312. ST. BERNARD. A. The order of those dedicated to continence is like passage over a bridge—and there is no one who does not appreciate that such indeed is the shortest way, an easy one, and the safest. . . . The way you are following, beloved brothers, is certainly straight and more secure than that of married persons, but even at that it is not absolutely free of risks. We must be fearful of a threefold danger: that an individual bring himself down to the level of others, that he look backward, or that he wish to halt or sit down halfway across the bridge —for the narrowness of the bridge will not permit any of these three. . . . Let us every one pray against the first danger, saying with the

* *Carmen de contemptu saeculi,* vers. 25 sq., *PL* 158:689. Deest in Schmitt, *Op. Om.*

Prophet: *Let not the foot of the proud overtake me nor the hand of the wicked disquiet me. See how the evildoers have fallen* (Ps. 35:12–13). Then, he who has once put his hand to the plow and afterwards turns back, falls immediately, and the waves wash over his head. . . . It is also necessary that he who seeks to stand still, while apparently not abandoning the course on which he has entered, but making only a pretense of advancing, be carried along and pushed forward by those who follow. The passage is narrow and he prevents the progress of even those who want to push ahead. They are constantly arguing with him and scolding him, being impatient with his slowness and lukewarmness. They urge him on as with goads and shove him with their hands. One of two things necessarily follows: he must either go forward, or stop altogether. So one should not halt at all, much less pay any attention to or compare himself with others; but we must run and hasten with all humility (*Serm. de div., Serm. 35, de tribus ordinibus Ecclesiae,* n. 2, *PL* 183:635).

B. True virtue never comes to an end, it does not finish in this life. . . . The righteous man never considers himself as *having attained his goal* (Phil. 3:13). He never says: "It is enough," but always hungers and thirsts for righteousness, so that even if he were to continue to live forever, he would always try as hard as he could to be constantly more righteous, always try with all his strength to go from good to better. He does not give himself to the service of God for a year, or for a specified time, like a mercenary, but forever. Hear what one righteous man says: *Never will I forget your precepts, for through them you give me life* (Ps. 118:93), and *I intend in my heart to fulfil your statutes always, to the letter* (*ibid.,* v. 112). Not, therefore, for a time. Hence his righteousness endures not for a time, but forever. His everlasting hunger for righteousness merits everlasting consolation and, although his life may be completed in a short time, yet he can be reckoned to have fulfilled a long life by the perpetuity of his virtue. . . . But unwearied effort to progress, unflagging effort to be perfect, is accounted perfection. If, therefore, to apply oneself to perfection is to be perfect, then it follows that not to wish to be perfect is to fall away. Where then do they stand who say: "It is enough for us to be like our fathers, we do not wish to be any better"? Do you, a monk, wish to be better? No. Do you wish to become worse? Certainly not! You say then that you wish to live and to remain at the stage in which you have now arrived, without becoming any better or any worse. But this is to wish for an impossibility. What stands still in this life? Certainly it is especially true of man to say: *Like a flower that springs up and fades, swift as a shadow that does not abide, even so he wastes away like a rotten thing* (Job 14:2). The Creator of both man and the world, as long as he was in the world and lived among men, never stood still. According to the Scripture: *He went about doing good, healing all* (Acts 10:38). He went about not fruitlessly, not lazily, he did not potter, but like a giant, joyfully running his course (cf. Ps. 18:6). No one overtakes a runner without running himself. What good is it to follow Christ if one never reaches him? St. Paul says: *So run as to obtain* [the prize] (I Cor. 9:24). Fix the limit of your course, Christian, where Christ fixed his. He became obedient to death (cf. Phil. 2:8); therefore however far you run, if you do not keep on running until death, you will not obtain the reward. The reward is Christ. If you cease to run while he continues to run, you do not approach him but fall behind, and in that case it is much to be feared that you would be like those of whom David said: *They who withdraw from you perish* (Ps. 72:27). If to progress is to run, when you cease progressing you cease running, and when you cease running you fall behind. From this it is evident that to cease wishing to progress is nothing else than to fall away (*Ep. 254, ad abbatem Guarinum* [Warren] *Alpensem, quem laudat pro studio reformandi ordinem, PL* 182:460 f.; James, n. 329, p. 409).

C. In his dream Jacob saw upon the ladder angels ascending and descending (cf. Gen. 28:12); but was any one of them either sitting or standing still? A fragile ladder is no place for standing still, nor, in the uncertain condition of this mortal life, can anyone remain fixed in one position. We have not here an abiding city nor do we yet possess it, but we are still seeking the one that is to come. Either you must go up or you must come down; you inevitably fall if you try to stand still. It is certain that the man who does not try to be better is not even good; when you stop trying to be better, then you cease to be good (*Ep. 91, ad abbates Suessione congregatos,* n. 3, *studium profectus serio commendans,* col. 224; James, p. 141. This was one of the first general chapters of the Black Benedictines, of the Province of Rheims, held in 1130).

D. That you should have now begun again, is an indication that you had reached the end of your reckoning; that you should have considered you had not yet finished, indicates that you had already done so. No one is perfect who does not wish to be still more perfect; the more perfect a man is, the more he reaches out to an even higher perfection (*Ep. 34, ad Drogonem monachum, cui congratulatur quod ad strictiorem observantiam—Cisterciensium—transierit,* col. 140; James, p. 68).

E. May you always act thus, dearest brothers! A disciple who is intent on progressing is the pride of his master. Anyone who does not advance in the school of Christ is not worthy of his teaching. . . . For *Jesus,* the evangelist tells us, *advanced in wisdom and age and grace before God and men* (Luke 2:52). So he did not stand still, on the contrary . . . *like a giant, joyfully he ran the course* (Ps. 18:6). And we, too, if we are wise, will run in his footsteps, allured by the fragrance of his perfumes. If we are sluggards and allow him to draw away from us, we will only find the road more difficult and dangerous, and we will not be refreshed by his fragrance or sure of his way. . . . Because *we know that for those who love God all things work together unto good* (Rom. 8:28), we should be stirred by the example of worldly men. Who has ever known an ambitious man content with his position and not covetous for yet further honors? In the same way the eyes of the curious men are never satisfied with seeing, nor the ears ever filled with hearing. Does not the insatiable desire of the avaricious man, or of the man who lives for pleasures or of him who pursues the flattery of others, rebuke our own tepid and remiss lives? We should be ashamed to be found less desirous of spiritual goods. The soul now turned to God should blush to seek righteousness with less fervor than it had formerly pursued evil. The inducement is very different. *For the wages of sin is death but the gift of God is life everlasting in Christ Jesus our Lord* (Rom. 6:23). We should be ashamed to be less ardent in the quest of life than we are in the quest of death, less zealous in the acquisition of the pledge of life than we were in earning the wages of sin. For, so that we should be without any excuse, the faster we run in the way of life, the easier it is; the more we undertake of our Savior's light burden, the easier it becomes to carry (*Ep. 385, ad monachos S. Bertini,* nn. 1–3, col. 587).

F. *Walk while you have the light, that darkness may not overtake you* (John 12: 35). To walk is to make progress. The Apostle was making progress when he said: *I do not consider that I have laid hold of it already. But one thing I do: forgetting what is behind, I strain forward to what is before, I press on toward the goal* (Phil. 3:13–14). What does he mean by this "one thing"? It is to say: There is one thing remaining to me which serves at once as a remedy, a hope, and a consolation. And what is that? It is the forgetting of the past and straining forward to fresh endeavors in the future. It is a great source of confidence for us that even the great man who was *a chosen vessel* (Acts 9:15), did not regard himself as perfect, but earnestly desired to make a farther advance toward perfection. The danger, then, for us is that we should be surprised by the shadows of death when we are not in progress toward good, but are motionless and inert. And who is thus motionless except him who does not make any effort to advance? Take heed of this, and then, if you shall be surprised by death, you will be in a state of gradual amelioration. You will say to God: *Your eyes have seen my actions* (Douay: *my imperfect being*); nevertheless, continues the Psalmist: *In your book all men are written* (Ps. 138:16). Doubtless those who are found in earnest desire for progress (*Serm. 49 in Cant., Qualiter per discretionem ordinatur charitas,* n. 7, *PL* 183:1019; Eales, p. 301).

G. In almost every religous community there are to be found

certain members who are . . . pusillanimous and remiss; who sink under the burden, and require to be urged on with whip and spur; who grow lax in joy and cowardly in sadness; whose compunction is as infrequent as it is short-lived; whose thoughts are all carnal, and whose lives are all tepid; whose obedience is without devotion and whose speech is without prudence; who pray without recollection and read without profit. . . . (*Serm. de temp., Serm. V in Ascensione Dni,* n. 7, col. 318).

H. [After the first fervor of the novitiate, with some persons] the soul undergoes sudden vehement chills, its vigor is relaxed, a languor creeps over its powers, a horror of austerity is continually intensified, the fear of poverty troubles it more and more, the soul contracts, as it were, upon itself, grace ebbs away from it, life becomes wearisome, the reason is stupefied, the courage stifled, the recent fervor of the man rapidly grows cold, a fastidious and dainty lukewarmness gains ground in the soul, brotherly charity grows cold (*Serm. 63 in Cant. . . . De tentationibus monachorum novitiorum,* n. 6, col. 1083).

I. My brethren, that is what every one of us ought to fear most of all, lest perhaps we should ever go so far in offending God that we shall be manifestly rejected by him and vomited out of his mouth; or if shame prohibit a visible apostasy of the body, lest tepidity, little by little, should bring about in us an apostasy of the heart (*Serm. de temp., Serm. 3 in Ps. Qui habitat,* n. 5, col. 193).

J. In order that humility be preserved, divine piety usually disposes that the more one progresses, the less he believes himself to have advanced (*Serm. de div., Serm. 25 de verbis Apostoli,* n. 4, col. 607).

K. Let us rouse ourselves, let us repair the injuries we have done to our souls, let us recollect our spirits, and renounce forever this pernicious tepidity, if not because of its danger, if not because God is wont to vomit the lukewarm out of his mouth (cf. Apoc. 3:16)—of which we have at times seen miserable examples—then at least because it is so bitter, so full of misery and pain, and because it is rightly regarded as a vestibule of hell and the shadow of death (*Serm. de temp., Serm. V in Ascensione Dni.,* n. 7, col. 319).

313. WILLIAM OF ST. THIERRY. Be not heedless, therefore, nor loiter on the way, since the road that lies before you is long. For your profession is an exalted one, it ascends above the heavens, it is equal to the holy spirits, it is like to angelic purity. For you have vowed not only all sanctity, but the very perfection of all sanctity and end of all consummation. It is not for you to be slack concerning common precepts, nor to observe that only which God commands, but that which he wills, giving evidence of how good is the will of God, how acceptable, and perfect (cf. Rom. 12:2). Others have the duty of serving God, but you are to cleave to him; others are to believe in God, to know, love, and

fear him; but you are to savor him, apprehend him, enjoy him. This is a great goal, an arduous goal. But God is almighty and good: in you he promises lovingly, fulfils his promises faithfully, and succors unfailingly (*Ep. ad fratres de Monte Dei, Lib. I,* c. 2, *Quam ardua et sublimis sit eorum professio,* n. 5, *PL* 184:311).

314. ST. ANSELM. You know, dearest sons, my desires in your regard, and you have frequently heard what it is in you that gives me consolation in my troubles. That your hearts are intent on being dedicated to God; that you labor hard as good workmen in the vineyard of the Lord, fulfilling with fortitude the program that you undertook; that your life gives evidence that the world is crucified to you and you to the world; that you live not for yourselves but for God, that is, according to God's will, and not your own; that even in the least matters you fear God with a great fear; that you love the severity of your order —for if a monk hates that austerity, he has shown positively that he is given to vice and that he loves dissolution; that you preserve peace among yourselves and render obedience to your prior—this is my desire in your regard, this my consolation and comfort I find in you. Consider these matters, reflect on them, perform them, if you wish to make me happy, nay, if you wish to make God pleased with you! May the Holy Spirit convince you of these truths, and because of them, grant you the blessed vision of his glory. Amen (*Lib. III, ep. 76, ad Ernulphum priorem et monachos Cantuarienses, PL* 159:113; Schmitt, n. 286, *Op. Om.* 4:206).

315. ST. AUGUSTINE. Who can but admire and commend those who, spurning and abandoning the pleasures of this world, living together in a most chaste and holy society, unite in passing their time in prayers, in readings, in discussions, without any swelling of pride, or noise of contention, or sullenness of envy; but quiet, peaceful, modest, their life is one of perfect harmony and devotion to God, an offering most acceptable to him from whom the power to do all things is obtained? . . . Such customs, such a life, such arrangements, such a system I could not commend as it deserves . . . (*De moribus Ecclesiae catholicae, Lib. I,* c. 31, *Manichaeorum continentiae opponit anachoretarum et coenobitarum vitam,* nn. 67–68, *PL* 32:1338).

SECOND PRINCIPLE

The Work of God

CONTENTS: Common prayer — Its nature — It makes us the equals and companions of angels — Handed down by Christ and the apostles — Arranged by the holy father Benedict — Its excellence — The psalmody — Fruits of the Work of God — Praise of the sacred liturgy — Particular promise of meriting a hearing — Christ, the Head of those praying in choir — The choir is the hope of the Church and of the faithful — The blessed lot of the monk — The voice of the Spouse of Christ and of all creation.

I. STATEMENT OF PRINCIPLE

Common prayer

316. The monastery is a family of God, the monk an adopted son of God. Must he then not be about his Father's business (cf. Luke 2:49), that is, in the oratory, in choir? If all the other exercises of the monastery are performed in common, would it be suitable and right that the principal undertaking of the community be performed individually and privately? Surely the opposite is true: it is precisely in order to perform this duty becomingly that monks abandon the world and unite in the bond of a mystical body through monastic profession. Reflect then, dear confrere, on the nature, the fruits, and the power of common prayer.

Its nature

317. He who takes part in this prayer worships God with body and soul. He adores the Most High God not only in spirit, but in full reality and truth; for he serves him with all his powers, and dedicates the whole man to the due service of his Creator and Redeemer. In so doing, the spirit elevates the body, ennobles and transfigures it; the body, in turn,

urges on and inflames the spirit, so that together body and soul glorify the Incarnate Word of the Father.

The Divine Office, that is to say, the public and common worship of God, is Catholic in the fullest sense, and the distinctive possession of the Catholic Church. For it places before our eyes most vividly the Communion of Saints, in which we have placed our faith, and is a beautiful illustration of the Mystical Body of Christ. For, as the monastery is like the heavenly city, and a family of God, the monks *are as angels in heaven* (Mark 12:25) *who join together in celebrating their joy . . . in glorifying the majesty of the Father . . . and never cease to cry out with one voice, Holy, Holy, Holy* (*Miss. Rom.*, excerpts from various prefaces).

318. The monks are "contenders for the blessed Sion," privileged to perform on earth the august and glorious ministry of the citizens of heaven. Even more obviously, all who worship God in heaven and on earth, are in reality children of one and the same family, united forever and bound together in singing the divine praises. For this reason the angels sang their vigils at night to Christ in the presence of the shepherds of Bethlehem. Without doubt, too, they chanted to the Savior when he celebrated the first conventual Mass with the Apostles in the Cenacle—*after reciting a hymn* (Matt. 26:30; Mark 14:26). No doubt they also took part when with his Blessed Mother, St. John, and the pious women, he offered as High Priest while hanging on the cross, the bloody and most adorable pontifical Sacrifice. These considerations impelled Holy Church in her earliest beginnings to institute and to retain with utmost concern different forms of common prayers and worship. Her first converts *continued steadfastly in the teaching of the apostles and in the communion of the breaking of the bread and in the prayers* (Acts 2:42) . . . *continuing daily with one accord in the temple* (*ibid.*, v. 46; cf. *ibid.*, 12:5 f.).

Arranged by St. Benedict; its excellence

319. Now this is what the holy Patriarch of monks had in mind when he instituted and arranged the Work of God in such painstaking detail. You must, therefore, hold this sacred and principal duty of the monk in highest regard and love it with all your soul. Keep its unusual excellence before your mind. It is God himself who puts his own words, or the praises, canticles, and hymns of his saints upon your lips.

The psalmody

320. First of all, what should we say of the psalms, those immortal and precious canticles, which the Holy Spirit has drawn forth from the breast of the man who was *after the heart of God* (Ps. 88:2; Acts 13:22). His purpose was that through all the centuries they might carry up to

heaven the pious wishes and aspirations, the prayers and praises of all men, and bring back divine inspiration, consolations, and the aids of grace. Reflect intently in your heart on the truth of God's words: *He that offers praise as a sacrifice glorifies me; and to him that goes the right way I will show the salvation of God* (Ps. 49:23).

Fruits of the Divine Office for you

321. You must marvel at the numerous and great benefits that accrue to your own soul from the Divine Office. This blessedness of common effort in prayer floods your heart with tranquillity, consolation, and joy in the Holy Spirit. In a marvelous manner it purifies your soul, illumines it, and unites it with God. The divine praises open the heavens, as it were, so that manna rains down upon you. This is the perfection of delight, a heavenly banquet to nourish the heart and *transform you into his very image from glory to glory* (II Cor. 3:18). This uniting of brethren in prayer is like a sacred bath in the Jordan. Seven times each day you enter it in order to wash away stains. You renew the youth of your soul, as does the eagle (cf. Ps. 102:5). It is also an excellent aid to piety, a sure characteristic of virtue, a powerful antidote against the spirit of the world, a loving practice of obedience to Holy Church, and an abundant source of divine contemplation. *It is good to give thanks to the Lord, to sing praise to your name, Most High* (Ps. 91:1).

Fruits of the Divine Office for the faithful

322. Consider moreover what a power for edification derives for the faithful from prayer in choir. Does not the public worship of God thoroughly till the field of the soul, plow its soil, and smoothly harrow it: it then invites the Divine Sower to scatter his heavenly seed. Choir worship bedews the soul with the richest graces and at the same time is the most effective commendation of the Church's sacred liturgy, which is truly *a fountain of water, springing up unto life everlasting* (John 4:14); the *tree of life . . . yielding its fruits according to each month* (Apoc. 22:2) in the paradise of the Church. Would that all knew of this gift and realized that the Word-made-flesh, full of truth and grace, dwells among us in the sacred liturgy, pouring out upon his mystical members the Spirit of his life!

323. There is, moreover, the special promise of being heard that adorns prayer offered in common. For the Lord himself tells us: *For where two or three are gathered together for my sake, there am I in the midst of them. . . . anything at all for which they ask, it shall be done for them by my Father in heaven* (Matt. 18:20,19). Jesus Christ stands therefore among those praying in choir, as their Head, the Leader, and Mediator. He intercedes for them, and his *Spirit himself pleads for us with unutterable groanings* (Rom. 8:26). For these reasons the hope

and strong confidence which the Church and the Christian people repose in the canonical prayer is so well established that they call those who pray the Divine Office in choir the picked troops arrayed against the ancient enemy, a citadel of peace and salvation, a second Moses who by lifting up his hands on the holy mountain implores by his entreaties victory for his people (cf. Exod. 17:11).

The blessed lot of the monk

324. This common prayer, then, is your exalted duty, your blessed lot and special function. You are called a Benedictine: then you should, by reason of the very name you bear, bless God with a never-ending praise and in a special manner, receive blessings from him. "Monks are founded because of the choir" in order that the Spouse of Christ [the Church] may use their voice as her own. They become the chanters of all creation. They are representatives at prayer for the faithful, their mediators before the Most High. Now you have been accepted into the number of the elect of whom the Lord speaks: *This people have I formed for myself, they shall show forth my praise* (Isa. 43:21). Holy Church has assigned to you an angelic ministry of great responsibility. You hold a privileged place day and night in the palace of the Most High King. You are granted this privilege in order to offer the sacrifice of praise. Indeed, no duty must ever mean more to you than dedication to divine worship. It is the capital and stronghold of the monastic life, the heart of religion, the bond of harmony for monks, the crown of all occupations—that is to say, it is that first duty to which all others, because they are less worthy and honorable, are merely associated. To it nothing at all must ever be preferred.

325. Here you have the reason why our holy Patriarch devotes thirteen chapters of the holy Rule (*RSB,* cc. 8–20) to the arrangement of the Work of God, and parts of four other chapters as well (*ibid.,* cc. 43, 45, 47, 52). Therefore these golden words should be inscribed on every monastery: Let nothing be preferred to the Work of God (*ibid.,* c. 43). Your fatherly lawgiver desires you to fulfil this excellent duty with profound reverence and ardent love. You must realize that you are to resemble in a distinctive manner that *angel who stood before the altar, having a golden censer; and there was given to him much incense, that he might offer it with the prayers of all the saints upon the golden altar which is before the throne* (Apoc. 8:3). At the same time you must never forget that the holy Patriarch called this duty a work. For it is indeed a laborious task, to which you must devote your whole interest and effort. Be solicitous for the Work of God and employ diligence in preparing for it. When the bell sounds, say to yourself: This is the sign of the great King: let us go . . . (*Antiph. ad Magn., I Vesp., in festo Epiphaniae, Brev. monastic.* 1:322). Put aside whatever you have been

doing, hasten to the choir. Examine yourself at the Statio,* so that you may make certain that your disposition is worthy as you prepare to stand before the Lord in prayer, and that you may devote your whole being to the divine service. Enter the oratory, the heavenly court, so recollected and composed that you are intent solely on the adoration and acknowledgment of the presence of your King and Bridegroom. Perform the Work of God worthily, attentively, and with devotion, religiously observing the rites and ceremonies prescribed by Holy Church. For by your love and devotion to the Work of God you may measure your faith and your love of God, your esteem and reverence for your vocation, and your zeal for the house of God.

326. In your eagerness for God's adoration you will so take part in the recitation that the prayers in honor of the uncreated Word from whom all truth emanates will be well articulated, clear, and accurately pronounced. When you recite in this manner, the more profound meaning of the words is appreciated and the heart is suffused with light and unction. In the psalmody and the sacred chant of the Church make your mind correspond with the voice [that is, with the words uttered], and the voice with the mind. . . . *Let me* [the Bridegroom] *hear your voice, for your voice is sweet, and you are lovely* (Cant. 2:14). Let the pure melodies of the angels echo in the sacred hymns you sing, so that those who are present at the divine services may be edified as you yourself are. Then you can be certain that your heart and your senses are truly directed to God in joy.

327. When you act thus you are singing wisely (cf. Ps. 46:8, Douay version); you rejoice in fear and gladness, in simplicity and purity of heart, in the spirit of reverence, in humility, and the compunction of tears. You are indeed blessed, for if such ability to praise the Lord is bestowed on you, then these words of Holy Scripture are applicable to you as a blessed and true worshiper of God! *With his every deed he* [David] *offered thanks to God Most High, in words of praise. With his whole being he loved his Maker and daily had his praises sung; he added beauty to the feasts* (Sir. 47:8–9).

But it must be borne in mind that the Work of God is not made up of the Divine Office alone. It is, so to speak, only a precious covering uniting with a still more precious treasure in order to form a whole, or like a radiant crown surrounding the brilliant sun, the source of all light and splendor.

* Statio: the assembling and forming ranks by the choir members in a corridor or courtyard for a brief period of recollection before entering the abbey church in procession. The unabridged dictionary gives no anglicized equivalent for the word, which is, so far as is known, always used in Latin about monasteries. Because the Statio can be dispensed with as not essential, and because of architectural limitations and the intense activity of many monks in the service of the Church, it is not so commonly observed in the United States as in Europe. [*Tr.*]

The Sacrifice of the altar

328. The sacrifice of praise only adorns and embellishes the Sacrifice of the altar, the most sacred and adorable mystery. In the Sacrifice of the altar there takes place before our eyes, under a mystical veil, the same oblation that is made without interruption on the sublime altar of heaven at the hands of the chief High Priest and in the presence of the Divine Majesty, amid the rejoicing of the whole heavenly court. The same Divine Victim offers himself to the Eternal Father on the throne of God and upon our altars, as an atonement for the living and the dead.

The conventual Mass

329. It would scarcely be possible to describe adequately the purity, the chaste and angelic devotion and love, and the sentiments of joy with which you should assist at the solemn conventual Mass, which is sung daily, as well as personally offer the holy Sacrifice. With perfect right this most sacred "mystery of faith" is considered the terminus and center of our entire religion and of all worship of God. Therefore with the most profound and ardent love you should adore the august Eucharist, the heavenly Emmanuel dwelling in the tabernacle, who gives himself to you as a most lovable companion, to be your nourishment and consolation, to feed and strengthen your soul with divine power, ever refreshing it with holy and constantly new delights, truly the Bread of the strong, the bond of charity, and the pledge of future glory.

330. You see now the intimate connection between the Holy Sacrifice of the Mass and the Divine Office; you readily understand too how appropriate is the proximity of the choir to the altar. The altar is the heart of the choir, and the choir or the presbyterium * is the complement of the altar. On both together, as on a heavenly stage, the divine drama of our blessed redemption and sanctification is enacted and actually effected through the sacred liturgy, by which divine life is diffused through the Church. For this reason also you rejoice that your abbot, who holds the place of the Eternal High Priest, presides in choir, and solemnly celebrates the august Sacrifice at the altar, enjoying pontifical dignity. Who could be considered more fortunate than yourself, my brother, whom God has summoned to take part in this heavenly drama and to be so abundantly filled with the divine life of Holy Church?

331. You are, in truth, a man of God in a special sense of the

* Presbyterium: Best observed in churches of the basilical style of architecture: the row of stone benches on either side of the bishop's throne, in the apse, immediately behind the altar; a sort of corona of attending priests about the altar and the bishop, at a pontifical Mass.

phrase, or—the thought is the same—a man of the Church, a man of faith, a man of prayer, a man dedicated to the sacred liturgy. Your whole life is supernaturalized. You must, accordingly, examine and weigh everything that goes to make up your life, in the scales of the sanctuary, with a divine appraisal, gradually penetrating more and more into the treasury of faith until finally you will live altogether by faith. Wisely distrusting your own judgment and inclinations, you will set your heart on God alone, firm in your dedication to the contemplation of things divine. You will carefully avoid dissipation of the powers of your mind in idleness, distractions, and the lack of custody of your senses. By perseverance in the habit of prayer and meditation, you will learn to walk in the presence of the Divine Majesty.

332. Second to your devotion to the loving Heart of Jesus, to which no devotion is ever to be preferred, you will cultivate a tender affection for your heavenly Queen and Mother, the Immaculate Virgin Mary. Make it your delight to promote her honor, extol her prerogatives, and place yourself confidently under her unfailing protection. You should, moreover, foster a fervent devotion to the angels, and the saints who followed in the footsteps of Christ and now reign gloriously with him in heaven. Animated with the spirit of the genuine ascetical life, love Holy Church in reverence and obedience. This means too that you must have a distinctive love for her head, the Roman Pontiff, the infallible teacher and shepherd of the world, who truly holds the place of Christ, having been appointed to watch over grace and truth, justice and salvation. Remaining attached to him by the bond of filial piety and duty, be ever prepared to serve him unto death, so that you keep in your heart his pronouncements and desires, his aims and achievements. From time immemorial monasteries have always been regarded as citadels of the Supreme Pontiffs.

333. Make it a policy to hold steadfast and dear whatever the Apostolic See recommends in the way of devotional practices such as pious recitation of the Rosary, the Way of the Cross, and other indulgenced prayers. Make your prayerful intentions for the increase and triumph of Holy Church, the growth of religion, the extirpation of heresy and schism, the conversion of pagans and infidels, the repentance of sinners, the perseverance of the just, and the relief of the poor souls. Your whole life, spent in intimate attachment to your Mother, the Church, should be a continuous Work of God, the *fragrance of Christ* (II Cor. 2:15). This is the true spirit of religion, that unfailing source of solid peace and sweet unction, the assurance of eternal salvation, and the only way in which God may be glorified in all things (*RSB*, c. 57). In this way alone is it possible for us being *delivered from the hands of our enemies, to serve him without fear, in holiness and justice before him all our days* (Luke 1:74).

II. EVIDENCE FROM THE RULE OF ST. BENEDICT

Common prayer

334. Let [the abbot] employ a still greater thing, namely the prayers of himself and all the brethren, that God, who can do all things, may effect the cure of the sick brother (*RSB,* c. 28). On Sunday, immediately after Lauds, the incoming and outgoing servers shall prostrate themselves before all the brethren in the oratory and ask for their prayers (*ibid.,* c. 35). After Mass and Communion let the incoming reader ask all to pray for him, that God may preserve him from the spirit of pride (*ibid.,* c. 38). Let the brethren who are to be sent on a journey commend themselves to the prayers of all the brethren and of the abbot (*ibid.,* c. 67). And before you call upon me, I shall say to you, *Lo, here I am* (Isa. 65:24, Douay version). What can be sweeter to us, brethren, than this voice of the Lord inviting us? (*Ibid., Prolog.*)

The Work of God

335. Let nothing be preferred to the Work of God (*RSB,* c. 43). The indicating of the hour for the Work of God by day and by night shall be the concern of the abbot . . . that everything may be fulfilled at its proper time (*ibid.,* c. 47). . . . Rising at the signal without delay, let all hasten to forestall one another to the Work of God; yet this with all gravity and self-restraint (*ibid.,* c. 22). The Prophet says: *Seven times a day I praise you* (Ps. 118:164). We shall observe this sacred number of seven if we fulfil the duties of our service in the Hours of Lauds, Prime, Terce, Sext, None, Vespers, and Compline; for it was of these Day Hours that he said: "Seven times a day I praise you." But of the Night Office the same Prophet says: *At midnight I rise to give you thanks* (*ibid.,* v. 62). At these times, therefore, let us render praise to our Creator for his just ordinances (cf. *ibid.,* v. 164; *RSB,* cc. 8–18 are devoted to the arrangement of the prayers and the specification of the hours for performing the Divine Office: that so large a proportion of the Rule's seventy-three nicely balanced chapters should be devoted to detailed instruction is significant of the question's importance in Benedict's estimation).

The Statio

336. As soon as the signal for None has been given, let them all abandon their work and hold themselves ready for the sounding of the second signal (*RSB,* c. 48).

The Work of God as a work

337. Let the oratory be what its name implies (*RSB,* c. 52). Let them perform the Work of God in the place where they are working, bending their knees in reverence before God . . . and not neglect to pray the due measure of their service (*ibid.,* c. 50). . . . Let the reader chant the *Gloria.* And as soon as he has begun it, let all rise from their seats in honor and reverence of the Holy Trinity (*ibid.,* c. 9). The abbot shall read the lesson from the book of the Gospels, all standing with fear and reverence (*ibid.,* c. 11). If we wish to prefer a petition to men of high rank, we do not presume to do it without humility and respect; how much more ought we to supplicate the Lord God of all things with all humility and pure devotion! (*Ibid.,* c. 20.) If anyone make a mistake . . . and does not make humble satisfaction there before all, let him undergo greater punishment, because he would not repair by humility the fault that he committed through carelessness (*ibid.,* c. 45). We believe that God is present everywhere and that *The eyes of the Lord are in every place keeping watch on the evil and the good* (Prov. 15:3); but let us especially believe this without any doubting when we are performing the Divine Office. Therefore let us ever remember the words of the Prophet: *Serve the Lord with fear* (Ps. 2:11); and again: *Sing ye wisely* (Ps. 46:8, Douay version); and *in the presence of the angels I will sing your praise* (Ps. 137:2). Let us then consider how we ought to behave ourselves in the presence of God and his angels, and so sing the psalms that mind and voice may be in harmony (*ibid.,* c. 19).

Psalmody and chant

338. The psalter with its full hundred and fifty psalms shall be chanted every week . . . for those monks who sing less show themselves very slothful in their sacred service (*RSB,* c. 18). The brethren are not to read or sing each in his turn, but those only who give edification to the hearers (*ibid.,* c. 38). Let no one presume to sing or read, unless he can fulfil the office to the edification of his hearers. Let it be done with humility, gravity, and reverence, and by him whom the abbot has appointed (*ibid.,* c. 47).

Choir and altar

339. Let the brethren, therefore, receive the kiss of peace, go to Communion, intone Psalms, and stand in choir according to the order which the abbot has determined, or which they have of themselves (*RSB,* c. 63). When the Work of God has been finished, let all go out in deep silence, and let reverence for God be observed (*ibid.,* c. 52).

Life of St. Benedict: [The man of God] was seized with a violent fever that rapidly wasted his remaining energy. Each day his condition worsened until finally on the sixth day he had his disciples carry him into the oratory, where he received the body and blood of the Lord to gain strength for his approaching end. Then, supporting his weakened body on the arms of his brethren, he stood with his hands raised to heaven and breathed forth his last in the act of praying (*S. Greg. Magn. Dialogorum Lib. II,* c. 37, *De prophetia sui exitus fratribus denuntiata, PL* 66:202).

Prayer

340. Whatever good work you undertake, ask God with most instant prayer to perfect it . . . so that where our nature is powerless, he will give the help of his grace (*RSB, Prolog.;* also cc. 37, 58). Instruments of good works are: To apply oneself frequently to prayer. Daily in one's prayer, with tears and sighs, to confess one's past sins to God. To pray for one's enemies in the love of Christ (*ibid.,* c. 4, nn. 57–58, 71). Let us be sure that we shall not be heard because of our much speaking, but because of purity of heart and tears of compunction. Our prayer, therefore, ought to be short and pure, unless perchance it is prolonged by the impulse and inspiration of divine grace (*ibid.,* c. 20). If anyone wishes to pray privately, let him go into the oratory and pray; not in a loud voice, but with tears and fervor of heart (*ibid.,* c. 52).

Life of St. Benedict: [The man of God] usually wept when praying (*S. Greg. Magn. Dialogorum Lib. II,* c. 17. *PL* 66:168). In the meantime the saint devoted himself to prayer with his accustomed fervor (*ibid.,* c. 27, col. 184). On his way to the oratory of St. John . . . Benedict met the ancient enemy of mankind, and having scorned the threats of the evil one, continued on his way and after his prayer hurried back (*ibid.,* c. 30, col. 188). Long before the Night Office began, the man of God was standing at his window, where he watched and prayed, while the rest were asleep. In the dead of night he suddenly beheld a flood of light shining down from above, more brilliant than the sun (*ibid.,* c. 35, col. 198).

Meditation

341. Those brethren who need a better knowledge of them, should devote the time that remains after Matins to the study (*meditationi*) of the Psalms and lessons (*RSB,* c. 8). Let him ever remember all the commandments of God, and how hell will burn for their sins those that despise him; and let him constantly turn over in his heart the eternal life which is prepared for those who fear him (*ibid.,* c. 7, first degree). The forty-sixth instrument of good works is: To desire eternal life with all spiritual longing (*ibid.,* c. 4). [The monk] should always ponder the guilt of his sins, and consider that he is about to be brought before the dread judgment seat of God (*ibid.,* c. 7, twelfth degree). Let us open

our eyes to the divine light, and let us hear with attentive ears the warning that the divine voice cries out daily to us (*ibid., Prolog.*).

Life of St. Benedict: At the regular hour, after the brethren had finished chanting the Psalms, they devoted themselves to private prayers (*S. Greg. Magn. Dialogorum Lib. II,* c. 4, *De monacho vagae mentis ad salutem reducto, PL* 66:142).

Life of faith

342. Let us therefore gird our loins with faith and the performance of good works, and following the guidance of the Gospel walk in the path [of Christ]. . . . But as we progress in our monastic life and faith, our hearts shall be enlarged, and we shall run with unspeakable sweetness of love in the way of God's commandments (*RSB, Prolog.*). The forty-ninth instrument of good works is: To know for certain that God sees us everywhere (*ibid.,* c. 4). Let the monk consider that God is always beholding him from heaven, that his actions are everywhere visible to the eye of the Godhead, and are constantly being reported to God by the angels. . . . So, if *the eyes of the Lord are keeping watch on the evil and the good* (Prov. 15:4), and the eyes of *the Lord look down from heaven upon the children of men, to see if there be one who is wise and seeks God* (Ps. 13:2); and if our deeds are daily, day and night, reported to the Lord by the angels assigned to us, then, brethren, we must constantly beware, as the Prophet says in the Psalm (52:4) lest God some day behold us *having gone astray and become perverse* (*ibid.,* c. 7, first degree). Let the monk keep the fear of God before his eyes, altogether shunning forgetfulness (*ibid.*).

Liturgy of the Roman Church

343. But on other days let there be a canticle from the prophets, each on its own day and [in general let it be done] according to the custom of the Roman Church (*RSB,* c. 13).

Love and praise of God

344. Let monks prefer nothing whatever to Christ (*RSB,* c. 72; *ibid.,* c. 4, twenty-first instrument). When all these degrees of humility have been climbed, the monk will presently come to that perfect love of God which casts out all fear; whereby he will begin to observe without labor, as though naturally and by habit, all those precepts which formerly he did not observe without fear: no longer from fear of hell, but for love of Christ and through good habit and delight in virtue (*ibid.,* c. 7, last paragraph) . . . that in all things God may be glorified (*ibid.,* c. 57).

Life of St. Benedict: Do we not read in St. John that *God is love* (I John 4:16). Surely it is no more than right that [St. Scholastica] had greater influence than Benedict, since hers was the greater love (*S. Greg. Magn. Dialogorum Lib. II,* c. 33, *De miraculo Scholasticae sororis ejus, PL* 66:196).

III. DECREES AND DOCUMENTS OF THE CHURCH

345. CATECHISM OF THE COUNCIL OF TRENT. But vocal prayer has also its advantages and necessity [as well as mental prayer]. It quickens the attention of the mind, and kindles the fervor of him who prays. "We sometimes," says St. Augustine in his letter to Proba, "animate ourselves to intensify our holy desire by having recourse to words and other signs; filled with vehement ardor and piety, we find it impossible at times not to express our feelings in words; for while the soul exults with joy, the tongue should also give utterance to that exultation" (*Ep. 130,* c. 9, § 18, *PL* 33:501). And surely it becomes us to make to God this complete sacrifice of soul and body, a kind of prayer which the Apostles were accustomed to use, as we learn from many passages of the Acts and from the Apostle [Paul] (*Catechismus ex Decr. Conc. Trid., Pars IV,* c. 8, *quae ratio in orando requiratur,* II, p. 368; *Catechism of the Council of Trent,* McHugh and Callan, p. 497).

346. PROV. COUNCIL OF VIENNA (1858). Assembling large numbers of the faithful to offer praise and thanks to God is an efficacious means for nourishing and strengthening the spirit of piety. As fire spreads when new flames are added to it, so our faith and devotion increase by the example of the Christian people gathered together to pray to the Lord. Moreover, the human race has the sacred duty of publicly and corporately paying homage to the Creator of all goods (*Decr.,* tit. 4, c. 1, *de divino cultu publico et pietatis Christianae operibus, CL* 5:177).

Common and public worship

347. PROV. COUNCIL OF COLOGNE (1860). In countless passages and with great force, Sacred Scripture inculcates how serious is man's duty of worshiping God. And certainly it could not be sufficiently commended that man acknowledge the Supreme Majesty of God and honor him by devoted submission of soul, for a more just title than that by which we are obliged to render such homage is simply unthinkable. The Supreme Majesty of God shines forth, and man is caught up in it by virtue of his soul and his body, since both are gifts from God. Moreover, it is only right that he who is to be made wholly, body and soul, partaker of heavenly joy, should merit the same with his whole being, soul and body. Nor can that be true and sincere worship which remains locked away in the confines of the heart and which never breaks forth externally. What is not kindled and roused by outward acts can-

not long be fostered in the mind. Public worship, too, must be joined to that which is internal and external, because man, made a member of society, and a religious society at that, owes honor to God and good example to his fellow man. This public worship in common, which the Catholic Church, divinely instructed, has so strenuously fostered and promoted since its very beginning, and which the Christians of the first centuries so zealously and courageously sought to offer to God that they were not deterred even by the danger of death, must be all the more stressed by shepherds of souls because of the widespread religious indifference which tries to hold it up to ridicule and destroy it (*Decr.*, tit. 2, c. 19, *de cultu divino sacrisque caeremoniis, CL* 5:355).

348. POPE ST. INNOCENT I (d. 417). For, as you know well, we accomplish more by prayers in common and those recited in alternating choirs than by individual and private prayers (*Ep. 10, Aurelio et Augustino episc., PL* 20:513).

349. PROV. COUNCIL OF ALBI (France, 1850). Because God created all things for himself, certainly the first and greatest commandment is that we adore him in spirit and truth (cf. John 4:24), love him with all our heart, and serve him faithfully. On the observance of this precept depends not only what is for God's glory and honor, but also the happiness of the individual person and of society. If it were observed faithfully, all would easily be drawn to the fulfilment of other commandments (cf. *Catechism, Conc. Trid., Pars III,* c. 4, *De tertio Dei praecepto,* II, p. 293). Contempt and forgetfulness of this law shatters and overthrows the foundation of the whole moral order: it unleashes all evils on peoples, especially darkness of mind, moral corruption, and unrestrained greed for temporal possessions. It breaks asunder the bonds of all societies, religious, civil, and even domestic (*Decr.*, tit. 4, *de cultu divino fovendo, CL* 4:424).

350. PROV. COUNCIL OF AVIGNON (1849). All know well into what a profound abyss of evil today's society has been plunged: in it all principles of order have been called into question; the very foundations of family life and property rights are shaken. In their desire to offer a remedy for the situation let priests, the ministers of God, not seek elsewhere for the causes of these great evils than in forgetfulness of God and neglect of the worship due to him. It follows of necessity that everything must totter, since the rights of Divine Majesty, to which all honor and glory is owed, and whose supreme government over himself man is bound to acknowledge and profess, have not merely been violated but impudently trampled upon. Hence priests prompted by zeal for the divine law are to neglect no means by which people may be led to know, venerate, and adore God, in spirit indeed, for the Spirit is God, and it behooves those who adore him to do so *in spirit and in truth* (John 4:24), but also by external manifestation of the interior

worship. It is highly improper that men who take pride in paying their respects to the majesty of earthly princes with expressions of deep reverence, should disdain to show their profound sentiments, their love and veneration for the majesty of the Supreme God.

But let these same pastors of souls particularly bear in mind that while it is their duty to exhort others to God's adoration, they must strengthen their preaching by example, showing by their own reverence, piety, and accurate observance of the rites in performing their sacred duties, and by their intense zeal in beautifying the churches, how greatly the Supreme Lord of heaven, who dwells in our temples, is to be honored (*Decr.*, tit. 2, c. 1, *de divino cultu, CL* 4:327).

The Divine Office

351. PROV. COUNCIL OF PRAGUE (1860). A. All must consider as their first duty the religious performance of the divine praises, for from the Work's excellence and dignity monasteries are ennobled above others; it is that by which they are turned to God without interruption like Moses on the holy mountain, whereas in the valley below others must carry on the warfare against the enemy of salvation (*Decr.*, tit. 7, c. 3, *de obligationibus regularium, CL* 5:575). B. Rising at night, let us all keep watch; let us always meditate on the psalms, and with one voice sweetly sing hymns to the Lord. And when the darkness of the night is waning and the light shines forth, let us humbly pray to the Lord of all things. . . . In this way may the praise of all who chant the Office in this whole province be full and joyful, truly a fitting jubilation of the mind (*ibid.*, tit. 1, c. 5, *de sanctificatione clericorum*, p. 422).

352. COUNCIL OF SENS (France, 1528). Let it be the great care of priests and clerics to invite others to devotion and stir up in them the spirit of compunction by their moderate and fitting gravity of the chanting of the Office (c. 17, *Mansi* 32:1190).

353. POPE BENEDICT XII (d. 1342). Although it is adequately provided both in the Rule of St. Benedict and in other laws how monks are to assemble in churches, monasteries, and other conventual establishments for the divine offices, both for the day and the night hours, and how they are to sing at the same . . . We ordain that all monks must assemble for these sacred services with gravity and proper decorum, with humility and devotion, and celebrate them with devotion, slowly, distinctly, becomingly, reverently, not slurring over syllables or cutting words short . . . but attending to the divine utterances with complete dedication. . . . For the rest, those who cannot come to the choir or the church at the proper hours because they are engaged in works of piety (with the required permission) must, as far as is possible, gather together as groups in an appropriate place at the prescribed

hours and say the Divine Office properly, and thus fulfil their daily allotted service (*Const. Apost. Summi Magistri*, c. 27, 20 Jun., 1336. *Ordinationes et reformationes pro bono regimine monachorum Nigrorum O.S.B., BR* 4:382).

354. COUNCIL OF BASLE (1431–1439). Every man who bears the name of Christian is under obligation to praise and glorify his Creator. This is particularly true of religious who are bound more than others by this sacred duty because of their profession. Hence they must bestow their worthiest efforts on sacred worship in order to derive therefrom rich graces in this life and the reward of eternal happiness in the next. For these reasons we establish and ordain that the Divine Office, both in the Night and Day Hours, shall everywhere, but more particularly in choir, be performed devoutly by all the monks at the appointed hours, as prescribed in the Rule of the holy Father Benedict. The Office shall be prayed with reverence, seriousness of conduct, and careful, complete pronouncing of the words. It is to be recited slowly, and with the required pauses. All discordant noises, and those made by the student body, are to be excluded from the reading and singing (*Stat. et ordinationes ad monachos congregationis Mellicensis directae, ex manuscr. Salisburgensi*).

355. PROV. COUNCIL OF UTRECHT (1865). The passage, *Before prayer prepare thy heart* (Eccles. 18:23, Douay version), must be understood as commended chiefly to all who have the duty of praying the Divine Office. Let them zealously and diligently consider how great is its dignity. They are appointed by the Church, in whose name they act in fulfilling the Canonical Hours, to be the intercessors for the people; more than that, in rendering the due tribute of praise they are associated with the angelic choir.

They are to recite the divine psalmody at a fitting time and in a proper place; they should direct their whole effort not only in order to make their external attitude of body and general reverence harmonize with the sacred nature of what they are doing, but also to lift their minds to God and offer praise to the Divine Majesty worthily, attentively and devoutly, in psalms, hymns, and canticles.

They are to follow with great care the admonition of St. Augustine: "If the Psalm prays, pray; if it sighs, sigh; if it expresses joy, rejoice; if it hopes, hope; if it fears, fear . . ." (*Enarr. in Ps. 30, Serm. 3*, § 1, *PL* 36:248).

The most excellent of all are the prayers pronounced by us in the Sacrifice of the Mass and in the Canonical Hours, which we do not choose for ourselves, but which God, through the Church, proposes and offers for fostering our spirit of religion and for imparting his mercy to us. If we cultivate a heartfelt attachment to them, these prayers certainly furnish choice food for our soul. Freed by them from earthly desires and lifted up to things heavenly, we can in all sincerity say with David: *You have loosed my bonds. To you will I offer the sacrifice of thanksgiving, and I will call upon the name of the Lord. My vows to the Lord I will pay in the presence of all his people, in the courts of the house of the Lord, in your midst, O Jerusalem* (Ps. 115: 8–10; *Decr.*, tit. 8, c. 2, *de Missae celebratione et horarum canonicarum recitatione, CL* 5:902).

356. PROV. COUNCIL OF COLOCZA (Hungary, 1863). For whom is it more appropriate to be a man of prayer than for him who has been chosen to represent the whole world by interceding with God, so that standing between the porch and the altar, he prays and laments for his own sins and those of the people? (cf. Joel 2:17.) Let them unite meaning to the words they use, affection to the understanding, and exultation to affection. For they are not alone, but the whole Church prays in common with them, and unites their voice to that of the angels, who praise God unceasingly, thus making the Work of prayer performed on earth a prelude to the heavenly psalmody. . . .

The prayerbook [which contains the Divine Office] is by far the most excellent book of all for its antiquity, the integration of its parts, the arrangement of the Psalms, and their adaptation to the Church year. Through this book heaven and earth are joined in friendly union, the blessed spirits of heaven and the souls of the saints are venerated with devotion, the suffering Church receives solace and support, and the ministers of the Church Militant enter into a sacred covenant for mutual assistance and praise of God (*Decr.*, tit. 4, c. 10, *de Breviario, CL* 5:678, 677).

357. POPE CLEMENT XIV (d. 1774). It behooves religious to cultivate a great love for [the Divine Office], for such devotion makes them rivals of the holy Sion, of those blessed spirits, that is, who continually chant the divine praises in the heavenly Jerusalem. When the signal has sounded, let all respond promptly, take part humbly, chant with the others in a reverent manner, and piously reflect on what they are chanting. Let there be one common voice, and that a voice of harmony, one pause of uniform observance, one spirit, one heart, one mind addressed to the merciful God . . . so that the faithful who hear you are touched with remorse and their hearts directed to God (*Const. Apost. In vinea Domini,* § 10, 4 Jul., 1772, *confirmatio decr. pro Cappuccinis prov. Subalpinae, BR* 5:462).

358. SWABIAN CONGR. OF ST. JOSEPH (statutes approved by Benedict XIII, 1725). The celebration of the Divine Office, which our holy Father Benedict designates with the special title of "the Work of God" is by far the most excellent among the duties which our Rule and our profession demand of us. From it shines forth the distinctive happiness and the great dignity of our vocation, in that what is the proper function

of the heavenly spirits has been made our daily occupation, namely to praise God continually, as do the angels, to take our place before him day and night, and to sing his glories with heartfelt devotion and joyous words of praise. By God's singular gift we are granted in this vocation that one only request which David, the most devoted King, petitioned: to dwell in the house of the Lord all the days of our life, to gaze on the loveliness of the Lord and contemplate his Temple (cf. Ps. 26:4).

We are to direct all zeal and diligence in order to attain this goal: to perform the Divine Office with the worthiest devotion of which we are capable, and manifest our gratitude for the great favor by which the Divine Majesty daily condescends to admit us into his presence. The great care and solicitude with which our holy Father Benedict sought the perfection of divine worship is evident: he devotes no fewer than seventeen chapters to defining the manner of fulfilment and the times for celebrating the Divine Office.

In the spirit of his law, therefore, the abbot and all superiors must place concern for sacred worship foremost among their cares, and by every means possible see that in their monasteries the recitation of the Canonical Hours be daily performed to the glory of the Divine Majesty at the proper time, attentively, devoutly, to the edification of outsiders, and with no tolerance for confusion and error. They will also be zealous in seeing to it that the rubrics of the Breviary, as well as the rites and ceremonies prescribed by our Congregation for the celebration of the Divine Office are observed exactly by all (*Const. et declar., Pars I, Praef. et* c. 1, *punctum* 1, fol. 1).

359. CASSINESE CONGR. (approved 1409). Those who are to read or sing must go over the lessons and prepare the books in good time. Both in choir and in the refectory they are to read in a loud, clear voice, so that they may be understood by all unto edification and spiritual profit. This is all the more to be observed in the celebration of Mass, lest our priests cause scandal rather than instill sentiments of devotion in the hearts of their neighbors by reason of their excessive and unbecoming speed. The superiors are to exercise all vigilance in checking on this matter, and severely reprimand those who disregard these regulations. Let them see to it that the monastic inflections be observed also in the Gospels, Epistles, and other sung excerpts, so that uniformity in chant and ceremonies will be practiced by all. He who has disobeyed will, in punishment for a first offense, eat off the floor of the refectory; * for subsequent violations he will be subject to graver penances according

* This is not so bad as the literal translation of the Latin text may lead some to imagine. Personal experience (not at Montecassino—and for other infractions), as well as abundant observation show that the phrase has the following meaning: A tray with the full monastic meal is placed on a stool in the center of the refectory, and the monk under penance eats in a kneeling position in the sight of the whole community. [*Tr.*]

to the superior's judgment (*Declar. in c. 47 RSB;* in: *Regula S. Benedicti Abbatis, Monachorum Patriarchae, cum Declar. et Const. Patrum Congr. Casinensis, Motu Proprio confirmatis a SS. D.N. Innocentio XI, Papa,* 1680. *Typis Rev. Camerae Apostolicae,* 1680, p. 89).

360. CONGR. OF HIRSCHAU (approved by Pope St. Greg. VII, circa 1083). When the signal for a regular hour is heard during recreation, the monk in the cloister will not complete the word he has on his lips, but will observe silence forthwith, and betake himself to prayer (*Const. Hirsaugienses S. Wilhelmi abb., Lib. I,* c. 63, *PL* 150:992).

361. CONGR. OF STRASBURG (1624). We must make it a matter of principle to participate in the divine praises with vigor and purity of intention: with vigor in the sense that we are to stand before the Lord reverently and zealously, being neither lazy nor drowsy nor yawning, not sparing the voice nor cutting syllables in half, not passing over whole words, not pronouncing what we recite with weak and delicate voices, so that it sounds like something recited by women, . . . but giving expression to the utterances of the Holy Spirit with manly voice and disposition; with purity of intention in the sense that while we are engaged in the sacred chant we think of nothing else than what we are singing. At that time the Holy Spirit will not be pleased with whatever else we may offer at the expense of neglecting that which we are under obligation to perform.

Let us sing together, make the pauses in unison, always paying attention to one another. Do not stand in choir supporting your head on your hand, or leaning it to one side, or holding it lifted up on high, but bowed down modestly, with the eyes cast down or directed to your book, or to anything else that necessarily engages your attention. Never stand in choir with your feet spread apart. Do not keep your hands hanging in a slovenly attitude, but hold them properly folded under your scapular (*Declar. in c. 19 RSB,* fol. 25).

362. THE BREVIARY. O Lord, open my mouth that I may bless your Holy Name. Cleanse my heart of all vain, evil, and wandering thoughts; enlighten my understanding, kindle my affections, that I may pray to you, and praise you with attention and devotion, and may worthily be heard before the presence of your Divine Majesty. Through Christ our Lord. Amen. Lord, in union with that divine intention wherewith you yourself praised God while you were on earth, I offer these Hours to you (*Oratio ante Divinum Officium. Breviar. Monastic.,* 1:lx).

Chant unites us with the angels

363. ROMAN MISSAL. A. It is truly meet and just, right and availing unto salvation, that we should at all times and in all places give thanks unto you, O holy Lord, Father Almighty and everlasting God (*Praef. de SSma. Trinitate, Miss. Rom.,* p. 300). B. And therefore with the

angels and archangels, with thrones and dominations, and with all the heavenly hosts, we sing a hymn to your glory, saying without ceasing: *Holy, Holy, Holy!* (*Praef. de Nativitate Dni.*, p. 273.) C. Through whom the angels praise your Majesty, the dominations worship it, and the powers stand in awe. The heavens and the heavenly hosts, with the blessed seraphim join together in celebrating their joy. With these we pray you to join our voices also, while we say in humble praise: *Holy, Holy, Holy!* (*Praef. de Quadr.*, p. 281). D. The angels and archangels sing your glory, as do the cherubim also and the seraphim, never ceasing to cry out as with one voice: *Holy, Holy, Holy!* (*Praef. de SSma. Trinitate*, p. 301.)

364. ROMAN BREVIARY.

That abode of the blessed,
Resounds forever with praises;
And with ceaseless song extols the Triune God;
To it we rivals of holy Sion,
Are joined by virtue of our song.*

365. MONASTIC BREVIARY.

To you, O Christ, splendor of the Father,
You who are our life and strength of soul,
In the presence of the angels we sing our praises
With words and solemn promises,
Alternating from side to side of the choir.†

366. MONASTIC MISSAL. With his whole being he [David, applied to St. Benedict] loved his Maker and daily had his praises sung; he added beauty to the feasts and solemnized the seasons of each year with string music before the altar, providing sweet melody for the Psalms, so that when the Holy Name was praised, before daybreak the sanctuary would resound (*Epistola Missae votivae de S.P.N. Benedicto*, 18 Jul., *Missae propriae et Kalendarium*, p. 28).

367. ROMAN BREVIARY. With all our heart and soul, let us sing praise to Christ on this solemn feast-day of Mary, the mighty Mother of God (*In Nativ. B.V.M.*, 8 Sept., *Antiph. IV ad Laudes, Breviarium Rom.*, 4:585).

368. COUNCIL OF AACHEN (816). The great concern of chanters must be not to disfigure with vices but rather to embellish with humility and chastity, with sobriety and the ornaments of other virtues the gift bestowed on them from heaven. May their chant lift the hearts of the

* *Hymn. ad Laudes*, vers. 2, *Commune Dedicationis Ecclesiae, Breviar. Rom.* 1:87*.

† *In Dedicatione S. Michael. Archangeli, hymn. ad Vesp., Breviar. Monastic.* 2:647.

faithful who attend services to mindfulness and love of heavenly things, not by the sublimity of the words alone, but also by the beauty of the singing itself. . . . The Psalms should be recited in church not rapidly, nor with voices that are too high, or too loud, or lacking in harmony, but rhythmically, clearly, and in compunction of heart. In this way their recitation will fill with sweetness the minds of those who pray them, and will be pleasing to the ears of those who hear them (*Concilii Aquisgranensis, Lib. I, qui est de institutione canonicorum,* c. 137, *Mansi* 14:241).

369. ST. CHRODEGANG (d. 766). Such individuals are to be appointed for reading, chanting, and reciting the psalter in church, who will fulfil the debt of praise to the Lord not in a proud manner, but humbly, so that the appeal of what is read or sung will touch the heart of the learned and teach those who are not so well instructed (*ibid.,* c. 133, p. 238).

370. POPE JOHN XXII (d. 1334). With learning and authority the holy Fathers of the Church have decreed that in the offices of divine praise which we offer as the submission of homage due to God, all minds be intent on seeing to it that the pronunciation be not defective and that the chanting of the calm and peaceful melodies be performed with modesty and gravity. For we read: "From their lips came sweet sounds" (*Commune Dedicationis Eccl., Resp. I ad Matutin., Breviar. Monastic.* 1:168*).

It is indeed a sweet sound that comes from the mouths of the chanters, because it is through the pronouncing of words that they welcome him into their own heart and through their chant that they stir up the devotion of others, for him. It is precisely for this purpose of kindling the devotion of the faithful that the chanting of the psalmody in the churches of God is prescribed. To achieve this same end, the Day and Night Hours, and the solemnity of the Mass are constantly sung by the clergy and the faithful according to compositions that are solemn in nature, but varied in expression, so that whereas they have cause for pleasure in diversity, they also find their delight in solemnity.

Now certain disciples of the new school, in their great concern for accurate measurement of time, are turning their attention to a new system of notes; in so doing they have taken it upon themselves to prepare new compositions which they prefer to the singing of the ancient melodies. The Church's texts are now sung in "semibreves" and "minimas," and with grace notes of repercussion; the melodies are broken up with "hochetis"; * they are made to glide along smoothly

* The peculiar breaking up of a melody among two voices . . . *Guillaume de Machaut, Great religious composers,* by Siegmund Levarie. N.Y.: Sheed and Ward, 1954, p. 33.

with "discanti" [two parts]; in some instances they are filled up with "triplis" [three parts] and "motectis."

Meanwhile these practices have led to the result that they have come to look down upon the principles of the Antiphonary and the Gradual: by reason of the greater number of notes they employ, the simple, modest ascending notes and well-regulated descending notes of plain chant, by which the character and theme (mode) is emphasized, are thrown into utter confusion. . . . We hasten to cast out and banish all such [abuses] from the Church of God (*Extravag. commun. Lib. III,* tit. 1, *de vita et honestate clericorum CJC* Richter 2:1169; *Romita, Jus Musicae Liturgicae,* Turin: Marietti, 1936, p. 47; *White List of the Society of St. Gregory of America,* ed. 4, N.Y., 1954, p. 3; H. E. Woodridge, *The Oxford History of Music,* London: Oxford Univ. Press, 1929, 1:294 f.).

Gregorian chant

371. PROV. COUNCIL OF COLOGNE (1860). After the many corruptions that have been introduced into sacred music, no one will readily deny that the most ancient chant, which is called Gregorian, is truly ecclesiastic and the very source of all the Church's chant, not to be supplanted by any other. Those who possess great skill and authority do not deny that Gregorian chant possesses something holier and more sublime than all the varieties of composition which have been introduced through the centuries, and which are employed by non-sacred or profane music. We prescribe and command, therefore, that Gregorian chant be restored to its rightful place, and be cultivated more and more. . . . This is not a matter to be dealt with superficially. Unless a person is thoroughly trained in ecclesiastical and religious law, and acquainted with the mysteries of the kingdom of heaven, he can make no real progress in sacred music, nor will he be able to promote its cause or teach it. Hence we ordain and command that in cathedral and collegiate churches . . . training centers of chant . . . be set up in which men are to be appointed teachers who are well trained in the sacred sciences and disciplines and are genuinely pious. This is to be done so that the tradition of sacred chant, which has been interrupted, unfortunately, for too long a time, can be restored, and its proper and holy principles and the correct manner of singing it be taught in all the churches of the dioceses (*Decr., Pars II,* tit. 2, c. 20, *de cantu ecclesiastico, CL* 5:357).

372. POPE PIUS IX (d. 1878). Gregorian chant is to be taught to the exclusion of all other methods of singing (*Litt. Apost. quibus Seminarium Pium instituitur,* tit. 5, *Acta Pii IX* 1:485).

373. POPE BENEDICT XIV (d. 1758). Nothing is more inimical or harmful for the Church's discipline than to perform the divine psal-

mody in the churches of God in a contemptuous or negligent manner. . . . It follows of necessity that diligent care must be exercised that the chant be not sung too swiftly or recited more rapidly than is proper; that the pauses be made at their proper places; and that one side of the choir does not begin a verse of a Psalm until the other side has completed the preceding verse. . . . In order for the sacred text to be sung in unison, the choir is to be directed by those who are trained in ecclesiastical chant, which is also known as *cantus firmus,* and plainsong. This is the chant on which St. Gregory the Great, Our predecessor, bestowed great effort in directing and drawing up according to the rules of musical art. . . . This is the chant which stimulates the hearts of the faithful to devotion and piety. It is also that which is more willingly heard by pious persons and is deservedly preferred to that which is called harmonic or measured. . . . The fact that this chant is accurately and lovingly employed by monks and sung in their functions, is the principal reason that the churches of regulars are attended more by the Christian people, as J. Eveillon has well remarked in his treatise: *De recta ratione psallendi,* c. 9, art. 9, p. 99: "In comparison with this plainsong and the poetic beauty of the simple psalmody, when it is properly rendered, all the titulation of musical composition is offensive to the ears of pious persons. This is the reason that the faithful abandon parish and collegiate churches and flock to those of monks who, making devotion their mistress in adoring God, sing reverently, modestly, and, as the Prince of Psalmists expressed the thought in ancient times, wisely; and with supreme reverence serve their Lord as Lord and God" *(Ep. Encycl. Annus qui,* § 2, 19 Febr., 1749, *Ben. XIV, Op. Om.* 17:17).

374. PROV. COUNCIL OF PRAGUE (1860). Gregorian chant is to be restored and fostered (*Decr.,* tit. 3, c. 7, *de cantu et musica sacra, CL* 5:475).

375. PROV. COUNCIL OF ROUEN (1850). Ecclesiastical chant is to be retained or restored after the manner of the Church's pristine dignity and simplicity. All . . . are to be exhorted to join their voices in piety and simplicity to the choirs of angels and to the groups of priests chanting the divine praises (*Decr. II, de cultu Dei et sanctorum,* nn. 5–6, *CL* 4:521).

The power of plain chant

376. PROV. COUNCIL OF BORDEAUX (1850). The chant which is truly and properly ecclesiastical is plainsong or *cantus firmus,* instituted and marvelously adapted to the purpose of lifting the minds of the hearers to adoration of the Divine Majesty and to the fervor of devotion. . . . By its subdued and gently modulated melody the mind of the singers is nourished with the sweet appeal of the words, and the ears of those

who are listening are pleased with the recitation (*Decr.,* tit. 2, c. 5, *de cantu eccl.,* n. 1, *CL* 4:561).

377. PROV. COUNCIL OF BOURGES (1850). Mindful of the pleasure and spiritual benefit the faithful derive from skillful and religious rendition of Gregorian chant, the Provincial Synod earnestly desires that all take a holy pride in devoting themselves to this sacred art (*Decr.,* tit. 4, n. 1, *CL* 4:1111).

Proper conduct in chanting

378. CONGR. OF MOUNT OLIVET (Olivetan Benedictines, approved by Pope John XXII, 1324). In choir no one is ever to laugh, speak, keep his gaze lifted up for extended periods of time, read books or letters, give cause for laughing, or use a voice out of harmony with the singers. Rather, let all be so composed as to facial expression, actions, and general conduct that their attitude in singing will be an example of reverence, humility, devotion, and attention to prayer. While one side of the choir is chanting, those who are not at the moment singing will remain silent and attentive, and not begin to sing until the other side has finished. They are to use neither falsetto nor counterpoint, as it is called, but plain chant only. They will observe the monastic order of seniority and avoid all confusion in standing before the lecturn. The abbot will take the lead in these observances. Anyone acting to the contrary is to be corrected with a sharp reprimand (*Const., Pars II., ad c. 20 RSB,* p. 40; *CR* 5:36).

Holy Eucharist, Mass

379. ROMAN MISSAL. Grant to us, we beseech you, Lord, worthily to frequent these sacred mysteries: for as often as this saving Victim is offered up, so often is furthered the work of our redemption (*Dom. IX p. Pent., Secreta, Miss. Rom.,* p. 472).

380. COUNCIL OF TRENT. Our Savior . . . wished that this sacrament should be received as the spiritual food of souls (cf. Matt. 26:26 f.), whereby they may be nourished and strengthened, living by the life of him who said: *He who eats me, he also shall live because of me* (John 6:58; *Sess. 13, de Euch.,* c. 2, *de ratione institutionis, Can. et decr.,* Richter, p. 64; Schroeder, *Trent,* p. 74).

381. COUNCIL OF BASLE (1431). Relying on the authority of the Constitution of Pope Benedict XII (*Const. Apost. Summi Magistri,* § 27, 20 Jun., 1336, *BR* 4:382), we prescribe that all monks who are not priests must confess at least once a week, and receive Holy Communion especially on Sundays and the principal feasts (*Stat. et ordinationes ad monachos congregationis Mellicensis directae, ex manuscr. Salisburgensi*).

Purpose of the liturgy

382. COUNCIL OF TRENT. And since the nature of man is such that he cannot without external means be raised easily to meditation on divine things, holy Mother Church has instituted certain rites, namely, that some things in the Mass be pronounced in a low tone and others in a louder tone. She has likewise, in accordance with apostolic discipline and tradition, made use of ceremonies, such as mystical blessings, lights, incense, vestments, and many other things of this kind, whereby both the majesty of so great a sacrifice might be emphasized and the minds of the faithful excited by those visible signs of religion and piety to the contemplation of those most sublime things which are hidden in this Sacrifice (*Sess. 22, de Sacrificio Missae,* c. 5, *de Missae caeremoniis et ritibus, Can. et decr.,* Richter, p. 126; Schroeder, *Trent,* p. 147).

383. PROV. COUNCIL OF UTRECHT (1865). The whole liturgy of the Church serves the high purpose of giving testimony of our subjection to God as well as our gratitude and love for him; of publicly professing what we believe; of elevating our mind by visible signs to the meditation of invisible things and of inflaming it with the fire of devotion; of binding the members of the Church more closely and of putting Catholic unity before the eyes of all; and, finally, of manifesting the religion established by Christ the Lord—for just as it consists solely of the truth of faith, so also does it shine only by the splendor and majesty of true worship (*Decr.,* tit. 5, c. 1, *de cultus necessitate ac decore, CL* 5:848).

Meditation

384. POPE CLEMENT XIV. We exhort you, beloved brethren, to be vigilant always in prayer, and especially in that form which is called meditation. By meditation, St. Laurence Justinian tells us, temptation is banished, sadness put to flight, virtue recovered, fervor kindled, . . . and the flame of divine love intensified (*De casto connubio Verbi et animae,* c. 22, *Op. Om.* 1:247). This is the lamp by which your mind is enlightened, the fire at which your heart is warmed in God, the food by which your soul is nourished. In a word, "consideration" [meditation], says St. Bernard, governs the affections, directs action, and corrects excesses (*De Consideratione, Lib. I,* c. 7, *PL* 182:737). Draw near to it, brethren, and be enlightened. Pray without ceasing, and your way of life and the virtues which you will build up will be excellent. . . . Nor is this manner of prayer to be neglected because of other exercises, even though they are pious and religious, nor can the superior dispense the whole community from the prescribed meditation. Even with regard to individual brethren, the superior is to act with great prudence.

Reasons for dispensing from prayer are rarely justifiable. One may say: "I cannot fast, I cannot rise at night for the singing of the psalter." But can he ever say: "I cannot be brought heart and mind into the presence of God, and induced to adore his Majesty"? Those who are truly spiritual know what the royal Psalmist meant in saying: *I will bless the Lord at all times* (Ps. 33:2). . . . *Bless the Lord, all his works, everywhere in his domain. Bless the Lord, O my soul* (Ps. 102:22). . . . Believe Us, brethren, if the fervor of prayer [meditation] grows cool, the piety and zeal of the religious is gradually lessened, and the holy institute destroyed. . . . When a man neglects to be lifted above himself in prayer, God permitting it, he is cast down below his proper level by the worst crimes (*Const. Apost. In vinea Domini,* § 9, 4 Jul., 1772, *Confirmatio decr. pro Cappuccinis Prov. Subalpinae, BR* 5:461).

Precept and virtue of prayer

385. CATECHISM OF THE COUNCIL OF TRENT. A. In the first place the necessity of prayer should be insisted upon [by the pastor, preacher]. Prayer is a duty not only recommended by way of counsel, but also commanded by obligatory precept. Christ the Lord declared this when he said: *We must pray always* (Luke 18:1; Sir. 18:22). This necessity of prayer the Church points out in the prelude, if we may so call it, which she prefixes to the Lord's Prayer: "Admonished by salutary precepts and taught by divine instruction, we presume to say: Our Father . . ." (*Pars IV,* c. 1, § 2, *Usus orandi ad salutem necessarius est,* p. 353; *Catechism of the Council of Trent,* tr. by McHugh, O.P., and Callan, O.P., p. 478). B. Another pleasing and valuable fruit of prayer is that it is heard by God. "Prayer is the key of heaven," says St. Augustine. "Prayer ascends, and the mercy of God descends. High as are the heavens, and low as is the earth, God hears the voice of man" (*Serm. 47, In Append., de Beato Tobia,* § 1, *PL* 39:1838). In a word, there is in prayer an accumulation of spiritual joy; and hence the Lord said: *Ask and you shall receive, that your joy may be full* (John 16:24; *ibid.,* c. 2, § 2, p. 354; McHugh and Callan, p. 479).

386. ROMAN MISSAL. May you, O God, who have prepared for those who love you such good things as eye has not seen, pour into our hearts so great a love for you, that, loving you above all things, we may obtain your promises, which exceed all that we can desire (*Dom. V p. Pascha, Oratio, Miss. Rom.,* p. 412).

The monk: a man of God, of the Church, of the Holy Roman See

387. POPE PIUS IX (d. 1878). Because the monk is a "man of God," as you have so clearly pointed out, he is, by that reason, a man also of the Church, and in a special way a man of that See established by God for governing the Church and for being the mistress of truth and the

center of unity for all (*Bref a mons. Freppel, l'évêque d'Angers a l'occasion de son discours sur l'ordre monastique prononcé au service anniversaire du T.-R.P. Dom Prosper Guéranger, abbé de Solesmes, La Semaine du fidèle,* 1876, pp. 430–431).

388. POPE ST. GREGORY VII (d. 1085). Prompted by divine love, We have chosen to show Our love of your monastery in a particular manner, to aid it, and defend it against all attacks, inasmuch as it is in a special way attached to the Roman See (*Lib. VII,* ep. 8, *ad monachos Massilienses, PL* 148:552).

389. POPE URBAN II (d. 1099). A. Although the favor of Apostolic charity must come to the assistance of all the faithful in their petitions and necessities, its kindness and indulgence are especially shown to those whom the Church of Rome joyfully regards as her favored children. Among such devoted sons the Congregation of Cluny, more richly endowed with the divine charism (charity) than others, shines upon earth like another sun (*Ep. 214, in qua monasterii Cluniac. libertates, et privilegia confirmat augetque, PL* 151:486). B. We beg you to impress vividly upon the entire community of holy brethren to pray for Us and for Holy Church, that Almighty God in his mercy will deign to restore to her pristine state her who is now exposed to very grave dangers. Know that We consider that this responsibility rests more specially with you than with all others (*Ep. 2, ad Hugonem abb. Cluniacens.,* col. 285). C. Although by reason of the authority and benevolence of the Apostolic See Our obligation extends to all parts of Holy Church, the urge of charity inclines Us more strongly toward communities and persons who have in a particular manner remained intimately attached to the Church of Rome, and whom We know to excel in deeper sentiments of religious devotion (*Ep. 66, ad Petrum abb. Cavensem,* col. 347). D. With all the powers of mind and heart you should, beloved sons in Christ, most earnestly and devotedly long for perfection according to the demands of regular discipline. Especially should you strive to observe the venerable decrees of the Church of Rome, under whose patronage you are, with the Lord's approval, protected from every bond of submission . . . (*Ep. 129, monasterium Hirsaugiense sub protectione Sedis Apost. recipitur,* col. 403). E. Beyond all the general obligations of charity, beyond the unique prerogative of your monastery, which was established by the Lord as the cradle of all the monasteries of the West through the teachings on the monastic life by the lawgiver Benedict, the splendid good will which your community has always offered to the Holy Roman Church, even more particularly so in Our times, has placed Us under the obligation of deep gratitude to your monastery. Your abbey has always been and remains now the support of our poor, a sanctuary for those seeking refuge, an unwearingly offered haven of rest for those sons who have worn themselves out in

the service of the Apostolic See (*Ep. 219, Sacrum Casinense coenobium sub Ecclesiae protectione confirmat,* col. 492). F. Your blessed monastery has always in a particular manner remained intimately and devotedly bound to the Apostolic See, ever on the alert and with the offer of assistance in the time of persecution (*Ep. 247, Bulla pro Casinens. monasterio,* col. 515).

390. POPE PASCHAL II (d. 1118). . . . The constant oneness of charity by which you have clung steadfastly to the Apostolic See throughout all storms forcefully prompts Us to deep concern, nay, urges Us and compels Us to zealous action in providing for your tranquillity (*Ep. 34, ad Hugonem abb. Cluniac., PL* 163:56).

391. POPE GELASIUS II (d. 1119). The prudence in religion and the religious prudence of the monastery of Cluny, both before Our time and during the same, have placed the Church of Rome under serious obligation to it (*Ep. 8, ad Pontium abb. Cluniac., PL* 163:492).

392. POPE INNOCENT III (d. 1216). Because this venerable place has been the sole refuge for the children of the Church of Rome in their adversities and has persevered as a tirelessly offered haven of rest during the great prosperity of the Church, you have made Us beholden to your monastery of Montecassino (*Ep. 133, in qua abbatiae privilegia confirmat* (*Supplementum*), *PL* 217:186).

IV. WRITINGS OF SAINTS AND DOCTORS

Common prayer

393. ST. IGNATIUS, martyr, bp. of Antioch (d. 107). At your meetings there must be one prayer, one supplication, one mind, one hope in love, in joy that is flawless, that is Jesus Christ, who stands supreme (cf. Eph. 4:3–6; *Ep. ad Magnesios,* c. 7, *PG* 5:667; Kleist, S.J., p. 71).*

394. TERTULLIAN, priest of Africa (d. circa 245). We meet together as an assembly and a congregation as before God, as though we would in one body plead our cause to him by our prayers. This violence is pleasing to God (*Lib. apologetic. adversus gentes,* c. 39. *PL* 1:532).

395. ST. AMBROSE, bp. of Milan, Doctor of the Church (d. 397). A. The Lord said through Isaias, *Behold, I will lay a stone in the foundation of Sion* (Isa. 28:16). This means Christ as the foundation of the Church. For Christ is the object of the faith of all; but the Church is, as it were, the outward form of justice; she is the common right of all. For all she prays, for all in common she works, in the temptations of all is she tried (*De officiis ministrorum, Lib. I,* c. 29, n. 142, *PL* 16:70). B. Although they are indeed very small, many become great when

* The word "that" before "Jesus Christ," sums up the preceding clause. "That" is the whole, the true, the genuine Jesus Christ. Kleist, p. 128, note 24.

united in oneness of mind, and it is impossible that the prayers of many so united will not obtain their request (*In Ep. ad Rom.* [15:30], *In Append., PL* 17:186).

396. ST. AUGUSTINE, bp. of Hippo, Doctor of the Church (d. 430). A. Many members, therefore, of him, under one Head, our Savior himself, being united through the bond of love and peace . . . are one man; and of the same, as of one, many; the voice is ofttimes heard in the Psalms, and thus one cries out through all, because all in One are one (*Enarr. in Ps. 69,* § 1, *PL* 36:866). B. Our Lord Jesus Christ, the Son of God, prays for us and prays in us, and is prayed to by us. He prays for us as our Priest; he prays in us as our Head; he is prayed to by us as our God (*ibid., in Ps. 85,* § 1, *PL* 37:1081). C. What our spirit, that is to say our soul, is to our members, that the Holy Spirit is to the members of Christ, the Body of Christ, which is the Church (*Serm. 268, in die Pentecostes,* II, § 2, *PL* 38:1232).

397. ST. HILARY, bp. of Poitiers, Doctor of the Church (d. 368). Christ was so desirous for the harmony of peace among men that he assured them that all things which are to be prayed for to God would be granted if the prayers possess the merit of oneness and concord (*In Matt.,* c. 18 [vers. 19], § 9, *PL* 9:1021).

398. EMPEROR JUSTINIAN I (d. 565). If monks offer prayer to God for the Republic, lifting up hands that are pure, and [offering their prayer] with souls that are unstained, it is certain that the armies must fare well and the cities prosper. For God is propitious and benevolent. How can it be other than that everything will be in perfect peace and the observance of the laws; that the earth will produce its fruits and the sea furnish what it has to offer, since their prayers will draw God's benevolence on the entire Republic? Even the general welfare of the people will be more religious and prosperous, for they hold the purity of the monks' lives in reverence.

This united effort of all will mean that everyone is cooperating as far as possible, for these same results, and for the extirpation of all ill will. We are convinced that we are doing what is of benefit to the state in working for this higher goal and enlisting worthier and holier efforts, and harmonizing them with favorable conditions (*Novella 133, De monachis et sanctimonialibus et vita eorum,* c. 5, in: *Corpus Juris Civilis, III, Novella, recognovit Rudolphus Schoell; opus Schoellii morte interceptum, absolvit Guglielmus Kroll;* Berolini: apud Weidmannos, 1954, 3:674).

399. ST. BASIL THE GREAT, bp. of Caesarea in Cappadocia, Doctor of the Church (d. 378). A. The psalter is the one voice of the whole Church (*Hom. 1 in Ps. 1, In Append. PG* 31:1725). B. I call that the perfect community of life from which personal possession of all things whatsoever is excluded, which is free from dissension and all disturbance, as

well as of all striving against one another, and all discord. And in which, by way of contrast, all things are common—hearts, minds, bodies, and all the means we use to sustain life and offer worship: God possessed in common, the common performance of the works of piety, common welfare, trials borne in common, common labors, common rewards, and the crowns for the victory gained in struggles—where many are one, and the individual is not alone, but is one of many (*Const. monastic.*, c. 18, *ad canonicos in coenobio viventes,* n. 1, col. 1382). C. . . . Even prayer itself which does not come from persons praying together is much feebler, the Lord having declared that he will be in the midst if two or three call upon him with oneness of mind (cf. Matt. 18:20). The Lord even undertook the Incarnation in order that through the blood of his cross he might be a peacemaker both on earth and in heaven. As a result, because of all these things, we pray that our remaining days may be spent in peace, and we beg that our death may be in peace. For the sake of this peace, therefore, I have determined to leave no labor whatsoever undone, to omit nothing as too humble to say or to do, to take no account of the length of journeys, and to shrink from no other irksome trials, so that I may meet with the reward of the peacemaker. And if anyone follows us as we point out this way, that is excellent, and my prayer attains its end; but, if he draws away to the opposition, I shall not, in consequence, withdraw from my decision. But, each one himself on the day of retribution will recognize the fruits of his own labors (*Ep. 97, Senatui Tyanorum, PG* 32:494; *Way,* p. 215; Roy J. Deferrari 2:163 f.).

400. ST. JOHN CHRYSOSTOM, abp. of Constantinople, Doctor of the Church (d. 407). A. That one [the bishop] should entreat for many, is exceedingly bold and requires much confidence; but that many having met together should offer supplication for one is neither difficult nor burdensome. For everyone does this not trusting to his own virtue, but to that of the multitude, and to their unanimity, which God everywhere views with favor and in which he takes delight (*In Ep. II ad Thessalon.,* c. 3, Hom. 4, § 4, *PG* 62:491). B. Common prayer is the favorable moment for salvation, the means of achieving immortality of the soul, the rampart of the Church which cannot be broken down, the unshakable fortification; it strikes terror into demons, but is extremely beneficial to us (*De praecatione, Oratio 2, inter dubia, PG* 50:784). C. Do you wish to learn how great is the strength of prayer offered by the Church? *Peter was being kept in prison; but prayer was being made to God for him by the Church without ceasing* (Acts 12:5), and forthwith freed him from prison. Now, what could be stronger than this prayer which helps the pillar of the Church and its tower? . . . Do not say: "I scarcely dare pray for myself; how shall I make bold to pray for others?" For in the Church something greater is present, the prayers

of the priests, which are most powerful . . . If the petitions of those who are weak are joined with these, they mount to heaven with them (*Ecloga de oratione,* Hom. 2, *PG* 63:586). D. It is impossible for you to pray so well at home as you do in church, where there are so many fathers, and where the acclamations voiced by the blessed assembly is directed to God. You do not obtain the object of your prayers so well when you pray alone to the Lord as you do when you unite with your brethren. For in the latter case something new is realized, namely oneness of heart, concord, the bond of love and charity, and the powers of the priestly prayer are all united. For the priests preside over the assembly precisely in order that the prayers of the people, which are by nature weaker, may be lifted up to heaven united with those which are stronger. For that prayer has great force which is offered up in the united effort and persevering oneness of heart of a number of persons (*De incomprehensibili Dei natura,* Hom. 3, § 6, *PG* 48:725).

401. ST. ATHANASIUS, bp. of Alexandria, Doctor of the Church (d. 373). This was the better course [the assembly of all the worshipers in preference to isolated groups], for this showed the unanimity of the multitude: in this way God will readily hear prayer. For if, according to the promise of our Savior himself (cf. Matt. 18:20) where two or three shall agree about anything at all for which they ask, it shall be done for them, how shall it be when so great an assembly of people with one voice utter their "Amen" to God? (*Apologia ad Constantinum Imperatorem,* § 16, *PG* 25:615.)

402. CASSIODORUS, abbot of Vivarium in Calabria (d. circa 570). Throughout the whole Psalm [118] the chorus of all saints who have existed from the beginning of the world, who are now existing, and who are believed to come in the future, speaks out. Among these are found apostles, prophets, martyrs, confessors, members of ecclesiastical orders, and all who serve the Lord in holiness. . . . But the text always represents only one person as speaking, in order that the strength of unity may be recognized in the Church united in harmony (*Expos. in Ps. 118, Prooem., PL* 70:835).

403. ALCUIN OF YORK (d. 804). Great in God's sight is prayer offered in common, great the oneness of charity. It is far better to pray in common with the brethren, to eat with them, and sleep under the same roof with them than to remain with danger alone in a separate dwelling (*Ep. 16, ad fratres ecclesiae S. Petri, PL* 100:168).

404. ST. ANTONINUS, O.P., abp. of Florence (d. 1459). Prayer that is offered with the community is more quickly heard, for common prayer is more efficacious than that of the individual (*Summa Theol., Pars IV,* tit. 5, c. 8, de oratione, 4:206).

405. DENIS THE CARTHUSIAN, monk of Roermond (d. 1459). He who prays for all in the community shares in all the good works that are per-

formed, and the more a good is commonly bestowed, the more divinely is it bestowed. Hence every individual should humbly and fervently petition the prayers of others and beg them to pray for him. The more humbly and fervently we ask them to pray for us, the more we are made capable of the fruit of their prayer. More particularly is the intercession of devout and deeply virtuous men to be sought. Hence it is added: *For the unceasing prayer of a just man is of great avail* (Jas. 5:16; *Enarr. in c. 5 Ep. Cath. B. Jacobi,* art. 7, *Op. Om.* 13:609).

406. THOMAS À KEMPIS, canon regular (d. 1471). A cold lump of coal thrown on a blazing fire becomes hot and glowing: in like manner a tepid religious joined with one who is fervent and devout often becomes fervent himself (*Hortulus rosarum,* c. 1, *Op. Om.* 4:3).

Vocal prayer

407. ST. THOMAS AQUINAS, O.P., Doctor of the Church (d. 1274). A. We need to praise God with our lips, not for his sake indeed, but for our own sake; since by praising him our devotion is aroused toward him, according to Psalm 49:23: *He that offers praise as a sacrifice glorifies me; and to him that goes the right way I will show the salvation of God* [replacing the Douay wording]. And for as much as man, by praising God, ascends in his affections to God, by so much is he withdrawn from things opposed to God (*II–II.* q. 91, art. 1, *Utrum Deus sit ore laudandus, Op. Om.* 9:294; Am. ed. 2:1589). B. Wherefore whatever is useful in conducing to this result [arousing man's devotion to God] is becomingly adopted in the divine praises. Now it is evident that the human soul is moved in various ways according to various melodies of sound; . . . hence the use of music in the divine praises is a salutary institution (*ibid.,* art. 2, p. 295; p. 1590).

408. ST. LAURENCE JUSTINIAN, can. regular, protopatriarch of Venice (d. 1455). Vocal prayer is altogether commendable. By the testimony of experience we know that it is extremely useful as the introduction and guide to acquaintance with mental prayer, and to prayer generally that is offered in truth and in spirit (*De perfectionis gradibus,* c. 12, *Op. Om.* 2:446).

409. HUGH OF ST. CHER, O.P., cardinal (d. 1263). It is the duty of religious to praise God (*Sup. Ps. 34:8, Comment.* 2:88).

410. THOMAS À KEMPIS. A. How pleasing and praiseworthy is that gathering of men devoted chiefly to the praise of God, where there are as many resounding trumpets as there are voices cheerfully singing in choir (*Serm. ad novitios I, Op. Om.* 6:9). B. Nothing is more wholesome, nothing sweeter, nothing more pleasant than to praise God in hymns and Psalms (*ibid., Serm. 28,* p. 288). C. There is nothing better for you: nothing more salutary; nothing more delightful; nothing more agreeable; nothing more worthy; nothing more high-minded; nothing more

fruitful; nothing more perfect; nothing more blessed, than to love God most intensely and to praise him with all the ardor of which you are capable. This I will state a hundred times, and repeat a thousand more, there can be no effort more judicious, no undertaking that is loftier than to love and serve God (*Vallis liliorum,* c. 26, *Op. Om.* 4:109). D. Here on earth join all the saints in glorifying God whom the angels adore in heaven! In praising him you become like the angels (*Hortulus rosarum,* c. 19, *ibid.* p. 49). E. He who is indolent in performing the praises of God, or remains silent, or absents himself from choir, is not a friend of God nor a citizen of heaven (*De disciplina claustralium,* c. 8, *Op. Om.* 2:300).

411. ST. LAURENCE JUSTINIAN. Divine praise is a salutary sacrifice, a clean oblation, a sweet-smelling incense, an acceptable gift, a pleasing libation, a fragrant odor; a spotless host, especially when it is produced by purity of heart, cleanness of mind, ardor of desire, the secret recesses of humility, fervor of spirit, light of faith, knowledge of truth, purposes of charity, fulness of devotion, purity of conscience, contemplation of the heavenly fatherland, longing for the future life, and union with Eternal Wisdom (*De spirituali et casto Verbi animaeque connubio,* c. 25, *Op. Om.* 1:261).

412. ST. AUGUSTINE. To praise God is the salvation and joy of the soul . . . (*Lib. Meditationum,* c. 32, *In Append., PL* 40:925).

413. ST. BERNARD, abbot of Clairvaux, Doctor of the Church (d. 1153). The offering of praise, which is immolated to God, must have a threefold nature: it must be full of affection, that is, prayer in the manner that harmonizes with the words pronounced; it must be fruitful, so prayed that it will be an edification to him who beholds it; and complaisant, in the sense of being produced by the zeal for perfection, so that it will be pleasing to the Creator who freely granted it (*Lib. Sententiarum,* n. 14, *In Append., PL* 184:1158).

414. PHILIP OF HEINSBERG, bp. of Cologne (d. 1191). Monk: When our convent was invited to the mountain of Stromberg by Archbishop Philip, some of the provincials remonstrated with him because they were alarmed for their heirs. To these he made a good and worthy reply: "Would," he said, "that there were in every township of my diocese a convent of the just, who might praise God continually, and pray for me and those committed to my charge! So, I think, the condition of my province would be much better than it is now, for they would harm none, and would profit many" (*Dialogus miraculorum,* Dist. 4, c. 64, in: *Caesarii Heisterbacensis monachi Ord. Cisterc. Dialogus miraculorum . . . accurate recognovit Josephus Strange,* 2 v; Coloniae: Heberle, 1851, 1:233).

415. THOMAS À KEMPIS. The Divine Office was arranged as the work

and by the wisdom of the Holy Spirit (*De disciplina claustralium,* c. 8, *Op. Om.* 2:299).

416. ST. JOHN CHRYSOSTOM. Man is created for the purpose of praising God. The Lord demands nothing else in the same manner that he requires praise and thanksgiving of us. For that reason he made us rational beings and distinguished us from animals by our power of speech, so that we might praise and glorify him continually (*Comm. in Ps. 116*).*

417. ST. PETER DAMIAN, abbot of Fonte-Avellana, cardinal, Doctor of the Church (d. 1072). When we are hastening to the church to chant and pray, it is, if I may so describe it, as though we were marching into battle in the formation of soldiers. . . . The analogy from military life is a beautiful comparison, really, particularly at the night hours when the brethren, roused from sleep as by the sound of a trumpet, form ranks and in orderly battle-array, march together, inspired to readiness for the divine combat. The boys' wing of the army goes first; the troops of younger men are next, as though they were the infantry; and in the last place, following after them, the group of older men, the real strength in battle, to protect the whole army from the rear, lest anyone lie in ambush or a concealed enemy approach to attack. . . . Thus Christ's soldiers hasten to eat the heavenly manna. It is thus that the Israelite legions marched to take possession of the land flowing with milk and honey (cf. Josh. 1:1 f.). They hasten, as though to the sound of trumpets, to the tabernacle of the Covenant, there to partake of the banquet of the heavenly word, perform the sacrifice of praise in God's honor, and fulfil their vows (*Opusc. 13,* c. 17, *de significatione horarum, PL* 145:316).

418. NICETAS OF REMESIANA, bp. (d. after 402). What could be more profitable for us than the benefit we derive, what more pleasant than the delight we experience—for certainly we find delight in the Psalms, strength in the prayers, and nourishment in the readings that are inserted among them. Truly, as persons who enjoy a good meal are highly pleased with rich courses, so our souls are feasted with the numerous readings and hymns (*Opusc. 2, de psalmodiae bono,* c. 3, *PL* 68:374).

419. ST. BASIL THE GREAT. What, then, is more blessed than to imitate on earth the choirs of angels; hastening at the break of day to pray, to glorify the Creator with hymns and songs, and, when the sun is shining brightly and we return to our tasks, to accompany them everywhere with prayer, seasoning the daily work with hymns as food with salt? For,

* Wolter offers no other reference for this passage than that indicated. There is no such commentary under the exposition of the Psalms by Chrysostom. Similar statements, however, are quite frequent, e.g., in *Hom. 52 in Gen., PG* 54:460; *Expos. in Ps. 150, PG* 55:495 f. [*Tr.*]

the inspirations of the sacred songs give rise to a joyousness that is without grief (*Ep. 2, ad Gregorium Nazianzenum,* § 2, *PG* 32:226; Way, p. 7; Deferrari, 1:13).

420. ST. JOHN CHRYSOSTOM. A. Monks, those lights of the world, as soon as the sun is up, or rather, even long before its rise, leave their beds, healthy, and wakeful, and sober (for neither does any sorrow and care, nor headache and toil, nor multitude of business, nor any other such thing trouble them, for they live like the angels in heaven). Having risen then straightway from their bed cheerful and glad, and having made one choir, with the conscience bright, with one voice, all, as though only one mouth were speaking, sing hymns to the God of all, honoring him and thanking him for all his benefits, both particular and common. Let us put Adam aside for the moment and inquire what is the difference between angels and this company of them who on earth sing and say: *Glory to God in the highest, and on earth peace among men of good will* (Luke 2:14). Then, after they have sung these songs, they kneel down and entreat God, who was the object of their hymns and songs, for things to whose very suggestion some persons do not easily arrive. For they ask nothing of things present (since they have no regard for these); they plead only that they may stand with confidence before the fearful judgment seat, when the Only-Begotten Son of God comes to judge the living and the dead, and that no one of them may hear the fearful voice which will say: *I do not know you* (Matt. 25:12). They petition also that with pure conscience and many good deeds they may pass through this toilsome life, and sail over the stormy sea with a favorable wind. And he who is their father and ruler leads them in their prayers. After this, when they have risen up and finished those holy and continual prayers, at sunrise, they depart each one to his work, gathering from the same a large supply for the needy (*In Matt. Hom. 68,* § 3, *monachorum vita, PG* 58:644). B. We, therefore, need arms; and prayer is a powerful weapon. We need favorable winds; we need to learn everything, so as to go through the length of the day without shipwrecks and without wounds. For every single day the rocks are many, and often the boat strikes and is sunk. Therefore we have especially need of prayer early in the morning and at night (*In Ep. ad Hebr. 8:2,* Hom. 14, § 4, *PG* 63:116).

421. ST. JOHN CLIMACUS. Devote the first-fruits of your day to the Lord, because the whole day will belong to whoever gets the first start. It is worth hearing what an expert told me: "From my morning," he said, "I know the course of the whole day" (*Scala paradisi, Grad. 26, de discretione cogitationum, PG* 88:1035; Moore, n. 104, p. 217; Robert, p. 364).

422. ST. MACARIUS, monk (d. c. 390). Love the Divine Office of the

monastery above all else. He who desires to pray frequently will find the mercy of Christ more abundantly (*Reg. S. Macarii Alexandrini ad monachos,* n. 9, *CR* 1:20; *PL* 103:449).

423. CASSIODORUS. A. . . . so that any person who does not enjoy the pleasantness of this duty may with good reason believe that he is a stranger to the true life (*In Psalterium, Praef., PL* 70:10). B. What is more blessed than to be engaged now in doing what you hope to perform in the future blessedness? (*In Ps. 146:1,* col. 1034.)

The Statio

424. ST. PACHOMIUS, monk (4th century). When the brother hears the sound of the trumpet summoning him to the *collecta* [Work of God], he will forthwith leave his cell, and meditate on some passage of the Scripture on the way to the door of the church (*Reg.,* n. 3, *CR* 1:26; *PL* 23:65).

425. ST. AURELIAN, bp. of Arles (d. 551). When the signal has been given, all tasks are to be set aside . . . (*Reg. monachorum,* n. 30, *CR* 1:151; *PL* 68:391).

426. RULE FOR VIRGINS BY AN UNKNOWN AUTHOR (7th century). When the signal for the Divine Work has sounded, day or night, having set aside whatever work they were engaged in, they must bestir themselves in great haste, as though the King's herald had summoned them, so that nothing is preferred to the Work of God (*Reg. cujusdam Patris ad virgines,* c. 8, *CR* 1:398).

427. DENIS THE CARTHUSIAN. A. When the bell for rising has sounded, master immediately all tendency to delay, overcome all drowsiness, and trample laziness under foot. We are to get up promptly and with alacrity, as though we were answering the trumpet of the Supreme King, summoning us and inviting us to the glorification of the Creator, and to spiritual battle. Let the monk be ashamed to delay for even a moment, or to hide his head under the covers. Even though it is intensely cold let him joyfully rise at once . . . to speak to, and praise, and adore the Lord his God (*De fructuosa temporis deductione,* art. 1, *Op. Om.* 40:55). B. We must begin the Divine Office with the worthiest devotion of which we are capable, pursue its recitation with eagerness, and bring it to its close joyfully (*ibid.*). C. In going to and returning from choir, conduct yourself reverently (*Exhortatorium noviciorum,* art. 2, *Op. Om.* 38:529). D. In church and in choir during the time of the Divine Office and other prayers, you are to discipline your eyes and place a guard over them, lest they force upon your heart some obstacle to your devotion and spirit of interior recollection (*De profectu spirituali et custodia cordis,* art. 5, *Op. Om.* 40:477).

Divine Office replete with mysteries

428. DURANDUS, bp. of Mende, France (d.1296). The ceremonies and rites which constitute liturgical offices are filled with divine symbols and mysteries: for the diligent and reflective person who performs them, who knows how to live off the products of the fields, giving them honey to suck from its rocks and olive oil from its hard, stony ground (cf. Deut. 32:13), every one of them abounds in heavenly sweetness (*Rationale Divinorum Officiorum, prooemium,* n. 1; Venetiis: per Symonem Bevilaqua Papiensem, 1494, fol. 1).

429. LETTER OF THE BISHOPS OF DENMARK TO THE COUNCIL OF BASLE (1434). There are many monasteries [as a result of the influence of St. Birgitta] in which fervent and affective devotion of the conventual sisters and brothers is thriving, and the practice of the regular life instituted according to the order is observed to perfection, both by continual preaching and by the worship and homage of the Divine Majesty, that is, by the solemnity of the Mass and the chanting of the Divine Hours. Because of this, countless sinners * are, under divine inspiration, converted from day to day, and once converted, make rapid progress, intensify the practice of virtue in their life, and lead lives of greater spirituality, having trampled the cares of the world under foot (*Acta Sanctorum Bolland., Oct. tom. IV,* die 8, n. 177, p. 411, *Prolog. in vitam S. Birgittae*).

430. ST. BONAVENTURE, Franciscan general, cardinal, Doctor of the Church (d. 1274). Attentive fulfilment of the Office is the most solid foundation of the religious state; its neglect is the worst corruption of the life, the complete deordering of the religious institute (*Speculum disciplinae ad novitios, Pars I,* c. 16, *Op. Om.,* ed. Quaracchi 8:597).†

431. SUAREZ, FRANCISCO, S.J. (d. 1617). It is clear, first of all, that the form of the religious life established by Benedict is properly and perfectly monastic. Its purpose is personal perfection directed toward divine contemplation and prepared thereto by the employment of the means distinctive to the monastic life, as is evident from the study of the Rule. In this Rule the prescriptions which govern the divine and canonical Office and the chanting of the psalms are set down in greater

* Sinners: not so much in the sense that the monastic life is one of avowed penitence, but that all seeking of God (*RSB,* c. 58) is a return to him through the labor of obedience from whom we have wandered through the sloth of disobedience (*ibid.,* first sentence of *Prolog.*). [*Tr.*]

† It is certain that this minor work is not the actual composition of St. Bonaventure, but most probably that of Fr. Bernard a Besa, O.S.F., companion or secretary of the Saint. It seems, however, to have been written at the command and with some supervision of St. Bonaventure, and is included, in reduced type, in the definitive Quaracchi edition of St. Bonaventure's collected works, 8:583–622, with this explanation.

detail and with more accuracy than in the rules of other religious institutes approved by the Church; nevertheless the crafts, works, and manual labors of the monks are commended in it, for in the Rule the assumption is that the state was not created for the ministrations of clerics, but for the purely monastic life, as had been the custom prior to Benedict's time (*Tract. IX, de varietate religionum, Lib. II, de varietate rel. in specie,* c. 2. *quae fuerit religionis S. Benedicti institutio et progressus,* n. 5, *Op. Om.* 16:504).

432. ST. JOHN THE ALMONER, bp. of Alexandria (d. 616). John was desirous of participating in the praise and merits of the holy solitaries, for whose manner of life he had conceived the highest esteem, although he himself had never been a solitary. To this end he assembled a number of saintly anchorites from the desert, distributed them into two groups, assigning them cells in two chapels which he had constructed, one in honor of Our Lady, the Mother of God, and the other in honor of St. John. He also furnished them with all necessaries of life from his own farms. He addressed the monks, who are most beloved of God, in these terms: "After God, I shall provide for your material needs, and you will have the care of my spiritual well-being. At Vespers and during the night vigil, let your prayer go forth to God for me; whatever parts of the Office you pray in your cells will be for your own souls" (*Vita S. Joannis Eleemosynarii a Leontio Neapolitano episc.,* c. 44, *PG* 93:1652).

Psalmody makes us equals and companions of angels

433. HILDEMAR, monk of Milan (d. 843). When we sing God's praises, we chant with the assistance of the angels, for God is not without his messengers and ministers (*Comm. in S.P.B. Reg.,* c. 19, *PL* 66:478).

434. ST. AMBROSE. For this is the service of angels [and of monks, living an angelic life], to be occupied always in the praises of God, and to propitiate and entreat the Lord with frequent prayers (*Ep. 63,* § 82, *PL* 16:1262).

435. ST. JOHN CHRYSOSTOM. A. Do you not realize that you are standing in company with angels, that with them you chant and with them sing hymns? (*In Act. Apost., Hom. 24,* § 4, *PG* 60:190.) *B.* When I behold the progress you are making, I rejoice always, as one who has not planted in vain, nor borne labors fruitlessly, but as one who has sown seed in soil that is fertile and rich and good for producing fruit. Now, by what means can I expect such a harvest? How do I perceive that the sermons contribute to the work? From these considerations: that you zealously fill the church, the mother of all; from these meetings at night, held constantly; from this, that in imitation of the choirs of angels you offer without ceasing praises and hymns to the Creator. O wonderful gifts of Christ! In heaven the armies of angels chant the glory of God, and on earth men forming choirs in imitation of those

angels, chant the same canticles of praise in their churches! In heaven the Seraphim sing loudly their thrice holy hymn, on earth the multitude of men chant the same. The festive choirs of both the heavenly spirits and of men on earth join together: there is but one act of thanksgiving, one hymn of exultation, one religious meeting of a choir chanting joy (*Hom. sup.: Vidi Dominum sedentem in solio excelso, Isa. 6:1, PG* 56:97).

436. ST. JEROME. In Sion [Jerusalem, signifying the Church: cf. *hymn. ad Vesp. et Laudes, Commune Dedic. Eccl.*], which symbolizes the heavenly paradise, there should be nothing but joy and gladness, the acknowledgment of God and the voice of praise, so that the saints on earth may meditate in continual glorification of the Lord what they are to do in heaven in union with the angels of God (*In Isaiam, Lib. 14,* c. 5, *PL* 24:483).

437. ST. BERNARD. A. That the angels deign to be present, and to associate themselves with the praises of those who sing Psalms, is shown with great plainness by the Psalmist: . . . *the singers lead, the minstrels follow, in their midst the maidens play on timbrels* (Ps. 67:26). Wherefore he says also: . . . *in the presence of the angels I will sing your praise* (Ps. 137:1). When you are engaged in prayer, or the chanting of the psalms, have some thought of your fellow-singers, the angels; perform that in which you are occupied with reverence and according to the Rule, and you may glory in the thought that your angels in heaven always see the face of the Father (Matt. 18:10; *Serm. 7 in Cant.*, n. 4, *PL* 183:808). B. The angels are wont to draw nigh to men when they pray, and to rejoice at the prayer of those who raise pure hands to heaven. It is a pleasure for them to offer to God, as an odor of sweetness, the holocaust of their fervent devotion (*Serm. de temp., Hom. 3 super Missus est,* n. 1, col. 71). C. When your breasts are beaten with penitent hands, and your pavements are worn with your knees, your altars heaped with vows and devout prayers, your cheeks furrowed with tears; when groans and sighs resound on all sides and the sacred roofs echo with spiritual songs instead of worldly pleadings, there is nothing which the citizens of heaven more love to look upon, nothing that is more agreeable to the eyes of the heavenly King. For is this not what is said: *He that offers praise as a sacrifice glorifies me* (Ps. 49:23). O, if anyone had his eyes opened, as were those of the prophet's servant at his prayer: *The singers lead, the minstrels follow, in their midst the maidens play on timbrels* (Ps. 67:26). We should see, I say, with what care and ardor they assist at the chants, and at their prayers how they unite themselves with those who meditate; they watch over those who repose, they preside over those who order and care for all. The powers of heaven fully recognize their fellow-citizens; they earnestly rejoice, comfort, instruct, protect, and provide for all those who take the her-

itage of salvation, at all times (*Ep. 78, ad Sugerum abb. S. Dionysii,* § 6, *PL* 182:194; James, p. 114).

438. ST. LAURENCE JUSTINIAN (d. 1455). Holy angels are present in the choir of those who are glorifying God; they rejoice exceedingly in the praises of the chanters, but they do so only when these praises are uttered with the proper care; attentively, zealously, fervently, harmoniously, humbly. They move about among the members of the choir like fellow-citizens having an equal share in the kingdom of God. They suppress attacks of unclean spirits, and, as faithful protectors, will not tolerate the wild fury of the demons. They ascend and descend for the progress of those in choir. They are always and everywhere alert, bright, and solicitous that there be no interruption in the divine praises, and that the heavenly canticles be not defiled. But if only for a brief time affection grow lukewarm, distraction lay hold of the mind, or the eyes grow heavy with sleep, they consider such yawning persons unworthy, and finding nothing to offer, withdraw their presence. It is shameful and very harmful, therefore, to chant irreverently in the sight of such noble spirits (*De disciplina et perfectione monasticae conversationis,* c. 17, *Op. Om.* 1:140).

439. ST. NICETAS. No one must doubt that if it is celebrated with becoming faith and true devotion, this duty of the holy vigils is joined with the angels, whom we know are ceaselessly glorifying God and blessing the Redeemer in heaven without sleep, without distraction (*Opusc. 2, de psalmodiae bono,* c. 3, *PL* 68:373).

440. JOHN BONA, Cistercian, cardinal (d. 1674). Monks are to emulate the joys of the heavenly Jerusalem, throughout whose choirs the festive Alleluia is chanted with never an interruption (*De divina psalmodia,* c. 1, § 4, n. 7, *Op. Om.,* p. 394).

441. HAEFTEN, BENEDICT, provost of Affligem (d. 1648). The divine psalmody is in truth the sweet canticle of the Church Militant in which she finds solace in this exile of separation from her heavenly Bridegroom. It is a daughter of that hymnody which is zealously chanted before the throne of God and the Lamb. It is the most pious undertaking of the clergy and the daily cause of rejoicing for monks (*Disquisitiones monasticae, Lib. VII, tract. 6, de nocturnis vigiliis,* disq. 6, p. 743).

Seven times a day . . .

442. ST. BONAVENTURE. The Holy Spirit ordained that the Divine Office be offered in the Church for five reasons. . . . Secondly, that we should render thanks to God at certain hours, mindful of his blessings, and praying for his grace. From time to time turn to him who was born of the Virgin Mary at night; was dragged before the council in the early morning hours; arose at daylight; was scourged at the third hour; and

a little later sent the Holy Ghost upon the Apostles; was crucified at the sixth hour; died upon the cross at the ninth; and, being at supper in the afternoon, gave us the Sacrament; and was buried at the close of day (*Opusc. VIII, de sex alis Seraphim*, c. 7, §§ 5–6, *Op. Om.*, ed. Quaracchi 8:148).

443. RUPERT, abbot of Deutz (d. 1135). Anyone who does not wish to appear empty-handed and displeasing in the sight of God must not omit through negligence the seven Canonical Hours of the day. They bear our praises to the Creator and are a sort of tribute of thanksgiving for his certain and great blessings on us. Christ, the true Sun and eternal Day, having twelve hours, and ever standing with him, has enlightened and dedicated these seven Hours with the most brilliant rays of his mercy (*De divin. officiis per anni circulum, Lib. I*, c. 1, *de horis canonicis, PL* 170:13).

444. ST. PETER DAMIAN. The seven Canonical Hours are like seven baptismal fonts set up in the bosom of the Church in order that we may be intent on the expiation of the seven stains of offense [lighter faults, paralleling the seven capital sins, treated previously], which we contract in our daily way of life, and may expiate them by the streams, so to speak, of daily prayer (*Opusc. 10, De horis canonicis*, c. 1. *Peccatorum effectus, PL* 145:223).

Excellence of the psalter

445. ST. AMBROSE. A. Although all of the Divine Scripture breathes the grace of God, this is true in particular of the sweet book of the psalms (*Enarr. in Ps. 1*, n. 4, *PL* 14:965). B. The Historical Books instruct; the Law teaches; the Prophetic Books foretell; that which is reproof corrects errors; and morality appeals by persuasion; but in the Book of Psalms spiritual progress is found for all, and a certain medicinal protection for human salvation. Whoever reads it finds there a special remedy with which to heal the wounds of his own particular human weakness. As in a sort of public gymnasium of souls, or a kind of racecourse of virtues, with different contests available, anyone who desires to understand can choose for himself the contest for which he knows himself to be most capable, in order that he can the more easily win the crown. . . . Or, if he desires to be fortified against the attacks of spiritual evil, what does he know that is more beneficial than the chanting of the Psalms? David as a young man *took his harp, and played with his hand, and Saul was refreshed, and was better, for the evil spirit departed from him* (I Kgs. 16:23; *ibid.*, n. 7, col. 967). C. In the Psalms we are taught not only that Jesus was born, but also that he took upon himself that saving bodily passion, rested [in the tomb], arose from the dead, ascended into heaven, and sits at the right hand of the Father . . . (*ibid.*, n. 8, col. 968). D. What, then, can be more pleasing than the

Psalms? David himself stated the matter beautifully: *Praise the Lord, for he is good* [Douay: *because the psalm is good*]; *sing praises to our God, for he is gracious* (Ps. 146:1). In truth the Psalms are a blessing of the people. They are the glorification of God, the acts of praise by the people: the clapping of hands of all; the speech of all men; the voice of the Church; the pleasing acknowledgment of faith; full devotion of authority; the joy of freedom; the shout of happiness; the reverberation of joyfulness. The Psalms soothe away anger, cast worry aside, lift up from sadness. They are the weapon for the night, protection for the day, a shield in the time of fear; joy in holiness, the pattern for tranquillity, the pledge of peace and harmony. . . . The Psalms unite those who are separated, make companions of those who are in discord, reconcile the embittered. For who will not forgive him with whom he addresses God in united voice? It is a great bond of unity, to combine all people into one huge choir. . . . The Psalms are the occupation of the night; restfulness after the day's toil; instruction for beginner; the strengthening of the more advanced; the ministry of angels; the heavenly service; the spiritual host. The Psalms will prove a match for a rock: for when a Psalm is chanted even hearts of stone are softened. We see those who are hard of heart weep, and those who are wanting in mercy, bowed down (*ibid.,* n. 9, col. 968 f.). E. Doctrine and grace vie with each other in the praying of the Psalms; for we sing out of joy, and learn for our instruction (*ibid.,* n. 10). F. What, then, is the psalter other than an organ of virtues, which the venerable prophet, striking with the baton of the Holy Spirit, makes the sweetness of the heavenly melody to resound upon the earth? . . . The Lord, praising the minister of so great a blessing, says: *I have found David . . . a man after my heart* (Ps. 88:21; Acts 13:22; *ibid.,* n. 11).

446. ST. JOHN CHRYSOSTOM. The word . . . is not that of David, but of divine grace. True, the prophet is the one who actually spoke, but it was the Paraclete that stirred his tongue to speech. For that reason David says: *My tongue is nimble as the pen of a skillful writer* (Ps. 44:2: Douay: *of a scrivener that writeth swiftly*). As a pen does not write of itself, but by the power of the hand that moves it, so also the tongue of the prophets did not speak of its own power, but by the grace of God. But why does he not say merely: My tongue is the pen of a scribe? Why does he add: the pen of one that *writeth swiftly?* He does so in order that you may learn that wisdom is spiritual; therefore it has great ease, tremendous swiftness (*In Ps. 145,* § 2, *PG* 55:520).

447. ST. AUGUSTINE. A. Christ was in David; in David was Christ prefigured (*Serm. 175, in I Tim. 1: 15,* c. 7, n. 8, *PL* 38:948). B. It is Christ's voice that ought by this time to be perfectly known, and perfectly familiar to us, in all the Psalms; now chanting joyously, now sorrowing; now rejoicing in hope; now sighing at its actual state, even

as if it were our own (*Enarr. in Ps. 42,* § 1, *PL* 36:476). C. *In the presence of the angels I will sing your praise* (Ps. 137:2). Not before men will I sing, but before the angels. My song is my joy; but my joy in things below is before men, my joy in things above before the angels (*ibid., in Ps. 137,* 1, § 3, *PL* 37:1775). D. God has praised himself, that he might be properly praised by man; and because he has deigned to praise himself, man has discovered how to praise him (*ibid., in Ps. 144,* § 1, col. 1869).

448. ST. BASIL THE GREAT. The book of the Psalms is a storehouse of good instructions, diligently providing for each what is useful for him. For it heals the ancient wounds of souls and to the newly wounded brings prompt relief; it ministers to what is sick and preserves what is in health; and it wholly removes the ills, however great and of whatever kind, that attack souls in our human life; and this by means of a certain well-timed persuasion which inspires wholesome reflection.

For when the Holy Spirit saw that mankind was ill-inclined toward virtue and that we were heedless of the righteous life because of our inclination to pleasure, what did he do? He blended the delight of melody with doctrines, in order that, through the pleasantness and softness of the sound, we might unawares, receive what was useful in the words, according to the practice of wise physicians who, when they give the more bitter draughts to the sick, often smear the rim of the cup with honey. For this purpose these harmonious melodies of the Psalms have been designed for us, that those who are of boyish age or wholly youthful in character, while in appearance they sing, may be educating their souls.

. . . A Psalm is the tranquillity of souls, the arbitrator of peace, restraining disorder and turbulence of thoughts, for it softens the passion of the soul and moderates its unruliness . . . so that the singing of the Psalms brings love, the greatest of good things, contriving harmony like some bond of union and uniting the people in the symphony of a single choir.

A Psalm drives away demons, summons the help of angels, furnishes arms against nightly terrors, and gives respite from daily toil. . . . It peoples solitudes, it chastens market places. To beginners it is a beginning; to those who are advanced, an increase; to those who are concluding, a support. A Psalm is the voice of the Church. It gladdens feast days, it creates the grief which is in accord with God's will, for a Psalm brings a tear even from a heart of stone.

A Psalm is the work of angels, the ordinance of heaven, the incense of the Spirit. Oh, the wise invention of the teacher who devised how we might at the same time sing and learn profitable things, whereby doctrines are somehow more deeply impressed on the mind! What is learned unwillingly does not naturally remain, but things which are received with pleasure and love fix themselves more firmly in our minds. For what can we not learn from the Psalms? Can we not learn the splendor of courage, the exactness of justice, the dignity of self-control; the perfection of prudence, the habit of repentance, the measure of patience, or whatever good things you may name? Here is perfect theology; here is foretold the Incarnation of Christ; here are the threat of judgment, the hope of resurrection, the fear of punishment, the assurance of glory, the revelations of mysteries. All things are brought together in the Book of Psalms as in some great and common storehouse (*Hom. in Ps. 1*, §§ 1–2, *PG* 29:211; Strunk, *Source Readings in Music History*, pp. 64–66).

449. ST. NICETAS. In the Psalms a baby finds that which serves as milk to suck; a boy something to praise; a youth that with which to correct his ways; a young man an ideal to follow; an older man something to petition. A woman learns modesty; orphans find a father, widows a judge, the poor One who understands; strangers a protector, kings and judges that which makes them fear. The Psalms console the sorrowing; restrain the joyful; tame the angered; restore the poor to good condition; warn the rich to know themselves and admonish them not to be haughty; bestow effective medicine upon all who take them up. Nor do the Psalms disdain sinners, but in a most salutary manner constantly offer them a remedy to be obtained through tearful repentance. . . .

Whatever the prophets, in fact, whatever the Gospels themselves command, is contained in these hymns . . . : God is made known in order that we may fear him; idols are ridiculed; righteousness is constantly taught; evil forbidden; mercy praised; disbelief renounced; truth sought; lies condemned; deceit reprobated; innocence praised; pride cast down; humility exalted; penance commended; peace presented as an ideal.

Against enemies, protection is petitioned, vengeance promised, certain hope fostered. But what is more excellent than all these considerations: in the Psalms the mysteries of Christ are celebrated in song: for his generation is described; the rejection of the impious people and the inheritance of the Gentiles announced; the virtues of the Lord praised; the sacred passion prophesied; Christ's glorious Resurrection foretold; and even his being seated at the right hand of the Father is not omitted. Finally, the fiery Second Coming of the Lord is made known, the terrible judgment of the living and the dead unfolded. Is there still more? Yes, the sending forth of the creative Spirit, and the renewal of the face of the earth are set forth; after which there will be the eternal kingdom of the just in the glory of the Lord, and the everlasting punishment of sinners (*Opusc. 2, de psalmodiae bono,* c. 1, *PL* 68:371).

450. CASSIODORUS. The Psalms are vessels of truth, like spiritual casks preserving the wine of the Lord in its unspoiled flavor (*In Ps. 70: 23, PL* 70:503).

451. RADULPH OF RIVO, dean of Tongres (d. 1403). As formerly the manna possessed all delight and the taste of all sweetness, so the Psalms have the efficacy of all prayers and accommodation to every intention. In the choir of the chanters they are the words of men praising God; in the mouth of the just man they are the words of one offering his thanks; in the mouth of the sinner, the words of him who implores pardon; when prayed for the deceased, they are the voice of a soul crying out to God from the region of suffering. Whithersoever the chanter's intention is directed, the meaning of the Psalms will adapt itself to his affection. . . . As you devote yourself to the thought of the Psalms, Christ dwells in your mind; as you reflect on the Psalms, you will receive Christ as the fruit of your meditations; as you chant the Psalms with your lips, Christ is in your mouth, so that in these Psalms both the Old and the New Testaments come to you. The roots of the Psalms are fixed not on earth, but in heaven; for that is where Christ is, the subject and the intention of all the Psalms; there too is the way of life of the Church, which is the body of Christ (*De canonum observantia lib., Propositio IX.* in: Radulph de Rivo, *der letzte Vertreter der altrömischen Liturgie, von Cunibert Mohlberg, O.S.B.;* Louvain, 1911, 2:55).

452. ST. JOHN CHRYSOSTOM. A. We all bear David about with us as our ointment. Vigils are celebrated in church, and in them David is first, middle and last. In the morning hymns, again David is first, middle and last. . . . If public processions are held for the funerals of the deceased, if cloth is woven in the homes of virgins, David is first, middle and last. O unheard of phenomenon! Many who have never been taught their letters, not even the first principles according to the standards of the educated man, have learned David entirely by heart! He is conspicuous not only in the cities and in churches, and among people in all stages of life, but in the very midst of the forum. Even in the solitude (desert) and the uninhabitable land he zealously incites the people to the adoration of God. In the holy monasteries, in the choirs of angelic battle array, in the convents of virgins imitating Mary, David is first, middle and last. . . . And while everyone is deep in sleep during the night, David alone keeps watch; and assembling the servants of God into angelic choirs, prevails on them with the full intent of his mind. He changes earth into heaven, and makes men the equal of angels. He thus adorns our life with all manner of gifts, having become all things to all men (cf. I Cor. 9:22). He renders our whole life angelic; he grows up with boys; exhorts young men to prudence; bestows modesty on virgins; gives constancy to older persons; invites sinners to repentance;

. . . prompts those who have received benefits to gratitude; . . . recalls to confession those who have sinned repeatedly; . . . instructs those who seek God's mercy; . . . strengthens those who have been called to the priestly state.

He instructs those who are summoned to judgment; . . . gently admonishes in the spirit of fear those who have been converted; stirs up to more generous thanksgiving those who hope for favors and those who are grateful for the favors they have received. . . . What a huge zyther, striking the souls of men of the whole world, like strings that unite to produce one melody, one hymn of glory! (*De poenitentia et in lectionem de Davide et de uxore Uriae, Inter spuria, PG* 64:12.) B. We have all chanted only one song—youth and old men, wealthy and poor, women and men, slaves and freemen. For if the zyther player, skillfully plucking different strings, makes one melody of many sounds, what is there remarkable if the power of the Psalm and the spiritual canticle does the same? . . . The Psalm does more: it unites the dead with the living. The blessed Prophet praises God with us. . . . The inequality of the world is banished, and earth imitates heaven. Such is the very nobility of the Church (*Hom. 5, de studio praesentium,* n. 2, *PG* 63:486).

453. ST. BASIL THE GREAT. Among us the people come early after nightfall to the house of prayer, and in labor and affliction and continual tears confess to God. Finally, rising up from their prayers, they begin the chanting of Psalms. And now, divided into two parts, they chant antiphonally, becoming master of the text of the scriptural passages, and at the same time directing their attention and the recollectedness of their hearts. Then, again, leaving it to one to intone the melody, the rest chant in response; thus having spent the night in a variety of psalmody and intervening prayers, when day at length begins to dawn, all in common, as with one voice and one heart, offer up the Psalm of confession to the Lord, each one making his own the words of repentance (*Ep. 207, ad clericos Neocaesarienses,* § 3, *PG* 32:763; Way, 2:83; Deferrari, 3:187).

454. ST. GREGORY OF NAZIANZUS. The station in which you will presently stand after your baptism before the Great Sanctuary, is a foretype of future glory. The psalmody with which you will be received as members of the Church is a prelude of the psalmody of heaven (*Oratio 40, in sanctum baptisma,* n. 46, *PG* 36:426).

455. RULE OF MONASTERY OF TARNADAE (St. Maurice), circa 570. When we pray to the Lord in Psalms and hymns, let the thoughts that are uttered by the voice be planted in the heart. Let the farmer sing "Alleluia" as he holds the plow handle; the sweating sower entertain himself with Psalms; and as he cuts the young branches with sickle, let

the vine-dresser sing something of David's. Make these your songs . . . these the shepherd's whistling, these the elements of your culture (*Reg. monast. Tarnatensis,* c. 8, *CR* 1:182; *PL* 66:981).

456. ST. EPIPHANIUS, bp. of Salamis (Cyprus, d. 403). For a man to be a monk in truth he must, without interruption, have the spirit of prayer and psalmody, and the praising of God in his heart (*Apophthegmata,* in: Cotélier, Jean-Baptiste, *Ecclesiae Graecae monumenta;* Lutetiae Parisiorum: Muguet, 1677, 1:428).

457. ST. ISIDORE, bp. of Seville, Doctor of the Church (d. 636). The advantage of chanting the psalter is that it brings consolation to hearts that are sad; makes minds more attentive; pleases those who are inclined to be disdainful; stirs the lazy to activity; and invites sinners to repentance. For, however hard the hearts of carnal men, as soon as the Psalm's sweetness is sounded, it turns their souls to dispositions of piety (*Sententiarum Lib. III,* c. 7, *de oratione,* § 31, *PL* 83:678).

458. VEN. LOUIS DE BLOIS (Blosius). You will be happy indeed if you devote yourself zealously to the psalmody and deserve to taste the sweetness and the gift of peace which it contains. For psalmody is the most precious peace of mind, joyful serenity of heart, tender comfort for them who mourn, and the becoming attitude of the joyful. Psalmody puts demons to flight, summons angels, opens heaven and, as it were, compels God to have mercy (*Canon vitae spiritualis,* c. 18, n. 5, *Op. Om.* 1:18).

Preparation for the Work of God

459. ST. AUGUSTINE. My lips would not praise you, unless your mercy were to go before me. It is by your gift and through your mercy that I praise you. For I should not be able to praise God, unless he gave me to be able to praise him (*Enarr. in Ps. 62:4,* § 12, *PL* 36:755).

460. ST. BERNARD. A. When anyone prays, he summons the Holy Spirit to himself (*Lib. de modo bene vivendi, ad sororem,* c. 49, *de oratione,* n. 117, *In Append., PL* 184:1271).

B. When you enter the church to pray or to chant the psalter, leave behind all the hurry of wandering and tumultuous thoughts; utterly forget your concern for external things, in order that you may be distracted by no intruding object, but may fix your mind entirely on God. For it is not possible for a man who is all the while secretly chatting with the whole world to converse with God (*Meditationes piissimae de cognitione humanae conditionis,* c. 6, n. 16, *In Append.,* col. 495).

C. For by our Rule [*RSB,* c. 43], nothing must be preferred to the Work of God, which is the name that our Father Benedict desired to be given to the solemnities of divine worship, which are offered day by day in our oratory, thus showing more clearly how desirous he was that we should apply ourselves with all our heart to that holy work. Therefore I warn you and entreat you, beloved, always to occupy yourselves in the praises of God with pure hearts and earnest minds. With earnestness, so as to present yourselves at the worship of the Lord, as well with willingness and gladness as with reverence; not with laziness and sleepiness, not yawning, not keeping silence, not cutting your words short, or even passing over some altogether, not chanting through the nose or between the teeth, with broken and lowered voice, in a lazy and effeminate manner, but pronouncing the words of the Holy Spirit with manly and earnest voices, which correspond to the dignity of the subjects of which they speak. And purely also—that is to say, to occupy your thoughts while chanting with nothing else than the words which you are chanting (*Serm. 47 in Cant.*, n. 8, *PL* 183:1011; Eales, p. 291; Luddy, p. 237).

D. Now what else must a brother who enters to pray have in mind than that which the Prophet stated: *I went with the throng and led them in procession to the house of God, amid loud cries of joy and thanksgiving* (Ps. 41:5). Certainly it is most appropriate for us, during the time of prayer, to enter into the celestial court, even into the court in which the King of kings is seated on a throne of stars, surrounded by an indescribable army of countless blessed spirits. Hence he who had beheld this court in vision, being unable to find a number to express his vision, stated: *Thousands of thousands ministered to him, and ten thousand times a hundred thousand stood before him* (Dan. 7:10). With what reverence, then, and fear, and humility, should a despicable little tadpole approach there after having ascended from its little pond! How trembling, how suppliant, how humble, how solicitous, and how completely attentive to the glorious Majesty should the little man stand in the presence of the angels, before the assemblage of the just, before all the saints!

It is true, of course, that we need vigilance in all our actions, but this is particularly true at the time of prayer. As we read in our Rule: "Although the eyes of the Lord at all times and in every place behold us, let us especially believe this to be true when we are engaged in prayer" (*RSB*, c. 19). It is true also that we are seen at all times, but when we are praying we actually present and show ourselves, speaking, as the expression words the thought, face to face with God. Therefore, although God is everywhere present, he must be prayed to in heaven and thought of there while we are engaged in prayer, in such a way that our mind does not feel itself confined by the roof of the oratory, nor the height of the sky above, nor the thickness of the clouds, but we must pray according to the formula that Christ gave us when he said: *In this manner therefore shall you pray: Our Father who art in heaven . . .* (Matt. 6:9). Let him who prays do so as though he had been lifted up and presented to him who is seated on a throne, held on high by the angels who did not fall, surrounded by the lowly whom he raises up from the dust and the poor whom he lifts up from the dunghill (cf. Ps. 112:7). In this manner, I repeat, he is to consider himself and attend as though he were presented to the Lord of Majesty, so that he can say with Abraham: *I have ventured to speak to the Lord though I am but dust and ashes* (Gen. 18:27). And because, Lord, you commanded me with your precept, and have taught me by your instruction, I make bold to do just that, Lord, font of mercy! (*Serm. de div., de verbis Apostoli, Volo primum fieri obsecrationes,* nn. 7–8, col. 609.)

E. I believe that they are the holy angels who are present with human beings and pray, and offer to God their prayers and vows, since they are known to lift up pure hands unto heaven without anger or avarice. . . . Associate yourselves, then, with the sweet singers of heaven to chant in common the praises of God, since you are yourselves *citizens with the saints and members of God's household* (Eph. 2:19); and *sing wisely* (Ps. 46:8). As food is sweet to the mouth, so are Psalms in the heart. Only let the soul that is faithful and prudent grind them, as it were, between the teeth of his intelligence, for fear lest if they be swallowed in great fragments, and not masticated, the palate be defrauded of their sweetness, which is above honey and the honeycomb. Let us offer a honeycomb, as did the Apostles, at the table of the Lord (Luke 24:42). Honey in the comb, that is, spiritual devotion in the letter of the scripture. *The letter,* says the Apostle elsewhere (II Cor. 3:6) *kills* if it be swallowed down without the seasoning of the Spirit. If then, with the Apostle, you will sing with the Spirit, sing also with understanding (cf. I Cor. 14:15), and then you, too, shall know the truth of that saying of Jesus: *The words that I have spoken to you are spirit and life* (John 6:64); and also of that which we read as from the mouth of wisdom: *You will remember me as sweeter than honey* (Sir. 24:19; *Serm. 7 in Cant.,* nn. 4–5, col. 808).

461. ST. NILUS OF SINAI, monk (d. 430). If you have not yet received the gift of prayer or psalmody, ask persistently, and you will receive (*De oratione, tract.,* c. 87, *PG* 79:1186; *Philokalia,* p. 137).

462. ST. EPHRAEM. When you come to the Lord's house for divine and spiritual worship, show yourself eager and prompt for the sacred psalmody. For if you remain silent, then I too shall be silent, and our neighbor will keep silence; hence it necessarily follows that the chant will cease. They who greet a prince or a king coming from the theater with acclamations of approval and joy, and who see among them one who stands silently apart, not joining their chorus, drive him away from the crowd as one unworthy. It behooves us not to conduct ourselves sluggishly or negligently at prayer and hymns (*Consilium de vita spiritali ad monachum novitium,* c. 16, *Op. Om.* 1:49).

463. ORIGEN, priest of Alexandria (d. 253). The Lord is to be implored . . . that the Lamb of the tribe of Juda come and that he deign to open the sealed book. It is he who, opening the scriptures, kindled the hearts of the disciples [at Emmaus], so that they exclaimed: *Was not our heart burning within us while he was speaking on the road and explaining to us the Scriptures* (Luke 24:32; *In Exod., Hom. 12,* § 4, *PG* 12:385).

We must chant in a disciplined manner

464. GILBERT, abbot of St. Mary of Hoiland. My brethren, if you consider the order of your whole life and the course of observance of the Rule, it is no insignificant amount of good example that you build together. For if you begin with the night vigils [Matins] which you offer with zeal as a kind of first fruit, giving yourself with all generosity to God at the beginning of the vigils, if, as I say, you wish to consider in an orderly manner and from the beginning, the individual steps of the divine way of life, what will you find that does not demand discipline, that does not harmonize with our faith, that does not either exhaust the body or lift up the mind, and direct it after it has been lifted up? In singing the psalter, how great is the discipline for the body and for some there is even greater need of discipline for the mind, to keep it from wandering at all, or certainly as little as possible, from the meaning of the words. For they fix their mind on the words that are chanted, or they permit it to go to related matters, but never to anything at variance with the text. Should this last actually happen—for the human mind has a tendency to wander—how quickly they discipline it with correction and demand usury [even greater effort] of themselves for this lapse! But not even the intervals between the common hours of the night are without their claim. O good God! How that prayerful hour of the night is without night! How night shines as the day (cf. Ps. 138:11). The prayers that are offered privately do not petition private favors. Although the voice is lowered, the mind is more intense, and silent prayers have a greater understanding (*Serm. 23 in Cant. 4:1 Salomonis, PL* 184:120).

465. ST. CYPRIAN, bp. of Carthage, martyr (d. 258). A. When we pray, our words must be governed by discipline. They must have quietness and modesty in them. We must consider that we stand in God's presence. The carriage of the body and the measure of the voice must find acceptance in God's sight (*Lib. de Oratione Dominica,* c. 4, *PL* 4:538). B. Let the breast be shut against the adversary, and opened to God alone, not suffering the enemy of God to approach during the time of prayer (*ibid.,* c. 31, col. 557).

466. ST. BONAVENTURE. A. Both interior and exterior reverence are to be preserved in choir; interior, so that we sing in fear and humility,

as though God were visibly present; . . . exterior, so that we stand and kneel with devotion (*Speculum disciplinae ad novitios, Pars I,* c. 15, *Op. Om.,* ed. Quaracchi 8:595). B. Virtuous conduct in choir can be taken to mean seriousness and composure of external acts, fitting posture, and uniform disposition (*ibid.*). C. Uniformity in choir will refer particularly to kneeling and bowing together, although it is to be observed generally with regard to other acts. . . . They who love virtuous conduct in divine services diligently guard their eyes from all inordinate glancing about in choir (*ibid.,* c. 24, § 1, p. 606).

Personal worthiness in prayer

467. CASSIODORUS. *He that offers praise as a sacrifice glorifies me; and to him that goes the right way I will show the salvation of God* (Ps. 49:23). Now this is stated against those unworthy persons who presume to chant the praises of the Lord. He that offers praise as a sacrifice glorifies me—not as those chant who are guilty of sin, but as the pure of mind are accustomed to offer. That *praise as a sacrifice* glorifies the Lord which is immolated in the purity of faith and the worthiness of moral life. There follows the phrase *to him that goes the right way.* He explains whither this way leads with the words: *I will show the salvation of God.* It is a glorious path that leads to the Creator of heaven and earth. But this way, as it is called, is not traveled with our feet, but with holy minds. If we proceed along it with a pure heart, it leads us to Christ, and becomes for us that ladder of Jacob which led those who ascended it to heaven (Gen. 28:12; *In Ps. 49:23, PL* 70:357).

468. ST. EPHRAEM. When you stand in God's presence in prayer, put yourself before him in fear and trembling. Root out of your heart all thought and concern for the things of earth. In the time of prayer, let your entire person be like an angel of heaven; and your whole effort that your prayer be holy and pure, spotless and unblamable, so that when the gates of heaven see it rising they will be opened to it with delight (cf. Sir. 35:16 f.), and angels and archangels on beholding it will welcome it with joy and offer it before the holy and elevated throne of the Immaculate Lord (*Serm. de virginitate, Op. Om.* 1:129).

469. ST. AMBROSE. The mirror of our mind often enough reflects its image in our words. Sobriety weighs out the sound even of our voice, for fear that too loud a voice should offend the ear of anyone. Even in singing itself the first rule is modesty, and the same is true in every kind of speech, too, so that a man may gradually learn to praise God, or to sing songs, or even to speak, in that the principles of modesty grace his advance (*De officiis ministrorum, Lib. I,* c. 18, n. 67, *PL* 16:47).

Attention to the text of the prayer

470. ST. JEROME. *Do not be drunk with wine, for in that is debauchery; but be filled with the Spirit, speaking to one another in psalms and hymns and spiritual songs, singing and making melody in your hearts to the Lord, giving thanks always for all things in the name of our Lord Jesus Christ to God the Father* (Eph. 5:18–20). Let young men hearken to these admonitions; let those whose duty it is to sing in church pay attention to them, for God wills not to be praised with the voice, but with the heart. Do not sing after the manner of tragedians, who smear the throat and cheeks with sweet-smelling preparations, as though theatrical melodies and songs should be heard in church, but rather sing in fear, in deed, and in knowledge of the Scriptures. . . . Let the servant of Christ so chant that it is not the voice of the singer, but the words which are read, that are pleasing: so that the evil spirit which was upon Saul (cf. I Kgs. 16:23) may be cast forth from those who are similarly possessed, and may not be introduced into them who have made a public stage of the house of God (*In Eph. 5:19, Lib. III, PL* 26:528).

471. ST. JOHN CHRYSOSTOM. A. When you approach God, be mindful of whom you are approaching; faith in him from whom you expect your grace is sufficient to make you attentive to what you are saying. Look up to heaven and think of whom you are addressing (*In Ps. 145,* § 6, *PG* 55:527). B. Let him who devotes himself to prayer pray in the sight of God . . . collecting his thoughts from wheresoever they have wandered, breaking off all concern with the world, and entering with his whole being before God himself; all preoccupation about human needs having been expelled from the mind (*De Anna, Serm. II,* § 2, *PG* 54:645).

472. VEN. LOUIS DE BLOIS. Pronounce and sing all the sacred words of the divine offices in their entirety, with reverence, and in the spirit of religion; do this in the firm belief that if you are watchful in spirit, if your intention is right and your motivation pure, neither the shortest syllable, nor the chanting of a single note, nor the slightest bow will go unrecorded before God (*Vita Ven. Blosii abb.,* c. 18, *Exhortationes Laetiensibus datae,* n. 70, *Op. Om.* 1:lxiiii; *Acta Sanctorum,* Bolland., Jan., tom. 1, die 7, p. 445).

473. RULE OF THE MASTER (7th century). So great must be the serious reverence or the discipline of chanting the psalter, that it will be more lovingly heard by the Lord than it is said by us, as Scripture says: *The farthest east and west you make resound with joy* (Ps. 64:9). Again: *Sing to him a new song; pluck the strings skillfully, with shouts of gladness. For upright is the word of the Lord* (Ps. 32:3–4). And elsewhere: *Serve the Lord with fear, and rejoice before him; with trembling pay*

homage to him (Ps. 2:11–12). Likewise: *Sing wisely* (Ps. 46:8, Douay version). Therefore if he commands that he is to be sung to wisely and in fear, it behooves the singer to stand with head bowed and with unmoving body, and to chant the praises of the Lord modestly; he fulfils his duty before the Divine Majesty, according to the Prophet's teaching, when he says: *In the presence of the angels I will sing your praise* (Ps. 137:1; *Reg. Magistri ad monachos,* c. 47, *CR* 1:265; *PL* 88:1008).

474. ST. THOMAS AQUINAS. It must be observed, however, that there are three kinds of attention that can be brought to vocal prayer: one, which attends to the words, lest we say them wrong; another, which attends to the sense of the words; and a third which attends to the end of prayer, namely, God, and to the thing we are praying for (*II-II,* q. 83, art. 13, *Utrum de necessitate orationis sit quod sit attenta, Op. Om.* 9:206; Am. ed. 2:1548).

475. ST. CYPRIAN. When we stand praying, dearest brethren, we ought to be fully alert and intent on our prayers, with the whole heart. Let all carnal and secular thinking be put away from us; let the mind dwell on no thought except the prayer that it is offering. It is for this cause that the priest before worship uses the Preface, and prepares the brethren's minds by saying: "Lift up your hearts," that while the people answer, "We lift them up to the Lord," they may be reminded that there is nothing for them to think of except the Lord. . . . How can you petition God to hearken to you when you do not pay attention to what you yourself are doing? Do you wish God to remember you in your supplication when you are forgetful of yourself? (*De Oratione Dominica,* c. 31, *PL* 4:557.)

476. HUGH OF ST. VICTOR, canon regular of the monastery of St. Victor of Paris (d. 1141). At all Hours let there be one voice of heart and mouth. The voice of the choir is pleasing when the heart harmonizes with what the mouth utters (*Serm. 13, in anno novo, In Append., PL* 177:927).

477. HUGH OF FOLIETO (d. 1149). Some allow their minds to wander, are inquisitive of eye, slovenly of attitude, gazing intently at the surface of the walls; they chant one thing, but think of something else. Physically they are in choir, but their mind is in the market place. . . . About the altar let there be severe simplicity and worthiness of reverence (*De claustro animae, Lib. II,* c. 22, *abusio undecima in choro, PL* 176:1080, 1086).

478. ST. BONAVENTURE. To achieve perfection in prayer it is necessary that . . . during the prayer your mind dwell on nothing other than what is being prayed. It is most unbecoming for a person to speak with God with his lips while in his heart he is dwelling on something else, or that half his heart be turned toward heaven and half kept here on earth. Such prayer is never heard by the Lord. Hence the *Glossa*

states with regard to the passage of the psalm: *I call out with all my heart; answer me, O Lord* (Ps. 118:145), "A divided heart receives no answer" (*S. Aug., Enarr. in Ps. 118, vers. 145, Serm. 29, PL* 37:1585). When at prayer, the handmaid of God must recollect herself and banish from her heart all worldly desires, and turn to that which is interior. With her whole heart and mind she must devote herself to him alone to whom she addresses her prayer. Jesus, your Spouse, gave you this counsel in the Gospel, saying: *When thou prayest, go into thy room, and closing thy door, pray to thy Father* (Matt. 6:6). You have then gone into your room when you have recalled all your thoughts, all your desires, all your affections to the secret recesses of your heart. And you have closed your door when you guard your heart so zealously that you cannot be hindered in your devotion by any wandering thoughts. For devotion, as St. Augustine says, is the raising and turning of the mind to God in loving and humble affection (*De spiritu et anima,* c. 50, *In Append., PL* 40:816; *Opusc. VI, de perfectione vitae, ad sorores,* c. 5. *De studio orationis,* § 4, *Op. Om.,* ed. Quaracchi 8:118).

479. ST. AMBROSE. Let your prayer, then, be no mere pronouncing of words with the lips. Devote your whole attention to it, enter into the retreat of your heart, penetrate its recesses as deeply as possible. May he whom you seek to please not find you negligent. May he see that you pray with your whole heart, so that he will deign to hear you when you pray with your whole heart (*De sacramentis, Lib. VI,* c. 3, § 13, *PL* 16:476; Bernard Botte, p. 101).

480. ST. AUGUSTINE. A. It is an outstanding quality of noble minds to love the truth in words and not the words themselves. Of what use is a golden key if it cannot open what we desire? Or what objection is there to a wooden one if it can? We are asking only that what is closed be opened (*De doctrina Christiana, Lib. IV,* c. 11, § 26, *PL* 34:100; Gavigan, p. 192). B. David teaches us and warns us to sing praises with understanding, not to seek the sound of the ear, but the light of the heart (*Enarr. in Ps. 46:8,* § 9, *PL* 36:529). C. If the Psalm prays, pray; if it laments, lament; if it expresses joy, rejoice; if it hopes, hope; if it fears, fear. For all that is written here is a mirror for us (*ibid., in Ps. 30, Serm. 3,* § 1, col. 248). D. When you pray to God in psalms and hymns, let that dwell in your heart that you pronounce with your voice (*Ep. 211, ad monasterium monacharum,* § 7, *PL* 33:960).

481. JOHN CASSIAN, abbot of Marseilles (d. 480) . . . He will make his own all the thoughts of the Psalms, and will begin to sing them in such a way that he will utter them with the deepest emotion of heart, not as if they were compositions of the Psalmist, but rather as if they were his very own utterances and prayer; or at least he will certainly take them as aimed at himself, and will recognize that their words were not only fulfilled formerly in the person of the prophet, but that they

are fulfilled and carried out daily in his own case (*Collatio* X [*coll. II Abb. Isaac*], c. 11, *de perfectione orationis, PL* 49:838).

482. ST. BASIL THE GREAT. Stand at attention before the Lord during the time of prayer or the psalmody. Do not allow drowsiness to overwhelm your soul. Let not your thoughts and the words you pronounce be at variance, but let them be in harmony. Let what you say be the expression both of the prayer and of your thought. As it is impossible to serve two masters, neither can a double prayer [one expression by the lips and another by the mind] ascend to the Lord (*Admonitio ad filium spiritualem,* c. 12, *De vigiliis, CR* 1:460; *PL* 103:693).

483. ST. JOHN CHRYSOSTOM. David in his day sang Psalms, and we today with him. He had a harp made of dried animal skins, but the Church has a harp strung of living tissues. Our tongues are the strings of the Church's harp, which gives forth different sounds but a worship that is in harmony (*Comm. in Ps. 145,* § 2, *PG* 55:521).

Avoidance of distraction

484. ST. LAURENCE JUSTINIAN. To stand physically in God's presence during prayer and let the mind wander about fields of unprofitable thoughts is unworthy (*Lignum vitae, tract. de oratione,* c. 9, *Op. Om.* 1:92).

485. ST. GREGORY THE GREAT. For often in the very sacrifice of praise urgent thoughts press themselves upon us, that they should have force to carry off or pollute what we are sacrificing in ourselves to God with weeping eyes. Whence when Abraham at sunset was offering up the sacrifice, he was troubled by birds of prey sweeping down on the carcasses, but he diligently drove them off, so that they might not carry off the sacrifice which had been offered up (cf. Gen. 15:11). So let us, when we offer a holocaust to God upon the altar of our hearts, keep it from birds of prey that the evil spirits and bad thoughts may not seize upon that which our mind hopes it is offering up to God to a good end (*Moral., Lib. 16,* c. 42, § 53, *a pravis cogitationibus nemo immunis, PL* 75:1146).

486. ST. ADALARD, abbot of Corbei (d. 826), when entering the church for the Divine Office, as he was wont to remark pleasantly, promptly put aside all thoughts and temporal concerns at the door, and entered the church wholly in possession of himself, in order that he could devote full attention to God and to what he himself was doing (S. Paschasii Radberti, abb. Corbeiens., *De vita S. Adalhardi,* § 27, *PL* 120:1522).

487. RULE OF THE MASTER (7th century). Let that be in the mind of the chanter which is expressed in the words [cf. *RSB,* c. 19]. Let our voice and our minds be one in our chanting, as the Apostle says: *I will*

pray with the spirit; but I will pray with the understanding also (I Cor. 14:15; *Reg. magistri ad monachos,* c. 47, *CR* 1:265; *PL* 88:1009).

488. ST. ISIDORE OF SEVILLE. Monks should meditate on or sing something while they are working, in order to lighten the burdens of their labor with the pleasure of the song or the word of God. For if secular laborers never cease singing love songs and salacious passages during their work, and thus pass their time with songs and stories in order to keep at their tasks, how much more fitting it is for the servant of God so to work with his hands that he always has the praise of God in his heart, and his tongue is made to serve for Psalms and hymns! (*Reg. monachor.,* c. 6, *de opere monachorum, CR* 1:191; *PL* 83:874.)

The Office to be appreciated

489. VEN. LOUIS DE BLOIS. A. Make haste to the choir, as to a place of refuge and the garden of spiritual delights. . . . In the performance of the Divine Office, have a care to pronounce and hear the holy words reverently, perfectly, thankfully, and attentively, that you may *taste and see how good the Lord is* (Ps. 33:9), and many feel that the word of God has incomprehensible sweetness and power. For whatever the Holy Ghost has dictated is indeed life-procuring food and the delightful solace of a chaste, sober, and humble soul. Remember, therefore, to be faithfully attentive. . . . Persevere with a gentle, quiet, and watchful spirit in the praise of God, avoiding all singularity (*Speculum monachorum,* div. 2, *Op. Om.* 3:653). B. When St. Birgitta [of Sweden] was harassed by temptations during prayer, Mary, the Mother of God, said to her: "With malicious watchfulness the devil seeks to hinder the good from praying. Whatever the temptation that may assail you during prayer, remain steadfast, O daughter, in your desire and good will, and in your holy endeavors as best you can; because your pious desires and efforts will be considered as effectual as your prayer. Even if you are not able to cast out the base and evil thoughts that come to your mind, yet for those endeavors you shall receive a crown in heaven; thus these troubles will be of profit for you, provided that you do not consent to the temptation, but are displeased with whatever is unbecoming" (*Conclave animae fidelis, Pars II, Monile spirituale,* c. 3, *Op. Om.* 2:594; cf. *S. Birgittae Revelationes, Lib. VI,* c. 94).

Devotion

490. ST. THOMAS AQUINAS. A. Hence devotion is apparently nothing else but the will to give oneself readily to the things concerning the service of God (*II-II,* q. 82, art. 1. *Utrum devotio sit actus specialis, Op. Om.* 9:187; Am. ed. 2:1535). B. Prayer must be prompted by devotion, for the fatness of devotion makes the sacrifice of prayer acceptable to

God (cf. Ps. 62:5; *Opusc. 5, in Orationem Dominicam,* c. 1, *Op. Om.,* ed. Parma 16:123).

491. ST. AUGUSTINE. The more fervent the desire, the more worthy the effect which ensues (*Ep. 130, Probae praescribit quomodo orandus sit Deus,* c. 9, § 18, *PL* 33:501).

492. PETER DE ROYA. The more diligently I study their life from day to day, the more thoroughly I am convinced that these men who profess evangelical poverty are in all things perfect lovers and followers of Christ and true servants of God. . . . But when they are more publicly occupied in praising God with psalmody at the Canonical Hours, it is then above all that the fervor and devotion of their minds are revealed by their bodily postures, suggestive of holy fear and reverence; while their slow articulation of the syllables and their manner of singing the Psalms make it clear that the words of God are sweet to their palate above honey (Ps. 118:103; *Ep. 492 In Append. ad Ep. S. Bernardi, a Petro de Roya novitio Clarae-Vallensis ad C. praepositum Noviomensem,* n. 8, *PL* 182:710).

493. HUGH OF ST. CHER. A. When offering the sacrifice of praise our concern must be to join understanding to the recitation of the psalmody, love to understanding, rejoicing to love; seriousness to rejoicing, humility to seriousness, and freedom to humility. This psalmody must be properly performed in such a way that the mind is directed toward things heavenly, and not bent down toward what is of earth (*Sup. Ps. 32:3, Comm.* 2:80). B. It is not what is uttered by the voice, but longing and devotion; not musical flourishes, but disposition of heart; not the volume of sound, but the spirit of love, that makes its strong appeal in God's hearing (*Sup. Isa. 33:3, ibid.,* 4:72).

494. ST. VALERIAN, bp. of Cémèle, near Nice (d. circa 450). In order to present to your Creator every day the small gifts fashioned by your lips in the spirit of joy, fulfil the sacrifice of his praise in sweet words; hasten in the spirit of devotion to the duty of the work assigned to you. Hearken to the prophet as he says: *Accept, O Lord, the free homage of my mouth* (Ps. 118:108; *Hom. 3, de arcta et angusta via,* n. 4, *PL* 52:701).

495. THOMAS À KEMPIS. Stand in choir, then, as though you were standing among angels. . . . Place Jesus in the choir to your right, and Mary to your left, and all the saints about them. . . . A devout choir member is intent only on God and himself, as though he had been translated and elevated to the choir of heaven itself. . . . It is no light fault to stand in the presence of God and his saints with a distracted mind (*De disciplina claustralium,* c. 8, *Op. Om.* 2:297).

496. ST. NICETAS. . . . Brethren, let us faithfully fulfil with complete confidence the mystery of the hymns, in the conviction that we

have received a great grace from God, for it has been granted to us to proclaim the miracles of the eternal God, joining our voices to those of great and wonderful saints, prophets, and martyrs. Here with David we give glory to the Lord, *for he is good* (Ps. 105:1). With Moses we cry aloud the words of the great canticles, magnifying the power of the Lord. With Anna, once sterile, later blessed with child, who is a symbol of the Church (cf. I Kgs. 1:5 f.), our hearts are strengthened in the praise of God; we chant with Isaias, watching through the night; by our prayer we sing with Habacuc, with Jeremias, with Jonas, those holy prophets; we chant with the three boys as though placed with them in the furnace, having summoned every creature, blessing the Creator of all (*Opusc. 2, de psalmodiae bono,* c. 3, *PL* 68:373).

Sing wisely

497. ST. BASIL THE GREAT. A. During the time of the psalmody, sing wisely, my son, and attentively chant the spiritual songs in the sight of the Lord, in order that you may the more easily acquire the strength of the psalms. Let all hardness of heart be softened in their sweetness. Then with tenderness and rejoicing you will sing: *How sweet to my palate are your promises, sweeter than honey to my mouth* (Ps. 118:103). But you cannot experience this spiritual joy except by singing with complete attention and wisdom. The mouth will relish the food, but it is the understanding that discerns the words. For as the flesh is nourished by carnal food, the interior man is fed and nourished with divine words (*Admonitio ad filium spiritualem,* c. 12, *CR* 1:461; *PL* 103:693). B. What flavor is to the quality of foods, such is understanding for the words of Holy Scripture. The taste judges foods; the mind, words by understanding them (cf. Job 12:11; 34:1). If then one is as affected by the force of each word as he is for its quality by the taste of each food, he is completely satisfying the command, *sing ye wisely* (Ps. 46:8, Douay version; *Reg. brevius tractatae, Interrog. 279, PG* 31:1279).

498. ST. NICETAS. Beloved, breaking off all unnecessary concerns, let us chant the psalter with concentration and alertness of mind, in such wise that we shall not displease God. The Psalm itself exhorts us with these words: *For God is the King of all the earth; sing ye wisely* (Ps. 46:8, Douay version). That means intelligently, singing not with our breath or the sound of our voice only, but with understanding, dwelling reflectingly on what we sing, lest the mind, absorbed with preoccupations and distracting thoughts, perform its task without fruit (*De psalmodiae bono,* c. 3, *PL* 68:374).

499. ARNULPH, monk of Bohéries. When you have recited the verse on your side of the choir, silently pronounce what is being prayed on the other side: sprinkle each verse with a bit of pepper—that is, with

some spiritual reflection—for you have a delicate mind, whose food must be chosen carefully (*Alia documenta vitae religiosae, alias Doctrina B. Bernardi, PL* 184:1177).

500. EDMUND MARTÈNE, monk of Cong. of St. Maur (d. 1739). Certainly if, according to St. Bernard's teaching (*Serm. 85 in Cant.*, n. 9, *PL* 183:1192), he is wise who finds his delight in God, then he must be said to sing wisely who finds his delight in God through chanting. The Master in his Rule (seventh century) seems to follow the same explanation (*Reg. Magistri*, c. 47, *CR* 1:265; *PL* 88:1008 f.; *Comm. in c. 19 RSB;* Parisiis: Muguet, 1690, p. 328; *PL* 66:477).

Sing with perseverance

501. ST. GERTRUDE THE GREAT, abbess (d. 1302?). Once as Gertrude prayed for a sister under similar circumstances [for one excessively fearful in approaching to receive the Eucharist], our Lord replied: "I would that my elect should not consider me so severe, but rather believe that I receive as a welcome offering any least service they render me at their own expense. For example, he offers a sacrifice to God at his own expense who, although he finds no sweetness in devotion, never omits the service of God either by prayers, prostrations, or other acts of devotion, always hoping in God's mercy, that he will accept the fulfilment of these duties" (*Insinuationes divinae pietatis, Lib. III*, c. 18, § 12, p. 205; *Life and Revelations*, p. 174).

502. DAVID OF AUGSBURG. Do not give way to despair, as though God had abandoned you, or as though your good works were not acceptable to him, if the comfort of interior joy is taken from you. Have recourse at such times to the assurances that true doctrine gives, and place your consolation in that: namely, in God's faithfulness to his promises. As long as you do not withdraw from him by consenting to violate his laws, he, in his mercy will never abandon you (*De profectu religiosorum, Lib. II*, c. 1, ad n. 4, *Op. Om. S. Bonaventurae*, ed. Peltier 12:364).*

503. VEN. LOUIS DE BLOIS. True devotion consists in submission, resignation, self-denial, and humble-mindedness rather than in any sensible delight and sweetness (*Speculum spirituale*, c. 13, § 1, *Op. Om.* 2:581).

504. DENIS THE CARTHUSIAN. If [sensible sweetness at prayer] is granted, let it be received gratefully, and let him to whom it is given use it in a reasonable manner. But if it is denied him, or if he is deprived of it for any cause whatever, he is not to be downcast or overwhelmed with sadness, provided that he has not turned away from the spiritual desire of always pleasing and serving God: and if for a while

* This work is definitely assigned by the editors of the Quaracchi edition of St. Bonaventure's works to David of Augsburg (d. 1272), German Franciscan mystical writer and preacher (*Op. Om.* 10:17).

he does not long for this desire so fervently as he should, he will humbly and discreetly repent of his imperfection, and with the Psalmist seek to desire ardently, saying: *My soul is consumed with longing for your ordinances at all times* (Ps. 118:20; *De gaudio spirituali et pace interna, Lib. I,* art. 21, *Op. Om.* 40:548).

505. ST. LAURENCE JUSTINIAN. A. As the sun is not seen when the sky is overcast with heavy clouds, and as a disturbed pool cannot reflect the image of the one gazing into it as would the placid surface of the water; so a restless mind is unable to contemplate the love of God in the mirror of prayer (*Lignum vitae, tract. de oratione,* c. 5, *Op. Om.* 1:89). B. He who cultivates the soil must keep busy digging up weeds and brambles in order to reap a more abundant harvest; so too anyone eagerly desirous of experiencing the sweetness of devotion in prayer must employ every effort to overcome its obstacles (*ibid.,* c. 4).

The sacred chant and its effects

506. ST. JOHN CHRYSOSTOM. A. You were like a flute or a zyther in the hands of the Holy Spirit; for while others were dancing to the devil [in their drunkenness and revelry on the preceding day's festival], by the very fact that you remained here in church, you presented yourselves as organs and vessels to the Spirit. You offered your souls as musical instruments for the Holy Spirit to strike and through which to breathe his grace into your hearts. In so doing you have rendered a musical harmony that is pleasing not only to men, but also gives delight as well to the heavenly virtues (*De Lazaro, concio 1,* § 1, *PG* 48: 963). B. Wishing to make the labor more pleasing and to take away all tediousness in it, he blended melody with prophecy in order that, delighted by the modulation of the chant, all might with great eagerness give forth sacred hymns to him. For nothing so uplifts the mind, giving it wings and freeing it from earth, releasing it from the chains of the body, affecting it with love of wisdom, and causing it to scorn all things pertaining to this life, as modulated melody and the divine chant composed of number. To such an extent, indeed, is our nature delighted by chants and songs that even infants at the breast, if they be weeping or afflicted, are lulled to sleep by it. . . . Inasmuch as this kind of pleasure is thoroughly innate to our mind, and lest demons, introducing lascivious songs should overthrow everything, God established the Psalms, in order that singing might be both a pleasure and a help. . . . From the spiritual Psalms, however, proceeds much of value, much utility, much sanctity, and every inducement to wisdom, for the words purify the mind, and the Holy Spirit descends swiftly upon the mind of the singer (*Expos. in Ps. 41,* § 1, *PG* 55:156; Strunk, *Source Readings in Music History,* p. 68).

The chant is a work of love

507. ST. AUGUSTINE. A. Singing is for one who loves. The voice of this sacred song is the fervor of holy love (*Serm. 336, In Dedic. Eccl.*, § 1, *PL* 38:1472). B. What cries did I utter to you in those psalms and how was I inflamed toward you by them, and on fire to set them sounding through all the world, if I could, against the pride of man! (*Confessionum Lib. IX,* c. 4, § 8, *PL* 32:766; Sheed, p. 188.) C. The days were not long enough for me as I meditated, and found wonderful delight in meditating, upon the depth of your design for the salvation of the human race. I wept at the beauty of your hymns and canticles, and was powerfully moved at the sweet sound of your Church's singing. Those sounds flowed into my ears, and the truth streamed into my heart: so that my feeling of devotion overflowed, and the tears ran from my eyes, and I was happy in them (*ibid.,* c. 6, § 14, col. 769; Sheed, p. 193). D. Now David was a man skilled in songs, who dearly loved musical harmony, not with a vulgar delight, but with a believing disposition, and by it served his God, who is the true God, by the mystical representation of a great thing. For the rational and well-ordered concord of diverse sounds in harmonious variety suggests the compact unity of the well-ordered city (*De civitate Dei, Lib. 17,* c. 14, *PL* 41:547; Dods, p. 595).

508. ST. BERNARD. Where there is love, there is no effort, but delight (*Serm. 85 in Cant.,* § 8, *PL* 183:1191; Eales, p. 521).

The chant stirs minds to intensity of prayer

509. JOHN CASSIAN. For sometimes a verse of any one of the Psalms gives us an occasion of ardent prayer while we are singing. Sometimes the harmonious modulation of the voices has stirred up the minds of dullards to intense supplication (*Collatio IX, Abbatis Isaac I,* c. 26, *PL* 49:802).

510. ST. GERMAIN, bp. of Paris (d. 576). When King Solomon adorned his celebrated temple, he appointed chanters for it to sing the glories of God to the accompaniment of a variety of instruments, so that among the other ornaments which were resplendent in the temple, the divine utterances would be rendered with great beauty. The intention was that the word of God would be all the more pleasing the more elegantly it would be chanted by beautiful voices. For the custom of singing in churches was established because of the carnal man, not the spiritual man, in order that they who are not brought to compunction by words may be moved thereto by the sweetness of melody, thinking of themselves how beautiful must be the song of heaven when in the dwelling of this world the Church resounds so beautifully with

the praises of Christ (*Expos. brevis antiquae liturgiae Gallicanae, Ep. II, de communi officio, PL* 72:95).

The chant lightens the hardships of discipline

511. ST. BERNARD. A. Consider that silence and constant quiet from all stir of secular things disposes the soul to meditation on things above. And the laborious exercise of the religious life and the rigor of abstinence are lightened by the sweetness of Psalms and hymns (*Ep. 78, ad Sugerum, abb. S. Dionysii,* n. 4, *PL* 182:193; James, p. 113). B. The chant of the Psalms in church gives joy to men's minds, is pleasing to the fastidious, stirs the lazy to action, invites sinners to bewail their sins; for however hard the hearts of worldly men, as soon as they hear the sweetness of the Psalms, they are converted to the love of devotion (*Lib. de modo bene vivendi, ad sororem,* c. 52, n. 122, *In Append., PL* 184:1274).

The chant invites the Holy Spirit

512. ST. JOHN CHRYSOSTOM. A. Demons congregate where there are licentious chants, but where there are spiritual ones the grace of the Spirit descends, sanctifying mouth and mind (*Expos. in Ps. 41,* § 2, *PG* 55:157; Strunk, *Source Readings in Music History,* p. 68). B. Learn to sing the Psalms, and you will see the delightfulness of the employment. For they who sing Psalms are filled with the Holy Spirit, just as they who sing satanic songs are filled with an unclean spirit (*In Eph.,* c. 5, *Hom. 19,* § 2, *PG* 62:129). C. Blessed David's spiritual harp, played for us by the Holy Spirit, has given its heavenly notes, not so much for pleasing the ear, as for instructing the soul. The purpose of that sacred harp [the psalmody] is to make souls holy. For it is always the praise of psalmody, a solemn celebration for those who are rejoicing, the comfort of the sorrowful; a holy enchantment which is not produced by the recitation of fables: but as though it were dealing with wild beasts, it calms evil desires; casts forth licentiousness; destroys iniquity; kindles the spirit of righteousness; overthrows blasphemous doubts; banishes impure thoughts; repeatedly gives expression to the Divine Law; makes God known to us; interprets the faith; holds heretics in check; and builds up the Church (*Expos. in Ps. 96,* § 1 (*inter spuria*), *PG* 55:603).

513. HUGH OF ST. CHER. The psalmody drives out demons, . . . summons angels, stimulates devotion, placates God, wins pardon, gladdens the heart, enlightens the conscience (*Sup. Ps. 91:1, Comm.* 2:244. Wolter gives only a summary of the topic headings in the commentary).

514. JOHN OF TRITHEIM. As dust is scattered when blown by the wind, so our adversary, the devil, is put to flight in confusion and terror by the voice of those who chant [the Divine Office] with humble devo-

tion (*Hom. 17, de somno et vigilia monachorum, Op. pia et spiritualia,* p. 486).

515. ST. AUGUSTINE. The pleasures of the ear did indeed draw me and hold me more tenaciously, but you have set me free. Yet still when I hear those airs, in which your words breathe life, sung with sweet and measured voice, I do, I admit, find a certain satisfaction in them, yet not such as to grip me too close, for I can depart when I will. Yet in that they are received into me along with truths which give them life, such airs seek in my heart a place of no small honor, and I find it hard to know what is their due place. At times it seems to me that I am paying them greater honor than is their due—when, for example, I feel that by those holy words my mind is kindled more religiously and fervently to a flame of piety because I hear them sung than if they were not sung: and I observe that all the varying emotions of my spirit have modes proper to them in voice and song, whereby, by some secret affinity, they are made more alive. It is not good that the mind should be enervated by this bodily pleasure. But it often ensnares me, in that the bodily sense does not accompany the reason as following after it in proper order, but having been admitted to the aid of reason, strives to run before and take the lead. In this manner I sin unawares, and then grow aware.

Yet there are times when through too great a fear of this temptation, I err in the direction of over-severity—even to the point sometimes of wishing that the melody of all the lovely airs with which David's Psalter is commonly sung should be banished not only from my own ears, but from the Church's as well: and that seems to me a safer course, which I remember often to have heard told of Athanasius, Bishop of Alexandria, who had the reader of the Psalm utter it with so little modulation of the voice that he seemed to be saying it rather than singing it. Yet when I remember the tears I shed, moved by the songs of the Church in the early days of my new faith; and again when I see that I am moved not by the singing but by the things that are sung—when they are sung with a clear voice and proper modulation—I recognize once more the usefulness of this practice (*Confessionum Lib. X,* c. 33, §§ 49–50, *PL* 32:799; Sheed, p. 242; Strunk, *Source Readings,* pp. 73–74).

516. ST. AELRED, abbot of Rievaulx, Diocese of York, England (d. 1165). Melody is never to be given precedence to the meaning of the text, but taken together with the meaning of what is sung, melody is usually acknowledged to be a stimulus to sentiments of greater love. Hence the melody must be of such a nature that in its moderation and gravity it does not carry away the soul into complete forgetfulness of self, but leaves the major portion of the attention to the understanding of what is sung. St. Augustine says: ". . . I feel that by those holy words

my mind is kindled more religiously and fervently to a flame of piety because I hear them sung than if they were not sung" (cf. preceding number). But if the pleasure in listening to the chant yearns more for the melody than for the meaning of the words, such an attitude is reprehensible (*Speculum charitatis, Lib. II,* c. 23, *de vana aurium voluptate, PL* 195:571).

What is to be sung, and how it is to be sung

517. ST. BERNARD. A. Such occasions [solemn liturgical functions] require something venerable and beyond question orthodox, something redolent with holy gravity that would edify the people. But if you want to hear something new and if the occasion demands it, then let something be chosen that would both please and profit the hearers by the dignity of its diction and the authority of its author. Furthermore, the sense of the words should be unmistakable, and they should shine with truth, tell of righteousness, incite to humility, and inculcate justice; they should bring truth to the minds of the hearers, devotion to their affections, the cross to the vices, and discipline to their senses. If there is to be singing, the melody should be grave, and not flippant or uncouth. It should be sweet but not frivolous; it should both enchant the ears and move the heart; it should lighten sad hearts and soften angry passions; and it should never obscure, but enhance the sense of the words. Not a little spiritual profit is lost when minds are distracted from the sense of the words by the frivolity of the melody, when more is conveyed by the modulation of the voice than by the variations of the meaning. This is what should be heard in churches and the sort of man the composer should be (*Ep. 430, ad Guidonem abb. et fratres Arremarenses* [Montier-Ramey], nn. 2–3, *qui rogaverunt S. Bernardum ut Officium de S. Victore ipsorum patrono componat, PL* 182:610; James, p. 502). B. It seemed altogether unworthy that they who had vowed to live according to rule should sing their praises to God without a definite rule. Hence by common agreement you will find the chant has been corrected through the elimination of errors and the rejection of improper additions; and that it is now supported fully by corrected interpretation of the rules. It is now more easily read and sung than are the chants of others, to which it was formerly inferior (*Sup. Antiphonarium Cisterc. ordinis, Praef., seu tract. de cantu,* n. 1, col. 1121).

The chant is pleasing to God

518. ORIGEN. Who, think you, possesses so melodious a voice and so pure a mind, who sings so worthily that his song can give delight to God's hearing? Certainly he whose voice has none of the harshness of sin, whose tongue is free of offense, and in whom there is no coarseness of spirit, who can say: *To the Lord will I sing my song, my hymn to the*

Lord, the God of Israel (Judg. 5:3; *In Lib. Judicum, Hom. 6,* § 3, *PG* 12:977).

519. ST. AUGUSTINE. A. We sing with the voice to arouse ourselves; we sing with the heart to please God (*Enarr. in Ps. 147,* § 5, *PL* 37:1917). B. But we who, in the Church, have learned to sing the praises of God, should at the same time strive to be what is written: *Happy is the people who know the joyful shout* (Ps. 88:16). Therefore dearest brethren, what we have sung with the voice of harmony, we ought also to know and understand with an undisturbed heart (*Enarr. in Ps. 18,* II, *Serm. ad plebem,* § 1, *PL* 36:157). C. Not everyone who sings with his lips sings a new canticle, but only the one who sings in the way advised by the Apostle when he says: . . . *singing and making melody in your hearts to the Lord* (Eph. 5:19). For this joy is within, where the voice of praise sings, and is heard; with this voice he is praised who is to be freely loved *with the whole heart, with the whole soul, the whole mind* (Luke 10:27), and who kindles his lover with love for himself by the grace of the Holy Spirit. What else is the new canticle but the love of God? (*Ep. 140, ad Honoratum,* c. 17, n. 44, *PL* 33:557.) D. Sing to him, but not unskillfully. He would not that his ears be offended. Sing skillfully, brother. Now, if you are afraid to sing in the presence of a good musician—when you are invited to sing in order to please such a person —lest you displease a master of the art, because what an unskillful person would not find amiss in you, a master will criticize—then, who can undertake to sing skillfully before God who so intently judges the singer, who examines every part minutely, who hears so accurately? How can you possibly show so nice a skill in singing as to displease in nothing ears that are so perfect? Now David gives, as it were, the melody for your song; do not seek words as though you could explain whereby God is pleased. Sing the joyful shout: for this is to sing skillfully before God. Now, what does "sing the joyful shout" mean? Not to be able to understand, or to express in words what is said in the heart. For singers in the harvest or in the vineyards, or in any other intense work, after they have begun to exult and rejoice in the words of their songs and are filled with so great a joy that they can no longer express it in words, turn from the actual words to sounds of joyful shouting. This "jubilee" is a sound signifying that the heart labors with what it is incapable of uttering. And to whom is that jubilation more becoming than the Ineffable God? For he is Ineffable, whom you cannot speak. And if you cannot speak him, and must nevertheless not keep silent about him, what remains for you but joyful shouting, in which the heart may rejoice without words, and the boundless extent of joy may have no limit of syllables? (*Enarr. II in Ps. 32, Serm. I,* § 8, *PL* 36:283.)

We must sing in harmony

E. A chorus is the union of singers. If we sing in chorus, let us sing in concord. If anyone's voice is out of harmony in the chorus of singers, it is offensive to the ear and throws the chorus into confusion (*ibid. in Ps. 149,* § 7, *PL* 37:1953). F. But the choir signifies concord, which consists in charity (*ibid. in Ps. 87,* § 1, col. 1109). G. Vie with one another in prayer, in mutual and holy rivalry, for you are not so contending against one another, but against the devil, the enemy of all saints (*Ep. 130, Probae,* § 31, *PL* 33:507; Parsons, p. 401).

520. ST. NICETAS. Your voices must all sound together in consonance, not dissonance. One person is not to draw his voice out foolishly, another lower his, a third raise his; but each one is urged to join his voice to the sound as the choir sings together, and to do this in humility —neither lifting the voice apart from the choir, nor dragging it out unbecomingly as though acting from foolish ostentation, nor with the thought of pleasing men. We must celebrate the whole as though in God's sight, and not with the desire of pleasing men. We have an example for this consonance of voices those three blessed youths about whom Daniel the Prophet relates: *Then these three as with one mouth praised, and glorified, and blessed God in the furnace, saying: Blessed art thou, O Lord the God of our fathers* (Dan. 3:51–52). You see, this is related for our instruction that the three boys praised God together, as with one mouth, in a humble and holy manner. And we also are all to pronounce together, as though with one mouth, with a harmonious recitation of the Psalms, one modulation of the voice. He who is unable to keep with the others, should rather either remain altogether silent or sing in a subdued voice, than chant loudly; for in so doing he will be fulfilling the office of his ministry, and in his humility he will offer no hindrance to the brethren who are singing. . . . If the community's voice is undisturbed or in harmony with the well-sounding cymbals (cf. Ps. 150:5), it will be pleasing to us, edifying to those who hear us, and our whole praise will be gratifying to God, who, as we read, *maketh men of one manner to dwell in a house* (Ps. 67:7, Douay version). When we sing, let us all sing; when something is being read, let it be listened to in the same way, by all, and in silence, so that while the reader is reading, no one is to make any kind of loud noise. All are to assemble before the reading begins; if anyone comes late, he will adore God alone, mark his forehead with the cross, and zealously accommodate his ear to the law of God (*Opusc. II,* c. 3, *de psalmodiae bono, PL* 68:374).

521. ST. MECHTILD. A. On one occasion when she had become extremely fatigued during the chant, a condition that was recurring frequently, and she was totally lacking in strength, it seemed that her every breath was drawn from the heart of God, and that thus it was not

so much by her own power that she sang as with an energy that was divine. It was her custom to sing the praises of God with all her strength and with a love so intense that the thought often came to her that even if she were to give up her spirit in the act, she could not quit singing. While it seemed to her that she was thus singing with such an intimate union with God, the Lord spoke to her: "As you yourself seem now to be drawing your breath from my heart, so every person who loves me and longs for me, will draw his breath not from his own, but from my Divine Heart, like a bellows that has no breath but that which it draws from the air."

During the chanting of the hymn, *Bless the Lord, all ye works of the Lord* (Dan. 3:57) in choir, she sought to know what glory God drew from such an invitation to all creatures to join in his praise. The Lord replied: "When anyone chants this or a similar hymn, summoning all creatures to the divine praises, they all appear spiritually as persons in my presence and praise me with all the blessings I have bestowed upon them, for this person [who summoned them] and for men in general (*Le livre de la grace spéciale, IIIe partie,* c. 7, p. 200). B. [During Mass, after the Elevation], she saw a harp emerge from the bosom of God. This harp was the Lord Jesus, whose strings were all the elect who became one in God through love. Then Jesus, the great Precentor of all the singers, played the harp and all the angels accompanied him in a most beautiful melody, and all the saints united in God, sang in sweet harmony . . . (*ibid., IIe partie,* c. 2, p. 168).

522. ST. GERTRUDE THE GREAT. A. In the Mass which the Lord Jesus sang for St. Gertrude [in a vision, Gaudete Sunday, as she was preparing to receive Holy Communion], . . . by the desire of her soul, she united all the affection ever experienced in human love, and at the first *Christe eleison* returned it from her heart to the Divine Heart as to the source from which all the joy of all creatures derives. In this offering there was a wonderful inflowing of God into her soul and of her soul into God, so that at the descending notes the Divine Heart communicated himself with indescribable joy to her heart, and at the ascending notes, the joy of her soul flowed back to God (*Insinuationes divinae pietatis, Lib. IV,* c. 62, p. 641; *Life and Revelations,* p. 478). B. On the feast of a certain saint as (St. Gertrude) was chanting the Canonical Hours to the glory of God and the praise of the saint with more than usual devotion, each word that she sang seemed to dart like a sharp arrow from her heart into the Heart of Jesus Christ, piercing it to the inmost recesses and producing in it indescribable pleasure. From the upper end of the arrow, rays of light like brilliant stars shot forth to adorn with new glory all the saints they touched. But in a particular manner the saint whose feast was being celebrated seemed thus honored with a distinctive splendor. From the lower end of the arrow shaft dripped copious drops [of

the Precious Blood] to be applied to those on earth as an increase of special grace and as a consoling support for the souls in Purgatory (*ibid., Lib. III,* c. 25, p. 221; *Life and Revelations,* p. 182). C. As [St. Gertrude] strove on a different occasion to attach an intention to each note and word of the chant and failed repeatedly through human frailty, she asked herself sadly: "What can I gain from effort in which there is so much instability?" Unable to behold her sadness, the Lord, with his own hands, presented her his Divine Heart, under the figure of a burning lamp, saying: "I present my most loving Heart, the organ of the adorable Trinity, to the eyes of your soul. You will trustingly confide in this Heart to supply for whatever you yourself cannot do. Thus all that you do will appear absolutely perfect in my sight. Like the faithful servant who is always eager to do the will of his Master, my Heart will henceforth be ready to supply at any hour for all your negligences" (*ibid.*).

Live a holy life in order to chant in a holy manner

523. JOHN BONA, Cistercian, cardinal (d. 1674). A. Persons whose lives are in harmony with what they chant and whose deeds echo what they pronounce, sing with a melody that is most pleasing to God. *Let me hear your voice, for your voice is sweet, and you are lovely* (Cant. 2:14). *My friends are listening for your voice, let me hear it!* (*Ibid.,* 8:13.) O beautiful words of love, O beautiful song of the soul in love! Can one then really believe that God takes such delight in the praises of humans that he invites the soul he loves, to sing? O heavenly music produced by the virtues, far surpassing all keenness of the senses, which resounds in the soul of the just man but which cannot be perceived by outsiders who are not friends. God directs this concert with his saints, each of whom contributes to the melody according to the variety of gifts he has bestowed on them—the heavy note of humility, the sharp note of lively faith, the extremely sharp note of charity (*Divina psalmodia,* c. 17, § 5, n. 3, *Op. Om.* p. 528). B. First we must preserve in its purity and entirety the chant which we have received from our ancestors. Otherwise, once we begin to wander from the old paths which our fathers laid out, the integrity of religion will gradually be destroyed by ill-advised changes. They who change the chant change the morality [of a people] (*ibid.,* n. 2, p. 527).

524. ST. ODO, abbot of Cluny (d. 942). There are other kinds of music, accommodated to other measures; but that which we have described above [Gregorian] is considered perfect in the judgment of the most skillful and the saintliest men of music, because of its more gentle, more appropriate and natural inflection. The most holy Father, Pope Gregory, whose prescripts Holy Church observes scrupulously, enriched the Church with the Antiphonary, a book admirably composed in this

kind of music; moreover he personally taught his disciples. Nowhere do we read that he learned this art by ordinary human methods of acquiring knowledge; in fact, it is accepted that he received the fulness of his skill from heaven. Certain it is that this kind of music, because of the divine manner in which it was bestowed upon St. Gregory, enjoys the support not only of human authority but also of that which is divine. . . . From these considerations [about St. Ambrose, St. Isidore, on the philosophy of music], it is evident that Pope St. Gregory, through grace received from heaven, was blessed with greater zeal for this art than all others. For it is truly remarkable, when you reflect on the matter, that in the Responses of the Night Office he seems by the music, to exhort us earnestly to wakefulness . . . as we would one who is drowsy; in the Antiphons, however, the composition calls for singing that is full-toned and gentle; in the Introits it invites us with the voice of a herald to share in the divine mysteries; it rejoices gently in the Alleluia; in the Tract and Gradual it seems to course along simply, at greater length, and in a lower register. In the Offertory and especially the Communion chants, with their verses, it reveals itself fully, as richly as music can express itself—for here we find the complete development of this art, the perfect presentation—a delight for those who appreciate it, and a real difficulty, it is true, for those who are still learning; its wonderful presentation differing from all other chants. . . . He stands altogether in opposition to the authority of the Church who entirely neglects the divine gift of Blessed Gregory in favor of other forms of singing *(Opusc. de musica, PL* 133:783–785).

525. MANUSCRIPT OF VERONA (10th century). When the most holy Father Gregory poured forth his prayer to the Lord to give him from on high the expression for his musical composition, the Holy Spirit descended upon him in the form of a dove and illumined his heart, and thus finally, he began to chant with the words: "To you I lift up my soul" (*Ad Te levavi animam meam,* Introit, First Sunday of Advent, Ps. 24:1; cited in: P. L. Lambillotte, S. J., *Antiphonaire de Saint Gregoire; fac-simile du manuscrit de Saint-Gall,* viii siècle . . . Paris: Poussielque-Rusand, 1851, p. 8).

526. RULE FOR MONKS, by Sts. Paul and Stephen, abbots (6th century). Let no one in this community presume to meditate upon or recite responsories or antiphons which are not taken from the canonical Scriptures, but which are nevertheless sung by some in ornate composition on their own initiative. Nor is any guest who arrives at the monastery to dare to meditate on such things except with the prior's permission. [This provision is made] lest, carried away as it were by the strange doctrine and the attractiveness of what is trifling, they become critical of the sobriety of simplicity and truth, and ensnared, as it were, by the melodies of frivolity, they either hasten, at the devil's suasion, to depart

from the community; or, remaining within the monastery, but puffed up with their knowledge, hold others in contempt. We should, strengthened by grace, imitate the one, simple, apostolic doctrine of our Fathers and subject our heart and conduct to discipline. We must chant, as St. Augustine says, what is written to be chanted, and not sing what is not so written. Nor must those things be said by us in his praise in a manner different from what the Lord himself has commanded to be revealed to men through his prophets and Apostles; lest we change what is to be chanted into a form of prose or reading, or presumptuously change what is written to be read into subjects for our art of singing. For if we must offer God the sacrifice of confession and praise, we must do so as he commanded; for the Lord seeks from us the sacrifice of obedience rather than of victims. Nor is he pleased with the exercise of skill in singing so much as by the observance of the commandments and purity of heart (c. 14, *CR* 1:141; *PL* 66:953).

527. ST. NICETAS. Let there be sung words and melody which are in harmony with religious thought, and not such as cry aloud of tragic difficulties, but rather that which gives testimony of our true Christianity—not something that smacks of the theater, but that which instills sorrow for sin (*Opusc. II, de psalmodiae bono,* c. 3, *PL* 68:374).

The Holy Eucharist

528. ST. JOHN CHRYSOSTOM. A. When you see the Lord, sacrificed and laid upon the altar, and the priest standing and praying over the Victim, and all the worshipers empurpled with that Precious Blood, can you think that you are among men and standing upon the earth? (*De sacerdotio, Lib. III,* § 4, *PG* 48:642.) B. At such a time [when the Sacrifice is being offered] angels stand by the priest, the whole rank of heavenly virtues cries out, and the sanctuary and the space round about the altar, is filled with the powers of heaven, in honor of him who lies thereon (*ibid., Lib. VI,* § 4, col. 681). C. For where Christ is, there are the angels too, and where Christ and the angels are, there is heaven; there is a light more powerful than that of the sun (*In Matt., Hom. 48,* § 7, *PG* 58:495).

529. ST. GREGORY THE GREAT. For who of the faithful can doubt that in the very hour of the Sacrifice, at the words of the priest, the heavens are opened; that choirs of angels are present in that mystery of Jesus Christ; that the lowest things are united with the highest; that those of earth are joined with the heavenly; and that one thing is made of visible and invisible? (*Dialogorum Lib. IV,* c. 53, *De virtute ac mysterio victimae salutaris, PL* 77:425.)

530. ST. IGNATIUS OF ANTIOCH, martyr (d. 107). Make an effort, then, to meet more frequently to celebrate God's Eucharist, and to offer praise. For when you meet frequently in the same place, the forces of

satan are overthrown, and his baneful influence is neutralized by the unanimity of your faith (*Ep. ad Ephesios,* c. 13, *PG* 5:655; Kleist, S. J., p. 65).

531. ST. AUGUSTINE. I make bold to state that God, although omnipotent, could grant no more; although infinitely wise, knew nothing more to give; and although possessed of all abundance, had nothing more to give.*

The holy Sacrifice: the priesthood

532. ST. JOHN CHRYSOSTOM. A. And when the priest invokes the Holy Spirit, and offers the most dread Sacrifice, and constantly handles the common Lord of all, tell me, what rank shall we give him? What great purity and what real piety must we demand of him! For consider what manner of hands they ought to be which minister in these things; and of what kind his tongue which utters such words; and ought not the soul which receives so great a spirit to be purer and holier than anything in this world? (*De sacerdotio, Lib. VI,* c. 4, *PG* 48:681.) B. Wherefore the consecrated priest ought to be as pure as if he were standing in the heavens themselves in the midst of those powers [angels] (*ibid., Lib. III,* c. 4, col. 642). C. The priest's authority is erected in heaven; therefore he has the authority to administer the things of heaven (*Hom. 5 in Isa. 6:1,* § 1, *PG* 56:131). D. If a person is standing before a king of this world, he strives in every manner possible to show the greatest reverence toward him, in order to draw greater favor to himself. Out of respect for the king he is careful not only about the way he holds his head, but strives to show his reverence also by his voice, the posture of his hands, the position of his feet, the attitude of his whole body. . . . That is the way we should stand, in fear and trembling, offering such glorification to God as though beholding him in person with the mind's eye (*ibid., Hom. 1,* § 3, col. 101). E. But when the priesthood is offered to me, which exceeds a kingdom as much as the spirit differs from the flesh, will anyone dare to accuse me of disdain [for declining the office]? (*De sacerdotio, Lib. III,* c. 1, *PG* 48:641.) F. Christ's priests are Christ's vicars and Christ himself; he who honors a priest of Christ honors Christ himself; he who harms a priest of Christ commits an injury to Christ himself . . . (*Opus imperfectum in Matt., Hom. 17, PG* 56:727).

* Wolter simply labels this passage "Inter apocrypha." One runs across it occasionally, usually in pious books. It was quoted, e.g. in *Instr. S.C.C. Saepenumero,* n. 3, 14 Jul., 1941, *A.A.S.* 33:390, as from *Tract. 84 in Joan.,* but it is not to be found there in available editions.Two unusually capable scholars have advanced the opinion that the excerpt is composed from St. Augustine's writings, each phrase taken from a different source. In violation of the principle not to use any unidentified quotations, this one is being retained because of its interest, especially for meditation and preaching. [*Tr.*]

533. ST. CYRIL OF ALEXANDRIA (d. 444). The priest is the figure and visible form of Christ (*De adoratione in spiritu et veritate, Lib. 13, PG* 68:882).

534. ST. EPHRAEM, monk, deacon, who from humility refused to receive the sacred priesthood (d. 378). O stupendous miracle! O ineffable power! O tremendous mystery of the priesthood, spiritual and holy, commanding reverence, beyond all censure, which Christ, coming into the world, bestowed upon even the unworthy! (*Sermo de sacerdotio, Op. Om.* 1:1.)

535. ST. ISIDORE PELUSIOTA, monk (d. 449). The priesthood is a divine thing, and among all others the most pre-eminent (*Lib. II,* ep. 52, *Theodosio episc., PG* 78:494).

Priesthood's dignity and power to be held in veneration

536. ST. LAURENCE JUSTINIAN. Exalted and admirable is the dignity of priests; exceedingly great the power bestowed upon them. When they pronounce the heavenly words, almost at their will, the Body of Christ takes substance from the material of bread, the Word comes down in the flesh from heaven, and is truly present on the table of the altar. By a grace never granted to angels, this prerogative belongs to priests: to serve God, touch him with their hands, give him to the faithful, receive him within themselves. But because they hold the place of angels both in adoring and in ministering, they must be considered as having an angelic rather than a human way of life (*Serm. 39, De Christi Corpore, seu de Eucharistia, Op. Om.* 2:122).

537. ST. BERNARD. A. O noble power that is yours, so deeply to be held in reverence! Surely after God no power is like yours. . . . To it nothing in heaven or on earth can be compared—this power to consecrate the body and blood of the Lord! . . . In the presence of so marvelous a miracle, and the great privilege of your dignity, heaven stands in awe, the earth is stupefied, man trembles, the angels themselves bow in reverence before such power. . . . Here in truth is the condescension of heaven itself, here is grace in its fulness, the glory of priests exceeding all others—for the priest to hold his God in his hands and to present him to others. O new and divine power by whose ministry the Bread of angels and of life is daily made available to mortal men! (*Serm. de excellentia SS. Sacramenti,* n. 3, *In Append., PL* 184:983.) B. Hearken, and stand in admiration in your astonishment! To none of the angels, to no heavenly spirits, but to men—not however to all men, but to your order only, O priests—has been commanded the celebration of so great a mystery at the altar, to do what Christ did with his own hands at the Paschal Supper (*ibid.,* n. 5). O sacred and heavenly ministry that is yours! O praiseworthy desire, wonder exceeding all others, solemn miracle! God, who is wonderful in all his crea-

tures, is more wonderful, certainly, in himself; and by working his miracle through you, shows himself more wonderful through you. Is there more to be considered? *O ye priests of the Lord, bless the Lord* (Dan. 3:84), striving always to offer worthy things to God, lest what is provided unto healing for those who receive the sacrament worthily, be for you unto destruction (*ibid.*, n. 16).*

538. PETRUS COMESTOR, priest of Paris, called "the Bookworm," possibly because of his avidity in reading (d. 1179). He willed to have helpers in the mystery of our Redemption, saying, *Do this in remembrance of Me* (Luke 22:19). Hence the priest is the assistant of the Redeemer, the representative of the Lord of Sabbaoth, on whose recommendation they who have been guilty of offense return to the grace of their God. He is the servant at Christ's table . . . (*Serm. 47, ad sacerdotes et praelatos, PL* 198:1837).

539. ST. BERNARD. [At the altar] Christ addresses his minister: . . . "The altar at which you are standing represents the cross that I bore for you; the chalice, the tomb in which I rested after death; the paten, the stone that was rolled before the tomb; the corporal of the altar, the head cloth; the altar linens spread beneath the corporal, the shroud in which I was wrapped. The host upon which you look is no longer bread, but my Body which hung on the cross for the life of the world" (*Serm. de excellentia SS. Sacramenti,* n. 11, *In Append., PL* 184:987).

Virtuous life of the priest

540. ST. JEROME. In a priest of Christ, mouth, mind and hand should be at one (*Ep. 52, ad Nepotianum, de vita clericorum et monachorum,* n. 7, *PL* 22:533).

541. ST. GREGORY THE GREAT. As the superior surpasses others in the dignity of his rank, so should he in the virtue of his conduct (*Reg. pastoralis Lib., Pars II,* c. 3, *PL* 77:28; Davis, p. 49).

542. ST. PETER DAMIAN. He who has no fear of handling the body of the Lord with soiled hands stands convicted of being among those who crucified Jesus (*Opusc. 26, contra inscitiam et incuriam clericorum,* c. 2, *PL* 145:501).

543. HUGH OF ST. VICTOR. Consider well, O priest, of what kind should be the hands that minister such great things; of what kind the tongue that pronounces such words; how much purer and holier than others should be the soul that receives of such a Spirit! (*De anima, Lib. III,* c. 50, *In Append., PL* 177:167.)

544. PETER DE BLOIS. The hands which touch the most spotless body and blood of Christ must themselves be perfectly spotless. Let your

* As indicated in Migne, this is certainly not the writing of St. Bernard, but that of one who was not ordained a priest, as is evident from the wording of these excerpts. [*Tr.*]

words to your subjects be fruitful: let your deeds be an example, for, as St. Gregory testifies, if you do what is wrong, you deserve as many deaths as were the examples of perdition given to your subjects (*Lib. reg. pastoralis, Pars III,* c. 4, § 5, *PL* 77:54; Davis, p. 97; *Ep. 157, ad G. vicarium suum, quem monet ut pro grege sibi commisso sedulam curam gerat, PL* 207:452).

Celebration of holy Mass

545. ST. AMBROSE. What searching of heart, what shedding of tears, what reverence, and what awe, what purity of soul and body are called for in offering God's heavenly Sacrifice, when your flesh is eaten indeed and your blood is drunk indeed, where the things of the highest are brought down to the things of the lowest; and things that are of God to the things that are of earth; where the holy angels are present, where you yourself are wondrously and unspeakably among us, at once the Sacrifice and the Priest! Who can worthily deal with this, unless you, O God almighty, make him worthy? (*Precatio I in praeparatione ad Missam,* § 4, *In Append., PL* 17:831; *Missale Rom.,* p. liii.)

546. ST. FRANCIS OF ASSISI. Hear ye, my brethren: If the Blessed Virgin Mary is so honored, as is indeed fitting, because she bore him in her most holy womb; if the Blessed Baptist trembled and did not dare to touch the holy forehead of God; if the sepulchre in which he lay for some time is venerated, how holy, just and worthy ought he to be who touches with his hands, who receives with his heart and his mouth, and proffers to be received by others him who is now no more to die but to triumph in a glorified eternity, on whom the angels desire to look. Consider your dignity, brothers, priests, and be holy because he himself is holy (cf. Lev. 11:44). It is a great misery and a deplorable weakness when you have him thus present to care for anything else in the whole world (*Ep. 12, ad sacerdotes totius Ordinis, Op. Om.,* p. 8).

547. JOHN OF TRITHEIM. Weigh well and examine most carefully what kind of life is most proper for the priesthood, how clean and holy it behooves you to be, how pure in mind, how wise in speech, and zealous in deed. . . . Standing at the altar, about to immolate the Son of God and of the Virgin, the very excellence of the Sacrifice reveals to you how devout and reverent you must be. . . . What kind of man do you think the priest of Christ should be? Does the ordinary way of life of Christians suffice for him? Certainly that is not enough! For he who excels in order, is also to be more perfect in his way of life; a higher rank demands a more elevated form of recognition, and it is only fitting that he who enjoys precedence over others by the dignity of honor, must excel by the perfection of virtue, those at whose head he stands (*Ep. 1, ad novum quemdam presbyterum, Opera pia et spiritualia,* pp. 919–918).

548. IMITATION OF CHRIST (Thomas à Kempis). Oh, how clean should be the hands, how pure the mouth, how holy the body, and how undefiled the heart of a priest, into whom so often the Author of all purity enters. Truly, there should proceed from the mouth of a priest, who so often receives the Sacrament of Christ, no word but what is holy, honest and profitable (*De imitatione Christi, Lib. IV,* c. 11, *Op. Om.* 2:123; Gardiner, p 225).

549. ST. AUGUSTINE. If a sacred action [in the office of bishop, priest, or deacon] is performed carelessly or in a manner to draw flattery, in God's sight there is nothing more wretched, more melancholy, or more worthy of punishment (*Ep. 21, ad episc. Valerium,* § 1, *PL* 33:88; Parsons, p. 48).

550. ST. LAURENCE JUSTINIAN. A. The priest is approached in the Church that he may bring grace to the just, pardon to the sinful, strength to the weak, joy to the sorrowful; encouragement to the faithful, hope to the wavering, peace to believers, victory to the struggling, freedom to prisoners, and eternal rest to the deceased . . . (*Serm. 39, De Christi Corpore, seu de Eucharistia, Op. Om.* 2:113). B. With what spirit of adoration must the priest stand at the altar, for on him is bestowed the authority to consecrate hosts, offer incense, and plead for the faithful, for his office is one of mediation (*ibid.,* p. 122). C. Let the priest ascend to the altar in the person of Christ himself, assist as an angel, minister to others as a saint, offer the prayers of the people as a pontiff, intercede for peace as a mediator; but pray for himself as a man! (*Ibid.,* p. 123.)

551. ST. BONAVENTURE. When a priest who is free of mortal sin, well-intentioned, detained by no legitimate impediment, and acting not out of reverence but through negligence, omits the celebration of Mass, he deprives, as far as lies in his power, the Most Holy Trinity of praise and glory, the angels of joy, sinners of pardon, just men of help and grace; the souls detained in Purgatory of consolation, the Church of Christ of spiritual benefits, and himself of the remedy against his daily sins and weaknesses (*De praeparatione ad Missam,* c. 1, § 9, *Op. Om.,* ed. Quaracchi 8:102).

Holy Communion

552. ARNOLD, abbot of Bonnevaux (d. circa 1161). A. This Bread of angels, endowed in itself with all delights, has the wonderful power of pleasing all that worthily and devoutly receive it, conforming to every taste (cf. Wisd. 16:20 f.). Far more than the manna of the desert, it fulfils and satisfies the appetites of those who eat it; it overcomes the appeal of all fleshly enjoyments and pleasures of all gratifications . . . (*Lib. de cardinalibus operibus Christi, VI, de coena Domini, PL* 189:1647). B. How excellent is this Chalice, how religious the drunkenness of its

drink, by which we withdraw to God and, having forgotten that which is past, strive forward to what is before (cf. Phil. 3:13); having no longer appreciation for the things of this world, but, despising the pleasures of the finely dressed rich man, embrace the cross (*ibid.*, col. 1646).

553. ST. CYRIL, bp. of Alexandria (d. 444). A. Just as when one mixes melted wax with other melted wax, a united whole results, so by the communion of the body and blood of Christ, he is in us, and we are united in him (*In Joan. Evang., Lib. X,* c. 2, *PG* 74:342). B. Therefore in the spirit of piety, resolve to live morally and worthily, and thus to be a sharer in the blessing, believing that [Holy Communion] has the power not only to dispel death, but our illness as well (*ibid., Lib. IV,* c. 2, *PG* 73:586).

554. ST. AUGUSTINE. O sacrament of piety! O sign of unity! O bond of charity! Whoever desires to live has where to live, and whereof to live. Let him approach, let him believe; let him be incorporated, that he may be quickened. Let him not shrink from the whole into which the members are compacted together, let him not be a rotten member that deserves to be cut off, nor a distorted member to be ashamed of; let him be a beautiful, a well-fitting, a sound member; let him cleave to the body, let him live to God, by God; let him now labor on earth, that hereafter he may reign in heaven (*Tract. 26 in Joan.,* § 13, *PL* 35:1613).

555. ST. THOMAS AQUINAS. A. And therefore, this sacrament does for the spiritual life, all that material food does for the bodily life, namely, by sustaining, giving increase, restoring, and giving delight (*III,* q. 79, art. 1, *Utrum per hoc sacramentum conferatur gratia, Op. Om.* 12:217; Am. ed. 2:2480). B. Secondly, inasmuch as it is a sign of Christ's Passion, whereby devils are conquered, it repels all the assaults of demons (*ibid.,* art. 6, *Utrum per hoc sacramentum praeservatur homo a peccatis futuris,* p. 225; p. 2484). C. The effect of this sacrament is not only the obtaining of habitual grace or charity, but also a certain actual refreshment of spiritual sweetness; which is indeed hindered if anyone approach this sacrament with mind distracted through venial sins (*ibid.* art. 8, *Utrum per veniale peccatum impediatur effectus hujus sacramenti,* p. 227;2485).

556. ST. BERNARD. If any of you is not now assailed so often or so violently by the passion of anger, or of envy, or of lust, or by other like failings, let him return thanks to the body and blood of Christ, because the power of the sacrament has been efficacious in him; and let him rejoice, for this awful sore is beginning to heal (*Serm. de temp., Serm. in Coena Domini,* § 3, *PL* 183:272).

557. ST. AMBROSE. If it [the Eucharist] is daily bread, why do you take it only once a year, as the Greeks in the East were accustomed to do? Take daily what is to profit you daily. So live that you may deserve to receive it daily. He who does not deserve to receive it daily, does not

deserve to receive it once a year. Holy Job offered holocausts daily for every one of his sons, lest perchance they should have done any sin in heart or word (cf. Job 1:5). That is why you hear that as often as the Sacrifice is offered, the Lord's death, the Lord's Resurrection, the Lord's Ascension, and the remission of sins is signified—and you do not take this Bread of life daily! (cf. I Cor. 11:26.) He who has a wound needs medicine. The wound is that we are under sin; the medicine is the heavenly and venerable sacrament (*De sacramentis, Lib. V,* c. 4, § 25, *PL* 16:471).

558. ST. AUGUSTINE. A. "I am the food of grown men; grow and you shall eat me. And you shall not change me into yourself as bodily food, but into me you shall be changed" (*Confessionum Lib. VII,* c. 10, n. 16, *PL* 32:742; Sheed, p. 145). B. If a precious garment is not put away into a box that is soiled, by what line of reasoning is the Eucharist of Christ received into a soul soiled with the stains of sins? (*Serm. 229, In Dedicatione Eccl. vel altaris consecr.,* § 5, *In Append., PL* 39:2168.)

559. ST. JOHN CHRYSOSTOM. A. How many now say: "I wish that I could see his form, the marks of his passion, his clothes, his shoes!" But you see him, you touch him, you eat him! And you desire to see his clothes, but he gives himself to you not to see only but also to touch and to eat and receive within yourself. Let no one approach it with indifference, no one fainthearted, but all burning with zeal, all fervent, all aroused (*In Matt., Hom. 82,* § 4, *PG* 58:743). B. That at which the angels tremble when they behold, to which they dare not so much as look up without awe because of the brightness which shines forth from it, is that with which we are fed, with which we are commingled; and thus we are made one body and one flesh with Christ (*ibid.,* § 5). C. Beware, therefore, lest you also become guilty of the body and blood of Christ. [The Jews] slaughtered the all-holy body, but you receive it in a filthy soul after such great benefits (*ibid.*). D. Let no one have evil thoughts within, but let us purify our minds; for we approach to the pure Sacrifice. Let us make our souls holy (*De proditione Judae, Hom. I,* § 6, *PG* 49:381). E. Let us all come to this awesome table, but provided that we approach it with due reverence and fitting vigilance. Let not another Judas be found there; let no evil one draw near; let none infected with poison approach (*ibid.,* col. 380). F. For *there came out blood and water* (John 19:34). Not without a purpose, or by chance, did those founts come forth, but because by means of these two together, the Church is established. This the initiate know, being by water indeed born again, and nourished by the blood and the flesh. Hence the Mysteries that take their beginning: to teach you that when you approach to that awful Cup, you may so approach as drinking from Christ's very side (*In Joan., Hom. 85,* § 3, *PG* 59:463). G. For this table is the sinews of our soul, the bond of our mind, the foundation of our

confidence, our hope, our salvation, our light, our life. . . . Make your soul clean, then, prepare your mind for the reception of these mysteries (*In Ep. I ad Cor., Hom. 24,* § 5, *PG* 61:204). H. When you see [the body of Christ] exposed, say to yourself: "Thanks to this body, I am no longer dust and ashes. I am no more a captive but a freeman; hence I hope to obtain heaven and the good things that are there in store for me, eternal life, the heritage of angels, companionship with Christ; death has not destroyed this body which was once covered with blood, pierced with a lance from which issued forth saving fountains upon the world, one of blood and the other of water. . . . This body he gave us to keep and eat, as a mark of his intense love" (*ibid.,* § 4, col. 203). I. Look, I ask you: a royal table is set before you, angels minister at that table, the King himself is there, and do you still stand there and gape? . . . If your garments are clean, fall down and partake! (*In Ep. ad Eph., Hom. 3,* § 5, *PG* 62:29.)

560. ST. ISIDORE OF SEVILLE. The flesh [of Christ] is the food of the saints (*Quaest. in Vet. Testam., In Gen.,* c. 31, § 48, *PL* 83:284).

561. ST. JEROME. Nothing must be more tranquil, nothing more pure, nothing more beautiful than the mind which is to be prepared as the dwelling of God (*Ep. 148, ad Celantiam matronam, de ratione pie vivendi,* § 19, *PL* 22:1213).

562. RUDOLPH OF BIBERACH, Franciscan mystic (d. 1360). A. [By the eating of this body] resurrection is promised, eternal life hoped for, the gates of heaven opened. The table of the divine repast is prepared. At it the body of Christ is truly eaten, and divinity is bestowed on us (*De septem donis Spiritus Sancti, Pars II,* sec. 3, c. 3, *Op. Om. S. Bonaventurae,* ed. Peltier 7:610). B. O what refreshment is there, where Christ serves at the table, and the Holy Spirit is the cup-bearer! Certainly the Father is the most bountiful host. Christ sets the repast before his guests and refreshes and satisfies them with his own self, as we learn from the Gospel of St. John (6:51). The Holy Spirit plies them with drink until they are permeated with his gifts, as the Acts of the Apostles show us (2:38–47). And in both of them the Father most frequently shows and communicates himself: in the person of the Son, that he may be seen and possessed, as Jesus spoke to Philip (John 14:8 f.); and in the Holy Spirit, that he may be received and enjoyed (*ibid.,* sect. 8, c. 11, p. 650).

563. ST. BONAVENTURE. Guard against approaching the holy table with too great tepidity, want of preparation, or thoughtlessness; for you receive [Christ's body] unworthily unless you approach with reverence, mature deliberation, and reflection (*De praeparatione ad Missam,* c. 1, § 8, *Op. Om.,* ed. Quaracchi 8:102).

564. ST. BERNARD. Glorious and lovable Bride [the Church]! Here on earth you have your Bridegroom in the Sacrament, in heaven you

are to have him without the veil [that calls for faith]. Both here below and there you have the Reality; only here it is cloaked, there it is fully revealed (*Serm. de excellentia SS. Sacramenti*, n. 7, *In Append., PL* 184: 985).

565. BL. OGER. Let whoever desires to sit at the humble table of Christ not approach without tears; and when he has approached, let him not depart without a sigh! (*Serm. XV de Sermone Domini in ultima coena, Prolog., PL* 184:879, *inter opera S. Bernardi.*)

566. ST. THOMAS AQUINAS. A. O how precious a thing, then, how marvelous, how life-giving, how furnished with all delicacies is the Supper [of the Lord] (*Opusc. 19, Officium de festo Corp. Christi ad mandatum Urbani Papae IV dictum festum instituentis, Lect. II ad Matut., Op. Om., ed. Parmae* 15:234). B. Can anything be more health-giving than this sacrament? . . . By it sins are purged away, strength renewed, and the soul fed upon the fatness of spiritual gifts (*ibid., Lect. III*). C. [The Eucharist is] . . . the greatest miracle which he ever wrought (*ibid., Lect. IV*, p. 235). D. The Eucharist is the sacrament of love (*Opusc. 51, De venerabili sacramento altaris*, c. 25, *ibid.*, 17:166).

567. HUGH OF ST. VICTOR. As we do not dare to approach the altar without vestments, so let us not presume to approach it without virtues (*Serm. 14, In synodo . . . de vestibus sacris, In Append., PL* 177:927).

568. PETER DE BLOIS. He who unworthily consecrates the body of Christ, betrays Christ, so that the Lord says, as he is betrayed: *The hand of him who betrays me is with me on the table* (Luke 22:21). . . . He is worthy of condemnation for his sin who approaches the body of Christ with the gall of an evil conscience and the vinegar of iniquity. Faith-breaking Jew, faith-breaking Christian: the former pours out the blood from the side of Christ, the latter from the Chalice. . . . Is he not to be judged, rather, an anti-Christian than a Christian who, so far as lies in his power, touches unworthily; who treats shamefully; who cruelly kills; who dishonorably buries Christ; who has already become impassible? (*Ep. 123, ad Richardum episc. Londinensem cui declarat se ex diaconatu ad sacerdotium progredi nolle, non ex contemptu sed ex reverentia, PL* 207:360.)

569. VEN. LOUIS DE BLOIS. A. No tongue can express, no heart can comprehend how boundless are the spiritual goods which come to the soul from the devout reception of this sweet sacrament of the Eucharist (*Speculum spirituale*, c. 12, n. 3, *Op. Om.* 2:580). B. For the three Persons of the one Godhead and Essence cannot be separated from one another. The whole Trinity, therefore, dwells in the body of Christ, because the whole Godhead is in it. The fruits, therefore, of the Blessed Sacrament are many and precious. 1) He who receives the body of the Lord with due devotion is cleansed of all crimes, and is even absolved of those mortal sins of which he is no longer conscious or does not remem-

ber to have committed; provided only that he is so disposed that if he were conscious of having committed them, he would confess them and do penance. 2) In like manner he is made a partaker in all the good things which Christ merited for us in his life, passion, and death; 3) in fact, he shares in all the good things which have ever been performed since the time of Adam or will ever be performed down to the time of the last of the elect; and 4) lastly, he is united to Christ and incorporated into him, from which union he receives the strength and the power to withstand vices and devote himself to deeds of virtue. Thus, adorned with a life of greater purity and excellence, he is transformed and changed into God, and is filled with all the grace of the most glorious Trinity (*Institutio spiritualis*, c. 8, § 1, *ibid.*, p. 312).

The sacred liturgy

570. BARTOLOMMEO GAVANTI, general of congregation of Barnabites (d. 1638). In the whole course of the year the Church seeks to represent in an orderly manner, the life, deeds and sufferings of Christ, from his first Coming in the flesh to his second Coming at the end of the world (*Thesaurus sacrorum rituum, Pars II,* tit. 16; Venetiis, 1630, 1:161, somewhat adapted by Wolter).

571. RUPERT, abbot of Deutz. They who faithfully and devoutly follow the mysteries and wonders of the Church are not deprived of benefit, even though they are unable to understand the meaning of those mysteries. They were instituted precisely for this purpose: that in a marvelous manner the hidden designs of God, which can be understood by few, can nevertheless be shared in by all. Though it is true that only the eyes can see what we are doing in the performance of a work, are the other members, which do not see, but which are also engaged in performing the work, deprived of their share? (*De divinis officiis per anni circulum, Prolog., PL* 170:13.)

572. ST. PETER DAMIAN. All that is done in the acts of worship under both the Old and the New Testaments, always seems to be presented to us almost entirely through the medium of mystical symbols or figurative representations. What did the whole elaborate construction of the Dwelling of the Commandments (cf. Exod. 26:1 f.), what the number of Levites (cf. Num. 1:47 f.), what the ceremonies of the priests signify; or, for that matter, what do the modern rites of Holy Church demand, except that which calls for a spiritual interpretation? And, if I may so speak, the mystery lies in the ministry, whereas the hidden sacrament of allegorical explanation is to be found in the exercise of external worship (*Opusc. 11,* c. 17, *PL* 145:245).

573. ST. AUGUSTINE. A. Whatever right worship is paid to God profits not him, but man. For no man would say that he was conferring a benefit on a fountain by drinking, or on light by seeing (*De Civitate*

Dei, Lib. X, c. 5, *PL* 41:282). B. They who engage in prayer assume physical postures that harmonize with their prayer. They kneel, they lift up their hands, cast themselves prostrate on the ground, and perform other similar external gestures. Although God knows their invisible wills and the intention of their heart, and although he has no need for such material gestures in order to see the human conscience, man nevertheless, in so acting, stirs himself by them to pray and bewail his sins with greater humility and fervor. As movement of the body cannot be produced except by an interior motivation of the soul, the exterior and visible acts nevertheless intensify in their turn—I do not know how—the interior and invisible act which sets them in motion. And it is thus that the affection of the heart which goes before them so that they can be at all, itself grows with their realization (*De cura pro mortuis gerenda,* c. 5, n. 7, *PL* 40:597).

574. SPANISH CONGREGATION (1640). If order that is well regulated and free of all disturbance adds beauty in all other things, certainly we, who day and night apply ourselves in God's house to the performance of sacred services, must make it our concern to execute those sacred rites correctly and in an orderly manner, lest we bear the illustrious name of "order" [of St. Benedict] in vain. The whole argument of the Book of Leviticus in reality is to make God comprehended through ceremonies. In fact, if you consider this book from beginning to end, you would not be incorrect in saying that God himself is a Master of Ceremonies. He is the Master of the nine choirs of angels singing in heaven. And the angel . . . stands before the altar, having a golden censer in his hand (cf. Apoc. 8:3). . . . Thousands of thousands minister to him, and ten thousand times a hundred thousand stand before him (cf. Dan. 7:10) . . . and the four and twenty elders fall down on their faces (cf. Apoc. 4:10). Here you have the reason that sacred ceremonies are always considered to be of great importance. . . . They stimulate and urge on minds that have been fatigued with work even to the point of drowsiness; they captivate the attention of onlookers; they lead those who are overwhelmed with awe before the Divine Majesty to the adoration of the Godhead; nay, they even go so far as to make it seem that angels rather than men are ministering to the Great God (*Caeremoniale monastic. Congr. Hispanicae, in Praef.*).

575. VEN. LOUIS DE BLOIS. This is the beauty, this the majesty of the house of God; that what is prescribed in the rubrics and solemn ceremonies of the Divine Office and the Sacrifice, be performed with devoted seriousness and serious devotion; that the Gregorian chant be rendered clearly, slowly, resonantly . . . and with proper modulation; that the whole Work of God be correctly and properly performed with interior delight and external modesty (*Vita Ven. Blosii abb.,* c. 20, *Op. Om.* 1:lxvii; *Acta Sanctorum,* Bolland, Jan., tom. 1, die 7, p. 447).

576. ST. AUGUSTINE. They celebrate the feasts of the Church worthily who acknowledge themselves to be the children of the Church (*Serm. 231, In Dedic. Eccl. vel altaris consecr.*, III, § 1, *PL* 39:2171).

577. ST. GREGORY THE GREAT. The present [Paschal] solemnity is but the shadow of the solemnity to come (*Hom. 26 in Evang.*, § 10, *PL* 76:1203).

578. ST. BERNARD. A special honor is offered to God in the observance of the holy solemnities (*Serm. IV in Antiph. Salve Regina*, § 4, *In Append.*, *PL* 184:1075).

579. THOMAS À KEMPIS. The external celebration of feasts is the incitement to internal joy, and a kind of foretaste of eternal bliss (*Serm. 3 de vita et passione Domini, Op. Om.* 3:77).

The monk, a man of God who lives by faith

580. ST. AUGUSTINE. A. The house of God is made secure by the practice of faith; it is built upon hope; and it is made perfect through love. It is now in the process of being built; it will be dedicated at the end of the world (*Serm. 27* [cf. Ps. 95:1], *contra Pelagianos*, § 1, *PL* 38:178). B. There is no greater wealth, no treasures, no honors, no possessions that this world offers that are greater than Catholic faith. For it makes sinful men whole, gives light to the blind, heals the sick, baptizes catechumens, gives justification to the faithful, restores the penitent; gives increase to the just, and the crown of victory to martyrs; preserves virgins, widows, and the married in chaste modesty, consecrates priests . . . (*Serm. 384*, c. 4, *Fidei Catholicae encomium*, *PL* 39:1690). C. When, with God's help, one lives by the true faith, God assists in giving light to the mind, in conquering evil desires, in enduring hardships (*Contra Julianum, Lib. V*, c. 3, § 9, *PL* 44:788). D. For understanding is the reward of believing. Then seek not to understand in order that you may believe, but rather believe that you may understand, since: *If you will not believe, you shall not continue* (Isa. 7:9; *Tract. 29 in Joan.*, § 6, *PL* 35:1630).

581. ST. AMBROSE. A. Where there is faith, there is an army of angels (*Oratio de obitu Theodosii*, § 10, *PL* 16:1452). B. You have entered upon the office of a bishop and, sitting at the helm of the Church, you are piloting the ship in the face of the waves. Take firm hold of the rudder of faith so that the heavy storms of the world cannot disturb you (*Ep. 2, ad Constantium episc. nuper electum*, § 1, col. 917). C. Where faith is whole and entire, there the Savior teaches, protects, rejoices; there one finds rest, tranquillity, and a healing power for all (*Serm. 37, de mirabilibus, In Append.*, *PL* 17:701). D. Our bodies are vessels of clay [that is, the Christian ministry is discharged by frail human beings, cf. II Cor. 4:7]: faith is our treasure. Perhaps even these very bodies of ours which carry this treasure are made golden because they are filled

with prudence; or like silver vessels, are made to glisten with the consolations of the divine commandments (*De Abraham, Lib. I,* n. 90, *PL* 14:476).

582. ST. FULGENCE, bp. of Ruspe in Africa (d. 533). Divinely inspired faith is the foundation of all goods. It is the beginning of man's salvation. Without it no one can attain to the number of God's children, for without it no one receives the grace of justification in this world, nor will he possess eternal life in the next; and if one does not walk by faith here, he will not arrive at the vision of God. Without faith all of man's work is in vain (*De fide, ad Petrum diaconum, Prolog., PL* 65:671).

583. ST. JOHN CHRYSOSTOM. A. Faith is a lamp, for as a lamp lights up the house where it is placed, so faith illumines the soul of him who possesses it (*Opus imperf. in Matt., Hom. 52,* § 1, *PG* 56:930). B. One man inflamed with the zeal of faith is sufficient to reform a whole community. But when not merely one, or two, or three, but so great a multitude are able to assume the care of the negligent, it is only because of our own supineness, and not from want of strength, that the majority perish and fail (*Hom. I de statuis,* § 12, *PG* 49:34).

584. ST. BERNARD. A. Faith, therefore, seems to say in our heart: "God has prepared a treasure of inconceivable happiness for his faithful servants." Hope: "It is for me that this happiness is prepared." And then charity: "As for me, I am already speeding to the enjoyment of that happiness!" (*Serm. de temp., Serm. 10 in Ps. Qui habitat,* § 1, *PL* 183:221.)

B. What is there that faith does not find? It attains that which was not reached, it discovers what is hidden, it comprehends what is unlimited, it apprehends the farthest depths; it even contains, after a certain manner, in its comprehensive bosom, eternity itself (*Serm. 76 in Cant.,* n. 6, col. 1153; Eales, p. 471).

C. *This is the victory that overcomes the world, our faith* (I John 5:4). For it is by faith that we have been made the adoptive children of God; it is the faith in us that the world, which is *in the power of the evil one* (*ibid.,* v. 19), hates and persecutes; and it is by faith also that the world is conquered, according to what is written: The saints *by faith conquered kingdoms* (Heb. 11:33). Why should not the victory of the just man be attributed to faith, since to it he owes even his life? *He who is just,* says the Apostle, *lives by faith* (Rom. 1:17). . . . Listen lastly to the admonition addressed to you by the divinely appointed pastor of the Lord's flock: *Your adversary, the devil, as a roaring lion, goes about, seeking someone to devour. Resist him, steadfast in the faith* (I Pet. 5:8; *Serm. de temp., Serm. I in Oct. Paschae,* n. 2, col. 293).

D. . . . *Who is there that overcomes the world, if not he who believes that Jesus is the Son of God?* (I John 5:5.) . . . Do you suppose that Jesus is really the Son of God to that man, whoever he may be, who is neither frightened by his threats nor attracted by his promises; who is neither obedient to his commands nor acquiescent to his counsels? Is not such a one of the number of those of whom the Apostle says: *They profess to know God, but by their works they disown him* (Titus 1:16). Besides: *Faith without good works is useless* (Jas. 2:2; *ibid.*, n. 3).

E. Perhaps you would like to know, my brethren, what is this faith that lives and triumphs? It is that faith, doubtless, whereby Christ dwells in our hearts (cf. Eph. 3:17). For Christ is both our strength and our life. *When Christ, your life,* says the Apostle, *shall appear, then you too will appear with him in glory* (Col. 3:4; *ibid.*, n. 4).

F. It is an infallible sign that the world has been overcome by you: if you *chastise your body and bring it into subjection* (I Cor. 9:27), lest by abuse of its liberty it should become the slave of pleasure; if you give up your eyes to mourning rather than to curiosity and arrogance; and if, finally, your hearts are so filled with divine love that there is no room left for the love of vanity (*ibid.*, n. 7).

G. As the life of the body is the soul from which it has its motion and sensibility, so charity is the life of faith, which exercises its activity through love, as you may read in St. Paul: *Faith which works through charity* (Gal. 5:6). Hence it is that faith dies when charity loses its fervor, as does the body at the departure of the soul. Whenever, consequently, you see a man who is strenuous in the performance of good works, and exhibiting in all his conduct a joyous and fervent devotion, have no doubt that faith is living in him, for it is proved to be alive by the most indubitable evidence (*ibid., Serm. II in tempore Resurrectionis,* § 1, col. 283).

H. I can never cease wondering at the fact that our faith, which seems so certain regarding the things of the future, is so wavering about the things of the present. . . . The Prophet tells us: *Eye has not seen or ear heard, nor has it entered into the heart of man, what things God has prepared for those who love him* (I Cor. 2:9). And we believe that, all of us. But he who is the Lord of prophets speaks: *Come to me, all you who labor and are burdened, and I will give you rest. Take my yoke upon you . . . and you will find rest for your souls. For my yoke is easy, and my burden light* (Matt. 11:28–30). And how many turn away the ear of the heart! In vain does Christ cry out to us that his burden is light; fruitlessly he preaches that his yoke is easy, for at times the burden of the devil and the yoke of the flesh and of this world are considered more pleasant. . . . Those, of course, who have tried both, know that *God is true, and every man a liar* (Rom. 3:4). . . . *The sensual man does not perceive the things that are of the Spirit of God* (I Cor. 2:14). . . . Miserable and unhappy you are, who have not found the way to an inhabited city . . . but wandered astray through a trackless waste (cf. Ps. 106:4–40; *Serm. de div., Serm. 111, de fide, vita et moribus contestanda,* nn. 2–4, col. 737).

585. ST. LEO THE GREAT. A mighty bulwark is a sound faith, a true faith, to which nothing has been added or taken away, because unless it is one, it is no faith; as the Apostle says: *One Lord, one faith, one Baptism; one God and Father of all, who is above all, and throughout all, and in us all* (Eph. 4:5). Cling to this unity, dearly beloved, with minds unshaken, and in it strive for all holiness (cf. Heb. 12:14); in it carry out the Lord's commands, because *without faith it is impossible to please God* (*ibid.,* 11:6), and without it nothing is holy, nothing is pure, nothing alive (*Serm. 24, In Nativ. Dni.,* c. 6, *PL* 54:207).

586. CLEMENT OF ALEXANDRIA (d. circa 220). Faith is the solid foundation and support of charity . . . the mother and the greatest of all virtues (*Stromatum Lib. II,* c. *VI et V, PG* 8:966, 958).

587. ST. PETER DAMIAN. Faith is the origin of virtues, the foundation of good works; the beginning of the whole process of man's salvation. Whoever does not proceed with caution along the path of faith will of necessity be caught in the snare of error. . . . He who has not learned to walk by faith will never be able to attain to the Beatific Vision. To put it briefly in the form of a conclusion: without a right faith no one will attain to the grace of justification, nor merit eternal life (*Opusc. 1, de fide Catholica, Prooem., PL* 145:21).

588. ST. BRUNO, cardinal and bp. of Segni in Campagna (d. 1123). The Church's first ornament is faith, which stands at the head of the whole battle array of virtues. All other virtues follow it, and without it, they simply do not enter into the palace of the kingdom of heaven. If humility, if patience, if chastity, even if charity itself, which is called the greatest of the virtues by the Apostle (I Cor. 13:13), present themselves, they are rejected and are not permitted to enter, if faith is wanting (*Sententiarum Lib. II,* c. 1, *de fide, PL* 165:901).

589. ST. BONAVENTURE. A. In a marvelous manner the mind takes delight in understanding what it believes with perfect faith *Sententiarum* (*Lib. I,* Prooem., q. 2, *Op. Om.,* ed. Quaracchi 1:11). B. The faith, therefore, by which we believe in God, must not only itself be called a gratuitous virtue, but also the rule and director of virtues, as Bernard claims for prudence in his book to Eugene (*De Consid.,* c. 8, nn. 9, 11; *ibid., Lib. III,* Dist. 23, art. 1, q. 1, *Utrum fides sit virtus, ibid.,* 3:471).

590. JOHN OF TRITHEIM. A. If you believe as your faith demands, but live in an evil manner, you are destroying yourself with your own hand, because *he who knows how to do good, and does not do it, commits a sin* (Jas. 4:17; *Serm. 1, Quod caute sit monachis vivendum, Op. pia et spiritualia,* p. 527). B. Without the shield of faith, the devil is not conquered, nor is the impure urge of the flesh overcome (*Hom. 3,*

Quae sit armatura militiae spiritualis, ibid., p. 419). C. O monk, serving Christ, whenever you may be tempted by the devil, immediately imprint the sign of the cross on your forehead, and say with St. John Chrysostom, as he mentioned in one of his homilies: "I renounce you, satan, with all your iniquities, and I unite myself to you, Jesus Christ, Son of the living God!" (*Ad illuminandos catechesis II, PG* 49:240; *ibid.*, p. 422.)

The presence of God

591. ST. THOMAS AQUINAS. A. Therefore God is in all things by his power, inasmuch as all things are subject to his power; he is by his presence in all things, as all things are bare and open to his eyes; he is in all things by his essence, inasmuch as he is present to all as the cause of their being (*I*, q. 8, art. 3, *Utrum Deus sit ubique per essentiam, praesentiam et potentiam, Op. Om.* 4:87; Am. ed. 1:36). B. Hence, as the soul is whole in every part of the body, so God is whole in all things and in each one (*ibid.*, art. 2, p. 86).

592. ST. AUGUSTINE. A. Nothing is more present than God, and nothing more secret than God (*Lib. de spiritu et anima*, c. 57, *In Append., PL* 40:822). B. We will have [God] more present to us in proportion as we are able to purify the love by which we draw near to him, for he is not spread through or confined by corporeal space. He is everywhere present and everywhere wholly present, and we go to him not by the motion of our feet but by our conduct; not by walking but by loving (*Ep. 155, ad Macedonium, docens vitam beatam et virtutem veram non esse nisi a Deo*, c. 4, § 13, *PL* 33:672; Parsons, p. 315).

593. LIVES OF THE HOLY FATHERS. A. God is everywhere; but he draws near to the pious and to those who are intent on their spiritual exercises; not to those who are adorned only by reason of their profession, but to those who are actually adorned with the performance of good works. Who can threaten or harm one where God is present? (*Lib. X*, c. 144, *Admonitiones unius ex senibus, PL* 74:191.) B. If you keep God before your eyes, the enemy cannot frighten you in any way, whether you are rising, walking, sitting, or engaged in any occupation whatever. Hence if this thought of God's presence remains with a man, the strength of God will cling to him (*Aegyptiorum Patrum Sententiae*, § 24, col. 386).

594. CASSIODORUS. A. . . . for only the humble and devout man seeks the presence of God (*In Ps. 104:4, PL* 70:743). B. O, what utter blindness, not to keep God before one's eyes! (*In Ps. 9:24*, col. 87.)

595. EVAGRIUS, monk, abbot of Ponticus (4th century). One should remember God more often than one breathes. . . . Join to every breath the sober invocation of the name of Jesus and the thought of death with humility. Both these practices bring great profit to the

soul. Do you wish to be known by God? Try as much as possible to be less known by men. If you will always remember that God is the Seer of all that you do with soul or body, you will not sin in any action, and will have found God as your Companion (cf. *RSB*, c. 7, first degree of humility; *De octo vitiosis cogitationibus*, § 9, *PG* 40:1275; *Philokalia*, p. 113).

596. ST. GREGORY THE GREAT. Where mindfulness of God enters into your consciousness, the powerful light of truth is present (*In Sept. Ps. Poenit., Expos. I*, n. 5, *PL* 79:555).

597. VEN. LOUIS DE BLOIS (Blosius). A. Happy indeed is the soul of that man who, loving God sincerely, knows how, with the help of his grace, to contemplate, in this exile, his presence with free, clear, calm and, simple intuition of mind (*Speculum spirituale*, c. 10, *Op. Om.* 2:573). B. God everywhere beholds you, and knows your most secret intentions and affections to perfection. He is so present to you, he is so within you, that without him you cannot so much as move a finger. Be firmly persuaded of this, believe this, and love and reverence his presence. Be ashamed to admit anything that might be displeasing to the eyes of so exalted and so intimate a beholder (*Canon vitae spiritualis*, c. 23, n. 2, *Op. Om.* 1:22).

598. ST. BASIL THE GREAT. A. Prayers, too, following reading [the lives of the saints], take hold upon a fresher and more vigorous soul already stirred to a longing for God. And prayer which imprints in the soul a clear conception of God is an excellent thing. Thus we become in a special manner the temples of God, when earthly thoughts cease to interrupt our continual remembrance of him, and unforeseen passions cease to agitate the mind; and when the lover of God, fleeing all these, withdraws with him and, driving out the passions which tempt him to incontinence, spends himself in the practices which lead to virtue (*Ep.* 2, *ad Gregorium Nazianzenum*, § 4, *PG* 32:230; Way, p. 9). B. The Christian should not murmur (cf. I Cor. 10:10) either because of the meagre care of his needs or because of fatiguing labors, since those entrusted with authority in these matters have the final decision over each. There should be no outburst, nor any angry demonstration or commotion (cf. Eph. 4:31), nor should there be any distraction of mind from the realization of the presence of God (cf. Heb. 4:13; *ibid., Ep.* 22, *De perfectione vitae monasticae*, § 2, col. 290; Way, p. 57; Deferrari, 1:133). C. We should watch over our heart with all diligence (cf. Prov. 4:23), not only to avoid ever losing the thought of God or sullying the memory of his wonders by vain imagination, but also in order to carry out the holy thought of God stamped upon our souls as an ineffaceable seal, by continuous and pure recollection (*Reg. fusius tractatae, Interrogatio V, de cavenda mentis evagatione*, § 2, *PG* 31:922; Wagner, 243).

599. ST. EPHRAEM. Nothing is worse or more serious than the guilt

of forgetting God himself. By constant mindfulness of God, shameful passions depart from the soul, as do criminals at the soldier's approach: hence the soul becomes the cleansed dwelling of the Holy Spirit. But where mindfulness of God is absent, darkness reigns with its foul stench, and every evil deed is practiced (*De virtute,* c. 10, *Op. Om.* 2:305).

600. ST. JOHN CHRYSOSTOM. Tell me, if you had to stand constantly near the person of a ruler, would you not stand there with fear? And how, then, standing in God's presence, do you laugh and throw yourself about, with no fear or dread? Let it never be that you despise his patient endurance, for it is to bring you to repentance that he is long-suffering. . . . Whether you are eating, or preparing for sleep, or giving way to anger, or robbing another, or indulging in luxury, or whatever you may be about, consider that God is present—for he *is* present—and you will never fall into laughter, never be inflamed with rage. If this is your continual thought, you will be constantly in fear and trembling in that you are standing beside the King (*In Ep. ad Philip.,* Hom. 8, § 1, *PG* 62:239).

601. ST. GREGORY OF NAZIANZUS, Doctor of the Church (d. 389). [As the body must be united with the soul, the branches of the tree with its trunk, the rays of light with the sun, in order that they may draw their power from these sources, so we too must be united with God by our minds.] *Look to him that you may be radiant with joy, and your faces may not blush with shame* (Ps. 33:6). . . . For we ought to think of God more often even than we draw our breath; in fact, we ought to do nothing else (*Oratio 27, Theologica I, adversus Eunomianos,* § 4, *PG* 36:15).*

602. ST. DOSITHEUS, monk of Palestine (6th century). Devote attention to prayer, see to it that you never abandon it. . . . Only be mindful of God and consider yourself in his presence (*Acta Sanctorum,* Bolland, Febr., tom. 3, die 23, p. 389).

603. ST. AUGUSTINE. . . . Thus, Lord, you behold the steps I take and the paths I follow. You watch over me day and night, protecting me, attentively noting all my ways, observing perpetually, as though, unmindful of your whole creation of heaven and earth, you were concerned with me alone, and had thought for no others. For the immutable light of your sight is neither intensified when you look at only one, nor lessened when you behold countless different objects. . . . Whatever my intentions as I work, whatever my thoughts, in whatever

* Wolter gives this excerpt as here translated. The first sentence, which we have placed in brackets, does not occur in the *Oratio* in available editions, nor has it been located elsewhere in St. Gregory's writings. The beauty of the imagery (the vine and the branches), and the laboriously learned respect for differences of editions, seemed to justify its retention. Wolter furnishes no bibliography, and often but meager references. [*Tr.*]

I find my delight, you see it all. Your ears hear it, your eyes look upon and consider it, you seal it and record it in your book, be it good or evil, in order afterward to bestow rewards for that which is good and punishments for what is evil (*Lib. Soliloquiorum animae ad Deum,* n. 14, *In Append., PL* 40:875).

604. ST. BONAVENTURE. Because, then, being is most pure and absolute, that which is Being simply, is first and last, and, therefore, the origin and final cause of all. Because eternal and most present, therefore it encompasses and penetrates all duration, existing at once as their center and circumference. Because most simple and greatest, therefore it is entirely within and entirely without all things, and, therefore, is an intelligible sphere whose center is everywhere and whose circumference nowhere. Because most actual and immutable, then, "remaining stable it causes the universe to move" (Boethius, *Cons.* 3, met. 9). Because most perfect and immense, therefore within all, though not included in them; beyond all, but not excluded from them; above all, but not transported beyond them; below all, and yet not cast down beneath them (*Itinerarium mentis in Deum,* c. 5, *De speculatione divinae unitatis per ejus nomen primarium, quod est ESSE,* § 8, *Op. Om.,* ed. Quaracchi 5:308; George Boas, *The Mind's Road to God,* New York: The Liberal Arts Press, 1953, p. 38).

605. ST. LAURENCE JUSTINIAN. I consider no measure so effectual for acquiring purity of soul, attaining the height of virtues, and subduing the pleasures of the flesh which are known to besiege the soul, as the realization that you are always standing in the sight of the Judge who perceives everything (*De perfectionis gradibus,* c. 6, *Op. Om.* 2:431).

606. ST. BERNARD. A. For he reigns everywhere as King, he rules everywhere as Lord, his Majesty is ubiquitous (*Serm. de temp., Serm. V pro Dom. I Novembr.,* § 5, *PL* 183:355). B. As there is never a moment when we are not actually availing ourselves of and enjoying God's loving-kindness and mercy, so there should never be a moment in which we do not keep his presence in mind (*Tract. de interiori domo,* c. 3, *In Append., PL* 184:511). C. For we should always set him before our eyes by whom it is that we are, and live, and are able to think at all (*Meditationes piissimae de cognitione humanae conditionis,* c. 6, *de attentione tempore orationis habenda,* n. 19, *In Append.,* col. 497).

607. ST. DIADOCHUS, bp. of Photice (d. after 458, before 486). Let us ever dwell in this deceptive life with the constant remembrance of God, searching the depths of our hearts, as though our eyes were held fast (*Centum capita de perfectione spirituali,* c. 56, *PG* 65:1185).

608. THOMAS À KEMPIS. Learn, man, to direct all your practices to the love and honor of Jesus; and everywhere, and at all times, to be attentive to him as though he were [physically] present. . . . This means Christ dwelling in your heart through faith and love; never

turning your mind's eye from his image; ever directing yourself according to his will; preferring nothing to his love; but reducing to him wholly, and referring to him finally, whatever you have heard or read or done that is good (*De disciplina claustralium,* c. 13, *Op. Om.* 2:310).

The monk's love of God: the love motive

609. ST. BERNARD. A. O blessed love! from which emerge intensity of zeal, purity of affection, depth of understanding, holiness of desire, heroic character of deeds, fruitfulness of virtue, dignity of merit, the very height of reward [Wolter gives an incorrect citation for this passage, or rather he joins it with the following section, but it does not belong there. Diligent search failed to produce the context from which the excerpt is taken. Similar passages abound. *Tr.*]

B. God, then, requires that he should be feared as Lord, honored as Father, but as Bridegroom loved. Which of these three is the highest and most to be preferred? Surely it is love. Without it fear is painful, and honor without attraction. Fear is servile as long as it is not rendered free by love; and honor which is not inspired by love is not truly honor but flattery. Certainly honor and glory are due to God, and to him alone; but neither of these will he receive, if they be not, as it were, seasoned with the honey of love. Love is alone sufficient by itself; it pleases by itself; and for its own sake. It is itself a merit, and itself its own recompense. It seeks neither cause nor consequence beyond itself. It is its own fruit, and its own object and usefulness. I love, because I love; I love, that I may love. Love, then, is a great reality, a very precious reality, provided that it recurs to the principle on which it rests, that it is kept in continual relation with him who is its origin, and draws from that pure source waters that flow continually in greater abundance. Of all the feelings, affections, and movements of the soul, love is the only one by which the reasonable creature is able to respond to its Creator, and even in some sort repay, though not upon equal terms, the goodness which it has received from him. . . . For when God loves us, he desires nothing else than to be loved, because he loves us that he may be loved by us, knowing that those who love him become blessed by their love itself.

Love, then, is a great reality, but there are degrees in it. The Bridegroom stands highest of all. For though children have affection for their parents, yet they think of their heritage, and in fear of losing that, they have more respect than love for him from whom they expect it. . . . The very being of the Bride, and her only hope, consists in love. . . . In this the Bride abounds; with this the Bridegroom is content. Thence it is that he is a Bridegroom, and she is Bride. . . .

It is true that *the King in his might loves justice* (Ps. 98:4), but the love of the Bridegroom, or rather of the Bridegroom who is himself love, requires only love and faithfulness in return. Let it be permitted, then, to the Bride to love in return. How could she do otherwise who is the Bride, and the Bride of Love? How can Love fail to be loved? . . . For when she has poured herself forth entirely in love, what would that be in comparison with the ever-flowing and inexhaustible source of love? Not with equal fulness of resource flows that stream from Love and from the creature that loves him, from the soul and from the Word, the Bridegroom and the Bride, the Creator and the creature; and the thirsty wayfarer might as well be compared with the fountain that satisfies his thirst. What then? Shall the vow of the Bride, the deep aspirations of her heart, her loving ardor and undoubting confidence, perish and become of no effect because she is unable to contend with a Giant who runs his course; to dispute the palm of sweetness with honey; of gentleness with the lamb; of whiteness with the lily; of brilliance with the sun; or charity with him who is himself Charity and Love? No. For although, being a creature, she loves less than he by whom she is loved, because she is less; yet if she loves with her whole self, nothing can be wanting where the whole being is offered. . . .

Happy is the soul whose favored lot it is to be prevented with the benediction of a delight so great! Happy is the soul to which is granted to experience the delight of that communion so sweet, which is nothing else than a love holy and pure, sweet and delightful, as calm as it is sincere; a love mutual, endearing, powerful, which makes of two, by their close union, not indeed one flesh, but one spirit, as St. Paul declares: *He who cleaves to the Lord is one spirit with him* (I Cor. 6:17; *Serm. 83 in Cant., Qualiter anima, quantumcumque vitiis corrupta, adhuc per amorem castum et sanctum potest redire ad similitudinem Christi,* nn. 4–6, *PL* 183:1183–1184; Eales, pp. 509–511).

C. The proper motive for loving God is that he is God; the measure in which to love him is to love him without measure. . . . I say, then, that there are two reasons for which God should be loved: because no one has a greater right to our love; and because no one can be loved to greater advantage. . . . Surely he deserves that we should love him in return, particularly when we call to mind who this Lover is, and the objects loved, and in what degree he has loved us. For who is he? Is he not the same to whom every spirit confesses: *My Lord are you. Apart from you I have no good* (Ps. 15:2). And this love of the Divine Majesty for his creatures is true charity, because *it is not self-seeking* (I Cor. 13:5). But who are the objects of such disinterested charity? Listen to St. Paul: *When we were enemies, we were reconciled to God by the death of his Son* (Rom. 5:10). God, therefore, loved us without any merit on our part, loved us when we were his enemies. And to what degree did he love us? Let St. John answer: *God so loved the world that he gave his only-begotten Son* (John 3:16). Hear also St. Paul: *He spared not even his own Son but has delivered him for us all* (Rom. 8:32; *De diligendo Deo,* c. 1, *Quare et quomodo sit diligendus Deus,* n. 1, *PL* 182:974; Luddy, p. 182; Gardner, p. 26).

D. You perceive, then, in what measure, rather how immeasurable, should be our love of God who first loved us and so boundlessly, in spite of the infinite distance between his greatness and our littleness. . . . *I love you, O Lord, my strength, O Lord, my rock, my fortress, my deliverer* (Ps. 17:2), yes, my all that is good and sweet and desirable. *My God, my rock of refuge* (*ibid.*), I love you according to your gift and my measure, less indeed than I ought, but as much as I can: for I cannot love you either as much as is due or beyond my capacity. I shall have power to love you more when you deign to bestow it, but never can I love you as much as you deserve (*ibid.,* c. 6, col. 983).

E. God is not loved without recompense, although he should be loved without any view to the recompense. True, charity cannot be unfruitful, although it is no hireling, for it *is not self-seeking* (I Cor. 13:5). It is an affection, not a contract; it is neither gained nor does it seek to gain by bargaining. It bestows itself freely and makes its possessor free. True love is content with itself. It has its reward indeed, but in nothing distinct from the object loved (*ibid.,* c. 7, n. 17, col. 984; Luddy, p. 188; Gardner, p. 72).

F. O holy and chaste love! O sweet and tender affection! O pure and perfect intention of the will! surely so much more perfect and more pure, as there is in it nothing now mixed of its own; the more sweet and tender, as all is divine that is felt. To be thus affected is to be deified. As a little drop of water mingled with wine seems to lose its own character in assuming the taste and color of the wine; as iron held in the fire until red-hot and glowing, appears to have put on the very nature of the fire; as the air all flooded with the light of the sun seems not so much illumined as light itself; not otherwise must every human feeling in the saints melt out of itself, in some ineffable manner, and be entirely absorbed into the will of God. For if anything that is human remains in man, how can God be all in all (cf. I Cor. 15:28)? Human nature, of course, will remain unaltered in essence, but utterly transformed in beauty and glory and power. When shall this be? Who shall see it? Who shall possess it? *When shall I go and behold the face of God?* (Ps. 41:3.) My Lord and my God, *of you my heart speaks; you my glance seeks; your presence, O Lord, I seek* (Ps. 26:9; *ibid.,* c. 10, *de quarto gradu amoris cum nec seipsum diligit homo nisi propter Deum,* n. 28, col. 991).

G. When, O Lord Jesus, will you *take off my sackcloth and clothe me with gladness, that my soul may sing praise to you without ceasing?* (Ps. 29:12–13.) The beginning of joy which we sometimes experience here below is only *a runlet from the stream that gladdens the city of*

God (Ps. 45:5). When will the time come when we shall be deeply immersed in the very font of divinity, where in perennial joys one wave simply follows another without interruption? . . . When shall I enter into the wonderful tabernacle, even into *the house of God?* (Ps. 41:5.) When, as we have heard, shall we see the city of the Lord of hosts, where *God reigns over the nations, where God sits upon his holy throne?* (Ps. 47:9.) . . . Forward, then, my brothers, let us concentrate with joy on that blessed end, and be ever mindful of the saying: *Friend, for what purpose hast thou come?* (Matt. 26:50.) We are come to sacrifice to the King, to serve, in his image, him who alone is blessed forever (*Serm. de div., Serm. 19,* n. 7, *PL* 183:592).

610. ST. THOMAS AQUINAS. A. Charity signifies not only the love of God, but also a certain friendship with him; which implies, besides love, a certain mutual return of love, together with mutual communion. . . . Now this fellowship of man with God, which consists in a certain familiar colloquy with him, is begun here, in this life, by grace, but will be perfected in the future life, by glory (*I-II,* q. 65, art. 5, *Utrum caritas possit esse sine fide et spe, Op. Om.* 6:427; Am. ed. 1:865). B. For thus charity is the mother and root of all the virtues, inasmuch as it is the form of them all (*ibid.,* q. 62, art. 4, *Utrum fides sit prior spe, et spes caritate, ibid.,* p. 405).

611. ST. AUGUSTINE. A. Accordingly, two cities have been formed by two loves: the earthly by the love of self, even to the contempt of God; the heavenly by the love of God even to the contempt of self. The former, in a word, glories in itself, the latter, in the Lord (*De civitate Dei, Lib. 14,* c. 28, *PL* 41:436; Dods, p. 477). B. Perfection lies in peace, where nothing is at war; and the children of God are peaceful for the reason that no resistance to God is present, and surely children ought to bear a likeness to their father (*De Serm. Dni. in monte, Lib. I,* c. 2, § 9, *PL* 34:1233; Jepson, p. 15).

Necessity of prayer (individual prayer)

612. ST. THOMAS AQUINAS. A. Now, after baptism man needs to pray continually, in order to enter heaven; for though sins are remitted through baptism, there still remains the *fomes* of sin assailing us from within, and the world and devils assailing us from without. And therefore it is said pointedly that *Jesus having been baptized and being in prayer, heaven was opened* (Luke 3:21), because, to wit, the faithful after baptism stand in need of prayer (*III,* q. 39, art. 5, *Utrum Christo baptizato debuerint coeli aperiri, Op. Om.* 11:392; Am. ed. 2:2231). B. [Hence after baptism], when one has been justified by grace, he still needs to beseech God for the aforesaid gift of perseverance that he may be kept from evil until the end of his life. For to many grace is given to whom perseverance in grace is not given (*I-II,* q. 109, art. 10, *Utrum*

homo in gratia constitutus indigeat auxilio gratiae ad perseverandum, Op. Om. 7:309; Am. ed. 1:1131).

613. ST. JOHN CHRYSOSTOM. A. If they who address the king and enjoy a position of honor in his presence can never suffer any want, it is far less possible that they who pray to God, conversing with him familiarly, have souls that are subject to death. For death of the soul is impiety and opposition to the Divine Law. Whence it follows that the life of the soul consists in the worship of God, and in the acts that are in harmony with holy religion. Now in a marvelous manner prayer harmonizes a devout life that is worthy of divine worship, intensifies its activity, and stores up a treasure of precious things in our souls. . . . For since God is the origin of all goods, the person who loves him receives every blessing (*De precatione, Oratio I, PG* 50:775).

B. Whoever does not pray to God, nor has the desire to devote himself often to converse with God is deprived of life, devoid of sanity. . . . As this body of ours, when the soul has departed it, is dead, and already subject to corruption, so the soul, which fails to bestir itself to prayer is dead, and pitiable, and has a foul stench. . . . But as the great prophet Daniel, who preferred to die rather than to be deprived of prayer for thirty days, teaches us, we must consider being deprived of prayer a more bitter loss than any form of death (cf. Dan. 6:10 f.; *ibid.*, col. 776).

C. I think that it is evident to all that it is simply impossible to live virtuously without the help of prayer. For how can one practice virtue unless he continuously approaches and falls to his knees in supplication before him who abounds in all virtues and bestows them upon men? (*Ibid.*, col. 777.)

D. If a person were to say that prayer is the sinews of the soul, he would, in my judgment, be stating the truth. For as the body is made into a unified whole, runs, lives, stands, and is compacted together by its sinews, in such wise that if you cut those sinews you disrupt the entire harmony of the body; so it is equally true that through holy prayer, souls are formed into harmonious units and easily fulfil the duties of devotion (*ibid., Oratio 2*, col. 781).

E. If you have deprived yourself of prayer you have acted as though you had taken a fish out of water; for as water is life to the fish, so prayer is to you (*ibid.*).

F. If you devote yourself to repeated prayer at intervals throughout the day, you give no occasion to the devil, and allow him no entrance upon your thoughts. As in preparing dinner, when there is need of hot liquids and the water has grown cold, we heat it by moving it nearer the fire, so also our mouth must be addressed to prayers, as though moved toward hot coals, in order that the mind again be stimulated to piety (*De Anna, Serm. IV*, § 5, *PG* 54:666).

G. Wherever you are, you have at hand an altar, a knife, and a victim; for you are altar, priest, and victim. Wherever you are, you may set up your altar, provided that you bring a serious mind and neither the time nor place impede you. Even though you do not kneel down, nor strike your breast, nor lift your hands to heaven, nothing is wanting to your prayer, if only you have presented a fervent mind (*ibid.*, § 6, col. 667).

H. As he was wont to accept sacrifices, although he had no need of them (for, as he said: *If I were hungry, I should not tell you, for mine are the world and its fullness* (Ps. 49:12), but leading men to the performance of his praise, so also he receives our hymns of praise, although he has no need for our glorification, but rather because he seeks our salvation. God's concern is that we grow in virtue. But nothing can so advance us in virtue as continually dwelling and conversing with God, ever offering him our thanks and praises (*Expos. in Ps. 7*, § 15, *PG* 55:104).

I. Prayer [for sinful men] is pleasing and acceptable to God, *who wishes all men to be saved, and to come to the knowledge of the truth* (I Tim. 2:4). Hence let us not abandon prayer that is offered in their favor; for it is a most effective weapon; a never-failing treasure; an inexhaustible wealth; a harbor of utter calmness; the reason for tranquillity; finally, it is the root, source, and begetter of innumerable blessings, a power exceeding that of a kingdom (*Hom. 5, De incomprehensibili Dei natura*, §§ 5–6, *PG* 48:743).

614. ST. JOHN CLIMACUS. A. Prayer by reason of its nature is the converse and union of man with God, and by reason of its action upholds the world and brings about reconciliation with God; it is the mother and also the daughter of tears, the propitiation for sins, a bridge over temptations, a wall against afflictions, a crushing of conflicts; work of angels, food of all the spiritual beings, future gladness, boundless activity, the spring of virtues; the source of graces, invisible progress, food of the soul, the enlightening of the mind, an axe for despair; a demonstration of hope, the annulling of sorrow, the wealth of monks, the treasure of solitaries, the reduction of anger; the mirror of progress, the realization of success; a proof of one's condition, a revelation of the future; a sign of glory. For him who truly prays, prayer is the court, the judgment hall and the tribunal of the Lord before the judgment to come. . . . When you are going to stand before the Lord, let the garment of your soul be woven throughout with the thread that has become oblivious of wrongs. Otherwise prayer will bring you no benefit. Let your prayer be completely simple. For both the publican and the prodigal son were reconciled to God by a single phrase (*Scala paradisi, Grad. 28, de sacra et virtutum procreatrice beata oratione*, *PG* 88:1130; Moore, p. 250, nn. 1–5). B. He who keeps con-

stant hold of the staff of prayer will not stumble. And even if he does, his fall will not be fatal. For prayer is a devout coercion of God. The benefit of prayer can be inferred from the assaults of the demons during the Divine Office; its fruit from the defeat of the foe (*ibid.*, nn. 53–54, col. 1139; Moore, p. 257, nn. 60–61). C. War proves the soldier's love for his king; but the time and discipline of prayer show the monk's love of God. Your prayer will show what condition you are in. Theologians say that prayer is the monk's mirror (*ibid.*, nn. 37–38; Moore, p. 255, nn. 33–34).

615. ST. AUGUSTINE. Prayer is the support of holy virtues, the ladder of godliness . . . kindred with the angels; the fountain of faith, the crown of monks (*Ad fratres in eremo Serm. 22, In Append., PL* 40:1272).

616. CASSIODORUS. A. We must also acknowledge and believe fully that prayer, when it is poured out by the Lord Christ is a sacred instruction of the faithful, the pattern of imitation by good persons, and an example of true humility; but when it is prayed by subjects, it is the reparation of offenses, the acknowledgment of crimes, the washing away of sins (*Expos. in Ps. 85, Prolog., PL* 70:611). B. By prayer the anger of God is suspended, pardon procured, punishment avoided, and an abundant reward obtained (*In Ps. 89, Prolog.*, col. 643).

617. ST. LAURENCE JUSTINIAN. A. As it would be incongruous for a soldier to march into battle without the protection of arms, so it would not be proper for the Christian to undertake anything without the defense of prayer (*Lignum vitae, tract. de oratione*, c. 6, *Op. Om.* 1:89). B. Prayer is the short road, the easy climb, the safe journey by which we attain knowledge of God sweetly and truly (*De disciplina et perfectione monasticae conversationis*, c. 18, *ibid.* 1:143).

618. ST. JOHN CHRYSOSTOM. A. A powerful weapon is prayer, a beautiful ornament, a protection, a port, a treasure of good things, wealth that cannot be stolen (*Expos. in Ps. 145*, § 6, *PG* 55:526). B. While you are praying, the enemy is held fast; when you cease praying, he is released. Continual prayer is the enemy's weakness (*Serm. in Moysen*). C. For not so much does the roaring of a lion put the wild beasts to flight as does the prayer of the righteous man put to flight evil spirits; let him but speak, and they cower (*In Act. Ap., Hom. 53*, § 5, *PG* 60:374). D. Nothing equals the power of prayer; for it is prayer that makes possible the things that are impossible, easy the things that are difficult, and straight those that are crooked. Blessed David also employed prayer and for that reason stated: *Seven times a day I praise you for your just ordinances* (Ps. 118:164). Now if the king, immersed in countless concerns and distracted by so many matters addressed himself so often to God in prayer each day, what excuse or pardon can we have who enjoy so much leisure and still do not pray to him continually, despite the fact that we would receive great benefits from so doing?

For it is impossible, I repeat, it is impossible for a man who prays with the ardor that he should bring to his prayer, and who implores God continually, ever to sin (*De Anna, Serm. 4,* § 5, *PG* 54:666).

619. VEN. LOUIS BARBO, monk of St. Justina, Padua, founder of the Congr. of St. Justina, which was later called the Cassinese Congr.; bp. of Treviso (d. 1443). . . . Without the practice of prayer, it is extremely difficult, nay almost impossible for human frailty to bear up under the harsh trials of religion, and to saturate the dryness of the spirit with the sweetness that is drawn from the well-source of the Savior. When the sap is dried out during a drought, a tree will cast off immature fruits and leaves; in the same way a soul without the fervor of prayer is unfruitful and imperfect in all its works (*Formula orationis et meditationis. Exordium. In: Exercitatorium spirituale cum Directorio Horarum Canonicarum a R. P. Garcia Cisnerio, OSB, et Formula Orationis et Meditationis, auctore Ludovico Barbo, Abb. Regensburg;* Joseph Manz, 1856, p. 279).

620. ST. GREGORY OF NYSSA, bp. (d. circa 403). Through prayer we guard our chastity, control our temper, rid ourselves of vanity; it makes us forget injuries, overcomes envy, defeats injustice, and makes amends for sin. Through prayer we obtain physical well-being, a happy home, a strong, well-ordered society. Prayer will make our nation powerful, will give us victory in war and security in peace; it reconciles enemies and preserves allies. Prayer is the seal of virginity, and a pledge of faithfulness in marriage; it shields the wayfarer, protects the sleeper, and gives courage to those who keep vigil. It obtains a good harvest for the farmer and a safe port for the sailor. Prayer is your advocate in lawsuits; if you are in prison, it will obtain your release; it will refresh you when you are weary and comfort you when you are sorrowful. Prayer is the delight of the joyful as well as the solace of the afflicted. It is the wedding crown of the spouses and the festive joy of a birthday, no less than the shroud that enwraps us in death. Prayer is intimacy with God and contemplation of the invisible. It satisfies our yearnings and makes us equals of the angels. Through it, good prospers, evil is destroyed and sinners will be converted. Prayer is the enjoyment of things present and the substance of things to come (*De Oratione Dominica, Oratio I, PG* 44:1123; Hilda Graef, *The Lord's Prayer, Oration 1,* p. 24).

621. ST. NILUS OF SINAI. Prayer makes a monk the equal of angels, for his desire is to behold the face of the Father who is in heaven (Matt. 18:10; *De oratione,* c. 113, *PG* 79:1191; *Philokalia,* p. 140).

622. ST. AMBROSE. A virtuous life makes prayer soar, and gives spiritual wings to the petitions by which the prayer of saints is lifted to God (*Expos. in Ps. 118:169, Serm. 22,* § 5, *PL* 15:1591).

623. ST. AUGUSTINE. A. He knows how to live properly who knows how to pray properly. For he petitions no treasures of worldly wealth,

nor his neighbor's property, nor longer years for living. Rather, he begs to be taught goodness and discipline. Goodness makes discipline lovable, and discipline makes goodness faultless (*Serm. 55, in Ps. 118:66, Bonitatem et disciplinam et scientiam doce me,* § 1, *In Append., PL* 39: 1849). B. Prayer is fasting's nourishment; it summons the grace of the Holy Spirit. Prayer softens hardness of heart, tempers severity, makes fasting pleasant. As there is really no complete nourishment without drink, so fasting without prayer can never perfectly nourish the soul. For what is prayer but the ascent of the soul from earthly regions to the heavenly, the search for things that are on high, the desire of things unseen? Put aside distractions of worldly concern with which the human mind is constantly weighted down. Prayer is union with the Holy Spirit—but only if the mind is intent on the prayer—as the prophet cried out: *For you my flesh pines and my soul thirsts like the earth, parched, lifeless and without water* (Ps. 62:2; *Serm. 73 in Matt. 17:20, Hoc genus in nullo ejicitur, nisi in oratione et jejunio,* § 2, *In Append.,* col. 1887).

624. JEAN RIGAUD (Joannes Rigaldi). A. Prayer resembles the armor the soldier carries—for without prayer we should not enter the struggle against temptations; the light that brightens the way—guiding us in every good work; the dove carrying the olive leaf (cf. Gen. 8:11)—signifying penance, reconciliation, the forgiveness of sins (*Diaeta salutis, tit.* 2, c. 5, *de oratione, Op. Om. S. Bonaventurae,* ed. Peltier 8:270). B. Prayer is like an incense offered to the Divine Mercy, which is ever most pleasing to the Divine Majesty; . . . a shield for protecting us from the divine displeasure; . . . a tribute to be paid to God's universal dominion (*ibid.,* p. 269).

624.[a] DAVID OF AUGSBURG. A. Prayer appeases the anger of God (cf. Exod. 32:14) . . . effects the forgiveness of sins (cf. Matt. 18:32) . . . calms the force of temptations (cf. Num. 11:2) . . . frees one in danger (cf. Ps. 49:15), and protects him from falling into dangers (cf. Matt. 24:20) . . . bestows familiarity with God (cf. Ps. 144:18) . . . obtains for one the gifts of the Holy Spirit, the gift of wisdom, the grace of preaching, the uncovering of secrets (cf. Acts 2:4) . . . restrains the force of everything opposed to salvation (cf. III Kgs. 8:22 ff.) . . . bestows, preserves, and perfects all that is necessary for salvation (cf. Rom. 8:26; *De profectu religiosorum, Lib. II,* c. 67, *Op. Om. S. Bonaventurae,* ed. Peltier 12:420). B. The whole fruit and purpose of prayer is to cleave to God and to become one spirit with him (*ibid.,* c. 73, p. 427).

625. ST. LAURENCE JUSTINIAN. A. Prayer is a most blessed nurturing of virtue, the destroying of vices, the forgiving of faults, the wiping away of sins. It is opposition to the world; it is man's welfare. It is the mother of charity, the strength of chastity, the norm of justice; the mir-

ror of prudence, the storehouse of wisdom, the servant of God. It is the confidence of the soul, the heartening of faint-heartedness, the joy of the heart, the trusted companion of this pilgrimage, the consolation of the sorrowful, the impenetrable shield of those under attack. It is a knowledge of the secrets of God, a norm for humility, a key of faith, a forerunner of an upright life, the fulness of obedience, the source of security. It is the imitator of angels, the rejoicing of the just, the mistress of temperance, . . . the dispeller of demons, the refuge of a tranquil mind; an ornament of conscience, the increase of grace, the motivation of love, the gateway of heaven, the messenger of petition, a zealous helper; the principal mediator, the best opener of the heavenly sacraments. In it there is nothing unclean, nothing devious, nothing defiled. Since it is so beautiful and blessed with all gifts, it always makes those who love it joyful and happy (*De disciplina et perfectione monasticae conversationis,* c. 18, *Op. Om.* 1:146). B. Prayer is the turning to God by the pious mind which is sustained by faith, hope, and love (*Lignum vitae, tract. de oratione,* c. 1, p. 85). C. Prayer . . . is the destroyer of vices, the mother of virtues, the comforting companion of this pilgrimage; a mirror of the soul, strength of conscience, the way of knowledge. It nourishes confidence, fosters charity, soothes labors, leads to compunction. It is the gate of heaven. It destroys evil thoughts; unites the forces of the distracted mind; serves as the receptacle of kindled affections; and excels as the intercessor of all spiritual blessings. . . . If one holds fast to it perseveringly, he can never be lost. . . . Evil spirits flee from prayer as from a scourge (*ibid.,* c. 2).

626. ST. THOMAS AQUINAS. Four conditions are laid down: namely, to ask—for ourselves—things necessary for salvation—piously,—perseveringly; when all these four concur, we always obtain what we ask for (ad 2). Faith is necessary in reference to God to whom we pray; that is, we need to believe that we can obtain from him what we seek. Humility is necessary on the part of the person praying, because he recognizes his neediness (Corpus). Prayer depends chiefly on faith, not for its efficacy in meriting, because thus it depends chiefly on charity, but for its efficacy in impetrating, because it is through faith that man comes to know of God's omnipotence and mercy, which are the source whence prayer impetrates what it asks for (ad 3; *II-II,* q. 83, art. 15, *Utrum oratio sit meritoria, Op. Om.* 9:208–209; Am. ed. 2:1550).

627. ST. AUGUSTINE. A. If prayer is pure, if it is chaste, it penetrates the heavens and will not return empty-handed [Wolter gives an incorrect citation for this passage: not found by *Tr.,* but retained for its interest]. B. Prayer is all the more poured forth as a spiritual work the more the mind, which pours it forth is withdrawn from carnal pleasures (*Serm. 210. In Quadr. VI,* c. 6, § 9, *PL* 38:1052). C. Prayer must be extensive, devoted, and pure: extensive, so that you will petition for

all,—even for those who persecute and calumniate you (Matt. 5:44); devoted, so that you will not petition negligently, but with entire dedication; pure, in order that it will be offered with cleanness of heart (*Ad fratres in eremo, Serm. 42, In Append., PL* 40:1316).

628. JOHN OF TRITHEIM. Nothing so effectively raises the mind from things of earth to heavenly love; nothing so quickly and powerfully banishes the pleasures of the flesh; nothing so illumines the mind; nothing so confuses the enemy as does prayer which is directed to God with the fervor of divine love, and is adorned with the testimony of a good conscience (*Hom. 8, Quod sine intermissione sit orandum, Op. pia et spiritualia,* p. 441).

629. ST. EDMUND OF CANTERBURY, abp. (d. 1240). We must have four things in our prayer: perfect love for him to whom we pray; certain hope of obtaining what we ask for; steadfast belief in him in whom we hope; and true humility in that we have no good of ourselves, and are far from the highness of him in whom we believe, whom we love, and in whom we hope (*Speculum ecclesiae,* c. 17, *The mirror of St. Edmund,* c. 17 in: *Religious Pieces in Prose and Verse;* ed. from Robert Thornton's MS, c. 1440, by George G. Perry; London: Early English Text Society, 1867, p. 36; *Coasts of the Country,* Clare Kirchberger; Chicago: Regnery, 1952, p. 5).

630. ST. PETER DAMIAN. Prayer must be diffident out of shame for our sins; . . . pure, in that we seek from God nothing but God himself; devoted, presenting our petitions out of the fulness of our heart; generous, including even our enemies; continual, lest it grow remiss through interruption; tranquil, so that it will not be submerged in the currents of distracting thoughts (*Serm. de S. Martino episc. et confess, PL* 144:822).

631. ST. JOHN CHRYSOSTOM. For he that prays with warmth of heart is set on fire, yet not consumed; but like gold that is tried by fire, becomes brighter (*In Ep. II ad Cor., Hom.* 5, § 4, *PG* 61:433).

632. ST. HILARY, bp. of Poitiers, Doctor of the Church (d. 367). Prayers that are trivial, wanting in confidence, prayer that is not useful [for praising and serving God], prayers which express anxiety about worldly cares, and are wrapped up in the desire of material things, prayers that are wanting in the recommendation of the fruitfulness of good works, are all despised. . . . The prayer of that person [who otherwise prays properly] is despised where there remains an attachment to evil (*Tract. in Ps. 54,* 2, § 4, *PL* 9:349).

633. CASSIODORUS. That man's prayer is perfect whose cause cries out as well as his tongue, as do his deeds and his speech, his way of life and his thought (*In Ps. 16:1, PL* 70:117).

634. ST. GREGORY THE GREAT. In order to make certain that your prayers reach the ear of God, you must strive zealously to make your

deeds bolster your words, for prayer is useless where action is evil (*Lib. 11, ep. 51, ad universos Siciliae episc., PL* 77:1170).

635. HUGH OF ST. CHER. Like a little bird prayer flies before God, and there in his presence fulfils the mission where the flesh cannot go. Its wings are fasting and almsdeeds; fasting makes prayer buoyant, so that it can fly rapidly; but almsdeeds make it strong so that it will not faint on the way (*Sup. Tob. 12:8, Comm.* 1:380).

636. ST. THOMAS À VILLANOVA, O.S.A., abp. of Valencia (d. 1555). He who is about to engage in prayer must call together, as though he were assembling them to a chapter, all his thoughts and affections, and say with St. Bernard: * *Come, and let us go up to the mountain of the Lord, and to the house of the God of Jacob, and he will teach us his ways . . . come, let us walk in the light of the Lord* (Isa. 2:3–5). Come, let us go up to the mountain of the Lord, all you my plans, schemes, purposes, attachments, and all that goes to make up my inner life; let us go up to where the Lord sees and is seen. *Stay here with the ass,* you, my body with its cares, solicitudes, worries, and sufferings, *while the boy* [Isaac] *and I* [Abraham]—that is, my mind and my will—*go there to worship; then we shall come back to you* (Gen. 22:5). We shall return to you: yes, how all too quickly we shall return! (*Serm. in Dom. XXI p. Pent.,* § 1, in: *Divi Thomae a Villanova, archiepiscopi Valentini . . . Op. Om., 6 v.,* Manila: Amigos del Pais, 1881–87, 3:281.)

637. PAUL THE DEACON (Warnefrid), monk of Montecassino (d. 784). Who ever spent his life with greater simplicity of vision, that is, with purer intention of heart [than the holy Father, Benedict]? Ever despising all things that are to perish, he fixed his mind on those which are of heaven. For that reason he was speedily granted what he longed for: he pleased God by his singleness of purpose which excluded all compromise (*Hom. 3, de S. P. Benedicto, PL* 95:1575).

638. ST. BERNARD. A. When a person engages in prayer, he must keep in mind what it is that he is asking for, him whom he is asking, and himself as the one who is asking. Concerning what he asks for, he must pay attention to two things: that his request be according [to the will] of God, and that he hold the object of his request as the most profound desire of his affection. . . . As examples, if he begs for forgiveness of sins, for the grace of the Holy Spirit, for virtue and wisdom, for faith, truthfulness, justice, humility, patience, meekness, and other spiritual charisms; and if in thinking of these things he is moved to a great love, such prayer is truly according to God, and well deserves to be heard. God speaks of this kind of prayer through Isaias: *And it shall*

* With few modifications, this passage is taken from *De contemplando Deo,* c. 1, which is commonly attributed to St. Bernard, but which Mabillon attributes to William of St. Thierry, near Rheims, afterward monk and abbot of Segni, as the legitimate author.

come to pass, that before they call, I will hear; as they are yet speaking, I will hear (Isa. 65:24). . . .

In like manner there are two considerations to be kept in mind concerning him whom he petitions, namely his goodness and his Majesty—his goodness, out of which he freely wills to grant what is petitioned, and his Majesty which can most certainly grant whatever is asked. But in praying one must also turn his attention upon himself in his role of petitioner, also on two points: namely, that he realize that he is to receive nothing by reason of his own merits, but must hope that he will receive whatever he has asked for only through the mercy of God. The heart is then called pure when the one praying thinks of these three matters which have been mentioned, and in the manner explained. Whoever prays with this purity of heart and intensity of desire must know well that he will be heard, according to the teaching of St. Peter: *Now I really understand that God is not a respecter of persons, but in every nation he who fears him and does what is right is acceptable to him* (Acts 10:34–35; *Serm. de div., Serm. 107, de affectionibus orantium,* n. 2, *PL* 183:734). B. *He shall call upon me, and I will answer him* (Ps. 90:15). Here manifestly we have a testament of peace, a pledge of piety, a compact of mercy and compassion. *Because he clings to me, I will deliver him* (*ibid.,* v. 14). . . . A most sweet law, this, which places the right to be heard in the very cry of petition. . . . The ardor of strong desire is a loud cry in the ears of God. On the other hand, a weak desire resembles the subdued sound of a whisper. How shall this penetrate the clouds? How shall it be heard in heaven? In order for man to know how he is to cry out, it is stated at the very beginning of the Lord's Prayer that the Father to whom we are about to address ourselves has his home in heaven, in order to remind us that we must cry aloud and that our petition must be, as it were, shot up to him by the impulsive force of spiritual fervor (*Serm. de temp., Serm. 16 in Ps. Qui habitat,* n. 1, col. 247). C. Otherwise you do not pray aright, if in prayer you seek some object other than the Word, or seek it otherwise than on account of the Word, since in him are all things [that you ought to seek]. In him are the remedies for the wounds of your soul, in him the help for necessities; supplies for all defects; abundance for the soul's progress in holiness; and, in a word, all things that man ought to have or to desire, all things that he needs, all things that are good for him (*Serm. 86 in Cant.,* n. 3, col. 1196; Eales, p. 527).

Faith, hope, love necessary for prayer

639. ST. AUGUSTINE. A. If faith fails, prayer perishes (*Serm. 115, in Luc. 18:1, Oportet semper orare,* § 1, *PL* 38:655). B. Pray in hope, pray with faith and love, pray instantly and submissively, pray like the widow in the parable of Christ . . . (*Ep. 130, ad Probam, cui praescri-*

bit quomodo sit orandus Deus, c. 16, § 29, *PL* 33:506). C. Faith, therefore, and hope, and charity, lead the praying soul to God (*ibid.,* c. 13, n. 24, col. 503). D. Thus we shall receive that which is so great, which eye has not seen because it is not color, nor ear heard because it is not sound, nor has it entered into the heart of man (cf. I Cor. 2:9) because the heart of man has to enter into it; and we shall receive it in fuller measure in proportion as our hope is more strongly founded and our charity more ardent (*ibid.,* c. 8, § 17, col. 501; Parsons, 389). E. These are your promises, and who need fear to be deceived when Truth gives the promise? (*Confessionum Lib. 12,* c. 1, *PL* 32:826; Sheed, p. 289.)

640. ST. JEROME. I stand to pray; I could not pray if I did not believe; but if I really believed, I should cleanse that heart of mine with which God is seen, I should beat my hands upon my breast, the tears would stream down my cheeks; my body would shudder, my face grow pale; I should lie at my Lord's feet, weep over them, and wipe them with my hair. I should cling to the cross and not let go hold on it until I obtained mercy. But, as it is, frequently in my prayers I am either walking in the arcades, or computing my interest, or am carried away by base thoughts, so as to be occupied with things whose mere mention makes me blush. Where is our faith? Are we to suppose that it was thus that Jonas prayed? or the three youths? or Daniel in the lions' den? or the thief on the cross? (*Dialogus adversus Luciferianos,* § 15, *PL* 23:169.)

641. ST. JOHN CLIMACUS. Faith gives wings to prayer, and without it we cannot fly up to heaven (*Scala paradisi, Grad. 28, PL* 88:1034; Moore, p. 254, n. 26; Father Robert, p. 406).

642. ST. BERNARD. For it is hope alone that can move you to compassion; it is only into the vessel of faithful confidence that you pour the oil of your mercy (*Serm. de temp., Serm. III in Annuntiatione B. M.,* § 3, *PL* 183:394).

643. ST. MECHTILD [heard these words from the mouth of Christ]: "I tell you in all truth: it gives me deep pleasure for men to expect really great gifts of grace from me with all confidence. And if anyone believes that after this life I shall reward him far beyond his merits, and as a consequence thanks me now during his life, he is so pleasing to me in thus acting that the more he can believe or presume, so much the more, and still beyond that, will I reward him beyond his just merits; for it is impossible for man not to receive that which he has firmly believed in and hoped for" (*Le livre de la grace spéciale, IIIme partie,* c. 5, p. 196).

Perseverance in prayer

644. ST. CYPRIAN. Wherefore let us continue instant and fervent in prayer and lamentation; for not long ago, my beloved brethren, I re-

ceived, as you know, a reprimand in a vision for our sluggishness in prayer, and for want of zeal in it. Now, *whom the Lord loves he reproves, and he chastises the son he favors* (Prov. 3:12). Whenever he chastises, he always does so for our amendment, in order to save us (*Ep. 7, ad clerum, de precando Deo,* § 5, *PL* 4:248).

645. RABANUS MAURUS, monk of Fulda, pioneer of religious studies in Germany, abp. of Mainz (d. 856). Whoever seeks to attain the object of his desires must not allow his mind to wander from concentration on prayer: rather, it behooves him to persevere in the intention with which he has begun. Hence that blind man of Jericho mentioned in the Gospel (Luke 18:35 f.), who heard Jesus passing by, petitioned that he would show him mercy; when he was ordered by the passersby to be quiet, he cried out all the louder: *Son of David, have mercy on me!* (*Expos. sup. Jer., Lib. 19* [Lam. 3:50], *PL* 111:1237.)

646. ST. HILARY, bp. of Poitiers, Doctor of the Church (d. 368). In questions about which we are in ignorance, the way for arriving at the truth is open to us: to obtain it nothing else is needed but perseverance in prayer. In order, then, for us to experience and believe all things, and to be hampered by no uncertainty of doubt, we must pray, we must seek, we must knock (cf. Matt. 7:7); in order to receive mercy by our prayer, progress as a result of our seeking, and admission by our knocking (*In Matt. 7:6–7,* c. 6, § 2, *PL* 9:951).

647. ST. JOHN CHRYSOSTOM. Let us be ashamed, beloved, let us be ashamed and groan over our excessive sloth. For thirty-eight years that man had been waiting without obtaining what he desired (cf. John 5:5), and still he did not depart. And he failed not through any carelessness of his own, but through being oppressed and suffering violence from others, and not even thus did he grow despondent; whereas we, if we have persisted for ten days in praying for anything, and have not obtained it, are too slothful afterward to employ the same zeal (*In Joan., Hom. 36,* § 2, *PG* 59:205).

648. ST. GREGORY THE GREAT. Now it is to be noted that the Psalmist does not say, "I cry out to you," but *I have cried out to you* (Ps. 129:1, Douay version). You have the pattern of perseverance in the phrase: if at first you are not heard, do not abandon your prayer; in fact, be all the more urgent in your petitions and cries. God wills to be implored; he wills to be forced; he wills to be overcome with a certain importunity. For that reason he says to you: *The kingdom of heaven has been enduring violent assault, and the violent have been seizing it by force* (Matt. 11:12; *In Sept. Ps. Poenit. expos., Ps. 6:129,* § 2, *PL* 79:633).

649. ST. BONAVENTURE. No soldier engaged in battle ever puts down his weapons until victory has been won. Now, our weapons are the prayers by which we carry on the battle against the adversary and

through which we obtain aid from heaven. We must, therefore, never abandon prayer until we have gained the victory (*Serm. V de uno confessore, Op. Om.,* ed. Peltier 14:76).

650. ST. LAURENCE JUSTINIAN. A. We must pray with perseverance; for anyone who has not implored with confidence and persevering effort does not deserve to be heard by the Lord. A runner who withdraws from a race before reaching the goal receives no prize: in the same way whoever is not importunate in prayer will be deprived of its fruit (*Lignum vitae, tract. de oratione,* c. 9, *Op. Om.* 1:92). B. Once a person has spurned the enticement to sin that this fleeting existence presents, and has chosen and has actually begun to relish the spiritual and heavenly delights of the everlasting banquet, if he entertains the hope of pleasing God and seeks to pass through the pilgrimage of this world with its hardships, he must dedicate himself to prayer, engage in it eagerly and willingly; take part in it before the Lord zealously and with heartfelt devotion, and persevere in it day after day (*De disciplina et perfectione monasticae conversationis,* c. 18, *ibid.,* 1:146).

651. ST. BERNARD. Pray with tears, beloved sister, and incessantly. Pray continually. Address yourself to God in prayer day and night. Let your prayer be without interruption; let it be frequent; see to it that your constant means of protection be those of prayer; let prayer never cease from your lips (*Lib. de modo bene vivendi, ad sororem,* c. 49, *de oratione,* n. 118, *In Append., PL* 184:1271).

652. SUAREZ, FRANCISCO, S.J., Doctor Eximius, Spanish theologian (d. 1617). I assure you of this: if anyone prays perseveringly, asking for perseverance in grace, he will infallibly receive it (*Tract. III, de gratia Dei, Lib. 12, de merito, quod est effectus gratiae sanctificantis,* c. 38, n. 16, *Op. Om.* 10:263).

653. ST. BONAVENTURE. A. Frequent prayer conquers the assault of vices; intense prayer obtains the forgiveness of sins, according to what is stated in the scriptures: *Has anyone persevered in his fear and been forsaken? has anyone called upon him and been rebuffed? Compassionate and merciful is the Lord; he forgives sins, he saves in time of trouble* (Sir. 2:10–11; *Comm. in Evang. Lucae,* c. 18, n. 1, § 2, *Op. Om.,* ed Quaracchi 7:448). B. Fervent and frequent prayer puts every evil to flight: flies stay away from a boiling pot (*Speculum disciplinae ad novitios, Pars I,* c. 2, § 4, *ibid.,* 8:585). C. (David of Augsburg): The oftener one prays, the more gratifying and efficacious prayer will become for him; the more rarely he prays, the more insipid and irksome it is . . . (*De profectu religiosorum, Lib. 2,* c. 70, *inter opera S. Bonavent.,* ed. Peltier 12:424).

654. ST. AUGUSTINE. A. For the effect following upon prayer will be excellent in proportion to the fervor of the desire which precedes its utterance. And therefore, what else is intended by the words of the

Apostle: *Pray without ceasing* (I Thess. 5:17) than "Desire without intermission, from him who alone can give it, a happy life, which no life can be but that which is eternal" (*Ep. 130, ad Probam,* c. 9, § 18, *PL* 33:501). B. Let your desire be before him: and *thy Father, who sees in secret, will reward thee* (Matt. 6:6). For it is your heart's desire that is your prayer; and if your desire continues uninterrupted, your prayer continues also. For not without meaning did the Apostle say: *Pray without ceasing* (I Thess. 5:17). Are we to be *without ceasing* bending the knee, prostrating the body, or lifting up our hands, that he should say, *Pray without ceasing?* If this is the sense in which we are to say that we pray, I believe that we simply cannot do it *without ceasing.* There is another inward kind of prayer without ceasing, which is the desire of the heart. Whatever else you are doing, if you but long for that Sabbath, you do not cease to pray. If you would never cease to pray, never cease to long for it. The continuance of your longing is the continuance of your prayer (*Enarr. in Ps. 37:10,* § 14, *PL* 37:404).

655. ST. NILUS, monk (d. 451). A. If you desire to be a temple of God, offer him the sacrifice of constant attendance, that is, of unremitting prayer (*Capita paraenetica,* n. 118, *PG* 79:1259). B. The altar of prayer is sacred; for it draws the holy of holies to us in a sacred manner (*Sententiae,* n. 40, col. 1243).

656. WALAFRID STRABO, Monk of Fulda (d. 849). The just man never ceases praying without ceasing to be a just man: he is always at prayer who is always acting virtuously (*Glossa ordinaria in I Thess. 5:17, PL* 114:620).

We are to pray with tears of compunction

657. ST. JOHN CHRYSOSTOM. Flowing currents of water do not make gardens so productive as fonts of tears watering them; making the small plants of prayer grow to their greatest height (*De Anna,* Hom. III, § 1, *PG* 54:652).

658. ST. LAURENCE JUSTINIAN. O humble tear of sorrow, yours is the power and the kingdom! You do not stand in awe of the Judge's tribunal; you impose silence on the accusers of your friends; no one can prevent your approach to God. Even if you enter before him all alone, you never return empty-handed. Have you still greater powers than these? You overcome him who is invincible; you fetter him who is omnipotent; you move the Son of the Virgin to mercy; you open the gates of heaven; you put the devil to flight. You are the food of souls, the strengthening of the senses, the purification of crimes, the expulsion of vices. You are the preparation for the life of virtue, the companion of grace, the nourishment of the mind, the bath where faults are washed away. You are the sweet fragrance of life, the relish of the spirit, the savor of forgiveness, the wholeness of recaptured innocence, the

joy of reconciliation, the sweetness of the calmed conscience, the well-founded hope of eternal salvation. Let him rejoice who desires to have you as the companion of his prayer; because after his prayer he may take his departure in security (*Lignum vitae, tract de oratione,* c. 9, *Op. Om.* 1:92).

659. ST. NILUS OF SINAI. Before all else pray to be given [the gift of] tears, that weeping may soften the hardness which is in your heart, and upon having acknowledged your sin to the Lord (cf. Ps. 31:5), you may receive the forgiveness of the sin from him (*De oratione tract.,* c. 5, *PG* 79:1167; *Philokalia,* p. 129).

We must pray faithfully in times of aridity

660. ST. BERNARD. A. Often we approach the altar and begin to pray with a heart lukewarm and dry. But if we steadily persist, graces come suddenly in a flood upon us, our breast grows full of increase, a wave of piety fills our inward heart; and if we press on, the milk of sweetness conceived in us will spread over us in a fruitful flood (*Serm. 9 in Cant.,* § 7, *PL* 183:818; Eales, p. 47). B. Pride has been found in me, and the Lord has turned away in wrath from his servant. Hence that barrenness of my soul and that defect in devotion which I experience. . . . Fear then, when favoring grace is with you; fear when it has departed; fear also when at length it returns; that is to say, fear always (*ibid., Serm. 54,* n. 8, col. 1042; Eales, p. 329).

661. GUIGES, prior general of Carthusians (d. 1188). The Lord takes his leave of us lest, being too readily approachable by his presence, he is esteemed lightly; and also in order that being absent he may be longed for the more, sought after more earnestly, and having been sought for a long time, the more gratefully found once more. If comfort were never wanting—and in comparison with the future glory which is to be revealed in us, the comfort which we now have is only a figurative representation and a part—we might think that we have a permanent state here below, and would be less zealous in longing for the state to come (*Scala claustralium, seu tract. de modo orandi,* c. 8, n. 9, *PL* 184:480, *inter opera S. Bernardi*).

662. ST. LAURENCE JUSTINIAN. Aridity produces humility; protects innocence; purifies offenses; rouses up the spirit; moves the soul to compunction; perfects prudence; shows the need of perseverance; makes one diligent in watchfulness; casts off all sluggishness; quenches the flames of concupiscence; stimulates the soul to go in search of consolation, and sufficiently instructs it as to how it is to be found (*De casto connubio Verbi et animae,* c. 15, *Op. Om.* 1:219). Light is understood by contrasting it with darkness; peace with war; sadness with joy; penury with abundance; good with evil; the darkness of despair with the brightness of hope; the torment of the Divine Word's absence with

the delight and intimate union of his presence. He, therefore, who, because he loved intensely, has suffered keenly the harm of separation, will go to all lengths to keep the Bridegroom of the soul near him (*ibid.*, p. 218).

Meditation

663. ST. BERNARD. Those two [disciples on their way to Emmaus (Luke 24:13 f.)] can be taken for prayer and meditation, which are united in companionship made necessary by their nature. For prayer illumines meditation, and it is through meditation that prayer becomes truly fervent. As often as we are suspended in the contemplation of the Lord's passion, we are goaded in prayer by the remembrance of so great and admirable a happening. Meditation dwells on the blood of the wounds, the imprint of the nails, the lance and the vinegar; the inhuman conduct of the persecutors, the flight of the apostles, the most shameful death, the burial. Prayer pours out its sighs, distills the perfume of loving devotion, and is completely dissolved in lamentations. *And it came to pass, while they were conversing and arguing together, that Jesus himself also drew near and went along with them* (Luke 24:15; *Serm. pro feria II Paschatis, de duobus discipulis euntibus in Emmaus*, § 2, *In Append., PL* 184:965).

664. ST. THOMAS AQUINAS. A. Consequently meditation must needs be the cause of devotion, insofar as through meditation man conceives the thought of surrendering himself to God's service. Indeed a twofold consideration leads him thereto. The one is the consideration of God's goodness and loving-kindness, according to Psalm 72:28: *But for me, to be near God is my good; to make the Lord God my refuge;* and this consideration wakens love which is the proximate cause of devotion. The other consideration is that of man's own shortcomings, on account of which he needs to lean on God, according to Psalm 120:1–2: *I lift up my eyes toward the mountains; whence shall help come to me? My help is from the Lord, who made heaven and earth;* and this consideration shuts out presumption whereby man is hindered from submitting to God, because he leans on his own strength (*II–II*, q. 82, art. 3, *Utrum contemplatio, seu meditatio, sit devotionis causa, Op. Om.* 9:189; Am. ed. 2:1536, substituting New Catholic ed. of the Bible). B. The fire of charity is ignited in the heart through frequent meditation (*In Ep. ad Eph.*, c. 5, *lect. 7, Op. Om.*, ed. Parma 13:494).

665. ST. AUGUSTINE. Meditation begets knowledge, knowledge compunction, compunction devotion; and devotion in its turn perfects prayer. . . . Devotion is a loving and humble attitude in our relation toward God; humble through realization of our own weakness; loving because of consideration of the divine clemency (*Lib. de spiritu et anima*, c. 50, *Meditatio quid . . . PL* 40:816).

666. ST. BASIL THE GREAT. That is why she who is united to Christ by the promise of her virginity, consecrating herself for life to the worship of the Truth and Wisdom, must be prudent and reasonable. She must keep at a distance all reproach of unreasonable conduct and foolhardiness by constant meditation on divine things; decking her spirit with the beauty of Wisdom to which she is united. For if it is proper to any other person who seeks to be blessed, it is most appropriate for the spouse of Christ to converse lovingly and without interruption with her Bridegroom, the Word of God, in the bridal chamber of the spirit which defies description; and to *meditate on his law day and night* (Ps. 1:2; *De virginitate,* c. 50. *In Append., PG* 30:767; Valliant, p. 55).

667. SPANISH CONGREGATION (1640). Mental prayer is the hinge on which the whole spiritual life turns (*Caeremoniale monastic., Pars II,* dist. 3, c. 8, p. 410).

668. ST. EPHRAEM. If you apply yourself to reading . . . after the manner of a wise bee busily gathering honey from flowers, you will draw fruit for the healing of your soul from what you read (*De recta vivendi ratione,* c. 36, *Op. Om.* 1:42).

669. ST. JOHN CHRYSOSTOM. A. Let us devote ourselves to reading with great devotion and attention, so that we may be led by the Holy Spirit to an understanding of what is written; and derive much fruit from that understanding (*In Gen., Hom. 35,* § 1, *PG* 53:322). B. For as a body will be in better health when enjoying the benefits of a pure air, even so will a soul be more imbued with practical wisdom when nourished in such exercises as these [meditation] (*In Matt., Hom. 2,* § 4, *PG* 57:29).

670. ST. AMBROSE. *Be not slothful in zeal* (Rom. 12:11). This is what the prophet Jeremias states: *Cursed be he that doth the work of the Lord deceitfully* (Jer. 48:10). The lazy man is without hope in the divine way of life. Therefore [Paul] adds: *Be fervent in spirit* (Rom., 12:11). That is, in the performance of the divine work or in the observance of the law, you must not be lukewarm, for as John states in his Apocalypse: *But because thou art lukewarm . . . I am about to vomit thee out of my mouth* (Apoc. 3:16). Daily meditation takes away such sluggishness and makes one vigilant. And the works of the Lord are those he commands to be performed for the benefit of the Church, that is, for the brethren *(In Ep. ad Rom. 12:11, In Append., PL* 17:166).

671. SMARAGDUS, abbot of St. Michael's, Verdun (d. 824). He who wishes to be always with God, must pray often and read often. For when we pray, we speak with God; but when we read, God speaks to us (*Comm., in c. 4 RSB,* n. 56, *PL* 102:784).

672. ST. AUGUSTINE. A. The soul ascends to God by meditation and contemplation; but God descends to the soul by revelation and divine inspiration (*Lib. de spiritu et anima,* c. 32, *PL* 40:802). B. How sweet

is your memory, Lord! The more I meditate on you, the sweeter and more lovable you are to me! (*Manuale*, c. 14, *In Append.*, col. 957.) C. The man who possesses the love of God often beholds God in contemplation, and in his contemplation is sweetly nourished: the more sweetly the more often it happens. For God is always sweet to be meditated on, always sweet to be loved and praised (*ibid.*, c. 28, col. 963).

673. ST. GREGORY THE GREAT. A. When anyone desires to meditate, he must first get the dust out of his eyes, and then the eyes must be refreshed. Dust is cast out of the eyes when pictures of everything physical are eliminated from the intent of the mind. The eye is refreshed when, by continual use of meditation, that same intent of the mind is lifted up to things eternal (*In I Reg. expos. Lib. I*, c. 2, § 4, *PL* 79:51). B. Among the elect, the purer the mind becomes by guarding the interior spirit of meditation, the more copious the infusion of divine gifts (*ibid., Lib. II*, c. 4, § 9, col. 130).

674. ST. PETER DAMIAN. Never is the devil's cleverness avoided so perfectly as when we die with Christ, as though we were rendered insensible to the temptations of the wily enemy. Now contemplation produces this new death, which makes the world dead to us and us dead to the world. It is necessary for every soul united by love to the heavenly Bridegroom to be inseparably bound to him as with a chain through tireless meditation on the scripture (*Opusc. 32, De Quadr.*, c. 6, *quod caro in tentatione subjienda sit spiritui, PL* 145:555).

675. ST. ANSELM, abp. of Canterbury, Doctor of the Church (d. 1109). Meditation about you, O God, is more than a pleasing food; to speak to you, complete nourishment; to know you, perfect consolation; to cling to you, eternal life; to be separated from you, everlasting death (*Oratio 10, ad Deum, pro vitiis resecandis et virtutibus obtinendis, PL* 158:883; not retained in Schmitt's critical ed.).

676. MICHAEL OF MEAUX, abp. of Sens (d. 1199). O blessed meditation, burning within, shining without, leading the heart on high! As an expression of love it kindles within; as a prayer, *a fire blazes out* (Ps. 38:4); as a sigh, it longs for the things that are above (*Altera expos. in Ps. 118, 143*, c. 9, *Inter opera S. Bonaventurae*, ed. Peltier 9:501. Definitely attributed by the editors of the definitive edition of St. Bonaventure's works to Michael).

677. GIOVANNI DA CALVOLI, Franciscan preacher of note (d. after 1376). Continual and diligent meditation on the life of Christ Jesus strengthens the mind and gives it firmness against vain and fallen things; . . . fortifies it for bearing trials and adversities; . . . and teaches it with regard to the things that are to be done, so that neither enemies nor vices can assault or deceive it (*Meditationes vitae Christi, Prooem., Inter Op. Om. S. Bonaventurae*, ed. Peltier 12:510).

678. ST. BONAVENTURE. Meditation stimulates zeal for prayer and

gives it its form (*Speculum disciplinae ad novitios, Pars I,* c. 12, § 2, *Op. Om.,* ed. Quaracchi 8:593).

679. ST. LAURENCE JUSTINIAN. In the pilgrimage of this life, nothing more agreeable is experienced; nothing more gratifying is ever undertaken; nothing truer is understood; nothing so detaches the mind from love of this world; nothing so strengthens the powers of the soul against temptation and the intellect against all error; nothing so stimulates man in all undertakings and aids him in laborious efforts as meditation on the words of God (*Lignum vitae, tract. 10, De perseverantia,* c. 4, *Op. Om.* 1:63).

680. DENIS THE CARTHUSIAN. The objective and fruit of every true meditation (prayer) is to cling to God and become one spirit with him (*De perfectione charitatis dialogus,* art. 38, *Op. Om.* 41:395).

681. HUGH OF ST. CHER. Meditation and prayer are the two wings of charity (*Sup. Ps. 54:7, Comm.* 2:139).

682. ST. JEROME. A. Such books [explanation of the Psalms, and St. Hilary's work on the Synods] must be the food of the Christian soul if it is to meditate on the law of the Lord day and night (cf. Ps. 1:2; *Ep. 5, ad Florentium,* n. 2, *PL* 22:337). B. The learned teaching of our Lord strikes the Pharisees dumb with astonishment, and they were filled with amazement to find that Peter and John knew the Law, although they had not learned letters. For to these the Holy Ghost immediately suggested what comes to others by daily study and meditation. As it is written: *They have learned from God* (I Thess. 4:9; *Ep. 53, ad Paulinum, episc. Nolae, de studio Scripturarum,* n. 3, col. 542). C. Let the Divine Scripture be always in your hands and give yourself so frequently to prayer that such shafts of evil thoughts as are always assailing the young may thereby find a shield to repel them (*Ep. 79, ad Salvinam, viduam, de educatione filiorum,* n. 9, col. 730). D. After the Holy Scripture you should read the sacred writings of learned men; and of those only whose faith is well known. You need not go into the mire to seek for gold; you have many pearls, but the one pearl [of great price] with these (Matt. 13:45; *Ep. 54, ad Furiam, de viduitate servanda,* § 11, col. 555). E. Love the Holy Scriptures, and wisdom will love you. Love wisdom and it will keep you safe. Hold wisdom in honor and it will embrace you round about. Let the jewels you wear be the gems of wisdom (*Ep. 130, ad Demetriadem, de servanda virginitate,* n. 20, col. 1124).

683. ST. GREGORY THE GREAT. A. The Emperor of heaven, the Lord of men and angels, has sent you his epistles for your life's blood; and yet, excellent son, you neglect to read these epistles ardently. Study, then, I beseech you, and daily meditate on the words of your Creator. Learn the heart of God in the words of God, that you may long more ardently for the things that are eternal; that your soul may be kindled

with more intense desire for heavenly joys. For a man will have the greater rest in those joys in the proportion that he now allows himself to rest in the love of his Maker. But, that you may act thus, may almighty God pour into you the Spirit, the Comforter; may he fill your soul with his presence, and in filling it, compose it (*Lib. IV, ep. 31, ad Theodorum medicum, PL* 77:706). B. Holy Scripture is set before the eyes of the mind like a kind of mirror, that we may see our inward person in it; for therein we learn the deformities; therein we learn the beauties that we possess; there we are made sensible of the progress that we are making; there too, we learn how far we are from proficiency (*Moral., Lib. II,* c. 1, n. 1, *PL* 75:553). C. Many indeed read, but they remain hungry after their reading; many hear the words of preaching, but return empty after the sermon (*In Ezech., Lib. I, Hom. 10,* § 7, *PL* 76:888).

684. GUIGES, prior of Grande Chartreuse (d. 1188). A. Spiritual reading is to be thought of as though it were a sort of foundation: it provides the material, and sends us on to meditation. Meditation, in turn, leads the soul to inquire diligently into what is to be grasped; this it discovers and makes manifest, almost like laying a treasure bare. But since [meditation] is not of itself capable of acquiring possession of it, it sends us on to prayer. Then prayer, lifting itself to the Lord with all its strength, implores this most desirable treasure, the sweetness of contemplation. Contemplation repays the labor of the previous three stages, since it intoxicates the thirsty soul with the dew of heavenly sweetness. Reading, then, is an external exercise; meditation is an act of inner intellect. Prayer is the work of longing, and contemplation is beyond all sensible existence. The first step is that of beginners; the second, that of him who is setting out on the way; the third, that of the devout; the fourth, that of the blessed (*Scala claustralium, sive tract. de modo orandi,* c. 10, *PL* 184:481). B. It is as the Lord says: *Seek and you shall find; knock and it shall be opened to you* (Matt. 7:7). Seek in reading, and you will find in meditating; knock in praying, and you shall enter through contemplation (*ibid.,* c. 2, col. 476). C. Now these rungs of the ladder of the cloistered [*scala claustralium,* namely reading, meditation, prayer, and contemplation, cf. c. 1], are so closely linked and so designed to be of mutual assistance that the first two [reading and meditation] are of little or no value without the latter [prayer and contemplation]. And these last two can rarely, if ever at all, be attained without the first two. For of what profit is it for us to spend our time in continually reading the lives and writings of the saints, unless we extract the essence from these sources by breaking them and chewing them in our minds, and store it up in the depths of our hearts? We do this in order to compare our lives diligently with the lives of the saints, and to strive to reproduce in our own lives the works of those whose

deeds we read so attentively. . . . In the same way, of what profit is it for a man to see in meditation what he is to do, unless he is enabled to perform that duty through the aid of prayer and God's grace? . . . From these considerations we may understand that reading without meditation is barren; meditation without reading, subject to error; prayer without meditation, lukewarm; and meditation without prayer, fruitless. Prayer and devotion lead to contemplation; but it is rare, in fact it would be miraculous, to attain contemplation without prayer (*ibid.*, cc. 11–12, col. 481–482). D. Reading is the diligent searching of the scriptures by the mind's concentrated effort. Meditation is a zealous operation of the mind which, under the guidance of one's own reason, investigates the significance of the hidden truth. Prayer is the devout turning of the mind to God for the purpose of banishing evils and acquiring what is good. Contemplation is the elevation of the mind to a state of suspension in God, wherein it tastes joys of eternal sweetness (*ibid.*, c. 1., col. 476). E. Reading, to use an analogy, puts solid food into our mouths, meditation chews it and breaks it up; prayer perceives its savor, and contemplation is the sweetness itself which gives pleasure and refreshes. Or, again, reading is like the outer rind; meditation, the meaty substance; prayer resides in the demands of longing; and contemplation is the delight of the sweetness obtained (*ibid.*, c. 2).

685. ST. BERNARD. A. The first effect of consideration [meditation] is to purify the mind which has given it birth. Then it regulates the affections, directs the actions, cuts away all excesses, forms the character, orders and ennobles the life, and lastly, endows the understanding with a knowledge of things divine and human (*De consideratione, Lib. I*, c. 7, n. 8, *PL* 182:737). B. The Holy Spirit admonishes us, he moves us, he instructs us. He admonishes our memory (cf. John 14:26), he moves our will, he instructs our reason. In so doing he takes complete possession of our soul (*Serm. de temp., Serm. I in fest. Pentecostes, PL* 183:325). C. Meditation shows what is lacking to us, and prayer obtains that it no longer be lacking. The former points out the way, the latter leads us along that way. Meditation, to sum up, makes known to us the dangers that threaten us, and prayer enables us to avoid them (*ibid., Serm. I in fest. S. Andreae Ap.*, 10, col. 509).

Life of Jesus to be meditated on

686. IMITATION OF CHRIST (Thomas à Kempis). Let all the study of our heart be from now on to have our meditation fixed wholly on the life of Christ (*De imitatione Christi, Lib. I*, c. 1, *Op. Om.* 2:5; Gardiner, p. 31).

687. GIOVANNI DA CALVOLI, Franciscan preacher (d. after 1376). If you desire to draw spiritual fruit from what the Lord Jesus is recorded as having said and done, you should make yourself so present as though

you were actually hearing with your own ears what he said, and seeing with your own eyes what he did; paying attention with the whole intent of your mind—diligently, joyfully, scrupulously noting every detail, setting aside for the time being all other cares and preoccupations (*Meditationes vitae Christi, Prooem., inter Op. Om. S. Bonaventurae,* ed. Peltier 12:511).

688. DAVID OF AUGSBURG, German Franciscan mystical writer and preacher (d. 1272). Prayer [meditation] is like a mirror, for it makes man see more clearly his failings or his progress; in meditating the conscience reveals itself more clearly than in other acts, whereupon, either because of the progress made, it joyfully is stimulated to the confidence of hope, or it is shamed by the realization of its failing. More than any other acts, too, this kind of prayer lifts the mind and places it at a distance from earthly concerns: for whereas these latter, in their activity, are preoccupied with Martha about much serving (cf. Luke 10:39 f.), the former, clinging to the Lord's feet with Mary, only begs him to be merciful (*De profectu religiosorum, Lib. II,* c. 67, *Op. Om. S. Bonaventurae,* ed. Peltier 12:421).

689. RUDOLPH OF BIBERACH, Franciscan mystic (d. 1360). In our meditations, our spirit addresses God, who deigns to speak to it. . . . It does so by faithfully adoring him as the most lovable God; . . . by admiring him with great intensity as the Creator; . . . by petitioning him confidently as the Father; . . . by humbly giving him honor as Lord; . . . by fearing him as Judge; . . . by speaking familiarly with him as its Companion; . . . by whispering sweetly to him as the Bridegroom (*De septem itineribus aeternitatis, iter* 2, dist. 4, *Op. Om. S. Bonaventurae,* ed. Peltier 8:412).

690. ST. BONAVENTURE. It is necessary to understand that there are three steps in mental prayer, or three parts which perfect it: the first is the lamenting of [sinful] misery; the second, supplication for mercy; the third, the offering of adoration (*Incendium amoris,* c. 2, § 2, *Op. Om.,* ed. Quaracchi 8:80).

691. VEN. LOUIS DE BLOIS (Blosius). The man of interior life should also beware of all lightness of character, inconstancy, and instability. Let him adopt exercises that are good, and persevere in what he has once begun, even though it cease to hold its appeal for him; provided only that what the Holy Spirit wills is followed in all that he does, and that he reject his own choice and schedule. For the Holy Spirit invites us, as it were, in different ways and leads us by different paths to the wine cellar and bed-chamber of divine love (cf. Cant. 2:4 f.). We must note and readily follow his inspirations in all things, laying aside all self-love (*Speculum monachorum,* div. 5, *Op. Om.* 3:664).

692. DENIS THE CARTHUSIAN. Both in the cave at Subiaco and outside it, St. Benedict entered into the sanctuary of God, that is, into the

abyss of uncreated wisdom; the secret recesses of contemplation, the depths of divine revelation. For the Most High made manifest to him uncertain and hidden things of his Wisdom (cf. Ps. 50:8, Douay version); revealed to him the secrets of hearts; and filled him with the spirit of prophecy, so that he was able to foretell to his saintly disciple Maurus, and not only to him, but to the evil King, Totila, exactly how long they were to live (*Serm. I, in fest. S. Benedicti abb., Op. Om.* 31:386).

693. ST. GREGORY THE GREAT. . . . . Benedict returned to his beloved solitude, and alone under the eye of God dwelt with himself. He kept a constant guard on himself, considered himself as under the eye of God; examined himself constantly, and never allowed his thoughts to be scattered and wander abroad; . . . but whenever he was rapt aloft in the ardor of contemplation, then undoubtedly he was lifted above himself (*Dialogorum Lib. II,* c. 3, *PL* 66:138).

The monk is a man of the Church and of the Holy See

694. ST. BEDE, the Venerable, monk of Jarrow, Doctor of the Church (d. 735). Peter, the first shepherd of the Church, received his name from that spiritual rock (*petra*) upon which the immovable and unshaken structure of the whole Church endures. . . . Let us employ all solicitude, beloved brethren, so that, clinging steadfastly to the protection of this rock, we shall be shaken from the solidity of the faith neither by the dreadful confusion at the perishing of things, nor by the deceptiveness of temporal prosperity (*Lib. II, Hom. 23, In nat. S. Andreae Ap., PL* 94:261).

695. ST. ANSELM, abp. of Canterbury, Doctor of the Church (d. 1109). A. God loves nothing so much in this world as the freedom of his Church. They who desire not so much to be of service to her as to dominate her, show beyond doubt that they stand in opposition to God. God wills his Bride to be a free person, not a servant. They who treat her and honor her as children do their mother, prove themselves to be her sons and God's sons. Contrariwise, those who dominate her as though she were a slave, make themselves not her sons, but strangers to her; and in consequence are justly excluded from their inheritance and the goods she is promised (*Lib. IV, ep. 9, ad Baldwinum regem Hierosolymorum, quem hortatur ut libertatem Ecclesiae noviter resuscitatae servet, PL* 159:206; Schmitt, *Op. Om.* 4:143). B. Do not believe for a moment, my lord, that the Church in your kingdom has been bestowed on you as an inheritance over which you are to domineer; but rather as an inherited obligation of showing her reverence and protection. Love her as your mother, honor her as the Bride and friend of God. Those who now trample her under foot will be cast forth from her and themselves trampled under foot with the demons; those who exalt her will be glorified in her and with her among the angels (*ibid.,*

Lib. III, ep. 65, ad Humbertum comitem, col. 103; Schmitt, 4:177). C. As the faithful friend of your soul and as one truly loved in God, I pray you, I beseech you, I warn you, I advise you, my lord, never consider that the dignity of your highness has been lessened if you love and defend the freedom of the Spouse of God, and your Mother, the Church. Do not think that you are humbled if you exalt her; do not believe that you are weakened if you strengthen her. Look about you. Examples of what I mean are readily at hand. Consider the princes who attack her and trample on her. What do they gain? How do they end? It is evident: there is no need for speaking about it. This is certain: they who honor her will be glorified with her and in her (*ibid., Lib. IV, ep. 13, ad Robertum comitem Flandriae,* col. 208; Schmitt, n. 248, 4:158).

696. ST. BERNARD. [Most holy Pope Eugene], let us examine with still greater diligence who you are, that is to say, what role you fulfil, according to the time, in the Church of God. Who are you? You are the High Priest, the Sovereign Pontiff. You are the Prince of bishops and the heir of the apostles. By your primacy you are an Abel; by your office of Pilot [in Peter's bark], a Noe; by your patriarchate, an Abraham; by your orders, a Melchiesedech; by your dignity, an Aaron; by your authority, a Moses; by your judicial power, a Samuel; by your jurisdiction, a Peter; and by your anointing, a Christ. You are he on whom the keys have been bestowed (cf. Matt. 16:19), and to whom the sheep have been entrusted (cf. John 21:17). There are indeed other gatekeepers of heaven, and there are other shepherds of the flock; but you are in both respects more glorious than they in proportion as you have inherited a more excellent name (cf. Heb. 1:4). They have assigned to them particular portions of the flock, his own to each; whereas you are given charge of all the sheep, as the one Chief Shepherd of the whole flock. Not only of the sheep, but of the other shepherds also, you are the sole supreme Shepherd. . . . Your prerogative, therefore, remains secure and inviolable, both by reason of the keys entrusted to your keeping and by reason of the flock committed to your care. . . . Accordingly, although each of the other bishops has his own ship to pilot, the largest ship of all is entrusted to you. For your ship is the universal Church, made up of all the particular churches, and extending round the world (*De consideratione, Lib. II,* c. 8, *de pontificiae dignitatis et potestatis excellentia,* nn. 15–16, *PL* 182:751).

697. ST. ODO, abp. of Cluny (d. 942). From the whole world one is chosen Peter. And he is placed at the head of the vocation of all peoples, over all the Apostles, and all the Fathers of the Church; so that, although there are many priests among the people of God, Peter governs all whom Christ governs principally. Upon this one man the divine benignity has bestowed a great and wonderful union with his

Power. . . . O inestimable and boundless goodness! . . . How near and how profound are the means of help at our disposal! The world has the kingdom of God close at hand, if only it has recourse to Peter! . . . See, at Peter's nod, the cloisters of the heavenly kingdom are thrown open (*Serm. I in Cathedra S. Petri, PL* 133:711).

698. ALCUIN OF YORK (d. 804). A. I offer myself wholly to your Holiness, most loving Father, to be cured by that healing power which has been granted to you through the long succession of Holy Fathers, and which is acknowledged to be bestowed through the succession of inheritance from Christ who is God; by your words of saving kindness, command that I may be freed from the bonds of sin. . . . Blessed is that tongue on which rests the remedy of eternal salvation, by whose words the heavens are opened to those who believe! May it never remain silent; let it ever continue to admonish and to heal, never ceasing to open the doors of everlasting bliss to those who have recourse to it! O Lord Jesus, grant him a long and fruitful life! May you, who have given your people so worthy a Shepherd, deign to preserve him for a long time by the loving power of your right hand (*Ep. 18, ad Adrianum Papam, PL* 100:171). B. I have always loved the blessed princes and pastors of the Holy Roman See, seeking to be numbered through their holy intercession among the sheep that, after his Resurrection, Christ, who is God, commended to Blessed Peter, Prince of the Apostles, to be fed. . . . The health of the flock is the glory of the shepherd, and its increase his eternal reward. . . . O most Holy Father, you are the pontiff chosen by God, vicar of the Apostles, heir of the Fathers, ruler of the Church. . . . In your fatherly compassion, through your holy prayers and tender exhortations, gather us children of the Holy Church of God, within the sheepfold of security, the Church's unshakable firmness. . . . With your holy vigils devoted to pastoral solicitude . . . we shall not hesitate to offer our aid in the angelic visitations from the heavenly throne; with this help we believe that you can obtain whatever you have petitioned from the Divine Goodness (*Ep. 24, ad Leonem III papam,* col. 178 f.).

699. POPE ST. GREGORY VII, former monk of Cluny (d. 1085). Do you not know that by endowing them with perpetual exemption from the authority of bishops . . . the Holy Fathers [popes] have often made the monasteries of religious inviolable by attaching them to the Holy See as the principal members of its head? (*Lib. II, ep. 69, ad Cunibertum episc. Taurinen., PL* 148:420.)

700. PETER THE VENERABLE, abbot of Cluny (d. 1158). . . . for we have our own bishop [the Roman Pontiff]. For who can be found who is more rightfully, more truly, more worthily a bishop than the Bishop of Rome? Is he not the one whom no human but the Divine Authority established to be placed over all others? Is it not he to whom it was

said: *And do thou, when once thou hast turned again, strengthen thy brethren* (Luke 22:32). Is he not the one to whom it was stated: *I will give thee the keys of the kingdom of heaven; and whatever thou shalt bind on earth shall be bound in heaven, and whatever thou shalt loose on earth shall be loosed in heaven* (Matt. 16:19). We glory in having him and him alone, who is supreme, as our Bishop. Him alone we obey in a special manner . . . and we desire to obey him—and never to judge of his judgments, a thing that is lawful for no mortal man (*Lib. I, ep. 28, Domno Bernardo Claraev., PL* 189:137).

701. ST. ANSELM. A. The many and oppressive sufferings that my heart has experienced—and they are known only to God and myself! —bear witness to the steadfastness of mind and the obedience with which I cling in reverence to the Apostolic See, to the utmost of my ability. From the very beginning of my episcopate I bore them for four years in England and for three years in exile, simply because I remained inseparably attached in subjection and obedience to the same See. I place my trust in God that nothing can ever dissuade me from this resolve (*Lib. III, ep. 48, ad Paschalem papam, PL* 159:79; Schmitt, *Op. Om.*, n. 217, 4:118). B. They who refuse to obey the decrees which the Apostolic [Pontiff] issues for the strength of the Christian religion, prove themselves disobedient: certainly to Peter the Apostle, whose place the Pope holds, nay, to Christ himself, who commended his Church to Peter. Let them, consequently, who contemn the Christian decrees of the Vicar of Peter, and in him, the pronouncements of Peter and of Christ, try other gates to the kingdom of heaven. For it is certain that they will not enter by those whose keys Peter the Apostle carries! (*Ibid., ep. 65, ad Humbertum comitem.*, col. 103; Schmitt, n. 262, 4:177.) C. I fear not exile, nor poverty, nor torture, nor death. Placing my confidence in the help of God, my heart is ready to suffer all these for obedience to the Apostolic See and for the freedom of my Mother, the Church of Christ (*ibid., ep. 73, ad Paschalem papam,* col. 111; Schmitt, 4:195). D. We do not cease to pray to God zealously for you in your trials, and for those of the Roman Church, which is also our Church, and that of all the faithful. We pray that he will *give you rest from evil days: till the pit be dug for the wicked* (Ps. 93:13; *Lib. II, ep. 33, ed Urbanum Papam, cum Anselmus erat adhuc abbas Beccensis, PL* 158:1184; Schmitt, n. 126, 3:267). E. You all know, and as a body, that to the best of my understanding I render obedience to the Vicar of Blessed Peter in those things which are of God, and to the King I render conscientious counsel and help in those matters that belong by law to his earthly dignity. . . . Whoever, then, seeks to prove that I violate the trust and sacrament that I owe to an earthly king because I cannot deny my obedience to the Supreme Pontiff of the venerable holy Roman Church, let him stand forth, and in the name of the Lord

he will find me ready to answer him as I must and where I must (*Eadmeri Cantuarien. monachi Historia novorum, Lib. I, PL* 159:382, 384).*

702. POPE URBAN II (d. 1099). In these evil times when almost all of Gaul lies immersed in the darkness of error, We are grateful to God for you in the grace that he has given to you; because that grace has illumined the eyes of your mind to the knowledge of truth, in order that by the fire of his Spirit, God might set your heart aflame with the love of justice and the defense of the Catholic faith. . . . With every expression of charity you have always come to the aid of others in their labors for the defense of truth and justice; joyfully and cheerfully you have ministered to the needs of the saints; you have attacked with the powerful arrows of your preaching the simoniacs and the Guibertists,† the new enemies of the Church; you have pounded their shaky wall of argument with the battering ram of the faith; you have strengthened the athletes of God who were growing weak in the battle array of the religion of Christ. . . . Now that Henry, who is intent on overthrowing Christian peace, has raised violent hands against the Holy, Roman, Apostolic Church, does it seem remarkable to you that the sword of his insanity reaches out to strike you as well? . . . Rejoice, rather, that God wills you to be sharers in the labors of his saints. . . . We humbly beseech you and the brethren with you, to be mindful of Us in your holy prayers, and to beg him who in his birth brought peace on earth, and who by his blood united the Church to himself, to grant peace to Us and to his Church (*Ep. 125, ad Beringerum, abb. S. Laurentii Leodien.* [Liège], 1094 A.D., *PL* 151:395).

703. POPE ST. GREGORY VII, former monk of Cluny (d. 1085). A. Through the all-powerful Lord, We beseech you, as We have asked from the beginning of Our reign, to exhort your brethren to pray continually to God in Our behalf; for unless We merit the divine assistance by virtue of their intercession and that of all the faithful, We shall not be able to avoid the dangers that threaten Us, and what We fear more, those that threaten the Church (*Lib. I. ep. 62, ad Hugonem abb. Cluniacen., PL* 148:338). B. Your father [abbot], truly loving the Prince of the Apostles, has clung to Us in Peter's army, and has rendered Us aid under Christ's leadership. . . . May the infinite love of Christ,

* Eadmer, monk of Canterbury, wrote his *History of Recent Events in England;* published twelve years after St. Anselm's death. He had been the close friend and secretary of St. Anselm. The quotation is from his account of the Primate's opening address at Rockingham Council, 1095, preached before a large congregation of bishops, abbots, princes, monks, clerics, and laymen. [*Tr.*]

† Guibertists: followers of Guibert, Abp. of Ravenna, invalidly elected 1080, enthroned as Clement III in St. John Lateran, Rome, Mar. 24, 1084; d. 1100; and Emperor Henry IV.

dearest brethren, move you to love Us as you love yourselves, and extend a helping hand to those who are caught in a violent storm (*Lib. VI, ep. 15, ad monachos Massiliens.* [*Marseille*], col. 524).

Exercises of piety

704. GAETANO, THOMAS À VIO, O.P., cardinal (d. 1534). Now from this kind of meditation, which must be performed daily by religious and spiritual persons, which is free of lengthy word forms of vocal prayers, the spirit of devotion and consequently other virtues result. A person who does not engage in such meditation at least daily can be called neither religious nor spiritual. For as there can be no effect without a cause, no end without the employment of means, no reaching an inland port without navigation, so also active practice of religion cannot be realized without the frequent employment of these causes and means (*Comm. Cardinalis Cajetani in II-II,* q. 82, art. 3, *Utrum contemplatio, seu meditatio, sit devotionis causa, Op. Om. S. Thomae,* ed. Leonina 9:190).

705. ST. AUGUSTINE. The Son of God, who is eternally in the Father, the Truth and the Life, became the Way by assuming man's nature. Walk by him as man, and you come to God. It is by him that you go, and to him that you go. Seek no other way whereby to come to him than himself. Had he not condescended to be the Way, we should always have wandered aimlessly. He became the Way then whereby you should come. I do not say to you: "Seek the Way." No, the Way itself has come to you. Arise and walk. Walk by worthiness of your conduct, not the physical walking with the feet (*Serm. 141, in Joan. 14:6, Ego sum via . . . PL* 38:777).

Devotion to Mary ever Virgin

706. VEN. LOUIS DE BLOIS. It is impossible that any assiduous and humble worshiper of Mary should ever perish (*Canon vitae spiritualis,* c. 18, § 3, *Op. Om.* 1:18).

707. ST. BONAVENTURE. He who wins Mary's favor will be acknowledged by the citizens of heaven, and he who bears her mark will be inscribed in the book of life (*Psalterium Majus B.M.V., Ps. 91, Op. Om.,* ed. Peltier 14:212. This work is generally considered spurious, although by some it is held to be a doubtful work of St. Bonaventure. Sometimes it is printed anonymously. Cf. *Op. Om.,* ed. Quaracchi 10:24).

708. CONRAD OF SAXONY, Franciscan preacher and ascetical writer (d. 1279). Among the many dangers they face, how can ships arrive safely in port? Certainly by reliance on two helps, namely the wood and the star; that is to say, by confidence in the cross, and by virtue of the

light which Mary, the Star of the Sea, bore for us (*Speculum B.M.V.*, Lect. 3, in *Op. Om. Bonaventurae,* ed. Peltier 14:238; cf. *Op. Om.,* ed. Quaracchi 10:24).

709. ST. ANSELM. Just as every person who turns away from you and is looked on without favor by you, most Blessed Virgin, will of necessity perish, so it is impossible for anyone who turns to you and is looked upon with favor by you, to be lost (*Oratio 52, ad S. Mariam Virginem, cum meditatione et laude meritorum ejus, PL* 158:956; Schmitt, *Op. Om.,* n. 7, 3:22. This thought is paraphrased by many writers, e.g., St. Antoninus, abp. of Florence, *Summa Theologica, Pars IV,* tit. 15, c. 14, § 7, *de salutatione angelica,* 4:1007).

710. ST. BERNARD. A. Never do you shudder at nor disdain the sinner, O Mary, no matter how revolting his state may be, if only he cries out to you and implores your intercession in true repentance. With loving hand you withdraw him from the very depths of despair, you support him, you will not turn away from him until you have rescued him in his misery from the dreaded Judge (*Serm. panegyricus ad B.V. Deiparam,* § 2, *In Append., PL* 184:1010. Considered probably the sermon of Egbert, abbot of Schoenau). B. *And the virgin's name was Mary* (Luke 1:27). Permit me to say something concerning this name also, which is interpreted to mean "Star of the Sea" and admirably suits the Virgin Mother. There is indeed a wonderful appropriateness in this comparison of her to a star, because as a star sends forth its rays without detriment to itself, so did the Virgin bring forth her Child without prejudice to her integrity. And as the ray emitted does not diminish the brightness of the star, so neither did the Child born of her, tarnish the beauty of Mary's virginity. She is, therefore, that glorious star which, according to prophecy (Num. 24:17), arose out of Jacob, whose light illumines the whole earth, whose dazzling splendor coruscates magnificently in the heavens and reaches even unto hell; a star which, enlightening the universe, and communicating warmth to souls rather than to bodies, fosters virtue and extinguishes vice. She, I say, is that resplendent and radiant star placed as a necessary beacon above life's *great and wide sea* (Ps. 103:25); glittering with merits, luminous with examples for our imitation.

Whoever you may be, if you perceive yourself during this mortal existence to be rather floating in the treacherous waters, at the mercy of the winds and the waves, than walking secure upon the solid earth, do not turn away your eyes from the light of this beacon star, unless you wish to be submerged by the tempest. When the storms of temptation burst upon you, when you see yourself driven upon the rocks of tribulation; look up at the star, call out to Mary! When buffeted by the billows of pride, or ambition, or hatred, or jealousy, look up to the star, call upon Mary! Should anger, or avarice, or carnal desire violently assail the little vessel of your soul, look up at the star, call out to Mary! If you are troubled on account of the heinousness of your sins, confounded at the filthy state of your conscience, and terrified at the thought of the awful judgment to come; you are beginning to sink into the bottomless gulf of sadness and to be swallowed up in the black abyss of despair, O then think of Mary! In dangers, in doubts, in all your difficulties, think of Mary, call out to Mary! Let her name never depart from your lips, never suffer it to leave your heart. And in order that you may the more surely obtain the assistance of her prayers, do not neglect to walk in her footsteps. With her for a guide, you will never go astray; whilst invoking her, you will never lose heart; so long as she is in your mind you are safe from deception; while she holds your hand you cannot stumble; under her protection you have nothing to fear. If she walks before you, you will never grow weary; if she shows you favor, you will certainly reach the goal. And thus you shall experience in yourself the truth of what is written: *And the virgin's name was Mary* (*Serm. de temp., Hom. II sup. Missus est,* 17, *PL* 183:70).

711. RAYMOND JORDAN, abbot, Order of St. Augustine (d. 1390). In the present life Mary aids both the good and the evil; the good by preserving them in grace, for which reason we address her, "Mary, Mother of grace"; the evil, by bringing them back to mercy, and hence we call her "Mother of mercy." In the hour of death she helps by shielding from the insidious assaults of the devil, which brings to our lips the cry, "Protect us from the enemy!" Even after death she helps by receiving souls, and therefore we pray: "Receive us at the hour of our death!" She helps the afflicted by giving them patience; those who struggle under temptation, by giving them victory; those who are hungry in the love of God, by giving them spiritual nourishment (*Contemplationes idiotae . . . contempl. de Virgine Maria,* c. 6, fol. 43).

712. ST. BERNARD. A. We read in the Old Testament that there were two arks, the one of the deluge, the other of the Covenant. . . . Noe's ark also foreshadowed the ark of grace, namely Mary's excellence. For as all escaped the deluge by the former, all avoid the shipwreck of sin by the latter. Noe built the former in order to be saved from the deluge; Christ, who is our peace and reconciliation, prepared the latter for himself in order to redeem the human race. By the former only eight souls were rescued; through the latter all are summoned to eternal life . . . (*Serm. de B.V.M. in Luc. 1:28, Ave Maria, gratia plena,* § 6, *In Append., PL* 184:1017). B. The sea is the source of springs and rivers; Mary is the producer of virtues and the wisdom of all sacred sciences. As the sun outshines all the luminous bodies of the heavens by the intensity and brilliance of its light, so, after her Son, Mary excels all rational creatures by the splendor of her virtues and knowledge (*Serm. I in Antiph. Salve Regina,* § 2, *In Append.,* col. 1062). C. Remove from the

heavens the material sun which enlightens the world, and what becomes of the day? Remove Mary, remove this Star of the Sea, this Star of life's *great and wide sea* (Ps. 103:25), and what is left us but a cloud involving gloom and *the shadow of death* (Job 10:22, Douay version), and a darkness exceedingly dense (*Serm. de temp., Serm. in Nativitate B.V.M.*, § 6, *PL* 183:441) . D. The presence of Mary illumines the entire world, so that even the heavenly city above has now a more dazzling splendor from the light of this virginal lamp (*ibid., Serm. I de Assumptione B.V.M.*, § 1, col. 415). E. No words, no language of any people under heaven can fully express the grandeur of your glory, O kind, powerful, most lovable Mary! It is neither possible to pronounce your name without your kindling one to sentiments of love, nor to think of you without your strengthening the very affection of those who love you (*Serm. panegyricus ad B.V.M. Deiparam,* § 6, *In Append., PL* 184:1013).

713. ST. FULGENCE, bp. of Ruspe (d. 533). . . . Mary became the heavenly ladder because, through her, God descended upon earth, in order that, through her, man may merit to ascend to heaven (*Serm. 36, De laudibus Mariae ex partu Salvatoris, In Append., PL* 65:899).

714. ST. ANTONINUS, O.P., abp. of Florence (d. 1459). He who petitions without Mary as his guide is attempting to fly without wings (*Summa Theologica, Pars IV,* tit. 15, c. 22, 4:1086).

715. ST. ILDEPHONSE, bp. of Toledo (d. 669). All the goods that the Supreme Majesty willed to bring into being, he also willed to commend to your hands, Mary. To you are committed the treasures of wisdom and knowledge, the charismata, the ornaments of virtues, and graces (*Libell. de corona virginis,* c. 15, *PL* 96:304).

716. ST. PETER DAMIAN. For you approach before the golden altar of the redemption of the human race, not only interceding, but also commanding; the Queen, not a handmaid. May your [created] nature impel you, may your power remind you; for the more powerful, the more merciful you must be! To desire not to take revenge when one could do so, is to employ power unto glory (*Serm. 44, in Nativitate B.V.M., PL* 144:746).

717. ST. ANTONINUS. It is not possible for the Mother of God not to be heard, according to that which Solomon spoke to his mother by way of a figure: *My mother, ask, for I must not turn away thy face* (III Kgs. 2:20; *Summa Theologica, Pars IV,* tit. 15, c. 17, § 4, 4:1029).

718. ST. EPHRAEM. No other confidence is ours, except that which we draw from you, Virgin most humble (*Serm. de SSae Dei Genetricis V.M. laudibus, Op. Om.* 3:706).

719. THOMAS À KEMPIS. O supremely venerable Virgin Mary, Mother and Daughter of the Eternal King, to be blessed by all mouths, to be reverenced with every honor; most spotless in virginity, most pro-

found in humility, most fervent in charity; most mild in patience, most full of mercy, most devout in prayer; most pure in meditation, most sublime in contemplation, most sweet in compassion; most prudent in counsel, most mighty in aid! You are the court of God, the gate of heaven, the garden of delights, the well-spring of graces; the glory of angels, the joy of men, the pattern of morals, the brightness of virtues; the light of life, the hope of the needy, the health of the sick, the mother of orphans! (*Serm. ad novitios, Serm. 25, Op. Om.* 6:235; Scully, p. 191.)

720. ST. BONAVENTURE. The heavenly paradise is filled with your mercies, O Mary: and the enemy from hell is confounded by the terror that you strike. . . . Glorify your name in the multiplication of the graces you bestow; and do not permit your servants to be threatened with dangers (*Psalterium Majus B.V.M., Pss. 86, 93, Op. Om.,* ed. Peltier 14:211–212).

721. ST. BERNARD. A. Let us, therefore, look more deeply into this matter, and let us see with what sentiments of tender devotion the Lord would have us honor Mary, in whom he has placed the plenitude of all good; so that if there is anything of hope in us, if anything of grace, if anything of salvation, we may feel assured that it has overflowed to us from her (*Serm. in Nativitate B.V.M.,* § 6, *PL* 183:441).

B. Honor indeed the purity of her flesh, the sanctity of her life; wonder at her motherhood as a virgin; adore her Divine Offspring. Extol the prodigy by which she brought into the world without pain, the Son whom she conceived without concupiscence. Proclaim her to be reverenced by the angels, to have been desired by the nations, to have been known beforehand by patriarchs and prophets; chosen by God out of all women and raised above them all. Magnify her as the medium by whom grace was displayed; the instrument of salvation, the restorer of the ages. And finally, extol her as having been exalted above the choirs of angels to the celestial realms (*Ep. 174, ad canonicos Lugdunenses, de conceptione S. Mariae,* § 2, *PL* 182:333; Gasquet, p. 301; James, p. 290).*

C. The rod [of Jesse] signifies Mary, the Virgin Mother of God, and the flower represents her Son. . . . O truly celestial plant, singularly holy, precious beyond all others and holy without compare. In truth you are the tree of life, which alone has been deemed worthy to bear the fruit of salvation. . . . The Virgin herself is the royal road

* Many have interpreted this letter as St. Bernard's statement of opposition to the doctrine of the Immaculate Conception of Mary. St. Bernard states only that the feast of the Immaculate Conception was new; that it rested on no legitimate foundation because it had not been proclaimed or formally taught by the Church, and that it should not be instituted as a feast without consulting the Apostolic See, to whose opinion he submits. [*Tr.*]

by which the Savior came to us, issuing forth from her womb "as a Bridegroom from the bride-chamber." Therefore, dearest brethren, walking faithfully in this way . . . let us endeavor to ascend by it to Jesus, who descended by it to us. Let us strive to go by Mary to share his grace who by Mary came to share our misery. Through you, O most blessed one, finder of grace, Mother of life, Mother of salvation, through you let us have access to your Son, so that through you, he may receive us who was given to us through you. Let your integrity excuse before him the foulness of our corruption; let your humility, so pleasing to God, make amends and obtain pardon for our pride; let your abundant charity cover the multitude of our sins; let your glorious fecundity supply in our behalf for a lack of merit. O you who are our Lady, our Mediatrix, and our Advocate, . . . present us to your Son. Grant, O most blessed one, by the grace you have found, by the prerogative you have merited, by the mercy you have obtained, that he who deigned to make himself, by your consent and through your cooperation, a partaker of our poverty and infirmity, may make us by your intercession, partakers of his own glory and happiness; Jesus Christ, your Son, and our Lord, who is over all things, God, blessed forever *(Serm. de temp., Serm. 2 in Adventu Dni,* n. 4, *PL* 183:42).

D. Mary is the only woman in whom integrity and motherhood have met together. In her was once accomplished what had never been done before nor shall be done hereafter: "Whose like had ne'er been seen before, nor shall appear for evermore" (Sedulius, *Serm. in vigilia Nativitatis Dni,* § 9, col. 99).

E. O happy Virgin, happy in that, alone of all women, you have escaped the curse and obtained the blessing; in that you alone have been delivered from the universal malediction, and freed from the sorrows of motherhood! (*Ibid., Serm. IV,* § 3, col. 101.)

F. What purity can be found anywhere, even among the holy angels, to compare to the purity of her who was deemed worthy to be made the living sanctuary of the Holy Spirit and the dwelling of the Son of God? . . . How sublime and how precious in her was the virtue of humility united with such transcendent purity, with such spotless innocence, with such sinless conscience, with such a fulness of grace! . . . Let him, O most blessed Virgin, let him refuse to extol your mercy who—if there be any—remembers to have invoked your assistance and to have found you wanting to him in his hour of need. . . . We praise your virginity, we admire your humility, but because we are so miserable, more consoling to us than either is your mercy: we love your mercy more tenderly, we recall it more frequently, we invoke it more often. And the reason is, that it is to your mercy we owe the restoration of the whole world and the salvation of all. For it is manifest that you were solicitous for the salvation of the entire human race when it was said to you: *Do not be afraid, Mary, for thou hast found grace with God* (Luke 1:30); the grace, that is, which you were seeking. Who, then, shall be able to *comprehend what is the breadth and length and height and depth* (Eph. 3:18) of your mercy, O Virgin most blessed? . . . For it is through you, Mary, that heaven has been filled, that hell has been emptied, that the breaches in the wall of the spiritual Jerusalem have been rebuilt (cf. Ps. 50:20), and that the life they had lost has been restored to miserable, expectant mortals. . . . Therefore dearest brethren, let us run with thirsting souls to this fountain of mercy, let our misery have recourse with all the eagerness of desire to this treasury of compassion (*ibid., Serm. IV in Assumptione B.V.M.*, nn. 6–8, col. 428).

Devotion to the angels

722. ST. BERNARD. A. *To his angels he has given command about you, that they guard you in all your ways* (Ps. 90:11). O my brother, with how much reverence, with how much gratitude, with how much confidence ought not these words inspire you! With how much reverence for a presence so august! With how much gratitude for a benevolence so great! With how much confidence in a keeping so secure! . . . We must show ourselves grateful to these celestial spirits; . . . let us give them love for love; let us honor them as much as we are bound to, as much as we can. . . . They are faithful, they are prudent, they are invincible; wherefore, then, should we fear? Only let us follow them, only let us cling to them, and we shall dwell in the aid of the Most High and abide under the protection of heaven. . . . As often as you feel the pressure of violent temptation, as often as bitter tribulation threatens to engulf you, invoke your guardian angel, call upon your guide, cry out to your helper in due times in tribulation (*ibid., Serm. 12 in Ps. Qui habitat,* nn. 6–9, col. 233–235). B. Here then, dearly beloved, you have the three-ply cord that is not easily broken (cf. Eccles. 4:12), which from the holy abode of heaven (cf. Deut. 26:15) draws down the inconceivable charity of the angels to console us, to visit us, and to help us in our need; and that for God's sake, because they desire to imitate the infinite mercifulness of his dealings with us; for our sake, because they recognize and compassionate in us a resemblance to themselves; for their own sakes because they long with most ardent desire to see the gaps in their ranks filled up. . . . Such being the case, consider, dear brethren, how solicitous we ought to be to show ourselves worthy of such noble company and so to live in the sight of the holy angels that they shall see nothing in our conduct to displease them (*ibid., Serm. I in festo S. Michaelis,* nn. 4–5, col. 449).

Devotion to the saints

723. ST. BERNARD. A. For it is a *true saying and worthy of entire acceptance* (I Tim. 1:15), that we ought to imitate the example of those whom we worship with solemn veneration; that we should hasten with all eagerness to participate in the bliss of those whom we pronounce most blessed; and that we should be supported by the patronage of those whose praises we delight to celebrate. And in truth we find the practice of keeping festivals in honor of the saints very useful as a remedy against languor, tepidity, and sloth; for our weakness is reinforced by their powerful intercession; our apathy is enlivened by the consideration of their reward; whilst their example serves to instruct our ignorance (*ibid., Serm. II in festo Omnium sanctorum,* § 1, col. 462).

B. In venerating the saints' memory, therefore, we profit not them but ourselves. . . . The thought of any one of these several orders of the blessed, is as a single spark, or rather as a flaming torch for kindling the devout heart and making it thirst to behold and embrace them. . . . Let us long for those who are longing for us, let us hasten to those who are waiting for us, let us anticipate with the desires of our heart those who are looking for our advent. . . . But, my brethren, it is not merely the society of the saints we should long for: their happiness also should be the object of our desire, so that we ought to seek with all ardor a participation in the glory of them for whose society we yearn. . . . Surely, then, in order that we may hope for such glory and aspire to such bliss, we ought to solicit most earnestly the suffrages of the saints, so that what our merit is insufficient to obtain may be granted to us through their intercession. *Pity me!* let us cry out to them, *pity me, O you my friends!* (Job 19:21.) You know the dangers to which we are here exposed; you know the clay of which we are fashioned; you know our ignorance; you know the cunning wiles of our enemies; you know their violence and our weakness (*ibid., Serm. V,* nn. 5–10, col. 478 f.).

C. There are three things, my brethren, which we ought to consider carefully on such solemnities, namely; the assistance of the saint; the example he has left us; and the humiliating contrast of his life with our own. With regard to his assistance, it is certain that he who had such power on earth is more powerful now in heaven, where he stands before the face of the Lord God. . . . Let us reflect on the humility of his works and the authority of his words, and in so doing you will see how by word and example he shone among men; and you will also see the footprints he has left for our guidance, that walking in them we may not wander from the right way. For as the Prophet says in all truth: *The way of the just is right, the path of the just is right to walk in* (Isa. 26:7). But let us consider likewise, and even more attentively, the humiliating contrast between our lives and the life of the particular saint whose feast we happen to be celebrating. For *he was a man like ourselves, subject to the same infirmities* (Jas. 5:17), *molded from the selfsame clay* (Wisd. 15:8) as ourselves. . . . In this way then we should be filled with both joy and confusion on the solemnities of the saints: with joy at the thought that we have sent such powerful advocates on before us; with confusion to think that we cannot imitate them. Thus our joy in this valley of tears is to be seasoned with *the bread of tears* (Ps. 79:6), so that *even in laughter the heart may be sad, and the end of joy may be sorrow* (Prov. 14:13; *ibid., Serm. in vigil. SS. Petri et Pauli App.*, nn. 2–3, col. 404).

724. PETER, abbot of Moustier-la-Celle, later bp. of Chartres (d. 1187). We should venerate the angels [the Cherubim] as brothers and friends, so that helped by their protection we may avoid the snares of scandal, and lifted up in their chariots, we may seek our fatherland again (*Mosaici tabernaculi mystica et moralis expos., Lib. I, in Ex. 25, 22, PL* 202:1066).

725. JOHN OF TRITHEIM. It is in vain that we glory in the holiness of the saints unless we strive to imitate their holy way of life (*De viris illustribus O.S.B., Lib. 3,* c. 337, *Op. pia et spiritualia,* p. 115).

726. THOMAS À KEMPIS. If you desire to be pleasing to God and the saints, examine carefully the lives of the saints, read the doctrine of the saints: in order that you may become saintly with the saints; be instructed by the saints; be aided by the saints; be heard by the saints; and crowned with the saints (*De disciplina claustralium,* c. 15, *Op. Om.* 2:315).

727. POPE PIUS XII. We should imitate the virtues of the saints just as they imitated Christ, for in their virtues there shines forth, under different aspects, the splendor of Jesus Christ. Among some of these saints the zeal of the apostolate stood out, in others courage prevailed even to the shedding of blood; constant vigilance marked others out as they kept watch for the Divine Redeemer, while in others the virginal purity of soul was resplendent and their modesty revealed the beauty of Christian humility: there burned in all of them the fire of charity toward God and their neighbor. The sacred liturgy puts all these gems of sanctity before us so that we may consider them for our salvation, and "rejoicing at their merits, we may be inflamed by their example" (*Miss. III pro plur. martyr. extra T.P., Collecta., Miss. Rom.,* p. 15).

It is necessary then to practice "in simplicity, innocence; in charity, concord; in humility, modesty; diligence in government; readiness in helping those who labor; mercy in serving the poor; in defending truth, constancy; in the strict maintenance of discipline, justice; so that nothing may be wanting in us of the virtues which have been proposed for our imitation. These are the footprints left by the saints in their journey homeward, that guided by them we might follow them into glory" (*S.Beda Venerabilis, Hom. 70 subditit., in solemnitate Omnium Sanctorum, PL* 94:456; *Litt. Encycl. Mediator Dei,* 20 Nov. 1947, *A.A.S.* 39:581; Vatican Library tr., N.C.W.C. pamphlet, § 167, pp. 57–58).

Devotion

728. DAVID OF AUGSBURG (d. 1272). A. The disposition of the love of God and holy fear, united to fervor of good will, exercised in the spirit of humility, the urge of piety and the joy of hope, must never be extinguished in the heart of the servant of God. It is principally in these that the virtue of devotion consists (*De profectu religiosorum, Lib. II,* c. 70, *de utilitate orationis, Op. Om. S. Bonaventurae,* ed. Peltier 12:423). B. This is man's most sublime perfection in this life: so to cling to God that the whole soul, with all its powers and forces, united in God, becomes one spirit with him—remembering nothing but God, feeling and understanding nothing but God, with all the dispositions united in the joy of love sweetly reposing in the enjoyment of its Creator (*ibid.,* c. 73, *de specialibus orationibus,* p. 429).

729. ST. BERNARD. A. When you have long been exercised in these virtues [humility and confidence], pray that the light of devotion may be granted you; that most serene day, that Sabbath of the soul, in which, like a soldier honorably discharged, you may live without labor in the midst of all labor, and deserve to have applied to you the words of the Psalmist: *I will run the way of your commands when you give me a docile heart* (Ps. 118:32). Then you will discover an ineffable sweetness and delight in those very practices which in the beginning you were wont to go through with bitterness and repugnance of mind (*Serm. de temp., Serm. III in Circumcisione Dni,* § 10, *PL* 183:140). B. For there are some who, as regards all the exercises of our rule of life, do not simply walk but run, or one might almost say fly to them, in the alacrity of their zeal; finding the long vigils short, the coarse food sweet, the poor clothes beautiful, and the hard toil not only bearable but actually pleasant. There are others less fervent, who with a cold heart and a reluctant will can scarcely be forced by shame or by fear of hell-fire to the performance of their religious duties. . . . Now the cause of this most dangerous tepidity will be found in an affection or will that is not yet purified; these persons have knowledge of the good, but no love for it, being *drawn away and enticed by their own passion* (Jas. 1:14). For their delight is in those little earthly consolations which flatter the flesh, whether they be words, or signs, or deeds, or whatever else. And although they sometimes interrupt their evil habit, they refuse to break it off altogether. There can be no fellowship between the spirit and the flesh, between fire and tepidity, particularly as the Lord is wont

to vomit what is lukewarm out of his mouth (cf. Apoc. 3:16; *ibid., Serm. III in Ascensione Dni,* n. 6, col. 307).

730. JEAN RIGAUD (Joannes Rigaldi), Franciscan theologian (d. 1323). As incense placed on burning coals breathes forth a sweet-smelling and strongly scented fragrance, so prayer kindled over the glowing coals of devotion ascends as a most pleasing odor before the Divine Majesty (*Diaeta salutis,* tit. 2, c. 5, *de oratione, Op. Om. S. Bonaventurae,* ed. Peltier 8:269).

731. DAVID AUGSBURG, Franciscan mystical writer and preacher (d. 1272). A. As the oil's fat is pressed from the heart of the olive, so devotion's pleasing character derives from a virtuous way of life, particularly from divine love, desire for heaven, and spiritual joy which is nobler and more effective than compunction or fear or sadness (*De profectu religiosorum, Lib. II,* c. 22, *Op. Om. S. Bonaventurae,* ed. Peltier 12:383). B. Without the spirit of devotion to which prayer leads, all religious observance is barren and undeveloped (*ibid.,* c. 70, p. 424). C. There can be neither virtue nor devotion that does not grow out of the root of the love of God (*ibid.,* c. 74, p. 432).

732. CASSIODORUS. If a person who is wanting in devotion addresses God in prayer, he seems to be asking for judgment rather than pardon (*In Ps. 74:1, PL* 70:536).

733. HUGH OF ST. CHER, O.P. Without devotion the human heart is barren and the soul thirsts (*Sup. Gen. 29:1, Comm.* 1:39).

734. ST. PETER DAMIAN. Place upon the altar of your devotion all that you enjoy, all that you are capable of doing, the whole of the life you live, all that you hope for; and then offer yourselves as a sacrifice to God, which is greater than all holocausts (*Lib. VIII, ep. 14, ad sorores suas Rodelindam et Sufficiam, PL* 144:493).

735. POPE ST. LEO THE GREAT. Devotion is then all the more efficacious and holy if in the works of piety of the whole Church there is oneness of affection and oneness of thought (*Serm. 89, De jejunio septimi mensis,* IV, c. 2, *PL* 54:445).

736. ST. BERNARD. We may . . . call faith the root of the vine; the various virtues the branches; good works the bunch or cluster of grapes which it bears; and devotion the wine they yield (*Serm. 30 in Cant.,* n. 6, *PL* 183:936; Eales, p. 195).

737. ST. LAURENCE JUSTINIAN. Devotion is the proper food for those who love, the gift of the humble, the reward of the meek, heavenly dew; a hidden manna, the buried treasure, a salutary nourishment; a most pleasing possession, a spiritual interchange, a foretaste of future blessedness (*De spirituali animae resurrectione, Lib. II, Op. Om.* 2:227).

738. JOHN OF TRITHEIM. With the passing of time the fervor of devotion grows weak unless it is daily renewed with the means fur-

nished by Providence (*Orationes . . abbatum O.S.B. Reformationis Bursfeldensis habitae, Oratio 2, in capitulo Erphordiae 1 Sept. 1492, Op. pia et spiritualia,* p. 852).

739. VEN. LOUIS DE BLOIS. A. Reasonable devotion is by far safer and more acceptable to God than great sensible devotion. Devotion is reasonable when we hate and execrate sin, and worship God with a ready will; and when we strenuously embrace and execute whatever we know to be pleasing to God. If you have this devotion, you will never fail to receive your reward, even if you are entirely without the other kind of devotion (*Canon vitae spiritualis,* c. 26, § 1, *Op. Om.* 1:24). B. The sensible sweetness of devotion is a dangerous thing for those who desire it for unworthy motives and employ it unworthily; that is, by seeking in it and through it their own delight, instead of their mortification and the honor of God (*Enchiridion parvulorum, Lib. I, documentum 2, Op. Om.* 3:679).

740. ST. AUGUSTINE. Brethren, let everyone among the members of Christ be consumed with zeal for God's house. Now, who can be spoken of as consumed with zeal for God's house? He who, whenever he sees anything wrong there, does all in his power that everything may be set aright; who is intent in his desire to see the matter corrected and does not sit idly by, doing nothing; who, if he is powerless to correct it, endures it patiently, and mourns its presence (*Tract. 11 in Joan.,* § 9, *PL* 35:1471).

741. ST. LAURENCE JUSTINIAN. A. By means of these exercises [the four ways of loving God], the soul takes flight to the fourth degree of love in which the sweetness that has been tasted draws one more powerfully to the pure love of God than does any urgency of human need. This is the perfection of those who love you perfectly, Lord; this is the joy you give, not to the wicked, but to those who love and adore you with all their heart. This is already the beginning of the blessed life: to rejoice about you in you (*Lignum vitae, tract. 6., de charitate,* c. 10, *Op. Om.* 1:37). B. We should be ashamed to allow those who love this world to excel us: for in order to attain their goals, they make themselves subservient to their superiors, eagerly expose their bodies to dangers and their souls to loss. They will rise with us at the Judgment and deservedly accuse us who serve as soldiers of Christ only according to external appearances, and not truly in spirit (*Lib. de obedientia,* c. 9, *Op. Om.* 2:318).

742. ST. EPHRAEM. When the Lord sees the soul protecting itself from evil influences, and, as far as possible, seeking always and waiting upon him, crying out to him day and night (since he has commanded that we pray always), he will quickly deliver it from its enemies, cleanse it from every stain and blemish, and make it a holy and immaculate bride to himself (*De vera et perfecta renuntiatione, Op. Om.* 1:61).

The monk is blessed in the spirit of religion

743. ST. JOHN CHRYSOSTOM. The monastery is a serene harbor. The monks are like lights shining from a lofty place to mariners afar off. They are stationed at the port, drawing all men to their own calm, and preserving from shipwreck those who gaze on them. . . . To go to the monastery of a holy man [the monasteries were in that day formed by those who gathered about a holy man] is to pass, as it were, from earth to heaven. There you do not see what you see in a private home. That group is free of all impurity. There is silence and profound quiet. The words "mine" and "thine" are not in use among them. . . . There, as soon as it is day, or rather before it is day, the cock crows, and you do not see what you see in a private home—the servants snoring, the doors shut, all sleeping like the dead, whilst the muleteer without is ringing his bells. There is nothing of all this. Immediately shaking off sleep, all rise reverently when their superior calls them, and forming themselves into a holy choir, they stand, lifting up their hands all at once, and sing sacred hymns . . . with much harmony and well-composed rhythm. Neither harp nor pipe nor any other musical instrument utters such sweet melodies as you hear from the singing of those saints in their deep and quiet solitude. And the songs, too, are appropriate, and full of the love of God. *During the hours of the night,* they say, *lift up your hands toward the sanctuary, and bless the Lord* (Ps. 133:2). *My soul hath desired thee in the night; yea, and with my spirit within me in the morning early I will watch to thee* (Isa. 26:9). And the Psalms of David, that cause fountains of tears to flow, they sing with the angels. . . .

And when day is coming on, they take rest again; . . . and later, having performed their morning prayers and hymns, they proceed to the reading of the scriptures. There are some too who have learned to write out books, each having his own apartment assigned to him where he lives in perpetual quiet. No one is trifling, no one speaks a word. Then at the third, sixth, and ninth hours, and in the evening, they fulfil their prayer obligations; having divided the day into four parts, and at the conclusion of each they honor God with psalms and hymns . . . All there is full of prayer, of hymns, spiritual in character. There is nothing carnal among them. They fear no attack of robbers, having nothing of which they can be deprived, no wealth; but a body and a soul, of which, if they are robbed, it is not a loss but a gain. For it is said: *To me to live is Christ, and to die is gain* (Phil. 1:21). They have freed themselves of all bonds. Truly, *the joyful shout of victory is in the tents of the just* (Ps. 117:15).

There is no such thing to be heard there as wailing and lamentation. Their roof is free from that melancholy and those cries. Death takes place there indeed, for their bodies are not immortal, but they do not know death as death. The departed are accompanied to the grave with hymns. This they call a procession, not a burial; and when it is reported that anyone has died, great is their cheerfulness, deep their pleasure; or rather, not one of them can bear to say that another has died, but that he has been perfected. Then there is thanksgiving, and great joy, and everyone praying that such too may be his own end; that so his own combat may terminate, and he may rest from his labor and struggles, and may be united with Christ.

And if anyone is sick, instead of tears and lamentations, they have recourse to prayers. . . . There is no wife tearing her hair, nor children bewailing their orphan state before the time, nor slaves entreating the dying man to give them an assurance that they will be committed to good hands. Escaping from all these, the soul looks to but one thing: that at its last breath it may depart in favor with God (*In Ep. I ad Tim., Hom. 14,* §§ 3–5, *PG* 62:575 f.).

744. ST. PETER DAMIAN. The enclosure is in truth a veritable paradise. In it are to be found the green pastures of the scriptures, the shedding of copious tears which heavenly love causes to flow forth from the most pure affections. In it . . . is the sublime Table at which God feeds and is the Food, rewards and is the Reward, offers and is the Offered, is table Companion and Banquet. In it are heaped together the riches of the Omnipotent God; in it is the manifest glory of the angels. Do you think, however, that there is no activity in it, and that the men of one manner who dwell in the house (cf. Ps. 67:7, Douay version) are given to idleness? Take a look at this monk intent on sacred reading, or at that one engaged in prayer, or another bewailing excesses in prayer, or exulting in the praises of God, or keeping watch, or fasting, or being devoted to the works of piety, all vying with one another in zeal. They rise at night to glorify God; evening, morning, and noon they recall and announce his praises; all the earnest zeal of their lives revolves about their dedication to divine praise (*Serm. 59, de S. Nicolao episc. Myrensi et confess., PL* 144:837).

THIRD PRINCIPLE

Poverty and Humility

CONTENTS: Religious poverty — Christ, its Model — The vow of poverty — Nothing of one's own; nothing superfluous — Observance with regard to food — Clothing — The cell — The spirit of poverty — The esteem in which it is to be held — Its fruits — The "hundredfold" — Poverty directs one on the way of peace — Humility, poverty's companion and the measure of holiness — The vice of pride — Humility to be learned from Jesus and the Blessed Virgin — Heaven is open to the poor and the humble.

I. STATEMENT OF PRINCIPLE

Religious poverty

745. A monastic community is a family of God; for that reason God himself is not only the Father of such a family, but also the lord and possessor of its goods. As sons of that family, the monks enjoy indeed the use of its property, but not the rights of ownership. They possess all things in common, a prerogative founded on their faith in common. Poor in the true sense of the word, they bear a likeness to Jesus Christ whose members and children they glory in being. For the Incarnate Son of the Eternal Father has shown himself to be the perfect model of holy poverty.* Born of Mary, the most poor Virgin, in a miserable cave and wrapped in swaddling clothes, he was placed in a crib. In later years, together with his parents in their humble condition, he labored with his hands and earned a meager livelihood in the

* St. Benedict never refers to poverty (or to humility, or chastity, or any other virtue) as "holy," although he reserves his strongest language for those who violate poverty's ideal. For him, one virtue alone in the monastic plan of life, obedience, is to be designated with the adjective "holy." The terminology is constant and eminently significant. Wolter's text is here, and elsewhere, retained as faithfully as it can be translated (cf. Sause, Bernard A., O.S.B., *The School of the Lord's Service*, 3 v.; St. Meinrad: The Grail Press, 1:77 f.). [*Tr.*]

sweat of his brow. During his public life he associated with the poor, lived on alms, and had not whereon to lay his head. Finally, stripped of his garments and laden with shame, he died on the Cross, and found his last rest in the tomb of another. Thus God's adorable Son willed to be utterly poor on earth, in order thereby to make man rich in heaven. He urgently invites you, my dear confrere, *"Come, follow Me!* As a poor man, follow me who am poorest of all; embrace poverty generously—poverty wonderfully adorned by me as a bride is adorned, ennobled, consecrated. It is a royal road of reparation and merit that lies open before you."

The cloister, poverty's sanctuary

746. Obedient to this invitation from God, you entered the enclosure, the sanctuary of evangelical poverty. Like the man who found a treasure hidden in a field, you joyfully sold all that you had and bought this field. Like the merchant who discovered a fine pearl, you sold all and bought it (cf. Matt. 13:45). Holy poverty is in truth a treasure, not recognized for what it is by the children of the world, a pearl trodden under foot. Mindful of the divine saying: *Everyone who does not renounce all that he possesses, cannot be my disciple* (Luke 14:33), you have not sought gold, nor trusted in wealth and treasures of the world. No, you have willed to lay up *treasures in heaven where neither rust nor moth consumes, nor thieves break in and steal* (Matt. 6:20).

The vow of poverty

747. Courage, dear confrere! Realize to what you have bound yourself by the holy vows of conversion of morals and obedience. You have forsworn for all time every kind of ownership and every right of possessing or acquiring anything in this world as your own. The Lord alone is your portion, your own inheritance. Through the eye of a needle, to use our Lord's simile, you have entered the enclosure of the monastery, stripped of all possessions. In truth, as the first Christians placed the price of the goods they had sold at the feet of the apostles (cf. Acts 4:35), you have trodden the goods of this world under foot, in order never again to be able to say of anything: "This is mine." You have abandoned personal possessions, have renounced Mammon, have disdained the possession of money, which is an accursed bait which ensnares souls as fish are caught on a hook. It is a bait which the prince of this world holds out to his followers after the manner of an infernal sacrament, a kind of hellish viaticum.

748. You must cut off by the root that most baneful vice of personal ownership, and detest every form of the so-called *peculium.**

* The *peculium* was a sum of money granted regularly to the religious as a kind of monthly allowance, to be used at the discretion of the individual religious,

For such practices are a sort of rear-door entrance through which the private ownership that we cast aside when we entered the enclosure by the vows, manages to sneak in again; this awful bane of monasteries, this blasphemous sacrilege and public perjury, which sacred councils have so often condemned and anathematized. Could anything be more disloyal and deplorable than for a monk to lie to the Holy Spirit in imitation of Achan, Giezi, Ananias, and Sapphira, and even Judas, and by retaining "private possessions" abandon God and heaven?

749. The profession of poverty, then, forbids you not only to possess anything as your own, but also deprives you of every free disposition of material goods. Nothing whatever belongs entirely to you. Nothing is so entrusted to you that you may convert it to another purpose of your choice, or so that you can give or lend it to another at your discretion. As representative of the Supreme Lord, your spiritual father alone has the authority to free your hands from this bond. On the other hand, it is your duty to employ all that has been assigned to you for your personal use as though it belonged to another and had been placed in your keeping and trust—hence to be used sparingly and circumspectly, so that nothing will be harmed, destroyed, or broken. For we must consider all the goods of the monastery as holy, as though they were sacred vessels dedicated to God's service (*RSB,* c. 31). Besides, whatever exceeds your actual needs should be given up as wanting in purpose and superfluous. *But having food and sufficient clothing, with these let us be content* (I Tim. 6:8). Make yourself a friend of simplicity, living in common-sense frugality, and avoiding all that is excessive.

Bodily nourishment

750. The table that is set, therefore, should, as far as possible, resemble that of poor people. Accept with a grateful bow of the head whatever is placed before you at the common table, as though an alms had been bestowed on you from the hand of the heavenly Father. Let the food and drink be plain and simple.

Garb

In like manner, let the poverty of Jesus be your model in clothing and care of the body. You should, indeed, hold the blessed habit you wear in far higher regard than the royal purple; you should never be ashamed of the leather belt of your habit nor of your capuche, for they are the insignia of soldiers in a holy warfare. You should be proud to

---

independently of the control of the superior, which was opposed to the very nature of the common life and of the vow of poverty. It was still openly in operation in Wolter's day in a few isolated instances, largely as the continued observance of customs of long standing. These abuses have long since been corrected through Apostolic visitations. [*Tr.*]

wear them and never put them off without reason. You are the friend of God, a member of his family, dwelling in the intimacy of his house, a spouse of Christ.

The cell

751. For this reason you can readily understand that poverty should be the monastic cell's most beautiful ornament. Let this small room be simple and sparingly furnished, so that the Bridegroom of the soul, who lived in utter poverty, may find pleasure and peace in it. A bed, a table, one or two chairs, a small wardrobe, a few books and pictures of a religious character, a holy water font, and a crucifix: that is all in your cell that reflects honor on you in life or that will give you consolation in death. These, then, dear confrere, constitute the legal aspects of the poverty that you have taken upon yourself.

But far more has been entrusted to you. By offering yourself at the altar, you have, through the vow of poverty, drawn a double-edged sword whose blade has struck not only your legal ability to possess, but also the very will and desire to own anything. For you have sacrificed private ownership and all will to possess. In so doing you have made poverty something sacred, and bestowed upon it the nature of a virtue. The heavenly Father wants not only hands that are empty but a heart that is free of detachments. He wills to embrace sons, not hirelings. With the surrender of all your desires you have destroyed the last vestiges of ownership and have given yourself wholly to God. For it is interior resignation which makes the external observances of poverty spirtual and animated, and which gradually leads you to the height of interior and perfect resignation.

752. In order to attain such a goal you must cut yourself free from all the subtle demands of avarice and possessiveness. Banish from your heart for all time every immoderate attachment, no matter how insignificant the objects may be—a garment, a particular cell in the monastery, a book, anything at all. Should you experience this sort of possessiveness, root it out immediately. If the superior, in keeping with monastic custom, visits your cell for the purpose of inspecting it, be on your guard against deceiving or misleading him, or keeping anything concealed from him. A person realizes how deeply a tooth lies imbedded only when it is extracted. Do not spare yourself, but strive manfully to attain to that blessed freedom and calmness of soul which neither offers objections when deprived of anything, nor fosters a desire for what it does not possess. Be like a statue which has no concern for the manner in which it is adorned.

"Mine" and "thine"

753. In order that you may hasten heavenward unimpeded, you must have the courage to attach no importance to things of earth. It is a venerable custom, approved by the Rule, that monks banish from their vocabulary the cold "mine" and "thine" terminology, and all similar designations of ownership. It is far more important, however, to eliminate from their thought as well, every trace that reflects private ownership. For the person to whom poverty is a constructive element in striving for holiness does not defraud God, to whom he is bound by vows. He considers himself truly a beggar and fortunate to be bound so intimately to holy poverty. He rejoices with the Apostle: *For his* [Christ's] *sake I have suffered the loss of all things, and I count them as dung that I may gain Christ* (Phil. 3:8). He dies so that he may become *the fragrance of Christ* (II Cor. 2:15). He accomplishes so perfect a re-evaluation of all earthly standards that riches are nothing to him, poverty everything.

The esteem of poverty

754. Make it a point to hold poverty in the highest regard and honor. Think of it always with deep reverence. From such respect there grows a profound and energetic love of the virtue, powerfully motivated by the incomparable example of the Savior who, *being rich, became poor for our sakes* (II Cor. 8:9), and endured the most bitter privations for us. Love poverty as a son loves his mother; you should not only accept it with a cheerful and calm attitude and embrace it wherever you actually encounter it; but you should purposefully search for it and desire to live only in union with it. Then you will be content in the depths of your being with the poorest and the most extreme [*RSB*, c. 7, sixth degree]. More than that, you must strive to go so far as to make an effort to prefer what is contemptible in the sight of others, and delight in whatever reproduces more clearly in you the image of your poor Bridegroom. If such is your love of poverty, you will certainly also welcome its consequences in spiritual joy: you will patiently and cheerfully endure all the discomforts and trials associated with it.

755. The soldier who fears to draw the sword and runs away from battle is charged with cowardice. In the same way he bears the name of monk undeservedly who vows poverty but refuses to be poor. A real monk considers it a matter of pride to keep the promises of his profession: when circumstances demand that he restrict himself in the use of something, or forego it completely, he blesses the Lord and does not murmur. And if, perchance, under God's dispensation, he must endure utter want, hardship, or contempt, he will direct his gaze toward heaven and say with unshakable confidence: *Blessed be the name of the Lord*

(Job 1:21). He attains the highest degree of this magnanimous and generous spirit who, in sickness, does not complain of the diet he is served nor the care he is given, nor in any manner grows alarmed or ill-humored about his illness, but rather leaves all in God's providence. Such, then, dear confrere, is the pattern of holy poverty in accord with the example of him who lived its spirit in the inimitable perfection of his own life for our sakes, and who divinely instills it into all who love it.

Advantages and fruits of poverty

756. Human language is incapable of expressing the excellence of this virtue and enumerating its blessed fruits. It is the first step of the man who would strive to become perfect, that is, the beginning of the monastic life (cf. Matt. 19:24). For it lays the first trap for the enemy by withdrawing that which fosters sin, namely concupiscence of the eyes; it is the first nail to fasten our sinful nature to the cross. For these reasons poverty is not undeservedly called the entrance to the cloister: where it is well observed, discipline thrives. It is the impenetrable wall of the religious life which separates monks from the world and assures a dependable protection against the enemy. It is, too, the foundation and stronghold of the monastic order. So long as poverty has been well observed, a person is justified in every hope. On the other hand certain downfall and destruction threaten a monastery in which poverty is not held in honor and rigorously practiced.

757. This virtue *lifts thee up above the high places of the earth* (Isa. 58:14); in fact, one can say that it raises you right up to heaven itself. When you actually practice it, you are attached to God alone, you despise the passing splendor of the world; having nothing you possess all things; in a certain sense you become lord and ruler of all things. With the Psalmist you rejoice: *The Lord is my shepherd: I shall not want* (Ps. 22:1). You can make your own the words: *On you* [O God] *the unfortunate* [poor] *man depends* (Ps. 9:35). You can say all this with the fullest right, for in a special manner the eternal Father takes under his protection any son of holy poverty who renounces all things for love of God. *The Lord is a stronghold for the oppressed* [poor] (Ps. 9A:10). Because you have left all, you will receive the hundredfold in return (cf. Matt. 19:29).

758. Do not be surprised at all this, for the omnipotent Lord who governs all things with his supreme will has taken you into his protection as his son, and in his goodness directs your destiny. He nourishes you, ministers to you, sustains you, and with a Father's love takes care of all your needs. He is the administrator of your goods; your staff and support; your storehouse and treasury. The experience of the centuries has proved that the poor in spirit have always been the specially loved

sons of divine Providence. When the apostles were asked: *When I sent you forth without purse or wallet or sandals, did you lack anything?* they had to say: *Nothing* (Luke 22:35 f.). They therefore are twice blessed, because they *seek first the kingdom of God and his justice, and all these things shall be given* [them] *besides* (Matt. 6:33). The Lord will not deprive his sons of their livelihood, his soldiers of their pay, nor his faithful laborers of their wages. Holy poverty procures for us the surest fruits and is, moreover, a source from which benefits flow to rich and poor alike. By the power of its example it holds back the rich from enslavement by earthly goods; it inspires the poor with courage in enduring their lot and consoles them in their need; it unites poor and rich in mutual charity and benevolence. It destroys hatred in minds that riches and poverty would separate, and unites hearts in love. From such reflections it is clear what significance [monastic] love of poverty can have for a peaceful adjustment of social conflicts.

Poverty directs our steps in the way of holiness

759. We must also examine the spiritual benefits of holy poverty. To him who is attached to it, it makes known the way of righteousness and holiness. It destroys numerous vices in the germ stage, and furnishes the best soil in which virtues may grow. For this reason masters of the ascetical life refer to it as the seed corn and source; mother and nurse; guardian and companion of the virtues. It awakens a delight in virtuous practices and intensifies zeal for them. It purifies the heart and unites it more closely to God. It fosters concord and lifts up the children of God to the holy freedom of the spirit of detachment.

He who practices poverty sets out on his journey unencumbered; he enters the combat without hindrance. The road he is traveling to the everlasting fatherland is thus cleared of obstacles. Rich in heaven's gifts he can enjoy in that peace of soul and lightness of heart, which *surpasses all understanding* (Phil. 4:7), an abundance of merit, and can hasten along the safe road to heaven. For Christ is his glorious inheritance. And the Lord's statement remains ever true: *Blessed are the poor in spirit, for theirs is the kingdom of heaven* (Matt. 5:3).

760. Recognize therefore in holy poverty your true wealth, an inestimable good, and excessively rich prize, for it is the price of heaven. *I am your shield; your reward shall be very great* (Gen. 15:1). Because you have abandoned all things, you shall sit upon a throne of glory; you shall receive a hundredfold here and eternal life. In all truth: *In your goodness, O God, you have provided* [the necessary rain] *for the needy* (Ps. 67:11).

Humility

761. The rose of heaven's reward must grow among the thorns of poverty; it can bear its flowers only in the fertile soil of humility. For this reason the holy Patriarch, Benedict, laid down such admirable precepts and regulations regarding humility. Poverty is the renunciation of personal ownership, but humility is, in a sense, the renunciation of oneself. And that denial constitutes the precise goal of the monastic life: that humility take deep and firm root in the heart, never again to depart from it. Or, to word the thought in the terminology of St. Paul: *Lest any flesh should pride itself before* [the Lord] (I Cor. 1:29). Our goal is, rather: *That in all things God may be honored* (I Pet. 4:11; *RSB*, c. 57).

762. Humility is the golden ladder leading to perfection and to God. It is the root, the support, and the basis of all virtues. Without humility, none of our prayers and works have value; it alone is the measure for progress and the standard of genuine holiness. Whoever, therefore, accurately recognizes and readily acknowledges his lowliness and abjection in a wholly unassuming manner before God, himself, and his fellow men; whoever despises only himself, takes no credit to himself, nor boasts of his deeds, but rather always considers himself beneath others, is truly humble. Such a man will advance in grace before God and man (cf. Luke 2:52).

He, on the other hand, who, in want of knowledge of himself, holds himself alone in esteem, who looks down on others and despises them as inferior to himself, and boasts with the Pharisee: *I am not like the rest of men* (Luke 18:11), who is ambitious and eager for acclaim, boastful and haughty, self-admiring and sensitive, harsh and unpleasant, is a proud man, *odious to the Lord and to men* (Sir. 10:7).

763. Hold this diabolical vice in abomination! Cast out of your heart every manifestation of pride that remains in you, and subject yourself under the yoke of thoroughgoing self-contempt. Learn of your Bridegroom, who is humble of heart; imitate the example of the Blessed Mother of God, whose admirable humility God was pleased to behold. Pray with St. Augustine: "Lord Jesus, that I may know myself, that I may know thee!" Then the blessed disposition of Christlike simplicity, which restores the candor of little children, will grow in you. Then you will be established in the spirit of peace and will taste the delights of the life *hidden with Christ in God* (Col. 3:3). *He who walks honestly walks securely* (Prov. 10:9). Poverty-humility is the passport we must present in order for the gates of heaven to be opened to us. *Happy is the people whose God is the Lord* (Ps. 143:15). *For lowly people you save but haughty eyes you bring low* (Ps. 17:28).

II. EVIDENCE FROM THE RULE OF ST. BENEDICT

Poverty

764. This vice especially ought to be utterly rooted out of the monastery. Let no one presume to give or receive anything without the abbot's permission, or to have anything as his own, anything whatever . . . for monks should not have even their bodies and wills at their own disposal. But let them look to the father of the monastery for all that they require, and let it be unlawful to have anything which the abbot has not given or allowed. And as the scripture says: *Not one of them said that anything he possessed was his own, but they had all things in common* (Acts 4:32). . . . But if anyone shall be found to indulge in this most wicked vice, let him be admonished; . . . if he does not amend, let him undergo punishment (*RSB,* c. 33). Let them always remember Ananias and Sapphira (cf. Acts 5:1 f.), and take care lest they . . . should suffer in their souls the death which they endured in their bodies. . . . Let not the sin of avarice creep in (*ibid.,* c. 57).

Material goods of the monastery

765. If anyone treat the property of the monastery in a slovenly or careless manner, he is to be corrected (*RSB,* c. 32). Let [the cellarer] look upon the utensils of the monastery and all its property as upon the sacred vessels of the altar. Let him not think that anything may be neglected (*ibid.,* c. 31). Let the outgoing server restore the vessels of his office to the cellarer clean and sound (*ibid.,* c. 35). On no account shall a monk be allowed to receive letters, devout tokens or any small gifts whatever, from his parents or other people, or his brethren; or to give the same, without the abbot's permission. But if he have been sent anything even by his parents, let him not presume to take it before it has been shown to the abbot. If the abbot allow it to be received, it shall be his to decide to whom it is to be given; and let not the brother to whom it was sent, be vexed thereat, lest occasion be given to the devil (*ibid.,* c. 54). If any brother be found to have anything that he has not received from the abbot, let him undergo the strictest punishment (*ibid.,* c. 55).

Food

766. We believe it to be sufficient for the daily meal . . . that every table should have two cooked dishes, on account of individual infirmities, so that he who perchance cannot eat of the one, may make his meal of the other. . . . And if any fruit or fresh vegetables are available, let a third be added. Let a good pound weight of bread suffice

for the day. . . . The abbot shall have the choice and power, should it be expedient, to increase this allowance. Above all things, however, gluttony must be avoided, so that a monk may never be surprised by a surfeit (*RSB*, c. 39).

Drink

767. Keeping in view the needs of weaker brethren, we believe that a hemina of wine a day is sufficient for each. But those upon whom God has bestowed the gift of abstinence should know that they shall have a special reward. . . . We do, indeed, read that wine is no drink for monks; but since nowadays monks cannot be persuaded of this, let us at least agree upon this, to drink temperately and not to satiety; for wine maketh even the wise to fall away (cf. Sir. 19:2; Eccles. *ibid.*, Douay version). But when the circumstances of the place are such that the aforesaid measure cannot be had, but much less or even none at all, let the monks who dwell there bless God and not murmur (*RSB*, c. 40).

Clothing

768. Let clothing be given to the brethren according to the nature of the locality in which they dwell and its climate. . . . We believe that in ordinary places the following dress is sufficient for each monk: a tunic, a cowl (thick and woolly in winter, but thin and worn in summer), a belt for work, and shoes and stockings for the feet. The monks must not complain of the color or the coarseness of any of these things, but be content with what is to be found in the district where they live and can be purchased more cheaply. Let the abbot see to the size of the garments, that they be not too short for their wearers, but of the proper fit. When the brethren receive new clothes, they are always to return the old ones at once, that they may be stored in the clothesroom for the poor. For it is sufficient if a monk have two tunics and two cowls, to allow for a change at night and for washing of these garments; more than that is superfluity and should be curtailed. . . . Those who are sent on a journey shall receive trousers from the clothesroom . . . and their cowls and tunics [shall be] somewhat better than the ones they usually wear (*RSB*, c. 55).

The cell

769. Let [the monks] sleep each one in a separate bed. Their beds shall be assigned to them in accordance with the date of their entrance into the monastery (*conversationis*), subject to the abbot's disposition (*RSB*, c. 22). For bedding, let this suffice: a mattress, a blanket, a coverlet and a pillow. The beds should be examined frequently by the abbot, lest any private property be concealed in them. . . . And in order that this evil of private ownership be rooted out utterly, let the abbot pro-

vide all things that are necessary . . . so that all pretext of need may be taken away. Yet the abbot is always to consider those words of the Acts of the Apostles: *Distribution was made to each according as anyone had need* (Acts 4:35). So too let the abbot consider the weaknesses of the needy (*ibid.,* c. 55).

The spirit of poverty

770. *Seek first the kingdom of God and his justice, and all these things shall be given you besides* (Matt. 6:33). Again: *Nought is lacking to those who fear him* (Ps. 33:10; *RSB,* c. 2). [Let the monk be content] with the meanest and worst of everything (*ibid.,* c. 7, sixth degree). A pilgrim monk shall be received for as long a time as he wishes, provided that he is content with the customs of the place as they are, and does not disturb the monastery by excessive wants, but is simply content with what he finds (*ibid.,* c. 61). Let him who has need of less thank God and not be discontented; he who has need of more shall consider his infirmity a humiliation and shall not be made proud by the mercy shown to him: so will all the members be at peace (*ibid.,* c. 34). Let the one who has come to the monastery to work at his conversion, if he possess any property, either give it beforehand to the poor, or make a formal donation bestowing it on the monastery. Let him keep back nothing at all for himself, knowing that thenceforward he will not have the disposition even of his own body (*ibid.,* c. 58).

771. *Life of St. Benedict:* The man of God, who had resolved to give all things in this world in order that he might keep all in heaven, gave orders that the little oil that remained should be given to the one who asked for it (*S. Greg. Magni Dialogorum Lib. II,* c. 28, *PL* 66:186). The monk who was sent, having delivered his sermon, was offered a present of some handkerchiefs by the nuns. These he accepted and concealed in his breast. No sooner had he returned to the monastery than the man of God began to rebuke him sternly, saying: "How has evil entered your breast?". . . The monk fell prostrate at his feet, and repenting his foolish act, cast from him the handkerchiefs which he had concealed in his breast (*ibid.,* c. 19, col. 179).

Humility

772. Holy Scripture cries out to us, brethren, saying: *Everyone who exalts himself shall be humbled, and he who humbles himself shall be exalted* (Luke 14:11). When it so speaks, it teaches us that all exaltation is a kind of pride; which, by these words the Prophet shows that he shunned: *O Lord, my heart is not proud, nor are my eyes haughty; I busy myself not with great things, nor with things too sublime for me. Nay, rather, I have stilled and quieted my soul like a weaned child, like a weaned child on its mother's lap, so is my soul*

within me (Ps. 130:1–2). Wherefore, brethren, if we wish to attain to the summit of humility and desire to arrive speedily at that heavenly exaltation to which we ascend by the humility of the present life, then must we set up a ladder of our ascending actions like unto that which Jacob saw in his vision, whereon angels appeared to him, descending and ascending. By that descent and ascent we must surely understand nothing else than this, that we descend by self-exaltation and ascend by humility. And the ladder erected is our life in this world, which for the humble of heart is raised up by the Lord unto heaven. . . .

773. The first degree of humility then, is that [the monk] keep the fear of God before his eyes at all times, altogether shunning forgetfulness. . . . The second . . . that he love not his own will, nor delight in fulfilling his own desires. . . . The third . . . that for the love of God he subject himself to his superior in all obedience. . . . The fourth . . . that, meeting in this obedience with difficulties and contradictions and even injustice, he should with a quiet mind hold fast to patience; and enduring, neither tire nor run away. . . . The fifth . . . that he humbly confess and conceal not from his abbot any evil thoughts that enter his heart, and any secret sins that he has committed. . . . The sixth, that a monk be content with the meanest and worst of everything, and esteem himself, in regard to the work that is given to him, as a bad and unworthy workman. . . . The seventh . . . that he should not only in his speech declare himself lower and of less account than all others, but should in his own innermost heart believe it, humbling himself and saying with the Prophet: *But I am a worm, not a man; the scorn of men, despised by the people* (Ps. 21:7); *I am afflicted and in agony from my youth* (Ps. 87:16); and again: *It is good for me that I have been afflicted, that I may learn your statutes* (Ps. 118:71). The eighth . . . is that a monk do nothing except what is commended by the common rule of the monastery and the example of his superiors. The ninth . . . that a monk restrain his tongue and keep silence. . . . The tenth . . . that he be not ready and prompt to laughter. . . . The eleventh . . . that a monk, when he speaks, do so gently and without laughter, humbly and seriously, in few and sensible words. . . . The twelfth, is that a monk should not only be humble of heart, but should also manifest his humility to those who look upon him . . . his head bowed and his eyes downcast, pondering always the guilt of his sins; and considering that he is about to be brought before the dread judgment seat of God . . . always saying what was said by the publican in the Gospel: "Lord, I a sinner am not worthy to raise mine eyes to heaven" (cf. Luke 18:13); and again, with the Prophet: *I am very much afflicted* (Ps. 118:107). Then, when all these degrees of humility have been climbed, the monk will presently come to that perfect love of God which casts out all fear *(RSB,* c. 7).

774. Instruments of good works are: To honor all men . . . not to be proud. . . . To attribute to God, and not to self, whatever good one sees in oneself. But to recognize always that the evil is one's own doing, and to impute it to oneself. . . . Not to wish to be called holy before one is holy; but first to be holy, that one may more truly be called so. . . . To shun vainglory (*RSB,* c. 4, nn. 8, 34, 42, 43, 61, 67). We ought to supplicate the Lord God of all things with all humility and pure devotion (*ibid.,* c. 20). Let the incoming reader, after Mass and Communion, ask all to pray for him that God may preserve him from the spirit of pride (*ibid.,* c. 38). Let [the craftsmen] practice their crafts with all humility . . . but if one of them be puffed up because of his skill in his craft . . . let him be removed from his work and not return to it unless he have humbled himself and the abbot entrust it to him again (*ibid.,* c. 57).

775. They will dwell in the tabernacle of the Lord who . . . fearing the Lord, are not puffed up on account of their good works, but judging that they can do no good of themselves, and that all comes from God, they magnify the Lord's work in them, using the word of the Prophet: *Not to us, O Lord, not to us, but to your name give glory* (Ps. 113B:1). So the Apostle Paul imputed nothing of his preaching to himself, but said: *By the grace of God I am what I am* (I Cor. 15:10). And again he says: *He who boasts, let him boast in the Lord* (II Cor. 10:17; *RSB, Prolog.*). Let the brethren give their advice with all deference and humility (*ibid.,* c. 3). Above all things the cellarer must have humility (*ibid.,* c. 31). . . . rather let [the priest] give to all an example of humility (*ibid.,* c. 60). But let the one who is ordained priest beware of elation or pride (*ibid.,* c. 62). In the greeting of all guests, whether they be arriving or departing, let the greatest humility be shown (*ibid.,* c. 53). Let him undergo greater punishment, because he would not repair by humility the fault that he committed through carelessness (*ibid.,* c. 45).

776. *Life of St. Benedict:* It is helpful in this connection to recall the friendly contest of humility which arose between Maurus and the holy Father Benedict, when the latter ascribed the miracle [Maurus had walked upon the water to save Placidus], not to any merit of his own, but to his disciple's obedience, and Maurus contended that it was the direct result of Benedict's order (*S. Greg. Magni Dialogorum Lib. II,* c. 7, *PL* 66:146). One evening as the venerable Father sat at supper, a monk who was the son of a distinguished family was holding a light for him by the table. While the man of God ate his meal, and the other stood there holding the lamp, the spirit of pride entered into the monk, and he began secretly to dwell on and indulge such thoughts as these: "Who is this man on whom I am waiting as he eats, serving him and holding a light for him? Who am I to be performing this kind of task?" Immediately the man of God turned to him and admonished him se-

verely, saying: "Sign yourself, brother, sign yourself! What is this that you are saying?" And then, summoning the brethren, he bade them take the lamp from his hands, and dismissed him from his waiting. . . . The brethren afterward asked the monk what he had had in his heart, and he told them plainly how he had been puffed up with pride and what words he had spoken against the man of God in the secrecy of his thoughts (*ibid.,* c. 20, col. 179).

Both (*RSB,* c. 7, on humility) the longest chapter of the Rule, and St. Benedict's entire life, and his whole law give ample evidence of the high esteem in which he held the virtue of humility. Out of the deepest spirit of the virtue he calls his admirable legislation, which far excels the institutions and rules of others, "This little Rule for beginners"! (*RSB,* c. 73.) But [these other rules] are all, for us slothful, ill-living, and negligent monks, reasons to blush for shame (*ibid.*).

III. DECREES AND DOCUMENTS OF THE CHURCH

Religious poverty

777. POPE BENEDICT III (d. 858). Who does not know that the poor of Christ, spurning the wealth of this world and following the footsteps of our Savior who, although he was rich, became poor for our sakes, consider the title of holy perfection to be their riches? (Ep. 1, *confirmatio privilegiorum Corbeiae, PL* 129:1004.)

778. PROV. COUNCIL OF VIENNA (1858). Eternal Wisdom replied to the young man who asked what was yet wanting to him: *If thou wilt be perfect, go, sell what thou hast, and give to the poor, and thou shalt have treasure in heaven; and come, follow me* (Matt. 19:21). And when the Holy Spirit had descended upon the apostles, and *with great power* [they] *gave testimony of the Resurrection of Jesus Christ our Lord . . . those who owned lands or houses would sell them and bring the price of what they sold . . . and distribution was made to each, according as anyone had need* (Acts 4:33 f.; cf. *ibid.,* 2:45). Imbued with this doctrine and trained by such an example, saints, men whose lives were pleasing to God, established the religious life, erected on the foundation of the three vows. Through their profession and the ideal of the regular discipline, their followers not only deny themselves pleasures and goods of this world, but even forego the hope and desire of possessing such things, in order that they may look forward with greater confidence to joys that are eternal. They renounce their own judgment and opinion, rendering perfect obedience to superiors in all that is not opposed to the divine law, in order to enjoy greater confidence in dwelling

under the leadership of the Lord (*Decr.*, tit. 4, c. 13, *de vita religiosa. CL* 5:188).

Foundation of the religious life

779. POPE CLEMENT XIV (d. 1774). You are daily to gain the victory, beloved brethren, in smaller matters, in order that you may not be easily overcome in those which are greater; and also in order that the common life which is, as it were, the head and foundation of religious holiness, may not be gradually done away with (Constit. Apost., *In vinea Domini,* § 6, 4 Jul., 1772, *confirmatio decretorum pro Cappuccinis prov. Subalpinae, BRC* 5:458).

780. MEETING OF BISHOPS OF AUSTRIA (Vienna, 1856). Perfection in the regular life is impossible without accurate observance of the vow of poverty. With regard to this most serious subject, perfection must be striven for (*V. Litt. ad Em. et Rev. mos Cardinales Schwartzenberg et Scitovsky, CL* 5:1257).

781. POPE INNOCENT III (d. 1216). Let no abbot think that he can dispense a monk with regard to holding property; for renunciation of private ownership, as is true also of the observance of chastity, is so identified with the monastic rule, that not even the Supreme Pontiff can grant any permission contrary to them (c. 6, *de stat. monachorum, III,* 35 [*abbati et conventui Sublacensibus*], *CJC* Richter 2:577).

782. POPE BENEDICT XII (d. 1342). Renunciation of private property is identified with the monastic rule (Const. Apost., *Fulgens sicut stella,* § 39, 12 Jul., 1335, *reformatio O. Cist., BR* 4:340).

783. PROV. COUNCIL OF PRAGUE (1860). Because perfection in the regular life consists before all else in observance of the vows, such observance must be most dear to individual religious and to superiors. Whereas chastity shows forth the beauty and splendor of the race that seeks for God (cf. Ps. 23:6), and obedience constitutes the greatest good and distinctive perfection of the regular life, by which not only material possessions and the body are brought under subjection, but the mind and heart as well (*c. 1, in Extravag. Joan.,* XXII, 14, *CJC* Richter 2:1137), poverty is particularly effective in removing the obstacles and dangers by which the mind is withdrawn from the holy vocation to useless and harmful desires of this world. Hence the Fathers assembled in the Synod beg from their heart and exhort regulars to foster and cultivate a great love for this precious virtue of religious self-denial. They urge this particularly with regard to poverty, appealing to the religious to employ all means for promoting perfection of the common life. Poverty is a most gratifying consolation to those who practice it, and is so easily observed in such a way that all material things are common to all; from such observance there will also be for all one heart and one

spirit (Decr., tit. 7, c. 3, *de obligationibus regularium, CL* 5:575).

784. CONGR. OF BURSFELD (1431). Poverty, which had a most zealous guardian in the holy Father Benedict, is the very foundation of the religious life (*Stat.*, dist. 5, c. 1, § 4, *de paupertate,* p. 120).

Prohibition of peculium and ownership

785. III LATERAN COUNCIL (1179). Monks are not to be received into the monastery for a sum of money, nor are they permitted to receive the peculium. . . . Should anyone have private property, except in the case in which it is permitted by the abbot for the administrative duties enjoined on an official, he is to be barred from Communion at the altar. And if in his final illness one is found to possess property and has not properly repented, no offering [of the Mass?] is to be made for him, nor is he to be buried among the brethren. We command that this be observed for all religious. Let an abbot who has not zealously taken proper steps in this matter know that he is to incur the loss of office (c. 10, Mansi 22:224).

786. SYNOD OF MONTPELIER (1214). We severely forbid that a certain sum of money be appointed for any monk or canon, or that he keep in his possession money allotted for clothing, because from such practices the occasion is given for retaining private property (c. 18, *ibid.,* p. 944).

787. POPE INNOCENT III (d. 1216). In virtue of holy obedience, and under the abjuration of the divine judgment, We severely forbid any monk to possess property in any manner. If a monk has any property, he is to abandon it immediately and entirely. If after this he is still found to hold property in possession, after the regular warning has been administered, he is to be expelled from the monastery; nor is he to be received back into the community without having done penance according to the monastic discipline. But if such property is discovered in anyone's possession at the time of his death, as a sign of perdition it will be buried with him in the dung beyond the confines of the monastery. . . . Therefore, if a gift is specially designated for an individual, let him not presume to accept it, but let it be handed over to the abbot or to the prior, or the cellarer (c. 6, *De stat. monachorum,* III, 35, *CJC* Richter 2:576. Similar provisions were made by Pope Nicholas IV and other Supreme Pontiffs).

788. COUNCIL OF BASLE (1431). Because this most baneful vice of personal ownership among religious carries with it both the temptation to indulge in and the means of gratifying other vices, do not let this accursed root grow and become strong, but as is prescribed in the Rule of St. Benedict, chapter 33, "It ought to be utterly rooted out of the monastery." We severely command that no religious is to possess any property or money as his own, nor secretly retain such in any manner. Ex-

ception is made in the case of officials for whom it is lawful because of the duties enjoined on them. Under no pretext may a monk acquire or appropriate anything, or, on his own authority accept gifts from friends, relatives, or others, but he is to turn over all individual donations in their entirety to be distributed at the discretion of the abbot. Thus the monk is to have nothing at all except what the abbot has given him, or justly and reasonably allowed him to retain. . . . In order to exclude occasions of this baneful vice from monasteries, with the same authority we seriously enjoin on abbots and other officials who have the administration of material goods—and we command this in virtue of holy obedience—that distribution of food and clothing be made in adequate provision for all the brethren according to the prescriptions of the Rule. Such provision is particularly to be taken care of before winter, by October 1 at the latest; and at other times of the year according to the abbot's arrangements. . . . Let frequent search of the beds be made by the abbot or the prior, in order to prevent the possession of private property. Should anything be found which the abbot has not distributed or permitted, but which a person has presumed to acquire for himself, he is to be punished severely (*Stat. et ordinationes ad monachos congr. Mellicensis directae, ex manuscr. Salisburgensi*).

789. POPE GREGORY IX (d. 1241). A. We prescribe that no monk or other person, of either sex, converted to the religious life, is to presume to hold property either personally or through agents, whether under the title of gifts, trusts, or other form of possession, with the exception of what the abbot has commanded or permitted one to have. . . . Nor is anyone to dare to send or receive even letters without the abbot's approval. . . . As a sign of his condemnation, anyone found at death to have held property is to be buried beneath a dung hill (Const. Apost., *Cum pro reformatione,* 1 Jul., 1228, c. 9, *approbatio Stat. abbatum O.S.B. in prov. Narbonen.* [Toulouse], *BR* 3:436). B. Everyone, simple monks as well as officials of the monastery, must avoid bestowing gifts without their abbot's permission (*ibid.,* c. 11). C. We prescribe that the monks' habits are to be closed [that is, not buttoned down the front to the hem of the cassock, but seamless], cut neither too skimpily nor too loosely, to be of not too fine a material, and that when the monks receive new garments they always turn their old ones in to the wardrobe for distribution to the poor. . . . We consider it forbidden to give money [that is, in the form of the *peculium*] to monks for food and clothing. If there is question of an inheritance or property left as a legacy of piety, either to the community or to an individual, the entire sum must be assigned for the common use, lest the occasion of retaining property be given to anyone (*ibid.,* c. 16).

Punishments

790. COUNCIL OF LONDON, celebrated under Bl. Lanfranc, bp. of Canterbury (1075). If at the time of his death anyone is discovered to have held private property without the permission that has been indicated previously, . . . the bells are not to be tolled for him, nor is the salutary Host to be offered for his absolution, nor is he to be buried in the cemetery (Mabillon, *Acta SS. O.S.B.*, saec. VI, Pars II, *Vita B. Lanfranci*, c. 12, n. 30, 9:652; *PL* 150:52).

791. COUNCIL OF LONDON (1268). Lest the vice of private ownership offer the occasion of satan increasing sinfulness through the ease of violating the vows of one's profession, we prescribe that when a monk needs clothing, shoes, or other necessities, the one who has the duty of providing such articles never give the monk money to buy them, but furnish rather the articles themselves (c. 42, Mansi 23:1252).

792. SYNOD OF COLOGNE (1280). Under penalty of excommunication to be incurred automatically, we command strict observance by all monks and nuns of the law of having no private property nor any money except in the case of him to whom it is permitted by reason of his office (c. 3, *de stat. claustralium et religiosorum,* Mansi 24:347).

793. POPE BENEDICT XII (d. 1342). Adequate provision has already been made in canonical sanctions against property-holding monks. Nevertheless, wishing to legislate more specifically against those monks and converse brothers who, heedless of their own salvation and acting in defiance of regular and canonical regulations, acquire money, titles, possessions, income, or annual payments, and who buy property or have it bought for them; sometimes in their own name, often under an assumed name, employing many subterfuges, . . . seeking to acquire filthy lucre, conceal and unlawfully retain personal property to the danger of their souls; We decree with Apostolic authority that all the property mentioned in the foregoing which is not subject to restitution to be made to others . . . is to be turned over to their monasteries and houses, and converted in its entirety to their account, all customs, or rather all abuses, to the contrary notwithstanding.

It is Our desire also that it be understood that superiors cannot grant any monk or converse brother permission to retain property; and that prelates, monks, and lay brothers committing any of the offenses enumerated, and other persons retaining or appropriating such property . . . or not making known the *peculium* that has been referred to, are automatically incapable of receiving any benefice, office, government, or administrative position in any order or religious institute. . . . We establish and ordain that according to the means available, food, clothing, and whatever else is needed by the monks, be furnished in sufficient quantity, but with the provision very carefully observed that money never be given for such necessities, either all at one time or repeatedly in smaller amounts, or that any pension or income be assigned (Const. Apost., *Summi magistri,* §§ 16–17, 20 Jun., 1336, *ordinationes et reformationes pro bono regimine monachorum Nigrorum O.S.B., BR* 4:373).

794. COUNCIL OF TRENT. To no regular, therefore, whether man or woman, shall it be lawful to possess or to hold as his own or even in the name of the convent any movable or immovable property, of whatever nature it may be or in whatever manner acquired; but the same shall be handed over immediately to the superior and be incorporated in the convent. Neither shall it in the future be lawful for superiors to grant immovable property to any regular, not even the usufruct or use, or the administration thereof, or as *commendam.* But the administration of the property of monasteries and convents shall belong to the officials thereof only, who are removable at the will of their superiors. Superiors shall so permit the use of movable goods that the furniture is consistent with the state of poverty which they have professed; there shall be nothing superfluous, neither shall anything that is necessary be denied them. But should anyone be discovered or convicted of possessing something in any other manner, he shall be deprived for two years of his active and passive voice and shall also be punished in accordance with the prescriptions of his rule and order (Sess. XXV, c. 2, *Proprietas regularibus omnino prohibetur, Can. et decr.,* Richter, p. 394; Schroeder, *Trent,* p. 218).

All things in common

795. COUNCIL OF MALINES (1570). No one is permitted to receive any form of regular income. Nor are monks permitted, by reason of their offices and duties to collect and save money, even though such sums are to be devoted to pious causes, but everything is to be converted to the community's use (Decr. 21, *de regularibus et monialibus,* c. 1, Mansi 34:604).

796. POPE ST. PIUS V, O.P. (d. 1572). Ownership is the root of all evils. Wherever it is found, it prevents every good in the Rule, however well established the practices may be (Const. Apost., *Ex innumeris curis,* § 19, 8 Mar. 1570, *reformatio totius ordinis Cisterciensis, BR* 7:816).

797. POPE CLEMENT VIII (d. 1605). In order for the decrees of the Council of Trent regarding the observance of the vow of poverty to be put into practice more faithfully, We command that none of the brethren, including superiors, may possess immovable or movable property; money, sources of income, rents, honorarium received for sermons or lectures or for celebrating Masses, whether these are offered in their own church or elsewhere, or any other money acquired for lawful work,

or for other reasons, under whatever title; including charitable offerings from relatives, donations from pious benefactors, legacies, or contributions. They are forbidden to possess all such property as their own or even in the name of the convent. All such money is forthwith to be handed over to the superior and put in the common fund along with other property and sources of income. The common board and clothing are to be supplied for all from these community goods. No one is to retain as proprietor or otherwise use as his own anything granted for his personal needs. . . . As regards possession of property, no dispensation of any superior, nor any form of permission can excuse the brethren from being subject to sin and punishment imposed and automatically incurred by the decrees of the same Council (Const. Apost., *Nullus omnino,* § 2, 22 Aug. 1604, *Decr. generalia pro reformatione regularium, BR* 10:663).

798. POPE CLEMENT XII (d. 1740). It is fitting for the monk to be wholly without private property. He is to appropriate nothing as his own. Nor is he to be attached by desire or actual use to anything that belongs to his parents or relatives. When some need occurs and something is bestowed upon him, he is so to understand, that what is given to him is not because of any right of family relationship, but just as though it had been given to other externs (Const. Apost., *Misericordiarum pater,* Pars I, c. 3, §§ 1–3, 17 Jan. 1740, *Confirmatio reg. et const. monachorum Maronitarum S. Antonii abb. Congreg. S. Isaiae in Syria, BR* 24:605).

Feigned poverty

799. POPE CLEMENT XIV (d. 1774). Let all pernicious ownership, which destroys the ideal of genuine poverty and only makes for observance of poverty in a deceptive sense, about which St. Bernard spoke: "They desire to be poor, but with the provision that they be wanting in nothing" (*Serm. de temp., De Adv. Dni.,* serm. 4, § 5, *PL* 183:49), be excluded from the community. . . . Let the religious keep nothing in his room except what is necessary. . . . We must be on our guard not to be numbered among those of whom St. Vincent Ferrer stated: "They profess to be the friends of poverty, but are careful to avoid as much as possible hunger, thirst, abjection, and contempt, which are the inseparable companions of poverty" (*De vita spirituali,* c. 1, *de paupertate,* p. 114; Morrell, *Treatise on the spiritual life,* p. 30). Like companions on a journey, illness, hardships, hard work, torments, derision, contemptuous treatment and opprobrium accompany poverty. All these are to be loved, or at least borne with calmness for a person to be able to glory in the observance of poverty, which merits the high regard in which it is held not by reason of any hard physical suffering, but because of the spiritual love for it. It is true love of poverty, St.

Bernard teaches us, and not poverty as such, which is considered a virtue (cf. *Serm. 1, in fest. Om. Sanct.*, § 8, *PL* 183:456; Const. Apost., *In vinea Dni.*, § 6, 4 Jul. 1772, *BRC* 5:458).

800. POPE PIUS VI (d. 1799). The vice of private ownership, which the holy Father Benedict describes with the term "most evil," is to be cut off not only with regard to actual material possessions, but also the brethren must devote all earnestness in rooting out of their heart the desire for perishable things. In this spirit they must be on their guard against becoming so attached to an object that they would resent its being taken from them. In order to prevent such an attitude from forming, superiors must avoid granting anyone the use of an object for life, because such permission greatly resembles outright ownership; hence whatever is allowed is to be given, subject to the prudent judgment of the superior. Under no pretext is a monk permitted to hold money in his possession, whether it be that of his parents or others, or to be used for business transactions. Neither are monks allowed to keep anything at all without the permission of the superior, but must turn over to him all the money that they receive (Const. Apost., *Apostolatus officium,* Pars II, c. 4, nn. 129–130, 15 Maii 1799, *Confirmatio const. ord. Cluniacens.*).

801. CARTHUSIAN ORDER. The professed monk must know that he can have nothing whatever without the permission of the prior, not even the staff with which he supports himself when walking on the road (*Const. Guigonis prioris Carthusiae,* c. 75, *CR* 2:330; *PL* 153:747).

802. CONGR. OF CAMALDULI (founded 1018, approved 1072). Regarding the chapter of the Rule in which the holy Father commands that the vice of private ownership be cut out by the roots (*RSB,* c. 33), the Fathers first demand that everything contained in it as well as everything decreed in the Sacred Council of Trent, and in the canons generally with reference to the same matter, be observed inviolably. In order to make the practice of these principles easier, they order all superiors to exercise diligent care to keep their monks from holding anything either in their personal possession or retained for them by others, that they would not readily, cheerfully and willingly give up to their abbot whenever he saw fit to ask for it (*Declar. 1 in c. 33 RSB,* p. 159).

Perfect poverty

803. CONGR. OF STRASBURG (founded 1624). A. The purpose of the Rule is that ownership be cut off not only as regards external observances of poverty, but also, when in the abbot's judgment, any object is possessed with an unreasonable attachment. . . . Consequently superiors are to be on their guard not to grant anyone use of an object for life, or for an extended period of time; a practice that greatly resembles ownership: they are to make all such concessions subject to the prudent

judgment of the superior (*Declar. 1 in c. 33 RSB,* fol. 42). B. We, therefore, forbid anyone to presume to lend or make donations from the property of the monastery, or to distribute pictures, rosaries, scapulars, medals, even to their relatives, without the permission of the superior (*ibid., declar.* 2). C. We forbid all religious priests, under grave penalty, to presume to keep the stipends offered to them for Masses (*ibid., declar. 3*).

804. SWABIAN CONGR. OF ST. JOSEPH (founded 1671). So intent was our holy Father on establishing the precise nature of religious poverty (*RSB,* c. 33), that he willed that superiors devote their worthiest effort to eradicating the vice of personal ownership from the monasteries of his order. Appreciating this objective full well, being mindful too of the obligations of our office, and taking into account the many great benefits bestowed through the religious fostering of poverty as well as the numerous detriments and evils that are brought on monasteries through its neglect, with all the vigor of mind at our command, we earnestly entreat and exhort all abbots to be solicitous in their care and watchfulness in seeing to it that the laws which our holy Father laid down for preserving poverty are observed to the letter without modification or extenuation by all assigned to their charge. Nor must they permit these laws to be violated with impunity.

Let no one dare to possess anything as his private property, nor treat, usurp, receive, or conceal anything as his own, for as St. Augustine says: "Not only he who receives something without the knowledge of his superior is a violator of poverty, but also he who hides and conceals what has been given to him for his use" (Reg. III, c. 29, *CR* 2:126).

In order for this purity of poverty to be preserved more effectively, let the individual monks strive to acquire the spirit of detachment and rid themselves of affection for perishable things; desire and long for nothing beyond the demands of necessity, according to the warning of the Apostle: *But having food and sufficient clothing, with these let us be content* (I Tim. 6:8).

Let no one, then, dare to give anything to another, receive from others, exchange or under any pretext appropriate an object for his personal use, without first having obtained express permission or consent of the superior. Each one must keep in mind that after having pronounced the vow of poverty, he has given up all material possessions, and no longer has a right to dispose of anything independently of the will and consent of the superior. Should something be bestowed on one of the brethren, he will, with complete resignation and detachment, explain the circumstances to the superior and hand the gift over to him. If the latter, as commonly and ordinarily must be the case, designates it for the common use of other brethren, or for some other reason decides that it is not to be granted to the one who received it, he is not therefore to be disturbed or saddened, but is to remind himself that out of love for God and for the sake of his own salvation he has abandoned far more precious gifts than these small objects—namely, himself and his own will.

Because our holy Father Benedict prescribed that all vessels of the monastery should be treated as objects consecrated and dedicated to God, a conscientious effort must be made by all monks to keep the things given to them for their personal needs as clean as possible, and, to the best of their ability, in good repair. In so acting they should remind themselves that they have only the use of these articles: consequently, they are to care for them just as if they were borrowed. If a brother has squandered the goods distributed by the monastery—food, clothing or other necessities—or has failed to keep the articles clean and polished, if he has been guilty of misuse, waste, wantonness, breakage, or other forms of loss, he is to be punished according to the prescriptions of the Rule.

We desire the observance of cleanliness. On the other hand we forbid and condemn all unbecoming finery and splendor which are so foreign to the perfection of religious poverty. No one has the right to retain objects of gold or silver; to wear or carry articles of greater value as their personal property, such as extravagantly bound breviaries, costly rosaries or medals; or to affect whatever savors of softness, delicacy or excessive cost in food and clothing. All such abuses are utterly foreign to the prescriptions of the holy Rule in which St. Benedict commanded and warned us to be content with the meanest and worst of everything (*RSB*, c. 7, sixth degree). Let everyone be intent on avoiding all superfluity and on being content with what is given him from the common store for his need and intelligent use; avoiding all excess, lest he should be counted among those whom the honey-tongued Bernard so sharply stigmatized with the words: "They want to be poor, provided that nothing is lacking to them" (*Serm. de temp., serm. 4, de Adv. Dni.,* § 5, *PL* 183:49).

Everyone, then, must guard against causing serious inconvenience and expense under the pretext of poor health or imaginary weakness, by affecting the need for special considerations in food, clothing and protracted use of medicines, which are either altogether unnecessary, or not particularly helpful. We certainly are not poor in any true sense of the word unless at times we feel the effects of poverty by a real want of certain goods.

The superiors will exercise special vigilance in seeing to it that the brethren do not want what pertains to their becoming and religious maintenance in food and clothing; on the contrary, they are to furnish all that is necessary for everyone with paternal, provident, and generous solicitude. In so doing they are to be considerate of persons as individuals; their state of health, the seasons of the year, the duties assigned, and other circumstances. The greater the care that the subjects see the superiors have in providing what is necessary, the better disposed they will be in manifesting prompt obedience (*Const. et declar.*, Pars II, c. 2, punctum 5, *de paupertate,* fol. 72–78).

Religious poverty

805. PROV. COUNCIL OF ESZTERGOM (Hungary, 1858). As is well known, religious possess no property at all, either in the form of clothing, books, pictures, money, or furniture. At any time he sees fit to do so, the superior can freely make other dispositions of anything that the subject has received for his personal use. It is necessary also that everyone submit all gifts, no matter from whom they have been received, to the disposition of the superior who will conduct the administration of the property of the monastery or convent through its officials (*Concil. Trident.*, sess. XXV, c. 2, *de regularibus, Can. et decr.,* Richter, p. 394; Schroeder, *Trent,* p. 218). These officials are removable at will. The greatest simplicity and perfect uniformity are to be observed in the furnishings of the cells and in clothing (*Decr.,* tit. 7, n. 1, *CL* 5:65).

806. CONGR. OF BURSFELD (1433). In virtue of the vow and the command of the holy Rule, not only is all actual possession prohibited, but the very desire of ownership is unequivocally forbidden as well. Consequently, as practices opposed to holy poverty, we must be careful never to give, sell, exchange, borrow, acquire or dispose of anything. Let us undertake nothing without the superior's blessing; and, as the poor of Christ, want nothing elegant, superfluous, showy or unnecessary. We should live in humility and simplicity, content with whatever is mean and poor, so that we can fulfil our vow as its nature requires (*Stat.,* dist. 5, c. 1, § 4, p. 121).

Measure of food and drink

807. COUNCIL OF AACHEN (817). Each brother will be given his allotted portion of food and beverage individually; he is not permitted to give of this portion to another (Pars II, *capitula monachorum,* c. 76, *PL* 97:392).

808. POPE CLEMENT VIII (d. 1605). All monks, including superiors, regardless of their rank, are to partake of the same bread, wine, and prepared meals, as well as the same pittance, as it is called, at the common table; both at the first and the second serving, unless prevented from doing so by illness (Const. Apost., *Nullus omnino,* § 4, 22 Aug. 1604, *Decr. generalia pro reformatione regularium, BR* 10:663).

Monastic garb

809. COUNCIL OF AACHEN (817). Religious habits worn by the various orders in the Church differ from one another in order that positive recognition of the particular way of life or the profession under which the wearer does battle for the Lord will be readily determined (Lib. I, *de institutione canonicorum, Reg. ab Amalario collecta,* c. 125, *PL* 105:921).

810. POPE BONIFACE VIII (d. 1303). In order to remove the occasion of wandering about, which is a [spiritual] danger for religious, We severely forbid that in future anyone, whatever the form of the religious life he has professed, either tacitly or expressly, fail to wear the habit of his order in schools or elsewhere. . . . If anyone rashly violates this law, he is automatically to incur the sentence of excommunication (c. 2, *Ne clerici vel monachi saecularibus negotiis se immisceant,* III, 24 in *VI°, CJC* Richter 2:1002).

811. CONGR. OF ST. MAUR. The material for your habit must be what is specified by the Rule, and harmonize with monastic humility and poverty (*Declar. 4 in c. 55 RSB,* p. 215).

812. CONGR. OF ST. BERNARD, Italian Cistercians (approved by Pope Urban VIII, 1644). It is always proper for monks to be becomingly garbed in the habit, but particularly when they are to take part in sacred functions, or when they prepare to offer to the sacred rites. They are to avoid the use of the biretta, both in choir and in proceeding from the sacristy to the altar, when about to offer Mass: in choir they are to use the capuche, and when they are vesting to go to the altar to celebrate Mass, they will have the head covered with the amice according to the custom of the order (*Const.,* n. 3).

813. SWABIAN CONGR. OF ST. JOSEPH. There are three things that we specially want to be observed with regard to clothing: (1) that all garments be uniform—we specially insist that all outer garments in future be cut to this common pattern; (2) that the material of the individual habits be in harmony with the religious state, proper, of good quality, and substantial; (3) that nothing of worldly fashion or secular levity be tolerated. Hence the garb with which we cover the body should be an indication of the religious humility which adorns the soul. Nothing is to be for vain show, costly out of pride, or different for the sake of novelty, but in keeping with the demands of the monastic state, humble, proper, and modest. Humility and modesty are to be its only distinguishing features. Fastidiousness in garb always betrays fastidiousness in mind: no one will commend a striving for vanity on the part of a person who has professed poverty. We impress upon all the saying of St. Bernard: "Novelty in clothing is an indication of a deordering of minds and manner in the same way that a vain heart impresses the note

of vanity on the body, and external superfluity is an indication of interior vanity. Soft garments indicate softness of mind. The care of the body would not be given so much attention unless a mind that is uncultivated in virtue had first been neglected" (*Apologia ad Guglielmum,* c. 10, 26, *PL* 182:913). Let the pattern of clothing, therefore, be uniform and fitting, in order that even from the similarity of garb we may strive for a common bond of unity in souls and moral conduct (*Const. et declar.,* Pars II, c. 4. punctum 1, fol. 133–135).

814. POPE CLEMENT VIII. The garb of the brethren and the furniture of the cells are to be perfectly uniform and in harmony with the state of poverty that they have professed, so that nothing superfluous is permitted, and nothing that is necessary is denied anyone (Const. Apost., *Nullus omnino,* n. 3, *BR* 10:663).

The cell

815. CONGR. OF ST. MAUR (Maurists). Let there be a small table in the cell, a few devotional books, the *Rule of St. Benedict* with its declarations, a wooden or cane bottom chair, a little oratory with a few pictures of modest value for fostering devotion . . . and a bed . . . (*Declar. 1 in c. 34 RSB,* p. 134).

816. CONGR. OF STRASBURG. Monks are forbidden to keep valuable pictures and rosaries, superfluous clothing, unnecessary books, and similar movable property in their cells. Such articles are forthwith to be returned to their respective places in the community and, when needed, to be asked for again. The cells of the monks are to be conveniently arranged and furnished with a small table, two chairs, a prie-dieu, a few pictures for inspiring devotion . . . (*Declar. in c. 33 RSB,* fol. 44).

817. SWABIAN CONGR. OF ST. JOSEPH. In conformity with the accepted custom which has been observed in our congregation for several centuries, individual cells are assigned to the brethren for good reasons . . . so that they will not be disturbed or interfered with during the day when they are reading, praying, or studying; nor during the nocturnal quiet when getting their necessary rest. Each cell will have its patron saint. At no time are the cells to be locked with a key on the inside, but free entrance is to be left to the superior at all times. Except for superiors, no one is allowed to enter another's room. Anyone disregarding this rule is subject to serious punishment.

If there is reasonable cause for speaking, the conversation is to be conducted briefly, in a subdued voice, at the door of the cell. Should the superior grant anyone permission to take either a religious or a layman into his cell, this will never be done except with the door open all during the time the guest is within. Particular effort is to be made to see to it that the cells of the brethren are uniform with regard to general equipment: furniture, pictures, chests of drawers, tables, bedding, drapes, chairs, kneeling bench, so that no one will seem to be better provided for than another. The brethren are rather to emulate one another and in a pious rivalry seek to excel in simplicity, humility, recollectedness, devotion, industry, and the general observance of the sacred Constitutions, for these virtues constitute the true ornament of the monastic cell. On being transferred to another cell one is not allowed to take any articles from the cell he is vacating; whatever has once been assigned to a given cell must always remain there. Hence superiors will frequently visit the cells of the individual monks, and correct whatever they find needs to be corrected (*Const. et declar.,* Pars II, c. 3, punctum 7, nn. 1–4, fol. 110–113).

Perfection of common life

818. CONGR. OF BURSFELD. In order to strive earnestly for holy poverty, none of our possessions, apart from those used in sacred worship, are to be of great value, or decorated with paintings, but simple and uniform. Hence anything calculated to attract attention, even under the pretext of devotion, and everything superfluous, is to be removed. Possessions that would come under such a ban are watches, perfume boxes, a personal seal, pictures that draw unusual attention, mirrors, birds, medals or objects made of precious materials, which no one is to dare to keep in his possession. To remove all temptation of acquiring such possessions, the superior in person, or someone appointed by him, in the company of the prior, will visit the cells and workshops of the brethren once or twice a year, to see to it that nothing is kept there which is not in accord with holy poverty (*Stat.,* dist. 5, c. 1, § 4, nn. 3–4, pp. 121–122).

819. CONGR. OF HIRSCHAU (approved by Pope St. Gregory VII, 1083). A brother is not to call anything his own, but always to designate everything as "our," except when he refers to his father, his mother, or his sins. In these instances he is free to use the word "my" (*Const. Hirsaugienses,* Lib. I, c. 60, *PL* 150:989). The same provision was made in the customary of the monastery of St. Benignus at Dijon, and elsewhere.

820. POPE PIUS IX. It is a matter of common knowledge that regular observance falls into ruin principally because the perfect common life which the saintly founders of regular orders, as though they had been erecting a building, have set upon the foundation of the ancient discipline of the Church and commanded to be observed by their followers, has fallen into desuetude among many religious orders. Where it has happened that they turned away from the path of perfection [by

disregarding the principles of the common life] designated by these holy men, gradually there has been a deviation from their true spirit, and from the pristine foundation, with great loss of discipline.

In order to remove the grave evils which result from this lack of observance of the common life, the Council of Trent (Sess. XXV, c. 1), Popes Clement VIII (Const. Apost., *Nullus omnino*), Urban VII (*Decr. de regularibus apostatis et dismissis*), Innocent XI (Const. Apost., *Cum non alias*), Innocent XII (*Decr. Sanctissimus*) and other pontiffs, Our predecessors, have endeavored to restore the common life as well as they could. It is, nevertheless, common knowledge that it is not everywhere observed. Convinced that nothing will contribute more effectively to the reformation of regulars than the promulgation of the obligation of the common life in the most serious terms and its protection with sanctions by this Sacred Ecumenical Council, We establish, with the approval of the Council, decree, and command the following:

. . . Everyone who pronounces profession in the future is bound by the precept of observing the common life in its perfection; therefore the aforementioned precept must be clearly explained to him who petitions admission to profession in any order, congregation, society, or institute . . .

Moreover, within a year from the termination of the Council, the common life is to be completely established in novitiates, professed houses, and houses of studies, insofar as it is not as yet introduced in them. . . . All religious, including those who have professed previously, who reside in these houses which have just been mentioned, are bound to observe it fully. . . .

Since the perfect common life consists in this: that every kind of possessions, income, honorarium, and all other material property which is received by individual religious under whatever title, are fully to be applied to the use of the religious family; and that they in turn receive in common their support, clothing, and other necessities. The superiors are to deny nothing necessary for religious, and the religious on their part are to exact nothing superfluous. Hence charity and solicitude are urgently commended to superiors, and religious moderation to the subjects (*Acta. et decr. Concil. Vaticani,* XVII Schema . . . *de vita communi, CL* 7:676 f.).

IV. WRITINGS OF SAINTS AND DOCTORS

Voluntary poverty

821. ST. BASIL THE GREAT, bp. of Caesarea, Doctor of the Church (d. 379). A. Christ's testimony is clear and undeniable in the words: *So likewise every one of you who does not renounce all that he possesses*

cannot be my disciple (Luke 14:33). And elsewhere, after the words: *If thou wilt be perfect, go, sell what thou hast and give to the poor,* our Lord adds: *Come, follow me* (Matt. 19:21). Again, to any thoughtful person, the parable of the merchant points clearly to the same idea. *The kingdom of heaven,* says Christ, *is like a merchant in search of fine pearls. When he finds a single pearl of great price, he goes and sells all that he has and buys it* (Matt. 13:45). It is evident that this precious pearl is meant to be an image of the heavenly kingdom, which the word of the Lord shows we cannot attain unless we give up in exchange for it all our possessions alike: wealth, fame, lineage, and anything else that is an object of desire for many (*Reg. fusius tractatae,* Interrogatio VIII, *de renuntiatione, PG* 31:938; Wagner, 235). B. I call that the perfect community of life from which personal possession of all things whatsoever is excluded, which is free from dissension and all disturbances, as well as of all striving against one another, and all discord. And in which, by way of contrast, all things are common: hearts, minds, bodies, and all the means we use to sustain life and offer worship: God possessed in common, the common performance of the works of piety, common welfare, trials borne in common, common labors, common rewards and the crowns for the victory gained in struggles, where many are one, and the individual is not alone, but is one of many (*Const. monasticae,* c. 18, n. 1, col. 1382).

822. ST. BERNARD, abbot of Clairvaux, Doctor of the Church (d. 1153). *And opening his mouth, he taught them, saying, Blessed are the poor in spirit . . .* (Matt. 5:3). Truly his mouth was open then, the mouth of him *in whom are hidden all the treasures of wisdom and knowledge* (Col. 2:3). . . . He had announced long before by his Prophet: *I will open my mouth in parables; I will utter things hidden since the foundations of the world* (Ps. 77:2; cf. Matt. 13:35). For what can be so hidden as the blessedness of poverty? Nevertheless it is Truth who speaks, and Truth can neither deceive nor be deceived; it is Truth that proclaims: *Blessed are the poor in spirit.* O senseless sons of Adam, are you still eagerly running after riches and yearning for wealth, even after the blessedness of the poor man's lot has been plainly announced by God himself, even after it has been preached to Gentiles and believed in the world? (Cf. I Tim. 3:16.) Let the pagan who *lives without God in this world* (Eph. 2:12) seek after the treasures of earth, and likewise the Jew, who received the promise of a temporal reward. But with what manner of countenance, or rather with what kind of conscience can a Christian pursue temporal riches after he has heard Christ declaring: *Blessed are the poor?* How long, O ye alien children (cf. Ps. 17:46), how long shall your mouth speak vanity (cf. Ps. 143:11), so as to call those persons happy who possess these things, these visible and transient treasures; whereas the Son of God, opening his mouth, has

beatified poverty and pronounced woes upon wealth (cf. Luke 6:24).

But note carefully that the Lord speaks of those who are poor *in spirit;* not the ordinary poor, whose poverty is caused by miserable want and not borne from praiseworthy choice. With respect to these indigent people, I hope indeed that the misery of their unhappy lot will avail to win them mercy from the divine goodness; nevertheless I know that it is not of them the Lord is speaking in this place, but only of such as can say with the Psalmist: *Freely will I offer you sacrifice* (Ps. 53:8). Yet, not even all voluntary poverty enjoys glory before God. For we read of philosophers who renounced all things in order that by being emancipated from worldly cares they might devote themselves more freely to the study of vanity; they were unwilling to abound in the goods of fortune that they might rather abound in their own self-conceit. These also stand apart from the blessed poor, who are called *poor in spirit;* that is, not only voluntarily, but with a spiritual will. Therefore the words, *Blessed are the poor in spirit,* were spoken only of those who are poor from a spiritual intention, from a spiritual desire; from a pure motive of pleasing God and saving their own souls: *For theirs is the kingdom of heaven* (*Serm. de temp., serm. 1, in fest. Omnium Sanct.,* nn. 7–8, *PL* 183:456 f.).

823. ST. THOMAS AQUINAS, Dominican theologian, Doctor Angelicus (d. 1274). Poverty of spirit . . . can be understood as the renunciation of worldly goods, which is done in spirit, that is, by one's own will, through the instigation of the Holy Spirit (*II-II,* q. 19, art. 12, *Utrum paupertas spiritus sit beatitudo respondens dono timoris, Op. Om.* 8:150; Am. ed., 2:1258).

824. DENIS THE CARTHUSIAN, monk of Roermond (d. 1471). Voluntary poverty is the virtue by which things temporal are despised out of love for the heavenly Bridegroom, so that one neither possesses nor desires to possess anything (*De professione monastica,* art. 11, *Op. Om.* 38:566).

825. ST. CYPRIAN, bp. of Carthage, martyr (d. 258). A man who has thus raised himself above the world will be eager in expecting, and importunate in seeking nothing from it. What a blessed state of tranquillity and safety is this! . . . Be diligent in prayer, and in reading the word of God: at some times you are to speak with God, at other times he will speak with you. Let him instruct you with his precepts, and form your mind by the guidance of his counsel. The man whom God has enriched in this manner, no one can impoverish; he who is filled with the fulness of God, cannot be empty (*Ep. 1 ad Donatum,* cc. 14–15, *PL* 4:225).

826. BENEDICT HAEFTEN, provost of Affighem (d. 1648). The essence of poverty is to be so content with the supreme good, which is God, so

as to forget for his sake all other goods, and not even look at them or deign to hold them as of any worth; saying with the Prophet: *Whom else have I in heaven? And when I am with you, the earth delights me not. Though my flesh and my heart waste away, God is the rock of my heart, and my portion forever* (Ps. 72:25–26; *Disquisitiones monasticae, Lib. IV,* tract. 8, disq. 7, p. 449).

Christ, the model of poverty

827. ARNOLD, abbot of Bonnevaux, dioc. of Chartres, friend and biographer of St. Bernard (d. 1156). A. [In the Birth of Christ] there is no pretentiousness of dwelling, but only a turning aside into a stable, the Mother lying on straw, the Child in a manger. Such were the quarters the Creator of the world chose; such was the luxury surrounding the Holy Virgin's Child-bearing. Swaddling clothes in place of the royal purple, and instead of linen for the adornment of a king, remnants were piled on him (*de cardinalibus operibus Christi,* c. 1, *PL* 189:1616). B. Christ, the poor, rejects wealthy disciples. The poor Mother, the poor Son, the destitute dwelling, were all an efficacious document for those who do battle in this school of the Church (*ibid.,* col. 1618).

828. ST. JEROME, Doctor of the Church (d. 420). He who appreciates that Christ came among us in the flesh that he had taken upon himself, in which he became poor and needy, out of love for us, understands the riches of heavenly blessings. For the Lord became poor, in that he had nowhere to lay his head (cf. Matt. 8:20), indigent in that he showed that his delight was to be among the indigent. *Happy is he who has regard for the lowly and the poor* (Ps. 40:2; *Breviarium in Ps. 40:1, In Append., PL* 26:946).

829. ST. EPHRAEM, deacon of Edessa (d. 378). Be zealous in practicing the poverty of Christ, in order that you may be enriched by his divinity in the heavenly homeland (*De jejunio, Op. Om.* 1:17).

830. ST. BERNARD. Rich beyond all riches and treasures is the poverty of Christ (*Serm. de temp., serm 4, in vigilia Nativ. Dni,* § 6, *PL* 183:102).

831. ST. THOMAS AQUINAS. It must be borne in mind that the attackers of poverty who have been mentioned in the foregoing, stand in no small degree in opposition to the doctrine of Christ and to his life; for he taught by word, that poverty is to be observed in all things, and gave evidence of the teaching by his example. For the Apostle says of him that *being rich he became poor for your sakes* (II Cor. 8:9), and in the Glossa we read: "He assumed poverty and lost not riches: interiorly rich, outwardly poor; lying hidden in riches, appearing as a man of poverty." From this it is seen that those who follow Christ in

poverty acquire a great dignity (Opusc. theol. 3, *contra pestiferam doctrinam retrahentium homines a religionis ingressu,* c. 15, *Op. Om.,* ed. Parma 15:121).

832. ST. FRUCTUOSUS, monk, bp. of Braga (d. 670). The poor of Christ have this way of life in common: They desire to possess nothing in this world, in order to be able to love God and their neighbor with a perfect love. . . . Hence the servant of Christ, who seeks to be a true disciple, ascends the bare cross dispossessed of everything, in order that he may thus die to the world and live for the crucified Christ (*Reg. monastica communis,* c. 1, *CR* 1:209; *PL* 87:1112).

833. PETER DE BLOIS, chancellor and archdeacon in England (d. circa 1200). The title of poverty is precious in the sight of the poor Christ. Christ was poor, Son of the poor Virgin; who chose poor men for his Apostles (Ep. 3, *ad G., virum nobilem quem increpat, PL* 207:8).

834. PETER COMESTOR (d. 1179). Consider the whole life of the Savior from the womb of the Virgin to the gibbet of the cross; you will find nothing in his whole existence but the stigma of poverty (*Serm. 9, in Purificatione B. Virginis ad claustrales, PL* 198:1746).

835. IMITATION OF CHRIST (Thomas à Kempis). Stand purely and firmly in me, and you will have me, and will be so pure in heart and in soul that darkness of conscience or slavery to sin will never have power in you. Endeavor, therefore, to gain this freedom of spirit of which I speak. Pray for it, study for it and always desire it in your heart —that is to say, that you may clearly be deprived and bereft of all possessions and of your own will, and that stripped of all worldly things, you may follow me (*De imitatione Christi, Lib. III,* c. 37, *Op. Om.* 2:213; Gardiner, p. 160).

836. ST. LAURENCE JUSTINIAN, can. regular, patriarch of Venice (d. 1455). The Lord was so poor that on coming into the world he was born not in his own, but in another's dwelling; during life he had nowhere to dwell; in death he had not wherewith to cover his nakedness; after death, neither cloth in which to be wrapped, nor tomb in which his body might be laid (*Lignum vitae,* tract. 10, *de paupertate,* c. 2, *Op. Om.* 1:67).

837. ST. ODILO, abbot of Cluny (d. 1049). Mary was poor in earthly possessions, but rich in those which are heavenly. She was descended from the royal race, but paid the humiliating tax of the indigent. She was poor in material goods, but filled with divine gifts. She was poor to the extremity of being unable to bring the lamb for a sin offering (cf. Levit. 12:6 f.), but so rich that, without the loss of virginity, she gave birth to the Lamb who takes away the sins of the world (Serm. 3, *de Purificatione B.V.M., PL* 142:1000).

Proprietorship among monks

838. JOHN CASSIAN, abbot of Marseilles (d. 430). Do you want to know how dangerously and harmfully incitement, unless it has been carefully eradicated, will shoot up for the destruction of its owner, and put forth all sorts of branches of different sins? Look at Judas! (*De coenobiorum institut., Lib. VII,* c. 23, *PL* 49:314.)

839. ST. AUGUSTINE, bp. of Hippo, Doctor of the Church (d. 430). A. Should anyone conceal a gift bestowed on him, he shall be judged guilty of theft (Ep. 109, *Reg. sanctimonialibus praescriptam continens,* c. 10, *CR* 1:351; *PL* 33:963). B. Let no one arrogate to himself anything as his own, be it with regard to clothing or anything else; for we desire to lead the apostolic life (*Reg. Secunda,* c. 2, *CR* 2:122; *PL* 32:1450). C. What can be sufficient for him for whom virtue and happiness are not enough? (*De civitate Dei, Lib. IV,* c. 21, *PL* 41:128; Dods, p. 126.)

840. ST. JEROME. One of the brethren, more thrifty than covetous, and ignorant that the Lord had been delivered [to the chief priests] for thirty pieces of silver (Matt. 26:15), left behind him at his death a hundred pieces of money which he had earned by weaving linen. As there were about five thousand monks in the neighborhood, living in as many separate cells, a council was held as to what should be done. Some suggested that the coins should be distributed among the poor; others thought that they should be given to the Church; while others were for sending them back to the relatives of the deceased. Macarius, Pambo, Isidore and the rest who were called Fathers, however, decided that they should be buried with their owner with the words: *Thy money go to destruction with thee* (Acts 8:20). Nor was this too harsh a decision (Ep. 22, *ad Eustochium, de custodia virginitatis,* n. 33, *PL* 22:418).

841. ST. ASTERIUS, bp. of Amasea (d. circa 400). Nothing whatever belongs to you. You are a slave, and everything you have belongs to the Lord. A slave has no private property of his own (Hom. 2, *de oeconomo iniquitatis, PG* 40:187).

842. POPE ST. GREGORY THE GREAT, Doctor of the Church (d. 604). . . . if private property is held by the monks, it will not be possible for either concord or charity to continue in this same congregation, for what is the monk's garb but a contempt of the world? (*Lib. XII,* ep. 24, *ad Joannem subdiaconum Ravennae, PL* 77:1233.)

843. ST. LEANDER OF SEVILLE (d. 595). You are to avoid, as a plague, private ownership, which is considered a serious offense in monasteries. It is certainly a form of adultery, for it stains the purity of conscience with the evil of something stolen. It is a crime of theft, for while everything that is possessed in the monastery is common to all, one presumes to retain secretly what is unknown to others, and publicly uses the

common possessions with all the rest while furtively concealing the appropriated object. The deceit is obvious, because the person does not put in the common fund what he possesses, but secretly hides a small amount. There is one offense but many evil results (*Reg., seu institutio virginium ad Florentinam, sororem*, c. 18, *CR* 1:416; *PL* 72:890).

844. RULE OF THE MASTER (7th century). Since everything we need has been given us by the Lord, and the abbot alone has the responsibility for the administration of all property before God, why should the disciple dare to make anything for himself; possess or claim property of whatever kind as his own? It is forbidden to possess anything as one's own because *no one serving as God's soldier entangles himself in worldly affairs, that he may please him whose approval he has secured* (II Tim. 2:4). Thus when he has subjected himself with all his possessions, to another's government, there will be no occasion for his self-will, which is always opposed to the will of God, to be exalted (*Reg. Magistri ad monachos*, c. 83, *CR* 1:279; *PL* 88:1032).

845. ST. FRUCTUOSUS. Private ownership, be it in the possession of tools or clothing or other goods, and regardless of how worthless or insignificant the object may be, must be avoided by all means. For monks to possess anything superfluous or to reserve anything as their own is an abomination and a disgrace (*Reg. monachorum*, c. 8. *CR* 1:204; *PL* 87:1104).

846. STS. PAUL AND STEPHEN, abbots (6th century). Without permission of the prior let the brethren not be allowed to exchange, even among themselves, as though out of private friendship, what they have received from the common store (*Reg.*, c. 27, *CR* 1:142; *PL* 66:956).

847. ST. BERNARD. A. Whether a secular person should hold property or not is a matter of indifference; but for a monk it is wholly evil, for he is not permitted to hold any property at all (Ep. 7, *ad Adam monachum*, § 4, *PL* 182:96; James, p. 28). B. It amounts to theft for the handmaid of God to have anything hidden or retained as her own, unknown to the others; it is a sin of theft. . . . She who appropriates as her own that which is common is a Judas, and will suffer the punishment of Judas in hell. . . . To hide something as one's own is theft, obvious deceit, a great sin, the way of hell. By this path thieves have gone down to hell. The Apostle Paul states: *Neither . . . thieves, nor the covetous . . . will possess the kingdom of God* (I Cor. 6:10; *Lib. de modo bene vivendi, ad sororem*, c. 48, n. 115, *In Append., PL* 184:1270).

848. ST. PETER DAMIAN, monk of Fonte-Avellana, cardinal, Doctor of the Church (d. 1072). A. He who endeavors to possess private property cannot follow in the footsteps of the Apostles (Opusc. 24, c. 4, *PL* 145:486). B. Just as he who honors Christ is deservedly called a follower of Christ, so he who serves money by hoarding it, is not undeservedly

called a worshiper of money. . . . For he who is Truth itself says: *You cannot serve God and mammon* (Matt. 6:24), as though he had said "No one can worship God and money at the same time" (Opusc. 12, *de contemptu saeculi,* c. 6, col. 256). C. The possessor of property will perhaps say to me: "Why do you accuse me so bitingly of holding riches? Do you not see that I am content with a very small sum and have only a few coins. I keep this amount only because of my weaknesses; I am looking forward only to relieving my future needs. I have no intention of 'abounding in riches.' " . . . See, our possessor of property, or better, our adorer of wealth, employs the defense of poverty itself. . . . Why do you boast as though you were safe because of the small amount of money involved . . . especially since it is the nature of the human mind to be quite as preoccupied with small amounts if one is indigent, as about many concerns if he is wealthy? (*Ibid.,* c. 7, col. 257.) D. Who, I ask you, forced Ananias and Sapphira to give up their property? But because by agreement they kept back part of the money (cf. Acts 5:1 f.) in order to support themselves as it were for a long life, they did not escape the sentence of sudden death. . . . We not only give up far nobler acquisitions and all earthly possessions, but we have professed their renunciation forever—and we have given them up, not to man, but rather to God. If therefore money is still found in our pouch, if even the smallest amount of money is held back to the offense of him who beholds our inner man, what shall we say to him when rendering our accounts? With what defense can we cleanse ourselves? (*Ibid.,* c. 3, col. 253.)

849. JEAN RIGAUD, Franciscan theologian (d. 1323). As a bat drinks oil in the church where others adore God, so a religious who retains possessions . . . steals the goods of the monastery where others are devoted to the praise and service of God (*Diaeta salutis,* tit. 4, c. 1, *Op. Om. S. Bonaventurae,* ed. Peltier 8:283).

850. DENIS THE CARTHUSIAN. A. Many sins grow out of ownership of private property as from a poisonous root (*De reformatione claustralium,* art. 16, *Op. Om.* 38:236). B. The vice of private ownership is detestable and dreadful in religious, for they have professed evangelical poverty (*Enarr. in c. 5 Act. Ap.,* art. 5, *Op. Om.* 14:114). C. As often as a religious person longs to possess something as his own, or actually acquires, or uses something as his own, just so often does he violate his profession and sins grievously (*De professione monastica,* art. 11, *Op. Om.* 38:567).

851. JOHN GERSON, chancellor of the University of Paris (d. 1429). A. Private ownership by monks is a greater apostasy than putting off the habit or going beyond the confines of the church [abbey] without the superior's permission (*Contra proprietarios Reg. Divi Augustini,*

n. 5, *Op. Om.* 2:777). B. The possession of private property, especially when it is united with hypocrisy, is a wild beast more ferocious than the lion (*ibid.,* pars 3, p. 792).

852. JOHN OF TRITHEIM, abbot of Sponheim (d. 1516). A. In this world I sought for nothing, I possessed nothing, I was attached to nothing earthly, but being poor, humble, and meek, I subjected myself to my Father's will in all perfection, at all times, in all things. Should you, O monk, living in the enclosure and professing a rule under an abbot or a prior, possess personal property or anything of your own in the monastery . . . I shall consider you not a monk, but a faithless fugitive, an apostate, a liar, a scoffer, a perjurer (*Hom. 2, de profectu militiae spiritualis, Op. pia et spiritualia,* p. 415). B. A monk who possesses private property is preparing the way to hell for himself (*Serm. 2, Quae sit ordinatio vitae monasticae bona, ibid.,* p. 535). C. By ownership, the agreement entered into with God is broken; the solemn vow profaned; the charity of fraternal unity spurned; theft committed; sacrilege perpetrated (*De vitio proprietatis monachorum,* c. 5, *ibid.,* p. 732). D. The divine law forbids the monk to have anything as his own; canon law absolutely proscribes ownership to religious; all the rules of the holy Fathers cry out that . . . possession of property by the monk is wholly unlawful (*ibid.,* c. 7, p. 736). E. O cursed property of monks, which possesses no less than it is possessed (*ibid.,* c. 8, p. 737).

853. ST. FRANCIS OF ASSISI. A. I implore the favor of being sealed with this privilege. I crave to be enriched with this treasure. I beg you, O Jesus most poor, that it may be the distinction of me and of mine for ever more, for your name's sake, to possess nothing under heaven as our own, and to be sustained, as long as our poor flesh lives, only with the closely restricted use of things given us by others (*In suis opusculis, oratio pro obtinenda paupertate: ad finem orationis, Op. Om.,* p. 19). B. To God's servants money is nothing but the devil and a venomous snake (*Apophthegmata,* n. 38, *ibid.,* p. 68).

The true common life

854. ST. BASIL THE GREAT. Whenever, therefore, a group of persons aiming at the same goal of salvation adopt the life in common, this principle above all others must prevail among them: that there be in all, one heart, one will, one desire; and that the entire community be, as the Apostle enjoins, one body consisting of many members (I Cor. 12:12). Now this cannot be realized in any other way than by the enforcement of the rule, that nothing is to be appropriated to anyone's exclusive use—neither cloak, nor vessels, nor anything else which is of use to the common life, so that each of these articles may be assigned to a need and not to an owner. . . . Bed, covering, warm clothing,

footwear, should belong to the one who is strictly in need of these things, and not to an owner. As he who is wounded uses medicaments, and not the one who is sound, so also he who is in need of the things designed for bodily ease should enjoy them, and not one who is living in luxury (*Serm. asceticus II,* § 1, *PG* 31:881; Wagner, p. 217).

No exceptions to the Rule

855. JOHN OF TRITHEIM. A monk can become an owner or possessor even when objects of very small value are involved, quite as well as another would be a proprietor in great possessions. . . . The Rule says: "The monk is not to possess anything whatever as his own" (*RSB,* c. 33). . . . They are in error, therefore, and guilty of violation of the Rule, who contend that monks may give or receive any kind of small objects such as tablets, pictures, and handkerchiefs without the prior's permission (*De vitio proprietatis monachorum,* c. 8, *Op. pia et spiritualia,* p. 738).

Wilfulness and dangers of violations of poverty

856. ST. ZENO, bp. of Verona, martyr (d. 381). He whose heart is filled with the consuming flame of insatiable cupidity, freely admits any wicked deed, crime, disgrace or wrong-doing (*Lib. I,* tract. 10, *de avaritia,* § 4, *PL* 11:336).

857. ST. JEROME. A. He who loves money cannot love God (Ep. 121, *ad Algasiam,* c. 6, *PL* 22:1020). B. Do you want to know how pernicious the love of possessing and the longing to acquire money really is? Judas betrayed the Savior out of this love (Ep. 32, *ad Pammachium et Oceanum,* § 5, *In Append., PL* 30:241).

858. ST. MAXIMUS, bp. of Turin (d. circa 465). You see, then, that he who longs for money loses appreciation for the faith, and that he who collects gold, squanders grace. For avarice is blindness, and induces mistaken ideas with regard to religion. I say that avarice is blind, but it has keen vision for all sorts of fraud; it does not see the things that are of God, but it considers carefully the things that are of its own longing (*Hom. 96, de avaritia II, PL* 57:476).

859. CLEMENT, priest of Alexandria (d. circa 220). A. Much more, then, is the scripture to be believed, which says: *It is easier for a camel to pass through the eye of a needle* (Matt. 19:24) *than for a rich man* to lead a philosophic life [a life devoted to wisdom]. On the other hand, the scripture blesses the poor (cf. Matt. 5:3); as Plato understands when he says: "It is not the diminishing of one's resources, but the augmenting of insatiableness that is to be considered poverty, for it is not slender means that ever constitutes poverty, but insatiableness, from which the good man being free, will also be rich" (*Stromatum, Lib. II,* c. 5, *PG* 8:954). B. Love of money is the stronghold of evil, or as the Apostle calls

it, *the root of all evils* (I Tim. 6: 10). . . . But the best riches is poverty of desire; and the truest magnanimity is not to be proud of wealth, but to despise it (*Pedagogi Lib. II*, c. 3, col. 439).

860. JOHN CASSIAN. A. It is a veritable nest of sins, and a root of all evils, and becomes a hopeless incitement to wickedness, as the Apostle says: *Covetousness,* that is, the love of money, *is the root of all evils* (I Tim. 6:10; *De coenobiorum institut., Lib. VII,* c. 6, *PL* 49:296). B. Judas, wanting to reacquire possession of the wealth which he had abandoned at the time he followed Christ, not only fell into betraying the Lord and lost his dignity as an apostle, but also was not allowed to close his life with the common lot of all, but ended in violent death (cf. Matt. 27:5). But Ananias and Sapphira, keeping back a part of that which was formerly their own, were at the Apostle's words punished with death (cf. Acts 5:1 f.; *ibid.,* c. 14, col. 304).

861. ST. CYPRIAN. Alas! a man in these circumstances has greater reason to look well about him and to be apprehensive of danger, than any other: he always fears more than he is feared. Let him fence himself in with guards and securities ever so numerous; whoever possesses it, pays dearly for his power. The more dangerous his power is to his subjects, the more dangerous they become to him; before it can strike terror on others, it strikes it first upon his own breast. It gives him pleasure and pain together; allures, exalts, and flatters him, only to deceive, depress, and destroy him (Ep. 1, *ad Donatum,* c. 13, *PL* 4:224).

862. ST. HILARY, bp. of Poitiers, Doctor of the Church (d. 368). A. There is a snare for us in idleness, money, ambition, and immorality. They are presented before us, they flatter, they deceive; and our will must be set in opposition against them all (*In Ps. 123:7,* § 8, *PL* 9:678). B. The root of evils is most of all in the desire of money, and he who longs for it is drowned in the shipwreck of a most violent storm (*ibid., in Ps. 61, 11,* § 8, col. 399).

863. ST. AUGUSTINE. Whoever serves mammon delivers himself over to a master who is harsh and malignant; caught by his own cupidity, he puts himself under the devil, yet does not love him; for who is there who loves the devil? (*De Serm. Dni. in monte, Lib. II,* c. 14, § 47, *PL* 34:1290; Jepson, p. 134.)

864. ST. JOHN CHRYSOSTOM. A. The devil has no knowledge of an open and fair fight: he conceals himself like a serpent among thorns, often lying hidden in the deceitfulness of riches (cf. Matt. 13:22; *In Ep. ad Rom., Hom. 8,* § 6, *PG* 60:463). B. I am astounded at the entire matter. There must be some trickery that should cause gold and silver to be so highly valued among us. Indeed we have no regard for our own souls, but to graven images on metal we attach great significance (*In I Thess., Hom. 10,* § 3, *PG* 62:458). C. He who is suffering from a fever cannot be satisfied, but with constant desire of drinking, is never filled,

and still suffers continual thirst; in like manner he who is mad after wealth never knows the fulfilment of his desire; whatever is bestowed on him, he is still unsatisfied, and will therefore never be thankful (*In II Tim., Hom. 8,* § 2, col. 638). D. Like an inhuman mistress, a harsh tyrant, a savage barbarian, or a public and expensive prostitute, [the love of money] debases and exhausts and punishes with innumerable dangers and torments those who have chosen to be in bondage to her. Even though she is terrible and harsh, fierce and cruel, and has the face of a barbarian, or rather of a wild beast, fiercer than the wolf or the lion, she seems to those who have been taken captive by her to be gentle and lovable (*Lib. Quod nemo laedatur nisi a seipso,* § 6, *PG* 52:467). E. For nothing so makes us fall under the power of the devil as does the insatiable desire of possessing, and being addicted to avarice (*In Matt., Hom. 13,* § 4, *PG* 57:212).

865. ST. PETER CHRYSOLOGUS, bp. of Ravenna, Doctor of the Church (d. 450). Money governs nations, prescribes policies for kingdoms, declares wars, pits combatants against one another; sells blood, deals death, betrays fatherlands, destroys cities; subjugates peoples, besets strongholds, molests citizens, rules the marketplace; wipes out justice, confuses right and wrong . . . profanes the truth, calumniates good names; pulls down uprightness of morals, breaks asunder the bonds of love, takes away innocence; buries the sense of duty, breaks all harmonious relations, undermines friendship (*Serm. 126, de villico iniquo, serm. II, PL* 52:547).

866. ST. GREGORY THE GREAT. A. It must be noted that the Lord says in explanation [of the parable about the sowing of the seed] that the cares and riches and pleasures of life stifle the word of God (cf. Luke 8:14 f.). They stifle the word because by their oppressive concerns they choke the mind, and by not allowing virtuous desires to enter the heart, cut off, as it were, life-giving breath (*In Evangel., Hom. 15,* § 3, *PL* 76:1133). B. It is a rare thing for them who have gold to advance to rest, for he who is Truth itself has said: *With difficulty will a rich man enter into the kingdom of heaven* (Matt. 19:23; Mark 10:23; *Moral., Lib. IV, Praef.,* c. 3, *PL* 75:635).

867. POPE ST. LEO THE GREAT, Doctor of the Church (d. 461). To the love of wealth, all affection is paltry; the soul that is avaricious for possessions is not afraid to be lost even for something of little value (*Serm. 60, de Passione Dni.,* IX, c. 4, *PL* 54:345).

868. PETER DE BLOIS, chancellor and archdeacon, Bath, England (d. circa 1200). A. The slave to material possessions is an apostate for money and in it becomes an idolator (*Serm. 42, in fest. Omnium Sanct.,* II, *PL* 207:691). B. O love of money! cankerworm of hearts, darkness of minds, craven sluggishness of souls, subversion of virtues, germ of vices which turns love into hate and God's grace into contempt! How blind

the hearts of the rich so that the more they possess the less they believe they have! (*Tract. de Jerosolymitana peregrinatione acceleranda,* col. 1068.)

869. POPE INNOCENT III (d. 1216). A. O unquenchable fire, O insatiable cupidity! Was there ever a covetous man who remained content with the realization of his first ambition? Having acquired that which he sought, he longs for more; his purpose is always determined by what is to be procured, not by actual possession. . . . The eyes of men are ever disturbed by desire. *The two daughters of the leech are 'Give, Give'* (Prov. 30:15; *De contemptu mundi, Lib. II,* c. 6, *PL* 217: 719). B. How many persons cupidity has misled, how many has avarice destroyed! The ass rebuked Balaam because, overcome by the desire of the things that had been promised to him, he had resolved to curse Israel (cf. Num. 22:28 f.). The people stoned Achan for he had taken gold and silver subject to the ban, and converted them to his own use (cf. Jos. 7:11 f.). Naboth was slain in order that Achab might possess his vineyard (cf. III Kgs. 21:15). Giezi was struck with leprosy because he petitioned and received gold and silver and garments under the name of Elisaeus (cf. IV Kgs. 5:27). Judas hanged himself with a halter for having sold and betrayed Christ (cf. Matt. 27:5). Sudden death destroyed Ananias and Sapphira, for they had defrauded the Apostles of the price of their field (Acts 5:1; *ibid.,* c. 9, col. 720).

870. ST. JEROME. We read in the Acts of the Apostles (4:35) how, while the blood of the Lord was still warm and believers were in the fervor of their first faith, they all sold their possessions and laid the price of them at the Apostles' feet to show that money should be trampled under foot, and that *distribution was made to each, according as any one had need* (Ep. 130, *ad Demetriadem, de servanda virginitate,* n. 14, *PL* 22:1118).

The true riches of monks

871. ST. BASIL THE GREAT. A. They who are monks in truth do not claim earthly possessions for themselves, but strive for heavenly goods; each gather them in certain individual portions. For it is the possession of virtue, the wealth of things well done, a commendable avarice, a plundering which causes no tears, an unquenchable desire that has been realized, which makes him guilty who has not used violence to acquire it. Everyone seizes and no one is injured, for it is peace itself which distributes these riches (*Const. monasticae,* c. 18, § 3, *PG* 31: 1383). B. [The monk] must be free of all private possessions of earthly goods. Otherwise he first destroys the precise and genuine concept of the society by his private possession; then he shows that he is lacking in faith, almost as one who puts no trust in God, as though he thought that God were not to sustain those whom he has gathered together in

his name. He has not hearkened to David the Prophet, who said: *Neither in my youth, nor now that I am old, have I seen a just man forsaken nor his descendants begging bread* (Ps. 36:25; *ibid.*, c. 34, § 1, col. 1423). C. There should be a common supply room for all, and nothing should be called private or personal to any individual: neither clothing, nor footwear, nor anything else required for the body. The use of these items should be under the authority of the superior, so that the articles from the common store may be allotted to each according to his need at the superior's direction (*Serm. asceticus I,* n. 5, col. 878; Wagner, p. 213).

872. JOHN CASSIAN. The monks are to keep the utensils of the monastery with the utmost care and solicitude, so that none of them may be harmed or destroyed; for they believe that even for the smallest vessels they must give an account as though of sacred vessels, not only to a present steward, but to the Lord. . . . Wherefore if anything has once been brought into the monastery they should hold, that it ought to be treated with the utmost reverence as a holy thing (*De coenob. institut., Lib. IV,* c. 19, *PL* 49:179, 180).

873. JOHN OF TRITHEIM. A monk who has a book, a picture, or any similar object in his cell with the prior's permission, is to understand that its *use* has been granted to him, and that ownership or proprietorship is forbidden (*De vitio proprietatis monachorum,* c. 9, *Op. pia et spiritualia,* p. 738).

Superfluity is to be cut off

874. CLEMENT OF ALEXANDRIA. The diet which exceeds sufficiency injures a man, deteriorates his spirit, and renders his body prone to disease (*Pedagogi, Lib. II,* c. 1, *PG* 8:390).

875. ST. AUGUSTINE. The superfluities of the rich are the necessities of the poor. You possess what belongs to others when you possess more than you need (*Enarr. in Ps. 147,* § 12, *PL* 37:1922).

876. ST. JOHN CHRYSOSTOM. A. For nothing so characterizes practical wisdom (*philosophiam*) as to be free from superfluities, and, as far as may be, from wants (*In Matt., Hom. 32,* § 5, *PG* 57:384). B. Let us not covet superfluous things, but keep to a sufficiency, and we shall always be rich (*In I Cor., Hom. 16,* § 6, *PG* 61:138). C. That which if it is done profits not, and which if left undone injures not, is certainly superfluous (*ibid., Hom. 20,* § 4, col. 166). D. We are not recommending all this [spirit of detachment] to overwhelm you men and lead you on to the lofty heights of poverty, but we do require of you to cut off superfluities and to desire a sufficiency alone. Whatever can be cut off, and leave us still able to lead our lives sensibly and honestly, must certainly be considered superfluous (*In II Cor., Hom. 19,* § 3, col. 534). E. That which is superfluous and unprofitable [excessive clothing, precious or-

naments], is nothing else than loss [in that it prevents winning Christ] (*In Philip., Hom. 10,* § 3. *PG* 62:259). F. For they who live in a spirit of thanksgiving, who seek nothing beyond a sufficiency; they whose philosophy is of this nature, live in perpetual joyfulness (*In Coloss., Hom. 1,* § 6, col. 307).

877. JULIANUS POMERIUS, priest of Arles (5th century). Whatever indeed one takes without which he can live, is taken not to sustain life, but to foster the luxury of the flesh (*De vita contemplativa, Lib. II,* c. 17, § 1, *PL* 59:462; Suelzer, p. 86).

878. ST. COLUMBAN, abbot (d. 615). The desire for material possessions is to be trampled under foot by monks to whom the world is crucified, and they to the world out of love for Christ. For not only actually to possess, but even to desire anything superfluous is in them worthy of condemnation. They are to seek not money, but submission of the will. Abandoning all things and following Christ the Lord with the cross of daily fear, they place their treasures in heaven. Hence as they are to have many things in heaven, they must be content with little, nay with the severity of extreme necessity on earth, knowing that the desire of material things is a leprosy for monks. . . . Therefore the first perfection of monks is dispossession and the contempt of wealth; the second, the purging of vices; the third, continued and more perfect love of God, and the love of divine things which flows from disregarding earthly things (*Reg. coenobialis,* c. 4, *de paupertate, ac de cupiditate calcanda, CR* 1:171; *PL* 80:211).

879. ST. BERNARD. A. We read that *distribution was made to each, according as any one had need* (Acts 4:35). It was not, therefore, a matter of what each one could foolishly wear in gratification of puerile vanity (*Apologia, ad Guglielmum S. Theodorici abb.,* c. 10, § 24, *PL* 182:912). B. Take away that which is superfluous, and that which is conducive to salvation will have vigorous growth. Whatever you take away from things which minister only to pleasure, you add to those which minister to the soul's benefit. Let us give to self-denial its perfect work, and cut off the satisfaction of our desires and lusts in order that virtue may be strengthened thereby (*Serm. 58 in Cant.,* § 10, *PL* 183:1061; Eales, p. 353).

880. HUGH OF ST. VICTOR, canon regular, Paris (d. 1142). Whatever [the brethren] possess that they do not need, is deadly for them (*Expos. in Reg. S. Augustini,* c. 9, *PL* 176:912).

881. HUGO DE FOLIETO, canon regular, abbot of St. Denis of Rheims, cardinal (d. 1149?). Superfluity, which appears exteriorly, is an indication of the mind's vanity. . . . Give what is sufficient to a delicate person, so that he will not faint; but do not give him that by which he will be made proud (*De claustro animae, Lib. II,* c. 18, *PL* 176:1070).

Abstemiousness in food

882. ST. BONAVENTURE. It is not for one who is poor according to the ideal of the Gospel to enjoy superfluities and to indulge in excesses, and to wish for that which is not always in the power even of wealthy men—to have all things plentifully and not to experience any want (*Speculum disciplinae ad novitios, Pars II*, c. 6, § 3, *Op. Om.*, ed. Quaracchi 8:621).

883. ST. ANTONINUS, O.P., abp. of Florence (d. 1459). A. Nothing so impedes the functioning of the senses and causes disorder in the imagination as does excess of food (*Summa Theol., Pars IV*, tit. 4, § 1, *de partibus subjectivis temperantiae*, 4:125). B. A small amount suffices for the necessary care of the body, and they who are voluntarily poor are content with that little (*ibid.*, tit. 12, c. 3. *de consilio paupertatis*, § 1, p. 624).

884. VEN. LOUIS DE BLOIS. Be sober in your apparel as well as in your diet. Reject, scorn, and detest whatever is contrary to monastic simplicity (*Speculum monachorum*, div. 7, *Op. Om.* 3:667).

885. JOANNES DE FANO, O.F.M.CAP. (d. 1539). That is superfluous which, if taken away, leaves an adequate amount; whatever is costly is excessive if something cheaper will serve the purpose (*Brevis discursus super observantia Fr. Minorum*. In: *Reg. et Testamentum Seraphici Patris Francisci*, 1631).

886. THOMÁS DE JESÚS, O.C.D. (d. 1627). We call those things superfluous which are necessary neither for supporting life nor for upholding the proper decorum of the religious state. But to call something superfluous, we must take into account all the circumstances of the religious person: the place, the time, the office he holds, and so on. What is considered moderation in one religious institute, therefore, may deservedly be rejected as excessive in another; and even within the same religious family what may be necessary for one would be judged superfluous in another's case; and what is fitting and proper for a religious during the time of illness would be a violation of true poverty once his health has been regained (*In cap. Non dicatis, Pars IV*, c. 6. In: Thomás de Jesús, *Commentaria in Cap. Non dicatis XII;* Antwerpiae: apud Gerardum Wolffchalium, 1617).

887. ST. FULGENTIUS, bp. of Ruspe, Northern Africa (d. 533). When you eat, do not make it an occasion for gratifying your pleasure, but rather for supporting your weakness (Ep. 2, *ad Gallam viduam*, c. 13, § 27, *PL* 65:318).

888. ST. JOHN CHRYSOSTOM. A. Do you wish to nourish the body? Take away what is superfluous; give what is sufficient, and as much as can be digested. . . . Nothing is so productive of health, nothing so insures acuteness of the faculties, nothing tends so much to keep disease

at a distance as does moderate eating. For a sufficiency is both nourishment, and pleasure and health; but excess is injury, unpleasantness and disease (*In Hebr., Hom. 29*, § 4, *PG* 63:208). B. Let our purpose in taking sustenance be that it harm us not, that it take away our hunger without injuring us; but let us seek nothing beyond that (*De fato et providentia, Oratio VI, PG* 50:772).

889. ST. GAUDENTIUS, bp. of Brescia (d. circa 420). The permission to eat is to be used, not abused; as you know, we were born not to eat, but to live virtuously (*Serm. 15, De natali Machabaeorum, PL* 20:954).

Simplicity of the cell

890. PETER DE BLOIS. In imitation of that house of which it is written: *In my Father's house there are many mansions* (John 14:2), each one of us has here his little cell and small mansion, in order to devote himself more freely to contemplation and prayer. In the school of the Gospel he who is Truth instructs us with the statement: *When thou prayest, go into thy room, and closing thy door, pray to thy Father in secret* (Matt. 6:6; Ep. 86, *ad Magistrum Alexandrum monachum Carthus., PL* 207:268).

891. ST. JEROME. Enclosed in the narrow confines of her cell, [the virgin Asella] enjoyed the whole expanse of paradise (Ep. 24, *ad Marcellam, de laudibus Asellae*, § 3, *PL* 22:427).

892. PETER THE VENERABLE, abbot of Cluny (d. 1158). Let your cell be without money, but filled with justice; totally wanting in wealth, but abounding with virtues. . . . Leave no room unoccupied in your cell, so that when God has filled it to fulness with his virtues, there will be no place left over for the devil, nor for laziness, nor for any other vices (*Lib. I*, ep. 20, *ad Gislebertum eremitam, PL* 189:95, 98).

893. VEN. JUAN DE JESÚS MARÍA, third superior general O.C.D. (d. 1615). A. If your desire is for an abundant and rich inheritance in my [God's] kingdom, son, devote your efforts to making yourself poor in spirit. Do not seek after superfluities in clothing, food, bedding, and other necessities in this mortal life, but only what is necessary; and that always in Christian moderation. More than that, accept it in good part if at times you experience want even in the things that seem necessary, for this is the manner of acting of the good religious who follow me in my poverty. Free yourself of the burden of this world's goods, and I will personally fill you with those which are heavenly unto your soul's supreme consolation (*Epistola Christi ad hominem*, c. 5, *de paupertate*. In: *Theologia mystica et Epistola Christi ad hominem;* Friburgi Brisgoviae: B. Herder, 1912, p. 146). B. The few who love you indeed acted wisely in not seeking to have their inheritance in the land of the dying, in order that they might have you for their inheritance! And I, wishing to be among these few, disdain all that the world holds desirable, so

that if honors, pleasures, and wealth are offered to me, I do not wish my heart to be attached to them. Like a pilgrim seeking the city to come, I shall pass by without comfort in this present world, and hasten to my most desired fatherland. I shall imitate the courageous fighters who had no desire to receive the deceptive freedom of the world, in order that they might find the better resurrection, and hasten to their rest (Soliloquia. 6, *de contemptu mundi.* In: *Stimulus compunctionis et Soliloquia;* Florentiae: Jo. Bapt. Stecchi, 1771, p. 116).

894. GERARD THE BELGIAN. From a monastic point of view all that is necessary to equip a cell is that it have a monk and a crucifix. . . . In no sense of the term is he poor who, apart from God, is attached to the little that he has, or desires the little that he does not have. . . . He who has retained anything of the world for himself has abandoned the world in vain. Only one thing is the monk allowed to retain, only one thing should he have, and that one thing no one can take from him—God and the practice of virtue (*Dicta et facta Gerardi monachi, Opusc. pia* 2:135).

The monastic garb

895. ST. HILDEGARDE, abbess (d.1179), was thus addressed by God the Father: "The clothing of monks * is not to be compared to the garb of other stations in life. It is symbolic of the spotless Incarnation of my Son, who entered upon his earthly life in a manner different from all other men. . . . For this monastic garb lifts its wearers aloft as on spiritual wings, after the manner of the brilliant heavenly spirits. It represents the Incarnation and the burial of my Son. For whoever offers himself for that obedience which demands such great fortitude, has the symbol of the Incarnation in his garb. And the man who undertakes the works of godliness, renouncing all worldly concerns, wears the symbol of my Son's burial in his habit" (*Scivias, Lib. II,* visio 5, *PL* 197:487; Boeckeler, p. 166).

896. ST. JOHN CHRYSOSTOM. The [monks'] dress is suitable to their manliness. For they are not garbed like those who parade through the streets with trailing garments, enervated and mincing men, but rather like those blessed angels, Elias, Elisaeus, John, and the Apostles . . . (*In Matt., Hom. 68,* § 3, *PG* 58:644).

897. ST. HILDEGARDE [was thus addressed by the Lord]: "The Holy Spirit then inspired the hearts of his chosen ones who possessed the longing for life, and as in the bath of baptism the people's sins are washed away, so [monks and nuns] renounce worldly pomps in the

* Both here and in following references, by the reception of the habit is understood the effectual admission into the monastic family through the pronouncing of vows, and not today's "clothing" or "investiture" as the formal legal entrance into the novitiate (cf. Boeckeler, p. 166).

symbol of my Son's passion. As in holy baptism man is withdrawn from the power of the devil by the washing away of former sins . . . so also in like manner [members of religious orders], by receiving the holy habit, abandon all worldly concerns, and in so doing receive the mark of the angels. How is this so? They are, according to my will, made the protectors of my people. Should they be found worthy in their way of life, they may, if the need arise, take upon themselves in addition, the priestly office, for the defense of the Church; for the angels too, who are touched with no stain of the things of earth, are guardians of my people" (*Scivias, Lib. II,* visio 5, *PL* 197:488).

898. ST. JEROME. A. We must either speak as we are dressed, or else dress as we speak. Why do we profess one thing and practice another? The tongue talks of chastity, but the rest of the body reveals incontinence (Ep. 54, *ad Furiam de viduitate servanda,* n. 7, *PL* 22:553). B. Your dress changes with the change in your convictions . . . (Ep. 58, *ad Paulinum de Nọla, de vita sancte et caste peragenda,* § 2, col. 580).

899. ST. EPHRAEM. Reflect, monk, on the habit you wear, and note the difference between it and the clothing of people in the world; diligently take into account what the religious garb signifies. It denotes abandonment of things worldly and carries with it awareness of dedication to spiritual works (*De virtute,* c. 9, *Op. Om.* 2:303).

900. POPE INNOCENT III. Let the bishop and the priest each examine diligently and pay studious attention to make certain that he does not bear the sign without bearing also that which is signified; that he does not wear the garb without the virtue, lest he be like the whited sepulchre outwardly, but inwardly filled with all uncleanness (cf. Matt. 23:27). Whoever is ornamented with the sacred vestments but is not marked with virtuous conduct, the more worthy he appears to men, the more unworthy he is made in God's sight (*De sacro altaris mysterio, Lib. I,* c. 64, *PL* 217:799).

901. ST. BERNARD. You see, our habit—I cannot say this without great pain—which was, in other times, a visible mark of the humility that the ancient monks professed, has now become a public manifestation of pride [statement against the Cluniacs, their fastidiousness and vanity] (*Apologia, ad Guglielmum S. Theodorici,* c. 10, n. 25, *PL* 182: 913; Luddy, p. 106).

902. ST. BASIL THE GREAT. With regard to clothing and shoes, it is not for us to go in search for what is more expensive, but we are to choose what is cheaper, in order that we may give evidence in this matter too of humility of mind. Nor are we to cultivate the good opinion of the fastidious, or of those who love themselves, while we are actually shuddering away from fraternal charity. Whoever desires the best in material things is quite separated from charity and humility (*Const. monasticae,* c. 30, *PG* 31:1419).

903. JOHN CASSIAN. Let the garb also of the monk be such as may merely cover the body, prevent the shame of nudity and keep off harm from cold, but let it not be such as may foster the seeds of vanity and pride (*De coenobitorum institut., Lib. I,* c. 3, *PL* 49:64).

904. ST. BERNARD. A heart that is vain makes the body don the badge of its vanity, and superfluity in externals is evidence of vanity that dwells within: love of fine garments is indicative of softness of spirit. Certainly we should not devote such great concern for the adornment of the body had we not first neglected to cultivate the soul with its virtues (*Apologia, ad Guglielmum S. Theodorici,* c. 10, n. 26, *PL* 182:913).

905. ST. THOMAS AQUINAS. . . . It is becoming for religious to wear coarse attire, since religion is a state of penance and of contempt for worldly glory (*II–II,* q. 187, art. 6, *Utrum liceat religiosis vilioribus vestibus uti quam caeteris, Op. Om.* 10:520; Am. ed. 2:1991).

906. ST. PACHOMIUS, abbot (4th century). The cowls of the individual brethren will bear the insignia of the monastery and of the house (*Reg.,* n. 99, *CR* 1:31).

907. BENEDICT HAEFTEN, provost of Afflighem (d. 1648). There are seven purposes for the distinctive garb of monks: (1) to serve as a sign of their religious profession and segregation from seculars; (2) to bind its wearers to live as religious even against their will; (3) to enable them to profit by the contempt of the world leveled at them because of the coarseness of their garb; (4) to make the change of habit signify the reformation of their lives according to monastic principles (*conversionem morum*); (5) to implant in the heart of the wearer appreciation of the vow of poverty according to the phrase of the *Rule of St. Benedict:* "Let him be clothed in the habit of the monastery" [*RSB,* c. 58]; (6) to instill the love and striving for virtues, which are mystically represented by the design and color of the habit; and (7) to make the religious, seeing themselves vested with the habit of the Patriarch and Founder, which so many saints of the same order have, as it were, honored and consecrated by their merits and holiness of life, first feel shame at their having remained so distant from their example, and then generously bestir themselves to their imitation (*Disquisitiones monasticae, Lib. V,* tract. 1, disq. 3, p. 457).

908. PETER THE VENERABLE, abbot of Cluny (d. 1158). It seemed to those great fathers that black as the color of the habit was more in keeping with humility, penance, and mourning. Because it behooves the monk to dedicate his whole life to these strivings, they decreed that, as far as possible, the color be associated with their conduct, and the habit with their virtues (*Lib. IV, ep. 17, ad S. Bernardum Claraevallensem, PL* 189:334).

909. ACTS OF THE MARTYRS STS. GALLACTIUS AND EPISTAEMIUS (3th

century). "They who are wearing the black pallium," he said, "are like angels, namely in that they have cut themselves off from the world and from the things of the world; they preserve virginity and have chosen to make their lives like to that of Christ" (Surius, Laurentius, *Historiae seu vitae sanctorum,* 13 v., Augustae Taurinorum: Marietti, 1875–1878, 11 [*Novembr.*]: 298).

910. BENEDICT HAEFTEN. The color black (1) impresses the thought of death on the mind; (2) keeps one aware of that other form of death, which is spiritual, namely, mortification; 3) serves as a symbol of penance and mourning; (4) implants lowliness of mind in the heart; and (5) signifies stability and religious perseverance, for black can never, under any circumstances, be changed into another color (*Disquisitiones monasticae, Lib. V,* tract. 10, disq. 2, p. 545). [Wolter here selects only the chapter headings of a longer mystical explanation.]

911. ST. HILDEGARDE. The capuche is the distinctive sign of the monk, signifying, since he wears it on his head, that he is not to look out upon the world from either one side or the other (*Explanatio RSB, PL* 197:1062).

912. ST. GILBERT OF HOILAND, English Cistercian, abbot of St. Mary's, diocese of Lincoln (d. 1172). The form of his habit was a tunic [cassock] and a pallium [scapular], sewed together instead of held in place with buckles, and having a capuche inseparably attached to the scapular (*Acta Sanctorum Bolland.,* Febr. tom. 1, die 4, p. 576).

913. ST. JEROME. The leathern girdle which St. John the Baptist (Matt. 3:4) and Elias wore about their loins, is a symbol of mortification (*In Evang. Matt., Lib. I,* 3:4, *PL* 26:29).

914. ST. DOROTHEUS, monk of Palestine (6th century). We wear a leathern belt about our loins. This is a symbol that we are also girded for work, so that we are ready at a moment's notice. For he who is setting out to work first girds himself, and then goes forth, as it is stated: *Gird your loins* (Ex. 12:11). It is also a symbol of a mortified body, for we must mortify our desires. As a belt is made from the skin of a dead animal's body, we too are to deaden all the desires and delights of the flesh (*Doctrina I,* § 13, *PG* 88:1633).

915. COELFRID, abbot of Jarrow, England (d. 719). Similarly monks who have taken vows or those who are in holy orders should bind themselves to stricter discipline for our Lord's sake. They should wear the tonsure in the form of the crown of thorns borne by Christ in his passion, so that Christ may bear the thorns and briars of our sins and take them away from us, wearing them on his own head. In this way they will openly proclaim themselves willing and ready to suffer ridicule and disgrace for his sake, always live in the hope of receiving the crown of everlasting life which God has promised to those who love him (cf. Apoc. 2:10), and demonstrate that in order to win this crown they re-

gard both adversity and prosperity of equal significance (*Ep. in Bedae Ven., Historia Ecclesiastica, Lib. V,* c. 21, *PL* 95:278).

Banishment of desire to possess

916. ST. PETER DAMIAN. Why do we, who are known as men who have abandoned the world, who glory in having escaped the shipwreck of the flood of this world, allow ourselves to be drawn into it again, as though we had been swallowed under by a violent whirlpool? Why do we, going backward and giving way to evil desire, grow enthusiastic and desirous again for the things which we spurned out of love of God? Why have we no shame in seeking with the importunity of an unworthy ambition those things which neither the laws of the earth nor the authority of the divine law had forbidden us to possess? Certainly we gave up what we had in order that the things already lawfully possessed should be ours no longer and that the things that belonged to us should be given over to another's ownership. What could have induced us to engage in so dangerous a struggle, so that it was now necessary for us to do battle against the decrees of all human and divine laws, whose tranquillity we formerly enjoyed? (*Opusc. 12, de contemptu saeculi,* c. 2, *PL* 145:253.)

917. ST. BERNARD. What folly, or rather, what madness for us, who have left so much, to cling to so little at so great a cost! If we have scorned the world, renounced the affection of our parents, shut ourselves up in monastic prisons, and chosen not to do our own will but to submit ourselves to other men, how very careful should we be not to lose the fruit of all this through folly (*Ep. 385, ad monachos eccl. S. Bertini,* n. 4, *PL* 182:589; James, p. 492).

918. VEN. LOUIS DE BLOIS. You have bound yourself to the observance of poverty, have you not? Then be poor. Poor—in what sense poor? Be poor as to the desire for wealth; but more than that, be poor with regard to the desires of the mind, *poor in spirit* (Matt. 5:3). . . . Whatever is not God, let it not abide in your heart by cleaving to it or inordinately loving it (*Speculum monachorum,* div. 8, *Op. Om.* 3:670).

919. ST. JOHN CHRYSOSTOM. No one is so rich as the man who chooses poverty of his own accord and with generosity of spirit. How is that so? I will tell you, and if you please, I will prove that he who chooses poverty of his own accord is richer than even the king himself. For the king indeed needs many things, and is in constant anxiety, and fears lest the supplies for the army should fail him; but the other has enough of everything, and fears about nothing, or if he fears at all, it is not about such great matters (*In Hebr., Hom. 18,* § 3, *PG* 63:138).

920. ST. AUGUSTINE. Such then is the common life of the brethren who live in a monastery: great and holy men live therein, with daily hymns, prayers, praises of God; their occupation is reading; they labor

with their hands, and by this means support themselves; they seek nothing covetously, but use with contentment and charity whatever is brought in for them by pious brethren; no one claims as his own what another has not; all love, all forbear one another mutually (*Enarr. in Ps. 99,* § 12, *PL* 37:1278).

921. ST. PETER DAMIAN. The monk's poverty is security of soul, and security is the mother of purity (*Opusc. 12, de contemptu saeculi,* c. 25, *PL* 145:278).

922. GILBERT, abbot of St. Mary, Hoiland. Monks are not concerned about the morrow, nor for that matter even for today, but *cast all their care upon the Lord* (cf. Ps. 54:23) who rules over them. They are seeking no present reward, but only the kingdom of God (*Serm. 23 in Cant. Salomonis,* § 2, *PL* 184:121).

Poverty, the mother of virtues

923. ST. JOHN CHRYSOSTOM. Let us ever follow after poverty, for it is a great good. But, you say, it makes one humble and of little account. That is true, of course, but we have need of such humiliation, for it benefits us much. *Poverty,* it is said, *humbles a man* (Prov. 10:4, LXX, Douay version). And again, Christ says: *Blessed are the poor in spirit* (Matt. 5:3). Do you grieve because you are upon a path that leads to virtue? Do you not know that this gives us great confidence? But, one says, *the wisdom of the poor man is despised* (Eccles. 9:16, Douay version). And again, another says: *Give me neither poverty nor riches, provide me only with the food I need* (Prov. 30:8), and *Deliver me from the furnace of poverty* (Isa. 48:10, Douay version).

Then, too, if riches and poverty are from the Lord, how can either poverty or riches be an evil? Why then were these things said? They were all said under the Old Testament, where there was great contempt of poverty, where poverty was looked upon as a curse and riches a blessing. But now this is no longer the case. But if you want to hear the praises of poverty: Christ sought after it, and said: *The Son of Man has nowhere to lay his head* (Matt. 8:20). And again he said to his disciples *Do not keep gold or silver . . . nor two tunics* (Matt. 10:9). And Paul said in his epistle: *As having nothing, yet possessing all things* (II Cor. 6:10). And Peter spoke to him who was lame from birth: *Silver and gold I have none* (Acts 3:6). Even under the Old Testament, where wealth was held in esteem, who were the admired? Was not Elias, who had nothing save his mantle? Was it not Elisaeus? Was it not John?

Let no man then be humiliated on account of his poverty. It is not poverty which humiliates, but wealth, which compels us to have need of many, and forces us to be under obligation to those many. . . . The rich man is a slave, being subject to loss, and in the power of every one wishing to do him harm. . . .

The poor man is strong and possesses nothing from whose attachment he may suffer loss or be treated in an evil way; but the rich man is assailable on every side. In the same way that one would easily catch a man who was dragging many long ropes after him, whereas one could not readily lay hold of a naked man, so it is true in the case of the rich man: slaves, gold, lands, countless preoccupations, innumerable cares, difficult circumstances, and necessities make him an easy prey to all.

Let no man, henceforth, then esteem poverty a cause for disgrace. For if he possesses virtue, all the wealth in the world, which is either clay or straw, has no comparison with it. Let us follow after poverty, if we seek to enter into the kingdom of heaven. For Christ says: *Sell what thou hast, and give to the poor, and thou shalt have treasure in heaven;* and again, *With difficulty will a rich man enter the kingdom of heaven* (Matt. 19:21, 23). Do you not see that even if we do not have poverty, we ought to draw it to us? That is how great a good poverty is. For it guides us by the hand, as it were, on the path which leads to heaven, it is an anointing for the combat, an exercise great and admirable, a tranquil haven. . . .

Let no man then accuse poverty of being the cause of innumerable evils, nor let him contradict Christ who declared it to be the perfection of virtue, saying: *If thou wilt be perfect* . . . (Matt. 19:21). This he proclaimed in his own teaching, demonstrated by his personal example, and taught through his disciples. Let us therefore follow after poverty. It is the greatest good to be sober-minded. . . . For they who are voluntarily poor have all good things . . . and what is greater than all else, they have confidence in God (*In Hebr., Hom. 18,* §§ 2–3, *PG* 63:136).

"Mine" and "thine"

924. ST. JOHN CHRYSOSTOM. A. Where "mine" and "thine" are in use, there one finds all kinds of quarrelling, and the very occasion of strife; where there is no use of "mine" and "thine," there peace and concord dwell securely (*In Gen., Hom. 33,* § 3, *PG* 53:309). B. In the monastery there is no use of "mine" and "thine." But this expression which has been the cause of countless wars is banned altogether (*In Matt., Hom. 72,* § 3, *PG* 58:671).

925. ST. BASIL THE GREAT. The Scripture absolutely forbids the words "mine" and "thine" to be uttered among the brethren, saying: *Now the multitude of the believers were of one heart and one soul; and not one of them said that anything he possessed was his own* (Acts 4:32). The parents or brothers of a member of the community, therefore, if they live piously, should be treated by all the brethren as fathers or other relatives possessed in common: *For whoever does the will of my Father in heaven, he is my brother and sister and mother,* says the Lord

(Matt. 12:50; *Reg. fusius tractatae, Interrogatio 32,* § 1, *PG* 31:995; Wagner, p. 295).

926. JOHN CASSIAN. In other monasteries as well, where some indulgence and relaxation is granted, we see that this rule is still most strictly kept, so that no one ventures to say even in word that anything is his own; and it is a serious offense if there drops from the mouth of a monk such an expression as "my book," "my tablets," "my pen," "my coat" or "my shoes." If by accident some such expression escapes his lips through thoughtlessness or ignorance, he must make satisfaction by a proper penance (*De coenob. institut., Lib. IV,* c. 13, *CR* 2:26; *PL* 49:168). Almost all monastic rules have similar provisions.

Poverty must be loved

927. ST. FRUCTUOSUS. The simplicity and sparingness of the food, the hardness of the bed, are to be welcomed. Private ownership, be it in the possession of tools or clothing or anything else, and regardless of how worthless and insignificant the object may be, must be avoided. For it is an abomination and a disgrace for monks to possess anything superfluous, or to serve anything for their own use, or keep it hidden; for such manner of acting does not differ much from the example of Ananias and Sapphira (*Reg. monachorum,* c. 8, *de obedientia et sessione monachi, CR* 1:205; *PL* 87:1104).

928. VEN. LOUIS DE BLOIS. Mindful of the poverty that your God took upon himself for you, and which he commended to you, be content with few things, and find your delight in those that are simple. You are the disciple, he the Master; you the slave, he the Lord. Let the disciple rejoice as he imitates his Master; let the slave exult as he follows his Lord (*Enchiridion parvulorum, documentum 12, Op. Om.* 3:688).

929. ST. BERNARD. What can be stronger than those persons [monks] for whom affliction is reckoned a comfort, ignominy a glory, and indigence abundance? (*Serm. de div., serm. 93,* n. 2, *PL* 183:716.)

930. ST. FERREOLUS, bp. of Usez in ancient Gaul (d. 558). *But having food and sufficient clothing, with these let us be content. But those who seek to become rich fall into temptation and a snare and into many useless and harmful desires, which plunge men into destruction and damnation. For covetousness is the root of all evils, and some in their eagerness to get rich have strayed from the faith and have involved themselves in many troubles. But thou, O man of God, flee these things; but pursue justice, godliness, faith, charity, patience, mildness. Fight the good fight of the faith, lay hold on the life eternal, to which thou hast been called, and hast made the good confession before many witnesses. I charge thee in the sight of God, who gives life to all things, and in the sight of Christ Jesus, who bore witness before Pontius Pilate to the good confession, that thou keep the commandment without*

stain, blameless until the coming of our Lord Jesus Christ (I Tim. 6:8–14). Strive, brethren, that this which is written to one man, namely to Timothy, will be observed by one community (*Reg. ad monachos,* c. 14, *CR* 1:159; *PL* 66:964).

931. ST. BERNARD. A. The title of poverty is a noble one, which God himself is pleased to commend through the mouth of his Prophet when he says: *I am the man that see my poverty* (Lam. 3:1). Poverty is a surer title to nobility than all the treasures of a king. . . . How can I refrain from praising one who has ceased to pursue gold and who now scorns to put his trust in money and treasures? Of such a man Scripture itself says: *Who is he, that we may praise him?* (Sir. 31:9.) . . . And why should he not deserve my praise, whom God has honored with the praises of his name, according to the words, *The poor and needy shall praise my name* (Ps. 73:21, Douay version; *Ep. 23, ad Attonem Trecinsem episc., qui in morbo mortem cogitans omnia sua distribuerat in pauperes,* nn. 1–3, *PL* 182:126; James, p. 57).

B. We learn how he desires to be received by us from the fact that he chose Bethlehem for his birthplace. Perhaps there were then some who thought that a magnificent palace should be made ready in which the King of Glory might be honorably welcomed. But it was not for earthly honor that the Almighty Word lept down from heaven from his royal throne, where *long life is in her* [wisdom's] *right hand, in her left are riches and honor* (Prov. 3:16). He possessed from all eternity an inexhaustible store of all such things in heaven. One treasure, however, he could not find there, namely the treasure of poverty, of which there was on earth an abundance and a superabundance, although man was without recognition of its worth. It was, therefore, for the sake of this poverty that the Son of God came down from on high, in order to choose it for himself and by his appreciation to teach us its value. Adorn then, O Sion, adorn thy bridal couch: but let it be with the ornaments of humility and poverty. These are the swaddling clothes which please him best; these, as Mary bears witness, are the silks wherewith he delights to be clothed (*Serm. de temp., I in vigilia Nativitatis Dni,* § 5, *PL* 183:89).

932. ST. PETER CHRYSOLOGUS. That poverty is akin to the virtues is attested to both by the practices of earth as well as the discipline of heaven itself. The athlete enters the wrestling match unclothed, the swimmer battles the waves in the nude. The soldier in battle array is but lightly clad, ready for action. And he who devotes himself to the pursuit of wisdom (*philosophiam*), must first have spurned all that is material. Poverty, therefore, is linked to the virtues; and if poverty is considered here below the source and companion of the virtues, it is fitting to be prudent with regard to it. For this reason the Lord chose poor men for the duty of the virtues. Peter, Andrew, James and John,

one in brotherhood, but doubly united in their poverty, are chosen leaders among the apostles. . . . They were poor in material goods, but rich in innocence of life; humble in their origin, but exalted in holiness; of mean accomplishment in the nobler arts, but wealthy in the merit of life (*Serm. 28, de Matthaei publicani ac divitis vocatione, PL* 52:278).

933. PETER DE BLOIS. In the sight of God the title of poverty is honored and glorious (*Serm. 43, in fest. Omnium Sanct. III, PL* 207: 693).

The hundredfold return

934. ST. LAURENCE JUSTINIAN. A. Poverty makes him who embraces it rich in spiritual gifts. "He who has abandoned carnal and earthly goods out of love for our Savior will receive spiritual possessions, which as far as merit is concerned, excel all other possessions a hundred to one by any standard of comparison" (S. Hieronymus, *in Matt., Lib. III,* c. 19, vers. 29, *PL* 26:139). But a holy man does not give up earthly goods in order to possess more abundantly in this world: by the hundredfold which is held out in promise by the Lord to the poor who abandon all things, perfection is meant (*Lignum vitae,* tract. 10, *de paupertate,* c. 2, *Op. Om.* 1:69). B. What, then, can be better than poverty? What safer? What more agreeable? Even though all others were to be sad, and everyone to bewail conditions, and the whole populace steeped in fear, poverty always remains joyful, always unperturbed, always of the same disposition. It looks forward to the possession of heavenly goods in heaven; it has nothing to lose on earth. It frequently takes flight in spirit to its homeland above, for it knows that its rewarder dwells there. Such is its beauty, such its treasure. This is precisely the character of holy poverty, by which those who desire to cling to God in interior sweetness and heavenly contemplation adorn themselves as with a gem; they choose poverty as the foundation of their spiritual program and the principal aid of their observance (*ibid.,* c. 4, p. 71).

935. ST. AUGUSTINE. We know that Peter was a fisherman; what then could he give up to follow our Lord? Or his brother Andrew, or John, or James, the sons of Zebedee, who were also fishermen: and yet, what did they say? *Behold, we have left all and followed thee* (Matt. 19:27). Our Lord did not say to him, "You have forgotten your poverty; what have you actually given up, that you should receive the whole world"? He, my brethren, who gave up not only what he had, but also what he longed for, gave up much indeed. For what poor man does not swell with the hope of this life? Who does not daily desire to increase what he has? That desire was cut off: it was exceeding all bounds, it received a limit, and yet was nothing given up? Peter did indeed give

up the whole world: and Peter received the whole world in return (*Enarr. in Ps. 103, v. 17, Serm. III,* § 16, *PL* 37:1371).

936. JOHN CASSIAN. He who for the sake of Christ's name disregards the love of a single father or mother or child, and gives himself over to the purest love of all who serve Christ, will receive in a hundredfold measure in brethren and kinsfolk. Instead of but one he will have many fathers and brethren bound to him by a still more fervent and admirable affection [of oneness in Christ]. He who has given up a single house for the love of Christ will also be enriched with an increased possession of lands, for he will then possess countless homes in monasteries as his own, so that to whatever part of the world he may betake himself, he may always do so as to his own house. For how can he fail to receive a hundredfold, and, if it is not wrong to add somewhat to our Lord's words, more than a hundredfold, who gives up the faithless and compulsory service of ten or twenty slaves, and relies on the spontaneous attendance of so many noble and freeborn men? (*Collationes, Coll. 24, Abbatis Abrahae III,* c. 26, *PL* 49:1325.)

937. ST. JOHN CHRYSOSTOM. Why do you not give to him, who will assuredly make return to you and make return in greater abundance? Is it perhaps because it is so long before he will repay? Yet surely he repays even in this life. For he who cannot deceive says: *Seek first the kingdom of God and his justice, and all these things shall be given you besides* (Matt. 6:33). Do you see this extreme munificence? Those goods, he says, have been stored up for you, and are not diminishing; but these here I give now by way of increase and surplus (*In Rom., Hom. 7,* § 8, *PG* 60:451).

938. ST. BERNARD. You will possess not only eternal life in the future, but will also receive the hundredfold in the present, not only in spiritual goods, but in those which are temporal as well, if your heart has not been attached [to material possessions, if you have been truly poor in spirit] (*Ep. 462, ad quosdam noviter conversos,* § 7, *In Append. ad ep. S. Bernardi, PL* 182:666).

939. ST. EUCHERIUS, bp. of Lyons (d. 454). The Lord once fed his people in the desert (cf. Ex. 16:4 f.), and he continues even now to feed them [desert in the sense of monastic life, withdrawal from men]; he fed the former for forty years, the latter, as long as there will be the succession of years (*De laude eremi, ad Hilarium Lirinensem ep.,* § 29, *PL* 50:707).

940. ST. PETER DAMIAN. Because of our very weak faith we force Christ to be tenacious; because want of trust on the part of the pusillanimous makes Christ poor, whereas complete confidence reveals him as wealthy and bountiful in bestowing gifts (*Opusc. 12, de contemptu saeculi,* c. 8, *PL* 145:260).

941. ST. ALBERT THE GREAT, O.P. (d. 1280). There is nothing dearer to God, nothing more pleasing to the angels, nothing more profitable to man than to bring one's life of poverty to a close in obedience (*Paradisus animae, Pars I*, c. 5, *de paupertate, Op. Om.* 37:456).

942. CASSIODORUS. A. Let us consider how glorious is that poverty, how blessed the indigence which, even when it is silent, praises God and extols the might of his power. If a proud man plays the harp, it is as though he were silent; but even when they seem to observe silence, the poor man and the indigent man praise God (*In Ps. 73, vers. 20, PL* 70:534). B. They are the poor of Christ who are chosen to intercede not only for the misfortunes they suffer personally, but also for the evils of the whole world; they endure want in this world, but are rich in God; wanting in vices, but filled with virtue; looked down upon by men, but acceptable in God's sight (*In Ps. 101, titulus Ps.*, col. 705).

943. ST. BASIL THE GREAT. Blessed is he who possesses things considered of great value and shares in those which can never be destroyed or stolen (*Hom. in Ps. 1*, § 3, *PG* 29:215).

944. ST. AUGUSTINE. Let your poverty be not displeasing to you; nothing richer can be found. Do you want to know how wealthy it really is? It buys heaven (*Serm. 99*, § 4, *In Append., PL* 39:1936).

945. ST. LAURENCE JUSTINIAN. Learn, O religious, to possess nothing in this world, in order that by so doing, you may merit to obtain the inheritance of heaven (*Serm. 37, In Dom. de ramis palmarum, Op. Om.* 2:107).

Poverty a daily martyrdom

946. ST. BERNARD. What does it mean that the same reward is promised to the poor and to the martyrs? Are we not hereby instructed to look upon voluntary poverty as in very truth a kind of martyrdom? . . . What indeed can you find more wonderful, what martyrdom can be more cruel than to be famished with hunger in the midst of banquets, to shiver in the cold, half-clad, to suffer the wants of poverty in the midst of wealth which the world offers, which the devil displays, which our own cupidity longs for? . . . In the Beatitudes the kingdom of heaven is promised alike to poverty and to martyrdom, but while it is truly purchased by poverty, it is given immediately to those who suffer death for Christ's sake (*Serm. de temp., Serm. I in fest. Omnium Sanct.*, § 15, *PL* 183:462).

Five kinds of poverty

947. PETER COMESTOR. The excellence of voluntary poverty becomes increasingly evident by comparison with other kinds of need. There are five kinds of poverty: the poverty of misfortune, the poverty of cupidity, the poverty of excessive possession, the poverty of artifice

and voluntary poverty. The first is that of a beggar; the second, that of an avaricious man; the third, that of him who is extravagant; the fourth, that of a whited wall; the fifth, that of the man who is fettered. The first is a scourge, the second poison, the third a winnowing fork, the fourth a parasol, the fifth a building. The first is wretchedness, for it torments; the second is a crime, for it slays; the third, full of wind, for it makes one arrogant; the fourth, deceitful, for it dissembles; the fifth is glorious, for it crowns its possessor (*Serm. 32, in fest. S. Augustini III, ad claustrales, PL* 198:1798).

Present rewards

948. ST. BERNARD. Evangelical poverty is a powerful wing which enables us to fly speedily to the kingdom of heaven. Observe that the other virtues which follow in the Beatitudes obtain only a promise of this kingdom, to be fulfilled at a future time; but in the case of poverty it is not so much promised as actually given. Hence the nature of the blessedness of the poor is expressed in the present, for theirs *is* the kingdom of heaven, whereas the future tense is employed in all the other instances, thus: *Blessed are the meek, for they shall possess the earth. Blessed are they who mourn, for they shall be comforted* (Matt. 5:3–9; *Serm. de temp., In Adventu Dni IV,* § 5, *PL* 183:49).

949. ST. LEO THE GREAT. Christian poverty is always rich, because what it has is more than what it has not. Nor does the poor man fear to labor in this world, for to him it is given to possess all things in the Lord of all things (*Serm. 42, de Quadr. IV,* c. 2, *PL* 54:276).

950. JULIANUS POMERIUS. A. Because no one possesses God save him who is possessed by God, let him first be the possession of God, and God will become his possessor and portion. And who can be more fortunate than he whose Creator becomes his wealth? (*De vita contemplativa, Lib. II,* c. 16, § 2, *PL* 59:460; Suelzer, p. 83.) B. What further does he seek whose Maker becomes his all? Or what suffices him whom he does not suffice? . . . Let him, then, who wishes to possess God, renounce the world so that God may be his blessed possession (*ibid.,* § 3; Suelzer, p. 84).

951. GEOFFREY, abbot of Vendôme, cardinal (d. 1132). No one ever made himself poor for the sake of God without being able to possess God (*Lib. V, ep. 10, Huberto archidiacono, PL* 157:194).

952. THEOFRID, abbot of Echternach (d. 1110). Oh, how excellent is the poverty which, after the death of the body, merits all the riches of heaven and earth (*Lib. II, Flores epitaphii sanctorum,* c. 6, *PL* 157:357).

953. ST. PETER DAMIAN. When we renounced the world we chose God for our possession; and we thereby became his property, in order that in a distinctive sense he might be our portion and we his inheritance (*Opusc. 12, de contemptu saeculi,* c. 4, *PL* 145:254).

954. PETER DE BLOIS. A. *Opening their treasures they offered him gifts of gold, frankincense and myrrh* (Matt. 2:11). Blessed are they who possess treasures from which they can draw forth gifts that are to be offered to the Lord. But have only the wealthy of this world the means to offer to Christ? What about poor people and the ragged disciples of Christ, the sons of Peter (cf. Matt. 19:27), whose statement was: *Silver and gold I have none* (Acts 3:6). But they, *having nothing yet possessing all things* (II Cor. 6:10), who in their destitution have followed Christ who was stripped of his garments, look upon poverty as their unlimited wealth. The Apostle says of them: *I give thanks to my God . . . because in everything you have been enriched in him, in all utterance and in all knowledge; even as the witness to the Christ has been made so firm in you that you lack no grace . . .* (I Cor. 1:4–7). O rich poverty! O honorable destitution which lays up inestimable riches in heaven, on which you can draw incessantly and from which you still have an abundant store to offer back to God! (*Serm. 9, in die Epiph. Dni., PL* 207:587.) B. Do you not actually possess all things if you have him who possesses all? Nothing is wanting to him to whom God is present, nothing is lacking to him for whom Christ is all-sufficient. . . . Are they whose *citizenship is in heaven* (Phil. 3:20) not already sharing in the first fruits of the heavenly kingdom? they who, having spurned earthly possessions, desire nothing at all but Christ, into whose safekeeping they have deposited all their goods? By vow and by desire, they are already in the heavenly kingdom, for *where thy treasure is, there also will thy heart be* (Matt. 6:21; *Serm. 42, in fest. Omnium Sanct. II,* col. 691).

955. ST. GREGORY THE GREAT. What are earthly possessions except clothing for the body? He therefore who sets out for battle against the devil must abandon everything superfluous lest he be overcome (*Lib. II in Evangel., Hom. 32,* § 2, *PL* 76:1233).

956. ST. BERNARD. After he has laid aside his garments the athlete wages the contest more forcefully; the swimmer divests himself in order to cross the river; having cast off his sandals the traveler proceeds on his way without hindrance (*Serm. in Coena Dni,* § 5, *In Append., PL* 184:951).

957. ST. ALBERT THE GREAT. One never has to render an account for anything he has denied himself (*Paradisus animae, Pars I,* c. 7, *de abstinentia, Op. Om.* 37:460).

958. VEN. LOUIS DE BLOIS. As gold naturally goes downward, and the flame of fire rises upward, if all interference is removed, so a mind that is purged and purified of the dross of self-love and seeks only God's will, is naturally elevated to her beginning, which is God, and is more freely united to him (*Speculum monachorum,* div. 8, *Op. Om.* 3:671).

959. ST. GREGORY OF NYSSA. Would you like to know who it is that

is poor in spirit? He who is given the riches of the soul in exchange for material wealth, who is poor for the sake of the spirit. He has shaken off earthly riches like a burden so that he may be lightly lifted up into the air and be borne upwards, as the Apostle says, in the cloud walking on high together with God (cf. I Thess. 4:16; *De Beatitudinibus, Oratio 1, PG* 44:1207; Graef, p. 95).

960. ST. BERNARD. The more detached the voluntary poverty, which consists in freedom from possession and freedom from all desire to possess, the more secure it is. This kind of poverty is the guardian and the mistress of virtues (*Serm. in Coena Dni,* § 3, *In Append., PL* 184:951).

961. JOHN OF TRITHEIM. Never is the monk's conscience safer than when it is completely freed of all attachment to worldly possessions. . . . The monastic way of life is recognized as having been instituted for this purpose: in order that the monks, set apart from worldly preoccupations, could devote themselves without hindrance to the contemplation of things divine (*De vitio proprietatis monachorum,* c. 8, c. 9, *Op. pia et spiritualia,* p. 738).

Humility must be joined with poverty

962. TERTULLIAN (d. circa 245). Surely no one is poor in spirit unless he is humble (*De patientia,* c. 11, *PL* 1:1378).

963. CASSIODORUS. They are God's poor who, after they have abandoned the pride of the world, give themselves up to humility in all things. For if even a man who is poor is proud, he is not a poor man of God, and if a wealthy man loves humility, he is not a wealthy man of the world. The purpose of such men must be attended to, not the names they bear (*In Ps. 71, v. 2, PL* 70:507).

964. ST. JEROME. A. Let your garments be squalid in order to show that your mind is spotless; and your tunic coarse to prove that you despise the world. But do not give way to pride in the matter, lest your dress and your language be found at variance (*Ep. 125, ad Rusticum monachum,* § 7, *PL* 22:1075). B. Practice humility, but not that which is shown or simulated by gestures of the body, . . . but that which is an expression of the love of the heart. For it is one thing to possess virtue, and something altogether different to have merely the semblance of virtue; one thing to pursue the shadow of things, quite another, the truth. It is always more hideous for pride to lurk under the pretense of humility (*Ep. 148, ad Celantiam matronam, de ratione pie vivendi,* § 20, col. 1214).

965. ST. AMBROSE. He who is content with poverty is not content if he suffers insult. And he who can bear the punishment of the lash is upset by the word of contumely. He that can despise the humiliation of being governed by other men is made sorrowful when another is

preferred to him in honor. It is a great thing for men to preserve the balance of humility (*Expos. in Ps. 118, Sermo 14,* § 20, *PL* 15:1472).

966. ST. BERNARD. If thus, I say, we despise other men and our betters with pharisaical arrogance, of what avail are the poverty of our dress, the coarseness and scantiness of our food, our hard and uninterrupted labor, our constant fastings and watchings, in a word, all the austerities of our life? Do we suffer all this in order to be seen and admired by men? Then we shall deserve that Christ should say of us: *They have received their reward* (Matt. 6:5). Surely *if with this life only in view we have had hope in Christ, we are of all men the most to be pitied* (I Cor. 15:19). But what hope can we have in him beyond the present life, if in his service we seek after temporal glory? Alas for us, who endure so much labor and pain in order to appear different from other men, only to merit thereby a more awful damnation! (*Apologia, ad Guglielmum, S. Theodorici abbatem,* c. 1, nn. 1–2, *PL* 182:899; Luddy, p. 99.)

967. ST. ANTHONY OF PADUA. Blessed is that poor man who takes humility to himself as his bride (*Serm. Dom. infra Oct. Nativitatis Dni. S. Francisci Assisiatis necnon S. Antonii . . . opera, Pars II,* p. 12).

Nature of humility

968. ST. THOMAS AQUINAS. A. Humility has essentially to do with the appetite, insofar as man restrains the impetuosity of his soul from tending inordinately to great things; yet its rule is in the cognitive faculty, in that we should not deem ourselves to be above what we are. Also, the principle and origin of both these things is in the reverence we bear to God. Now the inward disposition of humility leads to certain outward signs in words, deeds and gestures, which manifest that which is within, as happens also with other virtues (*II-II,* q. 161, art. 6, *Utrum convenienter distinguantur duodecim gradus humilitatis qui in Reg. S. Benedicti ponuntur, Op. Om.* 10:307; Am. ed. 2:1853). B. Humility considered as a special virtue regards chiefly the subjection of man to God, for whose sake he humbles himself by subjecting himself to others (*ibid.,* art. 1 ad 5, p. 293; *ibid.,* p. 1848). C. If we set what our neighbor has of God's above that which we have of our own, we cannot incur falsehood (*ibid.,* art. 3 ad 2, p. 298; *ibid.,* p. 1850). D. It is possible, without falsehood, to deem and avow oneself the most despicable of men as regards the hidden faults which we acknowledge to ourselves, and the hidden gifts of God which others have (*ibid.,* art. 6 ad 1, p. 308; *ibid.,* p. 1853).

969. ST. AUGUSTINE. A. Mark what I say: God, man, beasts: above you, you have God; beneath you, the beasts. Acknowledge him who is above you, that those may acknowledge you who are beneath you. Thus because Daniel acknowledged God above him, the lions acknowl-

edged him above them (Dan. 6:22; *In Ep. Joan. ad Parthos,* tract. 8, § 7, *PL* 35:2039). B. More praiseworthy is that mind which knows its own shortcomings than that which, oblivious of the same, studies the cities of the world, the paths of the stars, the depths of the earth, and the positions of the heavens (*De Trinitate, Lib. IV, Prooem.,* § 1, *PL* 42:885).

970. ST. LAURENCE JUSTINIAN. Humility is the certain knowledge of oneself learned in the infused light of truth (*De compunctione et complanctu Christianae perfectionis, Pars II, Op. Om.* 1:19).

971. HUGH OF ST. VICTOR, canon regular of monastery of St. Victor, Paris (d. 1142). A. Humility is contempt of the world and abasement of self (*De anima, Lib. IV,* c. 16, *In Append., PL* 177:189). B. The principal companions of humility are prudence, justice, fortitude, temperance, faith, hope and charity (*De fructibus carnis et spiritus,* c. 11, *PL* 176:1002).

Humility is virtue's foundation, protection, center

972. HUGH OF ST. CHER. A. True humility is the sense of one's own emptiness (*Sup. Ps. 130, 2, Comm.* 2:332). B. Humility is the recognition of one's unworthiness (*Sup. Prov. 16, 1, Comm.* 3:35). C. He gathers fruit who, although he is advancing in virtue, preserves humility in all that he does (*Sup. Levit. 19, 23, Comm.* 1:119). D. Humility is nourished with reproaches, patience under the lash, meekness under unjust severity (*Sup. Ezech. 22, 26, Comm.* 5:83). E. Humility is the foundation of the spiritual edifice; it is a kind of center of all virtues. In fact, humility as a virtue is a kind of circle whose center may be placed at any point, and whose circumference can never be defined. For wherever one may exercise humility, the heart remains always cast down, and is never elated (*Sup. Luc. 9, 48, Comm.* 6:190).

973. JOHN GERSON. Humility derives from true knowledge of God and true knowledge of self, and is the contempt of self (*Definitiones vocum ad theol. moral. pertinentium, Op. Om.* 3:118).

974. RICHARD OF ST. VICTOR (d. 1173). He is humble indeed who truly despises himself in the depth of his heart; but he is more humble who does not refuse to be despised even by others; but most humble of all is he who not only considers it of no consequence when he is held in contempt, but even eagerly desires to be so considered by others (*De eruditione interioris hominis, Lib. II,* c. 32, *PL* 196:1330).

975. ST. JOHN CHRYSOSTOM. A. He alone can be humble-minded who has persuaded himself that he has done no great thing, however many things he may have done well (*In Philemon., Hom. 2,* § 3, *PG* 62:712). B. Simplicity is the high road to true wisdom (*In Act. Ap., Hom. 7,* § 3, *PG* 60:67). C. This very thing took place in the instance of the pharisee. For even after he had arrived at the very summit, he

went back to his home having lost everything (cf. Luke 18:14), because he did not have the mother of virtues; for as pride is the source of all wickedness, so is humility the beginning of all wisdom. Wherefore also [Christ] begins at this point, pulling up all boasting by the very root from out of the soul of his hearers (*In Matt., Hom. 15*, § 2, *PG* 57:225). D. Let us everywhere observe moderation and lay humility as the foundation and support of our good works, so that we can securely build what pertains to virtue. For that is truly a virtue which has humility joined to it. He who has safely laid this foundation can go as high as he desires in building his structure (*In Gen., Hom. 35*, § 7, *PG* 53:330).

976. ST. BERNARD. A. I would draw your attention to the fact that in these words, *Learn from me, for I am meek and humble of heart* (Matt. 11:29), there are two kinds of humility, the one appertaining to knowledge [understanding], the other belonging to the affections [the will]. It is this latter which Christ calls humility of the heart. By the former we know that we are nothing; this humility we learn of ourselves and from our own infirmity. Humility of the will, or of the heart, enables us to trample under foot the glory of the world; but this can only be learned from him who *emptied himself, taking the nature of a slave* (Phil. 2:7), who fled when they sought to make him king, but who freely offered himself when they wished to make him suffer all kinds of ignominy and the shameful death of the cross (*Serm. de temp., In Adv. Dni. IV*, § 4, *PL* 183:48). B. For certainly the spiritual edifice cannot stand except on the firm foundation of humility (*Serm. 36 in Cant.*, § 5, col. 969; Eales, p. 237). C. Abase yourself that you may arise; accept humiliations in order that you may be raised up (*Lib. de modo bene vivendi, ad sororem*, c. 39, § 100, *In Append., PL* 184:1260). D. For when, on the occasion of the performance of any good, pride is wont to intensify itself in its assertions, humility alone, as a bulwark and a tower of defense for the virtues, courageously resists its malice and goes forth to combat its presumption (*Tract. de moribus et officio episcoporum, Ep. 42, ad Henricum archiepisc. Senonensem*, c. 5, *de humilitate omnibus quidem, sed praelatis imprimis necessaria*, § 17, *PL* 182:821). E. Thus humiliation is the way to humility, as patience is to peace, or as reading is to knowledge. If you long for the virtue of humility, you must not flee from the way of humiliation. For if you do not allow yourself to be humiliated, you cannot attain to humility (*Ep. 87, ad Ogerium Canonic. Regularem, in quo S. Bernardus improbat abdicationem curae pastoralis*, § 11, col. 217). F. The man who is truly humble wishes to be held in light esteem, not to be proclaimed and praised as being humble (*Serm. 16 in Cant.*, § 10, *PL* 183:853; Eales, p. 92).

977. HUGO DE FOLIETO. The site of the spiritual edifice is sought in

the lowest part, that is, in humility; the foundation is distributed over the breadth, that is, in charity; the walls are erected in the height of good works; the roof is placed above, under the hope of God's protection; but it is necessary that the building be completed in the length of patience (*De claustro animae, Lib. III,* c. 9, *PL* 176:1107).

978. ST. AUGUSTINE. To him, my dear Dioscorus, I wish you to submit with complete devotion, and to construct no other way for yourself of grasping and holding the truth than the way constructed by him who, as God, saw how faltering were our steps. This way is first humility, second humility, third humility, and however often you should ask me I would say the same, not because there are not other precepts to be explained, but if humility does not precede and accompany and follow every good work we do, and if it is not set before us to look upon, and beside us to lean upon, and behind us to fence us in, pride will wrest from our hand any good deed we do while we are in the very act of taking pleasure in it. It is true that other defects have to be feared in our sins, but pride is to be feared in the very acts of virtue; otherwise those praiseworthy acts will be lost through the desire of praise itself (*Ep. 118, Dioscoro,* § 22, *PL* 33:442; Parsons, p. 282).

Self-contempt

979. ST. GREGORY THE GREAT. It is a usual mark of the elect that they always think more meanly of themselves than they really are. . . . But he who does not as yet despise himself, does not lay hold of the humble wisdom of God. Hence the Lord says in the Gospel: *I praise thee, Father, Lord of heaven and earth, that thou didst hide these things from the wise and prudent, and didst reveal them to the little ones* . . . (Matt. 11:25). But with regard to the proud it often happens that if they ever perform one single good thing, however insignificant it may be, they immediately turn away the thought of their mind from all their faults, and ever look with all their attention at even this least good thing they may have done, and that from this they regard themselves as already holy (*Moral., Lib. 34,* c. 22, nn. 43–44, *PL* 76:742).

980. ARNOLD, abbot of Bonnevaux. This is the first step to be taken in religion, . . . that whoever wishes to live a life that is pleasing to God must think humbly of himself. Humility has always been the foundation of holiness, nor could proud loftiness [Lucifer] remain in heaven (*De cardinalibus operibus Christi,* c. 1, *PL* 189:1619).

981. ST. CYPRIAN. The rich are envied more intensely than the poor; the savage attack of robbers does not perturb the indigent, but the wealthy. More than common soldiers, commanders and leaders are singled out by the enemy to be struck in battle. The higher tree tops are most violently shaken in winds and storms. More and more, too, as each

one excels others he must know that he has to fear that he will be humiliated in some point (*De singularitate clericorum, inter supposititia, PL* 4:946).

982. ST. THOMAS AQUINAS. Humility holds the first place, inasmuch as it expels pride, which God resists, and makes man submissive and ever open to receive the influx of divine grace. Hence it is written: *God resists the proud but gives grace to the humble* (Jas. 4:6). In this sense humility is said to be the foundation of the spiritual edifice (*II-II,* q. 161, *Utrum humilitas sit potissima virtutum,* ad 2, *Op. Om.* 10:300; Am. ed. 2:1852).

983. ST. BERNARD. A. Now humility is the true and firm foundation of all virtues, and the result of its shaking would be the ruin of the whole spiritual edifice (*De consideratione, Lib. V,* c. 14, n. 32, *PL* 182:806). B. A most valuable estate is humility, for every spiritual edifice constructed in it grows up into a holy temple of the Lord (*ibid., Lib. II,* c. 6, n. 13, col. 750).

The purpose of humility

984. ST. GREGORY THE GREAT. The discovered treasure is hidden in the hope of its being preserved, for he is not capable of guarding the effort of his longing for heaven from the wicked spirits who does not conceal that effort from the praises of men. We are, as it were, in the present life, on a highway by which we are traveling toward our fatherland. Now the spirits of evil block our way as though they were highway robbers. He who carries his treasure openly on the highway is inviting being plundered. Our works should be performed in public in such a way that our intention remains hidden, in order that we may give our neighbors the benefit of good example by our virtuous deeds, and at the same time by our intention, in which we seek to please God alone, we always strive for secrecy (*In Evangel., Lib. I, Hom. 11,* § 1, *PL* 76:1115).

985. ST. BERNARD. A. No virtue is more indispensable for us all at the beginning of our conversion than humble simplicity (*Serm. de temp., Serm. II in Epiph. Dni,* § 8, *PL* 183:152). B. In truth I have learned by my own experience that there is nothing so efficacious in deserving grace, in preserving it, or in recovering it if lost, as to be found at all times not high-minded before God, but filled with holy fear. *Happy the man who is always on his guard* (Prov. 28:14; *Serm. 54 in Cant.,* § 9, col. 1142; Eales, p. 330).

986. JOHN CASSIAN. Humility is, therefore, the mistress of all virtues, the surest foundation of the heavenly building, the proper and magnificent gift of the Savior (*Collatio 15, Abbatis Nesterotis II, de charismatibus divinis,* c. 7, *PL* 49:1005).

987. MICHAEL OF MEAUX, abp. of Sens (d. 1199). Humility is called the first virtue, or the virtue of pre-eminence over all others, in that it

is the beginning and is the first acquired of all the virtues (*Expos. in Ps. 110, in Op. Om. Bonaventurae,* ed. Peltier 9:313).

988. JOHN CASSIAN. For no structure, so to speak, of virtue can possibly be raised in our soul unless first the foundations of true humility are carefully laid in our heart that they will be able to carry the weight of perfection and love (*De coenob. institut., Lib. 12,* c. 32, *PL* 49:474).

The pre-eminence of humility

989. ST. JOHN CLIMACUS. A. The sorrowful humility of penitents is one thing; the condemnation of the conscience of those who are still living in sin is another; and the blessed wealth of humility which the perfect attain by the action of God is yet another. Let us not be in a hurry to find words to describe this third kind of humility, for our effort will be in vain. But a sign of the second is the perfect bearing of indignity. Previous habit often tyrannizes even over him who deplores it (*Scala paradisi, Grad. 5, de accurata et sincera poenitentia, PG* 88:779; Moore, n. 29, p. 107; Father Robert, p. 127). B. Humility is the divine shelter to prevent us from seeing our achievements. Humility is an abyss of self-abasement, inaccessible to any thief. Humility is a strong tower against the face of the enemy (Ps. 60:4; *ibid., Grad. 25, de humilitate,* col. 994; Moore, n. 26, p. 195; Father Robert, p. 317). C. Humility is a heavenly siphon which from the abyss of sins can raise the soul to heaven (*ibid.,* col. 1003; Moore, p. 200; Father Robert, p. 329). D. The man of humble mind always loathes his own will as wayward, and in his requests to the Lord he studies with unwavering faith to learn and to obey. He does not direct his attention to the life of his masters but casts his care upon God who used an ass to teach Balaam his duty. A worker of this kind, although he does everything and thinks and speaks according to the will of God, yet he never trusts himself. Self-confidence for the humble is just as much a weight and a burden as another man's choice is for the proud (*ibid.,* col. 999; Moore, p. 198). E. All the contrary vices are born of parents contrary to these [lust, vainglory, pride, lack of fear of God, conceit, anger, self-satisfaction, wilfulness]. But without enlarging on the subject (for I should not have the time if I were to inquire into them all one by one), I will merely say that for all the passions mentioned above, the remedy is humility. Those who have obtained that virtue have won the whole fight (*ibid., Grad. 26, de discretione,* col. 1023; *Moore,* n. 49, p. 209; Father Robert, p. 346).

990. ST. ISIDORE OF PELUSIUM, priest and abbot of monastery situated near that town at the Eastern mouth of the Nile (d. circa 449). Give evidence of your humility by your attitude and spirit of love rather than in speech (*Lib. I, ep. 342, PG* 78:378).

991. ST. ANTHONY OF PADUA. A. The humble man considers himself

a slave, calls himself a slave, and casts himself at the feet of all, abases himself, and thinks more lowly of himself than he really is (*Serm. II Dom. III. Quadr. S. Francisci Assisiatis necnon S. Antonii Op., Pars II,* p. 153). B. If humility is destroyed, the whole structure of the other virtues collapses as well (*Serm. II Dom. III p. Pascha,* p. 201).

992. ST. GREGORY THE GREAT. Humility is the guardian of virtue. . . . He who is striving for virtues without humility is carrying dust in the face of the wind, and when he seems to derive some advantage by carrying something away from his efforts, is all the more blinded (*In Evangel. Lib. I, Hom. 7,* § 4, *PL* 76:1102).

993. ST. DOROTHEUS, monk of Palestine (7th century). A. The daughters of humility are: perpetual self-accusation, hatred of one's will, abomination of one's judgment and opinion (*Doctrina I,* § 9, *PG* 88:1627). B. Everyone knows that it would be just as impossible for the soul to be saved without humility as for a ship to be built without helm or rudder. Whatever good one sets about to do, let him perform it humbly, so that what has been done may be preserved by humility (*Doctr. 14,* § 2, col. 1775).

Lowly tasks and humility

994. ST. ALBERT THE GREAT. The truly humble man always fears lest any praise be shown to him; when it is offered to him, he is deeply and fearfully saddened. . . . Frequent undertaking of lowly tasks leads to true humility . . . but he who refuses menial works will never attain the virtue of humility (*Paradisus animae, Pars I,* c. 2, *de humilitate, Op. Om.* 37:451).

Humility is medicine and protection

995. JOHN OF TRITHEIM. A. Humility is the most salutary medicine for souls: it takes counsel with regard to all spiritual problems, reduces the swelling of the wounded spirit, strengthens weaknesses, corrects tendencies to depravity, and removes all unhealthy and diseased growths (*Hom. 19, de vera humilitate monachorum, Op. pia et spiritualia,* p. 496). B. Without true humility, no one can attain salvation (*ibid.,* p. 495). C. Suffice it to recall for the moment the holy Rule [*RSB*] according to whose text all of you freely vowed long ago, in order to appreciate that humility is not less necessary for your salvation than the very love of God and neighbor. Humility is said to be the greatest virtue of the monk, and as such is so necessary for his profession that without it he cannot be saved. A monk who is exalted in spirit and proud is the property of the devil, not of Christ, and will have no part with the Son of God in heaven, but will be tormented with the demons forever in hell. For Christ, the Master and teacher of humility, detests

all proud men and admits into his presence only persons who are humble, meek and gentle (*ibid.,* p. 499). D. True humility performs great things, but thinks of itself in lowliest terms; the more it progresses, the more deeply it recognizes its own weaknesses (*ibid.,* p. 496). E. Where there is true humility demons cannot abide, for as ice is melted by fire, so evil spirits are dispersed by the presence of humility (*ibid.,* p. 500). F. The solid foundation of all virtues is humility; whatever is built upon that foundation will not be overthrown even by the most violent storms (*Serm. 1, Quod caute sit monachis vivendum, ibid.,* p. 528). G. The devil is conquered by Christlike humility and is put to flight in defeat as though he had been struck with a heavy instrument (*ibid.,* p. 529).

Humility and the measure of holiness

996. LIVES OF THE FATHERS. Abbot Eupraxius used to say: "The tree of life which rises to the heights is humility." . . . A brother asked an old man: "What is the real perfection of the monk?" And the old man replied: "Humility, for when a man has once arrived at humility, he can reach forward to the goal" (*De vitis Patrum, Lib. V, libell. 15, de humilitate,* nn. 49, 77, *PL* 73:962, 966).

997. ST. NILUS, monk (d. 451). A. Once you have ascended to the heights of virtue, you stand in great need of protection; for he who is humble remains close to the earth, walks upon the ground, and does not fall easily or far, and when he does fall, rises quickly; but he who falls from a height, is in danger of death. It is proper that a precious stone be ornamented with gold, and man's humility shines with many virtues (*De octo spiritibus malitiae,* c. 19, *PG* 79:1163). B. Humility lifts man up to heaven and gives him a place among the choirs of angels (*ibid.,* c. 18, col. 1163). C. Rejoice in humility: its serenity is firm and cannot be shaken (*Capita paraenetica,* § 71, col. 1255).

998. ST. AUGUSTINE. A. If you are thinking of raising a high and noble edifice, then devote your first attention to the foundation of humility. When a man wishes to raise a solid structure, and prepares to do so, the larger the building is to be, the deeper he goes for the foundation (*Serm. 69, in Matt. 11, 28,* c. 1, § 2, *PL* 38:441). B. Christ humbled is the Way; Christ the Truth and the Life, Christ highly exalted, and God. If you walk in Christ humbled, you will reach Christ the exalted (*Serm. 142, in Joan., 14, 6,* c. 2, § 2, col. 778). C. Where there is charity, there is peace; and where there is humility, there is always charity (*In Tract. sup. Ep. Joan., Prolog., PL* 35:1977). D. Before all, then, confession; then love; for what is said of charity? *Charity covers a multitude of sins* (I Peter 4:8). Now let us see whether he commends charity with regard to sins which subsequently overtake us: because

charity alone extinguishes sins. Pride extinguishes charity; therefore humility strengthens charity; and charity extinguishes sins (*ibid.,* tract. 1, § 6, col. 1982).

999. ST. ISIDORE OF SEVILLE. A. Let no one consider himself better than others, but judging himself to be inferior to all let him excel by his humility in proportion as he is outstanding in the performance of virtues (*Reg. monachorum,* c. 3, *CR* 1:189; *PL* 83:871). B. Remember that you are dust and ashes (cf. Gen. 3:19), that you are corruption and a worm, and that although you may really be something, unless you humble yourself by as much as you are great, you will lose altogether what you are (*De conflictu vitiorum et virtutum, In Append., VII,* c. 6, col. 1133).

1000. ST. FULGENTIUS. Recognize that the grace of God has grown in you so much the more in proportion as you see humility of heart abound more in you (*Ep. 6, ad Theodorum Senatorem,* c. 9, § 12, *PL* 65:352).

1001. DENIS THE CARTHUSIAN. The whole discipline of Christian wisdom consists not in a profusion of words, nor in keenness of argument, nor in any desire of praise or glory, but in true and voluntary humility (*Enarr. in Phil. 2, 8, Op. Om.* 13:339).

1002. ST. DOROTHEUS. *When you build a new house, put a parapet around the roof; otherwise, if someone falls off, you will bring bloodguilt upon your house* (Deut. 22:8). Humility is that parapet; it crowns and preserves all virtues, and all the perfection of virtue stands in need of humility. The spiritual progress of all the saints is the approach to humility (*Doctrina 14,* § 2, *PG* 88:1775).

1003. ST. JOHN CHRYSOSTOM. A. Humility, [David] says, is a sacrifice that is pleasing and acceptable to God (Ps. 50:19). Since my heart, therefore, has been humbled and, as it were, reduced, I offer it to you as an acceptable victim. I will make an immolation of my mind's submission in place of a victim: only forgive my sin and bestow the Holy Spirit on me. For there is no doubt that this sacrifice, namely humility, is far more excellent than that of the Jews—not only now, but it was true also at that time (*Expos. in Ps. 50, inter spuria, PG* 55:587). B. For [virtue] too has a head and members more comely than any graceful and beautiful body. . . . Humility is its head. . . . Mark its color, how ruddy and blooming, and very attractive; observe its ingredients . . . modesty and blushing. . . . And if you wish to see the eyes also, note how exactly they are delineated by delicacy and temperance. That is why they are also so beautiful and sharpsighted, as to behold even the Lord himself, for *Blessed,* he said, *are the clean of heart, for they shall see God* (Matt. 5:8). . . . And her mouth is wisdom and understanding (*In Matt. Hom. 47,* § 3, *PG* 58:485). C. There can be no humility without greatness of soul, nor has conceit any other cause but littleness of soul (*In Joan., Hom. 70,* § 2, *PG* 59:387). D. There is nothing to equal humility: this is the mother, the root, the nurse, the foundation and bond of all good things; without it we are detestable and unclean (*In Act. Ap., Hom. 30,* § 3, *PG* 60:225). E. Nothing is so powerful as humility, since it is stronger even than rock and harder than adamant, and places us in a safety greater than that of towers and cities and walls, being too high for any of the artillery of the devil (*In Rom. Hom. 20,* § 4, col. 602). F. Nothing makes the Christian so admirable as humility (*In I Cor. Hom. 1,* § 2, *PG* 61:15).

1004. ST. GREGORY THE GREAT. For the less a person sees himself, the less he is displeased with himself; and the more he discerns the light of greater grace, the more blameworthy he acknowledges himself to be (*Moral., Lib. 35,* c. 5, § 6, *PL* 76:753).

1005. ST. BASIL THE GREAT. A. Humility is the treasure purse of all the virtues (*Const. monastic.,* c. 16, *de humilitate, PG* 31:1378). B. My son, above all things cultivate humility, which is more excellent than all virtue, so that you can ascend to the very summit of perfection. For just instructions are not fulfilled except in the spirit of humility, and the labors of many are regarded as valueless because of pride. The humble man is like to God, and in the temple of his breast bears God (*Admonitio ad filium spiritualem,* c. 10, *CR* 1:460; *PL* 103:692).

1006. ST. ANSELM, abp. of Canterbury (d. 1109). A. The first stage in ascending the mountain of humility is knowledge of oneself (*Eadmeri Cantuar. monachi Lib. de S. Anselmi similitudinibus,* c. 101, *PL* 159:665). B. Whoever is trying to reach the summit of humility must pay attention to his neighbor's virtues and not his vices, and to his own personal vices and not his virtues (*ibid.,* c. 111, col. 670). C. Humility is a high mountain, at whose summit there is brilliant light and a group of persons of great goodness, representing the holy virtues (*ibid.,* c. 100, col. 665).

1007. ST. JUSTUS OF URGEL (d. circa 546). The simplicity of spiritual persons is to be held in the highest regard, for they never attempt to gain their own recognition, but by conscious effort at purity seek to be pleasing to God rather than to men (*In Cant. explicatio,* c. 4, § 71, *PL* 67:976).

1008. ST. BONAVENTURE. A. According to the reply given to Antony, only the man who humbles himself evades the insidious temptations of the devil. . . . He who humbles himself more than others is greater than they; the one who humbles himself most is the greatest of all (*In Hexaemeron Collatio I,* § 24, *Op. Om.,* ed. Quaracchi 5:333; second sentence Wolter's paraphrase). B. The humbler we are, the freer we are of the swelling of pride; and the freer we are of the swelling of pride, the more filled we are with true love; and the more love we have, the greater we are (*Comm. in Luc. 9, 48,* § 89, *ibid.* 7:244). C. Humility is the key of knowledge (*ibid.*, 10, 21, § 37, p. 264). D. Without humility there can be no virtue, nor can any degree of perfection be acquired or preserved (*Speculum disciplinae ad novitios, Pars II,* c. 6, § 2, *ibid.* 8:621). E. The most exalted virtue of the religious is humility, for it nourishes him, perfects him, preserves him in the state of virtue (*ibid.*). F. Humility perfectly subjects man to God, makes God man's helper, and through God's aid enables man to contemn the fiery weapons of the enemy (*Serm. V de uno martyre, inter spuria, Op. Om.*, ed. Peltier 14:47).

1009. DAVID OF AUGSBURG. The greater and more natural a humiliation, and the more promptly it is submitted to, the fuller will be the recovery of grace [after man's sinfulness] and the reward of glory. The greatness of a humiliation is measured by the difficulty of the work enjoined; its purity by the simplicity of intention; the promptitude with which it is submitted to by the swiftness of the task's execution (*De profectu religiosorum, Lib. II,* c. 39, *Op. Om. S. Bonaventurae,* ed. Peltier 12:399).

1010. JEAN RIGAUD (Joannes Rigaldi), Franciscan theologian (d. 1323). Humility is a short ladder of devotion, a short-termed school of perfection, a short road to salvation; if you want to go up, the ladder is short; if you wish to learn, the school term is brief; if you desire to enter, the road is short (*Diaeta salutis,* tit. 7, c. 1, *ibid.*, 8:311).

1011. ST. JEROME. A. Hold nothing to be more excellent, nothing more lovable than humility; for it is the principal preserver and, as it were, a kind of guardian of the virtues (*Ep. 148, ad Celantiam matronam de ratione pie vivendi,* § 20, *PL* 22:1213). B. Men are perfect only insofar as they know themselves to be imperfect (*Ep. 133, ad Ctesiphontem, adversus Pelagium,* § 6, col. 1154).

1012. ST. LAURENCE JUSTINIAN. A. The humble man is submissive, knows himself for what he is, judges himself, is prostrate before all others, is faithful to God, and readily yields in service to his brethren (*De compunctione et complanctu Christianae perfectionis,* c. 2, *Op. Om.* 2:190). B. It is fitting that the truly humble person be perfect in every virtue insofar as human frailty permits, and that he so regulate what concerns his soul before God that his external acts will also be able to edify his fellow man (*De humilitate,* c. 14, *Op. Om.* 2:391).

1013. ST. BERNARD. A. It is without doubt a great and rare virtue to have no consciousness of greatness, although performing great actions; and that the sanctity of a man, while it is manifest to all others, should be hidden from himself. To appear admirable to others, and to think humbly of yourself, this I judge to be the most marvelous among the virtues themselves. You are truly a faithful servant if you can suffer nothing to remain with yourself of all the glory of your Lord, when that glory, though it does not come from you, yet passes through you or by your means (*Serm. 13 in Cant., De gloria et laude Deo semper attribuenda pro omnibus ejus bonis nobis impensis,* n. 3, *PL* 183:835; Eales, p. 69). B. Be sure of this, this virtue [humility] is the most splendid jewel that can shine in the pontifical tiara (*De consideratione, Lib. II,* c. 6, n. 13, *PL* 182:750).

1014. VEN. LOUIS DE BLOIS (Blosius). A. He who is truly humble wishes to be thought of as vile and abject, rather than humble and holy. For since he acknowledges himself before God to be an unprofitable, unworthy, and ungrateful sinner, he has no desire to appear anything else in the sight of men. When you are justly reproached, humble yourself; be ready to correct your faults and, commending the rest to God's care, remain at peace (*Canon vitae spiritualis,* c. 8, § 4, *Op. Om.* 1:10). B. In the counsels of his unsearchable wisdom God often allows the stains of these negligences to cling to us, in order that we may be ever more humbled; that utterly distrusting ourselves, we may place our hope in him; and that manfully resisting sin, we may be trained in virtue, and at length be gloriously crowned (*ibid.,* c. 3, § 2, p. 6). C. True humility must be sought in the inmost heart; without this the mere outer appearance of it is nothing but hypocrisy (*Speculum spirituale,* c. 8, § 1, *Op. Om.* 2:568). D. As a rule our Lord is pleased to allow some failing or imperfection to remain even in the souls of the elect who are most dear to him. These defects make them vile in their own eyes and keep them humble. In reality they have true health of soul and have arrived at so high a degree of virtue that they would far rather suffer death itself than knowingly and wilfully sin against God. Nevertheless, unaware of their good spiritual well-being, they are always fearful and anxious, and are convinced that their souls are sickly and weak (*ibid.,* c. 7, § 1, p. 566).

1015. JEAN RIGAUD. Humility is whatever is most precious in value, most delicate in fragrance, most pleasing in dignity. . . . [It] is gracious as a beautiful flower is gracious, radiant as a radiant star, flawless after the manner of a precious stone (*Diaeta salutis,* tit. 7, c. 1, *Op. Om. S. Bonaventurae,* ed. Peltier 8:312, 314).

1016. ST. GREGORY THE GREAT. A. There is nothing more happy than simplicity of heart, in that in proportion as it presents itself in innocence in its relations to others, there is nothing it dreads to meet with from others. For it has its simplicity as a kind of citadel of strength (*Moral., Lib. 12,* c. 39, § 44, *PL* 75:1007). B. Simplicity of conduct is an assurance of great security (*Reg. Pastoralis, Pars III,* c. 11, *PL* 77:65; Davis, p. 119). C. True simplicity of heart is like a day which deceit does not cloud over, which lying and jealousy do not darken, envy does not confuse, but which the sun of truth makes bright (*In Sept. Ps. Poenit. expos., Pars V. Ps. 101,* § 4, *PL* 79:605). D. Wherefore, dearest brother, love humility with all your heart, through which the concord of all the brethren and the unity of the holy universal Church may be preserved (*Lib. V, ep. 18, ad Joan. episc. Constantinopolit., PL* 77:739). E. Purity of heart and simplicity, Peter, have great force with almighty God, who is most singular in purity and most simple in nature (*Dialogorum Lib. III,* c. 15, *de Eutychio et Florentio servis Dei,* col. 256).

Humble persons pleasing to God and men

1017. ST. JOHN CHRYSOSTOM. A. What can be more joyful than the lot of the humble; what more blessed? for although they are most pleasing in God's sight, they are wont to enjoy great glory among men as well; all revere them as though they were fathers, embrace them as brothers, admit them as though they were their own members (*In Matt. Hom. 65,* § 6, *PG* 58:625). B. It is true modesty to give way to those who seem beneath us, and show respect to those who seem less honorable. In fact, if we judge correctly, we admit that none are inferior to us, and acknowledge that we are excelled by all men. And I say this not of those of us who are immersed in countless sins, but also of him who is conscious of having performed many good deeds. Unless he thinks of himself as the least of all, there is no advantage to be derived from all his goods and deeds (*In Gen., Hom. 33,* § 5, *PG* 53:312).

1018. POPE ST. LEO THE GREAT. A. There is great happiness in true humility for which God is love, God is wisdom, God is counsel, God is fortitude (*Ep. ad Demetriadem, seu de humilitate tract.,* c. 24, *In Append., PL* 55:179). B. It is a great strengthening of the spirit of love when, according to the teaching of the Apostle, men endeavor to *anticipate one another in honor* (Rom. 12:10), and love to serve mutually, each considering the other his superior, with no puffing up by those so honored (*ibid.,* c. 3, col. 163).

1019. ST. ANTHONY OF PADUA. As a magnet draws iron to itself, so humility attracts grace and heavenly encouragement (*Summa, Pars III,* tit. 6, c. 10, § 5).

1020. PETER DE BLOIS. Nothing stands before the Divine Majesty more intimately, with greater confidence, or more agreeably than genuine humility (*Ep. 134, ad Willelmum electum S. Mariae, PL* 207:399).

Humility is always joined with charity

1021. ST. FRANCIS DE SALES, bp. of Geneva, Doctor of the Church (d. 1622). In this respect (humility) resembles a certain tree in the islands of Tylos. At night this tree closes up its beautiful carnation flowers, and only opens them to the rising sun. Hence the inhabitants of the country say that these flowers sleep at night. In this way, too, humility covers over and hides all our virtues and human perfections and never displays them except for the sake of charity. Now charity, since it is not a human, but a heavenly, and not a moral, but a theological virtue, is the true sun of all other virtues, over which she ought always to have dominion. Hence we may conclude that those acts of humility which are prejudicial to charity are assuredly false (*Introduction à la vie devote, IIIme partie,* c. 5, *de l'humilité plus interieure, Oeuvres de S. François de Sales,* 21 v.; Annecy: Niérat, 1892–1923, 3:149).

1022. ST. ISIDORE OF SEVILLE. A. Be small in your own eyes in order to be great in the sight of God. You will be all the more precious before God the more you are despised in your own estimation (*Synonym. Lib. II,* § 23, *PL* 83:850). B. The conscience of the servant of God must ever be humble and given to mourning, in order that by humility he will be kept from growing proud, and by the fruitful spirit of sorrow his heart will not fall into licentiousness (*Sentent. Lib. III,* c. 19, § 3, col. 694).

1023. IMITATION OF CHRIST (Thomas à Kempis). The more humble a man is in himself, and the more obedient he is to God, the more wise and peaceful will he be in everything he will have to do (*De imitatione Christi, Lib. I,* c. 4, *Op. Om.* 2:12; Gardiner, p. 37).

Humility is modest and gracious

1024. THOMAS À KEMPIS. The truly humble person is a stranger to vanity, rejects all praise, rejoices in being held in contempt, and readily forgives injuries (*Hortulus rosarum,* c. 9, n. 4, *Op. Om.* 4:19).

1025. VALERIAN, bp. of Cémèle (5th century). Humility is always pleasing and obliging, kind in friendship, indifferent to insults and affronts. It is neither puffed up in success nor depressed by adversity. . . . Its kindness makes it first to extend a greeting, the last to be seated. . . . It does not vaingloriously yearn to be recognized; it seeks not the ready word of praise, nor awaits flattery. . . . Humility is hedged about with goodness. Just as it is incapable of inflicting injuries, so it seeks no reprisals for insults (*Hom. 14, de bono humilitatis,* n. 6, *PL* 52:737).

Humility and meekness

1025.[a] HUGO DE FOLIETO. A. *Learn from me, for I am meek and humble of heart; and you will find rest for your souls* (Matt. 11:29). Here you have the honey of humility with the sweetness of meekness. As honey combines with all kinds of herbs in the compounding of medicines, so all virtues are seasoned with the sweetness of humility (*De claustro animae, Lib. III,* c. 8, *PL* 176:1100). B. When we see those who were wealthy in the world become poor in the monastery, members of the nobility take their place among the lowly and serve as humble men, the powerful subject, the learned despised for their appearance and their habit, are not such men placed by the example of their goodness in the spiritual temple? They are transferred from the mount of pride to the mount of righteousness; from the forest of worldly confusion to virtuousness of life in the dwelling of holiness (*ibid.*, c. 11, col. 1113).

Humility is joyful

1026. ST. ATHANASIUS, bp. of Alexandria (d. 373). And so for twenty years Antony continued exercising himself in solitude, shut away from the sight of men. After this, when many eagerly wished to imitate his discipline, and others, his acquaintances, came and began to pound and wrench off the door by force, Antony, as from a shrine, came forth initiated in the mysteries and filled with the Spirit of God. . . . When they saw him, they wondered at the sight, for he had the same habit of body as before, and was neither fat like a man without exercise, nor lean from fasting and striving with the demons, but he was just as they had known him before his retirement from the world. . . . And again, his soul was free from blemish, for it was neither contracted as if by grief, nor relaxed by pleasure, nor possessed by laughter or dejection, for he was not troubled when he beheld the crowd, nor overjoyed at being saluted by so many. But he was altogether even as being guided by reason, and abiding in a natural state. Through him the Lord healed the bodily ailments of many present, and cleansed others from the evil spirits. And he gave grace to Antony in speaking, so that he consoled many that were sorrowful, harmonized the differences of those at variance, and exhorted all to prefer the love of Christ before all that is in the world. And while he exhorted and advised them to remember the good things to come, and the loving-kindness of God toward us, *who has not spared his own Son but has delivered him for us all* (Rom. 8:32), he persuaded many to embrace the solitary life. His appeal moved the hearts of many who heard him to despise the goods on which so great a value is placed by men, and to become the pioneers of those who people the desert (*Vita Beati Antonii abbatis, auctore S. Athanasio . . . interprete Evagrio*, c. 13, *PL* 73:134).

1027. LIVES OF THE FATHERS. And we observed their joy in the desert, with which nothing on earth, and no bodily delight, can be compared. For there was among them no man that was sorrowful or afflicted with grief, and if any man was found in affliction, our father Apollo knew the cause thereof, and was able to make known to him the secret thoughts of his mind. And he would say to such a one: "It is not seemly for us to be afflicted at our redemption, for we are those who are about to inherit the kingdom of heaven; let the Jews weep, and let men of iniquity be in mourning, but let the righteous rejoice . . ." (*De vitis Patrum, Lib. VIII*, c. 52, *Vita Abbatis Apollo, PL* 73:1161; Budge, *Stories of the Holy Fathers*, p. 460).

1028. JOHN CASSIAN. That sorrow which produces a steadfast spirit of repentance that leads to salvation is obedient, courteous, kindly, humble, gentle and patient, as it springs from the love of God . . . and somehow or other rejoicing and feeding on hope of its own profit preserves all the gentleness of courtesy and patience, as it has in itself all the fruits of the Holy Spirit of which the Apostle gives the list: *But the fruit of the Spirit is: charity, joy, peace, patience, kindness, goodness, faith, modesty, continency* (Gal. 5:22). But the other kind is rough, impatient, hard, full of rancor and useless grief and penal despair, and breaks down the man on whom it has fastened, hinders his energy and wholesome sorrow, as it is unreasonable, and not only hampers the efficacy of his prayer, but actually destroys all those fruits of the Spirit of which we spoke, which that other sorrow knows not how to produce (*De coenob. institut., Lib. IX*, c. 11, *PL* 49:358).

1029. GERARD THE BELGIAN. There, then, is solid peace in a monastery when each of the brethren is loved for God, and everyone conducts himself as though he were a servant in his relations to every other person in the community. Let no one look upon a monk without being touched with compunction; let him see in the monk, as in a mirror, what he seeks in heaven (*Dicta et facta Gerardi monachi, Opuscula pia* 2:156 f., modified by Wolter).

1030. SMARAGDUS, abbot of the monastery of St. Michael at Verdun (d. 820). The monk should speak slowly, that is, moderately and gently, for it is written: *The words of the prudent are carefully weighed* (Sir. 21:25). This slowness results from kindliness and peace. In the same sense Solomon says: *A kind mouth multiplies friends, and gracious lips prompt friendly greetings* (*ibid.* 6:5). Again, he says: *Pleasing words are a honeycomb, sweet to the taste and healthful to the body* (Prov. 16:24), for they give dignity to him who speaks them and minister to the pleasure of them who hear them (*In RSB*, c. 7, *de undecimo humilitatis gradu*, *PL* 102:825).

1031. ST. BERNARD. A. But the humility of the Bride is like sweet perfume, and diffuses its fragrance, warm with love and devotedness, and redolent of sweetness to all. The humility of the Bride is spontaneous, constant, fruitful, and is as unaffected by severity as by praises (*Serm. 42 in Cant.*, n. 9, *PL* 183:992; Eales, p. 264). B. The beauty of the soul is its humility (*ibid.*, *Serm. 45*, n. 2, col. 999).

1032. ST. WILLIAM. Having given up the generalship in the army and abandoned the world, William, former duke of Aquitaine, frequently knelt before the abbot and the brethren [of the monastery of Gellonne, which he had built], petitioning and prevailing upon them with loud cries that it should be granted to him, permitted for the mercy of God, to be even more abandoned, more humiliated, more despised, and that he be held in utter contempt. He desired that there be no dignity or glory in the memory he would leave behind him, but simply that within the blessed community [his abbey] he would be considered the *refuse* and *offscouring of all* (I Cor. 4:13). In like manner he pleaded with great insistence that when there were duties in the monastery that others looked upon as unworthy of their station, or as shameful or unbecoming,—regardless of whether they were inconsequential or difficult—such tasks would, in Christ's name, be imposed upon him, and he would accept their fulfilment in good spirit and with a good conscience. . . . Then turning to the brethren and addressing them privately and even in confession, he begged them collectively and individually to look upon him as a servant and always to treat him as though he were one of the hirelings. He sought to be considered a beast of burden . . . to carry the burdens of the brethren in that house of the Lord, according to spirit of the Psalmist's statement when he spoke of the holy soul eager for obedience: *I was like a brute beast in your presence. Yet with you I shall always be* (Ps. 72:22–23). . . . Not even awaiting their commands, if any of the brethren were engaged in the performance of a task commonly held in disdain, in which he would be looked upon as an object of derision, Brother William was presently beside him as his helper, the bearer of his burden, his humble workman, in fact, to all alike, a common hireling (Mabillon, *Acta Sanctorum O.S.B., Saec. IV, Pars I, circa ann. 812, Vita S. Willelmi ducis et monachi Gellon.,* § 26, 5:80).

Pride and vainglory

1033. ST. ISIDORE OF SEVILLE. A. The devil subjects the monk to himself principally through pride, so that he pulls down from the heights and makes subservient to himself through the swelling of pride him whom he was unable to conquer through love of the world. . . . The servant of God must employ prudence in protecting his heart lest he destroy himself even in his good works with vainglory, and be lost (*Sentent. Lib. III,* c. 22, §§ 8–9, *PL* 83:697). B. There is no greater iniquity for anyone than to seek glory in himself and not in God (*ibid., Lib. I,* c. 10, § 16, col. 556). C. Without humility and charity every other virtue is considered a vice. . . . As pride is the beginning of all sins, it is also the destruction of all virtues. It is first in sin, last in the struggle. For it either lays the mind low by sin in the beginning, or in the end casts it down from virtues. Hence it is the greatest of all sins because it destroys the soul of man both in his virtuous deeds and in his vices (*ibid., Lib. II,* c. 38, §§ 5, 7, col. 639).

1034. ST. GREGORY OF NAZIANZUS, Doctor of the Church (d. 389). From this time, then, having shaken off all ambition for worldly things as a hard master and a painful disorder, I resolved to practice philosophy and adapt myself to the higher life; or rather, the desire was earlier born, the life came later (*Oratio 7, in laudem Caesarii fratris,* § 9, *PG* 35:766).

Vainglory robs us of reward

1035. ST. BASIL THE GREAT. By every effort we must shun vainglory which does not prevent us from performing works (which would be a lesser evil), but rather robs us of our crown once the work has been performed, and . . . like one lying in ambush, threatening our welfare, strives to hurl virtues to the ground. Where [vainglory] sees that the merchant of piety has filled the ship of his soul with all different kinds of precious wares, it then strives by the violence of its storm to wreck and sink the ship. . . . Let us take flight from vainglory, that pleasant plunderer of spiritual riches, that flattering enemy of souls, that moth which not unpleasantly consumes our property (cf. Matt. 6:19). Vainglory smears with honey the poison of its deception and presents a deadly cup to men's minds in order that they may become insatiably acquainted with this vice. The praise of men is sweet indeed to the inexperienced [in the ascetical life], and it leads those whom it has overcome from sound judgment into error (*Const. monasticae,* c. 10, *quod non convenit bona aemulari vanae gloriae causa, PG* 31:1371).

1036. ST. AMBROSE. Once vainglory has completely taken possession of the soul, it soon gives birth to a sevenfold evil: disobedience, boastfulness, hypocrisy, quarrelling, obstinacy, dissension, and the longing for new enjoyments, even though they involve sin (*Precatio II, in praeparatione ad Missam,* § 3, *In Append., PL* 17:834).

1037. ST. LEO THE GREAT. The insidious temptations of the evil one lie in wait so that whenever devotion makes progress, pride may emerge, and man may glory rather in the good work that has been performed in himself than in the Lord (*Ep. ad Demetriadem,* c. 16, *In Append., PL* 55:175).

1038. ST. AUGUSTINE. A. The vanity of human praise will not satisfy the hungry spirit, because it gives nothing to eat but emptiness and air (*Ep. 118, Dioscoro,* c. 1, § 6, *PL* 33:434; Parsons, p. 267). B. We must lift up our hearts to the Lord. To lift up the heart, but not to the Lord, is called pride; to lift up the heart to the Lord is refuge. Here, brethren, you have a great mystery! God is on high; if you build yourself up, he will depart from you; if you humble yourself, he will come down upon you (*Serm. 177, In Ascensione II,* § 2, *In Append., PL* 39:2033).

1039. ST. NILUS, monk (d. 451). A. A jar with a hole in it will not retain anything that is poured into it; in the same manner vainglory pours out the rewards of virtue. . . . Through vainglory the monk, despite all his labors, is deprived of reward; he performs the labor, but forfeits its rewards (*De octo spiritibus malitiae,* c. 15, *de vana gloria,*

PG 79:1159). B. Vainglory is like a rock lying beneath the surface of the water; if you dash your ship against it, you have suffered shipwreck (*ibid.*, c. 16, col. 1162).

1040. ST. GREGORY THE GREAT. For other sins assail those virtues only by which they themselves are destroyed, as for example anger assails patience, gluttony abstinence, or lust continence. But pride, which we have called the root of vices, far from being satisfied with the extinction of one virtue, raises itself up against all the members of the soul, and as a universal and deadly disease corrupts the whole body. Whatever, then, is being performed when it makes its assaults, even if it appears to be a virtue, vainglory alone, and not God is served thereby. . . . The mind is sometimes brought to such haughtiness, as in its pride to be unrestrained even in boastfulness of speech. But ruin follows the more easily, the more shamelessly a man is puffed up in his own mind. Hence it is written: *Pride goes before disaster, and a haughty spirit before a fall* (Prov. 16:18). For that reason too, Daniel said: *Nabuchodonosor . . . was walking in the palace of Babylon. And the king answered, and said: Is not this the great Babylon, which I have built to be the seat of the kingdom, by the strength of my power, and in the glory of my excellence?* (Dan. 4:26 f.). But when vengeance, once it had been aroused, swiftly repressed this pride, Daniel immediately added: *And while the word was yet in the king's mouth, a voice came down from heaven: To thee, O king Nabuchodonosor, it is said: Thy kingdom shall pass from thee, and they shall cast thee out from among men, and thy dwelling shall be with cattle and wild beasts: thou shalt eat grass like an ox, and seven times shall pass over thee* (*ibid.*, v. 28 f.; *Moral., Lib. 34*, c. 23, § 48, *PL* 76:744).

1041. JOHN CASSIAN. A. Vainglory is the soul's harmful nourishment, which gratifies it as with a delicious meal for a time; but afterward strips it clear and bare of all virtue and dismisses it barren and void of all spiritual fruit, so that it makes it not only lose the rewards of its hard labors but also causes it to incur heavy punishments (*De coenob. institut., Lib. 5*, c. 21, *PL* 49:239). B. The crafty cunning of our adversary lies in the fact that where he cannot overcome the soldier of Christ by the weapons of a foe, he fells him on his own spear (*ibid., Lib. 11*, c. 7, col. 406). C. They who in the conflict of battle have escaped the danger of death fall down before their own trophies and triumphs (*ibid.*, c. 11, col. 410). D. The athlete of Christ who desires to devote himself lawfully in this true and spiritual combat, should strive by all means to overcome this ever-changing monster of many shapes [vainglory] (*ibid.*, c. 18, col. 418).

1042. ST. JOHN CHRYSOSTOM. A. He who is puffed up with his own importance . . . has nothing solid and substantial, and glories in those things which pass by more quickly than the very waves (*In c. 9 Gen., Hom. 28,* § 3, *PG* 53:256).

B. If you seek to attain glory, then despise the glory of men, and you shall be held in greater glory than any other (*In Matt., Hom. 4,* § 10, *PG* 57:51).

C. [Vainglory] is the moth which consumes those treasures that are laid up for heaven; this is the thief of our wealth in heaven; this steals away the riches that cannot be spoiled; this mars and corrupts everything (*ibid., Hom. 71,* § 3, *PG* 58:666).

D. Almost every kind of evil plagues the servants of the devil; but the desire of vainglory attacks not only the servants of the devil, but the servants of God and faithful men as well—in fact, the servants of God even more than the slaves of the devil (*Opus imperfect. in Matt., Hom. 13,* § 4, *In Append., PG* 56:704).

E. This passion [of vainglory] is a sort of deep intoxication, and makes it hard for him who is subdued by it to recover. . . . For nothing is so ridiculous and disgraceful as this passion, nothing so full of shame and dishonor. One may in many ways see that to love the honor [of men] is dishonor; and that true honor consists in the disregarding of the honor of men, in making no account of it, but in saying and doing everything according to what seems pleasing to God (*In Joan., Hom. 2,* § 6, *PG* 59:46).

F. A mad desire for glory is the cause of all evils. . . . Let us, then, beloved, avoid this passion [of vainglory]; for if we avoid this we escape hell. For this vice specially kindles the fire of hell, and everywhere extends its rule and tyrannically occupies every age and rank. This has thrown churches into great confusion, this is mischievous in state matters, it has subverted houses and cities and peoples and nations. Do you wonder at this? It has gone forth into the desert [that is, among monks] and manifested its power even there. For men who have bidden an entire farewell to riches and all the pomp of the world, who converse with no one, who have gained the mastery over the more demanding urges of the flesh, these very men, made captives by vainglory, have often lost all (*ibid., Hom. 29,* § 3, col. 170).

G. A dreadful thing is the love of glory, dreadful and full of many evils; it is a thorn that is hard to extract, a many-headed untamable wild beast armed against those that feed it; for as the worm eats through the wood from which it is born, as rust wastes the iron when it comes forth, and moths the fleeces, so vainglory destroys the soul which nourishes it (*ibid., Hom. 30,* § 1, col. 171).

H. If you must seek glory, then be intent on seeking that which is truly glory and comes from God. If in your love for this true glory you despise the glory of this world, you will see how ignoble this world's recognition is: but as long as you do not recognize the glory which God bestows for what it is, neither will you be able to see how foul and how ridiculous the glory of this world is (*In Act. Ap. Hom. 28,* § 3, *PG* 60:212).

I. Nothing can be worse than vainglory. . . . For vanity is the mother of hell, and greatly kindles that fire and stirs the venomous worm to action. . . . For the vain man is ever like persons in a storm, trembling and fearing, and serving a thousand masters (*In Rom. Hom. 17,* §§ 3, 5, col. 568, 572).

J. But [St. Paul] looked not to vainglory, that savage monster, that fearful demon, that pest of the world, that poisonous viper. As that animal tears through the womb of her parent with her teeth, so also this passion tears in pieces him that begets it (*In I Cor. Hom. 35,* § 5, *PG* 61:302).

K. Wild beasts are tamed by giving them much attention, but vainglory is just the opposite: only by being contemned is it made tame. By being honored with attention it is made savage and takes up arms against her honorer. . . . Vainglory is a shadow of glory, not glory (*In II Cor. Hom. 29,* § 5, col. 603).

L. The Church is nothing other than a house built of the souls of us men. Now this house is not of uniform beauty throughout, but some of the stones of which it is constructed are bright and shining, whereas others are smaller and more dull, and these in turn, superior to others. There we may see many who are like gold, the gold which adorns the ceiling. Others again we may see who possess the beauty and gracefulness of statues. Many we see standing like pillars—St. Paul called men also pillars (cf. Gal. 2:9)—not only on account of their strength but also because of their beauty, adding as they do much grace, their capitals adorned with gold. We may see a multitude, forming the wide middle space, and the whole interior of the building—for a large body occupies the space enclosed by those stones with which the outer walls are built. Or to go on to a still more splendid picture: this Church, of which I speak, is not built of stones such as we see around us, but of gold, silver and precious gems, and there is an abundance of gold dispersed everywhere throughout. But what bitter tears this construction has called forth! For the lawless rule of vainglory, that all-devouring flame, which no one has yet avoided, has often consumed all these things (*In Eph. Hom. 10,* § 3, *PG* 62:78).

M. Nothing is more worthless than the praise of men . . . nothing more empty. . . . Human glory is hollow and an imitation of glory; it is not true glory (*In Tit. Hom. 2,* § 4, col. 675).

N. It is impossible that one who is not purified from vainglory should be lofty and great and noble (*In II Cor. Hom. 29,* § 5, *PG* 61:603).

O. I would rather be the slave of a thousand savages than of vanity once. For even they do not put such demands upon their captives as this vice lays upon its votaries. Because it says you must be everyone's slave, be he nobler or be he lower than you. Despise your soul, neglect virtue, laugh at freedom, give up your freedom, and if you do anything good, do it not to please God, but to display it to the many, that for these things you may even lose your crown. And if you give alms, or if you fast, undergo the pains, but take care to lose the gain. What could be more cruel than such demands? (*In Rom. Hom. 17,* § 4, *PG* 60:569.)

1043. ST. JOHN OF DAMASCUS (d. 754). I am directed to God with great longing; but I fear myself, lest I perish by my self-seeking (*Sacra parallela,* tit. 7, *PG* 96:82).

1044. JOHN OF TRITHEIM. A. Whatever good the monk may have done, he is to seek no recognition from men; when praise is sought for any good work that has been performed, virtue is handed over to the enemy (*Comm. in c. 4,* n. 67, *RSB, Op. pia et spiritualia,* p. 312). B. The more that one seeks the glory of recognition in things external, the farther he wanders, as did the five foolish virgins, from true glory (*De triplici regione claustralium, Pars I,* tract. 1, art. 7, p. 581). C. The temptation to vainglory can indeed be conquered, but only with great difficulty can it be wholly rooted out, unless a person shall give up trying to live a virtuous life. For sin alone is free of temptation. Hence as we have said, all vices that have been subdued gradually lose their force and, once they have been overcome, grow weaker day by day, lose their appeal with regard to both time and place, and present little trouble. Being so unlike opposite virtues, they are more easily guarded against, or avoided altogether. But once this vice of vainglory has been subdued, it rises more vigorously to the combat, and just when you think that it has been destroyed, it grows stronger in the very act of dying (*De religiosorum tentationibus, Lib. II,* c. 5, *de tentationibus vanae gloriae,* p. 717).

1045. ST. GREGORY THE GREAT. A. When we are living virtuously, great care must be employed lest the mind, looking critically at others, be lifted up by the pride of standing alone. Hence it is that the blessing of union with others is appropriately called to mind in the words of the verse which follows immediately: *You shall be in league with the stones of the field, and the wild beasts shall be at peace with you. And you shall know that your tent is secure; taking stock of your household, you shall miss nothing. You shall know that your descendants are many* . . . (Job 5:23 f.; *Moral., Lib. VI,* c. 31, § 49, *PL* 75:756). B. The heart of the carnal man, by seeking the glory of this life, rejects humility (*In Evangel. Lib. II, Hom. 32,* § 5, *PL* 76:1236). C. And if at any time you should remember having offended against our Creator, in word or in deed, always recall these offenses to your memory, so that mindfulness of your guilt may keep down the rising glory of the heart (*Lib. 11, Ep. 8, ad Augustinum Anglorum episc., PL* 77:1140). D. Wherefore the very raising up [of sinners] is their fall, because while they rely on false glory, they are emptied of true glory. . . . When the sinner enjoys in this life the glory which he must leave behind, he falls from that which comes after this life (*Lib. 1, ep. 5, ad Theoctistam sororem Imperatoris,* col. 450). E. Let us all hearken to the words: *God resists the proud, but gives grace to the humble* (Jas. 4:6). Let us all listen attentively to the words: *Every proud man is an abomination before the Lord* (Prov. 16:5). Let all hear: *Why are dust and ashes proud?* (Sir. 10:9.) Against this plague [pride], let us all hear that which Truth, our instructor, teaches, saying: *Learn from me, for I am meek and humble of heart* (Matt. 11:29; *Moral., Lib. 34,* c. 23, § 53, *PL* 76:748).

1046. ST. BERNARD. A. We must, then, be very much on our guard against this form of presumption by which we think less perhaps of ourselves than we really are; but not less, but even more must we avoid that presumption through which we attribute more to ourselves than we really are, which happens when, deceiving ourselves, we think that a good in us is from ourselves. But more than either one of these forms of presumption must we avoid and abhor that by which, knowingly and of set purpose, you would dare to seek your own glory from goods which are not yours and would not fear to rob the glory of another [God], for what you know that you have not from yourself. The first is a kind of ignorance, and has no glory in it; the second has indeed, but not with God. But this third evil, because it is now knowingly committed, usurps from God himself. This arrogance is more grievous and dangerous than the latter form of ignorance, inasmuch as through such ignorance God is not known, but by this arrogance he is contemned. It is worse and more detestable than the first kind of ignorance because by it we are made fellows of cattle, but by this the fellows of demons. Assuredly it is pride, the greatest of sins, to use the gifts [God has given us] as though they were naturally ours, and to usurp the glory of the benefactor in the benefits we have received (*Lib. de diligendo Deo,* c. 2, § 4, *PL* 182:977; Gardiner, pp. 34–37). B. Woe to us because of this dragon [vainglory]! For this dragon is a monster of prodigious size, which kills whatever it touches with its fiery breath (*Serm. de temp., Serm. 13 in Ps. Qui habitat,* § 5, *PL* 183:237). C. Fear the flying arrow. This arrow speeds lightly, and lightly penetrates. But not light, I can assure you, is the wound it inflicts, for it quickly slays. It is, in fact, nothing else than vainglory (*ibid., Serm. 6,* § 3, col. 198). D. Vainglory can kill only such as do not see it, the blind and the negligent, who expose themselves to it and present themselves before it; who do not rather fix their eyes upon it, observe it, study it, and perceive how silly a thing it is, how transitory, how vain, how worthless (*ibid., Serm. 14,* § 7, col. 242). E.

How foolish are the sons of Adam to lose both peace and glory by despising peace and craving for glory! (*Ep. 126, ad episc. Aquitaniae contra Gerardum Engolismensem,* n. 7, *PL* 182:276; James, p. 195.) F. As the eagle descends from great heights to eat, so by hunger after vainglory man is plunged from the elevation of a virtuous life to moral indignity (*Lib. de modo bene vivendi, ad sororem,* c. 38, § 98, *In Append., PL* 184:1259). G. Pride has only one foot to stand on: love of its own excellence. And so the proud man cannot stand for long, because he is like a man standing on only one foot. . . . Therefore to stand firmly, you must stand humbly. In order that your feet may never stumble, you must stand, not on the single foot of pride, but on the two feet of humility. Humility has two feet: appreciation of the divine power and consciousness of personal weakness. How fair are these feet and how strong, neither involved in dark ignorance nor defiled by deceitful excess! (*Ep. 393, ad W. Patriarcham Ierosolymorum,* § 3, *PL* 182:602; James, p. 296.) H. Can anything be more hateful than language of this kind, which has been used by some: *Our own hand won the victory; the Lord had nothing to do with it* (Deut. 32:27; *Serm. 54 in Cant.,* § 9, *PL* 183:1043; Eales, p. 330).

1047. PETER DE BLOIS. A. Do they not resemble the spider, which spins the web from its own body [hence, the idea of sacrifice], in order to catch a common fly? What is vainglory that miserable men seek after but a common fly, buzzing, sordid, stinging . . . (*Ep. 14, ad sacellanos aulicos Regis Anglorum, de eorum periculis, PL* 207:46). B. How deceptive and vain is the glory that men seek after and receive from one another! And to think that they seek not the glory which is from God alone! (*Ep. 102, ad Radingensem abbatem,* col. 316.) C. Unhappy he is indeed who, for the wind of vainglory, snuffs out his soul, piling up on himself infinite and insoluble debts (*Ep. 120,* col. 354).

1048. ST. FRANCIS OF ASSISI. Often that on which a value cannot be placed is lost for the meager reward of vainglory, and he who bestowed the gift is easily provoked not to give another (*Apophthegmata,* n. 28, *S. Francisci Assisiatis . . . Op. Om.,* p. 67).

1049. WALAFRID STRABO, abbot of Reichenau (d. 849). We must be on guard lest perchance after we have cast sins out from our body, the spiritual beast of . . . vainglory rise up, which is far more difficult to banish than carnal vices (*Glossa ordinaria in Deut. 7, 22, PL* 113: 460).

1050. ST. BONAVENTURE. A. The more one is humbled the less he holds in esteem the glory of the things of earth; and the less he holds it in esteem, the more will he trample it under foot; and the more he tramples on it, so much the more is he lifted up to higher things, and thus made greater (*Expos. in Luc. 14, 11,* § 25, *Op. Om.,* ed. Quaracchi 7:366). B. What is vainglory but decaying wood which glows brightly in the night? . . . The glory of this world flows past like a ship plowing the waves, like a bird flying swiftly through the air, like a torrent leaping rapidly only to disappear (*Serm. 1 de S. Andrea, Op. Om.,* ed. Peltier 13:494).

1051. ST. ANTHONY OF PADUA. A. The charity you have performed is like a daughter whom you sell to the brothel of the world for the price of vainglory. What a miserable exchange! To barter the reward of the kingdom of heaven for a puff of air from the mouths of men! (*Serm. Dom. III p. Epiph. Sancti Francisci Assisiatis necnon S. Antonii . . . Op., Pars II,* p. 22.) B. Good works are seeds that dry up in the sun's heat of vainglory; for whatever you do out of vainglory, you forfeit entirely (*Serm. Dom. III p. Pascha, ibid.,* p. 197).

1052. ST. ANTONINUS, O.P., abp. of Florence (d. 1459). Vainglory is the firstborn daughter of pride. . . . It is the first to take the field in order to wage war against those who are virtuous, and the last to withdraw from the battle; no one escapes being wounded by it at times (*Summa Theol., Pars II,* tit. 4, c. 1, 2:543 f.).

1053. HUGH OF ST. VICTOR. Anyone who is puffed up because of that which he has done well falls by the very same path by which he progresses. A good act done with pride does not raise one up but weights him down (*Expos. Reg. S. Augustini,* c. 2, *PL* 176:890).

1054. RAYMOND JORDAN, Augustinian abbot (d. circa 1390). Like a mighty wind vainglory hampers the wayfaring man, and forces him into the confusion of hell (*Contemplationes idiotae, contempl. de amore divino,* c. 17, fol. 18).

1055. THOMAS À KEMPIS. If you desire to overcome vainglory, give heed to each of your shortcomings as something known to all, and the inclination to vainglory will cease (*Serm. 14 ad novitios, Op. Om.* 6:110; Scully, p. 91).

1056. IMITATION OF CHRIST (Thomas à Kempis). A. Truly, vainglory is a perilous sickness, a grievous pestilence, and a very great vanity, for it draws a man away from the true joy he should have in God and robs him of all heavenly grace (*De imitatione Christi, Lib. III,* c. 40. *Op. Om.* 2:217; Gardiner, p. 163). B. Those who are greatest in heaven are least in their own sight, and the more glorious they are, the humbler they are in themselves, full of truth and heavenly joy, and not desirous of any vainglory or the praise of men (*ibid., Lib. II,* c. 10, p. 79; Gardiner, p. 91).

1057. HUGH OF ST. CHER. A. They are indeed miserable men who through their labors feed and give drink to demons when they turn their deeds into a seeking of vainglory (*Sup. Isa. 62, 8. Comment.* 4:157). B. It is great folly indeed to seek the recognition of men, which is nothing but dung and worms, and to reject the glory that God offers (*Sup. Joan. 5, 44, ibid.,* 6:322). C. Only he who has declared war on it can know the power for evil possessed by love of the praise of men (*Sup. I Thess. 2, 4, ibid.*, 7:197).

1058. ST. AUGUSTINE. A. *Who can detect failings? Cleanse me from my unknown faults! From wanton sin especially, restrain your servant; let it not rule over me. Then shall I be blameless and innocent of serious sin* (Ps. 18:13–14). And what would this be, but from pride? For there is no greater sin than apostasy from God, which is the beginning of man's pride (cf. Sir. 10:12 f.). And he shall indeed be undefiled, who is free from this offense also; for this is the last among those who return to God, which was the first as they departed from him (*Enarr. I in Ps. 18, 14, PL* 36:156). B. Do you seek to know how great that offense [pride] is, which cast down an angel, which made a devil of that angel, and forever closed the kingdom of heaven against him? This is the great offense and the head and cause of all offenses (*ibid., Enarr. II,* v. 15, col. 163). C. Woe to the man whose charioteer is pride, for he must needs go headlong! (*In Ep. Joan. ad Parthos, tract. 8,* § 9, *PL* 35:2041.) D. Jealousy is soon present to the servant of God whom pride has captured; for one cannot be proud without also being jealous (*Serm. 354,* c. 5, § 5, *PL* 39:1565). E. Where there is a puffing up there is emptiness; and where the devil discovers that which is empty he sets about building his own dwelling place (*ibid.,* c. 8, § 8, col. 1567).

Pride the beginning of all sin

1059. ST. LEO THE GREAT. Both in the fall of the devil and in the prevarication of man the beginning of the sin is always pride (*Ep. ad Demetriadem,* c. 9, *In Append., PL* 55:168).

1060. ST. GREGORY THE GREAT. A. It is written that *pride is the reservoir of sin, a source which runs over with vice* (Sir. 10:13). For by it [the devil himself] fell, and by it he overthrew men who followed him. with which he destroyed the life of his own blessedness (*Moral., Lib.* He assaulted the blessing of our immortality with the same weapon *34,* c. 23, § 47, *PL* 76:744). B. When pride assaults the mind, a kind of tyrant closely surrounds, as it were, a besieged city; the wealthier the person whom he has seized, the more harshly does he assert his authority; because the greater the effort at practicing virtue without humility, the more widely does pride exercise its sway. Anyone who has with enslaved mind admitted [pride's] tyranny suffers this loss first: his mind's eye is closed, and he so loses the equitableness of judgment that all virtuous deeds of others are displeasing to him. He always looks down on the good deeds of others, he always admires what he himself does, because whatever he has done, he believes that he has done with singular skill; he is partial to himself in his thought with regard to what he performs through the desire of recognition. And since he thus thinks that he surpasses others in all things, he walks with himself along the broad spaces of his thought, and silently utters his own praises (*ibid.*, § 48, col. 745). C. For to all who swell within with proud thoughts there is noisiness in their speech, bitterness in their silence, dissoluteness in their mirth, wrath in their sorrow, unseemliness in their conduct, comeliness in their appearance, erectness in their gait, rancor in their reply (*ibid.*, § 52, col. 747).

1061. ST. AUGUSTINE. A. There is no vice which is more resisted by God and in which the proud spirit [the devil] acquires a greater right of governing than the pride of those who think that they can purify themselves on their own power for seeing God (*De Trinitate, Lib. 4*, c. 15, § 20, *PL* 42:901). B. Let profound humility trample elation and pride under foot; for humility makes men like the holy angels, and pride made demons out of angels (*De salutaribus documentis*, c. 18. *In Append.*, *PL* 40:1053). C. Pride is the beginning and end and cause of all sins; because pride is not only a sin in itself, but no sin could ever have been, or can be, or will be, without pride (*ibid.*, c. 19).

D. The proud man is hateful in God's sight and like the devil. . . . The pride and levity of the proud man are always recognized by his words, his actions, his countenance, and his bearing (*ibid.*, c. 32, col. 1058). E. By joining humility to their holiness of life those persons who praise God have taught us that the holier one's profession and way of life, the more intent he must be on avoiding the deceptions of pride (*De sancta virginitate*, c. 56, § 57, col. 428). F. Pride is the stepmother of all virtues, the mother of vices, the gateway to hell, the mistress of error, the devil's head, the beginning of vices (*Ad fratres in eremo, Serm. 31, In Append.*, col. 1291). G. While the proud man is pursuing the goods of earth, the blessings of heaven depart from him; while longing for things transitory, he loses those that are eternal (*ibid.*, *Serm. 62*, col. 1346). H. If there were no pride, there would be neither heretics nor schismatics (*De vera religione*, c. 25, § 47, *PL* 34:142). I. The proud man puts God far from himself—not in the sense of distance, but by the affection of his heart (*De musica, Lib. 6*, c. 13, § 40, *PL* 32:1185).

1062. ST. EPHRAEM. The proud man is like a tall but decayed tree, whose branches are easily broken; anyone who climbs up into it will fall quickly (*De recta vivendi ratione*, c. 3, *Op. Om.* 1:40).

1063. ST. NILUS. Pride is a tumor of the spirit, filled with corruption, which if permitted to grow unchecked, will break out into a large open sore (*De octo spiritibus malitiae*, c. 17, *PG* 79:1162).

1064. ST. ISIDORE OF SEVILLE. A. Pride is the queen and mother of the seven capital sins (*Sentent. Lib. II*, c. 37, § 8, *PL* 83:639). B. Humility is the monk's highest virtue, pride his worst vice. Let each one then consider himself a real monk when he holds himself to be the least, even after he has performed the greater works of virtue. They who have abandoned the world, and nevertheless practice the virtues of the commandments without humility of heart, fall more heavily from their heights, for they are cast down more forcibly because of this pride in their virtue than they could have fallen by their vices (*ibid., Lib. III,* c. 19, §§ 1–2, col. 694).

Pride incurable

1065. ST. JOHN CLIMACUS. A. He whose will and desire in conversation is to establish his own opinion, even though what he says is true, should recognize that he is sick with the devil's disease. And if he behaves like this only in conversation with his equals, then perhaps the rebuke of his superiors may heal him. But if he acts in this way even with those who are greater and wiser than he, then his malady is humanly incurable (*Scala paradisi, Grad. 4, de beata . . . obedientia, PG* 88:706; Moore, p. 83, n. 48; Fr. Robert, p. 74). B. It often happens that when a worm becomes fully grown it gets wings and rises up on high. So too when vainglory increases it gives birth to pride, the origin and consummation of all evils (*Grad. 22, de multiforma vana gloria, ibid.,* col. 955; Moore, p. 179, n. 45; Father Robert, p. 284). C. Pride is denial of God, an invention of the devil, the despising of men, the mother of condemnation, the offspring of praise, a sign of sterility, flight from divine assistance, the precursor of madness, the herald of falls, a foothold for satanic possession, source of anger, door of hypocrisy, the support of demons, the guardian of sins, the patron of unsympathy, the rejection of compassion, a bitter inquisitor, an inhuman judge, an opponent of God, a root of blasphemy (*Grad. 23, de . . . superbia, ibid.,* col. 996; Moore, p. 179, n. 1). D. Pride is utter penury of soul, under the illusion of wealth, imagining light in its darkness. The foul passion not only blocks our advance, but even hurls us down from the heights (*ibid.,* col. 970; Moore, p. 182, n. 29; Father Robert, p. 291).

1066. POPE INNOCENT III. A. O pride, insupportable and hate-inspiring to all men, always first among all vices, always last as well! (*De contemptu mundi, Lib. II,* c. 31, *PL* 217:729.) B. Pride overthrew the tower [of Babel] and cast the whole earth's speech into confusion (cf. Gen. 11:1 f.), hurled Goliath to the ground in death (cf. I Kgs. 17:48 f.), and hanged Aman (cf. Esther 7:9 f.). It slew Nicanor (cf. II Mac. 15:28 f.), and struck King Antiochus with a wretched death (cf. II Mac. 9; *ibid.,* c. 32, col. 730).

1067. HUGO DE FOLIETO. Four forces draw the chariot of pride: desire to dominate, love of one's own praise, contemptuousness, and disobedience. The wheels are boastfulness, arrogance, talkativeness, and levity. The coachman is the spirit of pride. Lovers of the world are drawn in this carriage; the horses untamed, the wheels fast-moving, the coachman perverse, and he who is carried, weak (*De claustro animae, Lib. I,* c. 6, *PL* 176:1029).

1068. JEAN RIGAUD. The higher smoke rises, the more it thins out; the same is true of the proud man, for the more he is exalted, the more he comes to nothing and vanishes like smoke (*Diaeta salutis,* tit. 1, c. 3, *Op. Om. S. Bonaventurae,* ed. Peltier 8:251).

1069. ST. VINCENT FERRER, O.P. (d. 1419). Pride is the foundation of all sins (*Serm. 1 Dom. I Advent., de triplici adventu Christi in: S. Vincentii Ferrerii ex S. Praedicatorum Ordine concionatoris celeberrimi Opera, seu sermones de tempore et sanctis. Opera et studio Caspari Erhard;* Augustae Vindelicorum: Sumptibus Joannis Strötter, 1729, p. 2).

1070. ST. BERNARD. Therefore, dearest brethren, keep away from pride. Shun it, I beg you, with all possible diligence, for pride is the beginning of all sin, that pride which so swiftly overcast with a cloud of eternal darkness the glory of Lucifer, whose brightness had eclipsed the very stars of heaven, that pride which changed into the devil not an ordinary angel but the first and highest of all angels (*Serm. de temp., In Advent. Dni. I,* § 3, *PL* 183:36).

1071. ST. ANTHONY OF PADUA. A. The proud man is abusive, contemptuous, and insulting. He abuses his inferior almost as though he were dirt under his feet—a word, incidentally, derived from the verb *tero,* meaning to crush. He acts contemptuously toward equals, as though they were persons bound to him by close intimacy: for a proud man readily contemns and scandalizes those with whom he associates familiarly. He mocks his superiors with the same effrontery with which he would act in his own father's house (*Serm. in Quinquag. Sancti Francisci Assisiatis necnon S. Antonii . . . Opera, Pars II,* p. 34). B. Pride shuts off the warmth of divine love and the brightness of eternal light and truth (*Serm. in Dom. II p. Pascha, ibid.,* p. 194). C. It usually happens that he who does not realize that he is blinded by concealed pride learns to know of it to his shame and consternation through the vice of luxury (*Serm. II Dom. III Quadrag.*).

1072. JOHN OF TRITHEIM. Proud monks should give way to confusion, for in the garb of the school of humility, they are imitators of the devil in his pride; and as God did not spare him in the heavens, neither will he spare them in the cloister (*Comm. in c. 7 RSB, prooem. Op. pia et spiritualia,* p. 336).

Pride condemned by divine doctrine and example

1073. ST. GREGORY THE GREAT. It is written: *God resists the proud, but gives grace to the humble* (Jas. 4:6). Again: *Every proud man is an abomination to the Lord* (Prov. 16:5). Against the man that is proud it is written: *Why are dust and ashes proud?* (Sir. 10:9.) Truth in person says: *Everyone who exalts himself shall be humbled* (Luke 14:11). In order to bring us back to the way of life through humility, he deigned to exhibit in himself what he teaches us, saying: *Learn from me, for I am meek and humble of heart* (Matt. 11:29). For to this end the only-Begotten Son of God took upon himself the nature of our weakness; to this end the invisible appeared not only as visible, but even as despised; to this end he endured the mockery of contumely, the reproaches of derision, the torments of suffering; that God in his humility might teach man not to be proud. How great, then, is this virtue of humility, for in order that it also might be taught correctly, he who is great beyond compare became little even unto the suffering of death! Since the pride of the devil was the origin of our perdition, the humility of God has been found the means of our redemption. Our enemy, having been created among all things, desired to be exalted above all things; but our Redeemer, remaining above all things, deigned to become little among all things. . . . We know that our Creator descended from the summit of his loftiness that he might give glory to the human race, and we, created of the lowest, seek glory in the lessening of our brethren! God humbled himself, even to the dust which we are; and human dust sets its face as high as heaven, and with his tongue wishes to rise above the earth, and blushes not, neither is afraid to be lifted up—all this by *man who is but a maggot, the son of man, who is only a worm* (Job 25:6). . . . Let us then be humbled in mind, if we are striving to attain real loftiness. By no means let the eyes of our heart be darkened by the smoke of pride, which, the more it rises, the more it vanishes away (*Lib. V, Ep. 18, ad Joannem episc. Constantinop., PL* 77:741).

1074. ST. BERNARD. Woe, double woe, to them who bear the cross of Christ [that is, the hardships of the monastic life], yet not unto the following of Christ; who share in his passion, but have no part in his humility. Such persons are crushed with a double affliction—for on the one hand they torment themselves in this life for temporal glory, and in the future they are hurled into eternal sufferings for their pride of heart. They have labored with Christ, but will not reign with him; they have followed Christ in his poverty, but will not accompany him to glory; they have drunk of the torrent on the way, but will not lift up their heads in the fatherland (cf. Ps. 109:7); they mourn now, but they will not be comforted then. This is all strictly just, for what business has pride in the clothing of humility of Jesus? Could human malice not find something with which to cover itself other than with the swaddling clothes with which the Infant Savior was wrapped? Why does disguised arrogance have to try to hide itself within the crib of the Lord? (*Apologia, ad Guglielmum, S. Theodorici abb.*, c. 1, nn. 2–3, *PL* 182:899.)

1075. ST. BONAVENTURE. See, in Christ you have an example of humility, a ready remedy for pride. . . . Your leader is humble, and will you be proud! Would you have the head humble and the member arrogant? Such a deordering would be monstrous, something contrary to nature, as though you were to subject heaven to earth, and place the head beneath the feet (*Serm. IV de uno martyre, Op. Om.,* ed. Peltier 14:45).

Christ the model of humility

1076. ST. AUGUSTINE. A. On account of this vice, on account of this great sin of pride, God came in humility. This cause, this great sin, this mighty disease of souls, brought down the Almighty Physician from heaven, humbled him even to the form of a servant, treated him most shamefully, hung him on a tree; that by the saving strength of so great a medicine this swelling of pride might be cured. Let man now at length blush to be proud, because for his sake God has become humble (*Enarr. II in Ps. 18, 15, PL* 36:163). B. We are Christian men, beloved, as I suppose I need not go to great lengths to prove to you; and if Christian, then of course, by our very name, belonging to Christ. We bear his sign on our forehead; of this sign we are not ashamed if we bear it as well in our heart. His sign is that of his humiliation. The wise men knew him by a star. And this was a sign given by the Lord, heavenly and glorious. But such a star he would not have on the forehead of his believers, as his sign, but his cross. That by which he was humbled is that by which he is glorified. He lifts up the humble by the very same means by which being humbled, he himself had descended (*In Joan. Evangel.,* tract. III, § 2, *PL* 35:1396). C. *For the Son of Man came to seek and to save what was lost* (Luke 19:10). Lost by following the pride of the deceiver, let him follow the lowliness of the Redeemer, being found (*ibid.,* tract. 55, § 7, col. 1787). D. It is thus that pride, in its perversity, mimics God. It abhors equality with other men under him; but instead of his rule, it seeks to impose a rule of its own upon equals (*De civitate Dei, Lib. 19,* c. 12, § 2, *PL* 41:639; Dods, p. 689). E. *Take my yoke upon you, and learn from me* (Matt. 11:29): not to raise the fabric of the world, not to create all things visible and invisible, not in the world so created to work miracles and raise the dead; but that *I am meek and humble of heart.* You wish to be great; begin from the least. You are planning to construct some mighty fabric of great height; first think of the foundation of humility (*Serm. 69,* c. 1, § 2, *PL* 38:441). F. O holy, venerable humility! It was you who caused the Son of God to descend into the womb of the holy Virgin Mary! It was you that caused him to be wrapped in swaddling clothes, in order that he might clothe us with the ornaments of virtues. You, humility, caused him to be circumcised in the flesh, in order to purify us in our soul. You caused him to be scourged in his Body, in order to free us of the scourge of sin. You crowned him with thorns, in order that he might crown us with his everlasting roses. You made him weak who was

Physician for all men, healing all at a single word, in order that he might cure us all who are ill (*Ad fratres in eremo, Serm. 12, In Append., PL* 40:1255).

1077. ST. ANTHONY OF PADUA. Nothing humbles the proud sinner so much as does the humility of Christ's humanity (*Serm. Dom. in Quinquag., S. Francisci Assisiatis necnon S. Antonii . . . Opera, Pars II,* p. 34).

1078. JOHN OF TRITHEIM. Humility made the Son of God man; it will make Christ's servant the equal of the holy angel (*Hom. 19, de vera humilitate monachorum, Op. pia et spiritualia,* p. 500).

1079. ST. JEROME. However low you may abase yourself, you will never be more lowly than Christ (*Ep. 66, ad Pammachium,* n. 13, *PL* 22:646).

1080. POPE ST. LEO THE GREAT. It is in vain that we are called Christians unless we are imitators of Christ, who called himself the way in the sense that the Master's manner of life would be the pattern for the disciple, and that the servant choose the humility that his Lord followed (*Serm. 25, in Nativitate Dni. V,* § 6, *PL* 54:212).

1081. ST. HILARY, bp. of Poitiers, Doctor of the Church (d. 367). Christ's humility is our nobility; the insults borne by Christ, our honor (*De Trinitate, Lib. II,* c. 25, *PL* 10:67).

1082. ST. LAURENCE JUSTINIAN. Our Lord practiced every kind of humility, in food, in going about as a stranger, in the choice of disciples, in subjection to needs, in poverty, in persecutions, in reproaches and taunts, in his sufferings and death (*Lignum vitae, tract. de humilitate,* c. 2, *Op. Om.* 1:78).

Mary's humility and virginity

1083. ST. BERNARD. Therefore the angel Gabriel was sent from God into this city of Nazareth. To whom was he sent? *To a virgin betrothed to a man named Joseph* (Luke 1:27). And who is this Virgin, so venerable that she is saluted by an angel, yet so humble that she is betrothed to an artisan? We have here a beautiful alliance of virginity with humility. In no ordinary degree is that soul pleasing to God in which humility commends virginity and virginity adorns humility. . . . You have learned that she was a virgin and you have learned that she was humble. If you cannot imitate the virginity of her who is humble, at least imitate the humility of the Virgin Mary. Very praiseworthy is this virtue of virginity, yet humility is more necessary. We are counseled to embrace the former, the latter is a matter of precept. To the one you are invited, to the other you are constrained.

Concerning virginity the Savior says: *Let him accept it who can* (Matt. 19:12), whereas he speaks thus of humility: *Unless you turn and become like little children, you will not enter into the kingdom of heaven* (Matt. 18:3). The first therefore is commended with the promise of a special reward, the second is exacted as a debt. You can be saved without virginity, but without humility you cannot. The humility which laments the loss of virginity may be pleasing, but I make bold to state that the virginity even of Mary would not be pleasing apart from her humility. God has said by his prophet Isaias: *To whom shall I have respect* [St. Bernard: Upon whom shall my Spirit rest], *but to him that is poor and little, and of a contrite spirit, and that trembleth at my words?* (Isa. 66:2.) Notice that it is not upon virginity that he has promised that his Spirit shall rest, but on humility. Consequently, had Mary not been humble, the Spirit of the Lord would not have rested upon her. . . . For how could she have conceived by him without his cooperation? It is evident then that as she herself declares: *God has regarded the lowliness of his handmaid* (Luke 1:48), rather than her virginity, in order that she might conceive by the Holy Spirit. But although she was pleasing on account of her virginity, still it was her humility that made her a mother. And hence it may be said that her humility was the true reason that the Lord took complacence in her virginity (*Serm. de temp., Hom. I super Missus est,* § 5, *PL* 183:58).

1084. ST. BERNADINE OF SIENA, Franciscan (d. 1444). A. For the grace of sanctification, which filled her with every virtue, so established her soul from the very beginning in the abyss of humility that, as no creature apart from the Son of God, ascended to so high a dignity of grace, so no one descended to so profound a level in the abyss of humility as did the Blessed Virgin Mary. Nor is it granted to any pure creature in this world to taste so deeply of the nothingness of the creature, nor so to humiliate and annihilate itself according to the will of the divine Majesty, as it was granted to the Blessed Virgin (*Serm. IV pro festivitatibus B.V.M., de Imm. Conceptione,* art. 1, c. 3, *Op. Om.* 4:84). B. The Virgin preserved a continual actual relation to the Divine Majesty and to her own nothingness (*ibid.,* art. 3, c. 2, p. 88).

1085. ST. BIRGITTA of Sweden, foundress of Order that bears her name (d. 1373). [The Mother of God spoke thus to St. Birgitta]: "What is more contemptible than to be considered a fool, to stand in need of everything, to believe and hold oneself more unworthy than all others? Such, daughter, was my humility. This was my joy, my whole will, to think of pleasing none but my Son. . . . To what purpose did I humiliate myself to so great a degree? Why did I merit so great a grace—except that I thought and knew that of myself I was nothing and had nothing? I sought not my own praise, therefore, but the praising of him who is the giver and Creator of all" (*Revelationes, Lib. II,* c. 23; Cumming, pp. 101, 103).

1086. ST. AUGUSTINE. O truly blessed humility of Mary, which gave birth to God for men, bestowed life on the mortal . . . opened paradise, and freed souls from hell (*Serm. 208,* § 10, *In Append., PL* 39: 2133).

1087. ST. ODILO, abbot of Cluny (d. 1049). The most holy Virgin began to inquire by questioning, or rather by demanding to know how the angel should presume to announce so unusual and unheard-of thing with so great an authority. . . . O unheard-of and admirable example of unparalleled humility! She who rejoiced at having conceived her Lord and God, and who doubted not at all that he was to be born of her, since she could acknowledge herself to be the Queen of all the faithful without the loss of her most pure humility, did not hesitate to call herself the handmaid of her Lord, saying: *Behold the handmaid of the Lord, be it done to me according to thy word!* (Luke 1:38.) There, brethren, you have the humility of the Virgin, conceiving the Word of God! (*Serm. IV, de Incarnatione Dominica, PL* 142:1003.)

The fruits of humility

1088. ST. AUGUSTINE. A. What pride can be cured, if it is not cured by the humility of the Son of God? What avarice can be cured if it is not cured by the poverty of the Son of God? What anger can be cured, if it is not cured by the patience of the Son of God? What ungodliness can be cured, if it is not cured by the charity of the Son of God? Finally, what want of courage can be cured if it is not cured by the resurrection of the body of Christ the Lord? (*De agone Christiano,* c. 11, § 12, *PL* 40:297; Russell, p. 329.) B. O Medicine making provision for all: deflating what is distended; renewing what is wasting away; cutting away what is superfluous; preserving what is necessary; restoring what has been lost; curing what is corrupted! Who will now raise himself up against the Son of God? (*Ibid.,* col. 298.) C. O holy humility, how you differ from pride! For pride, my brethren, cast Lucifer forth from heaven, but humility vested the Son of God with flesh. Pride drove Adam forth from the [earthly] paradise, but humility admitted the thief into the heavenly paradise. Pride separated and confused the tongues of the giants; humility reunited those who had been disbanded. Pride changed Nabuchodonosor into a beast; but humility made Joseph the prince of Israel (*Ad fratres in eremo, Serm. 12, In Append.,* col. 1225).

1089. HUGH OF ST. CHER. Humility is the guardian of all virtues, the restorer of all good works. For humility takes flame when other virtues grow tepid, is enriched by poverty, is fulfilled to abundance through imperfections, rejoices on occasions of sorrow, and takes new life after death (*Sup. Prov. 26, 12, Comm.* 3:58).

1090. ST. ANTHONY OF PADUA. As he was engaged in prayer, Blessed Antony of the desert, beholding in a vision, the world so filled with temptations that they were intertwined, cried out: "Who indeed shall escape such dangerous trials?" Reply was made: "Humility alone can do so" (*Pars I,* tit. 5, c. 4, § 1).

1091. ST. GREGORY THE GREAT. And what is more sublime than humility which, in debasing itself to the lowest, joins itself to its Maker who remains above the highest? (*Reg. pastoralis, Pars III,* c. 17, *PL* 77:78; Davis, p. 142.)

1092. ST. BERNARD. A. Humility must always be considered the guardian of modesty and the mother of patience (*Tract. de ordine vitae,* c. 6, n. 20, *In Append., PL* 184:573). B. The virtue of humility alone can make restoration when charity has been violated (*Serm. de temp., serm. II in Nativitate Dni,* n. 6, *PL* 183:122). C. When you see yourself humbled, take it as a definite sign and even for a certain proof, that some grace from God is drawing near to you. For as *pride goes before disaster* (Prov. 16:18), so before honor comes humility (*Serm. 34 in Cant.,* n. 1, col. 960; Eales, p. 225).

1093. ST. LAURENCE JUSTINIAN. As ignorance begets presumption, and presumption, ruin; so knowledge produces humility, and humility, the increase of grace, greater light, perseverance in good, the delightful joy of hope, desire to progress, a relish for wisdom, constancy in faith, love of suffering, rejoicing of the spirit, uprightness of mind, zeal for justice, and thirst for virtue (*De institutione et regimine praelatorum,* c. 9, *Op. Om.* 2:256).

1093.[a] ST. BERNARD. A. A noble tree was the blessed Benedict, tall and fruit-bearing, *like a tree planted near running water* (Ps. 1:3). Now, where do we find running water? In the valleys, undoubtedly, because, as the Psalmist sings: *You send forth springs into the water-courses that wind among the mountains* (Ps. 103:10). Who does not know that even the mountain torrents shun the heights and always flow down to the low-lying valleys between them? It is thus, my brethren, it is thus that *God resists the proud, but gives grace to the humble* (Jas. 4:6). . . . Therefore choose the valley to walk in, choose the valley to plant in. . . . But in the valleys is found fertility of soil: there our plants shall prosper, there we shall reap the fine ears (Gen. 41:26), there our seed shall *yield fruit a hundredfold* (Matt. 13:8), according to what is written: *The valleys are blanketed with grain* (Ps. 64:14). You notice, my brethren, how the valley is everywhere praised, how humility is everywhere applauded. Let this, accordingly, be the place of your planting, where you shall find running waters . . . (*Serm. de temp., Serm. in natali S. Benedicti abb.,* § 4, *PL* 183:377). B. What can be richer, what can be found more precious than Christian humility wherewith the kingdom of heaven may be purchased and grace of God acquired? Hence it is written, *Blessed are the poor in spirit, for theirs is the kingdom of heaven* (Matt. 5:3; *ibid., Serm. IV in vigilia Nativitatis Dni.,* § 6, col. 103).

1094. ST. AUGUSTINE. Those disciples [the apostles James and John] were, of course, seeking glory, who wished to sit, the one at his right hand, the other at the left: they fixed their regard on the goal to which, and not the way by which they should go. The Lord, then, recalled to them the way, in order that they might reach their homeland in an orderly manner. That country is on high, lowly the way. That country is the life of Christ; the way, the death of Christ. That country, the mansion of Christ, the way, the passion of Christ. Why does he seek the country who refuses the way? (*In Joan. Evangel.,* tract. 28, § 5, *PL* 35:1624.)

1095. ST. JOHN CHRYSOSTOM. There is one table for all, both for them that are served, and for them that serve; the same food, the same clothes, the same dwellings, the same manner of life. Among them he is oustanding who takes on the more menial labors. There is no "mine" and "thine" among them, but this expression, which has been the cause of countless wars, is completely ruled out. And why do you marvel if there be one manner of life and table and dress for all, since indeed there is even one soul for all, not in the sense of substance only, for this is true with regard to all men, but in the spirit of charity. How then should it ever be lifted up against itself? There is no wealth and poverty there, honor and dishonor; how then should haughtiness and arrogance find entrance? (*In Matt., Hom. 72,* §§ 3–4, *PG* 58:671.)

FOURTH PRINCIPLE

Mortification and Chastity

CONTENTS: Religious chastity — The monk the spouse of Christ — Excellence, veneration, fruits, and preservation of chastity — Its patrons — Chastity, a condition for the monastic life — Mortification sustains it — Mortification is the monk's profession — Mystical death — Monastic discipline of the refectory — Fasting and abstinence — Discipline of the chapter of faults — Faults and the satisfaction for them: manifestation of conscience — Discipline of the cell — Mortification of body and mind — Physical bearing — Custody of the senses — The qualities that mortification must possess — Its fruits — Peace, joy, patience, hope.

I. STATEMENT OF PRINCIPLE

Religious chastity

1096. Monks are a family of God, selected from among the multitudes of the faithful. For that very reason, much more than these latter, they become an image of God's purity and holiness. God is pure Spirit. Therefore the monk needs be a man of the spirit, holy in body and soul. He must live in virginal chastity, in order to become, in all things, *conformed to the image of his Son* (Rom. 8:29), who is the first-born and the head of all the children of the Father. For that reason you also, dear confrere, can say with St. Peter: *I have left all* (Matt. 19:27); I am poor in spirit; I love holy chastity; I have followed you, the Immaculate Lamb. Jesus Christ has espoused you forever (cf. Osee 2:19). For that reason you can preserve chastity intact; you have the power to pray to the Lord without distraction (I Cor. 7:35).

1097. How blessed you are in this! The Lord has stationed you a little below the angels (cf. Ps. 8:6). He has, indeed, even made you the equal of the heavenly princes. For he has in great love chosen you and overwhelmed you with graces that in the flesh you may live a heavenly life. Your life is, therefore, transfigured after the manner of the brightness of angelic purity, a joyful prelude to the life of heaven, a sign of predestination. When the Word of God took our flesh upon himself, he accepted poverty from the earth, and by way of compensation gave it heavenly virginity. *Better is childlessness with virtue* [*chaste generation with glory,* Douay version]; *for immortal is its memory; because both by God is it acknowledged, and by men* (Wisd. 4:1).

In a way chastity restores paradise, for it restores to man his pristine place of honor and his dignity; it adorns the Church with a brilliant crown, resplendent with shining jewels; it fills the whole earth with a sweet fragrance before the Lord. Impurity, on the contrary, corrupts, defiles, and degrades both body and soul, completely overthrows the divinely established order, and shamefully disfigures the image of God, at the same time depriving man of all his beauty and honor, and subjecting him to eternal disgrace and punishment.

1098. It is wholly different with the glorious virtue of chastity. Once it erects its throne in the soul, it governs from there with mildness and power all the acts of the spirit, all its desires and demands; it holds the body in a holy discipline, and makes it an obedient instrument of the reason and of the Divine Will. In the innermost sanctuary of the soul it anoints the celestial Bridegroom with precious ointment and *fills the house*—that is, the body—*with the odor of the ointment* (John 12:3). We are not unmindful of the words of the Apostle: *Do you not know that your members are the temple of the Holy Spirit, who is in you, whom you have from God, and that you are not your own? For you have been bought at a great price. Glorify God and bear him in your body* (I Cor. 6:19–20).

1099. From these considerations you perceive clearly how exalted an esteem chastity merits. It frees you from a heavy yoke and bestows upon you rich treasures of grace, wisdom, and holiness. For it relieves you of the countless cares with which men are oppressed, it marks out for you an unobstructed and glorious way to perfection, and imbues your soul with pure and heavenly joys. And what can we say of the eternal reward with which it will be reimbursed? A pure heart is the best soil for yielding the hundredfold fruit. Virgins are permitted to ascend to a sublime degree of heavenly glory, where they *follow the Lamb wherever he goes, and sing as it were a new song . . . which no one could learn except those hundred and forty-four thousand, . . . who are without blemish* (Apoc. 14:3–5).

1100. The chaste and virginal monk is already admitted while still on earth into the ranks of the soldiers and courtiers of the highest King, one day to triumph forever at the side of his immortal Leader, under the white standard of the most glorious Queen of Virgins. Courage, then, dear confrere. Guard the prerogatives of holy purity in secure and faithful shelter; protect and defend it. With the utmost zeal be intent on seeing that it suffer not the slightest harm or ever be brought into danger. Shun with extreme caution all causes and occasions that might endanger this lovable and delicate virtue. *He who loves danger will perish in it* (Sir. 3:25). Chastity finds its refuge and salvation in seclusion; its victory lies in flight, and in humble diffidence with regard to its own strength. *The Lord keeps the little ones; I was brought low and he saved me* (Ps. 114:6).

1101. The sting of the flesh is called for that reason an angel of Satan, the spirit of him whom pride cast forth from heaven. Flee the world, therefore, and especially woman, who is, as it were, the symbol of the world and the most insidious danger for chastity. *Flee, save your lives: and be as heath in the wilderness* (Jer. 48:6). Be a man of unbroken dedication to labor, *forcing your slave to work that he may not be idle, for idleness is the apt teacher of mischief* (Sir. 33:28).

To this alertness employed interiorly and exteriorly—for *from out of the heart come evil thoughts* (Matt. 15:19)—join assiduous prayer, and be firmly convinced that *you can not be continent except God give it* (Wisd. 8:21). Above all, repose full confidence in the help of your Eucharistic Lord, the protection of the holy and immaculate Virgin and her spouse, St. Joseph, and of our holy Patriarch, the patron of heroic chastity. As a blessed son of St. Benedict, constantly hold the lamp of virginity in your right hand, awaiting the eternal nuptials; day and night beg the heavenly alms of grace with which, as with oil, to nourish the pure flame of chastity.

Chastity a condition for the monastic life

1102. But why is there scarcely any mention in the monastic law of this angelic virtue which with its heavenly fragrance brings the monk such joy and honor and confidence? The answer is not difficult to find. Holy chastity is so fundamental a law or condition, so indispensable to the very concept of monasticism, that it scarcely need be stated. It is hidden in silence, much in the same way that the foundation of a house lies below the level of the ground and out of sight. For the entire structure of the Holy Rule is, in a sense, built on chastity, supports itself on it, and is, at the same time, supported by it. Certainly the point is clear to all that the protecting and nourishing of purity of body and soul is the principal purpose of the monastic discipline of mortification. Nearly all the precepts of the sacred law are directed toward the one purpose of keeping intact purity of heart and body, and ascending by the aid of this detachment to the higher degrees of charity and contemplation. The monk, then, who preserves a chaste holiness of spirit and senses, can be compared to the Ark of the Covenant, covered with gold within and without, in which the law was preserved, and on which the majesty of God was enthroned.

The lily of purity flourishes only among the thorns of mortification. The more, therefore, a person holds himself in discipline, the purer he is, the better the discipline of the monastery, so much the more gloriously will the purity of its monks shine forth. Discipline and a prudent severity are the way to chastity, and the hedge that protects it. In reality, mortification is co-extensive with the universal law of Christian life. As long, namely, as we are pilgrims on earth, *the spirit indeed is willing, but the flesh weak* (Matt. 26:41); for ever since man rebelled against God's supreme dominion, he lost dominion over himself.

1103. *The flesh lusts against the spirit; and the spirit against the flesh; for these are opposed to each other* (Gal. 5:17). That ardently desired peace and harmony in which soul and body had worked in co-operation as mistress and servant, has been entirely disrupted—so much so that this free gift of integrity can be restored neither by baptism nor by profession. Hear the complaint of the Apostle: *I see another law in my members, warring against the law of my mind* (Rom. 7:23). For that reason he admonishes us: *Do not let sin reign in your mortal body so that you obey its lusts* (Rom. 6:12). *Is not man's life on earth a drudgery?* [*warfare,* Douay version] (Job. 7:1.) If he desires to escape sin, he must fight unceasingly against the wicked impulses of the flesh. *The kingdom of heaven has been enduring violent assault, and the violent have been seizing it by force* (Matt. 11:12).

1104. This law of mortification applies to all the sons of Eve, but binds monks in a special way. The whole monastic life rests on mortification and the spirit of penance. You entered the cloister and took vows to do constant violence to nature, to repress the desires of the flesh, master inordinate affections and impulses of the heart, break and overcome evil passions—in brief, daily to mortify the deeds of the flesh by the spirit, and in the process to die to this world and all things in it, and to yourself. *Unto this you have been called, because Christ also has suffered for you, leaving you an example that you may follow in his steps* (I Pet. 2:21).

1105. This constant self-mortification is your special obligation, your duty and program of asceticism, your warfare, your vocation. It is indeed your cross, according to the words of the Lord: *If anyone wishes to come after me, let him deny himself, and take up his cross, and follow me* (Mark 8:34). With the Psalmist therefore you can sing: *For your sake we are being slain all the day; we are looked upon as sheep to be slaughtered* (Ps. 43:23). Yes, for your sake, Lord! I am a victim, an expiatory sacrifice, a lamb following you, the Lamb. *No disciple is above his teacher, nor is the servant above his master* (Matt. 10:24).

Mystical death

1106. The constant zealous effort at practicing mortification is that mystical death which you have professed. It is precious in the Lord's sight, the tribute you owe him, your endeavor at imitating him, his life in you. Lifted up from the earth, he draws all things to himself (cf. John 12:32). Moreover, *The love of Christ impels us, because we have come to the conclusion that, since one died for all, therefore all died; and that Christ died for all, in order that they who are alive may live no longer for themselves, but for him who died for them* (II Cor. 5:14–15). Is there, then, a higher honor, a greater dignity and blessing, than this death, which is truly life, *hidden with Christ in God* (Col. 3:3), this ideal of monasticism? "Behold," exclaims our holy Father, "in his loving mercy the Lord shows us the way of life!" (*RSB, Prolog.*). He left us his example, and there will shine forth in his glorified flesh forever the marks of his passion and death. Go forward, then, in strength, brother!

1107. Put on the Lord Jesus Christ, you who are called a Christian, that is, another Christ! Learn the eminent science of the Crucified One! Bear the stigmata of the Lord Jesus in your body! In your every thought and act, in all your words and speech, may Christ live in you, for he is your delight and the model for your imitation. Follow closely in his footsteps, stained with his precious blood. Has not *the spouse of blood* (Exod. 4:25), by the most cruel death he suffered for you, deserved that you should at least mortify yourself for him?

1108. You must, then, hold monastic discipline in high esteem and love it. It is the sacred norm for the exercises of mortification. That these are observed in common by your monastic community renders them easier of performance and more meritorious. They effect the reformation of life and that purity of soul which unite us most intimately with God. Anyone who zealously and wholeheartedly applies himself to this discipline, endures in truth a martyrdom of love. At every moment he is condemning the old man within him to death, with the sentence: "Away with him! Crucify him!" (cf. Luke 23:18). By contrast there is the monk who practices no mortification, who deserves only to be likened to a whited sepulchre.

Monastic discipline in the refectory

1109. These considerations, dear confrere, must convince you to take up with a strong and generous spirit the discipline which you have vowed, and to do so everywhere—in the refectory, in the chapter of faults, in the cell, in your whole life. Let us consider the refectory first. Not unmindful of the words: *Brethren, we are debtors, not to the flesh, that we should live according to the flesh* (Rom. 8:12), our holy lawgiver laid down the principles of fast and abstinence as they are to be observed in the monastery. Although these have been mitigated with the approval of the Holy See, and we no longer observe them in their original severity, it would not be permissible for the monk to neglect them or to relax their severity to the extent that would reduce them to the common precepts that are binding on all the faithful. Lent's solemn observance deserves particularly to be retained in a most religious practice in monasteries. Keep in mind the praise with which the saints extol and recommend the discipline of fast and abstinence. In a way it conquers at its very source concupiscence of the flesh, and calms the blood, the hearth of lust.

Fast and abstinence

1110. Undisciplined eating and gluttony wholly destroy and take away the spirit of religion. The monk who yields to such gratification summons back the unclean spirit that had been driven out by prayer and fasting (cf. Matt. 17:20), and grants him welcome entrance. Be moderate and temperate, therefore, refraining from all luxuries and delicacies in food, and declaring all-out war on greediness. It is useless to take up arms against the external enemies of salvation as long as a crafty traitor lies concealed within the very walls. In your every meal let the strict meaning of the words apply: "Let each one, over and above the measure prescribed for him, offer something to God of his own free will in the joy of the Holy Spirit. That is to say, let him stint himself of food . . ." (*RSB*, c. 49).

1111. No matter how small a sacrifice it is, you can offer it as a token of love to Jesus and Mary, or in suffrage for the poor souls. Moreover, *Be not drawn after every enjoyment, neither become a glutton for choice foods* (Sir. 37:28), but in your inner person and in external moderation practice temperance, modesty, continence, self-control. Always pay close attention to the table reading. It elevates the mind above the senses and serves as a holy seasoning for the meal. In fear of God, in holy obedience, in simplicity and gratitude, eat what is placed before you, without being selective and without finding fault. The common meal of the monastery should be for you a reminder of the Lord's Supper, or the everlasting banquet of heaven. In both the Heavenly Father blesses, breaks, and gives bread to his children. He is the lovable host who provides and presides at the meal. Hence let thanksgiving to him be ever on your lips. Even the partaking of food has no purpose for you apart from the praise of God; your body, refreshed by food and drink, should assist the soul in singing God's praises and in serving him with joy.

The chapter of faults

1112. Apart from sacramental confession, which according to the prescriptions of Holy Church should be made weekly (*Codex Juris Canonici,* c. 595, § 1, 3°; *Declarations and Constitutions of American Cass. Congr.,* § 49, p. 90), which "increases the merit of the pious and grants pardon to sinners" (*Hymn. ad Vesp. temp. Passionis, Breviar. monastic.* 1:513), there is hardly any practice which helps foster monastic discipline and the spirit of mortification more than the public acknowledgment of faults made in chapter. This chapter of faults is not undeservedly called the purgatory of the cloister, for in it offenses committed through carelessness are purged away in the expiatory flame of fatherly correction.

When your name is called by the superior,* confess humbly and sincerely whatever you have been guilty of in failing to observe monastic discipline. After a contrite and sincere accusation, be happy that you have appeared before so paternal a tribunal, and that you are able to atone for your faults with such mild humiliation and mortification, whether it is to be performed publicly in the refectory † or in some other prescribed manner. The same appreciation is merited with reference to other satisfactions made in choir or elsewhere, all of which should be performed in deep humility and the spirit of penance.

Manifestation of conscience

1113. We must refer also to the salutary custom, long in use in monasteries, of manifesting the state of one's soul to the spiritual father. He is appointed by God to be both your spiritual physician and your teacher. Hence open your heart to him, in a generous and simple spirit, and with truly filial confidence, concealing nothing that could be of help to him as a solicitous father in giving you salutary counsel. The rich fruits for personal sanctity and the great advantages that are produced by this practice for the conversion of morals and for successful struggle against the attacks of evil spirits are astounding. On the

* The more common practice in the United States is for the monks to present themselves in rotation, according to seniority, two or three at each chapter. Notification is served on the bulletin board in adequate time beforehand for proper preparation. In some monastic congregations the monks may confess spontaneously, or be summoned by the superior without having been notified in advance.

† Archabbot Maurus Wolter here refers to the custom which is regularly observed in the monastic congregation of Beuron: when a monk acknowledges in the chapter that he has broken something, he is regularly given the penance of kneeling for a few minutes in the refectory at the principal meal at noon, holding in his hands the object broken through carelessness. The presence of guests, who are rarely wanting in the monastery, adds to the humiliation to which Wolter refers. [*Tr.*]

other hand, he who presumes to be his own spiritual director is running a great risk as far as his salvation is concerned.*

Discipline of the cell

1114. The discipline of the cell also demands attention. As all your deeds are evident to the fatherly eye of God, they should also be manifest to the abbot, who holds God's place in your regard. For this reason there is an ancient custom in monasteries of having a small opening in the door of the cell.† Since no one but the spiritual father is permitted to close this small aperture, it reminds you that you are always in the sight of him who searches the hearts and reins, who knows all the secrets of the mind. Whatever you do in the sacred seclusion of your cell, therefore, do under the eyes of the Almighty and your beloved Bridegroom, whose beneficent presence you do not cease to enjoy as long as you do not abandon the holy exercises of mortification and devotion.

Never fail to appreciate his love, but rather respond with ever-increasing zeal in all sorts of services and sacrifices. In this way your cell should be the joyous witness of your assiduous prayer and study, as well as your uninterrupted application to mortification. It should witness your voluntary taking of the discipline, which, in accordance with pious tradition, monks undertake at a given signal of the bell [usually on Friday evening immediately after Compline], in which the body is chastised and humbled in penitential memory of the Lord's scourging. The cell should also witness your discreet night watches and, if necessary, the enduring of cold or heat or ill health. These are all so many means for serving your crucified Lord, in heeding the admonition of the Apostle: *Mortify your members which are on earth* (Col. 3:5).

* The *Code of Canon Law* (1917) both clearly eliminates any compulsory or induced manifestation of conscience to superiors and encourages the ideal about which Wolter speaks. "All religious superiors are strictly forbidden to induce their subjects, in any way whatever, to make a manifestation of conscience to them. Subjects, however, are not forbidden to open their minds freely and spontaneously to their superiors; nay more, it is desirable that they approach their superiors with filial confidence, and if the superiors be priests, expose to them their doubts and troubles of conscience also" (Canon 530, §§ 1, 2, *Canonical Legislation concerning Religious;* authorised English translation; Rome: Vatican Printing Office, 1919, p. 22). Certainly it would be hazardous and foolhardy to begin or continue the monastic life without the help of spiritual direction from a confessor, or a superior, or a chosen guide in matters of the spirit. [*Tr.*]

† This custom is preserved today in the Congregation of Beuron. At about eye level a small round window, fitted with glass, slightly larger than a silver dollar, with a shutter on the outside of the door, enables anyone to glance into the monk's room. [*Tr.*]

Monastic discipline

1115. Let us conclude these considerations with that which really crowns the whole monastic discipline: a carefully controlled and mortified state of mind and body, which is proper to the monk. You must subject the movements of your body and the habits of your mind to an integrating plan of holiness and rigorous discipline, and hence avoid everything opposed to monastic seriousness. It is altogether fitting that the body, as the temple of the Holy Spirit, and the instrument of the soul, should be kept holy out of reverence for its Divine Guest, and be trained to reveal beauty of soul in all its movements. Hence it should bear itself with such modesty and gravity that in all that it does it glorify God and edify neighbor.

Make scrupulous cleanliness adorn your poverty, for such neatness is the natural expression of a heart that is pure and clean. Let your carriage be manly and erect, in keeping with monastic discipline, but with the head bowed slightly forward, not nervously moving from left to right, nor sanctimoniously hanging to one side. The countenance should bear evidence of a holy and cheerful dignity, as the expression of a heart that is truly joyous. Care must be taken, however, not to burst forth in uncontrolled or frivolous laughter, nor to take part in buffoonery, *for as the crackling of thorns under a pot, so is the fool's laughter* (Eccles. 7:6). Do not distort or wrinkle the brow, for *a man's wisdom illumines his face* (*ibid.*, 8:1), but maintain on it, as well as on the lightly closed lips, a holy and modest serenity.

Custody of the senses

1116. The spirit of mortification should stand guard over all the senses. It should warn and shield them in the presence of all harmful influences, lest out of curiosity they violate the spirit of monastic discipline. The eyes, like lamps or windows, are mirrors of the soul, and should be constantly hedged about with diligent watchfulness. *One can tell a man by his appearance; a wise man is known as such when first met* (Sir. 19:25). Keep your heart's gaze directed on high, but your eyes cast down and covered with your cowl. Make propriety and simplicity the adornment of your eyes; keep your glance modestly lowered, never restlessly darting about, nor fixedly staring at anyone. If you fail to devote attention to the control of the eyes, *you are like one now lying in the depths of the sea, now sprawled at the top of the mast* (Prov. 23:34). *No creature is greedier than the eye* (Sir. 31:13).

1117. In like manner you must guard your tongue, ears, the sense of smell. Never allow a confrere to touch you except at the kiss of peace [at the time of the Communion during Conventual Mass]. Regularly keep your hands under your scapular. In no gesture of your body should there be anything unbecoming; it must be as though it were animated by the divine spirit of your heavenly Bridegroom. For the Spirit of the Lord is the spirit of holy discipline, and *holiness lifts up your house, O Lord* (Ps. 92:5). Except for cases of necessity, you should walk with gravity and restraint, shunning all levity, haughtiness, affectation, much as though an angel had descended from heaven.

1118. There, dear confrere, you have the broad field of exterior and interior mortification that lies before you in the monastery. If you seek to course through it religiously, bestow greats pains in acquiring humility and discretion, leaving nothing to your own opinion, but subjecting every exercise of mortification to the control of holy obedience. Do not perform anything in the spirit of sadness or inconstancy: it is far better to undertake lesser tasks cheerfully and to persevere in them faithfully to the point of accomplishment than to begin those which are more pretentious, only to abandon them from want of perseverance. We must hold steadfast to mortification, no matter how much the tempter of our own heart in its cowardice may cry out: Come down from the cross! (cf. Matt. 17:42; Mark 15:30.) To such taunts never give any other than our Lord's own answer: *Shall I not drink the cup that the Father has given me?* (John 18:11.) Add to this the spirit of penance, which is a distinctive mark of monks, and the earnest desire of uniting all your efforts with the merits and bitter sufferings of Jesus Christ, and with the dolors of the most loving Queen of Martyrs, and you may glory with the Apostle: *Always bearing about in our body the dying of Jesus, so that the life also of Jesus may be made manifest in our bodily frame* (II Cor. 4:10). For then you are set as a seal on the Bridegroom's heart, and as a seal on his arm (cf. Cant. 8:6). Thus encircled with the girdle of purity, you lose your sinful soul only to find it anew, sanctified. And then in truth your life's little ship is really attached to the cross, and having life in joyful hope, you will reach the port of blessedness.

Fruits of mortification

1119. Finally, consider how blessed and excellent are the mature fruits of mortification. Because it subjects the body and its desires to the mastery of the spirit, it deals death to sin and brings truly divine life to the soul. More, it is, in a way, the beginning and germ of the future redemption and glory of the body. For under the controlling influence of victorious grace, the body itself is elevated to a higher state. And once every appetite of the body and all its effort are brought under reason's government, peace must sweetly dominate and flourish in the soul.

1120. Ultimately all sorrows, all anxieties, and quarrelling arise from concupiscence, and when concupiscence is properly checked and conquered, there results a delightful harmony between ourselves and our neighbors. Mortification makes you conciliatory and peaceful, amiable and pleasant. It turns you away from worldly desires and lifts you up to the heights of the perfect liberty of the children of God. It fills the heart with joy, spiritual motivation, and consolation. It so bathes you in the light of faith and holy contemplation that you will comprehend the true meaning of the words, *Blessed are they who mourn* (Matt. 5:5). For *as the sufferings of Christ abound in us, so also through Christ does our comfort abound* (II Cor. 1:5).

1121. Then, too, in an unexpected way the fervor of prayer, the strength of grace, the ardor of zeal, and consuming love will all be intensified in your life. Enlightened with the holy wisdom of the cross, you will be placing mortification like a cherub with a flaming sword before the paradise of your pure heart, awaiting your loving Bridegroom in confidence. Every sorrow, every temptation, every evil that falls to your lot will then conspire to good. Like gold, you will be tried in fire, but every tribulation will make you more pure, more chaste, more refined. Small wonder then that mortification will adorn you with the precious virtue of patience. *Tribulation works out endurance, and endurance tried virtue, and tried virtue hope. And hope does not disappoint, because the charity of God is poured forth in our hearts by the Holy Spirit who has been given to us* (Rom. 5:3–5).

II. EVIDENCE FROM THE RULE OF ST. BENEDICT

Religious chastity

1122. Instruments of good works are: To love chastity. To prefer nothing to the love of Christ. In the first place to love the Lord God with your whole heart, your whole soul, and with your whole strength (*RSB,* c. 4, nn. 1, 21, 64). Not to fulfil the desires of the flesh. Not to covet. When evil thoughts come into one's heart, to dash them at once on the rock of Christ (*ibid.,* nn. 6, 49, 59). Let the monk hasten to cut off the desires of the flesh that he may be careful regarding wrongful thoughts; let the good brother say constantly in his heart: *Then I shall be spotless before him, if I shall have kept myself from my iniquity* (Ps. 17:24, Douay version). Holy Scripture says: *Sometimes a way seems right to a man, but the end of it leads to death* (Prov. 16:25). We fear also what is said of the careless: *They are corrupt; they do abominable deeds* (Ps. 13:1). And in regard to the desires of the flesh, let us believe that God is always present to us, since the Prophet says to the Lord: *All my desire is before you* (Ps. 37:10). We must be on our guard, then, against evil desires, for death lies close by the gates of delight; whence Scripture gives this command: *Go not after your lusts* (Sir. 18:30; *RSB,*

c. 7, first degree). [He will dwell in the tabernacle of the Lord's kingdom] who takes the evil spirit that tempts him, and casts him and his temptation from the sight of his heart, and brings him to naught; who grasps his evil suggestions as they arise and dashes them to pieces on the rock that is Christ (*ibid., Prolog.*). Let no occasion be given to the devil (*ibid.,* c. 54).

1123. *Life of St. Benedict:* For he had once seen a certain woman whom the evil spirit now pictured to his imagination; the memory wrought so powerfully upon his mind that he could scarcely bear the fire of lust burning within him, and he was at the point of yielding to the temptation to leave his solitude. Then, suddenly mindful of the grace that was within him, he returned to himself, and seeing a thorny bush close at hand, cast off his garment, threw himself into the brambles and rolled about in them until every part of his body was suffering torture. Thus the wound of his soul was healed by the wounds inflicted on his body, since he conquered pleasure with pain, and while his exterior was burning from the sting of the thorns, his internal flame was extinguished. From that time, he afterward assured his disciples, he never experienced temptations of the flesh, so completely had he triumphed over lust. After this, many began to leave the world and hasten to receive instruction from him. Being now beyond the danger of yielding to temptation, he had become a worthy teacher of all virtues (*S. Gregorii Magni Dialogorum Lib. II,* c. 2, *de tentatione carnis superata, PL* 66:132).

Mortification

1124. Instruments of good works are: To deny oneself in order to follow Christ. To chastise the body. To avoid worldly conduct (*RSB,* c. 4., nn. 10, 11, 20). Do not at once be dismayed and run away from the way of salvation, of which the entrance must needs be narrow (*ibid., Prolog.*). Monks choose the narrow way, according to the Lord's words: *How narrow the gate . . . that leads to life!* (Matt. 7:14); so that not living by their own will, and obeying their own desires, but walking by another's judgment and orders, they dwell in monasteries and desire to have an abbot over them (*RSB,* c. 5). Let him who newly comes to be a monk be told all the hardships and trials through which we travel to God (*ibid.,* c. 58). The first [kind of monks] are the cenobites, that is, those who live in monasteries and serve under a rule and an abbot. The anchorites . . . have learned in association with many brethren how to fight against the devil, and go out well armed from the ranks of the community to the solitary combat of the desert (*ibid.,* c. 1). We are all one in Christ, and have to serve alike in the army of the Lord (*ibid.,* c. 2). Behold the law under which you wish to serve (*ibid.,* c. 58).

Life of St. Benedict: He never gave any thought to pleasure (*S. Greg. Magni Dialogorum Lib. II,* c. 1, *PL* 66:131).

Discipline of the refectory

1125. Let all say the verse and the prayers together and all at the same time go to the table (*RSB,* c. 43). *Each one has his own gift from God, one in this way, and another in that* (I Cor. 7:7). It is, therefore, with some misgiving that we determine how much others should eat or drink (*ibid.,* c. 40). He who needs less, let him thank God and not be discontented; he who needs more, let him be humbled for his infirmity (*ibid.,* c. 34). Love fasting (*ibid.,* c. 4, n. 13).

Lenten observance

1126. We urge that in these days of Lent the brethren should lead lives of greater purity, and should also in this sacred season expiate the negligences of other times. This will be worthily done if . . . we apply ourselves . . . to compunction of heart, and to abstinence. In these days, therefore, let us add something beyond the wonted measure of our service, such as private prayers, and abstinence in food and drink. Let each one, over and above the measure prescribed for him, offer God something of his own free will in the joy of the Holy Spirit. That is to say, let him stint himself of food, drink, sleep, talk, and jesting, and look forward with the joy of spiritual longing to the holy feast of Easter (*RSB,* c. 49).

Mortification in eating and drinking

1127. Instruments of good works are: Not to seek soft living. Not to be a wine-bibber. Not to be a glutton (*RSB,* c. 4, nn. 12, 35, 36). For the things that they need as they eat and drink, let the brethren so supply them to one another that no one shall need to ask for anything (*ibid.,* c. 38). We believe that it is sufficient for the daily meal . . . that every table should have two cooked dishes, on account of individual infirmities, so that he who perchance cannot eat of the one, may make his meal of the other. Therefore, let two cooked dishes suffice for all the brethren; and if any fruit or fresh vegetables are available, let a third be added. Let a good pound weight of bread suffice for the day. . . . But if the work chance to be heavier, the abbot should have the choice and power, should it be expedient, to increase this allowance. Above all things, however, gluttony must be avoided, so that a monk never be surprised by a surfeit; for there is nothing so unfitting for a Christian as surfeiting, according to our Lord's words: *Take heed to yourselves, lest your hearts be overburdened with self-indulgence* (Luke 21:34; *ibid.,* c. 39). Nevertheless, keeping in view the needs of weaker brethren, we believe that a hemina of wine [undetermined amount, which Paul Delatte (*The Rule of St. Benedict; a commentary;* London: Burns, Oates and Washbourne, 1921, p. 275) estimates at half a pint] a day is sufficient for each. But those upon whom God bestows the gift of abstinence should know that they shall have a special reward. But if the circumstances of the place, or their work, or the heat of summer require more, let the superior be free to grant it. Yet let him always take care that neither surfeit nor drunkenness supervene. . . . Let us at least agree upon this, to drink temperately and not to satiety. . . . But when the circumstances of the place are such that the aforesaid measure cannot be had, but much less or even none at all, let the monks who dwell there bless God and not murmur (*ibid.,* c. 40). At meals of the brethren there should not fail to be reading. . . . Let the [weekly] reader, having received his blessing, enter upon his reading. And let there be the greatest silence, so that no whisper, and no voice but the reader's may be heard there (*ibid.,* c. 38). Let no one venture to take any food or drink before the appointed hour or afterward (*ibid.,* c. 43). Let him not presume to eat while [outside the monastery] even though he be urgently pressed to do so, unless the abbot have bidden him to do so (*ibid.,* c. 51).

1128. *Life of St. Benedict:* It was the practice of the monastery that when the brethren went forth in response to some request, they did not partake of food or drink as long as they were away from the monastery. Now although this was conscientiously observed as a rule, several brethren were one day sent out upon some business of the monastery, and found themselves compelled to remain outside until a later hour . . . and they ate. [When they were reproved by the venerable Father, who had been divinely instructed of their disobedience], . . . they cast themselves trembling at his feet and confessed that they had done wrong. He at once forgave their fault, knowing that they would not offend again (*S. Gregorii Magni Dialogorum Lib. II,* c. 12, *PL* 66:156).

Discipline of the chapter of faults

1129. If anyone . . . shall commit any fault, or break anything, or lose anything, or fall into any transgression whatever, [let him come] at once to confess his offense to the abbot and the community and do penance for it and undergo punishment. However, should the matter be a secret sin of the soul, let him tell such a thing to the abbot alone, or to the spiritual father; for they know how to cure both their own wounds and the wounds of others without disclosing them and making them public (*RSB,* c. 46, slightly modified). The abbot should not allow evils to grow . . . but should eradicate them prudently and with charity, in the way which may seem best in each case (*ibid.,* c. 64). The abbot in his teaching ought always to observe the rule of the Apostle wherein he says: *Reprove, entreat, rebuke* (II Tim. 4:2). He must adapt himself to circumstances, now using severity and now persuasion, displaying the rigor of the master or the loving-kindness of a father. That is to say, he must sternly rebuke the undisciplined and restless; but he should exhort the obedient, meek, and patient to advance in virtue. As for the negligent and rebellious, we warn him to reprimand and punish them. And let him not shut his eyes to the faults of offenders; but as soon as they begin to appear, let him, as he can, cut them out by the roots, mindful of the fate of Heli, the priest of Silo (*ibid.,* c. 2; cf. also cc. 27, 28).

1130. *Life of St. Benedict:* Assembling the brethren, he reprimanded the monk [who out of selfishness had refused the alms of oil to Agapitus during a period of shortage of food] for his want of faith and for his disobedience (*S. Gregorii Magni Dialogorum Lib. II,* c. 28, *PL* 66:186).

If anyone makes a mistake [in the Work of God] and does not make humble satisfaction there before all, let him undergo greater punishment, because he would not repair by humility the fault he committed through negligence (*RSB,* c. 45).

Manifestation of conscience

1131. The fifth degree of humility is that he humbly confess and do not conceal from his abbot any evil thoughts that enter his heart, and any secret sins that he has committed. To this does Scripture exhort us, saying: *Commit to the Lord your way, and trust in him* (Ps. 36:5). And again: *Give thanks to the Lord, for he is good, for his kindness endures forever* (Ps. 105:1). And further: *I acknowledged my sin to you, my guilt I covered not. I said, I confess my faults to the Lord, and you took away the guilt of my sin* (Ps. 31:5; *RSB,* c. 7, fifth degree). An instrument of good works is: When evil thoughts come into one's heart, to dash them at once on the rock of Christ and to manifest them to one's spiritual father (*ibid.,* c. 4, n. 51).

Discipline of the cell

1132. Instruments of good works are: not to be somnolent; not to be slothful; to keep constant guard over the actions of one's life; to know for certain that God sees one everywhere (*RSB,* c. 4, nn. 37, 38, 48, 49). Being clothed, they will thus always be ready, and rising at the signal without delay may hasten to forestall one another to the Work of God (*ibid.,* c. 22).

Mortification of body and mind

1133. The twelfth degree of humility is that a monk should not only be humble of heart, but should also in his behavior always manifest his humility to those who look upon him. That is to say, whether he is at the Work of God, in the oratory, in the monastery, in the garden, on the road, in the fields, or anywhere else, and whether sitting, walking, or standing, he should always have his head bowed and his eyes downcast, pondering always the guilt of his sins, and considering that he is about to be brought before the dread judgment seat of God. Let him constantly say in his heart what was said with downcast eyes by the publican in the Gospel: "Lord, I, a sinner, am not worthy to raise my eyes to heaven" (Luke 18:13, in substance); and again with the prophet: "I am bowed down and humbled on every side" (Ps. 118:107, in substance; cf. *RSB,* c. 7, twelfth degree.) Honor all men (*ibid.,* c. 4, n. 8). In the reception of poor men and pilgrims special attention should be shown, because in them Christ more truly is welcomed (*ibid.,* c. 53). If the cellarer has nothing else to give, let him give a good word in answer, for it is written: *Sometimes the word means more than the gift* (Sir. 18:17; *ibid.,* c. 31). Not to love much or violent laughter (*ibid.,* c. 4, n. 55). The tenth degree of humility is that he must not be ready and prompt to laughter, for it is written: *A fool raises his voice in laughter* (Sir. 21:21; *ibid.,* c. 7, tenth degree). As for buffoonery and talk that is vain and stirs laughter, we condemn such things everywhere with a perpetual ban (*ibid.,* c. 6). Let the brethren who are sent on a journey commend themselves to the prayers of all the brethren. . . . When they return [let them] lie prostrate on the floor of the oratory and ask the prayers of all on account of any faults that may have surprised them on the road, by the seeing or hearing of anything evil, or by idle talk (*ibid.,* c. 67).

Discipline of mortification must be humble

1134. Let each one tell his abbot what he is offering [during Lent], and let it be done with his consent and blessing; because what is done without the permission of the spiritual father shall be ascribed to presumption and vainglory, and not reckoned meritorious (*RSB,* c. 49). Let the monk offer God [his abstinence] in the joy of the Holy Spirit (*ibid.,* adapted). Imitating the examples of discretion, the mother of virtues, let [the abbot] so temper all things that the strong may still have something to long after, and the weak may not draw back in alarm (*ibid.,* c. 64).

Patience

1135. Persevering in his teaching in the monastery until death, we shall share by patience in the sufferings of Christ, that we may deserve to be partakers also of his kingdom (*RSB, Prolog.*). Instruments of good works are: to bear persecution for justice' sake; not to render evil for evil; to do no wrong to anyone, and to bear patiently wrongs done to oneself. Not to render cursing for cursing, but rather blessing (*ibid.*, c. 4, nn. 33, 29, 30, 32). The fourth degree of humility is that, meeting in this obedience with difficulties and contradictions and even injustice, he should with a quiet mind hold fast to patience, and enduring, neither tire nor run away, for the Scripture says: *He who has persevered to the end will be saved* (Matt. 10:22); *Be stouthearted, and wait for the Lord* (Ps. 26:14). And showing how the true disciple ought to endure all things, however contrary, for the Lord, it says in the person of sufferers: *For your sake we are being slain all the day; we are looked upon as sheep to be slaughtered* (Ps. 43:23; cf. Rom. 8:36). Then, confident in their hope of the divine reward, they go on with joy to declare: *But in all these things we overcome because of him who has loved us* (Rom. 8:37). And again, in another place, the Scripture says: *You have tested us, O God! You have tried us as silver is tried by fire; you have brought us into a snare; you laid a heavy burden on our backs* (Ps. 65:10–11). And to show that we ought to be under a superior it goes on to say: *You let men ride over our heads* (vers. 12). Moreover, in adversities and injuries they patiently fulfil the Lord's commands: when struck on one cheek they offer the other, when robbed of their tunic they surrender also their cloak, when forced to go one mile they go two, with the Apostle Paul they bear with false brethren, and they bless those who curse them (*ibid.*, c. 7, fourth degree).

Life of St. Benedict: Read, in Chapter Three (*S. Gregorii Magni Dialogorum Lib. II, PL* 66:136), the account of St. Benedict's blessing of the deadly drink that had been prepared for him, and in Chapter Eight, of the loaf of bread that had been poisoned by Florentius (*ibid.*, col. 150).

Hope

1136. Instruments of good works are: to put one's hope in God, and never to despair of God's mercy (*RSB*, c. 4, nn. 41, 72). *Sustain me, O Lord, as you have promised, that I may live; disappoint me not in my hope* (Ps. 118:116: chanted by the novice in the ceremony of profession; *ibid.*, c. 58).

III. DECREES AND DOCUMENTS OF THE CHURCH

Chastity to be observed in a religious manner

1137. POPE CLEMENT XIV (d. 1774). "Chastity makes angels; he who preserves it intact is an angel; he who abandons it, a devil." These golden words of the blessed Father Ambrose (*De virginibus, Lib. I*, c. 8, § 52, *PL* 16:214), are to be meditated on intensely and often by religious men, in order that this excellent virtue may be kept undefiled.

Since you are under obligation of bearing here on earth, in a sense, the personality of angels, dearest brethren, in that you are assigned to work for the salvation of souls, it behooves you to cultivate before all others that virtue without which you can neither be angels nor perform their ministry. For that reason you must, each of you, exert yourselves to the utmost in taking flight, as you would from a serpent, from everything which to even the slightest degree, could tarnish the spotless beauty of this flower of all virtues. "A person can offer resistance to other vices," says St. Jerome, "but to this one, only flight" (*Contra Vigilantium,* § 16, *PL* 23:352).* If a struggle must be put up in other temptations to the sordid vice, this is particularly true with regard to the shunning of women. "Man and woman," states the same celebrated doctor, "are fire and straw to each other; and the devil never tires of blowing upon the straw to cause it to burst into flame." Usually this flame is ignited by conversations from which at first there easily arises a mutual affection, and afterward the vehement flame of love catches fire. Hence the same Father admonishes: "Kill the enemy while he is yet weak; the root is to be cut out immediately. Trust neither to your own nor to the other person's holiness . . . for you are not holier than David, nor stronger than Samson, nor wiser than Solomon." †

But the conversations, you will say, are spiritual—pious discourses on heavenly things. But let the devil blow on them, and a consuming fire, not indeed of divine charity, but of carnal love, will be ignited. "He later hurls headlong into the abyss," says St. Basil, "those who at first were attracted by a species of spiritual charity." But there are

* Although they are given in the form of direct quotations, none of Pope Clement's references in this excerpt are exact, nor does the Bullarium furnish helpful citations. The inserted references are the closest approximations that could be found: the translation is that of Pope Clement's text. [*Tr.*]

† Today's women may, I fear, bristle with indignation at these and subsequent passages of this Fourth Principle which deals with chastity. Modern authors seem occasionally to propose the thesis that a rather justifiable accusation of misogyny could be worked up against some of the Fathers and Doctors of the Church, several of whom are quoted in the numbers which follow. Whatever the respective Fathers said of women in general—and much of their thought is, understandably, beautiful and highly commendatory, and often far worthier than modern expression—any appreciation of the monastic life demands the consideration of the following: Almost all the excerpts here quoted are taken from the writings of men addressed to other men who were striving for the monastic ideal. That ideal concentrates on the sacrifice of attachments that are all admittedly in themselves good: the relinquishing of material *goods;* the forgoing of the *sacrament* of marriage; abandonment of one's will in obedience, which constitutes the most exalted sacrifice of which humans are capable. The sixth and ninth commandments, not our present concern, deal with what is evil. The other side of the coin (disconcerting statements regarding the dangers of association with men, as far as the ascetical ideal is concerned) is found copiously in such literature as sermons preached by saints to religious *women.* [Tr.]

women and girls, you contend, who constantly bear the mortification of the cross in their bodies and follow Christ with the whole intent of their heart. "It matters not," says the Angelic Doctor, "that they are holier, and for that reason less to be avoided; for the holier they are, the more attractive they are: to state it in a word, unless you take flight, you have lost" (This is a quotation, in substance, from St. Augustine, cf. *Opusc.* 57, *Op. Om.*, ed. Parma 17:317).

God forbid that a religious ever carry on conversations with women, alone with them in a room or other quarters attached to the church and hence accessible to women, behind closed and locked doors. Either let him arrange to have a witness present, or speak with the door remaining open, so that he can be seen by passersby (*Const. Apost. In vinea Dni,* § 7, 4 Jul., 1772, *confirmatio decr. pro Cappucinis provinciae Subalpinae, BRC* 5:459, 460).

1138. CONGR. OF BURSFELD (founded 1433). A. By virtue of the vow pronounced to God, chastity must be made to shine forth with all the spiritual forces at our command, since it is one of the principal glories of our order; we must preserve our heart and our bodies unsullied for God, and avoid whatever is opposed to purity and chastity. To this end we are to employ spiritual and physical means, some of which our holy Father Benedict prescribed in Chapters Four and Seven of the *Rule of St. Benedict,* such as prayerfully imploring the divine assistance, daily setting our intentions before our minds, annual renewal of vows, a loving reading of the Scriptures, mortification of the body, manual labor, flight from temptation, avoidance of persons who are perverse and impure in speech, and other means that the holy fathers and ascetical masters have recognized and prescribed as salutary (*Stat.,* dist. 5, c. 1, *de castitate,* § 2, n. 1, p. 118). B. As far as possible, the monks will try to avoid giving exhortations and conferences to women. Should necessity demand that they engage in such work, they are to strive for the greatest modesty in word and general conduct (*ibid.,* dist. 8, c. 4, *de fratribus in viam directis,* n. 9, p. 288). C. We forbid most severely that any of our brethren speak to a person of the other sex except for a just reason. Even then he may do so only after having obtained permission, and provided that the conversation be held in the presence of a witness, briefly, in a place and at a time above all suspicion. . . . No one is to presume to write to any person, send, or receive anything, without express permission. . . . In order to prevent, as far as lies in our power, that by his vicious conduct anyone incur the evil reputation of incontinence, thus bringing disgrace upon the monastery and the order, we forbid that anyone establish familiarity with women, even the most devout, go off with them to out-of-the-way places, or in any way lay himself open to suspicion, whatever the apparent justification; from the circumstances and his manner of acting he may be considered guilty. As our way of life must of its nature be most circumspect and conducted in the fear of God, a prudent and certain judgment about it must be formed in the fear of God, lest there be any detraction of the innocent and pure (*ibid.*, dist. 5, c. 1, § 2, n. 2, p. 118).

1139. SWABIAN CONGR. OF ST. JOSEPH (statutes approved by Pope Benedict XIII, 1725). Our holy Father Benedict offers five excellent aids in his holy Rule for preserving and defending the chastity to whose cultivation we are bound by solemn vow: (1) immediate and undelayed banishing of evil thoughts . . . (2) frequent calling to mind of the divine presence . . . (3) fear of God as the most severe punisher of sins . . . (4) avoidance of idleness . . . (5) moderate and discreet chastisement of the body and mortification of the senses. In order for us to escape unharmed so many grave dangers, we must, with unrelenting prayer, daily implore the aid of divine grace, and zealously observe these means that our holy Father has prescribed for purity's defense. When we have employed them we may confidently hope that under the assistance of divine grace, we shall happily ward off all the evil one's fiery weapons with which we are daily assaulted, and preserve inviolate and undefiled the treasure of spotless chastity that we have vowed to God. . . . Should it be necessary at times to speak with women, it should be done as briefly as possible, with utmost discretion, only in public places, and in the presence of others (*Const. et declar., Pars II,* c. 2, *punctum 4, de castitate,* fol. 66–70).

1140. PROV. COUNCIL OF GRAN (Ezstergom, Hungary, 1858). Since we bear this angelic virtue in extremely fragile vessels of clay, it is to be protected with utmost care and fortified with the worthiest means at our command against the dangers which constantly threaten it. Among these are to be reckoned daily examination of conscience, both general and particular; frequent sacramental confession; the celebration of the Sacrifice of the Mass. Daily prayer and meditation, the attentive and devout choral performance of the Canonical Hours in unison and aloud are likewise means for preserving and keeping unsullied the angelic virtue (*Decr.*, tit. 7, *de regularibus,* n. 3, *CL* 5:65).

1141. PROV. COUNCIL OF VIENNA (1858). Chastity is the excellent virtue, heavenly in character, which makes a clean man of an unclean one, a servant of an enemy [the body], and an angel of a man. It alone represents, to a degree, the state of immortal glory in this place of time and mortal nature, and takes upon itself the way of life of that blessed region where *they neither marry nor take wives* (Luke 20:35). But the more spotless the purity of chastity that adorns the man of the Church, the more miserably he sinks into degradation when it is violated (*Decr.*, tit. 5, c. 6, *de conversationis sacerdotalis honestate, CL* 5:197).

1142. PROV. COUNCIL OF PRAGUE (1860). A. Since chastity effects the beauty and honor of this holy race [that seeks God] (cf. Ps. 23:6), the

Fathers assembled in council, with all their heart beg and exhort religious to foster with deepest devotion and to practice this precious virtue of religious self-denial (*Decr.,* tit. 7, c. 3, *de obligationibus regularium, CL* 5:575). B. Since profession of the celibate life and virginal chastity is the distinctive and angelic ornament of the order of the priesthood, but since it is also a most fearful burden to place on human shoulders, the first and most zealous effort of clerics must be directed to the end that, being outstanding for the heavenly gift and their merit of chastity, they constitute, in the terminology of St. Cyprian, the senate of the Church. They must strive, with the help of the Lord, to be strangers to all pleasures of the flesh, and demonstrate by the splendor of their modesty the statement of Christ: *Things that are impossible with men are possible with God* (Luke 18:27). The ministers of the divine mysteries are so much the more to be drawn to the commendation of this chaste example because of the perversity of our times in which the number of unbelievers grows daily larger. These people are often slaves to their own carnal desires and refuse to believe that anyone else can remain chaste. Nor are there wanting great numbers of seducers who seek to involve clerics in desires of earth, in order that they can attack and contemn those who are faithless all the more vehemently (*ibid.,* tit. 1, c. 7, *de honesta clericorum vita et conversatione,* n. 1, col. 425).

1143. PROV. COUNCIL OF COLOCZA (Hungary, 1863). Jesus, the author of our religion, chose virgins for his mother and his foster father, and loved more than others the disciple who was particularly blessed with the prerogative of chastity. The Christian religion teaches universally the great dignity and singular blessedness that is reposed in purity of heart. Hence among the first Christians there began to develop a unique veneration for purity of life, and they demanded particularly this virtue, even in its highest degree, of those whom they wanted to be outstanding in all the virtues [the clergy], in conformity with the words the Lord addressed to them: *You are the salt of the earth . . . you are the light of the world* (Matt. 5:13–14). . . . Since this virtue is most certainly not lacking in difficulty, all who are called to the sanctuary of the Lord are by their ardent prayers to implore the grace from God, diligently employ the helps for fostering chastity, zealously strengthen themselves with the sacraments, and be cautious with regard to their relations with women. Let them avoid idleness, the great enemy of chastity, strengthen their heart by reminding themselves of the divine presence, cultivate a devotion to the Blessed Virgin in filial confidence, hold in veneration the more outstanding patrons of holy virginity, and so order their whole life that nothing be admitted into it that could become a temptation to chaste modesty (*Decr.,* tit. 4, c. 12, *de coelibatu, CL* 5:682–683).

1144. PROV. SYNOD OF UTRECHT (1865). A. The angelic virtue of virginal chastity, which is the highest nobility and glory of those who consecrate themselves without reserve to Christ, is to be guarded in faithfulness and holiness, and zealously to be shielded against all errors (*Decr.*, tit. 7, c. 1, *de perfectione religiosa, CL* 5:891). B. This virtue of virginal chastity is the greatest glory and the outstanding ornament of the priestly order. Hence not only must this excellent and angelic virtue so flourish among clerics that it may spread its fragrance far and wide, but everything from which there might arise even the least occasion of adverse suspicion or unfavorable comment must be prevented. Let clerics avoid all association and familiarity with women, not only with those whose reputation is perhaps not so good, but also with those who deservedly enjoy the praise of modesty and piety. Needless companionship with them cannot fail to lead to scandal and even danger. Whenever they are obliged by reason of their office to deal with women, priests should be mindful of St. Bonaventure's rule that all conversation with them must be kept brief and austere (*De modo confitendi et de puritate conscientiae*, c. 14, *Op. Om.*, ed. Peltier 7:575; actually this work is now attributed to Matthew of Cracow in the critical Quaracchi ed. of St. Bonaventure's works). . . . The companions of continence and purity, namely, temperance, mortification, and modesty, must also shine forth in the life of the cleric, unblemished by even the slightest stain. . . . For unless these are all preserved, it is impossible for clerical uprightness of life not to suffer. "Temperance makes a man temperate, abstemious, frugal, sober, moderate, chaste, silent, serious, modest. Residing in the soul, this virtue bridles lust, tempers the affections, multiplies holy desires and represses corrupt ones, sets in order all that is disordered within us, strengthens all that is well-ordered, removes wicked thoughts and implants holy ones, quenches the fire of lustful passion, kindles the tepidity of our soul by a desire of future reward, soothes our mind with peaceful tranquillity, and preserves it intact from every storm of vices (Julianus Pomerius, *De vita contemplativa, Lib. III*, c. 19, *PL* 59:502; Suelzer, p. 144). If the spirit of temperance is lacking, the priest has snuffed out the spirit of holiness (S. Petrus Chrysologus, *Serm. 26, de fideli dispensatore, PL* 52:273; *ibid.*, tit. 8, c. 4, *de honesta clericorum conversatione*, col. 904).

Virtues of the soul dedicated to Christ

1145. ROMAN PONTIFICAL. A. Blessed virginity, rival of the purity of angels, has acknowledged its Author; it has devoted itself to the dwelling place, to the bridal chamber of him who is the Bridegroom of virginity, as he is the Son of [Mary's] perpetual virginity (*De benedictione et consecratione virginum, praef., Pontificale Romanum* 1:199). B. May the Creator of heaven and earth bless you, God the Father Almighty, who has deigned to choose you for the companionship of Blessed

Mary, the Mother of our Lord Jesus Christ, in order that you may preserve unimpaired and immaculate that virginity which you have professed before God and his angels, and that you may be steadfast in your resolve, love chastity, preserve patience . . . (*ibid., Antiph. Annulo suo subarravit me,* p. 209). C. May there dwell in them chaste virginity; may they be adorned as well as strengthened with pure faith, unwavering hope, true charity. With their mind devoted to self-restraint, may they be granted the strength of grace with which to conquer all temptations of the devil and despise the goods of the present in order to attain those that are to come. May they prefer fasting to sumptuous dishes and place sacred reading before banquets and entertaining guests. Sustained by prayer and perfected by the truths they have learned, enlightened by their night watches, may they perform the works of virginal grace. Strengthen these your handmaids . . . with the arms of virtue; grant them the grace to complete the course of the virgin's vocation without hindrance (*ibid., Oratio, Deus plasmator corporum, versus finem consecrationis,* p. 213).

1146. ROMAN MISSAL. A. May the sacrament which we have received, O Lord, our God, heal us in the wounds of that sin from which, by singular privilege, you preserved immaculate the Conception of Blessed Mary (*In Conceptione Immaculata B.V.M.,* 8 Dec., *Postcommunio, Miss. Rom.,* p. 540). B. May this unspotted victim, with which we renew the great work of our Lord Jesus Christ's charity be, through the intercession of Blessed Camillus, our saving remedy against all infirmities of body and soul, and, in the last agony, our solace and protection (*Fest. S. Camilli de Lellis,* 18 Jul., *Secreta, ibid.,* p. 752). C. Make us, O Lord, to sit down to your heavenly banquet, clothed in the wedding garment which the pious preparation and constant tears of Blessed Aloysius adorned with priceless pearls (*Fest. S. Aloysii Gonzagae, 21 Jun., Secreta, ibid.,* p. 705). D. Grant, O Lord, that we, who have been fed with the Bread of Angels, may also lead lives of angelic purity, and, after the example of him whom we venerate today, pass our days in incessant giving of thanks (*ibid., Postcommunio*).

1147. MONASTIC BREVIARY. 1) O Jesus, Crown of virgins,/ Whom that Mother conceived / Who alone as Virgin gave birth to a Child,/ Graciously hear our praises. 2) You live among the lilies / Surrounded by choirs of virgins,/ As a Bridegroom adorned with glory,/ Dispensing gifts to brides. 3) Wherever you go,/ Virgins follow and / With songs of praise hasten after you,/ Causing sweet hymns to resound. 4) We suppliantly beseech you / To intensify that wherewith our senses / May know nothing whatever / Of all the wounds of corruption (*Commune virg., Hymn. ad Vesp., Breviar. monastic.* 1:128*).

1148. ROMAN BREVIARY. Virgin all excelling,/ Meek above all

others,/ Make us, freed from sin,/ Meek and chaste (*Commune fest. B.V.M., Hymn. ad Vesp., Breviar. Rom.* 1:213*).

1149. MONASTIC BREVIARY. 1) Gertrude, shrine of the Godhead,/ And united to the Bridegroom of virgins,/ Obtain for us to offer the chaste love / Of the bridal contract. . . . 3) Like a pure lily,/ Your fragrance sweetens the heavens,/ And by your chaste beauty,/ You draw the heavenly King to you (*Fest. S. Gertrudis virg.*, 17 Nov., *Hymn. ad Vesp., Breviar. monastic.* 2:770).

Self-denial

1150. PROV. COUNCIL OF VIENNA (1858). Interior self-denial is like the soul that animates the body of the religious life, the source and origin of all its honor and merit. The admirable victory of man over himself personally and over the world is the operation of the Holy Spirit, more wonderful indeed than the works of penance, which are directed to its preservation and perfection; in fact, it is for that reason that penance's fruits are an acceptable sacrifice in God's sight (*Decr.*, tit. 4, c. 13, *de vita religiosa, CL* 5:188).

1151. PROV. COUNCIL OF UTRECHT (1865). Men who set no purpose for themselves other than the goal of acquiring and storing up wealth, and who follow no law in their actions other than the unconquered cupidity of ministering to their own pleasure and advantage, especially in these times, inveigh against the religious orders with a bitter hatred, despite the fact that these orders have merited exceedingly well by their contributions to Christian and civil society, and to culture. These men babble about the orders having no legitimate reason for existing—and hence applaud the statements of heretics (*Decr.*, tit. 7, c. 1, *de perfectione religiosa, CL* 5:891; cf. Pius IX, *Ep. Encycl. Quanta cura*, § 4, 8 Dec., 1864, *Acta Pii IX* 3:691).

1152. PROV. COUNCIL OF COLOCZA (Hungary, 1863). When the Lord placed the first man and woman in possession of the garden of paradise, he gave them the command not to eat of the fruit of the forbidden tree, and sanctioned that law with the threat of death. The violation of that command opened the source of continual hardships which have endured ever since. Through his prophets the same Lord made it clear that fasting was a work acceptable to him. Although he had need of none of the helps of penance, our Savior fasted for forty days before he undertook the ministry of teaching publicly and foretold that his disciples were to fast when the Bridegroom would be taken away from them (Matt. 9:15). Hence the custom has grown up in the Catholic Church by which the faithful sanctify certain days with fasting, and by its means prepare themselves for celebrating the feasts. They devote themselves to the practice also in order more easily to conquer the pleasures of the flesh, and to be able to bestow alms more liberally upon the indigent.

The apostles led the way by their example, for the testimony of Holy Writ shows that they gave themselves to fasting with the other Christians; the holy Fathers composed entire works in praise of fasting; the Catholic Church has incorporated the discipline into its canonical prescriptions from the time of apostolic tradition, and legislated for a fast of forty days for all the faithful before Easter. Singular gifts from God show how greatly this practice has always been pleasing to him. At the prayers of those who undertook it, God freed cities from attack, received into his favor peoples that had been destined for destruction, and forgave the sins of souls humbled through fasting. Hence the Church sings in the Lenten Preface that by fasting God crushes vices, lifts up the mind, and bestows virtues and rewards (*Decr.*, tit. 7, c. 2, *de jejunio et abstinentia, CL* 5:716).

1153. PROV. COUNCIL OF COLOGNE (1860). It is impossible that what the Scriptures commend so often, what saints have never failed to practice, and what Christ himself made holy by his example, should not be pleasing to God and beneficial for men. The Church, which perpetuates the life of Christ on earth, has taught us how she considers her Master should be imitated, especially since he said: *The days will come when the bridegroom shall be taken away from them, and then they will fast* (Matt. 9:15). Since the Church is holy in herself and desires most ardently to lead her members to holiness, how could she do other than constantly recommend, in fact, prescribe, the most efficacious aids thereto? For she knows that fasting makes of man's body a victim for God; that it puts a restraint on his concupiscence; that he is humiliated when he is made aware of his weakness in fasting; that he atones for his former sins by fasting and more easily avoids future ones; that by repressing his earthly desires he is rendered more capable of longing after the things of heaven; and finally, that he acquires thereby great treasures of merit.

Hence the Church appropriately offers thanks to God, who "by the fasting of the body crushes vices, lifts up the mind, bestows virtue and reward" (*Praef. Quadr., Miss. Rom.*, p. 280). But the faithful must be reminded frequently, especially in our times, of the obedience they owe to holy Mother Church. They should be exhorted to observe her precepts on fasting and abstinence in a holy manner, all the more in that the loving Mother, by mitigating the precept of abstinence, has made this obedience easier for her children. In this connection, they who think that for special reasons they should be shown greater consideration, are to be admonished at least to petition, from those who are empowered to grant them, the dispensation and commutation of the fast into some pious work such as [added] prayer and almsdeeds, and zealously to fulfil the works enjoined. All are to be urged to seize this opportunity for professing their Catholic faith publicly, for such occasions occur often in the observance of this precept. In so doing they should be mindful of those words of the Savior: *Everyone who acknowledges me before men, I also will acknowledge him before my Father in heaven* (Matt. 10:32; *Decr., Pars II*, tit. 2, c. 22, *CL* 5:363).

1154. PROV. COUNCIL OF VIENNA (1858). The apostles and they who put their faith in the preaching of the apostles expended their holy efforts in order for the words of the Master to be fulfilled in truth (cf. Matt. 9:15). Afterward the sanction of law was added, lest the fervor should cool. Through dispensations that have been granted liberally, the severity of the ancient fasts has been so mitigated in our day that little remains of the love-inspired violence done to the body.

Nevertheless, to perform joyfully the small sacrifices that are still demanded, or to deny oneself anything out of the love of God, strengthens the will and lifts the mind up to our fatherland in heaven. To be so attached to anything to the point that it could not be looked upon as worthless, that to give it up out of love of God would seem too great a hardship, is an indication of a dead faith. Hence we must propose to the Christian people the merit to be gained by obedience to the laws of the Church, and by self-denial. Then, too, the nature of the ecclesiastical fasts adds greater dignity to the observance of the holy seasons; it is a profession of the Catholic faith from which no one can withdraw with safety. . . . Pastors and confessors should present these thoughts to the faithful with appropriate exhortations, so that they will be ashamed to prefer corruptible food to the welfare of their souls and to God's glory (*Decr.*, tit. 4, c. 11, *CL* 5:187).

1155. PROV. COUNCIL OF PRAGUE (1860). He will not be a just judge of things who doubts that the faithful, in fasting according to the precepts of the Church, perform a good work which is older than the law itself. It is also a good work which is completely in harmony with the human nature which was wounded in the sin of Adam (S. Basilius Magnus, *de jejunio Hom. 1*, §§ 3, 4, *PG* 31:167). It is, too, a work which is most acceptable to the merciful God who "by fasting of the body represses vices, lifts up the mind, bestows virtue and reward, through Christ our Lord" (*Praef. de Quadr., Miss. Rom.*, p. 280). The religious exercise of the fast was not unknown even to the Gentiles; to the children of Abraham it has always been the custom established by the divine law; and to the faithful of Christ, introduced by the august example and command of the Savior of mankind—in fact, to pious humility it has always been most agreeable.

We regret, therefore, that in these days there are many who are *enemies of the cross of Christ. Their end is ruin, their god is the belly, their glory is in their shame* (Phil. 3:18–19). Among them are children of the Church itself, although unworthy of the Catholic profession of faith, who delight only in what is of earth, and *deride whatever they do not know* (Jude 1:10), who even go to the extent of not being ashamed to hold the salutary discipline of fasting in ridicule. . . . We earnestly exhort the clergy, and priests in particular, to offer to God as a group their own fasting and the sacrifice of every self-denial they practice, in atonement for the many sins and negligences of those who hate the fast and who contemn the law of the Church, and thus offend the Divine Majesty. May God grant that the sacrifice of this atonement will, through Christ our Lord, be propitious for those for whom it is piously offered (*Decr.*, tit. 3, c. 9, *CL* 5:479).

1156. POPE BENEDICT XII (d. 1342). If moderation and modesty are seriously observed, they make a great contribution to progress in holiness. For that reason We desire that the doctrine presented by the *Rule of St. Benedict* on eating and on the observance of abstinence, as well as the prescriptions on the same subject in the Constitution of Innocent III of blessed memory, be adhered to. We prescribe and ordain that, with the exceptions to be made where unfeigned illness necessitates dispensation, all regulars of the order abstain from eating flesh meat from the first Sunday of Advent to Christmas, and from Septuagesima Sunday until Easter (*Const. Apost. Summi Magistri,* c. 26, 20 Jun., 1336, *BR* 4:381; *Ordinationes et reformationes pro bono regimine Monachorum Nigrorum O.S.B.*).

1157. POPE ST. GREGORY VII (in the Roman Synod of 1078). Saturday was always held in veneration in the observance of our holy Fathers. Following their authority and example, We earnestly exhort all who seek a share in the benefits of the Christian religion, to abstain from eating meat on that day, unless a major feast occur, or one is prevented from doing so through illness (c. 7, Mansi 20:510; *PL* 148:801).

1158. COUNCIL OF LONDON (1268). Regular observance, which leads to life by the narrow way, is attacked on all sides by the pride of the flesh once the reins of self-control have been permitted to slacken. For that reason the holy Fathers commendably restricted the eating of flesh meat, so that its sparing use would hold pride in check, and subdue the flesh by detaching it from the pleasures of this world, enabling the spirit to sing its praises of gratitude to the Lord (c. 45, Mansi 23:1253).

1159. CONGR. OF STRASBURG, O.S.B. (founded 1624). The brethren are to be mindful, as Hypocrates says, that food and drink should be consumed only in the quantity necessary to restore physical forces, not to oppress them. They must remember, too, that they are monks, not doctors; that they are not to be too concerned about health, but pay attention to their monastic profession; and that they are not to be delicate in selecting foods, nor murmur about their preparation. They are to consider, too, how detestable a perversion of the right order it is if in the monastery, where those who are zealous are spiritually rich, they are actually poor in their fastidiousness, now seeking in the monastery what they could not have had outside it—they who were poorer in the world than they now are in the cloister. Let them keep in mind also that our holy Father prescribed that the meals were to be prepared by brethren who certainly knew little of the art of cooking: hence that food was to be eaten to satisfy one's need, not for the pleasure of gratifying one's taste. As St. Jerome words the thought: "We are pouring oil on the fire when we minister to our delicate body what is fuel for the fire of its ardent passions" (*Ep. 22, ad Eustochium, Paulae filiam,* § 8, *PL* 22:399; *Declar. in c. 39 RSB,* fol. 53).

1160. CUSTOMS OF HIRSCHAU. A. If in taking a trip the prior is to return to the enclosure the same day, he must not, without permission, eat outside the monastery. Nor can he grant such permission to another if the abbot is at home, nor even in the abbot's absence except for a grave necessity (*Const. Hirsaugienses* [*S. Wilhelmi*], *Lib. II,* c. 16, *PL* 150:1057). B. A monk must observe the fast of the Rule while he is on a journey, unless at the time he set forth from the monastery he received permission to eat a full meal (*ibid.,* c. 18, col. 1062).

1161. CONGR. OF BURSFELD (founded 1433). A. Monks must only prevent hunger, not gratify the flesh nor be slaves to sensuality, but in keeping with the spirit of the Rule, be given to the observance of fast, abstinence and temperance (*Stat.,* dist. 5, c. 6, n. 4, p. 141). B. Let this norm be observed in a holy manner in the regulation of the fast: neither by excessive rigor nor immoderate indulgence are our abbots to render nugatory the provision of the Rule so characterized by discretion (*ibid.,* c. 7, n. 3, p. 143). C. Since the holy Father requires of us both special devotion and mortification of the flesh during Lent (*RSB,* c. 49), all are to strive to observe accurately everything that he has prescribed in the chapter of the Rule. Let the monks devote themselves to reading, compunction of heart, and other pious works; conform themselves to the sufferings of Christ; live for God alone in silence, so that as sons of Holy Mother Church and of the order, they may obey in all perfection the laws of the Church and the statutes of the order (*ibid.,* c. 9. n. 1, p. 145). D. Sympathizing with the weakness and even the necessity of its members, our congregation, drawing upon its long experience and acting after mature deliberation, supporting itself on the discretion of the holy Father [Benedict] and the power he granted so to temper everything that the strong would still have something to long after, and the weak would not be disheartened, dispenses its members so that on three days of the week, Sunday, Tuesday and Thursday, they may eat flesh meat in the spirit of gratitude to God. This decision has not been taken rashly, but on Apostolic authority, which has been petitioned humbly (*ibid.,* c. 6, n. 2, p. 140). E. The more indulgent the congregation, the greater should be the submission of our brethren to the principle of being "content with the meanest and worst of everything" (*RSB*, c. 7, seventh degree). Hence they are not to give way to the restlessness of murmuring or disgrace themselves by complaining if, in accordance with the Rule, common food and vegetables are served. Monks must be content with what is readily obtainable in the region and used by the common people, and not desire specially procured foods (*peregrina*) and those that gratify the taste rather than nourish the body (*ibid.*, n. 4, p. 141). F. If the brethren are working outside the monastery, they may drink there as often as the prior permits, because of the hard work and the excessive heat. But within the monastery they are never to have permission to drink except in the community room assigned for this purpose by the abbot (*ibid.*, c. 2, n. 8, p. 128).

1162. SWABIAN CONGR. OF ST. JOSEPH. Taking into account the weaknesses of many, and our constant labors, which are by no means light—in fulfilling parish duties, in our literary efforts, and in performing other regular tasks—we allow the eating of flesh meat, but with this restriction: it is permitted on only three days in the week, namely, on Sunday, Tuesday, and Thursday. On the other days all are to abstain, with the exception of the ill and those who are under doctors' care. All are to strive manfully for the virtue of moderation, and avoid as far as is possible any form of excess in opposition to the virtue of temperance. No one is to eat or drink outside the ordinary times. If someone needs food or drink because of illness, or the summer's heat, he is to seek the superior's permission, eat or drink what has been allowed him, and do so in the proper spirit of thanksgiving, in silence, and in the place assigned. During meals the brethren will conduct themselves with religious modesty, observe the silence, keep their eyes cast down, without bowing the head too low, and hold their elbows well away from the table. The meal is to be eaten at a reasonable pace, neither too rapidly nor too slowly. Should anyone come late to the table, he will kneel in the center of the refectory until he has received a sign from the superior ordering him to rise. In some places necessity demands, and edification usually recommends, that seculars be admitted to the common table in the monastic refectory; but this is to be done on the condition that there be no conversing with them, and that there be no dispensation from table reading (*Const. et declar., Pars II*, c. 3, punctum 3, *de refectione fratrum*, fol. 90–97).

1163. POPE PIUS VI (d. 1799). It is Our desire that all monks take their meals in the same place, that each be served his portion of food individually, and that everything be conducted in silence; without the superior's permission no one is to eat or drink before or after the common meal (*Const. Apost. Apostolatus officium, Pars II*, c. 20, n. 203, *BRC* 6:2078; *Confirmatio const. ordinis Cluniacensis*).

1164. ROMAN MISSAL. A. Grant, we beseech you, Almighty God, that, with the sacred fast to purify us, you may cause us to come with sincere minds to the holy things that are before us (*Feria VI p. Dom. II Quadr., Oratio, Miss. Rom.*, p. 113). B. Grant, we beseech you, Almighty God, that your household, which abstains from food in order to afflict the flesh, may, by following the ways of righteousness, abstain from sin (*Feria II, Oratio, ibid.*, p. 106). C. It is indeed meet and just, right and helpful for salvation, always and everywhere to give thanks to you, Holy Lord, Father Almighty, who because of the fasting of the body repress vices, lift up minds, and bestow strength and rewards (*Praef. de Quadr.*, p. 280).

Practice of mortification

1165. MONASTIC BREVIARY. A. 1) Now that the star of light has risen;/ Let us in humility beseech God / To preserve us from harmful things / In our actions during the day. 2) May he restrain the tongue, bridling it;/ Lest the dreadful discord of strife resound;/ May he lovingly veil the sight,/ Lest it drink in vanities. 3) May the heart's inmost recesses be pure;/ And unreasonable acts depart;/ May the sparing use of food and drink / Wear down the body's pride. 4) So that when the day has come to an end;/ And lot has brought back the night/ We may sing his glory;/ Cleansed by self-restraint (*Hymn. ad Primam, Breviar. monastic.* 1:2).

B. Stones that have been polished / By constant hammering, by pressure;/ Are chosen for their places / By the hand of the Builder / Arranged to remain there forever / In the sacred structure (*Commune Dedicationis Ecclesiae, Hymn. ad Vesp. vers. 4, ibid.*, 1:165*).

Discipline of the chapter of faults

1166. COUNCIL OF BASEL (1431). All practice of virtue and discipline will quickly be abandoned and disappear through negligence unless it is zealously maintained by the good example of the seniors and the correction of superiors. Superiors are held responsible not only for their own personal faults, but those of others as well. Hence in the daily chapter of faults the abbot is obliged personally to correct major transgressions, and through the prior, the minor infractions committed either in the recitation of the Divine Office or in other regular observances. Without any acceptance of persons he is bound to inflict a fitting penance, so that the fear of punishment will cause the transgressions and faults to cease (*Stat. et ordinationes ad monachos Congr. Mellicensis directae,* ex manuscr. Salisburgensi).

1167. COUNCIL OF AACHEN (817). A. When a monk has been corrected by the abbot or any other superior, he will first say "*Mea culpa.*" He will then cast himself on his knees at his superior's feet, with his cowl over his head . . . and request forgiveness. At the superior's command he will rise and humbly explain the matter for which he has been summoned (*Pars II, capitula monachorum,* n. 13, *PL* 97:382).

B. Should anyone cause a disturbance, through his negligence, or commit a fault in the refectory, he will forthwith ask the superior's pardon (*ibid.,* n. 41, col. 388).

1168. POPE BENEDICT XII. Since monastic discipline is strengthened and made to flourish by the well-conducted daily chapter of faults, We establish and ordain that this exercise be held regularly in all cathedral churches, monasteries, and other places of the order or of religious institutes where there are six members. In conducting the same, before proceeding to any other matter, the faults, transgressions and negligences of the monks and the brothers are to be corrected according to the monastic Rule and approved customs. The regular discipline and reformation of life are to be dealt with first. In this chapter no monk or brother is to presume to defend or support another in an irreverent or unbecoming manner. After the Rule has been read by the lector, the excerpt will be explained to the chapter in easily understood terms by the presiding superior or by another to whom he has assigned the task (*Const. Apost. Summi Magistri,* c. 5, 20 Jun., 1336, *BR* 4:356).

1169. CONGR. OF BURSFELD. The chapter [of faults] is conducted to strengthen the foundations of the religious life; renew zealous effort in serving God; correct faults; and train the monks in virtue (*Stat.,* dist. 6, c. 3, n. 1, p. 188).

1170. CONGR. OF STRASBURG. Since the chapter of faults is certainly not the least among the forces for preserving and fostering monastic discipline, it must not be omitted by the superiors except when an interference of a serious nature prevents. Hence we prescribe that the chapter of faults be held by the prior every Friday of the year, except on feasts of the first and second class (*Declar. 2 in c. 16 RSB,* fol. 21).

1171. SWABIAN CONGR. OF ST. JOSEPH. The place for administering public correction is the chapter of faults, so called from the acknowledgment and expiation of transgressions whereby defects are immediately amended. The more frequent the correction of even minor shortcomings, the less danger there is of their devolving into more serious offenses. . . . But because the chapter of faults was instituted precisely in order to strengthen the foundations of religious life, renew zeal in serving God, extirpate vices, and implant virtues, it is to be approached and celebrated with deep reverence, fear, and the desire to be disciplined and enabled to make spiritual progress.

They who have been guilty of a fault should willingly and readily acknowledge the same, not merely out of habit, nor prompted by the fear of a more severe punishment [if they do not publicly confess in this manner], but from true humility and the serious resolve to amend.

In the same way they should accept with resignation and patience the penances inflicted, even though the transgressions are neither serious nor willful. They must be convinced that by this act of regular discipline they will receive from God, the rewarder of all good deeds, the gift of many excellent virtues: humility in their spontaneous self-accusation; patience in their embarrassment; and obedience in the acceptance and fulfilment of the penance imposed. In correcting transgressions, shortcomings or other misdeeds, the superiors must be prompted to seek and intend nothing other than the observance of the holy Rule and our constitutions, and the offender's spiritual progress. The penances imposed on the brethren should be proportioned to the transgressions and errors of which they have been guilty—that is, they are to be lighter or more serious according to the nature and relative gravity of the offense.

He who is corrected by a superior outside the chapter of faults will humbly seek forgiveness on his knees, or even prostrate on the floor. Since this act of humility is best calculated to unite the souls of both superiors and subjects in mutual appreciation of what is being done, and is also specifically prescribed by our holy Father Benedict, we admonish and exhort all in the Lord not to omit it, even when they see that the superior is quite angry (*Const. et declar., Pars II,* c. 4, punctum 3, nn. 5–6, fol. 144–147).

Discipline of the cell

1172. POPE CLEMENT XII (d. 1740). A monk must not enter another's cell except at his invitation. If someone comes to visit him, the door is to be kept open while the visitor is present, and not to be closed until after he has left. The monk's cell is to be left closed in such a way that it can be opened with the master key for the cells of all the brethren. . . . The monk is personally responsible for cleanliness and good order in his cell (*Const. Apost. Misericordiarum pater, Pars I,* c. 8, nn. 3–6, *17 Jan., 1740, BR* 24:606; *Confirmatio reg. et const. monachorum Maronitarum O.S. Antonii abb., congr. S. Isaiae in Syria*).

1173. CONGR. OF STRASBURG. A. The dormitory is divided into separate cells in order to enable the brethren to devote themselves more freely to prayer and other spiritual exercises. We assign a cell to each of the brethren, so that they are to sleep in individual apartments (*Declar. in c. 22 RSB,* fol. 31). B. No brother is to enter another's cell whether he is in it at the time or not, without his permission, or without that of the abbot. As long as they are in the room together, with the required permission, the door is to be kept halfway open. Without permission from the superior, a brother is not to take anyone into a cell whether he be a layman or an ecclesiastic, regardless of his rank (*ibid., declar. 3*). C. Without the permission previously mentioned, let no brother dare to close the cell even for a brief time in such a way that it cannot be opened from the outside with the master key (*ibid., Declar. 4*). D. For the sake of cleanliness the dormitory is to be swept by the brethren every week (*Declar. 12,* fol. 32).

1174. CONGR. OF BURSFELD. A. In order that the brethren may devote themselves more freely to prayer and spiritual reading, the dormitories must be divided into separate cells (*Stat.,* dist. 6, c. 7, n. 1, p. 246). B. Let the cells be all alike, furnished with a simple bed and a table and uniform furniture, arranged in such a manner as to serve the purposes of meditating and sleeping, so that one will not easily be disturbed by another, and that the beds will be in conformity with our [religious] state (*ibid.,* n. 2). C. The doors of the cells must have a small grill so that passersby, and particularly superiors, can see how the monks are using their time (*ibid.,* n. 3). D. The doors are to be closed with locks that can be opened with the superior's master key. Let the person residing in the cell leave the key, so that it can easily be seen, and the room easily opened by the superior if he wishes to enter (*ibid.,* n. 4).

1175. MONASTIC BREVIARY. 1) Hail, meek dwellers of solitude and cloister,/ Who bore to the end the wicked hordes, of furious hell. 2) Gems and weights of gold, positions of importance and dignities / You trampled under foot, as you did the abominable pleasures the world has to offer. 3) Garden herbs and vegetables were your food / Pure water furnished your drink, the hard ground your bed. 4) You lived among vipers and with the wild dragons / And feared not the most dreadful threats of demons. 5) With the preoccupations of this mortal life kept at a distance, / Your fervent spirit took flight, and united with the hosts of the blessed in heaven (*In fest. Om. Sanctorum O.S.B.,* 13 Nov., *Hymn. ad Vesp., Breviar. monastic.* 2:761).

IV. WRITINGS OF SAINTS AND DOCTORS

Nature and purpose of holy chastity

1176. ST. BASIL THE GREAT, bp. of Caesarea, Doctor of the Church (d. 379). He who desires to be free of the cares of the world, foregoes the union of marriage as though it were a kind of fetter. Then, having sacrificed marriage, he consecrates his life to God and professes chastity, so that it no longer is permitted to him to return to [the possibility of contracting] marriage. Instead, he does violence to nature in its more urgent impulses, and dedicates himself to the struggle for perfect chastity. For he who has joined this community of men has become the lover of God, seeking to conquer his sloth, at least to some degree, and desiring to experience spiritual holiness and peace, quiet and gentleness, and the happiness and joy that result from such efforts. To this end he devotes himself to directing his thought far from all the pleasures of earth and body that disturb the mind. He goes farther: in pure contemplation of the mind, which is under no shadow of darkness, he meditates on things divine, and is insatiably inspired by the light emanating from such reflections. When he has for some time trained his mind to such habits, and to this way of life generally, he gradually grows more like God, as far as this is possible, and becomes most beloved and dear to him. Thus he who has endured the great and difficult battle, even though there remains the unwilled concern with material things, can come into most intimate union with God, his mind purified and detached from physical affections (*Const. monasticae, Prooem.,* § 2, *PG* 31:1323).

1177. ST. JOHN CLIMACUS, monk (d. 580). A. Purity means that we put on the angelic nature. Purity is the longed-for house of Christ and the earthly heaven of the heart. Purity is a supernatural denial of nature, which means that a mortal and corruptible body is rivalling the celestial spirits in a truly marvelous way (*Scala paradisi, Grad. 15, de castitate et temperantia, PG* 88:879; Moore, n. 1, p. 146). B. The beginning of purity is the refusal to have anything to do with bad thoughts and occasional dreamless emissions; the middle state of purity is natural movements due to excess of food, but without dreams and emissions; and the end of purity is the mortification of the body after previously mortifying bad thoughts (col. 882; Moore, n. 8, p. 147). C. With beginners, falls usually occur by reason of luxury; with intermediates, because of haughtiness as well as from the same cause which leads to the fall of beginners; and with those approaching perfection, solely from judging their neighbor (col. 883; Moore, n. 20, p. 148). D. Someone told me of an extraordinarily high degree of purity. He said: "A certain man [St. Nonus, Bishop of Heliopolis], on seeing a beautiful body, thereupon glorified the Creator, and from that one look he was moved to the love of God and to a fountain of tears. And it was wonderful to see how what would have been a cause of destruction for one was for another the supernatural cause of a crown." If such a person always feels and behaves in the same way on similar occasions, then he has risen immortal before the general resurrection (col. 891; Moore, n. 60, p. 155).

1178. ST. GREGORY THE GREAT, Doctor of the Church (d. 604). For the rest are not good things at all, if in the eyes of the secret Judge they be not approved by the testimony of chastity. For all the virtues lift themselves up in the sight of the Creator by reciprocal aid. And because one virtue without another is either not a virtue at all, or the very least one, they should be mutually supported by their alliance together (*Moral., Lib. 21,* c. 3, § 6, *PL* 76:192).

Companions of chastity

1179. ST. JOHN CHRYSOSTOM, abp. of Constantinople, Doctor of the Church (d. 407). Without its companions, namely fasting and temperance, chastity soon grows weary of its effort. . . . Chastity has nothing in common with discord, drunkenness, immodesty, anger, malice, flattery, eagerness for human praise, pursuit of pleasure, covetousness, avarice, dissension, jealousy, ill will or envy. Chastity is never joined with these (*Hom. super illud Zachar. 6, Ecce vir Oriens,* inter apocrypha. Wolter furnishes no further identification. Not contained in available sources).

1180. ST. PETER DAMIAN, monk of Fonte-Avellana, cardinal, Doctor of the Church (d. 1072). A. What does physical integrity avail, or mortification, or affliction of the flesh, if purity of the heart is wanting? (*Lib. VIII, ep. 14, ad sorores suas Rodelindam et Sufficiam, PL* 144:491.) B. That virginity is perfect which is encircled by the other virtues, and is seasoned with the true humility of the same (*Serm. 46, in Nativ. B.V.M.,* col. 759).

1181. ST. BONAVENTURE, Franciscan general, cardinal, Doctor of the Church (d. 1274). They who abstain from the act of the flesh are not to be called chaste unless by the effort of their will the mind is chaste, the affection is chaste, and all their faculties are kept chaste (*Serm. 1, de S. Ambrosio Ep., Op. Om.,* ed. Peltier 13:505).

Christ, the source of chastity

1182. ST. GREGORY OF NYSSA, bp. (d. circa 403). Christ . . . the seed of virginity (*In Cant., Hom. 13, PG* 44:1055).

1183. ST. AUGUSTINE, bp. of Hippo, Doctor of the Church (d. 430). Christ is the teacher of chastity . . . (*Serm. 125,* § 4, *In Append., PL* 39:1994).

1184. ST. JOHN OF DAMASCUS. Celibacy is, as we have said, an imitation of the angels. Wherefore virginity is as much more honorable than marriage as the angel is higher than man. But why do I say an angel? Christ himself is the glory of virginity, who not only was begotten of the Father without beginning or emission or connection, but also became man in our image, being made flesh of the Virgin for our sakes without connection, and manifesting himself the true and perfect virginity. Wherefore, although he did not enjoin that on us by law, for, as he said: *Not all can accept this teaching; but those to whom it has been given* (Matt. 19:11), yet in actual fact, he taught us that and gave us the strength for it. Surely it is clear to everyone that virginity is now flourishing among men (*De fide orthodoxa, Lib. IV,* c. 24, *de virginitate, PG* 94:1210).

1185. POPE ST. LEO THE GREAT. And because no virtues are worthier or more excellent than merciful loving-kindness and unblemished chastity, let us more especially equip ourselves with these weapons, so that, raised from the earth, as it were, on the two wings of active charity and shining purity, we may win a place in heaven (*Serm. 55, De passione Dni.*, IV, *PL* 54:325).

1186. ST. JEROME. A. As soon as the Son of God set foot upon the earth, he formed for himself a new household here, in order that, as he was adored by angels in heaven, angels [virgins] might serve him also on earth (*Ep. 22, ad Eustochium, Paulae filiam, de custodia virginitatis,* n. 21, *PL* 22:408). B. It is no earthly life but a heavenly one to live beyond the flesh in the flesh. To acquire an angelic life in the flesh is of greater merit than to have the life of an angel. To be an angel is a matter of blessedness; but to be a virgin is a question of virtue. . . . You have, virgins, the Bridegroom who is a virgin, the lover of virginity and chastity, who chose the Virgin as his mother, in order that she might be the exemplar of chastity for all (*Ep. 9, ad Paulam et Eustochium, de Assumpt. B.V.M.*, § 5, *In Append.*, *PL* 30:127).

1187. HUGH OF ST. CHER, O.P., cardinal (d. 1263). It is most of all among the lilies of virginity that Christ the Bridegroom is contented and delighted by the sight of beauty and the fragrance of sweetness (*Sup. Cant. 2, 16, Comment.* 3:120).

The soul is the foundation of chastity

1188. ST. BASIL THE GREAT. A. It is a matter of great importance that virginity, to state the matter briefly, makes man like the incorruptible God. It does not proceed from bodies into souls, but is the ornament of the spiritual soul, and it is by virginity that the soul, which is dear to God, preserves the body from corruption (*De virginitate*, c. 2, *In Append.*, *PG* 30:671). B. Thus, to sum up, virginity must be understood as something great and splendid; and it proves itself now to be the pure seed of resurrection and of incorruptible life. For if *at the resurrection they will neither marry nor be given in marriage, but will be as the angels of God in heaven* (Matt. 22:30; cf. Luke 20:36), and will become the *sons of God* (cf. John 1:12), they who now preserve their virginity are angels, passing through life with a flesh free of corruption; and they are angels not in any vague or obscure sense, but outstanding and noble angels (*ibid.*, c. 51, col. 771).

Praises of chastity

1189. ST. CYPRIAN, bp. of Carthage, Primate of Africa, martyr (d. 258). A. Virginity makes itself the equal of the angels, in fact, if we examine the question more searchingly, it even excels them, for it gains the victory against nature in the besieged flesh, which angels do not possess (*De disciplina et bono pudicitiae*, § 7, *In Append.*, *PL* 4:855).

B. Chastity is the unassailable defense of holiness and the powerful overthrow of bad repute; the strengthening of fortitude and the weakening of impudent licentiousness; the guardianship of goodness and the destruction of depravity; the victory of the soul and the conquering of the body. It is the abundance of praise and the absence of reprehension; the bridesmaid of holiness and the severing of all relationship with turpitude; the mark of purity and the removal of all scandals; the practice of continence and the complete avoidance of sinful excess; the peaceful security of virtuous living and the restless carrying the war to its victorious end; the summit of purity and the imprisonment of vice. Chastity is the tranquil port of goodness and the place of shipwreck of all degradation; the loving mother of virginity and the enemy of all uncleanness; modesty's armor of defense, the victory gained over all shamefulness, and the destruction of corrupt manners; the wall of rigor and the elimination of vulgarity; the sword of severity and the conqueror and slayer of dissoluteness; the equipping of strength with its armor and the disarming of reprehensible conduct. It is the dignity of purity and the disavowal of uncleanness; the high honor of virtue and the overthrow of infamy; the dedication to good works and the crushing of vices; the goal of modesty, the punishment of impudence, the gaining of triumphs, the defeat of crimes; the tranquillity of salvation and the banishment of perdition; the life of the spirit and the mortifying of the flesh; the state of angelic condition and the lot of human substance. All uncleanness is held in check by the reins of chastity; and by its fetters the footsteps of ungovernable inclination to sin are shackled (*De singularitate clericorum, In Append.*, col. 943).

C. Modesty is the dignity of the body, the ornament of manners, the honor of the sexes, the bond of propriety, the beginning of chastity, tranquillity in the home, the origin of harmony. Modesty does not bother about whom it pleases, other than to measure up to its own standards. Modesty is always diffident and temperate, for it is the mother of innocence. Modesty always has propriety for its sole ornament, and is rightly conscious of its beauty when it fails to please the wicked. Modesty seeks no ornament, for it is its own beauty. It commends us to the Lord, unites us with Christ . . . is blessed in itself, and blesses all among whom it deigns to dwell. Even those who do not possess it can never criticize it, for it is held in veneration even by its enemies who wonder at it all the more because they cannot conquer it (*De disciplina et bono pudicitiae*, § 3, *In Append.*, col. 853).

1190. ST. GREGORY OF NAZIANZUS, bp., Doctor of the Church (d. 389). An excellent thing is virginity and celibacy, something to be considered as of the order of angels and the simple nature—I shrink from calling it Christ's nature, who, though he willed to be born for our sakes who are born, by being born of the Virgin, enacted thereby the law of virginity, to lead us away from this life, and cut short the power of the world, or rather to transmit one world to another, the present to the future (*Oratio 43, in laudem Basilii Magni*, § 62, *PG* 36:575).

1191. ST. JOHN CHRYSOSTOM. A. Angels *neither marry nor take wives* (cf. Luke 20:35); neither are they composed of flesh and blood; nor do they inhabit the earth; nor are they subject to the disorders of passions and lustful desires. They need neither food nor drink. They are not of such a nature that sweet sounds or soft music or physical beauty can attract them; they are not captivated by any kind of charm. . . . But the human nature, although it is inferior to that of those blessed spirits, strives with might and main to become like them, as far as possible. How so? Angels neither marry nor take wives—but neither does the virgin. Angels stand forever before God, serving him—and so does the virgin. For which reason Paul would have virgins free from all cares (cf. I Cor. 7:32 f.), in order to serve God more diligently and constantly, and not be distracted from this duty by anything. Although virgins, as long as they are weighted down with the body, cannot ascend to heaven after the manner of angels, they compensate all the more with the comfort that if they are holy in soul and body, they now receive the King of heaven (*De virginitate*, §§ 10, 11, *PG* 48:540). B. Do you not see the virgin's pre-eminence, how it so affects inhabitants of earth that, although they are clothed with a body, it makes them the equals of those incorporeal spirits? . . . In what, I ask, did Elias, Eliseus and John, all true lovers of virginity, differ from angels? In no way at all, except that they were constituted of a mortal nature. For if one examines the question diligently, they will be found to be affected by that other nature of the blessed spirits; and that it is to be acknowledged to their great credit and praise that they are in so inferior a condition (*ibid.*, § 279, col. 591).

1192. ST. BERNARD. A. What is more beautiful than chastity, which alone can *clean of defilement* (Job. 14:4), which changes an enemy into a friend of God, and transforms a man into an angel? The difference between the chaste man and the celestial spirit is one not of virtue but of felicity. Nay, more than that, although the angelic chastity has more of bliss, human chastity has greater fortitude. Chastity stands alone in that here below, during this mortal life, it represents a certain condition of immortal glory. It stands alone here, where marriage is the ordinary way of life, by claiming unto itself the conduct of that blessed region where they neither marry nor take wives, thus presenting already on earth a kind of foreshadowing of the heavenly way of life. It is chastity which, as the Apostle admonishes (cf. I Thess. 4:4), teaches men to possess in holiness and honor the fragile vessel [body] that we bear about with us, and in which we are often exposed to danger. In the likeness of sweet-smelling balsam which preserves corpses from corruption, it contains and restrains the senses and limbs lest they grow negligent in idleness, become tainted by desires, or depraved by the pleasures of the flesh. . . . I would say that this is the ornament of great beauty that worthily honors the priesthood, which makes the priest beloved of God and men. For its memory is not to be found in carnal offspring begotten of the flesh, but in spiritual blessing. It renders the priest, although still dwelling in this region so dissimilar, similar to the saints in glory (*Tract. de moribus et officiis episcoporum,* i.e., *ep. 42, ad Henricum archiepisc. Senonensem,* c. 3, n. 8, *PL* 182:816). B. Yet beautiful as it is, without charity [chastity] has neither worth nor merit. This is not surprising, since apart from charity no virtue or good work is acceptable in the eyes of God. Faith? No, not even if it were strong enough to move mountains. Knowledge? Certainly not, even though one should have all knowledge and speak with the tongues of angels. Martyrdom? Listen to St. Paul: *And if I deliver my body to be burned, yet do not have charity, it profits me nothing* (I Cor. 13:1–3). Nothing is accepted that you offer without charity, nor is anything offered with charity refused. Chastity without charity is a lamp without oil (St. Bernard, *op. cit.,* c. 9).

1193. ST LAURENCE JUSTINIAN, can. regular, patriarch of Venice (d. 1455). The virtue of continence is so sublime that in a sense it renders man similar to the angelic nature. For the continence by which man becomes like angels surpasses the condition of human nature. In one way the victory of the continent is greater than that of the angels. For angels live without flesh, but the continent triumph over flesh. A pure man and an angel differ in that the virginity of the angel is more blessed, but man's purity is recognized as being the stronger. A pure man is the lovely and beautiful dwelling of Jesus Christ. Who could think of a greater beauty than the comeliness of a pure man who is loved by the King, commended by the Judge, dedicated to the Lord, and consecrated to God? This virtue protects man's dignity; the dignity of man lies in the freedom of the will, which can accept or reject what is presented to it. In brutes and in impure men slavery of the appetite stands in opposition to this freedom. . . . Continence is the distinction of the noble, the exaltation of the humble, the nobility of ignoble man, the beauty of men in their vileness, the consolation of the sorrowful, the intensification of all that is beautiful, the honor of all countries, the lessening of crimes, the increase of rewards, beloved of God the Creator of all, sister of the angels, victory over the lower passions, the school of virtue, and the possession of all good works. Whoever possesses it will have peace of conscience, light of mind, cheerfulness in his countenance, joy in his heart, security at his death, and reward in heaven (*Lignum vitae,* tract. 3, *de continentia,* c. 2, *Op. Om.* 1:17).

1194. ST. AUGUSTINE. Chastity or purity holds a glorious and brilliant place among the other virtues, for it stands alone in its power to enable the pure of soul to see God. He who is Truth itself says: *Blessed are the clean of heart, for they shall see God* (Matt. 5:8). It is as though he had said by way of contrast: "They are miserable in truth whose hearts are defiled with carnal desire, for they will be engulfed in eternal punishments" (*Serm. 291, de castitate et munditia,* § 1, *PL* 39:2296).

1195. EUSEBIUS, bp. of Emesa (d. circa 359). The promise [in reward of purity] is made to all, of course, but addresses more particularly those women who consecrate themselves to the holiness of virginity. They are like other women as far as nature is concerned, but by their resolve transcend nature, and in their holy way of life seek to be united to the Holy One. If some of them achieve their purpose, it calls for admiration; if one fails in her resolve, her ruin is miserable, for it is worse to be drawn down from on high than to fall at the level of the earth. The promise both surpasses nature and ascends to the heights of heaven, and hence dwells [now] with the angels in this way of life, as the Savior expresses the thought in giving testimony of its dignity, because *at the resurrection of the dead,* which is the hope of the saints, they who have been judged worthy of that resurrection and of the future blessings, *will neither marry nor be given in marriage, but will be as the angels of God in heaven* (Matt. 22:30). Hence the proposal of some persons [virgins] possesses by anticipation what is promised as the reward of the kingdom of heaven. In the fulfilment of the promise, when the body will have changed into another nature, there will be neither desires to disturb nor unlawful pleasures to excite, but reward in peace without struggles in combat (*Discursus 7, de virginibus,* § 5, *Discours,* Buyaert 1:178).

1196. ST. THOMAS AQUINAS. A. If a man abstain from bodily pleasures, in order more freely to give himself to the contemplation of truth, this is in accordance with the rectitude of reason. Now holy virginity refrains from all venereal pleasure in order more freely to have leisure for divine contemplation (*II-II,* q. 152, art. 2, *Utrum virginitas sit illicita, Op. Om.* 10:200; Am. ed. 2:1807). B. Virginity is directed to the good of the soul in respect to the contemplative life, which consists in thinking of the things of God (*ibid.,* art. 4, *Utrum virginitas sit excellentior matrimonio,* p. 204; p. 1809).

The frightful loss of chastity

1197. ST. AMBROSE. A. Why should I continue the praise of chastity with more words? For chastity has made even angels. He who has preserved it is an angel; he who has lost it, a devil (*De virginibus, Lib. I,* c. 8, § 52, *PL* 16:214). B. You were a virgin in the paradise of the Lord; in fact, you were a flower of holy Church, you were a bride of Christ, you were a temple of God, you were the dwelling of the Holy Spirit. And as often as I say *you were,* you should lament just so many times, for you no longer are what you were. You entered the church in procession like the dove about which it is written: *The wings of the dove shone with silver, and her pinions with a golden hue* (Ps. 67:14). As long as you walked with a pure conscience, you glistened like silver and shone like gold. You were like a shining star in the hands of the Lord; you were in dread of no storm, no darkness of struggle.

And how has this sudden change of conduct come about? How this sudden transformation? From the virgin of the Lord you have become the corruption of Satan; from the bride of Christ, an abominable courtesan; from the temple of God to a temple of uncleanness; from the dwelling of the Holy Spirit to a hovel of the devil. You who walked as secure as a dove now hide yourself in the darkness like a lizard. You who shone like gold by reason of the honorable distinction of virginity, have now become more vile than the mud in the streets to be trampled under foot even by the unworthy. You who were like a radiant star in the hands of the Lord have lost your light and have been changed into a burnt-out coal (*De lapsu virginis,* c. 2, §§ 6, 7, col. 384). C. Woe to you, miserable person, woe to you who have forfeited such great blessings for the pleasure of the moment! And what hope for yourself have you left with Christ, our Lord, from whom you have taken the members and made them the members of a harlot? (cf. I Cor. 6:15). How will the Holy Spirit, whom you have repudiated, still visit you—that Spirit who departs even from impure thoughts? (*Ibid.,* c. 3. § 8, col. 385.) D. And how, in that shameful act, did you not recall the virgin's habit, and how you marched into the church among the ranks of the virgins? Did not the light of the holy vigils burn before your eyes? Did not the chanting of the sacred hymns resound in your ears? Did not the powerful word of the sacred reading echo in your heart, where above all others the Apostle cries out to you: *Flee immorality. Every sin that a man commits is outside the body, but the immoral man sins against his own body* (I Cor. 6:18). In saying *against his own body* he indicates that the sin is also against Christ. In fact, he adds: *Do you not know that your members are the temple of the Holy Spirit, who is in you, whom you have from God, and that you are not your own? For you have been bought at a great price. Glorify God and bear him in your body* (*ibid.,* vv. 19, 20). And again: *But immorality and every uncleanness or covetousness, let it not even be named among you, as becomes saints* (Eph. 5:3). And setting all flattery aside, the Apostle states clearly: *For know this and understand, that no fornicator or unclean person, or covetous one (for that is idolatry) has any inheritance in the kingdom of Christ and God* (*ibid.,* v. 5; *De lapsu virginis,* c. 6, § 22, col. 389).

1198. HUGH OF ST. CHER. When once they have lost the beauty of chastity, souls no longer possess the force of charity from within, but deprived of the strength of defense with which they are blessed by the habit of virtue, wander aimlessly before the devil (*Sup. Jerem., Lament. 1:6, Comment.* 4:287).

In praise of virginity

1199. ST. JEROME. Virginity is a sacrifice to Christ where the virgin's mind has not been defiled by thought, nor her flesh by lust. . . . It is a mark of great faith and of great virtue to be a pure temple of God, to offer oneself a whole-burnt offering and, according to the Apostle *to be holy in body and in spirit* (I Cor. 7:34; *Adversus Jovinianum, Lib. I,* c. 13, § 12, *PL* 23:231).

1200. ST. ATHANASIUS, bp. of Alexandria (d. 373). Great is the virtue of continency, great the glory of chastity, great the praises of virginity! O virginity, immense riches! O virginity, unfading crown! O virginity, temple of God and dwelling of the Holy Spirit! O virginity, precious pearl hidden from many, found by the few! O continency, dear to God and praised by the saints! O continency, hateful to many, but known to those worthy of you! O continency, fleeing death and hell, and possessed of immortality! O continency, joy of the prophets, fortification of the apostles! O continency, life of the angels, crown of holy men! Blessed is he who possesses you, blessed is he who endures in patience, because after a little labor he will rejoice much in you (*De virginitate,* § 24, *In Append., PG* 28:279).

1201. TERTULLIAN, priest of Carthage (d. 245). Purity is the flower of moral conduct, the honor of our bodies, the true beauty of the sexes, the purity of blood, the foundation of holiness (*De pudicitia,* c. 1, *PL* 2:1031).

1202. ST. JOHN CLIMACUS. A. Purity is worthy of such great and high praise that certain of the Fathers ventured to call it freedom from passion. Some say that those who have tasted sin cannot be called pure. In refutation of this view I would say: If anyone is willing, it is possible and easy to graft a good olive on to a wild olive. And if the keys of the kingdom of heaven had been entrusted to one who had always lived in a state of virginity, then perhaps the teaching of those who maintain what I have quoted above would be right. But let them be put to shame by him who had a mother-in-law, and having become pure, received the key of the Kingdom (cf. Luke 4:38; Matt. 16:19; *Scala paradisi, Grad. 15, de . . . castitate et temperantia, PG* 88:894; Moore, nn. 66, 67, p. 156). B. Purity means that we put on the angelic nature. . . . Purity is a supernatural denial of nature, which means that a mortal and corruptible body is rivaling the celestial spirits in a truly marvelous way (*ibid.,* col. 879; Moore, n. 1, p. 146).

1203. ST. EPHRAEM, deacon of Edessa, Doctor of the Church (d.

378). O chastity, gift of God, full of mildness, discipline, knowledge, and wisdom! O chastity, tranquil harbor of greatest peace and security! O chastity, heavenly prudence and holiness of worship! O chastity, which gladdens the heart of him who possesses it, and furnishes the soul with the wings for flying to heaven! O chastity, which begets spiritual joy and banishes sadness! O chastity, which hates evil and clings to what is virtuous! O chastity, which weakens the force of the passions and frees the mind from disturbances! O chastity, which enlightens the just, surrounds the devil in darkness, and confidently runs the shortest course to the prize of exalted vocation with Christ! O chastity, which banishes laziness and bestows patience! O chastity, light burden that is not drowned in waters [martyrdom]; eternal riches, deposited in the soul of the person who loves Christ, which the possessor will find in the time of necessity. O chastity, beautiful ornament which is neither ravaged by wild beasts nor destroyed in fire [martyrdom]. O chastity, which holds in its hands the riches that are above reproach, and drives away sloth! O chastity, spiritual chariot which carries its possessor to sublime heights! O chastity, which dwells in the souls of the meek and the humble and makes man divine! O chastity, which blooms like a rose in the heart of soul and body, and fills the whole house with fragrance! O chastity, precursor and fellow-dweller with the Holy Spirit! O chastity, which placates God, merits his praise and promises, and finds favor among all men! All the saints have loved it; Saint John the Evangelist embraced it, and for so doing merited to recline on the breast of the Lord. O chastity, which is possessed and practiced not by virgins alone, but also by those who have been converted to penance! Let us blessed servants of the Savior love and embrace it with our whole heart, that we may fill with joy the Spirit of God dwelling within us (*De castitate, Op. Om.* 1:125).

1204. ST. CYPRIAN. A. From this point on this discourse will be directed specifically to virgins, from whom greater care is demanded, in proportion to the higher honor which is theirs. They are the flower of the Church's growth; theirs is the beauty and ornament of spiritual grace, a joyful nature, a virtuous and uncorrupted work of praise and honor. They are the image of God reflecting the holiness of the Lord; they are the nobler portion of the flock of Christ (*De habitu virginum,* § 3, *PL* 4:455). B. Virginity is the exclusive possession of neither sex; virginity is persevering childhood; virginity is the triumph over pleasure (*De disciplina et bono pudicitiae,* § 7, *In Append.,* col. 855).

1205. ST. BASIL THE GREAT. This fact, moreover, should specially be borne in mind: he who has chosen the way of angels by passing up the confines of human nature has taken up a spiritual mode of life. Now, this is the special character of the angelic nature: to be free from the marriage yoke, not to be distracted by any created beauty, but to be constantly intent on the divine countenance (*Serm. Asceticus I,* § 2, *PG* 31:874; Wagner, p. 209).

1206. ST. AUGUSTINE. A. Chastity is the angelic life, chastity unites man to heaven and makes him a fellow citizen of the angels (*Serm. 291,* § 3, *PL* 39:2297). B. O Chastity, mark of honor of noble persons, exaltation of the humble, nobility of the obscure, beauty of those who are of low estate, consolation of those who mourn, growth of beauty, ornament of our holy religion, the lessening of offenses, the increase of merit, friend of God, companion of angels, life of patriarchs, crown of prophets, cincture of the apostles, aid of martyrs, treasure of confessors, inspiration of virgins, refuge of widows, joy and comfort of all who are virtuous (*Ad fratres in eremo, serm. 16, PL* 40:1262). C. Chastity leads man to glory . . . lifts him up to heaven . . . unites him with the angels (*ibid., serm. 65,* col. 1351).

1207. ST. AMBROSE. You have adopted the warfare of chastity, which does battle for an everlasting reward (*De virginibus, Lib. II,* c. 4, § 29, *PL* 16:226).

1208. ST. ISIDORE OF SEVILLE. The beauty of chastity must be loved, for once its delight has been experienced, it is found to be sweeter than that of the flesh. Chastity is the fruit of sweetness and the beauty of the saints which is above all reproach. Chastity is tranquillity of mind and health of body (*Sententiarum Lib. II,* c. 40, § 5, *PL* 83:643).

1209. LIVES OF THE FATHERS. Virginity is a sign of the very first virtue [that is, the first evidence of the presence of virtue], likeness to God, similarity to the angels, the begetter of life, the friend of holiness, the way of tranquillity, the mistress of joy, the leader in virtue, nourishment and crown of faith, support and assistance of charity (*Vita S. Eugeniae virg. et martyr.,* c. 23, *PL* 73:617).

1210. ST. HILDEGARDE, in a vision, was thus addressed by the Lord: "All who have preserved their purity from motives of heavenly love will be called daughters of Sion by the resounding voice from the eternal home, for in their love for inviolate purity they have imitated my Son in his love of virginity. The heavenly multitudes rejoice with them: every kind of triumphant melody surrounds them. . . . They have received from my Son the right to join in the loud peal that proceeds from the throne, and thus the entire chorus of virgins sings with one accord, chanting the new song, as the beloved virgin, John, testifies: *And they were singing as it were a new song, before the throne, and before the four living creatures, and the elders* (Apoc. 14:3). What does all this mean? In those faithful persons, who virtuously embrace chastity, and from love of God preserve their virginity inviolate, their good will is, as it were, a wonderful praise of their Creator. In the dawn of virginity—whose dependence on the Son of God cannot be broken—there lies concealed a most powerful praise, which no earthly duty nor binding force of law can prevent from resounding to God's glory. When this new song, which had never before been heard, was first permitted to be sung, it rushed forth in a marvelous manner as the only-begotten Son of God, the true flower of virginity, returned from earth to heaven as the Son of Man, and took his place at the right hand of the Father. As new customs which have previously not been known are gazed at in astonishment, so this new, unheard-of mystery, resounding in heaven, was openly acknowledged to the honor of virginity in the presence of the majesty of God—for God alone was able to produce it; it was acknowledged too before the four wheels [that is, the Evangelists] which sped rapidly through the four parts of the world and had brought the truth of all justice and of the humanity of the Savior . . . and before the elders who, inspired by the Holy Ghost, had announced the way of justice to men already under the law of the Old Testament" (*Scivias, Lib. II, visio 5, PL* 197:481).

1211. HUMBERT OF ROMANS, fifth master general of the Order of Preachers (d. 1277). A. By the preservation of purity you are to make your heart a throne of ivory (III Kings 10:18), a verdant couch (cf. Cant. 1:16), a clear fountain, an enclosed garden (cf. Cant. 4:12), a paradise of pleasure (cf. Gen. 2:15), an ark overlaid with purest gold within and without (cf. Ex. 25:11), a delightful storehouse of virtues (*De tribus votis substantialibus,* c. 23. *De vita regulari,* p. 16). B. May God forbid that divine encouragement be poured into an unclean vessel! (*ibid.,* c. 25, *de delectatione,* p. 17.) C. Let us strive most zealously, brethren, to avoid evil with our whole heart, by hating sin; to turn to the Lord with our whole heart, by practicing penance; to seek the Lord with our whole heart, by imploring forgiveness; to cling to him with our whole heart, loving him above all things; to serve the Lord with our whole heart, praising him; to imitate our Lord with our whole heart, following his paths. We owe all this to the Lord in justice, for he bestows his blessings upon our heart. For God himself enlightens our hearts with wisdom, governs them with goodness, feeds them with sweetness, invites them with beauty, changes them with power, unites them in charity, draws them with promises, instructs them with stripes, strikes fear into them with threats, softens them with blessings. The most dear God searches our hearts by testing them, speaks to them by instructing them, touches them by stirring them [to good works], visits them by consoling them, bestows life by giving them justification, opens them by streaming light upon them. For all these gifts it is fitting for us to render our thanks to him unceasingly (*ibid.,* c. 51, *de ordinatione in se quoad dispositionem cordis,* p. 34).

1212. ST. BERNARD. And if those daughters of Belial are haughty, walk with stretched-out necks and mincing steps, got up and adorned like a temple (cf. Isa. 3:16), abuse you, answer them: *My kingdom is not of this world* (John 18:36). . . . Answer them: "My life is hidden with Christ in God. When Christ, my life, shall appear, then I too will appear with him in glory" (cf. Col. 3:3–4).

Although, if one must glory, you too can do so quite simply and quite safely, but only in the Lord. I will not mention the crown which the Lord has prepared for you in eternity. I will say nothing of the promises which he has given you, that as a happy bride you will be admitted to contemplate face to face the glory of the Bridegroom; that he will present you to himself in all your glory, not having spot or wrinkle or any such thing (cf. Eph. 5:27); that he will receive you in an everlasting embrace, will place his left hand under your head and his right arm embrace you (cf. Cant. 2:6). I will pass over in silence the special place reserved for virgins among the sons and daughters of the kingdom. I will not mention the new song which you will sing as a virgin among virgins, but with special and most sweet tones all your own, rejoicing in it yourself and giving joy to the whole city of God, whilst you sing and dance and follow the Lamb wherever he goes. Eye has not seen or ear heard, nor has it entered into the heart of man, what things God has prepared for you (cf. I Cor. 2:9), and for what you must prepare yourself. So I will pass over what is promised to you in the future and concern myself solely with the present, with what you have already, with *the first-fruits of the Spirit* (Rom. 8:23), the gifts of the Bridegroom, the pledges of betrothal, the abundant blessings with which he has met you on the way, he whom you await to follow you and complete what is lacking. May he come out into the open to be seen by his bride in all beauty and admired by the angels in all his glory. If the daughters of Babylon have anything like this, let them bring it forth, they whose *glory is in their shame* (Phil. 3:19). They are clothed in purple and fine linen, but their souls are in rags. Their bodies glitter with jewels, but their lives are foul with vanity. You, on the contrary, whilst your body is clothed in rags, shine gloriously within, but in the sight of heaven, not of the world. What is within delights because he is within you who is delighted, for you cannot have any doubt that Christ dwells in your heart (cf. Eph. 3:17); *all glorious is the king's daughter as she enters* (Ps. 44:14). . . . Therefore do not emulate evil-doers and those who borrow their beauty elsewhere when they have lost their own. . . . The true and proper beauty of anything needs no help from other sources. The ornaments of a queen have no beauty like to the blushes of natural modesty which color the cheeks of a virgin. Nor is the mark of self-discipline any less becoming. Self-discipline composes the whole being of a maid's body, and the temper of her mind. It bows her head, smoothes her brow, composes her face, binds her eyes, controls her laughter, bridles her tongue . . . calms her anger, and governs her steps. Such are the pearls that adorn the vestures of a virgin.

What glory can be preferred to virginity thus adorned? The glory of the angels? An angel has virginity, but he has no body. Without doubt he is more happy if less strong in this respect (*Ep. 113, ad Sophiam virginem,* nn. 2–5, *PL* 182:257; James, p. 175).

1213. JEAN RIGAUD (Joannes Rigaldi), Franciscan theologian (d. 1323). Chastity has a recompense above the value of gems, and holds a dominion above the stars. . . . Chastity is a treasure in an extremely fragile vase, therefore to be protected by all the means at our command. . . . It is a treasure to be defended against an enemy of great malignity, hence also a treasure to be possessed in fear (*Diaeta salutis,* tit. 4, c. 4, *Op. Om. S. Bonaventurae,* ed. Peltier 8:288–289).

1214. DAVID OF AUGSBURG, Franciscan mystical writer and preacher (d. 1272). Chastity keeps the body clean . . . frees the mind . . . gives joy to the conscience . . . and makes its possessor lovable and admirable to men as well as to angels. . . . Chastity is a virtue that is heavenly in origin (*De profectu religiosorum, Lib. II,* c. 52, *Op. Om. S. Bonaventurae,* ed. Peltier 12:408).

1215. ST. JEROME. We reckon the bearing of fruit in hundredfold (cf. Matt. 13:23) as belonging to virgins, the sixtyfold to widows and the continent, the thirtyfold to those living in chaste marriage (*Lib. II Comment. in Evang. Matt., PL* 26:89).

1216. JOHN CASSIAN. *This is,* says the Apostle, *the will of God, your sanctification.* And lest he should have left us with any doubt or obscurity about what he wanted to call sanctification, he adds: *This is the will of God, your sanctification; that you abstain from immorality; that every one of you learn how to possess his vessel* [body] *in holiness and honor, not in the passion of lust like the Gentiles who do not know God* (I Thess. 4:3–5). You see with what praise he honors chastity: he calls it the honor of the vessel, that is, of our body, and our sanctification (*De coenobiorum institut., Lib. VI,* c. 15, *PL* 49:285).

1217. ST. JOHN CLIMACUS. A monk is he who within his earthly and soiled body toils toward the rank and state of the incorporeal beings [angels, lit. "bodiless ones"] (*Scala paradisi, Grad. I, PG* 88:634; Moore, n. 4, p. 50).

1218. ST. AUGUSTINE. Chastity is necessary for all men, but more particularly than all others for the ministers of Christ's altar, for their lives must be an instruction for others and an assiduous preaching of the truths of salvation. It is fitting that the Lord have as ministers men who are defiled by no taint of the flesh, but who are distinguished for their continence of chastity (*Serm. 291,* § 3, *In Append., PL* 39:2297).

Hope of victory lies in flight

1219. ST. JEROME. I acknowledge my weakness. I would not fight in the hope of victory lest some time or other I lose the victory. If I flee [to the desert, the religious life], I avoid the sword; if I stand, I must either overcome or fall. But what need is there for me to forsake certainties in order to follow after uncertainties? I must avoid death either with my shield or with my feet. You who fight may either be overcome or may overcome. I who take flight do not overcome, inasmuch as I take flight; but I flee to make certain that I may not be overcome. There is no safety in sleep with a serpent beside you. Possibly he will not bite me, yet it is possible that after a time he may bite me (*Contra Vigilantium*, § 16, *PL* 23:352).

1220. ST. AUGUSTINE. A. If you desire to gain the victory, take flight whenever impurity thrusts its temptations at you; and feel no embarrassment at taking flight, if you seek to obtain the palm of victory in chastity (*Serm. 293, de incauta familiaritate extranearum mulierum*, § 1, *In Append., PL* 39:2301). B. Would any man, considering his own weakness, dare to attribute his chastity or his innocence to his own powers? (*Confess. Lib. II*, c. 7, § 15, *PL* 32:681; Sheed, p. 36.) C. The more that I see that this blessing [virginity] is great, the more I fear the thief of pride, lest the blessing be lost. No one but God, who granted it, guards this blessing [of virginity] and *God is love* (I John 4:8). The guardian therefore of virginity is love: but the place of this guardian is humility. It is there that he dwells who said that his Spirit rests on the poor and the little, on him who is contrite of spirit and on him who trembles at his words (cf. Isa. 66:2; *De sancta virginitate*, c. 51, § 52, *PL* 40:426).

1221. JOHN CASSIAN. A. In proportion to the sublime and heavenly reward of chastity, it is tormented by grievous and insidious temptations of its adversaries (*De coenob. institut., Lib. VI*, c. 17, *PL* 49:287). B. Corporal fasting alone does not suffice for securing and preserving the purity of perfect chastity . . . unless true humility is first firmly established; without humility the triumph over vice can never be secured (*ibid.*, c. 1, col. 268).

1222. ST. ATHANASIUS. Do not be too confident about your chastity, lest you fall; you should rather fear, for as long as you fear you will not sin (*De virginitate*, § 22, *In Append., PG* 28:278).

1223. ST. GREGORY THE GREAT. A. It is necessary to bear in mind that the strength of the righteous is of one sort, and the strength of the reprobate of another. The strength of the righteous is to subdue the flesh, to thwart our own wills, to annihilate the gratification of the present life, to be in love with the roughness of this world for the sake of eternal rewards, to set at nought the allurements of prosperity, to overcome the dread of adversity in our hearts. But the strength of the reprobate is to have the affection unceasingly set on transitory things, to hold out with insensibility against the strokes of our Creator, not even by adversity to be brought to cease from the love of temporal things, to go on to the attainment of vainglory even with the waste of life, to search out larger measures of wickedness, to attack the life of the good, not only with words and by behavior, but even with weapons, to put trust in themselves, to perpetrate iniquity daily without any diminution of desire (*Moral., Lib. VII,* c. 21, § 24, *PL* 75:778). B. For if either humility forsake chastity, or chastity abandon humility, before the author of humility and chastity, what does either a proud chastity or a polluted humility avail for our benefit? (*ibid., Lib. 21,* c. 3, § 6, *PL* 76:192.) C. All strength lies in humility, for all pride is weak. Wherefore the cleanness of chastity is to be preserved through guarding humility (*ibid., Lib. 26,* c. 17, § 28, col. 364).

1224. ST. AUGUSTINE. Beloved brethren, all unworthy and shameful familiarity must be shunned by all Christians, but especially by all clerics and monks; for without doubt anyone who does not wish to avoid familiarity that is subject to suspicion will soon fall into grave disorders (*Serm. 293,* § 1, *In Append., PL* 39:2301).

1225. ST. POSSIDIUS, monk at Hippo, later bp. of Calama (d. circa 440). When [St. Augustine] was requested on occasion to be visited or greeted by women, they were never admitted to him without clerics in attendance, nor did he ever speak with them alone, not even when matters of confidence were involved (*Vita S. Augustini episc.,* c. 26, *PL* 32:55).

1226. ST. JEROME. To all who are Christ's virgins show the same regard or the same disregard. Do not linger under the same roof with them, and do not rely on your past continence. You cannot be holier than David nor wiser than Solomon. Always bear in mind that it was a woman who expelled the tiller of paradise from his heritage. . . . If in the course of your clerical duty you have to visit a widow or a virgin, never enter the house alone. Let your companions be persons of such character that association with them can bring no discredit upon you. . . . You must not sit alone with a woman or see one without witnesses (*Ep. 52, ad Nepotianum, de vita clericorum et monachorum,* n. 5, *PL* 22:531).

1227. ST. ISIDORE OF PELUSIUM, priest, abbot (d. circa 449). As far as is possible, good man, avoid all companionship with women. . . . Should necessity force you to meet them, keep your eyes fixed on the ground. . . . And when you have spoken the few things that can occupy their attention or enlighten them, take flight immediately, lest perhaps protracted association with them weaken and break down your strength (*Lib. II, ep. 284, Palladio episc., PG* 78:714).

1228. ST. BASIL THE GREAT. We must first avoid all meetings and conversations with women, and never approach them except when so serious a necessity arises that it is impossible to act otherwise. If we are confronted with such a situation, we are to shun them as we would fire, and take our leave abruptly and quickly. Dwell in your mind on what Wisdom itself says on the matter: *Can a man take fire to his bosom, and his garments not be burned? Or can a man walk on live coals, and his feet not be scorched?* (Prov. 6:27–28; *Const. monastic.*, c. 3, *Quod non oportet incaute cum mulieribus colloqui,* § 1, *PG* 31: 1343.)

1229. HUMBERT OF ROMANS. Contacts must be avoided not only with women of licentious character, but also with those who are virtuous. Although the earth is good, and rain is good as well, mud is formed when they are mixed. In the same way, although a man's hand is good, and woman's hand is likewise good, sometimes evil thoughts or affections are generated from their union. *He who touches pitch blackens his hand* (Sir. 13:1; *Ep. de tribus votis substantialibus,* c. 30, *De vita regulari,* p. 19).

1230. ST. BONAVENTURE. Women are to be granted interviews only briefly and as it were fleetingly. "It is safer not to be able to perish than actually not to have perished in the face of danger" (St. Jerome, *Ep. 117, ad matrem et filiam in Gallia commorantes,* § 3, *PL* 22:955). I would call him neither chaste nor morally worthy who has no fear either to touch a woman or to admit her embrace. How can he touch that upon which he is not permitted to look? (Cf. Matt. 5:28; *Speculum disciplinae ad novitios, Pars I,* c. 30, § 4, *Op. Om.*, ed. Quaracchi 8:612.)

1231. ST. ANTONINUS, O.P., abp. of Florence (d. 1459). Looking at women, frequent conversations with them, or companionship with them, mutual acceptance and bestowal of gifts, are the destruction of chastity (*Summa Theologica, Pars IV,* tit. 4, c. 6, *de castitate viduali,* 4:143).

1232. JOHN OF TRITHEIM, abbot of Sponheim (d. 1516). I want you to listen to this thought carefully, and learn it well, my brethren, you who carry a great treasure in a weak body. Avoid idleness! Be always engaged in doing something good, so that no matter how often the devil approach to tempt you, he will find you busily occupied in doing something profitable. For the idle man is exposed to the snares of the tempter, whereas he who is preoccupied with a good work has denied all access to temptation. Hence the mind is to be kept engaged continually in some sort of activity, so that at no time will it be lacking in its interest. Blessed is the man who always keeps his mind occupied in worthy undertakings, never giving way to sluggishness or laziness. Blessed is the spiritual soldier of Christ who is ever on his guard in the fear of the Lord, and subdues all disturbances of the flesh at the very outset. Anyone who toys with impure thoughts as though he were deliberating about them, cannot preserve his chastity unsullied. At the first manifestation of evil thoughts he must take up the fight, for in a situation where delay brings danger, the battle must be fought fiercely from the outset. At all times we have to be on guard against the enemy of our salvation, who is never conquered more easily than when he is choked off at the very beginning. Continual practice of mortification is necessary, brethren, for a mind always devoted to the striving for holiness is like a massive tower in which the soldier of Jesus Christ, ever on guard, fears no insidious attack of the enemy. I beg you, therefore, brother, waste no time in idleness lest you increase the occasion of vice, for you certainly are not lacking in appreciation of the astuteness of the evil spirits (*Hom. 21, de continentia et vera castitate, Op. pia et spiritualia,* p. 509).

1233. ST. ISIDORE OF SEVILLE, Doctor of the Church (d. 636). Knowing that chastity is the beauty of the soul, and that by it man is made the equal in angelic gifts from which they themselves have fallen, and prompted therefore by the malice of envy, demons suggest through the bodily senses impurity of deed and desire, so that they can triumphantly lead to hell with them the souls of those whom they have overcome, now cast down from heaven (*Sententiarum Lib. II,* c. 39, § 22, *PL* 83:643).

1234. JOHN CASSIAN. Although the grace of God and [his gaining the] victory is necessary for all advance in virtue, and the conquering of all vices, God's very own favor and special gift are necessary in this matter [of preserving purity]. This is most abundantly evidenced in the sayings of the Fathers, and by the memory of personal trial in the case of those who have merited to possess it. For in a certain sense it is an escape from the flesh while still inhabiting the flesh, and a supernatural insensibility to its sting while still enclosed within the same weak flesh. It is impossible for man, if I may so express the thought, to fly with his own wings to so lofty and heavenly a prerogative unless the grace of God lift him up from the slime of the earth with the gift of chastity. For by no virtue are men in the flesh so distinctively made the equals of the spiritual angels through imitation of their conversation [manner of life], as by the reward and gift of chastity. Through it, while still dwelling on earth, they have, according to the Apostle, *citizenship in heaven* (Phil. 3:20), possessing here below in the weak flesh what is promised to the saints after they have laid aside this corruptible body (*De coenob. institut., Lib. VI,* c. 6, *PL* 49:272, 275).

1235. JOHN OF TRITHEIM. No one is chaste by his own power, because man in his frailty is unable to conquer nature, unless he who created nature and everything else grants the strength. As often as nature is overcome by chastity, God has obviously assisted man. . . . Therefore whenever the mind is assailed with temptations to uncleanness, divine assistance is to be invoked without delay. . . . Let prayer be always on the monk's lips; let the memory of the passion and death of the Lord Jesus Christ never depart from his reflection. Nothing is so able to strengthen the mind and soul against the demon of impurity as devout meditation on the passion of our Lord Jesus Christ (*Hom. 21, Op. pia et spiritualia,* p. 508, 510).

The help of the Most Holy Eucharist

1236. ST. JOHN CHRYSOSTOM. A. This blood, if worthily received, drives out devils, and keeps them afar from us, while it summons to us angels and the Lord of angels. For whenever they see the Lord's blood, devils flee and angels assemble (*Hom. 46 in Joan.,* § 3, *PG* 59: 261). B. Let us then arise from this table like lions breathing fire, having become terrible to the devil (*ibid.,* col. 260).

1237. ST. CYRIL, bp. of Alexandria (d. 444). Whilst Christ remains in us, he quiets the unruly nature of our members, strengthens piety, and calms the disturbances of the mind (*In Joan. Evangel., Lib. IV,* c. 2, *PG* 73:586).

1238. ST. BERNARD. If any of you is now not so often or so violently assailed by the passion of anger, or of envy, or of lust, or by other such domestic enemies, let him return thanks to the body and blood of Christ, for the power of the sacrament has been efficacious in him: and let him rejoice for this awful sore is beginning to heal (*Serm. de temp., Serm. in Coena Dni,* § 3, *PL* 183:272).

1239. ST. THOMAS AQUINAS. A. Although this sacrament is not ordained directly to lessen the *fomes* [literally: tinder, kindling-wood, hence vulnerability to sin], yet it does lessen it as a consequence, inasmuch as it increases charity (*III,* q. 79, art. 6, *Utrum per hoc sacramentum praeservetur homo a peccatis futuris,* ad 3, *Op. Om.* 12:225; Am. ed. 2:2484). B. Let this [Holy Communion] be to me the armor of faith and the shield of good will. Grant that it may work the extinction of my vices, the rooting out of concupiscence and lust, and the increase within me of charity and patience, of humility and obedience. Let it be my strong defense against the snares of all my enemies, visible and invisible; the stilling and calm of all my impulses, carnal and spiritual; my indissoluble union with you, the One and true God, and a blessed consummation of my last end (*Gratiarum actio post communionem, Miss. Rom.,* p. LIX).

1240. ST. AMBROSE. O you Holy Bread, you living Bread, you pure Bread, who came down from heaven and gave life to the world, come into my heart and purify me from every defilement, whether of flesh or of spirit (*Oratio in praeparatione ad Missam, Sabbato, Miss. Rom.,* p. LIV).

1241. WILLIAM OF AUVERGNE, bp. of Paris (d. 1249). *My flesh is food indeed, and my blood is drink indeed* (John 6:56). Here Christ speaks of the sacrament of the Eucharist, in which are contained the true flesh of Christ which was fastened to the cross, and his blood which was shed in his passion. The flesh and blood of Christ nourish the soul, which is immortal and incorruptible. Material food nourishes only the body, which is corruptible. Through eating and drinking men seek no longer to hunger and thirst. But this is not granted except by this food and this drink which render those who consume them immortal and incorruptible, and make them the companions of the saints, among whom there will be unity through spiritual participation: *He who eats my flesh, and drinks my blood, abides in me and I in him* (*ibid.,* v. 57; *In fest. Corp. Christi, Evangelium, Postilla,* fol. CXCIII; in, *Postilla super epistolas et evangelia;* Lugduni: Joannes de Vingle, 12 Febr., 1500, CCLV fol.).

Chastity, foundation of monasticism

1242. ST. BASIL THE GREAT. We do not recognize the professions of men, except of those who have enrolled themselves in the order of monks. These seem silently to have taken celibacy upon themselves. But, even in their case, I think that it is proper that this course of action should precede: that they be questioned and that a clear profession be received from them [explicit profession of the vow of chastity], so that, when they change to a carnal and voluptuous life, they may be subjected to the punishment of fornicators (*Ep. 199, ad Amphilochium, de canonibus,* § 19, *PG* 32:719; Way, p. 49).

1243. ST. JOHN CHRYSOSTOM. As I said earlier, if you were a private individual, no one would blame you for refusing to serve as a soldier. But you are now no longer your own master, engaged as you are in the service of so great a king. If the wife has not authority over her body, but the husband (I Cor. 7:4), far more they who love in Christ must be unable to have authority over their own body (*Adhortatio ad Theodorum lapsum, Lib. V, PG* 47:312).

1244. JOHN OF TRITHEIM. A. Chastity, a virtue of great beauty, through which, once the violent fury of inclination to evil has been conquered and the body is preserved in complete probity, all the force of the urge to impurity is subjected to the domination of reason, belongs in a special way to those who live within the enclosure. . . . There are three things without whose perpetual observance no one can be considered a monk: the first is the humble obedience of true submission; the second, abandonment of all ownership; the third, the guarding of perpetual continence and inviolate chastity. . . . Chastity is the greatest ornament of monks; those who are decorated with it will be admitted to the companionship of angels (*Hom. 21, de continentia et vera castitate, Op. pia et spiritualia,* p. 507). B. You are monks, separated from the world by your own voluntary promise and dedicated to the service of our Lord Jesus Christ. Hence under the necessity of your salvation you are bound to lead a more elevated and holier life than your fellow Christians, and to conquer all tendencies to evil in body and soul. You must always be perfectly pure in mind and body, never stained by any of the filth of corruptible flesh. An incontinent monk is an apostate . . . like one who violates an oath (*ibid.*, p. 509).

The lily of chastity among the thorns of mortification

1245. ST. JEROME. A. The preservation of chastity involves a martyrdom of its own (*Ep. 130, ad Demetriadem, de servanda virginitate,* § 5, *PL* 22:1110). B. To be as the martyrs, or as the apostles, or as Christ, involves a hard struggle, but brings with it a great reward. . . . Look to yourself and glory in your own success, not in others' failure (*Ep. 22, ad Eustochium, Paulae filiam, de custodia virginitatis,* § 38, col. 422). C. By rigid fast and vigil she must *quench all the fiery darts of the most wicked one* (Eph. 6:16; *Ep. 54, ad Furiam, de viduitate servanda,* § 7, col. 553). D. Therefore, if experience gives me the right to advise, or clothes my words with credibility, I would begin by urging you and warning you as Christ's spouse, to avoid wine as you would avoid poison. For wine is the first weapon used by demons against the young. Greed does not shake, nor pride puff up, nor ambition infatuate so much as does wine. . . . Wine and youth between them kindle the fire of sensual pleasure. Why do we throw oil on the flame, why do we add fresh fuel to a miserable body which is already ablaze? (*Ep. 22, ad Eustochium,* § 8, col. 399.)

1246. ST. AMBROSE. A. Virginity is not praiseworthy because it is found among the martyrs but rather because it itself makes martyrs (*De virginibus, Lib. I,* c. 3, § 10, *PL* 16:202). B. It is a distinguished army that does battle for the kingdom of heaven (*De virginitate,* c. 6, § 28, col. 287). C. Self-denial is the discipline of chastity: we learn to abandon dissipation, to conquer carnal impulses, banish covetousness, and rid ourselves of bodily pleasures (*De Jacob et vita beata, Lib. II,* c. 10, § 43, *PL* 14:663).

1247. ST. AUGUSTINE. The Lord's virgin must devote herself to fasting and abstinence in order to extinguish the flames of lust and of all evil impulses; she must be devoted to prayer day and night if she desires to avoid the snares and temptations of the devil in his deceptiveness and to obtain the rewards promised for virginity. The Lord's virgin must be given to self-denial with regard to all pleasures of taste, and always adorned with a proper spirit of recollection (*De sobrietate et castitate,* c. 2, *In Append., PL* 40:1108).

1248. ST. BASIL THE GREAT. The virgin must at the outset acquire a mastery over the sense of taste, prudently regulating from above the sources of pleasure of the stomach, and the causes of disorder that spring from them. Having once chosen to follow the virgin's life, she must not thoughtlessly betray her virginity in taking this pleasure through lack of discretion in the use of food. For even the taste must be virginal in the virgin. She must not allow herself to be tainted with anything that seduces her to the pleasure of eating . . . but prudently sustain her body for the duties of her soul (*De virginitate,* c. 7, *PG* 30: 683; Valliant, p. 11).

1249. ST. GREGORY THE GREAT. A. Chastity issues into the perfect radiance of purity when the flesh is spent with abstinence (*Regula pastoralis, Pars II,* c. 3, *PL* 77:30; Davis, p. 51). B. If the body is not worn down by the infliction of abstinence, the flame of lust kindles itself against the soul (*Moral., Lib. 13,* c. 16, § 19, *PL* 75:1026).

1250. ST. BERNARD. A. Although to mortify the deeds of the flesh by the spirit is a kind of martyrdom, and is done with a spiritual weapon which does not, indeed, excite so much horror as that with which the limbs of the body are mangled and cut, it is not less painful, since its action continues much longer (*Serm. 30 in Cant., . . . de prudentia carnis, quae est mors,* § 11, *PL* 183:939; Eales, p. 199). B. The first enemy of our abstinence or continence is *the flesh which lusts against the spirit* (Gal. 5:17). See how domestic an enemy we have here! how perilous a combat! how intestine a war! A most cruel antagonist is the flesh, O my soul, which we can neither flee nor put to flight; we have to bear it about with us everywhere, because it is firmly bound to us. And what adds to the danger and the misery, we are ourselves obliged to support and are forbidden to destroy our enemy. See, then, brethren, how watchfully we must guard ourselves against a foe that dwells in our very bosom.

But my flesh is not my only adversary: I have another, an adversary that encompasses and assails me on every side. If you do not know what I mean, let me inform you that I am referring to *the wickedness of this present world* (Gal. 1:4). This enemy *hath shut up my ways* (Lam. 3:9), and through the five gates of the soul, that is, through the five bodily senses, he wounds me with his arrows, and *death is come up through my windows* (Jer. 9:21). These two adversaries would certainly be enough for me, yet *behold a whirlwind came out of the north* (Ezech. 1:4), whence proceeds all manner of evil. Alas, what resource remains to me now but to cry out with the apostles: *Lord, save us, we are perishing!* (Matt. 8:25.) . . . For the wrestling of those who desire to keep themselves continent—continent, I mean, not alone from carnal pleasures, but also, as should be, from all other sins and vices—*their wrestling is not against flesh and blood, but against the Principalities and the Powers, against the world-rulers of this darkness, against the spiritual forces of wickedness on high* (Eph. 6:12). . . . I think you now understand in some degree the difficulty of abstinence from sin, so that, according to the Apostle's counsel, *you may know the things that have been given you by God* (I Cor. 2:12). And beyond a doubt it is only *under God we shall do valiantly*—with regard to this virtue in particular—it is he who will tread down our foes (Ps. 59:14; *Serm. de temp., serm. 3 pro Dom. VI p. Pent.,* § 5, col. 343).

1251. BLESSED OGERIUS, Cistercian abbot (d. circa 1200). In order for chastity to be vigorous in mind, the flesh must be immolated with the knife of abstinence (*Serm. de verbis Domini in coena.,* serm. 8, *in Joan. 14, 15–17,* § 4, *PL* 184:912).

1252. JEAN RIGAUD, Franciscan theologian (d. 1323). As soup stops boiling when we take away the wood or the fire from under it, so temptation of the flesh ceases when we deprive the body of food (*Diaeta salutis,* tit. 2, c. 6, *Op. Om. S. Bonaventurae,* ed. Peltier 8:270).

1253. JOHN OF TRITHEIM. A. The more familiar the weakness of the flesh is to you personally, the harder the struggles for chastity. Hence you must be very much on your guard, since we carry about with us a domestic enemy, and support, as it were, a domestic impeller to vice. As long, therefore, as we live in this mortal flesh, we must ever fear the corrupter of chastity. We are to avoid everything that can excite the feelings of lust and, as far as we can do so, flee sloth and idleness. . . . Arm yourselves with the shield of perfect confidence in Jesus Christ. . . . Be ever of one mind, all of you, in fraternal charity, and harmonious without pretense in the observance of the regular discipline. Be devoted to fasting and continence, pray always and without intermission. Love silence, and do not flee the monastic solitude, if you seek to attain to true purity of body and mind. Exercise a continual custody of the eyes, the ears, and of speech, lest through these windows death enter into the soul (*Hom. 21, de continentia et vera castitate, Op. pia et spiritualia,* p. 511). B. Eagerly direct your steps to enter into life by the narrow way: that means, not to fulfil the desires of the flesh, to hate the world, to live by the spirit. You have been called to do battle for God against the vices of the flesh. Seek no rest before gaining the victory, seek not to abandon the fight, for no one is crowned but the victor. In this life there is no certainty of victory, but only constant struggle. . . . *Is not man's life on earth a drudgery?* [Douay, *a warfare.*] *Are not his days those of a hireling?* (Job 7:1.) You are a soldier of the Supreme King, not free to desert his combat. . . . Work hard as a good soldier of Jesus Christ: let no allurement of carnal pleasures touch your mind (*Institutio vitae sacerdotalis,* c. 7, p. 782).

Mortification the law of Christian life

1254. ST. AMBROSE. A. What is death or mortification but the burial of vices and the bringing of virtues to life. . . . Mortification is the forgiveness of sins, the acquittal of the charges against us, the forgetting of faults, the receiving of graces (*De bono mortis,* c. 4, § 15, *PL* 14:575). B. To chastise the body is to cause it to feel pain with fasting and to give to it those things which are conducive to life, and not to excess (*Comment. in I Cor.*, c. 9, vers. 26, *PL* 17:246). C. What is more noble and splendid than to train the mind, keep down the flesh, and reduce it to subjection, so that it may obey commands, listen to reason, and in understanding labors readily carry out the intention and wish of the mind? (*De officiis ministrorum, Lib. I,* c. 36, § 10, *PL* 16:82.) D. Let then our flesh die to lusts, let it be captive, let it be subdued, and not war against the law of our mind, but die in subjection to a good service, as in Paul, who chastised his body that he might bring it into subjection (cf. I Cor. 9:27), in order that his preaching might become more approved. . . . For that which hurts the body benefits the spirit (*De poenitentia, Lib. I,* c. 13, § 61, col. 506).

1255. ST. AUGUSTINE. A. You must die in order to live; you must be buried in order to rise (*Serm. 169,* c. 13, § 16, *PL* 38:924). B. But the soul of one who does not die to this world and begins to be fashioned according to the image of Truth is drawn, by the death of the body, into a more serious death and will be restored to life, not in order to change to a heavenly home, but to undergo punishment (*De doctrina Christiana, Lib. I,* c. 20, § 19, *PL* 34:26). C. When we hear it said: *If by the spirit you put to death the deeds of the flesh, you will live* (Rom. 8:13), let our spirit not take the credit for itself, as though it could gain so great a victory by itself. For, in order that we should not understand the matter in so carnal a sense, the spirit being dead rather than that which puts others to death, [St. Paul] added immediately: *For whoever are led by the Spirit of God, they are the sons of God* (v. 14). Therefore for our spirit to mortify the deeds of the flesh, we are led by the Spirit of God, who gives the continence wherewith to curb, tame, and overcome lust (*De continentia,* c. 5, § 12, *PL* 40:357). D. For then [in heaven] there shall not be anything lacking to their desire, when God shall be *all in all* (I Cor. 15:28). Such an end has no end. No one dies there, whither no one comes unless he dies to this world, not by the death that is common to all men, wherein the body is deserted by the soul, but by the death of the elect, whereby even one who still abides in mortal flesh, has his heart set on high (*In Joan. Evangel.,* tract. 65, § 1, *PL* 35:1808). E. Let us here deprive death of its strength by dying to sins (*Serm. 252,* § 3, *In Append., PL* 39:2212). F. This is our work in this life, through the Spirit to mortify the deeds of the flesh; day by day to afflict, to diminish, to bridle, to kill it (*Serm. 156, in Rom. 8, 12–17,* c. 9, § 9, *PL* 38:854). G. There are two difficult things prescribed by our Lord for us in this life—to be continent and to be patient. We are commanded to be continent in those things which are called good in this world, and to be patient in bearing the many evils that abound in this world. This continence and this patience are called the two virtues which purify the soul and make us capable of the divine life (*Serm. 38,* § 1, col. 235).

H. Man received a body to be his servant, having God as his Lord, his body as his servant: having above his Creator, beneath him that which was created below him; while the reasoning soul, set in a sort of middle ground, has a law laid upon it, to cling to him who is above it, to rule that which is below. It cannot rule that which is below unless it is ruled by him that is better than it (*Enarr. in Ps. 145,* § 5, *PL* 37:1887). I. Since then the majority of men are what their loves are, and since there ought to be no other care for the regulation of our lives than the choice of that which we ought to love, why do you wonder if he who loves Christ, and who wishes to follow Christ, for the love of him, denies himself? For if by loving himself man is lost, surely by denying himself he is found (*Serm. 96, in Marc. 8, 34,* § 1, *PL* 38:585). J. By this covetousness the devil rules within man and takes possession of his heart. Such are all the lovers of this world. But the devil is cast out when we renounce this world with all our heart. The devil, who is the prince of this world, is thus renounced when we renounce his corruption, his pomp, and his angels. Therefore, when the Lord himself was already invested with his victorious human nature, he said: *Know that I have overcome the world* (John 16:33; *De agone Christiano,* c. 1, § 1, *PL* 40: 291; Russell, p. 310).

1256. ST. JEROME. The way of the Lord, by which he comes among men, is penance; it is the way by which God descends to us, and we ascend to him (*In Evangel. sec. Marc.,* c. 1, ad vers. 3, *PL* 30:591).

1257. POPE ST. LEO THE GREAT. A. If we are raised up, [the demons] are prostrated; if we are strengthened, they are weakened. Our cures are their blows, because they are wounded by our wounds' cure. . . . When the outer man is somewhat subdued, let the inner man be somewhat refreshed; and when bodily excess is denied to our flesh, let our mind be invigorated with spiritual delights (*Serm. 39, de Quadr. I,* cc. 4, 5, *PL* 54:265–266). B. The holy life of the saints, during which the nail of continence fastens the desires of the flesh, is never foreign to the cross of Christ, which by the strength of the Spirit dwelling within itself, destroys the passions of the body. For it is difficult for one not to have in himself that which should be destroyed—anger to be overcome, pride to be humiliated, excesses to be weakened . . . (*Serm. 45, de Quadr. VII,* c. 4, col. 291). C. By voluntary sufferings the flesh dies to its desires, the spirit is renewed with virtues (*Serm. 13, De jejunio decimi mensis,* col. 172). D. Taking up the cross means the slaying of lusts, the killing of vices, the turning away from vanity, and the renunciation of all error (*Serm. 72, De Resurr. Dni. II,* c. 5, col. 393). E. Since that which delights the outer man does most harm to the inner man, the more one's carnal substance is kept in subjection, the more purified is the reasoning soul (*Serm. 78, De jejunio Pentecostes,* c. 1, col. 416).

1258. ST. CYRIL, bp. of Alexandria. It was necessary that we, who were to be called children of God, should be made rather according to the image of the Son, in order that the nature of sonship would be fitting for us [in order to imitate Christ] (*Adversus anthropomorphistas,* c. 6, *PG* 76:1090).

1259. EUSEBIUS, bp. of Emesa. They restrain the flesh with fasts, exhaust it with night watches, and mortify it with prayers. They bedew the soul with psalmody and nourish it with divine readings. These efforts are mutual protections of soul and body. The attacks of youth are only of short duration. The bridle for them is the fear of God, shamefacedness before men. The one helps the other, and each protects the other. For those whom the love of God has once possessed, concupiscence is dead, unlawful pleasure mortified, the flesh crucified with its passions and desires (Gal. 5:24). Such flesh no longer suffers what you suffer. If I may so word the thought, you no longer have the same nature with it. It has changed its purpose. Its nature is no longer on earth with you. It has lifted up its desire to the Desired; it keeps company with angels; it dwells among the saints; it beholds what is above; it has forgotten what is here below (*Discursus 7, de virginibus,* § 13, Buytaert 1:184).

1260. ST. NILUS, hermit (d. circa 450). Cast forth whatever is inspired with malice, and intensely mortify the members of your body. As an enemy that has been dispatched no longer strikes fear, so the mortified body no longer disturbs the soul (*De octo spiritibus malitiae,* c. 3, *PG* 79:1147).

1261. ST. BASIL THE GREAT. *Would dust give you thanks or proclaim your faithfulness?* (*truth,* Douay version; Ps. 29:10). How will the man of earth, the man of flesh, acknowledge you, O God? How can he proclaim truth, he who has devoted no effort to the works of discipline, and possesses his very soul weighted down and overcome with so heavy a burden of flesh? It is only right that I weaken and emaciate my body and have no mercy on my blood which strengthens the flesh—lest it be a hindrance to the acknowledgment and understanding of truth (*Hom. in Ps. 29,* § 6, *PG* 29:319).

1262. ST. GREGORY THE GREAT. Unless a person renounces himself he cannot draw nigh to that which is above him. He cannot grasp what is beyond him if he has not learned to sacrifice what he is (*In Evangel., Lib. II, Hom. 32,* § 2, *PL* 76:1234).

1263. ST. AUGUSTINE. A. You have promised to renounce [the devil]: in your profession you said, not to man, but to God and his recording angel, "I renounce!" Well, then, renounce, not only in words but also by your deeds, not so much in the utterance of the tongue as by your way of life, not only with the lips, but by your works (*De Symbolo, ad Catechumenos serm. alius,* c. 1, *inter dubia, PL* 40:661). B. Let everyone be vigilant, lest, not having really renounced the devil and his pomps in their entirety, the devil recognize his own garments on him after profession; and he whom Christ willed to free through the operation of his grace, begin to be held forever in guilt (*Contra Judaeos, paganos et Arianos, serm. de Symbolo,* c. 4, *In Append., PL* 42:1119).

1264. THALASSIUS, Syrian abbot (d. 650). Destroy the evil in your life, lest when you are dead you will not rise, and pass from this brief death into an eternal one (*Centuria, IV,* § 51, *PG* 91:1463).

1265. SALVIAN, priest of Marseilles (d. circa 490). Deny yourself, lest you be denied by Christ; disown yourself, in order that you may be received by Christ; lose yourself, lest you perish. As the Savior says: *He who loses his life for my sake will save it* (Luke 9:24). Love this loss, which is so profitable, therefore, that you may obtain true gain. You will not be completely set free by God unless you renounce yourself (*De gubernatione Dei, Lib. V,* § 11, *PL* 53:108).

1266. ST. PETER DAMIAN. A. The man who denies himself is a follower of Christ (*Opusc. 11,* c. 19, *PL* 145:251). B. A dry string produces a sharp tone on the harp, whereas one that is damp makes only a dull sound; a tambourine too makes only an indistinct sound if any moisture has dampened it. In somewhat the same way the human mind necessarily must be detached from pleasures of the flesh in order for its prayer to be clear-sounding to the ears of the all-powerful God (*Lib. I, ep. 15, ad Alexandrum II Summum Pont., PL* 144:227).

1267. PETER THE VENERABLE, abbot of Cluny (d. 1158). It behooves you so to order your life in moderation as to withdraw from your body whatever can contribute to its pride, and to grant it only what can satisfy nature's needs. If you grant it more than is proper, it well become unmanageably haughty and be lifted above its proper rank, whereas if you deny it what properly belongs to it, it will be plunged in misery beneath the position it rightfully holds (*Lib. I, ep. 20, fratri Gisleberto eremitae, PL* 189:99).

1268. ST. BERNARD. *If anyone wishes to come after me, let him deny himself, and take up his cross daily, and follow me* (Luke 9:23). This is as though [the Savior] had said: "He who desires to possess me must despise himself, and anyone who is intent on doing my will must renounce his own" (*Serm. de temp., serm. II in fest. S. Andreae Ap.,* § 5, *PL* 183:511).

1269. PETER COMESTOR, priest of Paris (d. 1179). The flesh bent on pleasure has drawn us into sin, but on being punished draws us back toward pardon (*Serm. 45, ad sacerdotes, PL* 198:1829).

1270. HUGH OF ST. CHER, O.P. A. Evil men fatten their bodies here, but only that they may be eaten more sumptuously by the devil; but the good here torment their flesh so that it will not be fit to be eaten, but rather to be glorified. The cross in this life is a ladder to glory; but present glory is a ladder leading to an eternal cross (*Sup. Gen. 40:19,*

Comment. 1:58). B. Mortification of the flesh and prayer are the two things which force the devil to depart (*Sup. 1 Reg. 16, 23, Comment.* 1:232). C. It is justice to take vengeance on one's flesh (*Sup. Ps. 117, 14, Comment.* 2:301). D. The body is to be mortified, because living and impudent flesh is a mark of leprosy. We know that it is a greater merit in God's sight to be mortified frequently than to die (*Sup. Ps. 43, 22, ibid.,* p. 115). E. Mortification of the body terrifies demons and strikes them through and through (*Sup. Ps. 80, 3, ibid.,* p. 204). F. The cross is nothing other than ascent by mortification, or the ladder by which we mount from this pool of misery, from this mud of corruption, from this world to heaven (*Sup. Cant. 3, 9, Comment.* 3:122). G. Mortification of the flesh together with the exercise of virtues unite in harmony unto the praise of God (*Sup. Isa. 23, 16, Comment.* 4:53). H. It is not possible for him who is in love with this life to love the crucified life (*Sup. Joan. 5, 33, Comment.* 6:319). I. Evil desires are weakened by making the body suffer (*Sup. Rom. 8, 14, Comment.* 7:47). J. The body is punished, but the soul rejoices (*Sup. II Cor. 11, 26, ibid.,* p. 141). K. The mortification which is done within the community is pleasing to God (*Sup. Hebr. 2, 12, ibid.,* p. 242).

1271. ST. LAURENCE JUSTINIAN. It is fitting for our condition that while we are in pilgrimage in this vale of miseries and dangers, we fashion a cross of the carnal pleasures we must deny ourselves. . . . On this cross the Christian must hang continuously throughout his life. Now is not the time to dig out the nails (*Lignum vitae,* tract. 12, *de sobrietate,* c. 2, *Op. Om.* 1:73).

1272. ST. JOHN CHRYSOSTOM. A. Monasteries are indeed houses of mourning. There is sackcloth and ashes; there one finds no laughter, no pressure of worldly business. There is fasting, and lying upon the hard bed of the ground; there one finds no impure savor of rich food, no bloodshed [they commonly abstained from all flesh meat]; no tumult, no disturbance or crowding. There is a serene harbor. The monks are like lights shining from a lofty height to mariners afar off. They are stationed at the port, drawing all men to their own calm, and preserving from shipwreck those who gaze on them, and not letting those proceed in darkness who look thither (*In Ep. ad Timoth.,* c. 5, *Hom. 14,* § 3, *PG* 62:574). B. And now if you will come into the desert of Egypt, you will see this desert better than any paradise, and innumerable choirs of angels in human form, nations of martyrs, companies of virgins. There you will see all the devil's tyranny overcome, while Christ's kingdom shines forth in all its brightness. . . . In truth everywhere in that land may be seen the army of Christ, a royal flock, the very life of the powers above (*In Matt., Hom. 8,* § 4, *PG* 57:87).

Monasticism and martyrdom

1273. ST. JOHN CHRYSOSTOM. To have it in one's power to spend one's days in luxury and lavish spending, and yet to take up a life of toil and bitterness, and to mortify the body, is not this a whole-burnt offering, a holocaust? Mortify your body, and crucify it, and you will also receive the crown of martyrdom (*Hom. 11 in Ep. ad Hebr.*, c. 6, § 3, *PG* 63:93).

1274. ST. JEROME. As martyrs praise the Lord in purity in the region of the living, so also monks who sing the Lord's praises day and night must possess the same purity of the martyrs, because they are truly martyrs themselves. For what the angels do in heaven, that the monks do on earth (*Breviarium in Psalmos, Ps. 115, 17, In Append., PL* 26:1183).

1275. GERARD THE BELGIAN. "You know for certain, my brethren," he was wont to say to them, "that true monasticism is a continual martyrdom." He frequently stated the thought in these words: "There is no monk in heaven who is not a martyr" (*Dicta et facta Gerardi monachi, Opusc. pia* 2:157).

1276. ST. AUGUSTINE. Have mercy, then, and have compassion, and let me see in your works that you are not seeking in ease a ready subsistence, but through the straight and narrow gate of this way of life, are seeking the kingdom of God (*De opere monachorum,* c. 28, § 36, *PL* 40:576).

1277. LIVES OF THE FATHERS. For everyone to do violence to himself in all things—that is the way of God, and the duty of the monk (*Aegyptiorum Patrum sententiae,* n. 92, *PL* 74:392).

1278. JOHN CASSIAN. The aim of the cenobite is to mortify and crucify all his desires, and according to the salutary mandate of evangelical perfection, not to be concerned about the morrow (*Collatio 19, Abbatis Joan.,* c. 8, *de fine cenobitae, PL* 49:1138).

1279. ST. EPHRAEM, deacon of Edessa in Syria, Doctor of the Church (d. 378). For soldiers the battle is brief, but the warfare of the monk lasts until he sets forth to meet the Lord (*Adhortatio ad pietatem, Op. Om.* 1:72).

1280. ST. ANTONY, abbot. Light your lamp with the oil of your own eyes, that is, with your tears (*Reg. ad monachos,* c. 25, *CR* 1:4).

1281. ST. BASIL THE GREAT. There is but one escape from these distractions, a complete separation from the world. Withdrawing from the world, however, does not mean mere bodily absence, but implies a disengagement of spirit from sympathy with the body, a renunciation of city, home, personal possessions, love of friends, property, means of livelihood, business, social relations, and learning acquired by human teachings; also, a readiness to receive in one's heart the impressions produced there by divine instruction. And this disposition follows the unlearning of worldly teachings which previously held possession of the heart. Just as it is not possible to write in wax without first smoothing down the letters already engraved upon it, so it is impossible to impart the divine teachings to the soul without first removing from it the conceptions arising from worldly experiences (*Ep. 2, ad Gregorium Nazianz.,* § 2, *PG* 32:226; Way, 1:6).

1282. ST. JOHN CLIMACUS. A. A monk is he who strictly controls his nature and unceasingly watches over his senses. A monk is he who keeps his body in chastity, his mouth pure, and his mind illumined. A monk is a mourning soul that both asleep and awake is unceasingly occupied with the remembrance of death. Withdrawal from the world is voluntary hatred of vaunted material things and denial of nature for the attainment of what is above nature (*Scala paradisi, Grad. 1, de abdicatione vitae saecularis, PG* 88:634; Moore, n. 4, p. 50). B. Angels are a light for monks, and the monastic life is a light for all men. Therefore let monks strive to become a good example in everything, giving no occasion of stumbling in anything (cf. II Cor. 6:3) in all their works and words. For if the light becomes darkness, how much darker will be that darkness, that is, those living in the world (*ibid., Grad. 26,* col. 1022; Moore, n. 31, p. 206).

1283. ST. ODO, abbot of Cluny (d. 942). [Monks] avail themselves of this place of refuge as a traveler takes advantage of a shady spot or a bed; he stops to rest his body, but his mind, directed to a farther goal, hastens to be on the way. In much the same way, monks also refuse to arrest the progress of their desires at transitory things, lest, by reason of the delight they experience along the journey, they be detached from the abode of their everlasting dwelling. They desire to rejoice in their eternal home and hence refuse to be content in this place of their pilgrimage (*Collationum Lib. I,* n. 39, *PL* 133:546).

1284. ST. BERNARD. A. We are, as it were, baptized a second time by mortifying our *members which are on earth* (Col. 3:5), we put on Christ again; we are *united with him in the likeness of his death* (Rom. 6:5). But as in baptism we are rescued from the powers of darkness, and are transferred into the kingdom of eternal light, so in a kind of second regeneration of this holy plan of life, we also escape from darkness, not indeed of the one original sin, but of many actual sins, into the light of virtue (*De praecepto et dispensatione,* c. 17, § 54, *PL* 182:889). B. Fear not, man of God, to put off the earthly man who is holding you down to earth, and who would bring you down even to the regions under the earth. It is this which troubles, burdens, and aggrieves you. But why trouble about your clothing of the flesh, you who are about to put on the garb of immortality in heaven? It is ready for you, but it will not be given to you already clothed; it will clothe you, but not while you are still clothed in the flesh. Wait patiently, and be glad to be found naked and unclothed. God himself wishes man to be clothed, but not while he is still clothed in the flesh. The man of God will not return to God until what he has of the earth has gone back to the earth. These two, the man of God and the earthly man, are at variance one with the other, and there will be no peace for you until they are separated; and if there should be peace, it would not be the peace of God, nor would it be peace with God. You are not one of those who say: *Peace, and there is no peace* (Ezech. 13:10). The peace which surpasses all understanding is awaiting you, and the righteous are waiting for this peace to be given to you, and the joy of the Lord awaits you (*Ep. 266, ad Sugerum abbatem S. Dionysii, quem animat ut mortem intrepidus accipiat,* § 1, col. 471; James, *Letter 411,* p. 480). C. It is of little avail, therefore, to have pruned once; we must prune frequently, nay, if it were possible, always; because if you are honest with yourself, you will always find something within requiring to be sternly repressed. Whatever spiritual progress you may make while you remain in this body, you err if you suppose that sins and vices are dead because they have been suppressed (*Serm. 58 in Cant.,* n. 10, *PL* 183:1060; Eales, p. 352). D. You are indeed worthily dead to your own desires if you no longer are intent on living for yourself but for him who died for you (*Tract. de moribus et officio episcoporum, ep. 42, ad Henricum archiepisc. Senonensem,* c. 3, § 10, *PL* 182:818).

1285. PETER DE BLOIS, chancellor and archdeacon, Bath, England (d. circa 1200). A. The service of God by regulars has need of spiritual arms, for scarcely a half hour of the cloistral life is spent without some form of temptation (*Ep. 134, ad Willelmum electum S. Mariae, PL* 207:400). B. Let us wage war against Chanaan, against vices and spiritual evils, for our life upon earth is a warfare (cf. Job 7:1, Douay version). Let us do so in order that we may possess the land of our heart (cf. Matt. 5:4). Make my soul subject to you, O God, in order that I can subject the land of my body to you. *Only in God is my soul at rest* (Ps. 61:1); therefore I must possess my body in peace, and not as a power that is unmanageable, not lustful, but subdued and submissive to reason. O Lord, if I am unable to root out entirely my unlawful inclinations, at least grant me the grace to bring them under subjection. . . . [All this will be realized perfectly only when] the whole seed of Chanaan will be blotted out from our earth, when the creature also itself shall be delivered from its slavery to corruption, into the freedom of the sons of God (Rom. 8:21; *Serm. 43, in fest. Om. Sanct. II,* col. 694).

1286. IMITATION OF CHRIST (Thomas à Kempis). A. Go wherever you will, and reap whatever you desire, and you will never find, above you or beneath you, within you or without you, a more high, a more excellent, a more sure way to Christ, than the way of the holy cross (*De imitatione Christi, Lib. II,* c. 12, n. 3, *Op. Om.* 2:83; Gardiner, p. 95). B. If you gladly bear this cross, it will bear you, and it will bring you to the end you desire, where you will never afterwards have anything to suffer. But if you bear this cross against your will, you make a great burden for yourself, and it will be the more grievous to you, and yet it behooves you to bear it. And if it happens that you put away one cross, that is to say, one tribulation, another surely will come, perhaps heavier than the first one was (*ibid.,* n. 5). C. There is no other way to life and true inward peace but the way of the cross, and the daily submission of the body to the spirit [in mortification] (*ibid.,* n. 3). D. And if he has great virtue and fervent devotion, he yet lacks much, and there is especially one thing necessary to him. And what is that? It is that, forsaking all things and himself as well, he go clearly out of himself, and keep nothing to himself of any private love (*ibid.,* c. 11, n. 4; Gardiner, p. 93). E. "My son," says our Lord, "you will not have perfect liberty of mind unless you wholly forsake yourself" (*ibid., Lib. III,* c. 32, n. 1, *Op. Om.* 2:204; Gardiner, p. 152). F. Therefore it is no small thing for a man fully to forsake himself, though it be in very little and small things. Truly, the very perfection of man is a perfect denying and a complete forsaking of himself; such a man is very free and beloved of God (*ibid.,* c. 39, p. 215; Gardiner, p. 162). G. Forsake yourself and resign yourself wholly to me, and you will have great inward peace. Give all for all, and keep nothing to yourself after your own will (*ibid.,* c. 37, p. 212; Gardiner, p. 160). H. You must often do what you would not do, and you must forsake and leave undone what you would do. What pleases others will advance well, and what pleases you will go slowly (*ibid.,* c. 49, n. 4, p. 234; Gardiner, p. 177). I. My son, as much as you can abandon yourself and your own will, so much will you enter into me (*ibid.,* c. 56, n. 1, p. 252; Gardiner, p. 191).

1287. JOHN OF TRITHEIM. A. Our cross, my brothers, is denial of our self-will (*De vitio proprietatis monachorum,* 1, *Op. pia et spiritualia,* p. 724). B. Deny yourself with regard to your desires, in order to become a disciple of Christ (*Institutio vitae sacerdotalis,* c. 7, p. 782). C. The monk is always to be given to the spirit of penance, not only with regard to his own sins, for he is constituted an intercessor with God for the sins of others. A true monk never lives without the spirit of repentance (*Hom. 14, de vera poenitentia monachorum,* p. 468). D. The whole life of the monk must be penitential in character, even though he himself may seem to be free of sin. The just man who carries the difficult servitude of the flesh, always has cause for mourning in this life. If he has no personal sins of his own, he is to mourn those of others. We live on alms in the monastery; for that reason we are debtors for the sins of others. Let us so conduct our lives that we shall not fear death; a good life is not subject to death (*De viris illustribus O.S.B.*, p. 116).

1288. VEN. LOUIS DE BLOIS (Blosius), abbot of Liessies (d. 1566). You are called a monk; see that you are in truth what you are called. Do the work of a monk. Devote yourself to beating down and casting forth vice. Be always against the unruliness of nature, against haughtiness of mind, against the pleasures of the flesh and the enticements of sensuality. . . . Arm yourself against yourself, fight manfully against yourself, and as far as lies in your power, overcome and subdue yourself. . . . Go through this spiritual martyrdom with an invincible mind (*Speculum monachorum*, div. 1, *Op. Om.* 3:652).

1289. ST. BONAVENTURE, Franciscan general, cardinal (d. 1274). Blessed is that servitude—in reality it is a glorious state of liberty—in which of his own free will one is sold into a royal servitude and renounces his own will, choosing God and his representative rather than himself to rule over him (*Speculum disciplinae ad novitios, Pars I*, c. 4, § 12, *Op. Om.*, ed. Quaracchi 8:587).

1290. IMITATION OF CHRIST (Thomas à Kempis). Oh, how many and how grievous tribulations the apostles, martyrs, confessor, virgins and other holy saints suffered who were willing to follow the steps of Christ. They refused honors and all bodily pleasures here in this life that they might have everlasting life. Oh, how strict and how abject a life the holy fathers in the wilderness led. How grievous the temptations they suffered, and how fiercely they were assailed by their spiritual enemies. How fervent the prayer they daily offered to God, what rigorous abstinence they kept. What great zeal and fervor they had for spiritual profit, how strong a battle they waged against all sin, and how pure and entire their purpose toward God in all their deeds! In the day they labored and in the night they prayed, and though they labored bodily in the day, they prayed in mind, and so they always spent their time fruitfully (*De imitatione Christi, Lib. I*, c. 18, *Op. Om.* 2:30; Gardiner, p. 51).

1291. ST. AUGUSTINE. Thus man himself, consecrated in the name of God and vowed to God, is a sacrifice insofar as he dies to the world that he may live to God. . . . Our body, too, is a sacrifice when we chasten it by temperance, if we do so as we ought, for God's sake, that we may not yield our members to sin as weapons of iniquity, but present ourselves to God and our members as weapons for God (Rom. 6:13). Exhorting to this sacrifice, the Apostle says: *I exhort you therefore, brethren, by the mercy of God, to present your bodies as a sacrifice, living, holy, pleasing to God—your spiritual service* (Rom. 12:1). If then the body, which, being inferior, the soul uses as a servant or instrument, is a sacrifice when it is used rightly, and with reference to

God, how much more does the soul itself become a sacrifice when it offers itself to God in order that, being inflamed by the fire of his love, it may receive of his beauty and become pleasing to him, losing the shape of earthly desire, and being molded in the image of permanent loveliness? (*De civitate Dei, Lib. X,* c. 6, *PL* 41:283; Dods, p. 309.)

1292. JOHN OF TRITHEIM. A. It is obedience which reconciles the soul to God and which crowns the martyrs, quite apart from the shedding of their blood. The monk who binds himself of his own free will to the perpetual obedience of religion, and lives according to his vow, certainly bears a long-drawn-out martyrdom (*Hom. 20, de vera obedientia monachorum, Op. pia et spiritualia,* p. 505). B. Be diligent in exercising your mind in meditation on the passion of our Lord and Savior Jesus Christ. . . . The monk who does not at least every day recall with thanksgiving the sufferings of our Lord, who does not daily meditate on the Gospel law of the Lord, is deservedly considered the most ungrateful of men. For nothing is more powerful than prayer which is offered in union with and on the strength of the Lord's passion. . . . Let us do whatever we can out of the love of Christ. Let us endure all the adverse things that befall us in this world with contemplation of his passion and death; for the Lord Jesus who willed to suffer for us out of love, so that we may love him with our whole heart, has truly shown himself to be most worthy [of our love]. . . . Meditation on the Lord's sufferings excels all the exercises of this life . . . if it is continued for a long time with the fervor of deep devotion. . . . Blessed is the monk who can truthfully say with the holy martyr of Christ [St. Ignatius]: "My love is crucified, and therefore my heart receives none of the consolations of this world," or who can say with that other great lover of Christ, Paul: . . . *the world is crucified to me and I to the world* (Gal. 6:14). I assure you that among all the spiritual exercises of monks none can be holier, none more pleasing to God, none more profitable for you than that in daily meditation of the passion of our Lord Jesus Christ which is dwelt on in earnestness and in the compunction of deep love. Devout meditation on the passion of Christ makes us spurn all the pleasures of this world and to be afraid of no hardships or contradictions, whatever their severity. It banishes lust, conquers dissipation of mind and body, curbs greediness and gluttony, stirs sloth to action, appeases anger, and cuts out pride by the root. Moreover, no passion of carnal nature vexes the mind of the man which the passion of Christ has truly possessed. How greatly he is consumed whom the memory of the passion of Jesus has sweetly inflamed, and how blessedly the mind glows which embraces continual meditation on the death of Christ! (*Hom. 16, de quadragesimali jejunio monachorum,* p. 483 f.)

Monastic discipline

1293. JOHN CASSIAN. A. Renunciation is nothing but the evidence of the cross and of mortification. You must know that today you are dead to this world and its deeds and desires so that, as the Apostle says, you are crucified to this world and this world to you (cf. Gal. 6:14). Consider, therefore, the demands of the cross under whose sign you are, henceforth, to live in this life: because you no longer live, but he lives in you who was crucified for you (cf. Gal. 2:20). We must, therefore, pass our time in this life in that manner and form in which he was crucified for us on the cross, so that, as David says, our flesh shuddering with dread [of the Lord] (cf. Ps. 118:120), we may have all our wishes and desires not subservient to our own lusts but fastened to his mortification. For so shall we fulfil the command of the Lord which says: *He who does not take up his cross and follow me is not worthy of me* (Matt. 10:30). But perhaps you will object: "How can a man carry his cross continually? or how can anyone who is alive be crucified?" Hear briefly how this is: The fear of the Lord is our cross. As then one who is crucified no longer has the power of moving or turning his limbs in any direction as he pleases, so we also ought to affix our wishes and desires, not in accordance with what is pleasant and delightful to us now, but in accordance with the law of the Lord, where it constrains us. And as he who is fastened to the wood of the cross no longer considers things present, nor thinks about the things that are pleasing to him, nor is perplexed by anxiety and care for the morrow, nor disturbed by any desire of possession, nor inflamed by any pride or strife or rivalry, does not grieve at present injuries nor remember past ones, and while he is still breathing in the body considers that he is dead to all earthly things, sending the thoughts of his heart on before to that place whither he does not doubt that he is shortly to come: so we also, when crucified by the fear of the Lord, ought to be dead indeed to all these things, that is, not only to carnal vices but also to all earthly things, having the eye of our minds fixed there whither we hope at each moment that we are soon to pass (*De coenob. institut. Lib. IV*, cc. 34, 35, *PL* 49:194).

B. Everything should be done and sought after by us for the sake of this love, offering to God a perfect and pure heart kept clean from all disturbances. For this we must seek solitude, for this we ought to submit to fastings, vigils, toils, bodily nakedness, reading, and all other virtues, that through them we may be enabled to prepare our heart and keep it unharmed by all evil passions, and resting on these steps to mount to the perfection of charity. . . . These [practices] are not perfection, but they are aids to perfection: because the end of that science does not lie in these, but by means of these we arrive at the end (*Collatio I, Abbatis Moysis I, de monachi intentione ac fine,* col. 489).

1294. DENIS THE CARTHUSIAN, monk of Roermond (d. 1471). A. Mortification is nothing other than spontaneous self-denial . . . a preservative and spiritually-integrating breaking of self-will . . . a virtuous violence done to self (cf. Matt. 11:12), a hatred of sin and vice, a wholesome destruction of self (*De mortificatione vivifica et reformatione interna,* art. 2, *Op. Om.* 40:89 f.). B. This vivifying mortification is nothing other than the annihilation of self-love and the attainment of divine charity (*ibid.,* art. 3). C. Those who deny themselves through mortification are indeed dead to their own will—*for you have died and your life is hidden with Christ in God* (Col. 3:3)—but they are living for God in the spirit of the most ardent love (*De profectu spirituali et custodia cordis,* art. 13, p. 487).

1295. ST. JOHN CHRYSOSTOM. A. Therefore chastisement [discipline] is called "profitable"; therefore it is called a "participation in holiness." Yes, and this is abundantly true: for when it casts out sloth, and evil desire, and love for the things of this life, when it helps the soul, when it causes a light esteem of all things here (for affliction does this), is it not holy? Does it not draw the grace of the Spirit? (*In Ep. ad Hebr.,* c. 12, *Hom. 29,* § 3, *PG* 63:205.) B. So, then, chastisement is exercise, making the athlete strong, and invincible in combats, irresistible in wars (*ibid., Hom. 30,* § 1, col. 209).

1296. ST. AUGUSTINE. A. Let the patient bearing of unpleasant things be so alert that discipline will not be inactive (*Serm. 144,* c. 7, § 11, *PL* 38:900). B. As he is unhappy who abandons the way of discipline . . . so he who denies discipline is cruel (*Serm. 13,* c. 8, § 9, col. 111). C. He is fully alive in whom discipline is always in operation (*De immortalitate animae,* c. 1, *PL* 32:1021).

1297. VALERIAN, bp. of Cémèle (5th century). Discipline is the mistress of religion and of true piety, which, therefore, neither rebukes with the intention of wounding nor chastises in order to harm. . . . There is nothing that discipline will not either correct or heal. . . . All vices lie in fear of discipline . . . and unless a right order of living is established, nature of itself would never put an end to sin. . . . The sweet burden of discipline and the light burden of the Lord do not weigh heavily except on those who are already lost or are in the process of being lost. The prophet says: *He who rejects admonition* [*discipline,* Douay version] *despises his own soul* (Prov. 15:32). Let discipline accompany your life in its every act (*Hom. 1, de bono disciplinae,* nn. 1, 2, 4, 8, *PL* 52:691).

1298. BLESSED ALAIN DE LA ROCHE, O.P. (Alanus de Rupis) d. 1475. Discipline is the daughter of justice, the sister of religion, friend of the spirit of penance, mistress of humility, leader in the acts of fortitude, instructress of chastity, she who promotes devotion, bride of the saints, mother of all good persons, and the healer of all ills (*Opus aureum B.*

Alani de Rupe de Psalterio Christi ac Mariae, ejusque confraternitate, Pars V, c. 14, *Fructuosum est orare psalterium Virginis gloriosae, cum receptione disciplinae, in: Mare magnum exemplorum SS. Rosarii ex diversis auctoribus . . . quibus praemittitur opus aureum B. Alani;* Maioricae: apud Michaelem Capo, 1689, p. 161).

1299. PETER DE BLOIS. The austerity of discipline is the only key of innocence, the anchor of religion, the controller of the affections, and the destroyer of unlawful desires (*Invectiva in depravatorem operum Blesensis, PL* 207:1119).

1300. HUGH OF ST. CHER, O.P. A. Discipline is the royal road which leads to the City of God (*Sup. Prov. 4, 13, Comment.* 3:10). B. Discipline molds character and destroys vices (*ibid., 8, 10,* p. 16). C. Discipline is characterized by a certain harshness for the present, but even now begets joy and great happiness of mind; and for the future, the fruit of an eternal reward (*Sup. Hebr. 12, 11, Comment.* 7:272).

1301. ST. BONAVENTURE. A. When you are corrected by a wise man's discipline, you are adorned with a jewel of great beauty; when you contemn discipline, you trample a pearl under foot (*In Hexaemeron collatio 2,* § 4, *Op. Om.,* ed. Quaracchi 5:337). B. The cross for the flesh is severity of discipline: its four arms are night watches, abstinence [in food and drink], coarseness of garb, and the discipline of the lash. The cross by which the *world is crucified* [*to me, and I to the world*] (Gal. 6:14), is the spirit of poverty whose four arms are contempt of glory, of money, of fatherland, and of family. The cross of the spirit is fervor of devotion whose four arms are love, hope, fear, and suffering: hope [pointing] upward, fear downward, love to the right, and suffering to the left. Of these it is said: being rooted and grounded in love, may you be able to comprehend with all the saints what is the breadth and the length and the height and depth . . . (cf. Eph. 3:17 f.; *Comment. in Evangel. Lucae 23, 33,* § 40, *ibid.,* 7:576). C. If discipline is neglected, manifestations of insolent pride will increase (*Opusc. 19, Ep. officiales,* n. 2, *ad omnes Ordinis ministros provinciales, ibid.,* 8:470). D. Discipline is the imprisonment of evil desires, restraint of impure inclinations, the subjection of pride. Discipline tames intemperance, holds levity of conduct in check, chokes off all unregulated activity of the mind (*Speculum disciplinae ad novitios, Pars I,* c. 7, *ibid.,* p. 591). E. He who neglects discipline at the beginning of his turning to God will find it hard to be conformed to it afterward, for it is only with difficulty that one abandons a practice he has formed (*ibid., Prooem.,* § 1, p. 583). F. A religious whose life is without discipline exposes himself to serious harm (*Ad fratres Tolosates collationes octo, VII, Op. Om.,* ed. Peltier 14:644).

1302. JOHN OF TRITHEIM. You are called by the Lord to the perfection of the purest reformation of life according to monastic principles, but like an animal you grow foul in the dung heap of vainglory and negligence. You are called to the observance of God's commandments, but attached to the pleasures of the flesh, you think of nothing less than of Christ. You are invited to love the Lord Jesus above all things, but you pursue the evil desires of your heart, thereby showing your ingratitude toward your Savior. You who should live by the spirit, savor of the things of the world and, immersed in pride, spurn all the holy practices of the spiritual way of life.

And what are you going to answer on the day of judgment to the Judge who will say to you: "I, the Lord of all things, humbled myself for you, taking upon myself the form of a servant; and becoming man, I shed my blood for you; for you I suffered the lashes of the scourge; for you I voluntarily submitted to an exceedingly bitter death. I loved you, O monk, with my whole heart. In my blood I redeemed you from everlasting death. Out of love I called you to the heavenly kingdom, provided that you had kept my commandments.

"But you have lived in opposition to my commands and, what is more serious, since you had vowed according to my promises, you have not hesitated to make yourself an apostate and an impious traitor against me, your Lord. So now, render an account of your stewardship."

What will you then answer, lazy and indolent monk, you who are wasting the acceptable time which is now given you (cf. II Cor. 6:2), you who spurn the thought of living in true monastic purity according to the Rule? I ask you, what will you give in the way of an answer? . . .

The holy confessors who crucified their flesh in this world for love of the name of Christ, suffered a voluntary and long-lasting martyrdom, and were made glorious by their self-denial and humility. For they were ever patient and constant, ever ready to submit to physical martyrdom. Make it your effort, O monks, to be their imitators, as far as lies in your power. Since the enemies who put the body to death for the acknowledgment of Christ are no longer present, show that you are martyrs in mind and spirit by warring against the concupiscence of the flesh and by patiently bearing all hardships for love of God. This kind of martyrdom is the best in the peace of the saints: to afflict the flesh by self-denial for the love of God's name; to yearn for nothing in this world; to advance always in the performance of good works; and if anything evil befalls you, to bear it in patience, cheerfulness of mind, and joy. Live from now on, my brothers, according to this rule of patience if you desire to reign with Christ forever (*Hom. 18, de patientia et mansuetudine, Op. pia et spiritualia,* pp. 493–496).

Necessity of fasting

1303. JOHN CASSIAN. A. We ought first to give evidence of our freedom from subjection to the flesh, *for by whatever a man is overcome, of this also he is the slave* (II Pet. 2:19). . . . For it is impossible for a full belly to make trial of the combat of the inner man; nor is he worthy to be tried in harder battles who can be overcome in a slight skirmish (*De coenob. institut., Lib. V,* c. 13, *PL* 49:228). B. The first trial we must enter upon is that against gluttony, which we have explained as the pleasures of the palate (*ibid.,* c. 3, col. 205). C. Between their regular meals taken in common they are especially careful that no one should presume to gratify his palate with any food: so that when they are walking casually through gardens or orchards, when the fruit is hanging enticingly on the trees and not only knocks against their breast as they pass through, but is also lying on the ground and offering itself to be trampled under foot and, as it is all ready to be gathered, it would easily be able to entice those who see it, to gratify their appetite. The chance it offers, and the quality of the fruit should excite even the most severe and abstemious to long for it. Still, they consider it wrong not merely to taste a single fruit, but even to touch it with the hand unless it is put on the table openly for the common meal of all (*ibid., Lib. IV,* c. 18, col. 178).

1304. ST. PACHOMIUS, abbot (4th century). A. For the sake of order and discipline, no one is to dare to eat grapes or other fruits before the season. And no one is to eat anything at all in the garden or the orchard apart from the others, before they are made available to all the brethren alike (*Reg. monachorum,* n. 75, *CR* 1:30; Boon, *Pachomiana,* p. 34). B. Those who are placed in charge of the fruit trees and vineyards are not to eat of their fruits unless the brethren shall first have eaten. The overseer (prefect) of the brethren gathering the fruits will give them, individually, permission to eat a small amount of the fruit there in the orchard, and when they return to the monastery they will receive their share along with the other brethren. But if they find that fruit has fallen on the ground, they will not presume to eat it, but will place at the base of the tree what they have found while walking (*ibid.,* n. 78; Boon, p. 35, slightly different reading).

1305. ST. THOMAS AQUINAS. Abstinence . . . may be taken as regulated by reason, and then it signifies a virtuous habit or a virtuous act (*II-II,* q. 146, art. 1, *Utrum abstinentia sit virtus, Op. Om.* 10:150; Am. ed. 2:1784).

1306. ST. AUGUSTINE. A. He who recalls that he has been guilty of that which is unlawful, is to seek to abstain from those things which are lawful; and he who has committed that which is forbidden should wrench himself from those which are allowed (*De spiritu et anima,* c. 57, *PL* 40:822). B. The soul can examine itself more thoroughly when it is liberated from attachment to food and drink. For just as a man does not see himself as he really is in a soiled mirror, so also if he is weighted down with excessive eating and drinking, he certainly judges himself other than he is—for then the passions are excited, anger kindled, pride inflamed, coarseness adopted (*Quaestiones ex utroque Testamento,* q. 120, *PL* 35:2364).

1307. ST. GREGORY THE GREAT. A. Persons who abstain are, as it were, engaging in combat with a serpent, when with great force they repress their appetite in order not to be infected with the poison of luxury (*In I Reg. expositiones Lib. V,* c. 1, § 2, *PL* 79:314). B. Abstinence from food is powerful in combatting vice. For if the passions are fire, you are withdrawing fuel from the fire when you deny yourself food, and especially wine, wherein, according to the Apostle, is debauchery (cf. Eph. 5:18; *ibid.,* c. 4, n. 64).

1308. POPE ST. LEO THE GREAT. A. Abstinence is indeed a helpful observance which accustoms one to a meager diet, and checks the appetite against dainty foods: but woe to the dogmatizing of those whose very fasting is turned into a sin (*Serm. 42, De Quadr. IV,* § 4, *PL* 54:278). B. From abstinence there proceed chaste thoughts, will-acts in harmony with reason, more wholesome resolutions (*Serm. 13,* col. 172).

1309. ST. ISIDORE OF SEVILLE. Temptation does not inflame the body which abstinence subdues. . . . No one can easily expel the unclean spirits from himself except by fasting (cf. Mark 9:28; *Sententiarum Lib. II,* c. 42, §§ 7, 11, *PL* 83:648).

1310. ST. AMBROSE. Because they teach you to avoid the occasions of sin, sparing use of food and temperance in drink teach you not to fall into vices at all (*De virginibus, Lib. I,* c. 8, § 53, *PL* 16:214).

Observance of Lent

1311. ST. GREGORY THE GREAT. Since the year is made up of three hundred and sixty-five days, and we suffer for thirty-six days [during Lent], it is as though we were offering tithes of our year to God, so that we who have lived for ourselves through the year granted to us, should in his tithes mortify ourselves for our Creator by abstinence (*In Evangel., Lib. I, Hom. 16,* § 5, *PL* 76:1137).

1312. ST. JEROME. Moses fasted on Mount Sinai for forty days and forty nights, and showed even then that man does not live on bread alone, but on every word of God (cf. Matt. 4:4). The Lord complained that the people were depraved and had made for themselves a molten idol (cf. Deut. 9:9 ff.). Moses with empty stomach received the Law written with God's own finger. The people ate and drank and rose up to play, fashioned a golden calf and preferred an Egyptian ox to the majesty of the Lord (*Adversus Jovinianum, Lib. II,* § 15, *PL* 23:306).

1313. ST. AMBROSE. A. When the body grows weak through fastings, the soul is strengthened in purity. For the more that the strength of copious food is withdrawn from the former, the more the energy of the latter is increased (*Serm. 21, de S. Quadr. V,* § 2, *In Append., PL* 17:

666). B. Any Christian who shall not have consecrated Lent by fasting is to be considered guilty of violation of his duty, and of contumacy. . . . He observes Lent who approaches Easter by fasting and night watches; for as in the rest of the year to fast is to our advantage, not to fast in Lent is sinful (*Serm. 13*, §§ 2, 3, col. 670–671).

Fasting: its nature, advantages, and praise

1314. ST. AMBROSE. A. Gluttony drove man, while reigning supreme, from paradise; abstinence recalls him from his wandering to paradise (*Lib. de Elia et jejunio*, c. 4, § 7, *PL* 14:735). B. Fasting is the restoration of the soul, the food of the mind; fasting is the life of angels; fasting is the death of guilt, the destruction of sins, the means of salvation, the root of grace, the foundation of chastity (*ibid.*, c. 3, § 4, col. 733). C. Fasting is the instruction of continence, the discipline of modesty, humility of the mind, chastisement of the flesh, the mark of sobriety, the norm of virtue, purification of the soul, the expenditure of compassion, the foundation of gentleness, the allurement of charity, the grace of age, the protection of youth (*ibid.*, c. 8, § 22, col. 739).

1315. ST. BASIL THE GREAT. Fasting brings forth prophets, fortifies those who are strong. . . . Fasting is the virtuous guardian of the soul, the body's faithful companion, the weapon of those waging war fiercely, training for the athlete. It drives away temptations, anoints for piety, makes itself the companion of temperance, and dedicates itself to the observance of chastity. In wars it conducts itself with strength; in peace it trains to tranquillity. It makes the Christian (*Nazaraenum*) holy, and perfects the priest. And without fasting no one dares to approach the holy ministry. . . . To sum up all remarks: you will find that all who were holy were determined to a life in which fasting had made them worthy of God (*De jejunio Hom. I*, § 6, *PG* 31:171).

1316. ST. CYRIL OF ALEXANDRIA (d. 444). A. Fasting is a mirroring of the angelic life, the cause of temperance, the beginning of moderation, the abandoning of wantonness and passion (*Hom. Paschalis I*, § 4, *PG* 77:414). B. Let us embrace fasting as the parent of all that is good and joyful (*ibid.*, § 5, col. 418).

1317. POPE ST. LEO THE GREAT. A. What can be more efficacious than fasting, through whose observance we draw close to God and, contending with the devil, gain the victory over the allurements of the vices? (*Serm. 13, de jejunio decimi mensis II*, *PL* 54:172.) B. At all times fasting strengthens us against sin; fasting overcomes evil desires, repels temptations, abases pride, appeases anger, and nourishes all the fruits of good will to the maturity of perfection in virtue (*Serm. 15, de jejunio decimi mensis IV*, § 2, col. 175).

1318. ST. BASIL THE GREAT. Continency then, destroys sin, quells the passions, and mortifies the body even as to its natural affections and desires. It marks the beginning of the spiritual life, leads us to eternal blessings, and extinguishes within itself the desire for pleasure. . . . As plumpness and a healthy color betoken the athlete, so leanness of body and the pallor produced by the exercises of continency betoken the Christian, for he is the true athlete of the commandments of Christ. In weakness of the body he overcomes his opponent and displays his prowess in the contest of piety, according to the words, *When I am weak, then I am strong* (II Cor. 12:10). So beneficial is it merely to behold the continent man making a sparing and frugal use of necessities, ministering to nature as if it were a burdensome duty, and begrudging the time spent on it, and rising from the table in his eagerness for work, that I think no sermon would so touch the soul of one whose appetites are undisciplined and bring about his conversion as merely meeting with a continent man (*Regulae fusius tractatae, Interrogatio 17, quod oportet etiam risum continere,* § 2, *PG* 31:963; Wagner, 272–273).

1319. ST. NILUS, abbot, martyr (d. circa 430). The mind of a person who is fasting shines like a star in the night's calm, but that of the man who has eaten and drunk abundantly lies unknown, cast into oppressive darkness (*De octo spiritibus malitiae,* c. 1, *de gula, PG* 79:1145).

1320. ST. ATHANASIUS. Fasting cures illnesses, dries up the humors of the body, puts demons to flight, and drives out evil thoughts, thus rendering the mind fresher, the heart more purified, and the body more healthful (*De virginitate,* § 7, *In Append., PG* 28:259).

1321. ST. JEROME. How beautiful a thing is fasting which propitiates God, subdues lions [Daniel], and terrifies demons! (*Adversus Jovinianum, Lib. II,* § 15, *PL* 23:308.)

1322. ST. AUGUSTINE. A. Fasting is necessary for us in the same way that medicine is needed for wounds (*Quaestiones ex utroque Testamento,* q. 120, *PL* 35:2364). B. Our bodies need to be bridled with fasting much after the manner in which bridles are put on horses (*De salutaribus documentis,* c. 35, *PL* 40:1059). C. We must fast in order for the body to perform its service out of chastisement, and the soul to gain its victory by humility (*Serm. 210,* c. 2, § 3, *PL* 38:1049). D. Fasting purifies the mind, strengthens the senses for spiritual combat, subjects the flesh to the spirit, makes the heart contrite and humble . . . scatters the clouds of concupiscence, extinguishes the fire of the passions, lights the true light of chastity. Fasting has no love for loquaciousness, looks on riches as superfluity, contemns pride, makes humility agreeable, and grants man the grace to know himself (*Serm. 73,* § 1, *In Append., PL* 39:1887). E. By fasting vices are laid low, virtues intensified, the flesh humbled, and the power of demons overcome (*Ad fratres in eremo, Serm. 23, In Append., PL* 40:1273).

1323. ST. PETER CHRYSOLOGUS, abp. of Ravenna (d. 450). A. Fasting is the death of vices, life of the virtues, tranquillity of the body and the strength of its members, the distinction of life, power of minds, vigorous activity of souls, protection of chastity, defense of modesty, city of holiness, the training school of meritorious service, the teaching of teachers, the discipline of disciplines, the salutary equipment for the journey along the road of the Church, the unconquered leadership of Christian warfare (*Serm. 8, de jejunio et eleemosyna, PL* 52:209). B. We know that fasting is the fortress of God, the fortification of the spirit, the banner of faith, standard of chastity, the memorial of victory of holiness (*Serm. 12, de jejunio et tentationibus Christi,* col. 225). C. Fasting is the excellent plowshare of holiness, for it cultivates the emotions, roots out crimes, tears away evil deeds, digs out vices, sows charity, fosters abundance, and prepares the way for the harvest of purity (*Serm. 31, De Pharisaeorum et discipulorum Joannis jejunio,* col. 288).

1324. LIVES OF THE FATHERS. Fasting is for the monk like a bridle against sin; and like a spirited horse, whoever abandons the practice of fasting is seized by the desire of concupiscence (*De vitis Patrum, Lib. IV, libell. 4, de continentia,* n. 46, *PL* 73:870).

1325. ST. EPHRAEM, deacon of Edessa (d. 378). Fasting is a chariot to heaven (cf. IV Kgs. 2:11); fasting raises up prophets, teaches wisdom to lawmakers. Fasting is the guardian of the virtuous soul and the safe fellow-dweller of the body (*Serm. de jejunio, Op. Om.* 1:17).

1326. ST. JOHN CHRYSOSTOM. A. Nothing is mightier than a man who prays sincerely. . . . He who prays with fasting has his wings [for soaring to heaven] doubled, and is made lighter than the very winds. He does not gape, nor stretch himself at his prayers, nor grow torpid (*Hom. 57 in Matt.,* § 4, *PG* 58:563). B. Nothing is so productive of health; nothing so productive of acuteness of the faculties, nothing so tends to keep away disease [as does moderate fasting] (*In Ep. ad Hebr.,* c. 12, *Hom. 29,* § 4, *PG* 63:208). C. Fasting is the mother of all blessings, the teacher of modesty and all other virtues (*Hom. 1 in Gen.,* c. 1, § 1, *PG* 53:22). D. Fasting is the calm of souls, the charm of the elderly, the teacher of the young, master of the continent, which adorns all ages and sexes as with a jewelled crown (*ibid., Hom. 2,* § 1, col. 27). E. Fasting holds the body in check and restrains all inordinate inclination to lust; but it effects the greater purity of the soul . . . and makes the soul devoted and quick to respond to grace (*ibid., Hom. 10,* § 2, col. 83).

1327. ST. JOHN CLIMACUS. Fasting is the coercion of nature and the cutting out of everything that delights the palate, the prevention of lust, the uprooting of bad thoughts, deliverance from demons, purity of prayer, the light of the soul, the guarding of the mind, deliverance from blindness, the door of compunction, humble sighing, glad contrition, a lull in chatter, a means to silence, a guard of obedience, lightening of sleep, health of body, agent of dispassion, remission of sins, the gate of Paradise and its delights (*Scala paradisi, Grad. 14, de . . . gula, PG* 88:870; Moore, n. 23, p. 144; Father Robert, p. 212).

1328. ST. LAURENCE JUSTINIAN. Fasting is health of the body, physical strength, the death blow to sin, the cessation of crimes, remedy of salvation, source of grace, foundation of chastity, length of life (*Lignum vitae,* tract. 12, *de sobrietate,* c. 2, *Op. Om.* 1:72).

1329. ST. THOMAS AQUINAS. Fasting [and mortification of the body] are permitted for a threefold reason: first, in order to bridle the lusts of the flesh; . . . secondly, in order that the mind may arise more freely to the contemplation of heavenly things; . . . thirdly, in order to satisfy for our sins (*II-II,* q. 147, art. 1, *Utrum jejunium sit actus virtutis, Op. Om.* 10:153; Am. ed. 2:1785).

1330. ST. PETER DAMIAN. Love fasting, in order that while the body is wasted through lack of food the soul will be feasted on the strength of heavenly grace (*Lib. II, ep. 11, ad Desiderium abb. Casinensem, PL* 144:277).

1331. JOHN OF TRITHEIM. To love fasting is a matter of freedom; to observe fasting without loving it, slavery (*Comment. in c. 4. RSB,* § 13, *Op. pia et spiritualia,* p. 269).

1332. ST. BONAVENTURE. Fasting is the life of angels, death to sin, the cutting off of crimes, the remedy of salvation. . . . By fasting the perfect protection of holiness is obtained . . . as well as the perfect understanding of truth . . . and constancy of virtue. . . . Fasting is the sacrifice of reconciliation and the growth of virtue (*Opusc. 11, Apologia pauperum,* c. 6, § 15, *Op. Om.,* ed. Quaracchi 8:270).

1333. ST. BERNARD. A. Abstinence subdues and puts a restraint on the flesh; breaks the impetus of passionate desire; banishes the force of inclination to immorality (*Lib. de modo bene vivendi, ad sororem,* c. 24, *de abstinentia,* § 70, *In Append., PL* 184:1243). B. Abstinence quickens and torments: it quickens the soul, torments the body; it builds up virtues in the soul and destroys vicious habits in the body. . . . The body subdued by abstinence is not consumed by the fire of lustful desire (*ibid.,* n. 71).

1334. JOHN CASSIAN. A. A monk therefore who wants to proceed to the struggle of interior conflicts should lay down this as a precaution for himself at the very outset: that he will not in any case allow himself to be overcome by desire for delicacies, or take anything to eat or drink before the fast is over and the proper hour for refreshment has come, that is to say, he is never to eat or drink outside meal times; nor, when the meal is over, will he allow himself to take a morsel, however small (*De coenob. institut., Lib. 5,* c. 20, *PL* 49:236). B. For the nature of gluttony is threefold: first, there is that which forces us to anticipate the proper hour for a meal; next, that which delights in stuffing the stomach and gorging all kinds of food; third, that which takes pleasure in more refined and delicate feasting. And so against it the monk should observe a threefold watch: first, he should wait until the proper time for breaking the fast; second, he should not give way to gorging himself; third, he should be content with any of the commoner sorts of food (*ibid.*, c. 23, col. 240).

1335. ST. AUGUSTINE. They who refrain from meats in order to seek other foods that demand more difficult preparation and are more expensive are seriously mistaken, for this is not an observance of the fast, but a change of forms of extravagance (*Serm. 209, in Quadr. V.*, § 3, *PL* 38:1047).

Gluttony and overeating

1336. JOHN OF TRITHEIM. Self-denial (abstinence) preserves the monastic life; gluttony and overeating completely destroy it (*Comment. in c. 4 RSB,* n. 35, *Op. pia et spiritualia,* p. 289).

1337. ST. BASIL THE GREAT. Furthermore, we should prefer by all means whatever is more easily procurable and not concern ourselves with costly fare and seek to obtain extravagant foods with expensive sauces on the pretext of continency. On the contrary, we should choose whatever is easy to obtain in each region, cheap, and available for general consumption, and use only those imported foods that are necessary to sustain life, like olive oil and similar products (*Regulae fusius tractatae, Interrogatio 19, Quid sit continentiae modus,* § 2, *PG* 31:970; Wagner, p. 276).

1338. ST. ISIDORE OF SEVILLE. The eating of rich foods and meats gives rise to luxury of the flesh (*De eccl. officiis, Lib. I,* c. 45, § 2, *PL* 83:778).

1339. ST. LEANDER, monk, abp. of Seville (d. prob. 601). It is a hard situation to nourish him against whom you are waging battle, and to feed your own body to the point where you find it stubborn (*Reg., seu de institutione virginum et contemptu mundi, ad Florentinam sororem,* c. 15, *de indulgentia et prohibitione carnium, CR* 1:415; *PL* 72:889).

1340. ORIGEN, priest of Alexandria (d. circa 253–255). How does one make oneself a eunuch for the sake of the kingdom of heaven (cf. Matt. 19:12) except by cutting down on the amount of food and using abstinence as his servant? (*In Levit. hom. 10,* § 2, *PG* 12:528.)

1341. ST. GREGORY THE GREAT. The vice of luxury tempts us in five ways. Sometimes it anticipates the seasons of want. At other times it does not anticipate them, but seeks daintier food. Again it looks for those things which must be eaten, but wants them prepared more carefully. Then there are times when it agrees both with the quality of the food and the proper time for it, but exceeds in the quantity of what is taken, thereby violating the measure of moderate refreshment. On other occasions it longs for even baser kinds of food, and yet it sins more fatally through the intensity of unbounded desire. For Jonathan deserved in truth the sentence of death from the mouth of his father (cf. I Kgs. 14:44), because in taking honey he anticipated the time which had been fixed for eating. And the people which had been brought out of the bondage of Egypt died in the desert because they despised manna, and sought for fleshly food which was considered more delicate (Num. 21:5). And the first fault of the sons of Heli arose from this, that the servant, at their desire, would not receive cooked meat for the priest, after the ancient custom, but sought for raw flesh for him to serve up with greater daintiness (cf. I Kgs. 2:12 ff.). And when it is said to Jerusalem: *Behold, this was the iniquity of Sodom thy sister, pride, fullness of bread and abundance* (Ezech. 16:49), it is plainly shown that she forfeited her salvation, because with the sin of pride she exceeded the measure of moderate nourishment. And Esau lost the glory of his birthright because he desired a very ordinary food, namely lentils, with undue eagerness and longing (cf. Gen. 25:34); and when he preferred this, even to the selling of his birthright, he showed how intense was his desire for the food. For it is not the food, but the intensity of the longing that is in fault. Whence also we frequently take some delicate fare without blame, and take a taste of coarser food not without guilt of conscience. For this Esau, of whom we have spoken, lost his birthright through lentils, whereas Elias preserved the strength of his body by eating flesh in the desert (cf. III Kgs. 17:6). Whence also the ancient enemy, because he knew that it is not the food itself, but the desire of food that is the cause of damnation, both subjected the first man [Adam] to himself, not with flesh, but with an apple (cf. Gen. 3:6), and tempted the second Man [Christ] not with flesh, but with bread (cf. Matt. 4:3; *Moral., Lib. 30*, c. 18, § 60, *PL* 76:556).

1342. ST. THOMAS AQUINAS. Those vices are reckoned among the daughters of gluttony which are the results of eating and drinking immoderately. They may be accounted for either on the part of the soul or on the part of the body. On the part of the soul these results are of four kinds. First, as regards the reason, whose keenness is dulled by immoderate meat and drink, and in this respect we reckon as a daughter of gluttony dullness of sense in the understanding, on account of the fumes of food disturbing the brain. Even so, on the other hand, abstinence conduces to the penetrating power of wisdom. . . . Secondly, as regards the appetite, which is disordered in many ways by lack of moderation in eating and drinking as though reason were fast asleep at the helm, and in this respect, unseemly joy is reckoned. . . . Thirdly, as regards inordinate words, and thus we have loquaciousness. . . . Fourthly, as regards inordinate action, and in this way we have scurrility, that is, a kind of levity resulting from the lack of reason (*II-II,* q. 148, art. 6, *Utrum convenienter assignentur gulae quinque filiae, Op. Om.* 10:175; Am. ed. 2:1796).

1343. ST. JEROME. The eating of flesh and drinking of wine, and fullness of the stomach is the seed plot of lust. As the comic poet says, Venus shivers unless Ceres and Bacchus be with her (*Adversus Jovinianum, Lib. II,* § 7, *PL* 23:297).

1344. ST. JOHN CLIMACUS. Without preference for one food over another, he rejected nothing at all, but ate of whatever the teaching and laws on the religious life allowed him to eat, but always in the smallest quantity, so that he seemed rather to be tasting than eating the food. In so doing he conquered intemperance on the one hand by eating very little, and vainglory on the other by eating of everything put before him (*Isagoge ad Scalam Paradisi,* c. 3, *de vita S. Climaci, PG* 88:599).

1345. ST. AMBROSE. Let food be used to keep death at a distance, not to serve for delicacies (*De virginibus, Lib. II,* c. 2, § 8, *PL* 16:221).

1346. ST. ANTONINUS, O.P., abp. of Florence (d. 1459). A. Medicine is taken not for pleasure, but as a matter of necessity, to preserve the body from death, and it is taken with a certain fear, that it cause no harm; in much the same way, food must be eaten for the purpose of sustaining the body, to keep it from fainting, and with fear lest it offend from too much pleasure taken in it (*Summa Theologica, Pars II,* tit. 6, c. 1, *de gula,* 2:743). B. Nothing so impedes the proper function of the senses or causes such disorder in the imagination as excessive eating (*Pars IV,* tit. 4, c. 4, *de partibus subjectivis temperantiae, de abstinentia,* 4:125).

1347. ST. JOHN CHRYSOSTOM. A. Food, not feasting, drink, not drunkenness, constitute the object of the necessity of the body (*In Eph.,* c. 2, *Hom. 5,* § 3. *PG* 62:42). B. Consider what becomes of food, into what it is changed. Are you not disgusted at its even being mentioned? Why then be so eager for such accumulation? The increase of luxury is but the multiplication of dung. For nature has her limits, and what is beyond these is not nourishment, but injury, and the increase of ordure. Nourish the body, but do not destroy it (*In Ep. I ad Timoth.,* c. 5, *Hom. 13,* § 4, col. 569). C. For sufficiency is nourishment, pleasure, and health; but excess is injury, unpleasantness, and disease (*In Ep. ad Hebr.,* c. 12, *Hom. 29,* § 4, *PG* 63:208).

1348. ST. ISIDORE OF SEVILLE. A. Inclination to lust grows with the consumption of food; eating to the extent of repletion arouses the luxury of the flesh; by the vice of gluttony temptation of the flesh grows strong (*Synonymorum Lib. II,* § 14, *PL* 83:848). B. We must take food not to the point of eating extravagantly or to the state of being glutted, but only so that the body can be properly sustained. . . . The fires of lust increase with the excitation of food (*Sententiarum Lib. II,* c. 45, §§ 5, 7, col. 648).

1349. POPE ST. LEO THE GREAT. A. For by daily experience, beloved, it is proved that the mind's edge is blunted by over-indulgence of the flesh, and the heart's vigor is dulled by excess of food, so that the delights of eating are even opposed to the health of the body, unless reasonable moderation withstand the temptation and the consideration of future discomfort keep us from the pleasure (*Serm. 19, de jejunio decimi mensis, VIII,* c. 1, *PL* 54:186). B. But if it is taken with immoderate greed, it is the excess that disgraces the eaters and drinkers, not the nature of food or drink that defiles them (*Serm. 42, de Quadr. IV,* c. 4, col. 279).

1350. ST. NILUS. A. Eat those foods that are healthful, not those which are pleasant to the taste (*Capita paraenetica,* § 18, *PG* 79:1251). B. Richness of food overthrows and destroys the rampart of virtues. Like a catapult the tastefulness of condiments lays low the bulwarks that had been erected in the practice of virtue, and hurls to the ground what had been its firm and solid strength (*De monastica exercitatione,* cc. 58, 59, col. 791). C. Eat what you need, for moderate quantity of food is not forbidden. Eat in the spirit of thanksgiving, but do not gulp down your food (*Citat. in Joan. Damasc., Sacra parallela, Lib. III,* tit. 13, *PG* 95:1339).

1351. JULIANUS POMERIUS, priest of Arles (d. circa 498). Temperance makes a man temperate, abstemious, frugal, sober, moderate, chaste, silent, serious, modest. Residing in the soul, this virtue bridles lust, tempers the affections, multiplies holy desires and represses corrupt ones, sets in order all that is disordered within us, strengthens all that is well-ordered, removes wicked thoughts and implants holy ones, quenches the fire of lustful passion, kindles the tepidity of our soul by a desire of future reward, soothes our mind with peaceful tranquillity, and ever preserves it intact from every storm of vices (*De vita contemplativa, Lib. III,* c. 19, § 1, *PL* 59:502; Suelzer, p. 144).

1352. ST. THOMAS AQUINAS. A. The more the body is pampered with copious quantities of food and the softness of pleasure, the more its concupiscence is aroused (*Opusc. theolog. 2, de perfectione vitae spiritualis,* c. 9, *de his quibus juvatur homo ad continentiam servandam, Op. Om.,* ed. Parma 15:80). B. Excessive quantities of food and drink cause luxury (*In Eph.,* c. 5, lect. 7, *ibid.,* 13:494).

1353. DAVID OF AUGSBURG, Franciscan preacher and writer (d. 1272). Chastity is a daughter of sobriety. . . . Therefore he who seeks to be chaste must devote himself to the practices of sobriety, for without it chastity will not long be secure; purity progresses with him who is making progress [in the observances of sobriety], it is retarded with him who does not advance (*De profectu religiosorum, Lib. II,* c. 52, *de castitate, Op. Om. S. Bonaventurae,* ed. Peltier 12:408).

1354. HUGO DE FOLIETO, canon regular, abbot, cardinal (12th century). A flood of words so often accompanies an abundance of food (*De claustro animae, Lib. II,* c. 20, *PL* 176:1073).

1355. ST. GREGORY THE GREAT. A. From gluttony are propagated foolish mirth, scurrility, uncleanness, babbling, dullness of sense in understanding (*Moral., Lib. 31,* c. 45, § 88, *PL* 76:621). B. No one gains the palm of the spiritual contest without first having conquered the incentives of the flesh by afflicting the concupiscence of the stomach. For we cannot stand up to the conflict of the spiritual contest unless the enemy who is posted within, that is to say the appetite of gluttony, is first overcome; because if we do not overthrow those evils which are nearest to us, we doubtless proceed in vain to attack those which are farther off (*ibid., Lib. 30,* c. 18, § 58, col. 555).

1356. ST. AUGUSTINE. A. Placed amidst these temptations, I strive daily against greediness in eating and drinking. . . . For the reins of the throat are to be held somewhere between too lightly and too tightly. Who is he, Lord, that is not carried somewhat beyond the limits of necessity? If such a man there be, he is great. Let him magnify your name. But I am not he, for I am a sinful man (*Confessionum, Lib. X,* c. 31, § 47, *PL* 32:799; Sheed, p. 242). B. It is possible for a wise man to eat the most delicious food without any sin of sensuality or gluttony, while a fool is ravenous for the commonest food with a raging hunger that is most unseemly. Any sane man would rather eat fish as did the Lord (cf. Luke 24:13), than eat lentils as did Esau, Abraham's grandson (cf. Gen. 25:34; *De doctrina Christiana, Lib. III,* c. 12, § 19, *PL* 34:73).

1357. ST. BASIL THE GREAT. The vice of gluttony is wont to display its proper force not with regard to a great quantity of food, but in the appetite for a little taste (*Serm. de renuntiatione saeculi,* § 6, *PG* 31:639; Wagner, p. 24).

1358. ST. BERNARD. No man is ever so excessive in his demands as is the stomach, which forces you with its daily demands of hunger. Although we are sometimes born with other vices, sometimes we do not die with them; but with this one we are born, and with it we die. My father left me under obligation to many creditors, but I have been freed of all of them. There is only one from which I can never be freed, that is the stomach. It pays attention to no orders: it begs insistently, it demands (*Tract. de interiori domo, seu de conscientia aedificanda,* c. 26, § 54, *In Append., PL* 184:555).

1359. SMARAGDUS, abbot of St. Michael's in dioc. of Verdun (d. 826). The more that a gluttonous body grows fat, the more its soul is enfeebled through being deprived of virtues. . . . Gluttony brings on indolence; indolence, drowsiness; drowsiness, negligence, and negligence draws a curse upon itself, for it is written: *Cursed be he that doth the work of the Lord deceitfully* (Jer. 48:10). Gluttony produces a surfeit; surfeit, somnolence; and the somnolent person has no love for night watches, nor does he chant the psalmody at the proper time; . . . he is late to prayer, disinterested in reading, and hard of heart in understanding the word of God (*Comm. in c. 4, n. 36 RSB, non multum edacem, PL* 102:772).

1360. ST. CYRIL OF ALEXANDRIA. Grown fat and given to wantonness by excessive food, the body reveals itself to be difficult and obstinate, stubbornly struggling against the desires of the spirit, whereas in its weakness and unaided by the wealth that the spirit has to offer it, the body necessarily concedes the victory to the flesh (*Hom. Paschalis I,* § 3, *PG* 77:411).

1361. ST. AUGUSTINE. And while we eat and drink for the sake of health, yet a perilous enjoyment runs at the heels of health and often enough tries to run ahead of it: so that what I say I am doing and really desire for my health's sake, I do in fact for the sake of the enjoyment. For there happens not to be the same measure for both: what suffices for health is too little for enjoyment; so that often it is not at all clear whether it is the necessary care of my body calling for more nourishment, or the deceiving indulgence of greed wanting to be served. Because of this uncertainty my wretched soul is glad, and uses it as a cover and an excuse, rejoicing that it does not clearly appear what is sufficient for the needs of health, so that under the cloak of health it may shelter the business of pleasure (*Confessionum, Lib. X,* c. 31, § 44, *PL* 32:797; Sheed, p. 239).

1362. ST. BERNARD. A. The Christian man eats in order to live, and does not live to eat (*Vitis mystica, seu tract. de Passione Dni.,* c. 42, § 139, *In Append., PL* 184:719). B. If you afflict your body beyond due measure, you are killing your own citizen (fellow soldier), whereas if you nourish your flesh more than is proper, you are supporting your enemy (*Lib. de modo bene vivendi, ad sororem,* c. 24, *de abstinentia,* n. 72, *In Append.,* col. 1244).

1363. ST. ISAIAS, abbot who lived in desert of Scete (4th century). A. Reach out your hand to that which has been given to you as though you were forced to eat it (*Oratio 3,* § 1, *ad fratres juniores institutio, PG* 40:1108). B. If there is anything on the table for which one of the brethren has an intense dislike, let him not only not say that he cannot eat of it, but let him do violence to himself unto death, and God will comfort him (*ibid., Oratio 5,* § 1, col. 1121).

1364. ST. BERNARD. A. I will abstain from wine, because in it is debauchery (cf. Eph. 5:18); or, if I am weak, I will use a little, according to the counsel of St. Paul (I Tim. 5:23). I will abstain from eating flesh meat, lest it should too much pamper my flesh, and with it the lusts of the flesh. I will strive to take even bread in moderation that I may not, through fullness of stomach, stand wearily and reluctantly to pray, and that I may not be open to the reproach of the Prophet that I have eaten my bread in fullness (cf. Ezech. 16:49). I will not accustom myself to drink immoderately even of pure water, lest it may excite in me feelings that are corrupt (*Serm. 66 in Cant.,* n. 6, *PL* 183:1097). B. For food badly cooked and ill-digested generates unhealthy humors, and injures the body instead of nourishing it (*ibid., Serm. 36,* n. 4, col. 969). C. *You cannot drink the cup of the Lord and the cup of devils* (I Cor. 10:21). The cup of devils is . . . debauchery and drunkenness; the cup of Christ is . . . renunciation of the world and sobriety (*Ep. 2, ad Fulconem juvenem qui postea fuit Ligonensis archdiaconus,* § 10, *PL* 182:85). D. Lustfulness grows through eating and drinking. . . . Where there is a stomach filled with food, there the fire of lust has been ignited (*Lib. de modo bene vivendi, ad sororem,* c. 24, *de abstinentia,* n. 72, *In Append., PL* 184:1244).

1365. ST. PAULINUS OF NOLA (d. 431). Let us become the food of God, so that we will not become that of the serpent; may Christ consume us, lest the devil devour us. . . . We cannot be the food of Christ without doing his will, so that in turn he may be our food (*Ep. 23, Severo,* § 16, *PL* 61:268).

1366. WILLIAM OF ST. THIERRY. Upon food taken in moderation by a body held in restraint there follows the sobriety of sleep (*Ep. ad fratres de Monte Dei, Lib. I,* c. 11, n. 34, *PL* 184:330).

Table reading

1367. ST. AUGUSTINE. A. If the body alone is nourished without the soul being fed with the word of God, the servant is satisfied and the mistress tormented with hunger (*Serm. 141,* § 5, *In Append., PL* 39:2022). B. When you are at table, listen to what is being read according to your custom until it is time to leave, without disturbance or quarrelling. Do not let your jaws alone consume food, but let your ears perceive the word of God (*Ep. 211, Reg. ad monachos,* § 8, *PL* 33:960).

1368. ST. GREGORY THE GREAT. A. Bread is the nourishment of the body; the word, that of the mind; they who restore the forces of the body but not of the mind, are mentally dead (*In I Reg. expositiones, Lib. IV,* c. 4, § 47, *PL* 79:266). B. Gluttony is broken by abstinence, but he who does not fill his mind with spiritual foods cannot acquire abstinence from corporal foods (*ibid., Lib. V,* c. 4, § 9, col. 364).

1369. RULE OF STS. PAUL AND STEPHEN (6th century). Let us listen to the reading in the spirit of thanksgiving and in the fear of God while we are eating. Let us receive God's gift without quarrels, murmuring, manifestation of displeasure, talking aloud, shuffling of the feet, or making noise with the dishes, but in the spirit of charity, in silence and in the sweet restraint of discipline. Let us do so in fear of the example of the carnal Israelites (cf. Num. 11; Ps. 77). While they ate the bread of angels and quail flesh to the point that they were filled to nausea, and while their mouths were still stuffed with food and they were murmuring, *the anger of God rose against them and slew their best men* (Ps. 77:31; c. 18, *CR* 1:141; *PL* 66:954).

1370. THOMAS À KEMPIS. He who reads well and distinctly during the meal delights his companions at the table of Jesus with the heavenly cup, and inebriates the thirsty (*Hortulus rosarum,* c. 17, *Op. Om.* 4:41).

1371. WILLIAM OF ST. THIERRY. When you are engaged in eating, let your table, which of its very nature is already on the side of severity, be further adorned by your personal modesty. When engaged in eating, do not allow the whole man to devote himself to the task; while the body is taking its nourishment, let the soul not neglect hers, but meditate on some thought of the goodness of the Lord (*Ep. ad fratres de Monte Dei, Lib. I,* c. 11, § 33, *PL* 184:329).

1372. DAVID OF AUGSBURG, Franciscan preacher and writer (d. 1272). At table do not allow your eyes to wander about; you should not be glancing to either side, so that you do not know who is sitting at your side, what he is doing, or what he has before him. Direct your attention to your own affairs, or think on God, or listen to the reading. Eat with restraint, in the fear of God, in silence, and not with the gluttonous rapidity of a famished man. Neither should you glance about restlessly to see what is most tasteful on the table, seeking to feast your eyes before you satisfy your palate, but in the spirit of thanksgiving, let whatever you have received be sufficient for you. Always prefer to suffer some form of want than to abound in greater quantity. . . . Let poverty, Christ's intimate friend, be pleasing to you in all things, but particularly embrace it at table, in food, in drink. . . . Never allow any word of complaint to be heard from you regarding food, drink, or clothing. Judge yourself unworthy of what you actually have, for exterior want grows into increase of interior grace and the wealth of a good conscience (*De institutione novitiorum, Pars I,* c. 8, *Op. Om. S. Bonaventurae,* ed. Peltier 12:295).

1373. VEN. LOUIS DE BLOIS. You are called a monk. You must come, then, to the table to refresh your body with God's gifts, not to nourish the pleasures of the flesh. . . . Furthermore, beware that, while you refresh your body, your mind be not in the meantime hunger-starved. Therefore the mouth of your heart is to feed on the word of God, your ears to receive the wholesome doctrine and deeds of the saints (*Speculum monachorum,* div. 7, *Op. Om.* 3:667).

Discipline of the chapter of faults

1374. ST. DOROTHEUS, monk of Palestine (7th century). In Proverbs it is stated: *For lack of guidance a people falls; security lies in many counselors* (Prov. 11:14). Let us contemplate the force of that statement, brethren, and meditate on the Divine Scripture. It warns us to beware of trying to form ourselves without the aid of others lest we become sciolists, persuading ourselves that we are self-sufficient for our own direction. For we need the assistance of helpers besides God. There is nothing more miserable, nothing that can be more quickly overcome than those who have no leaders, no fathers in the striving for union with God. For it says: *for the lack of guidance a people falls* [like leaves]; the leaf that from the beginning was always green, always growing, always pleasing to the sight, shortly afterward withers and grows pale and on falling to the ground is disregarded and trampled under foot. In the beginning [of his conversion to God] he is fervent in fasting, in watching through the night, in observing silence, in obeying, and in practicing all other virtues. Not long afterward, when he has lost his first fervor, if he has no one to direct and exhort him, no one will stir up and kindle the fire that has burned low—and like the leaf, he will dry up and fall—left to himself he will be taken captive by his enemies who may then attack him at will. But in the case of those who do nothing precipitately, nothing rashly, but undertake all things with counsel, it says: *Security lies in many counselors* (*ibid.*). It does not say "in much counsel" (cf. Douay) in the sense that one consult just anyone at random, but him in whom he has reposed his whole confidence. Nor that he be silent about some things and speak of others, but that he manifest everything, and take counsel about them all; this indeed is safety in much counsel. . . . There is nothing that the devil detests so much and from which he takes flight so instantly as for his malice to be laid bare, leaving him nothing in the future that he can present in the form of insidious temptation. The soul thus protects itself by manifesting all its secrets. In acknowledging these difficulties to another person who is wiser, and who instructs him, he learns what he should do and what he should avoid, what is good and what evil, what is virtue and what is covetousness; that one time is propitious for an undertaking, another is not. In this way the devil will not at any time be able to harm him or trip him up, since he is directed in all matters, and hence perfectly safe and secure (*Doctrina 5*, §§ 1, 2, *PG* 88:1675).

1375. JOHN CASSIAN. If then anyone by accident breaks an earthenware jar, he can only expiate his carelessness by public penance; and when all the brethren are assembled for the service he must lie prostrate and ask for absolution until the service of the prayers is finished. He will obtain it when by the abbot's command he is bidden to rise from the ground. The same satisfaction must be given by one who, when summoned to some work or to the usual service comes rather late, or who, when singing a psalm hesitates ever so little [thereby causing distraction in the choir] (*De coenob. institut., Lib. IV,* c. 16, *PL* 49:172).

1376. ST. ISAIAS, Syrian abbot (4th century). Manifest your [spiritual] illnesses to your fathers, in order to receive aid by means of their counsel (*Reg. ad monachos,* n. 6, *CR* 1:6; *PL* 103:492).

1377. JOHN CASSIAN. True discretion, he said, is secured only by true humility. And the first proof of this humility is given by reserving everything (not only what you do but also what you think) for the scrutiny of the elders (*Abbatis Moysis coll. 2, de discretione,* c. 10, *PL* 49:537).

1378. ST. AUGUSTINE. For it is better to make acknowledgment of the sins of ignorance and negligence, that they may be done away with, than to excuse them so that they remain; and it is better to clear them off by calling upon God, than to cling to them, provoking him (*Enarr. in Ps. 105, 7,* § 7, *PL* 37:1410).

1379. ST. PETER DAMIAN. A. Pride makes the human mind as fragile as glass; because of his impatience the proud man cannot bear the blow of correction. . . . Even though he has acquired other virtues, anyone who is broken by impatience at the blows of correction shows that he possesses no stability of forces (*Lib. VI, ep. 9, ad Gebizonem abb., PL* 144:390). B. A wise person considers the harshness of a severe correction given to him as medicine for the wounds of his soul (*Opusc. 46,* c. 2, *PL* 145:706). C. If the reproach of correction is withdrawn from the sacred enclosure, all of discipline's strength is sapped, and the whole religious institute is destroyed. . . . Anyone in whom the fervor of the regular life is ardent, willingly welcomes correction (*ibid.,* c. 4, col. 708).

1380. DENIS THE CARTHUSIAN. The more praiseworthy it is to administer a paternal reprimand or a fraternal correction out of charity or justice, the more unjustifiable, unthankful, and stupid it is not to receive it in the spirit of obedience, patience, and filial or fraternal submission. Holy Scripture gives abundant evidence of this truth. It is written, for instance, in the Book of Proverbs: *Then they call me, but I answer not; they seek me, but find me not; because they hated knowledge, and chose not the fear of the Lord* (Prov. 1:28–29). . . . Since sin is death, the loss of the soul, and the way to hell, is he not incomparably more foolish who refuses to be corrected for his sins, to be reproved, and have his vices pointed out, than he who will not permit the wounds of his body to be seen, or treated, or cured? Let us cast this pestiferous disease from us with the words: Touch me not! . . . Inability to bear correction and excusing one's vices proceeds from the root of pride and is evidence of the want of heavenly illumination. The wise man (in the sense of a humble one) is fearful in all matters. Even though he is not conscious of having failed in the matters for which he is corrected, he knows that he has failed in many points that have escaped his own notice and that of the one correcting him. Hence with these thoughts in mind, the present correction is borne calmly. And even if he were conscious of no sin at all, he would cheerfully bear any correction out of the love of God, in union with the Lord's passion, for the increase of grace in this life, and glory in the next.

But there are those who are ashamed of being humiliated and belittled in the sight and in the hearts of others, a disposition that stems from shameless self-love. Once this attitude has been driven out and one has laboriously attained to a spiritual love, a person seeks to remain unknown, and as far as lies in his power, seeks to be despised, to be afflicted with humiliations; and desires, embraces, and readily seeks everything helpful in enabling him to progress in grace and glory, in pleasing God and rendering him honor.

We must not doubt that the rebukes and corrections of our superiors are rebukes and corrections of God himself. Hence patience is the test of all virtues. No matter how virtuous and devout one may pretend to be, if he does not observe patience in corrections, punishments, and hardships, he is definitely shown to be poor and weak. He is like a defective pot placed in the middle of the furnace, which jumps, cracks and is crushed. Hence it is written: *As the test of what the potter molds is in the furnace, so in his conversation is the test of man* (Sir. 27:5). . . . Imitation of the Son of God who taught us all humility, patience, and love, helps us greatly to bear calmly the humiliation of correction (*De modo judicandi et corripiendi,* art. 20, *Op. Om.* 40:46).

1381. ST. BONAVENTURE. Praiseworthy religious institutes differ from those in which the discipline is relaxed, not that in the former no one is found without sin, but that no one is suffered to sin unpunished, that the occasions of sin are zealously removed, that the incorrigible and those who wield an influence for evil are dismissed, and the good are helped on, encouraged to persevere, and advance always in virtue (*De sex alis Seraphim,* c. 2, § 13, *Op. Om.,* ed. Quaracchi 8:135).

1382. GILBERT OF HOILAND, English Cistercian, abbot of St. Mary's, diocese of Lincoln (d. 1172). Those who are called on in chapter [of faults] are subject to the abbot's judgment as though they were standing before the tribunal of Christ himself. In chapter each one is first of all to be his own accuser, thereby seizing from others the opportunity of accusing him (*Serm. 23 in Cant. Salomonis,* n. 3, *PL* 184:121).

1383. ST. MARY MAGDALEN DE PAZZI, Carmelite (d. 1607). Afterward she saw hordes of demons entering into different parts of the monastery to which she belonged, in order to tempt other sisters. But they could not enter into the chapter room because of the acts of humility and reverence performed there (*Acta Sanctorum Bolland. Maii tom. 6, die 25,* c. 7, n. 77, p. 198).

1384. ST. AUGUSTINE. It behooves him who has offended many by sinning to please many by his atonement (*De vera et falsa poenitentia,* c. 11, *In Append., PL* 40:1123).

1385. ST. BERNARD. Satisfaction, which is the remedy for a transgression of the law of God, which arose from pride, ought to be humble and shamefaced (*Serm. 4 in Cant.,* n. 2, *PL* 183:797).

1386. ST. FRANCIS OF ASSISI (d. 1226). Blessed is the servant who, on being reproved, cheerfully agrees, modestly complies, humbly confesses and readily makes amends (*Verba sacrae admonitionis B. Patris Francisci ad omnes fratres suos,* c. 22, *de correptione patienter suscipienda, Op. Om.,* p. 15).

1387. JOHN CASSIAN. A. For man is concerned with a daily and nightly conflict against no visible foes, but invisible and cruel ones, and a spiritual combat not against one or two only, but against countless hosts, failure in which is the more dangerous to all, in proportion as the foe is the fiercer and the attack more secret. And therefore, we should always follow the footsteps of the elders with utmost care, and bring to them everything which arises in our hearts, thus removing the veil of shame (*Collatio II, abbatis Moysis 2, de discretione,* c. 11, *PL* 49:541). B. And even before the sentence of discretion has been given, the foul serpent is by the power of confession dragged out, so to speak, from his dark underground cavern, and in some sense shown up and sent away in disgrace (*ibid.,* c. 10, col. 538). C. "Have faith, my child," he said. "Without any words of mine, your confession frees you from this slavery [of having eaten secretly outside meal times food that was stolen]. For you have today triumphed over your victorious adversary, by laying him low through your confession in a manner which more than makes up for the way in which you were overtaken by him through your former silence. . . . And therefore, after this exposure of him, that evil spirit will no longer be able to vex you . . ." (*ibid.,* c. 11, col. 540). D. The monks ought to be taught not to conceal through false shame any troublesome (*prurientes,* lit. itching) thoughts in their hearts but, as soon as ever such arise, to lay them bare before their superior (*De coenob. institut., Lib. IV,* c. 9, col. 161).

1388. ST. BASIL THE GREAT. Every subject, if he intends to make any progress worth mentioning and to be confirmed in a mode of life that accords with the precepts of our Lord Jesus Christ, ought not to conceal within himself any movement of his soul, nor yet utter any thoughtless word, but he should reveal the secrets of his heart to those of his brethren whose office it is to exercise a compassionate and sympathetic solicitude for the weak. In this way, that which is laudable will be ratified and that which is worthy of rebuke will receive the correction it deserves, and by the practice of such cooperative discipline, we shall by a gradual advance attain to perfection (*Reg. fusius tractatae, Interrogatio* 26, *quod omnia etiam cordis arcana sint praeposito detegenda, PG* 31: 986; Wagner, p. 288).

1389. ST. AUGUSTINE. Confession has a twofold meaning in Scripture. There is a confession of the one engaged in praising God, and there is that of him who groans in sorrow. . . . But does not this very act of confessing your sins pertain to the praise of God? Yes, truly it most fully pertains to God's praise. Why is this? Because the more desperate was the state of the sufferer, so much the greater is the honor of the physician. The more, therefore, you despaired on account of your iniquities, the more you must confess your sin; for so much greater is the praise of him who forgives as is the fullness of the penitent's confession more abundant. Let us not imagine that we have receded from the song of praise in understanding here that confession by which we acknowledge our transgressions. This too is a part of the song of praise; for when we confess our sins, we praise the glory of God (*Enarr. in Ps. 94*, 2, § 4, *PL* 37:1218, 1219).

1390. ST. AMBROSE. Let us place ourselves [in the hands of God's physician], prepared as he is to heal, with whatever medicine he chooses for curing us. . . . Consider him who seeks to be cured, willing to assent to his physician in everything. But note well the order of procedure. First he shows his wounds to the physician and says: "Heal me, I beg you, but do so not in anger, for my weakness will not suffer harsh medicine." Now here the medicine of Christ is reproof; for the Lord reproves him whom he wills to convert. For that reason Paul addresses the physician: *Reprove, entreat, rebuke* (II Tim. 4:2). He, therefore, does not refuse to be healed who requests to be reproved; but he wishes that the punishment be made lighter, lest he be reproved in anger and corrected in vengeance. Now, consider the process: first he asks to be reproved; next, what is more, he asks to be reproached. Then he not only confesses his sins, but also indicates their numbers, and accuses himself, for he wishes that his crimes remain no longer concealed. A fever which is most difficult to break gives hope of receding when it is brought to the surface: in much the same way, as long as it is hidden, the sickness of sin grows constantly more serious, but if made known in confession, disappears (*Enarr. in Ps. 37*, §§ 56, 57, *PL* 14:1086).

1391. ST. GREGORY THE GREAT. But those who rule others should show themselves such that their subjects are unafraid to reveal their hidden secrets to them. Thus when these little ones are enduring the waves of temptation, they will have recourse to the pastor's understanding as to a mother's bosom; and in the solace of his comforting words and in their prayerful tears they will cleanse themselves when they see themselves defiled by the sin that buffets them (*Reg. Pastoralis, Pars II*, c. 5, *PL* 77:33; Davis, p. 58).

1392. ST. FRUCTUOSUS, bp. of Braga, Portugal (d. 670). It is necessary that the monk always refer all his acts and occasions of sin—"thoughts, revelations, illusions, and negligences"—to the Father, so that relying on his discretion and judgment, he will know to what he should devote his attention (*Reg. monachorum*, c. 13, *CR* 1:204; *PL* 87:1105).

1393. ST. BONAVENTURE. A. Once they have entered into religion they must devote their time continuously to preparing for a general confession, and that of all that they have committed from childhood on in the world, insofar as they can recall it after diligent examination. The confession of evils is the beginning of virtues (*St. Augustine In Joan.*, tract. 12, § 13, *PL* 35:1491). The state of religion thus casts behind it past deeds together with their fault (*Speculum disciplinae ad novitios, Pars I*, c. 1, § 2, *Op. Om.*, ed. Quaracchi 8:584). B. Afterward acknowledgment is made of daily offenses, of which this life is never free—a secret confession of secret faults, a public one for public offenses which, however, may call for secret confession as well (*ibid.*, c. 9, § 1, p. 592).

Discipline of the cell

1394. LIVES OF THE FATHERS. A brother interrogated one of the seniors: "What shall I do, O my father, for I do nothing which the monks do? On the contrary, I am negligent, and I eat and drink and sleep, and I think filthy thoughts, and my mind is ever disturbed, and I depart from one work to another, and from one group of thoughts to another. What shall I do, then? For I am troubled, and my soul is little." Abba Sarmata said to him: "Sit in your cell, and do whatever you can, and do not trouble yourself. For I wish you to do now even a little, even as did Abba Antony great and wonderful things in the desert. I believe that by remaining in your cell for the sake of the name of God, you also will be found in the same place as Abba Antony" (*Lib. V., verba seniorum, libell. 7, de patientia et fortitudine*, n. 34, *PL* 73:901).

1395. JOHN CASSIAN. When the psalms are finished, and the daily assembly, as we have said above, is broken up, none of them dares to loiter ever so little or to gossip with another: nor does he presume even to leave his cell throughout the whole day, or to forsake the work which he is wont to carry on in it, except when they happen to be called out for the performance of some necessary duty (*De coenob. institut., Lib. II*, c. 15, *PL* 49:105).

1396. THOMAS À KEMPIS. A. Diligently guard your cell and it in turn will protect you. There is no safer place in this world for the servant of God than to dwell in secrecy where he can pray to the Father, with his mind free of all distractions, with the door of his cell closed (cf. Matt. 6:6). The danger is always in leaving the cell: remaining in it is the tranquillity of a devout life (*Libellus spiritualis exercitii,* c. 4, *Op. Om.* 2:336). B. He who loves his cell and dwells in it willingly is preserved from many sins and temptations. The more zealously it is dwelt in, the more pleasing it becomes, and the more it is loved. The more negligently it is treated, and the more infrequently it is entered, the more it will be shuddered at and the more intense the disgust it will cause. He is fortunate who cherishes and inhabits his cell, for the anointing of the Spirit will instruct him. Blessed is he to whom it is granted to inhabit his cell and persevere in it until the end of his life (*De disciplina claustralium,* c. 7, *ibid.,* p. 294).

1397. ST. PETER DAMIAN. When a brother knocks at the door of your cell, greet him forthwith . . . with calm countenance, and a pleasant brow that indicates your happiness (*Opusc. 51,* c. 10, *PL* 145:760).

1398. BENEDICT HAEFTEN, provost of Affighem (d. 1648). During the whole time that brethren are together in a cell, the door is to be kept ajar so that what they are doing can be seen. This also has the purpose of eliminating protracted conversation. Should necessity demand, it is wiser to assign another place for the purpose of visiting. In so providing, the quiet and silence of the dormitory building will not be disturbed by prolonged talking, nor will anyone be distracted in his prayer and study (*Disquisitiones monasticae, Lib. 12, de monachorum cellis,* tract. 3, disq. 6, p. 1056).

1399. WILLIAM OF ST. THIERRY. *Let all things,* says the Apostle, *be done properly and in order* (I Cor. 14:40). For propriety in action is a thing acceptable unto God and beloved of the angels. . . . And since the angels are without doubt both day and night with you in your cells, guarding you, rejoicing in your studies and efforts, and working together with you, it is their pleasure that all you do, even though no man see it, be done properly. . . . When you go to bed, bear with you ever in the memory or the imagination something wherein you may tranquilly pass to sleep . . . something that may await you when you awaken and restore you unto the state of yesterday's intention. In this way, then, for you, *darkness itself is not dark, and night shines as the day* (Ps. 138:12; *Ep. ad fratres de Monte Dei, Lib. I,* c. 11, nn. 32, 34, *PL* 184:329).

1400. VEN. LOUIS DE BLOIS. Every night before you go to bed, consider seriously, but without inordinately taxing the mind, in what you have offended that day, and ask pardon of the most merciful God, resolving to live more worthily and strive more carefully to avoid vice in the future. Then pray that God will vouchsafe to keep you that night from all defilement of body and mind, commending to him, to his Blessed Mother, and your guardian angel the custody of your soul and body. After you have gone to bed, arm yourself with the sign of the Lord's cross. Then, after having composed your body virtuously, tenderly address yourself to your beloved, dwelling on some pious thought until sleep gently overtakes you. If sleep is too deep and rather a burden than a refreshing of your body, or if the fantasies of the night bring with them anything which carries a threat to virtue, do not allow yourself to be greatly disturbed, but in humility sigh before the Lord and pray him to grant you sobriety of diet and of the senses, to which sobriety of sleep and purity of body are commonly companions (*Speculum monachorum,* div. 8, *Op. Om.* 3:673).

1401. BENEDICT HAEFTEN. The purpose of the monastic regulation [of having a small window in the door of each person's room] is that the superior may, at any time, even without previous warning, visit a room and see what is in it, or what its occupant is doing. He is presumed to be doing evil who shuns the superior's glancing into or entering the room. For, as Christ says: *Everyone who does evil hates the light* (John 3:20). Religious should cultivate frankness not only with regard to the cell, but even with regard to the secret recesses of the heart. Nothing is to be hidden from the abbot, not even the thoughts of the mind. The brethren are so to live as though everywhere they were seen by the abbot (*Disquisitiones monasticae, Lib. 12,* tract. 3, disq. 3, p. 1056).

The exercise of the discipline

1402. ST. ISIDORE OF SEVILLE. Every sinner must be made to suffer with scourgings during this life, so that he will be found purified of his sins at the judgment. . . . No eternal punishment can be meted out to those persons whom the discipline of penance has chastised here on earth. For if we are punished here below for our sins, we shall be freed from them there (*Quaestiones in Vet. Testament., in Deuteron.,* c. 22, § 2, *PL* 83:370).

1403. WILLIAM OF AUVERGNE, bp. of Paris (d. 1249). Taught by the Holy Spirit himself, the Fathers scourged themselves. By their intercession may they seek to obtain this great favor from the Lord: that the whole Church may preserve their spirit, doing penance with fastings, hairshirts, labors and even the discipline of scourging (*Rhetorica divina,* c. 28, *quod afflictio corporalis valet ad impetrationem lachrymarum;* in Guillaume d'Auvergne, *Rhetorica divina,* Freiburg in Breisgau; Kilian Fischer, ca. 1491–1493, no pagination, extremely small Gothic type).

1404. ST. PETER DAMIAN. A. Friday is appropriately dedicated to devotion of the life-giving cross, for it is the day which was purpled with the triumphant blood of the Lord hanging on the cross. In keeping with the very nature of the monastic life, all our brethren on this day add to the ordinary practices of their spiritual warfare that in the chapter they scourge themselves with whips made of thin branches and pass the day in observing a fast on bread and water. They thus give testimony to the fact that in such practices we share in the cross, we die with Christ, if on the day on which he suffered we too punish our bodies and torment them with fasting (*Opusc. 33,* c. 3, *PL* 145:565). B. Is there anything incongruous in the Church's now employing, during the time of peace, what it formerly used during persecutions? For the Apostle says: *I chastise my body and bring it into subjection* (I Cor. 9:27). And elsewhere: *Others* [of the martyrs] *had experience of mockery and stripes, yes, even of chains and prisons* (Hebr. 11:36). While the hand of the execution has, for the time being, been held from inflicting the scourge on the martyrs, what is to prevent sacred devotion itself from administering that by which it merits to become a sharer with the holy martyrs? For when I voluntarily use the discipline with my own hands in God's sight, as a longing of honest devotion, I show myself ready, should the executioner appear. For if from love of Christ the suffering is so sweet to me when the executioner is absent, with what zeal would it not be accepted if he were to inflict it? I would *desire* to suffer martyrdom for Christ; but since persecution has ceased, I have no opportunity for such grace: hence at least I can show the willingness of a fervent soul by inflicting the scourge on myself. Surely if the executioner were to summon me, I would scourge myself to prove to him that of my own free will I should be scourged. For if we meditate attentively on Scripture, Christ, the King of Martyrs, is found to have been handed over not only by Judas, but also by his Father, nay, even by himself. For of the Father the Apostle says: *He who has not spared even his own Son, but has delivered him for us all* (Rom. 8:32); and of the Son, elsewhere: *I live in the faith of the Son of God, who loved me and gave himself up for me* (Gal. 2:20). Whether my own hand wield the scourge, or an executioner strike the blow, I am in a special way responsible for the trial in which I voluntarily offer myself. Moreover, since the timbrel is a dry skin, he truly sings the praises of the Lord with timbrel and harp in accordance with the words of the Prophet (Ps. 149:3) who lashes with the discipline the body that has been prepared by fasting. . . . For the Psalmist says: *I was exercised and swept by my spirit* (Ps. 76:7, Douay version). If indeed I sweep the flesh and the spirit, I recall that I have sinned with both the flesh and the spirit. I sweep the latter free of reproaches, the former [the flesh] with other afflictions and even scourging with branches, so that because its delight led me into sin, it shall lead me back to pardon by its suffering. Man is enveloped with the flesh as with a shield, encompassed as it were with a breastplate studded with iron, protecting his members. He performs acts of penance only laboriously, and often casts the palm of victory to the ground. Why does he perform such acts [of penance] at all, except that while the body is chastised by such means, the consolation of the soul is procured? For by whatever means the body is wounded and hurled to the ground, man is in the process cleansed of the filth he had contracted in his guilt (*Lib. VI, ep. 27, ad Petrum Cerebrosum monachum, PL* 144:416).

1405. ST. MECHTILD. [Her spirit lifted up to heaven before the Lord seated on the throne, Mechtild] heard a most sweet sound in the vault of heaven, which came from the noise of the discipline which the sisters were taking at this hour for the common welfare of mankind. At this sound the holy angels applauded and danced with joy; the demons appointed to torture souls fled afar; and souls were delivered from punishments and the chains of their sins broken asunder (*Le livre de la grace spéciale, IIme partie,* c. 26, p. 167).

Discipline of soul and body

1406. JOHN CASSIAN. A. In order to preserve the mind and body in a perfect condition, abstinence from food is not alone sufficient; unless the other virtues of the mind as well are joined to it (*De coenob. institut., Lib. V,* c. 10, *PL* 49:225). B. For the soul also has its foods which are harmful, fattened on which, even without superfluity of food, it is involved in a downfall of wantonness (*ibid.,* c. 21, col. 238).

1407. ST. BASIL THE GREAT. True fasting is opposition to vices, control of the tongue, restraint of anger and the pruning of concupiscence, detraction, lying, and false swearing (*De jejunio, Hom. II,* § 7, *PG* 31:195).

1408. ST. JEROME. A. Like the Ark of the Covenant, Christ's spouse should be plated inside and outside with pure gold (cf. Exod. 25:11); she should be the guardian of the law of the Lord. Just as the Ark contained nothing but the tables of the Covenant (*ibid.,* vers. 16), so in you there should be no thought of anything that is outside. For it pleases the Lord to take possession of your souls as he met Moses, from above the propitiatory, between the two cherubim on the Ark of the Commandments (cf. Exod. 25:22; *Ep. 22, ad Eustochium, Paulae filiam, de custodia virginitatis,* n. 24, *PL* 22:410). B. What does it profit for your body to grow thin through abstinence if your mind is puffed up with pride? . . . What virtue is there in not drinking wine and to be drunk with anger and hatred? Self-denial is then admirable and chastisement of the body beautiful and splendid when the soul is rid of vices (*Ep. 148, ad Celantiam, de ratione pie vivendi,* n. 22, col. 1214).

1409. ST. AUGUSTINE. A. Of what use is it to drink no wine, but still to be filled up with the poison of anger? What benefit is there in abstaining from meat—which was created to be eaten—while still calumniating brothers with malevolent detraction? (*Serm. 143,* § 3, *In Append., PL* 39:2025.) B. There are two kinds of abstinence, or two kinds of crosses, the one physical and the other spiritual. The first consists in refraining from eating and drinking; in restricting the appetite with regard to pleasures and delicacies; and in manfully withholding consent and vigorously fleeing from those things which ensnare us through the senses of touch, taste, and sight. The other kind is more precious and sublime, and consists in controlling the emotions of the mind; in calming its disturbances with placid modesty; in controlling the impulses of anger and pride as though they were wild beasts; in striving daily against one's vices; in reproving oneself with a certain austerity of virtue; and in some manner or other in creating opposition to vices within the interior man (*Serm. 196,* § 7, *In Append.,* col. 2112).

Mortification of mind and senses

1410. ST. DOROTHEUS. Provided that he is sincere in wishing to do so, a person can in a brief space of time, prune his inclinations and easily learn to deny himself. I will show you how this is done. Let us say that a person is walking about and his attention is drawn to some object: he is instantly impelled to stop and examine it more closely. But if he is wise he will repress the curiosity and the inclination, reflect and say: "I will give it no attention, I will not even look at it." Or again, suppose that he comes upon a group engaged in trifling talk and the spreading of rumors, and his heart's impulse says to him: "Say something too; join in with them." But he denies himself such participation, and does violence to his inclinations. . . . If we deny ourselves often enough, it will soon result in our becoming accustomed to breaking away easily from whatever is drawn to our attention. We should begin however with small and less difficult tasks so that we may arrive at the ability to cut off major and more important things with complete calm. Thus finally we shall achieve the goal of having no [uncontrolled] will of our own at all (*Doctrina I,* § 14, *PG* 88:1635, slightly different reading than Wolter's text).

1411. ST. BERNARD. A. If the stomach alone has sinned, let it also fast alone, and that will suffice. But if other members have also sinned, why should not they also fast? Let the eye therefore fast, for it has ravaged the soul. Let the ear too be made to fast, and the tongue, and the hand, yes, and the very soul itself. Let the eye abstain from curious glances and wanton impudence so that, humbly disciplined, it may now be held in restraint by penance whereas in the past it made use of pernicious liberty to wander at large in sin. Let the prurient ear withhold itself from curiosity about news reports and idle gossip and from all that is vain and worthless with regard to salvation. Let the tongue fast from detraction and murmuring; from unprofitable, vain and useless words; and because of the great importance of silence, at times even from speech that might be considered necessary. Let the hands abstain from useless signs and every work that is not sanctioned by obedience. But more than all else, let the soul fast from vice and from its own will (*Serm. de temp., Serm. 3 in Quadr.*, n. 4, *PL* 183:176). B. For if my self-will is found, for instance in the fasts which I make, the Bridegroom [Christ] will not accept such fasting as that, because it savors not of the lily of obedience, but of the sin of my own self-will (*Serm. 71 in Cant. . . . de unitate Dei Patris cum Filio, et animae sanctae cum Deo,* n. 14, col. 1128). C. How lovely the flush which the jewel of inborn modesty colors a virgin's cheeks! Can the earrings of queens be compared to this? And self-discipline confers a mark of equal beauty. How self-discipline calms the whole aspect of a maiden's bearing! her whole temper of mind! It bows the neck, smoothes the proud brows, composes the countenance, restrains the eyes, represses laughter, checks the tongue, tempers the appetite, assuages wrath, and guides the deportment. With such pearls of modesty should your robe be decked (*Ep. 113, ad Sophiam virginem,* n. 5, *PL* 182:258; James, p. 177). D. The soul which is subject to such distractions [tepidity, attachment to things of earth] cannot be replenished with divine grace; this is infused in greater or lesser degree according to the measure in which the soul rids itself of these. . . . The oil can descend only so far as it finds the vessel empty (cf. IV Kgs. 4:6), and men will put new wine into none but fresh wine skins, so that both may be preserved (cf. Mark 2:22). Moreover, there can be no fellowship between the spirit and the flesh, between fire and tepidity (*Serm. de temp., Serm. 3, in Ascensione Dni,* n. 7, *PL* 183:308).

1412. ST. BASIL THE GREAT. But, in a single word, the body in every part should be despised by everyone who does not care to be buried in its pleasures, as it were in slime; or we ought to cleave to it only insofar as we obtain from it service in the pursuit of wisdom as did Plato, advising in a manner somewhat similar to Paul's when he admonishes us to make no provision for the body with thought for its lusts (cf. Rom. 13:14). Or, in what way do those differ, who are solicitous how the body may be as well off as possible, but overlook the soul, which is to make use of it as utterly worthless, from those who are much concerned about their tools but neglect the art which uses them for its work? Hence we must do quite the opposite—chastise the body and hold it in check, as we do the violent chargings of a wild beast, and by smiting with reason as with a whip the disturbances engendered in the soul, calm them to sleep; instead of relaxing every curb upon pleasure, and suffering the mind to be swept headlong, like a charioteer by unmanageable horses riotously running at large (*Serm. ad addiscentes de legendis libris Gentilium*, § 7, *PG* 31:583).

1413. WILLIAM OF ST. THIERRY. When [St. Bernard] was a novice, having no pity on himself, he forced himself in every way to mortify not only the pleasures of the flesh to which the bodily senses open the door, but the senses themselves, through which pleasure arises. . . . Through constant observance this mortification developed into habit, and in a sense the habit itself became second nature. . . . This nature was nothing other than grace. . . . He had received a good mind, a sensitiveness in no way subject to unwholesome curiosity, nor proudly rebellious, but taking delight in spiritual effort and in the things that pertain to God willingly submissive and at the service of the spirit. . . . His body too was a most apt instrument for serving the spirit (*S. Bernardi vita prima, auctore Guillelmo, Lib. I,* c. 4, §§ 20, 21, *PL* 185:238).

1414. JOHN OF TRITHEIM. A. He who is mortified as to his will desires nothing carnal, nothing evil (*Hom. 21, de continentia et vera castitate, Op. pia et spiritualia,* p. 511). B. Virtue is perfected when the flesh rebels; and how morally right the will is, is tested by the violence of the spirit (*De triplici regione claustralium, Pars I,* tract. 2, art. 6, p. 601).

Completeness of mortification

1415. VEN. LOUIS DE BLOIS (Blosius). A. By far the most excellent exercise is to have a mind always dying to things created, and to keep down and humble oneself below every creature. For he who always dies to himself is always beginning a new life in God. The resigned and mortified soul is like a bunch of grapes, ripe, soft, and sweet; but an unresigned soul is like a cluster that is unripe, hard and sour. . . . This constant mortification in the beginning is indeed difficult and troublesome. But if only one will persevere in it manfully for a time, it will afterward become, by the gift of God, truly easy and even delightful (*Institutio spiritualis,* c. 2, § 5, *Op. Om.* 2:304).

B. It should be clearly understood that true perfection does not consist in feeling much sweetness, nor in the enjoyment of abundant consolation; but it is attained by a man when he gives up himself and all things for the love of God; when he really denies and mortifies himself; and when, after completely pouring out his own will into the will of God, he remains free and calm in all that happens to him, and holds fast to God, being made one spirit with him. Therefore a man arrives at true perfection by entire resignation and mortification (*ibid.,* c. 7, § 2, p. 310).

C. Do you wish to know, in brief, in what mortification of yourself consists? . . . Put off all self-love (*proprietatem*): that is the essence of the process, put off all self-love. Abandon self-will and self-seeking, put off the old man. . . . Out of love of God utterly deny all things sensible; more than that, deny yourself. This is the same as saying: mortify yourself with regard to concupiscence, pleasures, anger, and natural indignation; in all matters, in adversity as well as in prosperity, be resigned to God's good pleasure, without any manifestation of contradiction on the part of your own will. Now, I have indicated this essential character of self-mortification and shown you in a general way in what it consists, that it is nothing other than the abandonment of self-love in all things, that is, humiliation of yourself in every manner. For perfect humility is the short way by which you attain to the heights of perfection. This summit is perfect charity or purity. . . . If, abiding in silence of heart as in a most tranquil haven, you lovingly direct and incline your mind to God, and preserve it from inordinate cares and affections, and from too lively an imagination of things beneath you, from all distraction and disturbances, so that your memory, your understanding, your will, in a word, your whole spirit, is happily united to God, you hold this summit of which we have spoken. This is the sum of all perfection. . . . When you are thus stirred up to true mortification of self, lay the axe to the root of the tree. What tree is this? It is the tree of self-love of which we have spoken. What is the axe, then? It is the fervor of spiritual and internal exercise. Particularly daily meditation on the Lord's passion, frequent aspirations to God, prompt obedience, and reasonable sobriety of diet are the axe. It is a sharp axe, a blessed axe, a golden axe studded with precious jewels. But the tree is cursed, laden with bitter fruit, a tree full of evils, a tree which produces and nourishes all disorders, a tree of obscurity and darkness. This tree is you (*Speculum monachorum,* div. 8, *Op. Om.* 3:670, 671).

Bodily deportment must be serious and modest

1416. ST. JEROME. A. The face is the mirror of the mind, and without a word a woman's eyes betray the secrets of her heart (*Ep. 54, ad Furiam, de viduitate servanda,* n. 12, *PL* 22:556).

B. Let there be nothing of scurrility or vanity in your conversation, but rather that which bespeaks seriousness and modesty, for the life of a Christian is reflected as in a mirror (*Ep. 41, ad Oceanum, de ferendis opprobriis,* n. 17, *PL* 30:287).

1417. ST. EPHRAEM. Act modestly and seriously; modesty and seriousness beget a peaceful and tranquil state of life (*Paraenesis seu adhortationes ad monachos, Paraen. 47, Op. Om.* 2:358).

1418. ST. BERNARD. Temperance is always to be observed. It is the measure of life in every word and deed. It is the companion of sobriety and propriety and is otherwise known as modesty. It guards the practices of humility, preserves peace of mind, loves continence and chastity, fosters moral dignity and honor, restrains the appetite with reason, spurns anger, and never seeks to avenge injuries (*Tract. de ordine vitae,* c. 7, *Quattuor virtutes cardinales,* n. 22. *In Append., PL* 184:575).

1419. POPE ST. LEO THE GREAT. The self-restraint of religious persons should not be gloomy, but sincere; nor murmurs of complaint should be heard from those who are never without the consolations of holy joy (*Serm. 42, de Quadr. IV,* § 2, *PL* 54:276).

1420. ARNOLD DE BOHÉRIES, Cistercian monk of Bohéries, dioc. of Laon, today's Soissons (12th century). It is prudence of soul . . . to hide with a smile, which must be modest, the glory of the interior man and seriousness of mind (*Speculum monachorum, PL* 184:1177).

1421. THOMAS À KEMPIS. Show in your conduct modesty with religious cheerfulness, as is proper for you (*Libellus spiritualis exercitii,* c. 4, *Op. Om.* 2:342).

1422. VEN. LOUIS DE BLOIS. It is commendable to be moderately cheerful, but never gloomy or forbidding among those with whom you associate (*Tabella spiritualis,* § 1, n. 12, *Op. Om.* 1:225).

1423. ST. BERNARD. It is proper for you to conceal your sadness, especially in the monastery, and present a certain cheerfulness of expression; but when you are by yourself, let your expression be unchangeable. When you are in the presence of others and are forced to laugh at something, let your laughter be not violent, for according to the Wise Man: *A man's attire, his hearty laughter and his gait, proclaim him for what he is* (Sir. 19:26; *Formula honestae vitae,* n. 4, *In Append., PL* 184:1169).

1424. ST. AUGUSTINE. If you are striving for purity of soul, keep as close a watch as you can on the allurements of the serpent: for if you are wanting in caution, you permit your five senses, like the five virgins, to be seduced by the serpent. Whatever is beautiful to the sight, or sweet to the taste, or flattering on being heard, or entices through the sense of smell, or is soft to the touch—through all these, if we are incautious, when evil desires arise, we permit the purity of the soul to be seduced, and what was said by the Prophet is fulfilled: *Death is come up through our windows* (Jer. 9:21; *Serm. 315,* § 3, *In Append., PL* 39:2350).

1425. WILLIAM OF ST. THIERRY. Let [the monk] have his outward senses not as his masters but as servants; and his inward being sober and diligent. Let him have the whole house and family of his thoughts so ordered and disciplined that he may say to one "Go," and it goes, and to another "Come," and it comes, and to his body, his servant, "Do this," and without contradiction it does it (cf. Matt. 8:9; *Ep. ad fratres de Monte Dei, Lib. I,* c. 11, n. 34, *PL* 184:330).

1426. ST. DOROTHEUS. The virtuous and unassuming disposition of the monk which is pleasing to God and men is this: first, hold your eyes in check and keep them from glancing about restlessly; but let them pay attention to and observe only what is before you. . . . When you enter the cell of your prior or master, or that of a friend or disciple, be on your guard not to examine curiously or pay attention to the objects that may be there (*Doctrina 24, PG* 88:1835).

1427. ST. BERNARD. As far as you can do so, avoid association with youths, especially the very young (*imberberes*). Never continue to gaze at anyone's face (*Formula honestae vitae,* n. 6, *In Append., PL* 184:1170).

1428. ST. BONAVENTURE. Those who love uprightness of life diligently guard their eyes from all inordinate glancing about or looking up especially when at table and in choir. For it is written: *The eyes of a fool are on the ends of the earth* (Prov. 17:24). . . . *Haughty eyes and a proud heart—the tillage of the wicked is sin* (*ibid.,* 21:4). The Prophet did indeed raise his eyes heavenward, but he did so in order to petition help; and the Lord did likewise, but only in order to grant help. I would find no fault in your conduct, in fact, I would frequently commend it, if, taking into account the proper place, the reason, and the time, you raise your eyes for your own or a brother's need, for in the former instance human misery, and in the latter, mercy, justifies your so acting. But apart from those, I would say that you are not making yourself an imitator of the Prophet, nor of the Lord, but rather of Dina or of Eve, or rather of Satan himself (*Speculum disciplinae ad novitios, Pars I,* c. 24, § 1, *Op. Om.,* ed. Quaracchi 8:606).

Modesty of speech and voice

1429. ST. BERNARD. A. Let the voice itself be not indifferent, feeble, or womanish, but let it maintain a certain character and principle and manly strength. . . . But on the other hand, while I do not approve of a weak and characterless voice, or slouchiness of person, neither do I think that rudeness and coarseness are to be imitated (*Tract. de ordine vitae,* c. 2, *Verecundiam esse praecipuam virtutem quae adolescentes ornet,* n. 9, *In Append., PL* 184:566). B. Let modesty regulate the very sound of your voice, lest an unduly loud voice offend anyone's ears (*ibid.,* n. 3, col. 563).

1430. VEN. LOUIS DE BLOIS. A. Do not lift the voice unbecomingly; nor so lower it that you can scarcely be understood, especially if the time, place, cause, or the person to whom you are speaking require that you speak somewhat more loudly than ordinarily; for, as the voice of a monk should always be modest, and for the most part low-pitched, according to the holy regulations of the religious life, so also at times it should be reasonably loud (*Speculum monachorum,* div. 7, *Op. Om.* 3:668). B. It is a good thing to accustom himself to advance his opinions with a certain hesitancy, saying, for instance, "I think," or "In my opinion it seems," or "Unless I am mistaken, this seems to be the case" (*Brevis regula tyronis spiritualis,* § 2, n. 1, *Op. Om.* 2:356).

1431. ST. PACHOMIUS. Let no one converse with another in the dark; nor sleep on the same mattress with another. Let no one hold the hand of another, but keep at a distance of one cubit from him, whether they are standing, walking, or sitting (*Reg.,* n. 94, *CR* 1:31; *PL* 23:78; Boon, p. 40).

Propriety, modesty, discretion

1432. HUGH OF ST. VICTOR, canon regular of monastery of St. Victor, Paris (d. 1142). Care is to be taken that each member of the body restrict itself to its distinctive function, and not usurp that of any other member. Also that each member fulfil its intended function with such propriety and modesty that the action cannot offend, through its lack of discipline, anyone who chances to observe it. . . . A proper relationship is to be observed in all actions, so that each member of the body perform that for which it is designed: the hand is not for speaking, nor the mouth for hearing, nor the eye for taking over the duties of the tongue. There are persons who seem incapable of listening except with their mouth open. . . . Others, while talking, point their finger, raise their eyebrows or, constantly glancing about in all directions or fixing their gaze intently as though on some profound consideration, convey the impression of concentration on some interior magnificence. Others carry their heads boastfully . . . or by shifting about restlessly or spreading their feet apart, present a ridiculous picture of ostentation. Still others, as though both ears had not been designed for hearing, always turn the same ear toward any voice directed to them, straining their neck to do so. . . . Others, when walking, swing their arms as though they were swimming; and with a kind of twin curiosity, at one and the same time walk with their feet on the ground and with the arms beating the air. What kind of monstrosity is this, I ask you, which combines the walk of a man, the rowing of a boat, and the flight of a bird? . . . The first concern of discipline in comportment, therefore, is that each member of the body confine itself to the function for which it was created. . . . The second, that what it performs it perform in the manner, no more, no less, nor otherwise than designed. To put the matter in a few words by way of illustration: One should laugh without showing the teeth, look without staring, speak without waving the hands or pointing a finger . . . walk without carelessly swinging the arms or shoulders, sit without crossing the legs, stretching them out, constantly moving them, and without slouching from side to side (*De institutione novitiorum,* c. 12, *PL* 176:941 f.).

1433. ST. AMBROSE. A. Modesty must further be guarded in our very movements of the body and gestures and gait. For the condition of the mind is often seen in the attitude of the body. For this reason the hidden man of our heart is considered to be either frivolous, boastful, or boisterous, or, on the other hand, steady, firm, pure, and dependable. Thus the movement of the body is a sort of voice of the soul (*De officiis ministrorum, Lib. I,* c. 18, § 71, *PL* 16:48). B. Some there are who in walking perceptibly copy the gestures of actors, and act as though they were bearers in a procession, and had the motions of nodding statues, to such an extent that they seem to keep a sort of time, as often as they change their step (*ibid.,* § 73). C. Nor do I think it becoming to walk hurriedly, except when some danger or real necessity demand it. For we often see those who hurry come up panting and with features distorted. If there is no need for such haste, it gives cause for just offense (*ibid.,* § 74). D. A suitable gait is that wherein there is an appearance of authority, weight and dignity, and which has a calm collected bearing. But it must be of such a character that all effort and conceit are wanting, and that it be simple and plain. Nothing counterfeit is pleasing. Let nature train our movements. If indeed there is any fault in our nature, let us mend it with diligence. And, to make certain that artifice be wanting, let not amendment be wanting (*ibid.,* § 75).

1434. ST. BERNARD. Do not walk with mincing steps, or throwing your shoulders from right to left, or holding your head high or your chest out, or even with your head bent to one side and resting on the shoulder, for all such practices smack of levity, show forth pride or hypocrisy. Whether walking, standing, or sitting, keep your glance lowered, reflecting in your mind that you are dust and will return to dust; keep your heart on high where Christ is sitting at the right hand of God the Father. Do not glance in any direction out of curiosity, but only when necessity forces you to do so (*Formula honestae vitae,* n. 4, *In Append., PL* 184:1169).

1435. ST. BONAVENTURE. They are to be mindful of discipline in walking as well, both with regard to their manner of walking and as a point of seriousness of conduct. The proper manner demands that they walk not with jerky and mincing steps, nor with the head held high, nor the chest thrust forward, nor the head leaning on one shoulder, nor the hands swinging loosely, for all these mannerisms are redolent of levity, pride, slovenliness or hypocrisy. In walking they must also give evidence of seriousness of conduct, lest they be included amongst those of whom the Prophet speaks: *There is no judgment in their steps* (Isa. 59:8). Certainly there is no judgment in the steps of those persons who pay attention neither to necessity nor order. Necessity excludes all useless running about, and order, the confusion of irregularity. . . . Order should be preserved in the religious community in such a way that one keep pace with the brother walking beside him in procession, and that he keep his place determined by his side of the choir, in the refectory and in the corridors when we go to the church for grace, and elsewhere. He should not cross over to the other side of the choir or change his place in the refectory or corridors, without reasonable cause for doing so. . . . There is also a certain observance of order dictated by reverence and propriety, according to which the younger brother should not go ahead of an older one, or, when it can easily be avoided, pass in front of him (*Speculum disciplinae ad novitios, Pars I,* c. 23, §§ 1, 5, 6, *Op. Om.,* ed. Quaracchi 8:606).

1436. DAVID OF AUGSBURG, German Franciscan writer and preacher (d. 1272). Let your manner of walking be mature. Do not run thoughtlessly and without necessity, nor carry yourself forcefully erect, but rather moderately stooped. Be not undisciplined in the custody of the eyes, nor carefree in swinging the arms, nor otherwise given to conducting yourself in the disorderly manner of worldlings, but act unaffectedly and humbly, as though you were returning from devout prayer (*De institutione novitiorum,* c. 19, *Op. Om. S. Bonaventurae,* ed. Peltier 12:298).

1437. ST. BERNARD. Let me pass over in silence the interior man in [St.] Malachy, for his whole character and life have adequately revealed its beauty and purity. In all his external acts he conducted himself with a uniformity of disposition that was ever modest and altogether proper: never was there anything in it that could offend anyone who chanced to observe him. And remember, *If anyone does not offend in word, he is a perfect man* (Jas. 3:2). Regardless of how intently he may have observed him, did anyone ever catch Malachy idle—I will not say in speech, but even in gesture? Who ever saw him in aimless action of hand or foot? On the contrary, what was there that was not edifying in his manner of approach, his appearance, posture, and general expression? Sadness never darkened the cheerfulness of his expression, but neither did laughter give it a tone of levity. Everything in his character was disciplined, everything a mark of virtue, everything the beauty of perfection. He was grave in all that he did, but never severe, good humored now and then, but never lax (*Vita S. Malachiae,* c. 19, *virtutum ejus insignia et mores vero praesule digni,* n. 43, *PL* 182:1097).

1438. GEOFFREY, abbot of Clairvaux (d. 1166). [St. Bernard] was calm of countenance, unassuming in disposition, circumspect in speech, reverent in work, pleasing in manner. . . . A certain grace, spiritual rather than physical, appeared in his body. A splendor, not so much something of earth, but heavenly in character, shone in his countenance; in his eyes there radiated an angelic purity and dove-like simplicity. So great was the beauty of the interior man that it would appear with certain unmistakable indications, and the great wealth of interior purity and abundant grace revealed itself also in the external man. . . . His manner of walking and general appearance were unpretentious and disciplined, giving evidence of humility, redolent of his piety, displaying his grace, eliciting the reverence of those who saw him and giving them joy (*S. Bernardi vita prima, Lib. III,* auctore Gaufrido, *monacho quondam Clarae Vallensi et S. Bernardi notario, postea abbate,* c. 1, § 1, *PL* 185:303).

1439. ARNOLD, abbot of Bonnevaux, dioc. of Chartres, friend and biographer of St. Bernard (d. 1156). The bishops wept; the Supreme Pontiff himself shed tears; they all marvelled at the calmness of his community at Clairvaux, that on so solemn an occasion of joy, everyone in the community kept his eyes fixed on the ground, none glanced about in idle curiosity, but with their eyes lowered, they looked at no one while they themselves were being looked at by all (*ibid., Lib. II,* auctore Ernaldo, c. 1, § 6, col. 272—giving an account of the visit of Pope Innocent II to St. Bernard at Clairvaux).

Mortification must be discreet and humble

1440. JOHN CASSIAN. A. The Apostle says: *And as for the flesh, take no thought for its lusts* (Rom. 13:14). He does not forbid care for it in every respect: but says that care is not to be taken in regard to its desires and lusts. He cuts away the luxurious fondness for the flesh; he does not exclude the care necessary for life; he does the former, lest through pampering the flesh we should be involved in dangerous entanglements of desires; the latter, lest the body should be injured by our fault and unable to fulfil its spiritual and necessary duties (*De coenob. institut., Lib. V,* c. 8, *PL* 49:223). B. We ought then with all our might to strive for the virtue of discretion by the power of humility, as it will keep us uninjured by either extreme, for there is an old saying: "Extremes meet." For excess of fasting and gluttony come to the same thing, and an unlimited continuance of vigils is equally injurious to a monk as the torpor of a deep sleep (*Collatio II, Abbatis Moysis 2, de discretione,* c. 16, col. 549). C. And so by the judgment of Blessed Antony as well as of all others it has been laid down that it is discretion which leads a fearless monk by fixed stages to God, and preserves the virtues mentioned above continually intact, by means of which one may ascend with less weariness to the extreme summit of perfection, and without which even those who toil most willingly cannot reach the heights of perfection. For discretion is the mother of all virtues, as well as their guardian and regulator (*ibid.,* c. 4, col. 526).

1441. ST. BASIL THE GREAT. A. It is serious and dangerous to turn aside into the intemperance of gluttony; it is wholly unreasonable also, to weaken the body with excessive abstinence; nor is the foregoing of the pleasure of taste to be desired for its own sake, but only in that it contributes to the acquisition of virtue. If, by moderate fasting, we neglect that for whose sake we abstain from food, we are acting contrary to our purpose. For if the instrument is broken or crushed, we can neither remain attached to God by the effort of reading and prayer, nor fulfil the duties of kindness in helping the brethren. Hence the care of the body is necessarily to be performed, not indeed for its own sake, but to enable us to employ the body's services in our striving for wisdom (*De virginitate,* c. 11, *In Append., PG* 31:691). B. It behooves the monk to be free of all haughtiness, and to proceed along the middle and truly royal course, never leaving that path on either side—neither giving himself to soft living, nor making his body useless by immoderate abstinence. For if there were any advantage for man to be broken of body and to lie dead while still breathing and living, the Lord would have created us that way from the beginning (*Const. monasticae,* c. 4, § 2, col. 1350).

1442. ST. ANTONY. Discretion is to hold the first place in everything we do . . . for discretion is the parent, the guardian, and moderator of all the virtues (*Vita S. Antonii Magni abbatis,* c. 3, *Acta Sanctorum Bolland, Jan. tom. 2, die 17,* p. 508).

1443. ST. GREGORY THE GREAT. A. But it is the great effort of discretion to give this exactor (the body) something, and yet to refuse it something; both to restrain gluttony by not giving, and by giving to support nature. . . . Pleasure so veils itself under necessity that a perfect man can scarce discern it. . . . But it is easy to discover when pleasure anticipates its necessity, though very difficult to discern when it secretly connects itself with that very eating which is necessary. . . . While the mind flatters itself on the necessity, it is deceived by the pleasure. . . . For frequently when the body is restrained beyond what is just, it is weakened even for the exercise of good works, so as to be unequal for prayer or preaching, while it hastens to put out entirely the incentives of vices within itself. For this very man whom we bear outwardly, we have as the assistant of our inward intention, and both the motions of wantonness are within, and there also abound in it the appliances of good works. But often, while we are attacking an enemy therein, we kill a citizen also whom we love; and while we spare, as it were, a fellow-citizen, we nurture an enemy for battle (*Moral., Lib. 30,* c. 18, §§ 61–63, *PL* 76:557).

B. Let us consider also that the string of the harp, if it is strung too little, makes no sound; if too much, it sounds harsh; because doubtless the virtue of abstinence is altogether nothing if a man does not tame his body as much as he is able; or it is very ill-ordered if he wears it down more than he is able to bear. For by abstinence the imperfections of the flesh are to be done away with, and not the flesh itself; and every one ought to rule himself with such great control that both the flesh may not carry itself high for sin, and yet that it may be supported in the practice of carrying out the works of righteousness (*ibid., Lib. 20,* c. 41, § 78, col. 185).

1444. DAVID OF AUGSBURG. It is difficult to assign an exact rule with regard to the amount to be eaten, except that you hold to the middle course between two extremes. Do not take so small a quantity that you will be wanting in strength or broken by the common work; on the other hand, do not eat so much that because of having taken a great amount of food you can neither pray nor read nor take an active part in the prescribed exercises. Between these two limits your own personal experience, coupled with good will, is your best table waiter (*De institutione novitiorum,* c. 8, *Op. Om. S. Bonaventurae,* ed. Peltier 12:295).

1445. ST. FULGENTIUS, bp. of Ruspe, Africa (d. 533). Moderation is so to be employed in fasting that on the one hand fullness will not rouse our body nor, on the other, will undue want of nourishment weaken it (*Ep. 3, ad Probam, de virginitate atque humilitate,* c. 13, § 21, *PL* 65:332).

1446. ST. DIADOCHUS, bp. of Photice in Illyria (5th century). A body filled with much food renders the mind dull and sluggish; excessive abstinence from food on the other hand makes for weakness, so that the part of the soul which engages in contemplation is cast into dejection and loathing for meditation. It is necessary, therefore, to accommodate food to the activities of the body, in such a way that when the body can bear it, it be appropriately chastised, and when it cannot bear it, the practices be mitigated moderately. He who wages the spiritual combat must not be weak of body, but strong enough to bear the struggle, and thus the soul as well can be fittingly purified with the efforts of the body (*Capita centum de perfectione spirituali,* c. 45, *PG* 63:1181).

1447. ST. JEROME. A. Yet even fasts must be kept moderate for, if they are carried to excess they weaken the stomach and then, by making greater quantities of food necessary to it, promote indigestion, which is the fruitful parent of unclean desires (*Ep. 125, ad Rusticum monachum,* § 17, *PL* 22:1075).

B. You must not go on fasting until your heart begins to throb and your breath fail, and you have to be supported and carried by others. No; while curbing the desires of the flesh you must keep sufficient strength to read Scripture, sing the psalms, and to observe the vigils no less than you are wont to do (*Ep. 130, ad Demetriadem, de servanda virginitate,* § 11, col. 1116).

C. A meager diet which leaves the appetite always unsatisfied is to be preferred to fasts three days long. It is much better to take a little every day than some days to abstain wholly and on others to surfeit oneself. That rain is best which falls slowly to the ground. Showers that come down suddenly and with violence wash the soil away (*Ep. 54, ad Furiam, de viduitate servanda,* § 10, col. 555).

1448. ST. HILDEGARDE OF BINGEN (d. 1179). A. The man who nourishes his body in moderation is pleasant and gentle of manner, whereas he who indulges himself to excess in eating and feasting gives way to every harmful vice to develop within him. The person in turn who tortures his body with too severe an abstinence is always irritable (*Ep. 115, ad N., abbatissam de Didenkirkim, PL* 197:336). B. Abstinence which is unreasonable in that it observes neither proper measure nor correct balance does harm to the body which is denied the strength and nourishment of which it stands in need. As a result the person is greatly weakened. When such a condition has been brought about, the precariously possessed virtues, namely humility and charity, those beautiful flowers of virtuous life, will cease, because excessive abstinence lacks the strength needed for virtues. In their place will appear the vanity of inactivity, and many errors, particularly in that such persons think that they are holy when in reality they are not (*Ep. 98, ad M., abbatissam in Wethderswinkele,* col. 320).

1449. ST. THOMAS AQUINAS. The mortification of one's own body, for instance by vigils and fasting, is not acceptable to God except insofar as it is an act of virtue; and this depends on its being done with due discretion, namely, that concupiscence be curbed without overburdening nature (*II-II,* q. 88, art. 2, *Utrum votum semper debeat fieri de meliori,* ad. 3, *Op. Om.* 9:239; Am. ed. 2:1568).

1450. ST. BERNARD. Bodily mortification must be practiced with secrecy, with prudence, and with due authorization. Your tender flesh, fostered hitherto in pleasure and ease, must be made to suffer a perpetual martyrdom, and henceforth you must abstain from even innocent enjoyments to atone for your guilty gratifications in the past. But this must be done secretly, so that your left hand shall not know what your right hand is doing (cf. Matt. 6:3). For it is not in the mouths of men but in the secret chambers of your own heart that so great a treasure should be deposited for safe keeping, in order that your boast may be the testimony of your conscience (cf. II Cor. 1:12). We are not saying that your light should not shine before men that they may see your good works and give glory to your Father who is in heaven (cf. Matt. 5:16). No, but that your intention should not aim at so poor and so perishable a reward as earthly glory. Surely nothing can be sadder than the lot of one who, after afflicting and torturing his flesh with rigorous fastings and watchings, consents to take human applause as his recompense in this life, and to have hell for his portion in the life to come.

I have said too that bodily mortifications should have the sanction of authority, because no offering can be acceptable in the sight of God unless it is made with the consent of the spiritual father (cf. *RSB*, c. 49): the Most High will accept nothing that is tainted with self-will, nothing but what is offered with submission to the will of the superior. The exclusion of self-will in this way helps us greatly toward the vanquishing of pride.

Our mortification needs also to be accomplished with discretion, lest through excessive zeal we should carry it so far as to injure our health, and should slay a friend, so to speak, in our eagerness to conquer an enemy. Consider how much your body can bear, and take account of your physical constitution, and let your severity be kept in proportion. It is a bounden duty to preserve our bodily health for the service of the Creator. How many have I seen chastising their bodies with such unsparing rigor at the beginning of their conversion to God, and carrying their practices of penance so far beyond the limits of prudence as to render themselves incapable of attendance in choir, and so languid that they had in consequence to be put on a special regime for many a long day (*Serm. de diversis, Serm. 40, de septem gradibus confessionis,* n. 7, *PL* 183:651).

1451. ST. JEROME. Guard against considering yourself already holy when you have begun to fast and abstain; this virtuous practice is a help toward holiness, not its perfection (*Ep. 148, ad Celantiam, de ratione pie vivendi,* § 22, *PL* 22:1214).

1452. BL. RABANUS MAURUS, monk of Fulda, abp. of Mainz (d. 856). The word of God is a sword which sheds the evil blood with which the sinful body is animated and, for our welfare, cuts away and amputates whatever it finds that is carnal or earthly that has clotted our members. It makes us live for God and by destroying vices makes us strong in spiritual virtues. It causes us to weep, not out of remembrance of the confessed sins of the past, but in the spirit of hope for future joys. It thinks not so much about past evils as about the goods that are to come. It sheds its tears not so much out of sorrow for sins as from eagerness for that everlasting happiness that is to be ours. Putting behind the things that are past, that is, the vices of the flesh, it stretches eagerly toward those that lie ahead, that is, the spiritual gifts and virtues (*Expos. sup. Jerem., Lib. 15,* c. 48, vers. 10, *PL* 111:1116).

1453. DENIS THE CARTHUSIAN. A. Choose the things which are more irksome to the body; seek to be governed, to obey, to be corrected, punished, and humiliated rather than to be a superior, to command, to be honored, praised, and treated with reverence (*Exhortatorium noviciorum,* art. 8, *Op. Om.* 38:541). B. Learn to subdue yourself; accustom yourself to find joy in subjection and abjection, and to glory in reproofs (*Expositio hymni Aeterne rerum Conditor, Op. Om.* 35: 113).

The spirit of penance

1454. ST. AUGUSTINE. He who repents sincerely effects nothing less than this: he does not allow his wrong-doing to remain unpunished (*Ep. 153, Macedonio,* c. 3, § 6, *PL* 33:655).

1455. ST. JOHN CHRYSOSTOM. It behooves us to have all our sins, great and small, recorded in our heart as though written in a book, to review them often, place them before our eyes, and deplore them as though they had been but recently committed. . . . Frequent remembrance of sin bestows a great good upon a person, as we see in the case of the Apostle Paul publicly referring to the sins of his life which had been forgiven and absolved. Since he had no sin in his actions at the time when he was preaching, he did so knowing that it was beneficial for his soul to call to mind and grieve and weep over his sins; hence he brings to memory that which he had committed through ignorance and which the grace of baptism and the profession of faith had wiped away (*De compunctione, Lib. II, ad Stelechium,* § 6, *PG* 47:420).

1456. ST. BASIL THE GREAT. We were wounded by sin; we are cured by penance; but penance without fasting is ineffectual and unfruitful (*De jejunio, Hom. 1,* § 3, *PG* 31:167).

1457. ST. ISIDORE OF SEVILLE. Out of shame for your sins, blush to lift up your eyes. Rather walk with your head bowed, with countenance cast down, with the mouth rather severe in expression, being humble of heart and somberly garbed. Let your body be wrapped in sackcloth and covered with haircloth, while you are given to mourning always, grieving always, always sighing from the depths of your heart [cf. *RSB,* c. 7, twelfth degree of humility] (*Synonymorum Lib. II,* § 23, *PL* 83:850).

1458. ST. BERNARD. A. The man who is truly repentant grieves and mourns for his past offenses and gives all diligence to avoiding their repetition in the future (*Meditationes piissimae de cognitione humanae conditionis,* c. 4, n. 13, *In Append., PL* 184:493). B. He who truly repents does not abhor the pain of penitence, but patiently and with quiet mind bears all that is enjoined on him for the guilt which he sincerely detests. In the exercise of his obedience he does not weary in suffering all that is inflicted on him, things contrary to nature and even at times unjust, so that he shows himself to be standing on the fourth step of humility (*Tract. de gradibus humilitatis et superbiae, Altera pars,* c. 18, n. 47, *PL* 182:967). C. For the spirit of penance three things are necessary: abstinence, by means of which the pride of the flesh is subdued; reading, through whose fruit the soul is to be renewed and nourished unto strength; and prayer, by the defense and protection of which virtues are shielded (*Lib. Sententiarum,* n. 27, *In Append., PL* 184:1141). D. Repentance without amendment will profit you nothing.

. . . In repentance the soul is warmed; in amendment it is set on fire; in solicitude [in which it may begin to walk carefully with God] it becomes all luminous and radiant, so that the whole man is renewed within and without (*Serm. de temp., Serm. 3 in vigilia Nativitatis Dni,* n. 4, *PL* 183:96).

1459. ST. THOMAS AQUINAS. Internal penance is that whereby one grieves for a sin one has committed, and this penance should last until the end of life, because man should always be displeased at having sinned (*III,* q. 84, art. 8, *Utrum poenitentia debeat durare usque ad finem vitae, Op. Om.* 12:295; Am. ed. 2:2536).

1460. ST. JEROME. The spirit of penance has no love for pleasures . . . but day and night prays, keeps watch, is given to fasting, rests upon a pallet of straw, not upon a featherbed, nor on silk (*Breviarium in Ps. 93, 20, In Append., PL* 26:1110).

1461. HUGH OF ST. VICTOR. When you are overcome, [O penance], you gain the victory; when you are crucified, you fasten to the cross; when you wound, you heal; when you submit to others for spiritual welfare, you triumph gloriously. You alone, O penance, all other powers remaining inactive, ascend to the throne of grace, bring forgiveness to David, reinstate Peter, illumine Paul, give the publican entrance from the tax collector's table into the group of apostles, out of the brothel unite Mary to Christ, introduce the thief into Paradise, still bloody from his death on the cross (*Adnotatiunculae elucidatoriae in Joelam prophetam 2, 19, PL* 175:349).

1462. ST. BONAVENTURE. A. Either continual sufferings will vex the life of penance, or eternal torments will torture the soul that is to be punished (*Serm. I, Dom. I Quadr., Op. Om.,* ed. Peltier 13:146). B. Ours is not indeed a true but a false penance—in fact, it is not worthy of the name of penance at all—if there are no hardships, but everything is pleasant (*Serm. II de S. Joan. Bapt.,* p. 571). C. After the manner of a physician who does not spare the man who is ill, in order that he may be cured, a person must punish himself in reality and not fictitously for his sins (*Serm. V de pluribus SS. Martyribus,* 14:59).

1463. VEN. LOUIS DE BLOIS. The best repentance and the most noble contrition is to have a humble mind, to turn the will from all sin and from everything which could stand in the way of the love of God, and fully to be converted to God himself (*Institutio spiritualis,* c. 8, § 4, *Op. Om.* 2:316).

1464. PETER DE BLOIS. Penance is the second table of the Commandments after shipwreck, the ladder to heaven, re-establishment of peace, intensification of life, destruction of vices, protection of bodies, medicine of souls (*De Hierosolymitana peregrinatione acceleranda, PL* 207: 1065).

1465. ST. PETER DAMIAN. How brilliant is the splendor of penance, which dispels the night of sin! (*Serm. 71, in dedicatione ecclesiae III, PL* 144:908.)

Mortification from love of the suffering Christ

1466. ST. JEROME. The things I have here set forth will seem hard to her who has no love for Christ. But one who has come to regard all the splendor of the world as offscourings, and to hold all things under the sun as dung in order that he may gain Christ (cf. Phil. 3:8); one who has died with his Lord and risen again, and has crucified his flesh with its concupiscences and lusts (cf. Rom. 4:4; Gal. 5:24), will boldly cry out: *Who shall separate us from the love of Christ? Shall tribulation, or distress, or persecution, or hunger, or nakedness, or danger, or the sword?* And again: *For I am sure that neither death, nor life, nor angels, nor principalities, nor things present, nor things to come, nor powers, nor height, nor depth, nor any other creature will be able to separate us from the love of God, which is in Christ Jesus our Lord* (Rom. 8:35, 38–39).

For our salvation the Son of God is made the Son of Man. Nine months he awaits his birth in the womb. . . . He who shuts up the world in his fist is contained in the narrow limits of a manger.

I say nothing of the thirty years during which he lives in obscurity, satisfied with the poverty of his parents (cf. Luke 2:51, 52). When he is scourged he holds his peace; when he is crucified, he prays for his crucifiers.

How shall I make a return to the Lord for all the good he has done for me? The cup of salvation I will take up, and I will call upon the name of the Lord. . . . Precious in the eyes of the Lord is the death of his faithful ones (Ps. 115:3–6). The only fitting return we can make to him is to give blood for blood and, as we are redeemed by the blood of Christ, gladly to lay down our lives for our Redeemer. What saint has ever won his crown without first contending for it? Righteous Abel is murdered. Abraham is in danger of losing his wife. And, as I must not enlarge upon my book unduly, seek for yourself: you will find that all holy men have suffered adversity. Solomon alone lived in luxury and perhaps it was for this reason that he fell. For *whom the Lord loves, he chastises; and he scourges every son whom he receives* (Heb. 12:6; Prov. 3:12). Which is best—to do battle for a short time, to carry stakes for the palisades, to bear arms, to faint under heavy bucklets, that afterward we may rejoice as victors, or to become slaves forever, just because we cannot endure for a single hour?

Love finds nothing hard; no task is difficult to the eager. Think of what Jacob bore for Rachel, the wife who had been promised to him. *Jacob,* the Scripture says, *served seven years for Rachel, and they seemed to him but a few days because of his love for her* (Gen. 29:20). Afterward he tells us what he had to undergo: *The heat wasted me by day, the cold by night* (*ibid.*, 31:40). So we must love Christ always and seek his embraces. Then everything difficult will seem easy. All things long we shall account as short; and with his arrows sunk deep in us (cf. Ps. 37:3), we shall say every moment: *Woe is me that I sojourn in Mosoch . . . all too long have I dwelt with those who hate peace* (Ps. 199:5–6). For *I reckon that the sufferings of the present time are not worthy to be compared with the glory to come that will be revealed in us* (Rom. 8:18). For *tribulation works out endurance, and endurance tried virtue, and tried virtue hope, and hope does not disappoint* (Rom. 5:3–5; *Ep. 22, ad Eustochium, Paulae filiam, de custodia virginitatis*, §§ 39, 40, *PL* 22:423 f.).

1467. ST. AMBROSE. Christ was tormented with physical miseries, in order to make men, who had been miserable, happy. . . . He was bowed down in order that we might be lifted up; he was made sorrowful in order that we might be joyful. . . . Let us also be bowed down to the very depths of our being, that is to say, bringing to Christ not only the expression of our faith but the persevering acceptance of our sufferings. More than that, let us rejoice in those sufferings as Christ rejoiced in his. For the love of the Lord let us submit to sufferings that he took upon himself for his servants (*Enarr. in Ps. 37*, § 32, *PL* 14: 1073).

1468. ST. AUGUSTINE. A. If the Passion of our Savior is kept before the mind, nothing is so difficult that it cannot be borne calmly (*De conflictu vitiorum et virtutum*, c. 9, *In Append.*, *PL* 40:1096). B. Nothing is so conducive to our well-being as to think daily how much he who is God and Man bore for us (*Ad fratres in eremo, Serm. 32. In Append. col. 1293*). C. If you delight in the way of Christ and are really a Christian—for he is in truth a Christian who does not shun, but rather delights in following Christ's way of suffering—do not follow a different path than that which he himself trod. It appears painful, but it is the very way of safety; another way is perhaps more inviting, but it is full of robbers. . . . He walked through painful paths, but promised great rewards. Follow him. Think not only of the way you must travel, but also of the destination at which you will arrive. Yes, you will have to endure temporal hardships, but you will come to eternal joys (*Enarr. in Ps. 36, 23*, § 16, *PL* 36:373). D. Relief that is safe from danger and powerful is found in the wounds of the Savior for the weak and for sinners. There I dwell in security; the bowels [of mercy] are open to me through the wounds. Whatever is wanting to me on my part I draw to myself from the mercy of my Lord, for it is abundant, and there are not wanting the wounds through which it may flow forth. . . . At these openings [that is, in the contemplation of his wounds], I may taste how tender in his mercies is the Lord my God. . . . Copious redemption, abundant sweetness, plenitude of grace, and the perfection of virtues are given to us in the wounds of Jesus Christ our Savior. When an impure thought assails me, I take my refuge in the wounds of Christ. When my flesh weighs me down, I arise by means of the remembrance of the wounds of my Lord. When the devil lays his temptations before me, I flee to the tender mercy of my Lord and [the tempter] departs. . . . In all sufferings and distresses I find no remedy so efficacious as the wounds of Christ. In them I can sleep and rest securely. Christ died for us. Surely then nothing is so [condemned] to death that it is not redeemed by the death of Christ. My whole hope is in his death. His death is my reward, my refuge, my salvation, my life and resurrection. . . . The more powerful he is in saving, the more secure I am (*Manuale,* cc. 21–23, *In Append., PL* 40:960).*

1469. ARNOLD, abbot of Bonnevaux, dioc. of Chartres (d. 1156). Grant, O Lord, that we may bear your cross without being forced to do so (cf. Matt. 27:32), and may understand with all the saints the true meaning of the breadth, the length, the sublimity, and the depth of this wood. Once it is understood, may the serpent not bite us before it is charmed (cf. Eccles. 10:11, and commentaries). May we follow you unharmed in all things, become as little children with you, submit to the circumcision with you, be baptized with you, fast with you, live crucified to the world with you, and, filled with the Holy Spirit, remain united body and soul with you forever, you who live forever to die no more (*De cardinalibus operibus Christi,* c. 9, *de passione Christi, PL* 189:1662).

1470. BASIL, bp. of Seleucia (d. circa 459). The way to salvation is that of suffering; it is the cross that procures the kingdom (*Oratio 31,* § 3, *PG* 85:350).

Contemplation of the sufferings of Christ

1471. ST. BERNARD. A. In the passion of the Savior there are three things in particular that demand our consideration: What he suffered, the manner in which he suffered, and the cause of the suffering. In the first we have patience commended to us; in the second, humility; charity in the third (*Serm. de temp., Serm. in Fer. IV Hebd. Sanctae,* § 2, *PL* 183:263). B. Surely it would be a shame for the members to seek after glory when they have seen their head overwhelmed with such ignominy. . . . Surely also it would be a shame for anyone to show

* As one might well suspect from the nature of this passage, this and several similar works attributed to St. Augustine were widely adopted for devotional practice. Early translations are available, but they are very free. The present text is as accurate as possible from the available Latin text. Cf. e.g., *Meditations of St. Augustine, His Treatise on the Love of God, Soliloquies, and Manual;* tr. by Geo. Stanhope, London, 1818, pp. 278, 279.

himself a delicate member under a thorn-crowned head (*ibid., Serm. V in fest. Omnium Sanctorum,* § 9, col. 480). C. Can anything be so bitter that it cannot be sweetened by calling to mind the life-giving passion [of Christ]? . . . Nothing so purifies our thought from the incitement and infection of all vices, and preserves it in that purity as does the continual remembrance of the cross and passion of Jesus (*Vitis mystica, seu tract. de passione Dni,* c. 44, § 154, *In Append., PL* 184:728). D. To meditate on [the wounds of Christ] I have called wisdom; in these I have placed the perfection of righteousness for me, the fullness of knowledge, the abundance of merits, the riches of salvation. There is among them for me sometimes a draught of salutary bitterness; sometimes again a sweet unction of consolation. In adversities they raise me up, and in prosperity repress my exuberant delight, and among the joys on the one hand, and the sorrows on the other, of this present life, they enable me to walk in safety along the royal road which leads to life by defending me from the perils on either hand. These conciliate on my behalf the Judge of all the world, showing to me him who is greatly to be feared, as one who is gentle and humble, and not only making him willing to receive and pardon, but even more, in giving me him who is far above all powers, and terrible among the kings of the earth, as a model for me to imitate (*Serm. 43 in Cant.,* n. 4, *PL* 183: 995; Eales, p. 268). E. Above all things it is the cup which you drank, O Jesus, merciful and kind, the great task of our redemption undertaken by you, which is a stronger motive than any other for love of you. It is this which easily draws to itself all the love I have to give, which attracts my affection more sweetly, which requires it more justly, which retains it by closer ties and a more vehement force. To this end the Savior endured many and great things, nor in the making of the world did its Creator take upon himself a task so laborious. For in that earlier work *he spoke, and it was made; he commanded, and it stood forth* (Ps. 32:9). But in the latter one he had to bear with men who contradicted his words, met his actions with ill-natured criticism, insulted his sufferings, and even reviled his death. Behold, then, how he loved us! . . . His love is tender, wise, and strong. . . . Learn, O Christian, from the example of Christ the manner in which you ought to love Christ. Learn to love him tenderly, to love him wisely, to love him with a mighty love! (*Ibid., Serm. 20,* nn. 2–4, col. 867; Eales, p. 110.) F. Who indeed can be so irreligious as not to be softened to sorrow during these blessed days? Who so proud as not to feel humble? . . . We are now approaching the passion of the Lord, which is as capable today as at the beginning of shaking the earth, rending the rocks, opening tombs (*Serm. de temp., Serm. in Fer. IV Hebd. Sanctae,* § 1, col. 263).

1472. ORIGEN. So great is the power of the cross that if it is kept before the eyes . . . no evil desire, no impure passion, no anger, no envy can survive: but immediately that whole army of sin and flesh takes flight in its presence (*In Ep. ad Romanos 6, 12, Lib. VI,* § 1, *PG* 14:1056).

1473. ST. PETER DAMIAN. Nothing is so effectual for rooting out attachment to pleasures as the recalling to mind of the wounds of Christ, who stood trial before the judge, who was scourged, spat upon, crowned with thorns, struck with blows, nailed to the tree and died on the cross (*Serm. 59, de S. Nicolao, episc. et confess.,* 6 Dec., *PL* 144:838).

1474. HUGH OF ST. CHER, O.P. From the passion of Christ eternal light is received, the soul satiated, wounds of sins healed (*Sup. II Reg. 15, 23, Comment.* 1:254).

1475. ST. BONAVENTURE. A. The devil can never be more overwhelmingly defeated than through the remembrance of Christ (*Serm. IV de Dom. 13 p. Pent., Op. Om.,* ed. Peltier 13:413). B. The memory of Christ's passion is the armor that we must put on in order to conquer all diabolical temptations (*ibid.*).

1476. THOMAS À KEMPIS. A. The passion of Christ is in truth the hidden treasure (Matt. 13:44) of God, the fullness of all virtue, the perfection of religion, the substance of all holiness (*Serm. de vita et passione Dni, serm. 24, Op. Om.,* 3:206). B. By the passion of Christ the devil is overthrown and confused, hell is despoiled, the thief converted, the world redeemed, heaven opened, the downfall of the angels repaired (*ibid., serm. 26,* § 4, p. 221). C. When presented to the mind the passion of Christ is an incentive to divine love, the lesson of patience, solace in hardships, avoidance of a dissolute life, the cause of holy compunction, the exercise of interior devotion. It is the banishment of despair, certain hope of forgiveness of sins, reconciliation of divine anger. It is the soothing of troublesome worries, the patient bearing of severe rebukes, expulsion of evil thoughts, repression of temptations of the flesh. It is the molding of humble subjection, alleviation of physical illness, disregard of worldly recognition, condemnation of abundant temporal goods. It is mature deliberation on voluntary poverty, abandonment of self-will, rejection of what is superfluous, the inspiration to arise from a tepid way of life, the kindling of fervent conversion. It is the reception of more abundant grace, the drawing of heavenly consolation upon oneself, approval of fraternal compassion, preparation for divine contemplation, increase of future blessedness. It is the alleviation of present punishment, and the clearing away of future fire (*ibid., serm. 24,* p. 204). D. Consider who it is that suffers these things, from whom he suffers them, how intensely he suffers, for whom he suffers, for how long a time he suffers, the places in which he suffers, the members of his Body in which he suffers (*ibid., serm. 26,* p. 218). E. He who is most high is oppressed; he who is most noble, dishonored; he who is most beautiful, defiled; he who is all-wise, derided; he who is most powerful, bound. He who is most innocent is scourged; he who is most holy is crowned with thorns; he who is most meek, struck with blows. He who is most rich is stripped of all possessions; he who is most generous, despoiled of everything; he who is most chaste, stripped to nakedness; he who is most worthy, blasphemed. He who is most longed for is condemned; he who is most learned, deemed a fool; he who is most loving, hated; he who is most truthful, contradicted; he who is most tender, offered gall to drink. He, the Blessed One, is cursed; he, the Bringer of Peace, persecuted; he, the Just, accused; he, the Innocent, condemned; he, the Physician, wounded; he, the Son of God, crucified; he, the Immortal, put to death (*ibid.*, p. 220).

1477. VEN. LOUIS DE BLOIS (Blosius). For the remembrance of Christ's most sacred passion . . . is the present extermination of passions and inordinate affections, a seasonable refuge in temptations and a sure safeguard in dangers, a tender refreshing in distress, a friendly rest from labor, a gentle repressing of distractions. It is the true door of sanctity, the only entry to contemplation, the sweet consolation of the soul, the unfailing flame of divine love, the salve of all adversities, the fountain from which all virtues flow to us. To conclude, it is the absolute example of all perfection, the haven, hope, reward, and salvation of all Christians (*Speculum monachorum,* div. 4, *Op. Om.* 3:658).

Fruits of mortification and penance

1478. CASSIODORUS. A. This is the certain formula for all penitents: they begin in tears and end in joy (*In Ps. 6, 11, PL* 70:65). B. O blessed lot of penitents, which makes just men of those who are guilty, men forever joyful of those who are sad, and men absolutely eternal of those who are destined to die! (*In Ps. 101,* col. 718.)

1479. ST. CYRIL OF JERUSALEM. As the dry tree, after partaking of water, puts forth shoots, so also the sinful soul, when it has been through repentance made worthy by the gift of the Holy Ghost, brings forth clusters of righteousness (*Catechesis 16, de Sp. Sancto I,* § 12, *PG* 33:934).

1480. ARNOLD, abbot of Bonnevaux. The fast is sustained with the delights of the Scriptures, refreshed with contemplation, supported by grace and nourished with the Bread of Heaven (*De cardinalibus operibus Christi,* c. 5, *PL* 189:1635).

1481. ST. JOHN CHRYSOSTOM. A. [Penance] cleanses the heart, enlightens the understanding, sanctifies minds, and prepares the body for receiving Christ (*Opus imperfect. in Matt., Hom. 3, PG* 56: 647).

B. Penance is the antidote to employ against crimes, the destruction of iniquities, payment in tears, trust in God, defense against the devil. . . . Penance is the hope of salvation and the destroying of despair. Penance opens heaven, leads to Paradise, conquers the devil (*De poenitentia, Hom. 8,* § 1, *PG* 49:337).

C. Penance is the medicine that heals sin, a gift bestowed from heaven, an admirable virtue, a grace transcending the force of laws (*ibid., Hom. 7,* § 1, col. 323).

1482. ST. ISIDORE OF SEVILLE. Penance is medicine to heal the wound, hope of salvation . . . which is measured not in terms of time, but by the profundity of grief, and by tears. . . . The tears of penitent persons are accounted before God as a baptism (*De ecclesiasticis officiis, Lib. II,* c. 17, §§ 2, 6, *PL* 83:802).

1483. JOHN GERSON. Do you seek health of soul, and of the body as well? Then you need temperance. Do you seek to be reconciled to God and to perform salutary penance for past sins? Adopt temperance. Do you wish to insure your rightful inheritance in paradise? Temperance is necessary for you. Do you desire to close the door on all vices? Then love temperance (*Serm. Dom. I Quadr., contra superbiam, Op. Om.* 3:1057).

1484. ST. LAURENCE JUSTINIAN. Sobriety shields from the fire of lust. . . . Sobriety governs the mind to prevent its being found wanting in firmness (*Lignum vitae,* tract 12, *de sobrietate,* c. 3, *Op. Om.* 1:74).

1485. THOMAS À KEMPIS. A. Where discipline is vigorously practiced one finds a richer blessing of peace and spiritual progress. Where discipline has disappeared, laxity is increased, vices prevail and virtue loses its force. Where discipline is preserved, heavenly grace abounds, devotion flourishes, divine reading is widely performed, meditation holds a great attraction, prayer is fervent (*De disciplina claustralium,* c. 1, *Op. Om.* 2:267). B. A religious who disregards discipline is seriously exposing himself to disaster (*ibid.,* c. 25).

1486. ST. BIRGITTA OF SWEDEN (d. 1373). The Mother of God spoke to her: "Daughter, it is written that he who had received five talents gained five more. Now, what is a talent but a gift of the Holy Spirit—for some are given the gift of wisdom, others wealth. . . . Thus that holy abbot, Benedict, multiplied the gift of grace that he had received when he spurned all that is transitory, when he subdued his flesh to serve the spirit, when he preferred nothing to the riches of charity. Fearing that his ears would be corrupted by hearing vain and idle talk, and his eyes by the sight of worldly pleasures, he fled to the wilderness, imitating [St. John the Baptist] who, as yet unborn, recognized while yet within his mother's body, the coming of his most loving Redeemer. . . . The world was dead to him [Benedict], and his whole heart was filled with love for God. . . . The body of this blessed man was like an earthenware furnace in which was closed the fire of the Holy Spirit, which excluded the diabolical fire from his heart. For the Spirit warms the soul for seeking God without burning it according to the flesh. It makes it bright with the purity of modesty without darkening the mind with malice. But the evil spirit heats the mind [that is, makes it desirous for carnal things], and makes it intolerably bitter. It darkens the soul as well by lack of care for itself, and beats it down inconsolably to things of earth" (*Revelationes, Lib. III,* c. 9).

1487. ST. AMBROSE. What a blessed life is this in which there is nothing to fear, and much to imitate! The hardship of fasting is compensated by tranquillity of mind, it is lightened by practice, it is aided by leisure, or beguiled by occupation; it is not burdened by the cares of the world, or occupied with the troubles of others, or weighted down by the distractions of the city (*Ep. 63, ad Ecclesiam Vercellensem. . . ,* § 82, *PL* 16:1263).

1488. ST. AUGUSTINE. A. The nourishing of [charity] is the lessening of cupidity; its perfection, the absence of all cupidity. . . . Whoever desires to develop charity, therefore, is to devote all his effort to the elimination of all greediness (*De diversis quaestionibus LXXXIII,* c. 36, § 1, *PL* 40:25). B. By your gift I had come totally not to will what I willed but to will what you willed. But where in all that long time was my free will, and from what deep sunken hiding-place was it suddenly summoned forth in the moment in which I bowed my neck to your easy yoke and my shoulders to your light burden (cf. Matt. 11:30), Christ Jesus, my helper and my Redeemer? How lovely I suddenly found it to be free from the loveliness of those vanities, so that now it was a joy to renounce what I had been so afraid to lose. For you cast them out of me, O true and supreme Loveliness, you cast them out of me and took their place in me, you who are sweeter than all pleasure (*Confessionum Lib. IX,* c. 1, *PL* 32:763; Sheed, p. 183).

1489. ST. JEROME. The sweetness of the fruit makes up for the bitterness of the root; hope of gain gives attraction to the dangers of the sea; desire of health soothes the pain caused by medicine. He who wants to get at the meat of the fruit sinks through the bitter rind. He practices penance who wishes to cling to the eternal good (*In Evangel. sec. Marc. 1, 15,* c. 1, *In Append., PL* 30:595).

1490. ST. GREGORY OF NAZIANZUS, Doctor of the Church (d. 389). For nothing seemed to me so desirable as to close the doors of my senses and, escaping from the flesh and the world, collected within myself, having no further connection than was necessary with human affairs, and speaking to myself and to God (cf. I Cor. 14:28), to live superior to visible things, ever preserving in myself the divine impressions pure and unmixed with the erring tokens of this lower world, and both being, and constantly growing more and more to be, a real unspotted mirror of God and divine things, as light is added to light;

and what was still dark grew clearer, enjoying already by hope the blessing of the world to come, roaming about with the angels, even now being above the earth by having forsaken it, and stationed on high by the Spirit (*Oratio 2, Apologetica,* § 7, *PG* 35:414).

1491. ST. BERNARD. Fasting gives us devotion and confidence at prayer. . . . Prayer obtains the strength for fasting and fasting merits the grace to pray. Fasting renders prayer more powerful, and prayer responds by sanctifying the fast (*Serm. de temp., Serm. IV in Quadr.,* § 2, *PL* 183:176).

1492. ST. BONAVENTURE. Let your soul refuse all comfort from others if you wish to delight in God's love (cf. Ps. 76:3). The consolation of God's love is tender and is not bestowed on those who admit any other form of consolation. . . . A mind that lovingly regards other forms of consolation and which does not refuse to find its solace in perishable and transitory things deprives itself of the grace of heavenly consolation. Whoever believes that there can be any alliance between that divine sweetness and this earth and ashes, between that celestial balsam and this poison, between those spiritual graces and these unworthy delights is most surely in error (*cf. S. Bernard. Serm. V in Ascens. Dni,* § 13, *PL* 183:321; *Ad fratres Tolosates Collationes octo, VI, Op. Om.,* ed. Peltier 14:644).

1493. VEN. LOUIS DE BLOIS. Believe me, the divine assistance will be present to your labors, and will lovingly aid you, comfort you when you fear, confirm you when you are wavering, defend you when you are being assailed, uphold you when you slip, raise you up when you fall, comfort you in your sorrow, and, now and then, infuse the most precious ointment of internal sweetness into you (*Speculum monachorum,* div. 8, *Op. Om.* 3:673).

Praise of patience

1494. ST. CYPRIAN, bp. of Carthage, martyr (d. 258). Patience restrains anger, bridles the tongue, governs the mind, guards peace, regulates discipline, breaks the impulse of lust, binds down the violence of pride, quenches the flame of hatred, controls the power of the rich, comforts the wants of the poor, maintains a blessed integrity in virgins, in widows a studious chastity, in the married a singleness of love. It makes men humble in prosperity, brave in adversity, mild toward injuries and contempt. It teaches us to pardon quickly those who have offended, and teaches the offender to make entreaty for a long time and often. It conquers temptations, bears persecutions, leads sufferings and martyrdoms to their consummation. It is patience which firmly fortifies the foundation of our faith; it is this that bears upward the growings of our hope; this patience guides our conduct in order that we may build the way of Christ, while we are walking according to his long-suffering; and makes us continue as sons of God, by imitating the patience of the Father (*De bono patientiae*, § 20, *PL* 4:659).

1495. ST. AUGUSTINE. A. Patience which is right and laudable and worthy of the name of virtue is understood to be that by which we tolerate evil things with an even mind, that we may not with an uneven mind desert good things, through which we arrive at better ones. Hence it is that the impatient, because they will not suffer ills, effect not a deliverance from ills, but only the sufferings of heavier ills. By contrast, they who are patient, who choose rather by not committing to bear, than by not bearing to commit evil, both make lighter through patience what they suffer, and also escape through patience, worse ills in which, through impatience, they would be submerged (*De patientia*, c. 2, § 2, *PL* 40:611). B. Patience is the companion of wisdom, not the handmaid of concupiscence; patience is the friend of a good conscience, not the foe of innocence (*ibid.*, c. 5, § 4, col. 613). C. Paul besought the Lord that the thorn of the flesh might leave him, and he was not heard for it to be taken away, and it was said to him: *My grace is sufficient for thee; for strength is made perfect in weakness* (II Cor. 12:9). His petition was not granted, but not unto folly, but unto wisdom, to the end that man may understand that God is a physician, and that tribulation is a remedy for salvation, not a punishment for condemnation (*Enarr. II in Ps. 21, 3*, § 4, *PL* 36:173). D. [The Lord] *scourges every son whom he receives* (Heb. 12:6)—and do you think, perhaps, that you will be the exception? If you are excepted from the suffering of the scourge, you are also excepted from the number of sons (*Serm. 46*, c. 5, § 11, *PL* 38:276).

1496. ST. GREGORY THE GREAT. A. When we are endeavoring to gain hold of the virtue of patience, we look at the examples of those who precede us. For what is more patient than Isaac, who carries the wood, asks about the burnt-offering, and is, shortly afterward, bound, and speaks not? is placed upon the altar, and offers no resistance (cf. Gen. 22:6 ff.; *Moral, Lib. 27*, c. 10, § 17, *PL* 76:408). B. Possession of one's soul is placed in patience, for it is the origin of all virtues, and their protector (*In Evangel. Lib. II, Hom. 35*, § 4, col. 1261). C. For me there is no doubt that the patience of so worthy a man did far excel in worth all his signs and miracles (*Dialogorum Lib. I, De Libertino praeposito monasterii*, *PL* 77:161).

1497. ST. EPHRAEM. Wretched and unhappy is he who is devoid of patience! He is fainthearted in adversities; he is easily taken prisoner in battle; he resists those who advise and instruct him. He is lazy at prayer, wanting in energy at night watches, sad on days of fast, negligent in observing self-restraint, dilatory in responses, bold in his actions, unsubdued in malice, tyrannical in commands, vehement in disputes, unable to master himself in quietude and silence (*Serm. de virtutibus et vitiis, serm. de impatientia, Op. Om.* 1:29).

1498. ST. JOHN CHRYSOSTOM. Patience is the foundation of all love of wisdom . . . the root of all self-denial . . . an impenetrable shield . . . an unshakable tower (*In I Cor., Hom. 33,* § 1, *PG* 61:276).

1499. DENIS THE CARTHUSIAN. This virtue [patience] is particularly necessary for the Christian who seeks to possess peace of heart and to serve God with a calm mind (*Enarr. in c. 10 Ep. ad Hebr.,* art. 10, *Op. Om.* 13:513).

1500. ST. THOMAS AQUINAS. A. The act of fortitude consists not only in holding fast to good against the fear of future dangers, but also in not failing through sorrow and pain occasioned by things present: and it is in the latter respect that patience is akin to fortitude. Yet fortitude is chiefly about fear, which of itself evokes flight, which fortitude avoids; whereas patience is chiefly about sorrow, for a man is said to be patient, not because he does not fly, but because he behaves in a praiseworthy manner by suffering (*patiendo*) things which hurt him here and now, in such a way as not to be inordinately saddened by them (*II-II,* q. 136, art. 4, *Utrum patientia sit pars fortitudinis,* ad 2, *Op. Om.* 10:104; Am. ed. 2:1752). B. Now, among the passions, sorrow is strong to hinder the good of reason, according to II Corinthians 7:10, *The sorrow that is according to the world produces death,* and Ecclesiasticus 30:25: *Sadness hath killed many, and there is no profit in it* (Confraternity ed., *Worry has brought death to many, nor is there aught to be gained from resentment,* Sir. 30:23). Hence the necessity for a virtue to safeguard the good of reason against sorrow, lest reason give way to sorrow; and this patience does (*ibid.,* art. 1, *Utrum patientia sit virtus,* p. 97; Am. ed., p. 1750).

Peace as the fruit of patience

1501. IMITATION OF CHRIST, Thomas à Kempis. Without battle you cannot come to the crown of patience, and if you will not suffer, you refuse to be crowned (*De imitatione Christi, Lib. III,* c. 19, *Op. Om.* 2:179; Gardiner, p. 132).

1502. ST. LAURENCE JUSTINIAN. He is truly patient who still loves the person at whose hands he suffers persecution; for neither mere toleration nor hatred have anything to do with the virtue of patience but are only a veil for fury (*Lignum vitae,* tract. 7, *de patientia,* c. 2, *Op. Om.* 1:44).

1503. TERTULLIAN. Patience . . . fortifies faith, is the pilot of peace, assists charity, establishes humility, waits long for repentance, sets her seal on confession, rules the flesh, preserves the spirit, bridles the tongue, restrains the hand, tramples temptations under foot, drives away scandals, gives crowning grace to martyrdom, consoles the poor, teaches the rich moderation, overstrains not the weak, exhausts not the strong, is the delight of the believer, invites the Gentile, commends the servant to his lord, and his lord to God, makes the man approved, is loved in childhood, praised in youth and looked up to in age (*De patientia*, c. 15, *PL* 1:1383).

1504. CASSIODORUS. It is patience that makes martyrs glorious, which guards the blessings of our faith, which overcomes all adversities. It does these things, not by struggling against evils, but by enduring them, not with murmuring but in the spirit of thanksgiving. It suppresses luxury in its deception, conquers the heat of anger, removes envy's devastation of the human race, makes men meek, is kindly disposed toward the liberal and prepares men's purified souls for future rewards. It is patience that wipes away the dregs of all pleasures; it cleanses souls. By it we serve Christ, by it we gain the victory over the devil, through it the blessed attain the kingdom of heaven, for it is written: *By your patience you will win your souls* (Luke 21:19; *In Ps. 32, 20, PL* 70:231).

In praise of hope

1505. ST. AUGUSTINE. A. O blessed, heavenly hope, you conquer fear of the world, root out dependence on the consolations the world has to offer . . . govern our thoughts. O hope, you make all things sweet and pleasant to bear. Forward, then, brethren, love this virtue, hold fast to it! But not without fear, for he who hopes and fears not is negligent; whereas he who fears and hopes not, is cast down and sinks to the depths like a stone (*Ad fratres in eremo, Serm. 10, In Append., PL* 40:1252). B. Our joy, therefore, brethren, is not as yet a reality, but in hope; but it is as perfect as though it were already realized. For we do not fear when Truth promises. For Truth can neither deceive nor be deceived. It is a good thing for us to cling to this hope; it frees us, but only if we have remained in his word. For we now believe, we shall then see; when we believe, it is hope, in this world; when we shall see, it will be reality, in a future world (*Enarr. in Ps. 123, 1*, § 2, *PL* 37:1640).

1506. ST. BASIL THE GREAT. Happy is he who has withdrawn himself from placing his confidence in the goods of this world and reposes all his hope in God! For as he is cursed who places his hope in man, so he is blessed who is supported by the Lord (*Comment. in Isa. 10, 20*, § 245, *PG* 30:550).

1507. ST. GREGORY THE GREAT. A. The hope of heavenly things makes the mind so firm that it will not be terrified by the flood of disturbances of this world's violence (*Hom. in Ezech., Lib. II, Hom. 5*, § 14, *PL* 76:994). B. Hope lifts itself the more firmly rooted in God in the proportion that man has suffered harder things out of love for God, because the joy of recompense in heaven is never gathered unless it has first been sown here in religious sorrowing (*Moral., Lib. X*, c. 19, § 36, *PL* 75:941). C. Holy men are very assured in their hope, but they always remain mistrustful regarding temptation, and consider as having been written for them: *Serve the Lord with fear, and rejoice before him with trembling* (Ps. 2:11), so that by hope, rejoicing should be produced, and by mistrust, "trembling" (*ibid., Lib. 20*, c. 3, § 8, *PL* 76:140). D. The more the flesh is kept down, the more fearlessly does the mind rejoice for the hope of heaven (*ibid., Lib. 31*, c. 38, § 77, col. 615).

1508. ST. JOHN CLIMACUS. Hope is a wealth of hidden riches. Hope is a treasure of assurance of the treasure in store for us. It is a rest from labors; it is the door of love; it is the superannuation of despair; it is an image of what is absent (*Scala paradisi, Grad. 30, de vinculo trium virtutum, fidei, nempe, spei, et charitatis, PG* 88:1159; Moore, p. 265, nn. 29–30).

1509. ST. BERNARD. *Our life, our sweetness, our hope. . . .* Hope lies in strength, like the spark in kindling wood. Unless you have kindling wood, the spark you have will not last. Remove the dry tinderwood and the spark sputters and dies; apply it, and the fire catches hold and burns. In the same way, hope that has no foundation will fall. . . . For hope without the life of virtue and the sweetness of devotion is not hope at all, but presumption. Hope is the mid-course between fear and security; hope is the name we give to a good that is uncertain. Life and sweetness banish the element of fear; they add strength to security, bestow beauty upon it. Hence [security] says to God: *As soon as I lie down, I fall peacefully asleep, for you alone, O Lord, bring security to my dwelling* (Ps. 4:9; *Serm. I in Antiph. Salve Regina*, § 6, *In Append., PL* 184:1064).

1510. HUGH OF ST. VICTOR. The companions of hope are: contemplation of the things above, joy, modesty, praise of God, patience, compunction, and long-suffering (*De fructibus carnis et spiritus*, c. 17, *In Append., PL* 176:1004).

1511. ST. THOMAS AQUINAS. As the anchor holds a ship motionless in the sea, so hope makes the soul secure in God in this world, which is something like the sea (cf. Ps. 103:25; *In Ep. ad Hebr. 6, 19*, c. 6, lectio 4, *Op. Om.*, ed. Parma 13:720).

1512. ST. LAURENCE JUSTINIAN. The hope of things to come provides rest for those who labor and perspire under the burdens of this present life. Hope of victory soothes the sufferings of those who are engaged in combat. Hope is like a pillar which supports the whole spiritual edifice; if it is taken away the whole building collapses and plunges into the depths of despair. Hope is the anchor of the soul preventing its destruction during the storms of temptations. . . . Hope is a most beautiful and pleasing gem; like gems it is translucent and bright (*Lignum vitae*, tract. 9, *de spe*, c. 2, *Op. Om.* 1:55).

1513. PETER DE BLOIS. I reverence the life of religious with the most heartfelt affection and embrace their feet in the spirit of the most devoted humility. For I know that more than all seculars, clergy as well as laity, they offer up more varied kinds of virtue as by their rules they have adhered to the footsteps of the apostles. . . . They oppress the flesh; lift up the spirit; living an angelic life on earth, they do battle for Christ in the simplicity of food, in the roughness of their garb, in their early rising for vigils, in psalms, hymns, and spiritual canticles, in their confessions, in their disciplines, and tears, and longing for heaven . . . (*Invectiva in depravatorem operum Blesensis, PL* 207: 1116).

FIFTH PRINCIPLE

Work Performed in Holy Obedience

CONTENTS: Man is born to work — Prayer and work — The lazy monk's injustice — Work produces blessings — Idleness is the mother of vices — Monastic work — Monks and lay brothers — Manual labor of monks — Study — Sacred Scripture, theology, philosophy, the arts — Work must be simple and performed with a pure intention — We must work joyfully, strenuously, with emphasis on discretion — Value of time — Work must be performed in holy obedience — St. Benedict, master of perfect obedience — The principal vow — Self-will — Fruits of holy obedience — Example of our Lord Jesus Christ — Obedience to be holy, simple, prompt, perfect, cheerful, strong — Obedience pleasing to the monk.

I. STATEMENT OF PRINCIPLE

The monk, God's servant, and son

1514. The monk is a most favored servant and child of God. His life must possess the greatest possible likeness to the divine, which is one of pure activity. He is a son by grace, and by nature the servant and slave of the Creator. As often as God sets up a monastic family he goes forth like the householder in the Gospel to hire laborers (Matt. 20:1 ff.). Reference to this simile should not be surprising to us, for *Man is born to labor and the bird to fly* (Job 5:7, Douay version). The Lord God took the man and *placed him in the garden of Eden to till it and to keep it* (Gen. 2:15; cf. Sir. 7:15).

Nature and purpose of work

1515. Hence the law of work comes from God and is given to men for the purpose of perfecting, strengthening, and increasing the powers of body and soul through work; of imitating the Creator himself, in whose image man is made; and of paying him as it were the creature's tribute. This duty of working was in man's origin a pleasant and honorable service, but by sin was changed into a punishment so that from that time man must eat his bread in the sweat of his brow (cf. Gen. 3:19). Thus work took on the nature of a yoke and a burden which weighs heavily on all. Even our Savior did not wish to remove this nature of work from us, although he made it sweet and light, in that he restored and even increased its dignity.

The monk a man of work

1516. For these reasons, then, the monk must not shun work. On the contrary, he is bound to it by holier ties than other men because he has in a unique way committed himself to God's service; and the greater the talent he has received, the greater the profit he must gain by its use. This is the origin of that venerable and celebrated motto of monks, "Pray and work."

Prayer and work

1517. The Work of God (sacred worship) and the work of obedience constitute the twofold service of the Lord, symbolized in the persons of Mary and Martha. These duties are the two wings by which men rise to the heights of perfection. Because the monk in his human weakness cannot as yet embrace the supreme good by continuous prayer and contemplation, he must prudently devote himself by turns to prayer and labor. When effort is so directed according to well-established principles, work bestows new strength on prayer, and prayer a new blessing on work.

Thus the soul will be purified by labor, more richly illuminated by meditation, and united to God by prayer. Add to these considerations what the Apostle, hinting at his own work-filled life, warns: *If any man will not work, neither let him eat* (II Thess. 3:10). For that reason, he says: *Neither did we eat any man's bread at his cost, but we worked night and day in labor and toil, so that we might not burden any of you (ibid.,* v. 8).

The injustice of the lazy monk

1518. It is perfectly true that every man is guilty of sin if he is lazy and neglects the duty of providing his own livelihood. The monk sins all the more grievously in not fulfilling this duty. He is a disgrace, a burden, and a hindrance for the whole monastic family to which he belongs. He is in reality a thief and a sponger, a parasite on the brethren earning their living by their sweat; he is like a corpse with which nothing can be done but bury it. He resembles the fig tree which the Lord cursed since it bore nothing but leaves so that it *withered from the roots* (cf. Mark 11:13–21).

Now we want to consider, dear confrere, the rich fruits which accrue to us from work, and the evils that have their origin in indolence.

Work subdues nature and restrains evil

1519. First of all, work subjects body and soul to the dominion of grace. It concedes not a moment to nature in its weakness and proneness to evil. As such it is a very important means for extirpating faults, avoiding sins, and escaping the temptations of the devil. Idleness, on the contrary, is the enemy of body and soul. It awakens evil desires, fosters gluttony, and brings forth from the union with the tempter all kinds of vice. The busy man, it is said, is tormented by one devil only, but the idle man's downfall is brought about by many.

1520. *Behold,* says the Prophet, *this was the iniquity of Sodom thy sister, pride, fullness of bread, and abundance, and the idleness of her* (Ezech. 16:49). The soul of the idle man is an uncultivated field, overgrown with thorns and briers, exposed to almost every evil, to every wickedness, to every misdeed, and to every temptation. It is like iron left lying on the ground, corroded with stagnant water whose nauseating stench infects everything. While the lazy man is asleep, his enemy comes and sows weeds (cf. Matt. 13:25).

Work is the source of many blessings

1521. Diligence at work, by contrast, puts vices to flight, permits virtues to grow, gathers a treasury made up of recognition, joy, merits, as it is written: *The diligent soul is amply satisfied* (Prov. 13:4). Those who sow the seed of labor *shall come back rejoicing, carrying their sheaves* (Ps. 125:6).

But the most precious fruit of industry is the illumination of the mind, tranquillity and confidence of soul, fraternal unity and charity. No one is more pleasant, amiable, peaceable, and happy than an industrious monk. Contrast him with the indolent man who is wasting his talent in idleness and inactivity. He is the wicked, irresponsible servant whose soul withers away more and more from sluggishness; it gradually loses all its merit and has nothing but the losses it has sustained; then, after this inglorious life has been spent, that terrible judgment will overtake it: "Cast the unprofitable servant into the darkness outside" (cf. Matt. 25:30).

The kind of work for the monk

1522. In what kind of work should the monk engage? The *Rule of St. Benedict* and monastic tradition show clearly that no work, either manual or intellectual, can bring the monk discredit or shame, provided that it does not stand in opposition to the purposes of the monastic life. The wisdom of the Creator has ordained that man, consisting of body and soul, should cultivate both his physical and spiritual powers. Nor should we forget that in the early ages almost all monks were laymen. Only one or the other, as circumstances required, was raised to sacred orders.

In the course of time, however, particularly after the ninth century, the monks proved themselves by their sacred learning and striving for virtue, to be well qualified for ecclesiastical offices; the Church insisted more and more that they should dedicate themselves to the sacred ministry of the altar and to working for the salvation of souls.*

1523. The natural result was that the number of laymen, or monks who were not formally trained in sacred sciences and who were occupied for the most part in manual labor and external duties, decreased more and more. Finally the Church, under the guidance of the Holy Spirit, determined that the monastic institute of our holy Patriarch should be an order of priests, and forbade anyone to be admitted among the choir monks who did not give promise of being promoted to sacred orders.†

1524. But in order that hands should not be wanting in the house of God for performing domestic and heavier works, a separate class of religious called converse brothers, or lay religious, or "bearded monks" was instituted in monasteries about the eleventh century. Although they are not monks in the strict sense of the term, they are religious in the fullest sense, and constitute an integral part of the monastic family.‡

* Pope St. Siricius (d. 398) is recorded to have written to Himerius, Bishop of Tarragona, already in 385: "We desire that monks whom seriousness of conduct, holiness of life, and practice of faith commend, be admitted to the duties of the clergy" (*c. XIII,* Mansi; 3:660). The Council of Poitiers (1078) summoned by Pope St. Gregory VII prescribed that: "Abbots and deans who are not priests must either receive the priesthood or resign their prelacies" (*c. 7,* Mansi, 20:498). And Pope Clement V, in the Council of Vienna (1311): "For the increase of divine worship, We prescribe that monks, at the notification of their abbots, must prepare themselves for all sacred orders, once legitimate excuses have been removed" (*Const. Apost. Ne in agro, I,* § 8, tit. 10, *de statu monachorum, in Clem., CJC* Richter 2:1086).

† Cf. Pope Clement VIII: "Whoever is received into an order of regulars . . . must possess such knowledge of letters or give unquestioned hope of acquiring such knowledge that he may receive minor orders, and in due season the major orders as well, according to the decrees of the Sacred Council of Trent" (*Const. Apost. Regularis disciplinae restitutione,* § 21, *19 Mar., 1603, BR* 10:773).

‡ Because of these considerations, converse brothers pronounce only simple vows, wear their own distinctive garb, pray an Office [or another form of prayer] specially prepared for them, and have no part in the deliberations of the conventual chapter. They are never to absent themselves from Compline, the chapter of faults, the conventual Mass, Vespers on Sundays and feasts, Benediction with the Blessed Sacrament, veneration of the sacred relics, ceremonies of investiture and profession,

They should show the choir monks filial and humble reverence. On their part the monks must consider the brothers cherished and helpful members of the monastic family, and love them with paternal affection and charity.

Manual work never to be despised

1525. Today's changed conditions demand that by far the greater part of domestic tasks and heavier work will be assigned, as a rule, to the brothers. But manual work has not ceased to be an integral part of the monastic vocation. Were anyone openly to scorn it, he would scarcely deserve the name of monk. For labor of the hands subjects the body to God, imparts a sense of stability to the restless of heart, and subdues pride. It is required, moreover, for perfect imitation of Jesus Christ. Our Lord spent only three years in preaching but had worked for nearly thirty years as a craftsman, and in so doing, adorned manual labor with an exalted dignity.

1526. In order to bear the name of monk with justification, you must be ready, dear confrere, to perform any manual work, even the most humble, cheerfully and with deep appreciation of its spiritual importance, be it assigned to you because of some particular skill you possess or because of some need of the monastery. Not less important is your duty to perform personally whatever work is involved in keeping your cell neat and your clothes clean, unless illness should excuse you from doing so. You must be eager to serve your brethren, especially those who are ill and, according to monastic custom, wait attentively on them at table when your turn comes round.

Principal work of the monk: priestly duties and studies

1527. Reading and devotion to sacred studies are the chief work that should occupy the monk after his priestly ministry. But these studies must be pursued in such a maner that they in no way interfere with either the Work of God, to which nothing is to be preferred (*RSB*, c. 43), or with monastic observance generally. On the contrary, both should derive help and advantage from such studies.

---

as well as other solemn functions which affect the monastic family as a whole. They should consider it the highest honor to assist in the functions at the altar. They will take their part in the annual retreat [many communities now arrange for a special retreat for the brothers, usually during the winter months when their work is less demanding]. They are to attend a spiritual conference weekly instead of the daily conference for the rest of the monastic family. The brothers' master or spiritual director is appointed by the abbot for instructing both the novices and the professed and training them in religion and in those observances which bind all the members of the community.

Purpose of monastic studies

1528. All followers of Christ, and particularly all religious, must in all their study seek one goal only, to glorify God and serve the Church. This is but another way of saying that all studies must be a fulfilment of St. Benedict's command: "Sing wisely." The monk must first of all devote himself humbly to the study of Sacred Scripture. From that source there gushes forth an inexhaustible wealth of sublime wisdom, which human intelligence can never completely absorb. The monk will devote the same effort to the study of the divine truths whose treasures are contained in the tried and proved sources of theology and philosophy, so admirably presented by the holy Fathers, and in particular by St. Thomas, the incomparable Angel of the Schools. Sacred theology, both mystical and speculative, is in perfect justification extolled as the queen of all sciences, for God himself has placed the crown upon her. The monk may devote himself to other sciences and the fine arts, such as painting and sculpture, provided that the spirit of the order suffer no harm, but rather that such efforts be made to serve the purposes of promoting the praise of God and the welfare of neighbor. In giving this advice we already touch on an important question that remains to be treated, namely, the qualities the monk's work must possess.

Work in the spirit of faith and simplicity

1529. Every work we undertake is like a body, to which the intention of the will gives form and life. No work of the monk, therefore, must be wanting in the purity and worthiness of intention to direct it to God alone. As our Lord says: *The lamp of the body is the eye. If thy eye be sound, thy whole body will be full of light. But if thy eye be evil, thy whole body will be full of darkness* (Matt. 6:22). Seek God in all sincerity, then, and look up to him as your work's witness and judge. When you thus regulate your work in the spirit of faith and simple humility, the heavenly Bridegroom will address you in these terms: *You are beautiful, my beloved, oh, you are beautiful; your eyes are doves* (Cant. 1:15).

In your humility you protest: "Beloved Master, only at your word will I lower the net (cf. Luke 5:5). For your glory alone, from pure love of you will I undertake my work. I shall do everything to serve you, to please you, in order to do honor to your Supreme Majesty, your holiness, your goodness." Such constant purity of intention is like a sanctuary lamp burning continually before Jesus in the Holy Eucharist. Once you adopt such constancy you can exclaim in all truth: I address all my works to the King (cf. Ps. 44:2, Douay version). Do not permit anything at all to draw your thought, your aspiration, your love away from him who is your sole purpose, your supreme good.

Prayer before work

1530. Before you begin a work, kneel in prayer asking God to come to your assistance, for you know that all the treasures of wisdom and knowledge are hidden in Jesus and in his Spirit and are distributed by them. During your work, too, frequently renew this good intention from the depth of your heart simply to love God for his own sake. Love of work grows from such a practice. You will begin and perfect all your works in a pure and holy intention and joyful spirit of willingness.

Your work united with Christ in the spirit of penance

1531. Be on your guard not to be influenced by reluctance or personal preference in your work: any such attitude lessens its worth and your merit in God's sight. Hence make every effort to unite what you do with the merits of Christ, and for his sake to take it upon yourself joyfully and as an exercise of penance. If you work with such supernatural motivation, you will be wanting neither in perseverance nor in the courageous and dependable constancy which will bring the work to its completion. Hearken to the divine admonition: *Keep control over all your affairs; let no one tarnish your glory* (Sir. 33:23). As a monk you work for God alone: *Cursed be he that doth the work of the Lord deceitfully* (Jer. 48:10), or slothfully or negligently.

God, your Father, is all-perfect and demands of you a striving for perfection; no half-hearted work is tolerated. Another incentive: do not deprive the Order of St. Benedict of its due honor. Its industry has been recognized as proverbial from time immemorial. Let your work be animated with constant diligence, indefatigable zeal, studious attention to even the most detailed considerations. With it all, however, you must not go beyond the proper measure, nor act imprudently, being *anxious and troubled about many things* (Luke 10:41). Distribute the portions of your day between prayer and work. Bedew your prayer with tears, your work with sweat.

Not a moment to be lost

1532. Put a high value on your time, and allow no moment to pass without producing something constructive as a sort of sacred usury. Time is an inestimable gift which God has entrusted to you, seed for the harvest of eternity, a string of pearls and gems of tremendous value for the purpose of making your crown in heaven beautiful. There clings to every moment of time a drop of the precious blood with which the Lord has bought it back and given it to you again. Time's value is that of your very soul, or of eternity, or even of God himself, for you gain or lose him by your use of time. Do not act as did the prodigal son, by irretrievably dissipating and squandering your patrimony on unprofitable ventures in which you only defraud yourself. Make the proper use of even the briefest moment, being *faithful over a few things* (Matt. 25:21). You dare not bury the valuable treasure which your Householder has placed in your keeping. Learn from avaricious and ambitious men to assess time at its proper worth—with this difference: by its use we acquire grace and merit the reward of eternal glory. Therefore, *while we have time, let us do good . . . for in due time we shall reap if we do not relax* (Gal. 6:10, 9).

Work is to be perfected in obedience

1533. Let us now turn our attention to that quality of work which alone gives value, force, and dignity to the monk's activity. That is holy obedience, which no man has explained more satisfactorily, taught more wisely, or exemplified more perfectly than our holy Patriarch.

Holy obedience is so essential and characteristic a mark of the monk that without it a work that he would perform would merit condemnation rather than reward. Among the religious vows it holds the place of pre-eminence indisputably. For although by means of poverty the monk forgoes the rights of ownership, and by chastity pleasures of the flesh, by obedience he sacrifices his very soul with all its powers and talents. Holy obedience chooses the best part in order to consecrate it to God, namely personal liberty and self-mastery. Religious obedience thus seals and crowns the monastic vows. It binds them into a oneness as the keystone holds the arch together: in so doing it perfects the noble offering of the vows as a whole. If obedience is refused, the entire sacrifice loses its value and the religious vocation deteriorates from a life of order to a sacrilegious destruction of the order.

Obedience unites man to God

1534. Obedience is the goal of the other vows; by its sacred bonds it unites the monk most intimately with God, binding his will and life with the divine. Through it he becomes a perfect child of God; through it he consecrates himself to the heavenly Father in most profound love and joyous zeal. Holy obedience is the reliable norm by which reformation of one's life according to monastic principles (*conversio morum*), personal holiness, and progress in virtue can be accurately measured. For that reason it is called the symbol of the religious life, the pillar of fire in which God's guidance and fatherly providence reveals itself, the monk's welfare, his sole ornament, the one service of which he is capable, in brief, the foundation and the soul, the beginning and end of the whole monastic life.

Obedience preserves from sin

1535. In very truth *an obedient man shall speak of victory* (Prov. 21:28, Douay version, used in the Alleluia of the Mass of St. Maur, January 15, *Missae propriae et kalendarium,* p. 3). By his obedience he is preserved from nearly all sins. It is not surprising that where self-will ceases, offense and punishment disappear. Man's free will is a gift that is as dangerous as it is precious, the root of death as well as of life, exercised in the love of God as well as in hatred of him. It is the key of heaven or of hell; it changes man into an angel or into a devil. This will ceases to be good at the point that it becomes an expression of self-will. What is more reasonable and more secure than to entrust so fateful an instrument into God's hand in order for him to employ it according to his wisdom and holiness, and to prevent it from turning to goods that are only deceptive and false? By virtue of this renunciation of self, the cloister becomes an ark which carries us in safety to the heavenly shores; a path of victory without insidious dangers; the precious pledge of your Bridegroom giving you the assurance that all your destiny is in his safekeeping. It is no wonder that in so close and strong a union with the Divine Will you are unconquerable, I might even go so far as to say incapable of sin.

Obedience guardian of the virtues

1536. Now if obedience averts sin and furnishes you powerful weapons which are the workings of God's own hand for overcoming the enemy of the soul, it follows from what has been said that it is a source, a guardian, and a treasure of virtues as well. It is the solid terrain over which we proceed to the perfection of love. In contrast, he who disregards obedience places himself out of contact with grace. Obedience roots out of the soul the most deeply hidden and rarely recognized growths of pride, and plants therein humility, the fertile soil of all holiness. In this way you will become more and more a child of God, a sheep of the Divine Shepherd who lovingly guides, nourishes and governs you by means of holy obedience. When you see your abbot's crosier, or rather the abbot himself, you can say: *I see* [God's] *rod watching* (Jer. 1:11).

Obedience inspires confidence, peace, joy

1537. Obedience will inspire you with deep filial confidence and bestow on you an indescribable tranquillity and joyfulness of soul. It is the wedding garment you must wear to be admitted to the banquet, the lovable interior light, the peace and serenity which are the properties of the perfect liberty of the children of God. Guided by God's wisdom, you walk without fear, you are pleasing to God and acceptable to men; even more than that, in a wonderful way you are made secure against the deceptions and artifices of obstinacy and self-love. Obedience leads you back to the mystical paradise from which disobedience had so unfortunately expelled man. Once you possess this excellent virtue, you become the support of your abbot, a help to your brethren, an honor and a treasure of your monastery, a delight and joy for all. *Obey your superiors and be subject to them, for they keep watch as having to render an account of your souls; so that they may do this with joy, and not with grief, for that would not be expedient for you* (Heb. 13:17).

Then, too, all your undertakings derive their value from obedience. It makes all that you do meritorious, perfect, pleasing to God. It acquires virtues in great numbers, perfects them, and makes them fruitful in your life. Thus it is an intensifier of all blessings and merits. Whatever it stamps with its royal seal acquires, in a certain degree, value before God, so that even the most insignificant service can become the seed of eternal glory and every step a step toward heaven.

1538. Obedience is the golden paten of the monk. Everything that he offers on it, all his prayer and work, all his zeal and mortification will without doubt find a pleasant reception in the presence of the Supreme King. If you cling steadfastly to holy obedience, you will always have God present. This realization will fill you with so serene a calmness that not even death has the power to disturb it. For the duty of rendering an account of your life will devolve not upon you but upon him into whose hands you have abandoned your will, dedicating it, by God's grace, to his service.

The spirit of obedience is the spirit of Christ

1539. Look then to Jesus as the perfect model of obedience. Then you can one day breathe forth your last breath of life, exclaiming with him: *It is consummated!* (John 19:30.) The Spirit of Jesus Christ is the spirit of obedience; our Savior could never repeat often enough: *I have come down from heaven, not to do my own will . . .* (*ibid.*, 6:38); *I seek not my own will, but the will of him who sent me* (*ibid.*, 5:30); *I do as the Father has commanded me* (*ibid.*, 14:31); *I do always the things that are pleasing to him* (*ibid.*, 8:29); *my food is to do the will of him who sent me, to accomplish his work* (*ibid.*, 4:34). . . . *Yet not as I will, but as thou willest . . .* (Matt. 26:39).

These words harmonized perfectly with his whole adorable life. He was subject not only to his parents (cf. Luke 2:51), but to every human creature (cf. I Pet. 2:13). Nothing was dearer to him than holy obedience, nothing more lovable; he longed for nothing more intensely, until, nailed to the cross and in the most horrible agony of death, he bowed his divine head as a token of his obedience, to give up his Spirit into the hands of the Father.

Jesus obedient unto death and beyond death

1540. Even with his death he did not finish his work of obedience. Perpetually under the veil of the Sacred Host he presents before our eyes the self-same obedience that he once joyously paid his pure and most blessed Mother. Look, dear confrere, upon this never-to-be-forgotten, glorious example of holy obedience which has been given as a shining pattern for your imitation at Bethlehem, at Nazareth, but particularly on Mount Calvary and at the altar. Do not remain indifferent to it; keep it constantly before your eyes, and make it a reality in your life.

The qualities of obedience according to St. Benedict

1541. In order to make good progress along the road of obedience, recall to mind the qualities which the holy Father Benedict demands in the submission of his disciples. First, it must be holy, as is proper for God's children, that is, it must be supernatural and heartfelt, not performed in hypocrisy or out of fawning human respect. It must be animated by so strong a faith that the spirit and the will of the divine head should be visible in you, for you belong to him as a member. *I know whom I have believed* (II Tim. 1:12). The command comes from God. *It is the Lord* (John 21:7) who speaks, the Beloved Son of the Eternal Father, of whom a voice out of the cloud said: *Hear him* (Matt. 17:5).

God governs you through your abbot

1542. The abbot to whom you are subject holds a divine authority; he is God's legate, ambassador, and representative. You must obey him *as you would Christ . . . giving your service with good will* (Eph. 6:5, 7). May he be for you, in a way, the veiled Ark of the Covenant from which the Most High made known his will, or, if the comparison is more pleasing, like the burning bush from whose flame the Lord spoke (cf. Exod. 3). He is in reality an instrument of divine providence for you and his commands are aids to your salvation. His word is the friendly voice of the Good Shepherd, a lamp to your feet, a light to your paths (cf. Ps. 118:105). The abbot can make mistakes, God, never; more than that, God can, in wonderful ways, turn a mistake to your advantage. Hence do not examine the orders given to you, nor pass judgment on them, or subject them to discussion, but obey them simply and humbly as God's commands.

Obedience must be simple and humble, without discussion

1543. Unless you become as submissive as a child, your obedience will fail to please God. Your duty is only to carry out the commands, not to judge the commander, unless he has ordered you to do something contrary to God's law. Holy obedience is an act of self-denial, hence the tomb of one's own judgment and will, an act through which in childlike devotion you gave yourself over to the judgment and authority of your father. Accordingly you should never expect to have the reasons for an assignment of obedience made known to you or seek to learn the same, but look only to Christ, who in his wisdom has given you the order. If your obedience is of such a nature, you will be like the wise man who knows how to combine in a skillful manner the simplicity of the dove and the prudence of the serpent. For then you have God's wisdom for your leader and guide on the way of salvation.

Obedience is not to be reluctant, but willingly and promptly offered

1544. In agreement with these qualities your obedience is to be willingly offered, not lazily, tardily, or indolently. Follow the steps of St. Maur who, at the command of the Father and with his blessing, went on his way, hastening at a fast run. Then it can always be said of you: He has left all things and followed the Lord. If you are summoned by holy obedience you should not even complete the letter that you have begun. *There is a stream whose runlets gladden the city of God* (Ps. 45:5). A person who obeys in a conscientious manner flies like an arrow toward its target. *I will whistle for them and I will gather them together* (Zach. 10:8), says the Lord of hosts.

The Mellifluous Doctor [St. Bernard] says beautifully in this connection: "The obedient man knows not what it is to delay. He never puts off until the morrow. Tardiness is unknown to him. He anticipates the one who commands him: he prepares his eyes for seeing, his ears for hearing, his voice for speaking, his hands for work, his feet for the journey. He gathers himself together in order that he may wholly compass the will of his superior" (*Serm. de diversis, Serm. 41, de virtute obedientiae, et septem ejus gradibus*, n. 7, *PL* 183:657).

Obedience must be perfect and all-embracing

1545. You must be fully ready to obey as if the Lord commanded you from his tabernacle. Accept the command literally and observe it as to time, place, the manner of execution, and the purpose of your superior. Do not deviate in any point in a given command, but carry it out fully. Then you can say with Tobias: *I will do all things, father, which thou hast commanded me* (Tob. 5:1), or with the Psalmist: *My heart is steadfast, O God, my heart is steadfast* (Douay version, *ready;* Ps. 56:8; 107:2).

Your abbot should never have to say to you: "What do you want me to do for you?" You must rather say to the abbot, in St. Paul's words: *Lord, what wilt thou have me do?* (Acts 9:6.) Be obedient in all things, with regard to all things, yes, even to all, becoming *subject to every human creature for God's sake* (I Pet. 2:13); first of all to the abbot, then to the officials of the monastery, and then to all the brethren. This obedience should be shown not timorously, but with happy disposition and cheerful countenance; for *God loves a cheerful giver* (II Cor. 9:7). Direct your gaze to the Lord always. If you place your hope in him, you will take wings as eagles, you shall run and not be weary, you shall walk and not faint (cf. Isa. 40:31). For the law of obedience so rests on the foundation of charity that it must be fulfilled with the whole heart and with a joyous spirit.

The vice of murmuring

1546. From these considerations it should be evident that murmuring is a most serious vice. For regarding superiors, he who is truth itself says: *He who rejects you, rejects me* (Luke 10:16). And *He that toucheth you, toucheth the apple of my eye* (Zach. 2:8). And the Apostle admonishes: *He who resists the authority, resists the ordinance of God, and they that resist bring on themselves condemnation* (Rom. 13:2).

Murmuring, either in the heart or by the spoken word, is an impious form of rebellion against God, a criminal denial of God's wisdom and authority, leprosy and death of the soul. A monk who murmurs is no longer what he must be, the support and staff of his abbot, but a scourge; the punishment meted out to the murmurers in the desert will overtake him. At the first intimation of the spiritual father's desires, without waiting for a formal command, you should do as he wishes, and with your whole being allow him to direct you.

Obedience must not be fearful

1547. With such willingness to be obedient and such zeal for childlike love, you will not obey in the spirit of timidity, but generously, resolutely and calmly, free of all confusion and pusillanimity. Then you belong to the number of those whom the Lord *led forth like sheep and guarded them like a herd in the desert. He led them on secure and unafraid, while he covered their enemies with the sea* (Ps. 77:52–53). Like a giant you will joyfully run your course (cf. Ps. 18:6). You will overcome all obstacles. Like Abraham, or rather like your heavenly Bridegroom who became obedient unto death on the cross, you will fulfill every command, with heroic and invincible courage, even though it is challenging to the understanding and opposed to your inclinations. You will remind yourself simply: "This is the Lord's command."

Obedience becomes sweet to the monk

1548. What Christ has done for me, I shall do for Christ! Obedience is dearer to me than life itself. The admirable and adorable example of my beloved Savior and childlike love of him and his representative, the abbot, will make the yoke sweet and the burden light.

I shall be a zither in the hands of Christ and of the abbot, which will produce a sweet melody before God; and I shall never forget the holy vow I pronounced on the day of my profession. May obedience be like the cowl of our holy Patriarch over my head, the cross on the breast of the abbot a standard marking a glorious path which I must follow. I shall rather die than be disobedient in order that in me Christ may gain the victory, Christ may rule, Christ may reign.

Forward then, dear confrere! May all these ideals be realized in you! May the cloister be for you *the mountain that God has chosen for his throne* (Ps. 67:17). In it may full days abound, until Christ's glorious kingdom comes, which unto eternity will have no end! *

II. EVIDENCE FROM THE RULE OF ST. BENEDICT

Work and idleness

1549. Hearken, my son, to the precepts of the master. . . . Freely accept and faithfully fulfil the instructions of a loving father, that by the labor of obedience you may return to him from whom you have strayed through the sloth of disobedience (*RSB, Prolog.*). Idleness is the enemy of the soul. The brethren, therefore, must be occupied (*ibid.*, c. 48); they must not be slothful (*ibid.*, c. 4, Instrument 38). Let them all work at the tasks appointed to them. . . . Let him be given some

* It is appropriate to insert, in this connection, the day's schedule or horarium as observed in the Congregation of Beuron, in conformity with the statutes approved by the Apostolic See: 4:15 A.M. (Sundays and feasts, 4:00 A.M.), the brethren assemble in choir for chanting Matins and Lauds. Private Masses are offered after Lauds; 6:30–7:00 A.M., Meditation, made individually, but in choir; 7:00 A.M., Prime, followed on Mondays and Fridays by the chapter of faults; 9:00 A.M., Terce, Conventual Mass, chanted daily, followed by Sext, unless the rubrics prescribe a different order; 12:00 noon, Dinner, followed by a brief adoration of the Most Holy Sacrament, after which there is common recreation for about an hour. Light manual labor may be added to this recreation; 3:00 P.M., None recited, Vespers chanted; 6:30 P.M., Spiritual conference in chapter; 7:00 P.M., Supper, followed by recreation in common; 8:00 P.M., Public common reading in the choir; Compline (recited); private devotions. At this time the brethren are free to retire; 9:15 P.M., Signal for all to retire.

work to perform, so that he may not be idle. . . . The brethren, therefore, must be occupied at stated hours in manual labor. . . . They will do the tasks that have to be done. . . . But if the circumstances of the place or their poverty require them to gather the harvest themselves, let them not be discontented; for then are they truly monks when they live by the labor of their hands, like our fathers and the apostles. Yet let all things be done in moderation on account of the fainthearted. But if there be anyone who . . . cannot study or read, let him be given some work to perform, so that he may not be idle (*ibid.,* c. 48). Let him not because of his priesthood forget the obedience and discipline of the rule (*ibid.,* c. 62). Let the brethren serve one another, and let no one be excused. . . . Let the rest serve one another in charity (*ibid.,* c. 35).

Sacred studies

1550. Let no one be excused from the kitchen service . . . unless he is occupied in some business of importance. For this service brings increase of reward and of charity (*RSB,* c. 35). The brethren must be occupied at stated hours . . . in sacred reading. . . . Let them apply themselves to their reading or to the study of the psalms. . . . Let them each receive a book from the library, which they shall read through consecutively. . . . But one or two senior monks should certainly be deputed to go round the monastery at the times when the brethren are occupied in reading, to see that there be no slothful brother who spends his time in idleness or gossip and neglects the reading, so that he not only does himself harm but also disturbs others (*ibid.,* c. 48). Let no one presume . . . to have anything as his own . . . whether book or tablets or pen (*ibid.,* c. 33). Listen gladly to the holy reading (*ibid.,* c. 4, n. 56). Let the abbot provide all things necessary . . . pen, tablets (*ibid.,* c. 55).

Sacred Scripture and the Fathers

1551. It behooves the abbot, therefore, to be learned in the divine law (*RSB,* c. 64). For him who would hasten to the perfection of the monastic life, there are the teachings of the holy Fathers, by observing which a man is led to the summit of perfection. For what page or what utterance of the divinely-inspired books of the Old and the New Testaments is not a most unerring rule of human life? Or what book of the holy Catholic Fathers is not manifestly devoted to teaching us the straight road to our Creator? The Conferences of Cassian and his Institutes, and the lives of the Fathers . . . (*ibid.,* c. 73).

Life of St. Benedict: Besides the many miracles that made him famous in the world he was eminent also for his teaching (*S. Gregorii Magni Dialogorum Lib. II,* c. 36, *PL* 66:200).

The crafts

The monastery should, if possible, be so arranged that . . . the crafts may be plied within the enclosure (*RSB*, c. 66).

Work must be performed in a holy manner

1552. If there be craftsmen in the monastery, let them practice their crafts with all humility, provided that the abbot give his permission. But if one of them be puffed up because of his skill in his craft . . . let him be removed from this work. . . . If any of the work of the craftsmen is to be sold . . . let the goods always be sold a little cheaper than they are sold by people of the world (*RSB*, c. 57); because of the holy service which they have professed . . . (*ibid.*, c. 5). . . . that in all things God may be glorified (*ibid.*, c. 57). *Not to us, O Lord, not to us but to your name give glory* (Ps. 113 B:1). . . . They magnify the Lord's work in them. . . . Let us ask God that he be pleased, where our nature is powerless, to give us the help of his grace. . . . Whatever good work you are about to undertake, ask him with most instant prayer to perfect it (*ibid., Prolog.*). There shall be appointed to this kitchen [for the abbot and the guests] by the year two brethren who can discharge the duty well. Let help be given them according as they need it, so that they may serve without murmuring. And, on the other hand, when they have less to do, let them go out to whatever task is assigned to them (*ibid.*, c. 53).

Use of time

1553. For we must always so serve him with the gifts which he has given us that he may never, as an angry father, disinherit his children, nor yet as a dread lord be driven by our sins to cast into everlasting punishment the wicked servants who would not follow him to glory (*RSB, Prolog.*). Let us consider how we ought to behave ourselves in the presence of God and his angels (*ibid.*, c. 19). If our deeds are daily, day and night, reported to the Lord by the angels assigned to us: then, brethren, must we constantly beware, as the prophet says in the Psalm, lest God some day behold us falling into evil ways and turned unprofitable, and spare us for this present time, because he is merciful and awaits our amendment, but should say to us in the future: *These things thou didst do, and I was silent* (the Confraternity ed. of the Bible has the far better reading: *When you do these things, shall I be deaf to it?* Ps. 49:21; *ibid.*, c. 7, first degree of humility). Sick or delicate brethren should be assigned a task or craft of such a kind that on the one hand they be not idle, and on the other be not overborne by excessive toil or driven away from the monastery. The abbot should have consideration for their weakness (*ibid.*, c. 48). Let help be given to them according as they need it, so that they may serve without murmuring. . . . To all the officials of the monastery, let the same consideration be shown and help given whenever it is needed (*ibid.,* c. 53). If the community is large, let helpers be given [to the cellarer], so that by their assistance he may fulfil with a quiet mind the charge that has been committed to him (*ibid.,* c. 31). Let the weak brethren have help provided for them, that they may not perform their office with sadness; and indeed let everyone have help, according to the size of the community or the circumstances of the locality (*ibid.,* c. 35). And let [the abbot] so arrange and ordain all things that souls may be saved and that the brethren may do their work without justifiable murmuring (*ibid.,* c. 41).

Life of St. Benedict: Then [Benedict] at once gave the tool back to the Goth with these words: "Work, now, and be sad no longer" (*S. Gregorii Magni Dialogorum Lib. II,* c. 6, *PL* 66:144).

St. Benedict, master of perfect obedience

1554. My words are now addressed to you, whoever you may be, that renouncing your own will to fight for the true King, Christ, you take up the strong and glorious weapons of obedience. . . . Therefore our hearts and our bodies must be made ready to fight under the holy obedience of his commands (*RSB, Prolog.*). It is proper for disciples to obey their master (*ibid.,* c. 3). Monks should not have even their bodies or their wills at their own disposal (*ibid.,* c. 33). Let no one in the monastery follow the will of his own heart (*ibid.,* c. 3). To deny oneself in order to follow Christ (*ibid.,* c. 4, n. 10). To hate one's own will (*ibid.,* n. 59). We are, indeed, forbidden to do our own will by Scripture, which says to us: *Turn away from thine own will* (Ecclus. 18:30, Douay version; *Go not after your lusts,* Confraternity edition). Moreover, we ask God in prayer that his will be done in us. And rightly are we taught not to do our own will, since we dread that sentence of Scripture: *Sometimes a way seems right to a man, but the end of it leads to death* (Prov. 16:25; *ibid.,* c. 7, first degree of humility). The second degree of humility is that a man love not his own will, nor delight in fulfilling his own desires, but carry out in deed that saying of the Lord: *I have come down from heaven, not to do my own will, but the will of him who sent me* (John 6:38). It is written also: "Self-will has its punishment, but necessity wins a crown" (*ibid.,* second degree). . . . "When the abbot has decided what is the better course, all are to obey" (*ibid.,* c. 3). "Let none follow what seems good for himself, but rather what is good for another" (*ibid.,* c. 72). "The third kind of monk is that detestable one of the Sarabaites. . . . Their law is their own good pleasure: whatever they think of or choose to do, that they call holy; what they do not like, that they regard as unlawful. The fourth kind of monks are called Gyrovagues, who . . . giving up to their own wills and the allurements of gluttony, are worse in all respects than the Sarabaites" (*ibid.*, c. 1).

The vow of obedience

1555. And let a senior be assigned to [the newcomers to the religious life] who is skilled in winning souls, that he may watch over them with the utmost care. Let him examine whether the novice truly seeks God, and whether he is zealous for the Work of God, for obedience, and for humiliations. . . . In the oratory, in the presence of all, he shall promise stability, conversion of his life, and obedience; and this before God and his saints (*RSB*, c. 58). The first degree of humility is obedience without delay. This becomes those who hold nothing dearer to them than Christ. Because of the holy service which they have professed, the fear of hell, and the glory of life everlasting, as soon as anything has been ordered by the superior, they receive it as a divine command and cannot suffer any delay in executing it. Of these the Lord says: *As soon as they heard me, they obeyed* (Ps. 17:45). And again he says: *He who hears you, hears me* (Luke 10:16).

Such as these, therefore, immediately abandoning their own affairs and forsaking their own will, dropping the work they were engaged in and leaving it unfinished, with swift obedience follow up with their deeds the voice of him who commands them. Almost in the same moment of time that the superior's order is issued, the disciple's work is completed in the swiftness of the fear of the Lord; the two things being rapidly accomplished together by those who are impelled by the desire of attaining life everlasting. Therefore they choose the narrow way, according to the Lord's words: *How narrow the gate and close the way that leads to life!* (Matt. 7:14.) Thus not living by their own will, and obeying their own desires and passions, but walking by another's judgment and orders, they dwell in monasteries, and desire to have an abbot over them. Assuredly such as these imitate that saying of the Lord in which he says: *I have come down from heaven, not to do my own will, but the will of him who sent me* (John 6:38).

But this obedience itself will then be acceptable to God and pleasing to men if what is commanded be not done timorously, or tardily, or tepidly, nor with murmuring or the raising of objections. For the obedience which is given to superiors is given to God, since he himself says: *He who hears you, hears me* (Luke 10:16). And disciples should give their obedience with a good will, because *God loves a cheerful giver* (II Cor. 9:7). For if the disciple obeys with an ill will, and murmurs not only in words but even in his heart, then even though he fulfil the command, his work will not be acceptable to God, who sees that his heart is murmuring. For such work as this he will gain no reward;

nay, rather, he will incur the punishment due to murmurers, unless he amends and makes reparation (*ibid.,* c. 5).

Holy obedience is to be perfect and all-embracing

1556. The third degree of humility is that a man for the love of God subject himself to his superior in all obedience, imitating the Lord, of whom the Apostle says: He became obedient even to death (cf. Phil. 2:8; *RSB,* c. 7). To obey in all things the commands of the abbot . . . (*ibid.,* c. 4, Instr. n. 60). Everything, therefore, is to be done with the approval of the abbot (*ibid.,* c. 49). Not only shall the virtue of obedience be practiced by all toward the abbot, but the brethren shall also obey one another, knowing that by this road of obedience they will go to God. The commands of the abbot or of the superiors appointed by him must rank first, and no unofficial commands take precedence over them; but, for the rest, let all the juniors obey their seniors with all love and diligence (*ibid.,* c. 71). Let [the cellarer] have under his care all those things which the abbot has assigned to him, but presume not to deal with what he has forbidden him. . . . Let him do all things with measure, and in accordance with the instructions of the abbot (*ibid.,* c. 31). Let the prior respectfully perform what is enjoined on him by his abbot, and do nothing contrary to the abbot's will or regulations (*ibid.,* c. 65). Let the monks vie in paying obedience to one another (*ibid.,* c. 72).

Holy obedience is to be strong and heroic

1557. If it happens that something hard or impossible be laid upon any brother, let him receive the command of his superior with all docility and obedience. But if he sees that the weight of the burden altogether exceeds the measure of his strength, let him explain the reasons of his incapacity to his superior calmly and in due season, without pride, obstinacy, or contentiousness. If after his representations the superior still persists in his decision and command, let the subject know that it is expedient for him, and let him obey out of love, trusting in the assistance of God (*RSB,* c. 68). The fourth degree of humility is that, meeting in this obedience with difficulties and contradictions, and even injustice, he should with a quiet mind hold fast to patience, and enduring neither tire nor run away; for Scripture says: *He who has persevered to the end will be saved* (Matt. 10:22); and again: *Be stout-hearted, and wait for the Lord* (Ps. 26:14). . . . And again in another place the Scripture says: *You have tested us, O God! You have tried us as silver is tried by fire; you have brought us into a snare; you laid a heavy burden on our backs* (Ps. 65:10–11). And to show that we ought to be under a superior, it goes on to say: *You let men ride over our heads* (v. 12; *ibid.,* c. 7, fourth degree of humility).

The punishment of disobedience

1558. Above all, let not the vice of murmuring show itself in any word or sign, for any reason whatever. But if a brother be found guilty in this, let him undergo strict punishment (*RSB,* c. 34). If a brother shall be found contumacious, or disobedient, or proud, or a murmurer, or in any way despising or contravening the holy Rule and the orders of his superiors . . . let him suffer excommunication (*ibid.,* c. 23). Do not be a grumbler (*ibid.,* c. 4, n. 35). And so at the last, for these sheep disobedient to his care, let death itself bring its penalty (*ibid.,* c. 2).

The example of the obedient

1559. The lives of the Fathers, their institutes . . . what else are they but tools of virtue for good-living and obedient monks? (*RSB,* c. 73.)

Life of St. Benedict: For Maur, having asked and obtained his Father's blessing, set off at full speed in obedience to his command and thinking that he was going on dry land, ran upon the water to the spot to which the current had carried the child, seized him by the hair of his head, and then returned quickly (*S. Gregorii Magni Dialogorum Lib. II,* c. 7, *PL* 66:146).

III. DECREES AND DOCUMENTS OF THE CHURCH

Idleness to be avoided

1560. COUNCIL OF BASLE (1431). Since every idle man is inclined to evil and more beset by demons than other men, we desire that the brethren . . . when not occupied with the recitation of the Divine Office or with sacred reading in their cells, do not engage in idle conversation or frivolous pursuits, but take up some form of manual labor, as is extensively provided for in the *Rule of St. Benedict,* chapter 48. Therefore no one is to be permitted to remain idle, and if anyone is found wasting time, he is to be corrected. All works, however, are to be imposed with discretion (*Stat. et ordinationes ad monachos Congregationis Mellicensis directae,* ex manuscr. Salisburgensi).

Manual labor

1561. CARTHUSIAN ORDER (founded 1086 by St. Bruno, approved by Pope Alexander III in 1176). They who are reluctant to engage at times in manual labor are blameworthy, for this is the way the question is stated in the *Lives of the Fathers:* At times occupy yourself with reading, at other times in prayer, and again devote your efforts zealously to work. Thus the hour will be short and the labor light (*Tract. Statutorum Ord. Carthusiensis pro novitiis, CR* 2:335).

1562. CONG. OF BURSFELD (founded 1433). A. In order for us to live according to the spirit of the holy Rule, as far as possible, it is in the prudent judgment of the superior so to regulate the different works according to the strength of the brethren and the needs of the monastery, that the prescriptions of the Rule will be observed, and all reasonable cause for complaining be removed; this is to be done, too, without prejudice to the Divine Office and other more necessary occupations (*Stat.*, dist. 5, c. 2, *de labore manuali,* n. 1, p. 124). B. The brethren assemble and proceed together to their appointed place and assigned work after having recited *Adjutorium nostrum in nomine Domini, Respice in servos tuos,* with the orations, *Dirigere et sanctificare* and *Actiones nostras.* In going out to their work and in returning they should not be separated, but walk in a group following the prior. As they walk they should not spend their time in talking, but should pray or meditate, as they are to do also while working, unless the prior shall have granted permission to speak of some pious and profitable subjects (*ibid.*, n. 3, p. 125). C. The abbot is to see to it that the individual brethren develop skills in manual work so that when tasks that are to be performed in common are wanting they will not grow lazy because they have no work in which to engage themselves profitably. Such skills are: writing, copying manuscripts [this was before the invention of printing], illuminating books, cultivating the garden within the walls of the monastery, making rosaries and similar employments, among which writing is considered the most useful insofar as it is closest to the spiritual order (*ibid.*, n. 9, p. 127).

1563. CONGR. OF CLUNY (12th century). We decree that the ancient and holy work of the hands be restored, to some degree, so that at least within the enclosure where it may be performed becomingly away from the gaze of seculars, the brethren will engage every day in some form of useful activity except on holydays when manual labor is not permitted (*Stat. Petri Ven., Congr. Cluniacensis,* c. 39, *CR* 2:185; *PL* 189:1036).

1564. CONGR. OF STRASBURG (founded 1624). The brethren will devote themselves to the manual labor to be assigned by the superiors. This work is always to be performed in perfect silence. Taking into account the regions in which the monasteries are situated and the seasons of the year, the superiors will arrange everything in a reasonable manner so as to assure answering the needs of the Church and of the people, and at the same time making certain that the monks will not be excessively burdened (*Declar. in c. 48 RSB,* fol. 61).

1565. SWABIAN CONGR. OF ST. JOSEPH (founded 1671). If some monks are less gifted and capable in the matter of studies, they are to be assigned to individual manual tasks which are respectable and in no sense unbecoming for the religious and priestly state, and that with the idea of removing the occasion of idleness, which is the mother of vices and the step-mother of virtues. Such works are: copying and printing books; correcting books already written and marking their chapter headings; cultivating gardens; extracting sap and juices from herbs for compounding medicines; preparing and taking charge of the medical remedies for the community; printing; sculpturing; illuminating books; making sundials and mathematical instruments, or even working at the lathe . . . so that they make what is needed and repair what has been broken, and thus they will always have at hand something with which to be usefully occupied (*Const. et declar., Pars II,* c. 3, punctum 2, fol. 89–90).

1566. PROV. CHAPTER OF ABBOTS celebrated at Northampton, England, 1343. Desiring to prevent idleness from leading anyone of our order into sin, we establish by this present constitution that abbots and priors see to it that the monks of their monasteries be engaged in exercises in place of manual labor according to their respective abilities: they are to engage in studying, reading, copying manuscripts, correcting, illuminating and binding books, or in other occupations, as they deem them to be expedient for their welfare (Haeften, *Disquisitiones monasticae,* p. 841).

1567. COUNCIL OF COLOGNE (1536). All monks and nuns must love knowledge of the Scriptures, and detest vices of the flesh. They must never allow the psalter to be out of their hands or out of their sight, but be devoted to prayer, be alert in guarding their senses, block the entrance to vain thoughts, tend toward God body and soul, conquer anger with patience. In a word, they must close the entrance to all such distractions which, once they have taken possession of the mind, lead to serious faults. They should continually be engaged in some form of work, so that the devil will find them always occupied. When there is no manual work in which they may engage, it is appropriate for them to copy sacred books, so that at times the hand will be busied with procuring food, and at others the soul will be nourished with reading. We learn that the Egyptian monasteries observed the policy of receiving no one as a monk unless he was qualified for work, not so much as a means of procuring the necessities for sustenance, as for the welfare of the soul, lest they be distracted with harmful thoughts (*Pars X,* c. 16, Mansi 32:1281).

Work to be begun with prayer

1568. MONASTIC BREVIARY. Look upon your servants, O Lord, and upon the works of your hands, and direct their children. And may the glorious beauty of the Lord our God be upon us and prosper the work of our hands; direct the work of our hands, O Lord. Glory be to the

Father, and to the Son, and to the Holy Ghost. As it was in the beginning, is now, and ever shall be, world without end.

Let us pray: O Lord God, King of heaven and earth, may it please you this day to direct and sanctify, to rule and govern our souls and bodies, our thoughts, words, and deeds according to your law, and in the fulfilling of your commandments, that now and forever we may, by your help, attain salvation and freedom, O Savior of the world, who live and reign forever and ever. Amen.

May the Almighty Lord order our days and deeds in his peace (*Versiculus, oratio et responsorium ad Primam, Breviar. monastic.* 1:6).

1569. ROMAN MISSAL. A. We beseech you, O Lord, assist our actions with the movements of your grace, and in their doing follow them up with your help, that every prayer and wish of ours may begin in you, and once we have begun them in you, we may finish them through you (*Oratio post Lect. IV Sabbato Quattuor temp., Miss. Rom.,* p. 101). B. O God, the strength of those who hope in you, graciously be present with us when we invoke you, and, because mortal infirmity can accomplish nothing without you, grant us the assistance of your grace that, in executing your commands, we may be pleasing to you both in our desires and in our deeds (*Oratio pro commen. Dom. I p. Pent., in festo SSmae. Trinitatis, ibid.,* p. 448).

Priest monks

1570. POPE ST. SIRICIUS (d. 398). We earnestly desire that monks who are commendable for seriousness of conduct, and holiness of life and faith, be admitted to the offices of clerics, so that those who have not yet reached their thirtieth year are to be promoted, one step at a time, to minor orders and, with the passage of time and the maturity of age, to the dignity of the diaconate and the priesthood (*Ep. 1, ad Himerium episc. Tarraconensem,* c. 13, n. 17, *PL* 13:1144; Mansi 3:660).

1571. COUNCIL OF AACHEN (8th century). The bishops decided, with the approval of the Lord Pope, that monks desist from heavy work and toil out of respect for the priesthood (*Fragmentum historicum de Concilio Aquigranensi,* Mabillon, *Vetera Analecta,* p. 149).

1572. POPE EUGENE II (d. 827). Abbots must also receive the dignity of the priesthood, in order that they can use all means to prevent the sins of their subjects and cut off those sins which have not been avoided, and thus observe that the prescriptions of the rules are not broken (*Synodus Romana, 826,* c. 27, Mansi 14:1007).

1573. COUNCIL OF POITIERS (1078). Abbots who are deacons, but not priests, must be ordained priests or forfeit their prelacies (*Concil. Pictaviense,* c. 7, Mansi 20:498).

1574. POPE BONIFACE IV (d. 614). Unsupported by dogma, some maintain, more boldly indeed, and incited thereto more with a bitter zeal than with charity, that monks, because they are dead to the world and live for God, are unworthy of the powers of the priestly office. . . . Nor was Blessed Benedict (cf. *RSB,* cc. 60, 62), the loving teacher of monks, in any degree opposed to the idea (of having priest monks), but stated only that they should be free from all worldly undertakings. . . . We, however, taught by the example of these great Fathers . . . believe that the office of binding and loosing, with God's help, is certainly not administered unbecomingly by priest monks (*Concil. Romanum III, 610, Decretum Synodi promulgatum in Concilio,* Mansi 10:504; *PL* 80:104).

1575. POPE CLEMENT V (d. 1314). For the increase of divine worship We command that all monks, when called by their abbot, prepare themselves for the reception of all orders, provided that there is no legitimate impediment (*c. Ne in agro, I,* § 8, tit. 10, *de státu monachorum, in Clem., CJC* Richter 2:1086).

1576. POPE CLEMENT VIII (d. 1605). Whoever is to be received in an order of regulars, even among the Mendicants, must be of the age required by the regulations and prescriptions of the order into which he is to be admitted. He must either already possess the degree of education required for receiving minor orders or give a well-founded hope of being able to acquire the same, and in due time also the major orders according to the decree of the S. Council of Trent. But if anyone more than twenty-five years of age petitions admission to the religious habit and is found to be wanting in such education, he is to be placed among the converse brothers, among whom formal literary training is not demanded. Converse brothers are not to be received before their twentieth year, and even then only if they know at least the principal teachings of Christian doctrine (*Const. Apost. Cum ad regularem,* § 4, 19 Mar., 1603, *BR* 10:773; *CJC Fontes,* n. 189, 1:359).

1577. CONGR. OF CELESTINES (approved 1629). Novices are to have such qualifications that they can properly and canonically be advanced to sacred orders. If they are more than twenty years old, they may be granted admission only by the chapter of definitors. If anyone who is more than twenty-five years old seeks admission to the monastery, and is found wanting in the necessary education, he is to be placed among the converse brothers and to be clothed with their habit (*Const. monachorum O.S.B. Congr. Coelestinorum,* tract. 1, c. 5, § 2, *CR* 4:501).

1578. CONGR. OF BURSFELD. When one who has converted from the world diligently seeks admission and perseveres when hardships are inflicted on him, he is to be questioned (among other things) as to whether he is prevented by an impediment from receiving orders. This interrogation can take place in the presence of the whole community, or privately. If he replies that he is bound by no such impediment, and if he is sufficiently well educated, a favorable answer to his request is not to be denied unless some other canonical impediment stands in the way. If there is a canonical impediment he is to be dismissed forthwith (*Stat.*, dist. 7, c. 1, *de susceptione novitiorum*, nn. 7–8, p. 263).

1579. SWABIAN CONGR. OF ST. JOSEPH. In the earliest beginnings of our glorious order only one or the other [monk] was promoted to sacred orders in each monastery. Later on, however, with the consent and even upon the command of the Supreme Pontiffs, our Fathers began to devote their efforts to the conversion of peoples and the welfare of their fellow man, and all of them who were capable of receiving sacred orders were ordained to the same (*Const. et declar., Pars II*, c. 3, punctum 3, *de laboribus et studiis fratrum*, fol. 87).

Laybrothers

1580. INSTITUTES [Statutes] OF CISTERCIANS (12th century). Since [the Fathers] realized that without help they would be unable to fulfil perfectly the precepts of the Rule day and night, they decided to admit unlettered men as laybrothers with the approval of the bishop and to treat them in life and in death as their own, except for [a share in] the monastic state (*Exordium coenobii et ordinis Cisterciensis*, c. 15, *PL* 166:1508; tr. by Robert E. Larkin, in *The White Monks*, by Louis J. Lekaio, O. Cist.; Okauchee, Wisc., 1953, *Append. I*, p. 263).

1581. GEN. CHAPTER OF CISTERCIAN ORDER (1224). Let such be received as converse brothers who will be so engaged in their work that it is certain and evident in the duty committed to them that they can take the place of one hired man (n. 1, Canivez, *Stat. Capitulorum Gen., O. Cist.* 2:31).

1582. CONGR. OF CAMALDULI. By their manual labor the converse brothers are to offer a constant reproach to idleness as a most dangerous enemy (*In Reg. divi Benedicti declar., Lib. I*, c. 48, p. 200; *CR* 2:256).

1583. ABBEY OF CLUNY. It has been prescribed that, in conformity with the customs of the past, no lay servant shall serve the sick brethren or anyone else eating in the infirmary; only monks or bearded converse brothers are to be employed for this purpose. The reason for this regulation was the more proper relationship to the monks on the part of the brothers than can be obtained by secular servants. . . . We also prescribe that those who are called servants living on monastery property, that is, who are neither monks nor brothers, and who have been the worst trouble makers of certain monasteries, are not to be received in other communities even for the greatest apparent advantage (*Petri Venerabilis Stat. Congr. Cluniacensis*, cc. 24, 48, *PL* 189:1032, 1038; *CR* 182, 186).

1584. CONGR. OF STRASBURG. With regard to our converse brothers . . . we prescribe that they are to be assigned to the more menial tasks by the superiors (*Declar. 10 in c. 57 RSB*, fol. 76).

1585. CONGR. OF BURSFELD. A. Since the Lord God wills everyone to be saved and to obtain the grace of conversion, and since the holy Father [Benedict] excluded no state in life from membership in the order, we also do not refuse to receive laymen, although they are bound neither to wear the habit nor to observe the full rigor of the discipline with others, and provided that they are otherwise of good repute, proper age, of service to the community and able to work (*Stat.,* dist. 9, *Introd., de conversorum susceptione,* p. 294). B. The abbot is not readily to receive anyone into the ranks of the converse brothers without being informed regarding his character, devotion to regular observance, and zeal for the works of the community (*ibid.,* c. 1, § 1).

1586. SWABIAN CONGR. OF ST. JOSEPH. Because they often aspire to the religious life from rather human motives or from an unbalanced attachment to some phase of the life rather than from the zeal of striving for perfection, converse brothers, who are to be received for performing domestic services, must be examined and tested rigorously with regard to their spirit, their general attitude, and the intention with which they have chosen the monastic life (*Const. et declar., Pars II,* c. 5, punctum 1, *de receptione saecularium,* § 7, fol. 176).

1587. POPE CLEMENT VIII (d. 1605). When the time of probation has ended, only those are to be admitted to profession who in a new and searching examination have given proof of being capable not only of continued striving for religious perfection, but also of performing manual labor. This presupposes, of course, that they have attained the required age, namely, that clerical candidates have reached their sixteenth birthday, and the converse brothers their twenty-first. Those who have once been clothed with the habit of the converse brothers are not permitted to transfer to the clerical state even during the time of probation (*Const. Apost. Cum ad regularem,* § 16, 19 Mar., 1603, *BR* 10:776; *CJC Fontes,* n. 189, 1:362).

1588. POPE INNOCENT II (d. 1143). Although they are not monks, once your [Cistercian] converse brothers have pronounced profession in your monasteries, no archbishop, bishop, or abbot must dare to receive one of them or keep one who has already been received, without your permission (*Ep. 352 inter Ep. S. Bernardi, seu Innocentii II Papae privilegium S. Bernardo concessum, PL* 182:555).

1589. GEN. CHAPTER OF CISTERCIAN ORDER (1188). A. Let the abbots see to it that they do not accept for the lay brotherhood zealous persons who can be of greater service in the office of monks than in the manual labor of the converse brothers; such individuals should rather be placed among the monks (*Stat. Capituli Gen. anni 1188,* n. 4, *CR* 2:406; Canivez, *O. Cist.* 1:108, n. 8). B. According to the statutes of the order, from the day that he has presented his petition for admittance, which is made in the chapter of the monks, no converse brother may become a monk (*Capitulum 1237,* n. 32. Canivez, *O. Cist.* 2:174).

1590. CONGR. OF CAMALDULI. The Fathers [in the chapter of Camalduli] forbade that any of the laybrothers be permitted to become a cleric or priest (*In Reg. divi P. Benedicti, declar., Lib. I,* c. 58, p. 236; *CR* 2:268).

1591. CONGR. OF BURSFELD. The probation of laybrothers who have been accepted will be the same as that for choir novices, except that no scrutinium is held with regard to their education, nor are they subject to investigation regarding impediments to sacred orders (*Stat.,* dist. 9, c. 1, *de conversorum susceptione,* p. 295).

1592. POPE CLEMENT X (d. 1676). No brother who has been received and admitted to the habit among converse brothers is to be admitted to the clerical state in the same order and promoted to holy orders (*Const. Apost. Exponi nobis nuper,* § 3, 9 Maii, 1675, *Prohibitio ne fratres laici Ordinis Eremitarum S. Aug. transeant ad statum clericalem, BR* 18:583).

1593. S. CONGR. OF BISHOPS AND REGULARS (decree of July 9, 1837). [Permission is granted] to the same superior [Abbot Prosper Guéranger, restorer of the Order of St. Benedict in France at the monastery of Solesmes in the diocese of Le Mans] whereby he may admit to solemn vows all who have dwelt with him for four years, provided that they have already pronounced simple vows and that they make a retreat, as well as those actually dwelling in the monastery who have completed eighteen months of novitiate, subject to the decision of the superior acting with the monastic chapter. Regarding converse brothers, however, the apostolic letter which gives approval to the Constitutions of the Solesmes Benedictines prescribes as follows: "At the termination of two years and a day from the public reception of the garb (*cappae*), they are to make profession, but their vows are to be only simple" (Reiffenstuel, Anaclet., O.F.M., *Jus Canonicum Universum,* ed. V. Pelletier; Parisiis: apud Ludovicum Vivès, 1868, 5:668).

Relation of brothers to monastic community

1594. GEN. CHAPTER OF CISTERCIAN ORDER (1181). We forbid absolutely that converse brothers be present * at abbatial elections (*Stat. Cap. Gen. an. 1181,* n. 2, *CR* 2:400; Canivez, *O. Cist.* 1:88).

1595. CONGR. OF CAMALDULI. With regard to their position in the community, the converse brothers will observe rank among themselves according to the time of their respective profession, taking their place

* This seems to be the most accurate translation of *interesse* in this instance: there could hardly have been serious discussion about the brothers actually casting votes at the election, since there is question of transmitting jurisdiction, for which laymen are incapable. [*Tr.*]

after all the cleric monks; in the refectory they will have their own table, but will be served the same food as others (*In Reg. divi P. Benedicti declar., Lib. I,* c. 58, p. 235; *CR* 2:268).

1596. CISTERCIAN RULE FOR CONVERSE BROTHERS. It is observed in our order, by reason of the pious custom that was confirmed already in the time of our Father [St. Bernard], that all the converse brothers are to conduct themselves in their own choir in the same way that the monks do in their choir (*Reg. conversorum Ord. Cist.,* c. 1, *CR* 2:426).

1597. CONGR. OF CAMALDULI. The converse brothers share in all spiritual works performed in the congregation, provided that instead of the Divine Office they recite the *"Our Fathers"* and *"Hail Marys"* prescribed for them, namely forty *"Our Fathers"* for Matins, ten for Lauds, and five for each other canonical hour. . . . The Fathers voted favorably on the motion that the abbot may grant permission for those of the laybrothers who can read to recite the Little Office of the Virgin and the Office of the Dead in place of their *"Our Fathers."* They will perform these devotions in their cells, or in some quiet place, lest they be motivated by the spirit of pride, or cause admiration or scandal (*In Reg. divi P. Benedicti declar., Lib. I,* c. 58, p. 235).

1598. HERMITS OF ST. JEROME (confirmed 1571). Instead of the Divine Office, laybrothers, who are not assigned a place in choir, will recite *"Our Fathers"* and *"Hail Marys"* in this manner: for Matins they will recite them thirty times, and ten times for all other hours (*Const. et reg. Fratrum Eremitarum O.S. Hieronymi, congr. B. Petri de Pisis,* c. 6, § 1, *CR* 6:96).

1599. CONGR. OF BURSFELD. A. Besides the manual work for whose performance they are admitted into the community, converse brothers must also at specified times praise and beseech God with their prayers. . . . Seven times a day, namely at the hours of Matins [Lauds], Prime, Terce, Sext, None, Vespers, and Compline, they are to offer their praises to the Creator as do the monks. If several of them are joined together while away from their choir, the senior among them will begin: *"O God, come to my aid . . ."* and the rest will continue, *"O Lord, hasten to my assistance."* For Lauds they say: *"O God, come to my aid, O Lord, hasten to my assistance,"* etc., in its entirety, then three *"Our Fathers,"* after which the *"Glory be to the Father"* is added. This they do thirty times. They stand up and bow for the *"Glory be to the Father."* After this they say *Kyrie eleison* three times, both at Matins and at all the hours, adding, *"Through our Lord Jesus Christ,"* etc., *"Let us bless the Lord . . ."* etc. (*Stat.,* dist. 9, c. 1, *De horis et modo orandi conversorum,* n. 1. p. 297). B. At the day hours, after they have said: *"O God, come to my assistance,"* etc., and the *"Glory be to the Father,"* everything is repeated as at Matins, except that they say the *"Glory be to the Father"* eight times at Lauds, ten times at Vespers, and five times at

Prime and the other minor hours. This manner of praying will be observed by them at all times (*ibid.*, n. 4, p. 298).

1600. CONGR. OF STRASBURG. Every day the laybrothers are to recite morning prayers or the Marian Office (*cursum*) as a distinct group. When they hear the signal for meditation, they are to apply themselves to spiritual reading or meditation. When they have completed this exercise, they will work at the manual tasks to which they have been assigned until summoned for being present at the first Mass (*Declar. 10 in c. 57 RSB,* fol. 76).

1601. SWABIAN CONGR. OF ST. JOSEPH. The master of the converse brothers will assign to his charges the prayers that they daily recite in place of the Canonical Hours, namely, thirty-three *"Our Fathers"* and *"Hail Marys"* for Matins and Lauds, twelve for Vespers, and seven for each of the Day Hours (*Const. et declar., Pars III,* c. 3, punctum 3, *de magistro novitiorum,* n. 12, fol. 240).

1602. CONGR. OF MOUNT OLIVET, Olivetans, (Statutes approved by Pope Gregory XIII, 1573). The converse brothers are distinguished from the clerics by these differences in the habit: their scapular is shorter, and does not reach more than a palm's breadth below the knee, nor is it to be made of a better grade of wool (*Const., anni 1568, Pars II,* c. 85, p. 76).

1603. CONGR. OF STRASBURG. The garb [of the converse brothers] is simple, brown in color, but like the clothing of seculars. The brothers are, however, to wear a smaller scapular, of the kind in which the monks sleep (*Declar. 8 in c. 57 RSB,* fol. 74).

1604. HERMITS OF ST. AUGUSTINE (statutes approved under Pope Gregory XIII, 1580). Under no condition are laymen or the brothers allowed to wear the tonsure (*Const. Ord. Fratrum Eremitarum S. Augustini, Pars II,* c. 8, § 1, *CR* 4:251).

1605. POPE CLEMENT VIII (d. 1605). Although major attention must be devoted to training clerics, the religious instruction of the brothers must also not be neglected, but must be undertaken in a program that is not to be disturbed, for it has often been well established that since they profess the same Rule, their rounded out education not only redounds to the credit and glory of the religious life, but also gives edification and good example, and contributes to the welfare of Christ's faithful. We order that a dormitory be assigned to the brothers apart from the clerical novitiate, if this can be arranged conveniently. Regardless of this separation they are to be subject to and obey the master of novices and the superiors of monasteries and convents, according to the statutes and constitutions of each order. They are to be tried and trained by the novice master not only with regard to observances of external discipline, but are also to be carefully instructed according to their capacity and the time available in spiritual matters, especially about the manner of meditating. In order for this to be accomplished more conveniently, they must be summoned and be present in church at the prescribed times for the chapters and spiritual conferences commonly given by the novice masters, unless at such hours they are actually at their assigned duties (*Const. Apost. Cum ad regularem,* § 33, 19 Mar., 1603, *BR* 10:775; *CJC Fontes,* n. 189, 1:361).

1606. CONGR. OF BURSFELD. After the candidate has been received, he is assigned to the master of the brothers, who will watch over him carefully, instruct him in religious doctrine, and teach him about the order (*Stat.,* dist. 9, c. 1, § 1, p. 295).

1607. CONGR. OF STRASBURG. We prescribe and insist firmly that, according to their capacity the laybrothers be instructed in spiritual doctrine, especially with regard to the manner of devoting themselves to mental prayer (*Declar. 17 in c. 58 RSB,* fol. 82).

1608. SWABIAN CONGR. OF ST. JOSEPH. He who has charge of laybrother novices must teach them the catechism, their prayers, the exercises to be performed morning and evening at the examination of conscience, the manner of making a reverent and accurate confession, the manner of communicating devoutly, the recitation of the Rosary, and other lessons that are within their grasp. . . . He will, moreover, instruct them on the benefit they should derive from listening to sacred reading which he will read and explain for them at the appointed times. For this exercise he will select German works on the life of Christ, or other simply written spiritual books. He must train them to formulate their intention so that they can perform their manual labor with greater merit and help them to learn to deny themselves, practice mortification, wage war against vices, and advance in the practice of virtues, particularly patience, obedience, and humility (*Const. et declar., Pars III,* c. 3, punctum 3, § 12, fol. 240).

1609. CONGR. OF STRASBURG. We seriously admonish all brethren, particularly priests, not to be unreasonable in imposing duties on laybrothers, nor to speak harshly to them. By admitting them to profession we granted them brotherhood in our religious family. Hence it is no more than proper that we embrace them in the spirit of brotherly love and bear their weaknesses as well as those of others. Failure in this obligation will result in that the brothers, overwhelmed with sadness, will have the impression that they have been reduced to a kind of servitude (*Declar. 13 in c. 57 RSB,* fol. 76).

Monastic studies

1610. POPE BENEDICT XII (d. 1342). Since the pearl of wisdom is acquired by the practice of reading, and the mind attains to a knowledge of the divine excellence through the study of the sacred books and is ennobled and more surely prepared for the living of a righteous life by the recognition of human law, We desire that the men of the order [of St. Benedict] who are working in the Lord's vineyard be instructed in the basic disciplines, and afterward in the sciences of divine and human law. We wish and firmly command that all adhere to the Constitutions of Pope Clement V, Our predecessor, about instructing monks in elementary disciplines within monasteries [next paragraph]. We prescribe and ordain, moreover, that all cathedral churches, monasteries, priories, and other conventual establishments which have the means for doing so, have a teacher of the order who will instruct the monks in these elementary disciplines, namely, grammar, logic, and philosophy. We also prescribe that no seculars be admitted with the monks for the purpose of being taught these disciplines (*Const. Apost. Summi magistri,* c. 6, 20 Jun., 1336, *ordinationes et reformationes pro bono regimine monachorum Nigrorum O.S.B., BR* 4:357).

1611. POPE CLEMENT V (d. 1314). Lest the opportunity for advancing in knowledge be wanting to the monks, let a capable master who will train them diligently in the basic disciplines be retained in all monasteries where they have the means of doing so (*Clementinarum Lib. III,* tit. X, *de statu monachorum,* c. 1, § 8, *CJC* Richter 2:1087).

1612. COUNCIL OF TRENT. In the monasteries of monks also, where this can conveniently be done, let there be instructions in the Holy Scriptures (*Sessio V,* c. 1, *de ref. Can. et decr.,* Richter, p. 17; Schroeder, *Trent,* p. 25).*

1613. POPE CLEMENT VIII (d. 1605). Twice a week, on fixed days, a lecture on Sacred Scripture or on cases of conscience will be held in each monastery, at which the brethren must all attend. When the lecture has been completed, they will all cooperate in conducting exercises for one another on the doctrine that has been explained (*Const. Apost. Nullus omnino,* § 1, 25 Jul., 1599, *Decreta generalia pro reformatione regularium, BR* 10:663; *CJC Fontes,* n. 187, 1:354).

1614. POPE GREGORY XVI (d. 1846). Since doctrine must be the inseparable companion and associate of uprightness of morals, integrity of life, and the observance of regular discipline, you will see to the restoration of studies in this monastery [Alta Comba, Cistercian order], particularly of those disciplines which pertain to the sacred ministry (*Litterae Apost. Maximas inter,* § 4, 19 Jun., 1832, *Archiepisc. Camberiensi, Acta Gregorii Papae XVI* 1:149, Romae: ex Typographia Polyglotta S. C. de Prop. Fidei, 1901. *In his litteris statuitur deputatio visitatoris apostolici qui collapsam disciplinam restituat in Cisterc. monast. Alta Comba*).

1615. CONGR. OF CAMALDULI. A. We must not remain silent regard-

* In the remaining portions of this long chapter there is question of a chair or lectureship in Scripture, a somewhat pretentious class assigned to more able scholars by general or provincial chapters. [*Tr.*]

ing some who think that the sentence of Blessed Jerome in the sacred canons (*c. XVI,* q. 1, c. 4, *monachus, CJC* Richter 1:654) where it is said that "the duty of the monk is not to teach, but to bewail" is an argument against us. The holy doctor speaks in this passage of those monks who dwelt in forests and were not educated in the sacred sciences. But who in his right mind would say that priests who now live in cities, perform sacred functions, hear the confessions of sinners, and are consulted by many concerning their souls' welfare should not be skilled in the sacred law and otherwise learned? Consider further that those about whom St. Jerome speaks could avoid idleness in other ways, devoting themselves to manual labor and the cultivation of fields, which is not true of the monks of our times. And who, pray tell, was Jerome? Was he not also a monk? Who, we ask, was Basil?—and Gregory? Where they not all monks? And nevertheless by their teachings they did much to contribute to the learning of the Church of Christ. Let all who offer their objections be silent, then. Moreover, our problems have come to the point where if they are not remedied by sacred studies, it will necessarily follow that all religious life will perish. Charity, the love of Christ, and devotion, have grown so cold that they have been cast forth from the monasteries to a large extent, and unless they are revived by reading sacred books and prayer, we have not served our purpose. Arise, therefore, men of Camalduli, ruthlessly cast off idleness, quicken your minds, lift up your souls, so devote yourselves to literary studies that you can no longer be called worthless coins and born to consume fruits (*In Reg. divi P. Benedicti declar., Lib. I,* c. 47, p. 195).

B. Since priests who are ignorant of Sacred Scripture are often seriously criticized, and the great and good God has threatened that he will reject those priests who cast aside his law and knowledge (Osee 4:6), it is impossible for unlettered religious to perform the Divine Office properly and to the spiritual benefit of the people. Therefore our Fathers, in commenting on that part of the Rule [of St. Benedict] which reads: "Let no one presume to sing or read . . ." following the example of well-established religious institutes, severely command the prelates of the undersigned monasteries to choose, on the advice of their seniors, those young men who are capable of learning, and assign them teachers who will diligently teach them first grammar, then rhetoric and the other liberal arts which are becoming to the religious man and contribute much to the understanding of Sacred Scripture. Finally, they are to devote themselves wholly to those studies without which it would be dangerous and almost impossible to hear confessions. If they do not have such teachers in their monasteries, they are to be procured from some other religious institute (*ibid.,* p. 193; *CR* 2:254).

1616. CONGR. OF BURSFELD. A. Because our holy order grew in piety and advanced doctrine, it bore most worthy fruits for the Church of God. Let us cling steadfastly to the traditions of our forebears and obey the command of our holy Father by being occupied every day at certain times in divine reading. Let the superiors, therefore, see to it that the monks lack nothing at all that would prevent them from being occupied with philosophy, theology, and other disciplines, especially those that lead to the understanding of Sacred Scripture according to the decrees of Pope Benedict XII and other Supreme Pontiffs (*Stat.,* dist. 1, c. 5, *de seminario et studio,* n. 1, p. 61). B. In charge of these studies are to be placed masters who are so endowed with prudence, maturity, and religious spirit that they are able to teach the doctrines by word and example, and would not dare to teach or defend novel opinions that are not commonly held and are less safe, in opposition to the mind of the Church or the explanation of the Fathers (*ibid.,* n. 2, p. 62). C. In every monastery courses are to be given in philosophy, theology, and particularly moral, in order not only that the brethren will spend their time profitably, but that they may perfect themselves in the literary studies and the understanding of Sacred Scripture for contributing to the growth of the Catholic Church (*ibid.,* n. 6, p. 63). D. Without the required testimonials of approval both of the Ordinary and the president [of the congregation], and the permission of his abbot, no one is to dare to publish anything (*ibid.,* n. 7, p. 64).

1617. CONGR. OF STRASBURG. It is contrary to monastic discipline to be listless and inactive, and abandon the principles of the Fathers of our order who in times past made their contributions to the Church in many fields of learning. Hence we are to flee all time-killing and avoid all laziness and trifling, which are the effective poison of the devil. We can then devote ourselves more intensely to the contemplation of Sacred Scripture, so that neither this gem of knowledge nor others will be lacking in our congregation. By this present regulation we prescribe that if possible in all monasteries where there are at least twelve monks, philosophy, scholastic and positive theology, and the sacred canons be taught, passing over all useless questions, and concentrating particularly on those matters which pertain to philosophy in its practical application, dogma, the direction of souls, Church history, and ethics (*Declar. 9,* c. 47, *RSB,* fol. 61).

1618. SWABIAN CONGR. OF ST. JOSEPH. During the hours set aside for that purpose, all must apply themselves with zeal and diligence to the study of letters. Summoning the Divine Judge to witness, we exhort in a particular manner those who have charge of instructing the religious youth in moral conduct and their studies. . . . We admonish all and exhort them earnestly never to allow the love of learning to cause neglect of spiritual exercises which for the religious must always hold the first place. As Gerson * states most correctly, on the day of judgment we will not be asked what we have read, but what we have done; not how well we have discoursed, but how religiously we have lived (cf. Thomas à Kempis, *de imitatione Christi, Lib. I,* c. 3, n. 5, *Op. Om.* 2:8; Gardiner, p. 35). We warn them also to devote themselves to subjects that are profitable and which can be of use to them, not to those that are empty or intended merely to gratify curiosity, or which are even altogether foreign to the religious way of life (*Const. et declar., Pars II,* c. 3, punctum 2, *de laboribus et studiis fratrum,* nn. 1, 3, fol. 88–89).

1619. PROV. COUNCIL OF PRAGUE (1860). Conferences and practical exercises in theological questions or other useful matters are to be held frequently and, according to the prescription of the Council of Trent, a professor of Sacred Scripture is never to be wanting (*Sess. V,* c. I, *de ref. Can. et decr.,* Richter, p. 17; Schroeder, *Trent,* p. 25). Monastic studies should not only equal in merit the efforts of others but should excel them (*Decr.,* tit. 7, c. 4, *de regularium studiis et cura animarum, CL* 5:577).

1620. PROV. COUNCIL OF UTRECHT (1865). Superiors must be most vigilant in seeing to it that the proper ratio studiorum be adhered to and encouraged in their monasteries, each according to the laws of his own order, and that conferences and practical cases on theological matters and helpful training in other disciplines be held frequently among the members of the religious houses (*Decr.,* tit. 7, c. 2, *de regularium regimine et disciplina, CL* 5:893).

1621. PROV. COUNCIL OF COLOCZA (Hungary, 1863). We are to be occupied especially with Holy Scripture . . . the monuments of tradition, the writings of the Fathers, the decrees of the councils, especially those of Trent, and the provincial councils, diocesan statutes, and the sanctions of the canons. Commentaries on the liturgy and ceremonies are to be reviewed and meditated upon (*Decr.,* tit. 4, c. 6, *de studiis in sacerdotio prosequendis, CL* 5:673).

1622. POPE PAUL V (d. 1621). By the constitution which is to bind perpetually, We sanction, prescribe, and order by the plenitude of Apostolic power bestowed on Us, that in the studies of every order and institute of regulars, however exempt they may be and immediately subject to the jurisdiction of the Apostolic See, there be teachers of all three languages, namely Hebrew, Greek, and Latin, and in the larger and more renowned houses Arabic as well. These teachers are to be regulars and belong to the house and order, if it has men possessing sufficient knowledge of these languages, otherwise, seculars or regulars

* The constitutions refer to Gerson as the author of the *Imitation of Christ,* according to the common opinion of the time in Germany. [*Tr.*]

of other orders (*Const. Apost. Apostolicae servitutis onere,* § 2, 31 Jul. 1610, *BR* 11:626).

The library

1623. CONGR. OF BURSFELD. The librarian is to have charge of all monastery books that are not for use in the Divine Office. He will keep a record of them according to authors and titles, and often check them to make certain that they are not torn apart, that no pages are worm-eaten, damaged, or otherwise harmed. He is frequently to go over them also for the purpose of seeing if any forbidden or heretical works are found there: such books are to be kept locked up and the librarian is not to withdraw them for anyone who has not obtained special permission to read them. A person who has not obtained such permission and is found reading these books will be punished severely (*Stat.,* dist. 3, c. 6, *de armario seu bibliothecario,* n. 1, p. 97).

1624. CONGR. OF CAMALDULI. Since it is impossible to devote oneself to studies without books, [the fathers of the general chapter] order superiors of the monasteries already mentioned to erect, each in his monastery, a library with those books that are considered necessary. One monk is to be put in charge of the library. Without his permission or that of the superior no one is to enter the library except the juniors who are studying there. The abbot will place a senior over them to keep them within the bounds of religious conduct, lest by the occasion of their studies they give themselves over to frivolity (*In Reg. divi P. Benedicti declar., Lib. I,* c. 47, p. 194).

1625. CONGR. OF STRASBURG. A. The librarian is to employ the utmost care in seeing to it that the books entrusted to him are not lost or damaged. He will bear in mind that he must give an account as of a violation of poverty if because of his negligence any loss is suffered. Since the library is one of the most attractive features of the order and its abbeys, we admonish the [abbots] and urge them not to be sparing in buying carefully selected books, so that those who visit our monasteries will be edified; will perceive that we cling to the traditions of our ancient Fathers for (the welfare of) the Christian state; promote studies according to our means; and furnish our monks with the things that are most becoming for religious men (*Declar. 10 in c. 48 RSB,* fol. 63). B. For the office of librarian let there be chosen a man who possesses prudence, scholarship, skill in languages and love of study (*ibid., Declar. 11*).

Example and intercession of the saints

1626. ROMAN MISSAL. A. O God, having deigned to provide for your Church Blessed Jerome, your confessor, a great Doctor, for expounding the Sacred Scriptures, may you grant, we beseech you, that through his merits we may be enabled by your assistance to practice what he has taught us in word and deed (*In fest. S. Hieronymi, 30 Sept., Oratio, Miss. Rom.,* p. 850). B. O God, may you who have enlightened your Church with the learning of Blessed Bede, your confessor and Doctor, mercifully grant your servants ever to be illumined by his wisdom and assisted by his merits (*In fest. S. Bedae Ven., 27 Maii, Oratio, ibid.,* p. 676). C. Hearken to us, O God, our Savior, that as we rejoice in the festival of Blessed Teresa, your virgin, so we may find food for the nourishment of our souls in her heavenly doctrine, and be instructed by the affection of pious devotion (*In fest. S. Teresiae, Virg., 15 Oct., Oratio, ibid.,* p. 868). D. O God, may you who enlighten your Church with the wondrous learning of Blessed Thomas, your confessor, and make it fruitful with his holy labors, grant us, we beseech you, both to understand what he taught and to imitate what he practiced (*In fest. S. Thomae de Aq., 7 Mar., Oratio, ibid.,* p. 600). E. As a teacher you both instruct and observe the law of the heavenly Divinity; merely to know the law avails not; we must diligently strive to fulfil it (*In fest. S. Joannis Cantii, 20 Oct., hymn. ad Vesp., vers. 2, Breviar. Roman.* 4:796).

The vow of holy obedience

1627. POPE JOHN XXII (d. 1334). Poverty is indeed an outstanding virtue, but chastity is greater, and, if it is kept inviolate, obedience is the greatest of the three. For the first is a mastery over material things, the second over the flesh, but the third over the soul and the mind, by which the humble man, by the operation of his own will, subjects that will, unbridled and free, to the government of another (*C. 1, Extravagantes Joannis XXII,* tit. 14, *de verborum significatione, CJC* Richter 2:1137).

1628. POPE CLEMENT XII (d. 1740). The monk must, without any rationalizing, consider his abbot as holding the place of Christ; obey him in all things, sin excepted; reverence him in honor and love, both interiorly and in external expression; decide nothing without having consulted him. He is not to pry minutely into the abbot's government with reference to the brethren. He must openly manifest to the abbot his own personal way of life, both with regard to his virtuous deeds, and those which are not what they should be. Without the abbot's knowledge and consent he is not to hold lectures, write treatises, preach or teach; nor is he to send or receive a letter without showing it to him beforehand; without consulting him the monk is not to assume any responsibility either by holding another's property in safe-keeping or retaining such property in trust, nor give or receive anything in the form of a loan, nor bestow or petition alms except with the abbot's approval, having observed in all these matters the formalities of law and having obtained the required permission from the proper superior (*Const. Apost. Misericordiarum pater, Pars I,* c. 1, *de obedientia,* nn. 1–10, 17 Jan., 1740, *Confirmatio reg. et const. monachorum maronitarum O.S. Antonii, congr. S. Isaiae in Syria, BR* 24:605).

1629. PROV. COUNCIL OF ESZTERGOM (Gran, Hungary, 1858). Obedience must be perfect in the sense that each person . . . offer complete submission to the laws, constitutions, and rules of his order as they have been confirmed by the Apostolic See. But everyone must also submit, and not with a lesser obedience, to the orders and appointments of the superior, in whom he is to behold God. For *there exists no authority except from God* . . . [and] *he who resists the authority resists the ordinance of God; and they that resist bring on themselves condemnation* (Rom. 13:1–2; *Decr.,* tit. 7, *de regularibus,* § 2, *CL* 5:65).

1630. PROV. COUNCIL OF PRAGUE (1860). Obedience constitutes the greatest good, and properly speaking, the very soul of the regular life, for by it religion governs not only exterior things and the flesh, but the mind and the spirit as well (*Decr.,* tit. 7, c. 3, *de obligationibus regularium, CL* 5:575).

1631. PROV. COUNCIL OF UTRECHT (1865). Obedience is the virtue most proper to those who have denied themselves in order to follow the Lord, for by it they have abandoned their own judgment and pleasure, and govern not only external things and the flesh, but the mind as well and the spirit (*Decr.,* tit. 7, c. 1, *de perfectione religiosa, CL* 5:891).

Obedience is the spirit of the Rule

1632. CONGR. OF BURSFELD. Obedience, which the holy Father [Benedict] commands of his disciples before all else, and which in the judgment of many doctors constitutes the very spirit of our Rule, is to be observed with the worthiest effort by all. The holy Father demands a will that is docile in obedience even when impossible things are commanded (*RSB,* c. 68); he desires this will to be swift, blind [*caecam:* nowhere is the word employed or implied by Benedict—*Tr.*], given with a good will (*RSB,* c. 5), patient and persevering (*ibid.,* c. 7, fourth degree of humility), and to be offered to the superior as to God (*ibid.,* c. 5). Hence this obedience is to be practiced most worthily by all the brethren in all matters. It is severely forbidden for anyone to presume to examine the commands of the superior to see whether they fall under obedience or not; rather, both in disposition and in deed, let obedience be offered humbly and simply by everyone in all observances that are not shown to be obviously opposed to the divine or the natural law (*Stat.,* dist. 5, c. 1, § 3, pp. 119–120).

1633. CONGR. OF STRASBURG. *I have come down from heaven, not to do my own will, but the will of him who sent me* (John 6:38). Monks are to be solicitous in seeing to it that they bear the likeness to the figure of Christ the Lord in all things. Therefore no one in the monastery is to follow the desire of his own heart, or his own judgment, but walking by another's judgment and orders, he is to do nothing, however insignificant it may be, without the command of the abbot, for what is done without the knowledge and permission of the spiritual father will be ascribed to presumption and vainglory and not reckoned meritorious (*RSB*, c. 49). But if anyone acts contrary to the orders and command of the superior, he is to accuse himself of his fault in the chapter and accept the punishment from the hands of the abbot or the prior according to the seriousness of the transgression (*Declar. unica in c. 5 RSB*, fol. 13).

1634. SWABIAN CONGR. OF ST. JOSEPH. Our holy Father demands of us not just any sort of obedience, but that which is perfect, absolute in its kind, not a timorous, nor a tardy, nor a tepid, nor a reluctant, nor a perfunctory obedience, nor a submission that consists in the mere physical performance of the work assigned, but rather that which conforms and subjects our judgment and our will entirely to the judgment and will of the superior, so that we judge, will, and refuse what the superiors judge, will, and refuse. In order to excite us to this ready generosity of obedience and submission of mind he wanted us to consider superiors not in the light of mere men liable to their own errors and weaknesses, but in their capacity of holding the place of God. St. Benedict was firmly convinced that no one could reflect that it is God who commands through the superiors, and who through their commands rightly and wisely orders all things to externally appointed ends of his divine providence (even though these remain hidden from us for the time being), who would not promptly and willingly render obedience and subject himself wholly to the divine will. "They are truly obedient," says our holy Father Benedict, "who live not by their own will, and obey not their own desires and passions, but walk by another's judgment and command . . . and with swift obedience follow up with their deeds the voice of him who commands them" (*RSB*, c. 5). Again he says: "But this obedience will then be acceptable to God . . . if what is commanded be not done timorously, or tardily, or tepidly, nor with murmuring or the raising of objections. For the obedience which is given to superiors is given to God" (*ibid*).

In order, therefore, that we may always and without difficulty conform ourselves to the will and judgment of our superiors—for such a disposition is required for the perfection of obedience—and in order that we may render our obedience readily and cheerfully, we must, according to our holy Father's command, recognize in the person of superiors, the authority and wisdom of Christ which is directing us, through their commands, to eternal salvation. To employ the words of St. Caesarius of Arles: "Accept whatever has been commanded of you by your superiors as coming from heaven, as though it had issued forth from the mouth of God. Do not refuse anything, do not criticize anything. For you came to the monastery to serve, not to rule; to obey rather than to command. Hence look upon every order given you or others by the superior as wholly sacred, entirely just, and useful for us (*S. Caesarii Arelatensis sermones . . . studio et diligentia D. Germani Morin . . . O.S.B., Serm. 233,* § 6, *Corpus Christianorum Series Latina 104:928*). In so acting we shall show ourselves to be genuine and truly obedient sons of our holy Father (*Const. et declar., Pars II,* c. 2, punctum 3, fol. 60–63).

1635. ROMAN-MONASTIC MISSAL. O God, who to give us a pattern of obedience to follow, made the blessed abbot Maur to walk dryshod on the waters, grant that we may become worthy to practice the teachings given to us by his virtues and to obtain a share in his reward (*In fest. S. Mauri abb., 15 Jan., Oratio, Missae propriae et kalendarium,* p. 2).

1636. ROMAN BREVIARY. Christ became obedient to death for us, even to the death on the cross; therefore God also exalted him and has bestowed upon him the name that is above every name (*Versiculus post "Benedictus" in Laud. Sabb. Sancti, Breviar. Rom. 2:592*).

Excellence of obedience

1637. POPE PIUS IX. The virtue of religious perfection lies principally in this: that they who embrace the regular life, besides the renunciation of material goods and the profession of chastity, are obliged to deny themselves and offer the perpetual holocaust of their self-will to God. Nothing, therefore, is so conducive to the restoration and preservation of regular discipline as a painstaking and faithful observance of religious obedience, for it implants other virtues in the soul and guards those it has planted (*S. Greg. Magni Moral., Lib. 35,* c. 10, *PL* 76:765). Poverty is indeed great, but integrity [chastity] is greater, and obedience, if preserved intact, is the greatest of the three; for the first governs material things; the second, the flesh; but the third the mind and the soul (*Joan. XXII, Extrav.,* tit. 14, c. 1, *de verb. signific., CJC* Richter 2:1137). Hence if the vow of obedience is neglected, the hearts of the religious become parched like soil without moisture; nor will they longer find their delight in humility, prayer, and meditation; rather, the religious family's bond of unity is shattered.

1638. Therefore, adhering to the decrees of the sacred Council of Trent, in order that religious discipline may be the more readily and firmly restored where it has collapsed, and may be preserved more constantly where it has been maintained, with the approval of the Sacred

Council, We command all regulars, men and women, of whatever religious family, society, congregation, or institute, to order and regulate their lives according to the prescript of the rule that they have professed, to observe the precepts and the vows, and especially to submit willingly in perfect obedience, with their gaze fixed on Christ, the crucified Lord, who in becoming obedient unto death (cf. Phil. 2:8), not only commanded this virtue, but left us the great example in his own person for us to imitate.

1639. And since there exists no authority except from God (cf. Rom. 13:1), all regulars are to recognize God himself in their superiors, and to be mindful that he who resists the authority not only resists the ordinance of God (*loc. cit.*), but also are bound by a distinctive obligation in virtue of the vow they have made to God in pronouncing their profession. Consequently, they are to obey all their superiors with due reverence and love, and fulfil whatever they enjoin according to the rule, completely, promptly, humbly, and without offering any excuses.

1640. We further exhort them to devote themselves with their whole heart to attaining perfection in this eminent virtue which is, in a sense, the mother and guardian of all virtues (cf. St. Aug., *De civitate Dei, Lib. 14,* c. 12, *PL* 41:420; Dods, p. 460); and that in every way and vigorously they guard against the evil spirit of the world which is the enemy of the cross of Christ and of all authority and submission * (*Acta*

* In both the Old and the New Testaments Holy Scripture frequently inculcates the necessity of the virtue of obedience. The holy Fathers of both the Greek and the Latin Church who were formed in this divine school, are in agreement. They not only show the necessity of obedience, but its excellence among the other moral virtues. Thus St. Gregory the Great: "Obedience is rightly preferred to sacrifices, because in the offering of sacrifice another's body is slain, whereas by obedience we slay our own will. . . . Hence it is said by Solomon with reference to obedience: *An obedient man shall speak of victory* (Prov. 21:28, Douay version). An obedient man speaks of victory in very truth, because when we humbly submit ourselves to the command of another, we overcome ourselves in our heart" (*Moral., Lib. 35,* c. 15, § 28, *PL* 76:765).

"Among the moral virtues," as St. Thomas points out, "the greater the thing which man contemns that he may adhere to God, the greater the virtue. Now there are three kinds of human goods which man may contemn for God's sake. The lowest of these are external goods, the goods of the body take the middle place; and the highest are the goods of the soul; and among these the chief, in a way, is the will, insofar as by his will man makes use of all other goods. . . . Wherefore even any other acts of virtue are meritorious before God through being performed out of obedience to God's will. For were one to suffer even martyrdom, or to give all one's goods to the poor, unless one directed these things to the fulfilment of the divine will, which pertains directly to obedience, they could not be meritorious: as neither would they be if they were done without charity, which cannot exist apart from obedience" (*II-II,* q. 104, art. 3, *Op. Om.* 9:387; Am. ed. 2:1643).

These explanations of the virtue of obedience in general terms apply in a special manner to religious who are bound by vow to observe it, and who must,

et decr. Concilii Vaticani: Schema XVI de regularibus, De voto obedientiae, CL 7:674).

IV. WRITINGS OF SAINTS AND DOCTORS

Man created for work

1641. ST. BASIL THE GREAT. A. When God created man, he willed not that man should be sluggish and lazy but that he be actively engaged and willing to undertake his tasks, for he commanded Adam to labor in paradise and to cultivate it (cf. Gen. 2:15). After Adam had been banished from this paradise, God proclaimed that he was to eat his bread in the sweat of his face (*ibid.,* 3:19). From the nature of the consideration, it is manifest that what was said to Adam was stated for all who were to take their origin from him. . . . For that matter, we can also confirm our statement by such testimony from the Divine Scriptures. . . . I give you a witness most worthy of belief, St. Paul, who says: *We have heard that some among you are living irregularly, doing no work* (II Thess. 3:11). In fact, he goes so far as to call sluggishness an abandoning of order: *For we were not unruly while with you, neither did we eat any man's bread at his cost, but we worked night and day in*

---

consequently, keep in mind that these praises through obedience are owed to God, whoever is the superior to whom it is offered, for he holds the place of God, from whom all right-ordered power descends. . . . But in order for obedience to be perfect, it not only demands that what is commanded by the superior according to the rule be performed with exactness and faithfulness, but also, that with regard to the matter commanded, as far as possible the will and the judgment of the subject be submitted and conformed to the will and judgment of the superior who governs as God's representative: for as Cassian states: "By no vice does the devil draw the monk so precipitately to death, as by neglecting the counsels of the seniors he induces him to repose his confidence in his own judgment and decision" (*Collatio 2, Abbatis Moysis, de discretione, PL* 49:541). St. Bernard addresses those who resent the commands that are less pleasing to them: "If you begin to receive such orders with a spirit of unwillingness, to judge the intentions of your superior, to murmur in your heart, even though you externally fulfil the duty imposed, such is not the virtue of obedience, but only a cloak for malice" (*Serm. de temp., Serm. III in Circumcis. Dni.* § 8, *PL* 183:140).

Now, when this perfect obedience shall flower in religious families, all other virtues will without doubt also flourish and will produce the fruits of holiness which are willed and demanded by the saintly founders who instituted the orders, by the Apostolic See which approved and confirmed them, and by the society which supports them. Experience proves this for us. In those orders in which the holy vow of obedience is kept accurately and faithfully, all other prescriptions are observed and all virtues are exercised: the spirt of unity and concord among the brethren; dedication to mental and vocal prayer; zeal for divine worship; contempt of things of this world; self-denial, meekness, humility, interior and exterior mortification, love of neighbor, for whose welfare each one generously spends himself (*Schema constitutionis super voto obedientiae Patrum examini propositum, ibid.,* pp. 672, 673).

labor and toil (*ibid.*, vv. 7–8). And elsewhere: *Such persons we charge and exhort in the Lord Jesus Christ that they work quietly and eat their own bread* (v. 12; *Const. monasticae*, c. 4, *PG* 31:1347). B. But why should we dwell upon the amount of evil there is in idleness, when the Apostle clearly prescribes that he who does not work should not eat (cf. II Thess. 3:10). As daily sustenance is necessary for everyone, so labor in proportion to one's strength is also essential. . . . The Lord couples sloth with wickedness, saying: *Wicked and slothful servant* (Matt. 25:26). . . . We have reason to fear, therefore, lest, perchance, on the day of judgment this fault also may be alleged against us, since he who has endowed us with the ability to work demands that our labor be proportioned to our capacity; for he says: *Of him to whom they have entrusted much they will demand the more* (Luke 12:48; *Reg. fusius tractatae, Interrogatio 37*, col. 1011; Wagner, p. 307).

1642. ST. JOHN CHRYSOSTOM. When Moses wrote: *The Lord God took the man and placed him in the garden of Eden,* he added: *to till it and keep it* (Gen. 2:15). Since those who dwelt there were to enjoy all delights, both in the pleasure given by everything that they beheld and in the joy of the things given for their use, God commanded man *to till and keep it* in order to prevent him from becoming haughty through having everything too much to his liking (for it is through idleness that man learned all evil). But why, one will ask, did paradise stand in need of this care that man was to give it? I am not saying that paradise needed man's care, but rather that God willed man to bestow some care on it proportioned to his strength, both by keeping it and by tilling it. For if he were altogether without toil, man would forthwith have fallen into laziness from too much leisure. But now that he is engaged in working, which would carry with it neither pain nor hardships, he would have to be more temperate and moderate in his desires (*In c. 2 Gen., Hom. 14*, § 2, *PG* 53:113).

1643. ST. BERNARD. When we read that Adam was put into the paradise of pleasure to till it and keep it (cf. Gen. 2:15), who would reasonably maintain that his children have been put in this place of trial in order to rest from work? (*Serm. de diversis, serm. 15, de quaerenda sapientia*, § 1, *PL* 183:577.)

Work is also in punishment of sin

1644. JOHN OF TRITHEIM, abbot of Sponheim (d. 1516). *For you shall eat the fruit of your handiwork,* says the Prophet of the Lord. *Happy shall you be, and favored* (Ps. 127:2). If all who eat by the labor of their hands are considered blessed, certainly no idle person can eat bread without a sense of guilt and sin. For the all-powerful God inflicted this penalty upon his creature Adam for the transgression of the original command, assuring him that in the sweat of his brow he should produce his food from the earth with his hands. Now, since we all sinned in Adam, we are necessarily subject to the same punishment, to which we are taught he was subjected (cf. Gen. 3:17 f.). He produced his food with his hands and did not eat his bread in idleness (*Hom. 7, de labore manuali monachorum, Op. pia et spiritualia,* p. 434).

The monk a man of work

1645. ST. EPIPHANIUS, bp. of Cyprus (d. 403). Monks labor in their individual monasteries, both in Egypt and in other lands where they are found, as though they were bees, holding the wax of their labor in their hands, and with drops of honey in their mouth, for according to their understanding they praise the Lord of all things with their hymn-pronouncing voices (*Adv. haereses, Lib. III,* tom. 2, *Haeresis 80,* § 4, *PG* 42:762).

1646. ST. AUGUSTINE. I would much rather every day at certain hours, as much as is appointed by rule in well-governed monasteries, do some work with my hands, and have the remaining hours free for reading and praying, or some work pertaining to divine letters, than have to bear these most annoying perplexities of other men's problems about secular matters, which we must either by adjudicating bring to an end, or by intervention cut short (*De opere monachorum,* c. 29, § 37, *PL* 40:576).

The evil of idleness

1647. JOHN OF TRITHEIM. A. Our holy Father Benedict, in abomination of idleness among monks, states in the Rule which is his legacy to us: "Idleness is the enemy of the soul. The brethren, therefore, must be occupied at stated hours in manual labor, and again at other hours in divine reading. . . . For then they are truly monks when they live by the labor of their hands, like our fathers and the apostles" (*RSB,* c. 48). Hence, too, St. Paul, that great lover of Christ, says in his epistle: *If any man will not work, neither let him eat* (II Thess. 3:10).

In the origins of the monastic state it was the custom to admit no one into the brotherhood without the performance of manual labor, not so much as a matter of necessity to support themselves as for their spiritual welfare, lest the occasion for evil thoughts be given through idleness. The monks in those days had no property, no tithes, no support received from rentals, no annual income, but procured food and clothing by the mutual cooperation of all in manual labor, not burdening anyone with the payment of their support. Although they enjoyed the right of living by the preaching of the Gospel, the holy Apostles of our Savior preferred to work with their hands, lest they seem to burden the faithful, and also so that they would not only have sufficient for supporting themselves, but could minister as well what was necessary for the needy. . . . *Man,* Scripture tells us, *is born to labor as the bird is to fly* (cf. Job 5:7, Douay version). Hence lest you eat your bread in idleness you should always be engaged in some worthy and useful work in which the mind will be relieved of the tedium of regular observance and through which serious want will be to some degree forestalled. We have the custom of going outside the enclosure of the monastery to work only at harvest time and in Autumn to the vineyard, when, namely, the need of labor is great and the scarcity of day laborers increases the wages of servants. We have ruled the rest of the time the monks are to remain in the abbey (*Hom. VII, de labore monachorum manuali, Op. pia et spiritualia,* p. 434). B. If they who live by their manual labor are truly monks (*RSB,* c. 48), it follows that they are not monks in truth who, living in idleness, spurn work. He who is not a true monk in the abbey, what, I ask you, *is* he? He is not a monk who is not a true monk, for whatever stands in opposition to truth is not what it should be. But whatever is not what it should be contradicts the Supreme Truth who established the right order of being for all things. And therefore, it is in reality not what it should be. Hence we must labor, brethren, so as not to offend the Apostle by eating in idleness; and also so as not to cease being that which we entered the enclosure of the monastery to be (*De laude scriptorum manualium,* c. 5, p. 747). C. Idleness is the mother, the source of all vices, the death of all virtue. For it fruitlessly and shamefully squanders "the acceptable time" (cf. II Cor. 6:2); it abandons the fostering of virtues; it suggests lustful imaginations; it decreases one's forces; it kills the soul. Flee idleness, you who desire to attain everlasting life, for this life is promised not to the idle but to those who work in the proper manner. Slothfulness is particularly reprehensible in monks, for they have not been summoned from activity to ease, but from sloth to labor: ". . . that by the labor of obedience you may return to him from whom you have strayed by the sloth of disobedience" (*RSB, Prolog.*). You vowed the reformation of your life according to monastic principles (*conversionem morum tuorum*), which so prescribe that monks work that it even denies that the idle are monks at all (*ibid.,* c. 13, pp. 758, 759).

Work to be joined with prayer

1648. ST. BASIL THE GREAT. Because some use prayer and psalmody as an excuse for neglecting their work, it is necessary to bear in mind that for certain other tasks a particular time is allotted according to the words of Ecclesiastes: *There is an appointed time for everything* (Eccles. 3:1). For prayer and psalmody, however, as also, indeed, for some other duties, every hour is suitable, that, while our hands are busy at their tasks, we may praise God sometimes with the tongue (when this is possible, or, rather, when it is conducive to edification) or, if not, with the heart, at least, in psalms, hymns, and spiritual canticles, as it is written (cf. Col. 3:16). Thus, in the midst of our work we can fulfil the duty of prayer, giving thanks to him who has granted strength to our hands for performing our tasks and cleverness to our minds for acquiring knowledge, and for having provided the materials, both that which is in the instruments we use and that which forms the matter of the arts in which we may be engaged, praying that the work of our hands may be directed toward its goal, the good pleasure of God. Thus we acquire a recollected spirit—when in every action we beg from God the success of our labors and satisfy our debt of gratitude to him who gave us the power to do the work, and when, as has been said, we keep before our minds the aim of pleasing him. If this is not the case, how can there be consistency in the words of the Apostle bidding us to *pray without ceasing* (I Thess. 5:17), with those others, *we worked night and day* (II Thess. 3:8; *Reg. fusius tractatae, Interrogatio 37,* nn. 2, 3, *PG* 31:1011; Wagner, 307 f.).

1649. JOHN CASSIAN. The aim of every monk and the perfection of his heart tends to continual and unbroken perseverance in prayer and, as far as it is allowed to human frailty, strives to acquire an immovable tranquillity of mind and perpetual purity. For the sake of these two blessings we seek unweariedly and constantly to practice all bodily labors and to exercise ourselves in contrition of spirit. And there is between these two a sort of reciprocal and inseparable union (*Collatio 9, Abbatis Isaac prima, de oratione,* c. 2, *PL* 49:771).

1650. ST. NILUS, monk of Sinai (d. circa 430). When you put your hand to labor, let your tongue chant and your mind engage in prayer, for God demands that we be always mindful of him (*Capita paraenetica,* § 80, *PG* 79:1255).

1651. ST. BONAVENTURE. "Always be engaged in doing something good, so that the devil will always find you occupied" (*St. Jerome, Ep. 125, ad Rusticum, juvenem monachum,* § 11, *PL* 22:1078). Train yourself especially in these things: frequent and fervent prayer, reading, and the performing of services for others. Let your whole life be made up of these three so that you are always engaged in prayer, or reading, or in fulfilling some task, especially in helping the aged, the poor, the sick. After you have rendered these services, do not stand idly by with the brethren, but go straightway to your cell (*Regula novitiorum,* c. 8, § 1, *de otio fugiendo, Op. Om.,* ed. Quaraccchi 8:484).

1652. DAVID OF AUGSBURG, Franciscan mystic (d. 1272). In order that it may not easily be broken you braid the rope [of good thoughts with which the vessel of your soul is made fast in life's storms to the immovable rock, Christ] with triple strands, namely, with devout reading of Sacred Scripture, the compunction of zealous prayer, and the humble performance of virtuous works. Reading furnishes the material: it is a kind of seed for good thought. Prayer waters the plant and makes it grow strong and brings it to maturity—that is, it gives the heart light for understanding, and nourishes its love of God to the delight of expressing itself. A virtuous deed, particularly one seasoned with charity or obedience or any other virtue, makes the conscience joyful and gives the confidence of hope in God. If at the moment the deed seems to interrupt the quiet of devotion it afterward merits a greater infusion of delight in prayer and the grace of purity (*De institutione novitiorum, Pars II,* c. 4, *Op. Om. S. Bonaventurae,* ed. Peltier 12:306).

1653. JOHN OF TRITHEIM. As idleness is the enemy of the soul, so moderate manual labor is a preserver of spiritual life. Because he is a soldier of the Eternal King, the monk must never allow himself to be given to idleness. For idleness produces sloth, and sloth in turn exposes the soul to a pernicious spiritual anemia that is deadly. But the works undertaken by monks are to be so regulated that they are never unaccompanied by words of divine praise: meditation on the Scriptures should give fervor to the spirit during the manual labor, and, once it has brought the mind into the sweet realm of the spirit, this meditation should be transformed into devout prayer. Let the monk, the soldier of Christ, be like the clean animal of God which ruminates: always keeping in the mouth of his heart the nourishment of the Scriptures, he is to guard his mind from vain and harmful thoughts, and his lips from all unworthy and idle speech. At his work he is ever to be mindful of that Scripture passage: *Happy is the man . . . who meditates on the law of the Lord day and night* (Ps. 1:2). For everyone who loves the Lord Jesus in truth daily dwells in his heart in tears and prayer on his teaching and his passion (*Hom. 7, de labore monachorum manuali, Op. pia et spiritualia,* p. 436).

1654. ST. HILDEGARDE. In his admonition the Lord addresses men in these terms: "I will render to everyone according to his deeds" (cf. Ps. 61:13). Now, some persons expend their efforts in the praise of God, but others grow weary with the unpleasantness of tedium. They who give honor to God speak thus: "We acknowledge that we have sinned through the temptations in the testing of Adam on this pilgrimage, and are afflicted with many vices in our works. Tearfully we deplore our transgressions. But we promise, for the glory of your name, to strive to preserve ourselves from all sin. Lovingly we cherish [the seeking of] your honor, the fulfilling of your justice, and the Scriptures that you gave us." And the Lord, whose ways are beyond all comprehension, praises them and sets them over many goods (cf. Matt. 25:21). He does not condemn them, for they invoke his name in the spirit of repentance. But they who grow weary in the performance of their divinely appointed tasks speak in this manner: "The striving for your honor has discouraged us; the seeking of your justice has wounded us; the multitude of your Scriptures suffocated us; the appealing strength of your Spirit rules out the pleasures our minds delight in; the pouring out of zeal [for your glory] has wearied us, so that we cannot behold you in joy, and we know that we cannot excuse ourselves." And the Lord calls them wicked servants and tells them that he has no need of their help or their works of justice, saying: "Why have you no shame to complain to me in your heedless words?" Hence they are to be bound and cast forth in punishment, where they will dwell on and realize their vices. But you, soldier of Christ, must understand that these reflections are applicable to yourself. . . . When you were in the world, you did little that was truly meritorious; but the warning of the Holy Spirit touched you and converted you to a life of virtue. See to it that you do not imitate the slothful servant. . . . Always love God in the spirit of good will and sound judgment; hold fast to him in love and you will live! (*Ep. 31, ad H., monachum Mulenbrunnensem, PL* 197:359.)

Idleness is the enemy of the soul

1655. ST. AUGUSTINE. A. Forward, then, my beloved brethren, you who are my crown and my joy! Avoid all idleness; be always engaged in doing something good; let him who has been fatigued in the chanting of the psalms and praying not fail to turn to manual labor. Let him remember that as long as David was engaged in military campaign, temptations of lust did not taunt him, but afterward, when he remained idle in his house, he gave way to adultery and committed murder (cf. II Kgs. 12:2–9). Consider also that while Samson waged war against the Philistines, he could not be taken by the enemy; but after he slept in the arms of a woman and remained with her in idleness, he was captured and blinded by the enemy (cf. Judg. 16:15 ff.). Solomon, too, while building the temple, remained untroubled by luxury, but once he withdrew from the work, he felt the temptations of lust deeply and, having given way to the same, upon the woman's temptation to idolatry, worshiped Astarthe and Moloch (cf. III Kgs. 11:1 ff.). Be on your guard, therefore, my brethren, and do not abandon your course, for I know that you are neither holier than David, nor stronger than Samson, nor wiser than Solomon (*Ad fratres in eremo, Serm. 17, In Append., PL* 40:1264). B. It is through idleness, my brethren, that we develop a dislike for the severity of the holy solitary life of religion; through it we are often tempted to abandon the desert; through it, also, we are frequently incited to luxury; through it we are encouraged to pride; through it we are led to seek the glory of this world (*ibid.*, col. 1263).

1656. ST. JEROME. A. Always have something to do, lest when our hand gives up working, the field of our heart be overrun with brambles of evil thoughts (*Comm. in Ezech., Lib.* 5, c. 16, n. 49, *PL* 25:155). B.

Always have some work on hand that the devil may find you busy (*Ep. 125, ad Rusticum, juvenem monachum*, § 11, *PL* 22:1078).

1657. ST. JOHN CHRYSOSTOM. A. Indolence is the source and baneful root of evil. For idleness is the teacher of all vice (*Hom. 16, § 1 in c. 4 Eph., PG* 62:112). B. But what can be less pleasant than the lot of a man who has nothing to do; what more wretched or miserable? Is such a condition not worse than all the fetters in the world? . . . Nothing is more hurtful than leisure in which one has nothing to do. . . . But just as inaction is evil, so also is activity in things that ought to be left alone. . . . Therefore let us avoid both inaction and the activity which is worse than inaction (*Hom. 35, § 3 in Act. Ap., PG* 60:257).

1658. JOHN CASSIAN. A. *Strive to live peacefully, minding your own affairs, working with your own hands* (I Thess. 4:11), that is to say, keep to your cells, and take no part in exchanging rumors, which generally spring from the curiosity and gossip of idlers: otherwise you not only waste your own time but become a disturbance to others as well. When St. Paul uses the phrase, "minding your own affairs," he means that you should not inquire with curiosity about the concerns of the outside world or pry into the lives of others, thereby spending your strength not on bettering yourselves and aiming at virtue, but in depreciating your brethren. . . . He cannot possibly walk in a manner becoming to the monk, not even according to the standards of men of the world, who is not content to cling to the seclusion of his cell and work with his hands; but he is certain to be lacking in virtue even while he is engaged in seeking his own needed food—for he will take pains to flatter, to follow up news and gossip, to seek for opportunities for chatting and relating stories as a means for gaining a footing and obtaining an entrance among others (*De coenob. institut., Lib. 10, de spiritu acediae*, c. 7, *PL* 49:373). B. The mind of the idler cannot think of anything but food and the belly, until the companionship of some man or woman equally lacking in zeal is secured, and it loses itself in their affairs and business, and is thus little by little ensnared by dangerous occupations, so that, just as if it were bound up in the coils of a serpent, it can never disentangle itself again and return to the perfection of its former profession (*ibid.*, c. 6, col. 370). C. This saying has been handed down from the Fathers in Egypt: a monk who works is attacked by but one devil; but an idler is tormented by countless evil spirits (*ibid.*, c. 23, col. 394).

1659. ST. GREGORY THE GREAT (d. 604). For when anyone who is worn out with fatigue relaxes himself at his ease, he abandons his mind without restraint to the corruptor. But if, by the dispensations of mercy from above, the stroke of temptation falls upon him in such wise as not to overwhelm him with sudden violence, but to warn him by a certain measured approach, then he is awakened to foresee the snares, so that with a cautious mind he girds himself to face the enemy in combat (*Moral., Lib. II*, c. 49, § 79, *PL* 75:594).

1660. WILLIAM OF ST. THIERRY. The stinking source of all evil temptations and unprofitable thoughts is idleness (*Ep. ad fratres de Monte Dei, Lib. I*, c. 8, § 21, *PL* 184:321).

1661. PETER DE BLOIS, chancellor and archdeacon, Bath, England (d. circa 1200). To be weakened by idleness and to become sluggish through laziness is nothing other than to choke off virtue, foster pride and build yourself a road to hell (*Ep. 9, ad quemdam desertorem vitae scholasticae, PL* 207:27).

1662. ST. BERNARD. For idleness, the mother of frivolous conduct and the step-mother of virtue, there ought to be no toleration at any time (*De consideratione, Lib. II*, c. 13, *PL* 182:756).

1663. JOHN GERSON, chancellor of University of Paris (d. 1429). There is no thought so foul, so abominable, so evil and execrable to which idleness, which is so detestable, will not lead. For the heart of a man given to idleness is like a mill which, having no good grain to grind, but being nevertheless in continual motion, grinds on and wears itself out, even unto total destruction, unless such ruin is prevented by someone's diligence. And it chops up dirty insects flying about just as readily as choice kernels of grain (*Tract. ad mysticam vitam, Pars III, de exercitiis discretis devotorum simplicium, Op. Om.* 3:614).

1664. ST. JOHN CHRYSOSTOM. A. If the eye does not perform its work —or the mouth, or the belly, or any member that one could mention —it falls into the worst state of disease: but this is true of no member so much as it is of the soul (*In Act. Ap., Hom. 35*, § 3, *PG* 60:258). B. Which is the useful horse, the pampered or the exercised? which the serviceable ship, that which sails, or that which lies idle? which the best water, the running or the stagnant? which the best iron, that which is much used, or that which does not work? Does not one shine bright as silver, whereas the other becomes all rusty, useless, and even loses some of its own substance? Something similar happens also to the soul as the consequence of idleness: a kind of rust spreads over it and corrodes it both in brightness and all other qualities (*ibid.*, § 2, col. 256). C. Thus a body also, being idle and without exercise, is sickly and unsightly; but that which is exercised and suffers labor and hardships is more comely and healthy: and this we should find to hold also in the case of the soul (*ibid., Hom. 54*, § 3, col. 378).

1665. ST. JEROME. In Egypt the monasteries make it a rule to receive none who are not willing to work; for they regard labor as necessary not only for the support of the body but also for the salvation of the soul, lest the mind stray into harmful thoughts (*Ep. 125, ad Rusticum, juvenem monachum*, § 11, *PL* 22:1079).

1666. GUERRICUS, Cistercian abbot of Igny, diocese of Rheims (d.

1157). Manual work is a burden by which tranquillity and seriousness are bestowed upon the restless of heart in much the same manner as a ship is stabilized by its cargo (*In Assumptione B. M., Serm. III, de quiete spirituali,* § 5, *PL* 185:196).

1667. ST. THOMAS AQUINAS. The study of letters . . . helps us to avoid the lusts of the flesh (*II-II,* q. 188, art. 5, *Utrum sit instituenda aliqua religio ad studendum,* ad 3, *Op. Om.* 10:527; Am. ed. 2:1998).

1668. THOMAS À KEMPIS. Go to your tasks and work in the vineyard of God for the denarius of eternal life, lest the lord of the household reprove you: *Why do you stand here all day idle?* (Matt. 20:6.) The Scriptures praise the man who works well. Christ rewards the faithful servant, reproves the lazy and negligent and commands that the talent placed in his custody be taken away from him and given to the one working more industriously. For the time will come when because of your weakness you will no longer be able to work, nor even to pronounce a single word. You must think of this now, and always be fearful of that last hour, lest it find you empty-handed. In this sense the Lord Jesus spoke to his disciples: *I must do the works of him who sent me while it is day; night is coming, when no one can work. As long as I am in the world I am the light of the world* (John 9:4–5). Take your example of performing good works from Christ Jesus, from Sts. Paul, Anthony, Augustine, Jerome, Benedict, Francis, Dominic, and from all the Fathers who wrote rules for monks and established religious families (*De disciplina claustralium,* c. 6, *Op. Om.* 2:292).

1669. ST. ISIDORE OF SEVILLE. If they who are physically able and of sound health are lazy at work, they are known to be guilty of double sin, for they not only do no work themselves, but also corrupt others and lead them on to imitate their conduct (*Reg. monachorum,* c. 6, *CR* 1:190; *PL* 83:874).

1670. JOHN OF TRITHEIM. Work like a good soldier of Jesus Christ, putting your hands diligently to whatever labor is enjoined on you under obedience. . . . No work must seem heavy, no time drawn out, no observance harsh to the monk when the glory of eternal happiness is acquired through it (*Hom. 7, de labore monachorum manuali, Op. pia et spiritualia,* p. 437).

Spiritual works preferable

1671. ST. THOMAS AQUINAS. Accordingly, those who devote themselves publicly to the aforesaid spiritual works are thereby exempt from manual labor. . . . On the other hand, those who devote themselves to such works not publicly but privately, as it were, ought not on that account to be exempt from manual labor (*II-II,* q. 187, art. 3, *Utrum religiosi manibus operari teneantur,* ad. 3, *Op. Om.* 10:511; Am. ed. 2:1986).

1672. PETER THE VENERABLE, abbot of Cluny (d. 1158). Does it not seem unbecoming, in fact altogether improper, that brethren who are commanded to dwell constantly within the enclosure, to devote their efforts with all intensity to silence, prayer, reading, and meditation, and to the other demands of the Rule, to services as ministers of the Church, should set all these aside and take up country life and common manual labor; that they who should adorn the interior of the tabernacle as costly and fine-textured silk—that is to say, by the profundity of their contemplation of heavenly things—should put on rough outer garments of goat's hair, expose themselves to the violence of the wind, the torrents of rain and all the disturbances of outdoor life—that is to say, to excessive attention to worldly works which draw them forth from occupations that are most interior in character? (*Lib. I, ep. 28, ad* [S.] *Bernardum Claraevallensem abb., PL* 189:144.)

1673. JOHN OF TRITHEIM. A. If you tell me, "I cannot write; I cannot remain in a cell all day long; I shall willingly go outside to work; I would not refuse to dig or to haul rocks, just so that I am not cramped up with duties that are displeasing to me. . . ," I reply briefly: You simply are not making much of a comparison if you set aside progress in worthier matters. To write is better than to dig; to read sacred books is better than to carry stones. . . . If you were a true monk you would have no horror of the privacy of the cell which is most in conformity with your way of life. The devotion of monks in our age is not so great that they can profit by the example of those of former times in the works of agriculture. . . . Freed from these labors as from certain bonds of distraction, turning our minds to interior things, let us love the privacy of the cell, devote ourselves to frequent prayer and reading, copy the books of the holy Fathers with devotion, and seek the foods that will nourish the soul (*De laude scriptorum manualium,* c. 13, *Op. pia et spiritualia,* p. 758). B. There is no work in the monasteries which is more suitable for us or comes closer to the ideal of our profession than writing. For being dedicated to divine duties we cannot dig; we are not able to bear the hard and heavy work of the fields, because if we tire ourselves out in farm work during the day, the divine service would perish from the choir. Since divine service is to be preferred to all other works (*RSB,* c. 48), it would be most inappropriate for monks to immerse themselves in external occupations while neglecting their interior life (*ibid.,* c. 5, p. 748).

1674. RUPERT, abbot of Deutz (d. 1135). A. It is manifest that manual labor, particularly of such a character as that by which a livelihood is obtained, such as plowing, planting, harvesting and cutting down forests, is not commanded, but only permitted by St. Benedict (*Sup. quaedam capitula RSB, Lib. III,* c. 5, *PL* 170:513). B. The Father of monks, St. Benedict, did not prescribe an orderly schedule of manual labor for monks as though he wished to disturb the leisure for holy meditation which is made possible by the bounty of wealthy faithful, concerning whom it is mystically stated in the Psalm: *Well watered are the trees of the Lord, the cedars of Lebanon, which he planted; in them the birds build their nests* (Ps. 103:16–17). We are, or we should be, those birds, small in our own eyes, but flying into the very heights of contemplation. God furnishes for such birds the trees of the forest and the cedars of Lebanon, that is, the wealthy men of the world, in order that we, whoever we may be that have this spiritual goal [the contemplative life], may find our rest in their property (*ibid.*, c. 7, col. 515). C. Hence it is indeed a good thing for monks to perform manual labor and thus avoid idleness which is the enemy of the soul, but it is better to avoid idleness and sanctify the leisure with the holy word of God. *Martha, Martha, thou art anxious and troubled about many things; and yet only one is needful* (Luke 10:41). And what is that one thing which is necessary? It is to sit at the feet of the Lord and hearken to his words. But where will we find his feet except in the sacrament of his altar? For these are the footprints [memorials] of his Passion, his Resurrection, his Ascension. Therefore to devote oneself to the service of the sacrament of the altar, and to this end to be freed of all other preoccupations, in order to give oneself to meditation on the sacred mysteries of our salvation, his *saving deeds on earth* (Ps. 73:12), is to sit at the feet of the Lord and hear the words from his mouth. You will object: But you admit into the monastery many laymen who are lacking in knowledge and experience for such meditation, men who could not be taught to live the contemplative life. Are they, then, not idle among you?

When Israel waged war against Amalec, Moses and Aaron and Hur climbed to the top of the hill (Exod. 17:10). *As long as Moses kept his hands raised up, Israel had the better of the fight, but when he let his hands rest, Amalec had the better of the fight. Moses' hands, however, grew tired; so they put a rock in place for him to sit on. Meanwhile Aaron and Hur supported his hands, one on the one side and one on the other, so that his hands remained steady till sunset* (*ibid.*, vv. 11–12). Could we say that Aaron and Hur were idle on that occasion? Certainly not, for although they did not actually pronounce the words of the prayer, they made it possible by their efforts that the arms of him who was praying should not grow weary. In much the same way—and in this I submit to holier intellects—unlettered monks, who because of their lack of education are not qualified for priestly and clerical duties, are also not idle when they furnish, as far as lies in their power, the daily support for priests and clerics in their divine offices, and work at their crafts within the enclosure of the monastery (*ibid.*, c. 8, col. 515 f.). D. For the best part is the dignity of sacred orders, for whose most sacred function no one can better prepare himself to be worthy of the sacred orders than by living under monastic discipline. . . . It is a perfectly correct and well-regulated arrangement for one first to learn the holy and celibate life under the yoke of obedience and then only to receive the crown of his obedience, namely the priestly stole. . . . In these men who are simply monks we behold that humble beginning which St. Benedict declared his Rule to be; whereas in the former [the priests of the monastery], who are both monks and clerics, we have apostolic perfection. I am not speaking of perfection as far as their personal merit is concerned, but perfection of their office (*ibid.*, c. 9, col. 516–517). E. There were many holy Fathers who were lacking in knowledge. . . . But now there is another state [priest-monks] in the Church; . . . there is the fulfilment of that which of old in the Canticle of Canticles the Bridegroom promising to his spouse, Christ to the Church, said: *Come from Lebanon . . . come! Descend from the top of Amana, from the top of Sanir and Hermon, from the haunts of lions, from the leopards' mountains* (Cant. 4:8; *ibid.*, c. 11, col. 519, 520).

1675. BENEDICT HAEFTEN, provost of Affilghem (d. 1648). Just as the blood sisters Martha and Mary dwelt in the same house, so in monasteries some monks are assigned to prayers and choir, or to the exercises of the contemplative life, whereas others devote themselves in obedience to external works, the service of others and the demands of the active life. We commonly call these latter laybrothers, as representing the people, whereas the former in times past represented the clergy, and now as a rule actually belong to the clergy. These laybrothers are like hands and feet to the body of the monastic community. For St. Dorotheus, comparing the monastery to a body and accommodating the various functions to its different members says: "They who are engaged in performing duties are like the hands; they who reply to the commands and are sent hither and thither to their appointed tasks represent the feet of the community" (*Doctrina 6,* § 8, *PG* 88:1695). Exhorting these latter he adds: "Are you a hand? Then work, and keep going manfully! Are you a foot? Be submissive, and fulfil your appointed duty! Let each of you serve the common body and perform his duty, not slothfully, but each according to his ability!" (*Disquisitiones monasticae, Lib. III,* tract. 1., disq. 8, p. 276.)

Laybrothers

1676. JEAN MABILLON, monk of congregation of St. Maur (d. 1707). A. The brethren whom we call converse brothers and who are assigned to external labors were not admitted to monastic communities before the eleventh century (*Annales O.S.B., Lib. 3,* n. 8, tom. 1:51). B. According to the Rule of St. Isidore, the duties of the monastery were in the hands of the abbot, the provost [prior], sacristan, porter, cellarer, hebdomadarian, and laymen. These laymen were attached to the monastery after the manner of our converse brothers or as oblates, and were consequently not considered lay monks (*ibid., Lib. 12,* n. 42, 1:332). C. Besides the choir monks, laymen were also admitted by John [St. John Gualbert, d. 1072]. ". . . As far as excellence of life was concerned, they differed but little from the monks, except for the quality of their garments, and the silence which, because of their external occupations they were unable to observe fully. The Father directed the tried and tested converse brothers on business assignments and other external duties." These words of the author of John's life seem to refer to the first converse brothers whom he admitted to his community (*ibid., Lib. 58,* n. 40, 4:411). D. The monks of the Cistercian Congregation . . . began to deliberate on the practices and arrangement by which they could provide the services for their own needs, the reception of guests, and the care of the poor. And because the monks, dedicated to the Divine Office and other duties of a spiritual character, were unable to render so many services themselves, they decided to admit converse brothers, or "bearded brothers," as they called them, into the monastic family for managing their farms and cultivating the fields, and to treat them like themselves in life and in death, with the exception of admission into the monastic state, that is, by pronouncing monastic profession (*ibid., Lib. 70,* n. 1, 5:403). E. In the privilege of exemption from paying tithes on their farms granted to the Cistercians by Pope Innocent in 1132, the converse brothers are stated not to be monks. This statement is so worded because they are assigned to external duties of the active life and not to the contemplative and solitary life as are the monks. But after they have pronounced their profession, they are numbered among the religious (*ibid., Lib. 75, n.* 152, 6:194).

1677. MARIAN BROCKIE, monk of St. James at Regensburg (d. 1756). Since the Rule of St. Benedict was most strictly observed throughout this congregation [of Vallumbrosa, St. John Gualbert] . . . did not allow any of his monks to leave the monastery to conduct business affairs, but entrusted the care of the guests and of the ill and the management of all temporal goods to the laybrothers. Hence he is said to be the first who instituted these brothers in monasteries. For in all the abbeys of the Vallumbrosian family, there was a hospital and a guest house, apart from the monastery itself, always presided over by such brothers. Although they are true religious, bound by the three monastic vows, they were not destined for choir service and the Divine Office, lived apart from the clerical monks and priests . . . and were often distinguished from them by a distinctive habit. . . . Thus among the Vallumbrosians these laybrothers did not put on the monastic cowl (*cuculla*) nor the capuche (*caputium*), but wore a long rust-colored tunic, with a broad scapular, and for the covering of the head, a cap made of lamb skin (*Observatio critica in Const. Ordinis monachorum Bened. Vallis-Umbrosae, CR* 4:361).

1678. HEYMO, monk of Hirschau (d. 1091). William, the faithful and prudent servant of the Lord . . . appointed religious monks to live with the laybrothers. In his great zeal for souls the beloved Father was the first to arrange for monks to employ the faithful service of the laybrothers in the administration of external affairs, complemented by the services of the monks in matters pertaining to the care of souls for these laymen. His purpose was that they should achieve their cloistral discipline, as far as possible, so that apart from the distinctive duties of the enclosure they would imitate the monks in the reformation of their life (*Vita S. Guillelmi abb.,* § 23, *PL* 150:914).

1679. BENEDICT HAEFTEN. In our order, among the Cistercians, and the congregation of Bursfeld, the converse brothers are considered religious in the strict sense of the term, as is also the case among the Carthusians, the Premontré Fathers, the Dominicans, and the Carmelites. In all instances there are certain differences between the monks and the converse brothers as regards the monastic garb, respective duties and monastic observances. [All these orders] state specifically that these converse brothers are in reality brothers, that they form part of the monastic family, and that they enjoy most fully all indulgences and exemptions in the same manner as the monks. . . . There are reasons for which they can be dismissed and for which they may be released from their vows, which are considered only simple (*Disquisitiones monasticae, Lib. III,* tract. 1, *de nomine monachorum,* disq. 8, p. 278).

Manual labor is not unbecoming for monks

1680. CASSIODORUS, former statesman, abbot of Vivarium (d. circa 570). It is not unbecoming for monks to cultivate gardens, till the fields, and be pleased at the abundance of the harvest. For we read: *You shall eat the fruit of your handiwork; happy shall you be, and favored* (Ps. 127:2; *De institutione divinarium litterarum,* c. 28, *PL* 70:1142; Jones, p. 130).

1681. ST. ISIDORE DE SEVILLE. The monk is always to work with his hands so that he devote effort to different skills and labors of craftsmen in imitation of the Apostle who says: *Neither did we eat any man's bread at his cost, but we worked night and day in labor and toil;* and again: *If any man will not work, neither let him eat* (II Thess. 3:8, 10). Through laziness, evil inclinations and food for bad thoughts grow, but by dedication to work vices disappear. The monk must never scorn taking part in any work that is necessary for the service of the monastery. . . . Peter himself, Prince of the Apostles, was a fisherman, and all the apostles performed manual labor in order to support their bodily needs (*Reg. monachorum,* c. 6, *CR* 1:190; *PL* 83:873).

1682. ST. BERNARD. Work, separation from the world, and voluntary poverty are the insignia of monks; these are the things that make monastic life so excellent (*Tract. de moribus et officio episcoporum,* c. 9, § 37, *PL* 182:883).

1683. ST. DOROTHEUS. Manual labor humbles and wears down the body. And in the process of humbling and fatiguing the body, the soul likewise is made humble. Hence it is properly stated that the soul is directed and led to humility by means of manual labor (*Doctrina II,* § 9, *PG* 88:1651).

1684. ST. JUSTIN, martyr (d. 166). And when Jesus came to the Jordan, he was considered to be the son of Joseph the carpenter; and he appeared without comeliness, as the Scriptures declared; and he himself was deemed a carpenter, for he was in the habit of working among men, making plows and yokes, by which he taught the symbols of righteousness and an active life (*Dialogus cum Tryphone Judaeo,* § 88, *PG* 6:687).

1685. ST. BASIL THE GREAT. Let us pass on to the life of our Savior himself who, when dwelling among men, presented his own life as the form and pattern of virtue to all who seek to spend their lives in a holy manner in order that, on beholding his example they might imitate it in their own lives. . . . Subject to his parents in his younger years, he bore together with them all manual toil in a gentle and obedient disposition (*Const. monasticae,* c. 4, §§ 4, 6, *PG* 31:1351).

The monk's principal work: sacred studies

1686. ST. PACHOMIUS, abbot of Tabenna, Thebes (d. 346). The unlettered man who has entered the monastery will first be taught the things he must observe as a monk; and when he perseveres in his desire to be a monk after he has been taught all he will have to do, they will assign him twenty Psalms and two epistles of the Apostle [Paul] or some other portion of the Scripture. If he does not know how to read, he will at the first hour [roughly, 6:00 A.M.], the third [9:00 o'clock], and the sixth hour [noon] go to him who is qualified to teach and who has been appointed for him. He will stand before this teacher and give himself to the task of learning with earnest zeal and in the spirit of gratitude. Afterward the rudiments [letters?], syllables, and words will be written for him. Even if he is unwilling, he will be forced to read, for there is to be no one in the monastery who does not learn to read and know something of the Scriptures—as a minimum, the New Testament and the Psalter (*Reg.,* nn. 139, 140, *CR* 1:32; *PL* 23:82; Boon, *Pachomiana Latina,* pp. 49–50).

1687. ST. JEROME. A. The roots of learning are bitter, the fruits sweet (*Comm. in Jerem. Lib. I,* c. 1, *vers. 12, PL* 24:685). B. I would much prefer honest ignorance to learned evil-mindedness; for in the one instance there is a certain honor, even though it is on a lower level, but in the other greater punishments in proportion to the increase of knowledge (*Comm. in Ep. ad Eph., Lib. III, Prolog., PL* 26:515). C. The science of piety is knowledge of the law, understanding of the Prophets, belief in the Gospel, full acquaintance with the Apostles. . . . Without religious piety knowledge is gratifying for the time being but it carries no eternal rewards (*Comm. in Ep. ad Tit., 1, 2,* col. 558).

1688. ST. AUGUSTINE. *Knowledge,* says the Apostle, *puffs up* (I Cor. 8:1). Well, then, must you avoid knowledge and choose rather to remain in ignorance than to be puffed up? To what purpose do we address you if ignorance is preferable to knowledge? Why do we reprove you for not knowing and exhort you to know, if knowledge is to be avoided lest it puff up? Love knowledge, but give charity the first place! Knowledge puffs up where charity does not edify; but where it does edify, knowledge is made stable. There is no puffing up where a rock is the foundation (*Serm. 354,* c. 6, *PL* 39:1566).

1689. ST. LEANDER OF SEVILLE. Let your reading be zealous, your prayer constant. Arrange your schedule and your duties in such fashion that after you have read you may pray, and after having prayed you may read (*Reg., sive institutio virginum et contemptus mundi ad Florentinam,* c. 6, *CR* 1:412; *PL* 72:883).

1690. ST. FERREOLUS, bp. of Uzès (Depart. Gard, France), d. 581. A. All who desire to merit the name of being a monk must not be ignorant of letters (*Reg. ad monachos,* c. 11, *CR* 1:158; *PL* 66:963). B. Reading and writing are an important part of the work of monks (*ibid.,* c. 28, p. 162).

1691. RULE OF THE MASTER. A brother sent on a longer journey should take with him from the monastery a small book with various readings in it, so that whenever he stops on the way he can engage for a while in reading (*Reg. Magistri ad monachos,* c. 57, *CR* 1:270; *PL* 88:1018).

1692. ST. BEDE, monk of Jarrow (d. 735). The man who is lacking in doctrine will everywhere suffer darkness (*Proverbia, sub littera "e," PL* 90:1096).

1693. RICHARD OF ST. VICTOR (d. 1173). What is knowledge of holiness without a good intention other than a figure devoid of life? What is knowledge alone, which does not produce holiness and love of goodness, but an empty, lifeless imitation? (*De eruditione hominis interioris, Lib. I,* c. 38, *PL* 196:1292.)

1694. HUGH OF ST. VICTOR (d. 1142). A. [The monk] must know that it in no manner is conducive to his purpose if, carried away with the vain desire of knowledge, he searches for and dwells on obscure passages of Scripture which call for profound study, in which the mind is more preoccupied than edified (*Lib. V, eruditionis didascalicae,* c. 7, *PL* 176:795). B. He who seeks knowledge must always be on his guard not to neglect discipline (*ibid., Lib. III,* c. 13, col. 773). C. The spirit of study sharpens the mental powers, dispels laziness, begets a love of learning, preserves the knowledge acquired, turns the mind away from vain and useless things, fosters a hatred of sin, seeks quiet and peace (*De bestiis et aliis rebus, Lib. IV,* c. 17, *In Append., PL* 177:161).

1695. ST. GREGORY OF NAZIANZUS, Doctor of the Church (d. 389). Nothing is so magnificent in God's sight as pure doctrine, and a soul perfect in all the dogmas of truth (*Oratio 42, Supremum vale,* § 8, *PG* 36:467).

1696. ST. EPHRAEM, deacon of Edessa (d. 373). When you devote yourself to reading, be on your guard carefully against following what pertains only to haughtiness and elegance of expression; let your study extend only to the point where the spirit of arrogance is not allowed to wound your heart (*Serm. de recta vivendi ratione,* c. 36, *Op. Om.* 1:42).

1697. ST. ISIDORE OF SEVILLE, bp., Doctor of the Church (d. 636). A. In reading it is not the form of words but the truth they express that we must love (*Sententiarum Lib. III,* c. 13, § 8, *PL* 83:687). B. It is wholesome to know much and to live virtuously; but if we are unable to do both, it is better for us to devote our efforts toward living as we should than to the pursuit of knowledge (*ibid., Lib. II,* c. 1, § 11, col. 601). C. Love of worldly knowledge achieves nothing but to raise man up for the praises he will receive (*ibid., Lib. III,* c. 13, § 9, col. 688). D. Knowledge wards off evils. . . . It is the greatest good to know what you are to avoid; the greatest misery not to know whither you are tending (*Synonymorum Lib. II,* c. 66, col. 860).

1698. ST. GREGORY THE GREAT. A. A teacher's effort is altogether useless if the heavenly building is not enlarged by that which he is doing on earth (*In I Reg. expositiones, Lib. III,* c. 5, § 32, *PL* 79:218). B. When men who are learned and arrogant do not live rightly, but are nevertheless compelled by the force of doctrine to say what is right, they become in a measure the heralds of their own condemnation, because while they enforce in their preaching that which they scorn to do, they proclaim with their own voices that they are condemned. Against them it is well said by the Psalmist: *They recoiled like a treacherous bow* (Ps. 77:57). For a treacherous bow strikes the very person who aims it; in this way the tongues of arrogant men are in their very sayings like a treacherous bow, because when they speak in their pride, they really fix their arrows on themselves as a target. Hence we must watch with the utmost care lest the wisdom we receive should take away the light of humility in the very act of its illuminating the darkness of ignorance, and should cease to be wisdom any longer. For though it shines forth in might of speech, it obscures the heart of the speaker with a covering of pride (*Moral., Lib. 27*, c. 46, § 75, *PL* 76:442). C. With God it is more tolerable that a man should be prostrated in weakness and in ignorance, together with humility, than that he should understand lofty themes with self-exaltation (*ibid., Lib. 17*, c. 11, § 15, col. 18). D. Every proud man thinks that he must play this role: at least to make a show of knowledge if he does not actually possess it (*ibid., Lib. 23*, c. 10, § 17, col. 261). E. It is perfect wisdom to know all things, and yet in a certain way to be ignorant of one's knowledge; for although we already know the precepts of God, although we are now weighing with anxious attention the power of his words, although we are doing those things which we believe we have understood; yet we still do not know with what strictness of examination these deeds will hereafter be investigated, nor do we as yet behold the face of God, nor see his hidden counsels (*ibid., Lib. 27*, c. 37, § 62, col. 436). F. Real knowledge influences without puffing up; and makes those whom it has filled not proud, but sorrowful. For when anyone is filled with such knowledge, he is first of all anxious to know himself; and being conscious of his own state, he thereby acquires a greater savor of strength, the more truly sensible he is of his own weakness (*ibid., Lib. 23*, c. 17, § 31, col. 270).

1699. ST. JOHN CHRYSOSTOM, bp. of Constantinople, Doctor of the Church (d. 407). A. The very sight of books makes us more reluctant to commit sin. And if we should dare to sin, our conscience condemns us more roundly when we return home and behold our books; and we become more firm in restraining ourselves against repeating such sins. If we continue in our holy way of life, we are made safer and more constant by books. For as soon as one touches the Gospel, he calms his mind and withdraws himself from the things of this world, and that just from touching the book. If diligent reading is added, the soul, devoting itself to divine things just as it does in the sacred assemblies, is cleansed and made worthier, for God converses with it by means of the Holy Scriptures (*De Lazaro, concio 3*, § 2, *PG* 48:994). B. It is good to know what contributes to one's edification; but to know that which does not benefit one is rather harmful and superfluous (*Opus imperfect. in Matt., Hom. 50, in Matt. 24, 36, PG* 56:922).

1700. BL. RABANUS MAURUS, abbot of Fulda, abp. of Mainz (d. 856). That the Philistines, in order to subdue the Hebrews more easily, forbade that there be a smith [ironmonger] in the land of Israel lest the Israelites should make swords and spears (cf. I Kgs. 13:19 ff.), signifies that the devil, by means of pagans, heretics, and false Christians, strives to prevent learned men in the Church from fashioning spiritual weapons with which to equip militant Christians. The pagans forbade the Christians to be taught the liberal arts, as we read in history, for they valued these disciplines most highly. We read in like manner that the heretics convinced the rulers to banish the defenders of the Catholic faith into exile in order that they could more easily turn the people from the truth, once they were deprived of their shepherds. The same enemy of old is now striving, in this period of the Church's lack of persecution, to turn those who are the spiritual leaders of the people from dedicating themselves seriously to learning, so that they will not employ the dogmas of truth in governing their subjects, whom he may more easily deceive if they remain unguarded (*In Lib. I Reg.*, c. 13, *PL* 109:42).

Charity is always the goal of knowledge

1701. ST. AUGUSTINE. A. Knowledge which is used to promote love is useful, but in itself and separated from such an objective, it turns out to be not only useless but even harmful (*Lib. II, ep. 55, ad inquisitiones Januarii,* § 39, *PL* 33:223; Parsons, p. 293). B. God is the source and origin of all knowledge; the more one drinks from this source, the more he will thirst (*De triplici habitaculo,* § 5, *In Append., PL* 40:996).

1702. WILLIAM OF ST. THIERRY. A. These [undertakings enumerated by St. Paul] and others like them are the holy strivings and exercises recommended by the Apostle (II Cor. 6:4–10), wherein the mind searches itself, finds and amends itself, cleanses itself from all defilement of flesh and spirit, accomplishes its sanctification in the fear of God (*Ep. ad fratres de Monte Dei, Lib. II,* c. 2, *de secundo statu vitae religiosae, id est, rationali,* § 6, *PL* 184:342). B. The love of God, which is produced in man by grace, is nourished by reading, fed by meditation, strengthened and enlightened by prayer (*ibid., Lib. I,* c. 14, col. 335).

1703. GILBERT OF HOILAND, English Cistercian, abbot of St. Mary's, diocese of Lincoln (d. 1172). A. For me, any teaching which employs no reference to Christ, which does not renew my strength with his sacraments, nor instruct me with his precepts, nor excites in me the love of his promises, is open to suspicion, and certainly to be shunned (*Serm. 5 in Cant. Salomonis,* § 3, *PL* 184:33). B. Reading must minister to prayer and predispose the affections; it is not to be indulged in to snatch away the hours nor to while away periods of time. When you read, you are being instructed about Christ; but when you pray you engage in familiar converse with him. How much sweeter is the grace of speaking with him than speaking about him! (*Ibid., serm. 7, in Cant. 3, 4,* § 2, col. 43.)

1704. PETER DE BLOIS. The work of study is in truth a leisure, but a well-occupied leisure, and one which renders the mind solicitous for virtuous pursuits (*Ep. 9, ad quemdam desertorem vitae scholasticae, PL* 207:25).

1705. HUGH OF ST. CHER, O.P., cardinal (d. 1263). The ship of religion is grounded when there is little depth of water, that is, doctrine, beneath it. For then it strikes ground, that is, the love of things of earth, and is broken (*Sup. Ps. 106, 30, Comment.* 2:285).

1706. THOMAS À KEMPIS. Books of learned men are the clergy's treasure: they instruct the ignorant, censure the lazy, stimulate the listless, rouse the somnolent, correct the erring, lift up the falling, cast fear into those who laugh at serious things, console the mourning, encourage the humble, offer serious criticism to the proud, and strengthen the weak (*Opusc. 11, doctrinale juvenum,* c. 3, *de thesauro eloquiorum divinorum, Op. Om.* 4:184).

1707. ST. BIRGITTA OF SWEDEN (d. 1373). A. Jesus addressed St. Birgitta: "Some of my friends [from the context: priests, religious] are my disciples, possessing three things: first, a conscience which understands beyond the nature of the intellect; second, a wisdom not imparted by man, for I personally instruct them interiorly; third, they are filled with sweetness and divine charity by which they conquer the devil. But now, on the contrary, men devote themselves to study: first, they want to be learned out of pride, so that they may be called good clerics; second, they want to be learned in order to possess and acquire riches; third, they want to be learned in order to obtain dignities and honors. For that reason when they enter their schools, I take leave of them, for they study out of pride, whereas I taught them humility; they enter the schools out of cupidity, whereas I had not whereon to lay my head; they enter upon [their studies] in order to obtain dignities, to be jealous of others, to be superior, and I was judged by Pilate and derided by Herod. Therefore I take my leave of them, for they do not devote themselves to my doctrine.

"But because I am meek and good, I give to each one what he asks. He who asks bread of me, will have it; if he asks for straw, that will be given to him. My friends request bread, they seek and learn divine wisdom in which is my charity. But others seek straw, that is, worldly wisdom. For in straw there is no benefit for self or for others, nor nourishment for the soul, but only a little recognition and meaningless striving. For when such a man dies, all his wisdom is wiped away, and is no longer recalled by those who praised it.

"I am like a great lord having many servants who distribute in the lord's name all that is necessary for all; thus good and evil angels stand at my command. The good angels minister to those who apply themselves to my wisdom, that is, to those who strive to please me, nourishing them with consolation and with work in which they find great pleasure. Evil angels on the other hand minister to those who are wise according to the world's standards, furnish them with the motives they seek, inform them according to their desires, and instill thoughts as a result of great effort. If only they would look to me, I would give them bread without labor, and the things of this world unto their satisfaction—but they are never content with what I offer, for they turn sweet into bitter" (*Revelationes, Lib. I,* c. 33). B. "Wisdom in things divine is not to be found only in letters, but in the heart and in a good life. Whoever zealously thinks of the way that leads to death, on the nature of death itself, and the judgment after death, is a wise man. Whoever casts from himself the vanity of the world and superfluous things, whoever is content with only what is necessary, and spends himself in the works of the love of God as far as he may, has the condiment of wisdom by which [the bread of] a good will and [the drink of] meditation on divine things are better tasting.

"For when a man thinks on death and his nakedness in death; when he dwells on the terrible judgment of God in which nothing will remain concealed or go unpunished; when he thinks on the uncertainty and vanity of the world, does he not rejoice and sense a delight in his heart at having abandoned his will to God and having avoided sin? Is not his body then strengthened and his blood purified, that is, all spiritual weakness, all sloth and lack of moral energy are cast forth, for he sees that it is more reasonable to love those things that are eternal than those that are to perish?

"Therefore the wisdom of divine things is not only to be found in letters, but in good works. For many are wise according to the world and for their own desires, but totally lacking wisdom with regard to the commandments of God and his will, and in subduing their body. These men are not wise, but stupid and blind, for they know the things that perish and which are useful only for the moment, but contemn and forget those that are eternal. Others are lacking in the wisdom regarding the pleasures of this world and its honors, and are wise in their appreciation of the things of God, and are fervent in praising him. These are wise in truth; for the command of God and his will have a strong appeal for them. These are the truly enlightened, and have eyes that are open, for they make it their concern always how they will attain the true life and the true light. Others walk in darkness, and it seems more pleasant to them to be in darkness than to seek the way by which they could come to the light" (*ibid., Lib. II,* c. 25, § D). C. "They who are now called wise [according to the estimation and terminology of the world] sin more grievously against me. For I gave them talent and intellect and wisdom so that they would love me. But they can appreciate nothing except what is for their own temporal advantage. Their eyes are in the back of their head; they are looking only for the things that are gratifying to them. They are blind for rendering thanks to me who gave them everything, for whether good or wicked, none could feel or understand anything without me, although I allow the wicked to turn their will to whatever they wish" (*ibid., Lib. I,* c. 19).

1708. ST. BERNARD. A. Perhaps you consider me unduly severe and narrow in my views on human knowledge, and suppose that I am censuring the learned and condemning the study of letters. God forbid that I should do so! I am well aware how much her learned members have benefited and still benefit the Church, both by refuting her opponents and by instructing the ignorant. And I have read what the Lord says by the mouth of his prophet Osee: *Because thou hast rejected knowledge, I will reject thee, that thou shalt do no office of priesthood to me* (Osee 4:6; *Serm. 36 in Cant., Quod scientia litterarum sit bona ad instructionem, sed scientia propriae infirmitatis sit utilior ad salutem,* § 2, *PL* 183:967).

B. Zeal without knowledge is insupportable. Where zeal is eager, there discretion, which is the rule of charity by order, is most of all indispensable. Without knowledge zeal is found to be always less useful and less effectual; and most often it is even very dangerous. The more fervent zeal is, the more eager the temper, the more profuse the charity, the more need there is of a watchful knowledge, which moderates zeal, tempers the warmth of the disposition, and regulates the gushings of charity (*ibid., serm. 49, Qualiter per discretionem ordinatur charitas,* § 5, col. 1018).

C. For there are those who wish to learn merely in order that they may know, and such curiosity is blamable. There are others who wish to learn for no other reason than that they may be looked upon as learned, which is ridiculous vanity. . . . Others, again, desire to learn only that they may make merchandise of their knowledge, for example, in order to gain money or honors; such trafficking is ignoble. But there are those who desire to learn that they may edify others; that is charity. And lastly, there are some who wish to learn that they themselves may be edified; and this is prudence (*Serm. 36,* § 3, col. 968; Eales, p. 235).

D. But, I pray you, what proof of virtue is it, what instance of self-control, what advantage in knowledge or artistic skill, to tremble with fear where no fear is needful, and to lay aside even the fear of the Lord? How much more wholesome the knowledge of Jesus and him crucified —a knowledge, of course, not easy to acquire except for him who is crucified to the world. You are mistaken, my son, quite mistaken, if you think that you can learn in the school of the teachers of this world that knowledge which only the disciples of Christ, that is, such as despise the world, attain; and that by the gift of God. This knowledge is taught, not by the reading of books, but by grace; not by the letter, but by the spirit; not by learning, but by the practice of the commandments of God. . . . You see that the light of knowledge cannot be duly attained except the seed of righteousness first enter the soul, so that from it may grow the grain of life, and not the mere husk of vainglory. What then? You have not yet sown to yourself in righteousness, and therefore you have not reaped the sheaves of hope; and do you pretend that you are acquiring the true knowledge? (*Ep. 108, ad Thomam de S. Audomaro, post transgressionem promissionis suae veniendi ad conversionem,* § 2, *PL* 182:250; Gasquet, p. 162; James, p. 166.)

E. Many are profoundly learned in a variety of arts and sciences, and all the while continue profoundly ignorant of themselves; they are inquisitive about the affairs of men, and perfectly void of thought or care for their own (*Meditationes piissimae de cognitione humanae conditionis,* c. 1, n. 1, *PL* 184:485).

F. Many seek knowledge (*scientiam*), but few strive to acquire a right conscience (*conscientiam*); if conscience were sought after with the same earnestness and care as is worldly and vain knowledge, it would be more easily attained and more profitably preserved (*Tract. de interiori domo,* c. 9, *In Append.,* col. 516).

G. The wine of worldly knowledge inebriates indeed, but with curiosity, not with charity; it fills, but does not nourish; it puffs up instead of edifying; it gluts, but strengthens not (*Serm. 9 in Cant.,* § 7, *PL* 183:818; Eales, p. 47).

1709. MICHAEL OF MEAUX, abp. of Sens (d. 1199). Studies of worldly knowledge are unproductive, in fact, dangerous (*Altera expos. Ps. 118,* c. 2, *vers. 3,* art. 2, *Op. Om. S. Bonaventurae,* ed. Peltier 9:343).

1710. ST. BONAVENTURE. A. He is never to be considered idle who devotes himself to the study of God's word; nor does he acquire greater merit who works externally than he who engages in the work of learning about the divinity (*Serm. 2 Dom. I in Quadr., Op. Om.,* ed. Peltier 13:148). B. And this is the fruit of all sciences, that in all, faith may be strengthened, *God may be honored* (I Pet. 4:11), character may be formed, and consolation may be derived from union of the Spouse with his beloved, a union which takes place through charity, to the attainment of which the whole purpose of Sacred Scripture, and consequently, every illumination descending from above, is directed—a charity without which all knowledge is vain because no one comes to the Son except through the Holy Spirit who teaches us all the truth, who is blessed forever. Amen (*De reductione artium ad theologiam,* § 26, *Epilog., Op. Om.,* ed. Quaracchi 5:325; St. Bonaventure's *De reductione artium ad theologiam;* a commentary with an introduction and translation by Sister Emma Thérèse Healy, 1955, p. 41).

1711. IMITATION OF CHRIST (Thomas à Kempis). A. We ought to seek in Holy Scripture spiritual profit rather than elegance of style, and to read simple and devout books as gladly as books of high learning and wisdom. Do not let the authority of the author irk you, whether he be of great learning or little, but let the love of every pure truth stir you to read. Ask not: Who said this; but heed well what is said. Men pass lightly away, but the truth of God endures forever (*De imitatione Christi, Lib. I,* c. 5, *Op. Om.* 2:12; Gardiner, p. 37). B. The more knowledge you have, the more grievously will you be judged for its misuse, if you do not live according to it (*ibid.,* c. 2, p. 7; Gardiner, p. 33).

1712. JEAN MABILLON, monk of the Congregation of St. Maur (d. 1707). Books are so to be used that by their help piety is fostered, the mind engaged with serious concerns and not what is inconsequential, and that it be rendered more fit for action. If we deprive the body of food and nourishment, it will soon grow weak and become incapable of performing its tasks. Reading is the food of the soul, and unless you provide it continually and generously, the soul will be hungry and weak in all its operations. If the mind is not invigorated by the practice of pious reading, no experience, no physical work, nor even the divine things themselves will have any appeal. Then the heart will become unresponsive and unproductive; the desire for spiritual things will be inactive, for it will be snuffed out like a flame from which the oil and fuel of reading have been withdrawn. . . . A person is to know that he has then finally arrived at the goal of true wisdom when he is refreshed by the taste of the Divine Scriptures alone. All studies of religious persons tend strongly in that direction and sharpen the mind, among which the principal should be the concern for understanding the psalms which they recite regularly, the reading and meditation of the Gospel, and Paul's epistles, which embrace the perfection of Christian doctrine (*Breve scriptum de monasticorum studiorum ratione ad juvenes studiosque Congregationis suae, inter op. posthum,* In, Bernardi Pezii . . . *Bibliotheca ascetica* 9:654–660).

Sacred Scripture, the reading of monks

1713. ST. JOHN CHRYSOSTOM. A. [The monks] are a pleasing spectacle to those who behold them not only when they are singing and praying, but also when riveted to their books. For after they have ended the choir, one takes Isaias and discourses with him, another converses with the Apostles, and another goes over the works of other men and seeks wisdom concerning God, concerning the universe, concerning the things that are seen, concerning the things that are not seen, concerning objects of sense and objects of the intellect, concerning the vileness of this present life and the greatness of that to come. They are fed on a food that is most excellent, not setting before themselves cooked flesh of beasts, but the oracles of God, sweeter than honey and the honeycomb—a honey far superior to that on which John fed in the wilderness. No wild bees collect this honey from flowers, but the grace of the Holy Spirit forms it, stores it up in the souls of the saints rather than in honeycombs and hives, so that he who desires to do so, may eat thereof continually in security (*In Matt., Hom. 68,* § 4, *PG* 58:646). B. The more that aromatic spices are rubbed with the fingers, the stronger the fragrance they give forth. The same is usually the case with the Scriptures. The more one becomes familiar with them, the more he can see the hidden treasure and gather the fruits of indescribable riches (*In c. 2, Gen., Hom. 13,* § 1, *PG* 53:106). C. There is not a syllable or a letter in the Sacred Writings in whose depths there is not some great treasure (*ibid., Hom. 21,* § 1, col. 175). D. There is no suffering of body or soul in human nature that cannot find its alleviation in the Sacred Scripture (*ibid., Hom. 29,* § 1, col. 261). E. The Scriptures are not like ores that must be dug out by laborers, but furnish a ready-provided treasure for those who seek their hidden riches. It is enough for them to have studied them closely to depart filled with every fruit; it suffices only to have opened them in order for them to see the splendor of the gems (*In illud Isa. Vidi Dominum, Hom. 2,* § 2, *PG* 56:110). F. Ignorance of the Scriptures is a high precipice over a deep chasm; and to know nothing of God's law, the great loss of salvation (*De Lazaro, concio 3,* § 3, *PG* 48:995). G. For the Divine Scriptures are a treasury of all kinds of medicines, so that whether it be needful to quench pride, conquer lustful desires, tread the love of money under foot, despise pain, inspire confidence, gain patience, from them one may find abundant resources (*In Joan., Hom. 37,* § 1, *PG* 59:207).

1714. ST. AMBROSE. Eat the foods of the heavenly Scriptures; eat so that they may remain with you unto eternal life; eat them daily so that you will never suffer hunger; eat in order to be filled; eat so that you may give to others the solid food of divine words (*Expos. in Ps. 118, Serm. 22,* § 17, *PL* 15:1595).

1715. ST. AUGUSTINE. A. Let us nourish the mind and give it drink by means of meditation and extended reflection on the Divine Scriptures (*De vera religione,* c. 51, *PL* 34:165). B. Christian learning is so deep a study that I might have made some progress in it if I had daily tried to apply myself to it exclusively from my earliest childhood to extreme old age, spending on it all my time, all my effort, and a better gift of mind. I do not say that it is too difficult to attain a knowledge necessary to salvation, but whoever remains firm in the faith, without which one cannot live religiously and uprightly, finds so many truths which have to be learned, shrouded in the manifold darkness of mystery, he finds such a depth of wisdom lying hidden, not only in the words in which the truths are expressed, but also in the truths themselves which are to be known, that even the most advanced in years, the most penetrating in mind, the most ardent in zeal for learning, might find himself described by what the same Scripture says elsewhere:

When a man ends he is only beginning (Sir. 18:5; *Ep. 137, ad Valusianum,* § 3, *PL* 33:516; Parsons, 412). C. But Scripture commands only charity and censures only lust, and in that manner molds the character of men. Also, if a belief in some fallacy has impregnated their minds, men consider whatever Scripture has maintained differently as figurative. But it teaches only the Catholic faith in relation to things past, future and present. It is a history of the past, a prediction of the future and a delineation of the present. All these are effective in cultivating and invigorating charity and in vanquishing and destroying lust (*De doctrina Christiana, Lib. III,* c. 10, § 15, *PL* 34:71; Gavigan, p. 130). D. Whatever a man has learned apart from Scripture, if it is harmful, it is censured there; if it is useful, he finds it there. And although everyone may have found there everything which he learned profitably somewhere else, he will discover there, in much greater profusion, things which he can learn nowhere else at all, except in the admirable profundity and surprising simplicity of the Scriptures alone (*ibid., Lib. II,* c. 42, col. 65; Gavigan, p. 116). E. The Scriptures speak in such a way that they ridicule the proud by their sublimity; frighten by their depth those who read them diligently; feed the grown up with their truth, and nourish children with their kindness (*De Gen. ad litteram, Lib. V,* c. 3, § 6, *PL* 33:323). F. Believe me, whatever there is in these Scriptures, is lofty and divine; there is in them altogether truth, and a system of teaching most suited to refresh and renew minds; and clearly so ordered in measure, that there is no one but may draw from them all that he needs, if only he approach to draw with devotion and piety, as true religion demands (*De utilitate credendi,* c. 6, § 13, *PL* 42:74). G. There too, in one city, heaven, which is Christ's body, dwell the angels, who are our fellow-citizens. We toil, because we are as yet pilgrims; while they are within that city awaiting our arrival. Letters have reached us too from that city, apart from which we are wandering; those letters are the Scriptures, which exhort us to live virtuously. Why do I speak of letters only? The King himself descended, and became the way to us in our wanderings (*Enarr. in Ps. 90, serm. 2,* § 1, *PL* 37:1159). H. For there are in Holy Scripture deep mysteries, which are for this reason hidden, lest they should be held cheap; for this cause are sought, that they may engage our efforts; for this cause opened, that they may feed us (*ibid., in Ps. 140,* § 1, col. 1815). I. Great is the treasury of the Divine Scriptures, for they contain many wonderful precepts, which are like so many gems or precious jewels and valuable metals. But who is able to examine this treasury, use it, and make his own all that it contains? (*De disciplina Christiana,* c. 2, *PL* 40:670.) J. The reading of Sacred Scripture is in itself no insignificant foretaste of divine blessedness; in them man can examine himself as in a sort of mirror and see what kind of person he is, and whither he is tending. The assiduous reading of the Scriptures purifies all things; it inspires the reader with fear of hell; it moves his heart to heavenly joys. . . . As the body is nourished with carnal food, so the inner man is supported and fed with the divine utterances . . . most blessed is he who translates the teaching of the divine Scriptures into act (*Serm. 302,* § 2, *In Append., PL* 39: 2324). K. By this piety he will also become worthy to understand why Jesus made this answer [to Mary at Cana: . . . *My hour has not yet come* (John 2:4)], if by prayer he knocks at the gate of truth rather than by approaching it in the spirit of argument (*In Joan. Evangel.,* tract. 8, § 7, *PL* 35:1454).

1716. ST. JEROME. A. What honey can be sweeter than to know the wisdom of God? . . . Let others possess riches, if they will, drink from a jewelled cup, be resplendent in silks, take delight in the applause of men, and try in vain to exhaust their wealth in the most varied pleasures. Our riches are to meditate in the law of the Lord day and night (cf. Ps. 1:2), to knock at the closed door (cf. Matt. 7:7), to receive the three loaves of the Trinity (cf. Luke 11:5–8; *Ep. 30, ad Paulam,* § 13, *PL* 22:444). B. . . . Love knowledge of the Scripture and you will no longer love sins of the flesh (*Ep. 125, ad Rusticum, juvenem monachum,* § 11, col. 1078). C. The divine word is most rich, containing in itself all delights. No matter what you may desire, the wish is begotten of and answered in the Scriptures, as the Jews taught us: for when they ate the manna in the desert it was endowed with all delights and conformed to every man's taste (cf. Wisd. 16:20; *Breviarium in Ps. 147, 14, PL* 26: 1259). D. Keep the Scriptures always in your hands, and constantly dwell on them in your mind; do not consider that it is sufficient for you to know God's commandments by heart, and to disregard them in your deeds (*Ep. 148, ad Celantiam, de ratione pie vivendi,* § 14, *PL* 22:1210). E. Read often, learn all that you can. Let sleep overcome you with the roll [book] still in your hands; when your head falls, let it be on the sacred page (*Ep. 22, ad Eustochium, Paulae filiam, de custodia virginitatis,* § 17, col. 404). F. By constant reading and long-continued meditation [Nepotianus] has made his breast a library of Christ (*Ep. 60, ad Heliodorum, Epitaphium Nepotiani,* § 10, col. 595). G. Let her treasures be not silks and gems but manuscripts of the Holy Scriptures; and in these let her think less of gilding and Babylonian parchment and arabesque ornamentation than of correctness and accurate punctuation. Let her begin by learning the Psalter, and then let her gather rules of life from the Proverbs of Solomon. From the preacher let her gain the habit of despising the world and its vanities (Ecclesiastes). Let her follow the example of virtue and patience set in Job. Then let her pass on to the Gospels, never to be laid aside when once they have been taken in hand. Let her also drink in with a willing heart the Acts of the Apostles and the Epistles. As soon as she has enriched the storehouse of her mind with these treasures, let her commit to memory the Prophets, the Heptateuch, the Books of Kings and Chronicles (Paralipomenon), the Books of Esdras and Esther. When she has done these things she may safely read the Canticle of Canticles, but not before; for, were she to read it at the beginning she would fail to perceive that, though it is written in fleshly words, it is a marriage song of a spiritual bridal. And not understanding this she would suffer hurt from it. Let her avoid all apocryphal writings (*Ep. 107, ad Laetam, de institutione filiae,* § 12, col. 876). H. It is the greatest help toward justice to fill the mind with divine utterances, and always to meditate in the heart what you seek to execute in your deeds (*Ep. 148, ad Celantiam, de ratione pie vivendi,* § 15, col. 1210). I. Ignorance of the Scriptures is ignorance of Christ (*Comm. in Isa., Prolog., PL* 24:17).

1717. ST. GREGORY THE GREAT. Sacred Scripture far excels all other knowledge and all doctrine, to say nothing of the fact that it tells forth what is true; that it summons us to the heavenly country; that it changes the heart of him that reads it from earthly desires to the embracing of the things above; that by its more obscure statements it exercises the strong, and by its humble strain speaks gently to the little ones; that it is neither so shut up that it should be dreaded, nor so open to view as to become contemptible; that by use it removes weariness and is the more delighted in the more it is meditated on . . . (*Moral., Lib. 20,* c. 1, § 1, *PL* 76:135).

1718. ST. ISIDORE OF SEVILLE. A. The more industriously one devotes himself to the reading of the divine utterances, the greater the understanding he derives from them, just as soil which has been better cultivated yields a more abundant harvest (*Sententiarum Lib. III,* c. 9, § 2, *PL* 83:681). B. Externally, the sacred utterances appear in unpolished phrases, but they shine within with the wisdom of mysteries (*ibid.,* c. 13, § 3, col. 686).

1719. ST. PETER DAMIAN. Keep the Scriptures always in your hands; find your whole being in them; tarry in them; always seek your tranquillity in them; do not place your delight in conversation and concern about worldly matters, a practice that often casts back its own influence [that is, reacts by shaping the mentality along worldly lines] and confuses one's outlook (*Lib. 6, ep. 29, ad Stephanum monachum, PL* 144:420).

1720. HUGO DE FOLIETO, canon regular, abbot, cardinal (12th century). In this refectory three tables are set forth, the three meanings of the divine Scriptures, namely the historical, the mystical and the moral. The first is for simple people, the second for the learned, the third for both. On the first table coarser food is placed, on the second that which is more delicate, the most appetizing on the third. The first draws people to it by the attraction of examples, the second by the power of mysteries, the third by the attraction of a morally good life. At the first Christ serves wine, at the second he breaks bread, at the third he becomes the teacher. The first nourishes us with the account of miracles, the second with figures, the third by means of doctrine. The examples of miracles strengthen faith; the fulfilment of the figures strengthens hope; the doctrine of morality strengthens charity (*De claustro aimae, Lib. III*, c. 8, *PL* 177:1097).

1721. HUGH OF ST. VICTOR. A. Certain passages of the divine Scripture can be understood only with effort, as in eating bread; other parts are more easily understood, like drinking wine; but in all its passages, as it is taken, the Scripture heals as though it were medicine and oil for the soul (*Miscellanea, Lib. III,* tit. 56, *In Append., PL* 177:672). B. Wherefore, it is apparent how much divine Scripture excels all other writings in subtlety and profundity, not only in its subject matter, but also in its method of treatment, since in other writings words alone are found to have meaning, but in it not only words but also things are significant (*De sacramentis, Lib. I, Prolog.*, c. 5, *PL* 176:185; *Hugh of St. Victor on the Sacraments of the Christian faith,* tr. by Roy J. Deferrari; Cambridge: The Medieval Academy of America, 1951, p. 5).

1722. HUGH OF ST. CHER, O.P. A. All of Scripture is directed to this objective: to recall from evil through fear, and to urge on to good by love (*Sup. Lib. Judicum, Prolog., Comment.* 1:195). B. Holy Scripture is a vessel containing the spiritual food and drink by which the souls of saints are nourished and their thirst slaked (*Sup. Prov. 25, 4, Comment.* 3:55). C. Read the Holy Scripture religiously and acquire a perfect knowledge of it, for through it God is known. He reads religiously who reads with devotion and zealously searches for understanding (*Sup. Sapientiam 1, 1, ibid.*, p. 139).

1723. ST. THOMAS AQUINAS. A. The author of Holy Scripture is the Holy Spirit, not only as regards the words themselves, but also of the thing (*Prolog. in scriptum sup. libris Magistri Sententiarum,* art. 5, *Op. Om.,* ed. Parma 22:6). B. The authority of Sacred Scripture is superior to all reason (*ibid., Lib. I,* dist. 2, q. 2, art. 1, p. 13).

1724. ST. ODO, abbot of Cluny (d. 942). In his great mercy God sent into the world the Holy Scripture, which can never pass away, so that, as Peter says, it may, *as a lamp shining in a dark place* (II Pet. 1:19), shed light upon our action, and in Paul's phrase, grant *patience and consolation* (Rom. 15:4) in all adversity. If there is anything at all that can sustain the wise man in the spirit of equanimity in the disturbances of this world, I think it must be more than anything else meditation on the Scriptures. All the means by which we are to know God and know ourselves are contained in the divine books. In this we are far removed, not only from other animals, but also from unwise and foolish men, and, as Solomon expressed the thought, our advantage is in knowing how to conduct ourselves in life (cf. Eccles. 6:8), that is, through having a knowledge of the Scriptures. The Lord himself testifies that life is in the Scriptures, saying: *The words that I have spoken to you are spirit and life* (John 6:64). The holy text is also a mirror through which we now see the divine mysteries in an obscure manner (I Cor. 13:12), and consider ourselves for what we are, so that in it there appears the progress we have made in virtue, or how far we have failed. There all things that destroy are laid bare; all that build up are made known to us. Despite all this many men listen more willingly to drollery than to this pattern of conduct which God has given them. Being negligent in the matter of holy reading is the same as a man refusing light in blindness, shade in summer, or medicine in illness (*Collationum Lib. I, prooemium, PL* 133:519).

1725. WILLIAM OF ST. THIERRY. For the Scriptures demand to be read in that spirit in which they were written; and in the same spirit they are to be understood. You will never attain to an understanding of Paul until you drink in his spirit by employing a good intention in reading him and studying him through continual meditation. You will never come to an understanding of David until you put on the very affections of the psalms by personal experience; and so with the rest. . . .

In the course of reading, affective thoughts are frequently to be expressed, and prayer composed as an interruption of the reading, not so much in the sense of discontinuing the thought as of restoring the mind to greater purity and to the understanding of what you read. Reading serves the intention. If he who reads truly seeks God through his reading, then all that he reads works for his good, and his understanding gathers and orders all the meaning of his reading unto the service of Christ. But if his mind wanders to other things, it draws everything after itself, and finds nothing so holy and sacred in the Scriptures but he will turn it—either through vainglory, or perversity of mind, or a corrupt understanding—to wickedness and vanity. For in reading all parts of the Scriptures the beginning must be fear of the Lord, wherein the purpose of the reader is first firmly established; from this purpose there must proceed and be ordered the understanding and meaning of all that is read (*Ep. ad fratres de Monte Dei, Lib. I,* c. 10, *officia et exercitia cellitae,* n. 31, *PL* 184:327).

1726. GILBERT OF HOILAND, abbot of St. Mary, diocese of Lincoln (d. 1172). Diligently hollow out a tomb for yourself in the rock, a new monument into which no one has been placed. For Christ is the rock. New places can always be found in Christ. You can always penetrate to new depths. There are many recesses in him, innumerable treasures of wisdom. He is not content to be led to the shearers only once; he can be sheared repeatedly. Abundant clippings are the mystical meanings, the profundity of sacred love. Jesus abounds in such: he can never be despoiled or plundered. *I will rejoice,* he says, *at your promise, as one who has found rich spoil* (Ps. 118:162). Clothe yourself with this spoil, wrap yourself in the wool that has been sheared, in order to keep yourself warm (*Serm. 14 in Cant. Salomonis,* § 1, *PL* 184:68).

1727. THOMAS À KEMPIS. A. A cleric without sacred books is like a soldier without weapons, a horse without a bridle, a boat without oars, a writer without pens, a bird without wings . . . an archer without arrows, a traveler without a staff, a blind man without someone to lead him. All such clerics can do little or nothing, nor will they make any progress without the means and without good teachers. In the same way a cloister or a congregation of clerics without sacred books is like a table without food, a well without water, a river without fish, . . . a garden without flowers . . . a vineyard without grapes, a tower without defenders, a house without furnishings (*Opusc. 11, doctrinale juvenum,* c. 7, *de indocto clerico sine sacris libris, Op. Om.* 4:189). B. When you take a book into your hands to read, be like the just Simeon when he received the Child Jesus into his arms, to hold and embrace him. After you read, close the book with thanksgiving for every word from the mouth of God, for you have discovered a hidden treasure in the field of the Lord. This treasure of the Church, worked out for us at great pains and made public by the holy Doctors, written and gathered together by good writers [copyists, before printing], provided by God for the consolation of many, is to be preserved from all stain (*ibid.,* c. 5, *de firma custodia librorum,* p. 186).

1728. ST. ISIDORE OF PELUSIUM, priest, abbot (d. circa 449). The sacred volumes which contain the testimony of the divine Scriptures are a ladder by which we climb to God. Hence accept all the things that are stated in the Church as genuine gold, and that which has been purified in fire by the Spirit of divine truth (*Lib. I, ep. 369, Cyro, PG* 78:391).

1729. JOHN OF TRITHEIM. A. Two practices have preserved the order [of St. Benedict] in its observance, namely the love of God and study of the Scriptures; where these have been wanting, the monks also have abandoned the holiness of their pursuits. . . . Some uneducated men, untried, and without knowledge of the Scriptures, since they had nothing [of a sacred nature] to which they could attach their heart in delight, have turned to love of the world, and miserably destroyed the discipline of the order (*De viris illustribus O.S.B., Lib. I,* c. 8, *Op. pia et spiritualia,* p. 23). B. Sacred knowledge, *like David's tower girt with battlements; a thousand bucklers hang upon it, all the shields of valiant men* (Cant. 4:4) possesses so great a power and fortitude as to render almost invincible him who truly loves it, by detaching his mind from all worldly pleasure. . . . O how sweet, Lord, is your Spirit, which through love of the Sacred Scriptures is drunk in by the purity of the humble heart! (*Ibid., Lib.* 2, c. 145, p. 62.) C. It is a deception of the devil to commend negligence in the matter of study under the guise of piety and to assign the title of humility to ignorance. Without this sun of doctrine from religious orders, what can you hope for but chimeras and Egyptian darkness? Without the arms and the sword of God's word for Christ's soldiers, how can they stand strong in faith against the battle arrays of the divided sects? (*Disciplina monastica,* tract. 4, *de lectionis disciplina,* n. 2.) *

1730. ST. EPHRAEM. When you read, do so with intense concentration and diligence, deliberating upon a verse twice or three times, and penetrating its meaning. Repeat the same verse, as I have said, twice or three times, or even oftener, so as to arrive at its full understanding. When you prepare to sit down to read or to listen to someone else read [this was more than a thousand years before printing was invented], pray to God in these words: "Lord Jesus Christ, open the ears and eyes of my heart that I may understand your words, and perform your will, O Lord" (*Serm. de patientia et consummatione saeculi, Op. Om.* 1: 166).

The study of secular subjects

1731. CASSIODORUS. Nevertheless, the holy Fathers have not decreed that the study of secular letters should be scorned, for these letters are not the least important means of instructing our minds in the understanding of the Sacred Scriptures; they have decreed, on the other hand, that, if the knowledge of these matters is sought soberly and reasonably with the support of the divine grace, we should not only hope to be advanced spiritually by reading them, but in the course of our reading we should desire to have profitable and advantageous wisdom granted to us by *the Father of Lights* (Jas. 1:17). How many philosophers through eager reading of secular letters alone have failed to arrive at the font of wisdom and, deprived of the true light, have been plunged into the blindness of ignorance! For, as someone has expressed it, that can never be fully discovered which is not sought in the proper manner.

Again, many of our Fathers, trained in letters of this sort and living by the law of the Lord, have attained true wisdom, as blessed

* This work is not included in the very large *Opera pia et spiritualia,* which otherwise contains all the excerpts from John of Tritheim used by Wolter, nor has it been found in the other works available, in any of the libraries visited. Father Suso Mayer, O.S.B., of Maurus Wolter's archabbey of Beuron reports that no such work is found in that monastery's excellent ascetical library. Contrary to the policy of not presenting uncontrolled passages, this excerpt is retained with Archabbot Wolter's citation because of its compelling significance for modern monastic life. [*Tr.*]

Augustine relates in his work, *On Christian Learning,* saying: "We see, do we not, with how much gold and silver and clothing Cyprian, a most agreeable teacher and a most blessed martyr, was enriched when he went out from Egypt? With how much Lactantius, and Victorinus, and Optatus, and Hilary were enriched?" (*De doctrina Christiana, Lib. II,* c. 40, § 61, *PL* 34:63.) We add Ambrose, and the aforesaid Augustine, and Jerome, and the many others included in the words "countless Greeks" (*loc. cit.*). Likewise enriched was that most faithful servant of God, Moses himself, concerning whom it is written that he *was instructed in all the wisdom of the Egyptians* (Acts 7:22). And imitating them carefully, but unhesitatingly, let us hasten to read both bodies of doctrine, if we can (for who could venture to doubt after the many examples of men of this sort?) with clear knowledge, as it has often been said before now, that the Lord can grant true and genuine wisdom, as the Book of Wisdom says: *All wisdom comes from the Lord and with him it remains forever* (Sir. 1:1; *De institutione divinarum litterarum,* c. 28, nn. 3, 4, *PL* 70:1142; Jones, p. 129).

1732. ST. WILLIAM, abbot of Hirschau (d. 1091). It is permissible and altogether proper for us in the investigation of secular philosophy to dig for gold in the mud, to plunder Egypt, to gather fragrant fruits among thorns, provided that we carry the gold that we have dug out to the treasury of the sacred word; provided too that we transplant in their proper order the young shoots we have gathered among the trees of the plentiful field which the Lord has blessed (cf. Gen. 27:27).

It is abundantly evident that to all Catholics who have knowledge of the arts and sciences that, with the exception of the Son of Man, who stands apart from all others in the human race, no one ever was or ever will be holier than Adam, the first man created. Before his sin he knew good by the order of nature, and had no knowledge of evil. So great was his holiness indeed that after he had been condemned to the exile of this world because of his sin, and the unbegotten purity of his mind began to be corrupted by the evil of his posterity, the loving Creator, regretting that he had withdrawn his creature from the original dignity of divine reason, began first through the patriarchs, then by means of the Law of the prophets, and finally by his Son with his Gospel, his signs and wonders, as well as those of his disciples, followed by the teaching and example of the doctors of the Church, to invite the human race to acquire once more the heavenly perfection of the breath of life and likeness to God by means of the hereditary strength of mind. Not only is it permissible by study to follow the acuteness of knowledge of him whose unborn holiness we must imitate; it is not allowed, for those who, living an active life, have received the talent of natural ability from the Lord, to abstain from its exercise.

Now let us see if this discipline about which we are to treat, has been wanting to man's wisdom. In the Book of Conferences, which is held in high repute, it is written: "Men have departed from that true discipline of the philosophy of nature which the first man, who followed in the very footsteps of the creation of all nature, could clearly understand and also transmit to his posterity with certainty—for he had beheld the world itself when it was struggling in its infancy, and was uncultivated in its first stages of development. In him, too, there was not only the fullness of wisdom, but also the grace of divine prophecy transmitted by that divine breathing into his soul by which he could not only distinguish the wildness and poisons of all animals and serpents, but also shared in the virtues of herbs and the nature of trees and stones, and changes of seasons not as yet known, so that he could say: *For* [the Lord] *gave me sound knowledge of existing things, that I might know the organization of the universe and the force of its elements, the beginning and the end and the midpoint of times, the changes in the sun's course and the variations of the seasons. Cycles of years, positions of the stars, natures of animals, tempers of beasts, powers of the winds and thoughts of men, uses of plants and virtues of roots—such things as are secret I learned, and such as are plain; for Wisdom, the artificer of all, taught me* (Wisd. 7:17–22).

There you see from what a pure source we are drawn even against our wills by natural inclination, even by a kind of inspiration, to the discipline of the whole quadrivium.* Hence, against all who speak evil things, and to their confusion in the name of him who *tells the number of the stars and calls each by name* (Ps. 146:4), let us develop our treatise on astronomy by means of dialogue discussion (*Praefatio in sua Astronomica, PL* 150:1641).

1733. JOHN OF TRITHEIM. While St. Benedict was still living and his order was being spread to different regions, many noblemen and well-educated youths who were skilled not only in Divine Scripture but also in profane literature, submitted to the teaching of monasticism according to his Rule. The most brilliant of these was the Senator Cassiodorus [not a follower of Benedict], a man most learned in many fields of endeavor, who became a monk living within the enclosure after he had given up the senatorial dignity [cf. modern patrology manuals]. As time went on the monks' study of Scriptures held the highest place, but the love of learning in all fields was constant. For those who were well educated at the time of their conversion to monasticism profitably taught the younger brethren the canons of learning. Youth was not allowed to interfere with the progress, since the program was conducted under the authority of masters. To mention a few of the many, let us glance at Boniface and Rabanus, both archbishops of

* The four higher liberal arts, arithmetic, music, geometry and astronomy, which were complemented by the trivium, grammar, logic, and rhetoric.

Mainz, and Bede, the priest. . . . Whatever these holy men, skilled teachers of the Scriptures as well, knew of the sacred writings, they learned in the monasteries under the Rule of the order. They were not sent elsewhere for the purpose of learning, for they always had masters of the arts in their own monasteries. I will pass over many others of great learning who had come to the monastery in boyhood and later shone as outstanding examples of erudition and holiness. . . . The younger brethren were instructed in scholastic disciplines, each according to his need—some in grammar and orthography, others in rhetoric and logic; certain ones in music and arithmetic or in the art of computing; others again in philosophy; and finally, those who had been trained in all these disciplines were introduced to a systematic study of the Scriptures. There was no occasion for idleness in the monasteries, but the individual brethren pursued their studies and work. Hence many became outstanding for their holiness and learning in every branch of knowledge of the Scriptures to the great recognition given to them personally and to the order (*De viris illustribus O.S.B., Lib. I,* c. 6, *Op. pia et spiritualia,* p. 20).

1734. VEN. LOUIS DE BLOIS. We thus permit the brethren, in keeping with the spirit of the age, to devote their efforts to literature, but in such wise that they do not through its study bring the stain of pride or vainglory upon themselves, but in simplicity refer all to the honor of God. Otherwise it is preferable for monks to remain unlettered than to be highly educated (*elegantes*). Simplicity also is quite salutary: through it humility is better preserved (*Coll. ex vita S. Birgittae,* c. 4).*

Prayer before work

1735. ST. FRUCTUOSUS, abbot, bp. of Braga, Portugal (d. circa 670). When the signal has been given and they have gathered together their iron tools, they will form a unit, say a prayer and go out to work until the third hour [about 9:00 A.M.], reciting prayers on their way (*Reg. monachorum,* c. 6, *CR* 1:203; *PL* 87:1102).

1736. ST. DUNSTAN, monk, abp. of Canterbury (d. 988). If they have work to perform, the prior will, after having given the signal, first invoke the divine assistance by repeating three times, *O God, come to my assistance* (*De regimine monachorum,* c. 1, *PL* 137:483).

1737. ST. FRANCIS OF ASSISI. Those brethren to whom the Lord has given the grace of working should labor faithfully and devoutly, so that in banishing idleness, the enemy of the soul, they do not extinguish the spirit of holy prayer and devotion, to which all temporal

* This is the only reference furnished by Wolter. In *Acta Sanctorum, Bolland., Octobr.,* tom. 4, *Vita S. Birgittae viduae,* c. 4, p. 508 f., comparable statements are made, of which the present excerpt seems to be a résumé. [*Tr.*]

things should be subservient (*Reg. II pro Fratribus Min.*, c. 5, *de modo laborandi, CR* 3:32).

1738. BENEDICT HAEFTEN, provost of Affligham (d. 1648). The Seraphim whom Isaias once beheld in vision had six wings (cf. Isa. 6:2). The works of Benedictine monks who, by their habit (as Boniface IV and others have said) represent the six-fold wings of the Seraphim, must be adorned according to the mind of St. Benedict, with a like number of qualities so that they may take flight to heaven and be acceptable before the Divine Majesty.

The first wing is that the manual labors must be [consciously] performed in God's presence, as the holy Father says: ". . . let him consider that God is always beholding him from heaven, that his actions are everywhere visible to the eyes of the Godhead" (*RSB*, c. 7, first degree of humility).

The second wing is that the work be performed in the spirit of diffidence with respect to one's own powers: "Let the monk esteem himself, in regard to the work that is given him, as a bad and unworthy workman" (*ibid.*, sixth degree).

The third . . . that trusting in divine assistance, he implore God's help, which thought the holy Father proclaimed in these words: "Whatever good work you undertake, ask him with most instant prayer to perfect it" (*ibid.*, *Prolog.*, § 2).

The fourth wing, or quality, of monastic work, is that it be performed in the spirit of humility, an ideal inculcated in many parts of the Rule, but particularly in Chapter Seven. In another place the Rule reads: "If there are skilled workmen in the monastery, let them work at their crafts with all humility" (*ibid.*, c. 57).

The fifth is that the work be performed in obedience. "Everything, therefore, is to be done with the approval of the abbot" (*ibid.*, c. 49).

The sixth and last wing of our works is that the religious, abandoning any credit that might be attributed to him and, as it were, divesting himself of his work, attribute it wholly to God, direct it to his glory, and offer it to him. St. Benedict teaches this practice in the *Instruments of Good Works:* "To attribute to God, and not to self, whatever good one sees in oneself" (*ibid.*, c. 4, n. 42). He expresses the thought even more clearly in the Prologue: "Fearing the Lord, they are not puffed up on account of their good works, but judging that they can do no good of themselves and that all good comes from God, they magnify the Lord's work in them, using the word of the prophet: *Not to us, O Lord, not to us, but to your name give glory . . .*" (Ps. 113 B:1).

This last disposition is the most sublime purpose of all that the worker can have in mind—to refer everything he does to God's glory—

just as the blessed in heaven refer all that they do to it. In fact, God himself, in all the works he undertakes apart from himself, to use the language of the theologians, always acts for the sake of his glory and with the intent of increasing it. For God's glory is a more excellent good than that of the creature. It is, therefore, a high degree of perfection to acknowledge that God is working in us, and that the work he produces is not ours but his, and to direct it to his glory and offer it to him.

With these six wings, our works, which otherwise crawl upon the ground, take flight to heaven and become spiritual (*Disquisitiones monasticae, Lib. IX,* tract. 2, *de laboris qualitate,* disq. 3, p. 848 f.).

1739. ST. BASIL THE GREAT. For the rest, everyone should be devoted to his own trade, applying himself to it enthusiastically and accomplishing it blamelessly with ready zeal and careful attention, as if God were the overseer, so that he may ever be able to say in all honesty: *Behold, as the eyes of servants are on the hands of their masters, . . . so are our eyes on the Lord, our God* (Ps. 122:2); but one should not work now at one kind of task, now at another (*Reg. fusius tract., Interrogatio 41, de auctoritate et obedientia,* § 2, *PG* 31:1023; Wagner, p. 315).

1740. ST. JOHN CHRYSOSTOM. A. It is a sad and most disgraceful situation to be in love with glory even in civil affairs. But when even in spiritual matters you are in the same plight, what excuse is there left remaining for you, when you are not minded to yield God even as much honor as you receive yourself from your servants? For even the slave looks on the hands of his master (cf. Ps. 122:2), and the hireling to his employer who is to pay him wages, and the disciple to his master. But you do just the contrary. Having left the God that hired you, even your Master, you look to your fellow servants; and this, knowing that God remembers your good deeds even after this life, but man only for the present (*In Ep. ad Rom., Hom. 17,* § 5, *PG* 60:570). B. But we ought not to do anything good for the hope of the kingdom, but simply because it is pleasing to God, which is more than any kingdom; what does he deserve who, because he does not receive his recompense here, becomes remiss concerning virtue? (*In I Cor., Hom. 43,* § 4, *PG* 61:372.)

Work must be from pure love of God

1741. ST. BERNARD. A. For it is not without reward that God is loved, although he ought to be loved without looking for reward. And this is because true love cannot be empty of effect, nor yet is it mercenary. We know that it *is not self-seeking* (I Cor. 13:5). It is a disposition of the emotions, not a legal contract; it is neither acquired by mutual agreement, nor does it acquire after such a fashion. It affects a man freely and it makes him free. True love finds satisfaction in itself. It has its reward, which is the object of its love. For whatever you appear to love for the sake of something else, it is plain that what you really love is not the mere means of loving, but the final object of your love. Paul does not preach the Gospel in order that he may eat, but he eats in order that he may preach the Gospel (cf. I Cor. 9:18), for the reason that he loves not food but the Gospel. True love does not seek a reward, but it does deserve one. In fact, it is when a man has not yet learned to love that a reward is set before him; when he loves, it is due to him; when he perseveres it is given to him. Finally, when persuading people in quite little matters, it is the reluctant and not the eager whom we entice by promises of rewards. For who would think that a man must be tempted by rewards in order that he may do what of his own accord he desires to do? (*Lib. de diligendo Deo,* c. 7, § 17, *PL* 182:984; Watkin Williams, p. 58.) B. God, then, demands that he should be feared as Lord, honored as Father; but as a Bridegroom, loved. Which of these three is the highest and most to be preferred? Surely it is love. Without it fear is painful, and honor without attraction. Fear is servile as long as it is not rendered free by love; and honor which is not inspired by love is not truly honor, but flattery. Certainly honor and glory are due to God, and to him alone; but neither of these will he receive if they be not, as it were, seasoned with the honey of love. Love is alone sufficient by itself; it pleases by itself, and for its own sake. It is itself a merit, and itself its own recompense. It seeks neither cause, nor consequence, beyond itself. It is its own fruit, and its own object and usefulness. I love, because I love; I love, that I may love. Love, then, is a great reality, and very precious, provided that it recurs to the principle on which it rests, that it is kept in continual relation with him who is its origin, and draws from that pure source waters that flow continually in greater abundance (*Serm. 83 in Cant., Qualiter anima, quantumcumque vitiis corrupta adhuc per amorem . . . potest redire ad Christum,* § 4, *PL* 183:1183; Eales, p. 509). C. It is expedient for every man to be always attentive to God, considering him not only as his helper in necessity, but also as the witness of his conduct. For how could negligence ever take hold of him who never forgets that the eyes of the Lord are upon him? Or how could he fail to regard God as peculiarly his own when he beholds him so watchful of himself that he never ceases, even for a moment, to consider both his interior disposition and his exterior work, and to scrutinize and examine the most secret movements of his soul as well as his external actions? (*Serm. de temp., serm. 2 in Ps. Qui habitat,* § 3, col. 190.)

1742. ST. AUGUSTINE. To persons who love what they are doing, no labors are burdensome; in fact, they are even a delight, as in the case of those who are hunting, fowling, fishing, gathering grapes, conducting business, or delighting themselves in some game. The principal concern, therefore, is what is loved. For, in the case of what is loved, either there is no labor, or the labor itself is loved. And consider how it should be matter for shame and grief if there be pleasure in labor in order to capture wild beasts, to fill cask and purse, to play ball, and there be no pleasure in labors to win God! (*De bono viduitatis,* c. 21, *PL* 40:448.)

1743. ST. CYRIL OF JERUSALEM. The root of all good works is in the hope of the resurrection; for the expectation of the recompense stirs the soul to good works. For every laborer is ready to endure the toils, if he sees their reward in prospect; but when men weary themselves for nothing, their heart soon sinks as well as their body (*Catechesis 18 illuminandorum,* § 1, *PG* 33:1018).

1744. HUGH OF ST. CHER, O.P. In order for work to be appealing to us, the Lord adds the condiment of three spices: granting dutifulness in intention, enthusiasm in the affection, and humility in the execution of the work (*Sup. Gen. 48, 8, Comment.* 1:68).

1745. ST. BERNARD. A. . . . *they are free from the burdens of mortals, and are not afflicted like the rest of men. So pride adorns them as a necklace* (Ps. 72:5–6), that they should not be humbled and made penitent, but be condemned because of their pride, with the devil, who is proud, and with his angels. For those who have no part in the trouble of men shall assuredly have part in that of demons, and shall hear that terrible sentence from the mouth of the Judge: *Depart from me, accursed ones, into the everlasting fire which was prepared for the devil and his angels* (Matt. 25:41; *Serm. 23 in Cant.,* § 13, *PL* 183:891; Eales, p. 140). B. *This is my commandment, that you love one another, as I have loved you* (John 15:12). He who imposes this commandment is good and gentle. That which love commands us to do, and which love attracts us to perform always seems pleasant and delightful. For there is no hardship where there is charity, no labor where there is real love (*Serm. 14, in verbis Dni in Coena,* § 2, *In Append., PL* 184:944).

1746. ST. JEROME. Does toil frighten you? No athlete wins a crown but in the sweat of his brow (*Ep. 14, ad Heliodorum monachum,* § 10, *PL* 22:354).

1747. ST. AUGUSTINE. Diligence is the mother of every good work (*Ad fratres in eremo Serm. 16, In Append., PL* 40:1262).

Time is irrevocably spent

1748. ST. JOHN CHRYSOSTOM. A. You should be more sparing in spending time than anything else. If you have spent gold, you may recover it, but if you have spent time, you shall hardly regain that (*In Joan., Hom. 57,* § 5, *PG* 59:321). B. For it is not we who know the due time, but he, the Maker of time and the Creator of the ages (*In Coloss., Hom. 4*, § 4, *PG* 62:331).

1749. ST. JEROME. Consider that you have lost the whole period of time in which you know that you have made no progress (*Ep. 13, Virginitatis laus*, § 16, *PL* 30:175).

1750. ST. AUGUSTINE. Let us run while we have the light, lest we neglect the times of salvation that are passing by (*Serm. 252*, § 3, *In Append., PL* 39:2212).

1751. ST. BEDE, monk of Jarrow (d. 735). Every day is to be spent as though it were one's last (*Proverbia, sub litt. "o," In Append., PL* 90:1104).

1752. ST. BERNARD. Let none of you consider as a matter of no consequence, brethren, the time wasted in idle talking, for now is the acceptable time, now the day of salvation. The spoken word passes speedily on, not to be recalled; time runs swiftly, never to return, and the unthinking man pays no attention to what he is losing. "We shall chat," they say, "until the hour has passed." * Until the hour has passed! Until one hour has run its course. Until the hour has gone which the mercy of the Creator grants you for doing penance, for obtaining pardon, for acquiring grace and meriting glory! Until the hour has run its course—for you, who should be spending your time in making the divine goodness propitious to you, in advancing to companionship with the angels, in longing for the lost inheritance, aspiring to the promised blessedness, awakening the weakened will, bewailing the evils you have committed. Is that the way that farmers act—seeking diverting pursuits and passing the day irresponsibly—when the long-awaited chance for planting has finally arrived? Do vine dressers, when the pruning time for which they have been hoping comes at last, rejoice that they have found interesting diversion and pass the day without work? Do peddlers, at market time, contrive delays and seek opportunities for chatting which prevent them from drawing advantage from their actions, unless they see some benefit to themselves from so acting? Do beggars act in this way when, after their prolonged shouting the almoner finally appears: do they engage in amusing distractions, seek to enjoy recreations and remain in hidden corners of the square, while their companions run to the almoner?

But would that it were only the time that belongs to this life that were lost in chatting! But many are known to lose life itself in idle words. Not only do they lose it; they also take it—and that from their

* Although there was generally a zealous observance of silence, some interpreters conclude from this passage that the Cistercians were granted an occasional hour for conversing, as is gathered from a subsequent remark in the same sermon: "after protracted conversation . . ." (§ 5).

brothers. Do not those who are guilty of detraction, which is hateful to God and odious to life, destroy life? Life flees those whom it hates; and they from whom life flees, must die (*Serm. de diversis, Serm. 17, de triplici custodia manus, linguae, et cordis,* §§ 3, 4, *PL* 183:584).

1753. MICHAEL OF MEAUX, abp. of Sens (d. 1199). A. Time passes by like flowing water (*Expos. in Ps. 76, 18, Op. Om. S. Bonaventurae,* ed Peltier 9:250). B. Nothing can be more precious than time, neither for the repentant sinner, nor for him who is making spiritual progress, nor for him who has attained to a higher degree of perfection (*Altera expos. in Ps. 118, 14, ibid.,* p. 479).

1754. ST. BONAVENTURE. God will demand an explanation of how you spent (*expensum*) all the time that he bestowed (*impensum*) on you. How inimical is the devil to man in this time, and he becomes all the more hostile as the time for attacking man grows shorter (*Serm. I Dom. I in Quadr., ibid.,* 13:145).

1755. IMITATION OF CHRIST (Thomas à Kempis). Now the time is very precious, but, alas, that you should spend so unprofitably the time with which you should win life everlasting! The time is to come when you will long for one day or one hour in which to make amends, but I do not know whether the day or hour will be granted to you (*De imitatione Christi, Lib. I,* c. 23, *Op. Om.* 2:46; Gardiner, p. 64).

1756. ST. BERNARDINE OF SIENA, Franciscan preacher (d. 1444). A. The just man retains the time that he has spent well. To him who possesses this time, time is given at the end for a period for examining and cleansing his conscience; and he will abound, namely with true repentance, great pardon, abundance of grace, and infinite glory. But he has none who, by living in an evil manner, has lost this most precious time (*Serm. 13, Fer. IV post Dom. I Quadr.,* art. 3, c. 4, *Quartum periculum est quod multis divino judicio insperate aufertur penitentiae tempus, Op. Om.* 1:55). B. So great is the precious value of time, that in a brief period a man can gain pardon, grace, and glory; therefore, Bernard (*Serm. de div., Serm. 17,* § 3, *PL* 183:584) states: "The loss of time is supreme, for you lose, man, what divine mercy bestowed on you for meriting, increasing, and preserving God's grace" (*Serm. 42, Dom. de Passione, infra diem,* art. 2, c. 2, p. 197).

1757. ST. LAURENCE JUSTINIAN. A. What is more precious than time? What, I ask you, is more productive? What dearer, or more excellent? What more lovable? But regrettably, scarcely anything is considered more cheaply by almost all men, nothing used more unprofitably, nothing possessed more unworthily. Not one moment of time passes in which eternal merits cannot be accumulated (*De vita solitaria,* c. 10, *Op. Om.* 2:142). B. Nothing is so much ours, nothing so advantageous for gaining the rewards of heaven as time; it is granted to us in mercy so that using it in the performance of praiseworthy deeds, we may merit eternal life (*De compunctione et complanctu Christianae perfectionis,* c. 2, p. 16).

1758. JOHN OF TRITHEIM. No work should seem hard for the monk, no time long, no observance forbidding, for all these are the means by which the glory of eternal blessedness is acquired. Consider well the shortness of this life, brethren, and perform your good deeds as long as you can; for he who now sows sparingly will also reap sparingly after death; and each is to receive the appropriate reward for his own efforts and not those of another (cf. Ps. 61:13). The time for working is short indeed, but that which is due for good work is everlasting. Consider, brethren, the men who are immersed in worldly pursuits, and all who love this present life—how strong they are in regard to things earthly and fallen, how weak and infirm in things heavenly. Surely you should at least be as intent on pleasing God as they are in working continually in order to appear rich and renowned before the world. For many do not hesitate to work hard until death for temporal recognition, but spurn to do anything or to suffer even a little for the hope of future blessedness. They will put up with any hardships in all patience in order to gain earthly goods, but refuse to submit to the contumely of even the slightest word in order to obtain a heavenly reward. They can be strong all day long in assisting an earthly king or prince or judge, but cannot continue for an hour in prayer before the almighty Lord. They willingly tolerate many adversities in order to acquire perishable wealth, but neglect to seek heavenly goods with the same zeal with which they are captivated when there is question of goods of earth (*Hom. VII, de labore monachorum manuali, Op. pia et spiritualia,* p. 437).

St. Benedict's example

1759. BENEDICT HAEFTEN, provost of Affligem (d. 1648). The personal observance of the Rule by its lawgiver is manifestly something unique, about which St. Gregory the Great wrote in these terms: "[St. Benedict] wrote a rule for monks, a book commendable both for its good sense and its attractive style. If anyone wishes to study his character and manner of life more closely, he will find it embodied in the precepts of that rule, for he could not have taught otherwise than he lived" (*S. Greg. Magn. Dialogorum Lib. II,* c. 36, *PL* 66:200). In these words the Supreme Pontiff clearly indicates that St. Benedict personally was adorned with all the virtues which he prescribed and commended in the Rule for his followers. St. Gregory adduces this consideration as a sufficient reason for his having purposely omitted parts of the life of the venerable Father, in that his life, virtues, and personal monastic observance are most clearly shown forth in the Rule, as in a flawless mirror. What more can I say of exact observance of the Rule than that "this is the way by which Benedict, the beloved of the Lord, ascended into heaven"? (*Ibid.*, c. 37, col. 202.) What, asks St. Bernard, is this way, leading from his cell, but the order which the blessed man instituted, and the pattern of life which had its beginning in him? "The beloved of the Lord ascended by this way," says St. Gregory, "because he could not teach other than he lived" (*Comment. in vita S. Benedicti, auctore S. Greg. Magn.*, c. 37, *Disquisitiones monasticae*, p. 191).

Obedience the supreme virtue

1760. ST. JEROME. A. To be a perfect and complete Christian it is not enough to despise wealth or to squander and fling away one's money, a thing which can be lost and found in a single moment. Crates the Theban did this; so did Antisthenes and others whose lives show them to have had many faults. The disciple of Christ must do more for the attainment of spiritual glory than the philosopher of the world, than the venal slave of rumors and of the words of men. It is not enough for you to despise wealth unless you follow Christ as well (*Ep. 66, ad Pammachium . . . qui statim post mortem uxoris Paulinae monachi propositum arripuerit,* § 8, *PL* 22:644). B. The Lord wills to have you as a living sacrifice, pleasing to God. Note that I say "you," not what belongs to you (*Ep. 118, ad Julianum,* § 5, col. 964). C. The first principle of union among monks is to obey superiors and to do whatever they command (*Ep. 22, ad Eustochium,* § 35, col. 419).

1761. ST. THOMAS AQUINAS. A. Man can give nothing greater to God, than by subjecting his will to another man's for God's sake (*II-II,* q. 186, art. 5, *Utrum obedientia pertineat ad perfectionem religionis,* ad 5m, *Op. Om.* 10:495; Am. ed. 2:1977). B. The vow of obedience is the chief of the three religious vows (Corpus). . . . It is to be preferred to virginity observed even as a vow (*ibid.*, art. 8, *Utrum votum obedientiae sit potissimum inter tria vota religionis,* ad 3m; p. 499; p. 1979). C. Therefore, properly speaking, the virtue of obedience, whereby we contemn our own will for God's sake, is more praiseworthy than the other moral virtues, which contemn other goods for the sake of God (*II-II,* q. 104, art. 3, *Utrum obedientia sit maxima virtutum, Op. Om.* 9:387; Am. ed. 2:1643).

1762. JOHN OF TRITHEIM. Among all the virtues of the monastic life the greatest is obedience, without which no one can be a monk, for it is the first and the principal vow for those promising to observe the Rule, that is to say, to direct their lives according to its maxims. For if obedience is lacking, neither chastity nor poverty makes one a monk. As Wisdom declares, it is the most noble kind of triumph to gain the victory over self; but having conquered himself the truly obedient monk does precisely that in fulfilling the commands of another (*Comm. in c. 7, Grad. 3 RSB, Op. pia et spiritualia,* p. 316).

1763. ST. AUGUSTINE. This it was in [Mary] that the Lord magnified, that she did the will of the Father, not that flesh bore flesh (*In Joan. Evangel.,* tract. 10, § 3, *PL* 35:1468).

1764. THOMAS À KEMPIS. By obedience man becomes beloved of God, and on such friendly terms with Christ as to merit to be his brother. *For whoever does the will of my Father in heaven, he is my brother and sister and mother* (Matt. 12:50; *De disciplina claustralium,* c. 4, n. 4, *Op. Om.* 2:285).

1765. ST. LAURENCE JUSTINIAN. Whoever seeks to serve God must choose obedience for his particular love. . . . Especially is obedience to be steadfastly cherished in monasteries and communities dedicated to God (*De disciplina et perfectione monasticae conversationis,* c. 7, *Op. Om.* 1:111).

Obedience is the norm of perfection

1766. THOMAS À KEMPIS. A. He makes greater spiritual progress and becomes more acceptably pleasing to God who fulfils more quickly and readily that which the will of the superior declares should be done. And if he knew better and the precept were more clearly made manifest to him, without any wavering, he should show himself most prompt to obey God and his vicar (*Serm. ad novitios, serm. 7, Op. Om.* 6:56). B. The more humbly one subjects himself to superiors, the more he will advance in virtues and the wiser he will become (*Dialogus novitiorum,* c. 2, *de contemptu mundi, Op. Om.* 7:8).

1767. IMITATION OF CHRIST (Thomas à Kempis). My son, says our Savior Christ, he who labors to withdraw himself from obedience withdraws himself from grace; he who seeks to have private possessions loses the things that are in common. If a man cannot gladly submit himself to his superiors, it is a sign that his flesh is not yet fully obedient to the spirit, but that it often rebels and murmurs. Therefore if you desire to overcome yourself, and to make your flesh humbly obey the will of the spirit, learn first gladly to obey your superiors. The outward enemy is the sooner overcome if the inner man, that is, the soul, is not enfeebled or weakened (*De imitatione Christi, Lib. III,* c. 13, n. 1, *Op. Om.* 2:168; Gardiner, p. 123).

The perfect obedience of the monk

1768. ST. BONAVENTURE. Before everything else religious must strive with most intense effort to deprive their self-will of its liberty. For what does it profit those living under the command of one person to give up their property unless they have abandoned their wills, since it is more excellent to abandon the will than to give up material goods. The whole perfection of the religious life consists in the abdication of self-will. . . . Now the proof of a submissive will is to be found in two things: if a person reverently obeys in the things enjoined on him, and if he does not fail to have the authority of obedience in all his deeds. . . . For whatever man orders as God's representative, which is not known to be certainly displeasing to God, must be accepted as though the Lord himself commands it. Obedience is also better than sacrifice as far as merit is concerned: it is proved that nothing is more acceptable to God than the sacrifice of holy obedience.

No one is more unencumbered for pursuing the course of perfection than the truly obedient man. For the sons of obedience show themselves completely given to obeying, and as soon as they hear the superior's voice they receive his order as though it were divinely commanded; they cannot suffer delay, but leaving all things, rise promptly and reverently to the faithful performance of all that is enjoined, so that with swift obedience they follow up with their deeds the voice of him who commands them [cf. *RSB,* c. 5].

Perfect obedience simply leaves unfinished the tasks at hand. In fact, the obedient man does not even await the spoken word if he is certain of the superior's wishes. "I would call that the perfect degree of obedience when work that is assigned is received in the same spirit in which it is commanded, that is, when the purpose of the one performing the deed depends on the will of the one commanding" (*S. Bernard., de praecepto et dispensatione,* c. 7, § 16, *PL* 182:870). "Let those whose duty it is to obey and fulfil what is ordered never pass judgment on the superior's purpose" (*S. Hieronymus, Ep. 125, ad Rusticum,* § 15, *PL* 22:1081). If they seek to attain to real progress in virtue through obedience, they must firmly resolve to be reverently submissive in all matters at all times. If perchance anything difficult or even impossible should be ordered, they will receive the order with all meekness [cf. *RSB,* c. 68]. . . .

Not only shall the virtue of obedience be practiced toward superiors, but the brethren shall also obey one another in the spirit of emulation [*RSB,* c. 71]. It is the duty of Christ's disciple to accede to the wishes of all who request something of him (cf. Luke 6:30). In imitation of the example of the Apostle they should make themselves the willing slaves of all. They should be, as it is written, *subject to one another in the fear of Christ* (Eph. 5:21).

The power of holy authority must always be present in all the works of obedience, for without it not even good works are good. . . . Hence the new followers of Christ [the novices], completely denying themselves in all they do, that is, in their works, their conversations, and in the use of all things whatsoever, must follow not their own will, but their superior's direction in everything.

No permission is necessary for performing the works of the monastery which benefit the community as a whole. . . . For special works touching an individual brother's need and causing no hindrance to the common life or the fulfilment of particular commands that have been given, I should say that there is no need to have recourse to superiors for permission, since according to the Apostle, we are bound to bear one another's burdens and serve one another in the spirit of charity (cf. Gal. 6:2).

For unusual services for the benefit of an individual, whether these be of the nature of bodily mortification, such as protracted night watches, unusual abstinences, or the exercise of manual labor to be performed personally or through another, permission is to be sought, for without it the religious must not undertake anything for his own advantage, because he has not the disposition even of his own body [*RSB,* c. 58]; and whatever is done without the permission of the spiritual father will be ascribed to presumption and vainglory, and not reckoned meritorious [*RSB,* c. 49]. . . . He is not allowed to work for himself on his own initiative, either by writing, undertaking other kinds of work, or substituting other articles for those assigned for his use, such as books, clothing, bedding, and the like. . . . I would not deny that the general permission of superiors suffices in insignificant or unimportant matters. . . .

There is no law governing the charity of lending objects according to the needs of those dwelling in the community. I may bestow an object on a brother who requests it, provided I do not give it with the attitude of claiming it as my own. . . . It is not permissible to appropriate something assigned for another's use, without his knowledge. That is a kind of theft, and a frequent cause of trouble—to keep something given for a brother's use, without his knowing it.

Taking the circumstances of time and place into account, the faithful and prudent servant can do certain things with the tacit or reasonably presumed permission of his superiors, which he will report as having been performed with such permission. For the rest, whatever a religious does or says that is good, and which he knows is not displeasing to his superior, is not deprived of the reward of true obedience. Blessed indeed is this slavery, which is in reality a glorious freedom, by which one is voluntarily sold into the royal servitude, choosing God and his representatives rather than oneself to govern one's acts, and renouncing wholly one's self-will (*Speculum disciplinae ad novitios, Pars I,* c. 4, *de captivatione propriae voluntatis,* §§ 1–12, *Op. Om.,* ed. Quaracchi 8:585–587).

1769. ST. GREGORY THE GREAT. A. For obedience is justly preferred to sacrifices, because by sacrifices the flesh of another, but by obedience our own will is offered up; a person, therefore, appeases God the more quickly, the more he represses before his eyes the pride of his own will, and immolates himself with the sword of the commandment (*Moral., Lib. 35*, c. 14, § 28, *PL* 76:765).

B. *For obedience is better than sacrifices; and to hearken rather than to offer the fat of rams* (I Kgs. 15:22), because it is of far higher merit always to subject one's will to the will of another than to wear down the body with excessive fasting or to punish oneself by means of compunction in secret sacrifice. What is the *fat of rams* other than the rich and interior devotion of one who is doing what he has chosen? He offers the fat of rams who possesses the love of devoted prayer in his striving for his secret way of life. Obedience is better than sacrifice and the offering of the fat of rams; for he who has learned to fulfil perfectly the will of his master, will in the heavenly kingdom excel those who have denied themselves in abstinence and those who mourn. All other good works are to be esteemed less highly than those which are commanded (*In I Reg. expos., Lib. V*, c. 2, § 23, *PL* 79:431).

Obedience a glorious victory, a share in the martyr's crown

1770. THOMAS À KEMPIS. A. It is a great struggle to overcome oneself, a noble triumph to bow the neck of pride, to give up one's own opinion, to lay aside one's own wisdom, to seek to conquer all assertiveness. Every man who freely obeys for God's sake does the work of a mighty warrior, because he fights against himself and slays the motions of his own will with the sword of the fear of God. And so he shall receive the crown of everlasting glory with the martyrs because he has manfully struggled and conquered. Whoever, therefore, humbly obeys a superior, or even an inferior, and willingly submits his own opinion to that of another, loses nothing, but yielding to the other, gains the more. Every man who thus overcomes and humbles himself treads upon the head of proud Lucifer, who suggests things contrary to humility—that a man do not submit to another, but turn to cunning arguments. Why this? Lest keeping silence he be lowered outwardly, and seem to be a fool or an ignoramus because he knows not how to defend himself, or allows himself to be vanquished. How blind and foolish pride always is, how far it wanders from the kingdom of God and rushes headlong to the gates of hell! What good and praiseworthy things have been said of you, holy humility, always ready to obey! For the gates of heaven open before you, enabling you to see the glorious countenance of Jesus Christ (cf. Acts 7:56). Let it not, therefore, be considered burdensome to anyone nor seem unworthy to obey another man for God's sake in things lawful and righteous, for Christ has been made obedient even to the shame of the cross (*Serm. 7 ad novitios, Op. Om.* 6:54; Scully, pp. 45–46). B. If he obeys in all that is enjoined on him, he shall be recompensed with the martyrs whose hands were fettered with chains and whose feet were hung in the rack. The obedient brother ought to reflect that he has not command over his own body, but the superior to whom he has freely resigned himself for God's sake to go and do whatever he shall order for the salvation of his soul. For thus shall he gain the palm of patience with the martyrs and the crown of life eternal, by the gift of our Lord Jesus Christ, who reigns forever and ever. Amen (*ibid., serm. 11,* p. 82; Scully, p. 68).

1771. JOHN OF TRITHEIM. A. There is no doubt that the monk who for love of God subjects himself . . . to the superior in all obedience . . . and desires to have a superior placed over him everywhere and at all times, imitates the Lord, who became obedient to God the Father unto death. . . . How much such a man resembles the holy angels, who at the slightest intimation obey God in all things! (*Comm. in c. 7, Grad. 3 RSB, Op. pia et spiritualia,* p. 316.) B. Obedience is the tree of eternal salvation that grows in the garden of monastic humility. Obedience is the dwelling place of the Holy Spirit and the tranquil tomb of self-will. Obedience is action that merits the reward of eternal blessedness, and the sole test of monastic discipline. It is the wiping out of all haughtiness and pride, the relentless pursuing of every vice. It conquers all malice and quenches all inordinate pleasures of the flesh. It makes the conscience pure and clean and protects true humility of heart. It is the healing of the wounded soul and the foundation of all monastic observance.

Obedience is the faithful guardian of all good works and the discipline of the sincere mind. It is the beginning of mortification and the splendid ornament of the monk. It preserves peace and concord, without which all vigor of monastic discipline is abandoned. It always directs the keenness of the intellect to God, for he who is truly mortified in mind spurns all that the world has to offer. Obedience draws the monk close to God and makes him a stranger to all meanness. It is loveliness of soul, the garment of beauty without which no one enters into the kingdom of eternal light. It is the mother of victory, for he who has learned to be humbly submissive for the honor of God will receive the crown of martyrdom in heaven.

Obedience separates the monk from the world; he who embraces it with his whole heart will be great before the Most High. It is the consummation of Christian perfection: the more a monk advances in it, the holier he becomes. It is security at the hour of death, for the more willing and prompt the monk has been in obeying, the more securely will he depart this life.

Obedience is the rewarder of the humble and the outstanding

quality of actions worthy of merit. Obedience is the pattern of Christian meekness, the powerful support of charity within the community. It is the protector of chastity, the ornament of innocence and purity. Obedience is the wisdom of monks; submission to the commands of superiors, the noble philosophy of those living in the cloister.

Obedience and humility are the resources and wealth of monks: to keep the memory of the Lord's passion in mind through them is sweetness with which all the rejoicing of the world cannot compare. Obedience and humility make the monk what he must be: he who is rebellious and proud wears the monastic habit without justification.

Obedience is the voluntary mortification of members by an alert mind; so great is its dignity that man has nothing greater that he can offer in God's honor. Let each one offer what he can out of the love of God: without doubt he will have offered most who by obedience has slain his own will out of love of God.

It is indeed a great good to distribute one's possessions in helping the poor out of love of Christ, and to give alms to relieve the hunger and helplessness of the indigent. But as the whole exceeds the part, as the use of free will is nobler than acting from necessity, as the heavens are distant from the earth, so much more does he offer who forever spontaneously gives himself up out of love of God than he who offers an alms. For whatever you offer to God out of your temporal goods is not yours, but someone else's, and is of lesser value and of lesser reward than that which is truly yours. You have one thing that is wholly yours which if offered to God pleases him more than anything else. What is this, other than your free will which the almighty Creator placed in your power? A good will is greater than all wealth; nothing more valuable can be offered to God; nothing more acceptable can be consecrated to him (*Hom. 20, de vera monachorum obedientia,* p. 502).

Self-will is the source of evils

1772. ST. EPHRAEM, deacon of Edessa, Doctor of the Church (d. 378). As much as one subdues his own will in the spirit of submission, so much the more does he progress. The more obstinately he persists in his own will, so much the greater harm and injury he inflicts on himself (*Consilium de vita spiritali ad monachum novitium,* c. 12, *Op. Om.* 1:48).

1773. ST. ANSELM, abp. of Canterbury, Doctor of the Church (d. 1109). A. Self-will is correctly called pride (*superbia*) for the very reason that it is not subjected to God's will but is exalted above it (*Eadmeri monachi Cantuar. Lib. de S. Anselmi Similitudinibus,* c. 7, *de superbia, PL* 159:607). B. As the crown belongs to the king alone, so self-will belongs to God only; and just as anyone would dishonor a king by taking his crown from him, so man dishonors God by usurping what belongs to him alone, in assuming the privilege of self-will. As self-will in God is the foundation and source of all that is good, self-will in man is the beginning of all evil (*ibid.*, c. 8). C. All [vices] belong to the family of self-will and obey her as their queen (*ibid.*, c. 36, col. 617).

1774. JOHN CASSIAN. Those who have learned by long experience say that a monk—and this is especially true of younger monks—cannot bridle the desires of his concupiscence unless he has first learned by obedience to mortify his wishes. And so they lay it down that . . . the man who has not learned to overcome his desires cannot preserve lasting unity with the brethren or a stable and continuous concord, nor remain for any length of time in the monastery (*De coenob. institut., Lib. 4*, c. 8, *PL* 49:160).

1775. ST. DOROTHEUS. A. When we insist on having our own way, the devil grows stronger, causes greater harm, accomplishes more, and under pretext of good, deceives us more than ever, nor do we realize that we are being led to ruin. How can we even know the will of God or seek it when we place our confidence in ourselves and follow our own will in everything? (*Doctrina 5*, § 1, *PG* 88:1675.) B. Destruction is justice mixed with self-will, the supreme danger to be feared more than all else; then the unhappy man is exposed to the gravest dangers, in fact, he perishes in them. For who can persuade him who sees for himself what he is doing, to believe that something else is more profitable for him, if he is more forcefully drawn to cling to his own will? (*Ibid.*, § 2.)

1776. ST. PETER DAMIAN. Sometimes no other burden is heavier for man than man himself. What tyrant is more cruel to man, what power harsher than man's own self-will? . . . Self-will has this peculiar power that the more obedient he is who obeys himself, the more this very obedience fetters him with its cruel bonds. It alone is loved, whereas it alone deserves to be hated—for it is the beginning of iniquity, the begetting of death, the great destroyer of virtue (*Serm. 9, de S. Benedicto, PL* 144:549).

1777. ST. BERNARD. A. We exhort you in all charity and admonish you with all the earnestness of pastoral solicitude not to love out-of-the-way corners, frequent hidden spots, or withdraw to places apart, *for everyone who does evil hates the light, and does not come to the light that his deeds may not be exposed* (John 3:20). . . . Therefore I earnestly beg and implore you, brothers, to shun all pretenses and all the hiding corners of self-will; avoid restlessness and the spirit of levity; flee obstinacy and that wretched vice of singularity (*Serm. de temp., Serm. I pro Dom. VI p. Pent.*, § 3, *PL* 183:338). B. With regard to the spirit of discretion, it is clear enough that nothing is so calculated to destroy it as self-will, which corrupts the hearts of men and blinds the eye of reason (*ibid., Serm. II in temp. Resurrectionis,* § 8, col. 286). C. The heart is infected with two kinds of leprosy [the sermon is on Naaman, bathing in the Jordan, cf. IV Kgs. 5:10], namely, self-will and obstinate attachment to one's own judgment. Both species of leprosy are most malignant, and so much the more dangerous because they are interior and hidden. . . . If self-will ceased to be, there would be no hell. . . . How cruel and abominable is that malice which could wish to see God deprived of his wisdom or of his power, or of his justice! This self-will then is a cruel beast, a treacherous wild animal, a rapacious wolf, the fiercest of lionesses (*ibid., Serm. III,* § 3, col. 289). D. We must, then, be on our guard against self-will as we would against a most vicious and poisonous snake, and that which alone can condemn our souls (*Serm. de div., Serm. 11,* § 3, col. 571). E. The summit of all humility seems to consist in this alone—that our will be subject to the divine will in conformity with what the Prophet says: *Only in God is my soul at rest* (Ps. 61:1; *ibid., Serm. 26,* § 2, col. 610). F. The way of sinners is the spirit of the world, or self-will, which is nothing other than pride, from which all evils proceed, whereas all goods come from the community (*ibid., Serm. 72,* § 3, col. 693). G. [Self-will] is that which teaches you not to show any forbearance toward your nature, not to listen to reason, not to listen to the advice of the example of your seniors, not to obey me [St. Bernard, as abbot]. Do you not know that *obedience is better than sacrifices?* (I Kgs. 15:22.) Have you not read in your Rule that what is done without the permission of the spiritual father shall be ascribed to presumption and vainglory and not be reckoned meritorious? (*RSB,* c. 49; *Serm. 19 in Cant.,* § 7, col. 866.) H. Whence do scandals arise, whence come disturbances, except that by following our own self-will, and rashly considering as true what we have set our hearts on, we encounter some obstacle which in one way or another forbids or prevents us from doing what we want to do, which in turn causes in us impatience, or murmuring, or the giving of scandal? In so acting we forget that *all things work together unto good for those who, according to his purpose, are saints through his call* (Rom. 8:28), and that what appears to us to be a failure is really a sign from God which makes known his will to us (*Serm. de div., Serm. 26,* § 3, col. 611).

1778. HUGH OF ST. CHER, O.P. To do battle against our enemy, which is self-will, the Lord sends us reproaches, disgrace, and persecution (*Sup. Eccles. 9, 17, Comment.* 3:97).

1779. ST. LAURENCE JUSTINIAN. A. Self-will is the beginning of sins, the tinder of crimes, and the motivating force of all evils. . . . Without it no one has ever fallen; with it no one has ever remained standing (*Lignum vitae, tract. de obed.,* c. 1, *Op. Om.* 1:49). B. He has freed himself of a very heavy burden who has rejected his own will; for self-will stands perennially in opposition to God. . . . It is always insolent, unrestrained in speech, disorderly in conduct, inordinate in its attachments, lacking in self-knowledge, averse to the love of neighbor (*De disciplina et perfectione monasticae conversationis,* c. 7, 1:111). C. Nothing is known to be so opposed to humility as the ambitious grasping of self-will (*Lib. de humilitate,* c. 19, 2:402). D. Nothing is to be considered more harmful than self-will, nothing more destructive of man's well-being (*Lib. de obed.,* c. 27, 2:356).

1780. JOHN OF TRITHEIM. A. The monk who has not given up his own will is not what he is called; in fact, he incites the anger of God. . . . The first tool that the monk must acquire is abandonment of self-will, without which no one is a monk. . . . Anyone who desires to offer an acceptable sacrifice to God will have nothing more precious to present than his own self-will. . . . It is damnable in a monk not to have ceased to do his own will (*Comm. in Prolog. RSB, Op. pia et spiritualia,* p. 158). B. There is nothing worse in a monk than to reclaim the will that he has once given up in sacrifice (*ibid.,* p. 204). C. Nothing more detestable can be found in a monk than self-will, for he is to be governed not by his own, but by another's authority: he came to the monastery to be governed, not to govern (*ibid., in c. 3,* p. 259). D. It is something great indeed, so great that man can offer nothing more precious to God, than to give up his own will out of love for him (*ibid., in c. 4,* n. 59, p. 308). E. Nothing so corrupts a man as does carnal self-will, which is not led by the Spirit of God (*ibid.,* c. 7, *Grad. 1,* p. 348). F. Let each one out of the love of God offer what he can; beyond all doubt he offers more than all others who makes an immolation of his self-will (*Hom. 20, de vera obedientia monachorum,* p. 502).

1781. ST. JOHN CLIMACUS. The man of humble mind always loathes his own will as wayward, and in his requests to the Lord he studies with unwavering faith to learn and to obey. He does not direct his attention to the life of his masters but casts his care upon God who used an ass to teach Balaam his duty. A worker of this kind, although he does everything and thinks and speaks according to the will of God, yet he never trusts himself. Self-confidence for the humble is just as much a weight and a burden as another man's choice is for the proud (*Scala paradisi, Grad. 25, de . . . humilitate, PG* 88:999; Moore, n. 54, p. 198; Fr. Robert, p. 324).

1782. ST. BERNARD. He who makes himself his own master subjects himself to a fool for a master (*Ep. 87, ad Ogerum canonicum regularem,* § 7, *PL* 182:215; Gasquet, p. 102; James, p. 133).

1783. ST. JOHN CLIMACUS. A. Obedience is absolute renunciation of our own life, clearly expressed in our bodily actions. Or, conversely, obedience is the mortification of the limbs while the mind remains alive. Obedience is unquestioning movement, voluntary death, simple life, carefree danger, spontaneous defense by God, fearlessness of death, a safe voyage, a sleeper's progress. Obedience is the tomb of the will and the resurrection of humility. A corpse does not argue or reason as to what is good or what seems to be bad. For he who has devoutly put the soul of the novice to death will answer for everything. Obedience is the abandonment of discernment in a wealth of discernment. The beginning of the mortification both of the soul's desire and of the bodily members involves much hard work. The middle sometimes means much hard work and is sometimes painless. But the end is insensibility and insusceptibility to toil and pain (*Scala paradisi, Grad. 4, De beata semperque laudanda . . . obedientia, PG* 88:679; Moore, nn. 3–4, pp. 66–67; Fr. Robert, p. 106). B. If anyone has his conscience in the utmost purity in the matter of obedience to his spiritual father, then he daily awaits death as if it were sleep, or rather life, and is not dismayed, knowing for certain that at the time of his departure, not he, but his director, will be called to account (*ibid.,* col. 706; Moore, n. 50, p. 83; Father Robert, p. 74). C. Just as trees swayed by the winds drive their roots deeply into the earth, so those who live in obedience get strong and unshakable souls (*ibid.,* col. 728; Moore, n. 124, p. 97; Fr. Robert, p. 106).

1784. ST. PETER DAMIAN. Our first parent . . . had received the command to recognize the Creator's will above his own, but by his wilfulness in using, or more correctly in abusing his will, in that he sought to make himself happy, he destroyed himself. Driven out from that blessed inheritance, man's lot became one of exile instead of homeland, death in place of life, disgrace where formerly there was glory. Hence, if you seek to return to your inheritance (cf. *RSB,* opening sentence of *Prolog.*), deny your will. . . . Denial of the will is the regaining of the inheritance (*Serm. 48, De exaltatione S. Crucis,* 14 Sept., *PL* 144:764).

1785. ST. LAURENCE JUSTINIAN. *Obey your superiors and be subject to them, for they keep watch as having to render an account of your souls* (Heb. 13:17). . . . This is an excellent counsel indeed, to place your burdens on the shoulders of others and to make another accountable to God for yourself (*Lib. de obed.,* c. 12, *Op. Om.* 2:324).

1786. ST. AUGUSTINE. By the precept he gave, God commended obedience, which is, in a sort, the mother and guardian of all the virtues in the reasonable creature, which was so created that submission is advantageous to it, whereas the fulfilment of its own will in preference to the Creator's is destruction (*De civitate Dei, Lib. 14,* c. 12, *PL* 41:420; Dods, p. 459).

1787. POPE ST. GREGORY THE GREAT. Obedience is the only virtue that implants other virtues in a soul, and preserves them (*Moral., Lib. 35*, c. 14, § 28, *PL* 76:765).

Necessity for spiritual guidance

1788. ST. JEROME. A. For my part I should like you to dwell in the society of holy men so as not to be thrown altogether on your own resources for your instruction. For if you set out upon a road that is new to you without a guide, you are sure to turn aside immediately either to the right or to the left, to lay yourself open to the assaults of error, to go too far or else not far enough (*Ep. 125, ad Rusticum juvenem monachum*, § 9, *PL* 22:1077). B. It is a good thing, therefore, to defer to one's superiors, to obey those set over one, to learn not only from the Scriptures but from the example of others how one ought to order one's life, and not to follow that worst of teachers, one's own presumption (*Ep. 130, ad Demetriadem, de servanda virginitate*, § 17, col. 1121).

1789. ST. VINCENT FERRER, O.P. (d. 1419). I should go still further and say that our Lord, without whom we can do nothing, will never bestow his grace on one who having at his disposal a man capable of instructing and directing him, neglects this powerful means of sanctification, believing himself to be self-sufficient and that, by means of his own powers, he is capable of seeking and discovering the things necessary for salvation. This way of obedience is the royal road leading man securely to the summit of that mysterious ladder over which the Lord seems to be leaning (*De vita spirituali*, c. 4, *Quod per instructorem idoneum citius et facilius pervenitur ad perfectionem, Speculum parvum religiosorum*, p. 134; Morrell, p. 92).

1790. IMITATION OF CHRIST (Thomas à Kempis). It is a great thing to be obedient, to live under authority and to seek our own liberty in nothing. It is a much surer way to stand in the state of obedience than in the state of authority. Many are under obedience more out of necessity than of charity and they have great pain and easily murmur and complain; they will never have liberty or freedom of spirit until they submit themselves wholly to their superiors. Go here and there where you will, you will never find perfect rest, save in humble obedience, under the governance of your proper superior (*De imitatione Christi, Lib. I*, c. 9, *Op. Om.* 2:16; Gardiner, p. 40).

The rewards of obedience

1791. ST. BASIL THE GREAT. A greater reward, moreover, is accorded to obedience than to the virtue of continency (*Serm. asceticus II*, § 2, *PG* 31:883; Wagner, p. 219).

1792. JOHN CASSIAN. They must put obedience not merely before manual labor and reading and silence and quietness in the cell, but even before all virtues, so that they consider everything should be secondary to it, and are content to undergo any amount of inconvenience if only it may be seen that they have in no way neglected this virtue (*De coenob. institut., Lib. IV,* c. 12, *PL* 49:165).

1793. ST. PETER DAMIAN. By the right of inheritance eternal salvation belongs only to the obedient (*Serm. 9, de S. Benedicto, PL* 144: 549).

1794. BENEDICT HAEFTEN. Let us bear in mind that it is better to do what we are summoned to do than to continue with what we have in hand and what we are called to abandon for the sake of obedience. If you recognize the voice of God in the superior's summons or in the signal for the community, who can question that it is for you to obey the signal, having set aside what you were doing. At that moment an act is commanded in such a manner that the superior demands nothing else of you, even though what you had been engaged in doing were objectively better than what you are called upon to do. Acts which are objectively better can and must be broken off at the superior's command for those which are, in themselves, less good. For what is commanded is made excellent by obedience, which is better than sacrifice (*Disquisitiones monasticae, Lib. VI,* tract. 2, *de obedientia,* disq. 8, p. 579).

1795. CORNELIUS À LAPIDE, S.J. By reason of its object religion is a more excellent and greater virtue than obedience. But obedience is called the better for it is more necessary and in practice preferred to religion. For what God has commanded is to be performed absolutely, and he is to be obeyed; whereas the acts of religion, such as victims and sacrifices are free; hence they must give way to obedience (*Comment. in I Reg. 15, 22, Comment. in Scripturam Sacram* 3:358).

God is always the object of obedience

1796. ST. BERNARD. For if my own self-will is found, for instance, in the fasts I observe, the Bridegroom [Christ] will not accept such fasting as that, because it savors not of the lily of obedience, but of the sin of my own self-will. The same is to be said, not only of fasting, but of silence, of vigils, of prayer, of reading, of manual labor and, in short, of every observance of the monastic life where there is found in it, not obedience to a superior, but the prompting of our own self-will. I should consider that those observances, although good in themselves, are not to be numbered among the lilies, that is, among virtues (*Serm. 71 in Cant.,* § 14, *PL* 183:1128; Eales, p. 440).

1797. ST. THOMAS AQUINAS. Wherefore even any other acts of virtue are meritorious before God through being performed out of obedience to God's will. For were one to suffer even martyrdom, or to give all one's goods to the poor, unless one directed these things to the fulfilment of the divine will, which pertains directly to obedience, they could not be meritorious (*II-II,* q. 104, art. 3, *Utrum obedientia sit maxima virtutum, Op. Om.* 9:387; Am. ed. 2:1643).

1798. THOMAS À KEMPIS. A. Truly, brethren, if a man will obey and serve a brother for the love of God, he shows God the greatest honor in his submission: and in the end he will have Christ as the recompense of his labor and the rewarder of his holy subjection, who will address him thus: *As long as you did it for one of these, the least of my brethren, you did it for me* (Matt. 25:40). For without obedience and brotherly love, our works are either little or nothing. But if performed with humble obedience, even worthless and small services rendered a brother please God. A truly and perfectly obedient man does not tarry when called; he does not excuse himself when busy or wearied; for he fears to incur the displeasure of God if he follow not the voice of him that commands according to his power. Whether, therefore, the obedient man toils or prays, whether he reads or writes, whether he is silent or speaks, whether he watches or rests, whether he eats or fasts, all things are accounted to him unto good from the merit of holy obedience. For in performing or in leaving all his acts he merits equally well, if he fully resign himself within; if herein he truly seek and aim at the good pleasure and honor of God (*Serm. 7 ad novitios, Op. Om.* 6:55). B. When a person has been reading the Scriptures zealously or transcribing manuscripts diligently closes his book or lays his pen aside on being summoned, and, rising immediately at the sound of the bell, hastens without delay to choir or to the common labor of the monastery, through the operation of the Holy Spirit, new flowers spring up, blossom, become beautiful in the garden of his heart, and produce the fruits of obedience. These will be entered to his credit as a great merit and a beautiful ornament of his crown (*ibid., Serm. 27,* p. 266; Scully, p. 216).

1799. ST. BASIL THE GREAT. As the smith, when he is forging an axe, for example, thinks of the person who commissioned the task, and with him in mind calculates its shape and size, suiting his work to the wish of him who ordered it done (for if he is unmindful of this, he will fashion something quite different from what he was ordered to make), so the Christian directs every action, small and great, according to the will of God, performing the action at the same time with care and exactitude, and keeping his thoughts fixed upon the One who gave him the work to do. In this way he fulfils the saying: *I set the Lord ever before me; with him at my right hand I shall not be disturbed* (Ps. 15:8; *Reg. fusius tractatae, Interrogatio 5, de cavenda mentis evagatione, PG* 31:922; Wagner, p. 244).

1800. ST. BERNARD. Obedience is the virtue which makes the soul to be perfectly subject to God and to live securely under the shadow of his wing (*Serm. 64, de div.*, § 2, *PL* 183:687).

The admirable example of Jesus

1801. ST. BASIL THE GREAT. The Apostle shows us to what lengths one must go in the observance of obedience if he seek to fulfil the command of pleasing God [this is the wording of the *Interrogatio*]. He proposes for us the obedience of the Lord who became *obedient to death, even to death on a cross* (Phil. 2:8), having first, however, set forth the words: *Have this mind in you which was also in Christ Jesus* (v. 5; *Reg. brevius tractatae, Interrogatio 116, PG* 31:1162).

1802. ST. HILDEGARDE, abbess of Rupertsburg near Bingen (d. 1179). [St. Hildegarde heard these words from God the Father]: "O my most valiant and loving people! I behold in them the suffering that my Son endured in the flesh, for they too die in imitation of his death in that, abandoning their own will and subjecting themselves to the government of others out of love of eternal life, they proceed at the command of their superiors" (*Scivias, Lib. II, visio 5, PL* 197:487).

1803. ST. BERNARD. A. Certain it is that from the standpoint of time, obedience places its limit in the monk's last moment, so that obedience and life itself have the same terminus. And it is precisely to this quality that the example of the Son of God exhorts us—for he became obedient to his Father, to death (cf. Phil. 2:8; *De praecepto et dispensatione*, c. 6, § 12, *PL* 182:868). B. Learn, O man, to obey; learn, O earth, to bear the yoke; learn O dust, to be submissive. It is of your Creator that the evangelist is speaking when he says: *He . . . was subject to them* (Luke 2:51), namely to Mary and Joseph. Blush for shame, proud dust! He who is God humbles himself, and do you exalt yourself? God subjects himself to men, and do you, by striving to subject men to yourself, prefer yourself to your Maker? Would to God that, whenever such ambitious thoughts possess my soul, the Lord would deign to address to me the words with which he once replied to the Apostle whom he rebuked: *Get behind me, satan, thou art a scandal to me; for thou dost not mind the things of God, but those of men* (Matt. 16:23; *Serm. de temp., Hom. I super Missus est*, § 8, *PL* 183:60).

1804. THOMAS À KEMPIS. A. Thus Christ left the temple and the doctors of the Law, and like a good son subject to his parents, obeyed his Mother and Joseph, as an example for all religious (*Serm. 7 ad novitios, Op. Om.* 6:53; Scully, p. 44). B. O blessed and venerable obedience which our Lord Jesus Christ, the Eternal Wisdom of the Father, preached and practiced, saying: *I have come down from heaven, not to do my own will, but the will of him who sent me* (John 6:38). And when he approached the place of agony, he prayed thus, with complete denial of his own will: *My Father, if this cup cannot pass away unless I drink it, thy will be done* (Matt. 26:42). The Blessed Mother of Jesus, the Virgin Mary, manifested most promptly and expressed most fully the same obedience, addressing the angel in these terms: *Behold the handmaid of the Lord: be it done to me according to thy word* (Luke 1:38). It is altogether fitting, nay, it is obligatory for the good subject to strive to do and also to state humbly and reverently before his superior: "My father, I shall willingly do whatever you command and recommend, to the best of my ability" (*De disciplina claustralium,* c. 4, *de obedientia humilis subditi erga praelatum suum, Op. Om.* 2:284).

1805. LIVES OF THE FATHERS. Abbot Hyperichius stated: "Since obedience is the duty of the monk, he who possesses it will be granted what he asks for and will stand with confidence before the Crucified; for the Lord came to the cross in the same manner, namely, *becoming obedient to death, even to death on a cross*" (Phil. 2:8; *De vitis Patrum, Lib. V, libell. 14, de obedientia,* n. 11, *PL* 73:950).

1806. BERNARD, abbot of Montecassino and cardinal (d. 1282). As the sheep which is destined for the slaughter is fed, fattened, and sheltered in order later on to be slaughtered, so the monk is also looked upon by others and must consider himself as fed in the refectory, served in the infirmary, and cared for in the cloister for no other purpose than to be Christ's host and victim, and to die under the sword of obedience (*In c. 7 RSB, PL* 66:387).

1807. JOHN OF TRITHEIM. *It is now no longer I that live, but Christ lives in me* (Gal. 2:20), by obedience, that is, so that I no longer do that which I will, but what the abbot, the vicar of Christ, has commanded. For Christ, after whom we are called Christian, in that we are bound to follow him, taught us by his example, to obey our superiors, when he said, as recorded in the Gospel, *I seek not my own will, but the will of him who sent me* (John 5:30). And lest you think that he only desired this and did not actually perform it—as though he had expressed a love for obedience without performing it himself, hear what he says to the Father when suffering in his agony: *Father, if it is possible, let this cup pass away from me; yet not as I will, but as thou willest* (Matt. 26:39). Again: *My Father, if this cup cannot pass away unless I drink it, thy will be done* (*ibid.,* v. 42). And lest you consider this as of little significance at the end of his life, hear what he did at the beginning of the same life: *He was,* says the Evangelist, *subject to them* (Luke 2:51). If the Creator of all things, Christ, our Savior, became obedient not only to the Father, but also to men, for us, what answer shall we miserable creatures give who make light of obedience to the men that God placed over us? God obeyed an inferior, and man refuses to obey an equal! (*Comm. in c. 7, Grad. 2, RSB, Op. pia et spiritualia,* p. 352.)

1808. BENEDICT HAEFTEN. Let us look upon Jesus, *the author and finisher of faith* (Heb. 12:2), who became, for those who obey him, the cause of eternal salvation. On Mount Calvary he gave the whole world the most magnificent example of obedience. Although no one doubts that in this renowned prototype of all acts of submission there are found all twelve degrees, and many more that our feebleness could never comprehend, it will be helpful for those who are following this way of obedience to study the prints of the Savior in each step he took, and to follow them, even though we are unable to take steps of equal length, for St. Benedict repeatedly presented this very obedience of Christ for imitation.

1. The first step is to subject oneself to the superior in all obedience (*RSB*, c. 7, *Grad. 3*). That Christ observed this in relation to his heavenly Father, of whom he said: *The Father is greater than I* (John 14:28), is perfectly known to all.

2. He also obeyed even those beneath him, both Mary and Joseph, about which obedience it is written: *He . . . was subject to them* (Luke 2:51); He obeyed the wicked judges and executioners as well.

3. He obeyed in a supremely difficult matter, one in fact which was almost impossible, *becoming obedient to death, even to death on a cross* (Phil. 2:8), prodigal of life and honor as well. . . . Obedience then made God suffer, made Life die, and stripped of honor him who is the splendor of the Father's glory, crowned with praise and honor.

4. No one ever strove for obedience to a superior in all deeds so perfectly as did Christ to his Father, for he said: *I do always the things that are pleasing to him* (John 8:29), and *I do as the Father has commanded me* (*ibid.,* 14:31).

5. He obeyed without delay, because in the first moment of his Incarnation Christ had the use of the intellect by means of which he recognized the will of God, as well as the power of his will of obedience and of offering, with which he offered himself, his life, and his death to God as the price of our redemption, and it is by that will that we are made holy. This truth is drawn from these words of the Apostle: *Therefore in coming into the world, he says, Sacrifice and oblation thou wouldst not, but a body thou hast fitted to me: in holocausts and sin-offerings thou hast had no pleasure. Then I said, Behold, I come . . . to do thy will, O God* (Heb. 10:5–7). Hence the obedience of Christ began with the very beginning of his life, and already at that moment he rejoiced like a giant running its course (cf. Ps. 18:6), running that hard and difficult course of our redemption.

6. He abandoned his own will who said: *I have come down from heaven, not to do my own will, but the will of him who sent me* (John 6:38). In like manner: *Yet not my will but thine be done* (Luke 22:42).

7. He abandoned his judgment, for he acceded in all things to the decree of his Incarnation that had been pronounced in the council

of the Most Holy Trinity, and conformed himself with complete exactness to it in every point. This is learned from the Prophet, speaking in the person of Christ: *The Lord God hath opened my ears, and I do not resist: I have not gone back* (Isa. 50:5). The meaning of the passage is this: When God, at the first moment of my conception, opened my ears, that is, when he made known his will, the mandate of the whole plan of my Incarnation, and showed me what I was to do and to suffer, I did not resist. St. Thomas teaches that Christ, according to his will, which is by means of reason, always willed what God wills (*III*, q. 18, art. 5, ad 2, *Op. Om.* 11:235; Am. ed. 2:2129). And, as Suarez explains in this same connection, Christ willed for the same reason for which God willed, to whose will his was identical not only in what was formally willed, but in what was materially willed as well. Hence St. Bernard says so beautifully: "How blessed is the man who says: *The Lord God hath opened my ear, and I do not resist: I have not gone back* (Isa. 50:5). There you have a model of voluntary obedience, an example of perseverance. For he who does not contradict works voluntarily, and he who has not turned back perseveres" (*Serm. 28 in Cant.*, § 6, *PL* 183:924; Eales, p. 180). Both dispositions are necessary because *God loves a cheerful giver* (II Cor. 9:7); and, *Whoever perseveres to the end shall be saved* (Matt. 24:13).

8. The Apostle bears witness to how humbly Christ obeyed: *He humbled himself, becoming obedient to death, even to death on a cross* (Phil. 2:8).

9. In this testimony we also have an appreciation of Christ's patience in his obedience. Has anyone ever suffered graver evils for the sake of obedience? Has anyone ever suffered with greater tranquillity of spirit, willing acceptance and patience? *And he, Son though he was, learned obedience from the things that he suffered* (Heb. 5:8), that is to say, he experienced obedience in a new and more demanding manner in his passion than in all the rest of his life, namely, what obedience is, how difficult and challenging it is to submit in all things.

10. How fearlessly did he carry out the obedience to his Father? *He was offered because it was his own will* (Isa. 53:7). He went voluntarily forward to meet his enemies, by whom he knew he was to be apprehended, asking whom they sought, and thus gave himself over into their hands. And he said: *No one takes* [my life] *from me, but I lay it down of myself. I have the power to lay it down, and I have the power to take it up again* (John 10:18).

11. All tepidity was lacking in his obedience. The fervor of love was present, which he expressed in these terms: *I have a baptism to be baptized with; and how distressed I am until it is accomplished!* (Luke 12:50.) Again: *I have greatly desired to eat this passover with you before I suffer* (*ibid.*, 22:15).

12. These words reveal his cheerfulness: *My food is to do the will of him who sent me, to accomplish his work* (John 4:34). To obey the Father, and to complete the work of the Redemption is pleasing to me as food is to a hungry man. St. Benedict put obedience with the disposition of murmuring or the raising of objections in opposition to cheerfulness: such attitudes were far removed from the Savior, of whom the Prophet had said: *He shall be led as a sheep to the slaughter, and shall be dumb as a lamb before his shearer, and he shall not open his mouth* (Isa. 53:7; *Disquisitiones monasticae, Lib. VI,* tract. 2, *de obedientia,* disq. 4, p. 571 f.).

Obedience according to the Rule of Benedict

1809. ST. BIRGITTA OF SWEDEN (d. 1373). Christ the Lord thus addressed St. Birgitta: "He is a monk of Benedict who obeys the Rule rather than flesh" (*Revelationes, Lib. IV,* c. 127).

1810. ST. BERNARD. It is in truth a praiseworthy degree of obedience to be submissive according to the mind of our master, St. Benedict, from fear of hell, or in appreciation of the holiness of the profession that has been made (*RSB,* c. 5); but it is a still greater perfection to obey out of the love of God (*ibid.*), since necessity produces the former, but charity the latter (*De praecepto et dispensatione,* c. 7, § 16, *PL* 182:870).

1811. JOHN OF TRITHEIM. As our holy Father Benedict teaches, these are the degrees by which obedience is made acceptable to God and pleasing to men: "This obedience will then be acceptable to God [that is, as far as reward is concerned], and pleasing to men [namely, with reference to the edification of good example], if what is commanded [by the abbot or the prior], is fulfilled not timorously [meaning doubtfully, hesitantly, timidly], not tardily [that is, not lazily, for laziness in works points to dullness of heart], nor tepidly [which signifies not indolently nor slowly], but manfully and readily" (*Comm. in c. 5 RSB, Op. pia et spiritualia,* p. 326).

Obedience must be based on faith

1812. ST. BASIL THE GREAT. The superior is no other than the one who holds the place of the Savior, since he has become a mediator between God and men, and offers to God the salvation of those who obey him (*Const. monasticae,* c. 22, *de obedientia uberius,* § 4, *PG* 31:1407).

1813. JOHN CASSIAN. And so they hasten to fulfil, without any discussion, all those things that are ordered by him [the superior], as if they had been commanded by God from heaven; so that sometimes, when impossibilities are commanded them, they undertake them with such faith and devotion as to strive with all their powers and without the slightest hesitation to fulfil them and carry them out; and out of reverence for their senior they do not even consider whether a command is an impossibility (*De coenob. institut., Lib. IV*, c. 10, *PL* 49: 162).

1814. ST. JOHN CLIMACUS. Once when we were sitting together in the refectory, this great superior put his holy mouth to my ear and said: "Do you want me to show you divine prudence in extreme old age?" And when I begged him to do so, the righteous man called from the second table one named Laurence, who had been about forty-eight years in the community and was second priest in the monastery. He came and made a prostration to the abbot, and took his blessing. But when he stood up, the abbot said nothing whatever to him, but let him stand by the table without eating. Breakfast had only just begun, and so he was standing for a good hour, or even two. I was ashamed to look this toiler in the face, for his hair was quite white and he was eighty years old. And when we got up, the saint sent him to the great Isidore whom we mentioned above to recite to him the beginning of the 39th Psalm (*I waited patiently for the Lord, and He inclined to me and heard my cry*).

And I, like a most worthless person, did not miss the chance of tempting the old man. And when I asked him what he was thinking of when he was standing by the table, he said: "I thought of the shepherd as the image of Christ, and I considered that I had not received the command from him at all, but from God. And so I stood praying, Father John, not as before a table of men, but as before the altar of God; and because of my faith and love for the shepherd, no evil thought of him entered my mind, for love does not resent an injury (cf. I Cor. 13:5). But know this, Father, that if anyone surrenders himself to simplicity and voluntary innocence, then he no longer gives the devil either time or place to attack him" (*Scala paradisi, Grad. 4, de beata semperque laudanda . . . obedientia, PG* 88:691; Moore, nn. 25–26, pp. 74–75; Fr. Robert, p. 56).

1815. ST. GENEBALDUS, bp. of Laon [today's Soissons] (6th century). "Even though the Lord Jesus Christ himself were to deign to come to me, the sinner, I would not go out from here until my superior [Blessed Remigius, bishop], who enclosed me here, in his name, should come; for, in obedience to my superior merit would not be wanting, whereas error or deception could enter into the apparition of Christ" (*Acta Sanctorum*, Bolland., Sept., die 5, tom. 2, p. 539. Genebaldus, appointed bishop, had returned to his wife, and she bore him a son. Bl. Remigius incarcerated him for seven years of penance. On the vigil of Holy Thursday an angel appeared to free him, and to him St. Genebaldus spoke the words recorded).

1816. ST. WILLIAM, abbot of Hirschau (d. 1091). We believe that the abbot is the head and master of all our obedience as the one appointed in the place of Christ (*Praef. in Lib. II constitut., Hirsaug., PL* 150:1037).

1817. ST. BERNARD. A. For whether God himself, or a man who acts in his place, gives us a command, we must obey with equal care and submit to the latter with the same respect, provided only that man does not command anything contrary to God (*De praecepto et dispensatione,* c. 9, § 19, *PL* 182:871). B. God deigns in one certain sense, to make superiors equal to himself in the good and the evil treatment they receive, and he regards as offered to himself the honor and the contempt that is offered to them, expressly stating: *He who hears you, hears me; and he who rejects you, rejects me* (Luke 10:16). For that matter does not our Rule teach the same doctrine in stating that the obedience that is given to superiors is given to God himself? (*RSB,* c. 5.) . . . For all that the man commands as the representative of God, which we are not certain is displeasing to him, we are to execute with the same submission as if God himself had commanded it. For what difference does it make whether God makes his will known himself, or does so through his ministers, be they angels or men? (*Ibid.,* § 21, col. 875.) C. Do not allow an overbearing master nor indiscreetly used authority to disturb you, but remember that *There is no authority except from God* . . . and that *He who resists the authority resists the ordinance of God* (Rom. 13:1–2). Such obedience is the same whether given to God or to man, because whatever obedience is offered to superiors is offered to him who says: *He who hears you, hears me* (Luke 10:16; *Serm. de div., Serm. 41, de virtute obedientiae et septem ejus gradibus,* § 3, *PL* 183:655).

1818. ST. THOMAS AQUINAS. In natural things it behooves the higher to move the lower to their actions by the excellence of the natural power bestowed on them by God; and so in human affairs also the higher must move the lower by their will in virtue of a divinely established authority. . . . Wherefore just as in virtue of the divinely established natural order the lower natural things need to be subject to the movement of the higher, so too in human affairs, in virtue of the order of natural and divine law, inferiors are bound to obey their superiors (*II-II,* q. 104, art. 1, *Utrum unus homo teneatur alii obedire, Op. Om.* 9:383; Am. ed. 2:1641).

1819. ST. BONAVENTURE. A. In order that you may be more obedient, always think, when the voice of the one commanding sounds in your ears, that you hear the words coming not from a man, but from God himself (*Ad fratres Tolosates collationes octo, Coll. 3, de obedientia, Op. Om.,* ed. Peltier 14:643. This is definitely not the work of St. Bonaventure, cf. *Op. Om.,* ed. Quaracchi 10:23, but the author is undetermined). B. Whatever man commands as God's representative, which the subject does not know to be certainly displeasing to God, is to be received with the disposition as though God had commanded it (*Speculum disciplinae ad novitios, Pars I,* c. 4, § 2, *Op. Om.,* ed. Quaracchi 8:585).

1820. VEN. LOUIS DE BLOIS (Blosius). Be assured of this: in his eternal wisdom and goodness the Lord your God has foreordained and provided for you those superiors whom you have in the state you entered; he willed to grant you his grace through them rather than through others (*Sacellum animae fidelis, Pars III,* c. 8, § 3, *Op. Om.* 1:266).

1821. ST. IGNATIUS OF LOYOLA, founder of the Jesuits (d. 1556). A. It is first of all most advantageous for spiritual progress and also most necessary that all devote themselves to perfect obedience. Acknowledging the superior, whoever he may be, to hold the place of Christ our Lord, and treating him with interior reverence and love, they are all to obey not only in the external performance of those duties he commands, and that vigorously, promptly, courageously, with due humility, without excuses and murmuring, even though what he commands is difficult and repugnant to our sensual nature; even more, they are to strive for interior resignation and abnegation of their own will and judgment, completely harmonizing their own will and judgment with what the superior wills and thinks, in all matters where sin would not be perceived; having set for themselves the will and judgment of the superior as the norm of their own will and judgment, they will be more exactly conformed to the first and highest norm of all good will and judgment, which is the Eternal Good and Wisdom (*Reg. Societatis Jesu: summarium earum Constitutionum quae ad spiritualem nostrorum institutionem pertinent et ab omnibus observandae sunt,* c. 31, *CR* 3:125). B. All are to strive to hold obedience in the highest regard and to excel in it, not only in what is obligatory, but in other matters as well, even though it should seem to be nothing other than a manifestation of the superior's will, unaccompanied by any express command. God, our Creator and Lord, because of whom obedience is offered to man, must be before our eyes, and care must be taken to act in the spirit of love and not from irresoluteness of fear (*ibid.,* c. 33).

1822. JOHN LANSPERGE, Carthusian monk (d. 1539). Love the virtue of obedience from the bottom of your heart, and never abandon it as long as you live. Adopt this disposition not only as regards your superiors, but also yield, obey, and subject yourself—whenever you are not restrained by my will—in all things and to all men for my sake. And do this without being grieved by it, repining at it, or disputing about it. And in order that you may do this the more freely, do not regard the man who by my ordinance is your superior, whether he be learned or not learned, an excellent man or a base person. But have regard for this only: that by my providence he is made your superior, and it is through him that I will govern you, and it is through him too that you must hear me, ask counsel of me and obey me (*Jesu Christi ad animam Sibi devotam epistola sive alloquia, quae non aliud atque divinae sunt inspirationes, quae homini sui cognitionem infundunt, atque ad verae pietatis perfectionem instituunt:* in: *Divini amoris pharetra, etc.;* Coloniae: apud Petrum Horst, 1590, pp. 267–409; c. *de obedientia,* p. 332).

1823. FRANCISCO SUAREZ, S.J. First it must be established that in virtue of this vow [obedience], man is to be obeyed, or rather God who commands through the instrumentality of man. . . . God is the person to whom the vow is made; the superior is placed as the person whom we are to obey as God's representative, in virtue of the vow. . . . All founders of religious orders have so understood and interpreted this obedience, and the same is the intention of those professing it (*Tract. VII, de statu perfectionis, Lib. X, de voto obedientiae,* c. 11, § 2, *Op. Om.* 15:924).

1824. JUAN EUSEBIO NIEREMBERG, S.J. (d. 1658). Obedience is like a pastoral staff which God uses to govern and lead into salutary pastures his rational sheep, that is to say, the men who have become like beasts of burden and sheep before him. To us this obedience is a rod, a staff to help us proceed in safety and to guard us on the difficult paths of this life. In order for us to perform our obedience perfectly, we must never allow it to be directed except with the staff and rod placed in the hand of a man. The whole doctrine of obedience is appropriately symbolized by comparing it to a staff, so that seeing it we can say with Jeremias: *I see a rod watching* (2:11). Let us understand this rod to represent the rule of obedience. First of all we must consider obedience as the instrument by which divine providence has decreed that he will bring about our salvation. As a shepherd uses his staff to protect his sheep, to push them away from what is harmful and to draw them back to him, God uses our obedience and the commands of our superiors to protect us, preserve us from dangers, recall us from evil ways, and lead us to glory. God, who created us for eternal blessedness, has provided in obedience the means for each of us to attain to that blessedness: anyone who does not refuse this way must be believed to be predestined for glory. His superiors and their commands must be considered as the means of our salvation, the pastoral staff of God, inspirations from heaven, the rod of the Good Shepherd watching over his flocks (*Doctrina 8, de obedientia,* c. 47, *praelati sunt instrumenta Dei per quos nos dirigit et providet. Doctrinae asceticae sive spiritualium institutionum pandectae;* Augustae Vindelicorum: Sumptibus Matthaei Rieger, 1756, pp. 203–205).

1825. ST. JEROME. No art is ever learned without a master. Even dumb animals and wild herds follow leaders of their own. Bees have their kings, and cranes fly after one of their own number in the shape of the letter Y. . . . A ship has but one pilot, a house but one master, and the largest army moves at the command of one man. Lest I tire you by heaping up instances, my purpose in all these statements is simply this: Do not rely on your own discretion, but live in a monastery. For there, while you will be under the control of one father, you will have many companions; and you will learn from these, from the one humility, from another patience, from a third silence, and from a fourth meekness. . . . The superior of the monastery you will fear as a master, and love as a father. Whatever he may order you to do you will believe to be wholesome for you. You will not pass judgment on those who are placed over you, for your duty will be to obey them and to do what you are told according to the word by Moses: *Be silent, O Israel, and listen!* (*Ep. 125, ad Rusticum, juvenem monachum, de securitate vitae monasticae et non eremiticae pro juvenibus,* § 15, *PL* 22:1080.)

1826. JOHN CASSIAN. A. For if all the arts and contrivances discovered by man's ingenuity and those which are only useful for the conveniences of this temporary life, though they can be felt with the hand and seen with the eye, can yet not be understood by anyone without lessons from a teacher, how foolish it is to fancy that there is no need of an instructor in this one alone which is invisible and secret and can only be seen by the purest heart! Moreover, a mistake in this matter brings about no mere temporary loss or one that can easily be repaired, but the destruction of the soul and everlasting death (*Collatio II, Abb. Moysis, de discretione,* c. 11, *PL* 49:541). B. Make yourself, as the Apostle directs, a fool in this world that you may become wise (cf. I Cor. 3:18), without showing any preference or choosing between the duties which are commanded of you, but always rendering obedience with all simplicity and faith, judging that alone to be holy, useful, and wise which God's law or your superior's decisions declare to be such for you. For built upon such a system of instruction you may continue forever under this discipline, and not fall away from the monastery in consequence of any temptations or devices of the enemy (*De coenob. institut., Lib. IV,* c. 41, col. 200).

1827. ST. JOHN CLIMACUS. Obedience is absolute renunciation of our own life, clearly expressed in our bodily actions. Or, conversely, obedience is the mortification of the limbs, while the mind remains alive. Obedience is unquestioning movement, voluntary death, simple life, carefree danger, spontaneous defense by God, fearlessness of death, a safe voyage, a sleeper's progress. Obedience is the tomb of the will and the resurrection of humility. A corpse does not argue or reason as to what is good or what seems to be bad. For he who has devoutly put the soul of the novice to death will answer for everything. Obedience is an abandonment of discernment in a wealth of discernment. The beginning of the mortification both of the soul's desire and of the bodily members involves much hard work. The middle sometimes means much hard work and is sometimes painless. But the end is insensibility and insusceptibility to toil and pain. Only when he sees himself doing his own will does this blessed living corpse feel sorry and sick at heart; and he fears the responsibility of using his own judgment (*Scala paradisi, Grad. 4, de beata semperque laudanda . . . obedientia, PG* 88:679; Moore, nn. 3–4, pp. 66–67).

1828. ST. GREGORY THE GREAT. True obedience neither questions the purpose of superiors nor distinguishes between commands. . . . He who is intent on the good of obedience must consider not the work enjoined on him, but the fruit to be gathered (*In I Reg. expos., Lib. II,* c. 4, § 11, *PL* 79:131).

1829. ST. BASIL THE GREAT. A. Not even for a single moment must the monk be independent in the sense that he has control over his own private affairs. When a craftsman is absent, a tool cannot be moved, nor a member be separated from the whole body, even for a moment, or be moved independently of the will of the internal craftsman, or the superior power of the whole body. In like manner neither is it permissible for the religious to undertake or perform anything at all without the permission of his superior. If he says that he is unable to carry out the command because of bodily weakness, he will submit his inability to be judged by the superior, and urge himself on to fulfil what he is ordered to do (cf. *RSB,* c. 68), mindful of the scriptural passage: *You have not yet resisted unto blood in the struggle with sin* (Heb. 12:4; *Const. monasticae,* c. 27, *PG* 31:1418).

B. As sheep follow their shepherd and go along any path that he chooses, so they who are religious (*ascetae*) according to the will of God must submit to their superior, never examining his commands, provided that these commands are free from sin; rather they are to bring them to execution with great alacrity of spirit and effort. As the craftsman or builder uses the individual tools of the craft as he sees fit, and as there has never been a tool which did not readily present itself to be used and give way to the hand of the craftsman, regardless of the use to which he put it, so it is proper for the religious to be like a tool at the service of the builder in completing the spiritual edifice, to be obedient in all things in which the superior considers it right for him to serve. Otherwise, if he should refuse, he is a hindrance to the completion of the spiritual work. And as a tool does not decide for itself what it should do to serve the handicraft, neither is it proper for the religious to judge what work he will undertake, but he is to leave the direction of his work to the prudence and advice of his superior. For the intelligent director knows how to search out diligently each one's manners and attitudes and habits of mind, and also how to accommodate his own service in each case. Wherefore we must not in any way oppose his decisions, but firmly believe that it is most difficult to know and care for oneself, for everyone naturally loves himself and is therefore deceived in weighing the truth because he is much prejudiced in his own favor. On the other hand, it is easy to be known and directed by another, since self-love does not then hinder from recognition of the truth those who judge others (*ibid.*, c. 22, *de obedientia uberius,* § 5, col. 1410).

C. They must embrace the commandments of God and obey their masters for this is the very essence of the whole life of the institute. For as God, who is the Father of all, and wishes to be called Father, demands the highest form of obedience of his servants, so he who is the spiritual father among men, when he makes his commands harmonize with the prescriptions of God's law, also demands obedience that is free of all rationalizing and controversy (*ibid.*, c. 19, *de obedientia,* col. 1387).

1830. HUMBERT OF ROMANS, fifth master general of the Order of Preachers (d. 1277). A. In order for your obedience to be acceptable before God, strive for a submission that is prompt, without delay; simple, without discussion; regular, without deviation; joyful, without disturbance; zealous, without pusillanimity; universal, without exception; persevering, unto the end (*Epistola de tribus votis substantialibus,* c. 5, *qualis debeat esse obedientia, Op. de vita regulari,* p. 4). B. Consequently, beloved brethren, be as ductile as gold, and as flexible as the rod which can be supported upright or curved at the will of the craftsman. Be as adaptable as the wheels that were lifted up together according to the direction of the spirit (cf. Ezech. 1:21); be in God's presence like a beast of burden on whose back it makes no difference what burden is loaded (*ibid.*, c. 6, *obedientia debet esse prompta*). C. Let your obedience be simple, brethren, so that, performing without argument what is enjoined on you, you give evidence that there is nothing of your own will in what you do. He who passes judgment on the intentions of the person commanding, prepares a conflict within himself, for in arguing the reasons for the commands, which he does not know, he puts himself in a labyrinth of errors (*ibid.*, c. 9, *quod obedientia debet esse simplex,* p. 6).

1831. ST. BERNARD. A. *Lord, what wilt thou have me do?* (Acts 9:6.) A short word, indeed, but how full of meaning! how *living and efficient* (Heb. 4:12), how *worthy of entire acceptance!* (I Tim. 1:15.) How few possess such perfect obedience, how few have so renounced their own wills, that they seem no longer to have even desires of their own, but are forever seeking, not what pleases themselves, but what is pleasing to the Lord, saying without interruption, "Lord, what wilt thou have me do?" Or, in the words of Samuel, *Speak, Lord, for thy servant heareth* (I Kgs. 3:10). Unfortunately we have more imitators of that blind man mentioned in the Gospel to whom the Lord said: *What wouldst thou have me do for thee?* (Luke 18:41.) They are far more numerous than the imitators of the newly-made Apostle.

How great is thy compassion, Lord, how great thy condescension! Do you think that the Lord really sought to know the will of his servant in order to accomplish it? That man of the Gospel was in truth blind, for he did not consider, he did not tremble with holy fear, he did not cry out: "Far be such presumption from me, Lord! Rather tell your servant what it is you would have him do, for it is more becoming and proper that your will be sought and accomplished than that mine be done by you!" You perceive, my brethren, that in the case of this soul there was real need of conversion. Even nowadays, the same pusillanimity and perversity of many a religious make it necessary for a superior to inquire, "What do you want me to do for you?" Whereas it is the subject's duty to say, "Lord, what wilt thou have me do?"

Yes, the ministers and representatives of Christ must nowadays consider what their subjects wish them to command, instead of having their wishes inquired by the latter. The obedience of such subjects is far from perfect; they are not prepared to submit their will in all things; they have not made up their minds to imitate in everything him who came down from heaven not to do his own will but the will of his Father (cf. John 6:38). They distinguish and withhold judgment, determining for themselves in what they will obey the superior, or, to be more exact, determining in what the superior must render submission to their wills. And although such religious may find superiors willing to bear with them, willing to condescend to their weakness and to indulge there humors, I must earnestly entreat them to rise to worthier dispositions and feel shame at being always found *little ones in Christ* (I Cor. 3:1). Otherwise they will hear addressed to them the words of reproach, "What is there that I ought to do more for you that I have not done?" (cf. Isa. 5:4.) For, having abused the superior's patience and charity, they will finally incur a just condemnation, all the more terrible on account of the many mercies shown to them.

Lord, what wilt thou have me do? And the Lord said to him, Arise, go into the city, and it will be told thee what thou must do (Acts 9:6). O Wisdom of God, which in truth *governs all things well!* (Wisd. 8:1.) You send the man to whom you are speaking to another man for instructions concerning your will, in order to commend to us the advantages of community life, and also in order that Paul, thus instructed by a fellow-man, might learn in his turn to assist others according to the grace given him (cf. Rom. 12:6).

Go into the city. You see from this passage, my brethren, that it was not without special ordinance of divine wisdom that you came into the city of the Lord of virtues [that is, the monastery], in order to learn the will of God. For plainly he who first filled your hearts with wholesome fear, and so changed them that they began to desire the knowledge of his will, said then to you: *Arise, go into the city*. But hear how expressly simplicity of will and Christian meekness are commended to us in what follows: *But when his eyes were opened, he could see nothing. And leading him by the hand, they brought him into Damascus* (Acts 9:8). O blessed blindness, wherewith those eyes, heretofore sadly keen-sighted in persecution, are now at last happily clouded by the grace of conversion! (*Serm. de temp., serm. I de conversione S. Pauli,* §§ 6, 7, *PL* 183:364.) B. It is an indication of imperfection of spirit and weakness of will to examine with minute exactitude the commands of the superior, to call into question each order he issues us, always to be asking for reasons for everything, to harbor suspicion regarding all the precepts whose motive has not been made known, and never to obey until what is ordered corresponds to our own inclinations, or until we recognize for evident reasons or from the weight of unquestioned authority that there is either no advantage in acting otherwise or that it is not tolerated at all. Such obedience is, to say the least, very delicate or, to speak more correctly, unduly troubled. Certainly it is not the obedience prescribed by the Rule with the words "obedience without delay" (*RSB,* c. 5). To debate or hesitate about a command amounts to this: it is to obey in the cunning of the heart, not in the hearing of the ear (*De praecepto et dispensatione,* c. 10, § 23, *PL* 182:874).

1832. PETER DE BLOIS. A. It is a kind of obstinacy to inquire into the limits of a command, to hesitate and discuss, or put off the execution of the obedience. In the vow of obedience there is no place for argument or debate; for if you make the things that you have been commanded to do subject to investigation or scrutiny, you are stretching the hand of prevarication to the tree of the knowledge of good and evil. Such obedience is too delicate, which devolves into a sort of discussion of merits. This is not "obeying at the hearing of the ear"; this is not the Rule's obedience without delay, but stubborn craftiness and open pride (*Ep. 131, ad E., priorem de monasteriolo, PL* 207:389). B. Let him who professes the Rule perform what is enjoined on him without any show of preference and without any exception. Let him not draw any distinctions as to what is ordered, the nature of the work or how much is commanded. Otherwise he presumes to eat of the tree of the knowledge of good and evil. The decision in such matters resides with the spiritual father who judges all things without himself being judged by anyone. Let the subject, therefore, decide nothing; let him be without preferences, in order that he may understand; let him be a fool in order that he may be wise (*Ep. 134, ad Willelmum electum S. Mariae,* col. 401).

1833. IMITATION OF CHRIST (Thomas à Kempis). But what great thing is it to you, who are but dust and nothing, if you submit yourself to man for my sake, when I, who am Almighty and the Most High God, Creator of all things, submitted myself humbly to man for your sake? I made myself the humblest and lowest of all men, so that you would learn to overcome your pride through my humility. Learn, therefore, you who are but ashes, to be docile; learn, you who are dust and earth, to be humble for my sake; learn to break your own will and to be subject to all from the heart. Rise in great wrath against yourself, and do not suffer pride to reign in you, but show yourself to be in your own sight little and obedient. O vain man, what have you to complain of? O foul sinner, what can you justly say against those who rebuke you, since you have so often offended God and have so often deserved the pains of hell? Nevertheless, because your soul is precious in my sight, my merciful eye has spared you, so that you should thereby know the great love I have for you, and be the more thankful to me in return, and give yourself to perfect and true humility. Be ready in your heart patiently to suffer contempt and derision for my sake, whenever they happen to fall to your lot (*De imitatione Christi, Lib. III,* c. 13, *Op. Om.* 2:169; Gardiner, p. 124).

1834. ST. FRANCIS OF ASSISI. When he was asked on one occasion who was to be considered truly obedient, [St. Francis] proposed similarity to a corpse by way of illustration. Take a dead body, he said, and place it anywhere you please. You will see it offers no resistance against being moved, it complains not against its position, it will not cry out if you let it go. If you seat it on a throne it will not look up but down, and to clothe it in purple only makes it pale. This is the truly obedient man. He reasons not why he is sent; he minds not where he is placed, nor insists on being sent elsewhere. If he is promoted to office, he still remains humble; the more he is honored, the more he counts himself unworthy (*Acta Sanctorum,* Bolland., Octobr., tom. 2, die 4, *Vita altera S. Francisci, a S. Bonaventura conscripta,* c. 6, § 77, p. 757).

Obedience must be willing, ready, and swift

1835. ST. BASIL THE GREAT. With what disposition must one hearken to him who urges the fulfilling of the law [this is the *Interrogatio*].

With the attitude of a boy overcome with hunger answering his nurse when she summons him to eat, or like that of a man seeking sustenance, in obeying him who bestows on him what is necessary for life. In fact, we should be submissive with a far greater obedience, as much greater as eternal life surpasses in excellence that which is corporal. For the Lord says: *I know that his commandment is everlasting life* (John 12:50). What eating is in food, that the performance of the deed is in a command, in the words of the Lord himself once more: *My food is to do the will of him who sent me* (John 4:34; *Reg. brevius tractatae, Interrogatio 166, PG* 31:1191).

1836. JOHN CASSIAN. [The monks of Egypt] sitting in their cells and dividing their energies between work and meditation, on hearing the sound of some one knocking at the doors summoning them to prayer or some other work, eagerly dash out from their cells. Thus one who has been practicing the writer's art, although he may have just begun to form a letter, does not venture to finish it, but hurries forth as soon as the sound of the knocking reaches his ears, without waiting to finish the letter he has begun. Leaving the lines of the letter incomplete, he aims not at abridging and saving his labor, but rather hastens with the utmost earnestness and zeal to attain the virtue of obedience (*De coenob. institut., Lib. IV,* c. 12, *PL* 49:164).

1837. RULE FOR MONKS BY AN UNKNOWN AUTHOR (6th century). At the first word of the one addressing him, each one must rise as though a coal of burning fire had fallen on him. If this obedience is not such as we have described, it is dead and not acceptable to God. *For all that is not from faith is sin* (Rom. 14:23). We are always to act with joy: *Exult, you just, in the Lord; praise from the upright is fitting* (Ps. 32:1). Again, the Apostle says: *Rejoice in the Lord always; again I say, rejoice* (Phil. 4:4). If anything we offer to God is done with sadness, the gift will not be acceptable (*Reg. cujusdam patris,* c. 29, *CR* 1:223; *PL* 66:993).

1838. ST. AURELIAN, bp. of Arles (d. 551). When the signal has been given, all tasks are to be set aside, and like busy bees the monks must strive to get to the beehive as speedily as possible (*Reg.,* c. 30, *CR* 1:151; *PL* 68:391).

1839. ST. BERNARD. *Swiftly runs* [God's] *word* (Ps. 147:15), and it seeks to have a swift-running follower. See how quickly he runs who says: *I will run the way of your commands when you give me a docile heart* (Ps. 118:32). The faithful and obedient man knows not what it is to delay, he never puts off until tomorrow. Tardiness is unknown to him, he anticipates the one who commands him. He prepares his eyes for seeing, his ears for hearing, his voice for speech, his hands for work, his feet for the journey. He gathers himself together that he may wholly compass the will of his superior. Consider the example of the Lord commanding quick action and the ready obedience of the man he thus addressed: *Zacchaeus, make haste and come down; for I must stay in thy house today. And he made haste and came down, and welcomed him joyfully* (Luke 19:5, 6; *Serm. de div., serm. 41, de virtute obedientiae et septem ejus gradibus,* § 7, *PL* 183:657).

1840. ST. THOMAS AQUINAS. Wherefore obedience makes a man's will prompt in fulfilling the will of another, the maker, namely, of the request (*II-II,* q. 104, art. 2, *Utrum obedientia sit specialis virtus,* ad 3m, *Op. Om.* 9:385; Am. ed. 2:1642).

1841. ST. IGNATIUS LOYOLA. When the signal bell for the appointed hours has been heard, all are to betake themselves immediately to that to which they are called, even leaving the letter unfinished (*Reg. communes Societatis Jesu,* c. 15, *CR* 3:127).

Perfect obedience

1842. ST. FULGENCE, bp. of Ruspe, Africa (d. 533). They are monks in truth who, through the mortification of their desires, are now prepared to will nothing, and to refuse nothing, but only to obey the abbot's counsels and commands (*Acta Sanctorum,* Bolland., Jan., tom. 1, die 1, p. 42).

1843. BALDWIN, abbot, abp. of Canterbury (d. 1190). The blood of Christ, who suffered for us, leaving us an example that we may follow in his steps (cf. I Petr. 2:21), that is, that we may die unto him and with him, demands of us obedience unto death; it exacts from us suffering for suffering, death for death. O wonderful and stupendous consideration! We are bound in our obligations unto death by reason of the very source from which we were freed from death. Our debt of death is contracted from the same source as the payment of the debt of death. But now we are debtors to death from a new cause, for even though it remains exacted for sin as of old, it is from the new grace. . . . The death of the saints made precious through the death of Christ is a kind of act of thanksgiving for the death of Christ and a certain interchange; obedience unto death is this likeness to death (*De sacramento altaris, PL* 204:685).

1844. ST. BERNARD. A. Perfect obedience recognizes no law, oversteps all limits. Not content with the narrowness of obligation induced by profession, it generously passes forth into the spaciousness of charity, and without considering modes or measures, without exception or reservation, with all the ardor of a free and noble spirit, executes everything that is enjoined (*De praecepto et dispensatione,* c. 6, § 12, *PL* 182:868). B. Let obedience stand to you, my brethren, in place of discretion, so that you shall do nothing more, nothing less, nothing otherwise than has been commanded (*Serm. de temp., Serm. III in Circumcisione Dni,* § 11, *PL* 183:142). C. Are you seeking a pattern of perfect obedience? If so, be attentive. *As he was walking by the sea of Galilee, he saw two brothers, Simon, who is called Peter, and his brother Andrew, casting a net into the sea* (*for they were fishermen*).

And he said to them, Come, follow me, and I will make you fishers of men (Matt. 4:18, 19). That is to say, "I will make you change from one kind of fishing to another, or rather from catchers of fish I will make you preachers of the Gospel. *And at once they left the nets, and followed him* (v. 20). At once, observe, without discussion or hesitation, without concern as to how they would make sure of their livelihood, without considering how rough and uneducated fishermen could be formed into preachers, without either questioning or delay [they followed him]. Now bear in mind that it is for your instruction that these words have been written down (cf. Rom. 15:4), that it is for your instruction they are recited year after year in the Church, so that making known the form of perfect obedience, you may purify your souls in the obedience of charity (*ibid., Serm. 2 in fest. S. Andreae Ap.*, § 2, col. 509).

1845. ST. THOMAS AQUINAS. That obedience is perfect according to which the subject obeys simply, in all things which are not opposed to the law of God, or to the Rule which he has professed (*Comm. in Lib. II Sententiarum*, dist. 44, q. 2, art. 3, *Op. Om. Venetiis 1777*, 10:565. Not contained in the Parma ed.).

1846. ST. BASIL THE GREAT. It behooves the religious man to accept even the most menial tasks with alacrity and eagerness, knowing that nothing that is done for God is small, but is rather great, spiritual, worthy of heaven, and of such a nature as to win a reward for us. Even though we must follow beasts of burden with the performance of common services, we must not be reluctant, since we must remember the Apostles, and how eagerly they obeyed the Lord who ordered them to bring him the colt (Matt. 21:1 f.). We must remember that they also, for whose sake we have undertaken the care of beasts of burden, are brethren of the Savior, and that the kindness and zeal practiced in their favor are referred to the Lord, who said: *As long as you did it for one of these, the least of my brethren, you did it for me* (Matt. 25:40). Now if he considers as done for himself the things that are performed for the least, far more will he claim as done for himself those which are done for his elect, provided that the one performing the service does not consider it a matter of lukewarmness and laziness, but that he give himself with great alacrity in order that both he himself and those who are with him may receive benefit from the same. If then more menial tasks are to be performed, we must remember that the Savior himself served the disciples and did not disdain to perform lowly works, and that it is a great thing for a man to imitate God and to ascend through these humble tasks to the heights [of virtue]. But who would call any of the things that the Lord did humble or abject? (*Constit. monastic.*, c. 23, *Quod debeat asceta vilia etiam opera . . . suscipere, PG* 31:1410.)

Obedience must be cheerful

1847. ST. BERNARD. The third degree of obedience is to submit cheerfully, *not grudgingly,* as the Apostle says, *or from compulsion, for God loves a cheerful giver* (II Cor. 9:7). Calmness of demeanor, and pleasantness of speech greatly affect the subject's obedience. Hence even the pagan poet spoke thus: "More than anything else, sweetness of countenance increases the value of the gift . . ." (*Metamorphoses, Lib. VIII, lin. 677 in: P. Ovidii Nasonis Metamorphoses;* selections from the fifteen books . . . by George Stuart; New York: Hinds, Noble and Eldredge, 1882, p. 97). What chance has obedience when we see a person overcome with reluctance? External manifestations usually give evidence of the attitude of the mind, for it is difficult to change the will without changing expression (*Serm. de div., Serm. 41, de virtute obedientiae et septem ejus gradibus,* § 6, *PL* 183:656).

1848. ST. BASIL THE GREAT. To rebel or contradict, however, are indications of many evils: a weak faith, a doubtful hope, and a self-important and arrogant character. His disobedience, indeed, implies that he holds in contempt him who gave the order. On the other hand, one who trusts in the promises of God and keeps his hope fixed on these will never draw back from commands, however difficult to execute they may be, knowing that *the sufferings of the present time are not worthy to be compared with the glory to come that will be revealed in us* (Rom. 8:18). Furthermore, one who is convinced that *whoever humbles himself shall be exalted* (Matt. 23:12), and bears in mind that *our present light affliction, which is for the moment, prepares for us an eternal weight of glory* (II Cor. 4:17), obeys with greater alacrity than he who gives the order expects (*Reg. fusius tractatae, Interrogatio 28, Quomodo oporteat affici omnes erga immorigerum et inobsequentem,* § 2, *PG* 31:990; Wagner, p. 291).

1849. ST. THOMAS AQUINAS. Everyone who bestows a reward does so for those things which are worthy of reward . . . and hence God loves not the one who only gives, but the cheerful giver, that is, he approves and regards him, and not the one who is reluctant and given to murmuring in his giving (*In Ep. II ad Cor.,* c. 9, lectio 1, *Op. Om.,* ed. Parma 13:349).

1850. ST. BASIL THE GREAT. The work of such persons [given to murmuring and self-exaltation], even as a blemished sacrifice, should not be accepted (*Reg. fusius tractatae, Interrogatio 29, De eo qui cum animi elatione aut murmuratione agit, PG* 31:991; Wagner, p. 292).

1851. ST. JOHN CHRYSOSTOM. So that murmuring is left for unprincipled and stupid slaves; for, tell me, what kind of son would he be who would murmur at the very time that he is employed in the affairs of his father and is working really for his own benefit? . . .

It is better to do nothing than to do it with murmuring, for with such a disposition even the very things that are done are spoiled. . . . For murmuring is intolerable, most intolerable; it borders on blasphemy (*Hom. 8 in Ep. ad Philip.*, § 2, *PG* 62:241).

1852. ST. EPHRAEM. Murmuring is scandalous to all, destroys charity, breaks asunder the bond of unity, and disturbs peace. The murmurer contradicts those who govern him, and is incapable and useless in the performance of any good work. The murmurer is ever ready with excuses. When any work is assigned to him, he gives way to faultfinding, and soon draws others in his path (*Serm. de inobedientia et murmuratione, Op. Om.* 1:34).

1853. ST. GREGORY THE GREAT. It must always remain a matter for serious consideration that neither they who are set at the head offer examples of evil conduct to those under them and destroy their life by the sword of their evil doing, nor they who are subject to the control of others presume to judge lightly the deeds of their superiors, and from this, that they who engage in murmuring against those who are placed over them set themselves in opposition not to a human appointment, but against that divine arrangement which disposes all things (*Moral., Lib.* 22, c. 24, § 56, *PL* 76:248).

1854. ST. BERNARD. Is it not evident that a religious who by his impatience and murmuring *grieves the Holy Spirit of God* (Eph. 4:30) dwelling in his brethren, by scandalizing one of the little ones that believe in him (cf. Matt. 18:6), is also a persecutor of Christ? (*Serm. de temp., Serm. 1 de conversione S. Pauli*, § 4, *PL* 183:362.)

1855. BL. RABANUS MAURUS, monk of Fulda, abp. of Mainz (d. 856). What does it mean that the fire of the Lord burned among the complaining people (cf. Num. 11:1), but that it consumes those who with tongues kindled from hell are constantly murmuring? (*Enarr. in Lib. Num., Lib. II*, c. 6, *PL* 108:654.)

1856. ALCUIN OF YORK (d. 804). Let all be intent on seeking the same goal, striving to realize the excellence of obedience instead of gratifying the inclination of their own will. If Christ came not to do his own will, but that of his Father, as he himself declares in the Gospel (cf. John 5:30), how much more must the monk not fulfil his own will, but that of Christ! How much more must he strive not to be indolent, but rather zealous in the work of God; how much more he must consider not what is commanded, but rather how what is commanded may be fulfilled; how much more must he be intent on not permitting the evil of murmuring to grow in any group. If some of the people of God perished in the desert because of their sin of murmuring, how much more will the monk be punished in the monastery by spiritual penalties if by giving way to the evil of faultfinding he has not feared haughtiness of mind. Rather let him gratefully accept what the Shepherd's solicitude has appointed as sufficient for him (*Ep. 93, ad fratres Juvaven. ecclesiae, PL* 100:298).

1857. ST. BERNARD. A. But perhaps even now that you have been established in the way of obedience, you will still meet with trials that are painful and hard to endure. You will sometimes perhaps have commands laid on you which, although they are good and salutary, may nevertheless seem harsh. Now if you begin to submit to these with an ill-humor, if you criticize your superior and murmur in the secret of your heart, even though you outwardly fulfil what is enjoined, that is not true obedience, but rather a cloak for malice (*Serm. de temp., Serm. III in Circumcisione Dni,* § 8, *PL* 183:140). B. You see whose Majesty it is that is contemned [when a monk refuses to receive a correction]? You think that it is I only who have been scorned. But it is the Lord that has spoken [to you through me]; and what he said to the Prophet he said also to his apostles: *He who rejects you, rejects me* (Luke 10:16). I am not a prophet, I am not an apostle, and yet I am bold to say that I am fulfilling the duty of both the prophet and the apostle; though I am far from approaching their merits, I am charged and burdened with their cares. Though it be to my great confusion, though it even be to my extreme danger, yet I do, in fact, sit in the seat of Moses, though I am far from claiming that my life is such as his, or the grace committed to me is the equal of that which he enjoyed (*Serm. 42 in Cant., de duplici humilitate,* § 2, col. 988; Eales, p. 260). C. The counsel of St. Paul the Apostle in which he states: *Neither murmur, as some of them murmured, and perished at the hands of the destroyer* (I Cor. 10:10), is very necessary for us. It is dangerous then for us to murmur, lest perhaps we perish at the destroyer's hand right in the monastery, even as they perished in the desert (*Lib. de modo bene vivendi, ad sororem,* c. 47, *de murmuratione,* § 113, *PL* 184:1268).

1858. ST. JOHN CHRYSOSTOM. It is better to do nothing than to do something with murmuring, for even the very thing itself is spoiled. Do you not perceive that in our own families we are continually saying: "It were better for these things never to have been done than to have them done with murmuring"? And we had often rather be deprived of the services that someone owes us than to submit to the inconvenience of his murmuring (*Hom. 8, in Ep. ad Philip.,* § 2, *PG* 62:242).

1859. ST. COLUMBAN, abbot (d. 615). Also, anyone who has been guilty of murmuring is to be considered as being not obedient according to his vow, but rather disobedient; therefore, his work is to be cast aside until his good will is recognized (*Reg. coenobialis,* c. 1, *de obedientia, CR* 1:170; *PL* 80:209).

Obedience must be courageous and constant

1860. ST. BASIL THE GREAT. *The kingdom of heaven has been enduring violent assault, and the violent have been seizing it by force* (Matt. 11:12). By "violence" is meant the affliction of the body which the disciples of Christ voluntarily undergo in the denial of their own will, in the refusal of respite to the body, and in the observance of Christ's precepts. If then you wish to seize the kingdom of God, become a man of violence; bow your neck to the yoke of Christ's service (*ibid.*, vers. 30). Bind the strap of the yoke tightly about your throat. Let it pinch your neck (*Serm. de renuntiatione saeculi*, § 9, *PG* 31:646; Wagner, p. 30).

1861. ST. JOHN OF DAMASCUS, monk (d. circa 749). Monks gathered together in large numbers in one place, and range themselves under one superior and president, the best of their number, slaying all self-will with the sword of obedience. Of their own free choice they consider themselves as slaves bought at a price, and no longer live for themselves but for him to whom, for Christ's sake they have become obedient, or rather, to speak more properly, they live no more for themselves but Christ lives in them, whom to follow they have renounced everything (*Vita SS. Barlaam eremitae et Joasaph*, c. 12, *PL* 73:490).

1862. ST. BERNARD. The fifth degree of obedience is to fulfil the command manfully. *Take courage and be stouthearted, all you who hope in the Lord* (Ps. 30:25). It is not a sign of fortitude to be disobedient; fortitude consists in not being led away from obedience. If you encounter difficulties; if you suffer persecution; if sinners endeavor to lead you into sin; if wicked persons stand in the way of your progress, do not abandon the path of obedience, but say: *I was prompt and did not hesitate in keeping your commands* (Ps. 118:60). Of what benefit are the things that have been enumerated above [the fruits of obedience, mentioned in the preceding portions of the sermon], if you are wanting in that fortitude which establishes virtues in the stronghold of constancy and protects them with that fortification that the attack of the enemies cannot storm? You have put your hand to the things that call for strength, have you not? You must act instantly then, and obey with constancy. So royal a way is not to be deserted because of harshness of words or stripes; it is to be held to all the more tenaciously and ardently (*Serm. de div., Serm. 41, de virtute obedientiae et septem ejus gradibus*, § 8, *PL* 183:657).

Obedience the joy of the monk

1863. THOMAS À KEMPIS. A. When the disciples returning from the city encouraged Jesus to eat, he showed them that the bread of obedience, which sweetly nourishes the soul subject to God, is to be preferred to all corporal food. No drink is sweeter than heavenly grace which cleanses him who is defiled, gives drink to the thirsty, and eases the struggle of him who is tempted. Nor can more palatable food be tasted, nor a richer table be set before the eyes of the lover, than the fulfilment of the heavenly command, for Jesus himself, the most obedient, states: *My food is to do the will of him who sent me* (John 4:34). For to seek God's pleasure in our acts is most pleasing to the one who loves; it supports and fills the obedient disciples with spiritual joy because of the rewards of obedience. Thus Elias, penetrating the vast expanses of the desert and being completely alone, when exhorted by the angel, arose and ate, and drank [a hearth cake and a vessel of water], and, fulfilling the command of the angel, walked in the strength of that food forty days and forty nights unto the mount of God, Horeb (cf. III Kgs. 19:6 f.). True obedience leads by a short ladder to the heights of perfection, and to the mount of everlasting rest, where there will be complete repose from all the heat of the day and the labor, and the possession of all blessedness in the presence of the Father and his Son, Jesus Christ, with the joy of the Holy Spirit. Amen (*Serm. de vita et passione Dni., Serm. 18, Op. Om.* 3:166). B. Therefore the truly obedient man is always joyful and has great trust in God, whose will he desires to accomplish at all times, from whom he doubts not that he will receive a never-ending reward with the elect. Thus he sings in his heart and with his lips: *My heart is steadfast, O God; my heart is steadfast* (Ps. 56:8). And again: *I was prompt and did not hesitate in keeping your commands* (Ps. 118:60; *Serm. 7 ad novitios, Op. Om.* 6:56; Scully, p. 47).

1864. JOHN OF TRITHEIM. God gave us free will; but he who is governed by the command of another and has freely given up his will out of love of God restores to God what he received and rejoices to be the slave of the Lord—to serve whom is to reign. This he does not for a time, or for a few years, but into eternity (*Comm. in c. 5 RSB, Op. pia et spiritualia,* p. 322).

1865. HUGO DE FOLIETO, canon regular, cardinal (12th century). The Founder of our order came from the cloister of the Supreme Abbot, that is to say, from the bosom of God the Father. He came into this world and received the habit of humility, he put on the garment of this flesh; he called sinners to the enclosure of perfect religion. He gave his grace in advance, offered mercy, promised forgiveness. He gathered his community about him, determined their number, namely the twelve apostles and innumerable disciples who were more or less like converse brothers. . . . As the superior precedes others to labor, and leads them back to the tranquillity of the cloister after the work has been done, so Christ, after the toil of this world, will lead his [followers] to the rest of divine contemplation. They who have remained with him in his sufferings, will share with him in the future of eternal glory. And those who have followed him to labor will indeed follow him to rest. They will dwell with him in the cloister of perfect blessedness and will enjoy with him forever the sweetness of divine contemplation. They will read from the book of life, delighted with the flowers of everlasting pleasures. They will rest in the shade of the tree of life, as under the shadow of divine protection. *Sion is my resting place forever; in her will I dwell, for I prefer her* (Ps. 131:14; *De claustro animae, Lib. IV,* c. 43, *PL* 176:1181).

SIXTH PRINCIPLE

The Works of Charity, Zeal for Souls

CONTENTS: Love of God and of neighbor — Love of neighbor is part of the imitation of Christ — This love must be orderly — Charity toward the sick, the dying, and the deceased — Charity toward friends, the poor, guests — Apostolate of literature and the arts — Works of apostolic charity — Fruitfulness of the priesthood — Zeal for souls — The office of preaching — Conversion of peoples — Education of children — Monastic discipline must remain undisturbed by the works of charity — The monk as a man of God — He wages the battle of the Lord — The wondrous deeds of charity in the history of the monastic order.

I. STATEMENT OF PRINCIPLE

Charity is the perfection of religion

1866. The reformation of life based on the principles of monasticism (*conversio morum*) which you have professed is established on faith, confirmed in hope, and perfected in charity. *So there abide faith, hope, and charity, these three; but the greatest of these is charity* (I Cor. 13:13). Faith is like a root—it can almost be considered the beginning; hope is like the trunk of a tree, or it may be considered the way; but charity is the fruit-laden crown of the tree, or the perfection of grace. It is, therefore, rightly called the bond of perfection, the rule of all rules, the objective of every precept and the fulfilling of the law. This virtue is infused into the soul as the very fullness and excellence of all virtues. The purpose of the monastic life and of the virtue of religion is to intensify it, enlarge its scope and perfect it.

Perfect love of God

1867. There is a twofold charity: *Thou shalt love the Lord thy God with thy whole heart, and with thy whole soul, and with thy whole mind. This is the greatest and the first commandment. And the second is like it, Thou shalt love thy neighbor as thyself* (Matt. 22:37–39). The monastic law also rests entirely on these two commandments. In the foregoing sections of this work we have briefly explained the first commandment, by which you are admonished to love God, who is himself love, with the perfection of love. For what else can be the aim of your life in the monastic enclosure, devoted as it is to the work of God, to holy poverty, mortification, and perpetual obedience, than to embrace the highest good in the most pure manner and without interference? For you are freed from the many obstacles that stand in opposition to charity, and are helped with monasticism's innumerable aids. Surely, dear confrere, the statement of the Lord must be more compelling for you than for others: *This command which I enjoin on you today is not too mysterious and remote for you* (Deut. 30:11). And inflamed with the spirit of profound love, you dare hardly answer other than with the words: *My soul clings fast to you* (Ps. 62:9).

God is loved in our neighbor

1868. But we must now concern ourselves with the second commandment. It is like the first; it is, in fact, practically identical with it. Who would seek to love God without love for him whom God himself loves? For God is the Creator and Father of all men, their head and their Redeemer, so that you seek and love your God and Lord in them. For this reason the love of God is properly called the source, the norm, the foundation, and the purpose of love of neighbor. Nothing is to be preferred to the love of God and of Christ. Rather, all charity must take its source from the love of God and be returned by you to that source. There is another important consideration: God took our flesh upon himself and as man gave himself up to death for mankind by shedding his most precious blood.

Love of neighbor is imitation of Christ

1869. In so doing he gave an adorable and incomparable example of love by which you may understand that no small part of the imitation of Christ consists in loving your neighbor from the bottom of your heart. For he said: *By this will all men know that you are my disciples, if you have love for one another* (John 13:35). *This is my commandment, that you love one another as I have loved you* (*ibid.*, 15:12). Hence if you seek to become conformable to the image of the Son of God, learn of him as your Master and follow him as your leader. Put on the Lord Jesus Christ who loved you to the end, yes, even without end. *We know that we have passed from death to life* [that is, from sin and the world to the life of grace and the monastic life], *because we love the brethren. He who does not love abides in death. . . . In this we have come to know his love, that he laid down his life for us; and we likewise ought to lay down our life for the brethren* (I John 3:14–16). Charity, therefore, including under the term both your love for God and that for your neighbor, is the perfect imitation of Jesus. It is, in a sense, the complete incorporation of your person into him, so that it is not so much, then, you that live, as Christ lives in you. When such is the case, will not your heart burn with the same flame as that with which your most loving Savior was consumed when he suffered death for you on the altar of the cross? It is only by means of this twofold charity that your perfection is wholly established and confirmed; because through it God, the heavenly Father, dwells in you and through you, all in all. Consequently love all men without exception as you love the pupil of your eye, even as you love yourself—friends and enemies alike. Let your heart be open most kindly to all, so that there can be no one who can *escape its heat* (Ps. 18:7). Let your love thus be like the sun which lights up the whole world with the benign rays of its light, and warms it with its heat. You should be aglow with the desire of bestowing every work of mercy, corporal and spiritual, upon all, mindful of the Bridegroom admonishing you: *Set me as a seal on your heart, as a seal on your arm; for stern as death is love, relentless as the nether world devotion; its flames are a blazing fire* (Cant. 8:6).

Love must be orderly

1870. Indeed, your Bridegroom's emblem over you is love *(ibid.,* 2:4). You must not, therefore, disregard the order of love that he assigns for you, nor fail to carry it out. The first claim on your love belongs, after God, to the members of your monastic family, to your spiritual father, and the circle of your brethren. Both justice and charity bind you with regard to this special love. We have already dwelt at length on the weighty reasons for this obligation.

Charity toward the sick, the dying, and the deceased

1871. We must first devote our attention to the acts of charity which we must perform for the sick and infirm brethren. There is scarcely any obligation which our holy father Benedict has impressed so pointedly upon his sons as the solicitous care of the sick. In God's counsels illness is taken to be for persons of faith a wonderful help for purifying the soul and directing it toward heaven. When illness strikes, it is as though the sick man were let down into the pool called Bethsaida (cf. John 5:2), in order that through suffering of the body his soul may find new vitality in the waters of grace. Illness is really a treasured blessing from heaven; it presents an excellent opportunity to those who suffer to gain rich merit and an increase of reward through the practice of virtue. It is true, nevertheless, that the sick man is tormented by the most severe physical pains and anguish of soul: not infrequently he is wearied with sighing . . . and floods his bed with weeping (cf. Ps. 6:7). In the monastery not only the infirmarian but everyone must lend help in every manner possible, whether this calls for sitting up at night or performing other acts of charity. For your confrere is a chosen member of Christ and in a visible manner now shows forth his image. He is sharing in the Lord's passion: his condition re-enacts Calvary's drama of suffering. Hence it is only with holy reverence and love that you should approach to adore and embrace Jesus himself in the person of him who is ill, with every possible expression of love, attention, and willingness to serve. At one time you pour in wine upon your brother's wounds, and oil at another, according to the need of comforting him and buoying up his spirits. Like a guardian angel, like a friend eager to perform whatever service he may, make yourself available for any kind of help that may be required. When the illness takes a more serious turn, intensify the zeal of your fraternal charity, particularly as the death-struggle becomes more imminent. In that hour the soul experiences its greatest need, and cries out: *The terror of death has fallen upon me. Fear and trembling come upon me, and horror overwhelms me* (Ps. 54:5–6). *I am a man without strength . . . and with all your billows you overwhelm me . . . your furies have swept over me; . . . they encompass me like water all the day* (Ps. 87:5, 8, 17). *There is no health in my flesh because of your indignation; there is no wholeness in my bones because of my sin. . . . Because for you, O Lord, I wait; you, O Lord my God, will answer when I say, Let them not be glad on my account who, when my foot slips, glory over me* (Ps. 37:4, 16, 17), *and say to me . . . Where is your God?* (Ps. 41:11.)

In reality the eternal salvation of your confrere is in grave danger when he approaches this last encounter with the ancient enemy. Come forward to his assistance in this peril, stand by him as a helper in the struggle, strengthening his afflicted spirit, encouraging and consoling him, fortifying him with every aid, particularly with your prayer. And when the Lord, at last, yielding to the supplications of so many brethren, has granted victory to the soul, and comes as the merciful Judge to call it forth from this life to its destiny, cease not to show your loving concern for the soul even beyond the grave. Leave nothing undone until your confrere, liberated from purgatory, takes flight heavenward like a dove, and eternally triumphant, reposes at the feet of his beloved Bridegroom.

The works of charity

1872. Now let us turn to the consideration of those works of charity which the monk must exercise in behalf of other persons. According to the proper order of charity, parents, benefactors and friends hold the first place. After them you must direct a special charity toward all with whom you are linked by bonds of relationship, duty or gratitude. It is true that at God's call you left all things—house, brothers, sisters, father, mother (cf. Matt. 19:29). Like Abraham, you have gone forth out of your country, from your kindred, and out of your father's house (cf. Gen. 12:1). And it is equally true that the Lord's word applies to you: *He who loves father or mother more than me is not worthy of me* (Matt. 10:37). Now you must flee with a holy dread from anyone, no matter how well disposed he may otherwise be, nor how much he has done for you, who stands in opposition to your welfare and your vocation, for *no one, having put his hand to the plow and looking back, is fit for the kingdom of God* (Luke 9:62).

It follows from these principles that no one, not even the closest relative, must be allowed to influence you with an immoderate and purely natural love, so that he be preferred to God, to whom you belong. But the more evident this is, the more carefully you must see to it that your charity, sanctified in the Holy Spirit, is confirmed and increased, lest it fail in its application toward those to whom you are under obligation by reason of some bond of duty or gratitude. You must be careful to bestow a special share of your prayers and pious exercises upon your relatives and friends. And in the letters you write to them, in conformity with holy obedience, exhort them by means of kindness and holy love unto edification and spiritual progress.

Special love for the poor

1873. As with your relatives and those who have other claims on your charity, you must be earnest in your solicitude or the poor who are your associates in the observance of poverty. *He shall have pity for the lowly and the poor; the lives of the poor he shall save . . . and precious shall their blood be in his sight* (Ps. 71:13–14). They are clothed with the authority of the Supreme King, whose place and dignity they represent. For he has said: *Amen, I say to you, as long as you did it for one of these, the least of my brethren, you did it for me* (Matt. 25:40).

With every expression of religious care, kindness, and charity, you must honor Christ your Bridegroom, hidden under the unattractive and lowly appearance of the poor. May these poor people be your special charge, and most dear to your heart, lest you detract from that unanimously accorded and highly esteemed praise which from the earliest times has acclaimed monks the fathers, benefactors, and patrons of the poor. For here lies the chief source from which the most abundant blessings, both heavenly and earthly, have descended upon monasteries. *He who has compassion on the poor lends to the Lord* (Prov. 19:17). *To the poor man also extend your hand, that your blessing may be complete* (Sir. 7:32). *A man's goodness God cherishes like a signet ring, a man's virtue, like the apple of his eye* (*ibid.*, 17:18).

Courtesy to guests

1874. But it is not only to the indigent and the oppressed that the houses and hearts were opened wide, but also to guests, in accordance with the ancient traditions which have been preserved down to our own day. *I was a stranger,* says the Lord, *and you took me in* (Matt. 25:35). Our holy Patriarch exhorts us: "Guests are to be received as Christ" (*RSB,* c. 53). Hence anyone not undeserving of hospitality who knocks at the monastery door must be admitted in all kindness. He is to be treated with every expression of humility, reverence, charity, and politeness. If, in accordance with the praiseworthy custom which has the approval of the Holy See, he is taken along to the monastic refectory, care must be employed in assuring that the regular discipline does not suffer as a result. And the brother who is appointed to the care of the guests is to see to it that he fulfils his office [in which he acts as the representative of the community] in the spirit of holy obedience and simplicity, endeavoring in all that he does to edify those who are assigned to his spiritual charge.

Apostolate of literature and the arts

1875. Brief mention must here be given to those works of charity which have their origin in the solitude of the cell, which more than other works give evidence of the humility, industry, and zeal of monks. I am referring to the monumental works of sacred sciences and art which have been produced by the monks, scattering rays of divine truth and charity to the ends of the earth. For like two beacons these works of sacred learning and charity shine forth from the cloister, spreading their light far and wide, enlightening the minds and kindling the hearts of men, or like two Cherubim, hovering over the faithful with their shining wings. But it is only when it is animated with the spirit of humility and zeal for God's glory that science flourishes in the cloister. When such is not the case, the works of the writer recoil like a treacherous bow (cf. Ps. 77:57).

For *the inclination of the flesh is death, but the inclination of the spirit, life and peace. For the wisdom of the flesh is hostile to God, for it is not subject to the law of God, nor can it be. And they who are carnal cannot please God* (Rom. 8:6–8). For *this is not the wisdom that descends from above; it is earthly* (Jas. 3:15), which *shall perish from their wise men* (Isa. 29:14). He who is infinite wisdom has stated: *I am the way, and the truth, and the life* (John 14:6). Even with regard to knowledge, *other foundation no one can lay, but that which has been laid, which is Christ Jesus* (I Cor. 3:11), in whom are hidden all the treasures of wisdom and knowledge.

Therefore, dear confrere, in applying yourself to the study of the sacred sciences and the arts, you must follow the shining standard of your Master, never departing from allegiance to his kingly scepter. The holy cross is for the works that are performed in the cell, as well as for all others, the tree of true life, and the one unconquerable source of truth, from which your own salvation and that of others flows abundantly, in order that in all things God may be glorified (*RSB,* c. 57, which last phrase has been adopted as the motto of the order of St. Benedict). Only in a monastery where the monks *rate themselves according to moderation* (Rom. 12:3) does the library become the citadel of God and the cell of the scholar or of the artisan the workshop in which are produced the glorious weapons of the Church.

1876. We have enumerated some of the great number of works of charity by which the monk can give practical proof of his love of God with his whole heart, his whole soul, his whole mind, his whole strength, and with all his powers (cf. Mark 12:30; Luke 10:27). Add to this the inestimable spiritual blessing for the whole human society from the Work of God, from so many sacrifices, prayers, tears, and works of supererogation. Indeed, the charity of the monk *is kind, . . . is not self-seeking . . . never fails* (I Cor. 13:4, 5, 8). Blessed you are indeed, O son of St. Benedict, and privileged as well, in being able to bestow blessings on others far and wide! As often as you pour forth the blessings of charity, you yourself will be more and more enriched with the same blessings of charity by the Lord who repays with an infinite generosity. *He who confers benefits will be amply enriched* (Prov. 11:25).

Charity in the priesthood

1877. But even with all these considerations the subject of charity of the monks is by no means exhausted: in fact, the more distinguished part of the works of charity remains to be mentioned. For an immeasurable and glorious field of apostolic activity is opened to the monk who is raised to the priesthood. As soon as he has reached maturity as a monk and has grown to be a perfect son of the heavenly

Father, he himself is constituted a spiritual father of God's children. This is indeed an event of great wonder! For as the Holy Spirit came upon the Blessed Virgin, so he has come upon you. The power of the Most High has overshadowed you, and what is born through you is called a child of God. From the moment of your sacred ordination your whole life is nothing but a kind of continuous incarnation of the Eternal Word: incessantly you bring into being at the altar the real or the Eucharistic Body, and in the sacraments the Mystical Body of Christ; in the Eucharist the true Son of God; in the sacraments, sons by grace and adoption.

Paternal zeal for souls

1878. What a wonderful and truly unheard-of fruitfulness! It begets both head and members of the new heavenly family. It bestows the Son of God on men; it begets men for God. Not only does it beget these men for God, but it also nourishes them unto eternal life with maternal food of grace and truth. So richly, O son of St. Benedict, *has God blessed you forever* (Ps. 44:3). In this light consider the zeal with which your heart must be inflamed for the honor of God and the salvation of souls! As the father of the family, so should the servant and the master of the household be. Now you have been chosen helper and companion of the Supreme Shepherd of souls. Your duty is to cooperate with him in the divine work of mercy and redemption.

You must, therefore, imitate the adorable example by which he has loved us with his infinite love, and by which he came into this world to save all men. If you follow him with complete confidence, you will deserve to be called in all truth a man of blessing. For then nothing shall be preferred or ever be considered of greater value by you than that all men whom the Lord has redeemed shall be filled with every heavenly blessing and grace. *O God, your way is holy* (Ps. 76:14). And you, O priest of God, will be made holy in order that you may gain as many as possible for the thrice holy God.

Preaching

1879. Whenever obedience calls you to the duty of preaching, therefore, "gird yourself with the sword" of the word of God, for the battle against the kingdoms of darkness. Be like a lamp put *upon the lamp-stand, so as to give light to all in the house* (Matt. 5:15). Your mouth should become the very mouth of God, ever announcing his revelations, his promises, his threats, in order that the kingdom of the Most High may grow day by day. To make certain that you will always burn with a holy and persevering zeal to save men, recall to mind again and again the inestimable value of even one soul, to which nothing can ever be compared except the most precious blood of the Savior. For all men were called to become children of God and co-heirs with Christ in his glory.

Conversion of nations

1880. Fired with this zeal almost countless monks spared no effort, nor did they even hesitate to offer their very lives and shed their blood. With the Book of the Gospels in one hand and the *Rule of St. Benedict* in the other, they penetrated even the most remote regions, constantly adding new peoples to the family of Christendom. In so doing they established, spread, and confirmed the reign of the cross over almost the whole world. This success was all the more brilliant and rich, and the influence more powerful and real, in that the life of the monastic family and the celebration of the sacred liturgy, which is the principal duty of monks, contributed toward the conversion of these peoples. Well may the praise be applied to the glorious family of the holy Patriarch: *Your arrows are sharp; peoples are subject to you* (Ps. 44:6).

Education

1881. Another work of charity should be brought to our present reflections, a form of charity in which monks have engaged from earliest antiquity, the traditional task of educating the young. The monastic family joins the Church in proclaiming: *Let the little children be, and do not hinder them from coming to me, for of such is the kingdom of heaven* (Matt. 19:14). Let the monk, then, remember that the young are entrusted to him by God himself, in order that he may bestow a new life upon them and that Christ may be formed in them. Therefore, what the monk himself has had the good fortune to learn in the Lord's school of the cloister is what he should impart in holy reverence to these pledges that divine love has entrusted to him. For indeed, *No one can come to me unless the Father who sent me draw him . . .* (John 6:44). Hence, dear confrere, it is to your honor and credit to exercise the heavenly Father's authority and to hold his place, that in the work of education you show the way to Jesus, fashioning his holy and heavenly image in the young.

As the painter has his canvas, you have the minds and hearts of the young before you. On these you must depict, with the colors of grace and truth, the lovable and radiant likeness of the Sacred Heart, so that the young may be made to resemble him, light of Light, purity of Purity, all resplendent images and sons of God. Spare no labor, then, that the young, imbued with a true and enlightened faith, filled with piety and wisdom, be not of the world, but may rather abhor its spirit; that they may shine with the light of a genuine erudition whose end is the glory of God and the honor of the Church; and that they may know the way leading to the heavenly fatherland. In so doing you have the assurance that you are educating them in God and for God, and are in reality a helper and an associate in God's providence.

The works of monastic charity must harmonize with the monastic life

1882. These, then, are the sacred works of charity to which obedience binds the monk. One common and indispensable condition applies to them all: they must be, without exception, in complete harmony with cloistral life, and in no manner at variance with the demands of holy profession. Here, too, the divine doctrine applies: *Seek first the kingdom of God and his justice, and all these things shall be given you besides* (Matt. 6:33). For he who, despising the world, has entered the monastery in order to attach himself to the monastic family, is guilty of sacrilegiously betraying his trust if afterward he becomes involved in worldly occupations and radically departs from the Rule and the way of life he has vowed. *To whom will he be generous who is stingy with himself and does not enjoy what is his own?* (Sir. 14:5.)

1883. Hence there is always serious reason to fear that while preaching and counselling salvation to others, the monk may himself become a castaway. But it were a worse, a most dreadful situation if an entire monastery were to be so absorbed in external works that the conventual observance, the Work of God, and other basic elements of the monastic life should be shaken and gradually crumble. Such a state in a monastery would leave scarcely any hope of making a recovery. Therefore nothing must ever be allowed to take precedence over the Work of God, but rather whatever work is undertaken for the salvation of souls by the monastery should be made at the same time to tend toward the personal sanctification of the monk and the perfection and greater glory of the Work of God, in order that in all things God may be glorified (*RSB*, c. 57). Then all the works of charity and zeal for souls that they undertake will be wonderfully blessed, dignified and fructified with grace, since they will be built on the foundation of prayer, humility, obedience, and perfect self-denial. This should cause us no wonder, for it is in reality God's powerful arm that performs the work, not that of man. Nor is it the individual monk that performs these holy tasks, but rather the entire community through its united powers of prayer and charity that bring the work to perfection.

The monk is the servant of God

1884. The monk is the privileged son of God, his servant, his vassal, dedicated solely to his service and the performance of his will. By that token the entire monastic family is a picked band of troops of the Supreme King, his body-guard which is ever in readiness for him to appear. It is his joy to dwell in their midst. He tests them for his nobler works, which call for great courage, and ever demand heroic devotedness. And in reality, whenever this King or his Church summons a monk, or a whole battle array of monks, they march dauntlessly forth to his greatest battles with fearless and unshaken fortitude. Like the prophets and their disciples, they go before the chiefs and peoples, confidently proclaiming God's Law, his justice and his will, or defending them with ardent zeal, like Elias, of whom we read: *Like a fire there appeared the prophet whose words were as a flaming furnace* (Sir. 48:1).

1885. Let the monks be prepared for every work of zeal. Let them at the same time spurn all worldly considerations and prove themselves so magnanimous, resolute and willing in the service of the Church, that it will be manifest that they are fighting with a strength endowed by God, and are filled with the power of the Holy Spirit. Animated with this zeal a glorious throng has gone forth from cloistral solitudes in the past—apostles of nations, confessors, doctors, and martyrs; they have founded, preserved, and marvelously increased families of the followers of Christ; have given renowned pontiffs to the Apostolic See and holy bishops to the Church; wise counsellors to rulers; teachers, shepherds, peacemakers, and efficacious reformers to the faithful; in a word, lovable and faithful fathers to the spiritually reborn children of God. Who can ever worthily praise that innumerable offspring of the Holy Spirit, the monastic family, which has given to the heavenly Bridegroom and to the Church so abundant a harvest of virtues and souls? We salute you, glorious mother! May God grant you once again that holy fruitfulness of activity with which your numerous sons will never cease to work for true and assured peace and for the salvation of the tired human race!

II. EVIDENCE FROM THE RULE OF ST. BENEDICT

Love of God

1886. The first instrument of good works is: To love the Lord with all one's heart, all one's soul, and all one's strength. To prefer nothing to the love of Christ (*RSB,* c. 4, nn. 1, 21). Let them prefer nothing whatever to Christ. And may he bring us all alike to life everlasting (*ibid.,* c. 72). Then, when all these degrees of humility have been climbed, the monk will presently come to that perfect love of God which casts out all fear; whereby he will begin to observe without labor, as though naturally and by habit, all those precepts which formerly he did not observe without fear; no longer from fear of hell, but for love of Christ and through good habit and delight in virtue (*ibid.,* c. 7, concluding paragraph). But as we progress in our monastic life and in faith, our hearts will be enlarged and we shall run the way of God's commandments with unspeakable sweetness of love (*ibid., Prolog.,* concluding paragraph). Obedience without delay . . . becomes those who hold nothing dearer to them than Christ (*ibid.,* c. 5).

Life of St. Benedict: Nor should we marvel that [St. Scholastica], desiring to be with her brother as much as possible, should in that hour have had more power than he. For St. John says, *God is love* (I John 4:16); and it was right that she should prevail who had the greater love (*S. Greg. Magni Dialogorum Lib. II,* c. 33, *PL* 66:196).

Charity toward neighbor

1887. Instruments of good works are: To love one's neighbor as oneself; to honor all men; not to forsake charity; to love one's enemies; not to render cursing for cursing, but rather blessing; not to be a detractor; to hate no man; to pray for one's enemies in the love of Christ; not to do to another what one would not have done to himself (*RSB,* c. 4, nn. 2, 8, 26, 31, 32, 40, 64, 70, 9).

Life of St. Benedict: Our holy Father performed many of his miracles particularly from motives of the most ardent charity, as in the mending of the broken sieve (*S. Greg. Magni Dialogorum Lib. II,* c. 1, *PL* 66:128); the paying of the debt of the poor man (*ibid.,* c. 27, col. 184), and in other instances. He also gave an outstanding example of love for one's enemies when he received the message of the frightful death of the priest Florentius: he wept bitterly, both for the death of his enemy, and because his disciple had exulted thereat. He prescribed that Maurus should do penance for venturing by such a message to rejoice over the death of an enemy (*ibid.,* c. 8, col. 150).

Charity toward the weaker brethren

1888. Instruments of good works are: To visit the sick; to bury the dead; to help the afflicted; to console the sorrowing (*RSB,* c. 4, nn. 15–18). Before all things and above all things care must be taken of the sick, so that they may be served in very deed as Christ himself; for he said: *I was sick and you visited me* (Matt. 25:36). Again: *As long as you did it for one of these, the least of my brethren, you did it for me* (*ibid.*, v. 40). But let the sick on their part consider that they are being served for the honor of God, and not provoke their brethren who are serving them by their unreasonable demands. Yet they should be patiently borne with, because from such as these there is gained a more abundant reward. Therefore let the abbot take the greatest care that they suffer no neglect. For these sick brethren let there be assigned a special room and an attendant who is God-fearing, diligent and careful. . . . Let the abbot take the greatest care that the sick be not neglected by the cellarer and attendants; for he must answer for all the misdeeds of his disciples (*ibid.*, c. 36). [With regard to what is necessary] let there be no respect for persons, but consideration for infirmities (*ibid.*, c. 34). In assigning work the abbot should have consideration for the weakness of sick and delicate brethren (*ibid.*, c. 48). Let the brethren bear with the greatest patience one another's infirmities, whether of body or character (*ibid.*, c. 72).

Charity toward the poor and guests

1889. Let the cellarer take the greatest care of the sick, of children, of the guests, and of the poor, knowing without doubt that he will have to render an account for all these on the day of judgment (*RSB*, c. 31). Instruments of good works are: To relieve the poor; to clothe the naked (*ibid.*, c. 4, nn. 13–14). When the brethren receive new clothes, let them always return the old ones at once, that they may be stored in the clothesroom for the poor (*ibid.*, c. 55). Let all guests that come be received like Christ, for he will say: *I was a stranger and you took me in* (Matt. 25:35). And let fitting honor be shown to all, but especially to clerics and pilgrims. As soon, therefore, as a guest is announced, let the superior or some one of the brethren meet him with all charitable service. And first of all let them pray together, and then let them bestow the kiss of peace. This kiss of peace shall not be offered until after the prayers have been said, on account of the delusions of the devil. In the greeting of all guests, whether they be arriving or departing, let the greatest humility be shown. Let the head be bowed, or the whole body prostrated on the ground, and so let Christ be worshipped in them, for indeed he is received in their persons. When the guests have been received, let them be led to prayer, and afterward let the superior, or a monk appointed by him, sit with them. Let the law of God be read before the guest for his edification, and then let all kindness be shown to him. The superior shall break his fast for the sake of a guest, unless it be a special fast day which may not be violated. . . . Let the abbot give the guests water for their hands. . . . Special attention should be shown in the reception of poor men and pilgrims because in them Christ is more truly welcomed; for the fear which the rich inspire is enough of itself to secure them honor. The guest house shall be assigned to a brother whose soul is full of the fear of God. Let there be a sufficient number of beds ready therein. And let the house of God be administered by prudent men in a prudent manner. Let no one, without special instructions, associate or converse with guests. If he meet or see them, let him greet them humbly, as we have said, and ask a blessing; then let him pass on, saying that he is not permitted to talk with a guest (*ibid.*, c. 53). At the gate of the monastery let there be placed a wise old man, who understands how to give and receive a message, and whose years will keep him from leaving his post. This porter should have a room near the gate, so that those who come may always find someone to answer them. As soon as anyone knocks, or a poor man hails him, let him answer *Deo gratias*, or *Benedic*. Then let him attend to them promptly, with all the gentleness of the fear of God and with fervent charity. If the porter need help, let him have one of the younger brethren (*ibid.*, c. 66).

Life of St. Benedict: The man of God, who had resolved to give all things in this world [to the poor, during the famine], in order that he might keep all in heaven, gave orders that the little oil that remained should be given to the petitioner (*S. Greg. Magni Dialogorum Lib. II*, c. 28, *PL* 66:186).

Pastoral zeal and care of souls

1890. The reader's attention is drawn to the holy Rule's demands for superiors to possess knowledge, wisdom, discretion, solicitude and holiness of life:

"But let the abbot always remember that he has undertaken the government of souls, and will have to give an account of them. . . . Let him regard it as certain that he will have to give the Lord an account of these souls on the day of judgment, and certainly of his own soul also. And thus, fearing always the examination which the shepherd will have to face for the sheep entrusted to him, and anxiously regarding the account which will have to be given for others, he is made solicitous for his own sake also (*RSB*, c. 2). Let him so arrange and ordain all things that souls may be saved and that the brethren may do their work without justifiable murmuring (*ibid.*, c. 41). Let him adapt and accommodate himself to all in such a way that he may not only suffer no loss in the sheep committed to him, but may even rejoice in the increase of a good flock (*ibid.*, c. 2). The abbot is bound to use the greatest care, and to exercise all prudence and diligence, so that he may not lose any of the sheep entrusted to him (*ibid.*, c. 27) . . . then, if he sees that all his trouble is of no avail, let him employ a greater thing still, namely the prayers of himself and of all the brethren, that God, who can do all things, may effect the cure of the sick brother [who has been corrected and does not amend] (*ibid.*, c. 28). Let him imitate the merciful example of the Good Shepherd who left the ninety-nine sheep in the mountains, and went after the one sheep that had strayed; and had so great pity on its weakness, that he deigned to place it on his own sacred shoulders and bring it back to the flock (*ibid.*, c. 27). Let him remember that the bruised reed is not to be broken" (*ibid.*, c. 54).

The duty of preaching

1891. Therefore, when anyone has received the name of abbot, he ought to rule his disciples with a twofold teaching, displaying all goodness and holiness by deeds and words, but by deeds rather than by words. . . . And whatever he has taught his disciples to be contrary to God's law, let him show by his example that it is not to be done, lest while preaching to others he should himself become a castaway, and lest God should some day say to him in his sin: *Why do you recite my statutes, and profess my covenant with your mouth, though you hate discipline and cast my words behind you?* (Ps. 49:16.) *Why dost thou see the speck in thy brother's eye, and yet dost not consider the beam in thy own eye?* (Matt. 7:3.) . . . For the abbot in his teaching ought always to observe the rule of the Apostle wherein he says: *Reprove, entreat, rebuke* (II Tim. 4:2) . . . displaying the rigor of the master or the loving kindness of a father. . . . And let him not shut his eyes to the faults of offenders. . . . One he must humor, another rebuke, another persuade, adapting and accommodating himself according to each one's disposition and understanding (*RSB*, c. 2).

Life of St. Benedict: But the time was now come when Almighty God had willed . . . that Benedict's life should be displayed to men for their instruction, so that his lamp being placed upon a lamp-stand might shine brightly and illuminate the whole Church of God. . . . His name became known to the people of the vicinity, and from that time forward many began to visit him. These visitors brought him food for his body; they themselves took away in their hearts the spiritual food of his teaching (*S. Greg. Magni Dialogorum Lib. II*, c. 1, *PL* 66:129 f.). Even his everyday speech was weighted with miraculous power, for no words fell idly from the lips of one whose heart was fixed on God (*ibid.*, c. 23, col. 178). There was a village not far from the monastery in which a considerable number of people had been converted from the worship of idols to the true faith by Benedict's preaching, and among them were some nuns. Now the servant of God used frequently to send his monks to that place for their spiritual benefit (*ibid.*, c. 19, col. 169).

Conversion of peoples

1892. *Life of St. Benedict:* When the man of God arrived [at Montecassino], he broke the idol to pieces, overturned the altar and cut down the sacred groves. Of the temple of Apollo he made an oratory dedicated to St. Martin, on the site of Apollo's altar he built a little chapel in honor of St. John, and preaching continually to the people of the vicinity summoned them to the Christian faith (*ibid.,* c. 8, col. 152).

Education of youth

1893. [Chapters 31 and 37 of the holy Rule may well be re-read in this connection.] Boys are to be kept under discipline at all times and by everyone (*RSB,* c. 63).

Life of St. Benedict: Members of the nobility and persons of a religious way of life began to come to him from the city of Rome and to give him their sons to be brought up for the service of Almighty God (*S. Greg. Magni Dialogorum Lib. II,* c. 3, *PL* 66:140).

Monastic discipline must remain intact even in the performance of works of charity

1894. But let him who is ordained [to the priesthood] beware of elation or pride; and let him not presume to do anything but what is commanded him by the abbot, knowing that he will be all the more subject to the discipline of the monastery. Let him not because of his priesthood forget the obedience and discipline of the Rule, but make ever more and more progress toward God (*RSB,* c. 62). If a [priest who wishes to dwell in the monastery] perseveres firmly in his petition, let him know that he will have to observe the full discipline of the Rule and that nothing will be abated for him. . . . Let him presume to do nothing, knowing that he is subject to the discipline of the Rule (*ibid.,* c. 60).

Life of St. Benedict: So, temptation having departed from him, the man of God, like a field that has been cultivated and well tilled, brought forth a more abundant harvest of virtue. The praises of his holy way of life were in every mouth, and his name had become famous (*S. Greg. Magni Dialogorum Lib. II,* c. 3, *PL* 66:134). The holy man in that same hermitage of his had long been growing richer in virtue and miraculous power, and had gathered many disciples about him for the service of Almighty God (*ibid.,* col. 140).

III. DECREES AND DOCUMENTS OF THE CHURCH

Charity is the goal of the religious life

1895. PROV. COUNCIL OF PRAGUE (1860). A. With every resource at their command, religious must embrace the excellent vocation which they have chosen. With the unquenchable ardor of charity and with constantly increasing generosity they must pursue the course whose sweetness defies description and which, as a share in the passion of Christ, leads to being heirs of his kingdom [cf. similarity with concluding paragraph of *RSB, Prolog.*] (*Decreta*, tit. 7, c. 3, *de obligationibus regularium, CL* 5:575). B. They must be considered a cherished and powerful portion of the flock of Christ, the inheritors of the apostolic life, a gem of the Church Militant, as inseparably united with the holiness of the body of Christ as with the unconquered love of Christ, and the necessary spirit of repentance. In fact, never have both the Church and the world seemed to have been in greater need of the works and the example of the religious life than in the present era. May the humility and obedience of the regular life, which submits from love to the fatherly commands of superiors conquer domineering pride! May the austerity and voluntary poverty of community life give the lie to today's insatiable thirst for pleasure and wealth! And may that divinely inspired zeal by which religious persons seek only God and the welfare of souls, stand in opposition to worldly desires which war against the soul. Nor are the works of penance and virginal chastity the world's only spiritual requirements: it certainly needs also prayer and constant intercession before God that he grant internal and external peace; it needs the humble efforts of religious in the propagation of truth: finally, and most of all, it needs the sacrifices of charity, by which religious spend not only what they have, but themselves as well, on the welfare of their neighbors (*ibid.*, c. 1, *de status regularis dignitate et augmento*, col. 571).

1896. CONGR. OF BURSFELD (founded 1433). A. Our brethren are to excel one another in honor and charity, putting into practice all that the holy Father defined about order in the community (*RSB*, cc. 63, 70), so that no one ever strike another, or presume even to offend him. When the brethren meet they should salute each other by uncovering the head and bowing; they must avoid quarrels as violations of charity that cause scandal; they must guard against forming cliques, particular friendships, and everything else opposed to charity (*Stat.*, dist. 5, c. 11, *de pace et charitate inter fratres nostros*, § 2, p. 151). B. In order that this charity may be made firm according to our custom, besides being under obligation to seek reconciliation immediately according to the prescription of the Rule, those who have given offense to each other will mutually ask pardon before four major feasts. We desire that this practice never be neglected, even though the brethren have not offended by the spoken word (*ibid.*, § 5, p. 152).

1897. CONG. OF STRASBURG (founded 1624). Long ago the Fathers preached that fraternal charity is the ornament of sacred orders, the mainstay of regular discipline, the glory of monasteries, the bond of perfection, the incentive for good works, the integrating force of holy virtues. For these reasons superiors must exercise great solicitude and the subjects also make it their concern that peace and charity thrive and be preserved in monasteries (*Declar. 1 in c. 72 RSB,* fol. 111).

1898. SWABIAN CONGR. OF ST. JOSEPH (approved 1725). A. Observance of regular discipline can no more be maintained without charity than a house could be supported if the mortaring of the stones were removed (*Const. et declar.*, Pars I, c. 2, punctum 1, *de pace et caritate fraterna,* § 1, fol. 48). B. Let the subjects perform all duties of mutual charity promptly and willingly, offer offense to no one, bear their mutual defects in the spirit of charity, judge no one rashly, but always accept and interpret the statements and deeds of others in the most favorable light. And because charity demands that we rejoice at the happiness of others as well as our own, should it happen that a concession is made to one or the other because of the state of his health or for any other reasonable cause, they are not to resent the grant, murmur, or seek a similar dispensation in the spirit of envy. Rather they should offer thanks to God, the author of all gifts, for needing less because of their own robust health (*ibid.*, § 3, fol. 49). C. We do not wish fraternal charity to degenerate into individual and particular friendships, however. According to the mind of St. John Chrysostom (*Hom. 10 in Ep. 1 ad Thess.*, § 1, *PG* 62:456), such friendships are not the fostering of charity, but the separation of discord and the destructive rupture of discipline and regular observance (*ibid.*, § 12, fol. 54).

Charity toward brethren who are ill

1899. CONGR. OF BURSFELD. A. In all charity our brethren are to be furnished with every remedy, physical and spiritual, and according to the seriousness of the illness, shown every consideration short of superfluities (*Stat.*, dist. 6, c. 8, *de infirmitorio,* § 2, p. 252). B. The sick are to be mindful of their religious profession and not expect either what is excessive or what would have to be specially procured for them. If anything is wanting, let them humbly and without murmuring offer its lack to God, who denied it to test their virtue and increase their merit. The sick must obey the abbot and the infirmarian even in matters that concern the care of their health and life itself.

As soon as one has become ill he should forthwith be admonished in all charity to look to the welfare of his soul by receiving the sacraments of penance and the Holy Eucharist. He is not to neglect, at least on Sundays, the help of these sacraments, so that strength of soul will be perfected in the body's weakness. He is to be prayed for in public and in private Masses. The customary passages are to be read to him in order to help him spiritually. The infirmarian as well as the one whom the prior has appointed, are to speak to the sick brother of matters referring to his spiritual welfare and encourage and hearten him in the Holy Spirit (*ibid.*, § 3, p. 253).

1900. CONGR. OF STRASBURG. Should it be necessary to assign a separate cell to a brother who is ill, that is the superior's duty. If special food is required, he is to order it. It is he, too, who is to dispense from choir and the common exercises. On the same day that a brother enters the infirmary and goes to bed, he is bound at least to confess, and, if he remains there eight days, receive Holy Communion, even though serious danger is absent. First of all, let there be appointed an infirmarian who will diligently minister to the ill and give them their medicine at the prescribed times. The other religious will frequently visit sick confreres in the spirit of fraternal charity, ministering spiritual comfort, speaking of such spiritual topics as patience, penance, the vanity of the world, and the transitoriness of the present life. When danger of death is not imminent, these visits are to be made during recreation only, unless the superior provides otherwise. As the danger of death becomes greater, one or two will always remain with the sick brother to read spiritual works to him and assist him in eliciting acts of faith, hope, charity, and contrition (*Declar. 3, 4 in c. 36 RSB,* fol. 47).

1901. SWABIAN CONGR. OF ST. JOSEPH. A. Our holy Father strongly commends the care of the ill to the abbot (*RSB,* c. 36). Since his zealous provisions express a most unusual charity and paternal affection for his sons, we exhort and warn all abbots and superiors, collectively and individually, that if they are to strive to put into practice what is taught, then it is to be particularly with regard to those who are ill, a form of charity that was so dear to the loving father. Unless the superior of the community desires to take this charge upon himself personally, let one of the older fathers have care of the sick, visit them often, comfort them and provide whatever is necessary according to the nature and severity of the illness. He will pay special attention to make certain that there is no neglect, and that the medicines are given as prescribed by the physician. If there is need for him to do so, he will exhort the brethren to obedience, patience, and the true spirit of compunction. The superior must, moreover, see to it that the brethren who are ill suffer no want either with regard to the proper medicines, food or any other means conducive to regaining health and restoring strength (*Const. et declar., Pars II,* c. 3, punctum 8, nn. 1, 3, 4, fol. 113 f.). B. The other brethren will fulfil their duty of fraternal charity toward the ill by consoling and visiting them when permission to speak is granted. During these visits they are not to disturb them with gossiping or joking. Neither are they to approach them during the times when silence is to be observed, without special permission from the superior (*ibid.,* n. 9, fol. 119). C. Care of the sick is to be assigned to one of the brethren who is particularly well qualified for such work in that he is motivated by the spirit of charity and sympathy for their plight and will devote himself to repairing and restoring their health (*Pars III,* c. 4, punctum 9, n. 1, *de infirmario,* fol. 284). D. After Compline he will impart the blessing to them and sprinkle them with holy water. When the condition worsens and the illness takes a more serious turn, he will see to it that the one who is ill is forthwith commended to the prayers of the others by the superior in the chapter (*ibid.,* n. 6, fol. 287).

Charity toward the dying

1902. CONGR. OF STRASBURG. Whenever the sick are to receive Holy Communion, all the religious are to accompany the Most Blessed Sacrament with lighted candles, singing or reciting the *Pange lingua.* At a sign given with the silence bell, all will assemble to assist the dying brother and devoutly recite the prayers prescribed in the Breviary, during which time the superior will impart the absolution of the order and of the Confraternity [of the Dying?] (*Declar. 10 in c. 36 RSB,* fol. 49).

1903. SWABIAN CONGR. OF ST. JOSEPH. A. When he observes that the condition of the sick brother has worsened to the point that danger of death seems present, the infirmarian will notify the superior in good time and warn the sick brother to be fortified with the holy sacraments so that he can prepare himself to die well (*Const. et declar., Pars II,* c. 3, punctum 9, *de fratribus morientibus,* fol. 120). B. The infirmarian is then to prepare everything necessary for administering the sacraments properly, seek to arrange that some brethren remain constantly with the dying person to hearten him by their prayers to bear the agony courageously, to induce him by their pious exhortations to make acts of faith, hope, love, and contrition (*ibid., Pars III,* c. 4, punctum 9, n. 9, fol. 288).

Charity toward the deceased

1904. ST. ISIDORE OF SEVILLE. When brethren depart this life, the Sacrifice is to be offered for the remission of their sins before they are buried. The bodies of the brethren are to be consigned to a common cemetery in order that one place will hold in death those whom the bond of charity united in life. On the second day after Pentecost [this was centuries before the *Requiem* Mass and specifically composed devotions for the deceased], the Sacrifice will be offered to God for the deceased of the monastery in order that having been made sharers in the life of the blessed they will receive as more purified souls their bodies on the day of resurrection (*Reg. monachorum,* c. 23, *CR* 1:197; *PL* 83:888).

1905. PROV. COUNCIL OF VIENNA (1858). Unless they were stained with mortal sin at death, they who have died among us live in the Lord and remain united to us by the bonds of faith and charity. Those who have not as yet been admitted to the sight of God help us by their prayers; and they await the help we give them by our suffrages. May it never happen that they feel that we have forsaken them. They seek not tears but the aid of good works from us. The commemoration of the deceased in the awesome mysteries [Mass] was sanctioned by the Apostles themselves (*S. Joan. Chrysost., Hom. 3 in Ep. ad Philip.,* § 4, *PG* 62:204). Since we are still walking in the faith, the Divine Sacrifice is ours if we offer it to the Omnipotent Father without fear and in the spirit of love. Let us offer for the deceased in the prayer of faith the infinite ransom by which the world was redeemed, and they will be bathed in the heavenly dew. Let us add prayers, almsdeeds and other good works (*Decr.,* tit. 4, c. 16, *de pietate erga defunctos, CL* 5:191).

1906. CONGR. OF STRASBURG. As soon as a brother has died, the body is to be clothed with the religious habit and scapular, and the capuche is to be put up over the head. The body is then carried to the chapter and placed upon the bier. Candles will burn there until time for the burial (*Declar. 12 in c. 36 RSB,* fol. 49).

1907. SWABIAN CONGR. OF ST. JOSEPH. A. When a brother has departed this life . . . his body will be kept in a becoming manner between lighted candles. Two of the brethren will remain constantly in a nearby room, replacing one another hourly according to the order arranged by the superior. During this watch they will commend the soul of the deceased to God with fervent prayers (*Const. et declar., Pars III,* c. 4, punct. 9, n. 10, fol. 289). B. The day of the burial, as well as the third, seventh and thirtieth days, and the anniversary, are always to be celebrated with the nine-lesson Office of the Dead recited in choir on the preceding day, and a solemn Mass on the day itself (*ibid., Pars II,* c. 3, punctum 9, n. 3, fol. 121). C. Let the *Requiem* Mass be offered every day for an entire month for the repose of the deceased brother by a priest appointed for that purpose. If a double feast precludes the *Requiem* Mass, at least the fruit of the Sacrifice is to be applied for the deceased (*ibid.,* n. 4, fol. 122) .

A crucifix is to be put at the deceased brother's place in the refectory for the same period of a month. This place is not to be occupied by anyone. All the food that would have been given to the brother, together with his portion of bread and wine, will be distributed to the poor for the welfare of his soul (*ibid.*, n. 5, fol. 123).

Share in the community's good works granted to seculars

1908. ABBEY OF CLUNY (11th century). Many of the faithful of Christ, wealthy and poor men alike, when taken into our chapter, express the desire of having some share in our brotherhood. We readily grant them a share and communion in all the good works that are performed by way of prayers and almsdeeds, not only here at the monastery, but also in all the places subject to our jurisdiction. For all of them, as long as they live, Psalm 68 is specially chanted at all the Hours, and the Collect *Praetende, Domine, famulis* is applied for them as often as it is said at the high Mass or the morning Mass. After they die . . . suffrages are offered for them (*Consuetudines Cluniacen. Udalrici, Lib. III*, c. 33, *PL* 149:777).

Charity to the poor

1909. CONGR. OF STRASBURG. Superiors must be zealous in seeing to it that fitting alms are bestowed on the poor. They will not permit the porters to dismiss anyone on their own initiative, except in the case of persons who are obviously unworthy. They are to warn the porters to be gracious, listen to and report the difficulties and needs of the poor people, and to show any testimonial letters and recommendations they have to the procurator (*Declar. 12 in c. 53 RSB*, fol. 67).

1910. CONGR. OF BURSFELD. Our holy Father includes relief of the poor among the Instruments of Good Works (*RSB*, c. 4, n. 14). Hence in treating of the matters which pertain to fraternal charity we are also to devote our attention to the love of neighbor. We admonish superiors of monasteries, therefore, to be solicitous not only in seeing to it that the obligation of bestowing the customary alms is fulfilled, but also that . . . emulating the charity of the ancient fathers of our order, they make it their concern cheerfully to give additional alms according to the means of their monasteries, and to consider how acceptable God holds works of mercy, which he will reward as though they had been done for him (*Stat.*, dist. 5, c. 12, *de eleemosynis*, n. 1, p. 153).

Courtesy to guests

1911. CONGR. OF STRASBURG. A. Abbots are to guard against treating guests by imitating worldlings, and on the pretext of hospitality or regard for dignity, entertaining them lavishly or extravagantly. Toward all there should be proper consideration for the guest's state in life, as well as for monastic poverty and sobriety (*Declar. 10 in c. 53 RSB,* fol. 67). B. In performing the duties of hospitality superiors will keep specially in mind that with due regard for the person's social rank and dignity they show those evidences of charity, considerateness and politeness which will edify them and make them well disposed toward the superiors personally, their monasteries, and the order. But above all else they are to see to it that the signs of respect are given in the true spirit of charity and out of love of Christ whom they receive and worship in the person of the guests (*ibid., declar. 11*).

1912. CONGR. OF BURSFELD. A. In many passages Holy Scripture commends most highly the charitable reception of guests; we have, in addition, the example and teaching of our holy father Benedict. Hence we prescribe the following: Guests are to be announced by the porter to the abbot or the prior, if the abbot is absent. Either the abbot or the prior, or one of the brethren appointed by the abbot, will go immediately to receive the visitor, greet him with proper reverence, with head uncovered and bowed, and accompany him to prayer. After the prayer has been said, the kiss of peace is given. Then the visitor is taken to the guest quarters, and when the short lesson from the Scriptures * has been recited, the guest is asked the purpose of his visit. His presence in the house is then made known to the abbot, who will receive him humbly, as prescribed in the Rule (*Stat.,* dist. 5, c. 13, *de susceptione hospitum,* n. 1, p. 154). B. Younger children are not accompanied to the prayer (*ibid.,* n. 3, p. 155). C. In the guest rooms everything is to be kept clean, but simple, lest in striving too hard to please we displease. Without explicit permission none of the brethren is to visit guests; permission is not granted to anyone for visits after Compline (*ibid.,* n. 7, p. 157). D. An experienced man should be chosen guest master, a brother who will faithfully receive the guests who come to the monastery. He will show proper respect to all, particularly however to religious and pious persons. He is to be skilled in accommodating himself to their respective needs and in assisting them courteously, as religion demands (dist. 3, c. 19, *de hospitalario,* n. 1, p. 108). E. On Holy Thursday he will introduce into the enclosure the poor persons whose feet are to be washed. He will help them in taking their assigned places, remove their shoes, and prepare for the Mandatum (*ibid.,* n. 3, p. 109).

* This was simply the two-line blessing *Dies et actus nostros* pronounced by the abbot before the reading of the day's excerpt of the *Rule of St. Benedict* at the second half of Prime (*Breviar. monastic.* 1:6). Recently the whole second half of Prime has been dropped at the request of the abbots' congress (*Decr. S. Rit. C.,* 12 Nov., 1959).

1913. SWABIAN CONGR. OF ST. JOSEPH. A. Our holy Father desired that guests arriving at the monastery be received with every manifestation of politeness and benevolence (*RSB,* c. 53). As soon as a guest comes to the door of the monastery, therefore, the porter, after having acquainted himself with the guest's name and the general purpose of his visit, will request him to wait briefly in a properly appointed room. He will forthwith make the visitor's presence known to the abbot or his representative, who will permit nothing to delay him in greeting the guest in a polite and friendly manner, according to his state in life. He will welcome him in a proper and becoming manner and accompany him to the guest quarters (*Const. et declar., Pars II,* c. 3, punctum 11, n. 1, fol. 128). B. Superiors are to perform all duties of hospitality promptly and willingly according to the rank and dignity of each guest and in keeping with the means of the monastery (*ibid.,* n. 2).

1914. ABBEY OF CLUNY (11th century). The guest master receives with all politeness guests who are pilgrims or those who come to the monastery simply for their spiritual welfare. . . . When a guest is led to the entrance of the enclosure at meal time, he waits there until presented to the abbot, who will pour water over his hands [a practice from ancient Roman hospitality prescribed in the *Rule of St. Benedict,* Chapter 53, and still ceremoniously observed in some monastic congregations], and accompany him to the head table. . . . Whatever has been prepared for the brethren is to be served generously to the prior and the guest. . . . If guests request to be shown the various departments of the enclosure, the guest master will obtain the prior's permission and take them through the monastery during the time of one of the Masses while the community is in church. He will take them to the alms house, the store rooms, kitchen, refectory, novitiate, dormitory, and infirmary. When they encounter brothers who have no permission to speak, these brothers are not to break the silence (*Consuetudines Cluniacen. Udalrici, Lib. III,* c. 22, *PL* 149:764).

Zeal for souls, apostolic charity

1915. PROV. COUNCIL OF PRAGUE (1860). Patience and assiduous devotion to work must be distinguishing marks of regulars no less than fervor at prayer. For these dispositions, no less than silence or poverty, indicate a well-ordered monastery, one in which the zeal of holy charity is united to self-denial. The harvest is abundant but the laborers few; hence the world awaits the fervent works of religious. As these prerogatives have been theirs from time immemorial, so also in our day, the fire of love and zeal for the kingdom of God must continue to burn and glow more brightly in the families consecrated to God, so that no matter what need may be urgent in the world, men will find in the enclosure of the monastery their first and most willing helpers. Although the obligation of performing works of mercy and almsdeeds binds all, individual religious congregations take upon themselves as their special work the care of the sick and of children. The more spiritual ministry generally is left to other religious bodies—the cultivation of the Lord's field and the healing of spiritual ills. In order for them to carry on fittingly the cultivation of the Lord's field, literary studies must flourish in monasteries. We exhort religious most urgently to acquire with all zeal the knowledge with which they may fulfil their duties, whether they are called on for the instruction of youth, preaching the word of God, assistance in the care of souls, or furthering the advance and increase of truth through the cultivation of the sciences within the enclosure. Let the superiors in particular see to it that the novices are well educated and trained . . . so that when they become clerics in their aspirations for the priesthood, they may be imbued with solid, adequate, in fact, abundant knowledge of theology, although not wanting in other preparatory disciplines which are required for worthily fulfilling the office of teachers (*Decr.,* tit. 7, c. 4, *de regularium cura animarum, CL* 5:576).

1916. PROV. COUNCIL OF GRAN (Hungary, 1858). A. We seriously warn, exhort, and petition you, superiors of monasteries, that the religious men assigned to your care, seriously reflecting on the vocation to which they are called, walk worthy of it, and strive most earnestly to fulfil the vows they once made to God. See to it with all vigilance that . . . they fulfil their duties worthily, meditate on and master the principles needed for administering the sacrament of penance correctly, and know what the sacred canons wisely prescribe for the preaching of God's word with fruit, and for breaking the bread to children through catechetical instruction (*Decr.,* tit. 7, *de regularibus,* n. 3, *CL* 5:65). B. Let all devote themselves diligently to the study of Sacred Scripture and other sacred literature, in order that they can properly offer in the form of praise what they owe to God and zealously lead others on the way of the Lord (*ibid.,* tit. 6, c. 1, *de vita et honestate clericorum,* n. 12, col. 54). C. They who are bound to extirpate errors, resolve doubts, explain divine truths and teach the sure way of eternal salvation, must necessarily advance constantly in sacred learning. *Be ready always with an answer to everyone who asks a reason for the hope that is in you* (I Petr. 3:15). . . . *Because thou hast rejected knowledge, I will reject thee, that thou shalt not do the office of the priesthood to me* (Osee 4:6; *ibid.,* c. 3, *de mediis augendae doctrinae in clero,* col. 57).

1917. PROV. COUNCIL OF UTRECHT (1865). Dedication to the pursuit of learning, to the more exacting disciplines, and particularly to the sacred studies must flourish in monasteries, as it has in all ages past, in order that the Church may constantly have men who are eminent for learning and zealous in the cultivation of the Lord's field (*Decr.*, tit. 7, c. 2, *de regularium regimine et disciplina, CL* 5:892).

1918. CONGR. OF BURSFELD. A. Abbots must be particularly careful in seeing to it that, in the spirit of the fear of the Lord they choose for the care of souls only those of whose character they are certain, men who have been long trained in the religious life and are skilled in living for God, men who are working for their own and other people's salvation, who possess knowledge and doctrine, who have proved themselves to be zealous for the things of God and of the order, who are not restless in their monasteries, who have not been burdensome to their abbots and the brethren, but who are humbly and obediently intent on their vocation; men of whom it can confidently be hoped that they will fill the Church of Christ and the order of St. Benedict with the pleasing fragrance of a worthy way of life (*Stat.*, dist. 8, c. 1, *de expositis in genere,* n. 1, pp. 275–276). B. Anyone who takes upon himself the care of souls should possess such a disposition, as well as the moral training and knowledge, to equip him to win souls for God and foster and strengthen devotion. The greater his debt to the religious life and the more opportunity he has had in the monastery in preparing himself to work for the welfare of souls, the more he is to strive to be exemplary in his conduct and helpful to others (*ibid.*, c. 2, *de vice-curatis,* n. 2, p. 280).

1919. CONGR. OF STRASBURG. A. Because of the power of binding and loosing, for which both jurisdiction and knowledge are required, we enjoin on superiors to appoint for hearing confessions of lay people only those priest-monks of whose probity and adequate knowledge they are certain (*Declar. 7 in c. 62 RSB,* fol. 92). B. Upon the advice of the superiors of the monastery and of the professors, the abbot is to choose to be clerics those of whose life, moral conduct, and learning he is certain, or those who are living an upright life. He is to observe with accuracy the precept of the Blessed Apostle inspired by the Holy Ghost: *Do not lay hands hastily upon anyone, and do not be a partner in other men's sins* (I Tim. 5:22). . . . Let abbots also beware of promoting religious to orders before they have been trained in the regular discipline for some years (*ibid., declar.* 2, fol. 91).

1920. SWABIAN CONGR. OF ST. JOSEPH. A. Those who have the care of souls must not be remiss in the duties of their office, but must zealously dedicate their work, concern, and efforts in piety, prudence, and discretion to promoting the welfare of their neighbors by fostering and exhorting them to progress in religious virtue and Christian piety (*Const. et declar., Pars II,* c. 3, punctum 2, *de laboribus et studiis fratrum,* n. 2, fol. 88). B. They must frequently remind themselves that they have the care of souls that God willed to redeem from the bond of the devil's slavery and liberate for heaven by the most precious blood and through the bitter death of his sole-begotten Son. Hence, they are to recognize with what effort and zeal they should devote themselves to winning souls that the infinite goodness of God has pursued with so great a love (*ibid.*, punctum 1, *de parochis*, n. 1, fol. 227). C. Afire with love for God and his fellow man, let the zealous seeker of souls strive to fulfil the obligations of his office with eagerness and willingness from motives of charity and the holy intention of promoting God's honor and his neighbor's welfare. This will involve being ever ready to minister to all and always exemplifying the way of attaining eternal salvation both by word and worthiness of life (*ibid.*, n. 2, fol. 228). D. In the administration of the sacraments he is to observe all the ceremonies prescribed by the Ritual with exactness, and strive to confer them in a spirit of deep piety in order that the people in attendance will be edified and will themselves grow accustomed to manifesting due veneration for the sacraments (*ibid.*, n. 3, fol. 229). E. When his duty includes fortifying the dying with the holy sacraments of the Church, preparing them for their journey into eternity, and disposing them to die well, he is—always from the motive of Christian charity—to prepare and have at his command those exhortations and texts that will serve in a matter of so great an importance for eternal welfare, to console the dying and edify those who are present (*ibid.*, n. 9, fol. 232). F. Nowadays in the monasteries of our congregation great numbers of penitents usually desire to confess, particularly on Sundays and feasts. In addition to the confessors chosen for the monastery, therefore, the abbot is to appoint certain brethren who will spend themselves generously for God's honor and the welfare and edification of neighbor, hasten to the church as soon as they have been summoned, so that those who have come from a distance may be heard without delay and enabled to return to their homes with joy and consolation (*ibid.*, punctum 2, *de confessariis*, n. 1, fol. 232).

The duty of preaching

1921. PROV. COUNCIL OF COLOGNE (1860). The duty of the sacred orator is indeed most serious and exalted. If you consider its origin, it follows in the footsteps of the prophets, the apostles, and of Christ himself; if its purpose, it promotes the glory of almighty God and the salvation of souls; if what it expresses, it announces the mysteries of God; if those to whom it speaks, immortal souls redeemed by the blood of Christ hear its voice; if the enemies against whom it must wage war, the gates of hell present most powerful battle arrays against it; if the aids by which it is bolstered, the Church implores the divine aid, the grace of the Holy Spirit, and Christ himself is at hand; and if, finally, the reward of its labors, *They . . . shall shine as the brightness of the firmament . . . and they that shall instruct many to justice, as the stars for all eternity* (Dan. 12:3; *Decr.*, tit. 2, c. 21, *de verbi divini praedicatione, CL* 5:361).

1922. PROV. COUNCIL OF VIENNA (1858). St. Gregory of Nazianzus [d. 389], who holds an illustrious position among the Doctors of the Church, warns preachers of God's word: "To me it seems no light task, but one requiring no little spiritual power, to give in due time (cf. Luke 12:42), to each his portion of the word, and so to regulate with judgment the truth of our opinions, which are concerned with subjects like the world, or worlds [visible and invisible], matter, soul, mind, intelligent natures, good and evil, providence . . . especially before a large congregation, composed of every age and condition, and needing to be played on in various ways like an instrument of many strings: or to find any form of words able to edify them all, and illumine them with the light of knowledge" (*Oratio 2, apologetica,* nn. 35, 39, *PG* 35:443, 447). In this sacred and salutary ministry there is no question of seeking honor for oneself, but of feeding the flock of Christ. They are deserving of praise who zealously minister those things which are beneficial to the faithful (*Decr.*, tit. 4, c. 4, *de verbi divini praedicatione, CL* 5:181).

1923. PROV. COUNCIL OF COLOCZA (Hungary, 1863). It is indispensably necessary for priests to be prepared with solid and well-grounded knowledge of things divine for teaching, explaining clearly, and instructing all to whom they are sent, in order that these may receive the heritage of salvation. . . . It behooves those whom God has sent *into the whole world to preach the Gospel to every creature* (Mark 16:15), to be insistent on the ministry of the word in season and out of season, to hold to the form of sound teaching which they have heard in faith and love (cf. II Tim. 1:13), and seek the wisdom of all the saints, remembering their superiors who have spoken to them the word of God (Heb. 13:7). They must be armed with the shield of faith for extinguishing the fiery darts of the most evil one. With this shield, too, they are to explain clearly, rebuke, entreat, and with the whole doctrine at their command, refute those who, in St. Bernard's terms, shed darkness instead of light, and who administer poison in place of honey (*Decr.*, tit. 4, c. 6, *de studiis in sacerdotio prosequendis, CL* 5:672, 673).

The converting of nations

1924. POPE PIUS IX. The constant voice of history through the centuries, an argument that carries more weight than all others, shows how the Christian religion was spread abroad by the monks of St. Benedict; how through religion the barbaric peoples were brought into submission to civil order, their morals tamed, laws established and learning and knowledge propagated, the arts fostered, agriculture advanced, mutual contracts of friendship and relationships entered into, and countless other benefits imparted to men (*Bref a monseigneur l'évêque d'Angers a l'occasion de son discours sur l'ordre monastique prononcé au service anniversaire du T.-R.P. Dom Prosper Guéranger;* La Semaine du fidèle, 1876, pp. 430–431).

1925. ROMAN MISSAL. We beseech you, O God, who desire that all men should be saved and that all should come to know the truth, to send forth laborers to your harvest, and give them strength to proclaim your word with all confidence, so that your teaching may be received with honor throughout the world, and all nations may acknowledge you the true and only God, and him whom you have sent, Jesus Christ, your Son, our Lord (*Missa votiva pro Fidei Propagatione, Oratio, Miss. Rom.,* p. 93).

Education of youth

1926. POPE LEO XII (d. 1829). It is Our heart's earnest desire that from the founding of this new congregation of the monks of St. Benedict, numerous advantages and benefits, especially of a spiritual nature, may accrue to the whole nation of Brazil. We are strengthened in this well-founded hope that the sons of the order, pursuing the splendid traditions of those who have gone before them, by devoting themselves to the study of both human and divine letters, will dedicate themselves primarily to the instruction of youth in sacred studies. To this end We earnestly desire—and We assure you that such a course of action will be pleasing to Us personally and to this Holy See—that the abbey schools will be made available to extern students, so that they may readily enter the monasteries in Brazil for learning philosophy and theology, as has been done to great advantage in different countries of Europe where the sons of the Benedictine family have always had the custom of thus making their schools available (*Const. Apost. Inter gravissimas curas,* § 8, 1 Jul., 1827, *BRC* 8:544).

1927. ABBEY OF CLUNY. Repeatedly observing the solicitude with which boys are watched over day and night, I have said in my heart that it would be difficult for the son of a king to be reared with greater diligence in the palace than the smallest boy at Cluny (*Consuetudines Cluniacenses, Udalrici, Lib. III,* c. 8, *PL* 149:747).

The works of charity must be made to harmonize with the monk's vocation

1928. PROV. COUNCIL OF PRAGUE (1860). Whatever the needs that are pressing on the world, whatever the indigence of a brother man that cries out for help, he should find his first and most willing helpers in the cloisters. Lest their available strength prove insufficient, however, if they seek to embrace all forms of charity, regulars are first to determine accurately what works they are going to undertake according to the nature and foundation of their order; and then, to this work they are to dedicate themselves and spend themselves with all zeal (*Decr.*, tit. 7, c. 4, *de regularium studiis et cura animarum, CL* 5:577).

1929. POPE BENEDICT XII (d. 1342). We prescribe the rigorous observance of both the decree of the Lateran Council "About not appointing individual monks to remain alone in estates, villages, and parish churches" (*Concil. Lateran. III, sub Alexandro III, 1179,* c. 10, Mansi 22:224), and the Apostolic Constitution of Our predecessor Clement [V, 1311], promulgated in the Council of Vienna, according to which individual monks may not presume to dwell alone even in dependencies and priories to which they have been assigned. . . . Those who are dwelling in these priories or dependencies are to be with these superiors in the church at the appointed times, in other assignments according to schedule, and pray the Office in common with them. We desire also that they take turns in observing their week for celebrating [the conventual] Mass. We draw attention also to their obligation to offer Mass slowly, not rushing through it, but offering it humbly and devoutly, at the scheduled times. And wherever there are three or more monks, at least one Mass is to be sung, daily. The prior and the monks are to eat together. . . . They are not to deviate from the common norm and prescribed observance in clothing, bedding, and the wearing of the tonsure. . . . They are never to go out alone, but must always be accompanied by another monk or some upright person. In the villages where such priories or dependencies are located, they are not to presume to eat, drink or enter private homes except in the company of persons whose lives are above all suspicion, and then only with the special permission of the prior (*Const. Apost. Summi Magistri,* § 25, 20 Jun., 1336; *Ordinationes et reformationes pro bono regimine monachorum Nigrorum O.S.B., BR* 4:379 f.).

1930. PROV. COUNCIL OF UTRECHT (1865). This Synod considers it necessary to emphasize and impress upon those religious who are assigned to the parochial ministry never to forget that they are constantly and completely bound to observe not only their vows, but all the prescriptions of the rule they have professed, as far as the duty to which they have been appointed will permit. They are not to consider themselves dispensed from these obligations except insofar as the care of souls demands (*Decr.*, tit. 7, c. 3, *de regularibus parochiali animarum curae addictis, CL* 5:896).

1931. PROV. COUNCIL OF AVIGNON (1849). Regulars have long bestowed great helps on the Church Militant! Now they can continue to bestow the same and many other benefits on the Catholic religion by giving examples of all virtues, by pouring forth their prayers, undertaking and carrying into execution all kinds of works of mercy and charity, and carrying on their respective programs which are conducive to God's glory, zeal for souls and the cultivation of learning. For these reasons we exhort them all to prove themselves our pious and zealous helpers in cultivating the vineyard of the Lord (*Decr.*, tit. 7, c. 1, *de regularibus*, n. 1, *CL* 4:350).

1932. PROV. COUNCIL OF COLOCZA (Hungary, 1863). In these unhappy times on which we have fallen, the prince of this world is striving with all the forces at his command to establish his kingdom. Hence we need to wage the war of the Lord with every type of spiritual warfare. Like a well-ordered battle array, our forces must stand alert day and night upon the walls of Jerusalem, and while some engage in the battle at close quarters, others, after the manner of Moses on the holy mountain (cf. Exod. 17:8 ff.), with their eyes and hands raised to heaven, sustain, with help from on high, the strength of those engaged in battling, and hasten the victory of the cross which conquers the world (*Decr.*, tit. 5, *de regularibus generatim, CL* 5:688).

1933. PROV. COUNCIL OF VIENNA (1858). If God, our Redeemer, deigns to call a person who is eager to imitate Mary's love and to sit as she sat at the Lord's feet (cf. Luke 10:39 f.), we recognize that he has granted him the best part. In fact, such a person can be of greater help to the Church through his prayers and petitions than others engaged in more active ministry. God seeks for a man who will set up a hedge and stand in the gap before him in favor of the world, lest he destroy it (cf. Ezech. 22:30), and would that he find him! (*Decr.*, tit. 5, c. 3, *de vita contemplativa et activa, CL* 5:194.)

1934. PROV. COUNCIL OF BORDEAUX (1856). We bear testimony that the humble seed [the monastic orders] has grown into a great blessing for both civil society and the Church, and that the restoration of the orders has been gratifying and helpful to the people of the whole province. To behold once again the ancient symbol of the holy habit and the timeless beauty of monastic observance has been like a silent exhortation to obedience, poverty, and chastity. Through the help of these forces, the authority of those who govern has been increased, the poor given encouraging example and comforting help, and all others taught that which alone can serve as a remedy for the world in its illness—for it has given itself up to delights and pleasures—namely, to be fastened to the cross of Christ. For we know that both the more recently founded congregations and the older orders have been accepted by the faithful with the proper attitude, and that they have avoided these prejudices of the world: 1) that they have already served their usefulness, and that there is no place in today's scheme of things for the older orders. On the contrary, according to the testimony of holy religion and of the Church, the longer orders have flourished and the more widely they are diffused, the richer their contribution to the Church; 2) [nor have they encountered the argument] that the variety of religious orders interferes with the good of the Church. By that very variety is shown the richness of God's grace and the charismata more generously poured out for the purpose of winning souls; 3) [neither have they faced the prejudice] that a life dedicated to contemplation or the practices of penance is valueless. For, as the Angelic Doctor teaches, the contemplative life is more excellent than the active, because the contemplative life is according to divine things, whereas the active is according to the human (*II-II,* q. 182, art. 1, in corp., n. 7, *Op. Om.* 10:440; Am. ed. 2:1943; *Decr.,* tit. 1, c. 10, *de regularibus,* n. 2, *CL* 4:704).

The wonderful fruitfulness of the religious life

1935. COUNCIL OF RHEIMS (1849). The excellence of the religious life is attested to by its great antiquity which goes back to the earliest ages of the Church, as well as by that wonderful fruitfulness of the Church which in ever century has increased the number of these holy institutes. It is testified to by the countless works and merits of these sacred societies which through their prayers, mortification, teaching, labors, and even by the shedding of their blood, have in the past carried the name and the kingdom of Jesus Christ to the farthest reaches of the earth, and continue in our time to propagate God's kingdom day by day. It is testified to moreover by that most numerous choir of saints and blessed who either as founders or as sons and daughters of the religious life, have obtained the crown of eternal glory by their heroic virtues. We have nothing more worthy of veneration than these excellent groups of men and women, preserving intact or fervently renewing the spirit of their religious families, whose piety and charity have served so gloriously for the edification of the Christian people and for the consolation of the shepherds (*Decr.,* tit. 16, c. 1, *de ordinum monasticorum piarumque congregationum excellentia et utilitate, CL* 4:141).

1936. POPE PIUS IX (d. 1878). Surely no one can be ignorant of the fact that from their very beginning the religious families have shone with almost countless men illustrious for their teaching and learning in every field, outstanding in the practice of all virtues and the glory of their holiness, renowned for the high positions they have held, consumed with ardent love for God and men. *They have been a spectacle to the world, and to angels, and to men* (I Cor. 4:9). They knew no greater delight than to devote themselves day and night with all their effort to the meditation of things divine, to bear about in their body the dying of Jesus (cf. II Cor. 4:10), to propagate the Catholic faith and its teaching from the rising of the sun to its setting, to fight for it with fortitude. They have cheerfully borne every kind of hardship, torment, and suffering for the faith. They have even poured out life itself in order to rescue uncultured and barbarous peoples from the darkness of error, the wildness of their customs, and the chains of vices. They have won them over to the light of the Gospel's truth and to virtuous living in civilized society; they have cultivated among them learning, the disciplines, and arts. They have imbued the tender minds of youth with sound doctrine and molded their impressionable hearts in piety and uprightness of life. They have called the erring to the way of salvation. Animated by mercy, there is no heroic charity that they have not practiced, even with danger to their own lives, in order to be able to offer to slaves, to the imprisoned, the ill, the dying, and all others who were suffering, to the indigent, and to those exposed to danger, the appropriate helps of Christian charity and providence, to lighten their pain, wipe away their tears, and aid them in their needs with all assistance and work at their command (*Ep. Encycl. Ubi primum,* 17 Jun., 1847, *ad omnes supremos moderatores, abbates provinciales aliosque superiores regularium ordinum, Acta Pii IX* 1:47).

IV. WRITINGS OF SAINTS AND DOCTORS

Love of God and neighbor

1937. ST. BERNARD. In the first place observe in what measure, nay, indeed, how without measure God deserves to be loved by us, in that —to repeat briefly what has already been said—he himself first loved us (cf. I John 4:19), so great a Lover, so great a love, freely bestowed upon such menials and such sinners (cf. Rom. 5:8 f.). This is what I remember having stated at the beginning, that the measure in which to love God is to love him without measure. In a word, seeing that a love which has God as its object has as its object the immeasurable, the infinite—for God is both infinite and immeasurable—what, I ask you, ought to be the measure of our love? What of the fact that this love is not in our case spontaneous, but paid as a debt? Immensity, then, loves, Eternity loves, Charity surpassing knowledge (cf. Eph. 3:19) loves, God loves; God whose *greatness is unsearchable* (Ps. 144:3), to whose wisdom there is no limit (Ps. 146:5); whose peace surpasses all understanding (cf. Phil. 4:7)—do we repay our debt to him in a calculated measure? *I love you, O Lord, my strength . . . my rock, my fortress, my deliverer* (Ps. 17:2–3), in sum, everything to me which can be called desirable and lovable. My God, my helper, I will love you for your gift and in my measure, less indeed than I justly should, but certainly not less than I can; for, although I cannot love you as I ought, yet I cannot love you more than I can. But I shall be able to love you more when you deign to grant me the power to do so, though never as you are worthy to be loved. . . . It is clear enough, I believe, both in what measure God is to be loved, and by what desert of his own. By what desert of his, I say, for the greatness of it, who may fully see? Who may tell? Who may know? (*Lib. de diligendo Deo,* c. 6, § 16, *PL* 182:983; Watkin Williams, *St. Bernard, the Man and His Message,* p. 57; Gardner, p. 68 f.)

1938. PETER DE BLOIS, chancellor and archdeacon of Bath, England (d. circa 1200). From this ineffable union of which the Son says, *I and the Father are one* (John 10:30), there proceeded a sort of bond of love among the angels, through which they are strengthened by the Son and the Spirit, as it is written: *By the word of the Lord the heavens were made; by the breath of his mouth all their host* (Ps. 32:6). Hence among them they always will the same things; the same, too, they will not; hence too the individuals are all loved by the others, and the whole body is loved by all the individuals. In imitation of this angelic bond of union, *the charity of God is poured forth in our hearts by the Holy Spirit, who has been given to us* (Rom. 5:5). Thus the Lord in times past promised through the prophet Joel: *I will pour out my spirit upon all flesh* (Joel 2:28). This communication of the Spirit enters into the hearts of men, so that what properly belongs to one becomes, through charity, the common property of others. Hinting at this, Blessed Peter wrote: *According to the gift that each has received, administer it to one another as good stewards of the manifold grace of God. If anyone speaks, let it be as with the words of God. If anyone ministers, let it be as from the strength that God furnishes; that in all things God may be honored through Jesus Christ* (I Petr. 4:10).

This common bond took its derivation from the ineffable source of the Supreme and Undivided Trinity, and the primitive Church was founded in the unity of the Spirit, of faith and of baptism, as the Apostle, briefly touching the matter, states: *One Spirit, one faith, one soul, one baptism* (Eph. 4:2 f.). *The multitude of the believers were of one heart and one soul.* Here you have intimate bond of hearts and the identity of wills: *Not one of them said that anything he possessed was his own, but they had all things in common* (Acts 4:32; *Tract. II, de charitate Dei et proximi,* c. 35, *PL* 207:933).

1939. JOHN OF TRITHEIM, abbot of Sponheim (d. 1516). Nothing is so beneficial for the monk as the love of God; if he possesses it, if it is true and lasting, he is truly blessed. . . . Love sustains in adversities, tempers in prosperity, is strong in the time of difficult temptations, is cheerful in good works, abundantly wealthy in temporal goods, unrestrained in hospitality, joyful among good brethren, patient in bearing with those who are false. This love is joyful in Abel in offering the sacrifice, secure in Noe throughout the Deluge, dependable in Abraham in his wandering, exceedingly serene in Moses amidst all that he had to suffer, meek in David in his tribulations. In the case of the three youths, it innocently watches the harmless flames; in the Machibees it bears the raging fire. It is chaste in Susanna in conquering the temptations of men, in Anna in her widowhood, in Mary who knew not man. It is free in Paul for pleading the cause of Christ, humble in Peter for obeying, human in the followers of Christ for acknowledging him, divine in Christ for forgiving. What shall I say of charity? *If I speak with the tongues of men and of angels, but have not charity . . . I am nothing* (I Cor. 13:1–2). It is the soul of learning, the strength of philosophy, the efficacy of the sacraments, the firmness of knowledge, the fruit of faith, the wealth of the poor, the life of the dying. *God is love, and he who abides in love abides in God, and God in him* (I John 4:16). Charity, which is God, is salvation, peace of heart, joy of mind, strength of soul, tranquillity of conscience, the robe of the elect, the ornament of monks. No religious institute can continue to exist, no virtue be pleasing to God, no work be judged good unless it is rooted in charity. Charity then is the root of all goods, and therefore deservedly is placed first among the commandments of God (*Comm. in c. 4 RSB,* n. 1, *Op. pia et spiritualia,* p. 264).

1940. ST. GREGORY THE GREAT (d. 604). A. Some there are who are so filled with the love for God and their neighbor that they might deservedly be called cherubim. Because the word cherubim means fullness of wisdom, and we learn from Paul that *love is the fulfillment of the Law* (Rom. 13:10), all who excel others in the love of God and neighbor will receive their reward among the cherubim. Others burn like torches of divine contemplation, sustained solely with desire for their Creator; they wish for nothing at all that this world has to offer and are supported only by their longing for eternity; they abandon all things earthly and rise with their mind above everything temporal; they love and burn, and find their rest in the very flame of love. They are consumed with love and by their speech inflame others. Anyone whom they touch with their words they straightway cause to burn also with the love of God. Such persons will receive their reward of vocation among the Seraphim (*Hom. 34 in Evangel.,* § 11, *PL* 76:1253). B. When he loves another no one is forthwith to conclude that he has charity, without first examining the motivating force of his love. For if a person loves another, but without loving him for God's sake, he does not have charity, but only thinks he has (*ibid., Hom. 38,* § 11, col. 1289). C. Charity rises to sublime heights when it is drawn in pity by the lowly things of one's neighbor; the more kindly it stoops to infirmity, the mightier is its reach to the highest (*Reg. pastoralis lib., Pars II,* c. 5, *PL* 77:33).

1941. ST. BASIL THE GREAT, bp. of Caesarea (d. 379). He who loves the Lord loves his neighbor in consequence. *If anyone loves me, says* the Lord, *he will keep my word* (John 14:23). And again he says: *This is my commandment, that you love one another as I have loved you* (*ibid.,* 15:12). On the other hand, he who loves his neighbor fulfils the love he owes God, for he accepts this favor as shown to himself. Wherefore, Moses, that faithful servant of God, manifested such great love for his brethren that he wished his name to be struck off the book of God in which it was inscribed, if the sin of his people were not pardoned (cf. Exod. 32:32). Paul also, desiring to be, like Christ, an exchange for the salvation of all, dared to pray that he might be an anathema from Christ for the sake of his brethren who were his kinsmen according to the flesh (cf. Rom. 9:3). Yet, at the same time, he knew that it was impossible for him to be estranged from God through his having rejected his favor for love of him and for the sake of that great commandment; moreover, he knew that he would receive in return much more than he gave (*Reg. fusius tractatae, Interrogatio III, de charitate erga proximum,* § 2, *PG* 31:918; Wagner, p. 240).

1942. ST. LAURENCE JUSTINIAN, can. regular, first patriarch of Venice (d. 1455). The more closely one approaches the perfection of love, the more he abandons himself out of compassion to work for his neighbor's welfare. Anyone who is wanting in love for his fellow man certainly knows nothing at all of the love of God. We make greater progress in the love of God when, in the bosom of that love, we first rejoice in charity for our neighbor. Love of God produces love of neighbor and excites it to action. In a marvelous manner the love of God ascends to the heights of perfection when out of compassion it is drawn to the very depths of our neighbor's miseries, and the more charitably it descends to these depths, the more perfectly it returns to the heights (*Lignum vitae,* tract. 6, *de charitate,* c. 14, *Op Om.* 1:39).

1943. ST. BERNARD. In order that love of our neighbor may be perfect justice, it must be referred to God. How otherwise can he love his neighbor purely, who does not love in God? Surely he cannot love in God who does not love God. It is then necessary that God be loved first, in order that our neighbor, too, may be loved in God (*Lib. de diligendo Deo,* c. 8, § 25, *PL* 182:988; Gardner, p. 90).

1944. ST. GREGORY THE GREAT. As a tree's many branches spring from one trunk, so many virtues are begotten of charity alone. No branch will have vitality as a good work unless it remains attached to the trunk of charity (*Hom. 27 in Evangel.,* § 1, *PL* 76:1205).

1945. ST. LAURENCE JUSTINIAN. Where there is charity there is also the fruitfulness of good works: all virtues are ingrafted into charity as in their root. They have life in its fullness as long as they remain united to this root. Sever it and straightway the fruits and leaves of the branches wither (*De triumphali Christi agone,* c. 14, *Op. Om.* 1:385).

1946. RICHARD OF ST. VICTOR, canon regular (d. 1172). Charity is not so much to be called a powerful virtue as the power of all virtues, in the sense that all virtues derive from it that which makes them virtues. It is the life of faith, hope's strength, the interior force and marrow of all virtues. It is charity that regulates life, gives warmth to the affections, endows acts with their moral worth, corrects excesses, gives unity and integration to moral conduct, is capable of doing all things, prevails in all situations and even, in a sense, renders omnipotence impotent. For was it not charity by which Moses, in the face of divine justice and power, gained the victory in his fortitude? *Let me alone,* said the Lord, *that my wrath may blaze up against them to consume them* (Exod. 32:10). Note the expression: "Let me alone." Have no doubt about the matter; God is not bound by any power other than the strength of love (*Tract. de gradibus charitatis,* c. 1, *PL* 196:1197).

1947. ST. PETER DAMIAN, cardinal, Doctor of the Church (d. 1072). Beloved brethren . . . remain steadfast in fraternal charity, cooperate in the spirit of oneness in the efforts of mutual love against the temptations of the enemy of old. Erect the entire effort of your holy observance on the foundation of charity; let all that you build up mount with the living stones of virtues held together with the cement of sincere love. The divine voice commanded that the ark which housed the eight souls during the Deluge should be *covered with pitch inside and out* (Gen. 6:14). Holy Church, which is tending toward the glory of the resurrection, is covered with pitch inside and out so that externally it is made attractive with fraternal goodness, and interiorly is held together with the truth of mutual love. For anyone who interiorly has the spirit of love, but is separated from the brethren because of his antagonistic conduct has indeed the protecting pitch within, but not exteriorly. But he who appears affable, feigning friendship, but in the secret depths of his heart does not preserve true friendship, is separated from the brethren from within, although he seems to be united with them by the external semblance of being covered with the pitch. Neither will be saved from the Deluge because neither is fortified with the twofold covering of pitch as was divinely commanded. But he who is both exteriorly affable and interiorly motivated by the sincerity of love, shows the fruits of charity exteriorly with the branches of the word, and interiorly he plants the root deeply, for he loves in the depths of his being. Such a man is like the ark lined with pitch both interiorly and exteriorly, for he is bound with his neighbors by the double cement of charity (*Opusc. 13, de perfectione monach.*, c. 24, *PL* 145:326).

1948. VEN. HILDEBERT, monk, abp. of Turin (d. 1135). Nothing is so broad as charity. Charity is as broad as the world itself, as all-embracing as the ocean. Where love abides, charity receives friends in God, and enemies because of God. It does not stop loving when it ceases to be loved. It is mindful of all, and remains attached to all. Those whom it cannot aid with actual service it helps by means of a loving disposition; . . . it makes heaven and earth one commonwealth (*Lib. II, ep. 9, Anselmo archiepisc. Cantuar.*, *PL* 171:217).

1949. ST. JOHN CHRYSOSTOM. Nothing contributes so forcefully toward making us imitators of Christ as concern for our neighbor's welfare. Even though you were to do violence to the body by fasting or sleeping on the ground . . . without thought for your neighbor, you would have done nothing great, and are yet far from the imitation of Christ (*Hom. 25 in I Cor.*, § 3, *PG* 61:208).

1950. PETER THE VENERABLE, abbot of Cluny (d. 1158). You too have the same Benedict as the author of your institutes. He commanded that everything that he had written was to be made to tend toward the perfection of charity and serve the welfare of souls. . . . The Rule of the holy Father rests on that sublime and all-embracing principle of love of God and of neighbor, from which and on which, according to the words of Truth itself, *depend the whole Law and the Prophets* (Matt. 22:40). If the whole Law, then certainly the law of his Rule. The monk, therefore, who professes the Rule of the holy Father Benedict, then observes it in truth when he preserves the law of charity in all that he does (*Lib. IV, ep. 17, ad S. Bernardum Claraevallen.*, *PL* 189:330).

1951. BENEDICT HAEFTEN, provost of Afflighem (d. 1648). As though to put a noble crown upon his entire work, in the second to last chapter of his Rule Benedict treats once again of the love of God and of neighbor, in order to show that charity is the purpose and scope of the entire Rule. He entitles the chapter "The virtuous zeal which monks ought to have" (*RSB*, c. 72). But zeal, as the Angelic Doctor says, "is an intense love that seeks to remove everything that opposes it" (*I–II*, q. 28, art. 4, in corp., *Op. Om.* 6:200; Am. ed. 1:712). Hence our lawgiver wills that it be fulfilled in the most fervent love, in order that the brethren "may practice charity with a pure love; . . . fear God; love their abbot with sincere and humble affection; . . . prefer nothing whatever to the love of Christ" (*RSB*, c. 72). With these words St. Benedict indicates that charity is to be had toward equals, toward superiors, and toward the great and good God. It is as though St. Benedict, by closing his Rule with these prescriptions, attests publicly that all the previous commands have only served the purpose of leading to charity (*Disquisitiones monasticae, Lib. II,* tract. 7, *Regulae scopus,* disq. 1, p. 176).

1952. JOHN OF TRITHEIM. A. Charity toward the brotherhood is a beautiful ornament of the monk. . . . Let us love, then, not in word only, but in deed and in truth; for the proof of love lies in deeds. The holy Fathers, who so loved one another in the Lord that each would have preferred to be governed rather than govern, have left us this instrument of virtue, *for charity . . . is not self-seeking* (I Cor. 13:5), but seeks that which is Jesus Christ's. Let the monk, for whom these Instruments of Good Works are drawn up, strive to love all in the Lord, pray for them, and if he has the chance to do so, express the sentiments of his charity by his deeds, honoring the image of God in his fellow creature. Let him hate no one, but only vices; let him be burdensome to no one; rather, let him have love for all (*Comm. in c. 4 RSB, Instr. 2, Op. pia et spiritualia,* p. 265). B. Fraternal charity regulates the conduct of those who dwell within the enclosure and causes God to dwell in their midst. . . . Mutual charity strengthens obedience and makes fraternal correction fruitful. . . . In a most laudable manner charity creates oneness of mind and heart among the monks in all their virtuous works. . . . As far as possible charity is humble toward all and in a deep spirit of love serves the weak neighbor as though it were ministering to the Son of God. . . . Charity never finds fault with a neighbor, but patiently and perseveringly bears the infirmities of all out of the love of God. . . . Fraternal charity is the perfection of the law, for whatever is commanded over and above the worship of God is directed to the love of fellow man (*Hom. 22, de fraterna charitate monachorum., ibid.,* pp. 512–513).

Examples of monastic charity

1953. ST. ANSELM, monk, abp. of Canterbury, Doctor of the Church (d. 1109). A. Whenever I set about to write to you, soul most cherished of my soul, I am at a loss to know how I should most properly begin my address. For, all that I feel concerning you is pleasing and joyous to my spirit; whatever I desire for you is the best that my mind can conceive. What I saw in you made me love you in the manner that you know; what I hear of you makes me long for you—and only God knows how much! Wherever you go, my love follows you, and wherever I remain, my longing reaches out to embrace you. You eagerly inquire by your messages, exhort me in your letters, and stir me by your gifts to remember you. *May my tongue cleave to my palate if I remember you not* (Ps. 136:6), if I have not reckoned Gondulph first among my friends. I am not now referring to Gondulph, the layman, my father, but to the monk, Gondulph, my brother. How could I forget you?

How could he fade from my memory who is impressed upon my heart as a seal is upon wax? Moreover, why do you complain so bitterly, as I have heard, that you never receive a letter from me, and why do you ask with such affection to hear from me frequently, when your spirit and mine are one and the same? Now, when you are silent, I know that you love me, and when I am silent, you know that I love you (*Ep. 4, ad Gondulphum, PL* 158:1068; Schmitt, *Op. Om.* 3:104). B. How short is our life! How near the day when we will have nothing other to do than to felicitate ourselves on God's presence and on our own mutual affection, never more to be severed—but this will be on condition that, with God's assistance, we pass through this short life in complete submission to him in all things. Meanwhile, however near or far we may be from each other, may charity always fuse our souls into one (*ibid., Ep. 11, ad Rodulphum,* col. 1076; Schmitt 3:118).

Friendship

1954. PETER DE BLOIS. A. Friendship is to be fostered in such a manner that there is pleasantness in our conversation, cheerfulness in expression, politeness in our conduct, and a certain ingratiating and favorably impressive appearance. Let there be frequent discussion of matters which are virtuous, the disclosure of confidences, together with mutual compliance and respect for one another's wishes. He who is Truth itself gave us the pattern to follow, that we reveal our innermost thoughts to one another and mutually do the will of our friends when he said: *No longer do I call you servants. . . . But I have called you friends, because all things that I have heard from my Father I have made known to you* (John 15:15). In these words, as St. Ambrose states (*De off., Lib. III,* c. 2, § 13, *PL* 16:157), Christ gives us the pattern of friendship to follow, that we may make our secrets known to one another and fulfil one another's wishes. Hence friendship is fostered by mutual giving of pleasure, and if at times a friend's sternness expresses the seriousness of maturity, that very seriousness will be all the more commendable the more kindly it descends in the social level. For the law of friendship humbles the higher to the more lowly in order that they who stand higher in rank, dignity, or knowledge may be gracious to those below them in the full spirit of humility (*Tract. 1, de amicitia Christiana,* c. 18, *PL* 207:887).

B. We consider it worthy of note that in the love of neighbor the rank and dignity of both those who are loved and those who love, present many combinations. It is well known that some are placed over others; that some are subjects and others are equals; some again assist, others require assistance. In dealing with all these persons it is necessary to use judgment and discretion. The superior must correct the inferior and, if need be, compel him with severity, to practice virtue;

but there must be love in the correction and compassion in the severity employed. If a subject is living worthily according to his rank, he may be exhorted to strive for higher things, but he cannot be forced except by means of salutary exhortation and example, particularly if the superior knows that the subject is striving for the higher level by the desire of his own will. The subject has the obligation of seeking his superior's advice when in doubt, of cooperating with him reverently, of venerating him sincerely, and obeying him humbly. An equal should suggest what is virtuous to his equal, manifest his affection by sharing in the happiness of the joyful, show compassion to those who are sad, offer his assistance when he can be of service or can render aid to those in need; they should stimulate one another with holy conversation, and anticipate one another with honor (Rom. 12:10; *RSB,* c. 72). A friend is bound to love every person who has been good to him, that is, his friend, in the depth of his soul, out of the deepest love of his heart. He is to bear with his enemy, that is, with him who has done him evil, charitably overlook his faults, love him, and, from love of God, bestow necessities on him. One's neighbor is to be loved in such a way that the love be governed by the affection of charity with which you love God above your nature. For if you do not love God, neither do you love your neighbor, nor do you love yourself. Since then you are bound to love your neighbor as you love yourself, realize that by the measure of the love with which you love God you may determine how much you love your neighbor or yourself. He who does not love God, does not love himself. And if he does not love himself, neither does he love his neighbor as himself. Therefore from your love of God you can measure accurately the love you have for yourself and for your neighbor (*Tract. 2, de charitate Dei et proximi,* c. 39, col. 938).

C. Although in bestowing the primacy upon Peter the Lord set Peter up before John, he did not thereby withdraw the affection from the disciple whom he loved. He bestowed the keys of the kingdom of heaven on Peter, in order that he might open and close the gates of heaven (cf. Matt. 16:19), but reserved to John the privilege of disclosing the secrets of his heart to us. To Peter he committed concern for and government of his Church, but to John, the care and protection of his mother. Peter was, therefore, the more exalted, John, the more secure. Peter is committed to action, John to love. The Lord foretold Peter's martyrdom to him, indicating that another would gird him and lead him [to a place where he would not naturally wish to go, that is, to his martyrdom], but of John he said: *If I wish him to remain until I come, what is it to thee?* (John 21:18 ff.) Peter did not dare ask the Lord who it was that would betray him; John, however, at Peter's prompting, asks with confidence what the Prince of the Apostles was afraid to ask.

Kindness and services are so to be distributed among friends, in modesty and with such thoughtfulness that reason, not affection, govern all, and determine, according to the means of all, what can be borne by each and what is useful for all. Uniform affection is not to be shown to all, for a certain pattern of loving our neighbor is described for us according to customs, social relations, and the merits of individual persons. . . . Let there be among friends a reasonable bestowal of gifts according to a moderate dispensation. Let one be a hand to another, or an eye; let him be the staff of support, let there be a mutual calmness of spirit, and in great hardships the striving to offer a veritable sanctuary of assistance to others. Finally, let them so live in friendship that they may merit to ascend to that love in which Christ is loved with the whole heart, and in which they may derive maximum benefit from their love, so that when all fear and all the concern and worry which they now have for one another have passed, they will enjoy full and everlasting security (*De amicitia Christiana,* c. 21, col. 890).

1955. JOHN OF TRITHEIM. A chaste and prudent man who loves his neighbor walks securely in the light of the Holy Spirit, being neither disturbed himself by others nor allowing himself to trouble them. For true love of neighbor is meek, gentle, kind, and in all its relationships gracious, peaceful, and calm. In the case of superiors, the natural severity of discipline tempers graciousness, and the clemency of fraternal considerateness beautifully softens this severity. It is necessary that the one temper the other so that neither will the vigor be unyielding nor the love dissolute. . . . The friendship of monks among those who are zealously striving for the same goal must be mutual and devoid of carnal affection. Let it be pure, simple, upright, persevering, without offense to anyone, free of all suspicious conspiracy. It is not the rule of fraternal charity to seek little private meetings for secret encouragements and, without the prior's permission, to indulge in furtive and prohibited conversations. Whenever you are tempted to make allowances for human weakness in violation of the regular discipline, you are not showing love to your neighbor in the proper way, but rather perniciously.

The monk's love must be pure-minded and entirely free of all transgression of the regular discipline, for unless charity is devoid of carnal speech, it does not possess the fire of divine love. Examine your manner of life, brethren, and see whether your hearts are rooted in true charity. Charity which gives to one's neighbor or receives encouragements which are harmful to the spirit is never sincere. . . . He loves his brother in the proper manner who cherishes him out of love of God and for the common share in the kingdom for which we are hoping. Hence St. John the Bishop says: "Not only is he who baptized us one, but that by which he baptized us is one. For we are baptized not in order to become different bodies, but that we may all mutually preserve the carefully designed oneness of that one body through charity and harmony. In other words, we are baptized in order that we may form one body" (St. J. Chrysostom, *Hom. 30 in I Cor.*, § 1, *PG* 61:251). As no one can attain salvation outside the unity of the Catholic Church, so we believe that no one can be saved without brotherly love. Hence before all else charity is necessary for your salvation; without it other virtuous works are utterly fruitless. There can be no good, no salutary merit which does not derive its origin from it. Charity is the shortcut of virtuous living: he who walks this right path has no need of a guide's directions.

Charity, pure, simple, and upright, never harms a neighbor or inflicts evil. Charity gives to all the love that it knows to be beneficial to self: whatever it hopes will lead to its own salvation it desires to give to all men in Christ Jesus. Without any disturbance charity fulfils the duty of love, and in loving all men without measure, is never provoked to bitterness toward anyone. It is always composed, constant, stable, and firm, for it is neither troubled by passions nor disturbed by habits of restlessness. It gives itself uniformly to all and so manifests its affection toward every individual that each seems to be particularly favored. It does not neglect itself in matters that pertain to the mind and the soul, but in those which consult the convenience of the body it often places the welfare of others before its own advantage.

Truly great is that charity which compels a man to make another's convenience his own concern. You, therefore, my brethren, who are solemnly sworn to serve as soldiers of Christ, who are eagerly striving for eternal life along the difficult path of obedience, see to it that you keep fraternal charity always inviolate among you, unless you wish to run to no avail in so difficult a race. For unless you have unaffected and perfect charity for one another, your regular observance is without fruit. Abstaining from eating flesh meat will contribute nothing to the salvation of souls; the abandonment of all personal ownership will not help at all in acquiring eternal happiness if brotherly love holds no place in your hearts.

In your eagerness, therefore, to be saved through Christ, love one another in truth as Christ loved you. Let each one at all times bestow on his brother whatever he desires for himself—and that not in the spirit of envy, but rather out of love of God. Let this divine love gain the victory in you over all quarrels and dissensions; let not pernicious contention find any place where the fullness of charity must always dwell (*Hom. 22, de fraterna charitate monachorum, Op. pia et spiritualia,* pp. 513–514).

The uses of ill health

1956. ST. ISIDORE OF SEVILLE. Sufferings of the body are medicine for the spirit; illness wounds the flesh, but heals the soul. The fevers of the body in illness melt away vices and break the strength of the passions (*Synonymorum Lib. II,* § 26, *PL* 83:851).

1957. HUMBERT OF ROMANS, O.P., fifth master general of the Order of Preachers (d. 1247). Many considerations must motivate the brethren, and particularly superiors, in exercising deep solicitude for sick brethren, and in the manner in which we have been treating the question. The first is the very nature of mercy, which is evident, because of all the miseries to whose alleviation the works of mercy are usually directed, none is so great an affliction as sickness—be it hunger, or thirst, or nakedness, or the want of a home, or imprisonment—whether you consider them individually or with aggravating circumstances. None of these renders man so incapable of helping himself in his misery as does sickness. The hungry and he who is thirsty, the poorly clad and the wanderer can help themselves in relieving their distress; even the imprisoned can at times free himself. All these persons retain their physical powers; but the sick man can do nothing, or but little, because sickness deprives him of his strength. Then, again, there is no one of the miseries that have been mentioned that cannot be relieved more readily than illness. It is easy to feed a hungry man, give drink to him who is thirsty, clothe the naked, take in the stranger, free the captive, for all these depend solely on the good will of the helper. But sickness can, at times, not be relieved even with many doctors and all kinds of medicines, but only by God himself, for it is he who *wounds, but he binds up; he smites, but his hands give healing* (Job 5:18). Hence sickness is the misery of the greatest affliction, rendering one most helpless; it is also the most difficult to heal. That is the reason that David, seeking to induce the Lord to be merciful to him, presents this form of misery as the basis of his plea, saying: *Have pity on me, O Lord, for I am languishing* (Ps. 6:3). It is as though he had said: "Have mercy on me because I am grievously afflicted as is a sick man, and hence cannot help myself, nor can I expect help from any other source." Since mercy [*misericordia*] means being heartfelt in aiding those who are suffering misery [*miseris-cordans*], and also since it must be the more directed to those who are suffering the greatest affliction, if there is any spirit of mercy in religious persons, it must pour itself out more copiously on the sick than on others, as upon men suffering the greatest misery, by exercising special care for them.

The second motive is Christ's example. Nowhere do we read that Christ, our model, showed so great a solicitude for any other form of distress as he manifested toward the sick. We do not read that he clothed the naked, took in guests or visited prisons. It is true, of course, that he fed the hungry and gave drink to the thirsty, but he did so only rarely, for he fed the hungry only in the desert and gave drink to the thirsty only at a wedding. But in the case of the sick we read that he exercised diligent care, at times comforting them . . . at other times touching them with his own hand, even in the case of the leper; again, raising them up; on other occasions healing them completely, and performing countless similar deeds that are part of the care of the sick. . . . Then, too, there is the consideration of the obligation of one's office, and this applies to superiors. For they are shepherds, as stated in Ezechiel (cf. Chapter 34, entire chapter). But it is the duty of a good shepherd to have greater care of the sick sheep than of the rest of the flock. It is said by way of reproof: *The weak you have not strengthened, and that which was sick you have not healed* (Ezech. 34:4; *Expos. in Reg. S. Augustini,* c. 136, *De vita regulari,* p. 411).

1958. ST. BASIL THE GREAT. . . . Consequently we must take great care to employ this medical art, if it should be necessary, not as making it wholly accountable for our state of health or illness, but as redounding to the glory of God and as a parallel to the care given to the soul (*Reg. fusius tractatae, Interrogatio 55,* § 2, *PG* 31:1046; Wagner, p. 331).

1959. RUFINUS OF AQUILEA (d. 411). All keep to their cells, and there is preserved great silence and quiet among them. On Saturday and Sunday they come together in the church. . . . If anyone is absent from these common exercises, the others immediately understand that he has been kept away by some physical indisposition. All of them go to visit him, not of course together, but at different times, each taking with him, if he has anything to give, whatever seems likely to gratify the brother who is ill (*Historia monachorum,* c. 22, *PL* 21:444).

1960. HUMBERT OF ROMANS. The Lord commands us to be merciful, as also the heavenly Father is merciful (cf. Luke 6:36). But *The Lord is good to all and compassionate to all his works* (Ps. 144:9). There is no greater mercy than that which is performed in behalf of the sick. Therefore mercy in caring for them should prevail over all one's other deeds. For in this mercy shown to them he who is hungry is fed; the thirsty given drink; clothing prepared for the naked; a bed readied for one who is worn out as for a stranger; he who is held by the bonds of illness is visited in the spirit of charity; and, finally, the obligations of human decency are fulfilled with regard to the deceased. Thus in the care of the sick all the works of mercy (cf. Matt. 25:35 ff.) are practiced.

Then, too, in the works according to the strict observance of the religious life, God is served now with one, now with another faculty or member of the body. This is true, for example, with regard to taste in abstinence, sight in the keeping of vigils, touch in the wearing of coarse garments, the tongue in observing silence, and the feet in keeping the enclosure. But in the works of caring for sick persons the eye serves him in night duty and also sometimes in beholding the most revolting sights; the sense of smell by putting up with foul odors; hearing, by listening to harsh criticisms, often from the sick man himself; the sense of touch in ministering to the sick person; taste, by sometimes interrupting one's customary meal schedule; the tongue, in offering words of consolation; the feet, in running errands for those who are ill; in fact, the whole body by performing many different kinds of work. Now, what practice of the religious life can be compared with that in which a person thus binds himself anew and wholly to God, in order to serve him with his whole heart? In fact, he is serving both God and his neighbor, or rather God in his neighbor, and his neighbor in serving God.

The Lord himself gave us the pattern for following this practice of religion by showing himself so kind to the sick, visiting them, speaking to them, often healing them. Then, too, on sending the Apostles forth, he commanded them to seek out and heal the sick. And through the Apostle James, he instituted a special sacrament to produce its effects for all time, unto the alleviation of human illness (*Expos. in Reg. S. Augustini,* c. 67, *De vita regulari,* p. 205).

1961. WALTER HILTON (d. 1396). A. O my soul, why are you perturbed all the day long in seeking Christ? I will show you, O spouse, him whom your soul loves. See where he lies there in the infirmary? He is there sick and in pain. Make haste, then, and minister unto him, and compassionate his misery. . . . Let us not henceforward inquire of him, "Where liest thou, or where dost thou rest at noon?" (cf. Cant. 1:6, Douay version.) For we know the place. We know he is lying in the infirmary, and there remains nothing else for us but to go and serve him (*Stimulus amoris, Pars II,* c. 6, *inter Op. Om. S. Bonaventurae,* ed. Peltier 12:671; *Stimulus amoris,* formerly attributed to St. Bonaventure; now edited from manuscripts by Clare Kirchberger; New York: Harper and Brothers, 1951, p. 127). B. When he sees his neighbor sick in bed, therefore, he believes that he is seeing Christ, and for this cause nothing is difficult to him, nothing abominable, nothing loathsome; he esteems nothing as ignominious or disgraceful to him that he does for the sick, or for any others that are in misery or necessity, but judges all things to be sweet, pleasant, and delightsome when he thus ministers to Christ in his neighbor (*ibid.;* Kirchberger, p. 126).

1962. ST. PETER CHRYSOLOGUS, bp. of Ravenna (d. circa 450). He who does not share in the illness of the man who is ill cannot bestow health on him (*Serm. 50, de paralytico curato, PL* 52:340).

1963. CASSIODORUS. I salute you, distinguished brothers, who with sedulous care look after the health of the human body and perform the functions of blessed piety for those who flee to the shrines of holy men [saints]—you who are sad at the sufferings of others, sorrowful for those who are in danger, and always distressed with personal sorrow at the misfortune of others, so that, as experience of your art teaches, you help the sick with genuine zeal. You will receive your reward from him by whom eternal rewards may be paid for temporal acts. Learn, therefore, the properties of herbs and perform the compounding of drugs punctiliously; but do not place your hope in herbs and do not trust health to human counsels. For although the art of medicine be found established by the Lord, he who without doubt grants life to men makes them sound (cf. Sir. 38:1). For it is written: *Whatever you do in word or work, do all in the name of the Lord Jesus, giving thanks to God the Father through him* (Col. 3:17; *Institutio divinarum litterarum,* c. 31, *de monachis curam infirmorum habentibus;* Jones, p. 135).

1964. ST. ANSELM. In compliance with the order of our father, the Archbishop, we are sending to England Dom Maurice, my superior by merit, my brother in community life, my dearly loved son by reason of my spiritual charge. We place him in your hands so that out of love of God you will treat his illness, inspired thereto both by our friendship for you and the seriousness of his need. May your medicine, under God's assistance, restore his health; may temporal welfare be bestowed on him through your efforts, and that which is eternal be your reward through the divine mercy. And as for brother Anselm, whom you already possess as a friend, you will have bought as a slave (cf. Phil., v. 17; *Ep. 28, ad Albertum, medicum, PL* 158:1092; Schmitt, *Op. Om.* 3:144).

Charity for the deceased

1965. ST. GREGORY THE GREAT. If the sins [that remained unabsolved] after death are not unpardonable, then the offering of the Sacred Host is of great benefit to men's souls; for this purpose the spirits of those who have died sometimes appear in order to request this very offering (*Dialogorum Lib. IV,* c. 55, *Quid sit quod post mortem valeat ad absolutionem animas adjuvare, PL* 77:416).

1966. ST. AUGUSTINE. A. It is not to be doubted that the deceased are indeed aided by the prayers of Holy Church, by the Sacrifice of salvation, and by alms which are expended for their souls, that the Lord may deal more mercifully with them than their sins have deserved (*Serm. 172, de verbis Apostoli I Thess. 4, 12,* § 2, *PL* 38:936). B. We must always pray for the dead, and if our prayers are not of benefit to them either because they are blessed [already in heaven], or damned, the prayer will be converted to our bosom (*Ad fratres in eremo, serm. 44, In Append., PL* 40:1321). C. The Church receives the supplications to be made for all who have died in the Christian society, even without [specific] mention of names, under the general Commemoration for all; thus they who have no parents, children, relatives, or friends are presented by the one living Mother of all. We are all born equal, we live together, and die equal. Consider, therefore, O man of wealth, that the poor man and the wealthy man are born in the same manner and die alike. Do not despise them, do not turn away the hand of blessing from them (*ibid.,* col. 1319). D. Pray for the deceased, so that when they shall have attained to eternal life, they will not fail to pray for you. . . . They who are lying in torments cry out to us daily—and few answer them; they utter their mournful plea, and there is none to comfort them. How awful a cruelty! Truly, this is a great inhumanity! . . . Consider for a moment: if a man lying ill on his bed cries out in pain, his suffering is relieved by the doctor; a pig squeals, and all the other pigs squeal with it; a donkey falls, and all hasten to lift him up; but a member of the faithful cries out in torments, and none answers his plea! (*Ibid.,* col. 1320.)

1967. ST. ALBERT THE GREAT, O.P., bp. of Regensburg (d. 1280). True compassion should be shown for our neighbors who are detained in purgatory, so that God will deign to release them from the harsh torments they endure (*Paradisus animae, Pars I,* c. 12, *de compassione, Op. Om.* 37:467).

1968. JOHN GERSON, chancellor of the University of Paris (d. 1429). We must pray willingly for all the faithful departed, for this is a work of great charity and mercy. . . . I admonish myself as well as you, dearly beloved, that we frequently direct our pious regard to the memory of the deceased, in order to do with love's swiftness what we know is helpful for their liberation. We must remind ourselves of the seriousness of their torments; we must reflect that until they are cleansed they cannot enter into rest. Their hope is based primarily on the merits of Christ, but also on the intercession of the saints, and on the offerings of the faithful. As often as you prepare to receive the body of Christ, and after you have received it, remember, I pray you, the faithful departed, and implore the mercy of God all the more ardently as you have within you the Pledge of eternal salvation. Often of a morning and at nightfall, think of the death of your loved ones, what their condition is, and how you can do what will benefit them, and be no inconvenience for you. Do not partake of food without first directing a spiritual alms to the faithful departed (*Ep. de pia memoria defunctorum, Pars III,* n. 72, *Op. Om.* 3:756).

1969. HUGH OF ST. CHER, O.P., cardinal (d. 1260). Mercy shown to the deceased is greater than that shown to the living, for the living can to some degree help themselves, whereas the dead are unable to do so (*Sup. Ruth 3, 1, Comment.* 1:217).

1970. JEAN MABILLON, monk of the congregation of St. Maur (d. 1707). After a lapse of 144 years Abbot Cralo of St. Gall and Alavicus of Augie (diocese of Troyes), and the brethren of the two monasteries decided that the long-standing agreement according to which the monks of St. Gall and Augie had originally formed a mutual confraternity of prayer, should be confirmed with a new decree, with certain added provisions. When a brother of either monastery died, his corpse was not removed from the church for burial until all the Canonical Hours had been prayed at their appropriate times. At the first Mass offered for him by all the brethren, after the angelic hymn [the Sanctus] had been chanted three times, all were to lie prostrate on the floor until the *Pax Domini* was said by the priest, earnestly commending the soul of the brother to the Lord with sighs and tears. His portion of food was given in full as an alms to the poor until his anniversary day, and thereafter for thirty-seven added days. When notice was received of the death of a brother of the other monastery, vigils, Masses, and psalms were forthwith offered for him, and at the community Mass the brethren lay prostrate as described, and the portion of food as though for one of their own brethren was set aside and distributed to the poor for a period of thirty days. Finally, the whole community of each monastery, divided into six groups, on private days [De Ea?] and on the days assigned, offered Matins and the Mass for all the deceased of both monasteries (*Annales O.S.B., Lib. 44,* n. 87, tom. 3:446).

The works of charity

1971. ST. JEROME. You have other duties to perform: to clothe Christ in the poor, to visit him in the sick, to feed him in the hungry, to shelter him in the homeless, particularly such as are of the household of the faith (cf. Gal. 6:10), to support communities of virgins, to care for God's servants, and the poor in spirit who serve the same Lord as you day and night, who, although they are on earth, live the angelic life and speak only of the praise of God. Having food and raiment they rejoice and count themselves rich. They seek for nothing more, content if only they can persevere in their purpose (*Ep. 130, ad Demetriadem, de servanda virginitate,* § 14, *PL* 22:1119).

1972. ST. AUGUSTINE. This man cannot walk; he who can walk lends his feet to him who is lame; he who has sight lends his eyes to the blind; and he who is young and sound of body, lends his strength to the old or the infirm, and carries him; the one is poor, the other rich. Sometimes even a rich man is found to be poor, and something is bestowed on him by a poor man. For instance, a rich man comes to a river, more delicate in health even than he is rich. He cannot pass over, for if he were to pass over with bared limbs, he would take cold, become ill, and die. A poor man, more active in body, comes along and carries the rich man across. The poor man bestows an alms on him who is wealthy. Do not think, therefore, that they only are poor who have no money. Consider every man in his needs, for perhaps you are rich in that wherein he is poor, and have wherewith to help him (*Enarr. in Ps. 125,* § 12, *PL* 37:1665).

1973. CASSIODORUS. A. Before all things, therefore, receive the stranger, give alms, clothe the naked, *deal thy bread to the hungry* (Isa. 58:7), since that man is truly to be called comforted who comforts the wretched (*De institutione divinarum litterarum,* c. 32, *exhortatio ad monachos et abbates, PL* 70:1147; Jones, p. 136). B. When [delicacies] are prepared for strangers and for sick people they become heavenly, however earthly they may seem to be. What a deed it is to refresh the sick with sweet fruits or to feed them with young doves or to nourish them with fish or to soothe them with sweet honey! Since, indeed, the Lord directs that in his name even a cup of cold water be offered a poor man (cf. Matt. 10:42), how much more deserving of thanks will it be to give especially sweet food to the different ones who are destitute, in order that on the day of judgment you may receive your reward with interest! One should not fail to employ every available means when there is the possibility of aiding anyone (*ibid.,* c. 28, col. 1142; Jones, p. 130).

1974. ST. JOHN CHRYSOSTOM. For it is not so much to have fed him when he appeared in his own person, which would have been enough to prevail with a heart of stone, as simply on the strength of his word to wait upon the poor, the maimed, him that is bent down. . . . There is proof of greater reverence toward him, when at his mere word, waiting upon your fellow servant, you refresh him in all things (*Hom. 88 in Matt.,* § 3, *PG* 58:778).

1975. THOMAS À KEMPIS. Whatever you give up to the benefit of the brethren of Christ, the just Judge will return to you on the day of judgment. When you sacrifice self-will and forgo personal advantage, or postpone your spiritual reading in favor of the needs of others, you are really buying from Christ the inheritance of eternal life. Let him be your most precious and firmly founded Pledge of the reward of eternal glory. To the Father he spoke thus: *Father, I will that where I am, they also whom thou hast given me may be with me* (John 17:24).

O Martha,* you can perform many good works if you are willing and ready to do so. The servants of Christ stand in need of your ministrations; without your care they are really not free to dedicate their service to God. But if you want your work to be meritorious, perform it with goodness of heart, wholly free of unwillingness and repugnance. You can exercise a great charity toward the brethren and cause joy when they hunger and thirst and have nothing to eat. And you answer their needs by placing before them what the Lord has allowed for the weakness of the human body.

Hearken to what the Patriarch Isaac said to his son Esau: *Take up your weapons, quiver and bow; go out into the fields to hunt me some game. Prepare for me some savory food such as I like; bring it to me to eat, so that I may bless you before I die* (Gen. 27:3). Whoever has been nourished with food and drink in the name of Christ by your ministry will bless you too, Martha. Nor will the blessing be only a certain temporal return, but the enduring reception of eternal inheritance (*De fideli dispensatore,* c. 2, n. 4, *Op. Om.* 1:165; *ep. ad quemdam cellararium*).

1976. RUPERT, abbot of Deutz (d. 1135). It is worthy of note that there are six works of charity which have a certain resemblance to the six days in which God created the world and all that is in it. For these works of mercy also merit their Sabbath, so that he who has performed them may also rest from his labors, says the Apostle, as God rested from his (cf. Heb. 4:4). The first of these works of mercy is: *I was hungry and you gave me to eat;* the second, *I was thirsty and you gave me to drink;* the third, *I was a stranger and you took me in;* the fourth, *naked, and you covered me;* the fifth, *sick and you visited me;* the sixth, *I was in prison and you came to me* (Matt. 25:35–36). They who have performed these works will enter upon their Sabbath, that is, into the rest of the Lord, upon the invitation of him who rested after six days (cf. Gen. 2:2). He will address them: *Come, blessed of my Father, take possession of the kingdom prepared for you from the foundation of the world* (Matt. 25:34; *Comment. in Matt., Lib. V,* c. 6, *PL* 168:1423).

1977. ST. JOHN CHRYSOSTOM. Nothing is so pleasing or so dear to God as the welfare of souls, as the Apostle exclaims: *Who wishes all*

* In the monastic terminology of the day this allusion to Christ's addressing Martha (Luke 10:41) was sometimes oddly applied to cellarers in much the same manner that it is more commonly referred today to convent domestics and parish housekeepers. [*Tr.*]

men to be saved and to come to the knowledge of the truth (I Tim. 2:4). Elsewhere the Lord himself says: *I desire not the death of the wicked, but that the wicked turn from his way, and live* (Ezech. 33:11). . . . Having over us such a Lord, so merciful and benign, let us devote ourselves to our own spiritual care and that of our brethren. Just as the soul is superior to the body, so they who by admonishing and continually teaching lead the fallen and slothful along the right way, showing them the beauty of the divine virtues and the foulness and ill will of vices, merit a richer reward than those who offer money and worldly substance to the indigent (*Hom. 3 in Gen.,* c. 1, § 4, *PG* 53:36, 37).

1978. ST. THOMAS AQUINAS. Spiritual almsdeeds are preferable to corporal almsdeeds; . . . first, because the offering is more excellent since it is a spiritual gift which surpasses a corporal gift . . . ; secondly, on account of the object succored, because the spirit is more excellent than the body; . . . thirdly, as regards the acts themselves, by which our neighbor is succored, because spiritual acts are more excellent than corporal acts, which are, in a fashion, servile (*II-II,* q. 32, art. 3, *Utrum eleemosynae corporales sint potiores quam spirituales, Op. Om.* 8:252; Am. ed. 2:1326).

1979. ST. JOHN CHRYSOSTOM. A. If punishment lies in store for him who has the money and does not help with the same, shall there not be a greater punishment for him who has the opportunity to exhort and does not do so? In the former case the body is nourished, in the latter, the soul; there you prevent temporal death, here, that which is eternal (*Hom. 30 in Heb.,* § 2, *PG* 63:211). B. Do you wish to correct a brother? Then weep, pray to God. Take the brother aside, admonish him, counsel him, entreat him! That is what Paul did, *Lest,* as he said, *when I come again God should humiliate me before you, and I should mourn over many who sinned and have not repented of the uncleanness and immorality and licentiousness that they have practised* (II Cor. 12:21). Show your charity toward the sinner. Persuade him that it is from concern and anxiety for his welfare and not from desire to expose him, that you remind him of his sin. Cast yourself at his feet; embrace him; be not ashamed if you truly desire to cure him. Physicians too do things of this sort; frequently when their patients are hard to please . . . they at length persuade them to take a salutary medicine by their ingratiating manner and entreaties (*Ad populum Antiochenum, Hom. 3,* § 5, *PG* 49:54). C. Devote your effort that pious doctrine be sown and cultivated among the Arians. I desire, I beg of all of you to be teachers and not only hearers of what we have taught; carry our doctrine to others and go in search for those who have wandered away, in order that they may return to the way of truth. St. Paul tells you to do this: *Edify one another* (I Thess. 5:11) and, *Work out your salvation with fear and trembling* (Phil. 2:12). In this manner God will increase our number and you will enjoy the grace of heaven more abundantly, by exercising deep concern for the members of Christ's body. Nor does God will that the Christian be concerned for himself alone, but that he edify others, not only with his doctrine but also by his life and conduct (*Hom. 8 in Gen.*, §§ 4, 5, *PG* 53:73).

1980. CLEMENT OF ALEXANDRIA (d. circa 217). Mercy is not, as some of the philosophers have imagined, pain on account of the misfortune of others, but rather something good, as the Prophet says: *I desired mercy and not sacrifice* (Osee 6:6). And he means by the merciful not only those who actually perform works of mercy, but those who wish to do so, even though they are unable; who actually do so as far as intention and purpose are concerned (*Stromatum Lib. IV*, c. 6, *PG* 8:1250).

1981. ST. GREGORY OF NYSSA, bp. (d. circa 400). If, therefore, the term "merciful" is suited to God, what else does the Word invite you to become but God, since you ought to model yourself on the property of the Godhead (*De Beatitudinibus, Oratio 5*, § 2, *PG* 44:1250; Hilda Graef, p. 131).

Objectionable attachment to relatives

1982. ST. BERNARD. I have seen a man running well on his course, and then, a sudden hesitation and scruple arises in him. . . . "To how many," he says, "of my brethren and relations, of my friends and acquaintances should I be able, if I were living in my own country and neighborhood, to communicate of that good which I enjoy here alone! They love me and would readily follow my advice. Why is this waste made here? I will go thither, and in saving many of them I shall equally save myself. There is nothing to be feared in a mere change of place. What does it matter where I am so long as I am doing a good work? In fact, I am best placed where I am living the most useful and fruitful life." Why repeat more of his reasoning? He goes whither he desires and, unhappy man, he perishes; rather as a dog returned to its vomit than as an exile returned to his own land. He both comes to a miserable end himself and he fails to save any of his own people. Surely this was *a little fox* (Cant. 2:15); I mean the deceptive hope of gaining over his friends which he had been nourishing. You will be able to find out for yourself other and similar ideas in your own mind if you examine it closely (*Serm. 64 in Cant., de tentationibus monachorum provectorum*, § 2, *PL* 183:1084; Eales, p. 383).

1983. ST. BASIL THE GREAT. The Scripture absolutely forbids the words "mine" and "thine" to be uttered among the brethren, saying: *The multitude of believers were of one heart and one soul, and not one of them said that anything he possessed was his own* (Acts 4:32). The parents or brothers of a member of the community, therefore, if they live piously, should be treated by all the brethren as fathers or other relatives possessed in common. *For whoever does the will of my Father in heaven, he is my brother and sister and mother,* says the Lord (Matt. 12:50). . . . Besides the utmost effort must be made entirely to remove occasions of sin from those still in the training school of virtues—the chief of these occasions being the remembrance of their former life in the world—so that it may never be said of them that in their hearts they have returned to Egypt (cf. Num. 14:4). This very often happens in prolonged conversation with their relatives according to the flesh. In general, therefore, neither these relatives nor any other extern should be allowed to talk with the brethren unless we are certain that their conversation will bring about the edification and perfection of their soul (*Reg. fusius tractatae, Interrogatio 32,* §§ 1, 2, *PG* 31:995; Wagner, p. 295).

1984. RABANUS MAURUS, monk of Fulda, abp. of Mainz (d. 856). A. That reverence and honor be shown to one's father and mother here below is a commandment of God. The precept reads: *Honor your father and your mother; that you may have a long life in the land which the Lord, your God, is giving you* (Exod. 20:12). . . . Those who follow this commandment will receive a crown; those who spurn it will be punished. . . . He wisely stores up treasures for himself who honors his mother, because for keeping the commandments of God, who prescribed that we honor our parents, he will receive the reward of eternal life (*In Eccl., Lib. I,* c. 9, *PL* 109:777). B. He who honors his parents and teachers in obedience to God's precepts will rejoice in the increase of good deeds until the end of his days. And as the prayer of him who turns his ear away in order not to hear the law will be detestable, so the prayer of him who obeys God's commandments will come like incense before the Most High (cf. Ps. 140:2).

. . . Note that it states that subjection be shown with a certain intenseness: *In word and deed honor your father* (Sir. 3:8), that is, the parents who have begotten you. This is to show that the spiritual father is worthy of great honor. With this thought in mind the Apostle wrote to the disciples whom he had begotten through the Gospel: *We beseech you, brethren, to appreciate those who labor among you, and who are over you in the Lord, and admonish you. Esteem them with a more abundant love on account of their work. Be at peace with them* (I Thess. 5:12). And in writing to Timothy: *Let the presbyters who rule well be held worthy of double honor, especially those who labor in the word and in teaching. . . . The laborer is worthy of his wages* (I Tim. 5:17). The honor of a father, whether a spiritual father or a father according to the flesh, merits a blessing from the Lord; and it is appropriately said that *a father's blessing gives a family firm roots* (Sir. 3:9), for he will be rewarded with an eternal reward (*ibid.*, c. 10).

Gratitude toward benefactors

1985. ST. BERNARD. A. Blessed was that Samaritan who realized that he possessed nothing which he had not received (cf. I Cor. 4:7), and who therefore preserved what had been bestowed on him by returning to the Lord to express his thanks [the leper who was cleansed, cf. Luke 17:11 ff.]. Blessed is he who for each gift renders thanks to him in whom there is the plenitude of all graces, for by showing ourselves not ungrateful for the favors we have received, we are making a place for grace, in order that we may merit to receive yet greater gifts. Nothing other than our own ingratitude prevents us from making progress in our way of life, since in a certain manner the giver, considering as lost that which was received thanklessly, takes care for the future not to suffer greater losses by conferring benefits on a thankless person (*Serm. 37 de div., contra pessimum vitium ingratitudinis,* § 8, *PL* 183:615). B. Happy is he who with care and pains collects [the benefits which the Divine Goodness has bestowed] for himself, and sets them before the eyes of his mind with acts of thanksgiving proportioned to their greatness (*Serm. 10 in Cant.,* § 7, col. 822). C. Learn not to be slow and slothful in returning thanks to God; learn to render thanksgiving to him for each of his gifts. *Keep in mind who is before you* (Prov. 23:1), so as not to let pass any gift of God, whether great, or mediocre, or even very small, without rendering due thanks for it (*ibid., serm. 51,* § 6, col. 1027).

1986. ST. THOMAS AQUINAS. He is not worthy of receiving a favor who does not render thanks for the favors he has already received (*In Ep. ad Rom.,* c. 1, lectio 5, *Op. Om.,* ed. Parma 13:11).

Charity to the poor

1987. ST. CYPRIAN, bp. of Carthage, martyr (d. 258). What greater things could Christ pronounce to us? What stronger argument could he use to call forth our works of righteousness and mercy than to say that whatever is given to the needy and poor is given to himself; and in saying that he is offended if the needy and poor are not supplied? (*De opere et eleemosynis,* § 23, *PL* 4:643.)

1988. ST. JOHN CHRYSOSTOM. Certainly if you were now to behold Christ the Lord, no one of you would hesitate to bestow as alms everything he possesses. . . . Do you not hear him saying: *As long as you did it for one of these, the least of my brethren, you did it for me* (Matt. 24:40). There is really no difference whether you have given it to this poor man, or to Christ himself. Surely you have no less to offer than the women who at that time gave Christ to eat (*Hom. 88 in Matt.*, § 3, *PG* 58:778).

1989. ST. AUGUSTINE. Let no one among you be tempted to say: "Oh, how blessed were those people who were privileged to receive Christ into their own homes!" Do not be vexed and troubled because you live in times when you do not see our Lord in the flesh. He has not withdrawn this privilege from you, for he says: *As long as you did it for one of these, the least of my brethren, you did it for me* (Matt. 25:40; *Serm. 103, in Luc. 10, 38*, § 2, *PL* 38:613).

1990. ST. JEROME. A. *Happy is he who has regard for the lowly and the poor* (Ps. 40:2). Give to all who ask an alms of you, but particularly to those who are of the household of the faith; clothe the naked; give food to the hungry; visit the sick. As often as you stretch forth your hand, think of Christ. Be on your guard lest your Lord God seeking an alms from you, you increase the wealth of others (*Ep. 54, ad Furiam, de viduitate servanda,* § 12, *PL* 22:556). B. See to it that you render greater thanks to Christ when you have given an alms than the thanks of the poor man who received it from you. Poor people offer us the occasion of a great blessing. For an alms blots out the sins which we are otherwise unable to wash away (*Breviarium in Ps. 133, 2, In Append.*, *PL* 26:1225).

1991. ST. AUGUSTINE. Men of riches *sleep their sleep* [of death]; *the hands of all the mighty ones have failed* (Ps. 75:6). They have slept in their desires. These desires were their great delight. This life passes away, and they find nothing in their hands, because they have put nothing into the hand of Christ (*Enarr. in Ps. 75, 6,* § 9, *PL* 36:963).

1992. ST. JOHN CHRYSOSTOM. A. Do not consider the poor person who is receiving, but God who will reward; not him who accepts the alms, but him who binds himself to be your debtor (*De verbis Apostoli, Habentes eundem spiritum, II Cor. 4, 13, Hom. I,* § 8, *PG* 51:278). B. It is not for the lifting up of hands that we shall be heard! Stretch forth your hands, not to heaven, but to the poor. If you stretch forth your hands to the hands of the poor, then you will have reached the very summit of heaven. For he who is seated there will receive your alms. But if you lift up your hands without a gift, you gain nothing (*Hom. 1 in II ad Timoth.*, § 4, *PG* 62:606).

1993. ST. PETER CHRYSOLOGUS. A. The hand of a beggar is Abraham's bosom; there everything that the poor man has received is stored away. The hand of a beggar is the treasure of heaven: what it receives it stores in heaven, lest it perish on earth. *Lay up for yourselves treasures in heaven* (Matt. 6:20). The hand of the beggar is the treasury of Christ himself, for whatever a beggar receives, Christ accepts. Give the earth to the beggar, that you may receive heaven in return; give him a coin of the kingdom that you may receive the kingdom; give him a crumb that you may receive the whole [loaf]. Give to the beggar that you may give to yourself. For what you have given to the poor man you will have in that future day; what you have withheld from him, another will receive (*Serm. 8, de jejunio et eleemosyna, PL* 52:210). B. God eats in heaven the bread that the beggar receives on earth (*Serm. 42,* col. 320).

1994. ST. CYPRIAN. How exceedingly great, my brethren, will be the joy and triumph of those who will be found abounding in good works when the Lord shall begin to take account of his servants, and give them the reward he has promised for their practice of virtue: —to exchange with them heavenly things for earthly, eternal for temporal, great for little; to present them before his Father, to whose favor he has restored them by dedicating himself to that great and gracious work [of our redemption]; to introduce them to that life and immortality which, after their having forfeited it, he bought back for them with his life-bestowing blood; to lead them back to paradise, and to make good in fullest measure all his promises by opening to them the kingdom of heaven. These things should never be out of our thoughts and desires; but we must endeavor to secure our interest in them by a never-ceasing diligence in all good works. Great, my brethren, is their advantage, unspeakable the comfort which the faithful may derive from them. Their confidence in God's goodness, their hope and faith derive from these good works a mighty support. With such works they may sue for the pardon of their sins successfully. It is easy, and in our power, that which is of final and supreme importance: it has, in a way, all the advantages with none of the dangers attending martyrdom; it is one of the best and greatest gifts which God can bestow on man, being of the greatest necessity for such as are weak in the faith, and the greatest honor for those who are strong. With its help the Christian obtains more grace, makes Christ his Judge, and God his debtor (*De opere et eleemosyna,* § 26, *PL* 4:644).

1995. ST. PETER DAMIAN. O the power of almsgiving which like the torrent of a copious spring washes away the filth of sins and extinguishes the violent flames of passions! O blessed almsgiving which snatches sons of darkness from the abyss of hell and admits them as adopted sons of the perpetual light in the kingdom of heaven! You take flight from the hands of the poor man up to heaven and there prepare a dwelling place for them who love you. If you are in the form of wine you never turn sour; if bread, you never spoil; . . . if clothing, you never wear out. . . . You conduct business transactions far more prudently than any merchant, for you buy heavenly rewards with earthly goods, acquire eternal blessings for those which are transitory. Blessed indeed are your market days, on which hospitality is offered and a permanent habitation is thereby acquired; a bit of bread given, and a kingdom received; a coin bestowed, and the court of heaven procured (*Opusc. 9, de eleemosyna*, c. 8, *PL* 145:222).

1996. RUPERT, abbot of Deutz (d. 1135). An almsdeed is like pure gold of mercy when it is dug with one's hand from the vein or the mine of love; it is precious, for it ascends to heaven, and there in a most agreeable manner serves to feed the King of kings, and the Lord of lords, becomes his gratifying drink, and covers him with a garment. He will testify to all this with his own lips on the day of judgment: *For I was hungry, and you gave me to eat* (Matt. 25:35; *Comment. in Matt., Lib. V*, c. 6, *PL* 168:1423).

1997. POPE INNOCENT III (d. 1216). An almsdeed cleanses, frees, redeems, protects. It petitions and obtains, perfects, blesses. It justifies, restores, saves (*De eleemosyna*, c. 1, *PL* 217:747).

1998. HUGH OF ST. CHER, O.P. Eight considerations adorn an almsdeed: compassion of heart . . . kindness of speech, the disposition one manifests, one's cheerfulness, humility, discretion, willingness, and rightness of intention (*Sup. Matt. 6, 2, Comment.* 6:22. Wolter uses only the topic headings, arranging them as a sentence).

1999. ST. AUGUSTINE. A. The bestower's alms are to be weighed in the judgment of the heart; nor is great attention to be paid to how much is given, but with what disposition, what affection, and how much one was able to give (*De vera et falsa poenitentia*, c. 15, § 30, *In Append.*, *PL* 40:1125). B. God considers not the person to whom the gift is made, but the spirit in which it is made (*De civitate Dei, Lib. 21*, c. 27, § 3, *PL* 41:748; Dods, p. 806). C. If you have nothing in your cellar or barn to give, you can always bestow from the treasure of the heart. . . . The alms of the heart are far greater than the alms of the body. . . . An alms of charity, even without earthly substance, is sufficient unto itself; that, however, which is given physically, without the disposition of benevolence, will never suffice (*Serm. 271*, § 5, *In Append.*, *PL* 39:2252). D. Never scorn a man who asks an alms of you. If you cannot give what he requests, at least do not spurn him. If you can give, give; if you are unable to give, at least be affable. God rewards the willingness within, when he finds inability to actually give. No one should ever say, "I have nothing." Charity is not served out of a bag; because whatever we say, whatever we have said, and whatever we shall ever be able to say, either we, or any of us, or they that were before us, have no end other than charity because *the purpose of this charge is charity, from a pure heart and a good conscience and faith unfeigned* (I Tim. 1:5; *Enarr. in Ps. 103, serm. 1*, § 19, *PL* 37:1351).

2000. ST. GREGORY OF NAZIANZUS, Doctor of the Church (d. 389). Give a small sum to an indigent person; it is nothing small to him who lacks everything; nor is it small either in God's sight, if you have given according to your means. Promptness and willingness mean much. If you have nothing at all to offer, at least shed a little tear. Sympathy that comes from the heart is a great solace to the man who is sorely tried (*Oratio 14, de pauperum amore*, § 28, *PG* 35:895).

2001. ST. BONAVENTURE. The poor man possesses nothing, but would like to give to one in need, but has nothing to offer; he would like to build places of refuge (*hospitalia*), but is unable to do so. His desire is valued as though it had actually been fulfilled (*Collationes in Hexaemeron, Coll. 5*, § 5, *Op. Om.*, ed. Quarracchi 5:354).

The rewards of hospitality

2002. ST. AMBROSE. A. By the hospitality of one hour the widow who received Elias and fed him from her meager supply of food (cf. III Kgs. 17:11 f.), discovered an undiminishing store of nourishment for the whole period of the drought, receiving the miraculous reward that meal should never be wanting from the pot. In like manner Eliseus repaid the debt of hospitality by restoring life to the deceased (*De Abraham, Lib. I*, c. 5, § 35, *PL* 14:458). B. Do you not see that Abraham, in looking for guests, received God himself to entertain? (cf. Gen. 18:1 ff.) Do you not see that Lot received the angels? (*Ibid.*, 19:3.) And how do you know that when you receive men, you also do not receive Christ? Christ may be in the stranger that comes, for Christ is there in the person of the poor, as he himself says: *I was in prison, and you came to me, naked and you covered me* (Matt. 25:36; *De officiis ministrorum, Lib. II*, c. 21, § 107, *PL* 16:140).

2003. ST. AUGUSTINE. A. They who practiced hospitality toward their Guest [that is, the disciples journeying to Emmaus] recognized him in the breaking of bread whom they had not recognized as he opened the Scriptures to them (cf. Luke 24:13 ff.; *Quaestionum Evangeliorum, Lib. II*, § 51, *PL* 35:1362). B. Hearken attentively, you my brethren, who have no desire to practice hospitality, and who receive a guest as though he were an enemy. Consider Blessed Abraham, as he warmheartedly welcomed men and merited, in his striving for hospitality, to receive God himself (cf. Gen. 18:1 ff.). Christ also confirmed this in the Gospel, saying: *I was a stranger and you took me in* (Matt. 25:35). Do not, therefore, disregard pilgrims, lest perchance he whom you have refused to receive be Christ himself (*Serm. 5*, § 4, *In Append.*, *PL* 39:1748).

2004. ST. GREGORY THE GREAT. Consider, brethren, how great is the power of hospitality. Receive Christ at your tables so that you can be received by him at the everlasting banquet. Offer your hospitality now to Christ the pilgrim, so that at the judgment he will not, as it were, fail to recognize you, but will welcome you as his own to his kingdom (*Hom. 23 in Evangel., Lib. II*, § 2, *PL* 76:1183).

2005. ST. JEROME. A. Welcome poor men and strangers to your humble board, that with them Christ may be your Guest (*Ep. 52, ad Nepotianum, de vita clericorum et monachorum,* § 5, *PL* 22:531). B. Our intention and aim in the monastery is to exercise hospitality, and all who come to us are received with benign disposition, for we fear lest Mary and Joseph should not find shelter in our hospice [the monastery was in Bethlehem], and then Jesus, being cast out, should address us in these words, *I was a stranger and you did not take me in* (Matt. 25:43). It is solely heretics we do not receive, and these are alone those you receive. Our whole solicitude is to wash the feet of all who resort to us, but not to examine their merits (*Apologia adversus libros Rufini, Lib. III,* § 17, *PL* 23:469). C. I must confess that very long ago I promised to write the *Explanation of Ezechiel,* but I have been unable to fulfil the promise, owing to the duty of attending to those who come [to Bethlehem] from all parts of the world; because there is no hour or moment in which we have not to go forth to receive the companies of brethren [pilgrims]; and the solicitude of the monastery is exchanged for a continuous receiving of guests, to such a degree that either we must close the doors, or put aside the study of Sacred Scriptures—and from them we learn how we have to open those very doors. . . . Therefore it comes to this: that only at short moments and during the hours we steal from the night—and with the approach of winter these hours are becoming longer—that we proceed with our dictating, such as it is, by candlelight. We do not say this to vaunt ourselves, as some may think, for the hospitality we offer, but simply to confess the cause of our delay (*Comm. in Ezech., Lib. VII, prooem., PL* 25:199).

2006. BENEDICT HAEFTEN. Christ became poor for us, born in a poor hovel, of a poor Mother. Throughout his life he cultivated the spirit of poverty to the extent that he had not whereon to lay his head. Christ is therefore received more in the poor, simply because they represent him better. There can scarcely be any cause for receiving the poor other than Christ himself, for whose love they are admitted (*Disquisitiones monasticae, Lib. II,* tract. 1, disq. 2, p. 985).

2007. ST. ISIDORE OF SEVILLE. Although virtue demands graciousness to all guests, an especially rich honor of hospitality is to be shown to monks (*Reg. monachorum,* c. 21, *CR* 1:197; *PL* 83:892).

2008. SMARAGDUS, abbot of St. Michel (d. 824). Although a uniform spirit of love should motivate us interiorly in our attitude toward all men, it is fitting in actual practice to minister in one way to the poor, and quite differently to men of importance. It is not proper to assign the same place to all, nor to prepare the same food for them indiscriminately. It is necessary with charity's discretion to recognize each person's proper rank, and give him becoming food, lodging, and signs of recognition, so that as they have been welcomed by us in an intelligent way, they will return home as our friends and without complaint (*Comm. in c. 53 RSB, de hospitibus suscipiendis, PL* 102:890).

2009. ST. BASIL THE GREAT. Is it a secular person who has arrived? Let him learn through actual experience whatever things verbal instruction has not convinced him of, and let him be given a model and pattern of frugal sufficiency in matters of food. Let memories of Christian fare linger in his mind and of great poverty which, because of Christ, gives no cause for shame. If he will not learn this lesson, but adopts a mocking attitude, he will not discommode us a second time. . . . The Lord did not praise Martha for being anxious about much serving, but he said: *Thou art anxious and troubled about many things; and yet only one thing is needful* (Luke 10:41). "Many things," that is for the preparation of the meal, and "one thing," that is, the purpose, namely, to satisfy need. . . . In every case, care must be taken for a good table, yet without overstepping the limits of the actual need. This should be our aim in giving hospitality—that the individual requirements of our guests may be cared for. The Apostle says: *as if using this world and not misusing it* (I Cor. 7:31, cf. Confraternity edition); unnecessary expenditure, however, is misuse (*Reg. fusius tractatae, Interrogatio 20,* §§ 2, 3, *PG* 31:971; Wagner, p. 278).

Spiritual works of charity performed in the cell

2010. CASSIODORUS. Happy the scribe's * design, praiseworthy his zeal, to preach to men, with the hand alone, to unleash tongues with the fingers, to give salvation silently to mortals, and to fight against the illicit temptations of the devil with pen and ink. Every word of the Lord written by the scribe is a wound inflicted on Satan. And so, though seated in one spot [in his monastery], with the dissemination of his work he travels through different provinces. The product of his toil is read in holy places; people hear the means by which they may turn themselves away from base desire and serve the Lord with heart undefiled. Though absent, he labors at his task. I cannot deny that he may receive a renovation of life from these many blessings, if only he accomplishes things of this sort, not with a vain show of ambition, but with upright zeal. Man multiplies the heavenly words, and in a certain metaphorical sense, if one may so express himself, that which the virtue of the Holy Spirit utters is written by a trinity of fingers. O sight glorious to those who contemplate it carefully! With the gliding pen [reed, *arundine*] the heavenly words are copied so that the devil's craft, by means of which he caused the head of the Lord to

* These were copyists of manuscripts, who contributed so substantially toward saving the treasures of antiquity: Cassiodorus wrote a thousand years before the invention of printing. [*Tr.*]

be struck during his passion with a reed [*arundine*], may be destroyed. They deserve praise, too, for seeming in some way to imitate the action of the Lord who, though it was expressed figuratively, wrote his law with the use of his all-powerful finger (cf. Exod. 31:18; *De institutione divinarum litterarum,* c. 30, *PL* 70:1144; Jones, p. 133).

2011. JOHN OF TRITHEIM. A. They that instruct many to justice shall shine as stars for all eternity (cf. Dan. 12:3). We hope to make clear, with God's grace, that this is to be understood not only of those who unearth new treasures, but also of those who transcribe old books. For no matter how valuable a teacher's instruction, it is not made known to those after his time without the services of the copyist. For whatever good we do, whatever we teach profitably, is soon forgotten unless it is laboriously committed to writing. They who transcribe books, therefore, give value to words, memory to events, and strength to the times. Take them out of the Church and faith will be weakened, charity grow cold, hope vanish, the system of government perish, the law end in confusion, and the Gospel itself pass into oblivion. If writing were to disappear the people would be dispersed, devotion extinguished, and the peace of Catholic unity thrown into confusion. Without copyists even what has been written cannot long remain intact, for [documents, manuscripts] are destroyed by accident or consumed with age. . . . Hence the copyist enriches the Church, preserves the faith, destroys heresies, repels vices, teaches morality, and gives increase to virtue. The devoted writer, whom we are endeavoring to describe, praises God, gives joy to the angels and courage to the just, corrects sinners, extols the humble, preserves the good, wages war against the proud, condemns the obstinate. The writer who is outstanding in his piety is a herald of God, for he makes known the divine will to present and future generations, promising eternal life to the good, pardon to the repentant, punishment to the negligent, and condemnation to scorners of discipline. What is more salutary than this art, what more praiseworthy than its charity which God loves, angels cherish, and all the citizens of heaven venerate? This skill fashions weapons for the faithful against heretics, casts down the proud, robs demons of their strength, and sets up a pattern of life for Christians. It teaches the ignorant, strengthens the fainthearted, encourages the devout, and lovingly embraces peacemakers (*De laude scriptorum manualium,* c. 1, *Op. pia et spiritualia,* p. 742).

B. With their hand and their pen monks copying divine works make the Lord's will known to distantly future generations. The writer's charity is greater than the preacher's office, for the latter's exhortation ceases with time, whereas the former's announcing lasts for many years. The preacher speaks only to those who are immediately before him, but the writer preaches also to those who are yet to come.

The preacher's sermon, once heard, is soon exhausted of meaning, but the reading of the former is never lessened, even though it be repeated a thousand times. When the preacher dies, his career has ceased, but even after his death the writer's book continues to teach what is virtuous. The vocation of the preacher amounts to but little if it is not aided by the writer's service. For what will he preach unless the writer has made available what he may read? Therefore it is from the writer's zeal that the preacher's sermon derives its effectiveness. For unless he wrote, the preacher would have nothing to preach. The zealous monk will realize four principal benefits from his writing: his time, which is precious, will be spent to excellent advantage; his mind is enlightened as he writes; his whole interior disposition is warmed to devotion; and after this life, he is granted a distinctive reward. How could the monk spend the time allotted to him more fruitfully than by being intent on writing books from the love of God? For the Lord looks with favor on this occupation, angels second the work rejoicingly; and of its very nature it ministers to the devotion of all the faithful. While copying virtuous and religious materials, the monk is disturbed neither by idle nor evil thoughts, speaks no superfluous words, remains untouched by gossip, but in the quiet of solitude finds his delight among books and invites those who behold him to deeds performed in God's honor. As he copies these works he gradually penetrates mysteries and his mind is enlightened in a wonderful manner. We impress powerfully on the mind what we transcribe, because the very nature of writing and reading forces one to ponder the thought. Then, too, the writer is happily stirred to devotion, because careful weighing of what has been written often kindles the affections. The reward of heaven held in store for the devoted writer can readily be appreciated from the extent of his labors. We are convinced that, in the rewarding of the just, the pious and faithful writer who has instructed many in the faith with his pen will not be deprived of the preacher's crown. For what the preacher instills by word of mouth the writer teaches by his writing.

In a monastery of our order, not unknown to me, there dwelt a pious brother possessed of great zeal in writing books for the library. He copied many works of the saints. Years after his death his body was raised. The three fingers of his right hand with which he had copied so many books were found to be so well preserved that they were as incorrupt as though he had just been buried. The rest of the body was completely decomposed, and only the bones remained, as customarily happens. By this testimony we can see how sacred this duty is before almighty God who, in order to show its merit to the living, honors the members of writers in the corpses of the dead (*ibid.*, c. 6, p. 749).

Spiritual labor appropriate for the monk

2012. PETER THE VENERABLE. Because you are prevented by your unbroken observance of the enclosure you cannot plant shrubs, water crops, or perform other rural labors. But what is far more useful, you can turn your hand from the plow to the pen; in place of tilling the fields you can dig passages from the Holy Scriptures, thus sowing the seed of God's word on paper. Once this seed has matured, that is, in the books that have been written, and the fruits have been produced, they will nourish hungry readers, and, like heavenly bread, will ward off deathly hunger of the soul. In this way surely you can become a silent preacher of the word of God and although you continue in your rigorous observance of silence, the product of your hand will cry aloud to many people. Enclosed in the obscurity of your cell and immersed in your books, you will travel over lands and seas; as a watcher from on high you will cry aloud the word of God in the public assemblies of the Church. In the remote corners of cloisters and monasteries you will whisper the same to the silent servants of God. Your profession makes you a hermit, but your devotion will make you an evangelist, so that what you cannot do in person you may earn the right to do by your labors. Let your incentive in this work be the excellent reward that you will receive because of the progress of all those whom you have been able to help by your commendable efforts. For whatever they have accomplished in overthrowing pride, conquering luxury, spurning avarice, taming anger, or in avoiding or repenting evils through reading your books, will be so many sheaves that you gathered by your labors to fill the barn with the rewards of eternity. . . . By spending your whole blessed life with these and similar holy pursuits you leave no room in your heart or in your cell into which your adversaries can thrust themselves. In this way, since God has completely filled your cell with all his virtues, no room remains for the devil, or for sloth or for other vices (*Ep. 20, Fratri Gisleberto, eremitae, PL* 189:97).

Three degrees of charity toward neighbor

2013. ST. THOMAS AQUINAS. Thirdly, the perfection of brotherly love is considered from the point of view of its effect: for the more we expend greater goods in favor of our neighbors, the more perfect the love seems to be. Now there are three degrees to be considered with regard to this matter. For some give help to their neighbors in corporal works, for instance, those who clothe the naked, feed the hungry, minister to the sick, and perform other like services, which the Lord considers as done for himself (cf. Matt. 25:35 ff.). Others bestow spiritual goods, which however do not rise above the human level, as he who instructs the ignorant, counsels the doubting, and recalls the erring. Such a person is commended in Job: *Behold, you have instructed many, and have made firm their feeble hands. Your words have upheld the stumbler; you have strengthened his stumbling knees* (Job 4:3–4). Then there are others who bestow upon their neighbors spiritual goods which are divine and supernatural, namely the knowledge of divine things, the things that lead to God, and the spiritual administration of the sacraments. The Apostle makes mention of these gifts in his letter to the Galatians: *He . . . gives the Spirit to you, and works miracles among you* (Gal. 3:5). Again, in his first letter to the Thessalonians: *When you heard and received from us the word of God, you welcomed it not as the word of men, but, as it truly is, the word of God* (I Thess. 2:13). And in the second letter to the Corinthians: *I betrothed you to one spouse. . . . For if he who comes preaches another Christ whom we did not preach, or if you receive another Spirit whom you have not received, or another gospel which you did not accept, you might well bear with him* (II Cor. 11:2–4). Now the bestowal of this sort of gifts pertains to a distinctive perfection of brotherly love, for through these goods man is joined to his ultimate end, in which his supreme perfection consists, when for showing this perfection it is stated: *Do you know how the clouds are banked, the wondrous work of him who is perfect knowledge?* (Job 37:16.) According to St. Gregory by the word clouds are understood the holy preachers (*Moral., Lib. 17,* c. 26, § 36, *PL* 76:27).

These clouds, namely the ways of sacred preaching, lead them into most subtle paths. They realize full well that of their own merits they are nothing, and that the things which they bestow on their neighbors are above them.

Now there is still a greater perfection, namely, if such spiritual goods are bestowed upon not one or two, but upon a whole multitude, because even according to the philosophers, the good of a people is more perfect and divine than the good of an individual. Hence the Apostle says to the Ephesians: *He himself gave some men as apostles, and some as prophets, others again as evangelists, and others as pastors and teachers in order to perfect the saints for a work of ministry, for building up the body of Christ* (Eph. 4:11), that is to say, the whole Church. And in the first letter to the Corinthians: *So you also, since you strive after spiritual gifts, seek to have them abundantly for the edification of the Church* (I Cor. 14:12; *Opusc. theol., Opusc. 2, de perfectione vitae spiritualis,* c. 14, *de perfectione dilectionis proximi, quae cadit sub consilio, Op. Om.,* ed. Parma 15:88).

Care of souls neither to be sought nor rejected

2014. ST. AUGUSTINE. But brethren, we exhort you in the Lord to keep your resolution and persevere to the end and, if Mother Church has need of your help, do not accede to her request with eager pride, nor refuse it with slothful complacence; rather, obey God with a meek heart (*Ep. 48, Eudoxio abbati,* § 2, *PL* 33:188; Parsons, p. 232).

2015. ST. THOMAS AQUINAS. It is foolish to say that a man is rendered less fit for spiritual duties [preaching, teaching] through advancing himself in holiness; and consequently it is foolish to declare that the religious state is an obstacle to the fulfilment of such like duties (*II-II,* q. 187, art. 1, *Utrum religiosis liceat docere, praedicare, et alia hujusmodi facere, Op. Om.* 10:506; Am. ed. 2:1983).

2016. ST. JOHN CHRYSOSTOM. The priest is the common father, as it were, of the whole world; it is, therefore, proper that he should care for all, even as God does, whose priest he is (*Hom. 6 in I Tim.,* § 1, *PG* 62:529).

2017. ST. GREGORY THE GREAT. For it becomes the Lord's priest to shine by his moral conduct and life, to the end that the people committed to him may be able, as it were in the mirror of his life, both to choose what to follow and to see what to correct (*Lib. VIII, ep. 33, ad Dominicum, episc. Carthaginien., PL* 77:935).

2018. IMITATION OF CHRIST (Thomas à Kempis). Truly, there should proceed from the mouth of a priest, who so often receives the Sacrament of Christ, no word but what is holy, honest, and profitable (*De imitatione Christi, Lib. IV,* c. 11, *Op. Om.* 2:123; Gardiner, p. 225).

2019. JOHN OF TRITHEIM. Two things are necessary for priests of Christ: worthiness of life and purity of doctrine. Worthiness of life is necessary for you; doctrine, for the people. Let the life of the priest be blameless without offense, his doctrinal knowledge free from error. From these, therefore, you can appreciate what you are commanded to strive for in your priesthood. Above all things else, let this be your concern: that you show forth the salutary words you teach by the holiness of your conduct. For a good life without doctrine will not excuse the pastor who in assuming the care of souls was bound to distribute to them the nourishment of the saving word in the measure of wheat. And although it might be acceptable for the faithful simply to be well instructed by the priest, it is not enough for the priest himself if he does not manifest by his example what he teaches. He will have to render an account to God for the way he has used both his life and his doctrine, and the danger is with regard to both, if either his life were evil or his doctrine fruitless. Consider in searching examination the kind of life that is proper to the priesthood, how clean and holy you must be, how pure in mind, how wise in speech, how diligent in work. Standing at the altar to offer the Sacrifice of the Son of God and of the Virgin, the very excellence of the Sacrifice itself will make you realize how devout and reverent you must be (*Ep. 1, ad novum quemdam presbyterum, Op. pia et spiritualia,* p. 919).

The supreme worth of the human soul: works of the priestly ministry

2020. ST. BERNARD. O soul, sealed with the image of God, adorned with his holiness, betrothed to him by faith, endowed with the Spirit, redeemed by [the Savior's] blood, associated with angels, destined for blessedness, inheritor of goodness, sharer in the power of reason, what have you to do with the flesh, from which you suffer so many evils? . . . This whole world cannot be compared in value to one human soul. For God willed to give up his spirit (cf. Matt. 27:50), not for the whole world, but for the human soul. Therefore the value of the soul, which could be bought back only with Christ's blood, is greater than the value of the world. What can you, who have forfeited your soul for nothing, give in exchange to redeem it? Did not the Son of God, when he was in the bosom of his Father, descend from his royal throne for her, to deliver her from the power of the devil? When he beheld her bound by the chains of her sins, and on the point of being handed over to demons in order to be condemned to everlasting death, he wept for her who did not even know how to weep for herself. Nor did he weep only, but allowed himself to be slain, in order to redeem her with the precious price of his blood. Look to it, mortal man, for whom so great a sacrifice has been made; recognize the nobility of your soul; realize how grievous were her wounds, for it was necessary that Christ the Lord suffer wounds for her. If her wounds had not been unto death, yes, unto everlasting death, the Son of God would never have died in order to heal them (*Meditationes piissimae de cognitione humanae conditionis,* c. 3, *de dignitate animae et vilitate corporis,* nn. 7–9, *In Append., PL* 184:489–490).

2021. RICHARD OF ST. VICTOR (d. 1173). I do not know whether it is possible for man to receive anything greater from God in this life; I do not know whether God can bestow a greater grace than that sinful men are changed for the better through the priest's ministry, and from being children of the devil are made sons of God. Perhaps to some it would seem a greater grace to raise the dead to life. But would it really be more to resurrect the body that must die again than to restore to grace the soul that is to live eternally? Would it be truly greater to call the flesh back to the pleasures of the world than to give back the joys of heaven to the spirit? Would it be greater to restore to the body the transitory goods that will again be lost anyway, than to give to the soul the blessings which will last forever? O what an endowment, how great a dignity, to receive such a grace from God! The bride of God (the Church) needed to receive no other dowry from her Bridegroom, nor was it fitting that the heavenly Bridegroom bestow upon his bride any other dowry than that, by the grace of adoption, she could beget many children of God and from among children of anger destined for hell could enroll heirs of the kingdom of heaven (*Benjamin minor,* c. 44, *PL* 196:33).

2022. ST. JOHN CHRYSOSTOM. A. For nothing is so pleasing or so dear to God as the welfare of souls, as the Apostle exclaims: *Who wishes all men to be saved and to come to the knowledge of the truth* (I Tim. 2:4). Elsewhere the Lord himself says: *I desire not the death of the wicked, but that the wicked turn from his way, and live* (Ezech. 33:11). . . . Having over us such a Lord, so merciful and benign, let us devote ourselves to our own spiritual care and that of our brethren. Just as the soul is superior to the body, so they who by admonishing and continually teaching lead the fallen and slothful along the right way, showing them the beauty of the divine virtues and the foulness and ill will of vices, merit a richer reward than those who offer money and worldly substance to the indigent (*Hom. 3 in Gen.*, c. 1, § 4, *PG* 53:36–37). B. How many things Christ suffered for this flock [*Feed my lambs . . . feed my sheep* (John 21:15 ff.)]. He became Man; he took upon himself the form of a servant; he was spat upon; he was struck with blows; finally, he did not even refuse death, and a most ignominious death it was; he poured forth his blood on the cross! If anyone desires to stand high in his esteem, let him have care of his sheep, let his great concern be the welfare of many, let him work to procure the welfare of his brethren. No office is more precious in God's sight than this (*De beato Philogonio, Hom. 6,* § 2, *PG* 48:751). C. So that it is an angelic work to do all for the salvation of the brethren; or rather, it is the work of Christ himself, for he indeed saves as Lord, but they as servants (*Hom. 3 in Ep. ad Heb.*, § 2, *PG* 63:30). D. Care of the brethren is the whole of Christian life; by this mark one is recognized as a Christian; . . . it is the greatest evidence of faith; . . . it is genuine charity (*Serm. 9 in Gen.*, § 2, *PG* 54:623). E. For nothing contributes so much toward making us followers of Christ as caring for our neighbors (*Hom. 25 in I Cor.*, § 3, *PG* 61:208).

2023. ST. JEROME. Seeking men's welfare is a pleasing sacrifice to God (*Comm. in Evangel. Matt., Lib. II,* c. 12, § 3, *PL* 26:76).

2024. ST. GREGORY OF NAZIANZUS. God rejoices in nothing so much as in the amendment and salvation of man, on whose behalf every discourse is uttered and every sacrament administered; so that we may become lights to the world (cf. Phil. 2:15), a living form to all other men (*Oratio 39, In sancta lumina,* § 20, *PG* 36:359).

2025. ST. LAURENCE JUSTINIAN. There is nothing greater nor more pleasing to the Word than the sacrifice of working to win souls (*De casto connubio Verbi et animae*, c. 12, *Op. Om.* 1:207).

Priestly zeal for souls

2026. ST. AMBROSE. A. The priest who strives to preserve the purity of the Church incorrupt must possess zeal (*Expos. in Ps. 118, serm. 18*, § 11, *PL* 15:1532). B. By zeal Jerusalem is liberated, by zeal the Church is assembled, by zeal faith is acquired, by zeal purity is possessed (*ibid.*, § 15, col. 1533).

2027. ST. JOHN CHRYSOSTOM. A. For if each man's welfare depends on his neighbor's safety . . . and if our care that we exercise for our neighbor is the welfare of the whole body, it follows that our glory and our sadness must be common (*Hom. 31 in I Cor.*, §§ 2, 3, *PG* 61:260–261). B. For I am not myself able to believe that it is possible for one who has never done anything for the salvation of souls to be saved (*De sacerdotio, Lib. VI*, c. 10, *PG* 48:686).

2028. DENIS THE CARTHUSIAN (d. 1473). Let us seek always to be kindled with zeal for the honor of God and the welfare of our brother (*Enarr. in c. 5 Ep. B. Jacobi*, art. 7, *Op. Om.* 13:610).

2029. IMITATION OF CHRIST (Thomas à Kempis). First, therefore, have a zealous regard to yourself and your own soul, and then you may more righteously and with better ordered charity have zeal for your neighbor's soul (*De imitatione Christi, Lib. II*, c. 3, *Op. Om.* 2:64; Gardiner, p. 79).

2030. ST. LAURENCE JUSTINIAN. The commendably right order of zeal is this: first correct yourself, and then others (*De vita solitaria*, c. 4, *Op. Om.* 2:132).

2031. ST. BERNARD. Let charity render your zeal ardent, wisdom rule and direct it; let constancy make it enduring. Let it be free from lukewarmness, not timid, not wanting in discretion (*Serm. 20 in Cant.*, § 4, *PL* 183:868; Eales, p. 111).

2032. ST. ALBERT THE GREAT. True and perfect zeal for souls lies in the performance of good works for the welfare of souls by means of holy meditations, fervor of desire for their progress, tears, prayers, fasting, preaching, hearing confessions, giving counsel, teaching, and other virtuous efforts (*Paradisus animae, Pars I*, c. 26, *Op. Om.* 37:486).

Preaching

2033. ST. GREGORY THE GREAT. He who is preparing himself for the words of true preaching must of necessity derive the pattern of the appeals he is going to present from the pages of Holy Scriptures, so as to make everything that he speaks rest on a foundation of divine authority, and in that setting make firm the evidence of his own speaking (*Moral., Lib. 18*, c. 26, § 39, *PL* 76:58).

2034. GILBERT OF HOILAND, Cistercian abbot of St. Mary's, diocese of Lincoln (d. 1172). A. As you are a man of the Gospel, speak entirely as from the Gospel (*In Cant., serm. 16,* § 5, *PL* 184:83).

B. The word of God both enlightens and inflames (*Serm. 24,* § 2, col. 126).

2035. ST. PETER DAMIAN. The words of the Lord are like fire, for they cast coldness out of hearts and instill warmth; they are like a hammer, too, for they soften the hardness of obstinacy and stubbornness (*Opusc. 31, contra philargyriam,* c. 7, *PL* 145:541).

2036. ST. ISIDORE OF SEVILLE. The priest's preaching must be confirmed by his deeds, so that what he teaches by word he is to illustrate by example. That teaching is true which the preacher's manner of living puts into practice. For nothing is more shameful than for one to fail to practice in his deeds the good that he preaches by his words. A sermon is fruitfully preached only when it is effectively fulfilled (*Sententiarum Lib. III,* c. 36, § 2, *PL* 83:707).

2037. HUGH OF ST. CHER, O.P. He is a wise preacher who devotes greater attention to his deeds than to his words; for his actions are words heard in silence; after he ends his sermon, he continues to preach by his deeds (*Sup. I Thess., 1, 8, Comment.* 7:196).

2038. ST. PETER DAMIAN. Whoever incites others to take up the [spiritual] warfare by carrying out the duty of preaching that has been enjoined on him, but who does not engage in the combat himself, is like him who blows loudly on the trumpet to summon others to battle but does not have the courage to enter the fighting at close quarters. He who is a cowardly father does not beget a manly offspring (*Lib. IV, ep. 15, ad V., episc., PL* 144:330).

2039. ST. BONAVENTURE. All preachers are trained to devote their efforts, first to their own perfection, and then to the edification of their neighbor, because, as St. Gregory states, it follows logically that anyone's preaching will be held in contempt if his manner of life is despised (*Expos. in Luc.,* c. 2, *vers. 80,* § 144, *Op. Om.,* ed. Quaracchi 7:43).

2040. ST. THOMAS AQUINAS. No one should take up the office of preacher unless he be already cleansed, and perfect in virtue, according to what is said of Christ, that Jesus began to do and to teach (cf. Acts 1:1). Consequently immediately after his baptism, Christ began to adopt an austere form of life, in order to teach us the need of taming the flesh before passing on to the office of preaching, according to the Apostle: *I chastise my body and bring it into subjection, lest perhaps after preaching to others I myself should be rejected* (I Cor. 9:27; *III,* q. 41, art. 3, ad 1m, *Utrum tentatio Christi debuerit esse post jejunium, Op. Om.* 11:406; Am. ed. 2:2243).

2041. JOHN OF TRITHEIM. If you desire to be a sincere preacher, first do what God commands, then teach others; otherwise, if you should have presumed to teach [virtues] before you have practiced them, you shall be rejected. . . . Worthiness of life is to be sought in preference to doctrine, for a silent good man is more pleasing than a less virtuous one full of words (*Comm. in c. 2 RSB, Op. pia et spiritualia,* p. 229).

2042. ST. BERNARD. If you are wise, you will show yourself to be rather a reservoir than a canal. For a canal spreads abroad water as it receives it, but a reservoir waits until it is filled before overflowing, and thus communicates, without loss to itself, its superabundant water, knowing that there is blame to one who deteriorates that which he receives; and that you may not regard my counsel as to be despised, hear a wiser than I: *A fool uttereth all his mind, but a wise man keepeth it in till afterwards* (Prov. 29:11, Douay version). But in the Church at the present day we have many canals, few reservoirs. Those by whom the dew of heaven distills upon us are of a charity so great that they desire to pour it forth before they are themselves filled with it; they are more prepared to speak than to hear, are quick to teach that which they have not learned, and long to preside over others while they do not as yet know how to govern themselves (*Serm. 18 in Cant., De duabus operationibus Sp. S., quarum una vocatur effusio, altera infusio,* § 3, *PL* 183:860; Eales, p. 101).

2043. HUGH OF ST. CHER, O.P. A. When the truths revealed by the Lord have been chewed in meditation, consumed with love, and assimilated into the blood through the acids of penance and contrition, they give life to our whole being (*Sup. II Thess. 3, 1, Comment.* 7:207). B. The wealth of the Lord consists in poverty, want, hunger, contempt at the hands of others, humility, virtuous conduct, zeal for souls, and the nourishment of doctrine. The preacher must carry these about with him like riches to be bestowed on the poor. In so doing, the more his own life illustrates for his hearers what he preaches, the more quickly will he induce them to follow God. . . . Four things are necessary for a preacher: the example of deeds, the word of doctrine, the lily of chastity, and the perfection of faith (*Sup. Gen. 24, 10, ibid.,* 1:31). C. The preacher must be wise, eloquent, humble, and patient, or else he must not preach (*Sup. Josue 6, 20, ibid.,* 1:182). D. Unless a preacher is filled with virtues as the heavens are studded with stars, unless he is exemplary in his personal life, unless he is clear of doctrine and bowed down with humility, a rebuke from his lips will do more harm than good (*ibid., 10, 41,* p. 185).

2044. ST. JOHN CHRYSOSTOM. No one must undertake the lofty duty of preaching unless he is prepared to expose his soul to death and dangers a thousand times (*Hom. 6, de laudibus S. Pauli Ap., PG* 50:507).

2045. ST. GREGORY THE GREAT. A. He who does not have charity for his neighbor must never undertake the office of preacher (*Hom. 17 in Evangel.*, § 1, *PL* 76:1139). B. Unless he is able to ignite the spark of love, the words of the preacher are in vain (*ibid., Hom. 30,* § 5, col. 1223). C. It is often the case, as we have said previously, that hypocritical preachers are supported by scholarship in the sacred law, that they deliver lessons of instruction, that they substantiate with proofs every statement that they make. But they are not thereby seeking the spiritual life of their hearers, but applause for themselves. For they know how to put forth anything except that which will stir the heart of their hearers to the quick to pay the recompense of praise, not what will kindle them to shed tears [of repentance]. When the heart is preoccupied with external desires, it is not inflamed with the fire of divine love; words that issue from a cold heart can never warm their hearers to heavenly affection (*Moral., Lib. VIII,* c. 26, § 72, *PL* 75:845).

2046. ST. FRANCIS OF ASSISI (d. 1226). The office of preaching is more acceptable to the Father of mercies than any sacrifice, particularly if it is exercised in devotion to charity (*Opusc., collatio 17, de conditionibus et laude boni praedicatoris, Op. Om.*, p. 47).

2047. ST. BONAVENTURE. The teacher of the Gospel must be anointed with divine grace, trained in genuine obedience, inflamed with brotherly love (*Expos. in Evangel. S. Luc., prooem.*, § 3, *Op. Om.*, ed. Quaracchi 7:3).

2048. JOHN OF TRITHEIM. The preacher's sermon which the fire of divine charity ignites is never without fruit (*De regione claustralium, Lib. I, Op. pia et spiritualia,* p. 614).

2049. ST. GREGORY THE GREAT. A. Sacred orators have an exalted vocation, not only by reason of their actual task, but also because of the contemplation it calls for; the more profound part lies in the loftiness of the contemplation, the least part in the actual preaching (*Expos. in I Reg., Lib. V,* c. 4, § 4, *PL* 79:360). B. He is no perfect preacher who either from devotion to contemplation neglects work that ought to be done, or from preoccupation with external activities puts aside the duties of contemplation. . . . Hence it is that the Redeemer of mankind exhibits his miracles in cities during the day, and spends the night in devotion to prayer upon the mountain, namely, that he may teach all perfect preachers that they neither entirely leave the active life from love of the contemplative, nor wholly slight the joys of contemplation from excess in working. He would teach them to imbibe in quiet by contemplation what in their active work they may pour back to their neighbors by word of mouth. For by contemplation they rise into the love of God, but by preaching they return back to the service of their neighbor (*Moral., Lib. VI,* c. 37, § 56, *PL* 75:760). C. I beg you to dwell in daily meditation on the words of your Creator;

learn to know the heart of God in the words of God, in order that you may hope more ardently for things eternal and that your soul may be inflamed with more intense desire for heavenly joys (*Lib. VI, ep. 31, ad Theodorum medicum, PL* 77:706).

2050. ST. AUGUSTINE. A. If God does not by his own inward grace sway and act upon the mind, no preaching of the truth is of any avail (*De civitate Dei, Lib. 15,* c. 6, *PL* 41:442; Dods, p. 484). B. And so, an orator, in speaking of justice, sanctity, and virtue (for he should not preach on other topics), tries, as far as possible, when he is speaking of these matters, to make his words understandable, pleasing, and persuasive. And he should not doubt that he can do this, if it is possible, and as far as it is possible, more through the piety of his prayers than through the power of his oratory. Thus, in praying for himself and for those whom he is about to address, he should be a suppliant before he is a speaker. As the hour when he is to speak is at hand, before he uses his tongue in preaching, he should raise his parched soul to God, that he may utter only that with which he has become imbued and manifest what has inspired him (*De doctrina Christiana, Lib. IV,* c. 15, § 32, *PL* 34:103; Gavigan, p. 197).

2051. ST. FRANCIS OF ASSISI. A. The preacher must first draw from hidden prayer what he wishes to communicate afterward in holy discourse; he must first become inwardly warm himself, or he will afterward speak only cold words. . . . Let the preacher work more by tearful prayer than by extensive speech (*Opusc., collatio 17, de conditionibus et laude boni praedicatoris, Op. Om.,* p. 46). B. In preaching there is a kind of distribution of gifts received from heaven (*Coll. 14, Quid Deo magis placeat, orare vel praedicare,* p. 45).

2052. HUGH OF ST. CHER, O.P. The word of God offers medicine to the sick . . . sight to the blind, bread to the hungry, wine to the thirsty, warmth to him who is cold, protection for those who are under attack, and comfort to the forsaken (*Sup. Ps. 57, 6, Comment.* 2:147. Wolter uses only the topic headings for the paragraphs of the commentary).

2053. ST. BONAVENTURE. The word of God not only guides the mind, arouses the emotions, and makes work perfect, but by introducing to the heavenly glory, it fills up what it has perfected (*Serm. de SS. Evangelistis, II, Op. Om.,* ed. Peltier 14:35).

2054. POPE INNOCENT III (d. 1216). So great is the power of preaching that it calls back the soul from error to truth, and from vices to virtues. It changes what is wrong into what is right; what is harsh and difficult it converts into what is readily accepted. It instructs in faith, builds up hope, strengthens charity. It roots out what is harmful, implants what is helpful, fosters what is upright. It is the way of life, the ladder of salvation, the gate of paradise (*In prologo ad Serm. de temp., PL* 217:311).

2055. ST. JEROME. After the ninth hour [about 3:00 P.M.] they meet together to sing psalms and read the Scriptures according to the custom. Then when the prayers have ended and all have sat down, one who is called the Father stands up among them and begins to expound the [scriptural] passage of the day. While he is speaking the silence is profound; no man ventures to look at his neighbor or to clear his throat. The speaker's praise is in the weeping of his hearers. Silently tears roll down their cheeks, but no sob escapes their lips. Yet when he begins to speak of Christ's kingdom, of future bliss, and of the glory that is to come, everyone may be noticed saying to himself, with a gentle sigh and uplifted eyes: *Had I but wings like a dove, I would fly away and be at rest* (Ps. 54:7; *Ep.* 22, *ad Eustochium,* § 35, *PL* 22:420).

Conversion of peoples

2056. ST. JOHN CHRYSOSTOM. Let us not neglect to make the teaching of the Scriptures known to the peoples, but in so doing we are to devote all our effort in such a way that they are to be brought back to the truth from error. For although they are held captive by errors, they are our brethren, and it is proper that we exercise great solicitude for them, never giving way to sloth, but doing what lies in our power with all earnestness. Let us use an effective medicine for them, even though the illness is far advanced, so that at last they may return to true health. Nothing is so pleasing to God nor of so great a concern as the welfare of souls. . . . Having a Lord who is so merciful, so benign, so meek, let us be intent on working for our own and our brethren's welfare; for this is both a proof of our own salvation and the occasion for procuring it, if we are solicitous not only about ourselves, but are helpful to our neighbor as well, leading him to the way of truth (*Hom. 3 in c. 1 Gen.,* § 4, *PG* 53:36).

2057. ST. BONIFACE, monk, bp. of Mainz, and martyr (d. 755), when about to depart for Frisia, said to St. Lullus: "The day of my death is near at hand, that end at which, God granting, after I have cast off the burden of this flesh, I shall receive the reward of eternal recompense. Devote your efforts zealously, my dearest son, to instructing the people committed to you, in order that you may continue to withdraw them from the deceptive errors of pagan superstition" (*Vita S. Bonfacii,* c. 11, § 33, *PL* 89:626; Mabillon, *Acta SS. O.S.B., saec. III, Pars II,* c. 11, p. 20).

Education of youth

2058. ST. BASIL THE GREAT. A. Inasmuch as the Lord says: *Let the little children come to me* (Mark 10:14), and the Apostle praises him who has known the Holy Scripture from infancy (cf. II Tim. 3:15), and also directs that children be reared *in the discipline and admonition of the Lord* (Eph. 6:4), we deem every time of life, even the very earliest, suitable for receiving applicants. Indeed, those children who are bereft of their parents we should take in on our own initiative, so that we may become fathers of the orphans in emulation of Job (*ibid.,* 29:12). Those who are under their parents' care and who are brought to us by them should be received before many witnesses so as not to give occasion [for blame] to those who are desirous of this, but that every unjust tongue speaking falsely against us may be stopped (cf. Ps. 62:12). They should be received according to this method, but not immediately numbered and reckoned with the body of the community, in order that, in the event of their failing to persevere, they may not afterward heap reproaches on the devout life. They should be reared with all piety as children belonging to the entire community (*Reg. fusius tractatae, Interrogatio 15,* § 1, *PG* 31:951; Wagner, p. 264 f.). B. Their studies, also, should be in conformity with the aim in view. They should, therefore, employ a vocabulary derived from the Scriptures and, in place of myths, historical accounts of admirable deeds should be told them. They should be taught maxims from the Proverbs, and rewards should be held out to them for memorizing names and facts. In this way, joyfully and with a relaxed mind, they will achieve their aim without pain to themselves and without giving offense. . . . While the mind is still easy to mold and as pliable as wax, taking the form of what is impressed upon it, it should be exercised from the very beginning in good discipline. Then, when reason enters in and habits of choice develop, they will take their course from the first elements learned at the beginning, and from traditional forms of piety; reason proposing that which is beneficial and habit imparting facility in right action (*ibid.,* §§ 3, 4, col. 954). C. Is it proper that in a community of brethren there be a master of secular boys? Since the Apostle says: *You, fathers, do not provoke your children to anger; but rear them in the discipline and admonition of the Lord* (Eph. 6:4), if they who offer their children do so with this understanding, and those who receive them be such that they have perfect confidence that they can bring up the children thus offered in the discipline and admonition of the Lord, let that be obeyed which is commanded by the Lord in these words: *Let the little children be, and do not hinder them from coming to me, for of such is the kingdom of heaven* (Matt. 19:14). But without such an understanding and the hope of its being realized, I would consider such would be neither pleasing to God, nor suitable for us, nor helpful (*Reg. brevius tractatae, Interrogatio 292,* col. 1287).

2059. JEAN MABILLON. [Once he had arrived in Denmark to propagate religion], nothing seemed so opportune or useful to St. Anschar for the heralds of the Gospel as the erection of schools in which children might be instructed both in the literature of the region and the mysteries of the Christian faith (*Annales O.S.B., Lib. 29,* n. 79, 2:468).

2060. ST. BASIL THE GREAT. Moreover, one who is advanced in years should be placed in charge of these little ones, a person of more than average experience and who has a reputation for patience. Thus he will correct the faults of the young with fatherly kindness and give wise instruction, applying remedies proper to each fault, so that, while the penalty for the fault is being exacted, the soul may be exercised in interior tranquillity (*Reg. fusius tractatae, Interrogatio 15, § 2, PG* 31:954; Wagner, p. 266).

2061. ST. ISIDORE OF SEVILLE. The care of young boys who are to be taught will belong to him whom the father of the monastery appoints for the task, a holy and wise man of mature age, training the boys not only in the study of letters but also acquainting them with the sources and the doctrine of the virtues (*Reg. monachorum,* c. 19, *Quid ad quem pertineat, CR* 1:196; *PL* 83:891).

2062. ST. BONAVENTURE. It behooves him who assumes the office of striving to make others virtuous to have first learned the discipline of goodness by exercising himself in it zealously, and to have turned his observance into habit by constant practice. Hence we read that the Lord first practiced what he was afterward to teach: *Jesus did and taught* (Acts 1:1; *De sex alis Seraphim,* c. 1, § 1, *Op. Om.,* ed. Quaracchi 8:131).

Danger in the care of souls exercised outside the enclosure

2063. ST. PETER DAMIAN. It often happens that a man who is not satisfied with the good state of his own affairs and concerns himself with the well-being of another is rather, in so doing, forced to take new danger for himself. In a shipwreck, when someone reaches out his arm to a man who is thrashing about in the sea, there is danger that he too will be drawn into the whirling waves. It is safer, therefore, for us in the black-as-night darkness of this life to remain where we are on the shore, and throw out light to the shipwrecked, than to swim out to them in the spirit of compassion, thereby endangering our own lives. In pursuing this course of action, they will reach the sanctuary of a safe port through our directions, and the frothy waves will not claim us as would happen if we actually went out to them.

Moses prayed on the top of Mount Raphidim, while Josue led the

Israelites into battle in the valley below. But had Moses descended to the battlefield personally to aid his people, Amalec would undoubtedly have slaughtered the Jews from behind. If he had so much as begun to arm himself, his people would have been massacred and an easy victory would have fallen to their triumphant enemies. This can be readily seen in a careful reading of that passage of Holy Scripture where it is said: *As long as Moses kept his hands raised up, Israel had the better of the fight, but when he let his hands rest, Amalec had the better of the fight* (Exod. 17:11). His hands in prayer strengthened the hands of the warriors; his hands, although not engaged in the fighting, brought victory over the ruthless enemy to those hands which were in the thick of the fight. The warriors did the fighting, but the victory certainly belonged to Moses. It was given to them to conquer, but the victory was due to Moses' being found worthy of the divine favor. But on the other hand, Balaam, son of Beor, is executed with the sword because he came out with the Madianites, whom Moses had decreed to be slaughtered (Num. 31:8). And rightly so, for he who is not content with the duties of his own office, places himself in another's danger. That foolhardy man who was in a position of peace, deserved to die on an enemy's sword, who got caught in the wedge of hand-to-hand fighters after he had been stationed there to report the outcome of the battle (*Opusc. 12, de contemptu saeculi,* c. 27, *Ut monachus se a mundi implicatione custodiat, PL* 145:280).

Works of charity must not be in opposition to monastic profession

2064. JOHN OF TRITHEIM. We read many tributes of praise of the holy fathers of this religious order [of St. Benedict], which are proposed for our imitation. Great devotion burned in them; praiseworthy zeal for the regular discipline, which never permitted them to be idle, glowed in their hearts. Except for the Divine Office, at which all assisted devoutly, the monks dedicated themselves to study of the Scriptures. By the holy text they were not only enlightened in mind but moved to action. The love which summons the studious from reading to the vigilance of prayer is always vigorous in the exercise of monks.

For during the hours when they were free, those who would further train themselves in the Holy Scriptures devoted their efforts to study and explanation of the text, writing books and treatises, with which they daily stimulated the studies of their brethren and directed those studies to God. Other brothers, in conformity with the Rule, were not given to idleness, but after prayers spent their time in manual labor. Those who were capable of doing so, transcribed books and prepared clean copies of what had been edited by the learned monks on slips of paper. Some bound manuscripts artistically, others corrected them, others again ornamented the books with red coloring. No one failed to have his part in this sacred duty, and all rejoiced to be sharers in the studies conducted for explaining the Scriptures (*De viris illustribus O.S.B., Lib. I,* c. 6, *Op. pia et spiritualia,* p. 21).

2065. ST. JOHN CHRYSOSTOM. Come to me, and I will show you the places of refuge of these holy men; come and learn something useful from them. Shining lamps are these in every part of the earth. They are set as walls about cities. For this cause they have occupied the deserts, that they may instruct you to despise the tumult in the midst of the world. For they, as being strong, are able even in the midst of the raging waters to enjoy a calm; but you, who are disturbed on every side, need to seek tranquillity, and to take breath a little, after the successive waves. Go there continually, that, having purged away the abiding strain by their prayers and admonitions, you may both pass in the best manner the present life, and attain to the good things to come (*Hom. 72 in Matt.,* § 4, *PG* 58:672).

SEVENTH PRINCIPLE

Government of the Monastery, Spiritual Direction of the Individual

I. STATEMENT OF PRINCIPLE

Constitution and general character of the monastic family

2066. We now approach the final principle of the monastic life, the consideration of its form and constitution. The importance and seriousness of this study are evident in that the constitution of the monastic unit preserves and defends the whole life of the community which it ordains and establishes. For this reason the Lord willed to give his Church a constitution based on his own authority; the Church had to be just as firmly and divinely established as her truth and her means of grace. The enemies of the Church have striven no less stubbornly to overthrow or at least to upset her constitution than they have sought to destroy her doctrine: their policy has rested on the correct conviction that they could bring about the ruin of the Church through the destruction of her constitution.*

For this reason the Holy Spirit has, in the course of time, strengthened more and more and clarified both the doctrine and the constitution of the Church, the election of the Pope, the appointment of bishops, the infallibility of St. Peter's see.

Similarity of the monastic order's constitution with that of the Church

2067. Since the monastic order's whole way of life is so intimately bound up with that of the Church, one might readily assume that their forms of constitution would bear a marked resemblance and be intimately connected. But in order to perceive this relationship clearly we must examine accurately the precise nature of a monastery's government. In the holy *Rule of St. Benedict* there is concern with one community only, a single family. The character and law which St. Benedict gives to that family are such that they embrace every phase of the monastic life and constitution of the order. What is a monastery according to the mind and spirit of our lawgiver? It is nothing other than the Church in miniature. It bears its likeness to the Church in all points. The monastery is a family of God. With sharp clarity the holy Rule places this characteristic mark at the very center of all its considerations.

Appointment of the abbot as the father of the family

2068. The monastery is a group of sons who serve the Supreme King under their spiritual father. This father is not raised to the position and spiritual dignity of fatherhood without the intervention and special cooperation of God. Under the workings of divine grace he has long before been predetermined as it were in the hearts of the monks, for they consider him worthy of the dignity of spiritual fatherhood in preference to their other confreres and have already mani-

* Examples: Byzantinism, which led in the West to Gallicanism, "which tended chiefly to a restraint of the pope's authority in the Church in favor of that of the bishops and the temporal ruler" (A. Degert, "Gallicanism," in *Catholic Encyclopedia* 6:351); Josephinism, ". . . the craving among secular princes after an episcopal and territorial church . . . the supremacy of the State over the Church," (H. Franz, "Joseph II," § 3, *ibid.*, 8:509); Liberalism, ". . . a systematic persecution of Christianity and especially of the Catholic Church and her institutions, a frivolous disregard and even a mocking contempt of the Divine moral order . . ." (Herm. Gruber, "Liberalism," § 3, *ibid.*, 9:213).

fested their evidences of unusual esteem and respect for him. After the election has been held, the Church confirms their choice and seals it in heaven's name with a solemn blessing [modern terminology tends often to refer to the abbatial blessings as a consecration: the terminology of the *Pontificale Romanum* is here retained throughout]. This blessing communicates to the father of the monks, in the bestowal of jurisdiction and authority, a share in God's own paternity.

The most solid foundation on which the monastic family operates is thus laid and a strong and secure support given for discipline and the practice of charity. From the abbatial blessing there derives, in the first place, that venerable and sacred name of "abbot" for the father of the monastic community.* This form of address held a profound significance for the holy Patriarch; he admonished the abbot never to forget what his title implies (*RSB,* c. 2). He wants to indicate that in this word are contained essential and important considerations for the monastic state, so that the abbot fully measures up to his duty only if he is in reality the father of his monks.

The abbot is elected for life

2069. A further consequence follows: the abbot is elected for life and endowed with life-long authority and jurisdiction. Even in the natural order fatherhood is not for a given time only. It forms so lasting a bond of relationship and of belonging together that the relation between father and son can never be broken. This general law is of even greater validity in the case of spiritual fatherhood, since it stems not from physical considerations, but is rooted in the soul itself, whose immortality it is permitted to share. Hence not only the common father of all the faithful, the pope, whom the Christian world venerates and loves as a father, and after him bishops and pastors, but abbots too as fathers of monks, possess their fatherhood forever, in order that with full right the monastic family be not deprived of the very foundation on which it is built.

The abbot's fatherhood is divinely bestowed

2070. This life-long fatherhood of the abbot is not incorrectly called his stability. For father and son must both have stability of such a character that only death can sever the bond which unites them both to the monastery.† Were stability wanting to either father or son, it

* The abbot's title is one of holiness. "Abba" is one of the few words taken from the Gospel as spoken by the holy lips of Jesus, and preserved today in the same form and sound in which they were originally pronounced in Aramaic (cf. Mark 14:36).

† St. Benedict holds stability in such high esteem that he wishes it to be strengthened for his sons by a vow. That this vow has belonged from the beginning

would be impossible for a family of God to possess permanence. It could neither strike root nor flourish if the soil were constantly changed. The monastic fatherhood of the abbot, of which we are speaking, like the other *charismata* of the Church, and like *every good gift and every perfect gift is from above, coming down from the Father of Lights, with whom there is no change, nor shadow of alteration* (Jas. 1:17). This fatherhood with all its rights and duties is, in a sense, imparted from heaven and indelibly engraved as a spiritual grace in the hearts of monks and the abbot, shining with the light of faith.

Mutual love of father and son

2071. It is from these considerations that the mutual devotion of father and son derives which contributes so powerfully to the perfection of charity. It grows constantly until it attains to the full maturity of a sacred love. From the same source there flows abundantly that divine power which in great measure lightens the burdens and the obligations of monastic life, and bestows peace of soul, confidence, and delicacy of conscience, which are characteristic of monks. But most important of all, its holds pernicious ambition in check and keeps at a distance whatever can endanger harmony and tranquillity.* It gives the abbot the possibility of fulfilling his pastoral office with calmness and prudence, the opportunity of venturing on more important undertakings which call for greater time and sustained effort. Let us add further that the life-long tenure of the abbatial office about which we have spoken is both established by the definite authority of the holy Rule and the Doctors of the Church's law,† and follows of necessity from the very nature of the family.

---

of the order to the monastery or to the claustral community, which the holy Father calls a "congregation" is sufficiently evident (*RSB,* c. 4, concluding paragraph, and c. 58).

* Suarez, the great Jesuit Doctor, has this to say: "When superiorships (prelacies) are conferred by election, morally speaking, it seems more prudent for them to be permanent, or of quite long duration . . . because of the evils and dangers which seem so inherent in elections, granted human weakness and ambition, so that it seems more difficult to avoid them than those which result from the perpetuity or long protracted superiorship" (*Tract. 8, Lib. II,* c. 7, *An praelatio religionis perpetua sit, quantove tempore durare possit aut debeat,* § 7, *Op. Om.* 16:132).

Benedict brought the institute in which the abbot assumes his duties for life into the West from the Orient. An abbot appointed for a specific period of time could no more be imagined in that mentality than a temporary bishop. This understanding of the matter stood unchallenged for more than a thousand years. In the fifteenth century Louis Barbo made bold to abandon it, because, as he states, only in such a program could the monastic order escape the miserable and calamitous condition of *in commendam* abbeys (*cf.* Tamburinus, *De jure abbatum,* tom. 1, disp. 1, q. 2, n. 28).

† Then too, there was the added reason that at Venice the rise of the excessively republican form of government favored temporary appointments. The monastic

The abbot's first duty: the begetting and rearing of sons in the spiritual order

2072. His first obligation is the training of new sons of God for the family in the spirit of the Gospel and the holy Rule. Called by divine grace, the novice who enters the cloister must be born anew, so to speak, unto the monastic life and become a son of a particular abbot, a brother to a particular group of monks, a member of a particular family. With this objective in view, it must be the abbot's first duty and principal effort to see to it that the novice acquire the spirit and character of the family, impress its features on himself, and mold the talents and ability he brings to the monastic life into harmony with this character. For the monastery is the loving mother, *alma mater,* of the future monk, and the abbot is his father in a full and true sense. The abbot must, therefore, exercise care that the new sons adopt the monastic family's spirit in order to live with the brethren in the harmony of oneness of heart and soul.

2073. From these considerations it is manifestly appropriate for each monastery to have its own novitiate, in order that the novice may, so to speak, become the son of the abbot of his own distinctive monastic family.* Once he has become a monk by making holy profession, which

congregations of Spain and Portugal followed this example of Italy for similar reasons. But whenever the *in commendam* appointments were excluded and the free election of abbots was preserved intact, as in Germany, Switzerland, Holland, Hungary, and Poland, the perpetual character of the abbot's election ordinarily remained unquestioned. Even Van Espen, although most inimical to the liberty of monks, acknowledged: "In antiquity the prelates of monasteries or abbots seem to have been perpetual, or for life, nor is there mention in any ancient monastic rule or constitution about abbots or abbesses holding office for a period of three years" (*Zegerus Bernardus Van Epsen, Jus Ecclesiasticum Universum, Pars I,* tit. 31, *de monasteriorum superioribus,* c. 1, § 15, tom. 1:305; Coloniae Agrippinae: Metternich, 1777). From these considerations two points seem worthy of note: First, it is improbable that a number will be found in the claustral family who are possessed of all the virtues needed for fulfilling the office of abbot commendably well; secondly, an abbot chosen for life becomes more skilled and capable day by day for discharging his duties, more accurately appreciates the character and talent of his subjects, and grows in the ability to govern. He thus takes possession of his office and administers it as a father. The ring he wears is the symbol of lifelong and inviolable fidelity.

* It follows from what has been said that only when he is compelled by some real necessity can the abbot send to another monastery for their novitiate training the sons whom God has led to him. For it is well established that the holy Rule and the whole early history of monasticism demand that every monastery have its own novitiate.

It was only from the time when the simple, broad concept of the family began gradually to be forgotten that the institute of the common novitiate was adopted in some monastic congregations, or rather was introduced into them from outside the monastic environment. For the common novitiate derives its origin from the

the Fathers call a second baptism, and, to continue the symbolism, has been reborn and presented as a son to the monastery, the new monk is in no sense withdrawn from the care-laden direction of the abbot. For education follows upon birth, and in its process the newly-begotten son is only gradually trained unto the maturity of monastic asceticism and sacred studies. It is obvious that this education belongs also to the office of the spiritual father. Hence the abbot must both personally instruct the monastic family by means of frequent conferences and direct the scholasticate of the younger members and the whole program of studies with paternal concern. It is the duty of the father to lead the family with vigilant eye and heart, to ordain, direct, and dispose everything in the wisest manner in God's house. The abbot must bestow care not only on temporal concerns; as the father of the family he must preside at all regular exercises; but more than all else he must make himself available for aiding his sons in their spiritual life with counsel, solace, and help in whatever manner he can.

The quasi-episcopal dignity of the abbot

2074. The threefold office which holy Church enjoins on the abbot involves spiritual fatherhood, the duty of education and the power of government. To this abbatial office a still greater power is added today. The Church numbers the abbot among her prelates, honors him with a dignity which resembles that of bishops, and thereby exalts and ennobles his office in an extraordinary manner. This grants him a share in the threefold office of Christ, whose place he holds, namely that of priest, teacher, and king. He presides in pontifical vestments at the divine worship and fills the house with every blessing and grace, and leads his people like a flock under the care of Moses and Aaron (Ps. 76:21).

What kind of man the abbot should be

2075. The abbot must, first of all, be filled with the fear of the Lord. He must always remember that he must give a strict account of the administration of his authority—a consideration that the holy Patriarch impresses upon him repeatedly. He is not an absolute lord over his subjects, but the servant of God, the representative and steward of the Eternal Father before whom he must soon stand in judgment. Hence he is always to be guided by the will of God and not his own pleasure. The divine will is his sacred law and norm. It is by fulfilling it with complete fidelity that the abbot personally observes the

religious congregations which, since they are without personal stability, are set up, not so much as families, as military squadrons of spiritual troops specifically designed to wage war against the enemies of the Church. Obviously for them the common novitiate seems preferable.

monastic vow of obedience. "May God's kingdom, not my desires, become a reality; not my will, but yours be done!" Such is the mentality, the manner of speaking, and the prayer of the conscientious abbot. The mitre has far more in common with a crown of thorns than a symbol of honor for him. It is a warning to care for his flock rather than an incentive to preside over them. Since he is what he is by God's grace, he looks only to the Lord, the source of his fatherhood, and formulates his intention: "That God may be glorified in all things!" (*RSB*, c. 57.)

The abbot's humility and simplicity

2076. For this reason the abbot's office is founded on the perfect humility of mind and heart; it is characterized by holy simplicity, in order for him to seek only God's honor and to work for the cause of Jesus Christ and his Church. Because he thinks lowly of himself and avoids all ostentation, the more he is honored, the more he feels himself humbled. He must refer all marks of respect to him whose unworthy instrument he knows himself to be.

Love of God and solicitude for his own soul

2077. From this fear of the Lord and from unfeigned humility a holy love of God is certain to flower. More pointedly applicable to the abbot than to any other person is that saying of the Lord: *Seek first the kingdom of God and his justice, and all these things shall be given you besides* (Matt. 6:33). Even before care for his sons the father must seek God first, striving in all earnestness for his own personal sanctification and salvation. Like a shepherd watching over his sheep from an elevation, the abbot is to devote his efforts to guarding over his monks from the watchtower of prayer and vivid consciousness of God's presence. He must be a living example for his flock, as well as their protector. He must allow nothing to divert him from practicing faith, hope, and charity. Such must be his way of life that his sons may look to him and say: *He himself is our peace* (Eph. 2:14); he is in all truth *the fragrance of Christ* (II Cor. 2:15). He will then govern without disturbance, and like a good shepherd calmly lead his flock; in fact, he will be more like a guardian angel to them. *Dost thou love me?* the Lord asked Peter. And when Peter answered in the affirmative, the Lord commanded him: *Feed my sheep* (John 21:15–17).

The abbot's love for his sons

2078. If the abbot has a son's love for God, then he will love his own sons as a father. As God's chosen one, holy and beloved, he puts on a heart of mercy, kindness, humility, meekness, patience (cf. Col. 3:12). His pure love as a father, which impels him to guard his sons day and night with paternal concern, and even with the tender anxiety of a mother, has a certain similarity both with the eye of the dove and the sharp sight of the eagle. Austere toward himself only, the abbot becomes all things to all men. In union with the divine Shepherd the abbot calls out: *Come to me, all you who labor and are burdened, and I will give you rest . . . learn from me, for I am meek and humble of heart . . . For my yoke is easy, and my burden light* (Matt. 11:28–30). He reminds himself of the Apostle's warning: *It is God's minister to thee for good* (Rom. 13:4). His pastoral staff continually drips with the dew of heaven's blessing.

Fatherly correction

2079. If a wound is to be healed, the abbot must not neglect to pour on the oil of clemency after using the wine of correction. He tempers the severity of the master with the loving clemency of the father, in order that his son may mend his ways and be able to say rejoicingly: *Your rod* (which has chastized me) *and your staff* (which has defended me) . . . *give me courage* (Ps. 22:4).

Spiritual leadership

2080. To the virtues that have already been mentioned, the devoted abbot will add an out-of-the-ordinary wisdom, prudence, and moderation. He has the duty of teaching his sons the way of the Lord, by which they are to attain purity of heart, the light of wisdom, and mystical union with the Supreme Good. It is also his duty to explain correctly and fundamentally the meaning and spirit of the holy Rule. He must allow exceptions and grant exemptions from the observance of its precepts with a holy discretion and moderation. He is to imitate in all things the infinite mercy and loving kindness of Jesus and his heavenly Father. Finally, he must govern his family with all patience. He is to be the standard-bearer and the cross-bearer for his sons—a truth of which his pectoral cross must ever remind him—and seek first to implant in his own heart the symbol of salvation before he strives to bring others under its authority. In patience he will be the master of his own and his sons' souls, whose eternal salvation is best procured at the foot of the cross and before the tabernacle.

The paternal or domestic power of the abbot

2081. Let us examine the nature of the abbot's authority very briefly. From the fact that he is the father of his monks, it follows that he holds paternal authority in such a way that the entire government of the monastery depends solely on his judgment and power. The persons and property of the monastery repose in his fatherly hands. Every decision regarding them and all authority over them belongs to him alone. In making his decisions he is bound only by his own conscience.

Perfect monarchy

2082. It is understandable, therefore, that the whole monastic constitution is made to revolve about this paternal-monarchical perfection of authority. What is true of every family is eminently true of the family of God, whether we consider the one in heaven or the one on earth (the Church, the diocese, the parish, the monastery): it is always a perfect monarchy in which all are governed by one only authority, either by God personally or through his representative. Hence the abbot's authority is unrestricted, except by what God's law and the rules of the Church and the order impose on him. Surely it is evident that if the sons could give orders to their father or place limitations on his mode of action, the family life would be undermined and its well-being destroyed. From these considerations the system of government by which our holy Patriarch wants the monastery to be ruled can readily be appreciated.

The abbot freely appoints his officials

2083. It goes without saying that the abbot cannot in person fulfil all the offices required in the management of the community. Hence he appoints certain officials as helpers in his duties. Among these the prior holds the first place. He is the closest associate and assistant of the abbot in his works. When the abbot is absent or prevented from taking an active part in the life of the community, the prior presides over the monastery. He must watch over it with all care to make certain that regular observance suffer no harm. When the prior must have a substitute, the subprior of the monastery takes over for him.

For training and instructing the candidates the master of novices functions as a most trusted helper of the abbot. His appointment is of the gravest importance and significance in the sense that all future promise of harvest is in the seed. The novice master should be a sort of pattern for molding the hearts of the disciples entrusted to him and forming them into a likeness to the Sacred Heart of Jesus. Through a most conscientious observance of the holy Rule his life must be the worthiest possible example of what a monk should be. By the force of good example, with all humility and gentleness, in holiness and patience, he is to develop the novices into obedient and happy sons for God and for the abbot. He must be a man of great love for souls and dedicated to the task of impressing this truth on his charges: God is yours, and you are God's.

The cellarer

2084. The cellarer represents the abbot in conducting the temporal affairs of the monastery. It is his duty to administer the temporalities conscientiously, to procure, distribute, and properly care for everything needed for life in the monastery. He is to conduct all business transactions outside the abbey in the fear of God, and according to the principles of justice, religion, and prudence.

Other minor officials

2085. To help him fulfil his onerous duties cheerfully, the cellarer is given several assistants. Among them are the procurator,* the steward, the treasurer, the one who procures clothing, distributes it, and sees to its repair, the monk in charge of the kitchens, the overseer of farms and gardens, and others. To mention all the customary officials of the monastery we should include the infirmarian, the guestmaster, the almoner, the instructor and master of the converse brothers, the master of ceremonies, the head chanter, the sacristan, the secretary of the chapter, the archivist, the chancellor, and the librarian. Each of these monks must assume and perform his respective assignment as an obedient son, under the direction and leadership of his abbot. None of them should undertake anything except in accordance with the abbot's will.

Annual re-appointment of offices

2086. All these persons are removable from office, not only at the abbot's discretion, but in keeping with a well-established monastic custom by which all officials are formally released of their responsibilities once a year [usually at the time of the community's annual retreat: as far as is known this custom is nowhere in use in the United States]. After a few days new appointees are named, or the old ones confirmed, as the abbot sees fit. During these days of the vacancy of the offices, the whole government of the monastery actually resides in the abbot's hands. It is remarkable to observe how great a light and what sacredness this practice bestows on the authority of the father of the monastery.

2087. In addition to the support the abbot receives from all these persons in bearing his responsibilities, the abbot is provided another form of assistance. Although it remains true that he directs everything on his own authority, he nevertheless summons the members of the

* Monasticism in the New World has not yet got round to pinpointing all these tasks so nicely, although they are jealously retained in European abbeys. American men and women in charge of these duties would be astounded to hear themselves referred to as officials. They are given the responsibility of seeing that certain tasks are properly performed, usually in addition to their regular work: a teacher will double as guestmaster, the novice master may be sacristan, whoever can best get the job done will probably be put in charge of the choir, and so on. The indulgence of Latin purists is here (as elsewhere) petitioned in the endeavor to make these terms intelligible. [*Tr.*]

family for deliberation and counsel whenever a question of more serious concern arises. He is impelled to do so by the very nature of the family, by custom and by his fatherly concern which is bolstered in the unanimity and agreement of the brethren.

Council of the seniors

2088. Two monastic institutions have arisen as a result of the abbot's consulting the brethren: the ordinary council, and the extraordinary council of the abbot. The former has more or less the nature of a senate of the monastery. In the latter, or the council of the seniors (usually only five or six in number), half the members are appointed annually by the abbot, and the other half is elected by the community. The abbot regularly assembles these counselors, monks distinguished for their practical experience and wisdom, in order to deliberate on matters of necessity and practical utility for the family.* This senate bears a marked resemblance to the college of canons whom bishops have for their counsel.† In the other, the extraordinary council, the entire monastic family [that is, all monks permanently attached to the monastery through the profession of solemn vows], is assembled.

* Modern Statutes and Declarations to the Holy Rule confirmed by the Sacred Congregation of Religious since the publication of the *Code of Canon Law* specify these purposes accurately. Thus the Declarations of the American Cassinese Congregation state: "The seniors, or counselors, are five in number, namely: the prior, the subprior, the procurator, and two others to be elected annually by the chapter. In non-abbatial monasteries they are three in number: the subprior, the procurator, and one to be elected annually by the chapter. The superior shall hold counsel with the seniors about business to be proposed to the chapter, about more important matters, and expenditures of money over and above the ordinary needs in an amount to be determined by the general chapter [of the entire monastic congregation, which sum is currently fixed at amounts between $1,000 and $6,000]. About once a month the superior shall consult with the seniors regarding the furtherance of virtue and regular observance in the monastery. The seniors should realize that in this particular they ought to excel the rest. Matters requiring the consent of the seniors given by secret vote are: the dismissal of a religious in temporary vows; the dismissal of a religious in solemn vows in case of grave scandal (*Code of Canon Law*, canons 653 and 668 ff.); extraordinary expenditures; . . . the contracting of a debt in any amount; . . . the disposal of land not requiring the consent of the conventual chapter; investments in any amount (*The Holy Rule of our most holy Father Benedict . . . with Declarations and Constitutions of the American Cassinese Congr.*, pp. 19–20). [*Tr.*]

† This is another institution of the Church's common law (*Code of Canon Law*, c. 391 ff.) which has not as yet been introduced into the United States. In this country the diocesan consultors (*ibid.*, cc. 423 ff.), "priests excelling in piety, worthiness of life, learning, and prudence," substitute in all matters of giving counsel and consent, for the college of canons. [*Tr.*]

The brethren are summoned for counsel

2089. It is wholly reasonable, and for a good father it is a matter of necessity, to call together all his sons and seek their advice in sacred confidence and charity, when important and weighty matters affecting the family at large are under consideration. These sons should express their views with childlike and humble candor. They will take care to show all due respect and submissiveness to their father. If he governs in a truly worthy manner, and is dispassionate and calm, and if the spirit of the sons is in harmony with virtuous zeal and the hierarchical order of the family, then it will necessarily follow from such common discussion that minds will be united and hearts and souls formed into a unity.*

The abbot is the ordinary of the monks

2090. From what has been stated about the paternal authority of the abbot, it is evident that his power is not delegated, but ordinary, and that it is highly appropriate that he be immediately subject to the Supreme Pontiff.

Autonomy of the individual monastery

2091. With this thought we conclude the presentation of the bold lines of the sacred nature of the monastic government according to our understanding of the text and the spirit of the *Rule of St. Benedict.* As has already been stated, the Rule contemplates an individual monastery and gives it only one single, independent, complete system of government. Thus the monastery is a sole organism which contains within itself everything, both as to substance and form, that belongs to completeness and to the closed corporation character of the monastic life. It will also be recalled, in this connection, that the Patriarch, St. Benedict, prescribed that whatever is needed to sustain life should, as far as is possible, be found within the confines of the monastery it-

* Read the *Rule of St. Benedict,* Chapter Three, for St. Benedict's excellent statement of the principles involved. It is true, of course, that subsequent provisions of Canon Law have withdrawn certain matters from the exclusive control of the abbot and made them subject to the consent of the community manifested by means of secret ballot. This is the case particularly in connection with financial matters and in the admission of candidates to the novitiate and to temporary profession. These exceptions really serve rather to emphasize the general principle of the abbot's unrestricted authority than to lessen its force [or, to word the thought in technical language, it emphasizes the usually consultive- rather than the decisive-vote character of the conventual chapter's deliberations]. So foreign is it to the mind of the Church to restrict the free government by the abbot that these modifications [of *RSB,* c. 3] should be considered wise provisions to protect the monastic constitution from dangers and abuses.

self, thus emphasizing the thought of completeness even in externals (cf. *RSB*, cc. 57, 66).

Monasteries develop into monastic congregations

2092. But even with all these provisions, the constitution of the monastic way of life is as yet not brought to its fullest fruition. As in the case of the natural family, so in its counterpart, the supernaturally constituted cenobitic family, the monastery grows and spreads out. In time it sends forth members to found new families which remain, at least for a while, dependent on the mother abbey. This is the origin of the monastic congregation, or union of abbeys, in much the same manner as the gradual spread of natural families is the origin of clans or community relationship. The pattern of this growth takes us back to the very beginnings of the order's history. When God assigned St. Benedict to the high office of lawgiver for the monastic life, he sent so many disciples to him that his foundation at Subiaco was soon too small. The man of God then sent twelve of them forth to found a new monastery, and to set up the same discipline as that of the parent monastery. At the same time he appointed a father for them, conferring on him the rights and duties of an abbot.

2093. Our holy Father repeated this process of making foundations twelve times in and about Subiaco. In this action we have a sort of prototype of the monastic congregation. It consisted of a mother-abbey and a circle of daughter abbeys, a group of new abbots gathered about their common father, St. Benedict, the Patriarch. By virtue of having established a separate foundation, he was not thereby alienated from his former subjects, but remained their devoted father, holding in his heart a deep love for all his sons, and particularly for the abbots. He continued to watch over them all, prayed for them, continued to be solicitous for them, was ever ready to help them, instruct them, warn them, and, if the need arose, to lead them back to the right way when they had wandered from it. It hardly seems difficult to recognize in this first composition of the monastic congregation a pattern that monasteries must continue now to follow. Before all else it is definitely established that the monastic congregation arises from a real relationship of a sacred family and that it is wholly patriarchal in character, and not, as is so often the case in our day, merely constitutional and legal. For the monastic congregation to have hope for a fruitful life, it is necessary that it build on a sort of spiritual birth, or a spiritual rebirth.*

* We speak properly of a rebirth in the case of a monastery which unites itself to a mother abbey of a stricter observance and by that act is, as it were, reborn as its daughter to a new life of holiness.

It is obvious that Archabbot Wolter's concern in underscoring the essential

2094. A recently founded monastery needs to retain its spiritual dependence on the abbey from which it has taken its origin. Certainly no one can question the right of the mother abbey to be cherished with a filial attachment and regard. But this loving mother has for her spouse the abbot of the founding abbey. He is mystically united with her, and hence, together with the founding abbey, is the protector of its offspring. Since he is, in virtue of his mystical union with his abbey, truly the head of the congregation, and is thereby endowed with the dignity and authority of a father, who would not think it proper that he also be honored with the name of father?

2095. Let us direct our attention to Holy Church, the pattern and mirror of all spiritual and hierarchical order. In it the pope is the supreme bishop and father of all. The head of a province is the metropolitan or the archbishop, who is the father not only of the faithful who belong to the metropolitan see, but also of the suffragan bishops. And this relationship is already determined in the very process of setting up the ecclesiastical province. When he is sent by the Supreme Pontiff to spread the light of the faith far and wide, the first bishop makes provisions for new episcopal sees as they become necessary. The bishops of these new sees are subject to him as their archbishop, and his church is the metropolitan or mother church (cf. *Catech. Concil. Tridentini, Pars II*, c. 7, *de sacram. ordinis*, § 26, p. 247). The archbishop enjoys certain rights of authority over the suffragan churches. In much the same manner that an ecclesiastical province comes into being, a monastic province or congregation also arises, so that this relationship is another instance in which monastic life harmonizes with that of the Church.

2096. If, then, the abbots in the order have a certain similarity with bishops in the metropolitan province, it seems logical that the

---

nature of monastic congregations and declaring affiliations was a great deal more significant and practical when he was in the process of establishing Beuron than in today's well-defined legal status of the Confederation of Black Benedictines. This remark in no way intends to minimize the importance of the relationships which he stresses—for they are important. Whatever the logic and merit of his presentation, and both historically and ideally there is much to recommend it, generally accepted practice in a number of modern congregations rejects, with the full approval of the Sacred Congregation of Religious, any protracted claims to superiority and jurisdiction by the founding abbey. With the lapse of decades, the increased membership in a monastic congregation, wide separation of abbeys, and an all-engrossing concern with local problems, sentimental ties to the oldest monastery can wear quite thin, justifiably or not, and will usually give way to more democratic procedure in the choice of a superior for the congregation. Since the monastic congregation is of its nature somewhat artificial, *salva reverentia,* in the monastic scheme of things, it seems for present purposes inconsequential which method of electing an archabbot, or an abbot president, is followed. Certainly either system is defensible on practical grounds. [*Tr.*]

father of the congregation should be called an archabbot. Besides, the title of archabbot very nicely implies the paternal character of the archabbot's position at the head of the congregation, since the word abbot means father. Finally, this title presents no difficulty from the standpoint of monastic tradition. The archabbot of St. Martin, Pannonhalma, Hungary, is head of the venerable Hungarian Congregation [monastery founded by St. Stephen, 1001, first king of Hungary; erected into a congregation in 1514]. May the Supreme Pontiff, in whose hands rests all ecclesiastical jurisdiction, and as abbot of abbots, all monastic power, give his decision in this matter. No one will deny that titles that lately have come into vogue, such as "abbot president" or "praeses," "superior general," "abbot general," and the like, have little in harmony with the concept of the family ideal or with monastic simplicity, and have been introduced from outside the spirit of the order. Let it be agreed, then, for us to speak of the head of the congregation as the archabbot.

The "Charter of Charity," basic norm of monastic congregations

2097. The nature and extent of the archabbot's rights and duties are neither so undetermined nor so difficult of explanation as might at first seem to be the case. A very clear light is shed on these questions both by the statutes of the Congregation of Cluny and even more particularly by the Charter of Charity written by the Cistercian abbot St. Stephen [Harding, d. 1134]. Because of their zealous, prudently developed, sober, and skillfully presented principles of the cenobitic life, these two sources merit to be reckoned among the most important monuments of monastic tradition. But we have at our command other authorities on the matter. The Councils of the Church, such as the IV Lateran Council (1215) and the Council of Trent, as well as individual Supreme Pontiffs, especially Popes Innocent III (d. 1216) and Gregory IX (d. 1241), declared that the conducting of the general chapters of the Congregation of Cluny and all other monks should conform with the practices observed by the Cistercians.* It is probably right to conclude from these papal pronouncements that the whole character of that early Cistercian legislation reflects the mind of the Church regarding the true idea of a monastic congregation.

* *Concil. Lateran. IV*, c. 12, Mansi 22:999; *Concil. Trident., Sess.* 25, c. 8, *Can. et decret.*, Richter, p. 411; Schroeder, p. 232; Innoc. III, cf. c. 7, X, *de stat. monach., III*, 25, *CJC*, Richter 2:577; Greg. IX, *Const. Apost. Behemoth*, § 1, 13 Jan., 1233, *BR* 3:475.

The archabbot governs only his own monastery

2098. As the first conclusion of these considerations we desire to emphasize that although the archabbot is the father of the whole monastic congregation, he is superior of only the mother abbey over which he presides as abbot. Each monastery, therefore, is governed by its own abbot, so that the whole administration and management both as to temporalities and spiritual considerations lies entirely in his hands. Every abbot is in the fullest and most proper sense the father and head of his sons in his own abbey.

2099. Whether a monk should be transferred from his own abbey to another for a time, for the welfare of the congregation or of his own monastic family is a problem which the archabbot may not decide without the consent of the respective abbots who are concerned. The archabbot is rather the father of other abbots whom the monks of the several abbeys honor and reverence more as the patriarchal head of the congregation than as a father. Lest the dignity of the head become wholly meaningless, it must be emphasized that the archabbot must enjoy some jurisdiction and paternal recognition in the whole monastic congregation.

The mother abbey sets the pattern of observance for the whole monastic congregation

2100. Two prerogatives properly belong to the archabbot of the congregation. The first is a result of the seniority and pre-eminence of the mother abbey, which remains a kind of inspiration and model for the daughter foundations. The monastic life should in all the abbeys be patterned on its observance, so that it both furnishes the practical interpretation of the Rule * and determines the order and rite of the sacred liturgy so that certain general uniform customs are established. The second prerogative which belongs properly to the archabbot lies in his obligation to keep watch over the monastic observance of the whole congregation with paternal solicitude and regular authority. He is, in a sense, the lawful custodian, preserver, and defender of the way of life established by the holy Rule and the monastic discipline peculiar to the congregation.†

* "We wish and command that henceforward the [abbots and monks] observe the Rule of St. Benedict in everything, as it is observed in the New Monastery [Citeaux], and understand it in no other sense than that which our pious forefathers of Citeaux have given to it and maintained, and which we ourselves now understand and hold after their example" (*Charta Charitatis, PL* 166:1379; available in tr. in: *The White Monks,* by Louis J. Lekai, S.C. Cist.; Okauchee, Wisc.: Cistercian Fathers, 1953, Appendix II, c. 2, p. 268, tr. by Denis Murphy, S.J.).

† "And because we receive all monks coming from other monasteries into ours, and they in like manner receive ours, it seems proper to us, that all our monasteries

Vigilance as to regular discipline: 1) the visitation

2101. From these rights of the archabbot there arise two duties of gravest import. He must frequently conduct a visitation of the abbeys belonging to the congregation (usually these were prescribed as annual, e.g., *S.C. Trident., Sess.* 25, c. 20, *Can. et decr.,* Richter, p. 436; Schroeder, *Trent,* p. 229). Since he is their father, he cannot deny himself the paternal inclination to visit the houses of his beloved sons, namely the abbots, to visit them and rejoice with them in the progress of their abbeys he uses all means not only of strengthening the bond of filial love which attaches the daughter foundations to the mother abbey, but also to increase and foster the devotion of the monks toward their own abbot. When the archabbot enters an abbey he is to be received joyfully. In filial submission the local abbot surrenders to him the honor of presiding at all exercises and of giving the blessings. The archabbot supports the abbot with benevolent and wise counsel; if he finds a monk laboring under hardship or guilty of some serious fault, he helps him conscientiously or leaves him to be reprimanded by his own abbot.

2102. Whenever the archabbot judges that a condition in the monastery calls for improvement, correction, or restoration, he should seek to effect the betterment through the authority of the local abbot rather than by using his own authority. As the kindly disposed father visits his sons with pleasure, so these sons long to visit their mother and father in the mother abbey. A holy zeal impels them to express their veneration of the mother abbey and their filial love, reverence and devotion to the archabbot. They are delightful and festive occasions when father and sons dwell in the sacred companionship within the embrace of the mother abbey, each endeavoring to express every evidence of mutual love and zeal.

2) The general chapter of the congregation

2103. This last mentioned thought hints at that wholesome institution, the general chapter, which according to the decrees of the Church, is to be held periodically, as specified in the individual con-

---

should have the same usages in chanting, and the same books for the Divine Office day and night and the celebration of the Holy Sacrifice of the Mass, as we have in the New Monastery; and that there may be no discord in our daily actions, but that we may all live together in the bond of charity under one rule, and in the practice of the same observances" (*RSB,* c. 1, n. 2).

Wolter gives a series of quotations from the Charter of Charity as footnotes. Since they are largely in confirmation of his own exposition of the matter, and since the references to both the Latin text and the English translation are here furnished, it seems superfluous to repeat these passages. [*Tr.*]

stitutions. It is the duty of the archabbot to convoke these solemn sessions and to be their moderator. In such a setting he is truly a father in the midst of his sons. The status and aims of the family are there reviewed, the vicissitudes, hardships, and difficulties related. When any one of the abbeys encounters difficulties with regard to its property or its members, the help of the brethren is requested who endeavor with the utmost charity to remove the problem. All help one another as members of a family. Then matters of concern for the whole congregation are taken under consideration: the preservation of the blessing of peace and harmony; the maintenance of discipline; and regular observance. In this way the mutual exhortations of the father and the sons will wonderfully renew fraternal harmony and increase the love for the holy Rule.

3) The chapter of faults

2104. But even with all this the archabbot's duty is not completely fulfilled. The general chapter of the monastic congregation is also properly a chapter, and like the community chapter of the individual monastic community which every abbot conducts in his own monastery according to general law. Its name derives from the custom of publicly reading and explaining the recurrent chapter of the holy Rule during the meeting. It is usually terminated with a voluntary acknowledgment of faults. Hence in the general chapter of all the abbots of the congregation, the discussion should center not only on monastic observance in the abbeys, but a chapter of faults should also be conducted. In this chapter the archabbot holds the relation to the abbots that they themselves hold toward their own sons. Hence if the abbots have committed errors in their high office, they acknowledge their failures to their father in profound humility and gratefully accept from him paternal correction, admonition, and penance, happy for this brief opportunity of conducting themselves as simple monks once more.

Participants in the general chapter

2105. From what has been said, it seems to us reasonable and just to conclude that only abbots and conventual priors [the superiors of independent priories which have as yet not been elevated to the dignity of abbeys, not claustral priors, who function as assistants to governing abbots] should be admitted to the general chapter.* The presence of

* In some modern congregations, like the American-Cassinese Congregation, one delegate is elected from each abbey and each independent priory to represent their communities (*Rituale monasticum, pars ritualis,* c. 15, *sect. III,* § 402, pp. 763 ff.). This is no mere concession to democracy or ritual gesture. These delegates attend all meetings, are sworn to secrecy, present the communications of the members of

monks could perhaps be prejudicial to the exercise of the authority of the abbots. It is also self-understood that the archabbot, as father of the monastic congregations, conducts the election of every new abbot.

Election of the president of the congregation

2106. On the other hand it is no more than right that in the election of the archabbot the other families of the monastic congregation should exercise an influence. Finally, if a monastery of the congregation makes a new foundation, the abbot who erects the house exercises the same paternal authority over it as the archabbot. In the general chapter, however, this founding abbot remains in the same relationship of filial devotion to the archabbot as formerly.

Thus we have, or if I may be so bold as to make the statement, the Church has, in a certain sense, furnished a sort of over-all plan for the monastic congregation. It is wholly unnecessary to tabulate and label the rich benefits which the monastic life has derived from the monastic congregation. One consideration should be noted: Today it is no longer the custom for individual monasteries to be represented and have a vote in ecumenical councils: only the Abbot Primate in his capacity of representing the whole order; the monastic congregations, fifteen in number, through their abbots president; and the fifteen *abbates nullius dioeceseos,* that is, those prelates who not only govern a monastic family but have an assigned territory which is distinct from any bishopric, all of which is now accurately determined in the Church's common law (cf. *Code of Canon Law,* c. 223, § 1, nn. 3–4).

The Confederation of Monastic Congregations

2107. [*Translator's insertion*]: Although the principles presented by Archabbot Wolter are fundamental and comprehensive (and in some instances subject to differences of interpretation), there have been numerous developments since his work was originally published (1880). Some foundations have heavily emphasized the contemplative character of monasticism, almost to the point of complete exclusion of external works. Other abbeys and congregations have gradually allowed themselves, in answering the local needs of the Church, to become so immersed in activity that the ideals of monasticism have suffered in the process. Not infrequently this problem has carried to the extreme of becoming a serious concern for those who have the respon-

---

their abbeys to the definitors, enter into all discussions, and vote on all issues except the election of the abbot president, in which only abbots and conventual priors participate. In recent years a canonist has been appointed by the president of the congregation to be present at each general chapter and to attend all the sessions: this last assignment is purely advisory and does not include the right of voting on the issues raised. [*Tr.*]

sibility of preserving monasticism's way of life and distinctive contribution to the spirituality of the Church. As has been true through the long centuries of organized monasticism, uniformity is scarcely attainable, nor, considering the nature of the family, particularly desirable.

2108. After the crushing losses sustained during the French Revolution and the Period of Secularization, decades were required to begin the slow and painful rebuilding of the order, which really got under way only toward the end of the first half of the nineteenth century. Even then the struggle was for a long time discouragingly slow, and, more important for present considerations, made uneven by reason of environmental conditions. The new congregations of France (Solesmes) and Beuron could take up traditions of old established congregations (St. Maur, Bursfeld, Swabian Congregation of St. Joseph, the Strasburg Congregation), which were products of the soil and had been operative within the memory of living men; they were blessed with unity of language which was indigenous to the soil, a common cultural background and a fairly uniform and serious scholastic pattern; they were re-commencing in lands of long established monastic tradition; and, possibly most significant of all, they were blessed with scholarly leaders who had, or who were able to create the leisure that is indispensable for thorough study of so complicated a way of life. Almost the precise opposite was true in every detail in the houses of the English-speaking world. The English themselves had been away from their home for centuries, ever since the Reformation, and the American-Cassinese and Swiss-American congregations which grew up in a dominantly Protestant environment, were confronted with the task of transplanting a form of the religious life designed to answer the religious needs of other lands, and, despite their inadequate numbers endeavored to help meet the missionary problems created by a rapidly developing body of the faithful.

2109. Pope Leo XIII, who will for all time to come stand high among the great benefactors in the history of monasticism, recommended to the abbots through his friend, the Cassinese Joseph-Benedict Cardinal Dusmet, Archbishop of Catania, the establishment of an office with no precise counterpart in the history of monasticism, namely that of the Abbot Primate, a sort of super-abbot to reside in Rome and represent the order's interests there, while functioning also as the superior of the projected international college of the order, the Collegio di Sant'Anselmo, which was subsequently built through the munificence of the Supreme Pontiff.*

* All documents relative to the establishment of the Confederation of Black Benedictines, the development of the Abbot Primate's office, the founding of St. Anselm's international College, Rome, and the *Lex Propria* of the Confederation are collected, translated, and annotated in: *The Law proper to the Confederation*

2110. Pope Leo's proposals envisaged a Primate with the rather anomalous position of not really being a superior nor a spiritual father of monks professed to him, but rather the head of an international college whose entire personnel was, to a man, still subject to the abbots of the monasteries where they had pronounced their profession. The Abbot Primate functioned as a sort of chief co-ordinator, an on-the-spot consultant on things monastic pertaining to Benedictines, the accepted representative to the Holy See for the (now) fifteen monastic congregations. These were the basic lines on which the office of the Primate and the Confederation of Congregations were erected in the Apostolic Brief *Summum semper* of July 12, 1893.

2111. Because of the autonomy of the individual monastery, once it has been granted independence, and particularly after it has been raised to the dignity of an abbey, the juridical structure of the monastic congregations has little in common with the more familiar patterns of the centralized institutes (Dominicans, Franciscans, Jesuits, and practically all modern religious institutes), on whose juridical lines the *Code of Canon Law* (1917) lays down almost all general provisions for governing religious bodies in the Church.

2112. The eminently capable scholars of the Benedictine Order who collaborated in the codification of the *Code of Canon Law* * succeeded in obtaining repeated recognition of the distinctive nature of the monastic orders, together with their privileges (later to be subjected to revision), constitutions, and declarations to the holy Rule. It still remains abundantly evident, however, that the *Code of Canon Law* is designed chiefly to harmonize with the juridical constitution and to answer the needs of centralized orders.

2113. This lack of agreement between the monastic ideal and *modus operandi* and the Code is no serious handicap either to monastic congregations or to individual abbeys. It does, however, create the need of drawing up declarations to the *Rule of St. Benedict* and constitutions so that they will give legal and binding expression to the order's objectives. Once they are approved by the Sacred Congregation of Religious they become the distinctive law for the respective congregation. As has been comprehensively stated in the statutes of the Swiss

of Monastic Congregations of the Order of St. Benedict (cf. Bibliography, under "Benedictines").

* Justinian Serédi, of St. Martin's Abbey, Pannonhalma, Hungary, afterward Cardinal Archbishop of Esztergom (Budapest); Laurence Janssens, of Maredsous Abbey, Belgium, afterward bishop; and Peter Bastien, of the same abbey, all of whom were professors at Sant'Anselmo, are specifically mentioned by Father Joseph Noval, O.P., in his brochure, *Codificationis juris canonici recensio historico-apologetica* (Romae: Desclée et Soc., 1918, Appendix, pp. 76 ff.). Others, like Abbot Raphael Molitor, of St. Joseph's Abbey, Gerleve, Germany, contributed to the work.

Congregation: "The norms by which the regular life in our congregation is governed, are, besides the divine commands and the [general] law of the Church: (1) the Rule of our Father St. Benedict, which is the principal and fundamental law under which we have promised to do battle; (2) the declarations of the holy Rule approved by the Apostolic See, by means of which declarations the precepts of the holy Rule are accommodated, in conformity with the mind of St. Benedict, to the circumstances of time and place; (3) the constitutions, which embrace the form and life of the congregation and also certain features of monastic life not defined in the holy Rule—the declarations and constitutions taken together are called the "Statutes"; (4) the decrees of the chapter of the congregation by means of which matters pertaining to our congregation are decided, or norms approved by the Holy See are changed with the permission of the same; (5) the regulations and precepts of the chapter of the congregation, which are issued to provide for the needs of the congregation, often temporary in character; (6) definitions of the chapter of the congregation by means of which doubts regarding the text of the holy Rule, the declarations, constitutions, or other laws are interpreted; and (7) fatherly admonitions by means of which the chapter of the congregation exhorts the brethren to greater progress in virtue or to the avoidance of spiritual dangers" (*Statuta Congr. Helveticae O.S.B., Constitutiones,* c. 2, § 171, pp. 93, 94).

2114. The often repeated objective of Pope Pius XII, in his vast program of accommodating the efforts of all societies of religious men and women to the present-day needs of the Church, was to create a system of legal organization better equipped to devote itself to activity in the service of the Church, powered by deeper spiritual formation. The problem in the case of monastic institutes was to preserve the jealously guarded autonomy that flows from the nature of the family and the prelatial character of the father, both realized in even the smallest and poorest monasteries. This resulted in bestowing far greater authority on the Abbot Primate—at least potentially, given emergency conditions—than had been contemplated by Pope Leo XIII. The result has been the new concept of the Confederation, into which the Olivetan Benedictines have already (September 1959) been admitted, operating under the sweeping regulations of the *Lex Propria.*

2115. [Wolter's text, which continues at this point, now seems to have been prophetic]: May the great monasteries of the monastic order, outstanding for their antiquity, their great glory and merits, which still remain independent, join into congregations! Once united with other flourishing abbeys, they will experience a rebirth and be rejuvenated unto a holy fruitfulness of life. Then perhaps one day the Holy Father of the universal family of God, the Supreme Abbot, our Pope, will call together the heads of all the Benedictine congregations to a general monastic council in the Eternal City, in order that they can present to the Common Father the rejuvenated order as a holy leaven and an instrument in the great renewal of the Church. [All the abbots of the Confederation meet in congress every six years; the abbots president meet every three years.] What succeeded once under the leadership of St. Benedict, divine grace can produce again today, namely, that the monastic order will fight valiantly under the leadership of the Holy Father, the Pope, for all the people, carry on the battle of the Lord, and gain glorious victories over the enemies of Christ, that in all things God may be glorified!

II. EVIDENCE FROM THE RULE OF ST. BENEDICT

The election of the abbot

2116. In the appointment of the abbot let this rule always be observed, that he be made the abbot who is chosen unanimously in the fear of God by the whole community, or even by a minority, however small, if its counsel be more wholesome. Let him who is to be appointed be chosen for the merit of his life and his enlightened wisdom, even though he be the last in the order of the community. . . . Let them set a worthy steward over God's house. Let them be sure that they will receive a good reward, if they do this with a pure intention and out of zeal for God, just as, on the contrary, they will incur sin if they neglect to intervene (*RSB,* c. 64). Let the abbot, since he is believed to hold the place of Christ, be called lord and abbot, not for any pretensions of his own, but for the honor and love of Christ. Let the abbot himself be mindful of this, and behave so that he may be worthy of such honor (*ibid.,* c. 63).

What kind of man the abbot ought to be

2117. An abbot who is worthy to rule a monastery should always remember what he is called and realize in his actions the name of a superior. For he is believed to be the representative of Christ in the monastery, and for that reason is called by a name of his, according to the words of the Apostle: *You have received a spirit of adoption as sons, by virtue of which we cry, Abba! Father!* (Rom. 8:15.) . . . The abbot should always remember what he is and what he is called, and should know that to whom more is committed, from him more is required. Let him realize also how difficult and arduous a task he has undertaken, of ruling souls and adapting himself to many dispositions (*RSB,* c. 2). Let the abbot when appointed consider always what an office he has undertaken and to whom he must render an account of his stewardship; and let him know that it is his duty rather to profit his brethren than to preside over them (*ibid.,* c. 64). The abbot himself, however, should do all things in the fear of God and observance of the Rule, knowing that he will certainly have to render an account of all his judgments to God, the most just Judge (*ibid.,* c. 3). Yet the abbot must not disturb the flock committed to him, nor by an exercise of arbitrary authority ordain anything unjustly; but let him always consider that he will have to render God an account of all his judgments and deeds (*ibid.,* c. 63). Yet let the abbot bear in mind that he must give God an account of all his judgments, lest perchance his mind be inflamed by the fire of envy or jealousy (*ibid.,* c. 65). But in all his decisions let him think upon the retribution of God (*ibid.,* c. 55) . . . for [the abbot] must answer for all the misdeeds of his disciples (*ibid.,* c. 36). Let the abbot remember always that at the dread judgment of God there will be an examination of both these matters, of his teaching and of the obedience of his disciples. And let the abbot realize that the shepherd will have to answer for any lack of profit which the Father of the family may discover in his sheep (*ibid.,* c. 2). And let him know that he who has undertaken the government of souls, must prepare himself to render an account of them. And whatever number of brethren he knows he has under his care, let him regard it as certain that he will have to give the Lord an account of all these souls on the day of judgment, and certainly of his own soul also. And thus, fearing the examination which the shepherd will have to face for the sheep entrusted to him, and anxious regarding the account which will have to be given for others, he is made solicitous for his own sake also; and while by his admonitions helping others to amend, he himself is cleansed of his faults (*ibid.,* c. 2).

The abbot is to be the humble servant of God

2118. And especially let [the abbot] keep this present Rule in all things; so that having ministered faithfully he may hear from the Lord what the good servant heard who gave his fellow servants wheat in due season: *Amen I say to you, he will set him over all his goods* (Matt. 24:47; *RSB,* c. 64).

The abbot's loving care for his sons

2119. . . . Let the abbot [display] . . . the loving kindness of a father. . . . Let him not make any distinction of persons in the monastery. Let him not love one more than another, unless he find him better in good works and obedience . . . whether slaves or freemen, we are all one in Christ, and have to serve alike in the army of the same Lord. *Because with God there is no respect of persons* (Rom.

2:11). In this regard only are we distinguished in his sight, if we be found better than others in good works and humility. Therefore let the abbot show an equal love to all, and let the same discipline be imposed on all in accord with their deserts (*RSB,* c. 2). It behooves him, therefore, to be learned in the divine law, so that he may have a treasure of knowledge whence he may bring forth things new and old; and to be chaste, sober, and merciful. Let him always permit mercy to triumph over judgment (cf. Jas. 2:13), so that he himself may obtain mercy. Let him hate ill-doing, but love the brethren. . . . And let him study rather to be loved than feared (*RSB,* c. 64).

Life of St. Benedict: Let the loving-kindness of the holy Patriarch serve as an example. When the forthcoming destruction of the monastery was prophetically made known to him, he begged that at least the preservation of the souls of his disciples be granted to him out of that place. And for his consolation he obtained the lives of all his companions (cf. *S. Greg. Magni Dialogorum Lib. II,* c. 17, *PL* 66:168).

The abbot must have a zealous care for souls

2120. Let the abbot exercise all diligence in his care for erring brethren, for *it is not the healthy who need a physician, but they who are sick* (Matt. 9:12). He ought, therefore, as a wise physician, to use every remedy in his power. Let him send *senpectae,* that is, old and prudent brethren, who may, as it were, secretly comfort the troubled brother, inducing him to make humble satisfaction and consoling him *lest perchance he be overwhelmed by too much sorrow* (II Cor. 2:7). As the Apostle says: You should rather *assure him of your love for him* (v. 8), and let everyone pray for him. For the abbot is bound to use the greatest care, and to exercise all prudence and diligence, so that he may not lose any of the sheep entrusted to him. Let him know that what he has undertaken is the charge of weakly souls, and not a tyranny over the strong; and let him fear the threat of the prophet, wherein God says: "What you saw to be fat, that you took for yourselves; and what was feeble you cast away" (cf. Ezech. 34:3–4). And let him imitate the merciful example of the Good Shepherd, who left the ninety-nine sheep in the mountains and went after the one sheep that had strayed; and had so great pity on its weakness, that he deigned to place it on his own sacred shoulders and so bring it back to the flock (cf. Luke 15:4–5; *RSB,* c. 27). Above all, let him not have greater solicitude for fleeting, earthly, and perishable things, and so overlook and undervalue the salvation of the souls committed to him; but let him always remember that he has undertaken the government of souls and will have to give an account of them. And if he be tempted to complain of the lack of means, let him remember the words: *Seek first the kingdom of God and his justice, and all these things shall be given you besides* (Matt. 6:33). And again: *Nought is lacking to those who fear him* (Ps. 33:10). . . . If the abbot sees that all his trouble is of no avail, let him employ a greater thing still, namely, the prayers of himself and of all the brethren, that God, who can do all things, may effect the cure of the sick brother. But if he be not healed in this way, then let the abbot use the knife of amputation, as the Apostle says: *Expel the wicked man from your midst* (I Cor. 5:13). And again: *If the unbeliever departs, let him depart* (*ibid.,* 7:15), lest one diseased sheep contaminate the whole flock (*RSB,* c. 28).

The abbot's correction must be paternal

2121. In administering correction, let him act with prudent moderation, lest being too zealous in removing the rust he break the vessel. Let him always distrust his own frailty and remember that the bruised reed is not to be broken. By this we do not mean that he should allow evils to grow, but that, as we have said above, he should eradicate them prudently and with charity, in the way which may seem best in each case (*RSB,* c. 64). One he must humor, another rebuke, another persuade, according to each one's disposition and understanding, and thus adapt and accommodate himself to all in such a way that he may not only suffer no loss in the sheep committed to him, but even rejoice in the increase of a good flock (*ibid.,* c. 2).

Life of St. Benedict: Examples of fatherly and charitable correction may be found in St. Benedict's handling of the monk who could not stay at prayer (*S. Greg. Magni Dialogorum Lib. II,* c. 4, *PL* 66:142); of the monk who accepted a present of handkerchiefs against the regulations (*ibid.,* c. 19, col. 179); of the monk in whom the spirit of pride asserted itself as he held the light for St. Benedict at table (*ibid.,* c. 20). Finally, overcome by their prayer, he [became their abbot]. Taking charge of the regular observance, he would allow none of the monks to indulge in unlawful practices, by deviating either to the right or to the left from the straight path of their religious vocation, as they formerly had done (*ibid.,* c. 3, col. 134).

The abbot's teaching

2122. It behooves him, therefore, to be learned in the divine law, so that he may have a treasure of knowledge whence he may bring forth things new and old (*RSB,* c. 64). Therefore the abbot ought not to teach, or ordain, or command anything which is against the law of the Lord; on the contrary, his commands and teaching should be infused into the minds of his disciples like the leaven of divine justice. . . . Therefore when anyone has received the name of abbot, he ought to rule his disciples with a twofold teaching, displaying all goodness and holiness by deeds and by words, but by deeds rather than by words. To intelligent disciples let him expound the Lord's commandments in words; but to those of harder hearts and ruder minds let him show forth the divine precepts by his example. And whatever he has taught his disciples to be contrary to God's law, let him show by his example that it is not to be done, lest while preaching to others he should himself be rejected, and lest God should some day say to him in his sin: *Why do you recite my statutes, and profess my covenant with your mouth, though you hate discipline and cast my works behind you?* (Ps. 49:16–17.) And again: *Why dost thou see the speck in thy brother's eye, and yet dost not consider the beam in thy own eye?* (Matt. 7:3.) . . . For the abbot in his teaching ought always to observe the rule of the Apostle, wherein he says: *Reprove, entreat, rebuke* (II Tim. 4:2). He must adapt himself to circumstances, now using severity and now persuasion, displaying the rigor of a master or the loving-kindness of a father. That is to say, that he must sternly rebuke the undisciplined and restless; but the obedient, meek, and patient, these he should exhort to advance in virtue. As for the negligent and rebellious, we warn him to reprimand and punish them. And let him not shut his eyes to the faults of offenders; but as soon as they begin to appear, let him, as he can, cut them out by the roots, mindful of the fate of Heli, the priest of Silo. Those of gentle disposition and good understanding should be punished, for the first and second time, by verbal admonition; but bold, hard, proud, and disobedient characters should be checked at the beginning of their ill-doing (*RSB,* c. 2).

The abbot's prudence and discretion

2123. Let him be prudent and considerate in all his commands; and whether the work which he enjoins concern God or the world, let him always be discreet and moderate, bearing in mind the discretion of holy Jacob, who said: If I cause my flocks to be overdriven, they will all perish in one day (cf. Gen. 33:13). So, imitating these and other examples of discretion, the mother of virtues, let him so temper all things that the strong may still have something to long after, and the weak will not draw back in alarm (*RSB,* c. 64). That it is the abbot's duty to dispense in the regulations of the *Rule of St. Benedict* is evident in that, at his command, one is permitted to speak after Compline (*ibid.,* c. 42), partake of food before the appointed time or afterward (*ibid.,* c. 43), eat away from the monastery (*ibid.,* c. 51), and so on.

The abbot is to act in all patience

2124. Let him not be turbulent or anxious, overbearing or obstinate, jealous or too suspicious, for otherwise he will never be at rest (*RSB,* c. 64).

Paternal power of the abbot, perfect monarchy

2125. Everything, therefore, is to be done with the approval of the abbot (*RSB,* c. 49). [In all important business to be transacted] . . . let the decision depend rather on the abbot's judgment, so that when he has decided what is the better course, all may obey. However, just as it is proper for disciples to obey their master, so it is becoming that he on his part should dispose all things with prudence and justice (*ibid.,* c. 3). Therefore we have judged it expedient for the preservation of peace and of charity, that the abbot should have the appointment of all offices in his monastery (*ibid.,* c. 65). . . . As soon as anything has been ordered by the superior, they receive it as a divine command and cannot suffer any delay in executing it (*ibid.,* c. 5). If it be possible, let all the affairs of the monastery be administered by deans under the control of the abbot, as we have already arranged (*ibid.,* c. 65). The abbot must not disturb the flock committed to him, nor by an exercise of arbitrary authority ordain anything unjustly (*ibid.,* c. 63). Should [the pilgrim monk] reasonably, modestly, and charitably censure or remark upon any defect, let the abbot consider the matter prudently, lest perchance the Lord have sent him for this very end (*ibid.,* c. 61).

The officials of the monastery

2126. Let such men be chosen as deans that the abbot may without anxiety share his burdens among them; and let them not be chosen by order, but according to their worthiness of life, learning, and wisdom. Should any of these deans become puffed up with pride and be found worthy of censure, let him be corrected once, and a second time, and a third time; if he will not amend, then let him be deposed from his office, and another, who is worthy of it, put in his place. And we order the same to be done in the case of the prior (*RSB,* c. 21). And let the house of God be administered by prudent men in a prudent manner (*ibid.,* c. 53). . . . Let there be chosen out of the community brethren of good repute and observant life, and let them be appointed deans. They shall take charge of their deaneries in all things, observing the commandments of God and the instructions of their abbot (*ibid.,* c. 21). Let [the cellarer] have charge of everything; let him do nothing without the abbot's orders, but keep to his instructions (*ibid.,* c. 31). Let the abbot appoint as his prior whomsoever he may choose, with the advice of God-fearing brethren. Let the prior respectfully perform what is enjoined him by his abbot, and do nothing contrary to the abbot's will or regulations; for the more he is set above the rest, the more scrupulously should he observe the precepts of the Rule (*ibid.,* c. 65). For the ones who have newly come to the monastery let a senior be assigned who is skilled in winning souls, that he may watch over them with the utmost care. Let him examine whether the novice truly seeks God, and whether he is zealous for the Work of God, for obedience, and for humiliations. Let him be told all the hardships and trials through which we travel to God. . . . Let this Rule be read through to him . . . and re-read, so that he may know on what he is entering. . . . And let him be tested in all patience (*ibid.,* c. 58). Further regulations of the holy Rule on the appointment of officials may be found (e.g., *RSB,* c. 31, entire chapter). Let the abbot take the greatest care that the sick be not neglected by the cellarer and attendants; for he must answer for all the misdeeds of his disciples (*ibid.,* c. 36; similar provisions are found in *RSB* cc. 21, 32, 35, 53, and 66). But if the business to be done in the interests of the monastery be of lesser importance, let him use the advice of the seniors only. It is written: *Do nothing without counsel, and then you need have no regrets* (Sir. 32, 19). Let him [act] with the advice of God-fearing brethren (*RSB,* c. 65).

Calling the brethren to council

2127. As often as any important business has to be done in the monastery, let the abbot call together the whole community and himself set forth the matter. And, having heard the advice of the brethren, let him take counsel with himself and then do what he shall judge to be most expedient. Now the reason why we have said that all should be called to council, is that God often reveals what is better to the younger. Let the brethren give their advice with all deference and humility, nor venture to defend their opinions obstinately; but let the decision depend rather on the abbot's judgment, so that when he has decided what is the better course, all may obey. However, just as it is proper for disciples to obey their master, so it is becoming that on his part he should dispose all things with prudence and justice. In all things, therefore, let all follow the Rule as master, nor let anyone rashly depart from it. Let no one in the monastery follow the will of his own heart; nor let anyone presume to contend impudently with his abbot, or to contend with him at all when outside the monastery (*RSB,* c. 3).

Monasteries, the congregation

2128. *Life of St. Benedict:* The holy man in that same hermitage of his had long been growing richer in virtue and miraculous power, and had gathered many disciples about him for the service of almighty God. Thus he was able, with the all-powerful help of our Lord Jesus Christ, to build twelve monasteries there [Subiaco], to each of which he appointed an abbot and twelve monks (*S. Greg. Magni Dialogorum Lib. II,* c. 3, *PL* 66:140).

III. DECREES AND DOCUMENTS OF THE CHURCH

Ecclesiastical hierarchy based on Christ

2129. PROV. COUNCIL OF SENS (France, 1850). Individual pastors are to preside over their parishes. They will govern those parishes under the authority and sacred leadership of the bishop. . . . In this way the individual member of the faithful is subject to his parish priest, the parish priest to his bishop, the bishop to the Supreme Pontiff, and the Pontiff to Christ. This is the order of the sacred hierarchy, effected through obedience, submission, and love, which is ever visible to men of the world, from which order they see the Church's never-aging beauty and strength. . . . The constitution of the Church is like the cementing and joining together of the divine dwelling erected by Christ and having its cornerstone in Christ. . . . This Church, unshakable and always constant in its unity for eighteen centuries, is forever showing forth the miracle of an immense society scattered over the face of the earth, always troubled, constantly under attack, and although at times suffering, ever victorious; for although the cradles at times flow with her children's blood, and in every age numerous enemies dedicate themselves to her destruction, God who established her and made her firm, shields and protects her and will continue always to shield and protect her (*Litterae R.mi Archiepiscopi et episcoporum Prov. Senonen. quibus Concilii decr. promulgantur, CL* 4:942–944).

The Church is a family

2130. PROV. COUNCIL OF UTRECHT (1865). A. While we ourselves manifest and declare our union with the successor of Peter in terms of highest veneration, as is alone fitting, we commit to pastors the duty of zealously instructing the faithful concerning the necessity of this union, of fostering due reverence and obedience to the Roman See, and of exciting in them a filial love for the common father of all believers (*Decr.*, tit. 1, c. 7, *CL* 5:757). B. As the one body of the Church is made up of the sacred orders of the hierarchy and of the faithful people, in that there is one supreme head, one Bishop of bishops, the Roman Pontiff, so by union with their bishop, and his subjection to the one throne which was founded by the pronouncement of the Lord, the faithful themselves are joined and remain united to the Mystical Body of Christ. . . . By their appointment bishops are also fathers in the house of God and the family of saints. For it is their duty to embrace with paternal affection all who have been begotten in Jesus Christ through the Gospel and who have been born again of water and the Holy Spirit; to support the weak in their resolutions; give strength to the pusillanimous; call back the erring; strengthen the weak; reinstate the fallen; win back those who have been corrupted; seek those who have wandered away; and foster and practice charity toward all, especially the needy and the afflicted (*ibid.*, tit. 2, c. 2, col. 779–780).

The community of monks is a family

2131. ROMAN PONTIFICAL. Although it is true that we are all brothers in Christ and have one Father in heaven by virtue of the grace of baptism, if we obey his laws as well as we can, there is no doubt that we are then most united when we bind ourselves together by prayer and mutual assistance; as we read of the holy Fathers who were one in heart and soul having done in the infant Church. Many of them, inspired with love for Christ, sold their possessions and property, gathered together the money they had received, and presented it joyfully to the Apostles. On receiving it, the Apostles distributed to each according as anyone had need (*De benedictione abbatis* 1:129).*

The election of the abbot

2132. CONGR. OF HIRSCHAU. The election of an abbot enjoys this distinctive prerogative: absolutely no one may be present besides those who are professed for our monastery. Hence first of all the matter is to be commended to God by the zealous prayer of all the brethren. Having assembled the council of the seniors, the election is taken up and carried to its conclusion, as far as possible, with one sole purpose in mind—that it be done according to the Lord's will (*Constitutiones Hirsaugiens. S. Wilhelmi, Lib. II*, c. 1, *PL* 150:1037).

2133. CONGR. OF BURSFELD. With all the urgency at our command, we exhort the brethren that after they have implored the divine assistance in devout prayer, all are to give themselves completely to the election of the kind of abbot that our holy Father calls for in his holy Rule, one who is zealous for the glory of God and the welfare of the order, of the monastery, and the brethren (*Statuta*, dist. 2, *Introd.*, p. 67).

2134. CONGR. OF STRASBURG. A. Since it is not expedient for monasteries to remain without abbots, the prior and the chapter will see to it that the election of the new abbot is scheduled for the earliest time that can conveniently be arranged (*Declar. 4 in c. 64 RSB*, fol. 94). B. He who presides at the election of the new abbot is earnestly to warn the chapter members that setting aside all personal attachments, and being mindful of their duty in the present act of election, on which

* This is from the last prayer of the simple form of abbatial blessing, now no longer used. It immediately precedes *De benedictione abbatis auctoritate apostolica*, from which all subsequent excerpts are taken.

practically the whole welfare of the monastery depends, they keep before their eyes the glory of God and the common advantage of the monastery, seeking to elect him whom before God they consider most helpful to the monastery and most worthy both in spiritual and temporal matters (*ibid., declar. 12,* fol. 97).

2135. SPANISH CONGR. (1640). Since the abbot assumes the obligations of a father, it is proper that he be designated with the title of fatherhood and that he be called our father (*Caeremoniale monastic., Pars II,* dist. 1, c. 1, no. 2, p. 285).

2136. CONGR. OF STRASBURG. Fast and abstinence are to be observed on the day before the election of an abbot. On the day itself, let all who are to take part in the voting devoutly offer the most holy Sacrifice of the Mass and by most fervent prayer implore grace and the assistance of the Holy Spirit for blessed results in so important an undertaking (*Declar. 10 in c. 64 RSB,* fol. 97).

2137. SWABIAN CONGR. OF ST. JOSEPH. A. Since it is a matter of supreme importance for a monastery to have an abbot who possesses the skill of governing as well as prudence and blamelessness of life, each one is to endeavor to obtain by his daily prayer, his offering of the most holy Sacrifice, and by other works of piety, the kind of abbot that our holy Father described and desired (*Const. et declar., Pars III,* c. 1, punct. 1, n. 6, fol. 196). B. As regards the election of an abbot by "inspiration" or "quasi-inspiration," no other formality or solemnity is required except that, without previous discussion about electing a certain person, all agree unanimously on the same individual; in such a case the Holy Spirit is understood to have moved the minds to that kind of election, which supplies abundantly for any order or form of electing (*ibid.,* n. 19, fol. 205).

2138. ROMAN PONTIFICAL. A. It is fitting indeed and just, right and availing unto salvation, that we should always and in all places give thanks to you, holy Lord, Father almighty, everlasting God. Graciously hear our prayers and pour forth upon this your servant the bounteous spirit of your ✠ blessing. [At this point the bishop's hands are imposed upon the head of the abbot-elect]. That he who is today made abbot by the imposition of our hands, being made worthy by your ✠ sanctification, may remain your chosen one and never hereafter prove himself unworthy of your grace (*De benedictione abbatis auctoritate apostolica, Praefatio, prima pars,* 1:146). B. We humbly beseech you, that all the days of his life your goodness and blessing be upon this your servant whom you have called to assume the high pastoral office (*ibid., oratio 3a post praefationem,* p. 152).

The abbot's love must be paternal

2139. CONGR. OF BURSFELD. The abbot must remember what he is. He must be a father to the brethren and embrace his religious not only as brethren but with a truly paternal affection and strive more to be loved than feared by them, the holy Rule remaining intact (*Stat.,* dist. 3, c. 1, n. 1, pp. 77–78).

The monks' love for their abbot

2140. CONGR. OF STRASBURG. A. Religious subjects are frequently to call to mind that by reason of the burden imposed upon him by his office, the newly-elected abbot must devote himself almost wholly to the needs of his subjects, and after he has completed the course of his present life, render a rigorous account to the Supreme Judge of their progress or their lack of progress in the observance of the regular life. They should realize, then, that it is altogether right that collectively and individually they show him love and honor (*Declar. 21 in c. 64 RSB,* fol. 100). B. Let all manifest due reverence and obedience to their abbot in all places and at all times, not only when he passes by or when he is actually speaking to them. This they will observe by such practices as uncovering the head and making a polite bow, by rising if they chance to be seated, by religiously controlling their manners and actions when in his presence, obeying his commands promptly, not showing resentment at his admonitions and corrections, nor addressing him in the spirit of obstinacy, but rather asking his forgiveness and promising correction, always showing him filial love and by fostering and protecting his name and authority, especially among outsiders. Anyone who is found guilty in such points is obviously to be subjected to rather severe punishments (*ibid., declar. 22*). C. As often as the abbot has been absent from the monastery for fourteen days or longer the brethren will humbly and reverently assemble to meet him on his return home, and indicate by the happiness of their reception and the kindness of their greeting the love with which they venerate him (*ibid., declar. 23*).

2141. CONGR. OF BURSFELD. A. As the abbot has accepted a heavy burden in the name of the monastery and for the welfare of his fellow monks, the brethren must remain aware of their obligation of filial affection and respect, so that as the abbot is eagerly concerned for their spiritual and temporal well-being, they reciprocate in all things by showing him love and reverence (*Stat.,* dist. 3, c. 1, *de reciproca obligatione fratrum erga abbatem,* n. 1, p. 81). B. When the brethren see severity of discipline used against offenders, they must not lose their confidence in the abbot, but accept the correction after the manner of worthy sons; the mother hen (says St. Augustine, *Serm. 383,* c. 3, *PL*

39:1688) does not cease to be a mother if she presses with her foot in the time of distress the chick that she keeps warm (*Stat.,* n. 4, p. 82).

2142. ROMAN PONTIFICAL. Receive the ring, symbol of fidelity, that adorned with an unspotted faith, you keep inviolate the spouse of God, namely, his holy Church (*De benedictione abbatis auctoritate apostolica, impositio annuli* 1:155).

The abbot, the novice master, and the novices

2143. CONGR. OF BURSFELD. It is the abbot's duty to bless the novices [at their admission or clothing] and to receive their professions, as well as those of the converse brothers (*Stat.,* dist. 3, c. 1, n. 5, p. 72).

2144. COUNCIL OF BASLE (1431). When transplanted, young trees which are given proper moisture close to running water grow strong and in due season shoot forth branches, blossom in the spring, and finally bear sweet fruit. We ordain that the novices who are to be trained should be clothed with the monastic habit forthwith, but not before they have been determined on as worthy individuals through whom the praise of God can be performed in a proper manner. Let a mature brother be appointed their instructor who will zealously devote himself to winning their souls for God. He is to read and explain the Rule to them during the year of probation in the manner fully described in the *Rule of St. Benedict,* Chapter 58. When the year has been spent, the novices, if they desire to pronounce vows and are found to be without impediment, are to be received for profession (*Statuta et ordinationes ad monachos Congregationis Mellicensis directae, ex manuscripto Salisburgensi*).

2145. POPE CLEMENT VIII (d. 1605). A. The master of novices must be diligent in seeing to it that all novices are zealously trained in regular discipline; that they learn to appreciate the pre-eminence and excellence of the divine vocation to which they have been admitted; that they understand the true and perfect fulfilment of solemn vows and the necessity of observance of the constitutions of each order. [They are also to be taught] the method of persevering fruitfully in both vocal and mental prayer, the ways to repress their evil passions and vices, to which nature, weakened by sin, is always inclined and subject: by guarding the senses, by mortification, severity, fasts, and the use of the discipline; by purity of conscience through its frequent examination; by reception of the sacraments, especially confession, which is to take place at least twice a month; by the daily disclosing of interior struggles and the manifestation of conscience and temptations; by the practice of humility in the performance of menial tasks; by the observance of modesty in all acts, and continual silence (*Const. Apost. Cum ad regularem,* § 26, 19 Mar., 1603, *BR* 10:774). B. Let the novices devote themselves to manual labor, read and copy spiritual works, but also have provision in their schedule for a certain moderate relaxation of spirit. . . . This recreation is, however, always to take place in the presence of the master or of his companion, who will be on the alert to see to it that no two draw apart and remain away from the others. Recreation also furnishes a good opportunity for observing the inclinations toward which each one seems to be naturally drawn (*ibid.*, § 29). C. During the novitiate and the time of probation novices are not permitted to associate with the professed except in choir, in the church during the time of sacred services, in processions, or in the refectory at meal times. Neither are they allowed to be companions to the professed when these leave the enclosure (*ibid.*, § 30).

2146. CONGR. OF MOUNT OLIVET (Olivetans, constitutions approved by Pope John XXII, 1324). During their probation the novices must learn by heart, word for word, so that they can recite all from memory: all of Christian Doctrine, the Prologue to the *Rule of St. Benedict,* and Chapters 4, 5, 6, 7, 19, 20, 22, 33, 42, 49, 68, 71, 72, and 73 of the same Rule. They are also to study in a summary manner what is contained in the rest of the Rule. Moreover, they will learn plain chant and everything else that pertains to the monastic way of life. They are not to be admitted to vows without first having taken a test before the abbot and the seniors. . . . No one is to address a novice except in public and in the presence of the novice master. Novices are never to enter the cells of monks (*Constitutiones, Pars II,* c. 58, p. 90; *CR* 5:59).

2147. CONGR. OF STRASBURG. A. We do not absolutely exclude adults or even older persons from our order and congregation. Nevertheless, since each one ordinarily keeps rather constantly even to advanced age that plan of life to which he has been accustomed from tender years . . . we consider it far more advisable to adhere to the long-standing custom of our fathers, from which, as from a fruitful source of holiness and learning so many holy and erudite men have been produced from the beginning of the order. Boys of tender age who are attracted by love of the religious life and have completed at least their fifteenth year, are received into the novitiate in which, along with their studies, they are diligently trained in chant, practices of piety, and the discipline of the monastic life while they are in that innocent age which is impressionable for all that is good as a seal is impressionable on soft wax (*Declar. 2 in c. 58 RSB,* fol. 77).

B. The master of novices is to give them a spiritual conference every day, in which he will read and explain the Rule and the statutes, so that in conformity with the prescriptions of our holy Father they will have completed the reading of the Rule three times during the year of the novitiate. He is also to instruct them and train them in appreciation of how much it is to their advantage not to neglect the blessing of their vocation; with what reverence and devotion, fervor of spirit and cheerfulness they must approach the Divine Office, and with what great attention they must take part in the same; in what reverence they must hold their superiors; and with what charity they must conduct themselves toward their brethren. (He is to teach them) always and everywhere to practice piety and modesty, both in appearance and in conduct, to the edification of externs; to be patient in recreation; observe silence; be humble; love their cells and solitude; be subdued and modest in conversation; be temperate and moderate at table and pay attention to what is read there; to be zealous in daily exercises, moderate and calm in relaxation of spirit, chaste and modest in conduct, truthful, sincere, and faithful to their word (*ibid., declar. 12,* fol. 80).

C. Besides the holy Rule, he will also read the statutes of our congregation to them, explaining the same where there is need to do so. . . . He will train them with regard to all monastic ceremonies, bows, the manner of walking in procession, the signs of reverence to be shown to superiors, always admonishing them to seek to present a pattern of religious humility in all their actions. He will teach them not only monastic and ecclesiastical ceremonies, but also gradually instill their meaning and spiritual significance, their origin, nature, and the religious motives from which they are performed, lest they remain meaningless gestures; hence that they are to be fulfilled by them as an expression of the virtue of religion, the fruit of the spirit. Finally, in order to avoid, as far as can be, errors and confusion in the choir and in the refectory, he must make it a matter of deep concern that they practice in the novitiate and learn thoroughly whatever they are to perform, read, or sing in public (*ibid., declar. 13,* fol. 81).

D. And because our holy Father, Benedict, commands that "the novice be told all the hardships and trials through which we travel to God" (*RSB,* c. 58), in his explanation of the Rule the master of novices will zealously explain and show them how perfect and absolute an obedience our holy Father demands of his religious; how serious are the laws of Benedictine poverty; how great the obligation of preserving chastity and stability and of always striving for perfection. He must make it clear to them that in order to realize all these ideals, no other means can serve but mortification and devotion—the former as it were the hammer, and the latter the heat for shaping the iron of our heart (*ibid., declar. 14*).

2148. SWABIAN CONGR. OF ST. JOSEPH. A. The master is frequently to test the novices in the practices of self-denial, in renouncing their own inclinations and giving up their own will, in giving evidence of their contempt of the world, in facing embarrassments, and in performing acts of humiliation and penance. He will try their spirits by assigning them to more menial and unpleasant tasks; by taking from them those works which are more pleasing and easily performed; and by mortifying them in other ways. But in all this he is to observe moderation and confine his practices to that which is in harmony with [the traditions of] our order (*Const. et declar., Pars III,* c. 3, punctum 3, n. 9, fol. 238). B. Meanwhile, he will attentively observe what are the inclinations and manners of each individual. Should he note that some are opinionated, much attached to their own views, stubborn, proud, wanting in devotion, contumacious, quarrelsome, troublesome, or unable to bear the common burdens of our order, either because of physical weakness or other defect, he will inform the abbot as soon as possible in order that undesirable candidates may be dismissed in good season. Let him particularly note that in such cases the common welfare of the monastery is always to be preferred to the private good of anyone (*ibid.,* 10, fol. 239).

2149. SPANISH CONGR. (1640). The master must often place before the eyes of the novices the excellence of the state to which they have been called by God; the eminence of religion's four vows of obedience, chastity, poverty, and the enclosure [stability]; the perfection and sweet reasonableness of the holy Rule and the constitutions according to which our life is to be led. As often, moreover, as he addresses an exhortation to them, he will direct his remarks toward inspiring them with love for their state. It will contribute greatly to this end if they examine their conscience repeatedly during the day and everywhere remain conscious of God's presence. The master is to be present at the suitable recreation which is permitted to the novices from time to time. He will temper and blend all his commands with a deep love as the means of gaining them for God (*Caeremoniale monasticum, Pars II,* dist. 3, c. 4, n. 6, p. 386).

2150. CONGR. OF HIRSCHAU. The profession of anyone who comes from another monastery is to be deferred beyond that of other novices, and after the candidate has become acquainted with our customs, nothing is to be passed over unnoticed, no matter what he has done amiss, in order that it can be determined whether he truly seeks God. Those who have as yet no experience of our way of life—whether they be cleric or lay—must be told in all earnestness, as stated in the Rule, the harsh and difficult things that must necessarily be borne if they are to attain to our subjection. For this demands of them that they give up all power over their own will and be dependent on the judgment of another in all things (*Const. Hirsaugiens. S. Wilhelmi, Lib. I,* c. 2, *PL* 151:933).

2151. CONGR. OF FRANCE (Solesmes, 1837). During the novitiate the novices are particularly to be devoted, under their master's direction, to spiritual progress, the acquisition of monastic virtues, and the perfection of self-control. Consequently they must not be assigned to classes in subjects that are profane or calculated merely to gratify curiosity. They are zealously to take up, each according to his ability, the manual labor assigned to them. They are to seek earnestly to learn those things which mark the true monk, namely the holy Rule, on whose spirit and letter they will have their principal conferences, besides the one which is held every day for all in the monastery. They will make their culpa [acknowledgment of faults] every Wednesday to their master, in the presence of others. They are to study Gregorian chant, ceremonies, and rubrics. They will strive to develop the memory in order to prevent it from being lost or growing weaker (*Reg. SS. P.N. Benedicti una cum Const.,* art. 67, p. 161).

2152. POPE LEO XII (d. 1829). The standing and honor of every religious family depends to the greatest extent on the excellence of the novitiate training; if this is neglected or allowed to become indulgent, the honor of the order will necessarily decline and collapse (*Const. Apost. Lectissimam,* § 2, 20 Jul., 1827, *Coenobium S. Sabinae de Urbe in Aventino erigitur in domum tirocinii pro Dominicanis, BRC* 8:547).

2152 [a]. PROV. COUNCIL OF UTRECHT (1865). The observance of those regulations that ecclesiastical sanctions demand with regard to the admission of novices to the habit and to profession is of utmost importance, for it is beyond all doubt that the welfare or disaster of every religious institute depends upon this observance. The superiors of orders are free to receive postulants for the habit and to admit to profession those who have been tried, according to the statutes of the order and the precepts of the Holy See; but first they must make diligent inquiry with regard to the candidate's character, talent, and habits, and try to learn on what counsel, with what spirit, and for what motives they are drawn to the regular life. In fulfilling these requirements they are to keep before them the prescript published January 25, 1848 (*Decr. Romani Pontifices, CJC, Fontes,* n. 4375, 6:961), regarding testimonial letters of the Ordinary to be petitioned before reception for those who request to be admitted to the habit. Another Apostolic decree of March 19, 1857 (*Neminem latet, ibid.,* n. 4381, 6:973; Bizzarri, *Collectanea,* p. 853), is also strictly to be observed: according to its provisions, upon termination of the novitiate, simple vows are to be pronounced for at least three years before solemn vows may be made.

For the rest, novices are not to be admitted to profession before they have been tried in the *tyrocinium* (novitiate) for the entire period that the sacred canons, as well as the constitutions of the religious institute prescribe. This trial itself is to be conducted in the manner which is determined in the instructions published at the command of Pope Clement VIII for the reception and training of novices in monasteries and convents already designated or to be designated (*Const. Apost. Cum ad regularem,* 19 Mar., 1603, *ibid.,* 2:358). Hence we admonish and earnestly request superiors of regular orders to employ personally, or see to it that others employ, the most exacting diligence and care in trying the novices. Let them rather act with severity in trying and in admitting the candidates to the profession of vows than admit with excessive ease those who, not having been drawn by a divine vocation, may prove to be an embarrassment and disgrace to the religious institute and a scandal to the faithful (*Decr.*, tit. 7, c. 2, *de regularium regimine et disciplina, CL* 5:893).

Training of professed religious

2153. CONGR. OF ST. BERNARD in Italy, Cistercians. With regard to the education of the newly professed, the Apostolic Constitution of Pope Clement VIII [see preceding number] is to be observed in all its provisions. No custom to the contrary (which should rather be called a corruption of the law) is to be admitted as an excuse. Therefore, after they have pronounced profession, those who are not forthwith to be sent to college, and others, are to be kept in the novitiate department under the regulations and following the manner of life prescribed for novices until such time as they are actually sent to college, or, if need be, until they are transferred to another monastery where they have the facilities for training professed clerics according to the prescriptions of the Apostolic Constitution of Pope Clement VIII. There they will remain until they have attained the age required for receiving sacred orders, or at least for three years after profession, devoting themselves to their studies, each according to his ability. During this time they will be under the direction and government of the superior, who is to possess the same qualifications as are demanded for the master of novices (*Const.* approved by Pope Urban VIII, 1641).

2154. SWABIAN CONGR. OF ST. JOSEPH. As in the case of the novices, individual attention is also to be directed to the professed, so that they will not grow remiss in anything they have learned in the practices of the novitiate, but will daily make greater progress in the virtues of religion (*Const. et declar., Pars III*, c. 3, punctum 3, n. 11, fol. 239).

2155. SPANISH CONGR. (1640). Juniors who have not yet completed three years after their clothing with the habit [that is, profession], are to remain under the discipline and instruction of the master whom the abbot has appointed for them. As regards their spiritual exercises, he will follow with them the routine prescribed for the novices and zealously see to it that they do not lose the sound doctrine and spiritual fruit they have acquired in the novitiate. They are daily to make an examination of conscience, and as men who are seriously intent on acquiring virtues, deliberate with themselves and see whether they are making progress (*Caeremoniale monast., Pars II,* dist. 3, c. 6, n. 1, p. 402).

The abbot's paternal government of the monks

2156. SWABIAN CONGR. OF ST. JOSEPH. A. The abbot is to watch over the welfare and progress of his monks with scrupulous care and by his paternal exhortations is personally to encourage earnest striving for genuine obedience, fraternal charity, humility, mortification, and religious perfection itself; he is likewise to see to it that this zealous effort is seconded by others (*Const. et declar., Pars III*, c. 1, punctum 2, n. 2, fol. 209). B. In keeping with the admonition of our holy Father Benedict, the abbot must maintain as his first and most important charge the constant and prudently zealous preservation in his monastery of the splendor of divine worship and the observance of monastic discipline, in harmony with the nature of the institute and the prescriptions of our congregation. He must earnestly implore by daily prayer and sacrifice the aid of divine grace, that he may foster and promote the increase of this splendor and observance (*ibid.*, n. 1, fol. 208).

2157. PROV. COUNCIL OF BOURGES (1850). Superiors of religious communities must know that the houses assigned to them are so to be governed that the glory of God will be promoted; the honor of the Church and the benefit of civil society itself, which religious families so happily foster by their prayers and works of charity, will be furthered; the welfare of souls will be increased; and the edification of the people in the territory advanced (*Decr.*, tit. 2, *II, CL* 4:1100).

2158. PROV. COUNCIL OF GRAN (Hungary, 1858). We seriously warn, exhort and petition you, superiors of monasteries, to see to it that the religious men assigned to your charge, seriously reflect on the vocation to which they are called, walk worthy of it, and strive in a most religious manner to fulfil the vows which they have made to God (*Decr.*, tit. 7, n. 3, *CL* 5:65).

2159. PROV. COUNCIL OF PRAGUE (1860). Let all superiors bear in mind that as they have the power not only of governing but also of judging their subjects and punishing them, they are bound in conscience to foster and perfect in every way possible the regular life among those subjects, to remove abuses, and promote the internal and external prosperity of the order and of their community (*Decr.*, tit. 7, c. 2, *de regimine regularium, CL* 5:572).

The abbot is adorned with quasi-episcopal dignity by the Church

2160. POPE ST. THEODORE (d. 649). We are prompted by the obligations of charity and moved by the benevolence of the Apostolic See to honor brethren and bestow favors of special privileges on the children of the Roman Church, in order that, enjoying distinction in the eyes of men, and being supported by such expressions of Apostolic love, they may more securely govern the churches assigned to them. We do this too in order that their subjects may show them greater reverence and honor. We are pleased to grant this privilege to the monastery [of Bobbio] and its church, to be preserved with perpetual authority: it is permitted for the abbot of this venerable place to use the miter and other pontifical insignia. And since we have so disposed by favor of Blessed Peter's and Our own love, We grant the monastery itself and its church the additional honor that the abbot of the same monastery, in the act of performing the sacred mysteries, may be fortified with the sign of the Holy Cross (*Ep. 6, ad Bobiense monasterium privilegium, an. 643, PL* 87:99).

2161. CONGR. OF HIRSCHAU. The abbot's throne is to be placed to the right of the altar facing the choir. But if he himself desires to chant the Mass, a cope is to be brought to him, in order that the choir can be conducted by him. . . . After the Gospel the book is presented to him to be kissed, and the *Pax* is given to him. Whenever he assists at Mass, the priest or the deacon, who is about to chant the Gospel turns toward him to receive the blessing, unless he is at too great a distance (*Const. Hirsaugiens., S. Wilhelmi, Lib. II,* c. 12, *PL* 150:1049).

2162. ROMAN PONTIFICAL. A. Graciously strengthen by the grace of your protection him whom the common choice of your servants has chosen abbot over your sheep. Grant that he may so rule his subjects and the sheep entrusted to his care that together with them he may attain the kingdom of heaven. With your help, O Lord, and ever supported by the Apostolic teaching may he, with fruit a hundredfold, joyfully enter the gates of paradise. And may he merit to hear from you, Lord, the words of your praise: *Well done, good and faithful servant; because thou hast been faithful over a few things, I will set thee over many; enter into the joy of thy master* (*De benedictione abbatis auctoritate apostolica, Oratio 2a post litanias sanctorum,* 1:145). B. We beg you, Lord, grant to me, your servant, that by means of worthy doctrine and works I may, by my example, instruct the minds of my subjects, and may receive from you, the most loving Shepherd, an everlasting reward. Through the same Lord Jesus Christ . . . (*Ibid., Oratio 2a Missae, sub unica conclusione,* 1:136). C. May he, O Lord, this day receive through your bounty perseverance in good works, constancy in adversity, patience in tribulation. May he find pleasure in fasting, show mercy to wrongdoers, exercise authority with humility, hate pride, be a lover of the faith, be vigilant in doctrine, chaste, abstemious. May he employ moderation on all occasions; may his own life show forth his teaching. Grant, O Lord, that he may persevere in his ministry even as St. Stephen, chosen a Levite by the Apostles, merited to persevere. May he, from this day forward, despise attachment to worldly ways. May he, Lord, by virtue of your blessing, hold as of little worth the things of the present, love those which are heavenly, and keep his desire fixed on eternity. May his faithful government in your Church be an example and pattern of justice. May he be for other abbots a worthy model of a superior. May he be outstanding in spiritual direction, diligent in reproving wrong, wise in his manner of discipline. By the operation of your grace, may he serve you, O Lord, with a clean heart and without blame in all your commands, and in so doing attain the reward of his high calling, and with fruit multiplied a hundredfold. May he be adorned with the crown of justice and enter upon the enjoyment of your heavenly treasures (*ibid., Praefatio, media pars,* 1:148 ff.). D. . . . Bestow upon him the gifts of your virtues of justice, temperance, fortitude, prudence, charity, sobriety, patience, long-suffering, invincible constancy, unfeigned faith, unshakable hope, a devout mind, perfect humility, right understanding, benignity, modesty, single-mindedness, peace, concord, chastity, abstinence, vigilance, discretion, uprightness, knowledge, piety, counsel, and irreproachable perseverance in all good works (*ibid., Oratio 3a post praefationem,* 1:152).

2163. POPE CLEMENT VIII (d. 1605). Let those especially be chosen for offices, positions of rank, and prelatial dignities who are able to observe and have actually been accustomed to observe the Rule of the order and the constitutions, particularly with regard to attendance at choir and the community distribution of clothing and food (*Const. apost. Nullus omnino,* § 23, 25 Jul., 1599, *BRC* 10:666; *CJC, Fontes,* n. 187, 1:356).

2164. CONGR. OF ST. MAUR. By means of attentive and frequent reading of this chapter (*RSB,* c. 2), let all superiors zealously reflect on the heavy burden they bear and be so watchful over the spiritual progress of the souls assigned to them that they excel in the example of virtue those over whom they preside by their authority (*Declar. 2 in c. 2 RSB,* p. 17).

2165. POPE INNOCENT III (d. 1216). See to it, my sons, that both by rooting out vices and by implanting virtues you who are abbots watch so vigilantly over your own lives and over the flock committed to your care that you may be able to present a worthy account at the severe judgment on the last day before the fearful Judge who will *render to everyone according to his deeds* (Ps. 61:13; *Ep. 91, universis Cluniac. ordinis abbatibus et prioribus ut monasteria eorum reformare studeant,* 15 Mar., 1214, *BR* 3:274).

2166. BURSFELD CONGR. A. The abbot must know that he is to render an account to God of his own manner of life and that of his subjects, and that he will incur the displeasure of the Shepherd if God finds any lack of profit in the sheep which the abbot's diligence could have gained. Hence he is never to fail to petition from God both the grace of enlightenment for himself and the disposition of eagerness to be directed on the part of his subjects. Nor should he fail to offer his subjects to God in Mass (*Stat.*, dist. 3, c. 1, n. 2, p. 76). B. He is, therefore, zealously to foster the practice of mental prayer, silence, fasts, fraternal charity, and similar observances, which are the foundation of the whole religious life (*ibid.*, n. 3).

2167. SWABIAN CONGR. OF ST. JOSEPH. Let the abbot, *becoming from the heart the pattern of the flock* (I Petr. 5:3), acquire and protect his authority with solid virtues. With the conviction that he is guilty of as many deaths as he has led others into sin by his evil example, let him solicitously guard against committing anything that could cause scandal to others or rightfully be considered a vice (*Const. et declar., Pars III,* c. 1, punctum 2, n. 4, fol. 211).

2168. ROMAN PONTIFICAL. We place on the head of this your servant, the abbot, O Lord, the helmet of salvation and protection, so that his face being adorned and his head armed with the might of both Testaments, he may appear terrible to the enemies of truth and, through the indulgence of your grace, may be their powerful adversary, you who marked the countenance of Moses, your servant, with the bright rays of your splendor and truth from his fellowship with your word, and ordered the tiara to be placed on the head of your high-priest, Aaron. Through Christ our Lord. Amen (*De benedictione abbatis auctoritate apostolica, impositio mitrae, paulo ante Te Deum,* 1:158).

2169. ROMAN MISSAL. Place upon my head, O Lord, the miter, which is the helmet of salvation, in order that I may proceed without hindrance in the face of temptations of the ancient foe, and all my enemies (*Praeparatio ad Missam; orationes dicendae ab episcopo quando in pontificalibus celebrat; . . . ad mitram. Miss. Rom.*, p. LVII).

The abbot must be a man of humility and simplicity

2170. SWABIAN CONGR. OF ST. JOSEPH. Let the abbot be particularly intent on practicing humility, but tempered with dignity and maturity of conduct (*Const. et declar., Pars III,* c. 1, punctum 2, n. 4, fol. 211).

2171. CONGR. OF BURSFELD. A. The abbot's garb is not to differ from that of the brethren as to form; in quality it must not exceed the demands of religious modesty and must exclude even the slightest note of vanity. Let his habit be determined by the respectability called for by his office and the religious modesty of his profession. . . . Neither within the monastery nor away from it is he to incur unnecessary expense by serving sumptuous banquets or permitting them to be served (*Stat.*, dist. 3, c. 1, § 5, p. 79). B. In dispensing the goods of the monastery according to the intention of the founders and of St. Benedict to the brethren, the poor, and the guests, he is to observe religious frugality and moderate liberality in everything. He must rigorously guard against what is superfluous, ostentatious and useless in buildings, garb and service (*ibid.*, § 3).

2172. POPE CLEMENT XII (d. 1740). Since abbots and all others appointed to share in governing are to work for the common welfare of the whole order, and since they know that their own powers are inadequate for bearing so heavy a burden, they are, more than all else, never to cease imploring the divine aid; they are particularly to have recourse to prayer when some necessity arises. They must realize that they have been chosen to work and exercise zealous care rather than to enjoy positions of honor; they must constantly remind themselves that they are to excel the brethren in example and virtuous works. Hence they will observe community regulations accurately and avoid, as far as possible, all singularity in food, clothing and the use of commodities. From the frequent reading of the constitutions as they apply to the community at large, themselves personally and other officials, they are to seek to acquaint themselves with the purposes of their office, and understand that they are never to act rashly or arbitrarily. Rather they are to realize that the order is to be governed and the brethren directed by the prescripts of the Rule, by the constitutions and accepted customs (*Const. Apost. Misericordiarum pater, Pars III*, c. 1, n. 1, 17 Jan., 1740; *confirmatio reg. et const. monachorum Maronitarum O.S. Antonii, Congr. S. Isaiae in Syria, BR* 24:624).

The abbot must be intent on his own sanctification

2173. CONGR. OF BURSFELD. A. An abbot must be distinguished by his personal observance of the Rule as well as by the honor he receives. When assignments that justify his absence cease, and he is not engaged in works that are necessary for the monastery, nor otherwise hindered, he will endeavor to be present in choir, at meditation, in the periods of recollection and at Mass. He will thus become the pattern of the flock and excel by his religious example in the things of God (*Stat.*, dist. 3, c. 1, n. 1, p. 71). B. Since he must be intent not only on the spiritual welfare of others but also have care for his own soul, the abbot will see to it that as far as the works of administration will permit, he will attend morning office and meditation frequently, so that he can both render his duty to God and inspire the brethren to observance (*ibid.*, § 5, n. 1, p. 79).

2174. CONGR. OF STRASBURG. In order to make their subjects more willingly submissive, prelates must become a pattern to the flock and leaders in all things that are to be done. Let them make an effort, therefore, to be present and take part in the regular exercises, insofar as their duties, the administration of temporalities, their physical health and bodily powers will permit. One commands most persuasively by example. Let them be on their guard lest, being forgetful of their own spiritual welfare and that of their subjects, and preferring earthly things to heavenly and the human to the divine (*Conc. Trident., Sess. VI, de ref., Can. et decr.,* Richter, p. 33; Schroeder, *Trent,* p. 47), they keep themselves occupied with the solicitudes of temporal matters to the neglect of the care of the sheep entrusted to them (*Declar. 2 in c. 2 RSB,* fol. 5).

2175. POPE CLEMENT XII. The superiors are to devote their efforts to governing others in spiritual matters and even in things temporal, in such a manner that they themselves do not grow negligent in the practice of virtue or in the concern for their own personal welfare. All things that pertain to religious perfection and which are prescribed for monks in their relations toward abbots and superiors, such as the manifestation of conscience, the withdrawal from common recreational activity for the purpose of making a retreat, and similar practices are to be understood as applying to abbots and other superiors as well (*Const. Apost., Misericordiarum pater, Pars III,* c. 1, n. 8, *BR* 24:624).

The abbot's filial love for his sons

2176. SWABIAN CONGR. OF ST. JOSEPH. The abbot is to strive for meekness and charity, and in order to win the reciprocal love of his subjects. He is to exercise foresight with paternal solicitude and care regarding each person's requirements and that not only in connection with their corporal needs, but even more so with regard to their spiritual necessities (*Stat., Pars III,* c. 1, punctum 2, p. 211).

2177. POPE CLEMENT XII. Let superiors be ever on their guard against offending others by familiarity and unwarranted considerations shown to certain individuals; they must take care not to give others any occasion for taking offense in this matter. They must be careful never to show themselves distant or unfriendly toward anyone, but must strive to be impartial and devoid of all acceptance of persons (*Const. Apost. Misericordiarum pater, Pars III,* c. 1, n. 3, *BR* 24:624).

2178. SPANISH CONGR. (1640). As a kind father let the abbot receive his sons with great tenderness and unaffected love when he must correct them, acting thus solely in order to win them for God and the order. In deep sorrow he is to realize that they have abandoned the royal road, and that he is to use all his powers to bring them back to it (*Caeremoniale monastic., Pars II,* dist. 2, c. 2, n. 9, p. 339).

The crosier is the symbol of fatherly correction and spiritual direction

2179. ROMAN PONTIFICAL. Receive the staff of the pastoral office and carry it before the flock entrusted to you, that in correcting vices you may be lovingly severe, and mindful of mercy when you are provoked to anger (*De benedictione abbatis auctoritate apostolica, traditio baculi pastoralis,* 1:155).

2180. POPE CLEMENT XIV. Be mindful, all you who are superiors, and whatever your rank, that in order to be able to fulfil the duties of prelate, judge, and father, as your office demands, to extirpate vices and foster the practice of virtue, you must continually practice prudence, justice, and charity (*Const. Apost., In vinea Dni,* § 14, 4 Jul., 1772; *confirmatio decr. pro Cappuccinis provinciae Subalpinae, BRC* 5:464).

2181. CONGR. OF STRASBURG. The Lord demands that prelates possess zeal for discipline, stating: *Seek not to become a judge if you have not strength to root out crime* (Sir. 7:6); thus teaching that he makes himself guilty of no light fault who, by reason of his office and the power vested in him, is duty bound to repress and correct vices, through dissimulation and conniving in reality encourages and increases them (*Declar. 3 in c. 2 RSB,* fol. 6).

2182. POPE CLEMENT XII. In giving corrections and imposing penances, let superiors avoid every expression of anger or any other unworthy attitude. Rather let them take into account the disposition of persons, having in mind both general and particular edification. Unless prudence dictates otherwise in individual instances, superiors are to proceed in this order in their corrections: they who have been guilty of fault are first to be dealt with in all charity, it is true, but in such a way that they are embarrassed and shamed, and then, if necessary, those things which strike fear are to be added to the love. The penance must be public for public violations (*Const. Apost., Misericordiarum pater, Pars III,* c. 1, n. 7, *BR* 24:604).

The abbot must instruct his subjects

2183. ROMAN PONTIFICAL. A. By the same authority [the ancient rule of the holy Fathers], we ask: "Will you observe your sacred promise and the Rule of St. Benedict, and diligently instruct your subjects to do the same?" The abbot-elect responds: "I will" (*De benedictione abbatis auctoritate apostolica, prima pars interrogationis, ante Missam,* 1:133). B. Show him the way in which he should walk; bestow on him the treasure of wisdom, so that he may know and possess whence to bring forth new things and old (*ibid., Oratio 3a post Praefationem,* 1:153).

2184. POPE CLEMENT VIII (d. 1605). We admonish all superiors in the Lord to be mindful of the accounting for the flock committed to them that they must render on the last day. With this thought before them, let them see to it that everything that has been prudently and piously prescribed in the rules and constitutions of their orders regarding mental prayer, silence, fasting, the chapter of faults, and other spiritual exercises be observed in all points to the letter of the law. They are to realize that whatever is built up in all religious orders can only be erected and enlarged on these foundations, and that it is highly appropriate for obtaining results more readily, and producing richer fruits in the souls of the brethren to have a sermon on religious discipline and regular observance every week in each monastery (*Const. Apost., Nullus omnino,* § 26, 25 Jul., 1599, *BR* 10:666; *CJC, Fontes,* n. 187, 1:387).

2185. CONGR. OF BURSFELD. [The abbot] "ought to rule his disciples with a twofold teaching, displaying all goodness and holiness by deeds and by words, but by deeds rather than by words" (*RSB,* c. 2), so that at the command of our holy Father he teach by his own observance more than with his lips (*Stat.,* dist. 3, c. 1, § 3, n. 4, p. 76).

2186. POPE CLEMENT XII. Let [abbots] arrange that at appointed times the brethren discuss their matters of conscience with them personally or with others assigned for that purpose by them. Nor are they to be negligent about the customary spiritual conferences, but they are to address their subjects frequently, and with profound spirit of charity. They are likewise to be paternally provident not only with regard to their physical needs, but much more those which are spiritual. When they realize that a brother is besieged by some serious temptation, they are to concern themselves with doing all they can for him, not only personally but if necessary through others, and to be on their guard against delay in employing the remedy, lest in so doing they make the cure more difficult. . . . They are to devote their efforts to watching over all the brethren with solicitude and to shielding them from harmful influences at home and away from it, both by prevention and, if any evil has already occurred, by employing a remedy, so that the honor and reputation of the individual brethren as well as of the order at large will be consulted (*Const. Apost., Misericordiarum pater, Pars III,* c. 1, nn. 5, 4, *BR* 24:624).

The abbot must act with prudence

2187. POPE HONORIUS I (d. 638). The norm set up by the traditions of our Fathers must be kept before both the eyes of the mind and those of the body. Let every superior realize how he must govern his subjects: the natural rigor must be moderated and severity toward the brethren be made one of solicitude (*Privilegium Bobiensi coenobio datum, PL* 80:484).

2188. CONGR. OF STRASBURG. Abbots must strive to realize the great prudence they need to govern their subjects, and the discretion they must possess to accommodate themselves to each one's nature in order to gain souls (*Declar. 4 in c. 2 RSB,* fol. 6).

2189. CONGR. OF BURSFELD. The abbot is bound to use the greatest care and to exercise all prudence and diligence to prevent losing any of the sheep entrusted to him. Let him know that what he has undertaken is the charge of weakly souls, not a tyranny over the strong (*RSB*, c. 27). Hence he is not to show a dislike by avoiding the imperfect, nor adopt an attitude of hopelessness regarding them, being mindful that it is not the well who need a physician, but those who are ill (*Stat.*, dist. 3, c. 1, § 4, n. 3, p. 78).

2190. ROMAN MISSAL. Deign to protect me, Lord Jesus Christ, with the sign of your most holy Cross, from all insidious temptations of all enemies; and deign to grant me, your unworthy servant, that as I carry this cross which contains the relics of your saints, on my breast, I may thus be ever mindful of the memorial of your passion and the victories gained by your holy martyrs (*Praeparatio ad Missam; orationes dicendae ab episcopo quando in pontificalibus celebrat: . . . cum accipit crucem pectoralem, Miss. Rom.*, p. LVII).

Entire government of the monastery belongs to abbot

2191. ROMAN PONTIFICAL. Receive the Rule handed down by the holy Fathers for the government and protection of the flock entrusted to you by God, insofar as God himself will strengthen you and human frailty will allow. Receive the office of paternally providing for the Lord's flock and of caring for their souls. Walk according to the precepts of the divine law, and thus be their guide to the pasture of their heavenly inheritance. With the help of our Lord Jesus Christ, who lives and reigns with the Father and the Holy Spirit, God, world without end. Amen (*De benedictione abbatis auctoritate apostolica, traditio Regulae*, 1:154).

Abbot personally chooses the officials of the monastery

2192. COUNCIL OF BASLE (1431). In order that the abbot may not personally be unduly burdened with the administration of temporal affairs, and all the more, in order that he may be able to devote immediate attention to spiritual concerns, We desire and ordain that, after having consulted the seniors, he appoint the officials of the monastery, namely, the cellarer, the infirmarian, the monk in charge of the wardrobe, the sacristan, the porter, and others whom he may need for all the necessary duties of the monastery. These officials will present an accurate report to the abbot and the seniors about the duties assigned to them, or the works that they have commissioned to others, as often as the abbot deems such a report advisable (*Stat. et ordinationes ad monachos congr. Mellicensis directae, ex manusc. Salisburgensi*).

2193. CONGR. OF BURSFELD. In order for the affairs of the order to be administered properly and fruitfully, the abbot is to appoint different religious as his officials and helpers. These men are not to be chosen in any given order of seniority or out of personal attachment, but solely for their fear of God, worthiness of life and personal ability. Other factors being equal, however, men of more mature age and long, continued observance are to be preferred for appointment to regular offices. But they too must be chosen solely for the greater good of the monastery and the welfare of souls. Neither in their appointment nor in their removal are votes of the brethren taken, for St. Benedict commits the government of the monastery to the abbot (*Stat.*, dist. 3, c. 1, § 3, n. 6, p. 77).

2194. CONGR. OF STRASBURG. A. The appointment of claustral superiors is the abbot's exclusive right; it is prudent, however, if he so desire, that the nomination of the prior be made upon having consulted two or three of the seniors (*Declar. 10 in c. 21 RSB,* fol. 30). B. Our holy Father grants the abbot full authority of putting the prior into office and also of deposing him, after he has consulted the seniors; in the same way, he is free to appoint and remove other religious officials, both in order that by so doing their humility may be tested, and that they who have been distracted for a year with numerous preoccupations, often to the neglect of their own personal religious duties, by reason of their obligations to others, may once more devote themselves fully to the spirit of recollectedness (*Declar. 1 in c. 65 RSB,* fol. 100). C. The abbot should appoint officials who are prudent, experienced, trustworthy, and obedient, men with whom he may safely share the burdens of his office (*Declar. 6 in c. 2 RSB,* fol. 7). D. Let the prelates choose as officials men whom they know observe the rules and constitutions of their order, as Pope Clement VIII prescribes (*Const. Apost., Nullus omnino,* § 23, 25 Jul., 1599, *BRC* 10:666), especially with regard to choir service, common food, and clothing, men of whose religious life and moral conduct they are certain, as Pope Innocent III warns, men who are faithful (c. 3, *Cum ad monasterium,* c. 6, *de stat. monachorum, CJC,* Richter 2:577). We exhort in the Lord officials who have been thus appointed to perform in all humility and obedience the duties enjoined, or any other obligations assigned to them by the superior. Should one of them become puffed up because of his skill in practical affairs or the quality of his work, or if he seems to think that he is conferring a benefit on the monastery, or if he murmurs against the instructions of the superiors when they prescribe something in connection with his work or office, he is to be called to render an accounting and is to be removed if he does not correct his ways after he has been admonished once or twice (*Declar. 3 in c. 32 RSB,* fol. 42).

2195. CONGR. OF CAMALDULI (founded in 1018 by S. Romuald, confirmed by Pope Alexander II in 1072). After he has thought over the matter carefully and has discussed it with the seniors, the superior will assemble all the monks in chapter and announce whom he has chosen as prior, if he is an abbot, or whom he has appointed subprior in a monastery which only has a prior. He also appoints the deans in proportion to the number of monks; then the sacristan, the priests for hearing confessions, infirmarians, guestmasters, porters, managers of the household, the ones in charge of the wine cellar, and the other officials of the monastery (*In Reg. divi P. Ben., declar.*, c. 21, p. 118; *CR* 2:229).

2196. POPE INNOCENT III. Only they who are trustworthy and discreet are to be appointed to the offices of the monastery. Nor is an assignment under obedience to be committed to anyone as though it were a possession to be held in perpetuity, or bestowed on him for life. When it becomes desirable that he be removed from office, he is to be changed without any show of opposition (*Lib. V. Regestorum, Ep. 82, Abbati et conventui Sublacens., PL* 214:1066).

2197. SWABIAN CONGR. OF ST. JOSEPH. A. Let the abbot appoint conventual superiors and officials whom he has observed to possess a deeper love of monastic discipline and to excel others in purity of life and prudence, and whom he has found that he can direct with his counsel and inspire and encourage with his authority (*Const. et declar., Pars III*, c. 1, punctum 2, n. 7, fol. 213). B. He will appoint men who are of good repute, experienced, prudent, loyal, and obedient to him personally, men with whom he can safely share his responsibilities (*ibid.*, n. 8). C. No appointee's tenure of office is permanent; any of them may be removed whenever it seems advisable, not only when some seem to fulfil their duties unsatisfactorily, but for any other reason as well (*ibid.*, n. 2, fol. 209).

The kind of man the prior should be

2198. POPE INNOCENT III. Second in rank only to the abbot, the prior must be conscientious and zealous in the practice of the religious life, strong in deed and word, so that he may instruct the brethren in virtue, both by his exemplary life and his doctrine, and win them away from evil by correcting and punishing the delinquent and by encouraging and strengthening the obedient (*Lib. V. Regestorum, Ep. 82, Abbati et conventui Sublacens., PL* 214:1066).

2199. POPE BENEDICT XII (d. 1342). Since the claustral prior must be a man powerful in deed and effective of speech, We desire and command, in virtue of holy obedience, that the most capable man available in the monastery . . . be appointed to that office, that he be fervent, discreet, and so dependable in character that he will reside continually within the community and be bound by the obligation of assiduously devoting himself to the spiritual care and government of all within the enclosure (*Const. Apost. Summi magistri,* c. 30, 20 Jun., 1336; *ordinationes et reformationes pro bono regimine monachorum nigrorum O.S.B., BR* 4:383).

2200. CONGR. OF HIRSCHAU. A. When a prior is to be appointed, the abbot will first discuss the selection with the seniors. He will afterward report his decision to the chapter, and all will commend the choice he has made (*Const. Hirsaug., Lib. II,* c. 16, *PL* 150:1056). B. Let all respect be shown to the prior by everyone in chapter. He must always be on his guard not to undertake matters that the abbot has reserved to his own decision. On the other hand he must be zealous in chapter and everywhere in handling with reverence and discretion the matters pertaining to his office (*ibid.,* c. 17, col. 1058). C. From the hour of his appointment the prior, after the abbot, is in charge of all the property and can conduct all the business of the monastery, with the exception of the treasury and safe of the church, which are reserved to the abbot's authority (*ibid.,* c. 16, col. 1057).

2201. CONGR. OF BURSFELD. A. Since the abbot cannot personally handle the entire administration, he is to select and appoint a prior according to the Rule, after having privately obtained the advice of God-fearing brethren. His choice must rest on one who is powerful in word and work, capable of leading the brethren by his example and teaching, qualified to govern, correct, encourage, inspire, and exhort all to regular observance. An inflexible observer of discipline, he must be neither quarrelsome nor domineering, but a model to the community, serious and moderate, able to win the minds and hearts of his brethren, most closely allied to the abbot in sincere and religious humility, and earnestly seeking to verify in his life everything that the holy Rule prescribes for the prior of the monastery (*Stat.,* dist. 3, c. 2, n. 1, p. 82). B. The prior is to relieve the abbot of the duty of examining the cells and beds of the brethren, of visiting and helping the sick and, in general, of granting those daily or frequently-recurring permissions for which the brethren have recourse to him, unless there should arise a matter of such importance that it should not be decided without the knowledge and special permission of the abbot (*ibid.,* n. 6, p. 85).

2202. COUNCIL OF BASLE (1431). We ordain that a prudent and discreet prior be appointed who will faithfully exercise the authority committed to him for the benefit of the community, continually reside in the monastery, constantly devote himself to the care and government of the brethren. As he is called prior (the first), he will everywhere be first, especially at the Work of God. He will see to it that the law of silence be diligently observed at the prescribed hours. Above all else he will devote himself with conscientious effort to the Divine Office. It is his duty to visit the cells, at least during the Ember weeks, to make certain that no weapons or private property are kept in them (*Stat. et ordinationes ad monachos Congr. Mellicensis directae, ex manuscr. Salisburgensi*).

2203. SWABIAN CONGR. OF ST. JOSEPH. The prior must render the abbot perfect obedience and every sign of reverence, and particularly in these obligations give an example to others, so that they will also be drawn to the abbot in the same spirit of veneration and love. The prior will frequently confer confidentially with the abbot on means to improve regular discipline; he must preserve secrets inviolably; nourish the Lord's flock in the same spirit as the abbot, lest conflicting commands render the sweet yoke of the Lord unbearable for the brethren. Let him be first not so much as a matter of title and rank as in observance, and hence in everything pertaining to regular discipline he is to excel others by his good example. . . . He is to be zealously alert in seeing to it that the Rule and our constitutions are constantly observed by all. . . . In his charity he is to provide for the needs of the community, particularly in those wants that make themselves felt daily, and in the matters where recourse must be had to him, unless there be question of so important a concession that it would not be proper to grant it without the knowledge and special permission of the abbot. . . . He will substitute for the abbot in his absence and decide everything as it seems to him most expedient in the Lord, but observe whatever restrictions the abbot has made before his departure (*Const. et declar., Pars III,* c. 2, punctum 1, n. 1, fol. 220–221).

2204. POPE PIUS VI (d. 1799). Those who are appointed priors must be priests, well trained in regular observance, men who have lived in the order in a commendable manner, possessing a reputation for their worthiness (*Const. Apost. Apostolatus officium,* § 97, *Pars II,* c. 1, 15 Maii, 1799, *BRC* 6:2066).

Subprior substitutes for prior when he is absent or impeded

2205. CONGR. OF HIRSCHAU. The claustral subprior is the vicar of the prior in all matters. . . . Whenever the abbot and the prior go away from the monastery, it is he who remains continually in the enclosure and assumes the responsibility for the entire community. . . . To sum up his office briefly: if neither the abbot nor the prior is at home, not only all subjects in the enclosure, but the deans as well, obey his orders, whatever the need that may arise. Hence it is necessary that such a person be appointed who is considered capable of handling so many and such important affairs. Whether he is actually governing the community or not, he is to be treated by all with honor and respect (*Const. Hirsaugiens. S. Wilhelmi, Lib. II,* c. 20, *PL* 150:165).*

* Although no such provision is ordinarily included in the Statutes, it has become a rather widely accepted practice to unite the offices of subprior and master of the converse brothers. The arrangement seems logical because as a member of

2206. CONGR. OF BURSFELD. If the community has a subprior, he must be closely united to the prior in spirit and interpretation of the Rule. Whenever the prior is away from the monastery, the subprior takes his place in all the duties that are of regular occurrence; and even in unforeseen contingencies which should not or cannot be postponed (*Stat.*, dist. 3, c. 3, n. 1, p. 89).

2207. SWABIAN CONGR. OF ST. JOSEPH. He whom the abbot appoints subprior must excel in maturity of conduct and the observance of the regular life no less than the prior. His duties are: to take the place of the prior in all matters whenever the prior is absent; . . . to correct discreetly all shortcomings and mistakes, both privately and publicly, in the chapter, with the same authority as the prior; more than that, he is to coerce the negligent with the imposition of penances proportioned to the seriousness of the offenses. As the prior's assistant he is to be closely bound to him in his manner of handling affairs and in his interpretation of the Rule. Between them there should be singleness of intent and harmony of action, both of them animated with the same solicitude and zeal for fostering and preserving observance of the regular life (*Const. et declar., Pars III,* c. 2, punctum 2, n. 1, fol. 225).

2208. POPE PIUS VI. Since he is next to the prior in the government of the monastery, if the prior is absent, or if he has died, or is so detained by illness that he is unable to take part in the common exercises, the subprior is to take over the government and care of the monastery and act with prudence in all matters (*Const. Apost. Apostolatus officium, Pars II,* c. 1, n. 105, *BRC* 6:2067).

The novice master's duty

2209. CONGR. OF CAMALDULI. The appointment of the novice master belongs exclusively to the abbot, who is to weigh the matter most seriously before he commits the charge of his small flock to anyone, for there seems to be no more difficult and no more important duty in the religious institute than that of the novice master. If such a one is available, he is to be chosen for this duty *whose hands are sinless, whose heart is clean* (Ps. 23:4; *In c. 58 Reg. divi P. Benedicti declar.*, pp. 237–238; *CR* 2:268).

2210. SPANISH CONGR. (1640). Novice masters are to be endowed with a high degree of zeal for the perfection of religious observance. They must take the lead in being dedicated to a way of life that is harsh and difficult. Day and night they are to be faithful and prompt in choir service.

It is highly desirable that the novice master have a command of

---

the abbot's board of seniors, the subprior-master can present necessary reports and furnish detailed information regarding this sizable portion of the community. [*Tr.*]

those things which he is to teach the novices, such as chanting, reciting in choir, reading and waiting at table, observing ceremonies in choir and elsewhere, and whatever else may be customarily practiced. He is to be held in high regard by all since he is the master of religious perfection. No one is to refuse this duty, even though he hold a higher rank in the monastery (*Caeremoniale monastic., Pars II,* dist. 3, c. 2, nn. 1–2, p. 377).

2211. CONGR. OF STRASBURG. Novice masters must be men who are mature in age and personal conduct, skilled in winning souls, well equipped to train monks in both natural and supernatural virtues, and to instruct in monastic and regular discipline the candidates who have converted from the world, and to teach them basic and necessary elements of the monastic life (*Declar. 11 in c. 21 RSB,* fol. 30).

2212. SWABIAN CONGR. OF ST. JOSEPH. Since the growth and firmness of monastic discipline depends mostly on the proper training of novices, the abbot must appoint for their direction and instruction in virtue him whom he considers most skilled for training both the natural and the supernatural man, because of his seriousness of conduct and zeal for the regular discipline. . . . The novice master must excel in good example and personally give expression to all the religious principles with which he seeks to imbue his charges. He must be dedicated to the reading of spiritual works, from which, however, he is to choose only those writings on the ascetical life which are in harmony with our order and by means of which the novices may be more solidly grounded in the Benedictine spirit (*Const. et declar., Pars III,* c. 3, punctum 3, fol. 234–235).

2213. CONGR. OF BURSFELD. The novice master must teach and diligently instruct in matters pertaining to the order those who enter the monastery for the conversion of their moral life. . . . He will direct and inform them, not according to the teachings of other institutes, but by insisting solely that they follow in the footsteps of the Fathers of our order (*Stat.,* dist. 3, c. 4, n. 1, p. 90).

2214. CONGR. OF FRANCE (1837). Let a man of mature years, skilled in the discernment of spirits, whether they be of God, a man qualified for winning souls and always intent on imparting fervor to the tepid, be appointed novice master. It is his duty to report the progress of the novices to the superior, if he is not personally superior; to hear their faults at "culpa" each week; to impose salutary penances on those who have been remiss; and inculcate the principles of the Rule (*Reg. SS. Patris, una cum Const.,* art. 67, p. 161).

The cellarer is appointed by the abbot

2215. CONGR. OF CAMALDULI. In every monastery the appointment of the cellarer belongs to the abbot, who will make it his concern to choose, as far as possible, one who has the qualities that the holy Father Benedict presents in the present chapter (*RSB*, c. 31). A more beautiful, considered, and complete statement would not be easy to find (*Declar. in c. 31 RSB*, p. 152).

2216. CONGR. OF BURSFELD. A. The cellarer must not be negligent in anything which according to the Rule and tradition pertains to his office, unless the abbot has made other arrangements in certain matters. He must conform himself to the abbot's will in all things (*Stat.*, dist. 3, c. 5, n. 3, p. 94). B. He must be kind and even-tempered toward all, and not disturb or upset the officials or the brethren with haughtily given orders or harsh and contentious words of rebuke. . . . He is to be humbly obedient to the abbot and the prior in everything and willingly give himself to recollectedness of spirit and the reading of ascetical works as far as possible, thus, so tempering the ministry of Martha that he does not lose the better part which belongs to Mary (*ibid.*, n. 10).

Other officials

2217. CONGR. OF CAMALDULI. In the management of a private home, neither the father, who is the head of the family, nor the mother, whose duty it is to have charge of the domestic arrangement, is self-sufficient. . . . So also in the monastery, the abbot, prior and cellarer cannot alone perform all that is to be done, but it is necessary to substitute other officials to help them. After them, therefore, let the abbot prudently choose those who are fitted for the duties assigned to them (*In Reg. divi P. Benedicti, declar. in c. 32*, p. 154).

Annual appointment

2218. CONGR. OF BURSFELD. A. After the celebration of the annual chapter, the prior and all other officials of the monastery must publicly request release from their offices, and the abbot, upon the advice of God-fearing brethren, is to do what he judges most expedient before God (*Stat.*, dist. 3, c. 2, n. 13, p. 88). B. Let the abbot assign an opportune time each year at which the cellarer and others who have charge of administering property, are to present detailed reports (*ibid.*, c. 1, § 2, n. 7, p. 75).

2219. CONGR. OF CAMALDULI. As soon as possible after the general chapter of the congregation, the abbot is to provide for his monastery by assigning all offices and obediences (*In Reg. divi P. Benedicti, declar. in c. 21*, p. 118).

The abbot is to consult the seniors only, or the whole chapter

2220. SWABIAN CONGR. OF ST. JOSEPH. A. In matters of lesser moment the abbot is to consult only the seniors, those brethren, namely, who are distinguished for prudence, religious observance, and experience in public affairs. They must never dare to make known to anyone else the matters treated of in these meetings. . . . It is not in the least our intention to deprive the abbots of their authority, as though to say that they do not have the power to decide for themselves, arrange, and order done the matters which arise daily and are not of major importance. It is rather for the sake of greater safety that they are to prefer to seek the advice of a few of the more prudent brethren, who enjoy their confidence to a greater degree, so that according to the warning of Scripture, having done nothing without counsel, they need have no regrets (cf. Sir. 32:19; *Const. et declar., Pars II,* c. 4, punctum 4, nn. 11–12, fol. 164–165). B. When more serious problems arise, the abbot is to bring into consultation the men he considers more prudent and skilled. Keeping the welfare of the community before their eyes, these men will make their recommendations to the abbot with becoming modesty and submissiveness. Should he decide and issue his orders in opposition to what one or the other of the men suggested, they too must conform themselves to his judgment. Afterward they are not to show by a critical attitude that they were not pleased at what the abbot decided, or that they held a different opinion, but are rather to commend and defend the abbot's judgment as not having been adopted rashly but as having been arrived at by thorough discussion (*ibid., Pars III,* c. 1, punctum 2, n. 9, fol. 215). C. With a circumspect and wise warning our holy Father Benedict prescribes that when grave matters are to be treated of to the monastery's advantage, all the capitular brethren are to be called for counsel. This practice is of supreme importance both for promoting the common welfare, and for strengthening and making firm the mutual harmony and confidence between the abbot and the community. Whenever, therefore, an issue of major importance is to be treated, a definite notice will be issued, and the abbot will summon all capitulars who can be present without undue inconvenience at the most opportune time and appropriate place. Having first invoked the grace of the Holy Spirit, he will humbly and energetically outline the matter to be discussed, present the motives for both sides of the question without distinction, call for the opinions and views of the individual chapter members according to seniority. In keeping with the prescripts of the holy Rule, they will present their recommendations with all reverence and humility, with fewness of words, and without digressions which have no bearing on the matter (*ibid., Pars II,* c. 4, punctum 4, n. 1, fol. 159).

The abbot is the ordinary of his monastery

2221. POPE BENEDICT III (d. 858). According to the Rule of St. Benedict (*RSB*, c. 65), the abbot is to have the free government of his monastery; the monks are to look to him alone as their shepherd (*ibid.*, c. 2), nor does episcopal administration obtain in their regard. Since the abbot is believed to hold the place of Christ in the monastery, he is recognized as having the shepherd's duty over the sheep entrusted to him. In order for him to exercise the ministry of his stewardship worthily, he must not be troubled or subject to anyone's power, but be free of all subjection to the bishop. He is to await as his judge Christ alone, to whom he will render an accounting for the sheep entrusted to him (*Ep. 3, ad episc. Galliarum, in confirmationem privilegiorum Corbeiae, PL* 115:696).

2222. POPE ST. GREGORY VII (d. 1085). The holy Fathers have frequently also cut off monasteries of religious from subjection to bishops . . . and endowed them with perpetual exemption by sanctioning their attachment to the Apostolic See as principal members to the head (*Registrum, Lib. II, ep. 69, ad Cunibertum episc. Taurinens., PL* 148:420).

2223. ROMAN PONTIFICAL. Receive the full and free power of governing this monastery and its community in all matters which pertain to its spiritual and temporal welfare either interiorly or exteriorly (*De benedictione abbatis auctoritate apostolica; traditio baculi pastoralis,* 1:159).

Union of monasteries into congregations

2224. SWABIAN CONGR. OF ST. JOSEPH. A. The welfare of our order is found not only in the discipline of the individual house, but also in the common bond of a number of fervent houses, for the zealous striving of many in the fostering of virtue is less liable to descent into laxity than the piety of a few that is developed in one place. Hence if every monastery of our congregation is aided by every other, as a brother is helped by his brother, the congregation will become like a strong city (cf. Prov. 18:19), which stands unshakable, supported by the aids of mutual charity (*Const. et declar., Pars IV, praefatio,* fol. 297). B. In all our monasteries a priest is to be appointed each week to offer his private Mass that virtue will progress in our congregation; that the undertakings and efforts on the part of the president and the other prelates for God's greater glory will produce the perfection of monastic discipline in all our houses; and that what has been prescribed from time to time will be fulfilled with constancy. Having implored God's aid with diligence and intense fervor, the abbots and all superiors of the congregation will devote their efforts with uniform zeal for souls to make accurate observance of the three vows and the keeping of even the most detailed regulations flourish as the foundation of all religious life and discipline, in order that our congregation will never grow slack in its observance, but will be recognized by all as the genuine offspring of our glorious Father. . . .

In particular, let all bear in mind that the constitutions and statutes of our monastic congregation do not constitute a distinct burden added to the Rule, but are in the nature of declarations which prescribe in greater detail how the monasteries must observe with uniformity of practice what the Rule legislates for in a general way. We must work with all diligence so that the whole congregation apply itself with uniform accuracy of observance so that there will not be excessive severity in one monastery and laxity in another, but, as far as is possible, a praiseworthy and long-desired-for uniformity which in itself can contribute much to the preservation and increase of our union. No one can doubt that monasteries can preserve worthy observance much more easily and effectively, and grow both temporally and spiritually, if they employ both the same manly discipline and course of action, and help one another when the need arises. This has been the experience of different congregations of our own and other orders. The earliest founders of this congregation had a profound appreciation for it (*ibid.,* c. unicum, punctum 1, fol. 300–301).

2225. CONGR. OF BURSFELD. A. Every month a solemn Mass is to be celebrated for the increase of our congregation and for the vigor of regular discipline (*Stat.,* dist. 1, c. 2, § 12, n. 4, p. 42). B. If a monastery suffers serious loss through an accident, or for any other cause, the abbot president, with the advice of the other visitators [lit. abbots president], announces a collection of money to the abbots, which will be presented to the monastery in need. All are bound to this assistance (*ibid.,* c. 1, § 8, p. 19).

2226. CONGR. OF FRANCE. The monastic congregation does not take away, in fact it presupposes as taken for granted the autonomy and individual character of the monasteries in harmony with the first foundations of the order and with the text of the holy Rule. The several monasteries have each their own economic program and their own abbots elected for life. To these abbots the entire administration and government is committed in conformity with the constitutions. This includes, of course, the duty of helping with mutual aids and charitable assistance whenever the need arises, which may easily and frequently be the case with regard to man power (*Reg. SS. Patris B., una cum const.,* art. 89, p. 191; earlier manuscript form, fol. 15).

2227. POPE CLEMENT XIII (d. 1769). We exhort you to elect him superior of your monastic family who is considered the most zealously dedicated and the worthiest in the sight of the Lord for promoting

Christian piety, carefully preserving monastic discipline, and piously and wholesomely fostering ecclesiastical study (*Breve ad monachos O.S.B., congregationis Bavaricae,* 30 Maii, 1759).

2228. CONGR. OF BURSFELD. A. All abbots and superiors of monasteries who have bound themselves by oath to our congregation, having invoked the Holy Spirit in the fear of God, are to elect according to majority vote one of the abbots who is capable of presiding over the congregation by reason of his learning and zeal for regular discipline (*Stat.,* dist. 1, c. 1, n. 12, p. 21). B. He will everywhere enjoy universal precedence among the fathers (*ibid.,* n. 13). C. The president, whom all are bound to acknowledge and reverence as the head and legitimate superior of the congregation, must do all in his power to see to it that regular discipline flourishes and progresses, and that the members of the congregation keep peace inviolate and grow in mutual charity. The abbots will cooperate with him by offering him their counsel; the religious, by their prayers; and all, by confidence reposed in the congregation and by humble obedience. In virtue of Apostolic authority the president has the power to summon the annual chapter. All are bound to obey its definitions, decrees, and regulations regarding the observance of the Rule, fraternal union, the fostering of peace, and government in both spiritual and temporal matters. The president orders and approves visitations; with the advice of the chapter he resolves doubts that have arisen; other matters pertaining to regular discipline are subject to his decision (*ibid.,* n. 1, p. 17). D. It is his care to see to it that not only the monasteries actually belonging to the congregation are preserved, but also that when the opportunity presents itself, those which have been confiscated in the iniquity of the times be recovered, so that the prosperity of the monasteries be furthered in spiritual and temporal matters (*ibid.,* n. 2). E. The president must keep a vigilant eye for the preservation of the order and the conservation of its property, and must exercise diligent precaution with regard to all matters that might cause the order harm (*ibid.,* n. 4). F. He will faithfully keep in his custody the great seal of the congregation which is affixed to letters sent out in its name (*ibid.,* n. 6). G. All business matters which pertain to the congregation that arise after the last chapter, are to be referred to him until the next chapter, so that he can take them up and provide for them according to his judgment: in order to expedite matters and guarantee greater security, he can use, if the case calls for it, the counsel of near-by abbots (*ibid.,* n. 9). H. In virtue of holy obedience we command the superiors and members of our union that in all judicial causes of our congregation that may arise, they acknowledge the president as the competent judge, revere him in that capacity, call upon his services, and religiously submit according to our statutes and customs, by virtue of their oath made to the congregation, avoiding all the intricacies of [civil? ecclesiastical?] law (*ibid.*, c. 4, *de judicio in causis regularibus*, n. 2, p. 59).

2229. SWABIAN CONGR. OF ST. JOSEPH. As president (and visitor) of the congregation is to be chosen a man of uncommon zeal and prudence for promoting the common and public good of the order and of our congregation, and for preserving and increasing monastic discipline. It is his duty to be constantly alert with distinctive care and concern in all matters affecting the welfare of the congregation as a whole, whatever their origin; to be watchfully intent on the preservation of the individual monasteries; to use his authority in offering advice and help to the abbots who have recourse to him; to proclaim the biennial meeting of the abbots; and to conduct the visitation of all the monasteries of our congregation every year. He has all the authority that the law grants for building up and preserving monastic discipline in the monasteries incorporated in our congregation (*Const. et declar., Pars IV,* c. unicum, punctum 2, fol. 304).

2230. CONGR. OF FRANCE. A. The Congregation of France of the Order of St. Benedict will have as its superior general the actual abbot of St. Peter's Abbey, Solesmes [Dom Prosper Guéranger], and at his death, or upon his removal from office, the senior abbot superior of the congregation until his successor, having been duly elected and confirmed by the Supreme Pontiff, shall have taken possession of his office. It will be the duty of the abbot general, personally or through a delegate, to conduct the visitation of all the monasteries of the congregation (with the exception of his own abbey at Solesmes, which the first abbots of the congregation will jointly visit with the same rights and under the same conditions). The superior general will also preside at the general chapters, and between times scheduled for chapters will decide urgent matters of an extraordinary nature. In decisions to be made for those outside his own monastery, he will discuss the problem with the abbots or conventual priors whose interests are involved. His decision will be binding until the following general chapter, which will then have the duty, if the need persists, of confirming or rejecting his decision (*Reg. SS. P.N. Benedicti una cum Const.*, art. 95, pp. 192–193). B. Either he, or another abbot of the congregation delegated by him with a special mandate, will preside at the election of an abbot (*ibid.*, art. 93).

Principal duty of the president of the congregation is the visitation of monasteries

2231. PROV. COUNCIL OF PRAGUE (1860). The Fathers assembled in this Council intensely desire and express their confident wish that all regular institutes which are subjected to their general and provincial superiors by virtue of their rule will either on their own initiative or at the command of the Holy See, unite into congregations; that in future they will be governed by the zealous and conscientious vigilance of the superiors of the [respective] order or the congregations just mentioned; and that they will be visited and corrected either by these superiors in person or by those deputed to conduct such visitations (*Decr.*, tit. 7, c. 2, *de regimine claustralium, CL* 5:572).*

2232. PROV. COUNCIL OF UTRECHT (1865). More than anything else the prescribed visitation of monasteries contributes by helping to foster and perfect the regular life, to remove and prevent abuses, and to promote internal and external well-being of both the order and of the individual religious house (*Decr.*, tit. 2, *CL* 5:892).

2233. CONGR. OF BURSFELD. A. Because the visitation, searchingly made, preserves regular discipline, closes the way to the decline of the order, resists the corrupting influences that endanger souls, and furthers the progress of those who are conscientious in their observance, we decree that every monastery of our congregation must be visited annually, or at least before each general chapter. Should this program be interfered with by some reasonable cause, the visitation will be conducted as soon as the impediment has ceased (*Stat.*, dist. 1, c. 3, § 6, p. 57). B. It is proper that the visitors be zealous for the order, mature persons, discreet, and, in harmony with the prescriptions of the Council of Trent (*Sess. 24,* c. 3, *de ref. Can. et decr.*, Richter, p. 330; Schroeder, *Trent,* p. 193 f.), careful and circumspect in conducting the visitation (*ibid.*, § 1, n. 1, p. 45). C. When the visitors arrive at the monastery, the community and abbot are to assemble in the chapter house at an hour that the visitors shall have appointed. . . . The prayer commonly used for the opening of the annual chapter [monastic ritual] is employed (*ibid.*, n. 3, p. 46). D. One of the visitors makes a brief exhortation about the observance of the monastic life, obedience, reverence for the superior, peace, fraternal charity, and similar topics. When the method of conducting the visitation has been presented, the visitors are to admonish the monks as a group and individually, and command, even in virtue of holy obedience, by the authority of the general chapter, that they are to answer whatever they are asked about the abbot, the prior, the brethren mutually, the converse brothers, or about the state of the community as a whole—whatever they know should be revealed and corrected (*ibid.*, n. 4, p. 46).

* This expressed wish of the council, which was celebrated in the city of the Abbey of Emmaus, subsequently of the Beuronese Congregation, is significant in that it antedates the formal establishment of that monastic congregation (1868), Pope Leo XIII's letter inviting the abbots of the order to form into a federation (January 4, 1887), and the actual erection of the Benedictine Confederation (1893) (cf. Bibliography: Benedictines: *The Law proper to the Confederation of Monastic Congregations,* pp. 61 ff., 67 ff.). [*Tr.*]

2234. CONGR. OF STRASBURG. Let it be the special care of the first visitor to be watchful over the legal concerns of the congregation, from whatever source they may arise; to be far-sightedly intent on the preservation of the individual monasteries; and, to use his authority in giving counsel and aid to the abbots who have recourse to him. He is annually to visit all monasteries of the congregation, according to the prescription of the Council of Trent: "They shall be bound to visit the monasteries of their congregation frequently, to apply themselves to their reform, and to observe whatever has been decreed in the sacred canons and in this holy council" (*Sess. 25,* c. 8, *Can. et decr.,* Richter, p. 411; Schroeder, *Trent,* p. 222 f.; *Stat. et const., Pars II,* c. 8, § 2, fol. 123).

2235. SWABIAN CONGR. OF ST. JOSEPH. Since frequent and diligently conducted visitation preserves the regular discipline of monasteries; closes the way to the decline of the order; resists those things which are dangerous to souls and productive of corruption; and is the means by which the advancement of those who are already progressing spiritually is best consulted, the individual monasteries of our congregation will be visited annually by the president at the time most convenient for him. He will notify by letter the abbot of each monastery to be visited regarding the day on which the visitation is to be held. . . . The visitation opens with the celebration of Mass by the president or the first visitor at the high altar in church, with the intention that the visitation may happily redound to God's greater glory, the increase of regular discipline, mutual peace, and the support of fraternal charity. All must take part in the Mass with devotion.

The visitor will question and examine the monks individually as to whether the keeping of the three vows, the observance of the Rule, and the keeping of our constitutions are in force; more specifically, whether the ordinances and decrees of the last visitation have been carried into execution; whether the Divine Office is daily celebrated at the prescribed hours with devotion and to the edification of externs; whether all who are not exempted for special reasons attend the Office diligently; whether the superiors fulfil their duties, correct and amend errors in the proper manner, and as far as lies in their power, strive to guard against and devote their attention to occasions of sins and dangers; whether the same superiors excel others by good example in regular observance; whether the appointed times are properly devoted to the exercises of religion; whether care be had with regard to the Masses to be celebrated; whether religious silence, particularly the night silence, is properly observed; whether there still are abuses and evil customs at variance with monastic discipline and the keeping of the vows; whether the superiors of the monastery are in accord with the abbot, foster discipline, strive to preserve charity and peace; whether there is concord among the superiors themselves.

The visitor is to note briefly, for the purpose of having a record, the points that he considers need correction, and will include them in his report of the visitation. But he must be careful to propose these and similar matters in such a manner that nothing will be derogatory to the authority of the superiors.

The president is to make no changes of officials without having consulted the abbot, and if he considers certain of the reasonable and grave causes impelling him to make changes, he will not personally announce them, but the abbot of the place, at the proper time after the visitors' departure, will make the new appointment as his own. The president will embody in his report those points of regular monastic discipline that he thinks need correction and promulgate them to the abbot and assembled community.

In order for them to be put into operation with exactness and observed by everyone, he presents the report to the abbot, to be employed again at next year's visitation of the monastery, seriously warning and commanding its use, with his authority and power, whenever and as often as it becomes necessary. He will then hold the concluding exhortation in which he is to stimulate the members of the community to progress constantly in the striving for religious observance. He terminates the visitation with the customary prayers.

If properly performed, visitations produce the greatest benefits in all monasteries; lest they be rendered odious, as the malign enemy strives with all his powers to effect, no one is to harbor hidden suspicions in his mind, but, taking the prudence and zeal of the visitors for granted, is to be convinced that it has been in the interests of his spiritual welfare to have been admonished.

For the rest, the abbots themselves must not consider that everything is to be left to the president and the visitors, but they too must be watchful over the flocks just as though there were no visitors. The accounting for the sheep that have been neglected, for the abuses and weeds that have grown up (cf. Matt. 13:28 f.) will not be made by the abbot president and the visitors, but will be demanded accurately and severely of the abbot, as our holy father Benedict repeatedly and with heavy emphasis warns in his holy Rule. If each abbot performs his duty as he should, he will acquire more authority and the greater love of his sons, and will rejoice more, both in this life and in the other, before God and men. The burden of the president and of the visitors will then be greatly lessened, and it will be a comfort to behold fields so well cultivated, in which they will then not be called upon so much to toil and sow, as to reap and recount, with deep joy of soul, the glory given to God. Then they will make shorter visits in the individual monasteries, and will thus be able to devote greater attention to their own spiritual needs and those of their subjects, a condition which doubtlessly everyone desires (*Stat., Pars IV,* c. unicum, punctum 3, p. 309).

2236. POPE PIUS VI. A. The visitors are bound to conduct the visitation of the monasteries once every three years before the celebration of the general chapter, in order that they can make an accurate report on the spiritual and temporal state of the monasteries in the general chapter (*Const. Apost. Apostolatus officium,* c. 12, n. 72, 15 Maii, 1799; *confirmatio const. ordinis Cluniacens., BRC* 6:2055). B. Before the visitors come to any monastery, they are to make known the time of their arrival. When they actually appear, and the superior and the monks have assembled, they will explain the purpose of their coming, and briefly exhort [the monks] to make known to them freely and sincerely those things that they consider need to be revealed to them for the good of the order and of the monastery. They then open the visitation with a visit to the most holy sacrament of the Eucharist, the church, the relics, the sacred furnishings and vessels, and the sacrarium. They are to be diligent in seeing whether all these are kept with becoming reverence. They are to hear the superiors and the monks individually and secretly. They are to inquire searchingly as to whether the Divine Office is performed reverently day and night. They will question about the number and kind of monks, about the fulfilment of their duties by the officials, about the observance of the statutes of the congregation, the Rule, the decrees of the general chapter, and the prescriptions of preceding visitations; about the spiritual and temporal state of the monastery. They will examine the account books carefully, visit the buildings and the cells of the monks, and correct those whom they find negligent (*ibid.,* n. 76). C. The visitors will zealously investigate whether uniformity with regard to clothing, and proper silence in the places prescribed by the Rule are observed; whether too frequent permission is granted for leaving the enclosure of the monastery. In fulfilling their office of visitor, let them always keep God before their eyes (*ibid.,* n. 77). After they have completed their interrogations on all these matters, without respect for persons, according to the *Rule of St. Benedict* and the statutes of the order, they are to correct what needs to be corrected, provide for the things that need to be provided for, and by the use of regular punishments, force the obstinate and reduce them to observance, as well as property holders and the disobedient. They are not to depart from the place of visitation until everything that can forthwith be corrected has actually been corrected (*ibid.,* n. 78).

The general chapter

2237. POPE INNOCENT III. Since decisions on general spiritual progress which are confirmed by the vote of many persons are usually very sound, such problems are best treated in general sessions. Hence you are to strive to take part in the general chapter of the annual meetings, setting aside all excuses, firmly resolving to observe the things there established according to God and the *Rule of St. Benedict* (*Lib. XVI, ep. 6, Universis abbatibus et prioribus Cluniac. ordinis, PL* 216:791).

2238. POPE GREGORY IX. We prescribe, first of all, that the general chapter of the abbots and priors . . . be celebrated at Cluny every year. In this chapter, without acceptance of persons, let the excesses of the delinquent be corrected and the welfare of souls be dealt with according to God, the *Rule of St. Benedict,* and the legal prescriptions of the order of Cluny. . . . They are to have no mercy on one another in this matter, but each one is charitably to propose publicly to the chapter or in private (as seems most appropriate to him), whatever he sees in another that needs correction, keeping the fear of God ever before his eyes. Nor is the one so corrected to bear this resentfully, but to receive the brother's correction in the spirit of patience (*Const. Apost. Behemoth non contentus,* § 1, 13 Jan., 1233; *reformatio monachorum Cluniac. O.S.B., BR* 3:475).

2239. POPE BENEDICT XII (d. 1342). For this kind of general chapter is held precisely in order that diligent discussion may be conducted regarding the status of monasteries . . . the reform of the order, and regular observance. Hence we know that all to whom such matters are pertinent act worthily in attending these chapters (*Apost. Const. Fulgens sicut stella,* § 18, 12 Jul., 1335; *reformatio ordinis Cisterciensis, BR* 4:335).

2240. CONGR. OF BURSFELD. A. In order that the congregation may be preserved in continual discipline; that difficulties which arise be resolved with higher authority; and uniformity in the service of Christ be maintained inviolate, annual chapters are to be celebrated at the time and in the place determined by the president of the Bursfeld Congregation (*Stat.,* dist. 1, c. 2, n. 1, p. 22). B. The matters to be treated of in the general chapter are: those which deal particularly with the observance of the Rule; that regulation of all phases of their own [the abbots'] life, and that of their subjects; and the preservation of the unbreakable bond of peace among them. They must also consider whether there is any monastery that stands in particular need, be it material or spiritual. All subjects are to be examined prudently and action is to be taken when needed (*ibid.,* c. 3, n. 6, p. 32). C. At the chapter's termination all [abbots] are to be reminded by the president that after they return to their monasteries they see to it that the prayers prescribed by the chapter are fulfilled faithfully; that they devote themselves to the preservation of the purity of the religious life, to the conscientious fulfilment of what has been professed, to peace, charity, and benevolence toward all, and particularly toward the officials whom we have appointed, to ever-watchful solicitude over their subjects, and to the other matters which are in keeping with the seriousness of monastic life, and which contribute to the welfare of souls (*ibid.*, n. 10, *de exhortatione finali praesidis*, p. 40). D. On an appropriate day after the abbot has returned home the report [of the general chapter] is to be read and, where necessary, explained, to the assembled community by the abbot personally or by the prior, and the reading is to be repeated a month before the celebration of the next general chapter, so that no one can excuse himself on the score of ignorance (*ibid.*, n. 12, p. 42).

2241. CONGR. OF STRASBURG. The resolutions are to be passed in the general chapter by vote in such wise that whatever is decided by a majority of the abbots is to be adopted. . . . No community has the right, under the pretext of appeal, to violate the statutes and decrees so passed, if they concern only matters of monastic discipline and the preservation of peace (*Reg. S.P. Benedicti . . . cum declar., Pars II*, c. 5, § 4, fol. 120).

2242. CONGR. OF FRANCE. If, on the advice of the abbots and conventual priors, the superior general [of the monastic congregation] should deem it necessary in future to draw up new articles or to declare [that is, explain legally] those articles that are already in force, these new articles and declarations must be approved by secret ballot by a three fourths' majority of the voters of the congregation. If such plurality is actually attained the new regulations will not bind beyond three years, after which time the issue will again be submitted to secret ballot. If the vote is again favorable, the superior general will then forward these articles to the Sacred Congregation of Bishops and Regulars * for confirmation (*Reg. SS. P.N. Benedicti una cum Const.*, art. 97, p. 193).

IV. WRITINGS OF SAINTS AND DOCTORS

The monastery is a family

2243. ST. BASIL THE GREAT. A. Permit me to present, as well as I can, the profundity and excellence of the establishment of the cenobites. What can compare favorably with such a blessing? Among the monks, one is a father, imitating the Heavenly Father; there, many are sons, who strive to excel one another in progress in kindness toward their superior, sons, I say, who maintain the spirit of concord among themselves and revere their father with manifestations of unusual love and respect, not basing their bond and close relationship on nature, but on a support more solid than nature and reverencing

* The S.C. of Bishops and Regulars was the forerunner of the present S.C. of Religious (1908).

him as the leader and guardian of their harmony, and uniting themselves in the bond of the Holy Spirit. What simile taken from things of earth can possibly express the excellence and dignity of so outstanding an institute? Certainly nothing earthly can do so: hence only that which is above is left. The heavenly Father is not subject to manifestations of preference [cf. Acts 10:34(?)]; this father [of the cenobites] too is immune from such influences, gaining all to himself by his word and teaching. The children of the heavenly Father are pure; their blamelessness of life makes these his adopted sons as well. Love unites the things above into a oneness; charity also is the bond that unites this group. The devil despairs in the face of an army of this kind, with so many soldiers warring against him, drawn up in so orderly and compact a battle array, shielded with the protection of so great a charity in their attack, so guarded and fortified by the Holy Spirit that they leave no smallest opening to his assaults. Consider for me, if you will, the united struggle of the seven Machabees. You will find among these brethren a harmony even more fervent. Of such as these the prophet David exclaimed in the psalm: *Behold, how good it is, and how pleasant, where brethren dwell at one!* (Ps. 132:1.) By the word "good" he expresses the innocence of this life; by "pleasant," the joy of harmony and unity. They who scrupulously and diligently cultivate this kind of life seem to me to emulate the very highest virtues (*Const. monastic.*, c. 18, § 4, *PG* 31:1386). B. If parents have left the world and betaken themselves to their son's way of life, they are then truly relatives, holding the place no longer of parents, but of brothers. For there is [in such a course of action] most truly a father; the first, the Father of all men, the second, after him, who holds the leadership in the institute of the spiritual life (*ibid.*, c. 20, § 1, col. 1390).

The abbot

2244. EDMUND MARTÈNE, monk of congr. of St. Maur (d. 1739). The election of the abbot belongs to the monastic community itself. This was the ancient discipline of the monastic order, confirmed by the rules of the first monks as well as by ecclesiastical and civil law (*Comm. in c. 64 RSB, Comment.*, p. 834; *PL* 66:881).

2245. ELIAS DE COXIDA, seventh abbot of Notre-Dame des Dunes, Bruges, O. Cist. (d. 1203). Since prelates are bound to strive for absolute perfection, whoever is considered worthy to be appointed pastor of the people of God in order to govern them and dispense the patrimony of the crucified Savior, must be approved with great diligence. No one must assume this honor on his own, . . . but only he who has been called by God, as Aaron was. He is called by God who has been chosen with the proper qualifications, in the proper manner, and by those who are empowered to choose him, namely, by those who have knowledge of the truth and are intent on a choice that is good. Knowledge of the truth does not permit the judgment to err; a worthy choice made through love causes them to cling to the dispositions of the divine will. He is called by God who is neither imposed on a community by a superior force, nor promoted because of a personal attachment, nor advanced out of ambition for the prelacy. These three things, namely, force, private affection, and ambition are usually the causes of the promotion of one who is unworthy (*Serm. 1, PL* 209:995).

2246. RICHARDUS DE S. ANGELO, monk of Montecassino (13th century). When they are elected abbots, they are called by God, even as was Aaron, and once so called, they receive from the pope, who is the representative of the true God, their authority and power to hold the place of Christ (*Comm. in c. 2 RSB, PL* 66:265).

2247. HUGO DE FOLIETO, canon regular, abbot, cardinal (12th century). Prelates must imitate Christ particularly in three things, for in those three things they hold his place, that is, in dignity, authority, and duty. Christ was priest, king, and servant—priest when he offered himself as a Victim on the altar of the cross; king, when he reigned from the cross; servant, when he washed Peter's feet. Dignity corresponds to the priest's nature, authority to the king's, and duty to the servant's. Reverence is owed to dignity, obedience to authority, and service to duty. Two of these are owed to prelates, the third to subjects: reverence and obedience are to be shown to prelates, pastoral care to be devoted to subjects by the superiors. Why? Must not the subjects imitate their superiors in these matters? No. But when they observe their superiors being humble in dignity, meek in the exercise of authority, and employing great zeal in the administration of the community's goods, let them too be humble, meek, and submissive in accepting the tasks assigned to them (*De claustro animae, Lib. II,* c. 10, *PL* 176:1057).

2248. ST. BERNARD. Reassure yourselves, be comforted. I will be to him a father, and he shall be to me a son, until *the God of patience and comfort* (Rom. 15:5) receive him from my hands. So do not mourn; do not weep. For your Geoffrey is hastening to joy, and not to grief. I will be to him father and mother, brother and sister. I shall make the crooked ways straight for him and the rough ways smooth (cf. Luke 3:5). I will so temper and arrange all things that his soul may advance and his body will not suffer (*Ep. 110, ad parentes Gaufridi consolatoria,* § 2, *PL* 182:253; James, p. 169).

2249. ST. BASIL THE GREAT. [The abbot] should be disposed toward the brethren like a nurse cherishing her own children (cf. I Thess. 2:7), ever desirous of giving to each according to God's pleasure, and to all for the common welfare of the community, not only the Gospel of God, but even his very life, according to the command of our Lord and God,

Jesus Christ, who said: *A new commandment I give you, that you love one another: that as I have loved you, you also love one another* (John 13:34). *Greater love than this no one has, that one lay down his life for his friends (ibid.,* 15:13; *Reg. brevius tractatae, Interrogatio 98, PG* 31:1151).

2250. ST. FRANCIS OF ASSISI. In order for a prelate to carry his subjects on his shoulders, it is necessary that he bear them in his heart, for he cannot tolerate those whom he has ceased to love (*Ep. 7, ad fratrem Eliam, Op. Om.*, p. 5).

2251. ALCUIN OF YORK (d. 804). A. Love your reverend father [Bonulphus, successor of St. Sturmius] as a father, for he is to render an account of your souls. He expends his efforts for your sake, traveling from place to place, that you may live in tranquillity, observe your regular life, and have what is necessary for your physical well-being. Fearing God, loving God, act as dearly loved sons, keeping your father's welfare in your prayers, asking that he may live with you happily in long-lived prosperity and that he may merit eternal life with you and you with him (*Ep. 142, ad fratres Fuldenses, PL* 100:384). B. [The abbot] must render an account of his solicitude for you, and in the same way, you must render an account of your obedience to him. For your sake he is placed in serious danger; with great charity be intent on interceding in his behalf, that he may receive a blessed reward before God because of his solicitude for you, and that you will attain to rest with him in God's kingdom. The children's discipline is the praise of teachers; the increase of the flock is the shepherd's reward (*Ep. 93, ad fratres Juvavensis Eccl.*, col. 299).

2252. ST. PACHOMIUS, abbot (4th century). If anyone comes to the door of the monastery with the intention of renouncing the world and joining the brotherhood, he will not be allowed to enter freely, but first will be announced to the father of the monastery, and will remain for a few days outside, before the entrance, where he will be taught the Lord's Prayer and as many of the psalms as he can learn. He will examine himself thoroughly whether perchance he has committed an evil and, disturbed for the time being, has left home out of a motive of fear, or is acting under someone's influence. He must examine himself as to whether he can give up his parents and despise his own will. If they decide that he is capable with regard to the prayers and for everything else, he will be taught the other rules of the monastery that he must observe, and what he must do, whom he must obey, both in the assembly of all the brethren and in the house to which he will be assigned, and as regards the rank to be observed at meals, so that he may be admitted among the brethren well instructed and well trained in all good works.

They will then take his secular garb from him, clothe him with the monks' habit, and assign him to the porter who will lead him at prayer time in the sight of all the brethren, and he will sit in the place that has been previously determined. Those who are assigned to this duty will take the clothing that he brought with him, put it in the common wardrobe, and from then on it will be in the power of the father of the monastery (*Reg. monachorum,* n. 49, *CR* 1:28; *PL* 23:73).

The novices

2253. LIVES OF EGYPTIAN FATHERS. A. Those who had recently come to serve the Lord were taught to be eager for all exercises of piety. Because he could no longer personally assume such cares [as their training], the blessed old man [St. Pachomius] admonished them not to be worried, saying: "Remain manfully steadfast in that to which you have been called; recite the psalms, and retain by memory other books and particularly the holy Gospels. You will become perfect in serving the Lord and loving one another according to his commandment. You will be a comfort to me especially if you fulfil the heavenly precepts zealously" (*Vita S. Pachomii abb. Tabennen.,* c. 22, *PL* 73:243). B. It was prescribed that whoever entered this monastery [of Tabenna] for the first time, with the intention of remaining there perpetually, was barred from all sacred studies for three years, and was kept at manual tasks, and only after the three years had elapsed, was admitted to his place in the combat (*ibid.,* col. 242).

2254. JOHN CASSIAN. [The senior] will first teach the novice to conquer his own desires; and, anxiously and diligently exercising him in this, he will purposely contrive to give him such orders as he knows to be contrary to his liking; for those who have great experience say that a monk, and especially one of the younger ones, cannot bridle the desire of his concupiscence unless he has first learned by experience to mortify his wishes (*De coenobior. institut., Lib. IV,* c. 8, *PL* 49:160).

2255. ST. BASIL THE GREAT. But you who aspire to become a lover of the celestial polity, an active participant in the angelical life, and a fellow soldier of Christ's holy disciples, brace yourself for the endurance of tribulations and manfully betake yourself to the company of the monks. Even in the beginning of your renunciation of the world show yourself a man, and, that you may not be dragged down by attachments to your blood relatives, strengthen yourself by exchanging mortal for immortal aspirations. Futhermore, when you make renouncement of the goods you possess, be adamant in your resolve, convinced that you are merely dispatching these goods to heaven in advance; for, although you are hiding them in the bosom of the lowly, you will find them again with God, greatly increased. Moreover, be not cast down at having divested yourself or friends and relatives, since you are thereby united with Christ who was crucified for you; and what greater proof of love can be conceived of than this? (John 15:13.) And when, with God's help, you will have gained victory over your enemy in this first onset, do not be careless of yourself as if you were a useless vessel—for, indeed, by the renouncement of earthly goods you have won honor with Christ—but with much care and forethought set about finding a man skilled in guiding those who are making their way toward God who will be an unerring director of you life. . . . If you should find such a one, surrender yourself to him, completely renouncing and casting aside your own will, that you may be found a clean vessel, preserving unto your praise and glory the good qualities desposited in you. For if you suffer any of your former vices to remain within you, those virtues that were placed in you will become contaminated and you will be cast out like a vessel unfit for use.

And now we shall consider the second contest against the enemy of our salvation. Good masters teach good doctrine, but that taught by evil masters is wholly evil. Whenever, therefore, our wicked adversary is not able to prevail upon us to remain amid the tumult and perdition of the world, he endeavors to persuade us not to devote ourselves to a life of discipline or surrender ourselves to a man who will place all our sins before our eyes and correct them. On the contrary, he urges us toward one who is bent on popularity and who puts a favorable light on his own vices under the pretext of indulgence to his associates, so that, when he has thus imperceptibly increased our vices a thousandfold, he may cause us to be fettered by chains of sin we ourselves have forged. But if you place yourself in the hands of a man rich in virtue, you will become the heir of the good qualities he possesses and you will be supremely blessed with God and men. . . .

If, then, with the grace of God, you find a teacher of good works (for if you really seek, you will find, cf. Matt. 7:7), keep a watch over yourself so as to do nothing against his will; for whatever is done without his consent is, as it were, a piece of thievery and a sacrilege leading not to your profit but to your ruin, however good it may seem to you (*Serm. de renuntiatione saeculi,* §§ 2–4, *PG* 31:630; Wagner, *Ascetical Works,* pp. 18–20).

2256. BENEDICT HAEFTEN. The novice must first of all realize that he is something like a rough log cut from the forest of the world. In order for this log to be carved into a beautiful religious statue representing a holy man, it needs to be cut down to size, and hewed on a great deal with axe and chisel. In place of the tools used in the example given, the novice must suffer wrongs, corrections, and reproaches. He is not to be disturbed by these, but consider them inflicted for the welfare of his soul (*Disquisitiones monasticae, Lib. IV,* tract. 3, *de novitiorum probatione,* disq. 7, p. 388).

2257. ST. BONAVENTURE. Hence it is necessary for the younger to be humbly submissive to a superior, for a patient cannot be cured of his illness unless he obediently follow the directions of his physician (*De sex alis Seraphim,* c. 1, § 2, *Op. Om.,* ed. Quaracchi 8:132).

2258. ST. LAURENCE JUSTINIAN. [Novices] are to believe their master as though he were an oracle in all that he teaches and obey his will in everything. They are not to concern themselves with discovering the reasons for what he prescribes: all they need know is what he has commanded (*De obedientia,* c. 20, *Op. Om.* 2:341).

2259. WILLIAM OF ST. THIERRY. The good and simple man and he that is new in the profession of religion and solitude has neither reason to guide him, affection to draw him, nor discretion to refrain him, but must use violence on himself as the potter uses violence on whatever he is making. Such a man is to be molded by the law of God's commandments as a vessel is fashioned in the potter's hands; he is to be molded into shape in all patience, and upon the wheel of swift obedience and in the fire of his probation to be subdued to the will of his molder and shaper (*Ep. ad fratres de Monte Dei, Lib. I,* c. 6, n. 17, *PL* 184:319).

The abbot's pleasure in worthy novices

2260. ST. BERNARD. We cannot say of [our novices] that our vine *has flourished* (Cant. 2:15, Douay version, cf. Confraternity), for it is blooming *now.* That which in the meantime you see appear in them is the flower, but the time of fruit has not yet come. The flower is their new and altered manner of life, their recently adopted rule, and stricter method of conduct. They have put on a mortified countenance, and a well regulated demeanor of their whole body. That which appears in them is, I confess, pleasing, for their outward man shows less care for dress and appearance, their speech is more sparing, their countenance more cheerful, their glances more modest, their movements more quiet and measured. But since they have practiced these rules of life for only a short time, this very newness obliges us to regard them, so to speak, as flowers, and their actions as the hope of fruit, rather than as fruit itself (*Serm. 63 in Cant.,* n. 6, *PL* 183:1083; Eales, p. 381).

The abbot has spiritual direction of all the monks

2261. BENEDICT HAEFTEN. The abbot is shepherd, guide, and leader, but he must not lead the sheep entrusted to him in one unvarying direction. He must lead them away from vices; withdraw them from dangers; summon them back from errors; lead them to the enclosure [sheepfold]; lead them out to pasture; guide them along the way; direct them to Christ; induce them to the performance of good;

lead them on to perfection; introduce them into the kingdom (*Disquisitiones monasticae, Lib. III,* tract. 5, disq. 5, p. 319).*

2262. ST. PACHOMIUS. A. When the superiors of the individual [smaller] houses instruct the brethren on the holiness of their way of life, none shall absent himself except for the gravest necessity (*Praecepta ac leges,* n. 188, *CR* 1:36; *PL* 23:85). B. When the signal has sounded for summoning the brethren to hear the commands of the superiors, none will remain away (*Regula,* n. 23; *CR* 1:27; col. 67). C. When they are seated at home, none is to be permitted to speak of anything secular; but if the superior has taught something from the Scriptures, they will discuss the matter among themselves and compare what each one has understood and what he has learned by heart (*ibid.,* n. 122, p. 32; col. 76). D. As a matter of obligation, let all be bound to review among themselves what they have heard explained in the assembly of the brethren, particularly during the seasons of the fast, when they are to be instructed by their superiors (*Praecepta ac leges,* n. 138, p. 32; col. 78). E. Each week two disputations, that is, catechetical sessions [questions and answers] are to be held by the superiors (*ibid.,* n. 156, p. 33; col. 80).

2263. ST. AUGUSTINE. At the day's end they gather together from their separate cells before breaking their fast, to hear their father, assembling to the number of at least three thousand for one father; for one may have even a much larger number than this. They listen with astonishing eagerness and in perfect silence, and give expression to the feelings of their minds as they are moved by the words of the preacher, in groans, or tears, or signs of joy, without noise of shouting (*De moribus Ecclesiae Catholicae, Lib. I,* c. 31, n. 67, *PL* 32:1338).

2264. ALCUIN OF YORK. You, fathers and shepherds of the holy community, make it your concern to teach with the utmost zeal and love for the brethren, the family you have been appointed to govern, and by your personal conduct give an example of worthiness of life. The *Rule of St. Benedict* is frequently to be read so that it can be explained in your own language and thus be understood by all in the assembly of the brethren (*Ep. 14, ad fratres Wirensis et Gyrvensis eccl., PL* 100:163).

The abbot honored with quasi-episcopal dignity by the Church

2265. PETER THE VENERABLE, abbot of Cluny. As the Roman Pontiffs are placed over all churches, and other pontiffs each over his own individual church, so also abbots govern their monks in all matters with a similar authority. . . . Even though these fathers should be wanting in personal holiness, the authority of their prelacy would

* The play on the verbs, each with a prefix of the root *ducere* cannot be reproduced in English. [*Tr.*]

suffice for demanding that obedience be rendered to them. As they have the right to command their subjects, so the subjects have the duty to obey these commands (*Lib. I, ep. 38, ad Bernardum Claraevallensem, PL* 189:153).

2266. PHILIP DE HARVENG, O.PRAE. (d. 1182). Those priests who have received the pastoral staff [crosier], either as abbots or bishops, enjoy a certain pre-eminence by reason of the dignity bestowed on them. The former must impart the discipline of their rule to their subjects within the enclosure; the latter must give both those dwelling in the enclosure and all others the example and doctrine for virtuous living. . . . It is precisely for this reason that certain persons are elevated by God in the Church, and others made subject to them in a divine hierarchy, so that the higher may bestow faithful care on those below them, and the subjects may obey their superiors in a becoming spirit of humility. For the former are to impart spiritual doctrine to their subjects with paternal solicitude; the latter are to render their superiors filial obedience. This mutual charity, a [spiritual] force far more powerful than physical generation, must make them fathers and sons to one another—for the terms are correlative (*Ep. 13, de virtutibus praelatorum, PL* 203:105).

What kind of man the abbot must be

2267. ST. BASIL THE GREAT. [The abbot] . . . must be a man skilled in guiding those who are making their way toward God, an unerring director [of the spiritual life]. He should be adorned with virtues, bearing witness by his works to his love for God, conversant with Holy Scriptures, recollected, free from avarice, a good, quiet man, tranquil, pleasing to God, a lover of the poor, mild, forgiving, laboring hard for the spiritual advancement of his clients, without vainglory or arrogance, impervious to flattery, not given to vacillation, and preferring God to all things else (*Serm. asceticus de renuntiatione saeculi,* n. 2, *PG* 31:631; Wagner, *Ascetical Works,* p. 19).

2268. ST. GREGORY THE GREAT. A. It is necessary, therefore, that [the prelate] should be pure in thought, exemplary in conduct, discreet in keeping silence, profitable in speech, in sympathy a near neighbor to everyone, in contemplation exalted above all others, a humble companion to those who lead good lives, erect in his zeal for righteousness against the vices of sinners. He must not be remiss in his care for the inner life by preoccupation with the external; nor must he in his solicitude for what is internal, fail to give attention to the external (*Regula pastoralis, Pars II,* c. 1, *PL* 77:26; Davis, *St. Gregory's Pastoral Care,* p. 45). B. He should not only do what is upright in the midst of the wicked, but also surpass the well-doers among his subjects, and as he surpasses them in the dignity of his rank, so should he in the virtue of his conduct (*ibid.,* c. 3, col. 28; Davis, p. 49). C. He must, therefore, devote himself entirely to setting an ideal of living. He must die to all passions of the flesh and by now lead a spiritual life. He must have put aside all worldly prosperity; he must fear no adversity. . . . In the affection of his own heart he sympathizes with the frailties of others, and so rejoices in the good done by his neighbor as though the progress made were his own. In all that he does he sets an example so inspiring to others, that in their regard he has no cause to be ashamed of his past. He so studies to live as to be able to water the dry hearts of others with the streams of instruction imparted. By his practice and experience of prayer he has learned already that he can obtain from the Lord what he asks for (*ibid., Pars I,* c. 10, col. 23; Davis, p. 38). D. No one must assume the height of government who does not possess the strength to devote himself to these great tasks, namely the knowledge of contemplation and the fervor of charity (*Lib. V in I Reg.,* c. 3, § 18, *PL* 79:458). E. If the leader of an army is not chosen until he has been tried in labor and carefulness, let those who desire with immature haste to ascend to the exalted dignity of the episcopacy consider, at least in the light of this comparison, the kind of men leaders of souls must be; and let them abstain from suddenly attempting untried labors, lest a blind ambition for dignity both be to their own penalty, and also sow seeds of pestiferous errors among others, they themselves not having learned what they have to teach (*Lib. IX, ep. 110, ad Theodoricum et Theodebertum, reges Francorum: quod multi per simoniam ordinentur, PL* 77:1040).

2269. JOHN OF TRITHEIM. A. You who undertake the government of souls are yourselves to be the pattern of the blessed life you desire your subjects to follow (*In c. 2 RSB, Op. pia et spiritualia,* p. 227). B. You are to exercise extreme care in seeing to it that he who is appointed superior over others is adorned with wisdom and the spirit of religion (*Oratio IV, de cura pastorali, habita in capitulo generali, coram abbatibus,* 1 Maii, 1496; *ibid.,* p. 865).

2270. ST. BERNARD. Therefore on these two commands of word and example, understand that the whole of your duty and the security of your conscience depends (*Ep. 201, ad Baldwinum abbatem Reatini monasterii,* § 3, *PL* 182:370; James, p. 340).

2271. ST. FRANCIS OF ASSISI. A. Be moderate in your demands, merciful to sinners, prompt in granting pardon, abstemious in eating, poor in garb, mild in speech, faithful to God and to your assigned duties (*Ep. 9, ad provinciales totius Ordinis Minorum, Op. Om.,* p. 6). B. He should be a man of the highest character, of great discretion and of praiseworthy reputation; a man without private attachments, lest the greater love he shows to some should scandalize the whole body

(*Opusc., collatio 26, De conditionibus quibus insigniri debet minister generalis, ibid.*, p. 49).

The abbot must act in humility and fear of God

2272. ST. BERNARD. A. Even though none of your brethren has been committed to your spiritual charge, there is one under subjection to you which demands watchfulness and discipline. I am speaking of your own body, over which your spirit is to exercise control. You owe your body watchfulness so that sin may not reign in it *so that you obey its lusts* (Rom. 6:12). You owe it discipline, too, that chastises the body and *brings it under subjection* (I Cor. 9:27), in order that it may produce worthy fruits of penance.

Yet far heavier and more perilous is the bond by which are held those who must render an account for many souls. Unhappy man that I am, what shall I do, whither shall I flee, if it is found that I guarded negligently this immense treasure, this priceless deposit, which Christ judged more precious than his own blood! Had I collected the blood of the Lord dripping [from his body] on the cross, had I retained it in my possession in a vessel of glass which I should be under necessity of carrying about with me, how terrible would be my anxiety amid so many dangers! Yet I have been made custodian of that for which no imprudent merchant but he who is Wisdom itself, shed that blood. More than that, I am keeping this treasure in an earthen vessel, which is exposed to greater and more numerous dangers than are vessels of glass (*Serm. de temp., Serm. 3 in temp. Advent. Dni*, § 6, *PL* 183:46). B. How good are the sentinels who watch while we sleep, as if to give an account of our souls! How good the guardians who are wakeful in spirit, and pass the night in prayer; who seek out wisely the devices of the enemies, forestall the designs of the evil-disposed, lay bare their snares, escape their entanglements, shatter their nets, frustrate their plots! These are lovers of the brethren and of the people of Christ, who pray much for the people and for all the holy City. These are they who, being careful and anxious for the sheep entrusted to them by the Lord, bear them on their heart at their waking, when the day breaks, to the Lord who made them, and offer intercession for them in the presence of the Most High. And though they thus watch and thus intercede, they do it as knowing their own insufficiency to keep the city safe, and being conscious that *unless the Lord guard the city, in vain does the guard keep vigil* (Ps. 126:1; *Serm. 76 in Cant.*, § 7, col. 1153; Eales, p. 471).

2273. ST. GREGORY THE GREAT. For superiors should know that if ever they do what is wrong, they deserve as many deaths as were the examples of perdition given to their subjects.* Wherefore, it is necessary that they should guard themselves against a fault, as by their misdeeds they not only perish themselves, but are responsible for the souls of those whom they ruin by their evil example (*Reg. pastoralis, Pars III,* c. 4, *PL* 77:54; Davis, p. 97).

2274. ST. ANTONINUS, O.P., abp. of Florence (d. 1459). A most exacting trial will be conducted in the case of those who have ruled the multitude (cf. Wisd. 6:2 ff.)—harsh indeed if they have failed to govern themselves well; more severe if they have failed to govern their own household well; most severe of all if they have not administered legal justice to all (*Summa Theol., Pars I,* tit. 5, c. 2, *de tribus novissimis,* 1:378).

2275. HUGH OF ST. CHER, O.P. A. Although [superiors] are placed before others [*prae-lati*] by reason of their authority, they are in reality subject to all others by reason of their ministry, and in this they are like the Lord who is above all prelates (*Serm. III, De spiritu Christi conviv.*). B. No one is worthy to be promoted to the superiorship unless he has first become aware of his own defects and has deplored them, so that he can preserve humility in his own regard and be better disposed to have compassion on others (*Sup. Isa. 7, Comment.* 4:186).

2276. ELIAS DE COXIDA, abbot. *Be as one of themselves* (Sir. 32:1). Here conformity of life is prescribed for the observance of charity. Nothing contributes so much to the observance of charity, nothing wins the favor and grace of others as does this disposition whereby, placed in a position of superiority, you do not think highly of yourself, but associate with the humble and live among them and in harmony with them, so that you conduct yourself as one of them. *Be as one of themselves,* so identifying yourself with them that you rejoice with the joyful, sympathize with the sorrowful, are weak with him who is weak and inflamed with him who is scandalized (cf. II Cor. 11:29). *Be as one of themselves,* by being pleasant always, helpful when you can, judicious in distributing favors, and just in all judgments, for all these seem to belong to the [superior's] conformity in living with others. Let your affability be such that you will have plenty of salt of soul when you must take action, and plenty of honey when you are approached for help. . . . Try to offer your aid to them so that you provide for their need in all things, as you would wish to be provided for in their circumstances (*Serm. 1, PL* 209:998).

2277. JOHN TAULERUS, O.P. (d. 1361). I give this counsel to all, regardless of the rank of superiorship to which they may be assigned: let them always abase themselves to the lowest level, to the very ground, not dwelling on their own status, but avoiding every manifestation of

* As noted by Father Davis, this stricture on superiors is cited by Gratian (*Decretum,* C. 11, q. 3, c. 3, *CJC,* Richter 1:550).

pride. When they have occasion to correct someone, let them first administer a correction to themselves. As far as possible, they should be intent on overcoming evil with good: for it is certain that Satan will not drive out Satan. In this spirit of meekness let them speak words that are kind or severe, as the matter under consideration and the occasion seem to demand. Let them enter into themselves in reflection repeatedly each day, particularly of a morning and at night, setting aside for the moment and banishing from their minds all problems and all temporal affairs of office, in order to review their own status. With the mind thus lifted to God they will welcome as from his hand whatever is contrary to nature and difficult to bear. They will make an offering of their subjects to him, bear them out of love for him, and through him rise above them. All this they will do with a disposition of loving generosity, addressing expressions of their love to the Lord, and renewing their spirit in him. For perfection is to be found not in an abundance of consolation but in the will's complete resignation to God's will in bearing the bitter with the sweet (*Serm. sup. illud, Ego sum pastor bonus, Dom. II p. Pascha, In: D. Joannis Thauleri . . . piissimae tam de tempore quam de sanctis homiliae, operaque ejus alia pietati quam maxime inservientia, a Laurentio Surgio recognita;* Coloniae: Joannis Quentel, 1553, p. 215).

2278. ST. BERNARD. It is profession that makes the monk; necessity, the abbot. And in order that this necessity may not become prejudicial to the point of making void the profession, the abbot must resemble his monks, not be exalted above them. Otherwise how will it be fulfilled: *Have they made thee ruler? be not lifted up: be among them as one of them* (Eccles. 32:1, Douay version; *Tract. de moribus et officio episcoporum,* c. 9, § 33, *PL* 182:831; Luddy, p. 163).

2279. LIVES OF THE FATHERS. Even this venerable Father [Pachomius], although engaged in spiritual exercises, would take over and perform by himself all duties like the servants of all whenever [the prior] to whom he had committed the government of the monastery chanced to be absent. This he did with none of the ostentation or vainglory which at times seems to mar the great virtues of spiritual men. For he edified all in the Lord with his great humbleness of mind, distributing all things profitably (*Vita S. Pachomii, Lib. I,* c. 25, *PL* 73:246).

2280. ST. CAESARIUS OF ARLES. Be an equal among those with whom you gather at the common table in the daily nourishment of the body, and in partaking of the common food. . . . You should justify the place of honor which you hold at this table by excelling others in the observance of moderation (*Ep. hortatoria ad virg.—superiorissam—Deo dicatam, PL* 67:1137; *CR* 1:490).

2281. ST. PETER DAMIAN. When you, Father abbot, are about to partake of food, do not avoid with repugnance the table of the brethren, nor find your delight in meals taken privately or away from the common refectory. Do not consider as unworthy of sharing with you in eating physical food those who enjoy the common table of the altar with you (*Opusc. 13,* c. 15, *PL* 145:314).

2282. ST. GREGORY THE GREAT. Consequently humility must be preserved in the heart, and discipline in action. Between these two, we must diligently beware not to relax the rights of government by immoderate adherence to the virtue of humility, for if the superior depreciates himself unduly, he may be unable to restrain the lives of subjects under the bond of discipline. Let rulers, therefore, uphold externally what they undertake for the service of others, and internally retain their fear in their estimate of themselves. Nevertheless, let the subjects themselves perceive, by signs becomingly manifested, that their rulers are humble in their own estimation. They should thus apprehend both what they ought to fear from authority, and what to imitate in the sphere of humility (*Reg. pastoralis, Pars II,* c. 6, *PL* 77:36; Davis, p. 64).

2283. ST. ISIDORE OF SEVILLE. He who has been set over others to govern them must so conduct himself with regard to maintaining the discipline of his subjects that he may excel others not only by reason of the authority vested in him, but also by his humility. But he must possess this virtue of humility in so high a degree that the way of life of his subjects will not devolve into vices; he must also exercise authority in such a manner that immoderate severity will not result from hardness of heart (*Sententiarum Lib. III,* c. 42, n. 1, *PL* 83:711).

The abbot must work at his own sanctification

2284. JOHN OF TRITHEIM. Let the abbot beware lest the Lord one day say to him in his sin: *Why do you recite my statutes and profess my covenant with your mouth?* (Ps. 49:16.) You are unworthy of the duty of preacher: you exhort others to virtuous deeds, but are piling up evils for yourself; you promise others heaven, but are yourself descending into hell; you wish others to be good, and you yourself have been rejected. To what purpose, then, do you recite my statutes? Are you ignorant of the fact that the kingdom of God is *not in the persuasive words of human wisdom, but in the demonstration of the Spirit and of power?* (I Cor. 2:4.) Worthiness of life is to be sought before doctrine. A silent virtuous man is more pleasing than an evil man full of words. What will it profit you if you gain all by your words, and suffer the loss of yourself? . . . If you seek to be a true preacher and disciple of Christ, do first what God commands, and then teach others, lest you be rejected if you presume to teach before you practice what you preach. And, whatever you command or teach, do not be wise in your own estimation, but let love of God, not your personal ambition, force you to teach, lest it be said of you: *You hate discipline and cast my words behind you* (Ps. 49:17; *Comment. in c. 2 RSB, Op. pia et spiritualia,* p. 229).

2285. SMARAGDUS, abbot (d. 824). It is fitting that he who is first in rank should also be first in action, that before he expects others to obey his commands he personally fulfil by his deeds what he preaches by word; and that he first carry on his own shoulder and neck the burden he places on the brethren to bear. It is up to him to know by personal experience whether the burdens he imposes on the brethren are light or heavy. Let him give evidence of his primacy in rank at table by the virtue of moderation; and he should have learned by his own personal practice the abstinence he teaches others (*In c. 64 RSB, PL* 102:919).

2286. PHILIP OF HARVENG, abbot, O.Prae. (d. 1183). Ecclesiastical discipline has providentially prescribed that some superiors carry a rod or staff (crosier) before them, to serve as their reminder, almost as though a book had been placed in their hands. When Joas [seven-year-old son of the king] was made king, he was given the book of the law to hold in his hand, as Joiada, the high priest, had ordered it to be offered to him, in order that Joas and all the rest might know that the king must be obedient to the divine law (cf. II Paral. 23:11), and to confirm by its testimony his hands, that is, whatever he did. So also when those among us are called by divine counsel to be abbots and govern, they receive into their hands the pastoral rod or staff, in order that they may constantly have a mystical reminder of their obligations. Its very form seems to hold no small mystical significance. For by its means, almost as though a book had been placed into the hands of the abbot, it does not cease to warn him how great must be the virtues he is to acquire, and by how great a grace of virtues he must excel in his outward conduct in the eyes of his subjects. For this staff is straight and smooth, so that in it there is no crookedness, no uneasy anxiety, but it is to be carried without any sin against charity (*Ep. 13, . . . de virtutibus praelatorum, PL* 203:109).

2287. ST. HILDEGARDE. Dear daughter in the Lord, enclose your land [that is, the range of your activities] within yourself, lest it dry up without bestowing fruitful benefit upon your daughters. Organize your spiritual powers and do not allow your soul to become attached to restless excesses, for otherwise you will drive your daughters from you. Be rather like good soil which is frequently watered with timely rain, and which consequently produces pleasing vegetables (*Ep. 115, ad N., abbatissam Didenkirkem, PL* 197:335).

The abbot is to avoid excessive concern for external cares

2288. ST. GREGORY THE GREAT. A. Let the ruler not relax the care of the inner life by preoccupying himself with external matters, nor should his solicitude for the inner life bring neglect of the external, lest, being engrossed with what is external, he be ruined inwardly, or being preoccupied with what concerns only his inner self, he does not bestow on his neighbors the necessary external care. For some persons, forgetting that they are superiors of their brethren for the sake of their souls, devote themselves with all concentration of heart to secular cares. . . . And so it happens that, while they rejoice in being weighed down with tumultuous worldly business, they disregard those interior matters which they ought to be teaching others. Consequently, the life of their subjects undoubtedly grows languid, because, though these wish to make spiritual progress, they are confronted with the stumbling block, as it were, of the example of their superior.

For when the head languishes, the members have no vigor. It is in vain that an army, seeking contact with the enemy, hurries behind its leader, if he has lost the way. No exhortation then uplifts the minds of the subjects . . . and [they] cannot see the light of the truth, for when earthly cares occupy the pastor's mind, dust, driven by the winds of temptation, blinds the eyes of the Church. When, to counteract this state of things, the Redeemer of the human race, wishing to restrain us from gluttony, appositely said: *But take heed to yourselves, lest your hearts be overburdened with self-indulgence and drunkenness,* he promptly added: *and the cares of this life* (Luke 21:34; *Reg. pastoralis, Pars II,* c. 7, *PL* 77:39; Davis, *Pastoral Care,* pp. 68–69).

B. Wherefore Paul withdraws the minds of religious persons from consorting with the world, by summoning, nay, rather by enlisting them, when he says: *No one serving as God's soldier entangles himself in worldly affairs, that he may please him whose approval he has secured* (II Tim. 2:4). . . . Hence Moses, who speaks with God, is judged by the reproof of Jethro, a man of alien race, on the ground that he devotes himself by his ill-advised labor to the earthly affairs of the people (cf. Exod. 18:17–18). At the same time counsel is given him to appoint others in his stead for the composing of strifes, so that he himself may be more free to learn the secrets of spiritual matters for teaching the people. Subjects, then, are to transact inferior matters, rulers to attend to the highest, so that the eye, which is set above for guiding the steps, may not be dimmed by annoying dust. For all rulers are the heads of their subjects, and surely the head ought to look forward from above, that the feet may be able to go onward on a straight path. Otherwise, if the body's upright posture becomes bent and if the head stoops toward the earth, the feet will drag in the way of progress. . . . This is contemplated and deplored by the Prophet Jeremias in the great grief of his charity, under the symbol of the destruction of the Temple, when he says: *How is the gold become dim, the finest color is changed, the stones of the sanctuary are scattered in the top of every street* (Lament. 4:1). . . . What is signified by the term streets but the expanse of this life? . . . Gold is dimmed when a holy life is corrupted by earthly deeds. . . . The stones of the sanctuary are scattered in the streets when those who have occupied themselves in the interior mysteries for the adornment of the Church, as it were in the secrets of the Tabernacle, wander outside in the broad ways of secular affairs . . . when persons in sacred orders, given over to the laxity of their pleasures, cling to earthly affairs. . . . Secular employments, then, are sometimes to be sympathetically put up with, but never sought after out of affection for them. Otherwise, when they oppress the mind of him who is attached to them, he becomes submerged by the weight and sinks down from the concerns of heaven even to the very depths. . . . Let pastors, then, give their entire devotion to the inner life of their subjects, yet not neglect to provide for the external life also. . . . In these matters, therefore, they must always fear and watchfully take heed lest, while engaged in external cares, they be weaned away entirely from aspirations of their inner selves. For it commonly happens, as I have said, that when the hearts of rulers are incautiously occupied with temporal cares, their interior love grows cold, and immersed in external affairs, they do not fear forgetting that they have undertaken the guidance of souls. Consequently, the care that is expended externally on their subjects is to be kept within defined limits. For that reason it was well said by Ezechiel: *The priests shall not shave their heads, nor wear long hair, but they shall only poll their heads* (Ezech. 44:20). For they are rightly called priests who preside over the faithful to afford them guidance in sacred matters. The hairs of their head are the thoughts about exterior matters. When these grow insensibly above the brain, they denote the cares of this life which, sometimes arising unseasonably for lack of advertence, issue forth, as it were while we are unconscious of them. Since, then, all who are placed over others should, indeed, have a care of external matters, but without being excessively occupied by them, priests are rightly forbidden to shave the head, or let their hair grow long . . . that is, care for temporal concerns must be displayed as much as need be, yet promptly reduced, lest it increase beyond measure (*ibid.,* col. 41 f.; Davis, pp. 71–74).

C. Let the ruler be neighbor in compassion to everyone and exalted above all in thought, so that by the love of his heart he may transfer to himself the infirmities of others, and by the loftiness of his contemplation transcend even himself in his aspirations for the invisible things. . . . Thus it is that Paul . . . reaches the heavens in contemplation, yet in his solicitude he does not ignore the couch of the carnal, for being united by the bond of charity to the highest and the lowest alike, though in person mightily caught up to the high places by the power of the Spirit, he is content in his loving-kindness to be weak with others in their weakness (cf. I Cor. 7:2; II Cor. 11:29; I Cor. 9:20). . . . Thus Moses frequently goes in and out of the Tabernacle; and while within he is caught up in contemplation, outside he devotes himself to the affairs of the weak. Inwardly he considers the hidden things of God, outwardly he bears the burdens of carnal men. In doubtful matters, too, he always returns to the Tabernacle to consult the Lord in front of the Ark of the Covenant. He thus, no doubt, sets an example to rulers, that when they are uncertain what dispositions to make in secular matters, they should always return to reflection, as though to the Tabernacle, and there, as it were, standing before the Ark of the Covenant, should consult the Lord. . . . Thus the Truth itself, manifested to us by assuming our human nature, engaged in prayer on the mountain and worked miracles in the towns (cf. Luke 6:12). He thus showed the way to be followed by good rulers (*ibid.*, col. 32; Davis, pp. 56–58).

2289. ST. BERNARD. A. It is against your will, I do not doubt, that you are called away so frequently from the embraces of your dear Rachel [that is, contemplation]. Now every time this happens to you, there is necessarily a renewal of your grief (*De consideratione, Lib. I,* c. 1, § 1, *PL* 182:728).

B. Do not rely too heavily on your present disposition, for nothing is so firmly established in the soul that it cannot be removed by time and neglect. A wound grows callous when not attended to in time, and becomes incapable of cure in proportion as it loses sensibility. . . . At first something will seem insupportable to you. After a while, when you have become a little accustomed to it, it will not appear so very dreadful. Later on it will shock you less; later still, it will have ceased to shock you at all. Finally, you will begin to take delight in it. Thus little by little, you may proceed to hardness of heart. . . . Yes, this is what I am most afraid of, that despairing of ever seeing the end of the multitudinous cares which distract you, you should begin at last to stifle your conscience, and thus little by little to deaden the sense of good and salutary discomfort. How much more prudent would it not be to withdraw from your occupations occasionally, even for a short time, instead of allowing them to overwhelm you and to *lead thee where thou wouldst not?* (John 21:18.) Where is that, you ask? To hardness of heart. . . . See now to what these accursed occupations are capable of dragging you, if you continue, as you have begun, to give yourself up entirely to them, reserving nothing of you for yourself. Besides, you are only wasting time in acting thus. And if I may venture to address you in the words of Jethro to Moses, know that you are spending yourself with foolish labor (cf. Exod. 18:18, Douay version) in these secular occupations, the only result of which can be, so far as you are concerned, affliction of spirit, vexation of mind, and loss of the grace of devotion. For does not the fruit of your toil resemble the worthless cobwebs? (*Ibid.*, c. 2, §§ 2, 3, col. 729.)

C. What slavery can be more degrading and more unworthy of the Sovereign Pontiff than to be kept thus busily employed, I do not say every day, but almost every hour of every day, in straining with sweat over such matters and for such [ambitious] persons? What leisure have you left for prayer? What time remains over to you for instructing the people, for edifying the Church, for meditating on the Law? . . . For certainly *the law of the Lord is perfect, refreshing the soul* (Ps. 18:8; *ibid.*, c. 4, § 5, col. 732).

D. For in the words of the Lord: *What does it profit a man, if he gain the whole world, and suffer the loss of his own soul?* (Matt. 16:26.) Wherefore, since everybody else enjoys a share of your solicitude, you likewise must participate therein. Why should you be the only one to be defrauded of the benefit of your zeal? . . . By all means let the waters of your well flow over into the public ways; only you also must with the rest slake your thirst at the fountain. . . . Remember, therefore, I do not say always, I do not even say often, but at least from time to time, restore yourself to yourself. Attend to yourself among others, or at all events, after the others (*ibid.*, c. 5, § 6, col. 734–735).

E. Let it suffice to have admonished you not to give yourself up completely or uninterruptedly to activity, but to reserve for consideration [meditation] something of yourself, of your heart, and of your time. . . . Devote yourself to consideration. . . . What, I ask, belongs more essentially to the worship of God than that which he himself exhorts us to do by the mouth of the Psalmist, saying, *Desist! and confess that I am God?* (Ps. 45:11.) Now this is the principal function of consideration. Besides, what can be so profitable to all things as that which, with a certain kindly presumption, usurps even the office of action, by forestalling, so to speak, and preordaining whatever has to be done? And such anticipation is very necessary. For otherwise actions which, if preconceived and premeditated, might have been of advantage, become rather a source of danger through being performed without forethought. . . . The first effect of consideration is to purify its very source, that is, the mind which has given it birth. Then it regulates the affections, directs the actions, cuts away all excesses, forms the character, orders and ennobles the life, and lastly, it endows the understanding with a knowledge of things divine and human. . . . It is consideration which preordains what we have to do, and passes in review what has been accomplished, so that nothing disordered may remain in the mind, nor anything requiring correction (*ibid.*, c. 7, § 8, col. 736–737).

2290. BARTHOLOMEW OF THE MARTYRS, O.P., abp. of Braga, primate of Spain (d. 1590). A. Duties are to be performed with diligence, but without anxiety. Bear in mind that all things serve the spirit; do not encourage your feet more than your head, nor subject your head to the convenience of your feet. Let your spirit ever remain free and receptive to the rays of the Lord's light, and after ardent prayer, let the glowing embers be devoted to the times set apart for duties. . . . We must exert our efforts most earnestly and beg God with an urgency that pours forth from the very heart that in the whirlwind of preoccupations, even though they seem to overwhelm the mind, it may ever remain free, secure, and generous of spirit before the Lord. We must therefore arrange our duties, and not allow ourselves to be immersed in them, but lift our eyes confidently, by praying the Psalm to ourselves: *I lift up my eyes toward the mountains* (Ps. 120:1). Ponder the words of the Acts of the Apostles, addressed to bishops: *Take heed to yourselves, and to the whole flock* (Acts 20:28). Note the order: to yourselves, first, and then to the whole flock. When difficulties and dangers appear, have immediate recourse with all your heart to prayer, addressing yourself to the Father of lights and consolations. This constant urge to pray is an excellent occasion for spiritual progress (*Stimulus pastorum, Pars II,* c. 4, *studium praelati in oratione, contemplatione ac Sacrificii oblatione,* p. 160). B. Especially when more important undertakings present themselves, be careful not to give your whole heart to them, but in their performance always preserve your longing for God. Tell me, is not God in every transaction? Is he not to be found there as the one for whom you are working, your Inspirer, your Commander, your Helper, your Adviser? Look to him, then, when you are performing your task. Then your heart will experience tranquillity and be blessed with generosity, inspiration, and joy. Strive with deepest longing to win this grace from God.

Woe to you if the font of devotion dries up within you. For what is devotion but the font of living waters irrigating all your practice of virtue, without which they soon dry up? It is also like a heavenly wine, giving joy to the heart of man; a balsam soothing all passion; food for the soul; the tongue with which we speak to God, in fact, without which man has no tongue with which to speak to God; it is a manna from heaven. It is devotion [wisdom] which says: *You will remember me as sweeter than honey* (Sir. 24:19). But such devotion is not granted to those who love worldly comforts at table, and recognition, and honors, just as the manna was not bestowed except by giving up onions and the other foods of Egypt (cf. Num. 11:5). Swine cannot produce the wonderful sweetness of the honeycomb; that is for bees hovering solicitously around the flowers of the life of Christ. . . . Even in the whirlwind of secular concerns, let there always remain a candle lighted in your heart. After these busy concerns let the shepherd of souls take refuge in the solace of prayer and in conversation with spiritual associates. Hence Blessed Gregory in his *Pastoral Care* states: "Actually the heart greatly deteriorates in the midst of human converse, and since it is undoubtedly manifest that, driven by the tumults of exterior occupations, it goes to ruin, it should ceaselessly make it its aim to rise again by the pursuit of instruction" (*Reg. pastoralis, Pars II,* c. 11, *PL* 77:51; Davis, *Pastoral Care,* p. 87). Since it is beyond all dispute that the heart driven from itself by the confusion of external preoccupations is bound to fall, it must strive constantly to rise by the effort of prayer and meditation. The ruler is never to abandon the pursuit of sacred reading. In Proverbs (5:15) it is stated: *Drink water from your own cistern, running water from your own well,* for, as St. Gregory says (*Reg. pastoralis, Pars III,* c. 24), it is proper that [the preacher] should drink first, and then give to others to drink by his preaching (*ibid.,* pp. 156 ff.).

2291. ST. BERNARD. A. Our spiritual mother [the Church] . . . gives words of consolation to one, to another exhortation, according as each seems to have need. For instance, if she sees that one of her children begotten of the Gospel has been taken unawares by some violent temptations so that he is rendered troubled and sorrowful, doubting and fearful, and is no longer able to bear up against the force of the temptation, how she condoles with him and soothes him! how she sorrows for him and gives him comfort, and finds many a pious reason to enable him to rise out of his state of depression. If, on the contrary, she sees one active, energetic, and making good progress in the spiritual life, she rejoices greatly, she plies him with beneficial advice, she animates him to advance still further, instructs him in what is requisite for perseverance, and exhorts him so that he may go on from strength to strength. To all she adapts herself, in her heart she reflects the feelings and dispositions of all, and, lastly, she shows herself the mother no less of the feeble and failing than of the strong and progressive (*Serm. 10 in Cant.,* § 2, *PL* 183:820; Eales, p. 49). B. Among your [Pope Eugene III's] predecessors there have been those who devoted themselves unreservedly to the care of their flocks, who gloried in the shepherd's name and functions, who thought nothing unworthy of them except what they regarded as prejudicial to the salvation of souls, who so far from seeking their own interests (cf. Phil. 2:21), rather sacrificed their personal well-being to the good of their people. They were sparing neither of their pains nor of their means, in fact, they were not even sparing of themselves. You hear one of them crying out to his sheep: *I will most gladly spend and be spent myself for your souls* (II

Cor. 12:15). . . . The only profit they sought from their subjects, the only glory, the only consolation, was this: if by any means they might of them *prepare for the Lord a perfect people* (Luke 1:17). For this they strove by all the means in their power, with much tribulation of mind and body, *in labor and hardships . . . in hunger and thirst . . . in cold and nakedness* (II Cor. 11:27; *De consideratione, Lib. IV,* c. 2, § 3, *PL* 182:774). C. O charity, the good mother who nourishes the weak, puts the vigorous to work, scolds the restless, using various expedients with various people, but always loving all her sons! When she scolds you it is with gentleness, when she praises, it is with simplicity. She rages lovingly, her caresses are without guile. She knows how to be angry without losing patience, how to be indignant without being proud. It is she who is the mother of men and of angels, and makes the peace not only of earth but of heaven. It is she who rendering God favorable to man, has reconciled man to God; she, my dear Fulk, makes those brethren, with whom you once shared pleasant bread, to dwell in one manner of life in a house (cf. Ps. 6:7, Douay version). Such and so honorable a parent complains of being injured, of being wounded by you (*Ep. 2, ad Fulconem puerum, qui postea fuit Lingonensis archidiaconus,* § 1, col. 80; James, p. 10).

2292. ST. GREGORY THE GREAT. A. Those who rule others should show themselves such that their subjects are unafraid to reveal their hidden secrets to them. Thus when these little ones are enduring the waves of temptation, they will have recourse to the pastor's understanding, as to a mother's bosom (*Reg. pastoralis, Pars II,* c. 5, *PL* 77:33; Davis, *Pastoral Care,* p. 58). B. He who has assumed the care of souls receives a fearful warning, when it is said: *My son, if you have become surety to your neighbor, given your hand in pledge to another, you have been snared by the utterance of your lips* (Prov. 6:1–2). . . . Consequently, to these words the exhortation is at once well added: *so do this, my son, to free yourself. . . . Go, hurry, stir up your neighbor! Give no sleep to your eyes, nor slumber to your eyelids* (vv. 3–4). . . . To give sleep to the eyes is to cease from care, and thus to neglect altogether the charge of subjects. The eyelids slumber when our thoughts, weighted down by sloth, connive at what we know should be reproved. . . . Those who are superiors must be warned to be earnestly on the watch, to have vigilant eyes within and round about (cf. Apoc. 4:8) . . . inasmuch as they aim at pleasing the Judge within, and while giving outwardly examples of living, should detect what is to be corrected in others (*ibid., Pars III,* c. 4, col. 54; Davis, pp. 97–99).

2293. RULE FOR MONKS BY AN UNKNOWN FATHER. What must be the senior's attitude toward the brethren? Like that of a nurse caring for her small ones, loving each, strengthening each, that is, he is to open to them the way of perfection, walk before them in all perfection and holiness of mind and body. And without any acceptance of persons he is, with his whole heart, to love all alike and with an affection as sincere as though they were his sons. If he sees one of them transgress the commandment of the Lord, he is not to be moved to anger toward him, but treat him with commiseration and compassion after the manner of him who said: *Who is weak, and I am not weak? Who is made to stumble, and I am not inflamed?* (II Cor. 11:29.) If he is negligent with matters which deal with the care of the body and the soul, he will without doubt be subjected to that sentence which is worded: *Depart from me, accursed ones, into the everlasting fire which was prepared for the devil and his angels. For I was hungry, and you did not give me to eat; I was thirsty and you gave me no drink . . .* (Matt. 25:41–42). And, *Cursed be he that doth the work of the Lord deceitfully* (Jer. 48:10; *Reg. cujusdam Patris ad monachos,* c. 24, *CR* 1:223; *PL* 66:992).

2294. HUGH OF ST. CHER, O.P. A. A superior must conform himself to two kinds of subjects, by giving an example of fortitude to the strong and by being compassionate to the weak (*Sup. Gen. 2, Comment.* 1:6). B. The prelate's discipline must be exercised with regard to his delinquent sons; otherwise in vain will he carry the pastoral staff, in which the three duties of the shepherd are symbolized: they are to be drawn by the upper portion, governed with the middle of the staff, and struck with its lower part (*Sup. Eccl. 7, ibid.* 3:184).

The abbot is to act from zeal and love in correcting the erring

2295. ST. BERNARD. The spiritual physician needs to mix the wine of fervid zeal with the oil of gentleness, since it behooves him not only to console the weak, but also to restrain the unruly. For if he perceives that the wounded man, that is, the sinner, is not at all amended by the gentle and kindly reprimands which he has first employed, but, on the contrary, abuses his forbearance, becomes more negligent because of his patience, and sleeps the more securely in his sin, then, the oil of his gentle remonstrances being shown to be of no use, it behooves him to employ more powerful remedies, and so to pour in the wine of penitence, that is, to have recourse to stern corrections and reproofs, and if need be, and the stubbornness of the offender be so great, to smite him with the staff of ecclesiastical censure (*Serm. 44 in Cant.,* § 3, *PL* 183:996; Eales, p. 272).

2296. ST. GREGORY THE GREAT. Wherefore, it is necessary that when the wound of sin in the subjects is repressed by correction, even the restraint must be most carefully moderated, lest the feeling of kindness be extinguished by the manner in which the principles of discipline are exercised against the sinner. For care must be taken that loving-kindness, like that of a mother, be displayed by the ruler toward his subjects, and correction given as by a father. In all such cases treatment must be bestowed with care and circumspection, lest discipline be too rigid, or loving-kindness too lax. . . . But rulers in their relations with subjects should be animated by compassion duly considerate and by discipline affectionately severe. . . . Thus it is necessary that he who sees to the healing of wounds should apply in wine biting pain and in oil soothing tenderness, for wine cleanses suppuration and oil promotes the course of healing. In other words, gentleness is to be mingled with severity; a compound is to be made of both, so that subjects may not be exasperated by too great harshness, nor enervated by excessive tenderness. This, says St. Paul, is well symbolized by that Ark of the Tabernacle, in which, together with the Tables, were the rod and the manna (cf. Heb. 9:4); because if with the knowledge of the Sacred Scripture in the breast of the good ruler there is the restraining rod, there should also be the manna of sweetness. Wherefore, David says: *Your rod and your staff give me courage* (Ps. 22:4). It is with a rod that we are smitten, but we are supported by a staff (*Reg. pastoralis, Pars II,* c. 6, *PL* 77:37–38; Davis, pp. 66–67).

The abbot must nourish his sons with his doctrine

2297. ABSOLON, canon reg. of St. Augustine, abbot of Holy Trinity Abbey, Sprinkirsbach, diocese of Trier (d. 1203). Prelates must feed with pabulum, that is, they must nourish the pusillanimous or those who are found to be less fervent in their sacred duties, with solid doctrine and spiritual exhortation. Do you wish to know what the prelate's doctrine must be? It is necessary that it have something in common with ordinary money. A coin must possess three qualities: matter, weight, and form. In much the same way the shepherd's doctrine must also possess three qualities; it must be approved, that is, it must be correct doctrine, so that it does not teach anything except what is right and just; it must be weighty, in the sense that he propose the doctrine with authority, which is to say that he must strive to do what he seeks to teach; likewise . . . it must be authentic, that is, in no point opposed to the authority of the holy Fathers, but that he teach what the saints have propounded, or which Christ himself promulgated (*Serm.* 27, *PL* 211:162).

2298. ST. BONAVENTURE. A. Of worthy prelates it is stated: *And I will give you pastors according to my own heart, and they shall feed you with knowledge and doctrine* (Jer. 3:15). Pastors then govern according to the good pleasure of the divine will when they feed their flock with knowledge by means of the word and with the doctrine of example,—for the example of deeds moves more effectively than do words (*Serm. 1 de Dom. I post Octav. Paschae, Op. Om.,* ed. Peltier 13: 239). B. A shepherd of souls who loves God feeds [his flock] with the word, he feeds them by his example, and he feeds them by helping them with the words of consolation or prayer, with the example of his own manner of life, and with the help of his assistance in material substance (cf. I John 3:17; *Serm. 3 Dom. 17 p. Pent., ibid.,* p. 441).

2299. JOHN OF TRITHEIM. We admonish you who are shepherds of souls that, if you love almighty God, you will lead the flocks he has entrusted to you, to the pastures of life. The norm to be employed in this holy solicitude has been indicated for every shepherd of souls in the holy Gospel where the government of the Universal Church is committed to the Prince of the Apostles with the threefold question (cf. John 21:16 ff.). One simple statement of love is not sufficient for a shepherd of souls from whom the Supreme Shepherd demands a threefold feeding. If you have professed your true love when you have been asked a third time whether you love the Lord, you have also been commanded a third time to assume the care of the sheep. It is as though the Lord were to say to you: "O abbot, if you love me, receive these my sheep, to be fed with a threefold nourishment: feed them with the word, feed them by example, feed them with nourishment." These three things are indispensably necessary for the shepherd of those who dwell within the cloister. If one of them is wanting, he becomes useless as a shepherd (*Oratio IV, de cura pastorali, habita in capitulo generali,* 1 Maii, 1496, *coram abbatibus, Op. pia et spiritualia,* p. 866).

The abbot must act with prudence and discretion

2300. BARTHOLOMEW OF THE MARTYRS, O.P. Prudence is the abbess of virtues; none of them performs anything well except under her direction. Remember the words of Job: *The cause which I knew not, I searched out most diligently* (Job 29:16, Douay version). In the prelate's manner of life, it is demanded that we be simple, agreeable, and pleasant as doves, but at the same time, as prudent as serpents, that is, protecting our head, by preserving charity. This means that we are to do nothing whatever that is unlawful—regardless of anyone's authority, the esteem in which he is held, the nature of the petition, the love we have for him, or the fear in which we hold him. We are to examine with a critical eye to see whether any poison lies concealed in what is requested—so that we may refuse with constancy what must be denied, acting always, however, with great politeness. We must also be sharp-eyed for the devil's cleverness. There is nothing that fails to present some appearance of reasonableness and which cannot be justified with arguments when presented by men of eloquence (*Stimulus pastorum, Pars II,* c. 11, *prudentia ac circumspectio pastoris in verbis et factis,* p. 256).

2301. ST. BERNARD. A. Discretion, then, is not so much a single virtue, as a certain moderator and conductor of all the virtues, a director of the affections, and a teacher of all the conduct of life. Without it, even virtue degenerates into vice, and the natural impulses themselves are changed into passions which disturb and destroy nature (*Serm. 49 in Cant.*, n. 5, *PL* 183:1018; Eales, p. 300). B. The virtue of discretion lies prone and helpless without the fervor of charity, while the vehement fervor of charity without the moderating influence of discretion, hurries on to the precipice. Therefore he is to be praised to whom neither is wanting, insomuch as fervor animates his discretion, and discretion regulates his fervor. So it behooves him to be constituted who rules over others (*ibid., serm. 23*, n. 8, col. 888; Eales, p. 136). C. I would not have you to be austere in your manner, but rather only grave. Austerity is wont to repel the timid, whereas the effect of gravity is to sober the frivolous. The presence of the former disposition would render you odious, the absence of the latter would make you contemptible. As in all things else, you will do best in this matter to observe moderation. Therefore avoid undue severity as much as excessive lightness. What can be more pleasing than such manners as are equally removed from the stiffness which freezes and from the familiarity which breeds contempt? (*De consideratione, Lib. IV*, c. 6, § 22, *PL* 182:787.)

2302. BERNARD, abbot of Montecassino (d. 1282). The abbot then adapts himself to circumstances (*RSB*, c. 2) when, because of a brother's anger or other manifestation of passion, he puts off to a more appropriate time the rebuke which, in his upset and disturbed condition he could not now bear, and which would not only not be of benefit to him, but could even be of great harm (*In c. 2 RSB, PL* 66:277).

2303. ST. ODO, abbot of Cluny (d. 942). Certainly he who does not rebuke his subjects, either because he is awaiting a more propitious occasion for doing so, or because he fears that if they were reproved they would only become worse and would harm even more those who are not strong, is guilty neither of negligence nor of manifestation of partiality, but is acting from motives of charity (*Collationum Lib. III*, n. 44, *PL* 133:629).

2304. ST. GREGORY THE GREAT. A. It should also be observed that at times the faults of subjects must be prudently overlooked, but they should be given to understand that they are being overlooked. Sometimes even what is openly known should be judiciously tolerated, while in other cases even hidden faults must be subjected to a closer scrutiny; and, as the case may be, they should be either gently reproved or sharply censured. Some things are, as we have said, to be prudently connived at, but the connivance indicated, so that when the delinquent sees that he has been discovered and tolerated, he may be ashamed to augment the faults which he realizes are tolerated in silence, and may punish himself in being his own judge, when the patience of the ruler mercifully excuses him. It was with such connivance that the Lord fitly reproved Judea, when he said through the Prophet: *Thou hast lied, and hast not been mindful of me, nor thought of me in thy heart. For I am silent and as one that seeth not* (Isa. 57:11). He, therefore, both connived at her faults and let her know that he was doing so. . . . For some things, even openly known, are to be judiciously tolerated, when, that is, the occasion is not suitable for public reprehension. For wounds are more inflamed by untimely incisions, and if medicaments do not suit the occasion, it is certain that they do not serve their purpose of healing. But while an opportunity is being sought for the correction of subjects, the patience of the ruler is tried under the burden of their faults, and so it is well said by the Psalmist: *Upon my back the plowers plowed* [understood to mean that "Israel was scourged like a slave"] (Ps. 128:3) . . . as though he meant to say in plain words: "Those whom I cannot correct I carry as a burden."

Some secret matters should, however, be closely investigated, so that from certain symptoms breaking out, the superior may discover all that lurks hidden in the minds of his subjects, and by timely reproof come to know from insignificant things what is more serious. . . . Some things, however, are to be reproved gently. Thus when sin is committed, not through malice, but through sheer ignorance or frailty, it is then, indeed, necessary to temper reproof of the sin with great forbearance. For, in truth, all of us are subject to the frailties of our corrupt nature so long as we remain in this mortal flesh. Each one, therefore, ought to infer from his own case to what degree he should have mercy on the weakness of others, lest he seem forgetful of his own estate while he violently rushes into reproof of the frailty of his neighbor. Wherefore Paul admonishes us, saying: *If a person is caught doing something wrong, you who are spiritual instruct such a one in a spirit of meekness, considering thyself, lest thou also be tempted* (Gal. 6:1) . . . that the spirit may moderate itself in its zeal for reproving, in fearing in its own case that which it reproves (*Reg. pastoralis, Pars II,* c. 10, *PL* 77:44 f.; Davis, pp. 79–82).

B. Nevertheless, there are some things which are to be reproved severely, so that when a fault is not recognized by the one committing it, he may appreciate its gravity by the verbal reproof. . . . It is, surely, the duty of the ruler to reveal the glory of our homeland in heaven by preaching, to show what great temptations of the ancient enemy are lurking in this life's journey, and to correct with severe and zealous asperity those evils in his subjects which cannot be treated with forbearance, lest, being too little incensed against such faults, he himself be held guilty of all (*ibid.,* col. 46; Davis, pp. 82–83).

C. Young people are to be admonished in one way, old people in another, because the former are for the most part guided to make progress by severe admonitions, while the latter are disposed to better deeds by gentle remonstrance, for it is written: *Do not rebuke an elderly man, but exhort him as you would a father* (I Tim. 5:1; *ibid., Pars III,* c. 1, col. 52; Davis, p. 92).

D. The wise of this world are to be admonished to stop knowing what they know [Davis: that they are not to show themselves proud of the knowledge they have]; and the dull are to be admonished to seek to know what they do not know. In the former the first thing to be got rid of is the persuasion that they are wise. In the latter, whatever heavenly wisdom they know, is to be built up, because as they are not proud their hearts are prepared to undertake the building. . . . The former are usually more readily converted by arguments from reason; the latter are often converted better by examples. To the former it is profitable to fall vanquished by their own allegations, but for the dull it is sometimes sufficient to learn of the praiseworthy deeds of others (*ibid.,* c. 6, col. 56–57; Davis, pp. 101–102).

E. The deeds of the insolent are to be subtly demolished by him who reproves, so that what they are complacent about may be shown to be displeasing to God. We best reprove the insolent when we show them that what they believe they have done well has been ill-done, so that a wholesome confusion may ensue from what they believe won glory for them. . . . [The fainthearted], too conscious of their weakness, commonly fall into despondency . . . and think that what they do is extremely despicable, and therefore their spirit is broken in dejection. . . . We are more apt to bring them back to the path of welldoing, if by way of indirect approach we refer to some of their good points. Thus by reproving and correcting some things, and approving and praising others, their sensitiveness is palliated by the praise they hear, though it is chastised by the rebuking of their fault. Generally we make more profitable progress with these people, if we also speak of their good deeds. And if they have done some deeds out of order, we do not reprove this as something actually done, but utter a prohibition against it as something not to be done. . . . Thus the favor shown them will encourage their zeal for the things which we approve, and the gentle exhortation will be the more effectual with the fainthearted against what we reprove in them (*ibid.,* c. 8, col. 58; Davis, pp. 104–105, slightly re-arranged).

F. The insincere are to be admonished to realize how burdensome is the business of duplicity which they guiltily bear. For in the fear of discovery they ever try to defend themselves even dishonorably, and are ever agitated with fear and apprehension. . . . For commonly, though they are discovered in their fault, they shrink from being known for what they are, and they screen themselves under a veil of deceit, and the fault which is quite obvious they try to excuse. The result is that often one who aims at reproving them, led astray by the mists of disseminated falsehood, finds that he has all but lost the certain conviction he had been holding concerning them. . . . *He who walks honestly walks securely* (Prov. 10:9); for sincerity of conduct is an assurance of great security. Let them be told what is said by the mouth of the wise men: *The holy spirit of discipline flees deceit and withdraws from senseless counsels* (Wisd. 1:5; *ibid.*, c. 11, col. 64; Davis, pp. 117–119).

G. The choleric pursue even those who shun them, stirring up occasions of strife, rejoicing in the trouble caused by contention. It is better, however, that in correcting these people we shun them when their anger is actually seething; for when they are aroused, they do not perceive what is being said to them. But when they have been restored to their senses, they the more willingly accept words of counsel, as they blush for having been peacefully borne with. For to the mind that is intoxicated with frenzy, everything said that is right appears wrong. . . . But when the choleric so attack others that it is impossible to shun them, they should not be smitten with open rebuke, but sparingly with a certain respectful forbearance. . . . For those who try to check them in their frenzy . . . should show all possible calmness; and let them suggest discreetly that which will, as it were, by a side stroke (of the spear) pierce their frenzied mind. . . . Of course, to smite with the sharp point is to oppose another with an attack of open rebuke, but to smite a pursuer with the reverse end of the spear is to touch the frenzied quietly and partially, and to overcome him, as it were, by sparing him (*ibid.*, c. 16, col. 76, 77; Davis, pp. 139, 140).

H. It is, however, to be observed that we often reprove the haughty to better effect, if with our reproofs we mingle a measure of conciliatory praise. We should introduce either some good qualities which they possess, or at least mention some such qualities that could be present, though they actually may not be; and then only should the evil in them that displeases us be cut away, when the good points which are pleasing to them have in advance rendered their mind well-disposed to listen to us. Thus, too, in the case of unbroken horses we first stroke them gently with the hand, so that afterward we may tame them completely even by using the whip (*ibid.*, c. 17, col. 78; Davis, p. 143).

2305. JULIANUS POMERIUS, priest of Arles (5th century). [Superiors] chastise those of whom they know that they can bear rebuke; and they feel their way with those who cannot bear reproof, as being weak, not by flattering them because they are such, but by compassionating the infirmities of such persons if it happens that they cannot be healed otherwise. But if the weak who cannot be cured by the application of reproof are debarred from communion with the Church, being burdened beyond measure by the weight of intolerable sadness, they either break down and shun the sight of all holy persons through whom they could be restored to God, or are certain to leap into every shameless sin if they are embittered. . . . On this account, then, those who cannot be reproved because of their weakness are to be tolerated with gentle compassion. And, truly, if you produce a healthy sense of shame in a sinner because you blush for him and if by the tender compassion of your heart you transfer to him the shame which you assume for his sins, you will easily repress in him all laxity with regard to sin and take from him all the observance which incites to wanton baseness. . . . There you see how one who thinks of nothing but the salvation of those he wishes to help treats all sinners gently, or rebukes them (*De vita contemplativa, Lib. II,* c. 5, §§ 1, 2, *PL* 59:449; Suelzer, p. 66).

The abbot is to direct his sons in all patience

2306. BENEDICT HAEFTEN. Subjects are to be borne. This is foreshadowed in the figure by which the Lord commanded that the names of the sons of Israel be engraved on the two onyx stones set on the shoulder straps of the ephod which covered Aaron's shoulders and that the same be inscribed on the stones to be placed on the rational or breastpiece (cf. Exod. 28). Now what else does this signify but that the superior must bear the souls committed to his charge—both in his heart by charity and on his shoulders as a constant burden? These obligations are so interrelated that the one follows upon the other. For he will bear with a subject in proportion to his love for him: if he ceases to love him, he will bear him no longer. This is the abbot's burden, which would be dreadful even for the shoulders of an angel (*Disquisitiones monasticae, Lib. III,* tract. 5, *de abbate,* disq. 4, conditio 3, p. 317).

2307. ST. ATHANASIUS, bp. of Alexandria (d. 373). You know, for you have read the Scripture, how great an offense it is for a bishop to desert his church [diocese], and to neglect the flocks of God. For the absence of the shepherd gives the wolves an opportunity to attack the sheep. And that was what the Arians and all the other heretics desired, —that during my absence they might find an opportunity to entrap the people into impiety. If then, I had fled, what defense could I have made before the true bishops? or rather, before him who has committed to me his flock? (*Apologia ad Constantium Imperatorem,* § 26, *PG* 25:627.)

2308. ST. LAURENCE JUSTINIAN. The pastoral office is nothing other than this, to lay down one's very soul for the sheep committed to one (*De institutione et regimine praelatorum,* c. 4, *Op. Om.* 2:241).

2309. BARTHOLOMEW OF THE MARTYRS. A. The infirmities and difficult dispositions of many must be borne. For that reason prelates are called gods, for there must shine in them a certain divine patience, magnanimity of soul, and prudence (*Stimulus pastorum, Pars II,* c. 11, *prudentia et circumspectio pastoris in verbis et factis,* p. 271). B. A twofold martyrdom is involved in the pastoral duty: one is penitential in character, which is primarily concerned with external works and with interior bitter experiences, the worries and trials connected with the office. The other arises from anxieties and perplexities about things to be done or not to be done—and in these instances we must hasten to the anchor of prayer. Pray thus: "Lord, you know all things. You know that on no account do I wish ever to be displeasing to you—that, in fact, I am ready to die rather than offend you. Illumine my eyes . . . and teach me to do your will, for you are my God" (*ibid.,* c. 10, p. 198).

2310. ST. PETER DAMIAN. Although you are under obligation to excel in all holy practices, in that you have been appointed over others as an example of a virtuous way of life, you must devote yourself even more specially to the cultivation of patience. Overcome the obstacles of all kinds of hardship by patience. Let patience show you to be a hard stone, in fact, an untouchable diamond. A diamond marks other stones whereas it itself admits the imprint of no other solid. If your mind remains unswayed when hardships appear, that is, if it does not receive into itself the image of another stone, in fact, if it imprints its own mark on others, whatever hardships befall are converted unto your own welfare, by your composure of mind and tranquillity of disposition (*Opusc. 15, De institutis ordinis Eremitarum,* c. 31, *PL* 145:363).

2311. ST. BERNARD. A. Therefore I say hold on to what you have, remain where you are, and try to benefit those over whom you rule. Do not try to escape the responsibility of your office while you are still able to discharge it for the benefit of your subjects. Woe to you if you rule them and do not benefit them, but far greater woe to you if you refuse to benefit them because you shirk the burden of ruling them (*Ep. 86, ad Guglielmum, abbatem S. Theodorici,* § 2, *PL* 182:210; James, p. 128). B. Yet it is for you to see if you have acted wisely in not following my advice about this matter [St. Bernard had counselled his close friend Ojer not to resign his abbacy, which advice Ojer had rejected]; it must be decided also by those wiser persons than I, on whose authority you have relied, whether you have acted according to reason. Let them tell you, I say, whether it is lawful for a Christian man to lay down the burden of obedience before his death, when Christ was made obedient to the Father even unto death. You will reply: "I have acted with permission, asked and received from the bishop." True, you have, indeed, asked for permission, but in a manner you ought not to have done, and, therefore, have rather extorted than asked it. But an extorted or compelled permission should rather be called violence. What therefore the bishop did unwillingly, when overcome by your importunity, was not to release you from your obligations, but violently to break them (*Ep. 87, ad Ogerum, Canonicum Regularem,* § 2, col. 212; Gasquet, p. 96 f.; James, p. 130).

2312. JULIANUS POMERIUS. Whatever progress they who place themselves under one person out of love for perfection . . . make by being freed from all occupation, becomes the fruit of him who alone has been occupied in behalf of many. And, consequently, he who bears responsibility for all who live under him advances in the advancement of his community with the result that, as his occupation has become the fruitful leisure of his subjects, so their glorious perfection may be considered the honor and glory of their superior (*De vita contemplativa, Lib. II,* c. 16, § 4, *PL* 59:461; Suelzer, *The Contemplative Life by Julianus Pomerius,* p. 85).

2313. ST. ANSELM, abp. of Canterbury, Doctor of the Church (d. 1109). Do cheerfully whatever you do, work cheerfully at your tasks, *for God loves a cheerful giver* (II Cor. 9:7). You complain also that because you are so occupied with your duties, the opportunity for praying and reading is interfered with. Be assured that you will find no small consolation in this thought: *charity covers a multitude of sins* (I Petr. 4:8). While you are being held back, another is drawn forward; while you are bowed down, another is helped to stand erect; while you are burdened, another is supported. Then too you should remind yourself that although the servant who returns home empty-handed travels more swiftly, the whole household runs with great rejoicing to him who is heavily burdened. Nor is anyone reproved because he returns a bit late, but he is urged to rest if he has been worn out in working profitably (*Lib. I, ep. 11, ad Rodulphum, PL* 158:1076; Schmitt, *Op. Om.,* n. 13, 3:118).

The abbot is the head of the monastic family

2314. ST. BONAVENTURE. The brotherhood is like a human body, with the [superior] at its head. As the other members are devoted to their respective functions, the head, by being placed over all, is to provide for all by means of the commands and concessions of holy obedience, something after the manner of the head in the human body as the nerve center over the whole body and imparting to all the senses the impulses and emotions (*De sex alis Seraphim,* c. 6, § 13, *Op. Om.,* ed. Quaracchi 8:145).

The officials of the monastery

2315. PETER THE VENERABLE. Cannot the abbot place his burdens on others, and fulfil through representatives what he personally, involved in many and divers duties, cannot perform? . . . We know surely that bishops could be without priests and ministers if they themselves were able to perform alone everything necessary for the welfare of their dioceses. In like manner the abbot also, if he were able to care for everything, would be cellarer, infirmarian, distributor of alms, and guestmaster, and hold the places of all the other officials, if he were able to perform these tasks alone. But because it is impossible, or at least extremely difficult, to divide his efforts among many duties, it is fitting for many to do what one cannot perform. Thus Jethro, remonstrating with Moses regarding such matters, says: *"You should also look among all the people for able and God-fearing men, trustworthy men, and set them as officers over groups of thousands, of hundreds, of fifties, and of tens. Let these men render decisions for the people in all ordinary cases. More important cases they should refer to you* (Exod. 18:19 ff.; *Lib. I, ep. 28, ad Bernardum Claraevall., abbatem, PL* 189:132).

2316. BENEDICT HAEFTEN. As in a large army a group is placed under one leader, who keeps the soldiers at their duties, so in religious orders, which constitute a kind of spiritual army, it is proper that there be several subordinate superiors for lending their assistance to the abbot in the government of the monks (*Disquisitiones monasticae, Lib. III,* tract. 6, disq. 4, p. 332).

The prior

2317. ST. BASIL THE GREAT. Since it frequently happens by reason of physical weakness, or the necessity of travel, or some other circumstance, that the superior is absent from the community, some other person approved by him and by others who are competent to judge should be selected to take charge of the brethren in his absence, that there may be one person to address words of exhortation and solace to those who remain at home. This will also ensure that, when the superior is away, the brethren will not adopt a popular system of government, as it were, to the abrogation of the rule and traditional discipline, but will preserve established and approved customs unto the glory of God (*Reg. fusius tractatae, Interrogatio 45,* n. 1, *PG* 31:1031; Wagner, p. 322).

2318. VIGILIUS, deacon and monk (d. circa 420). He who is placed by the abbot over the brethren according to the order of discipline and the recommendation and desire of all the brethren, will assume complete charge of the discipline and the work of the monastery, having the power in the abbot's absence to do all that the abbot does when present. He will practice patience, gentleness, humility, charity, and justice without distinction of persons, so conducting himself that he will neither cause the abbot trouble, nor will the brethren suffer as a result of his severity. The senior who is placed over the brethren will observe all this, referring everything to the abbot, particularly those matters that he personally hesitates to decide (*Reg. Orientalis ex patrum orientalium regulis collecta a Vigilio Diacono*, c. 3, *CR* 1:61; *PL* 50:375).

2319. RULE OF THE MONASTERY OF TARNADAE. It is the particular duty of the provost (prior) to refer to the abbot, whose authority is higher among you, anything that exceeds the power vested in him. . . . He will correct the restless, encourage the fainthearted, support the weak, exercise patience toward all, maintain discipline with a pleasant disposition, and instill fear. And although both dispositions are necessary, he is to seek rather to be loved than feared (c. 23, *CR* 1:186; *PL* 66:986).

2320. ST. PETER DAMIAN. The prior of the monastery then fulfils his office zealously when he does not personally stand in opposition to the will of his abbot and when, as far as lies in his power, he confirms the brethren in their sincere love for the abbot. . . . Just as the abbot himself must, in all that he does, incite a love for Christ in his sons, so the prior must strive to stimulate the brethren in their love for the abbot, to prevent any envy from manifesting itself, which God forbid! Let him, therefore, not show himself indulgent toward those who have been guilty of faults, intending thereby to make the abbot appear unduly severe. When the abbot is absent he is to reprove all evils, so that on his return the abbot may rest calm in the pleasure of rejoicing spiritual brethren as though in the tranquillity of a sheltered port. Let him be unyielding in his judgment with regard to the correction of those who have been guilty of faults. Nor is he to allow the traditional discipline of the regular life to grow lax. He must be severely just in order that the abbot may seem loving in his mildness. Let him be rather exacting in his demands so that there can be that which the abbot can remit in fatherly kindness. Moses, the faithful servant, handed down the Commandments of unadorned justice, but Christ, the loving Lord, tempered the Law's harshness. Aaron, on the other hand, who showed himself yielding to the people in their sinfulness, joined with them in making idols for sacrilegious rites.

Like the veil suspended before the Ark of the Covenant, the prior should serve as a sort of shield for the abbot in all external affairs. Let him always be exposed to the dust arising from contacts with the world, but the abbot, like the Ark of the Lord, protected in the cleanliness of its brilliance. Let the former, like Aaron, acting as the abbot's spokesman, address the people, whereas the latter, like Moses, pronouncing divine exhortations, is to act in the matters that pertain to God. When each thus complements the other unto a spiritual unity, they are to nourish such sons for God, if such a thing is possible, that no worthier can follow in the right of heavenly inheritance (*Opusc. 13, de perfectione monachorum*, c. 16, *PL* 145:314).

2321. BENEDICT HAEFTEN. The prior's duty is to render assistance to the abbot in all things: he is to serve as his eyes for keeping vigilance, his foot in the commitments that call for going about, his hand in performing duties, his consolation in worries, his support in weakness, his comfort in difficulties (*Disquisitiones monasticae, Lib. III,* tract. 6, disq. 3, p. 331).

The novice master

2322. ST. BERNARD. Because the way that leads to life is narrow and difficult, my sons, like little children in Christ, you need a teacher and guardian who will instruct you, draw you on, protect you and, as it were, cherish you as small children, and console you with encouraging words, lest the age of weakness be lost. Hence not I, but rather the Head and Pastor of the whole Church admonishes you: *Crave, as new-born babes, pure spiritual milk,* not indeed that you may remain in that state, but in order *that by it you may grow to salvation* (I Petr. 2:2; *Serm. 8 de div.,* n. 7, *PL* 183:564).

2323. JOHN OF TRITHEIM. The novice master should be the kind of person who is zealous for souls, skilled in healing the wounds of temptations—who knows when prudently and opportunely to pour in the wine of reproach, and the fitting moment to use the oil of encouragement. He should be mature in his manner of life, cautious in counseling, sparing of speech, firmly established in good habits, strong in the practice of the interior life, diligent and meticulous in observing the conduct of the novices. Let him shield them with the same holy solicitude with which he protects his own soul; let him omit nothing that pertains to their training in virtue, and show them by his own deeds that such goodness can be imitated. While their minds are so receptive, let him direct their manners according to the Rule, and from the very beginning train the kind of novices who will become the kind of monks he desires for the future. For the novice who is neglected at the beginning of his conversion will never again be turned to the observance of discipline, nor will he ever, as long as he lives, correct the laxity which has once taken hold of him. Anyone who is disobedient or opposed to the precepts of the Rule and of the seniors during the novitiate has already manifested clearly that he will not become a good monk in the future; lest he destroy good observance by his evil conduct, he is to be sent away from the monastery forthwith. You will never get a good monk from a bad novice. Hence a negligent training of novices carries with it the greatest disaster for religion, a result that can never be sufficiently guarded against (*Oratio quinta, . . . in capitulo annali, coram abbatibus,* Sept., 1496, *Op. pia et spiritualia,* p. 876).

The cellarer to devote paternal care to the brethren

2324. ST. BASIL THE GREAT. In his dealings with him by whom he has been appointed, let [the cellarer] be mindful of the Lord himself, who said: *Of myself I can do nothing* (John 5:30); but toward those whose care he undertakes, he is to consider each one's personal need. For it is written: *Distribution was made to each, according as anyone had need* (Acts 4:35). The same principles are to be applied in the case of all to whom similar duties are assigned (*Reg. brevius tractatae, Interrogatio 148, PG* 31:1179).

All officials must obey the abbot

2325. ST. AUGUSTINE. A. They hand over the product of their labors to the men who are called deans because they are placed over groups of ten, so that thus no one is preoccupied with corporal necessities, be it with regard to food or clothing, the daily requirements, or the needs that are felt in the time of common illness. These deans, arranging all things with great care, and distributing whatever this form of life demands because of bodily infirmities, render their accounts to the one whom they call Father. These fathers are men who are not only saintly in conduct, but are outstanding in their doctrine in things divine, and of excellent character generally. With no fault of pride they govern those whom they call sons, possessing great authority in directing them spiritually and accepting the ready obedience of those under their charge (*De moribus Ecclesiae Catholicae, Lib. I,* c. 31, *Manichaeorum continentiae opponit anachoretarum et coenobitorum vitam,* § 67, *PL* 32:1338). B. God spoke to Moses, did he not? (cf. Exod. 18:14 ff.). Yet Moses very prudently and humbly yielded to the advice of his father-in-law, foreigner though he was, with regard to governing and directing such a mighty nation. For he realized that no matter from what source right counsel proceeded, it should be attributed not to him who conceived it, but to him who is Truth, the immutable God (*De doctrina Christiana, prolog.,* § 7, *PL* 34:18; Gavigan, p. 23).

The abbot consults the brethren

2326. ST. BASIL THE GREAT. The works that pertain to God are, according to God, to be committed to those who have already shown that they can perform the task assigned to them in a manner pleasing to the Lord. And it is supremely necessary for the one placed over others to be mindful in every undertaking of Holy Scripture which says, *Do nothing without counsel* (Sir. 32:19; *Reg. brevius tractatae, Interrogatio 104, PG* 31:1154).

2327. ST. BERNARD. Cannot what the abbot decides, after consulting the seniors, be allowed to stand unless all the community agree to it? Have you forgotten, or are you ignoring, what your Rule says so explicitly, on the matter? It commands that the community should be summoned to council [whenever there is anything important to be decided], and that each monk should humbly give his advice, without presuming stubbornly to defend his opinion; but that the abbot, when he has heard what each monk has to say, shall do whatever he thinks best, and that all shall submit to his decision (*Ep. 397, ad Odonem abbatem Majoris-Monasterii* [Marmoutier, near Tours], n. 4, *PL* 182:608; James, p. 500).

The monastic family grows into a congregation

2328. JEAN MABILLON, monk of congregation of St. Maur (d. 1707). When the man of God, Benedict, had long observed silence [toward the end of his three years in the cave at Subiaco], had gained the victory over the temptations of the flesh, and had cultivated the fervor of the divine fire through meditation, reading, and intense prayer, this flame could not longer be restricted to the narrow confines of the cave at Subiaco. Under the impelling force of the Holy Spirit, it addressed itself to the spiritual formation of new men, and the drawing up of a complete rule of all monasticism. St. Gregory the Great thus relates the story: "When the holy man for a long time excelled in that lonely wilderness by reason of his virtues and wondrous deeds, a great number gathered about him as days passed, and he established twelve monasteries like so many schools of holiness, to each of which he assigned twelve monks under superiors." Thus from St. Gregory we learn that abbots were placed over the individual monasteries, all under the direction of St. Benedict, who remained the general master. He mentions that restless monk who had been repeatedly admonished by his abbot, whom the holy father [Benedict], invited thither because of his dignity, brought back to his senses by striking him with his staff. He appointed twelve monks in each of the little monasteries, not more, for all beginnings are small and weak, nor fewer, because below that number the monastic discipline can scarcely be maintained intact and given a chance to develop, with the waxing strong and maturing of the practice of religion. Those who have subsequently erected new foundations and established reforms have continued to employ this number, consecrated by our holy lawgiver; examples are particularly to be found among the Cistercian monks (*Annales O.S.B., Lib. II,* c. 1, 1:34, abbreviated).

Visitation of monasteries

2329. JOHN OF TRITHEIM. A. The most powerful force for achieving reform is to be found in the zeal of the visitors. Hence it is stated in the constitutions of the fathers that worthy men are to be chosen for the duty of conducting the visitation, men who by word and example can effectively teach the virtuous way of life to those who are to be visited. . . . The basic principle of the regular observance with the visitors is this: if it is continued, it will grow; if it is neglected, it will disappear. In other words, if the visitors have performed their duty diligently, they will preserve the reformed monasteries in regular observance, and will easily bring weakened monasteries to a worthier monastic life (*Lib. lugubris de statu et ruina monastici ordinis,* c. 10, *Op. pia et spiritualia,* p. 837).

B. The visitor must be learned in the divine law in order to be able to discern prudently between good and evil and to apply the proper medicine for each individual weakness. He is to be outstanding in personal holiness, inspired at all times with zeal for what is virtuous; cautious in giving advice; mature in speech; discreet in judgment. He should be meek, never cruel; merciful, not severe. Let him show by his humility that he is a companion to the good, while giving an example of zeal for good discipline to the impudent and disobedient. He should inaugurate the reform in his own life and among his own monks, and only then proceed to the conversion of others (*Oratio quinta, in conventu abbatum habita,* Sept., 1496, *Op. pia et spiritualia,* p. 885).

C. If it is properly celebrated, the provincial chapter is the greatest strength of our stability. For it is the distinctive stronghold of our order, without which our whole religious institute would be thrown into confusion. . . . For the chapter is the preservation of order, the increase of regular discipline, that which effects our unity. In it integrity is given to morals, purity is increased for minds, and uniformity of the regular life is instituted. The ultimate reason for the provincial chapter, therefore, is the preservation of the regular institute. The Roman Pontiffs and presidents of the general councils, seeing that our order could not long subsist without some sort of special remedy, chose to help it by means of the provincial chapter. . . . In the chapter of the abbots vices are to be corrected, exhortations to virtue given, so that the evil may find cause for fear, and the good may learn how to become better. . . . In the provincial chapter the governing abbot is instructed; in it he is admonished with regard to the dangers of pastoral work; in it he is commanded as to what he is to do; and, in the love of God, is forbidden the things he should avoid. Finally, when we assemble in this manner in chapter, many helpful points are brought to our attention which, if we are seeking the welfare of our souls, are very necessary. To pass over other points, it is shown by experience how significantly mutual charity contributes to love of regular discipline. By knowledge fraternal charity is preserved and increased, which would otherwise soon grow cold if it did not receive such warmth of mutual recognition. In the chapter there is an easy approach to uniformity, where from the united gathering of the fathers the motivation is prepared for exemplary observance; the assembly presents an example of holiness. Here we have a fortress of God, my fathers, and the fortification of our order by which all the clever attacks of our adversaries are reduced to nothing (*De statu et ruina monastici ordinis,* c. 8, p. 832).

D. Two practices give promise of perseverance with great hope of reform, namely the annual chapter and the office of visitation. If either were removed, the process of reforming [the order] would soon die out. . . . These two provisions are to our reform what the two eyes are to the head. If you pluck out the eyes of a seeing man, you blind and cripple him; if you discontinue the chapter or the visitation, you have reduced the reform to nothing. Preserve, therefore, fathers, these institutes of the ancients. Do not put an end to these two—if you desire the holy reform to continue inviolable (*Oratio secunda, coram abbatibus,* 1 Sept., 1492, p. 852).

2330. GUIGES, fifth prior of La Grande Chartreuse (d. 1188). Abundant fruits for the whole order [Carthusians] result from the congress of the venerable fathers at the annual chapter. . . . Let us not deny what is true—they come here to us not without arduous effort, but with intense devotion, with cheerfulness, alacrity, humility, simplicity, benignity, piety, and charity. And this is why they come: first, to show that they must render prompt and humble obedience to the ancient provision of the order; . . . second, that even corporeally they may see one another in all spiritual joy and increase more and more the brotherhood's mutual charity in the Lord; third, that by common counsel and agreement, employing zeal and knowledge, always reserving the first place for discretion, they may, according to their experience and ability, revive, consolidate, and strengthen in its good state the order in which they have professed. In intensely fervent solicitude and solicitous fervor according to God, they set as their purpose to destroy what is harmful and to build up what is profitable. In this twin program of salvation they are studiously to imitate him whom the Lord set for an identical purpose over nations and kingdoms, *to root up, and to pull down, and to waste, and to destroy, and to build, and to plant* (Jer. 1:10). Our fathers and prelates assemble united in Christ by a triple bond: the strength of profound humility, the sweetness of fraternal charity, and solicitude for the charge committed to them. Such a bond can be broken only with difficulty; in fact, if the Lord strengthens it and preserves it in its purity, it is impossible for it to be broken when it is possessed by men of holiness. It is manifest that the integrity of this bond cannot be in any degree dissolved among those in whom the perfection of fraternal charity has not been diminished. . . . While the shepherds were living in the fields and keeping watch over their flock by night, did not an angel of the Lord stand by them and the glory of God shine round about them (cf. Luke 2:8–9). It is evident that they who have the glory of God shining round about them can fear no harm. Whence this extraordinary blessing of the shepherds? Because they were in the fields guarding their flocks and keeping watch over them (*De quadripertito exercitio cellae,* c. 1, *PL* 153:804).

In praise of monastic union

2331. JOHN OF TRITHEIM. I sing your praises, O sacred brotherhood of monks! By an unbroken history of subjection you have praised God and preferred what is spiritual to things transitory. To the limits of human strength you have walked in sincere observance of the Rule; in your devotion you have spurned the vain pomps of the world, loved justice, and embraced oneness in charity. And because you have praised the Lord in simplicity of heart, he has blessed you with *dew from heaven and fruitfulness of the earth* (Gen. 27:28), so that the more zealously you have served in your eagerness for the regular observance, the more abundantly you have been blessed by him with those material goods of which you have need.

I beg you, fathers, let us be ever mindful of the pristine glory of our order, of how many saints it has produced, how many learned men have shone brilliantly in it, who have worked for our benefit as well as to their own advantage. Let us strive to imitate, as well as we can, those whom we venerate, if we desire to come to the glory they have attained. . . . We must look to the ancients who served the Lord in all sincerity in this most holy order, and take the pattern for our own progress from that which they made. They despised the world and longed for the things of heaven, and the Lord whom they loved, was solicitous for them, providing in abundance all the things they needed, as he has promised in the Gospel: *Seek first the kingdom of God, and all these things shall be given you besides* (Luke 12:31; *Oratio secunda, in capitulo annali, coram abbatibus,* 1 Sept., 1492, *Op. pia et spiritualia,* p. 852).

Encomiums, prayers

2332. ST. BERTHARIUS, abbot of Montecassino, martyr (d. 883). Rejoice, O virgin of God [St. Scholastica], you who have been honored with triumphs so great! Exult, O Benedict, holy Father of fathers, Doctor of doctors, so sweetly reasonable in your teaching, now that your holy works have been brought to their consummation, you delight together in the kingdom of heaven. Intercede for those committed to you; beg for us in our afflictions; pray for the forgiveness of our sins; intercede with Christ that the persons of every age, sex, and rank who have submitted to your precepts may despise the perishable things of this world, long for eternal joys, strive for the heavenly kingdom, and be blessed with what is beneficial to soul and body. May they not be molested by the deceptions of the devil, afflicted with incursions of evil spirits, nor destroyed by any catastrophe.

O blessed Father, be favorable to our petitions; give ear to the prayers of your servants; grant pardon to those who implore it; bestow gifts on those who request them; have mercy on sinners! For you are the shepherd, we the sheep. Hear the bleating of your flock, draw us after you so that we may come to you in order to find the proper nourishment, which for us is where there are true, eternal joys.

Present to God the talents we have gained with what was given to us; give an account of the fruits we have produced with the doctrines we have believed in—first in order that we may attain, with the whole flock committed to you, the rewards of eternal life, and second, that God may say to you: "*Well done, good and faithful servant; because thou hast been faithful over a few things, I will set thee over many; enter into the joy of thy master* (Matt. 25:21) together with all these who were committed to you," in fulfilment of the promise he has made of worthy joys to his servants, who lives and reigns forever and ever. Amen (*Vita S. Scholasticae virginis,* c. 18, *conclusio, PL* 126:987).

2333. ST. ANSELM OF CANTERBURY. O holy and blessed Benedict, grace from on high richly endowed you with the blessing of virtues, not only in order to raise you up to the longed-for glory and blessed rest of heaven, but also in order that your admirable life should draw countless others to the same bliss, urging them on by your tender admonitions, instructing them with your sweetly reasonable doctrine, rousing them to action by the example of your miracles! I have recourse to you, O blessed one of God, whom the Lord blessed so abundantly. My soul prostrates itself before you in abjection and deep humility; it pours out its prayer with all the affection at its command; it implores your assistance with intense desire. For my soul's need is exceedingly great and unbearable.

I professed the reformation of my life in monasticism. I vowed it, and proclaim this conversion by bearing the name and wearing the habit of the monk. But I am far removed from such a life. My conscience accuses me of lying before God and angels and men. Come to my aid, O kind Father! Hear my prayer! I beg you not to stand in horror of one who is so completely given to vicious habits and deception, but to look with favor upon him who humbly acknowledges his sin. Have mercy on my sorrow—far beyond anything I have deserved.

It is true that I joined your ranks, O glorious leader among the great captains of Christ's army, weak soldier that I am. I placed myself under your guidance, although I am an indolent disciple. I vowed, all too human monk that I am, to live according to your Rule. How perverse is my heart! hard and dry as a rock when there is question of deploring the sins I have committed, but weak and attentive to temptations that it should resist. My depraved mind is ever eager and untiring in accepting what is unprofitable and harmful, but full of aversion and sloth for thinking of that which is salutary. Blind and troubled, my soul is submissive and prompt in hurling itself into vices and wallowing in them, but too rebellious and lazy even to reflect on virtues.

It would take too long, beloved father, to mention each of my failings. It would be too tedious to enumerate gluttony, drowsiness, levity, impatience, vainglory, detraction, disobedience, and the other vices of which my unhappy soul has become the daily toy. At times they drag me this way and that, making sport of so pitiable a man, as though he were a beggar in rags. At other times they unite to insult him by trampling on him, and trample on him by insulting him.

Thus you can see, O blessed Benedict, how courageously this soldier of Christ wages the combat under your leadership! Look at the great progress this student of yours is making in your school! Consider the good monk who, having subdued his vices and the pleasures of the flesh by mortification, desires nothing else and lives for nothing else than the practice of virtue! Alas, see rather the false monk, devoid of virtue, overwhelmed by a whole array of vices, crushed by the weight of his sins!

For shame! O monk devoid of shame! How dare you call yourself a soldier of Christ, a disciple of St. Benedict? How can you so impudently display the tonsure and wear the garb of religion, when you do not live what you profess? How painful a situation! Difficulties confront me on every side. If I deny my Supreme King, and my good master, and the profession I pronounced, it means my death. But if I proclaim myself to be [Christ's] soldier, and Benedict's disciple, and a true monk, when my life shows me to be a liar, I am also condemned.

Be troubled, my spirit, be disturbed in the depths of your being, my heart. Rise up and cry aloud, my soul: "O Jesus, good Master, *put an end to my affliction and my suffering, and take away all my sins* (Ps. 24:18). Be my helper, O Lord! Do not abandon me, or despise me, but *teach me to do your will* (Ps. 142:10), so that my life will give evidence of that which my heart and lips pronounce so readily. *Heed my call for help, my king and my God* (Ps. 5:3), through the merits and the intercession of your beloved St. Benedict, who is my kind leader and master."

And you, my good leader, my gracious master, sweet and blessed father Benedict! I pray and beg you by the mercy that you have shown others and by that which God has shown you, have compassion on me in my misery, as I rejoice in your eternal blessedness. Come to the aid of him who venerates you as his patron; release him who is cast down by the weight of his sins; free him who is bound by the fetters of his crimes; disentangle him who is held fast by the habits of sin. Lift up the fallen one, sustain him in his wavering. Fortify with spiritual weapons him who is weak in his practice of virtue; instruct and protect him who enters the combat. *Fight, O Lord, against those who fight me* (Ps. 34:1). Raise me up for the victory, and lead me to the reward.

O advocate of monks, act with the strength of that charity which made you solicitous as to how we should live; make it your concern that we have the zealous desire and the efficacious will to live as we are bound to live by our profession, so that you may rejoice in our discipleship and we in your guidance, before God, who lives and reigns forever. Amen (*Oratio 72, ad S. Benedictum, PL* 158:1006; Schmitt, *Op. Om.*, n. 15, 3:61).

2334. ANCIENT PRAYER TO THE HOLY PATRIARCH. O loving father, Benedict, leader and ruler of monks, hope and refuge for all who cry out to you with their whole heart, I humbly commit myself to your holy protection. Through the excellence of your personal merits, deign to shield me from whatever can harm my soul. Out of the wealth of your compassion, obtain for me the grace of tearful compunction to bewail fittingly and copiously the many evils and offenses by which I have, from youth on, offended our Lord Jesus Christ, who is worthy of all my love. And may I merit to praise and venerate you as I should.

O olive tree! fruitful vine in the house of God! vessel of pure gold, ornamented with every precious stone! Chosen one, fashioned according to the will of God, adorned with countless charisms of grace as though they were so many glittering gems. Most kind father, beloved master, I pray you, I beseech you, I earnestly entreat you with all the love of my heart and all the longing of my soul: deign to be mindful of me, a miserable sinner, as you stand before God. Beg him in his mercy to forgive all my sins, preserve me in virtue, and, whatever the compulsion, never permit me to abandon him. Obtain for me, father, that God will admit me to the company of the elect in the beatific vision, as one of your followers. There, may I rejoice forever with you and with that exceedingly great number of monks enrolled under your banner. May this be granted through our Lord Jesus Christ, who with the Father and the Holy Spirit lives and reigns, God, forever and ever.

We beseech you, almighty God, by the merits and exemplary works of our blessed Father Benedict, his disciples Placid and Maur, his virgin sister Scholastica, and all the saintly monks who have done battle under his leadership, renew your Spirit within us. With the help of your Spirit, may we manfully wage war against the flesh, the world, and the devil.

Since there can be no palm of victory without laborious effort, grant us patience in adversities, constancy in temptation, counsel in dangers. Give us the purity of chastity, an eagerness for poverty, the rewards of obedience, and the firm resolve to be faithful in our observance. Strengthened by your consoling aid; united in the ties of brotherly love, let us serve in the common effort of all. Let us pass through these present times so as to merit to reach our everlasting home, crowned victors in the battle, to be numbered forever and ever in heaven's ranks of holy monks. Through Christ our Lord. Amen (Guéranger, *Enchiridion Benedictinum,* p. 294; Guéranger states simply that this prayer is to be found in ancient Breviaries).

Bibliography

Acta Sanctorum quotquot toto orbe coluntur, vel a catholicis scriptoribus celebrantur, quae ex latinis et graecis, aliarumque gentium antiquis monumentis collegit, digessit, notis illustravit Joannes Bollandus, S.J. . . . servata primigenia scriptorum phrasi; operam et studium contulit Godefridus Henschenius, S.J. Ed. novissima. 70 vols.; Parisiis: Palmé, 1863–1919.

Albertus Magnus, Saint, O.P., bp. of Ratisbon, 1193–1280, *Opera Omnia,* ex ed. Lugdunensi religose castigata; . . . cura ac labore Augusti Borgnet. 38 vols.; Parisiis: apud Ludovicum Vives, 1890–98.

Ambrosius, Saint, bp. of Milan, *Ambroise de Milan Des Sacrements; des Mystères;* texte etabli, traduit et annoté par Dom Bernard Botte, O.S.B.; *Sources Chretiennes,* collection dirigée par H. de Lubac, S.J. et J. Danielou, S.J., n. 25. Paris: Cerf, 1949. 139 pp.

——— *Saint Ambrose On the Sacraments and On the Mysteries;* tr. by T. Thompson; ed. with Introduction and Notes by J. H. Srawley. London: S.P.C.K., 1950. viii, 157 pp.

Anselm, Saint, abp. of Canterbury, 1033–1109, *Opera Omnia;* . . . ad fidem codicum recensuit Franciscus Salesius Schmitt, monachus Grissoviensis, O.S.B. 6 vols.; Seckau [Austria]: Abbey Press, 1938.

——— *Cur Deus Homo* by St. Anselm; to which is added a selection from his letters. London: Griffith, Farran Ideden and Welsh, 1897. xxviii, 244 pp.

——— *Eadmeri Historia Novorum in Anglia et opuscula duo de vita Sancti Anselmi et quibusdam miraculis ejus;* ed. from manuscripts in the library of Corpus Christi College, Cambridge, by Martin Rule. London: Longman & Co., 1884. cxxvii, 460 pp.

——— *Obras completas de San Anselmo;* traducidas por P. Julian Alameda, O.S.B. por primera vez al Castellano, texto latino de la edicion critica del P. Schmitt. 2 vols.; Madrid: Biblioteca de Autores Cristianos, 1952.

Antoninus, Saint, O.P., abp. of Florence, 1389–1459, *Summa Theologica* in quattuor partes distributa. 4 vols.; Verona: 1740. This extremely valuable work, generally considered to pioneer systematic moral theology, has recently been reprinted, 1959. Graz, Austria: Akademische Druck—u. Verlagsanstalt. The pagination remains the same throughout the work.

Antonio da Padova, Saint, 1195–1231, *Divi Antonii Patavini, vulgo dicti de Padua, Sermones Dominicales sive de tempore.* n. pr. 1528. [xxxviii], 340 fol. Alternate pages numbered.

——— See also under Francesco d'Assisi, *Opera Omnia.* Because of the rarity of the preceding work, all references have been made in the text to the more commonly available *Opera Omnia* by de la Haye. In all passages consulted the text is identical.

Augustinus Aurelius, Saint, bp. of Hippo, *The City of God by St. Augustine;* tr. by Marcus Dods, with an introduction by Thomas Merton. New York: The Modern Library (Random House, Inc.), 1950. xvi, 892 pp.

——— *The Confessions of St. Augustine;* tr. by F. J. Sheed. New York: Sheed & Ward, 1943. xxii, 354 pp.

——— *Letters;* tr. by Sister Wilfrid Parsons, S.N.D. 4 vols. (Fathers of the Church Series, nn. 12, 18, 20, 30). New York: Fathers of the Church, Inc., 1951.

——— *Oeuvres de Saint Augustin: 1re* Serie; *opuscules;* texte de l'édition Bénédictine, traduction, introduction et notes de Gustave Combes . . . 6 vols.; Paris: Desclée, de Brouwer et Cie., 1937.

Baronio, Cesare, Cardinal, 1538–1607, *Caesaris S.R.E. Card. Baronii Annales Ecclesiastici* denuo excusi et ad nostra usque tempora perducti ab Augustino Theiner. 37 vols.; Bari-Ducis, Parisiis: Guerin, 1864–1883.

Bartholomeu [Fernandez] dos Martyres, O.P., abp. of Braga, 1514–1590, *Stimulus pastorum, ex sententiis Patrum concinnatus,* in quo agitur de vita et moribus episcoporum, aliorumque praelatorum, per Reverendissimum D. D. Bartholomaeum a Martyribus, archiepiscopum Bracharensem et Hispaniae Primatem; nunc denuo ed. Dr. Joseph Fessler, Episcopus Sanhippolytanus juxta exemplar A. 1572 Romae impressum, ed. 2a. Einsidlae: Charles & Nicholas Benziger, 1869. xvi, 282 pp.

Basilius, Saint, the Great, abp. of Caesarea, 330c.–79, *Sancti Basilii re et nomine Magni Caesareae Cappadociae Archiepiscopi Opera quae ad nos latine pervenerunt Omnia,* denuo ad exemplaria Graeca reconsita, emendata, et Epistolis locupletata studio Andreae Schotti, Antverpiani, Soc. Jesu presbyteri. Antverpiae: apud Henricum Aertsium, 1616. [xl], 799 [liii] pp. Because of its far greater availability, references have consistently been made to Migne's *PG,* which is substantially the same text.

——— *Saint Basil, Ascetical Works;* tr. by Sister M. Monica Wagner, C.S.C. (Fathers of the Church Series, n. 9). New York: Fathers of the Church, Inc., 1950. xii, 525 pp.

——— *Saint Basil, Letters;* tr. by Sister Agnes Clare Way, C.D.P., with notes by Roy J. Deferrari. 2 vols.; New York: Fathers of the Church, Inc., 1951, 1955.

——— *Saint Basil, The Letters;* with an English translation by Roy J. Deferrari. 4 vols.; Cambridge: Harvard University Press, 1950.

——— *Saint Basil and his Rule; a study in early monasticism,* by E. F. Morison. Oxford: University Press, 1912. xii, 150 pp.

——— *De virginitate, de Saint Basile;* texte vieux-slave et traduction française par A. Vaillant; textes publiés par l'Institut d'Études slaves, n. 3. Paris: Institut d'Études Slaves, 1943. viii, 108 pp.

Basle, Council of, 1431–39, Statuta et ordinationes (quae etiam quandoque decreta vocantur) ad monachos Congr. Mellicensis directae, ex manuscripto Salisburgensi. The Translator's repeated effort failed to procure a copy of the original of this document, which was used at Salzburg by Archabbot Wolter, whose reading merits complete faith. This very important decree is in answer to a printed document: Ven. Martini de Senging, prioris Mellicensis *tuitiones observantiae Regulae S. Benedicti,* Patribus Generalis Concilii Basiliensis oblatae, ex MSS. Cod. Monasterii Mellicensis, n. 16 (in: Pezius, *Bibliotheca Ascetica* 8:503–550).

Benedictines: *The Law proper to the Confederation of Monastic Congregations of the Order of St. Benedict;* tr. and annotated by Bernard A. Sause, O.S.B. Atchison, Kansas: The Abbey Student Press, 1953. 85 pp.

——— American Cassinese Congregation, *The Holy Rule of our most holy Father Benedict,* tr. from the Latin by Boniface Verheyen, O.S.B., with *Declarations and Constitution of the American Cassinese Congregation.* Atchison, Kansas: The Abbey Student Press, 1949. xii, 184 pp.

——— American Cassinese Congregation, *Rituale monasticum;* complectens partem caeremonialem et partem ritualem juxta ritum Romano-monasticum. Collegeville, Minn.: Typis abbatiae S. Joannis Baptistae, 1942. xvii, 950 pp.

——— Bursfelder Kongregation, *Statuta Congregationis Bursfeldensis sub Reg. Divi P. Benedicti* secundum sacros canones, Romanorum Pontificum, et SS. Concil. Tridentini decreta renovata, secundum recessus capitulorum congregationis aucta et emendata. Paderborn: Joachim Fredericus Buch, 1700. 330 pp.

——— Congregatio Benedictino-Suevica S. Joseph, *Constitutiones et declarationes ad Reg. Sanctissimi Patris Nostri Benedicti,* Congregationis Benedictino-Suevicae S. Joseph, approbatae et receptae in conventu Rmor. DDrum. Abbatum, die 6 Oct., a. 1671, in monasterio Ochsenhusano celebrato. 331 fol. These statutes, among the most spiritual drawn up in the history of Benedictine monachism, were never printed. The copy used by the translator through the kindness of Dom Suso Mayer, O.S.B. at Beuron Archabbey, in Germany, was copied longhand in 1733, and bears the following note on the title page: "Ad usum superioris et compositoris, P. Aemiliani Neiner." This copy was employed extensively by Archabbot Maurus Wolter in the composition of the present work. It is corrected throughout and edited, in red ink, by him.

——— Congregatio Hispanica, *Caeremoniale monasticum congregationis Hispanicae O.S.P.N. Benedicti* ad Breviarium, a Paulo V.P.M. recognitum, et Missale accommodatum . . . opera vero P. F. Thomae Weiss, monachi Neresheimensis ex Hispanico latine versum et bono publico sacri ordinis publicae luci datum. Viennae, Austriae: typis Gregorii Gelbhaar, 1640. 470 pp. The title of this work is somewhat misleading. Only the first part of the book is a ceremonial in the usual sense of the term. The second half, pp. 285–458, from which Wolter quotes almost exclusively, is a sort of combination of constitutions and practical directives of an ascetical character, arranged principally according to the duties assigned to the various officials of the monastery.

——— Congrégation de France, *Regula SS. Patris nostri Benedicti unacum Constitutionibus Congregationis Sancti Petri de Solesmes.* Solesmes: E typographia S. Petri, 1901. viii, 216 pp. The translator was fortunate in finding, at the Archabbey of Beuron, Germany, Maurus Wolter's personal manuscript copy of the first draft of these Constitutions which antedated the formal establishment of the Congregation and the printed Constitutions. Wolter had collaborated with Dom Guéranger in their composition.

——— Congrégation de Saint Maur, *Regula S.P. Benedicti, cum declarationibus Congregationis S. Mauri;* jussu et authoritate Capituli Generalis ejusdem Congregationis. 1701. vi, 296 [xxv] pp.

——— Congregazione Cassinese, *Reg. S. Benedicti Abbatis, Monachorum Patriarchae, cum Declarationibus et Constitutionibus Patrum Congregationis Casinensis,* Motu Proprio confirmatis a Sanctiss. D.N.D. Innocentio Papa XI. Romae: Typis Reverendae Camerae Apostolicae, 1680. xii, 283 [viii] pp.

——— Kongregation von Elsasz [Strasburg], *Regula S.P. Benedicti abbatis et Patriarchae monachorum, cum declarationibus Patrum Congregationis Argentiniensis.* 137 fol. These constitutions and declarations to the Rule of St. Benedict, promulgated by the monastic congregation of Strasburg, established 1624, were never printed. The manuscript copy, complete with index, consists of 137 legal-size pages. It is underscored throughout and filled with marginal notes and corrections of the inaccurate Latin in Archabbot Wolter's handwriting. The copy bears the date of Jun. 18 1754, and is preserved in the archives of the Archabbey of Beuron, Germany.

——— Swiss Congregation, *Statuta Congregationis Helveticae Ordinis S. Benedicti . . .* jussu Rev.mi Ignatii Staub, abbatis praesidis edita. Monte Angelorum: typis abbatiae, 1932. 139 pp.

Benedictus, Saint, Abbot of Montecassino, 480–547, *Sancti Benedicti Regula Monasteriorum;* editionem critico-practicam adornavit D. Cuthbertus Butler, monachus monasterii S. Gregorii de Downside; ed. 2. Friburgi: Herder, 1927. xxiv, 223 pp.

——— *The Rule of St. Benedict, in Latin and English;* ed. and tr. by Abbot Justin McCann. London: Burns, Oates, 1952. 214 pp. Translations and editions of St. Benedict's Rule abound. There is even a wide variety of English versions. McCann's translation seems to excel in accurate rendition of the original text.

Bernard of Clairvaux, Saint, 1091–1153. *Obras completas de San Bernardo;* edicion espanola preparada por el R. D. Gregorio Diez Ramos, O.S.B. 2 vols.; Madrid: Biblioteca de Autores Cristianos, 1953, 1955. xxxv, 1190, 1260 pp.

——— *Cantica Canticorum: eighty-six sermons on the Song of Solomon,* by *St. Bernard, Abbot of Clairvaux;* tr. and edited, with notes, by Samuel J. Eales. London: Elliot Stock, 1895. xxxii, 535 pp.

——— *St. Bernard's treatise on consideration;* tr. from the original Latin by a priest of Mount Melleray. Dublin: Browne and Nolan, Ltd., 1921. xvi, 254 pp.

——— *On conversion, a sermon to the clergy by St. Bernard of Clairvaux;* a translation of the Anchin Manuscript with notes by Watkin Williams. London: Burns, Oates & Washbourne, Ltd., 1938. xvi, 60 pp.

——— *Letters of St. Bernard of Clairvaux;* newly tr. by Bruno Scott James. London: Burns, Oates, 1953. xx, 530 pp.

——— *Some letters of St. Bernard, Abbot of Clairvaux;* from the translation by the late Dr. Eales, selected, with a preface, by Francis Aidan Gasquet. New York: Benziger Brothers, 1906. xvi, 309 pp.

——— *The Book of St. Bernard on the Love of God;* edited with a translation and notes by Edmund G. Gardner. London: J. M. Dent & Sons, Ltd., 1915. 181 pp.

——— *St. Bernard's Sermons for the seasons and principal festivals of the year;* tr. from the original Latin by a priest of Mount Melleray. 3 vols.; Dublin: Browne and Nolan, Ltd., 1922–1925.

——— *The Steps of Humility, by Bernard, Abbot of Clairvaux;* tr. with an introduction and notes, as a study of his epistemology, by George Bosworth Burch. Cambridge: Harvard University Press, 1940. xii, 287 pp.

——— *St. Bernard, the man and his message,* by Watkin Williams. New York: Spiritual Book Associates, 1944. 72 pp. Appendix, pp. 50–72, contains the translation of St. Bernard's *De diligendo Deo, Why and how to love God.*

——— *Life and teaching of St. Bernard,* by Ailbe J. Luddy, O. Cist. Dublin: M. H. Gill & Son, Ltd., 1927. XVI, 774 pp. This extensive and very readable history of St. Bernard's life contains numerous excerpts from his writings in translation.

——— *The Life and times of St. Bernard;* by M. l'abbe Ratisbonne; tr. from the French with preface, by H. E. Manning. New York: P. J. Kenedy & Sons, n.d. xxiv, 487 pp.

Bernardino da Siena, Saint, 1380–1444, *Sancti Bernardini Senensis, Ordinis Seraphici Minorum Opera Omnia,* synopsibus ornata, postillis illustrata, necnon variis tractatibus, et eximiis, praecipue in Apocalypsim, commentariis locupletata, opera et labore R. P. Joannis de la Haye Parisiensis. . . . 4 vols.; Venetiis: Andrea Poletti, 1745.

——— *S. Bernardini Senensis, O.F.M. Opera Omnia;* jussu et auctoritate Rev.mi P. Pacifici M. Perantoni . . . edita. 5 vols.; Quaracchi: Ex typographia Collegii S. Bonaventurae, 1950.

Birgitta, Saint, of Sweden, d. 1373, *Revelationes.* Nuremberg: Anton Koberger, 21 Sept., 1500. No pagination, Gothic type.

——— *The Revelations of Saint Birgitta;* edited from the fifteenth-century MS in the Garrett Collection in the Library of Princeton University, by William Patterson Cumming. London: published for the Early English Text Society by Oxford University Press, 1929. xxxix, 135 pp. This text does not harmonize with the Latin, into which the original Swedish account was translated.

Bizzarri, Andreas, *Collectanea in usum Secretariae S. Congregationis Episcoporum et Regularium edita.* Romae: ex Typographia Polyglotta, S.C. de Propaganda Fide, 1885. xl, 881 pp.

Blois, François Louis de (Blosius), Abbot of Liessies, 1506–66, *Ven. Patris D. Ludovici Blosii monasterii Laetiensis Ordinis S. Benedicti in Hannonia abbatis Opera, cura et studio R. D. Antonii de Winghe abbatis et monachorum ejusdem monasterii aucta, ornata, illustrata.* 3 vols.; Antverpii: Balthasar Moreti, 1632.

——— *A mirror for monks (speculum monachorum), by Ludovicus Blosius;* in an old anonymous translation (Paris, 1676), revised and edited by Dom Roger Hudleston, O.S.B., monk of Downside Abbey. London: Burns, Oates & Washbourne, Ltd., 1926. xxiv, 93 pp.

——— *The paradise of the faithful soul (paradisus animae fidelis);* Part I, *A rule of the spiritual life (Canon vitae spiritualis),* by Ludovicus Blosius; in an anonymous translation, revised and edited by Bernard Delaney, O.P. London: Burns, Oates & Washbourne, Ltd., 1927. XXVI, 143 pp.

——— *A sanctuary of the faithful soul,* by the Ven. Ludovicus Blosius, O.S.B. (Louis de Blois), Abbot of Liessies; tr. from the Latin by the late Bertrand A. Wilberforce, O.P. St. Louis: B. Herder Book Co., 1905. xvi, 125 pp.

——— *A book of spiritual instruction (institutio spiritualis),* by Ludovicus Blosius; tr. from the Latin by Bertrand A. Wilberforce, O.P. London: Burns, Oates & Washbourne, Ltd., 1925. xlii, 214 pp.

Bona, Giovanni, Cardinal, 1609–74, *Eminentissimi Domini D. Joannis Bona, Cardinalis presbyteri, Ordinis Cisterciensis, Opera Omnia.* Venetiis: Ex typographia Balleoniana, 1752. xxiv, 668 pp.

Bonaventura, Saint, Cardinal, 1221–74, *Doctoris Seraphici S. Bonaventurae, S.R.E. Cardinalis, Opera Omnia,* jussu et authoritate Rev.mi P. Bernardini a Portu Romantino . . . edita, studio et cura PP. Collegii a S. Bonaventura, ad plurimos codices MSS. emendata. 10 vols.; Ad Claras Aquas [Quaracchi] prope Florentiam: Ex typographia Collegii S. Bonaventurae, 1872–1903. This critical, definitive edition excludes almost 100 works formerly attributed to St. Bonaventure, a number of them used by Wolter. These have been retained largely by reference to the following edition.

——— *S.R.E. Cardinalis S. Bonaventurae, ex Ordine Minorum Opera Omnia,* Sixti V jussu diligentissime emendata; accedunt selecta multa tum ex postrema veneta ed., tum ex prodromo eruiditissimo Fr. Benedicti a Cavalesio Ordinis Minorum Reformati. Ed. accurate recognita ad puram et veriorum testimoniorum biblicorum emendationem; denuo reducta cura et studio A. C. Peltier, canonici Ecclesiae Remensis. 15 vols.; Augustae Taurinorum; H. Marietti, 1874.

——— *The virtues of a religious superior (De sex alis Seraphim)*; instructions by the Seraphic Doctor, St. Bonaventure; tr. from the Latin by Fr. Sabinus Molitor, O.F.M. St. Louis: B. Herder Book Co., 1920. 112 pp.

Breviarium Monasticum; Pauli V. jussu editum; Urbani VIII et Leonis XIII cura recognitum; Pii X et Benedicti XV auctoritate reformatum; pro omnibus sub Regula S. Patris Benedicti militantibus. ed. 3. 2 vols.; Brugis: sumptibus et typis Societatis S. Augustini, Desclée, de Brouwer et Soc., 1941.

Breviarium Romanum, ex decreto Sacrosancti Concilii Tridentini restitutum; S. Pii V Pont. Maximi jussu editum aliorumque Pontificum recognitum; Pii Papae X auctoritate reformatum; cum Psalterio secundum novam versionem Latinam Pii Papae XII auctoritate edito, ed. 7 juxta typicam Vaticanam. 4 vols.; Novi-Eboraci: Benziger Brothers Inc., 1945.

Bullarii Romani Continuatio Summorum Pontificum. 14 vols.; Prati, 1835–1857.

Bullarium Diplomatum et privilegiorum S. R. Pontificum, Taurinensis editio. 20 vols.; Taurinensis, 1857–1872; Neapoli, 5 vols.; 1867–1885.

Camaldulese, *In Reg. Divi P. Benedicti declarationes et constitutiones PP. Ordinis Camaldulensis.* Florentiae: apud Bartholomaeum Sermatellium, 1572. xxxvi, 334 pp.

Canones et Decreta Concilii Tridentini, ex editione Romana A. MDCCCXXXIV repetiti; accedunt S. Congr. Card. Conc. Trid. interpretum declarationes ac resolutiones . . . ed. Aemilium Ludovicus Richter. Lipsiae: Typis et sumptibus Bernhardi Tauchnitii, 1853. vi, 665 pp.

Cassiodorus, Senator, Flavius Magnus Aurelius, circa 487–circa 580, *An Introduction to divine and human readings, by Cassiodorus Senator;* tr. with an introduction and notes by Leslie Webber Jones. New York: Columbia University Press, 1946. xviii, 233 pp.

Catechism of the Council of Trent for parish priests; issued by order of Pope Pius V; tr. into English with notes, by John A. McHugh, O.P. and Charles J. Callan, O.P. New York: Joseph F. Wagner, Inc., 1923. 603 pp.

Catechismus ex decreto Concilii Tridentini ad parochos, Pii V. et Clementis XIII pont. max. jussu editus, ad editionem Romae A. D. MDCCCXLV publici juris factam accuratissime expressus. ed. stereotypa 6a. Ratisbonae: G. J. Manz, 1905. iv, 463 pp.

Chrysostomus, Joannes, Saint, Patriarch of Constantinople, d. 407, *Saint Chrysostom on the priesthood;* tr. from the original Greek with notes and a life of the father, by Rev. Henry M. Mason, Philadelphia: E. Littell, 1826. 194 pp.

Cistercians, *Statuta Capitulorum Generalium Ordinis Cisterciansis ab anno 1116 ad annum 1786;* opus in lineamentis ab eximio A. Trilhe [d. 1930] non ita adumbratum suscepit, ampliavit, ad librorum manu scriptorum fidem recognovit, annotatione critica emendationibusque instruxit et edidit D. Josephus-Maria Canivez, Ord. Cist. Ref. 8 vols.; Bibliothèque de la Révue d'Histoire ecclésiastique, fasc. 9–14 b; Louvain: Bureau de la Révue, 1933–1941.

Codicis Juris Canonici Fontes; cura Emi. Petri Card. Gasparri [vv. 1–6], Emi. Justiniani Card. Serédi [vv. 7–9] editi. 9 vols.; Romae: Typis Polyglottis Vaticanis, 1923–1939.

Corpus Juris Canonici . . . post Justi Henningii Boehmeri curas . . . denuo edidit Aemilius Ludovicus Richter. 2 vols.; Lipsiae: sumpt. et typis Bernh. Taughnitz, 1839.

Cyprianus, Saint, bp. of Carthage, d. 258, *The genuine works of St. Cyprian, Archbishop of Carthage and Primate of all Africa . . . together with his life, written by his own deacon, Pontius;* all done into English, from the Oxford ed. . . by Nath. Marshall. 2 vols.; London: W. Bowyer, 1717.

Denis le Chartreux, Monk of Roermond, d. 1471. *Doctoris Ecstatici D. Dionysii*

Carthusiani Opera Omnia in unum corpus digesta ad fidem editionum Coloniensium cura et labore monachorum sacri ordinis Cartusiensis, favente Pont. Max. Leone XIII. 41 vols.; Monstrolli: Typis Cartusiae S. M. de Pratis, 1896.

Enciclopedia Cattolica. 12 vols.; La parte editoriale è curata dalla Casa editrice G. C. Sansoni, Firenze; Città del Vaticano, 1949.

Ephraem Syrus, Saint, *Sancti Ephraem Syri, Patris et Scriptoris Ecclesiae antiquissimi et dignissimi Opera Omnia,* quotquot in insignioribus Italiae bibliothecis, praecipue Romanis Graece inveniri potuerunt, in tres tomos digesta, nunc recens latinitate donata, scholiisque illustrata, interprete et scholiaste R. D. Gerardo Vossio . . . ed. 3a. Coloniae: apud Arnoldum Quentelium, 1616.

Eusèbe d'Émèse. *Discours conserves en latin; textes en partie inedits.* 2 vols.; par E. M. Buytaert, O.F.M. Spicilegium Sacrum Lovaniense, n. 26; Louvain: Spicilegium Sacrum Lovaniense, 1953, 1957.

Fathers of the Church, *The Ante-Nicene Fathers;* translations of the writings of the Fathers down to A.D. 325 . . . Roberts . . . and Donaldson, ed. 8 vols.; Buffalo: The Christian Literature Publishing Co., 1885–1886.

——— *A Library of the Fathers of the Holy Catholic Church, anterior to the division of East and West;* tr. by members of the English Church. 41 vols.; Oxford: John Henry Parker; London: J. G. F. and J. Rivington, 1845–1857.

——— *A Select Library of Nicene and Post-Nicene Fathers of the Christian Church;* tr. into English with prolegomena and explanatory notes, under the editorial supervision of Henry Wace and Philip Schaff. 14 vols.; Oxford: Parker and Company; New York: The Christian Literature Company, 1890.

Fathers of the Desert, *The Desert Fathers;* translations from the Latin with an introduction by Helen Waddell. New York: Sheed & Ward, 1942. viii, 295 pp.

——— *Early Fathers from the Philokalia, together with some writings of St. Abba Dorotheus, St. Isaac of Syria and St. Gregory Palamas;* selected and tr. from the Russian text *Dobrotolybiye* by E. Kadloubovsky and G. E. H. Palmer. London: Faber and Faber, Ltd., 1953. 421 pp.

——— *The Lives of the Fathers of the Eastern deserts;* tr. by the Rev. Dr. Challoner. New York: D. & J. Sadlier, 1852. 609 pp.

——— *Stories of the Holy Fathers,* being Histories of the Anchorites, Recluses, Monks, Cenobites and Ascetic Fathers of the deserts of Egypt, between 250 A.D. and A.D. 400 circiter; compiled by Athanasius, Archbishop of Alexandria; Palladius, Bishop of Helenopolis; St. Jerome, and others; now tr. out of the Syriac with notes and an introduction by Sir Ernest A. Wallis Budge. London: Oxford University Press, 1934. lxxxviii, 512 pp.

——— *The wit and wisdom of the Christian Fathers of Egypt; the Syrian version of the Apophthegmata Patrum by Haman Isho of Beth Habbe;* tr. by Sir Ernest Wallis Budge. London: Oxford University Press, 1934. viii, 445 pp.

Francesco d'Assisi, Saint, 1182–1226, *Sancti Francisci Assisiatis, Minorum Patriarchae, necnon S. Antonii Paduani ejusdem Ordinis, Opera Omnia,* postillis illustrata . . . opera et labore R. P. Joannis de la Haye. Lugduni: sumptibus Petri Rigaud, 1653. lxiv, 96, 744 [xli] pp. It is well known that this is not a critical edition of either saint's works, but it is apparently the source used by Wolter—who furnishes no bibliography, and few references—in the original composition of this work. Unless otherwise specifically indicated, excerpts from both writers are referred to this work.

——— *The ideals of St. Francis of Assisi* by Hilarin Felder, O.M. Cap.; tr. by Berchmans Bittle, O.M. Cap. New York: Benziger Brothers, 1925. xvi, 518 pp.

——— *Life of St. Francis of Assisi,* by Father Cuthbert, O.S.F.C. New York: Longmans, Green and Co., 1914. xiv, 536 pp.

——— *Opuscula Sancti Patris Francisci Assisiensis;* sec. codices MSS emendata et denuo edita a PP. Collegii S. Bonaventurae, ed. 3. Quaracchi: Typographia Collegii S. Bonaventurae, 1949. xvi, 209 pp.

——— *The Rule and General Constitutions of the Friars Minor;* tr. into English by a priest of the Province of the Most Holy Name. Paterson, N.J.: St. Anthony Guild Press, 1936. xxii, 195 pp.

——— *The Words of St. Francis;* an anthology compiled and arranged by James Meyer, O.F.M. Chicago: Franciscan Herald Press, 1952. viii, 345 pp.

——— *The writings of St. Francis of Assisi;* newly translated into English with an introduction and notes, by Father Paschal Robinson, O.F.M. Philadelphia: The Dolphin Press, 1906. xxxii, 208 pp.

Gerardus Belga, *Opuscula pia Gerardi Belgae,* monachi Ordinis S. P. Benedicti, opera et studio R. P. Gabrielis Butzlini, ejusdem Ord. monachi Weingartensis. 3 vols.; Augustae Vindelicorum: apud Johannem Praetorium, 1632–1641.

Gerson, Joannes, Chancellor of University of Paris, 1363–1429, *Joannis Gersonii . . . Opera Omnia,* novo ordine digesta et in V. tomos distributa. Antwerpiae: Sumptibus Societatis, 1706.

Gertrude, Saint, Abbess of Convent of Helfede, 1256–1302(?), *Insinuationes divinae pietatis, seu vita et revelationes S. Gertrudis Virginis et abbatissae Ordinis S. Benedicti;* a mendis quibus scatebant expurgatae studio et labore D.[omini] N.[icholai] C.[anteleu] B.[enedictini]. Parisiis: Frederick Leonard, 1662. XXIV, 800 pp.

——— *Der hl. Gertrud der Grossen Gesandter der göttlichen Liebe;* nach der Auggabe der Benediktiner von Solesmes übersetzt von Johannes Weissbrodt. ed. 12. Freiburg: Herder, 1955. xvi, 667 pp.

——— *Le Héraut de l'amour divin; révélations de Sainte Gertrude,* vierge de l'ordre de Saint-Benoit, traduites sur l'édition latine des Pères Bénédictins de Solesmes. 2 vols.; Nouvelle éd., revue et corrigée; Tours et Paris: Maison Alfred Mame, et Fils, 1921.

——— *The Life and revelations of St. Gertrude, virgin and abbess of the Order of St. Benedict.* London: Burns, Oates & Washbourne, Ltd., 1870. xlv, 565 pp.

Giustiniani, Lorenzo, Saint, Patriarch of Venice, 1380–1456, *Sancti Laurentii Justiniani Proto-patriarchae Veneti Opera Omnia.* 2 vols.; Venetiis: J. Baptista Albritius & Joseph Rosa, 1751.

Gregory of Nyssa, Saint, c. 335–95, *St. Gregory of Nyssa; The Lord's Prayer; The Beatitudes;* tr. and annotated by Hilda Graef. (Ancient Christian Writers, n. 18) Westminster, Maryland: The Newman Press, 1954. vi, 209 pp.

Gregorius I, the Great, Saint, Pope, 540c.–604, *The Dialogues of St. Gregory the Great;* an old English version; edited by Henry James Coleridge, S.J. London: Burns and Oates, 1874. xliv, 307 pp.

——— *The Life and miracles of St. Benedict, by Pope St. Gregory the Great;* tr. by Alexius Hoffmann, O.S.B. Collegeville, Minnesota: St. John's University Press, 1925. xiv, 94 pp.

——— *Morals on the Book of Job, by St. Gregory the Great,* the first Pope of that name; tr. by [C. M.], with notes and indices. 3 vols. (A Library of the Holy Catholic Church, nn. 18, 21, 23, 31); Oxford: John Henry Parker, 1844.

——— *St. Gregory the Great, Pastoral Care;* tr. and annotated by Henry Davis, S.J. (Ancient Christian Writers series, n. 11). Westminster, Maryland: The Newman Press, 1950. 281 pp.

Guéranger, Prosper, Abbot of Solesmes, 1806–1875, *Enchiridion Benedictinum complectens Regulam, vitam et laudes Sanctissimi Occidentalium monachorum Patriarchae; accedunt Exercitia S. Gertrudis Magnae et Blosii Speculum,* a Rev. mo Prospero Guéranger compilatum. Andegavi: Cosnier et Lachese, 1862. xxx, 647 pp.

Guillaume de Saint-Thierry, 1085 (ca.)–1148, *The Golden Epistle of Abbot William of St. Thierry to the Carthusians of Mont Dieu;* now first translated into English by Walter Shewring, and edited by Dom Justin McCann. London: Sheed & Ward, 1930. lvi, 120 pp.

——— *Un traite de la vie solitaire; lettre aux Frères du Mont-Dieu de Guillaume de Saint-Thierry;* traduction française precedée d'une introduction et de notes doctrinales, par M.-M. Davy (Études de Philosophie Medievale, Directeur, Etienne Gilson, n. 29). Paris: Libraire philosophique J. Vrin, 1946. 334 pp.

Haeften, Benedictus, van, 1588–1648, *S. Benedictus illustratus, sive Disquisitionum monasticarum libri xii, quibus S. Benedicti Regula et religiosorum rituum antiquitates variae dilucidantur.* Antwerpii: Petrus Bellerus, 1644. lx, 1103, xlii pp.

Hildegarde, Saint, *Der heiligen Hildegarde von Bingen Wisse die Wege, Scivias,* nach dem Urtext der Wiesbadener kleinen Hildegardeskodex in Deutsch übertragen und bearbeitet von D. Maura Boeckeler, O.S.B. Berlin: Sankt Augustinus Verlag, 1928. xxiv, 508 pp.

Holstenius, Lucas, 1596–1661, *Lucae Holstenii . . . Codex Regularum monasticarum et canonicarum quas SS. Patres monachis, canonicis et virginibus sanctimonialibus servandas praescripserunt;* collectus olim a S. Benedicto Anianensi abbate; nunc autem auctus, amplificatus et in sex tomos divisus . . . observationibus critico-historicis a Mariano Brockie . . . illustratus; eoque defuncto, ab alio ejusdem coenobii [S. Jacobi Scotorum, Ratisbonae] asceta ulterius continuatus et indicibus necessariis instructus. Augustae Vindelicorum: sumptibus Ignatii Adami et Francisci Antonii Veith, 1759.

Hugues de Saint Cher, Cardinal, ca. 1200–1263, *Hugonis de Sancto Charo, S.R.E. . . . Cardinalis, Primi Ordinis Praedicatorum . . . Commentarium in Libros S. Scripturarum . . .* in quo declarantur sensus omnes, literalis scilicet, allegoricus, tropologicus et anagogicus. 8 vols.; Lugduni: Joannes Anthonius Hegetan et Guglielmus Barhier, 1669.

Humbertus de Romanis, O.P., 1194(?)–1277, *Beati Humberti de Romanis, quinti Praedicatorum Magistri Generalis Opera de vita regulari,* ed. curante Fr. Joachim Joseph Berthier, O.P. 2 vols.; Romae: A. Befani, 1888. Vol. 1 continet *Epistolam de tribus votis substantialibus et Expositionem Regulae S. Augustini.* 643 pp.

——— *The religious vows and virtues by Bl. Humbert of Romans;* ed. by James Harrison, O.P., with a preface by Vincent McNabb, O.P. London: Burns, Oates & Washbourne, 1922. xvi, 93 pp.

Ignatius, Saint, bp. of Antioch, 1st. Cent., *The Epistles of St. Clement of Rome and St. Ignatius of Antioch,* newly tr. and annotated by James A. Kleist, S.J. Westminster, Maryland: The Newman Press, 1946. ix, 162 pp.

Joannes Climacus, Saint, *The holy ladder of perfection, by which we may ascend to heaven, by St. John Climacus,* abbot of the monastery of Mount Sinai; tr. from the Greek by Father Robert, Mount St. Bernard's Abbey, Leicestershire. London: Richardson and Son, 1858. xii, 473 pp.

——— *The ladder of divine ascent;* tr. by Archimandrite Lazarus Moore. London: Faber and Faber, 1959. 270 pp.

——— *La scala santa, ossia Gradi per salire al cielo, composti da S. Giovanni Climaco, abate del Monte Sinai e padre della Chiesa Greca, tradotti . . .* pel P. Agostino Ferrara. Napoli: Gabriele Sarracino, 1866. viii, 612 pp.

Jordan von Quedlinburg, d. 1380, *Contemplationes Idiotae,* de amore divino; de Virgine Maria; de vera poenitentia; de continuo conflictu carnis et animae: de innocentia perdita; de morte. Parisiis: in aedibus Henrici Stephani, 1519.

Julianus Pomerius, Priest of Arles, 5th Cent., *Julianus Pomerius, The contemplative life;* tr. and annotated by Sister Mary Josephine Suelzer (Ancient Christian Writers, n. 4). Westminster, Maryland: Newman, 1947. 220 pp.

Labbe, Philippe, 1607–67, *Conciliorum Collectio Regia Maxima;* ad P. Philippi Labbei et P. Gabrielis Cossartii e. Soc. Jesu labores haud modica accessione facta, et emundationibus plurimis additis, praesertim ex codicibus manuscriptis; cum notis et locupletissimis indicibus; studio Joannis Harduini ex eadem S.J. 12 vols.; Parisiis: ex typographia Regia, 1715.

Laurence Justianian, Saint. *See* Giustiniani, Lorenzo.

Mabillon, Jean, 1632–1707. *Acta Sanctorum Ordinis S. Benedicti in saeculorum classes distributa* . . . collegit D. Lucas d'Achery, Congregationis S. Mauri monachus, ac cum eo edidit D. Joannes Mabillon, ejusdem Congregationis. 9 vols.; Venetiis: Coleti et Bettinelli, 1733.

——— *Annales Ordinis S. Benedicti, Occidentalium monachorum patriarchae* . . . auctore D. Joanne Mabillon, presbytero et monacho ejusdem ordinis e Congr. S. Mauri. 6 vols.; Lucae: typis Leonardi Venturini, 1739–45.

Mansi, Joannes Dominicus. 1692–1769 (ed.), *Sacrorum Conciliorum nova et amplissima collectio.* 53 vols. in 59; Parisiis . . . Lipsiae, 1901–1927.

Mechtild of Hackeborn, 1241 or 2–1299(?), *Le livre de la grace spéciale; révélations de Sainte Mechtilde, vierge de l'ordre de Saint-Benoit;* traduites sur l'édition latine des Pères Bénédictins de Solesmes. Tours: Maison Mame, 1920. xxii, 419 pp.

Migne, Jacques Paul, 1800–1875, ed., *Patrologiae cursus completus, series graeca.* 161 vols. in 167; Parisiis: 1857–1866.

——— *Patrologiae cursus completus, series latina.* 221 vols.; Parisiis, 1844–1865.

Missae propriae et Kalendarium totius Ordinis S.P.N. Benedicti. Neo-Eboraci: Sumptibus et typis Benziger Brothers, Inc., 1944. vi, 56 pp. Bound into *Missale Romanum,* infra, with separate pagination, after p. 914.

Missale Romanum; ex decreto Sacrosancti Concilii Tridentini restitutum, Summorum Pontificum cura recognitum; juxta editionem VI post Typicam Vaticanam, ed. 5. Neo-Eboraci: Benziger Brothers, Inc., 1956. lxii, 914, (224), 35*, 14 pp.

Olivetans, *Constitutiones Congregationis Olivetanae,* determinatae in Capitulo Generali anno MDLXIIII, Reverendissimo Domno Barnaba Perusino existente Abbate Generali; his accessere ea quae a Reverendis Patribus delectis per capitulum Generale 1568 fuere sancita, qui etiam, authoritate sibi tradita, utraque in perpetuum rata, firmaque esse voluere. Romae: apud heredes Nicolai Mutii, 1602. [xii], 115 pp.

Perrin, J. M., *Virginity;* tr. by Katherine Gordon. Westminster, Maryland: The Newman Press, 1955. xiv, 161 pp.

Pachomius, Saint, *Pachomiana Latina; règle et épitres de S. Pachome, épitre de S. Theodore, et "liber" de S. Orsiesius; texte latine de S. Jérome;* édité par Dom Amand Boon de l'abbaye du Mont César, Louvain; avec appendice: La règle de S. Pachome; Fragments Coptes et excerpts Grecs; édités par L. Th. Lefort; Bibliothèque de la Revue d'Histoire ecclésiastique, fasc. 7. Louvain: Bureau de la Revue, 1932. lx, 210 pp.

Pez, Bernard, 1683–1735, *Bibliotheca Ascetica antiquo-nova,* hoc est, collectio veterum quorumdam et recentiorum opusculorum, quae hucusque in variis MSS codicibus et bibliothecis delituerunt. 12 vols.; Ratisbonae: sumptibus Joannis Conradi Peezii, 1723.

Pierre de Blois, fl. 1190, *Petri Blessensis, Bathomensis in Anglia Archidiaconi Opera Omnia* ad fidem manuscriptorum codicum emendata, notis et variis monumentis illustrata, ed. nova. Parisiis: Simeon Piget, 1667. xxxvi, 802, lxiv pp.

Because of the rarity of this work, references are made only to the more available *PL*.

Pius IX, Pope, 1792–1878, *Pii IX Pontificis Maximi Acta*. 8 vols.; Romae: ex typographia Bonarum Artium, 1857.

Pontificale Romanum Summorum Pontificum jussu editum et a Benedicto XIV Pont. Max. recognitum et castigatum. 4 vols.; Romae: Typis Rev. Camerae Apostolicae, apud Salvinccios, 1848.

——— *Ceremony of the blessing of the Rt. Rev. Cuthbert McDonald, O.S.B.*, coadjutor abbot of St. Benedict's Abbey. Atchison, Kansas: Abbey Student Press, 1943. 44 pp. This is a complete translation of *De benedictione abbatis auctoritate apostolica, Roman Pontifical.*

——— *The Consecration of virgins;* according to the *Roman Pontifical*. Clyde, Missouri: Benedictine Convent of Perpetual Adoration, 1952. 25 pp. Same pagination for facing Latin and English texts.

Schroeder, H. J., O.P., *Canons and Decrees of the Council of Trent*. St. Louis: B. Herder Book Co., 1941. xxxiv, 608 pp.

——— *Disciplinary Decrees of the General Councils;* text, translation and commentary. St. Louis: B. Herder Book Co., 1937. viii, 669 pp.

Strunk, Oliver, *Source readings in music history;* from classical antiquity through the Romantic Era; selected and annotated by Oliver Strunk [Princeton University]. New York: W. W. Norton and Company, 1950. xxii, 919 pp.

Suarez, Francisco, e Soc. Jesu, 1548–1617, *R. P. Francisci Suarez, e Societate Jesu Opera Omnia,* ed. nova a S. M. André . . . juxta editionem Venetianam XXIII tomos in F. continentem, accurate recognita. 26 vols.; Parisiis: 1856–1877.

Thomas à Kempis, 1380–1471, *Thomae Hermerken à Kempis, Canonici Regularis O.S. Augustini, Opera Omnia;* voluminibus septem edidit additoque volumine de vita et scriptis ejus disputavit Michael Joseph Pohl. Friburgi Brisigavorum: Herder, 1902–10.

——— *The Imitation of Christ;* a modern version based on the English translation made by Richard Whitford around the year 1530; edited with introduction by Harold C. Gardiner, S.J. New York: Image Books, a division of Doubleday & Company, Inc., 1955. 237 pp.

——— *Reden und Betrachtugen über das Leben und Leiden, die Auferstehung und Himmelfahrt Jesu Christi,* aus dem Lateinischen übersetzt . . . von Julius Meellendorff. Regensburg: Manz, 1907. xx, 277 pp.

——— *Sermons to the Novices Regular, by Thomas à Kempis,* Canon Regular of the Congregation of Windesheim; authorized translation from the text of the edition of Michael Joseph Pohl, by Dom Vincent Scully, C.R.L. London: Kegan, Paul, Trench, Truebner & Co., Ltd., 1907. xxvi, 255 pp.

Thomas Aquinas, Saint, 1225?–74, *Sancti Thomae Aquinatis, Doctoris Angelici, Opera Omnia,* jussu impensaque Leonis XIII, P.M., edita. 15 vols.; Romae: Ex Typographia Polyglotta S.C. de Propaganda Fide, 1882–1919.

——— *Sancti Thomae Aquinatis Doctoris Angelici Ordinis Praedicatorum Opera Omnia,* ad fidem optimarum editionum accurate recognita. 25 vols.; Parmae: Typis Petri Fiaccadori, 1852–73.

——— *Divi Thomae Aquinatis Doctoris Angelici Ordinis Praedicatorum Opera;* ed. altera veneta ad plurium exempla comparata et emendata. 28 vols.; Venetiis: cudebat Simon Occhi, 1775–88.

——— *Summa Theologica;* first complete American edition in 3 vols.; literally tr. by Fathers of the English Dominican Province. New York: Benziger Brothers, Inc., 1947.

——— *S. Thomae Aquinatis Opuscula Theologica* . . . cura et studio Fr. Raymundi A. Verardo, O.P. 2 vols.; Torino: Marietti, 1954.

——— *An Apology for the religious orders;* being a translation from the Latin of two minor works of the Saint, edited by . . . John Procter. London: Sands & Co., 1902. vi, 488 pp.

Trithemius, Joannes, O.S.B., 1462–1516, *Joannis Trithemii Spanhemensis primum, deinde D. Jacobi in suburbano Herbipolensi, Abbatis eruditissimi opera pia et spiritualia* . . . a R. P. Joanne Busaeo, S.J. Theologo in omnium religiosae vitae cultorum gratiam diligenti studio conquisita, et in unum volumen, mendis expurgatis, redacta. Moguntiae: Joan. Albini, 1605. xx, 1226 pp.

——— *Joannes Trithemii Abbatis Ordinis S. Benedicti ad monachos dehortationes,* curis monasterii S. Benedicti de Urbe iterum editae. Romae: Typis Vaticanis, 1898. 283 pp.

Vincentius Ferrerius, Saint, O.P., d. 1419, *S. Vincentius Ferrarius, Ordinis Praedic., de vita spirituali, et brevi methodo perveniendi ad perfectionem;* in: *Speculum parvum religiosorum.* Coloniae Agrippinae: apud Petrum Henningium, 1619, pp. 105–214.

——— *A Treatise on the Spiritual Life;* with a commentary by Ven. Mother Julienne Morrell, O.P. Westminster, Maryland: The Newman Press, 1957. 157 pp.

Wolter, Maurus, Archabbot, founder of Beuron Archabbey, *Praecipua ordinis monastici elementa,* e Regula Sancti Patris Benedicti adumbravit, testimoniis adornavit D. Maurus Wolter, Abbas S. Martini de Beuron et B.V.M. de Montserrato—Emaus, Pragae, superior generalis Congregationis Beuronensis O.S.B. Brugis: ex typographia societatis S. Augustini, Desclée, de Brouwer, et Soc. 1880. viii, 840 pp.

——— *Elementa; die Gründlagen des Benediktinischen Mönchtums von Maurus Wolter, O.S.B.,* Erzabt und Gründer von Beuron; aus dem lateinischen übersetzt und eingeleitet von P. Suso Mayer, O.S.B., Beuron. Beuron [Hohenzollern]: Beuroner Kunstverlag, 1955. 176 pp.

Index

(Entries refer to numbered paragraphs of text.)